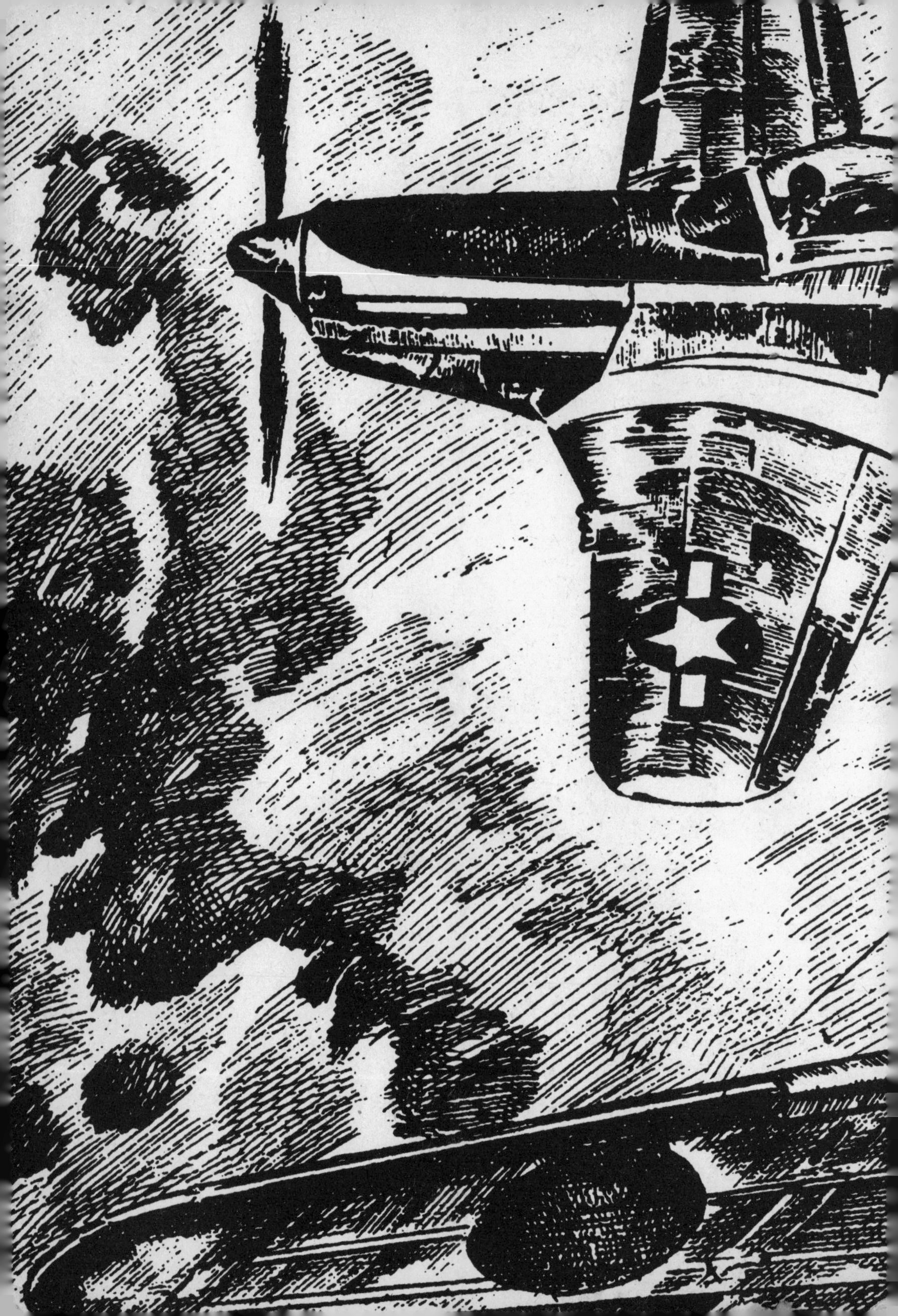

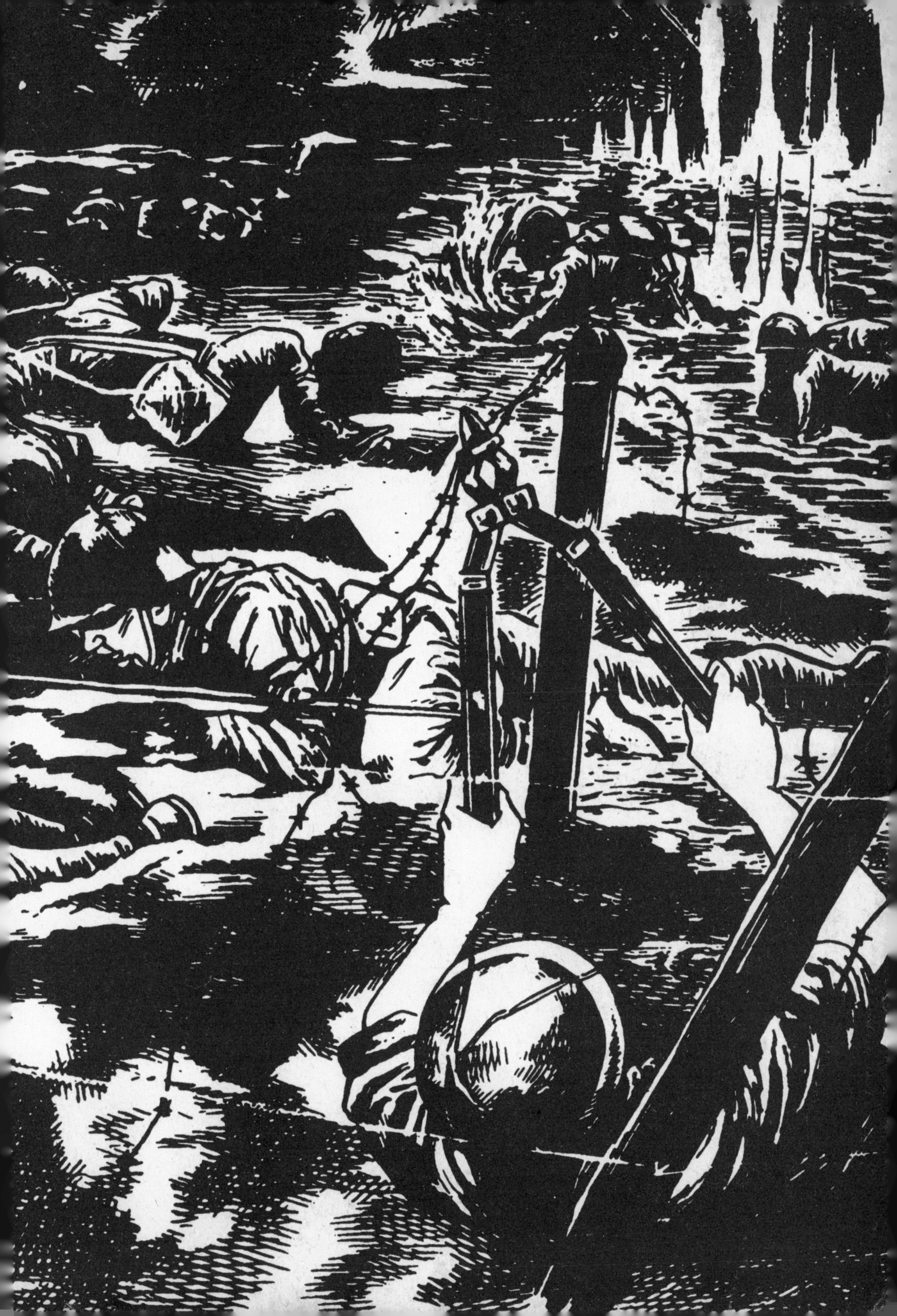

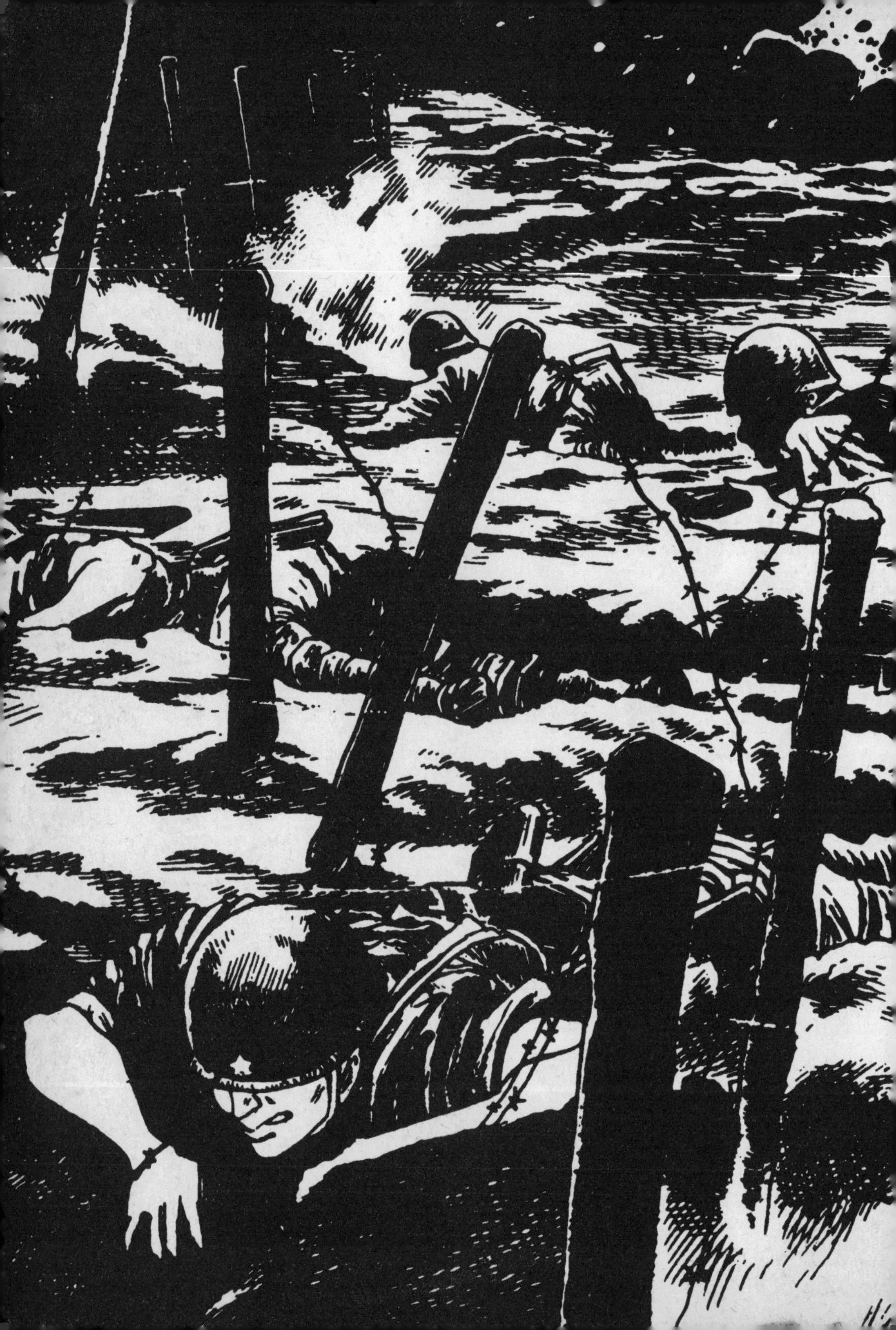

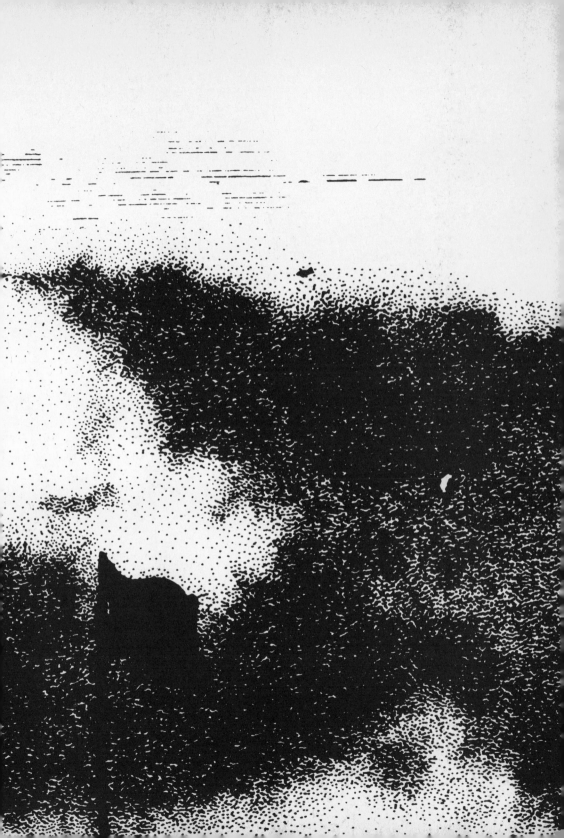

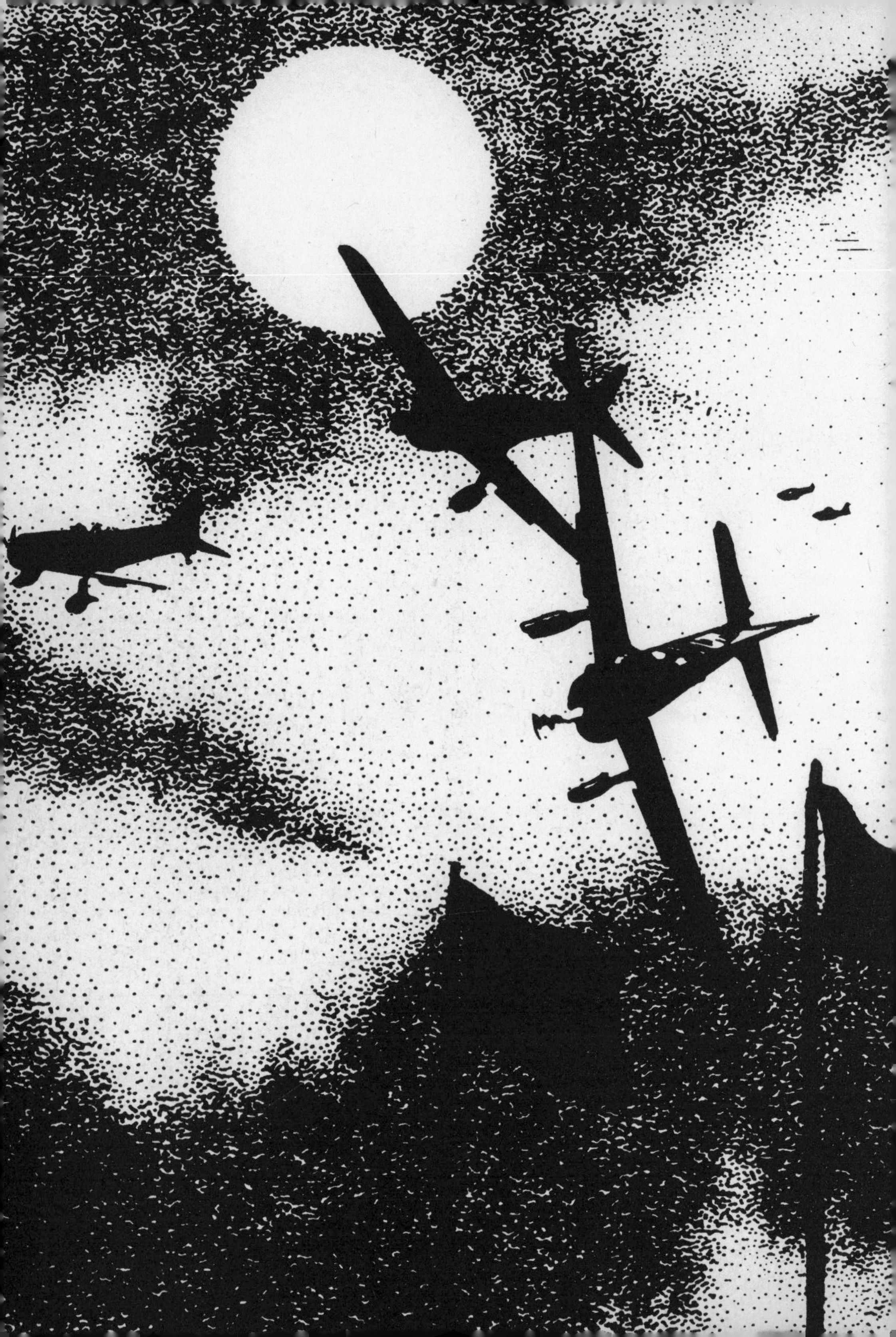

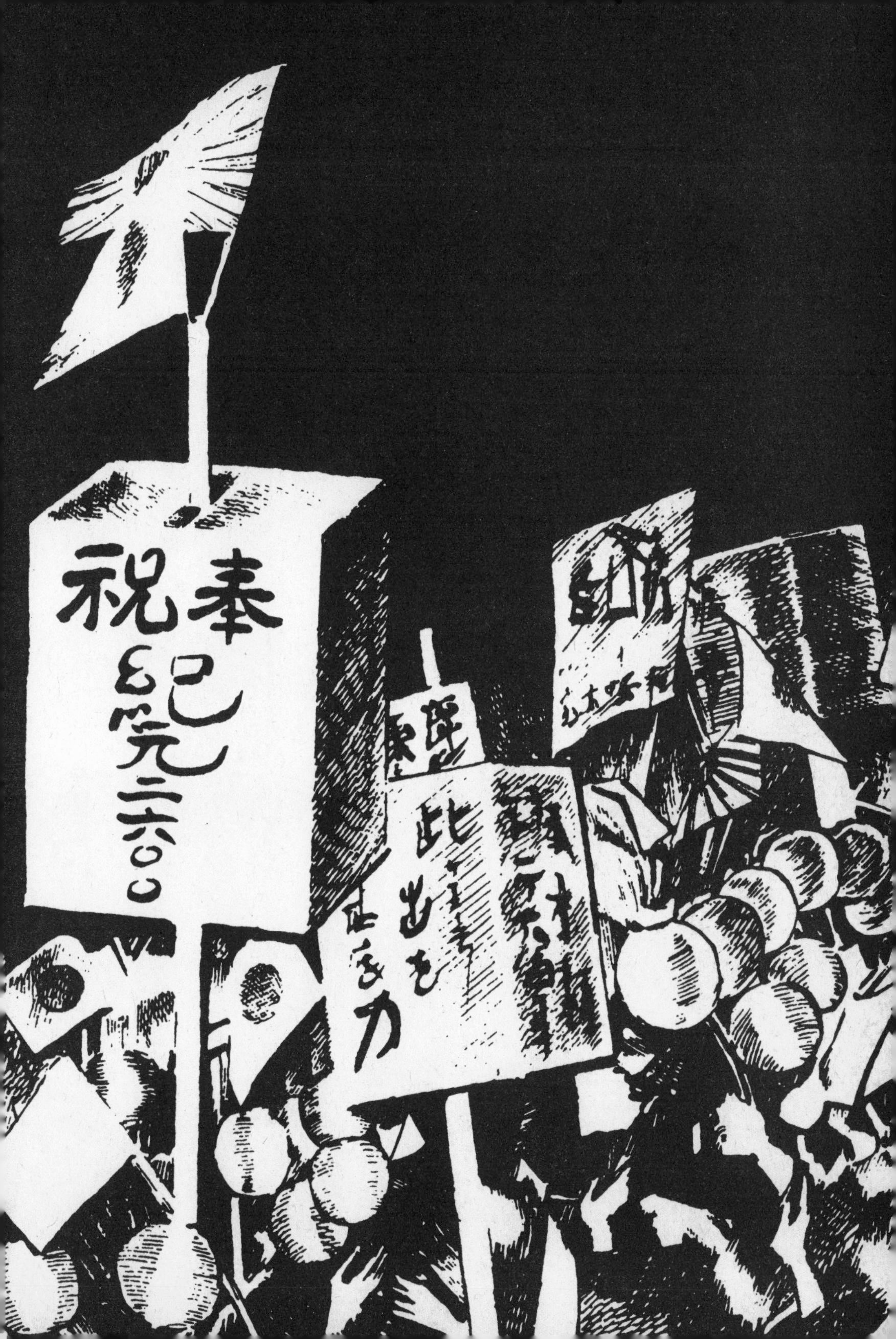
奉祝
紀元二六〇〇

SHOWA 1939–1944
A HISTORY OF JAPAN

SHIGERU MIZUKI

TRANSLATION BY ZACK DAVISSON

PUBLISHED BY
DRAWN & QUARTERLY

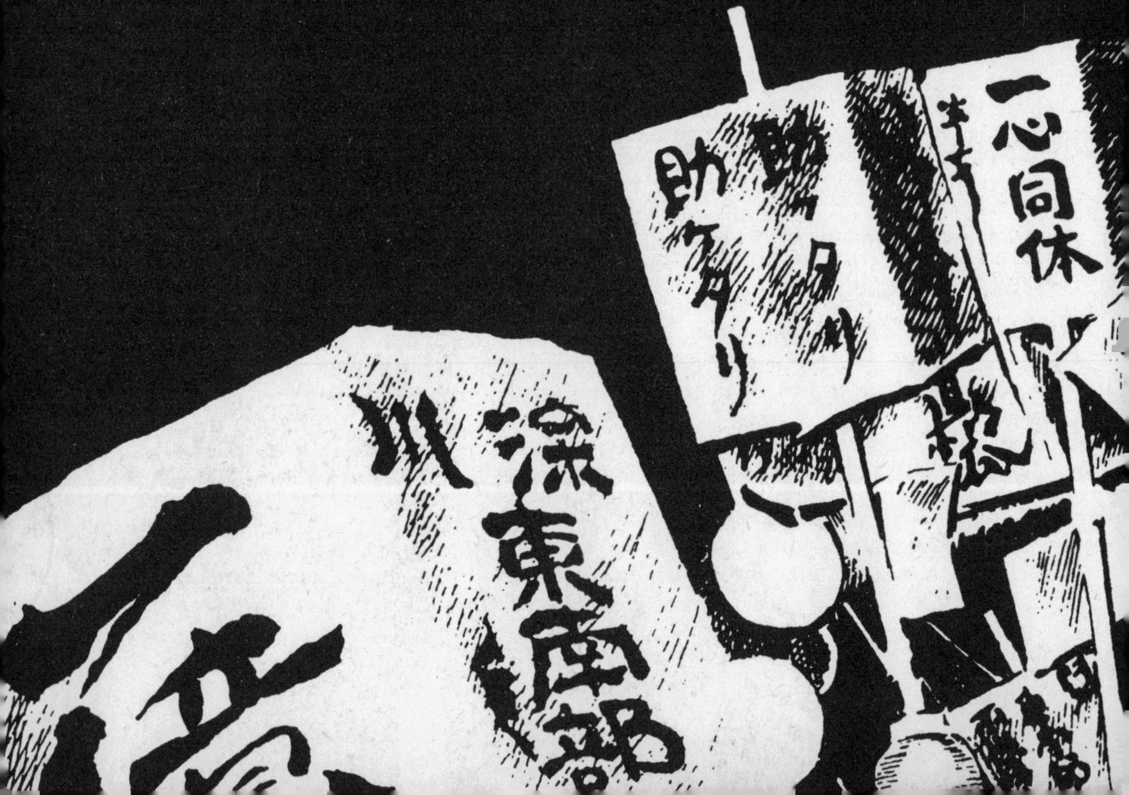
一心同体

ALSO BY SHIGERU MIZUKI

Showa 1926-1939: A History of Japan (2013)

Kitaro (2013)

NonNonBa (2012)

Onward Towards Our Noble Deaths (2011)

Story and art © copyright 2014 Shigeru Mizuki/Mizuki Productions. Translation © copyright 2014 Zack Davisson. Forward © copyright 2014 Frederik L. Schodt. This edition © copyright 2014 Drawn & Quarterly. All rights reserved. No part of this book (except small portions for review purposes) may be reproduced in any form without written permission from Shigeru Mizuki/ Mizuki Productions or Drawn & Quarterly. Font design: Kevin Huizenga.

Drawn & Quarterly gratefully acknowledges Presspop Inc. and Maki Hakui for their invaluable assistance with the publication of this book.

www.drawnandquarterly.com

First paperback edition: May 2014. Printed in Canada.

Library and Archives Canada Cataloguing in Publication: Mizuki, Shigeru, 1922–. [*Komikku Showa-shi*. English]. *Showa, 1939-1944: A History of Japan*/Shigeru Mizuki; translator, Zack Davisson. Translation of: *Komikku Showa-shi*. ISBN 978-1-77046-151-2 (pbk.) 1. Japan—History—1926–1945— Comic books, strips, etc. 2. Japan—Social life and customs—1912–1945—Comic books, strips, etc. 3. Graphic novels. 4. Mizuki, Shigeru, 1922— —Childhood and youth—Comic books, strips, etc. I. Davisson, Zack, translator II. Title. DS888.5.M59213 2014   952.03'3   C2013-906211-4

Published in the USA by Drawn & Quarterly, a client publisher of Farrar, Straus and Giroux; Orders: 888.330.8477. Published in Canada by Drawn & Quarterly, a client publisher of Raincoast Books; Orders: 800.663.5714. Published in the United Kingdom by Drawn & Quarterly, a client publisher of Publishers Group UK; Orders: info@pguk.co.uk.

SHIGERU MIZUKI'S SHOWA 1939-1944: A HISTORY OF JAPAN *FREDERIK L. SCHODT*

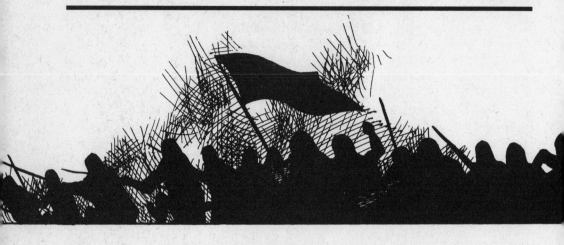

Many years ago, I interviewed a Japanese manga artist who had worked for the government during World War II, drawing propaganda leaflets—most of which were dropped on American and Australian troops in the Pacific to demoralize them. I had always been interested in how the Japanese government so successfully enlisted so many artists into its cause during the war. I knew that, in many cases, it was through oppression, because freedom of speech had been so radically curtailed and dissent so stifled, and it was impossible for artists to find work unless they worked for the government. But I knew there were other reasons, too.

I always felt grateful to this particular man, who has long since passed away, because he was so forthright and honest. He told me that many young people, like himself, had believed in the official government policy of Japan's Greater East Asian Co-Prosperity Sphere—a policy that, on the surface, was designed to counter Western imperial powers in Asia, liberate European colonies, and create a block of Asian nations that existed in solidarity with Japan. Given that the European nations and the United States had carved up and exploited large swathes of Asia for themselves, it was an idea that resonated with many intellectuals, not only in Japan but throughout Asia. For many proud Japanese, it helped to counter a deep-seated feeling of humiliation they felt had been inflicted upon them by Western powers, and satisfied a desire to catch up and surpass the West.

In *Showa 1939–1944*, the second volume of Shigeru Mizuki's series, we can see how this official policy, which may have initially had good intentions, started to go horribly awry—twisted out of shape by greed, delusion, and a superiority complex vis-à-vis other Asian powers that rivaled that of the Western imperialist powers. And we can also see how some of the internal contradictions in Japanese society manifested, especially in appalling strategic miscalculations on the part of the Japanese military brass. In *Showa 1939–1944*, Mizuki, too young and too uninterested to be a participant at the beginning, finds himself, like so many others, sucked violently into what rapidly became a global conflict.

In his own afterword to the Japanese edition of the series, Mizuki obliquely apologizes for devoting so much space to the war. And, in fact, the war years only constituted a small part of the long Showa era. But as Mizuki points out, for his generation these were the defining years, since the war was, in many senses, a gigantic trauma, a turning point in the long history of Japan, and a bloody point of no return. The war also lasted far longer for Japan than it did for Europe and America. Because of this, in the entire Showa series, Mizuki rarely uses the term World War II; for the Japanese people, the war really started on the Chinese mainland in 1931, when the Japanese army began charging out of control on the Asian continent, in Manchuria. Thereafter, the military gradually usurped the power of the Japanese civilian and parliamentary government and, as long as its ventures succeeded, enjoyed overwhelming support from ordinary citizens. As often happens with empires, the entire nation fell under the spell of its own initial victories and successes, thereby paving the way for a reckless expansion of the war, and for future disasters. In Japan, the war with China, which continued until 1945, is often referred to as the Fifteen Year War. What Americans might think of as the war with Japan, or simply part of World War II, the Japanese (and Mizuki) more specifically refer to as the Pacific War. Although Japan cooperated with far-away Nazi Germany and Italy in the Axis alliance, it did not do any real fighting in the Western hemisphere. Instead, in its wars in the Pacific and on the Asian mainland, Japan faced an astounding array of enemies, which only seemed to grow in number. What started as small conflicts in northern China quickly became an Eastern hemispheric war with the British, Australians, Dutch, Chinese, Americans, and Russians, to name only a few. And what began with spectacular Japanese tactical victories turned into spectacular strategic disasters.

As with the first volume of this series, in *Showa 1939–1944* Mizuki continues to take a macro and micro approach to telling his story, alternating between a traditional bird's-eye view of the build-up to war and a very human, personal account of the situation on the ground. And Nezumi Otoko, or Rat Man, continues to serve as the interlocutor and bridge between the two views. It is a structure that works well and allows Mizuki to weave in a dizzying amount of information—far more than most manga works can convey—while keeping the story gripping, factual, personal, entertaining, and educational.

In the first half of this volume, the young Mizuki is depicted as something of an idler or slacker—a nose-picking teenager with no particular motivation who floats in and out of schools and jobs and spends time at home doing nothing. It is part of an image that Mizuki likes to cultivate, even today, of himself as someone who is inherently lazy—a bit of a space-case who normally doesn't worry about the same things that most people do—and who, never the brightest in his class, is the constant victim of bullying.

As factual as Mizuki's story is, we do well to take his self-depiction with a grain of salt. In the first part of this volume, Mizuki describes what it was like to be a young man in his hometown of Sakaiminato during the war fever of Japan's early, successful years, feeling adrift and waiting to be drafted into the military. He and his friends all expected to die young, and as Mizuki notes, this created a mini-boom in the reading of religious and philosophical books, as well as European classics. As readers who pay close attention will surely notice with amazement, Mizuki claims to have read the New Testament five times and memorized it; he also read Buddhist texts and works of philosophy by the ancient Romans, such as Seneca. He was also a great fan of the

nineteenth century German Johann Wolfgang von Goethe, reading Johann Peter Eckermann's *Conversations with Goethe* over seven times, and memorizing it, too.

While Mizuki regularly espouses the virtue of being lazy—not worrying about material things too much and getting lots of sleep—his astounding work on the Showa series and his lengthy bibliography indicate he is far closer to what most people would consider a workaholic. What he is, in the story and in real life, both then and now, is also a bit of an eccentric—someone who marches to the beat of his own drum, and has an intense curiosity about life and the world. He is, moreover, someone with an extraordinarily tough physical and mental constitution, who as a young man had a voracious appetite for ideas, and food.

Many other histories in manga form or works of an expository nature about World War II have been published in Japan. But they are almost all—with the rare exception of works like Keiji Nakazawa's *Barefoot Gen* or Osamu Tezuka's *Kami no Toride* (*Paper Fortress*)—written by younger postwar artists who had no direct experience with war. And many of these newer manga tend to be didactic in their anti-war messages, peddling cheap thrills and displaying a fetishistic fascination with war machinery, or even—as is unfortunately and increasingly the case—promoting a revisionist and nationalistic version of the war that tries to absolve Japan of any guilt. For Mizuki, who was drafted into the Imperial Army and saw many of the worst aspects of combat and human behavior, the war proved to be an opportunity for an existential awakening. For him, the absurdities of what he witnessed, and the extraordinary luck that allowed him to survive, helped to connect him with a larger world, and ultimately to develop a vision that transcended the pettiness of nationalism, ideology, and human arrogance, and helped connect him further with both the natural and paranormal worlds.

In this volume, Mizuki guides readers through the early Showa years, showing us how the war in China developed, what life was like on the home front, and, finally, in the second half, what the beginning of the Pacific War was like for him first as a civilian and later as a draftee. For the young Mizuki, life was not yet too bad, but it was going to get a lot, lot worse.

Frederik L. Schodt is an award-winning author of numerous non-fiction books on Japan and a well-known translator. In 2009, he received the Order of the Rising Sun, Gold Rays with Rosette, for his work. His latest book is Professor Risley and the Imperial Japanese Troupe: How an American Acrobat Introduced Circus to Japan—and Japan to the West *(Stone Bridge Press, 2012).*

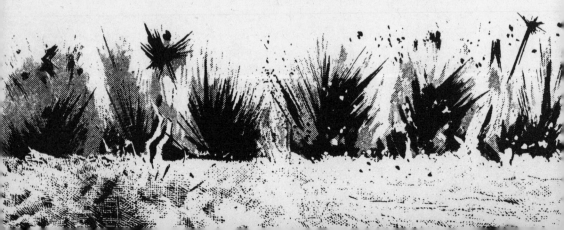

THE NEW ORIENTAL ORDER

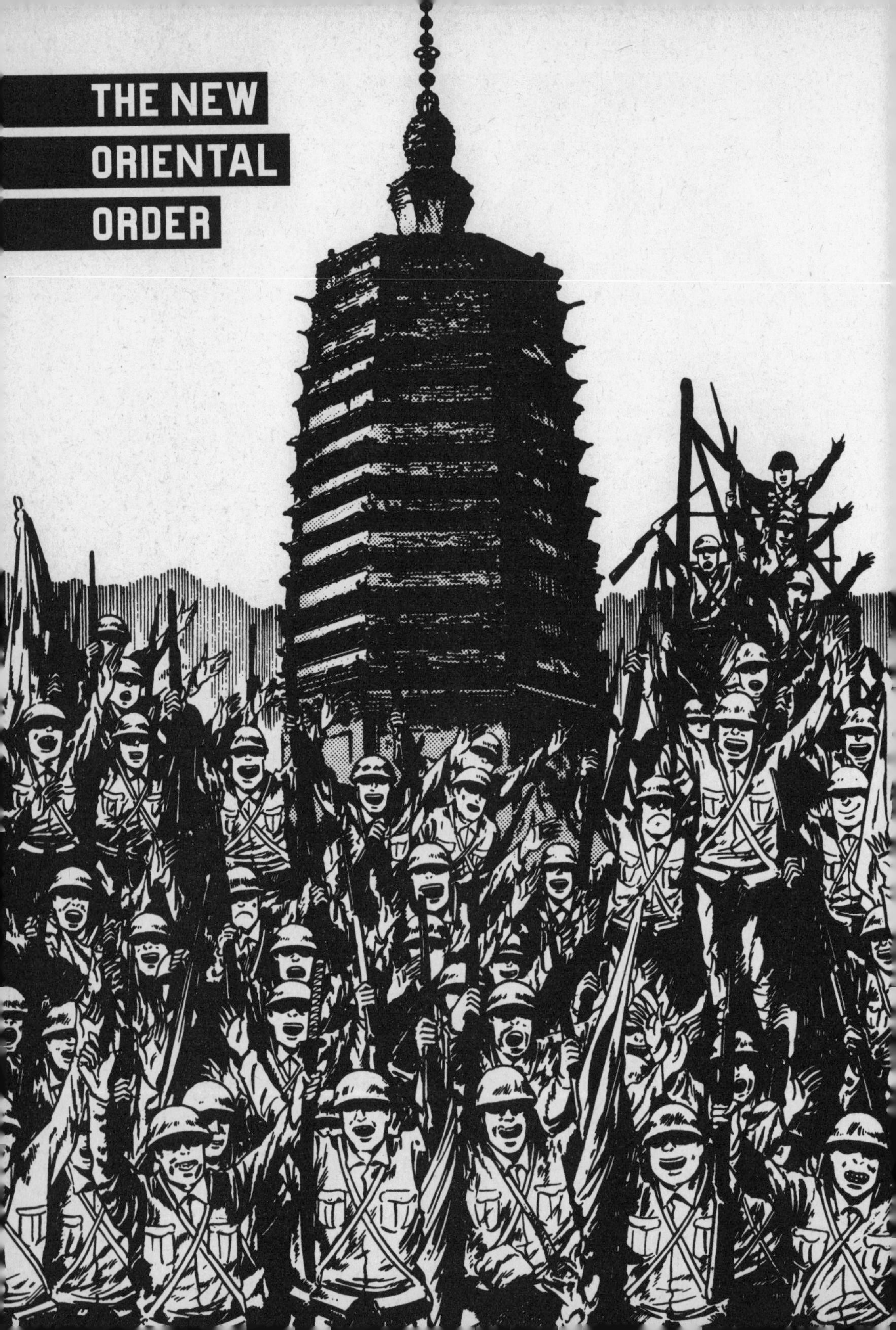

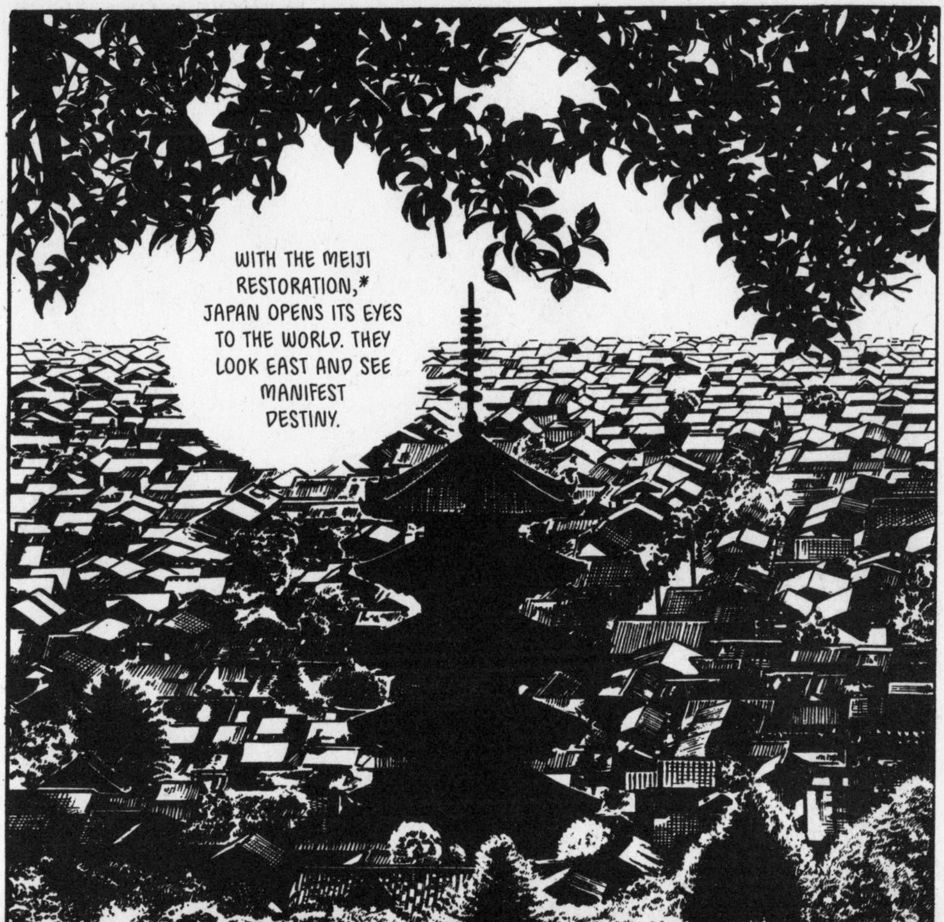
WITH THE MEIJI RESTORATION,* JAPAN OPENS ITS EYES TO THE WORLD. THEY LOOK EAST AND SEE MANIFEST DESTINY.

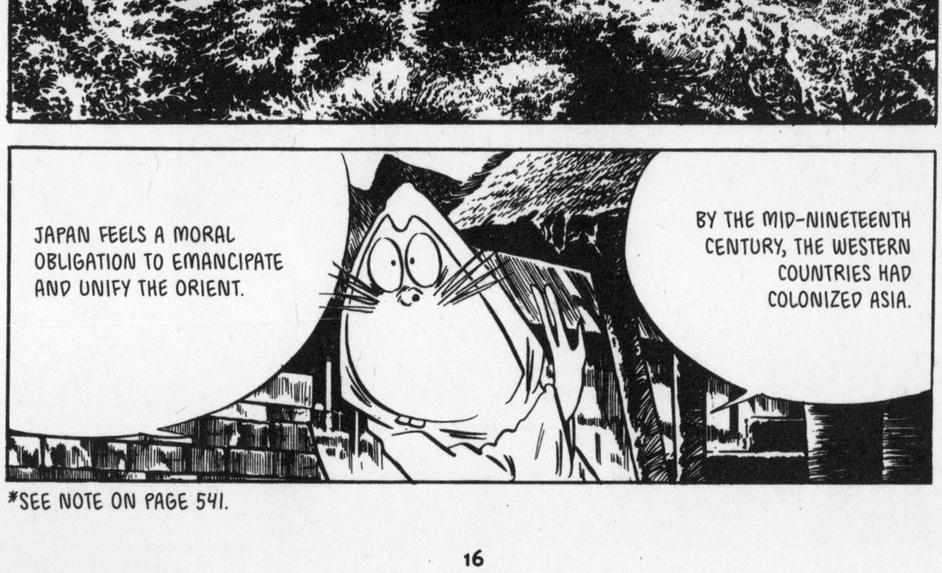
BY THE MID-NINETEENTH CENTURY, THE WESTERN COUNTRIES HAD COLONIZED ASIA.
JAPAN FEELS A MORAL OBLIGATION TO EMANCIPATE AND UNIFY THE ORIENT.

*SEE NOTE ON PAGE 541.

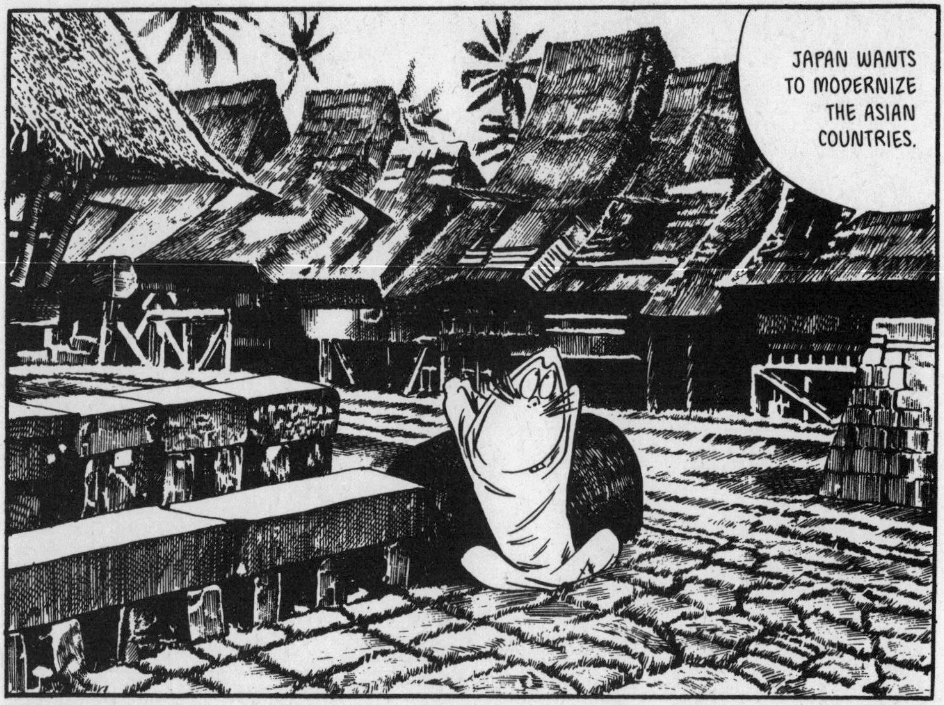
JAPAN WANTS TO MODERNIZE THE ASIAN COUNTRIES.

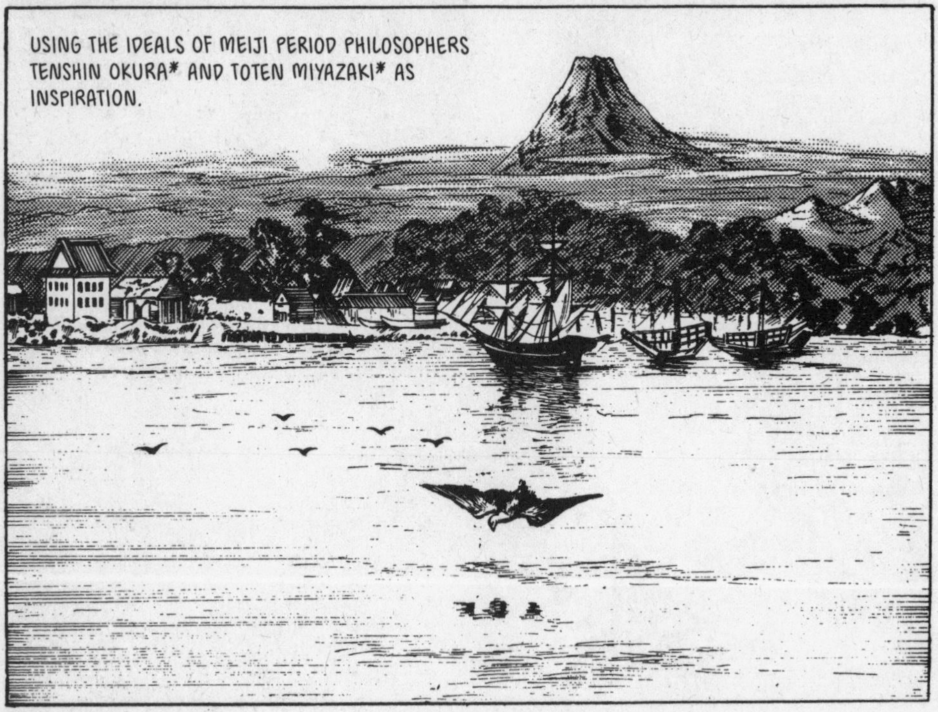
USING THE IDEALS OF MEIJI PERIOD PHILOSOPHERS TENSHIN OKURA* AND TOTEN MIYAZAKI* AS INSPIRATION.

*SEE NOTE ON PAGE 541.

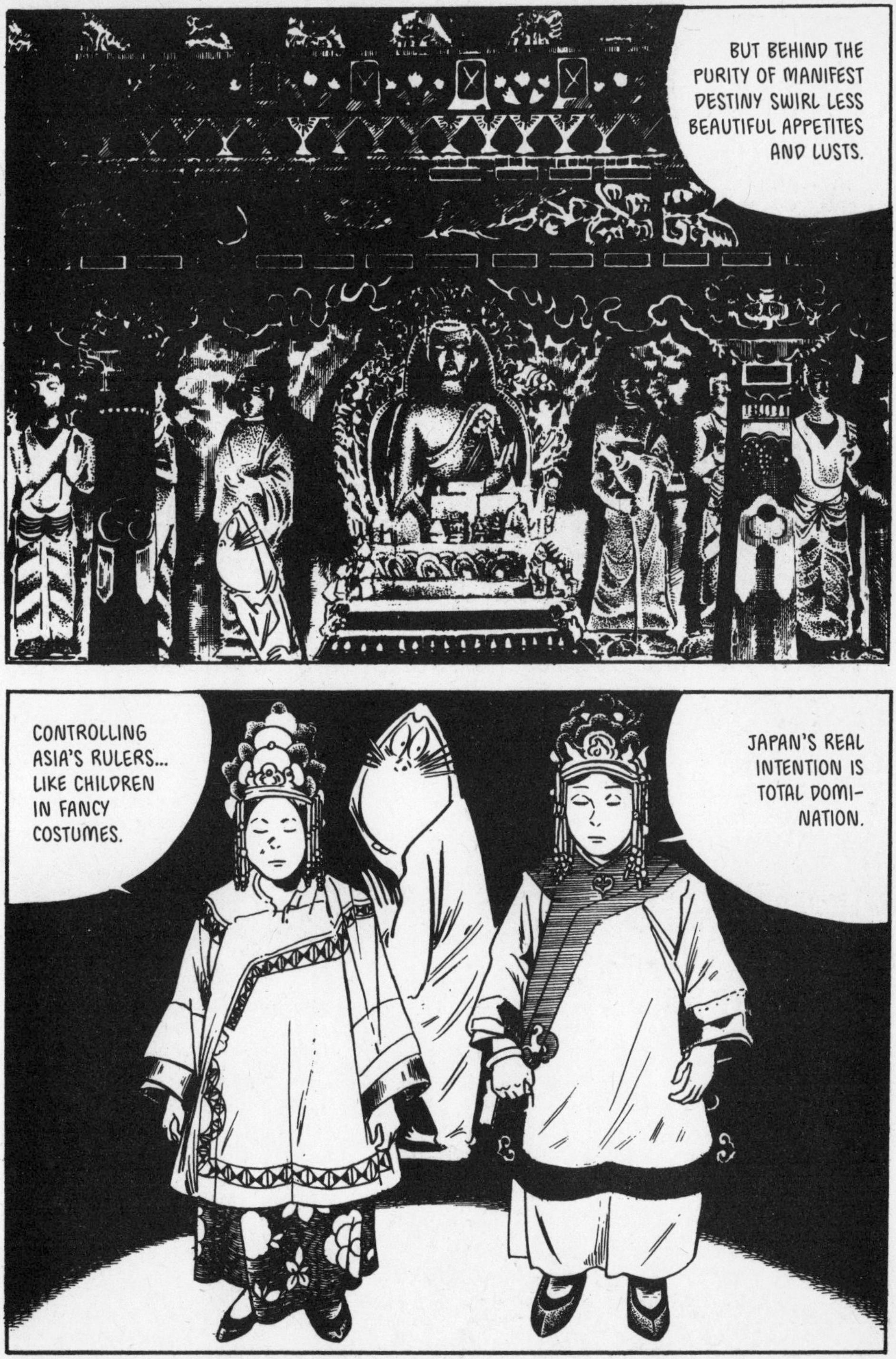
BUT BEHIND THE PURITY OF MANIFEST DESTINY SWIRL LESS BEAUTIFUL APPETITES AND LUSTS.
JAPAN'S REAL INTENTION IS TOTAL DOMI-NATION.
CONTROLLING ASIA'S RULERS... LIKE CHILDREN IN FANCY COSTUMES.

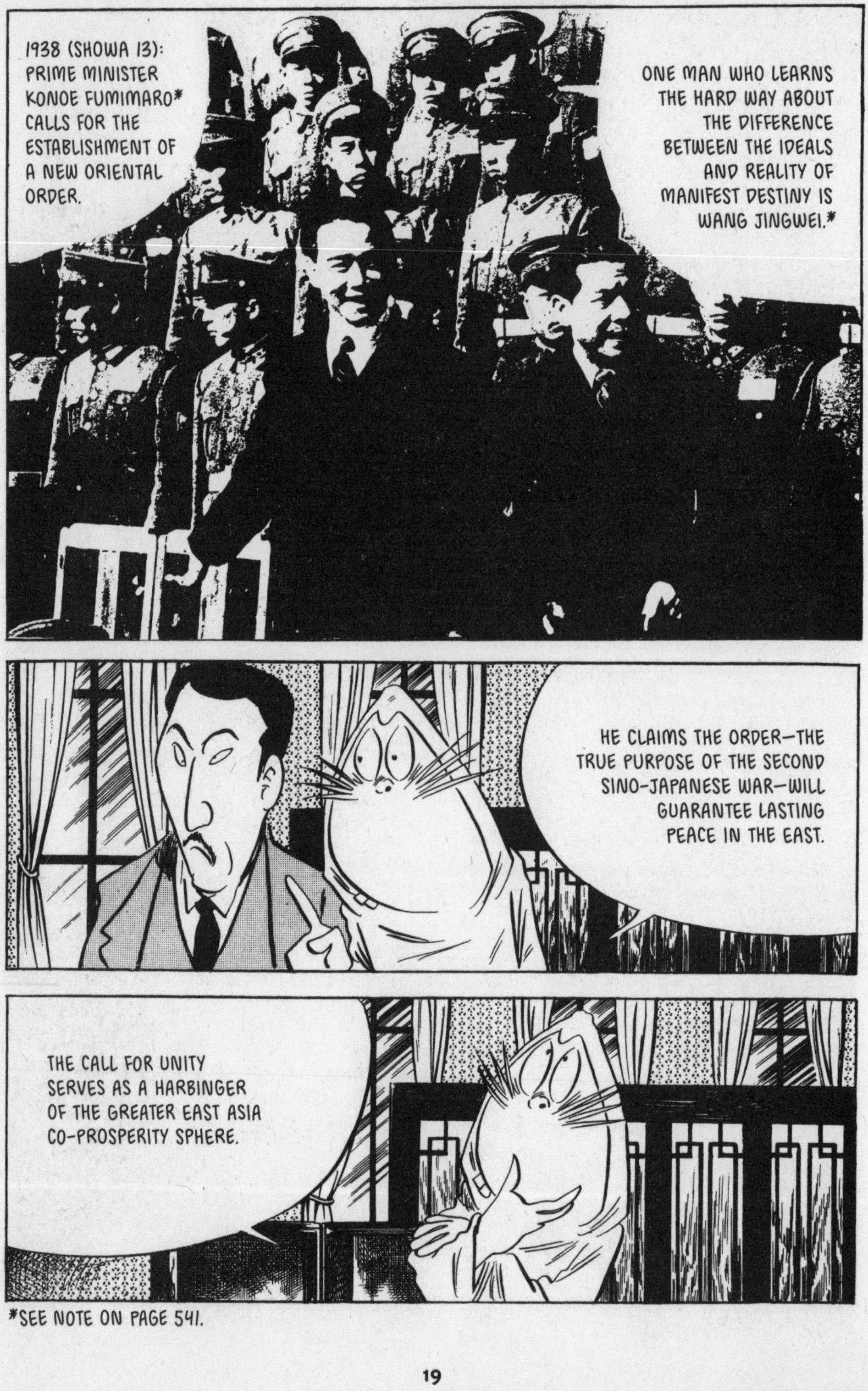
1938 (SHOWA 13): PRIME MINISTER KONOE FUMIMARO* CALLS FOR THE ESTABLISHMENT OF A NEW ORIENTAL ORDER.
ONE MAN WHO LEARNS THE HARD WAY ABOUT THE DIFFERENCE BETWEEN THE IDEALS AND REALITY OF MANIFEST DESTINY IS WANG JINGWEI.*
HE CLAIMS THE ORDER—THE TRUE PURPOSE OF THE SECOND SINO-JAPANESE WAR—WILL GUARANTEE LASTING PEACE IN THE EAST.
THE CALL FOR UNITY SERVES AS A HARBINGER OF THE GREATER EAST ASIA CO-PROSPERITY SPHERE.

*SEE NOTE ON PAGE 541.

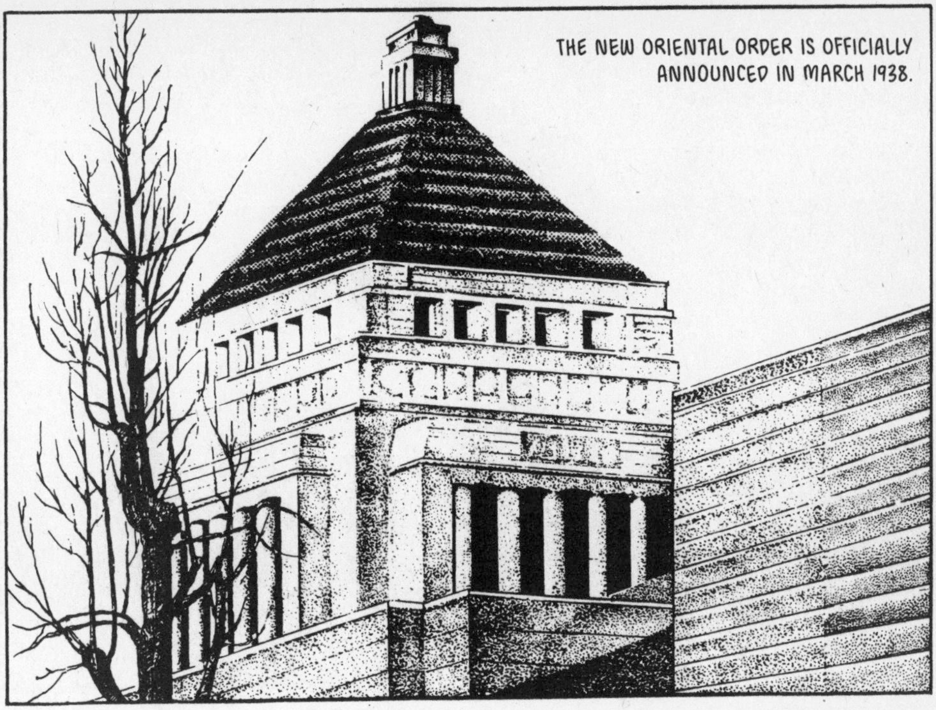
THE NEW ORIENTAL ORDER IS OFFICIALLY ANNOUNCED IN MARCH 1938.

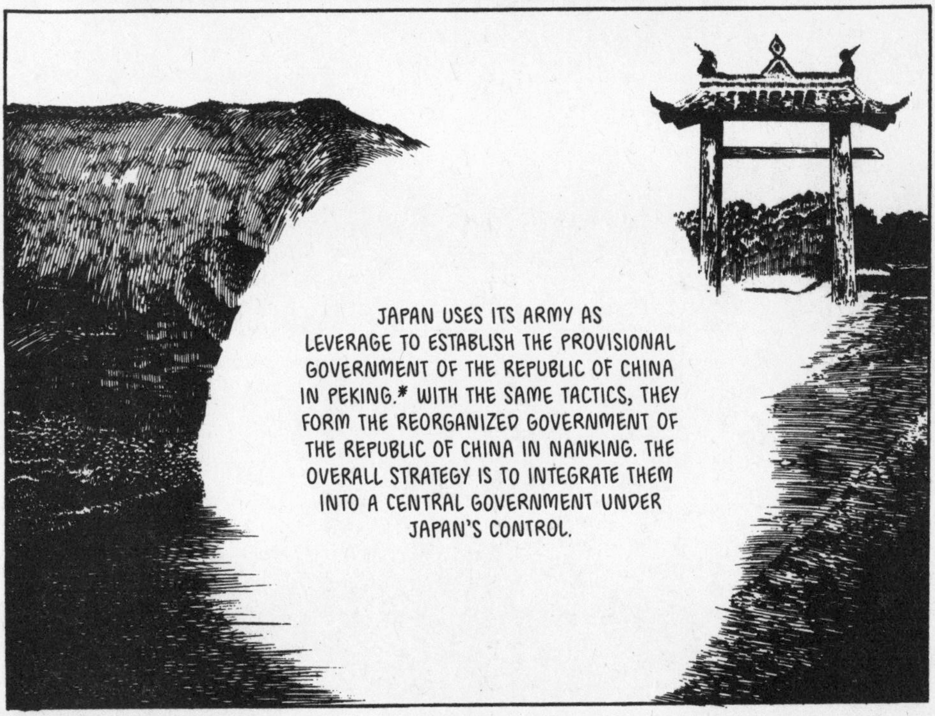
JAPAN USES ITS ARMY AS LEVERAGE TO ESTABLISH THE PROVISIONAL GOVERNMENT OF THE REPUBLIC OF CHINA IN PEKING.* WITH THE SAME TACTICS, THEY FORM THE REORGANIZED GOVERNMENT OF THE REPUBLIC OF CHINA IN NANKING. THE OVERALL STRATEGY IS TO INTEGRATE THEM INTO A CENTRAL GOVERNMENT UNDER JAPAN'S CONTROL.

*SEE NOTE ON PAGE 541.

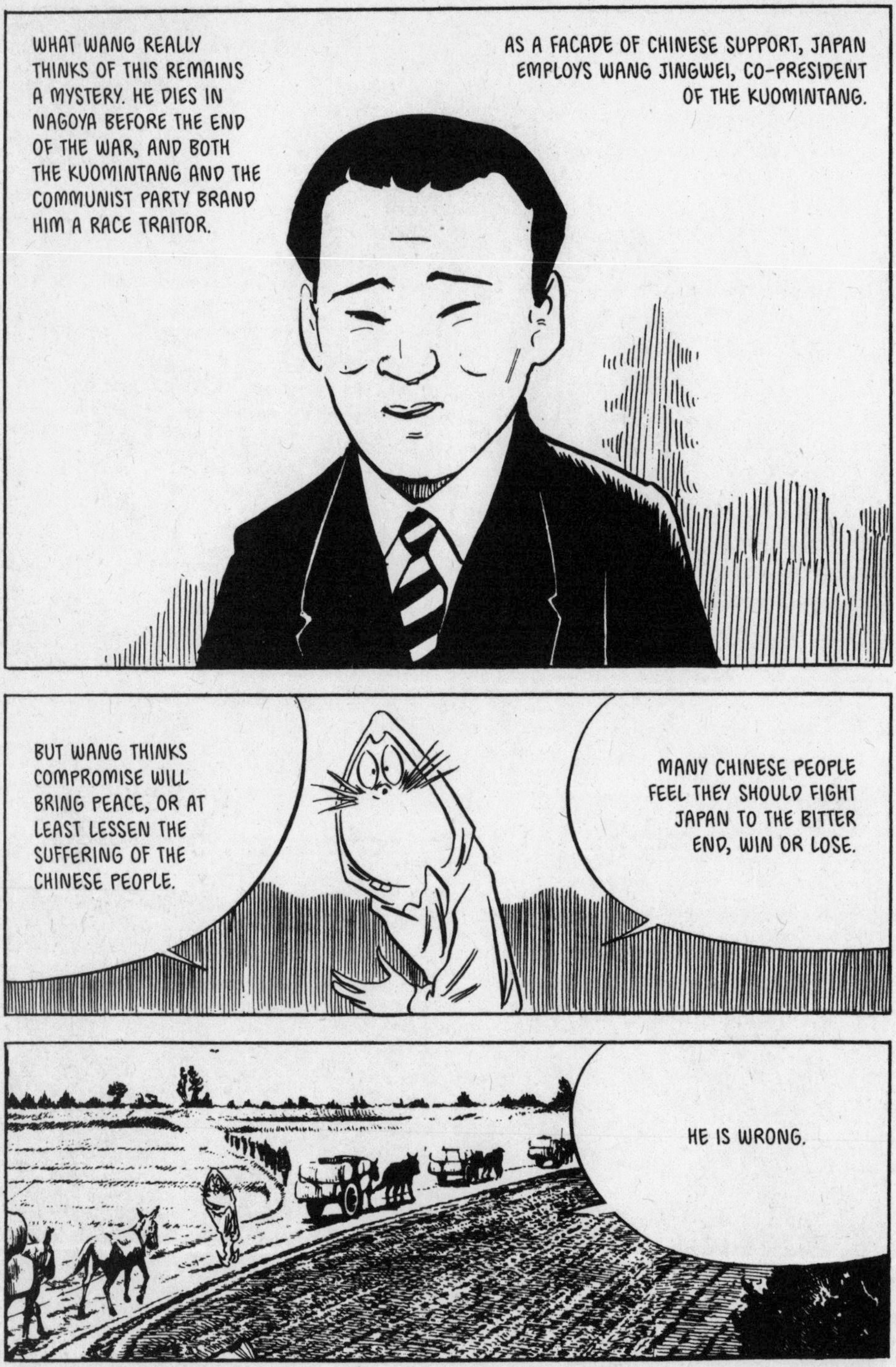
AS A FACADE OF CHINESE SUPPORT, JAPAN EMPLOYS WANG JINGWEI, CO-PRESIDENT OF THE KUOMINTANG.
WHAT WANG REALLY THINKS OF THIS REMAINS A MYSTERY. HE DIES IN NAGOYA BEFORE THE END OF THE WAR, AND BOTH THE KUOMINTANG AND THE COMMUNIST PARTY BRAND HIM A RACE TRAITOR.
MANY CHINESE PEOPLE FEEL THEY SHOULD FIGHT JAPAN TO THE BITTER END, WIN OR LOSE.
BUT WANG THINKS COMPROMISE WILL BRING PEACE, OR AT LEAST LESSEN THE SUFFERING OF THE CHINESE PEOPLE.
HE IS WRONG.

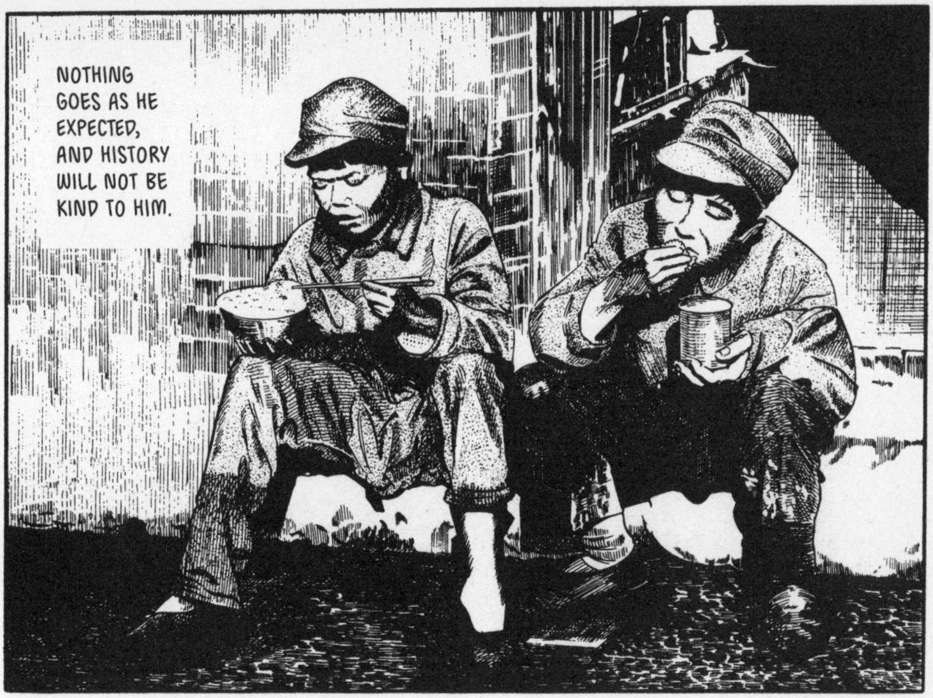
NOTHING GOES AS HE EXPECTED, AND HISTORY WILL NOT BE KIND TO HIM.

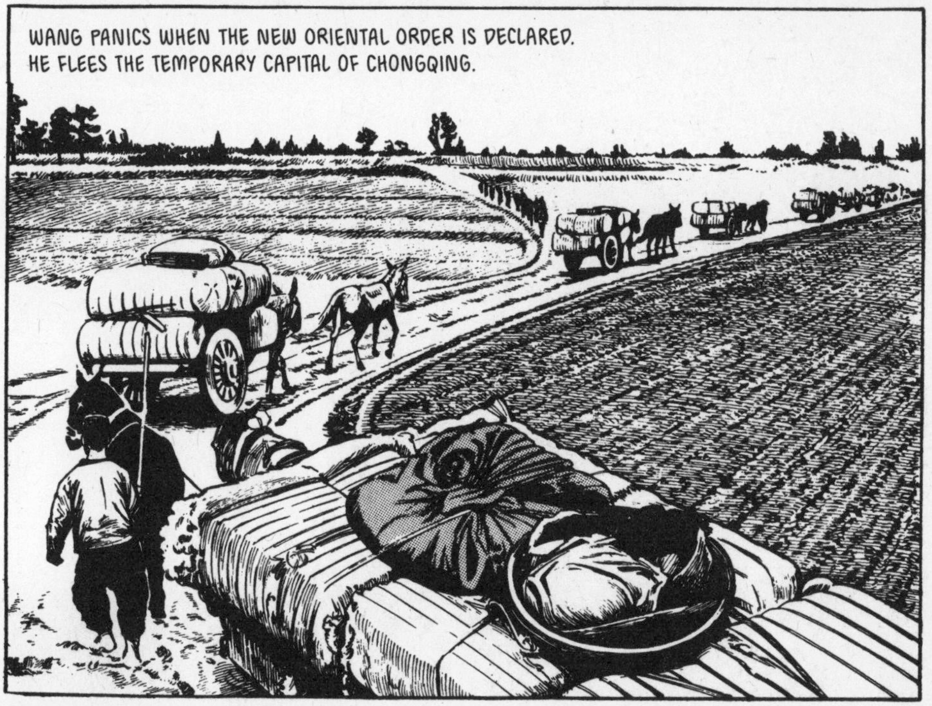
WANG PANICS WHEN THE NEW ORIENTAL ORDER IS DECLARED. HE FLEES THE TEMPORARY CAPITAL OF CHONGQING.

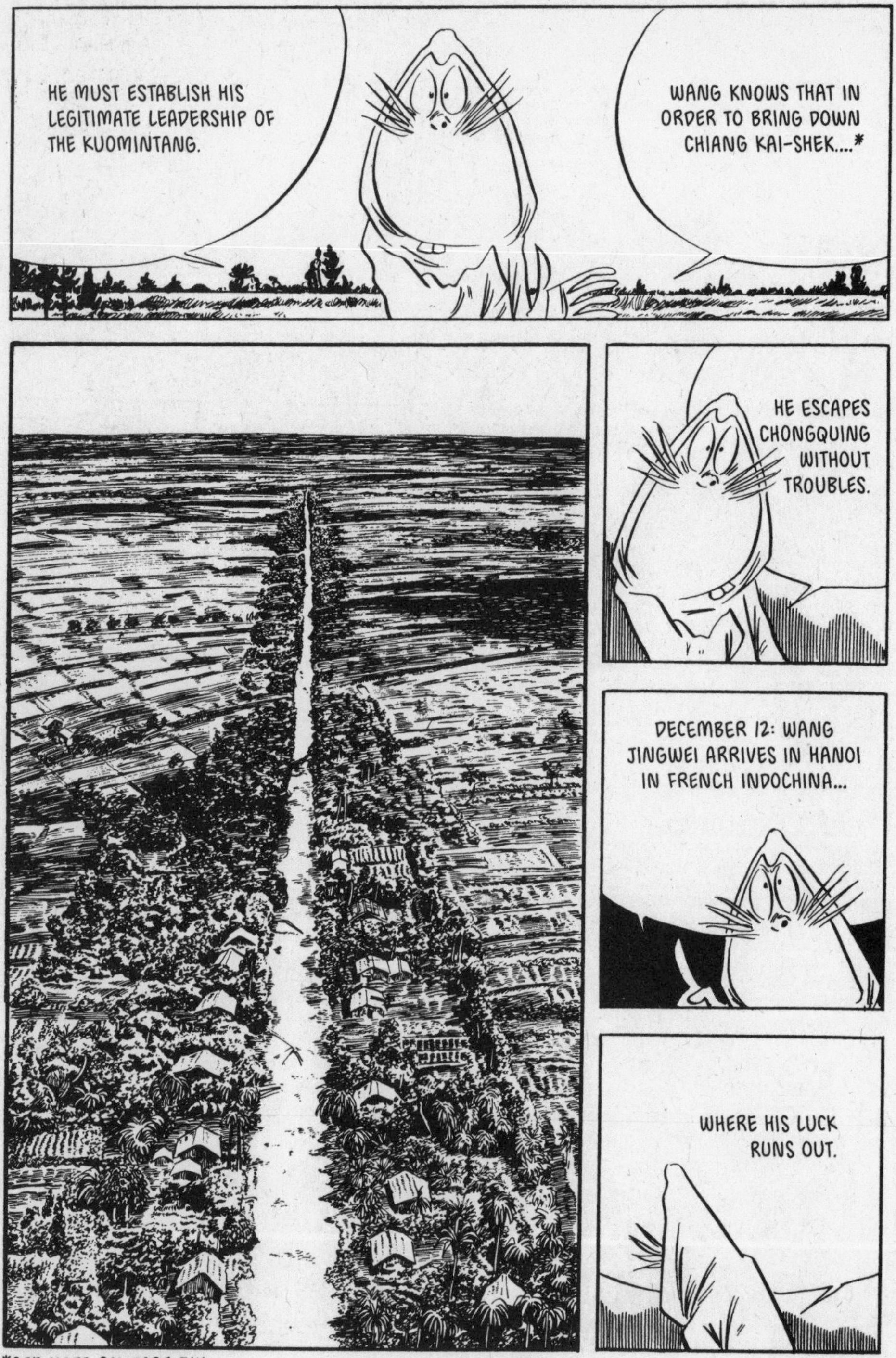
WANG KNOWS THAT IN ORDER TO BRING DOWN CHIANG KAI-SHEK....*
HE MUST ESTABLISH HIS LEGITIMATE LEADERSHIP OF THE KUOMINTANG.
HE ESCAPES CHONGQUING WITHOUT TROUBLES.
DECEMBER 12: WANG JINGWEI ARRIVES IN HANOI IN FRENCH INDOCHINA...
WHERE HIS LUCK RUNS OUT.

*SEE NOTE ON PAGE 541.

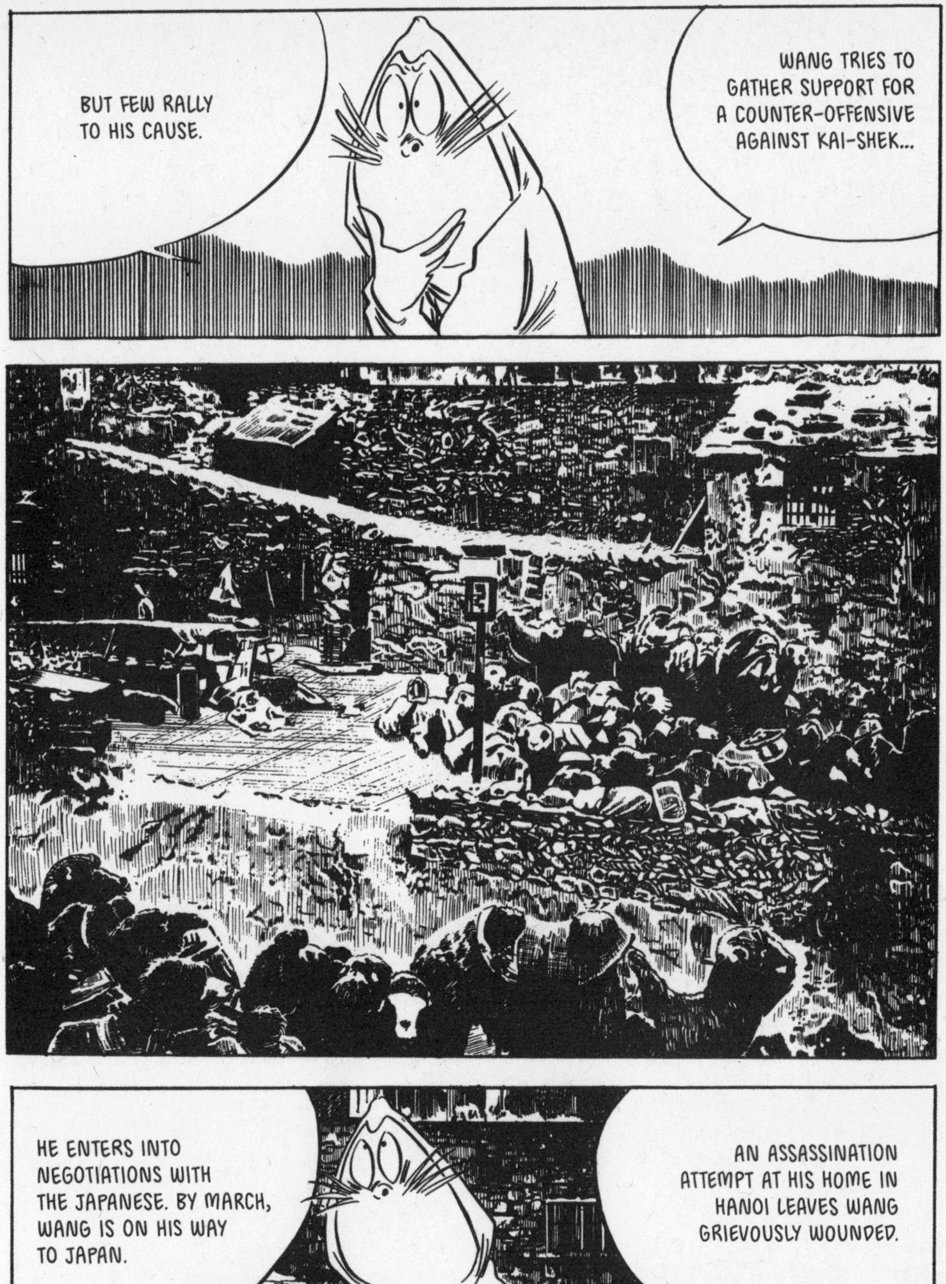
WANG TRIES TO GATHER SUPPORT FOR A COUNTER-OFFENSIVE AGAINST KAI-SHEK...
BUT FEW RALLY TO HIS CAUSE.
AN ASSASSINATION ATTEMPT AT HIS HOME IN HANOI LEAVES WANG GRIEVOUSLY WOUNDED.
HE ENTERS INTO NEGOTIATIONS WITH THE JAPANESE. BY MARCH, WANG IS ON HIS WAY TO JAPAN.

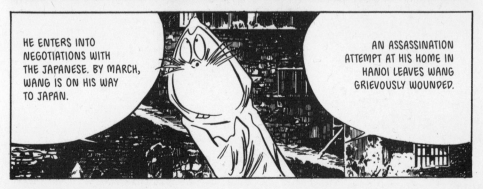

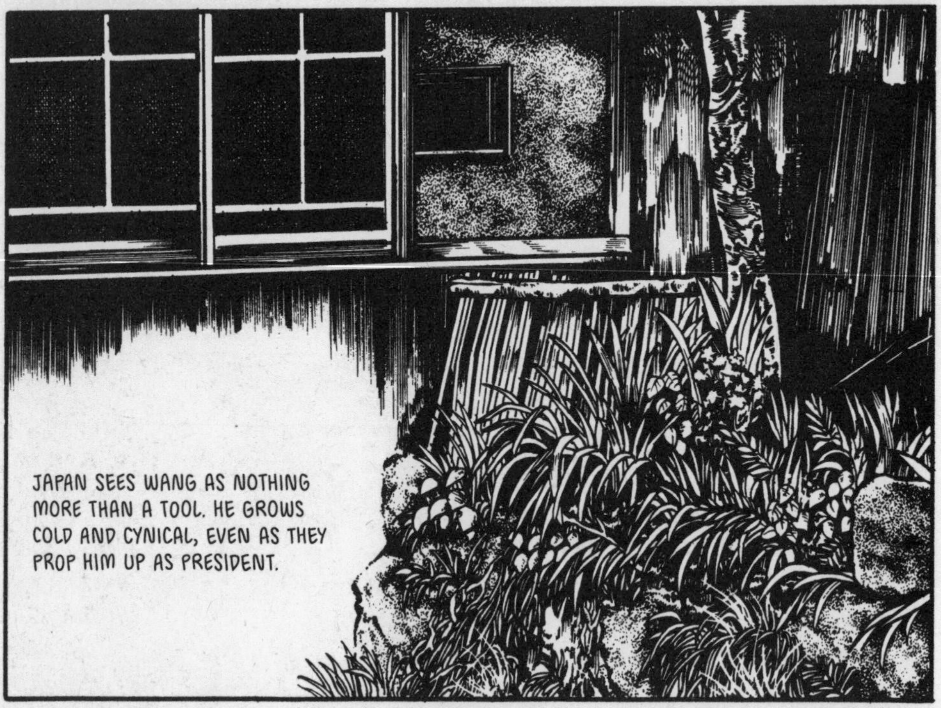
JAPAN SEES WANG AS NOTHING MORE THAN A TOOL. HE GROWS COLD AND CYNICAL, EVEN AS THEY PROP HIM UP AS PRESIDENT.

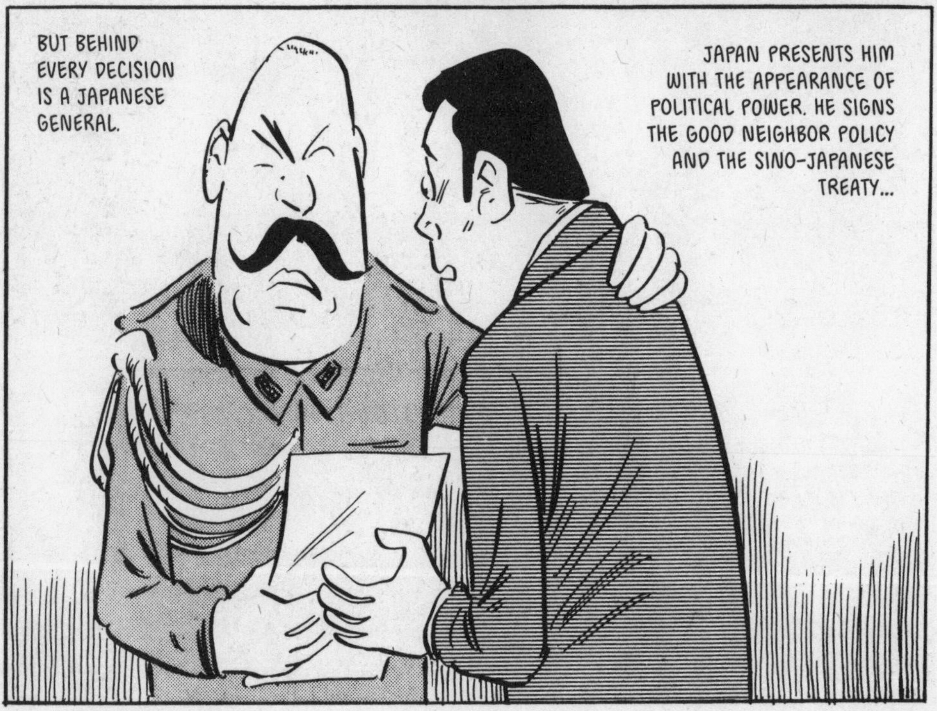
JAPAN PRESENTS HIM WITH THE APPEARANCE OF POLITICAL POWER. HE SIGNS THE GOOD NEIGHBOR POLICY AND THE SINO-JAPANESE TREATY...
BUT BEHIND EVERY DECISION IS A JAPANESE GENERAL.

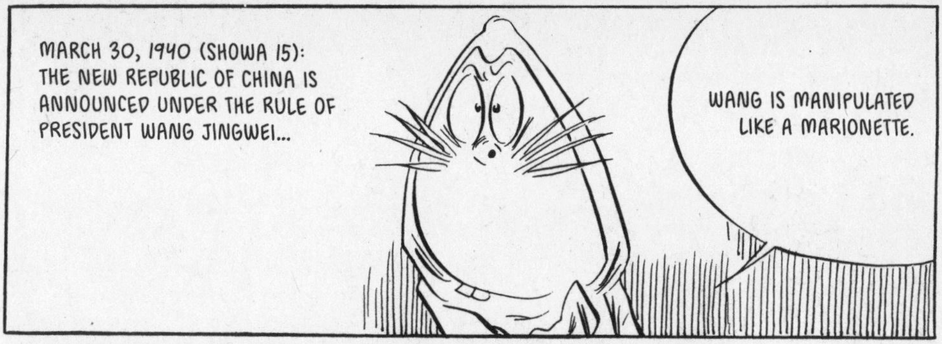
MARCH 30, 1940 (SHOWA 15): THE NEW REPUBLIC OF CHINA IS ANNOUNCED UNDER THE RULE OF PRESIDENT WANG JINGWEI...
WANG IS MANIPULATED LIKE A MARIONETTE.

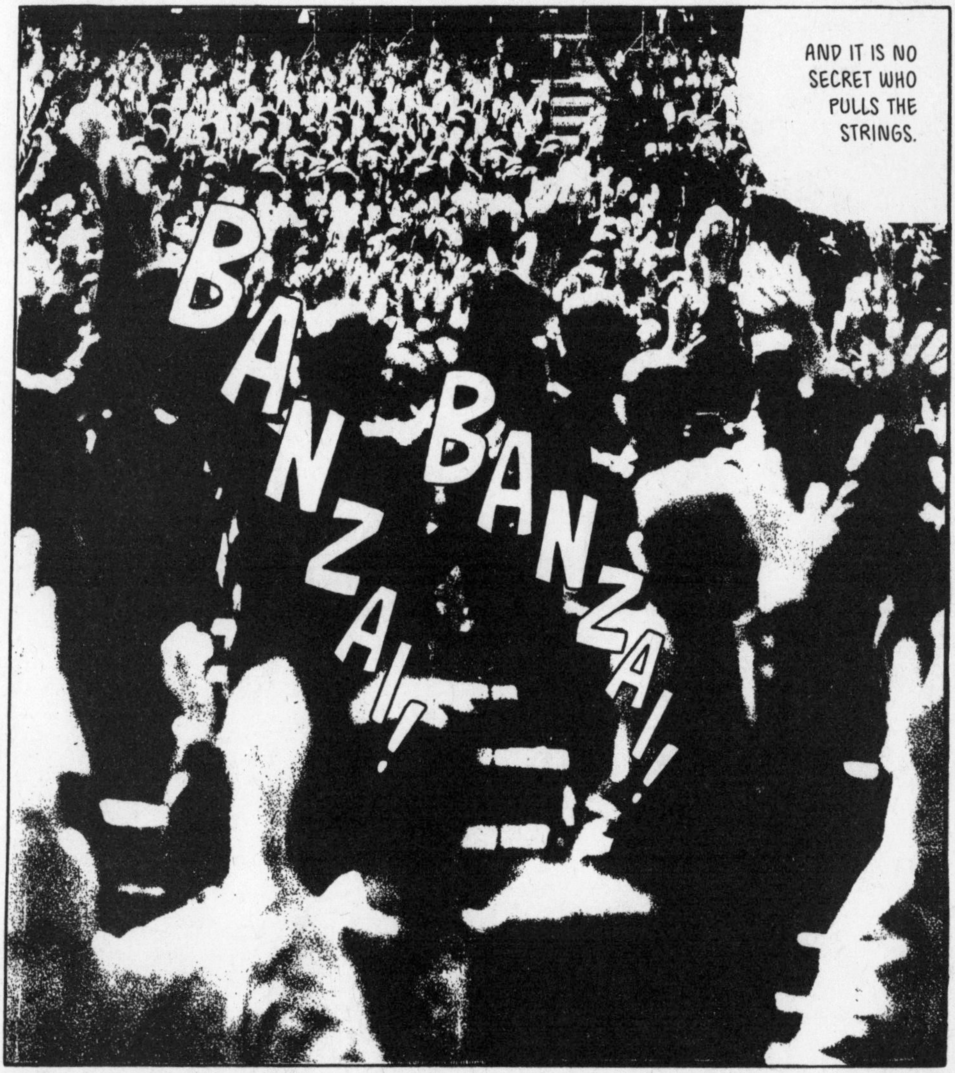
AND IT IS NO SECRET WHO PULLS THE STRINGS.
BANZAI!
BANZAI!

NEWSPAPER DELIVERY BOY

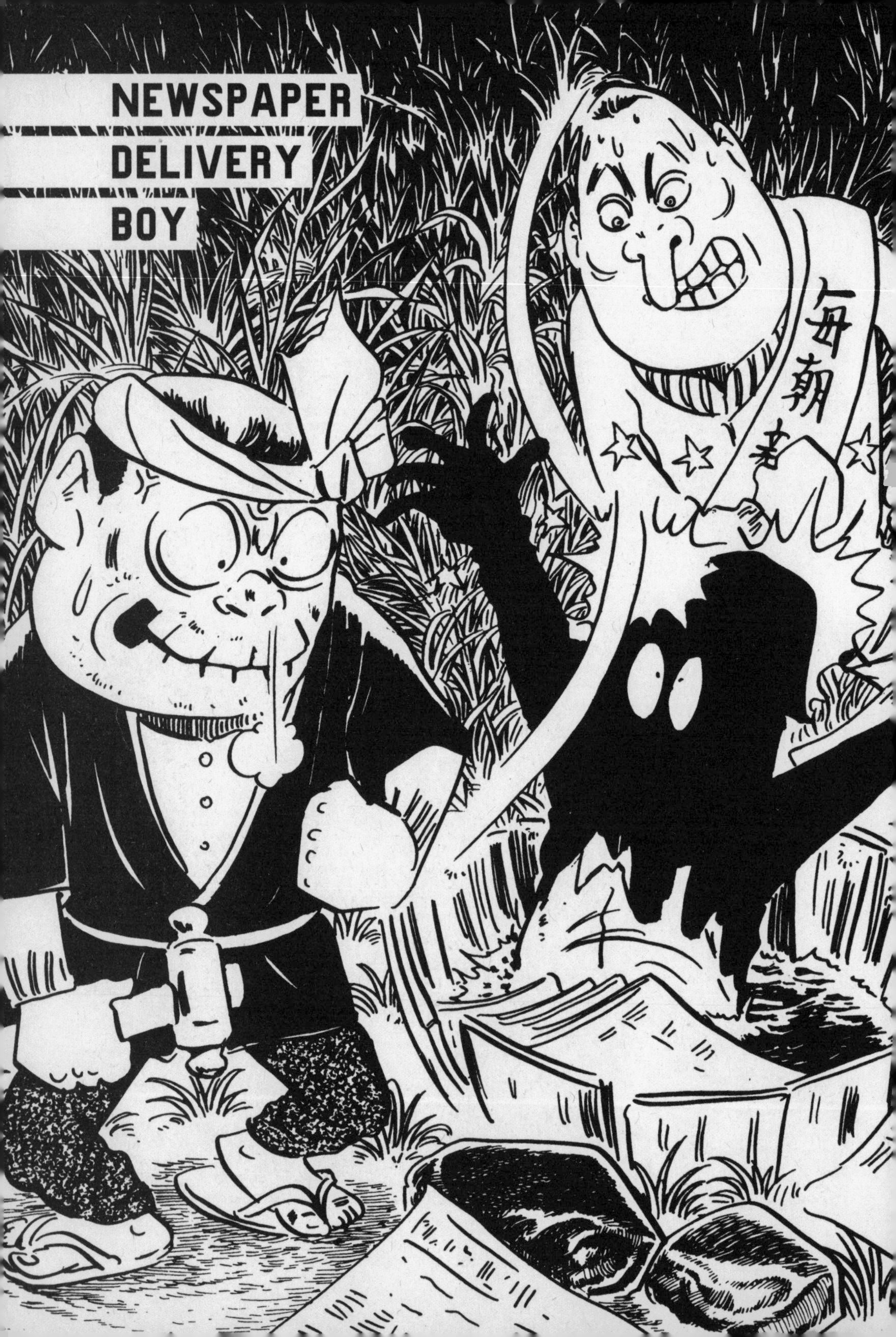

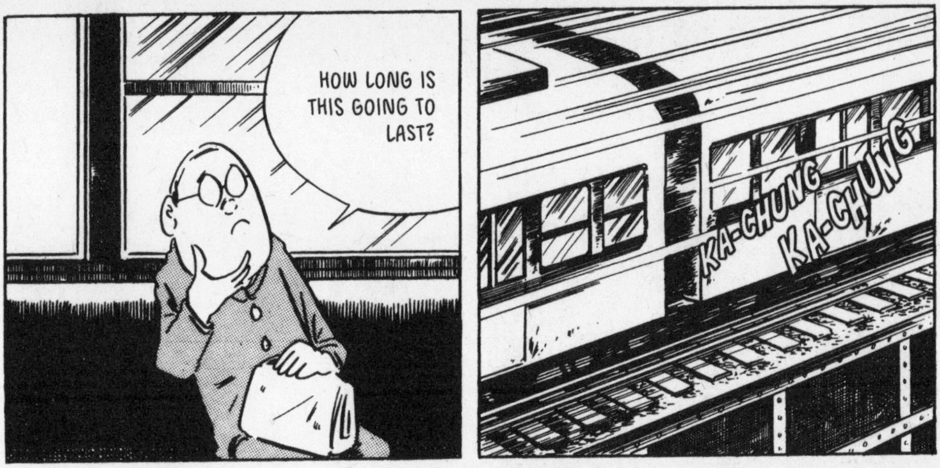
KA-CHUNG
KA-CHUNG
HOW LONG IS THIS GOING TO LAST?

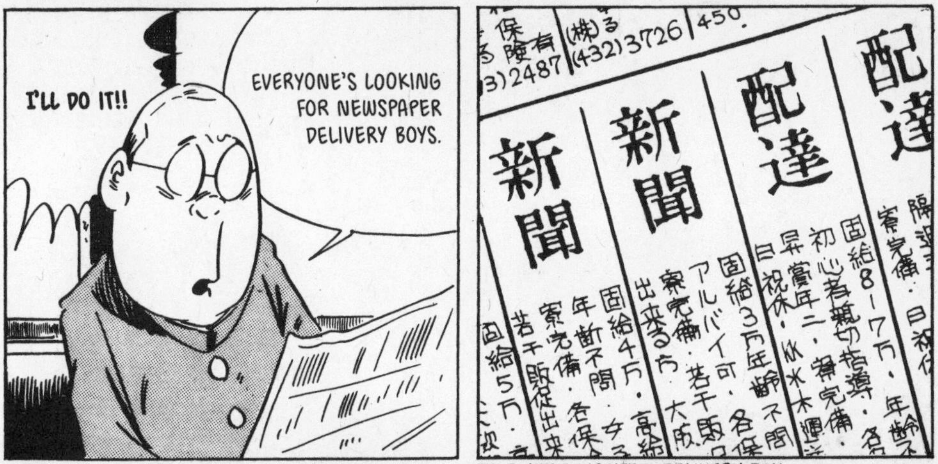
EVERYONE'S LOOKING FOR NEWSPAPER DELIVERY BOYS.
I'LL DO IT!!

TEXT: HELP WANTED—DELIVERY BOY.

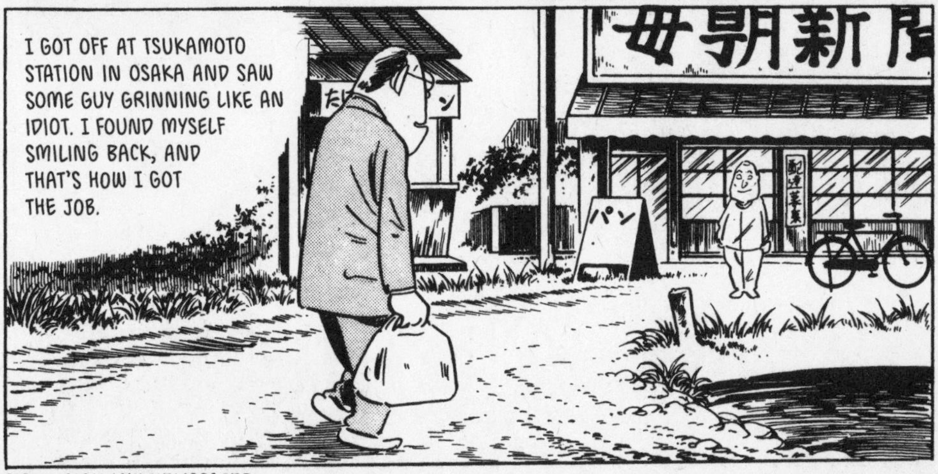
I GOT OFF AT TSUKAMOTO STATION IN OSAKA AND SAW SOME GUY GRINNING LIKE AN IDIOT. I FOUND MYSELF SMILING BACK, AND THAT'S HOW I GOT THE JOB.

SIGN: *MAINICHI* NEWSPAPER.

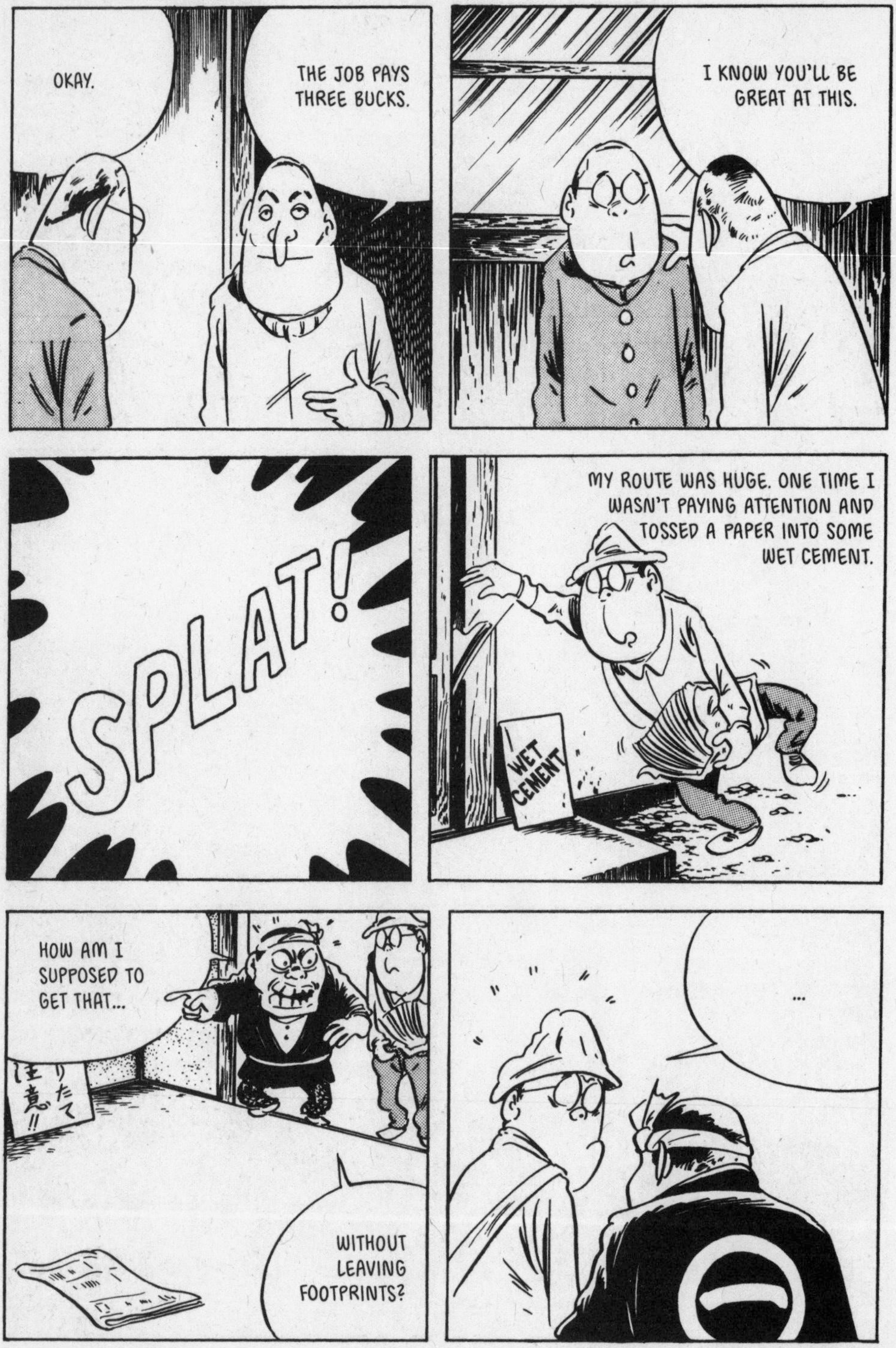
I KNOW YOU'LL BE GREAT AT THIS.
THE JOB PAYS THREE BUCKS.
OKAY.
MY ROUTE WAS HUGE. ONE TIME I WASN'T PAYING ATTENTION AND TOSSED A PAPER INTO SOME WET CEMENT.
WET CEMENT
SPLAT!
...
HOW AM I SUPPOSED TO GET THAT...
WITHOUT LEAVING FOOTPRINTS?

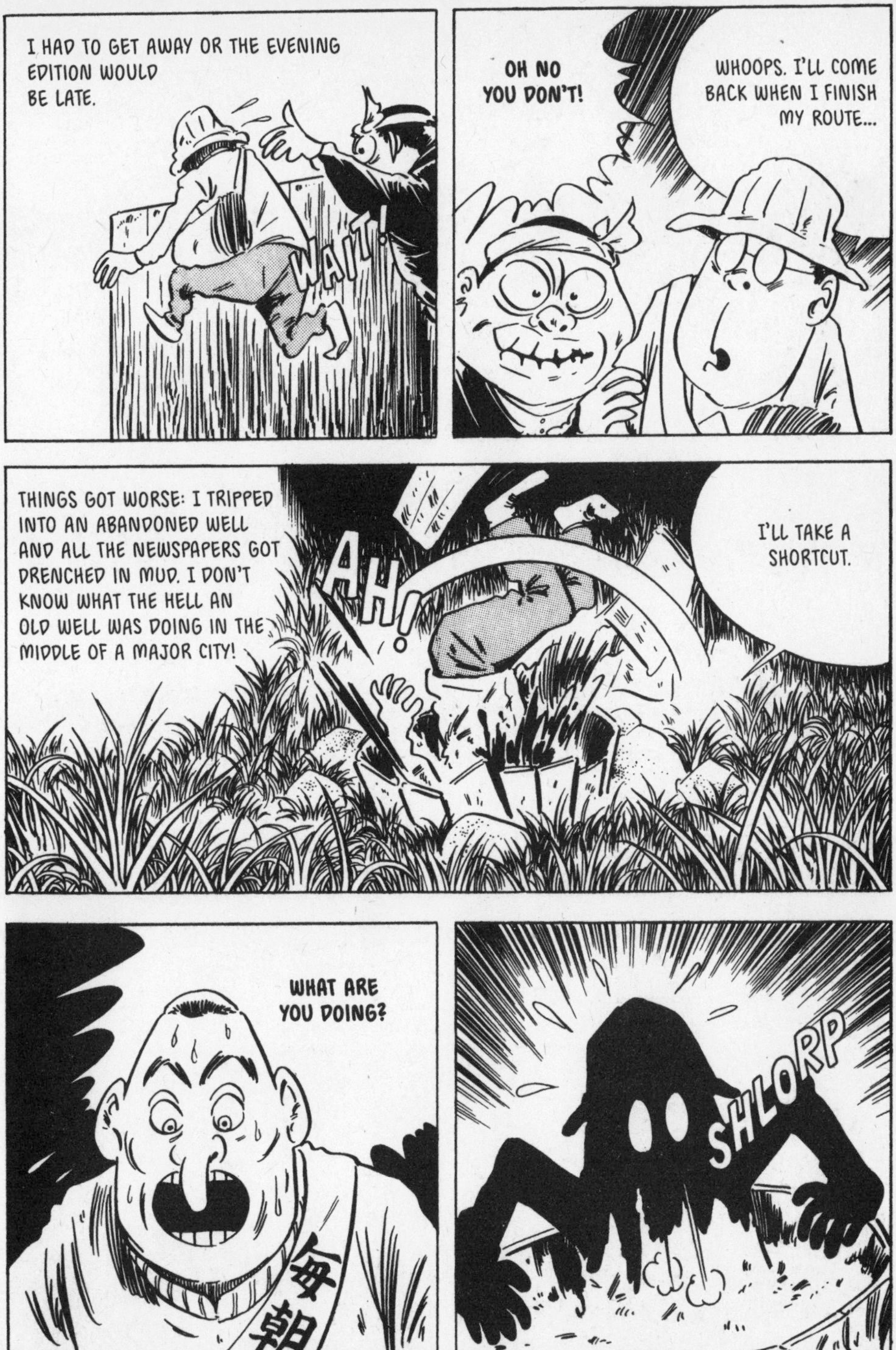
WHOOPS. I'LL COME BACK WHEN I FINISH MY ROUTE...
OH NO YOU DON'T!
I HAD TO GET AWAY OR THE EVENING EDITION WOULD BE LATE.
WAIT!
I'LL TAKE A SHORTCUT.
THINGS GOT WORSE: I TRIPPED INTO AN ABANDONED WELL AND ALL THE NEWSPAPERS GOT DRENCHED IN MUD. I DON'T KNOW WHAT THE HELL AN OLD WELL WAS DOING IN THE MIDDLE OF A MAJOR CITY!
AH!
SHLORP
WHAT ARE YOU DOING?
毎朝

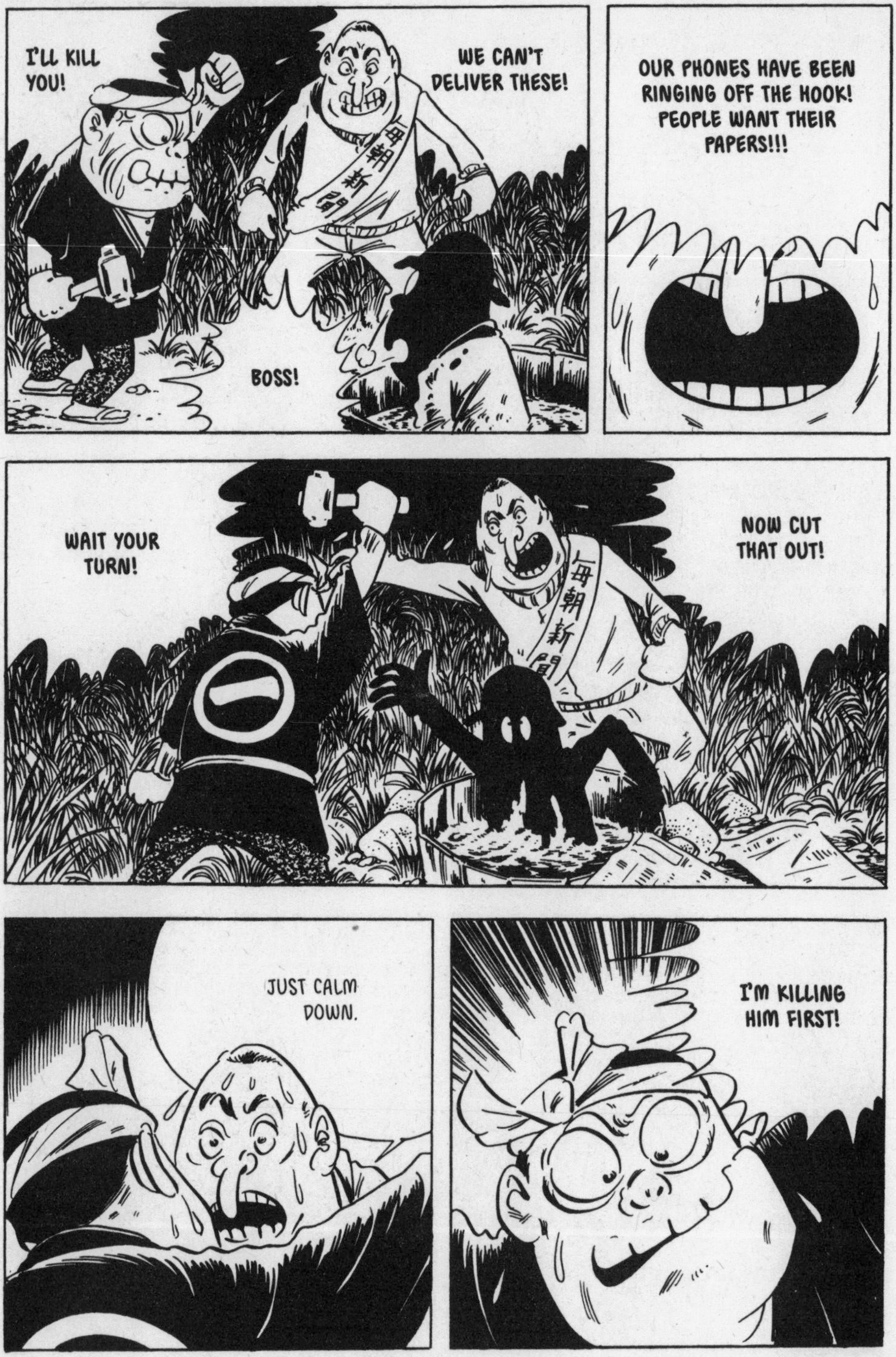
OUR PHONES HAVE BEEN RINGING OFF THE HOOK! PEOPLE WANT THEIR PAPERS!!!
WE CAN'T DELIVER THESE!
毎朝新聞
I'LL KILL YOU!
BOSS!
NOW CUT THAT OUT!
毎朝新聞
WAIT YOUR TURN!
I'M KILLING HIM FIRST!
JUST CALM DOWN.

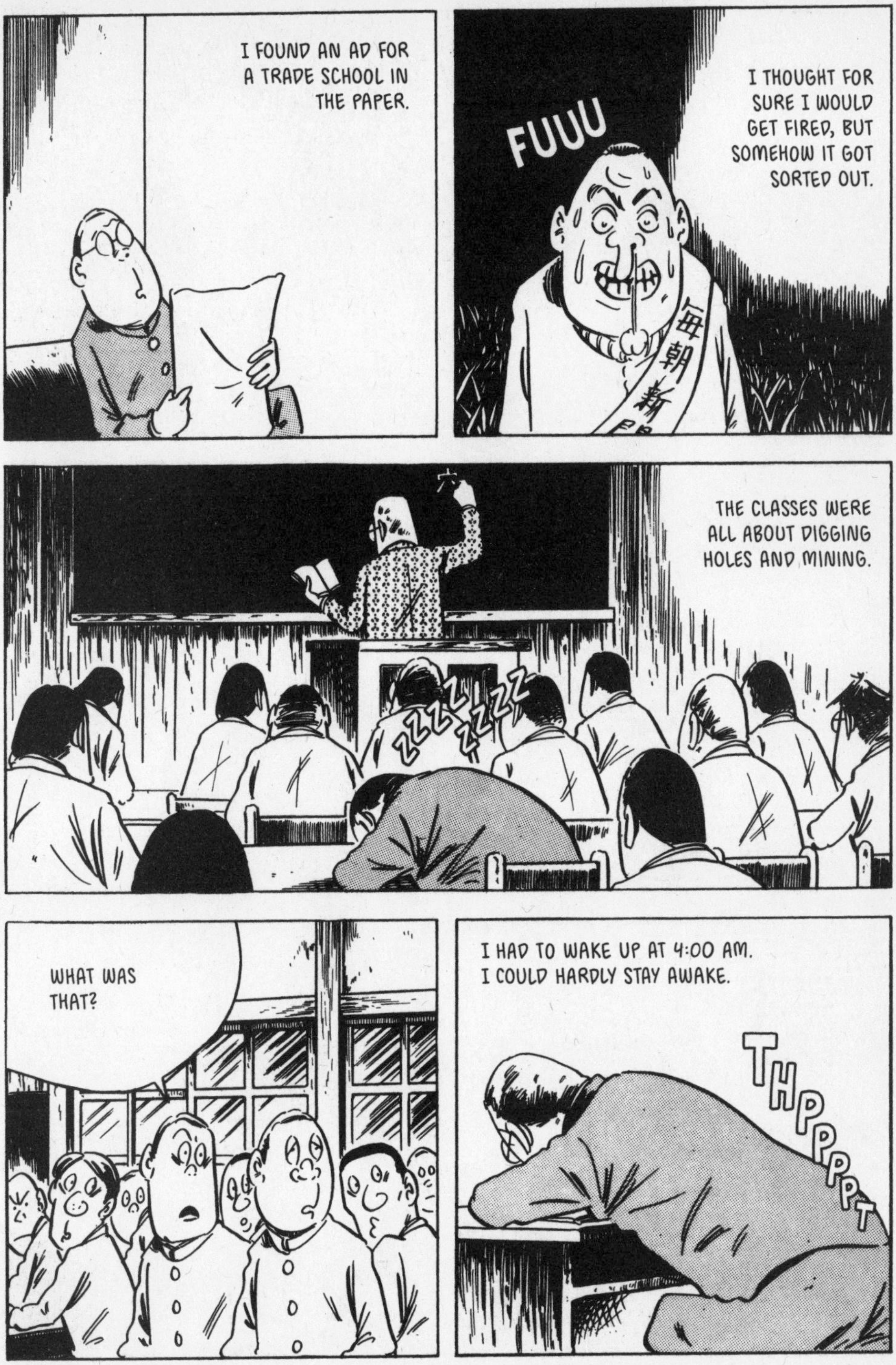
I THOUGHT FOR SURE I WOULD GET FIRED, BUT SOMEHOW IT GOT SORTED OUT.
FUUU
毎朝新
I FOUND AN AD FOR A TRADE SCHOOL IN THE PAPER.
THE CLASSES WERE ALL ABOUT DIGGING HOLES AND MINING.
I HAD TO WAKE UP AT 4:00 AM. I COULD HARDLY STAY AWAKE.
THPPPPT
WHAT WAS THAT?

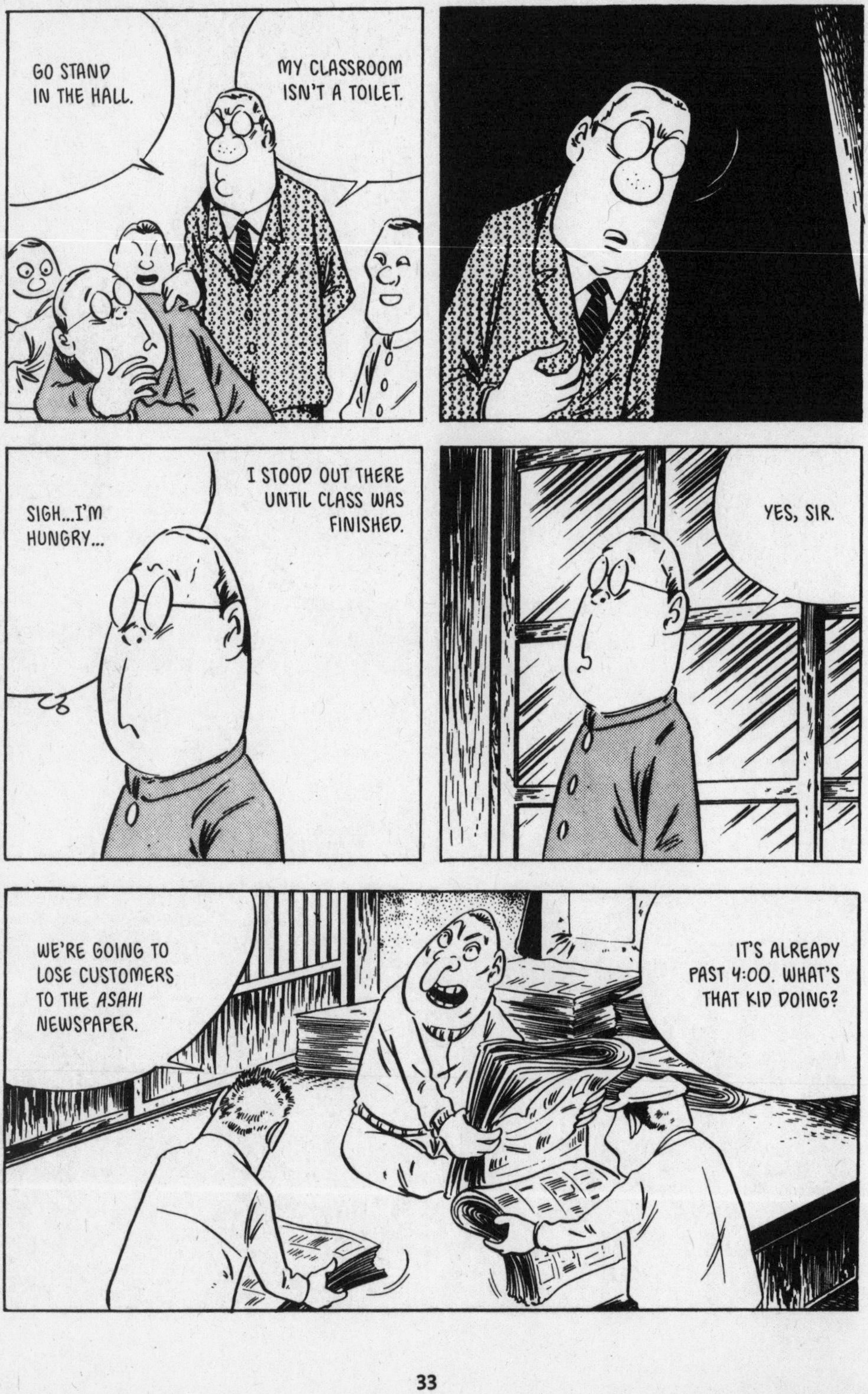
MY CLASSROOM ISN'T A TOILET.
GO STAND IN THE HALL.
YES, SIR.
I STOOD OUT THERE UNTIL CLASS WAS FINISHED.
SIGH...I'M HUNGRY...
IT'S ALREADY PAST 4:00. WHAT'S THAT KID DOING?
WE'RE GOING TO LOSE CUSTOMERS TO THE *ASAHI* NEWSPAPER.

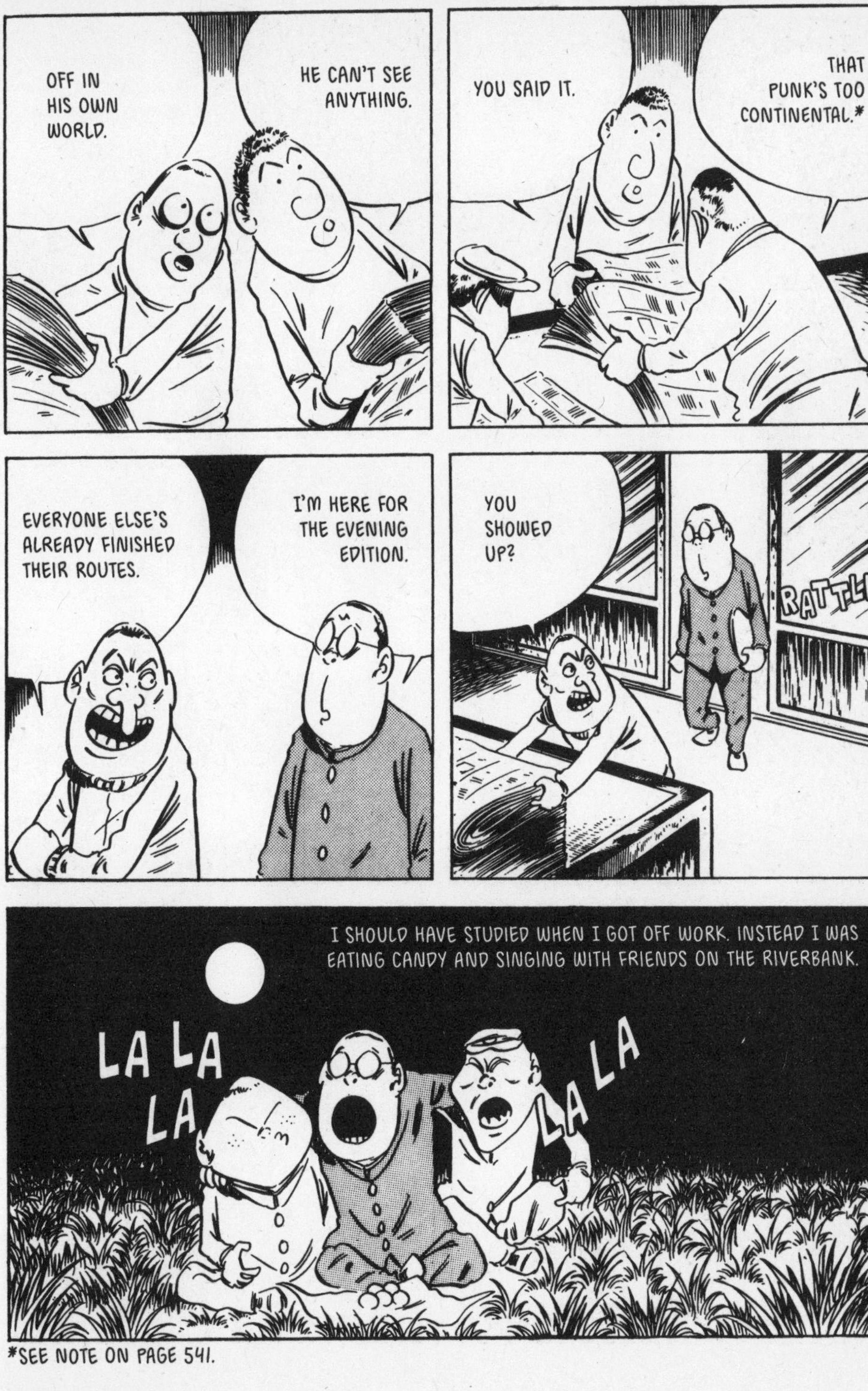
THAT PUNK'S TOO CONTINENTAL.*
YOU SAID IT.
HE CAN'T SEE ANYTHING.
OFF IN HIS OWN WORLD.
YOU SHOWED UP?
RATTLE
I'M HERE FOR THE EVENING EDITION.
EVERYONE ELSE'S ALREADY FINISHED THEIR ROUTES.
I SHOULD HAVE STUDIED WHEN I GOT OFF WORK. INSTEAD I WAS EATING CANDY AND SINGING WITH FRIENDS ON THE RIVERBANK.
LA LA
LA LA
LA LA

*SEE NOTE ON PAGE 541.

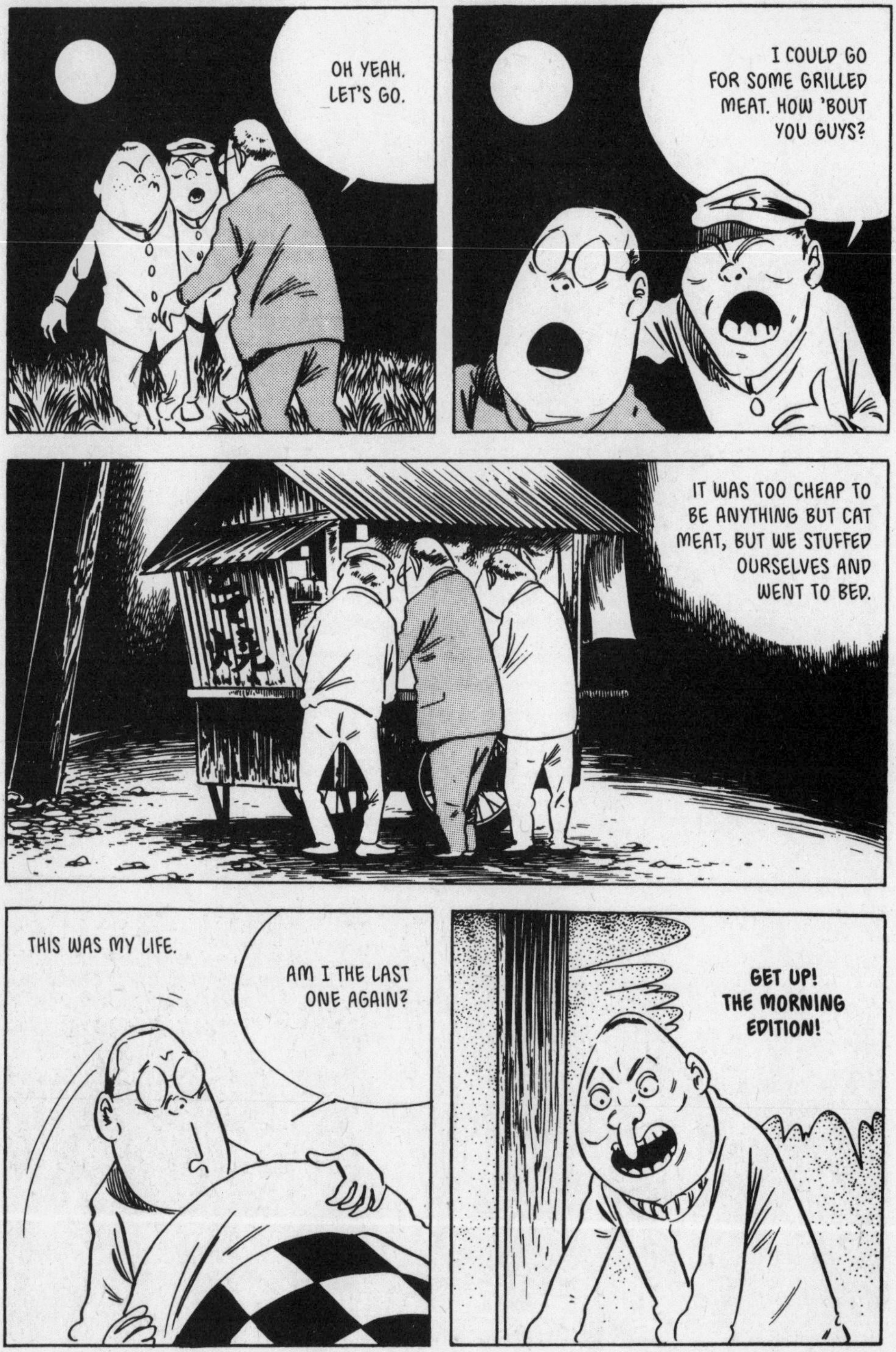
I COULD GO FOR SOME GRILLED MEAT. HOW 'BOUT YOU GUYS?
OH YEAH. LET'S GO.
IT WAS TOO CHEAP TO BE ANYTHING BUT CAT MEAT, BUT WE STUFFED OURSELVES AND WENT TO BED.
GET UP! THE MORNING EDITION!
THIS WAS MY LIFE.
AM I THE LAST ONE AGAIN?

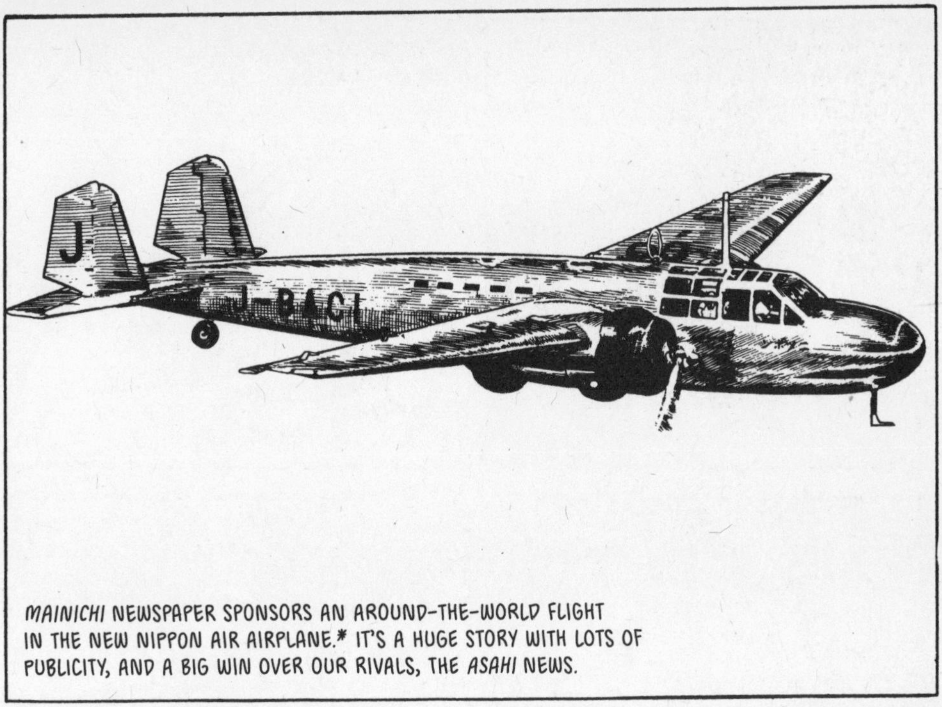
J
J-BACI
MAINICHI NEWSPAPER SPONSORS AN AROUND-THE-WORLD FLIGHT IN THE NEW NIPPON AIR AIRPLANE.* IT'S A HUGE STORY WITH LOTS OF PUBLICITY, AND A BIG WIN OVER OUR RIVALS, THE *ASAHI* NEWS.

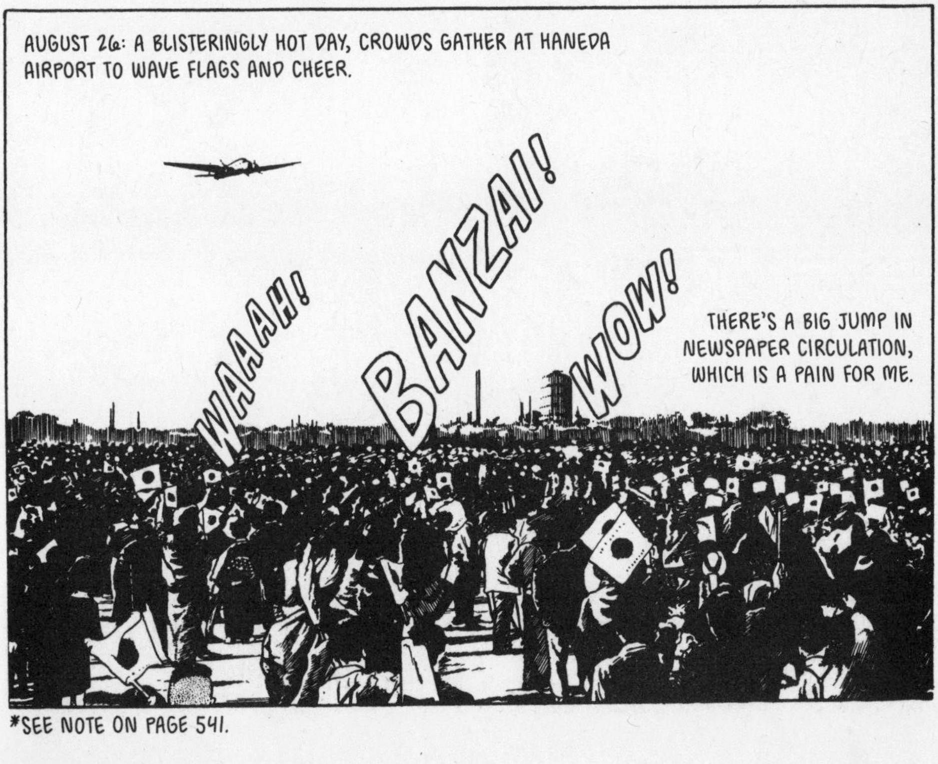
AUGUST 26: A BLISTERINGLY HOT DAY, CROWDS GATHER AT HANEDA AIRPORT TO WAVE FLAGS AND CHEER.
THERE'S A BIG JUMP IN NEWSPAPER CIRCULATION, WHICH IS A PAIN FOR ME.
WOW!
BANZAI!
WAAAH!

*SEE NOTE ON PAGE 541.

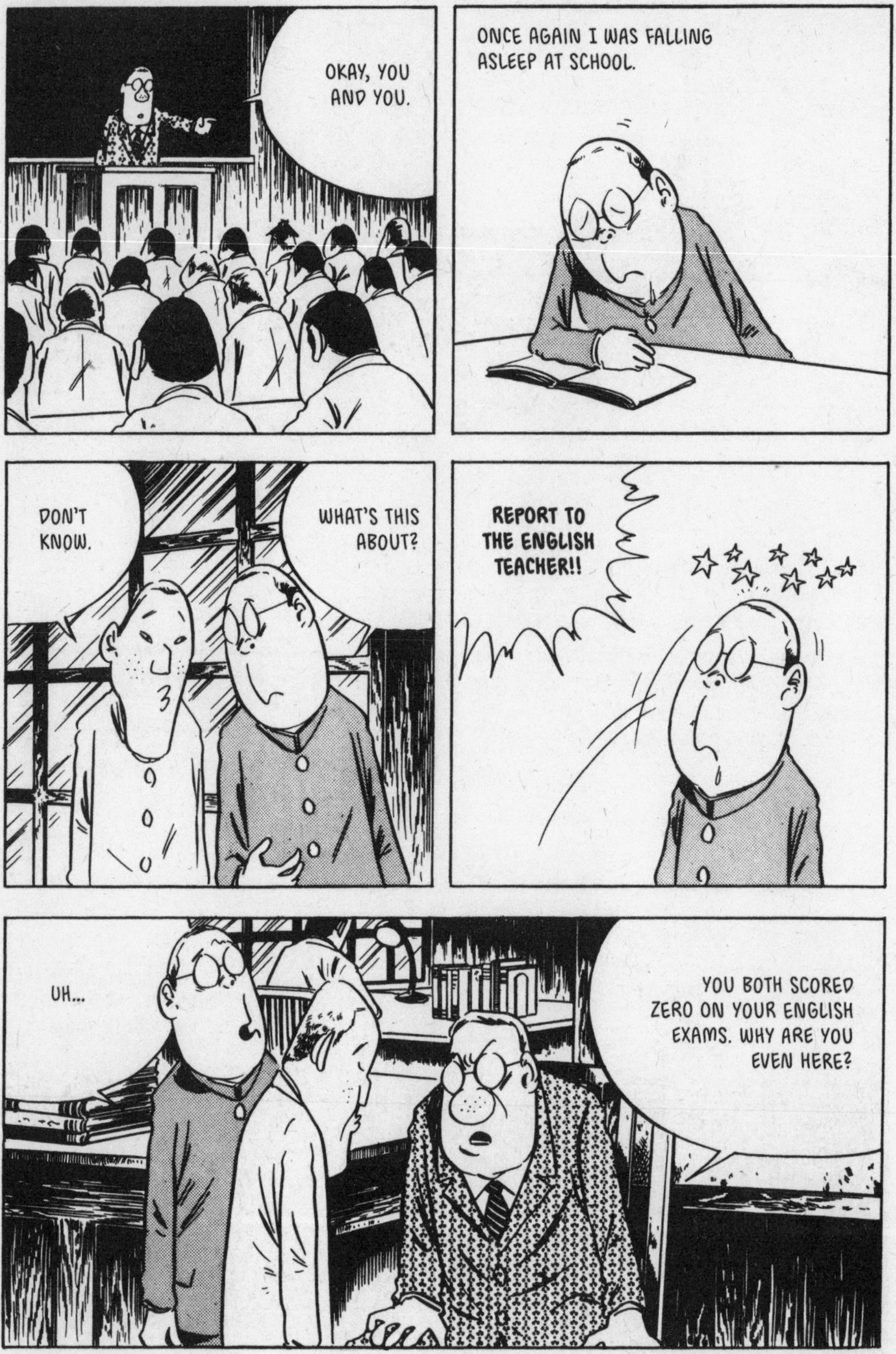
ONCE AGAIN I WAS FALLING ASLEEP AT SCHOOL.
OKAY, YOU AND YOU.
REPORT TO THE ENGLISH TEACHER!!
WHAT'S THIS ABOUT?
DON'T KNOW.
YOU BOTH SCORED ZERO ON YOUR ENGLISH EXAMS. WHY ARE YOU EVEN HERE?
UH...

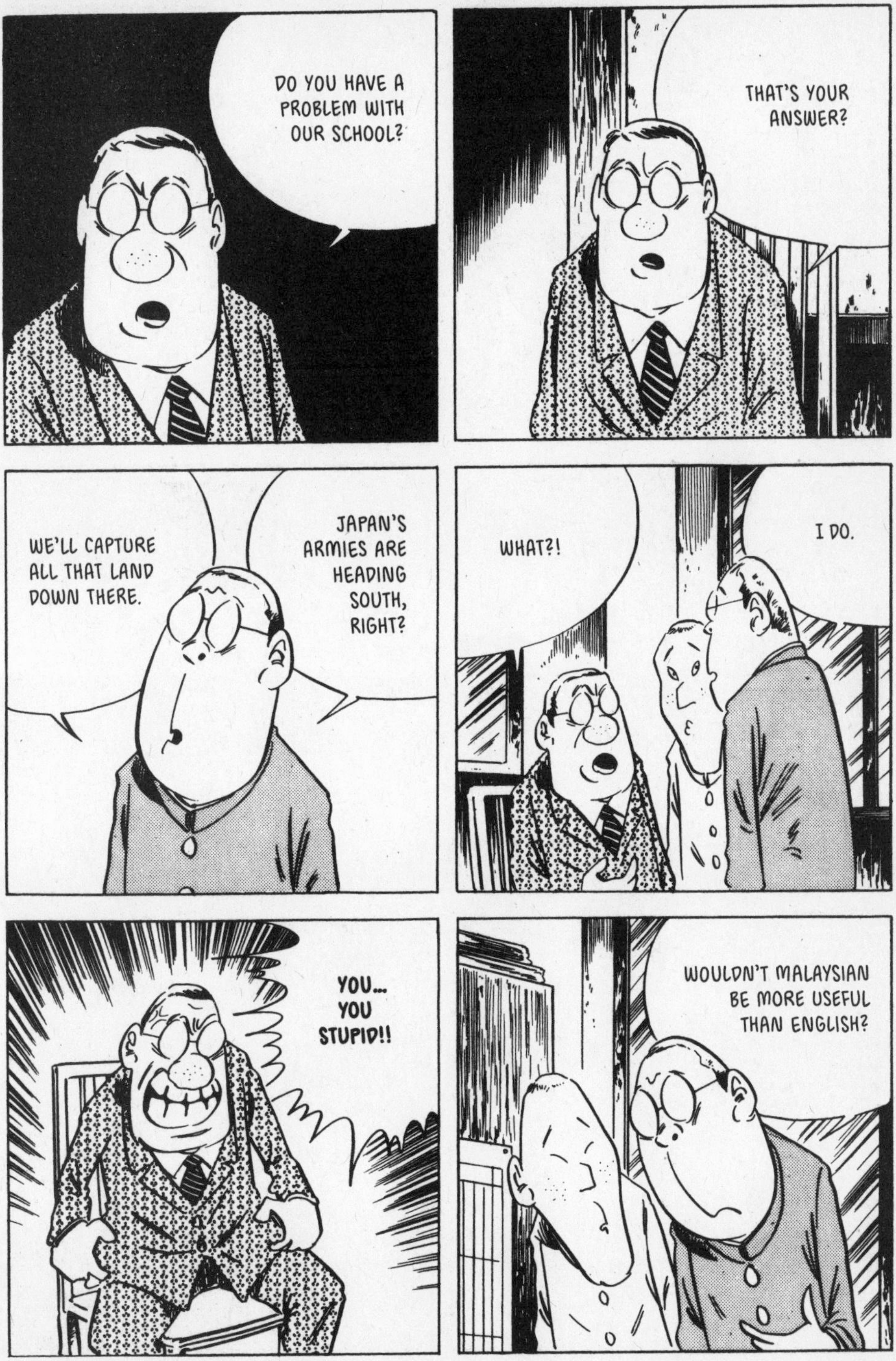
THAT'S YOUR ANSWER?
DO YOU HAVE A PROBLEM WITH OUR SCHOOL?
I DO.
WHAT?!
JAPAN'S ARMIES ARE HEADING SOUTH, RIGHT?
WE'LL CAPTURE ALL THAT LAND DOWN THERE.
WOULDN'T MALAYSIAN BE MORE USEFUL THAN ENGLISH?
YOU... YOU STUPID!!

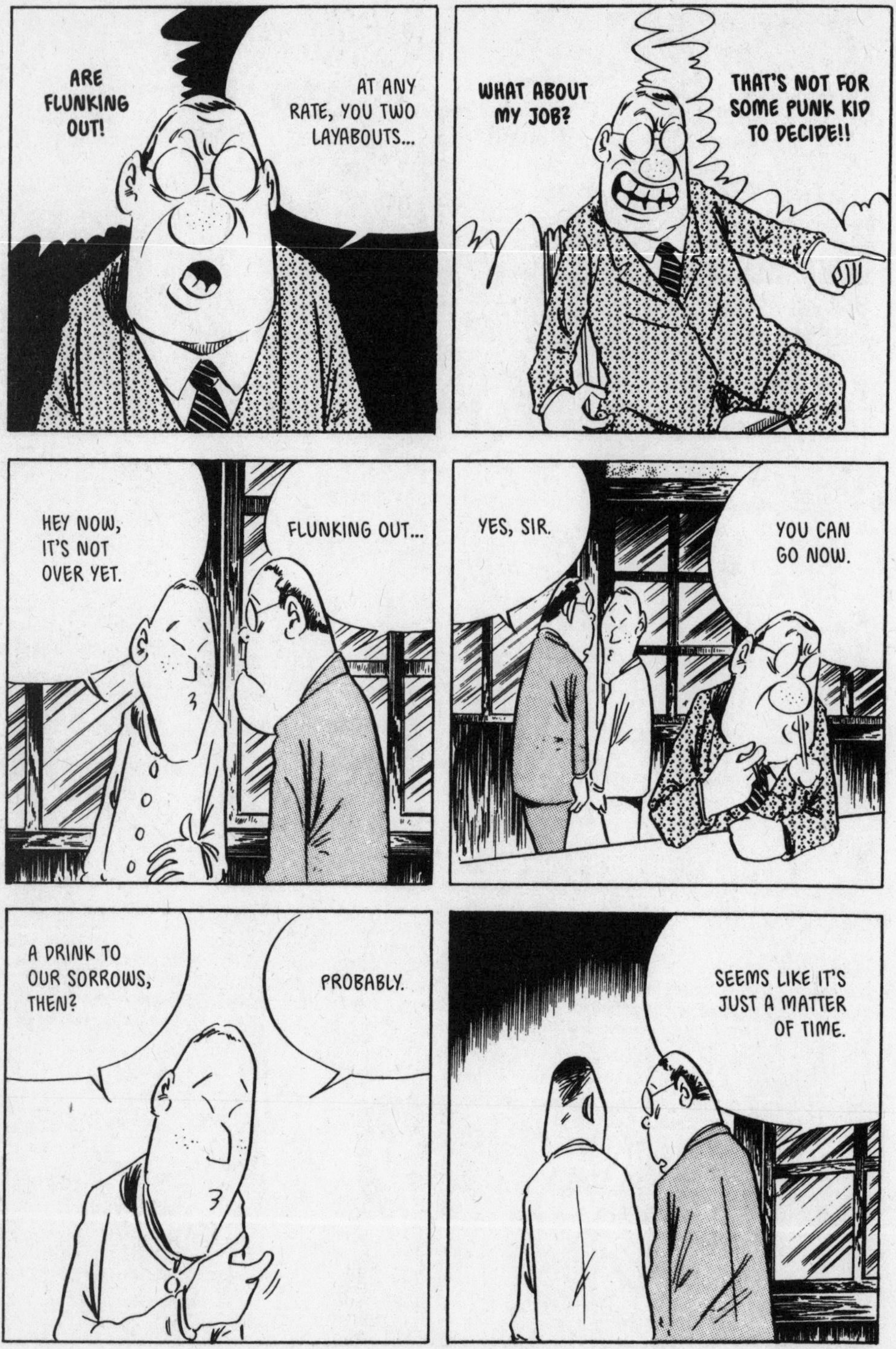
THAT'S NOT FOR SOME PUNK KID TO DECIDE!!
WHAT ABOUT MY JOB?
AT ANY RATE, YOU TWO LAYABOUTS...
ARE FLUNKING OUT!
YOU CAN GO NOW.
YES, SIR.
FLUNKING OUT...
HEY NOW, IT'S NOT OVER YET.
SEEMS LIKE IT'S JUST A MATTER OF TIME.
PROBABLY.
A DRINK TO OUR SORROWS, THEN?

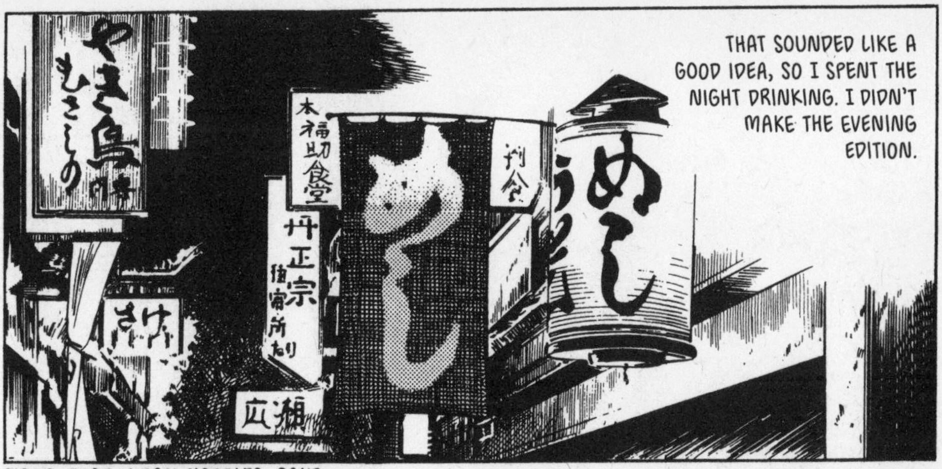
THAT SOUNDED LIKE A GOOD IDEA, SO I SPENT THE NIGHT DRINKING. I DIDN'T MAKE THE EVENING EDITION.

SIGNS: FOOD; UDON NOODLES; SAKE.

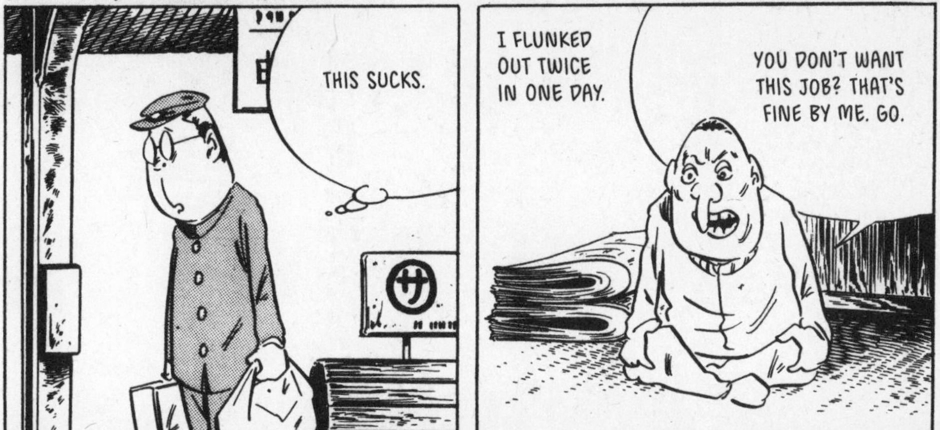
YOU DON'T WANT THIS JOB? THAT'S FINE BY ME. GO.
I FLUNKED OUT TWICE IN ONE DAY.
THIS SUCKS.

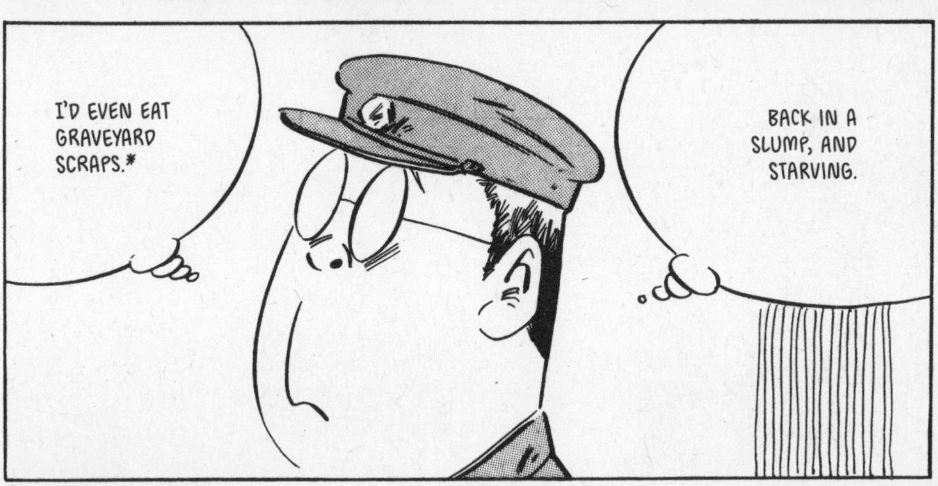
BACK IN A SLUMP, AND STARVING.
I'D EVEN EAT GRAVEYARD SCRAPS.*

*SEE NOTE ON PAGE 541.

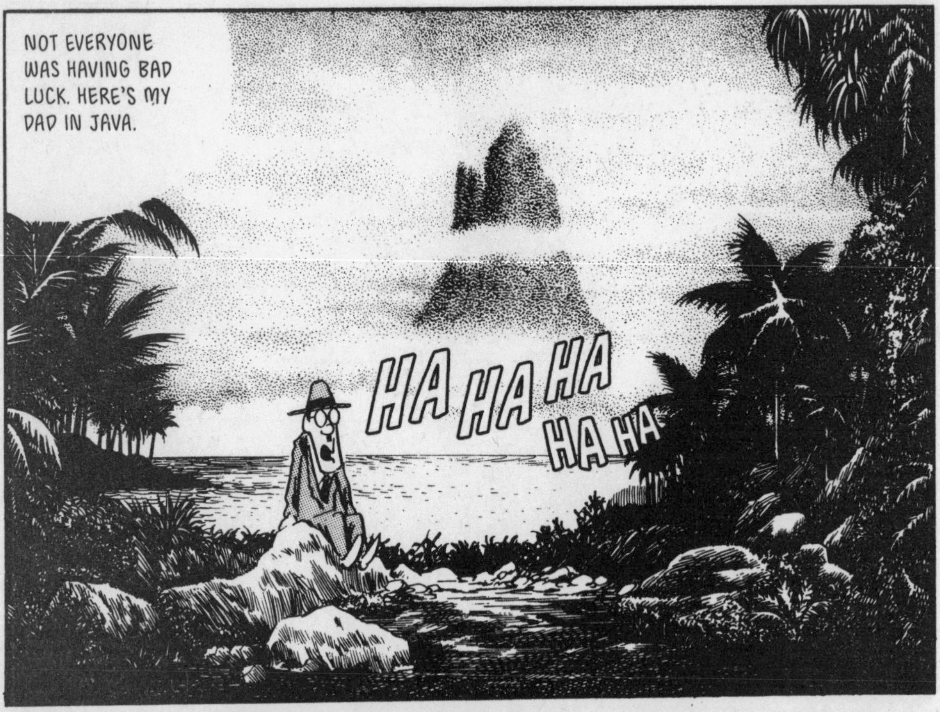
NOT EVERYONE WAS HAVING BAD LUCK. HERE'S MY DAD IN JAVA.
HA HA HA HA HA

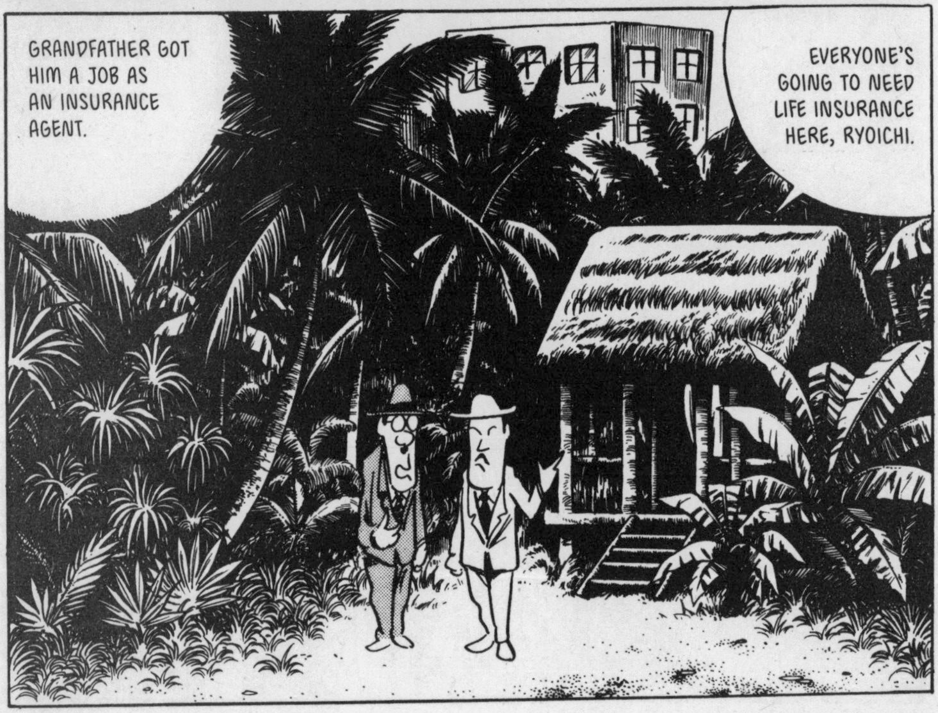
EVERYONE'S GOING TO NEED LIFE INSURANCE HERE, RYOICHI.
GRANDFATHER GOT HIM A JOB AS AN INSURANCE AGENT.

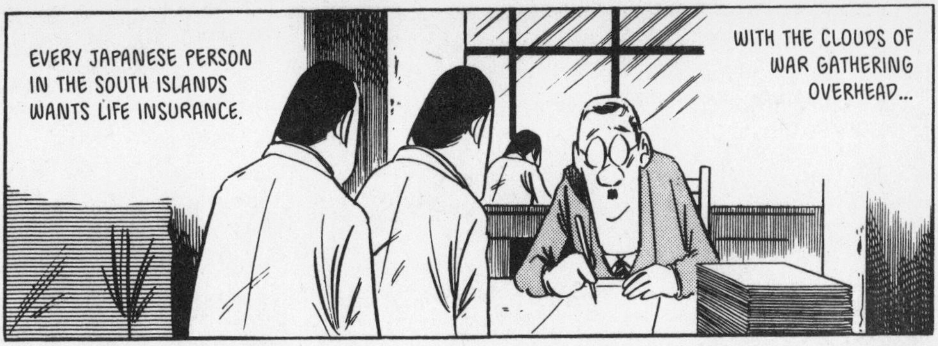
WITH THE CLOUDS OF WAR GATHERING OVERHEAD...
EVERY JAPANESE PERSON IN THE SOUTH ISLANDS WANTS LIFE INSURANCE.

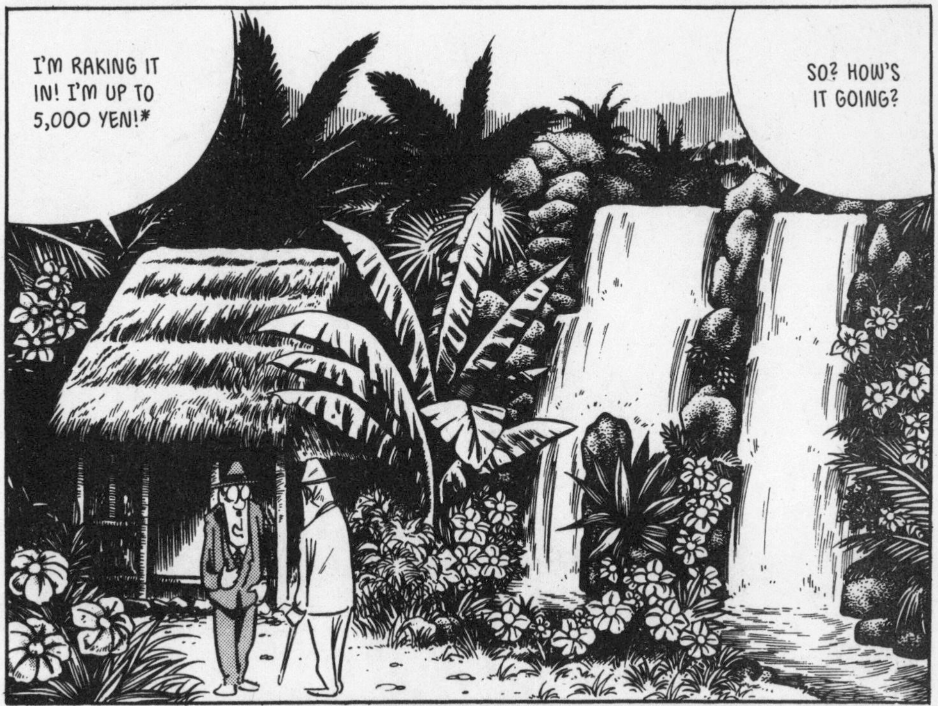
SO? HOW'S IT GOING?
I'M RAKING IT IN! I'M UP TO 5,000 YEN!*

*ABOUT 100,000 YEN ($1,270 WHEN ADJUSTED FOR INFLATION.)

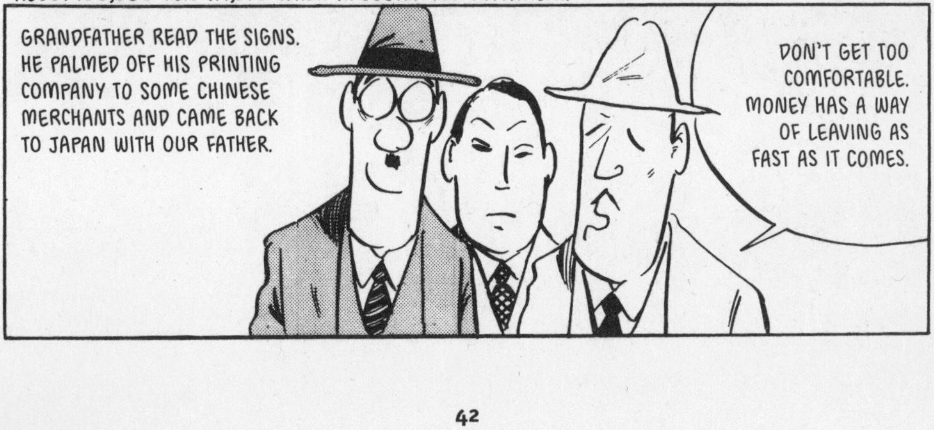
DON'T GET TOO COMFORTABLE. MONEY HAS A WAY OF LEAVING AS FAST AS IT COMES.
GRANDFATHER READ THE SIGNS. HE PALMED OFF HIS PRINTING COMPANY TO SOME CHINESE MERCHANTS AND CAME BACK TO JAPAN WITH OUR FATHER.

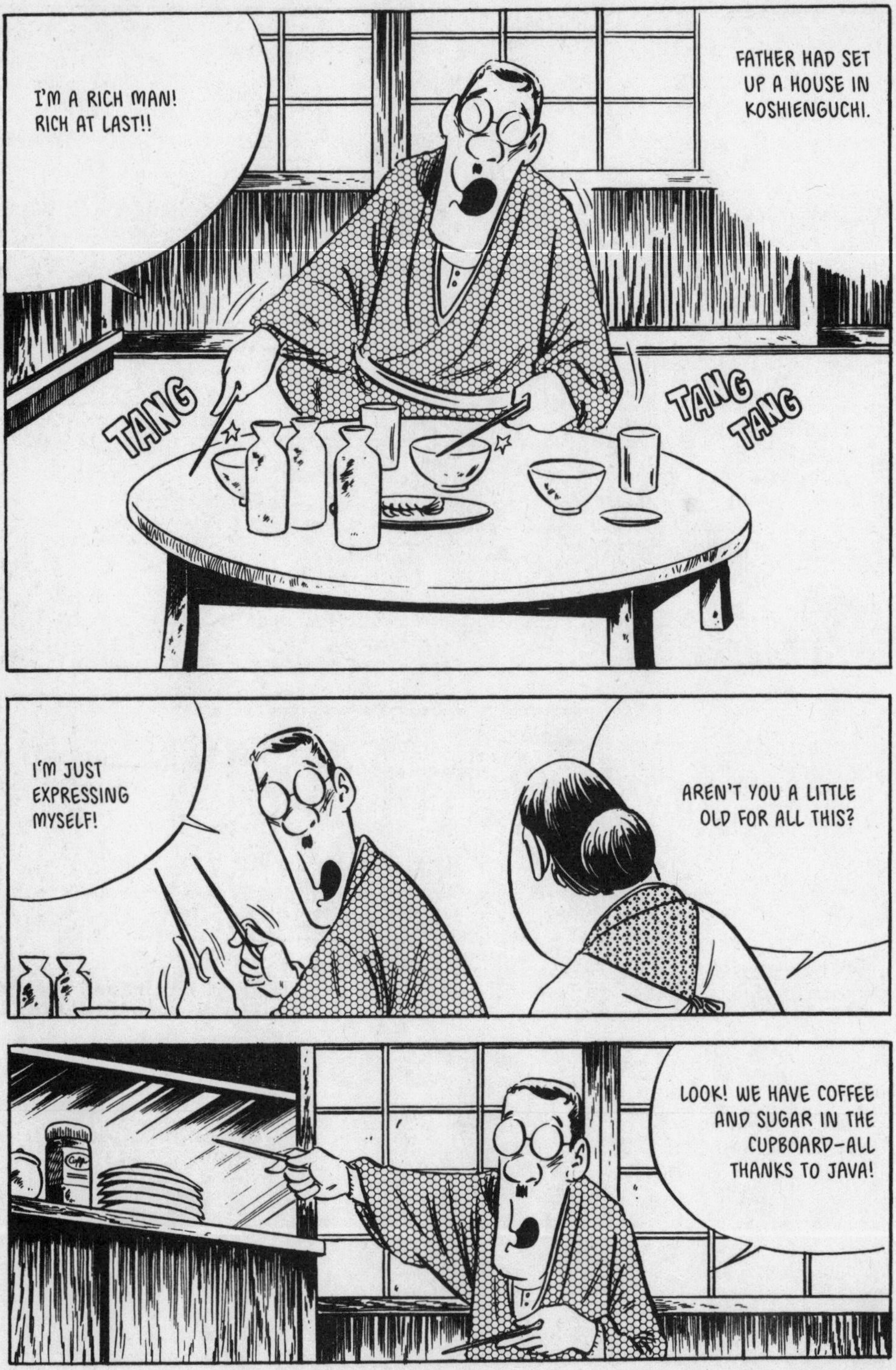
FATHER HAD SET UP A HOUSE IN KOSHIENGUCHI.
I'M A RICH MAN! RICH AT LAST!!
TANG TANG
TANG
AREN'T YOU A LITTLE OLD FOR ALL THIS?
I'M JUST EXPRESSING MYSELF!
LOOK! WE HAVE COFFEE AND SUGAR IN THE CUPBOARD—ALL THANKS TO JAVA!

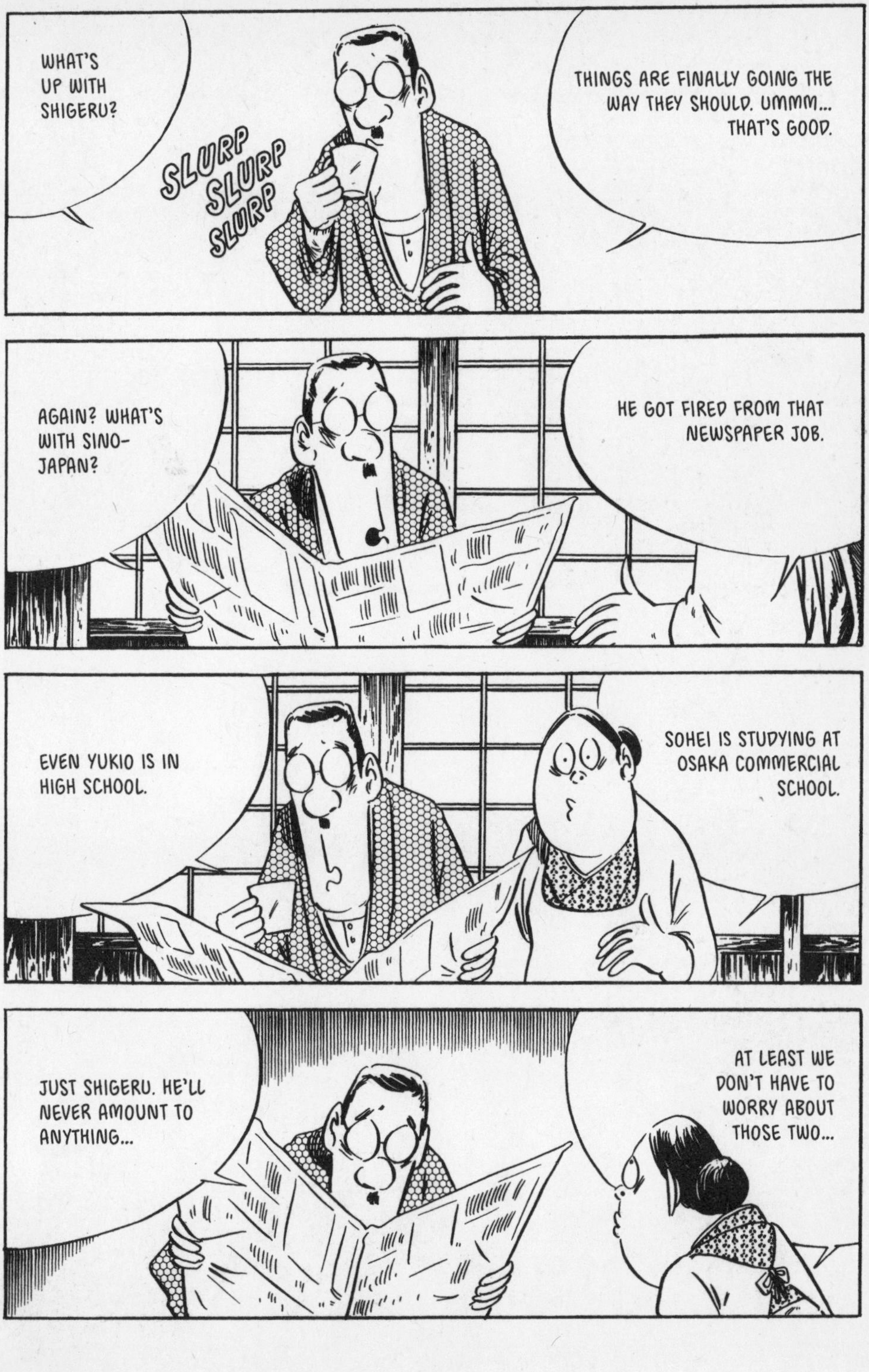
THINGS ARE FINALLY GOING THE WAY THEY SHOULD. UMMM... THAT'S GOOD.
WHAT'S UP WITH SHIGERU?
SLURP SLURP SLURP
HE GOT FIRED FROM THAT NEWSPAPER JOB.
AGAIN? WHAT'S WITH SINO-JAPAN?
SOHEI IS STUDYING AT OSAKA COMMERCIAL SCHOOL.
EVEN YUKIO IS IN HIGH SCHOOL.
AT LEAST WE DON'T HAVE TO WORRY ABOUT THOSE TWO...
JUST SHIGERU. HE'LL NEVER AMOUNT TO ANYTHING...

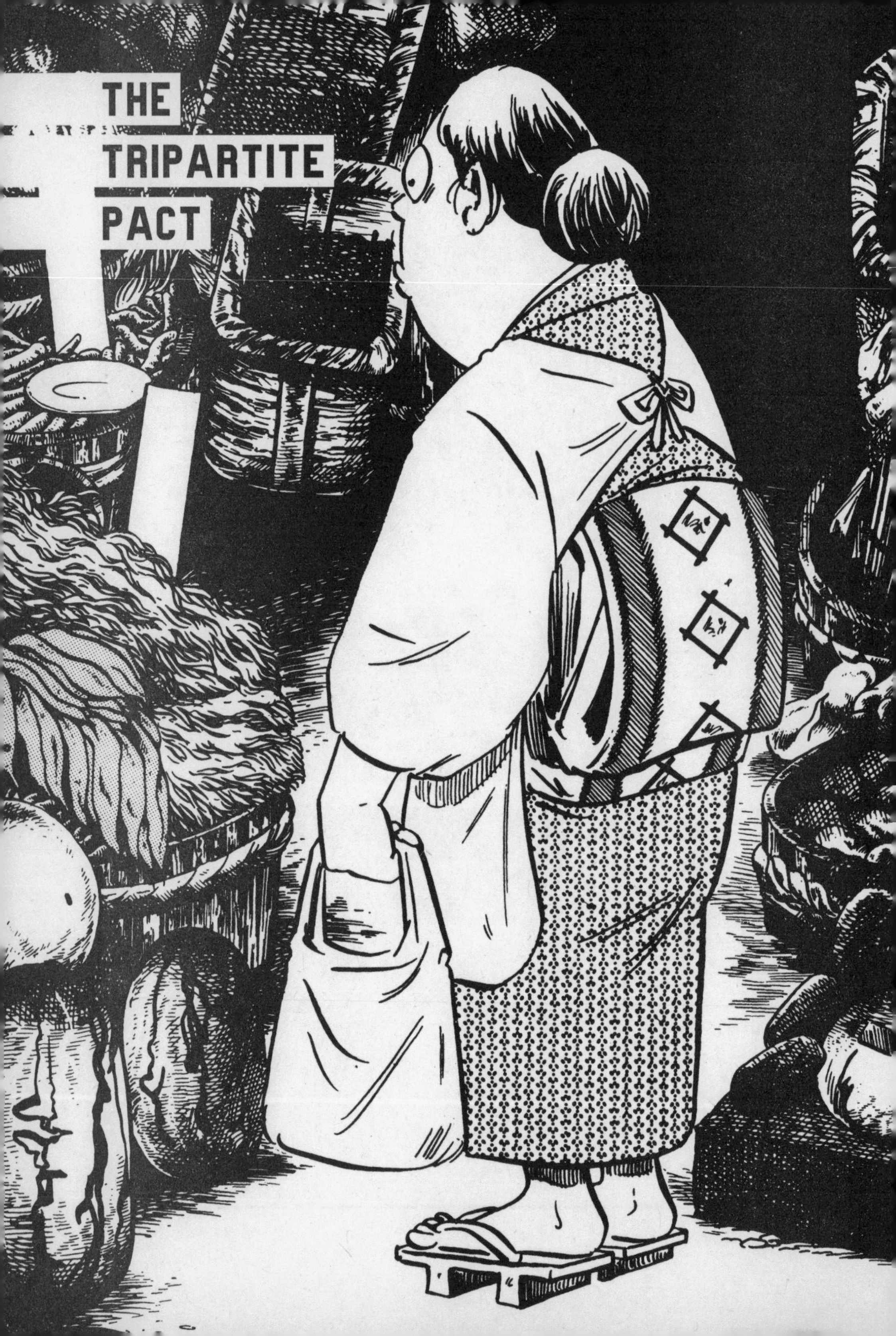
THE
TRIPARTITE
PACT

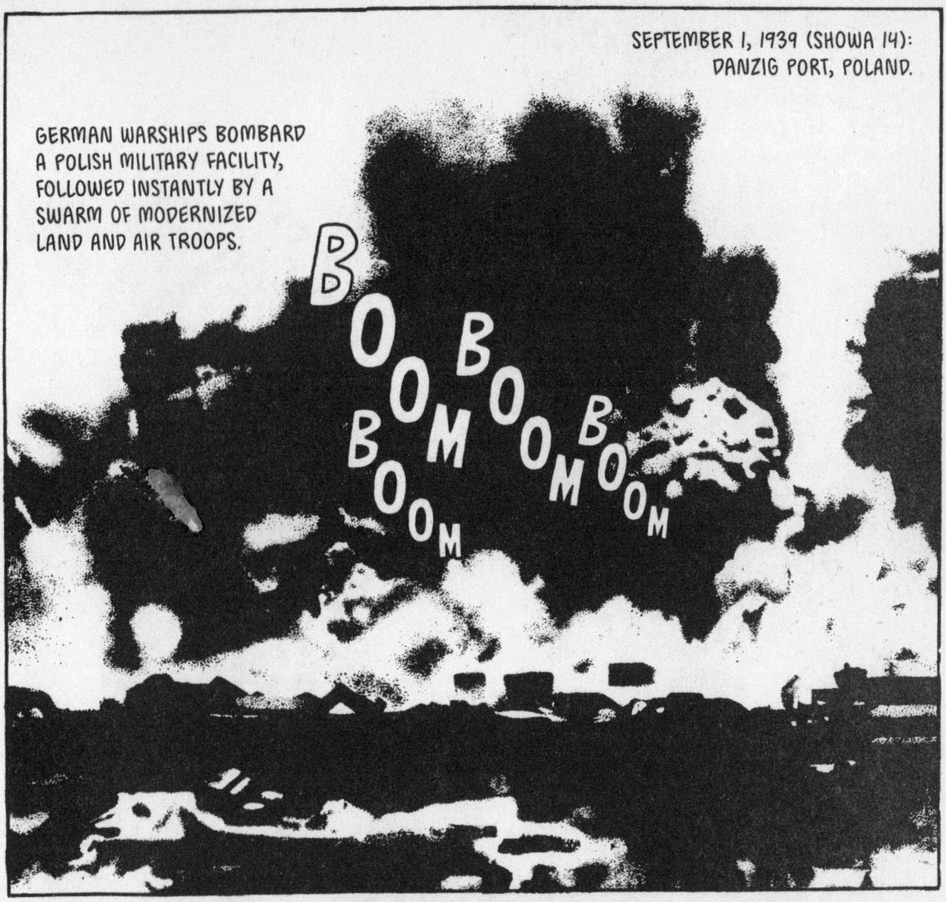
SEPTEMBER 1, 1939 (SHOWA 14):
DANZIG PORT, POLAND.
GERMAN WARSHIPS BOMBARD A POLISH MILITARY FACILITY, FOLLOWED INSTANTLY BY A SWARM OF MODERNIZED LAND AND AIR TROOPS.
BOOM BOOM BOOM BOOM

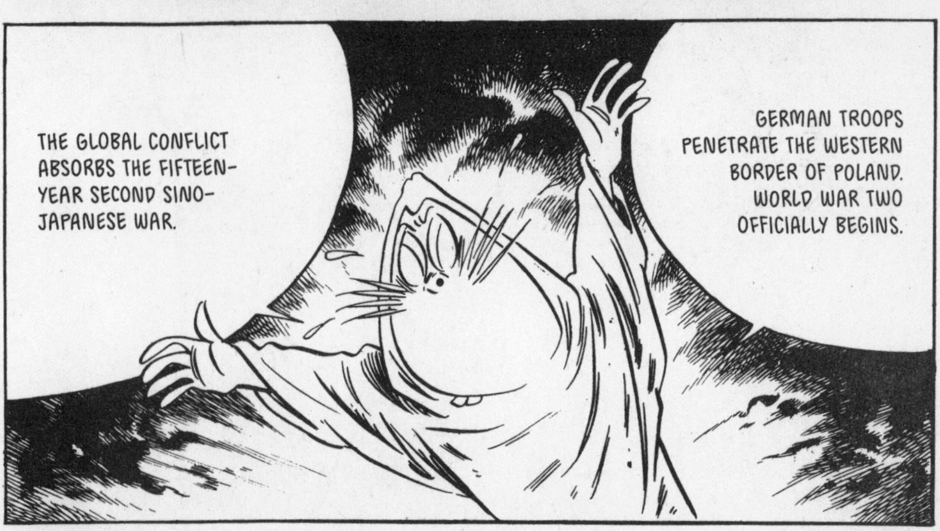
GERMAN TROOPS PENETRATE THE WESTERN BORDER OF POLAND. WORLD WAR TWO OFFICIALLY BEGINS.
THE GLOBAL CONFLICT ABSORBS THE FIFTEEN-YEAR SECOND SINO-JAPANESE WAR.

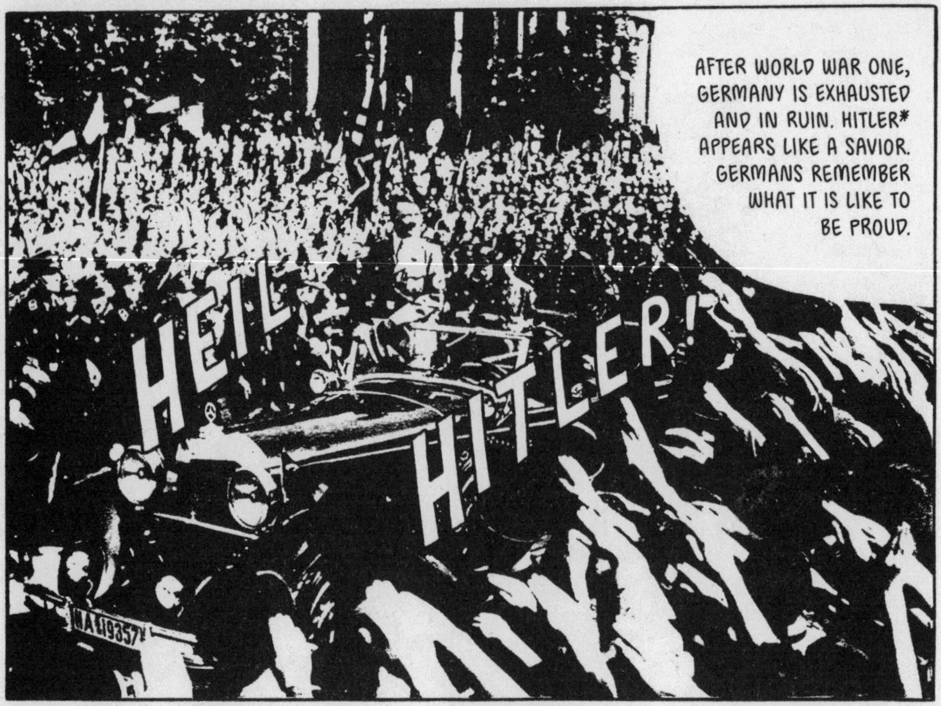
AFTER WORLD WAR ONE, GERMANY IS EXHAUSTED AND IN RUIN. HITLER* APPEARS LIKE A SAVIOR. GERMANS REMEMBER WHAT IT IS LIKE TO BE PROUD.
HEIL HITLER!

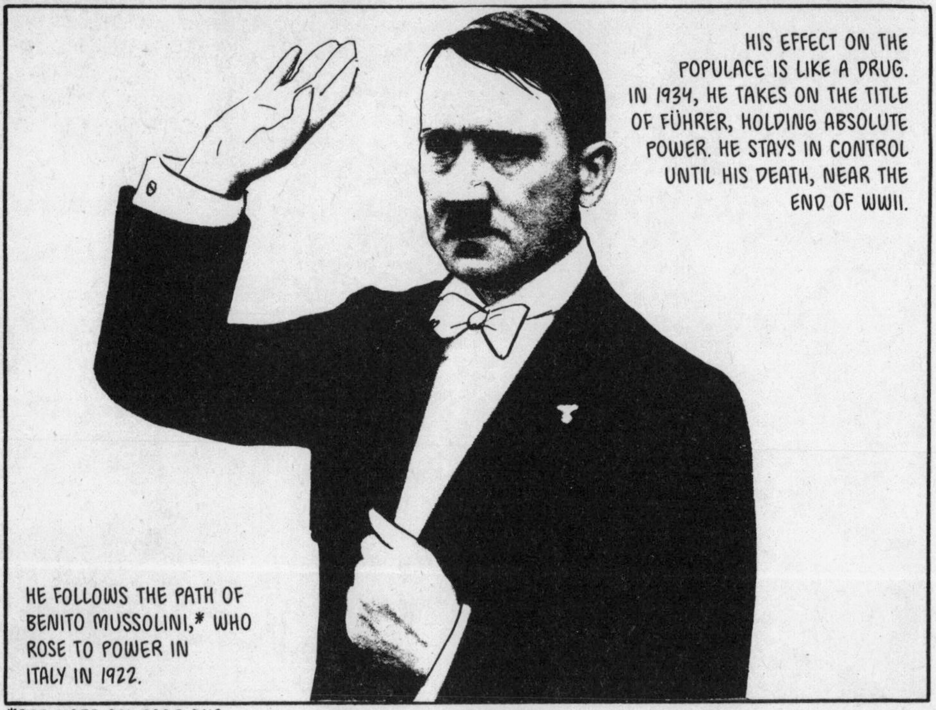
HIS EFFECT ON THE POPULACE IS LIKE A DRUG. IN 1934, HE TAKES ON THE TITLE OF FÜHRER, HOLDING ABSOLUTE POWER. HE STAYS IN CONTROL UNTIL HIS DEATH, NEAR THE END OF WWII.
HE FOLLOWS THE PATH OF BENITO MUSSOLINI,* WHO ROSE TO POWER IN ITALY IN 1922.

*SEE NOTE ON PAGE 542.

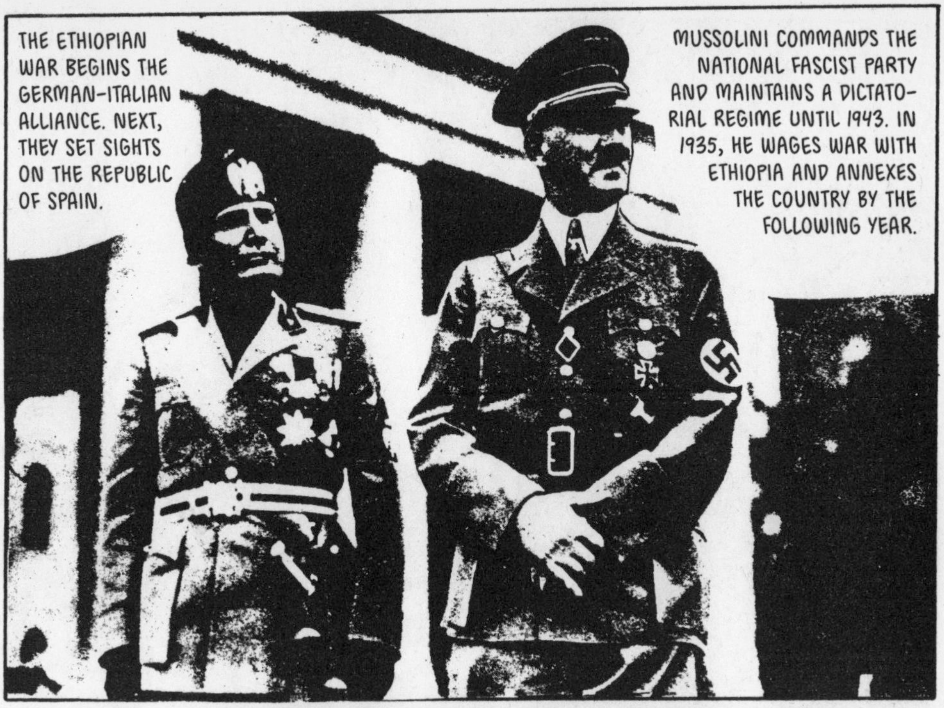
MUSSOLINI COMMANDS THE NATIONAL FASCIST PARTY AND MAINTAINS A DICTATORIAL REGIME UNTIL 1943. IN 1935, HE WAGES WAR WITH ETHIOPIA AND ANNEXES THE COUNTRY BY THE FOLLOWING YEAR.
THE ETHIOPIAN WAR BEGINS THE GERMAN-ITALIAN ALLIANCE. NEXT, THEY SET SIGHTS ON THE REPUBLIC OF SPAIN.

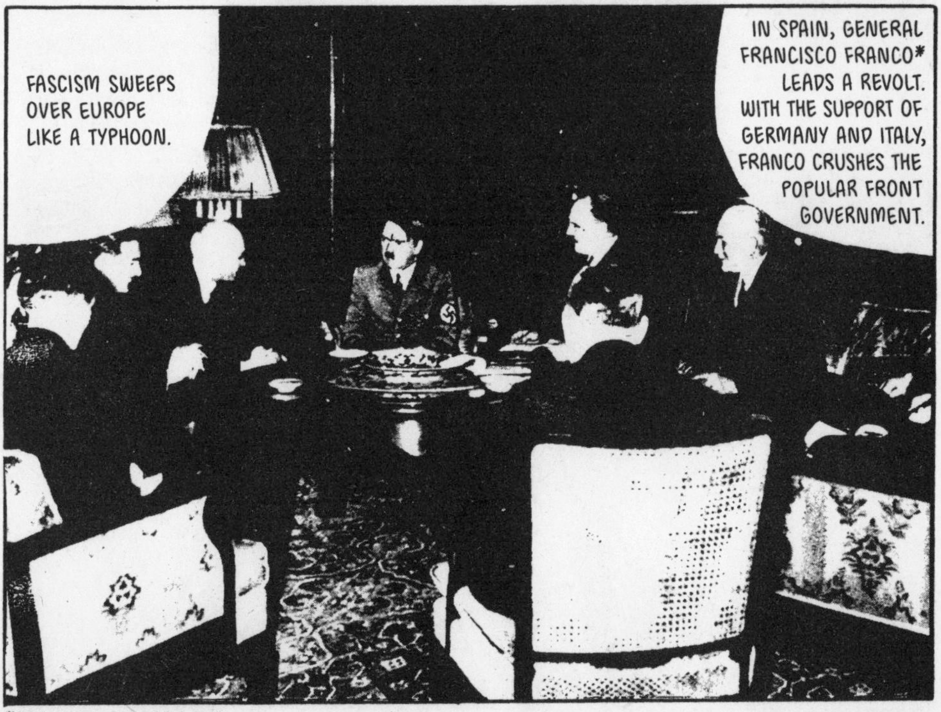
IN SPAIN, GENERAL FRANCISCO FRANCO* LEADS A REVOLT. WITH THE SUPPORT OF GERMANY AND ITALY, FRANCO CRUSHES THE POPULAR FRONT GOVERNMENT.
FASCISM SWEEPS OVER EUROPE LIKE A TYPHOON.

*SEE NOTE ON PAGE 542.

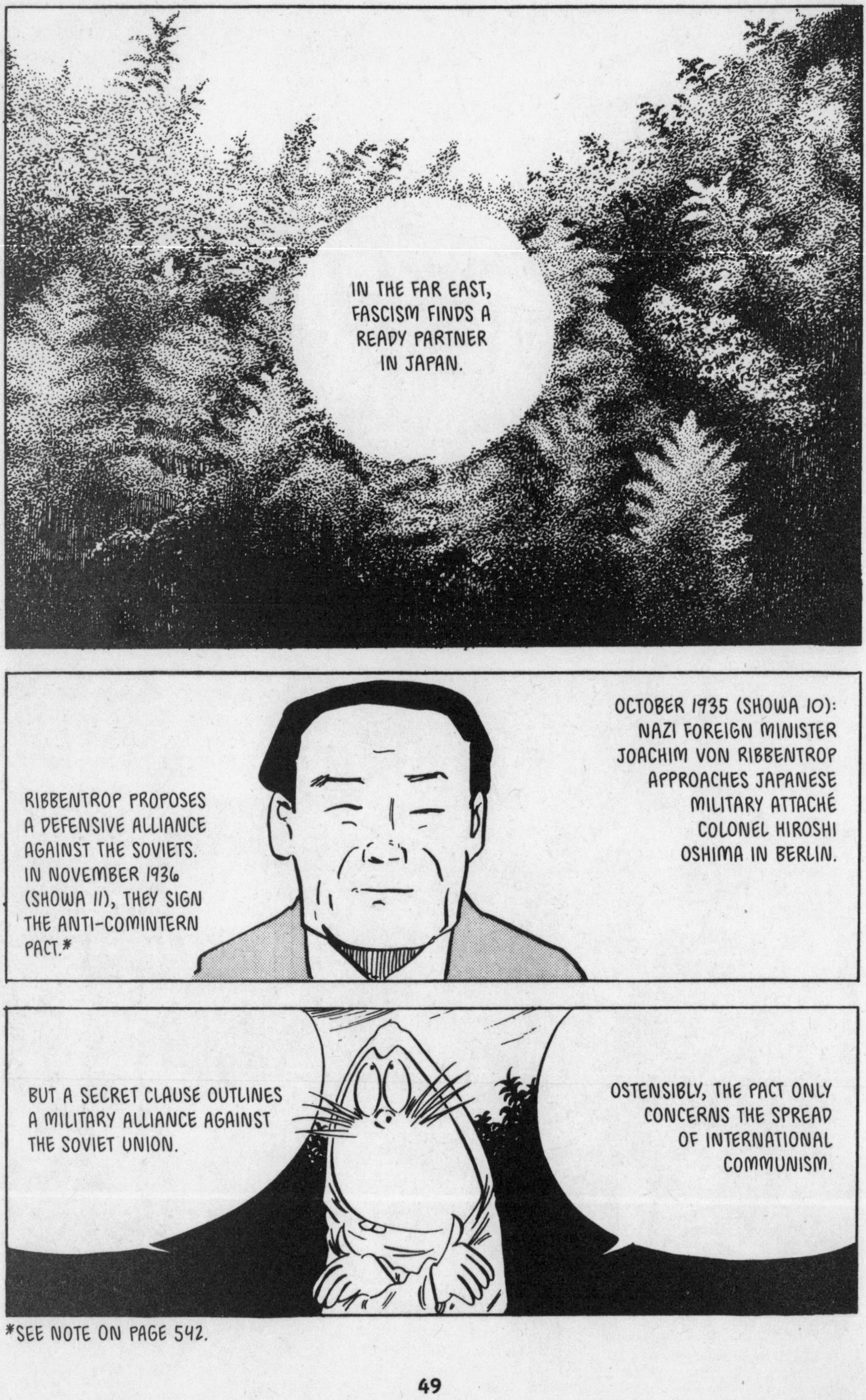
IN THE FAR EAST, FASCISM FINDS A READY PARTNER IN JAPAN.
OCTOBER 1935 (SHOWA 10): NAZI FOREIGN MINISTER JOACHIM VON RIBBENTROP APPROACHES JAPANESE MILITARY ATTACHÉ COLONEL HIROSHI OSHIMA IN BERLIN.
RIBBENTROP PROPOSES A DEFENSIVE ALLIANCE AGAINST THE SOVIETS. IN NOVEMBER 1936 (SHOWA 11), THEY SIGN THE ANTI-COMINTERN PACT.*
OSTENSIBLY, THE PACT ONLY CONCERNS THE SPREAD OF INTERNATIONAL COMMUNISM.
BUT A SECRET CLAUSE OUTLINES A MILITARY ALLIANCE AGAINST THE SOVIET UNION.

*SEE NOTE ON PAGE 542.

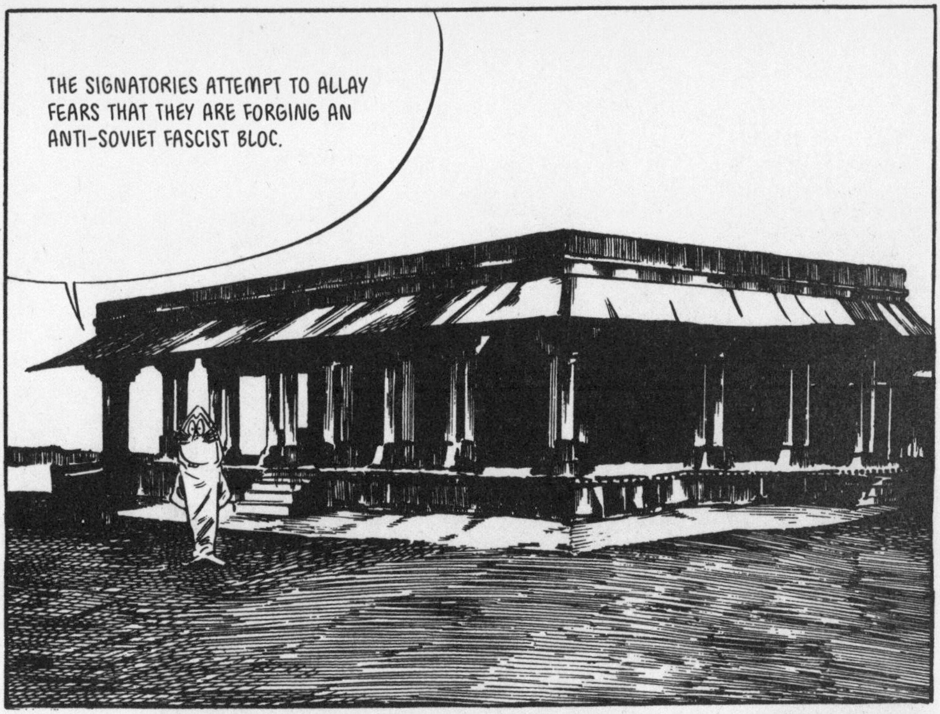
THE SIGNATORIES ATTEMPT TO ALLAY FEARS THAT THEY ARE FORGING AN ANTI-SOVIET FASCIST BLOC.

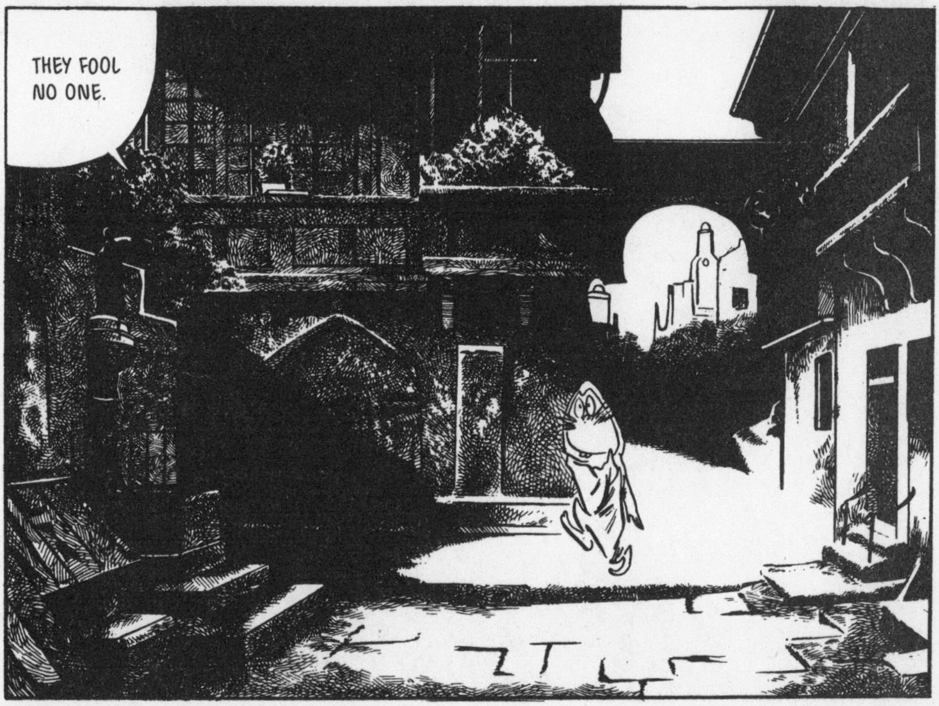
THEY FOOL NO ONE.

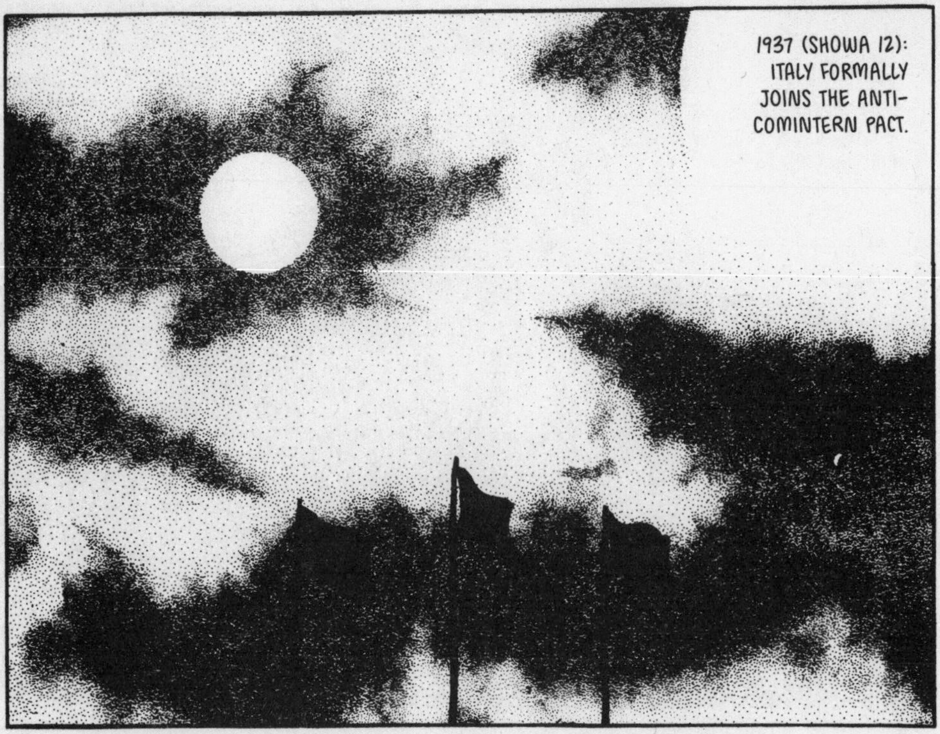
1937 (SHOWA 12): ITALY FORMALLY JOINS THE ANTI-COMINTERN PACT.
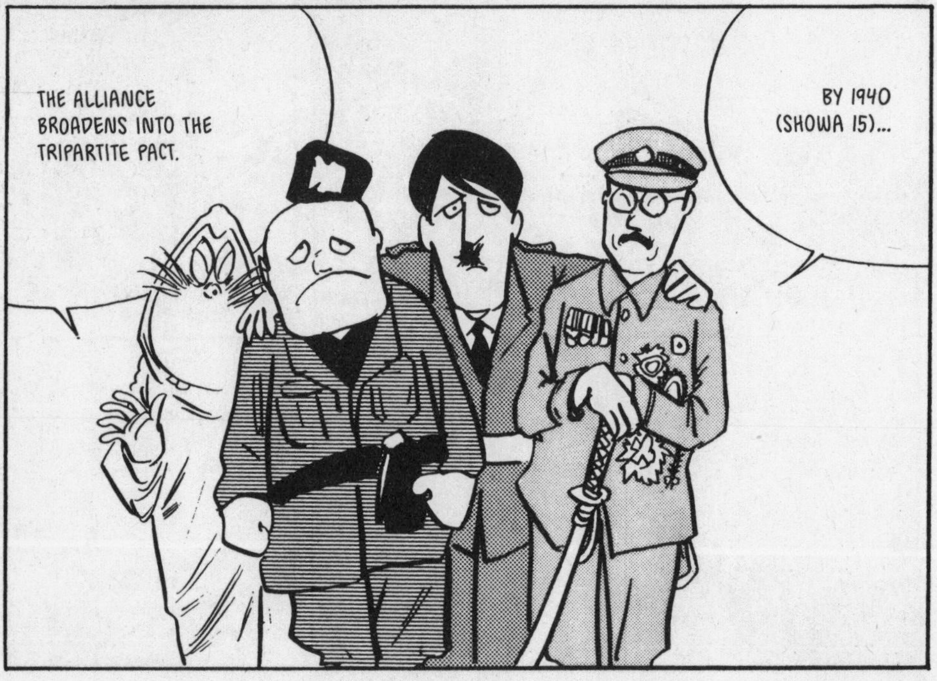
BY 1940 (SHOWA 15)...
THE ALLIANCE BROADENS INTO THE TRIPARTITE PACT.

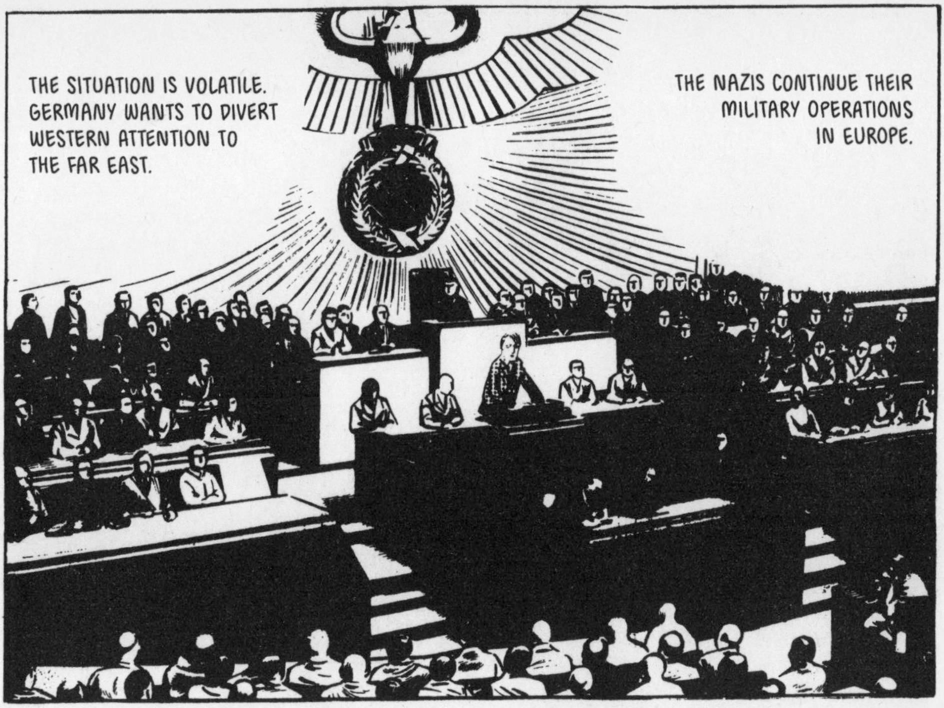
THE NAZIS CONTINUE THEIR MILITARY OPERATIONS IN EUROPE.
THE SITUATION IS VOLATILE. GERMANY WANTS TO DIVERT WESTERN ATTENTION TO THE FAR EAST.
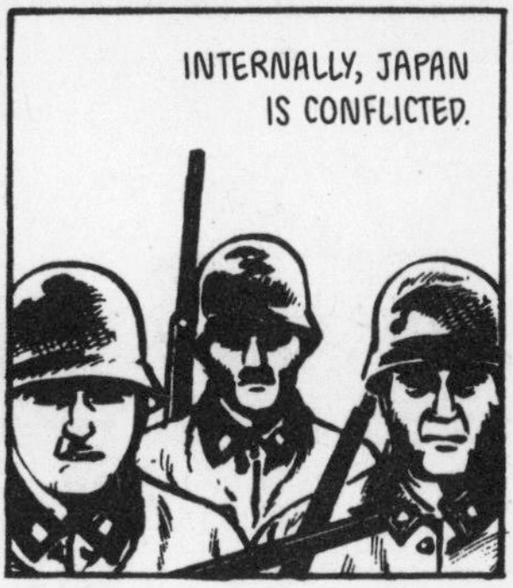
INTERNALLY, JAPAN IS CONFLICTED.
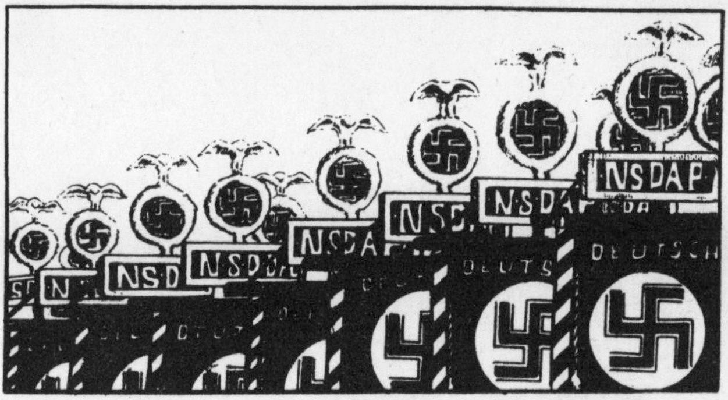
NSDAP
DEUTSCH
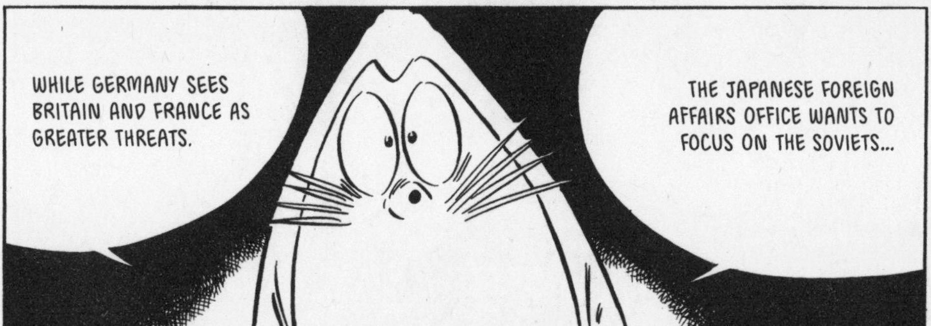
THE JAPANESE FOREIGN AFFAIRS OFFICE WANTS TO FOCUS ON THE SOVIETS...
WHILE GERMANY SEES BRITAIN AND FRANCE AS GREATER THREATS.

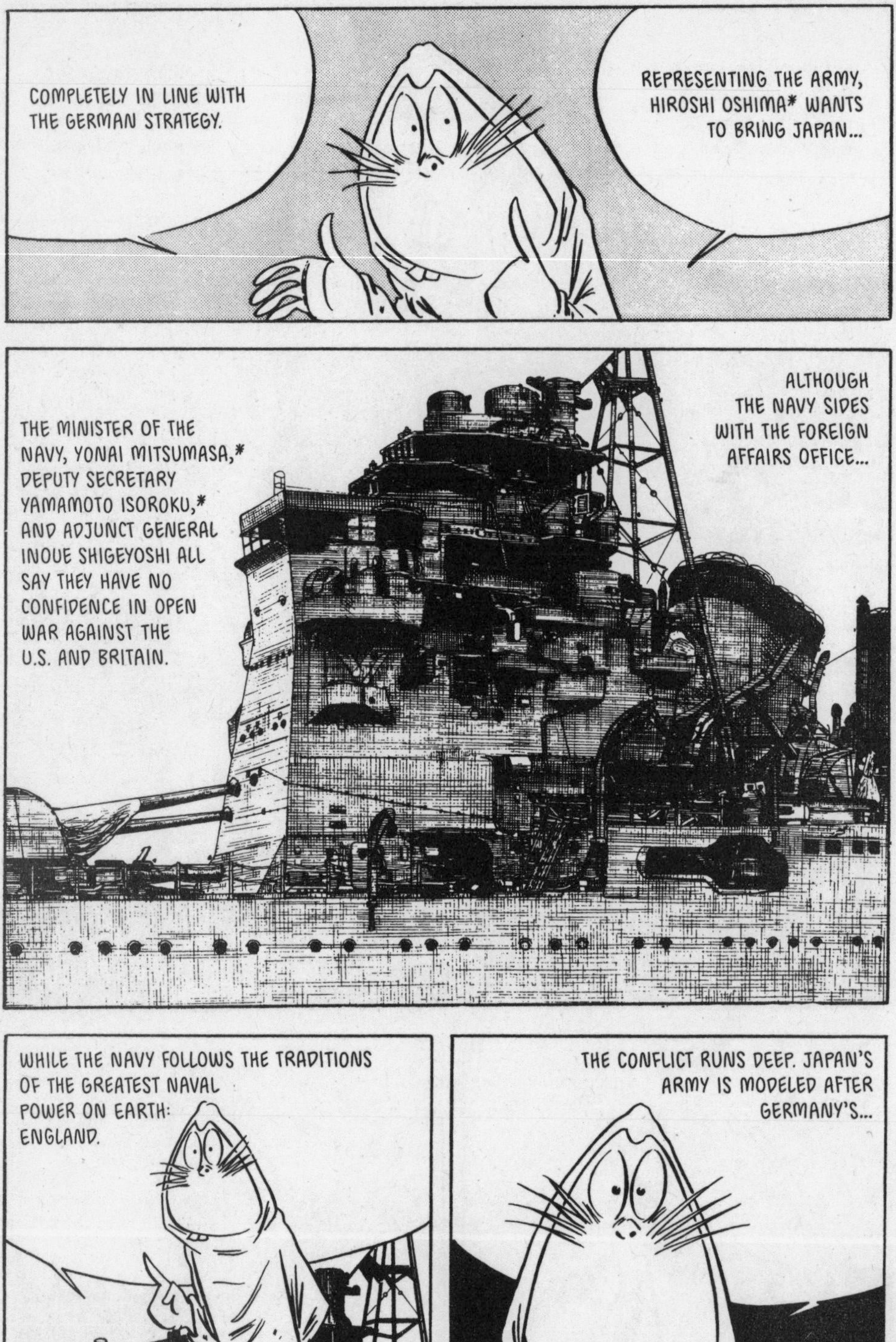
REPRESENTING THE ARMY, HIROSHI OSHIMA* WANTS TO BRING JAPAN...
COMPLETELY IN LINE WITH THE GERMAN STRATEGY.
ALTHOUGH THE NAVY SIDES WITH THE FOREIGN AFFAIRS OFFICE...
THE MINISTER OF THE NAVY, YONAI MITSUMASA,* DEPUTY SECRETARY YAMAMOTO ISOROKU,* AND ADJUNCT GENERAL INOUE SHIGEYOSHI ALL SAY THEY HAVE NO CONFIDENCE IN OPEN WAR AGAINST THE U.S. AND BRITAIN.
THE CONFLICT RUNS DEEP. JAPAN'S ARMY IS MODELED AFTER GERMANY'S...
WHILE THE NAVY FOLLOWS THE TRADITIONS OF THE GREATEST NAVAL POWER ON EARTH: ENGLAND.

*SEE NOTES ON PAGE 542.

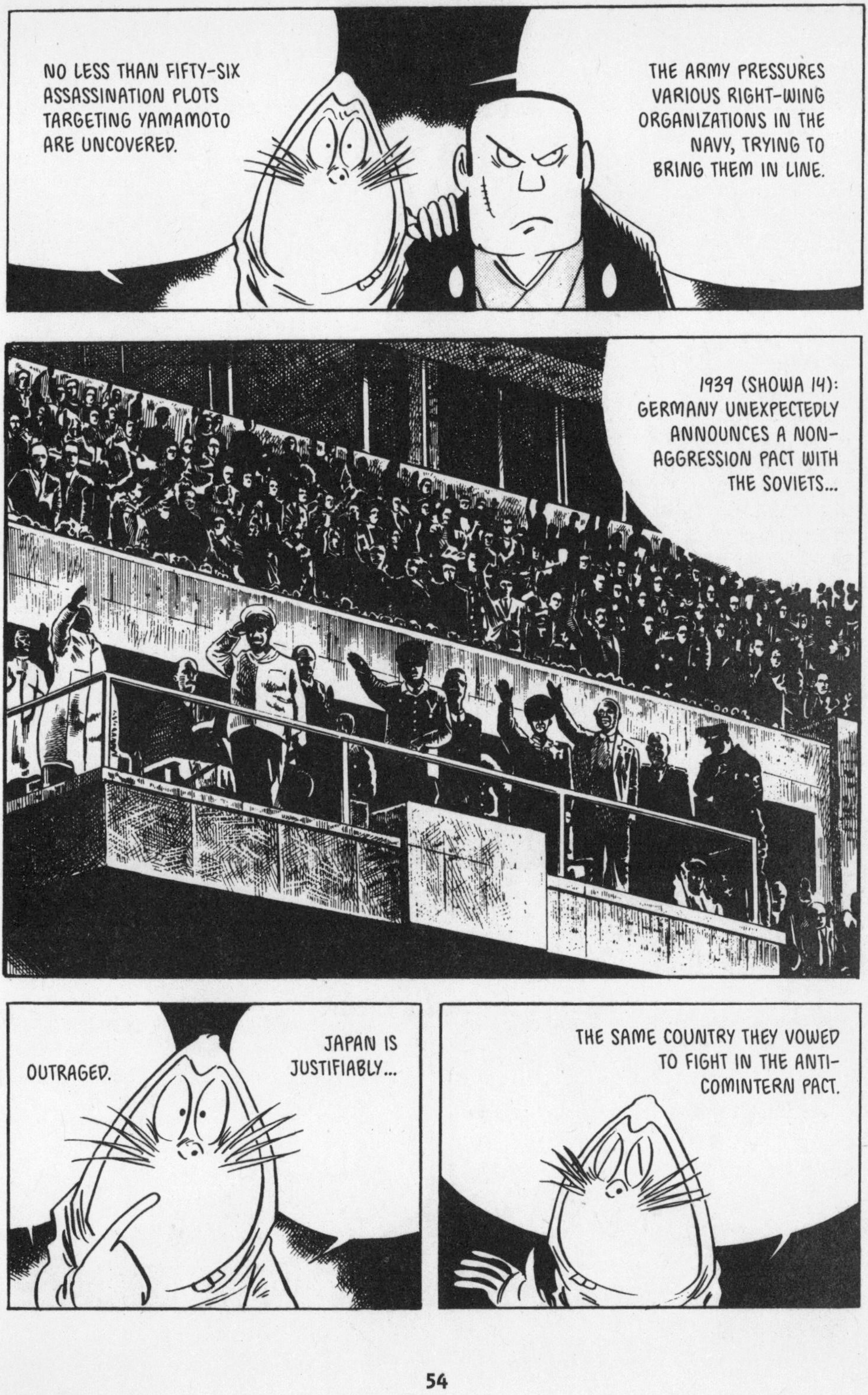

THE ARMY PRESSURES VARIOUS RIGHT-WING ORGANIZATIONS IN THE NAVY, TRYING TO BRING THEM IN LINE.
NO LESS THAN FIFTY-SIX ASSASSINATION PLOTS TARGETING YAMAMOTO ARE UNCOVERED.
1939 (SHOWA 14): GERMANY UNEXPECTEDLY ANNOUNCES A NON-AGGRESSION PACT WITH THE SOVIETS...
THE SAME COUNTRY THEY VOWED TO FIGHT IN THE ANTI-COMINTERN PACT.
JAPAN IS JUSTIFIABLY...
OUTRAGED.

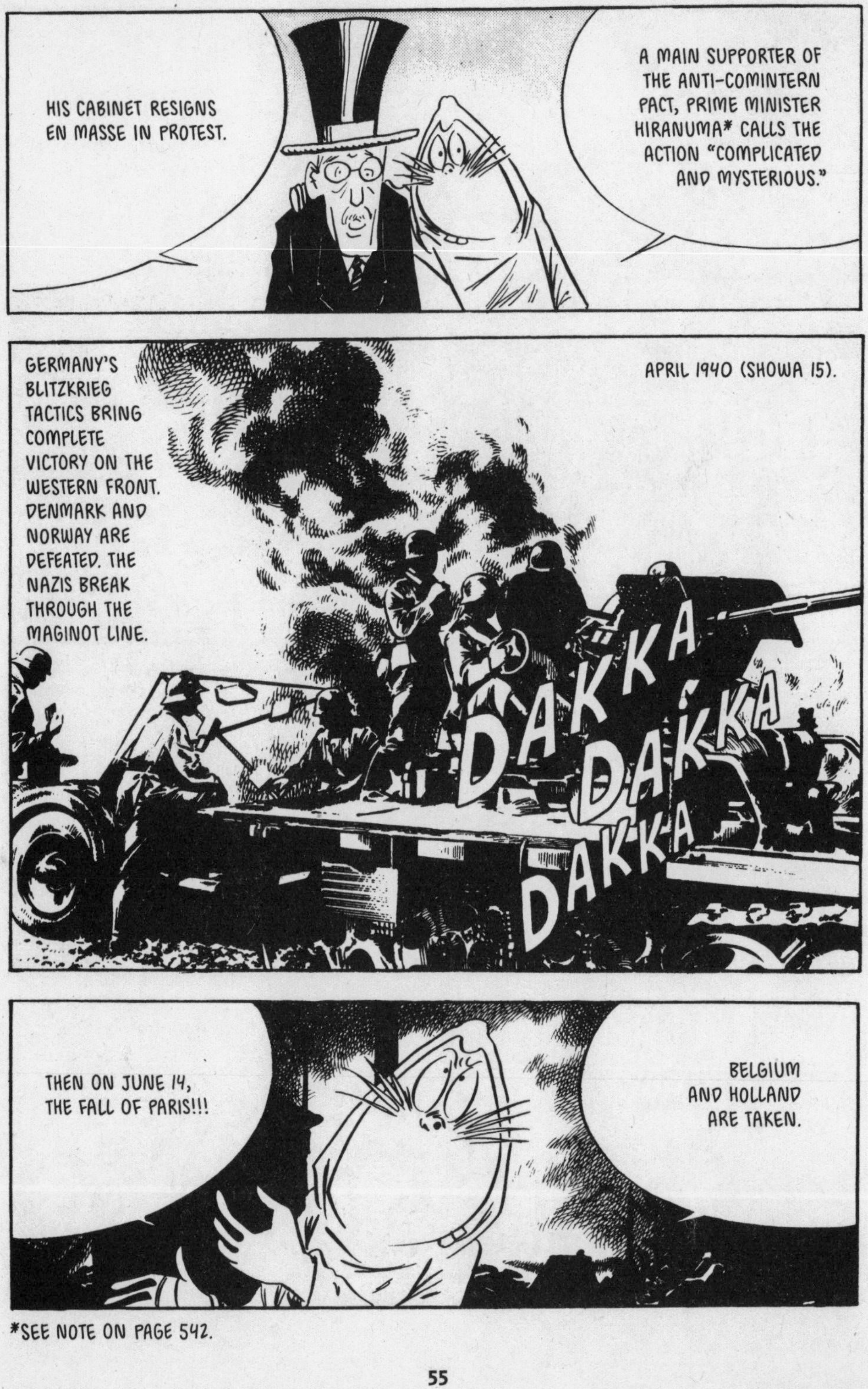
A MAIN SUPPORTER OF THE ANTI-COMINTERN PACT, PRIME MINISTER HIRANUMA* CALLS THE ACTION "COMPLICATED AND MYSTERIOUS."
HIS CABINET RESIGNS EN MASSE IN PROTEST.
APRIL 1940 (SHOWA 15).
GERMANY'S BLITZKRIEG TACTICS BRING COMPLETE VICTORY ON THE WESTERN FRONT. DENMARK AND NORWAY ARE DEFEATED. THE NAZIS BREAK THROUGH THE MAGINOT LINE.
DAKKA DAKKA DAKKA DAKKA
BELGIUM AND HOLLAND ARE TAKEN.
THEN ON JUNE 14, THE FALL OF PARIS!!!

*SEE NOTE ON PAGE 542.

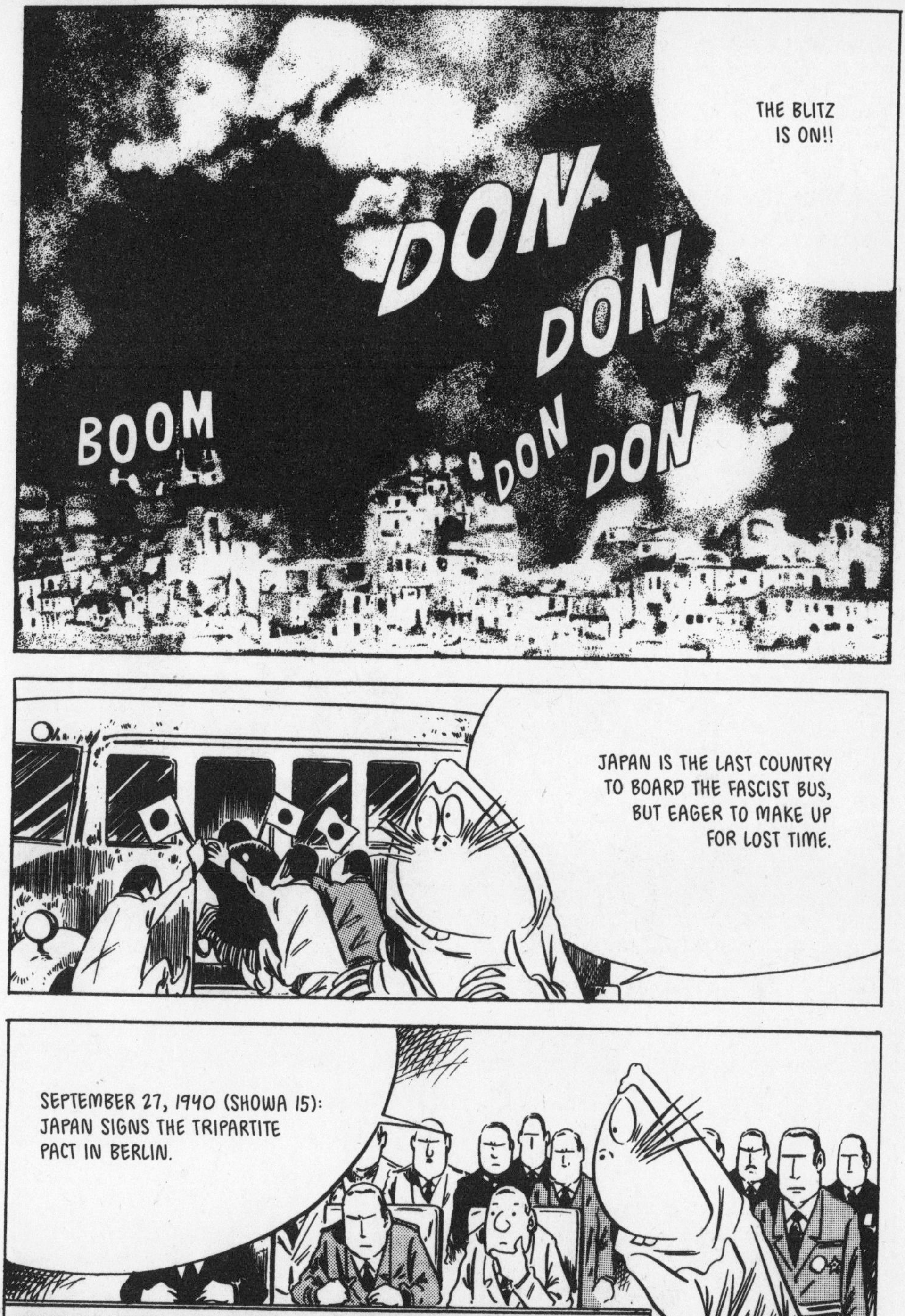
THE BLITZ IS ON!!
DON
DON
DON
DON
BOOM
JAPAN IS THE LAST COUNTRY TO BOARD THE FASCIST BUS, BUT EAGER TO MAKE UP FOR LOST TIME.
SEPTEMBER 27, 1940 (SHOWA 15): JAPAN SIGNS THE TRIPARTITE PACT IN BERLIN.

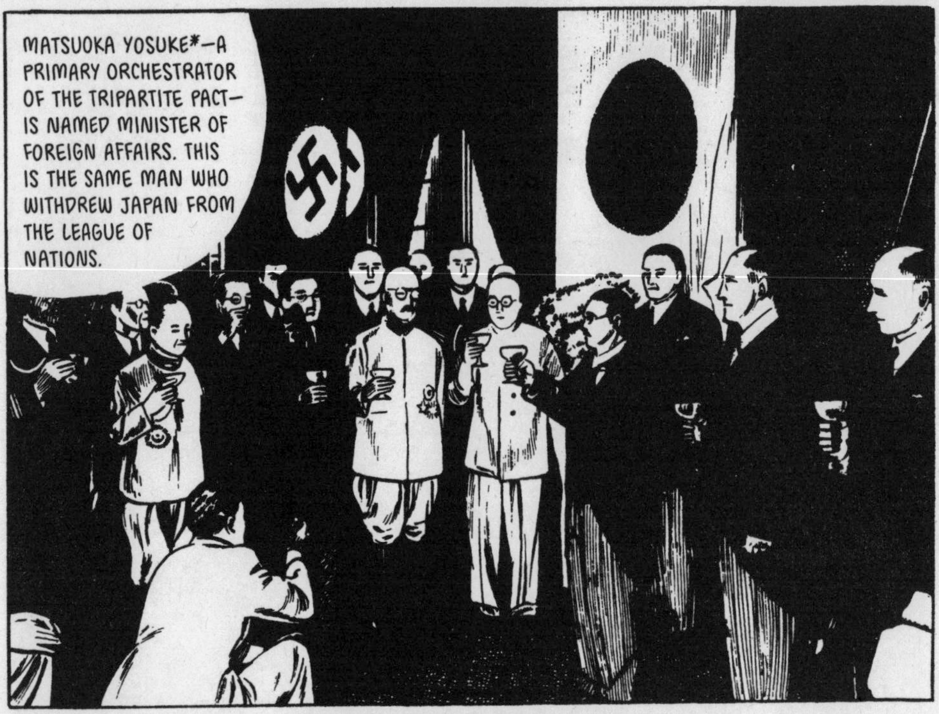
MATSUOKA YOSUKE*—A PRIMARY ORCHESTRATOR OF THE TRIPARTITE PACT—IS NAMED MINISTER OF FOREIGN AFFAIRS. THIS IS THE SAME MAN WHO WITHDREW JAPAN FROM THE LEAGUE OF NATIONS.

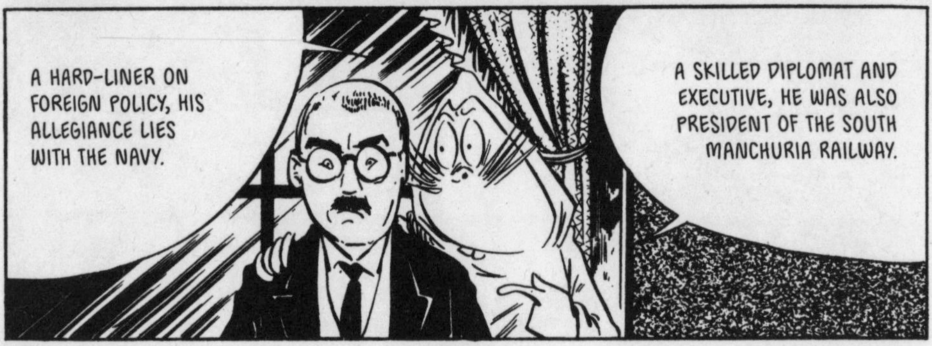
A SKILLED DIPLOMAT AND EXECUTIVE, HE WAS ALSO PRESIDENT OF THE SOUTH MANCHURIA RAILWAY.
A HARD-LINER ON FOREIGN POLICY, HIS ALLEGIANCE LIES WITH THE NAVY.

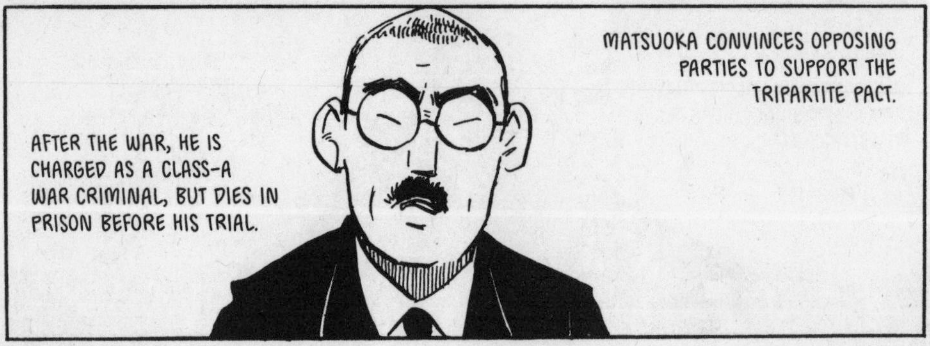
MATSUOKA CONVINCES OPPOSING PARTIES TO SUPPORT THE TRIPARTITE PACT.
AFTER THE WAR, HE IS CHARGED AS A CLASS-A WAR CRIMINAL, BUT DIES IN PRISON BEFORE HIS TRIAL.

*SEE NOTE ON PAGE 542.

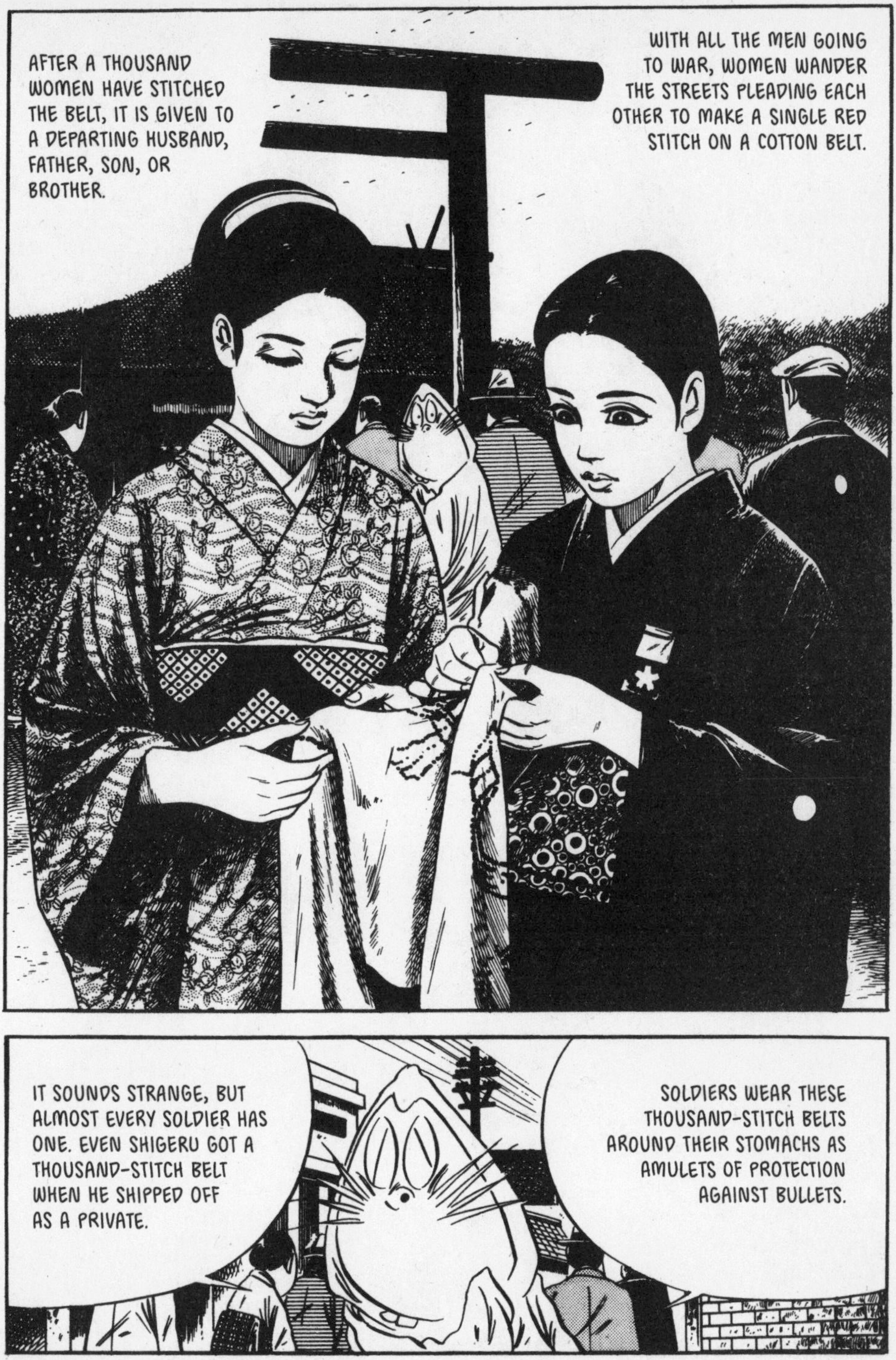
WITH ALL THE MEN GOING TO WAR, WOMEN WANDER THE STREETS PLEADING EACH OTHER TO MAKE A SINGLE RED STITCH ON A COTTON BELT.
AFTER A THOUSAND WOMEN HAVE STITCHED THE BELT, IT IS GIVEN TO A DEPARTING HUSBAND, FATHER, SON, OR BROTHER.
SOLDIERS WEAR THESE THOUSAND-STITCH BELTS AROUND THEIR STOMACHS AS AMULETS OF PROTECTION AGAINST BULLETS.
IT SOUNDS STRANGE, BUT ALMOST EVERY SOLDIER HAS ONE. EVEN SHIGERU GOT A THOUSAND-STITCH BELT WHEN HE SHIPPED OFF AS A PRIVATE.

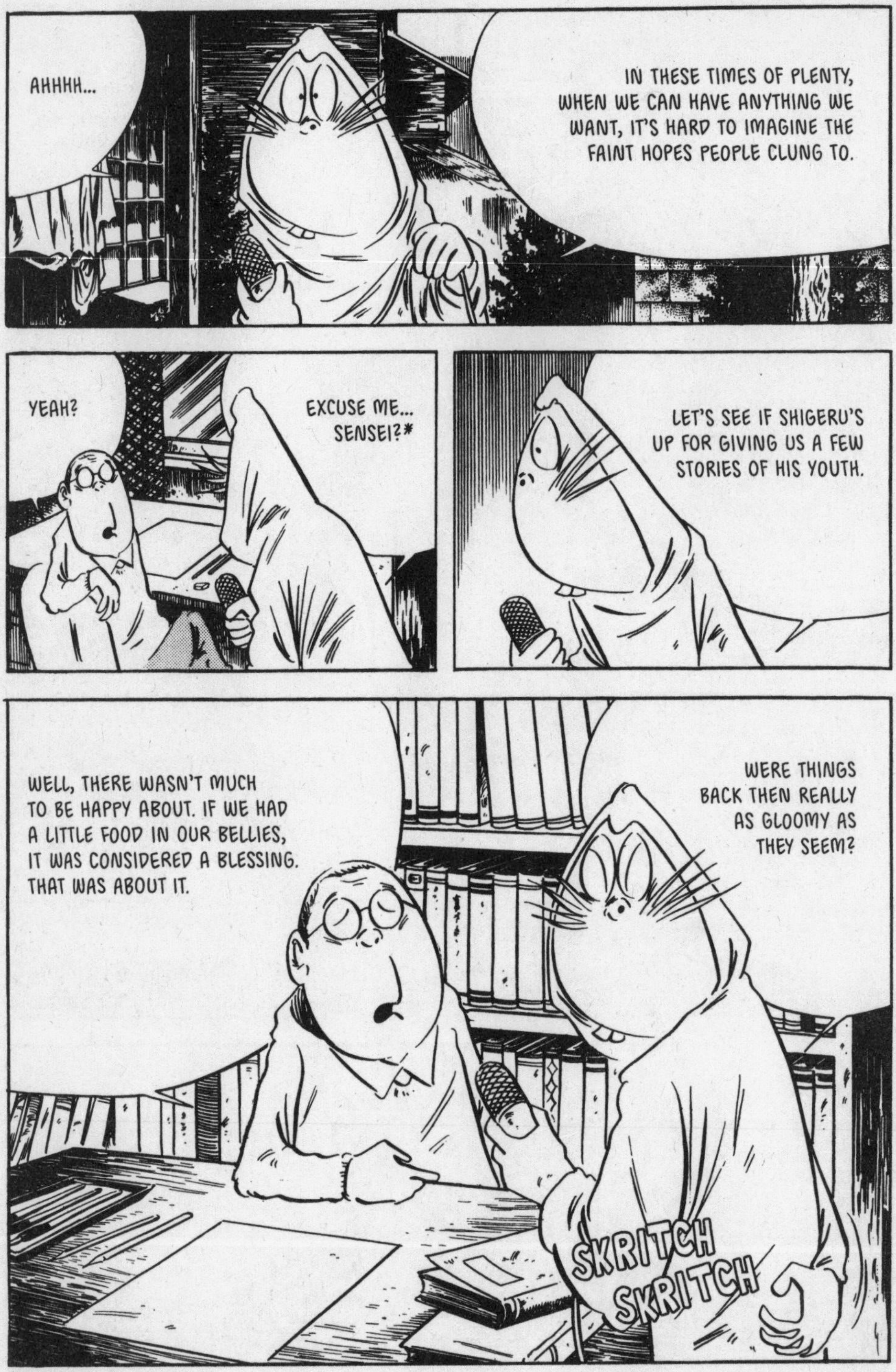
IN THESE TIMES OF PLENTY, WHEN WE CAN HAVE ANYTHING WE WANT, IT'S HARD TO IMAGINE THE FAINT HOPES PEOPLE CLUNG TO.
AHHHH...
LET'S SEE IF SHIGERU'S UP FOR GIVING US A FEW STORIES OF HIS YOUTH.
EXCUSE ME... SENSEI?*
YEAH?
WERE THINGS BACK THEN REALLY AS GLOOMY AS THEY SEEM?
WELL, THERE WASN'T MUCH TO BE HAPPY ABOUT. IF WE HAD A LITTLE FOOD IN OUR BELLIES, IT WAS CONSIDERED A BLESSING. THAT WAS ABOUT IT.
SKRITCH SKRITCH

*SEE NOTE ON PAGE 542.

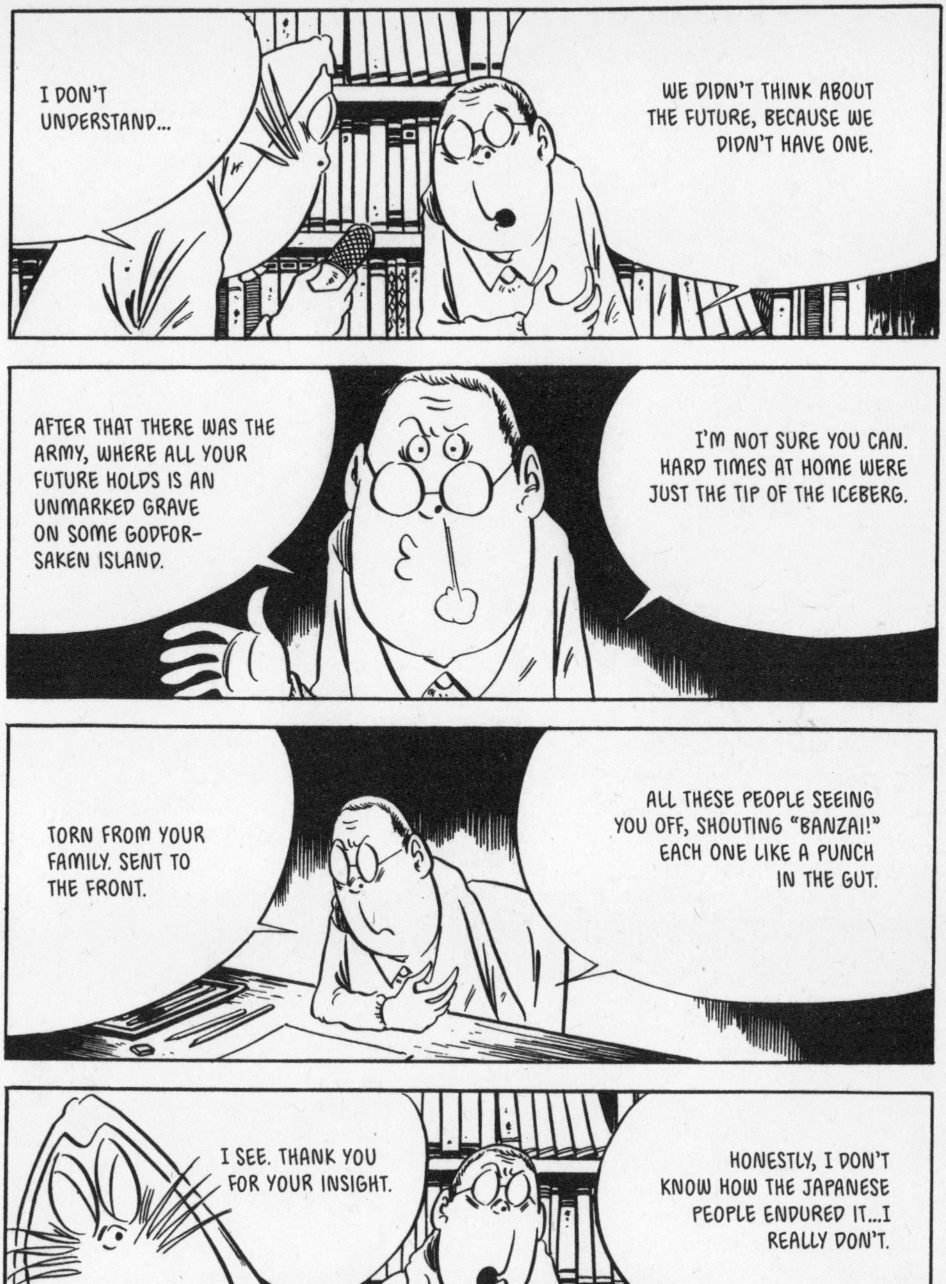
WE DIDN'T THINK ABOUT THE FUTURE, BECAUSE WE DIDN'T HAVE ONE.
I DON'T UNDERSTAND...
I'M NOT SURE YOU CAN. HARD TIMES AT HOME WERE JUST THE TIP OF THE ICEBERG.
AFTER THAT THERE WAS THE ARMY, WHERE ALL YOUR FUTURE HOLDS IS AN UNMARKED GRAVE ON SOME GODFOR-SAKEN ISLAND.
ALL THESE PEOPLE SEEING YOU OFF, SHOUTING "BANZAI!" EACH ONE LIKE A PUNCH IN THE GUT.
TORN FROM YOUR FAMILY. SENT TO THE FRONT.
HONESTLY, I DON'T KNOW HOW THE JAPANESE PEOPLE ENDURED IT...I REALLY DON'T.
BAM
I SEE. THANK YOU FOR YOUR INSIGHT.

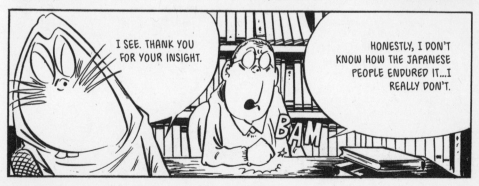

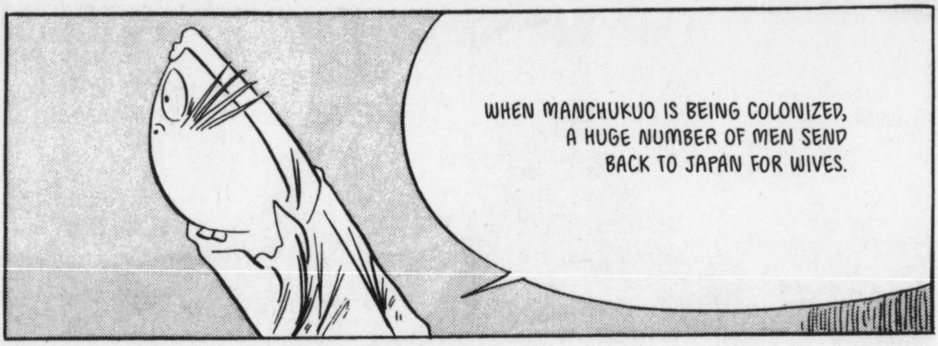
WHEN MANCHUKUO IS BEING COLONIZED, A HUGE NUMBER OF MEN SEND BACK TO JAPAN FOR WIVES.

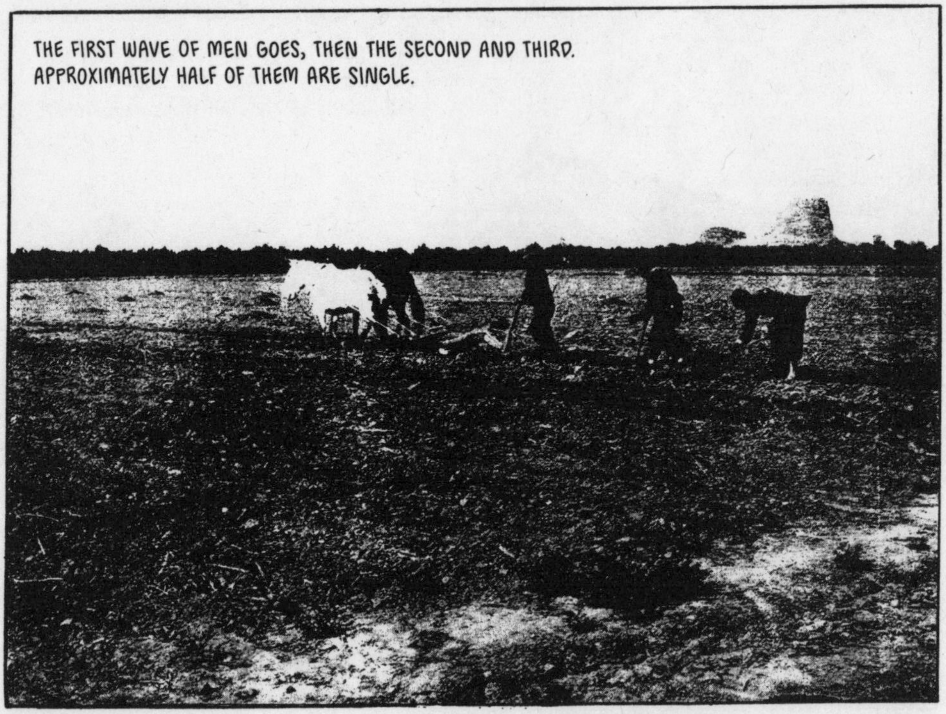
THE FIRST WAVE OF MEN GOES, THEN THE SECOND AND THIRD. APPROXIMATELY HALF OF THEM ARE SINGLE.

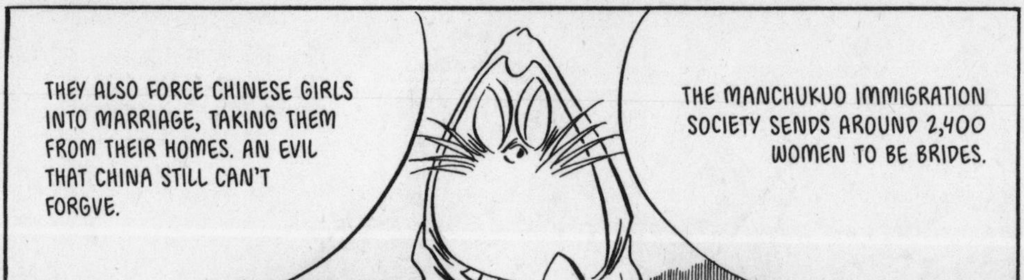
THE MANCHUKUO IMMIGRATION SOCIETY SENDS AROUND 2,400 WOMEN TO BE BRIDES.
THEY ALSO FORCE CHINESE GIRLS INTO MARRIAGE, TAKING THEM FROM THEIR HOMES. AN EVIL THAT CHINA STILL CAN'T FORGVE.

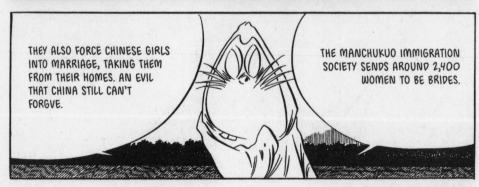

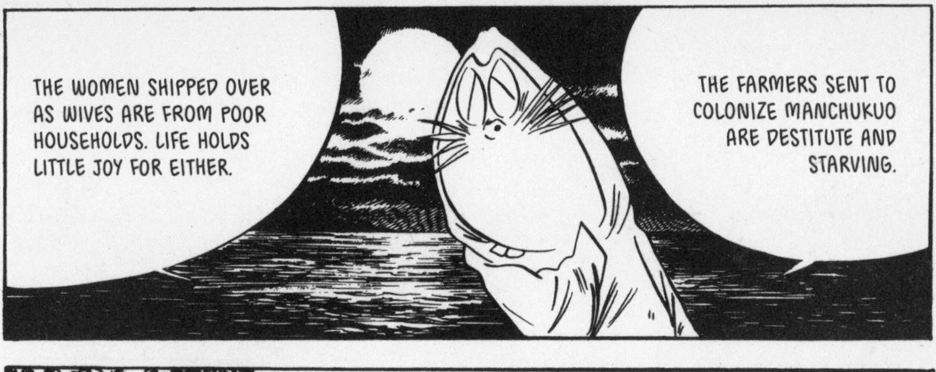
THE FARMERS SENT TO COLONIZE MANCHUKUO ARE DESTITUTE AND STARVING.
THE WOMEN SHIPPED OVER AS WIVES ARE FROM POOR HOUSEHOLDS. LIFE HOLDS LITTLE JOY FOR EITHER.

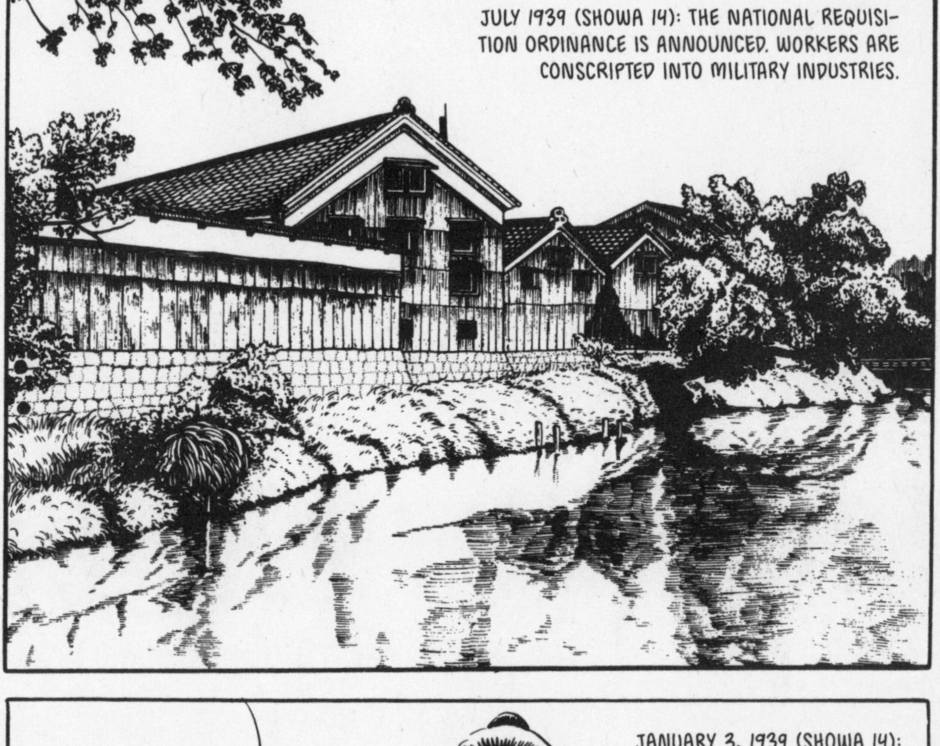
JULY 1939 (SHOWA 14): THE NATIONAL REQUISITION ORDINANCE IS ANNOUNCED. WORKERS ARE CONSCRIPTED INTO MILITARY INDUSTRIES.

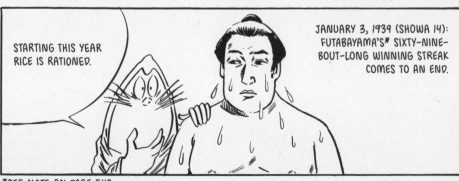

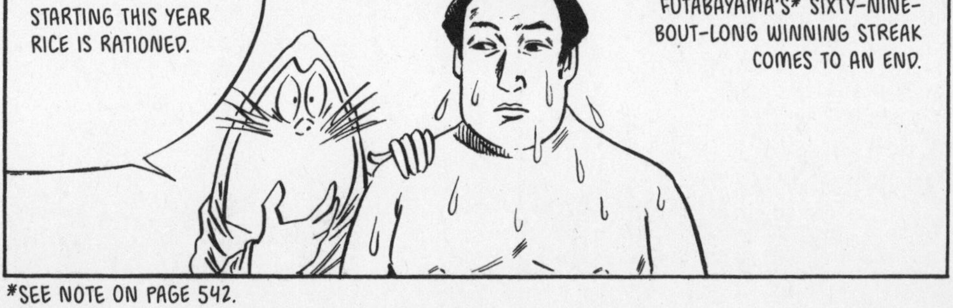
JANUARY 3, 1939 (SHOWA 14): FUTABAYAMA'S* SIXTY-NINE-BOUT-LONG WINNING STREAK COMES TO AN END.
STARTING THIS YEAR RICE IS RATIONED.

*SEE NOTE ON PAGE 542.

THE YEAR 2600

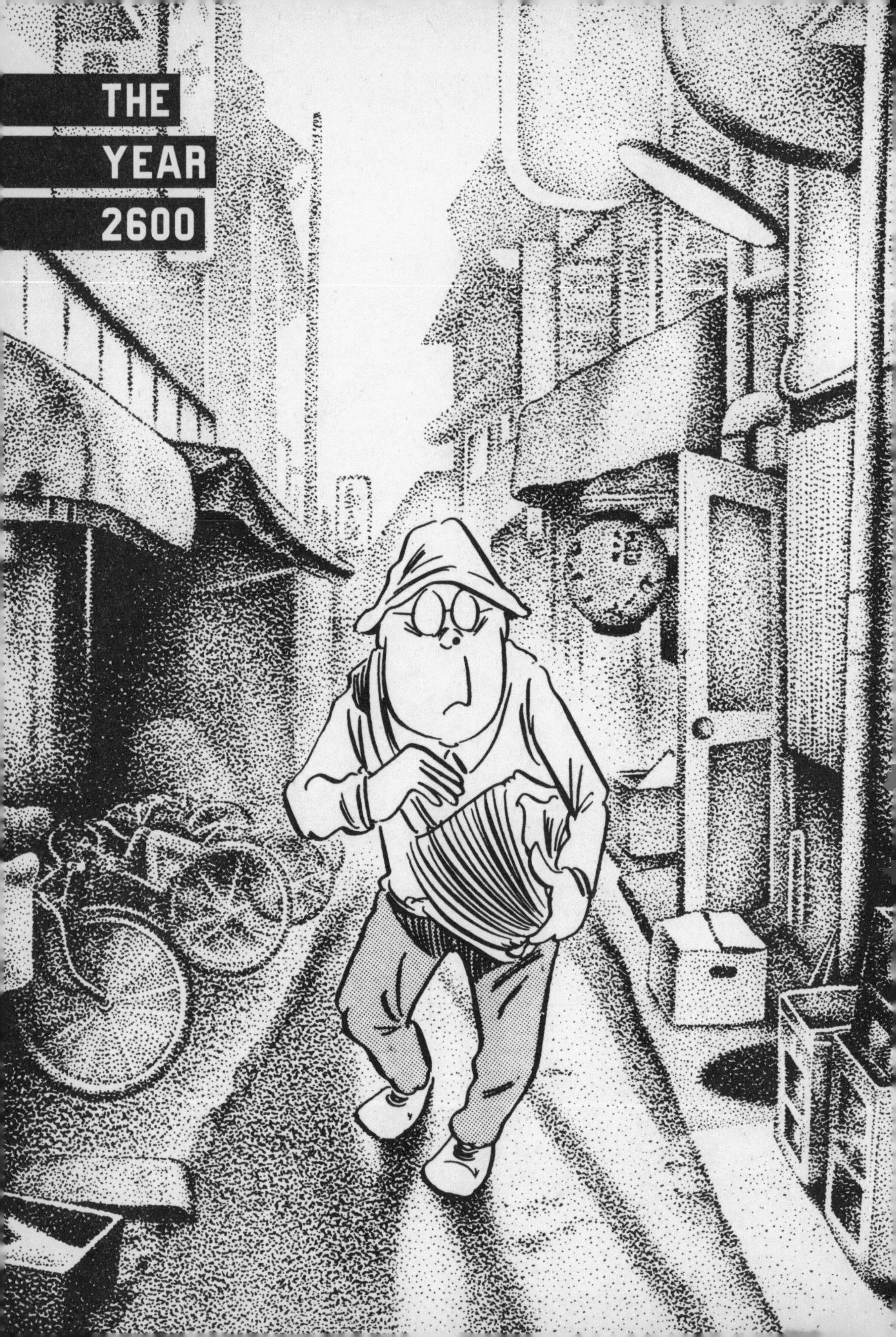

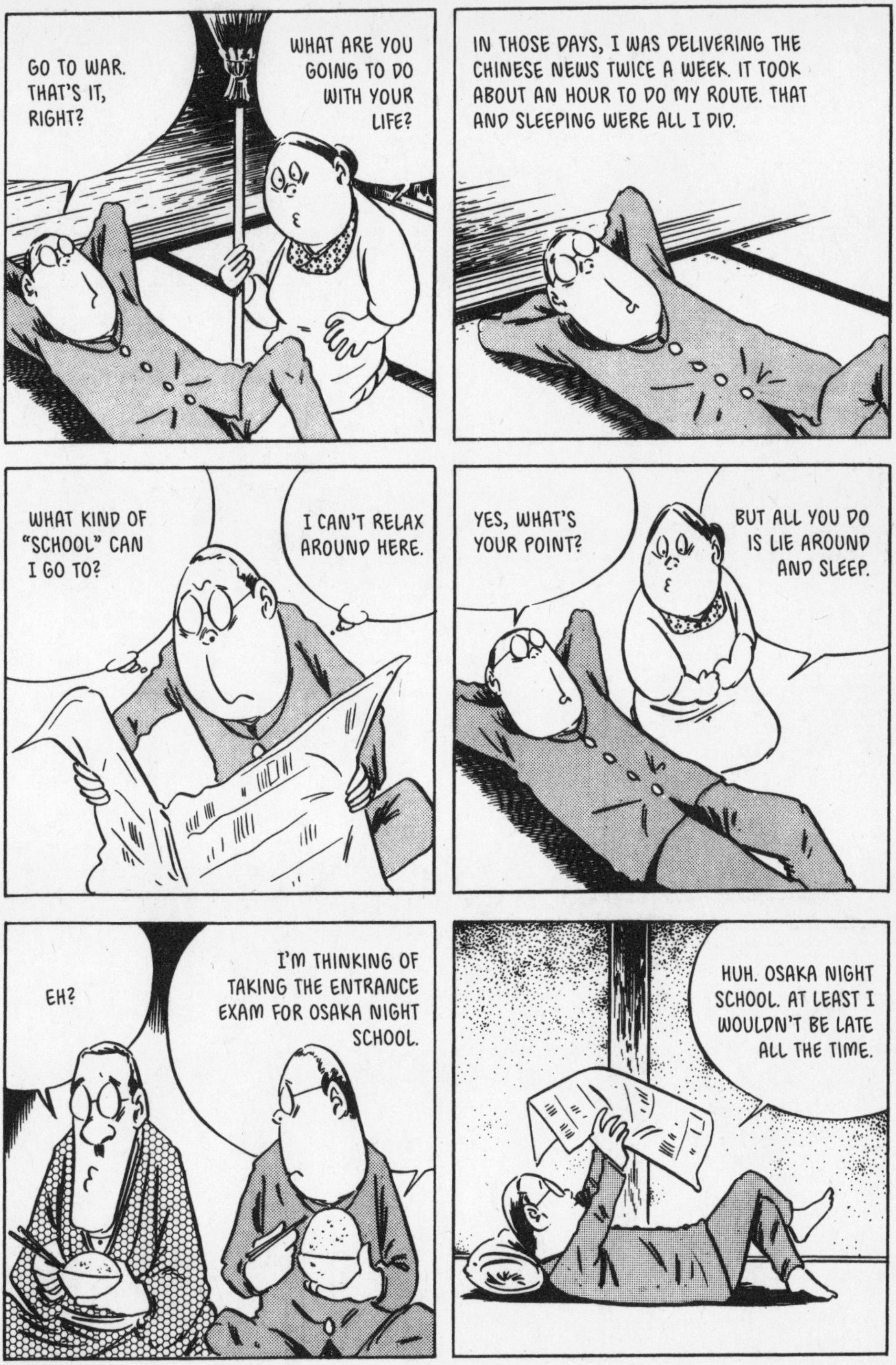
IN THOSE DAYS, I WAS DELIVERING THE CHINESE NEWS TWICE A WEEK. IT TOOK ABOUT AN HOUR TO DO MY ROUTE. THAT AND SLEEPING WERE ALL I DID.
WHAT ARE YOU GOING TO DO WITH YOUR LIFE?
GO TO WAR. THAT'S IT, RIGHT?
BUT ALL YOU DO IS LIE AROUND AND SLEEP.
YES, WHAT'S YOUR POINT?
I CAN'T RELAX AROUND HERE.
WHAT KIND OF "SCHOOL" CAN I GO TO?
HUH. OSAKA NIGHT SCHOOL. AT LEAST I WOULDN'T BE LATE ALL THE TIME.
I'M THINKING OF TAKING THE ENTRANCE EXAM FOR OSAKA NIGHT SCHOOL.
EH?

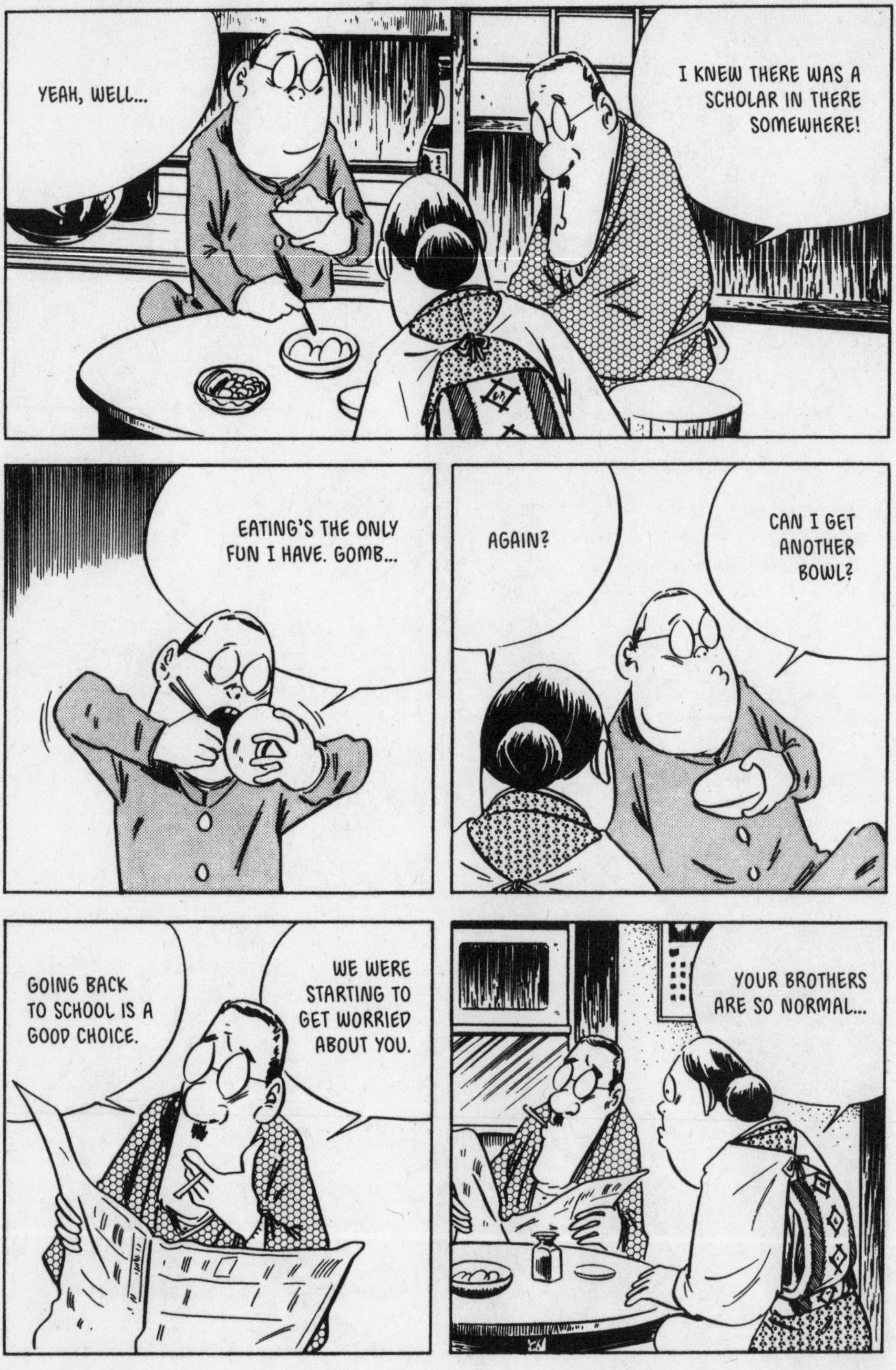
I KNEW THERE WAS A SCHOLAR IN THERE SOMEWHERE!
YEAH, WELL...
CAN I GET ANOTHER BOWL?
AGAIN?
EATING'S THE ONLY FUN I HAVE. GOMB...
YOUR BROTHERS ARE SO NORMAL...
WE WERE STARTING TO GET WORRIED ABOUT YOU.
GOING BACK TO SCHOOL IS A GOOD CHOICE.

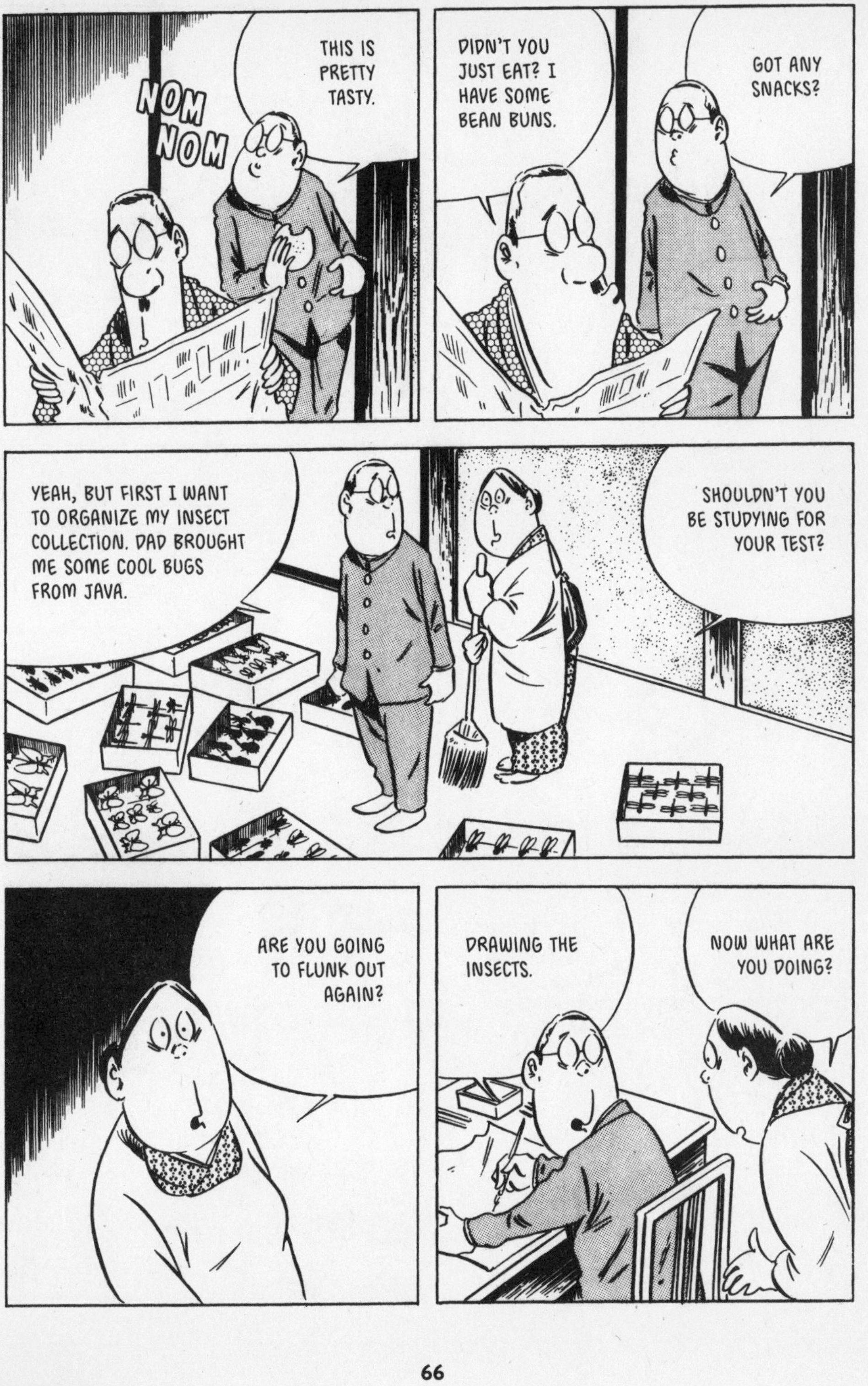
GOT ANY SNACKS?
DIDN'T YOU JUST EAT? I HAVE SOME BEAN BUNS.
THIS IS PRETTY TASTY.
NOM NOM
SHOULDN'T YOU BE STUDYING FOR YOUR TEST?
YEAH, BUT FIRST I WANT TO ORGANIZE MY INSECT COLLECTION. DAD BROUGHT ME SOME COOL BUGS FROM JAVA.
NOW WHAT ARE YOU DOING?
DRAWING THE INSECTS.
ARE YOU GOING TO FLUNK OUT AGAIN?

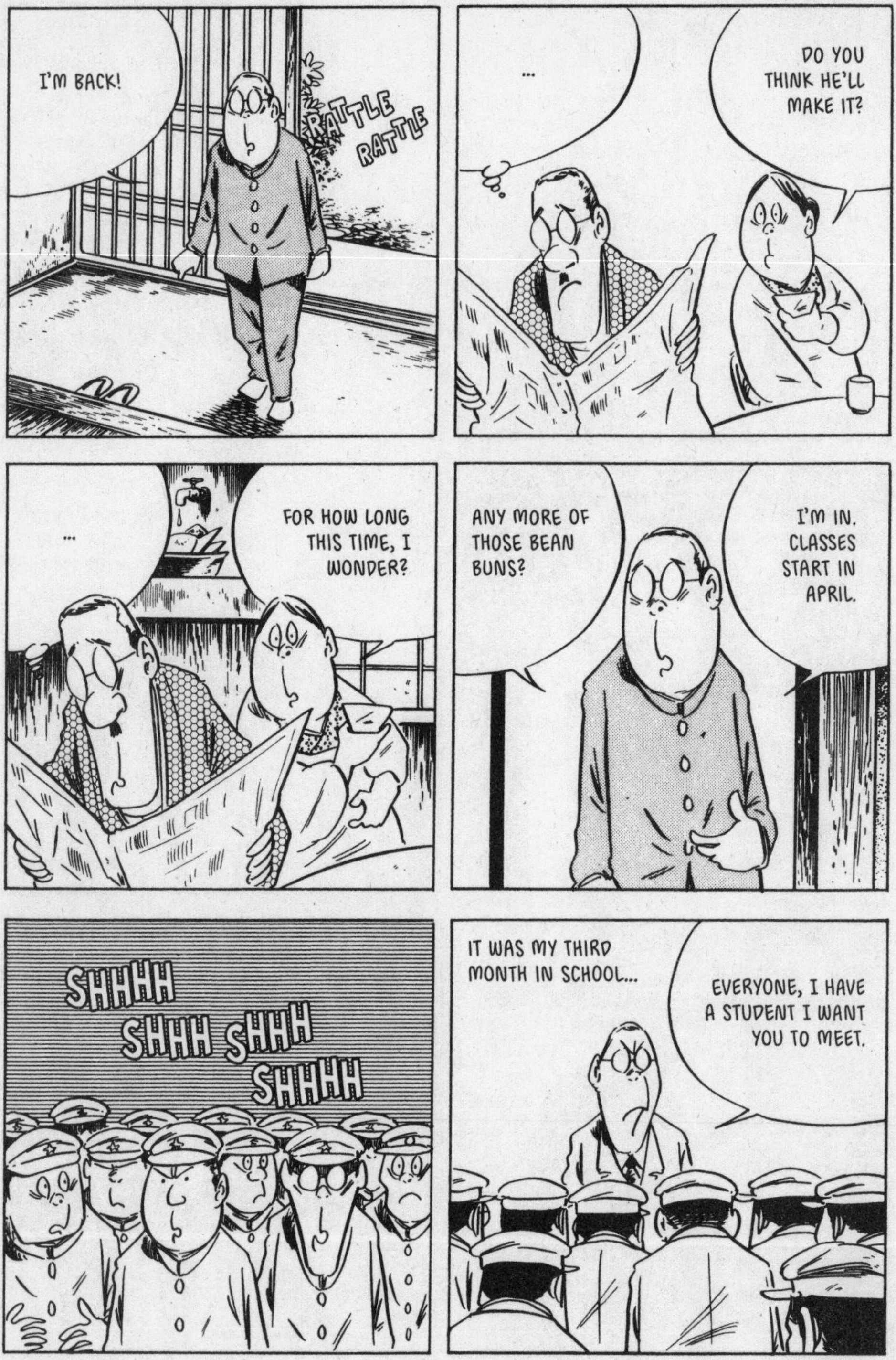
DO YOU THINK HE'LL MAKE IT?
...
I'M BACK!
RATTLE RATTLE
I'M IN. CLASSES START IN APRIL.
ANY MORE OF THOSE BEAN BUNS?
FOR HOW LONG THIS TIME, I WONDER?
...
EVERYONE, I HAVE A STUDENT I WANT YOU TO MEET.
IT WAS MY THIRD MONTH IN SCHOOL...
SHHHH
SHHH SHHH
SHHHH

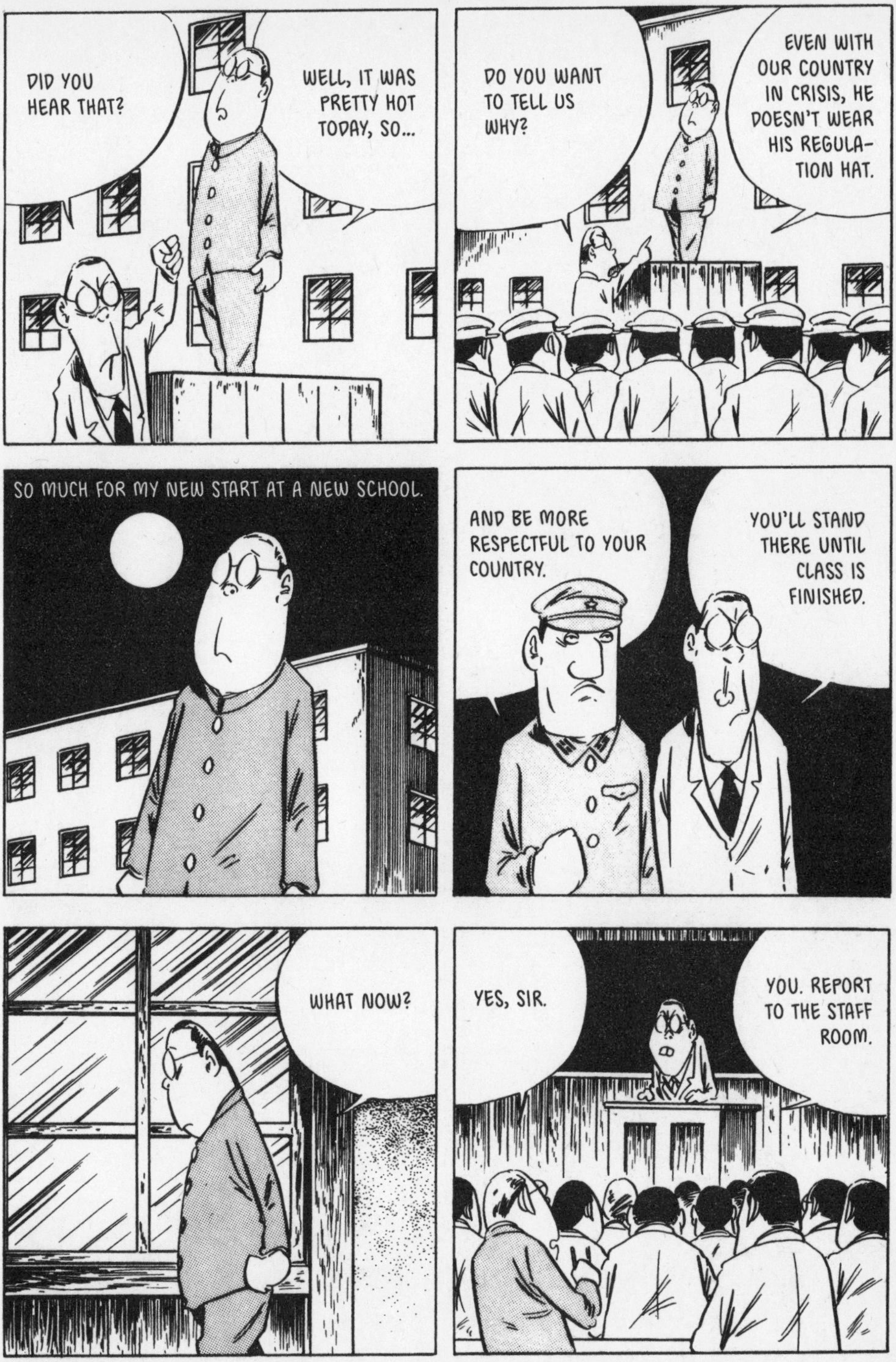
EVEN WITH OUR COUNTRY IN CRISIS, HE DOESN'T WEAR HIS REGULA-TION HAT.
DO YOU WANT TO TELL US WHY?
WELL, IT WAS PRETTY HOT TODAY, SO...
DID YOU HEAR THAT?
YOU'LL STAND THERE UNTIL CLASS IS FINISHED.
AND BE MORE RESPECTFUL TO YOUR COUNTRY.
SO MUCH FOR MY NEW START AT A NEW SCHOOL.
YOU. REPORT TO THE STAFF ROOM.
YES, SIR.
WHAT NOW?

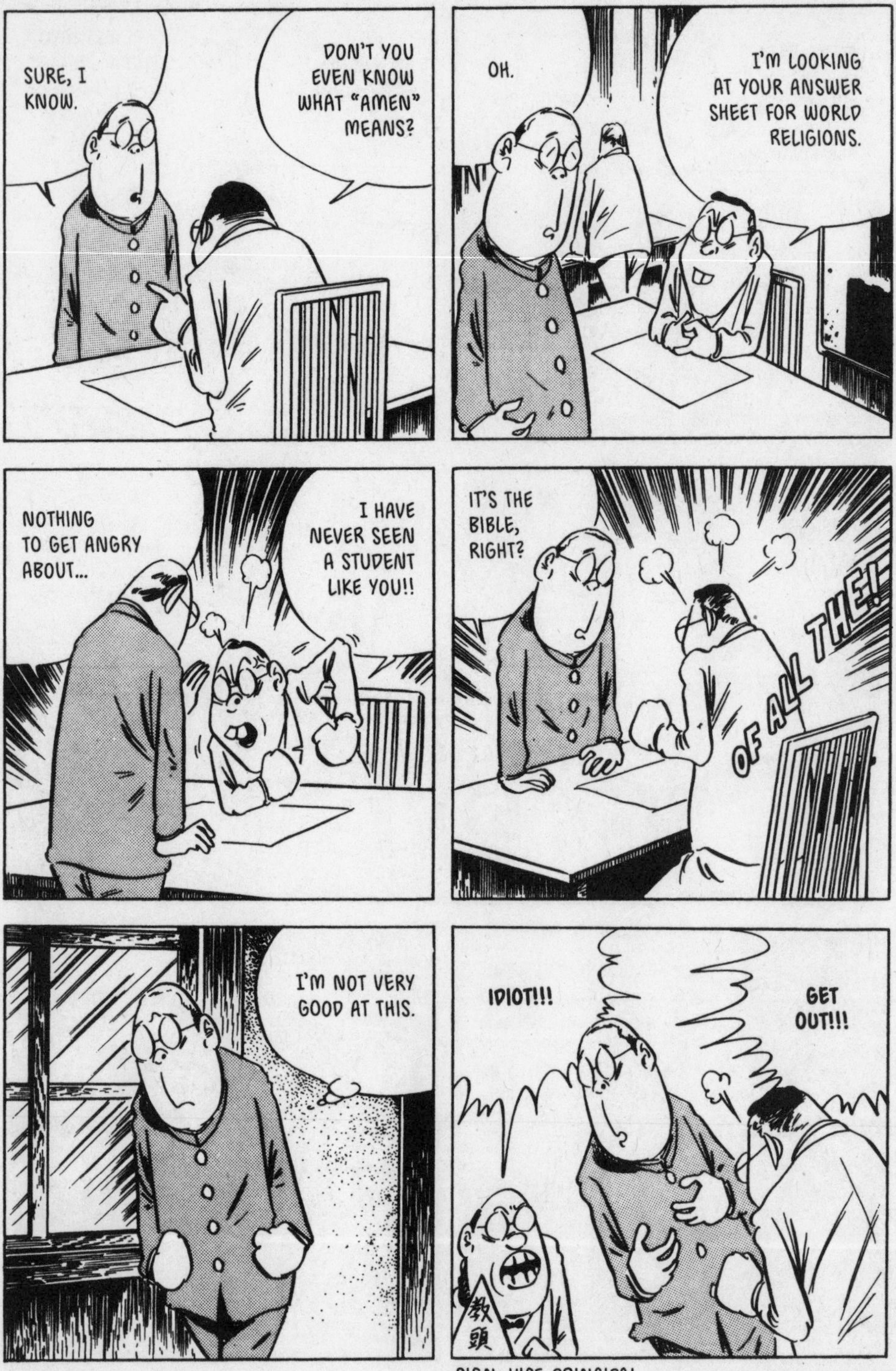
I'M LOOKING AT YOUR ANSWER SHEET FOR WORLD RELIGIONS.
OH.
DON'T YOU EVEN KNOW WHAT "AMEN" MEANS?
SURE, I KNOW.
IT'S THE BIBLE, RIGHT?
OF ALL THE!
I HAVE NEVER SEEN A STUDENT LIKE YOU!!
NOTHING TO GET ANGRY ABOUT...
GET OUT!!!
IDIOT!!!
教頭
I'M NOT VERY GOOD AT THIS.

SIGN: VICE PRINCIPAL.

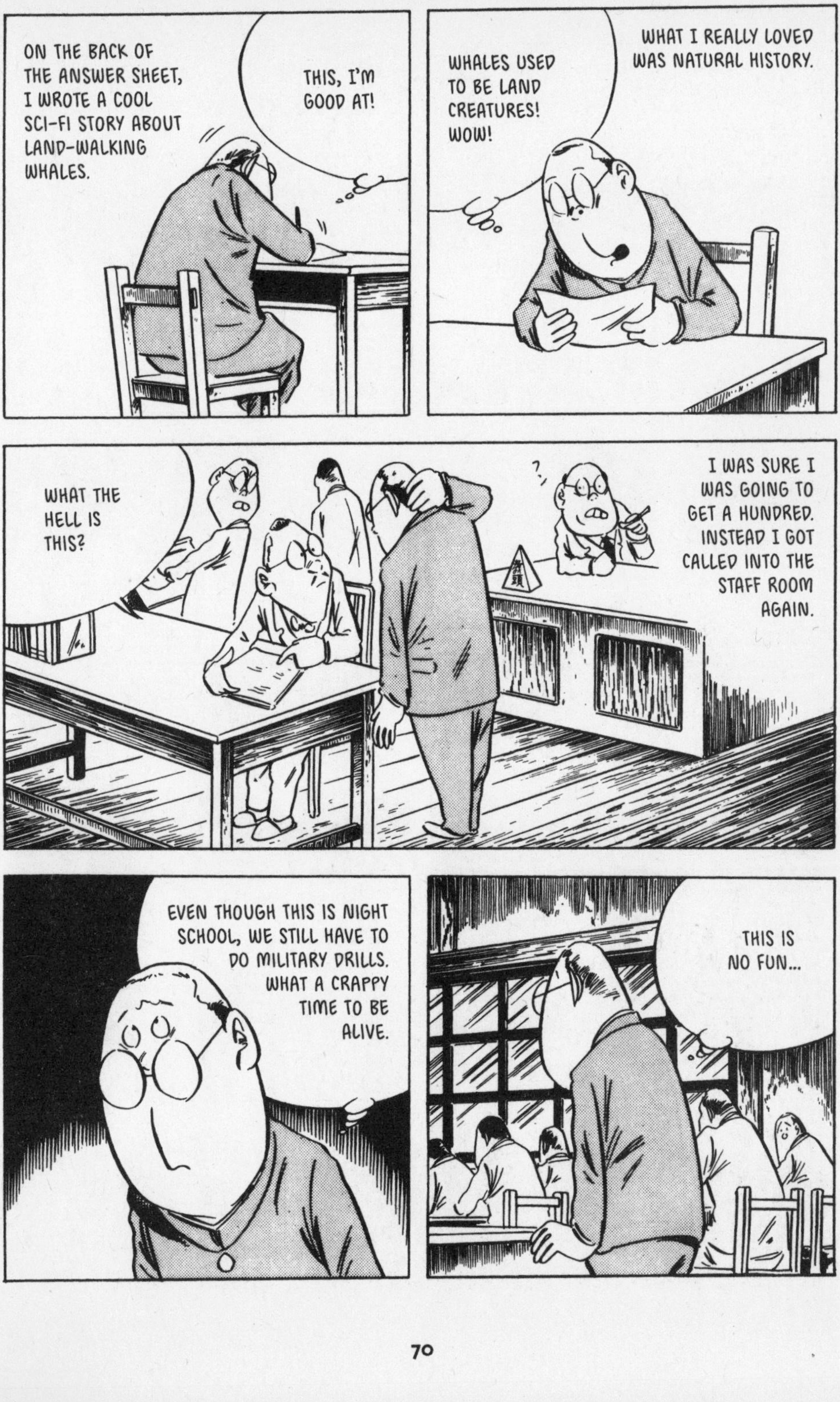
WHAT I REALLY LOVED WAS NATURAL HISTORY.
WHALES USED TO BE LAND CREATURES! WOW!
THIS, I'M GOOD AT!
ON THE BACK OF THE ANSWER SHEET, I WROTE A COOL SCI-FI STORY ABOUT LAND-WALKING WHALES.
I WAS SURE I WAS GOING TO GET A HUNDRED. INSTEAD I GOT CALLED INTO THE STAFF ROOM AGAIN.
WHAT THE HELL IS THIS?
THIS IS NO FUN...
EVEN THOUGH THIS IS NIGHT SCHOOL, WE STILL HAVE TO DO MILITARY DRILLS. WHAT A CRAPPY TIME TO BE ALIVE.

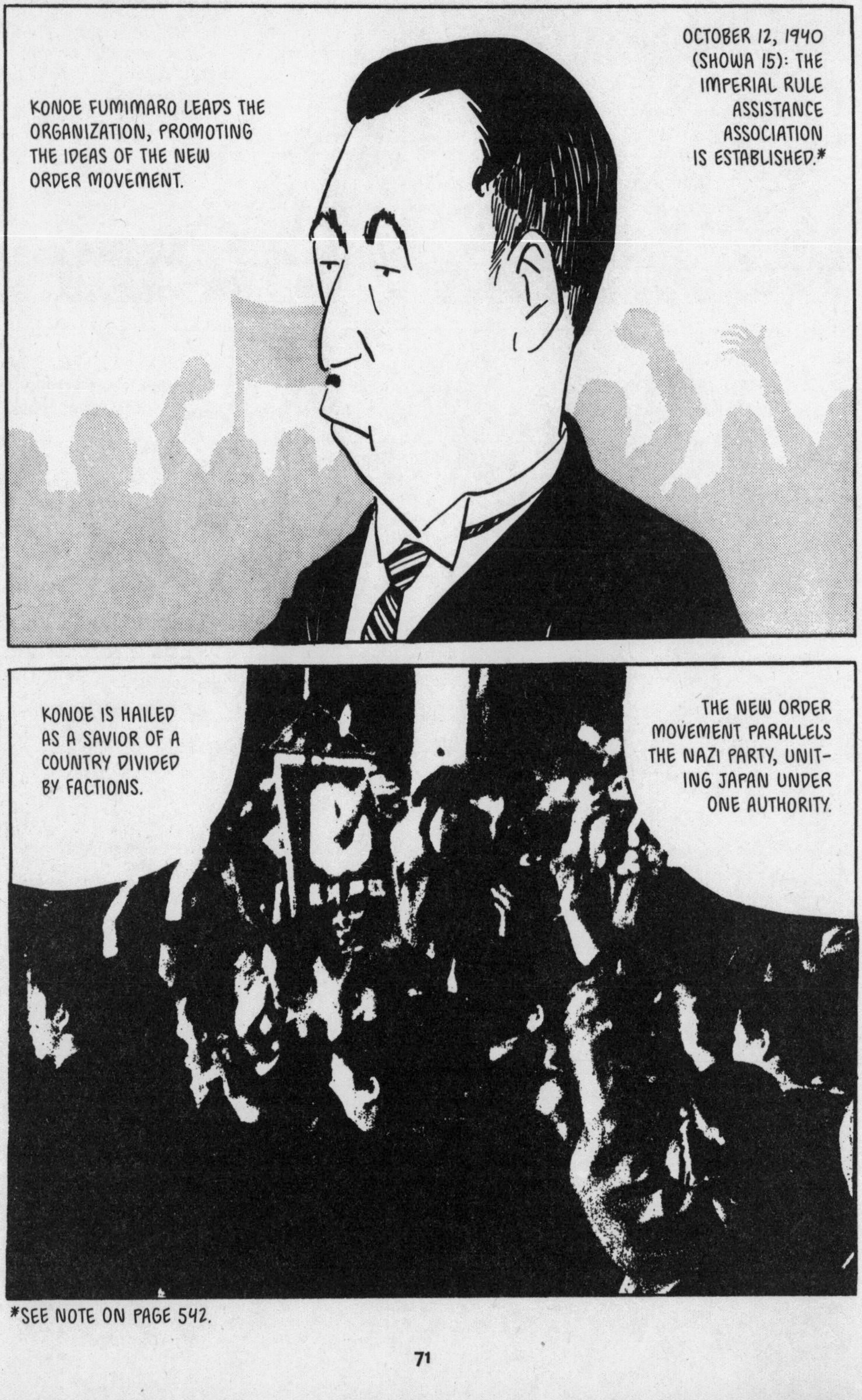
OCTOBER 12, 1940 (SHOWA 15): THE IMPERIAL RULE ASSISTANCE ASSOCIATION IS ESTABLISHED.*
KONOE FUMIMARO LEADS THE ORGANIZATION, PROMOTING THE IDEAS OF THE NEW ORDER MOVEMENT.
THE NEW ORDER MOVEMENT PARALLELS THE NAZI PARTY, UNIT-ING JAPAN UNDER ONE AUTHORITY.
KONOE IS HAILED AS A SAVIOR OF A COUNTRY DIVIDED BY FACTIONS.

*SEE NOTE ON PAGE 542.

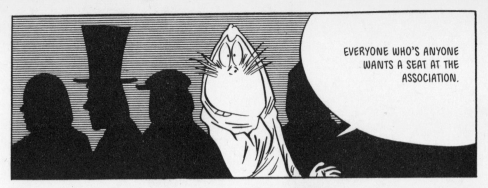

EVERYONE WHO'S ANYONE WANTS A SEAT AT THE ASSOCIATION.

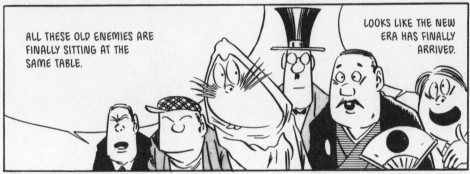

LOOKS LIKE THE NEW ERA HAS FINALLY ARRIVED.
ALL THESE OLD ENEMIES ARE FINALLY SITTING AT THE SAME TABLE.

MILITARY LEADERS PUSH FOR A FULL MILITARY DICTATORSHIP.
LOOK AT GERMANY!! WE DON'T WANT TO BE LATE TO THE BUS AGAIN!!!

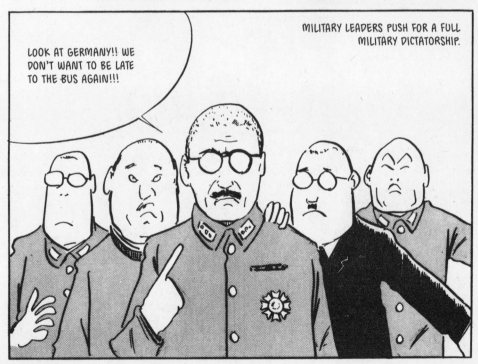

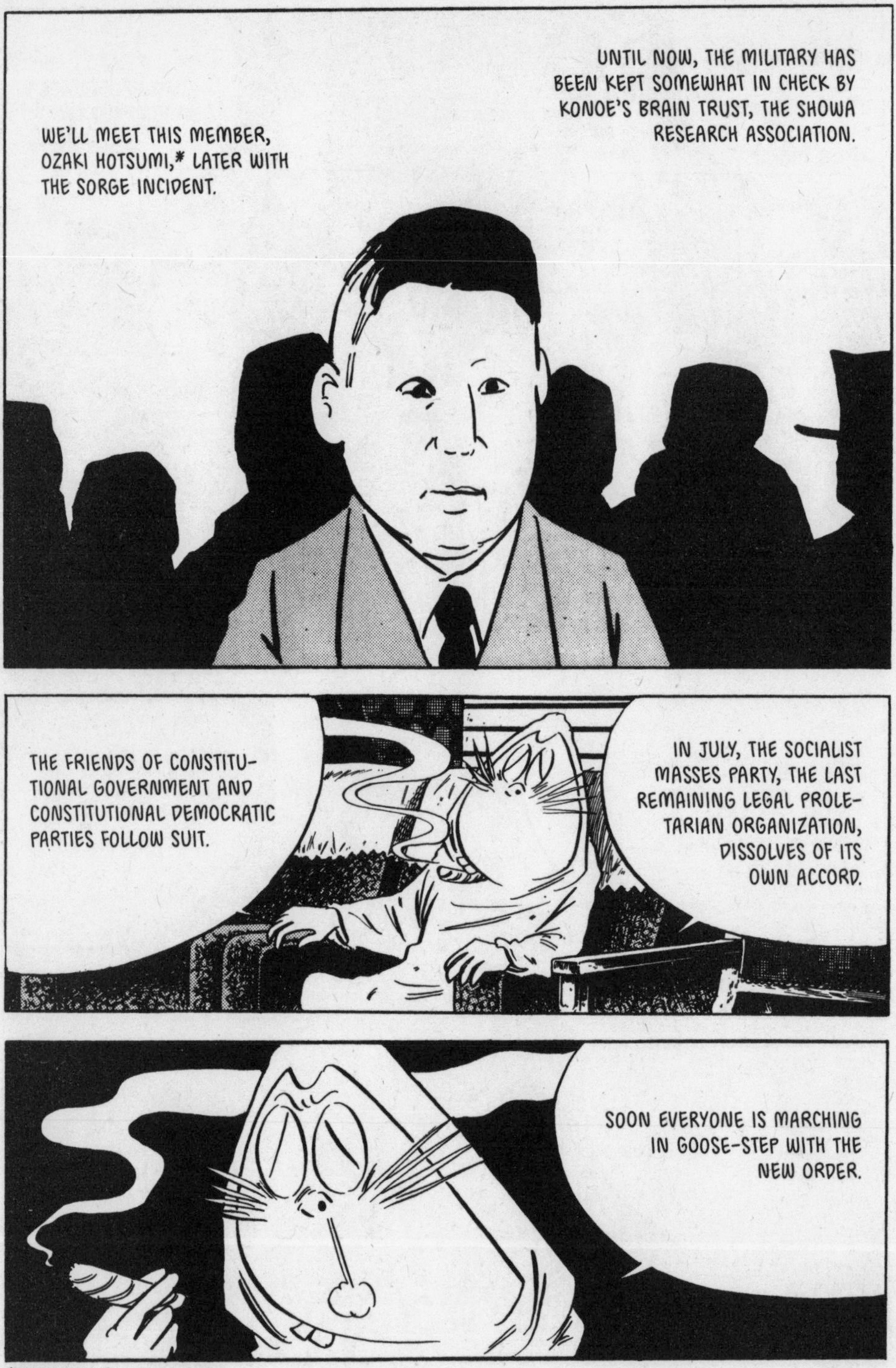
UNTIL NOW, THE MILITARY HAS BEEN KEPT SOMEWHAT IN CHECK BY KONOE'S BRAIN TRUST, THE SHOWA RESEARCH ASSOCIATION.
WE'LL MEET THIS MEMBER, OZAKI HOTSUMI,* LATER WITH THE SORGE INCIDENT.
IN JULY, THE SOCIALIST MASSES PARTY, THE LAST REMAINING LEGAL PROLE-TARIAN ORGANIZATION, DISSOLVES OF ITS OWN ACCORD.
THE FRIENDS OF CONSTITU-TIONAL GOVERNMENT AND CONSTITUTIONAL DEMOCRATIC PARTIES FOLLOW SUIT.
SOON EVERYONE IS MARCHING IN GOOSE-STEP WITH THE NEW ORDER.

*SEE NOTE ON PAGE 542.

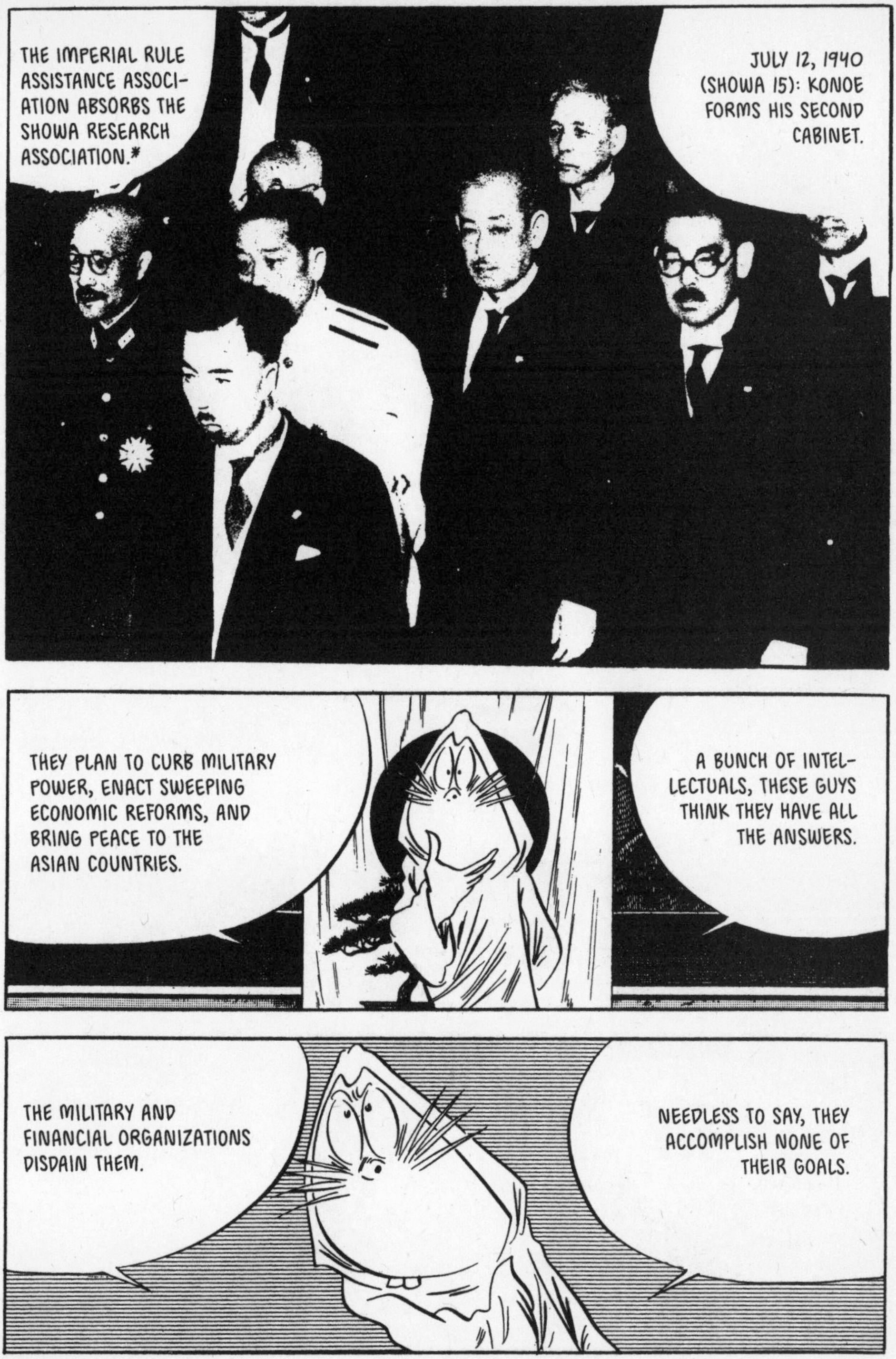
JULY 12, 1940 (SHOWA 15): KONOE FORMS HIS SECOND CABINET.
THE IMPERIAL RULE ASSISTANCE ASSOCIATION ABSORBS THE SHOWA RESEARCH ASSOCIATION.*
A BUNCH OF INTELLECTUALS, THESE GUYS THINK THEY HAVE ALL THE ANSWERS.
THEY PLAN TO CURB MILITARY POWER, ENACT SWEEPING ECONOMIC REFORMS, AND BRING PEACE TO THE ASIAN COUNTRIES.
NEEDLESS TO SAY, THEY ACCOMPLISH NONE OF THEIR GOALS.
THE MILITARY AND FINANCIAL ORGANIZATIONS DISDAIN THEM.

*SEE NOTE ON PAGE 543.

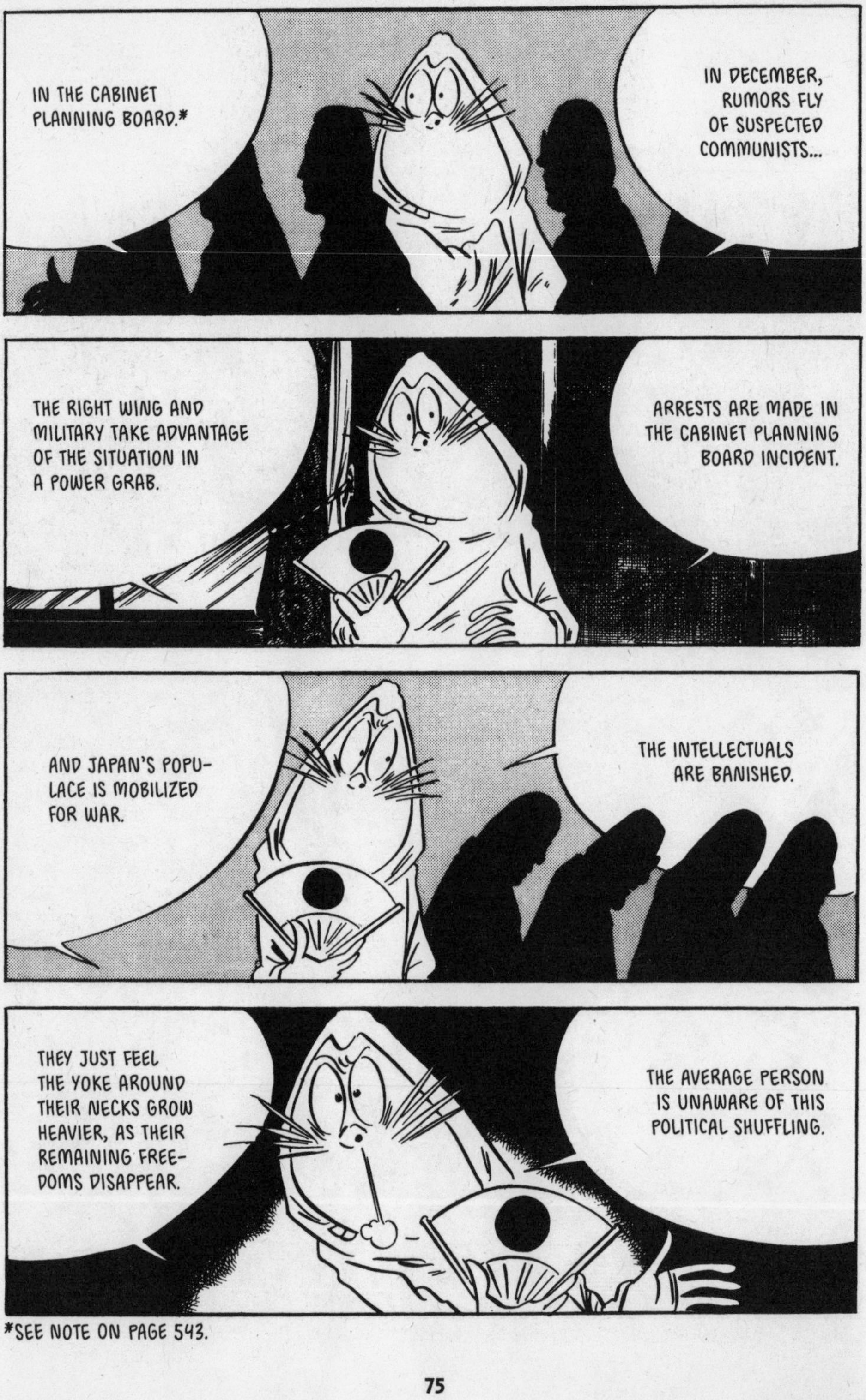
IN DECEMBER, RUMORS FLY OF SUSPECTED COMMUNISTS...
IN THE CABINET PLANNING BOARD.*
ARRESTS ARE MADE IN THE CABINET PLANNING BOARD INCIDENT.
THE RIGHT WING AND MILITARY TAKE ADVANTAGE OF THE SITUATION IN A POWER GRAB.
THE INTELLECTUALS ARE BANISHED.
AND JAPAN'S POPULACE IS MOBILIZED FOR WAR.
THE AVERAGE PERSON IS UNAWARE OF THIS POLITICAL SHUFFLING.
THEY JUST FEEL THE YOKE AROUND THEIR NECKS GROW HEAVIER, AS THEIR REMAINING FREEDOMS DISAPPEAR.

*SEE NOTE ON PAGE 543.

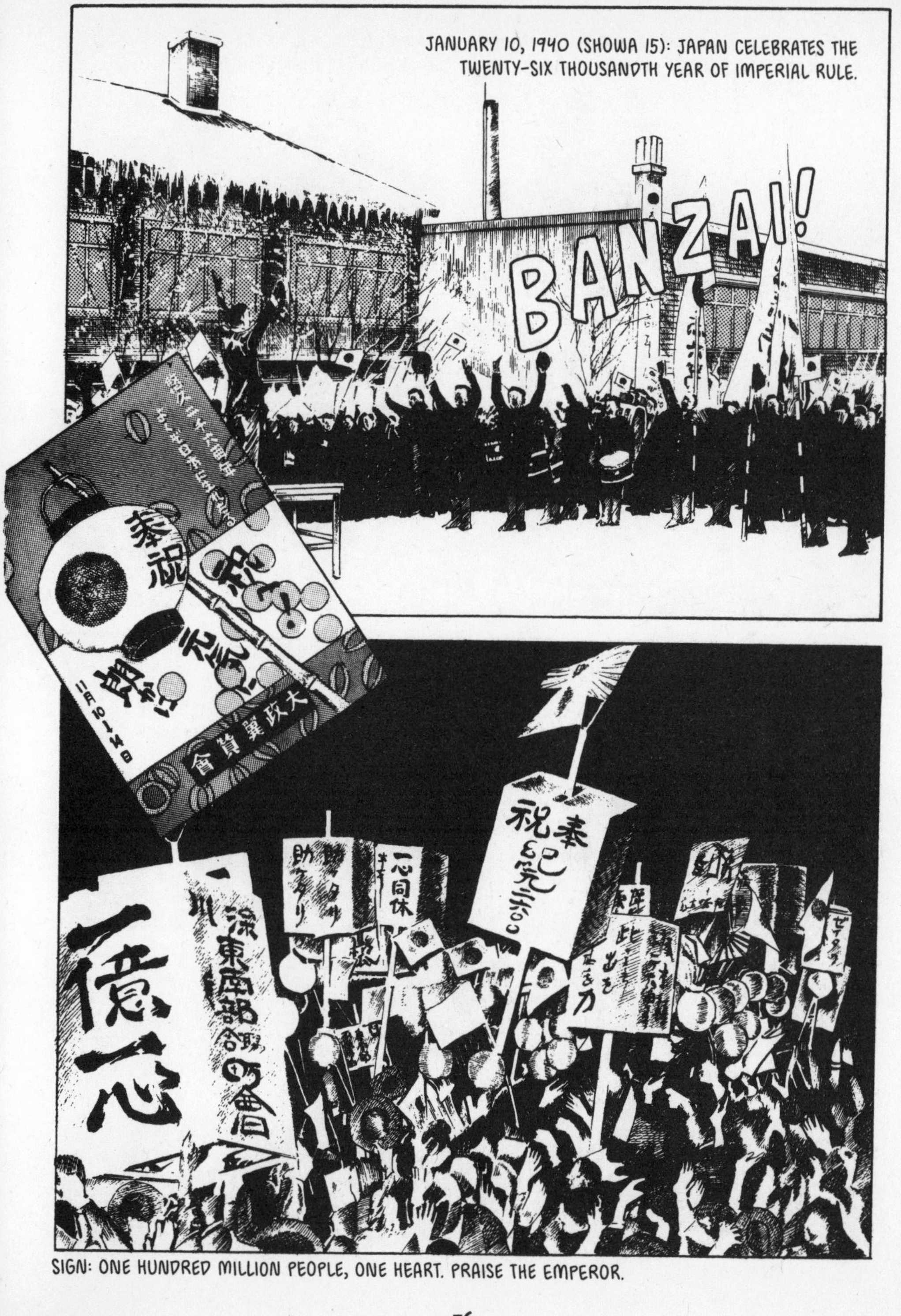
JANUARY 10, 1940 (SHOWA 15): JAPAN CELEBRATES THE TWENTY-SIX THOUSANDTH YEAR OF IMPERIAL RULE.
BANZAI!
一億一心
SIGN: ONE HUNDRED MILLION PEOPLE, ONE HEART. PRAISE THE EMPEROR.

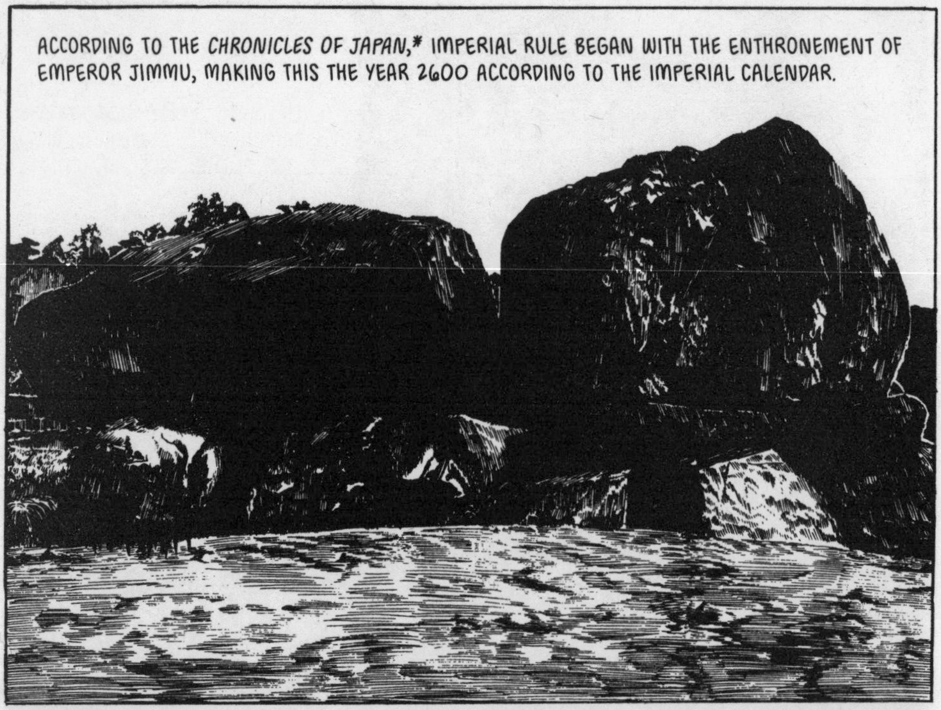
ACCORDING TO THE *CHRONICLES OF JAPAN*,* IMPERIAL RULE BEGAN WITH THE ENTHRONEMENT OF EMPEROR JIMMU, MAKING THIS THE YEAR 2600 ACCORDING TO THE IMPERIAL CALENDAR.

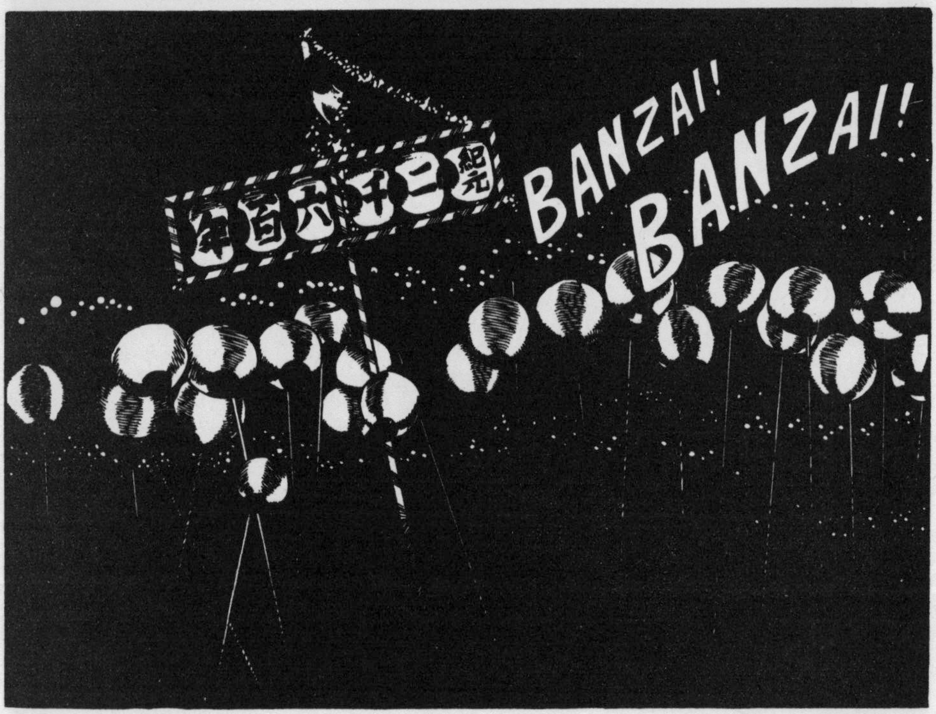
紀元二千六百年
BANZAI!
BANZAI!

*SEE NOTE ON PAGE 543.

SIGN: THE YEAR 2600.

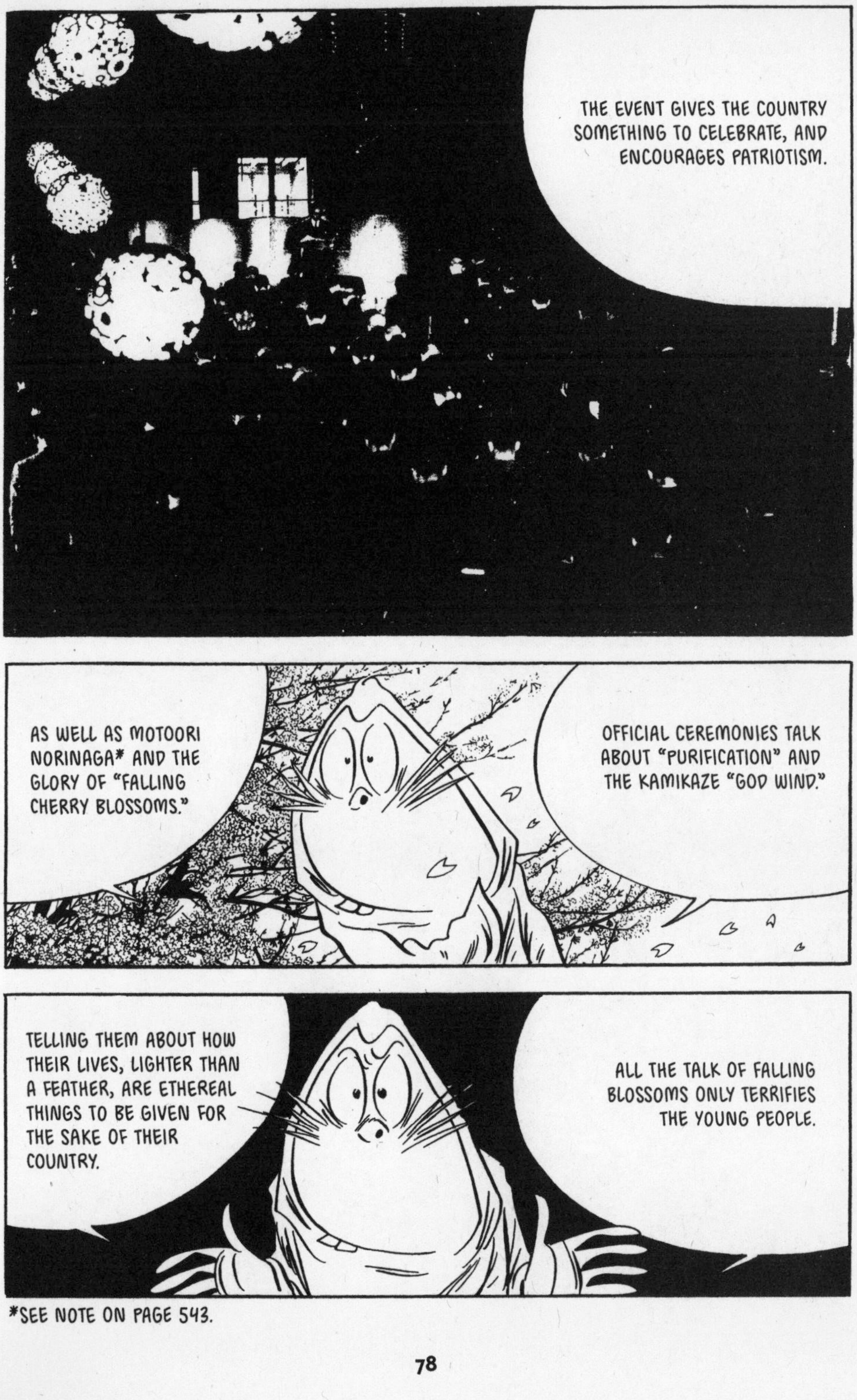
THE EVENT GIVES THE COUNTRY SOMETHING TO CELEBRATE, AND ENCOURAGES PATRIOTISM.
OFFICIAL CEREMONIES TALK ABOUT "PURIFICATION" AND THE KAMIKAZE "GOD WIND."
AS WELL AS MOTOORI NORINAGA* AND THE GLORY OF "FALLING CHERRY BLOSSOMS."
ALL THE TALK OF FALLING BLOSSOMS ONLY TERRIFIES THE YOUNG PEOPLE.
TELLING THEM ABOUT HOW THEIR LIVES, LIGHTER THAN A FEATHER, ARE ETHEREAL THINGS TO BE GIVEN FOR THE SAKE OF THEIR COUNTRY.

*SEE NOTE ON PAGE 543.

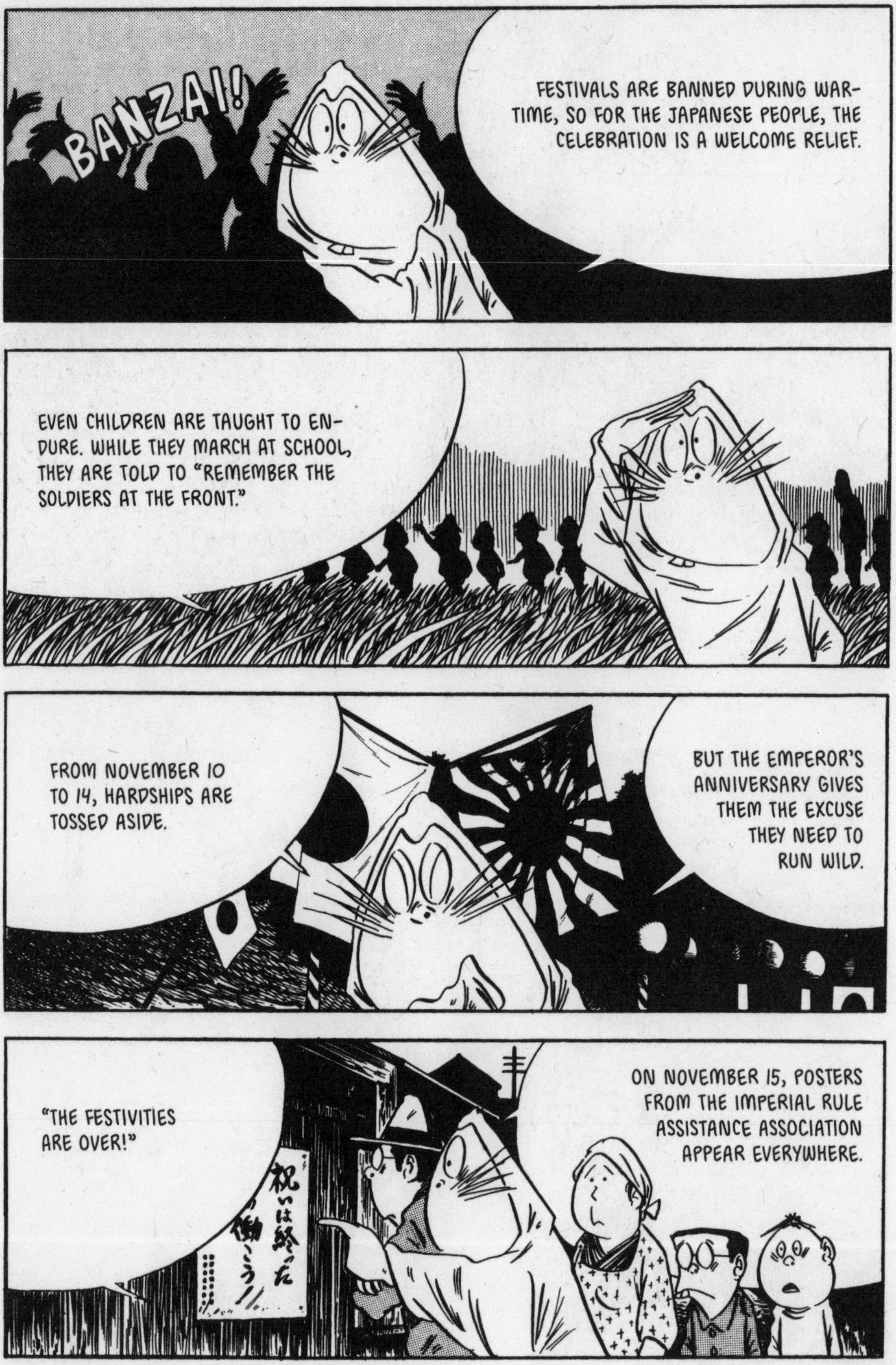
FESTIVALS ARE BANNED DURING WAR-TIME, SO FOR THE JAPANESE PEOPLE, THE CELEBRATION IS A WELCOME RELIEF.
BANZAI!
EVEN CHILDREN ARE TAUGHT TO EN-DURE. WHILE THEY MARCH AT SCHOOL, THEY ARE TOLD TO "REMEMBER THE SOLDIERS AT THE FRONT."
FROM NOVEMBER 10 TO 14, HARDSHIPS ARE TOSSED ASIDE.
BUT THE EMPEROR'S ANNIVERSARY GIVES THEM THE EXCUSE THEY NEED TO RUN WILD.
ON NOVEMBER 15, POSTERS FROM THE IMPERIAL RULE ASSISTANCE ASSOCIATION APPEAR EVERYWHERE.
祝いは終った 働こう!
"THE FESTIVITIES ARE OVER!"

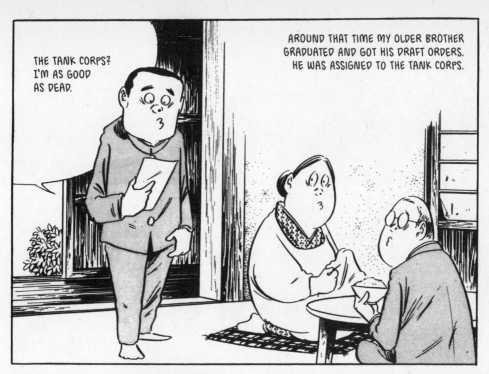

AROUND THAT TIME MY OLDER BROTHER GRADUATED AND GOT HIS DRAFT ORDERS. HE WAS ASSIGNED TO THE TANK CORPS.
THE TANK CORPS? I'M AS GOOD AS DEAD.
I READ SOMETHING ABOUT THE NAVY ACCEPTING PREPARATORY CANDIDATES. THERE WAS AN ANNOUNCEMENT IN THE PAPER.
NAVY PREPARATORY CANDIDATES? WHAT'S THAT?
WHATEVER IT IS, THE NAVY'S WAY BETTER THAN THE ARMY.
THAT'S TRUE. I GUESS I'LL GIVE IT A SHOT.

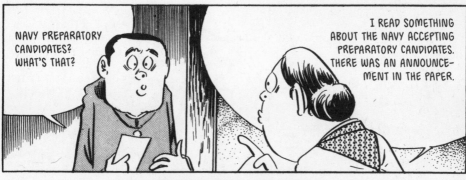

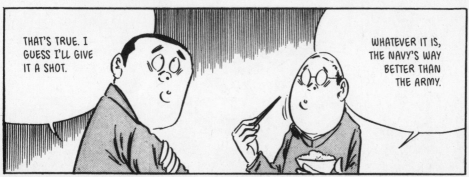

THE EVE OF WAR

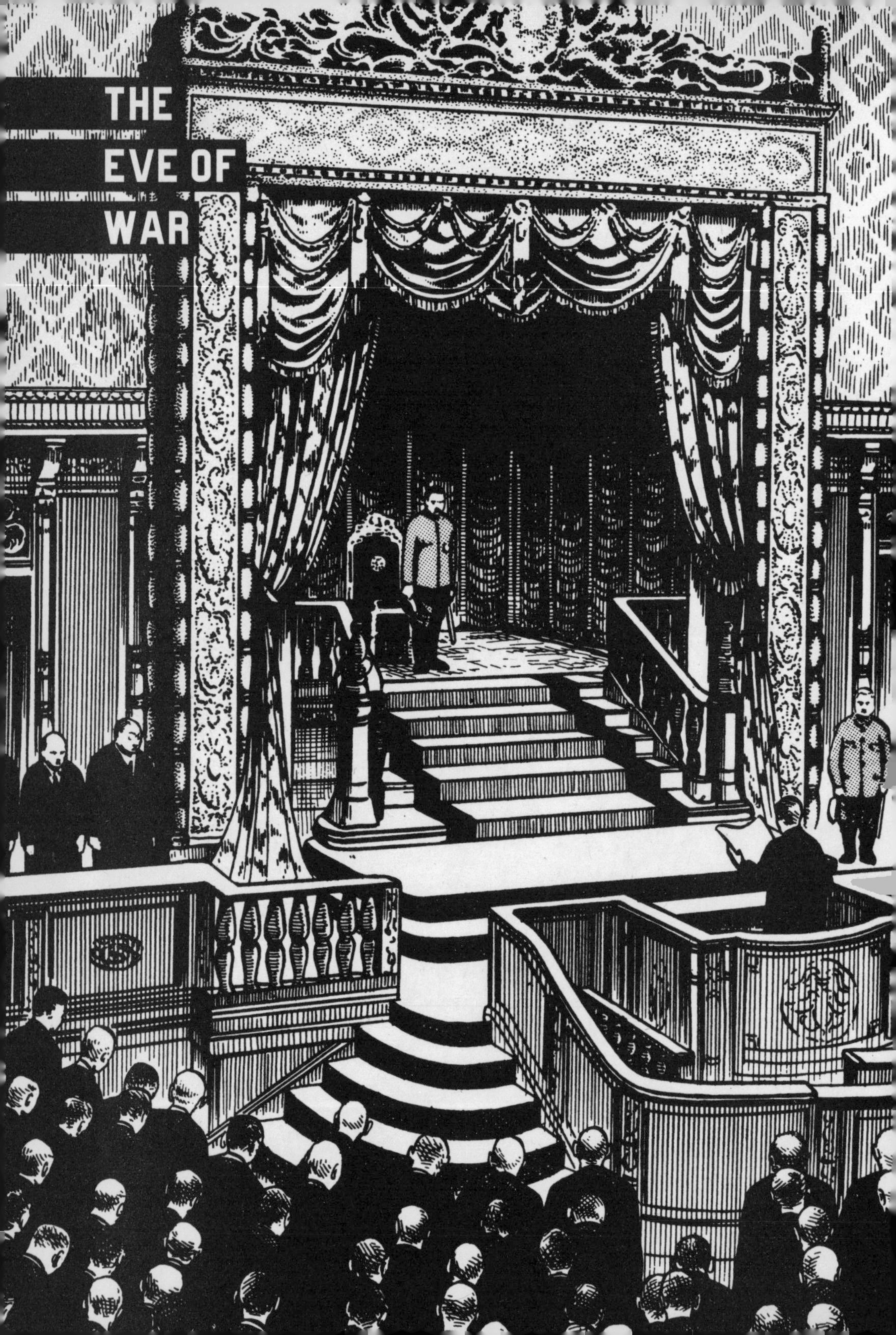

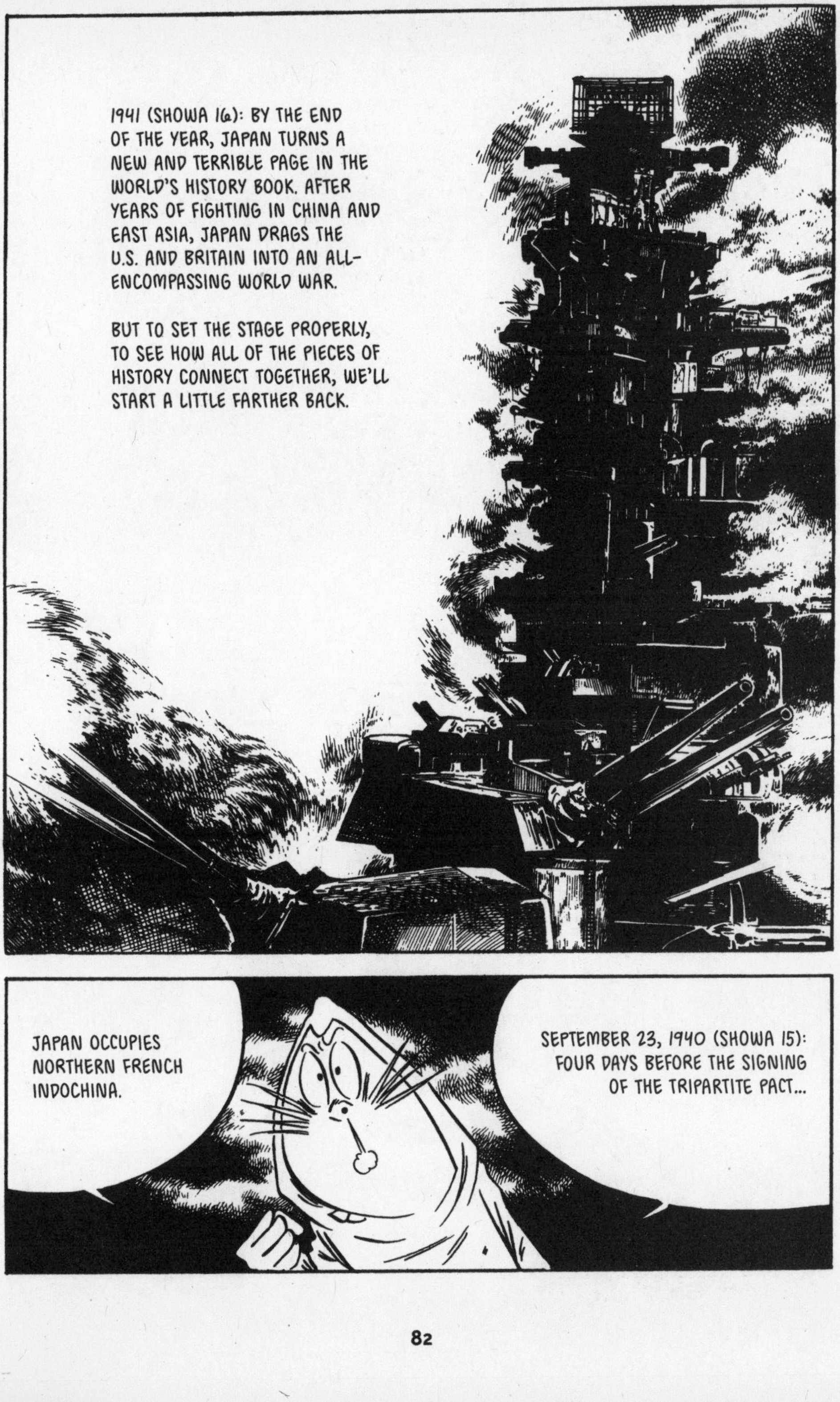
1941 (SHOWA 16): BY THE END OF THE YEAR, JAPAN TURNS A NEW AND TERRIBLE PAGE IN THE WORLD'S HISTORY BOOK. AFTER YEARS OF FIGHTING IN CHINA AND EAST ASIA, JAPAN DRAGS THE U.S. AND BRITAIN INTO AN ALL-ENCOMPASSING WORLD WAR.
BUT TO SET THE STAGE PROPERLY, TO SEE HOW ALL OF THE PIECES OF HISTORY CONNECT TOGETHER, WE'LL START A LITTLE FARTHER BACK.
SEPTEMBER 23, 1940 (SHOWA 15): FOUR DAYS BEFORE THE SIGNING OF THE TRIPARTITE PACT...
JAPAN OCCUPIES NORTHERN FRENCH INDOCHINA.

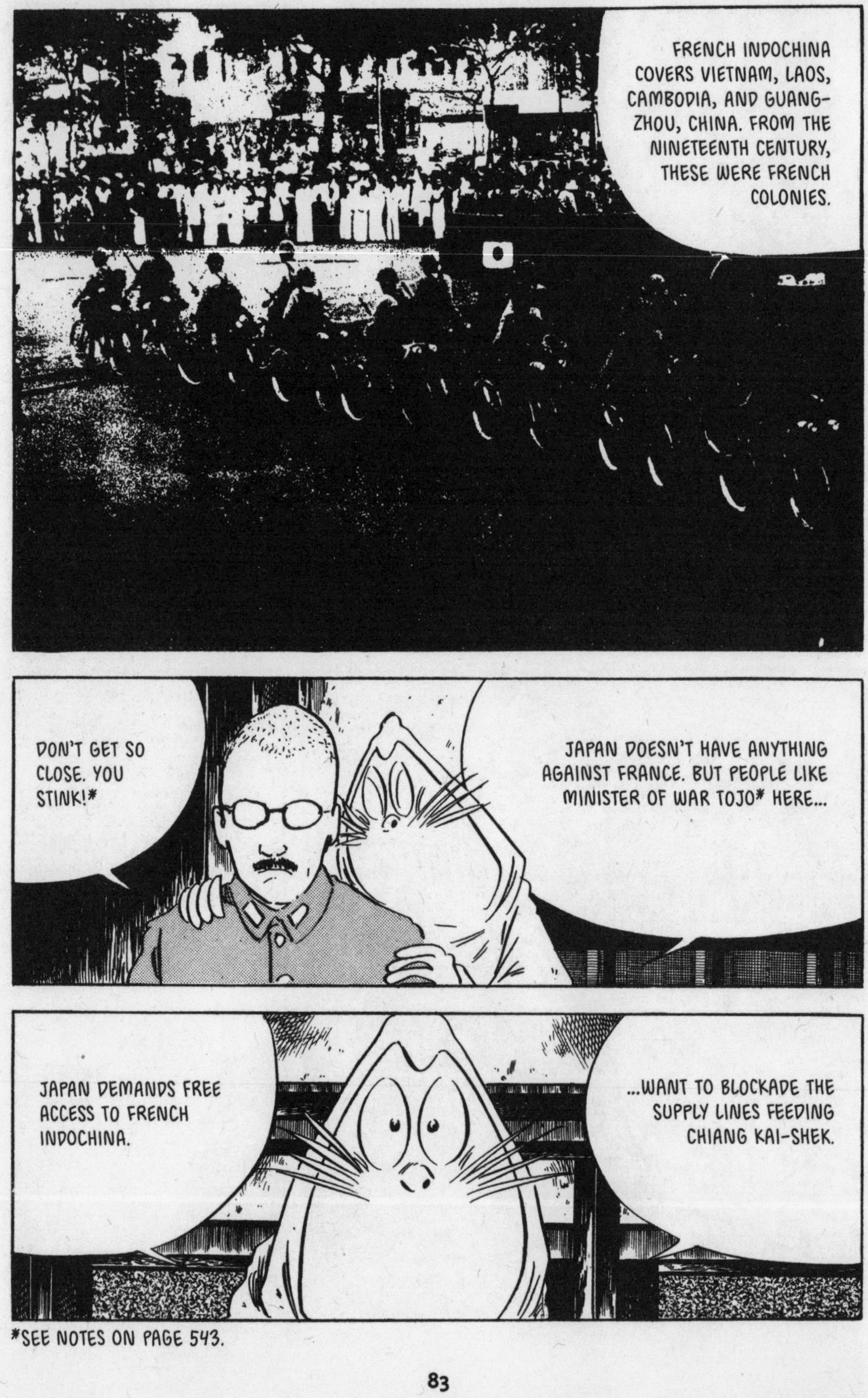
FRENCH INDOCHINA COVERS VIETNAM, LAOS, CAMBODIA, AND GUANG-ZHOU, CHINA. FROM THE NINETEENTH CENTURY, THESE WERE FRENCH COLONIES.
JAPAN DOESN'T HAVE ANYTHING AGAINST FRANCE. BUT PEOPLE LIKE MINISTER OF WAR TOJO* HERE...
DON'T GET SO CLOSE. YOU STINK!*
...WANT TO BLOCKADE THE SUPPLY LINES FEEDING CHIANG KAI-SHEK.
JAPAN DEMANDS FREE ACCESS TO FRENCH INDOCHINA.

*SEE NOTES ON PAGE 543.

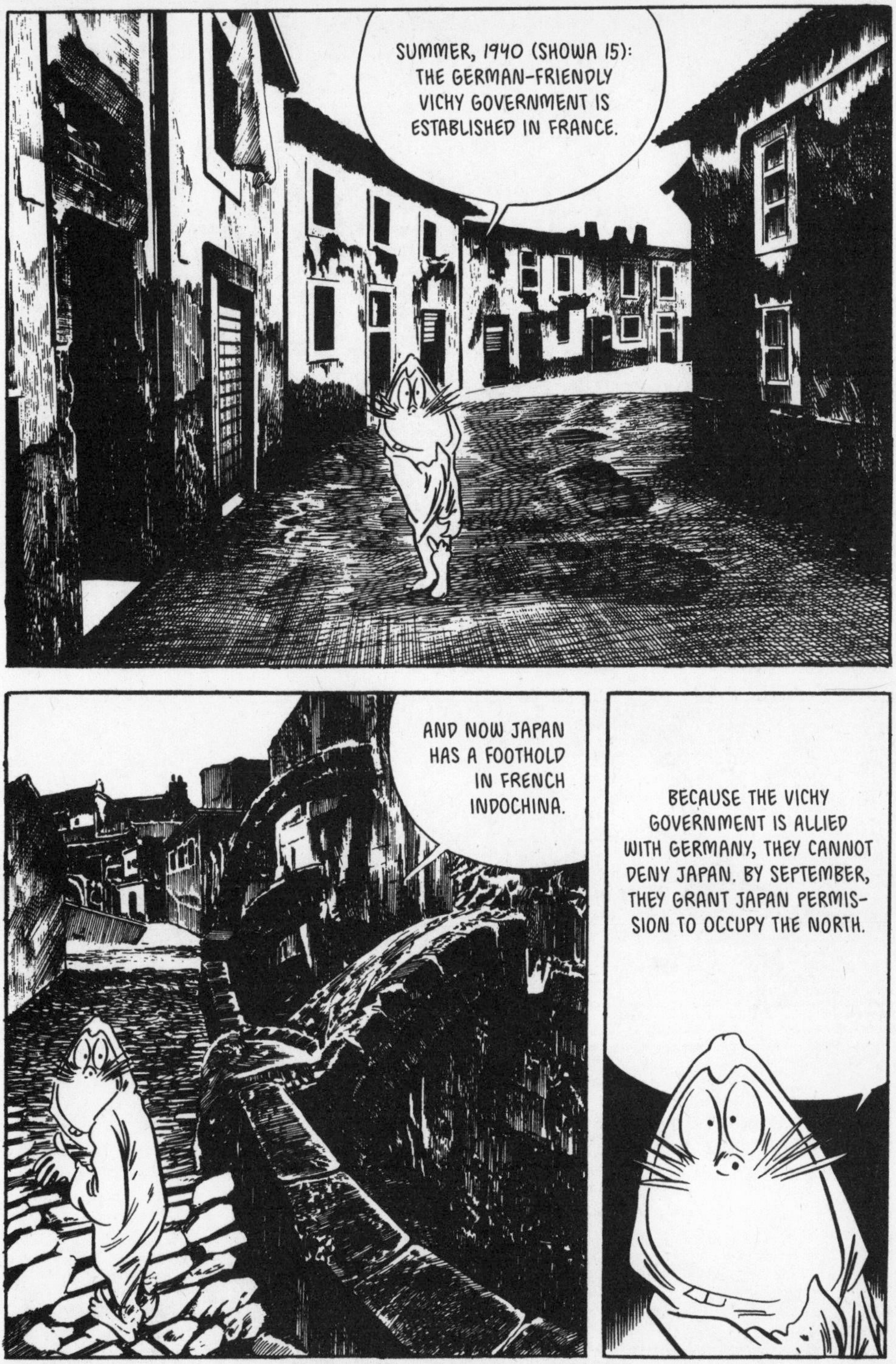
SUMMER, 1940 (SHOWA 15): THE GERMAN-FRIENDLY VICHY GOVERNMENT IS ESTABLISHED IN FRANCE.
BECAUSE THE VICHY GOVERNMENT IS ALLIED WITH GERMANY, THEY CANNOT DENY JAPAN. BY SEPTEMBER, THEY GRANT JAPAN PERMISSION TO OCCUPY THE NORTH.
AND NOW JAPAN HAS A FOOTHOLD IN FRENCH INDOCHINA.

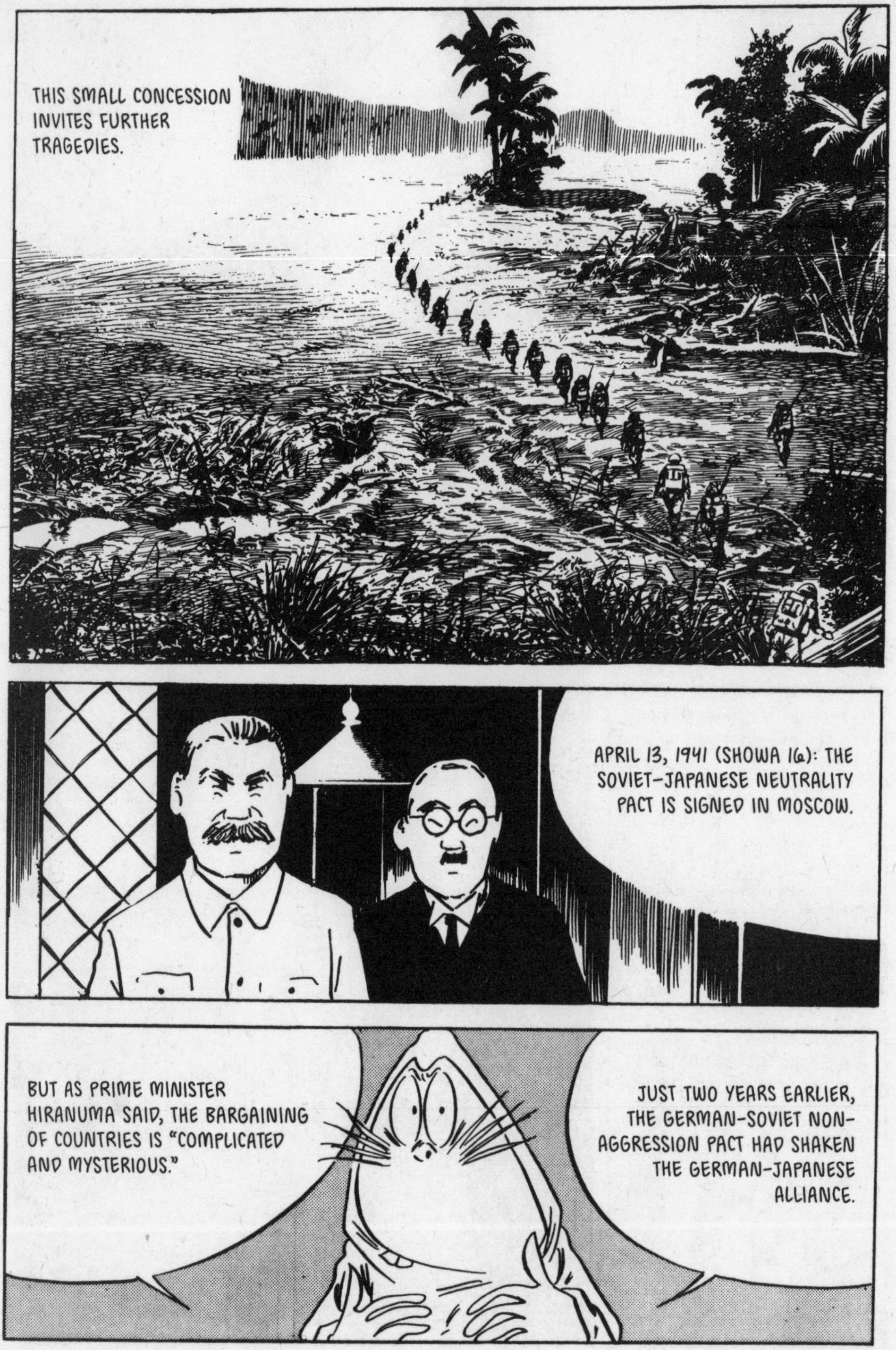
THIS SMALL CONCESSION INVITES FURTHER TRAGEDIES.
APRIL 13, 1941 (SHOWA 16): THE SOVIET-JAPANESE NEUTRALITY PACT IS SIGNED IN MOSCOW.
JUST TWO YEARS EARLIER, THE GERMAN-SOVIET NON-AGGRESSION PACT HAD SHAKEN THE GERMAN-JAPANESE ALLIANCE.
BUT AS PRIME MINISTER HIRANUMA SAID, THE BARGAINING OF COUNTRIES IS "COMPLICATED AND MYSTERIOUS."

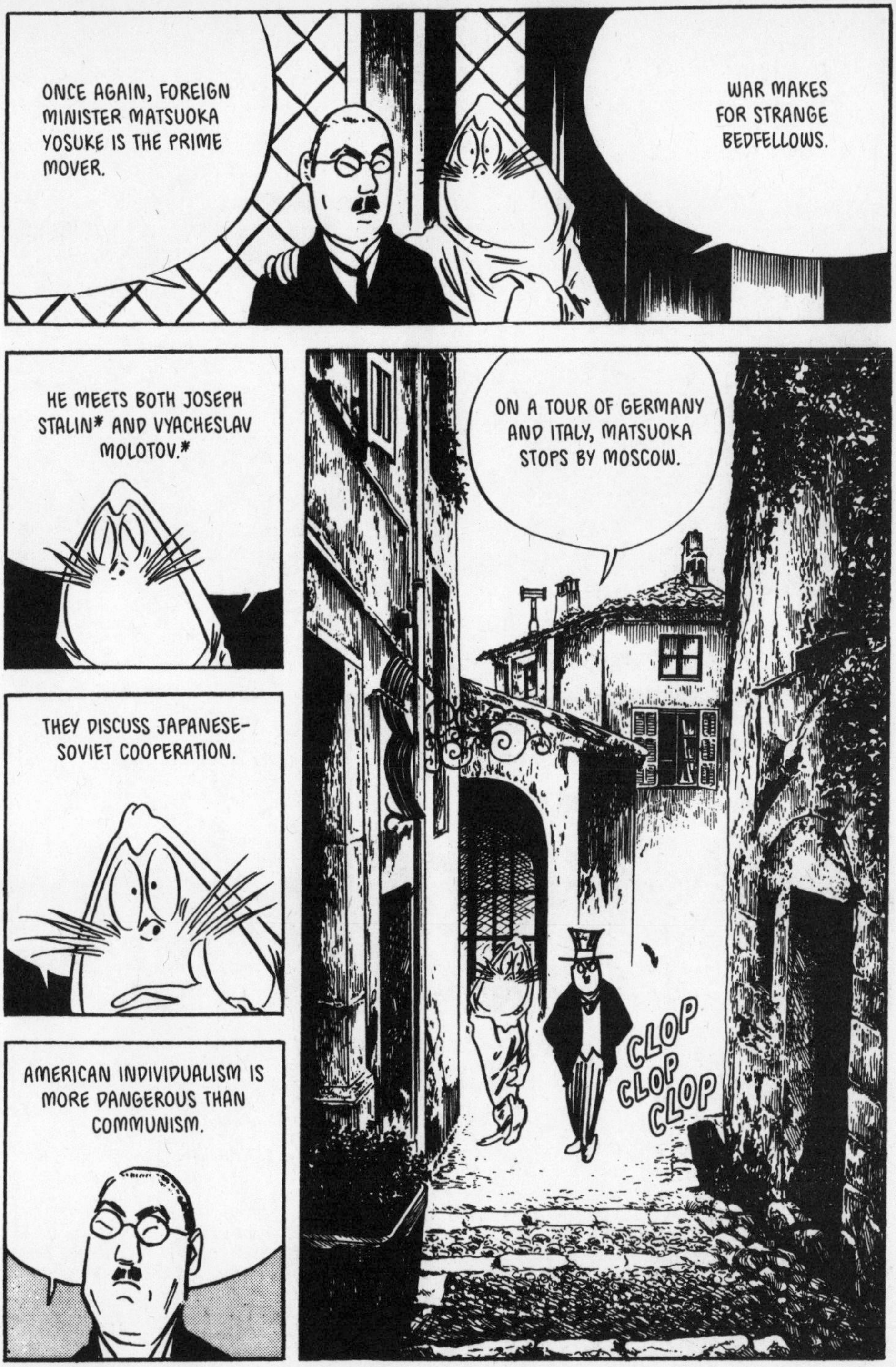
WAR MAKES FOR STRANGE BEDFELLOWS.
ONCE AGAIN, FOREIGN MINISTER MATSUOKA YOSUKE IS THE PRIME MOVER.
ON A TOUR OF GERMANY AND ITALY, MATSUOKA STOPS BY MOSCOW.
CLOP CLOP CLOP
HE MEETS BOTH JOSEPH STALIN* AND VYACHESLAV MOLOTOV.*
THEY DISCUSS JAPANESE-SOVIET COOPERATION.
AMERICAN INDIVIDUALISM IS MORE DANGEROUS THAN COMMUNISM.

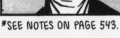

*SEE NOTES ON PAGE 543.

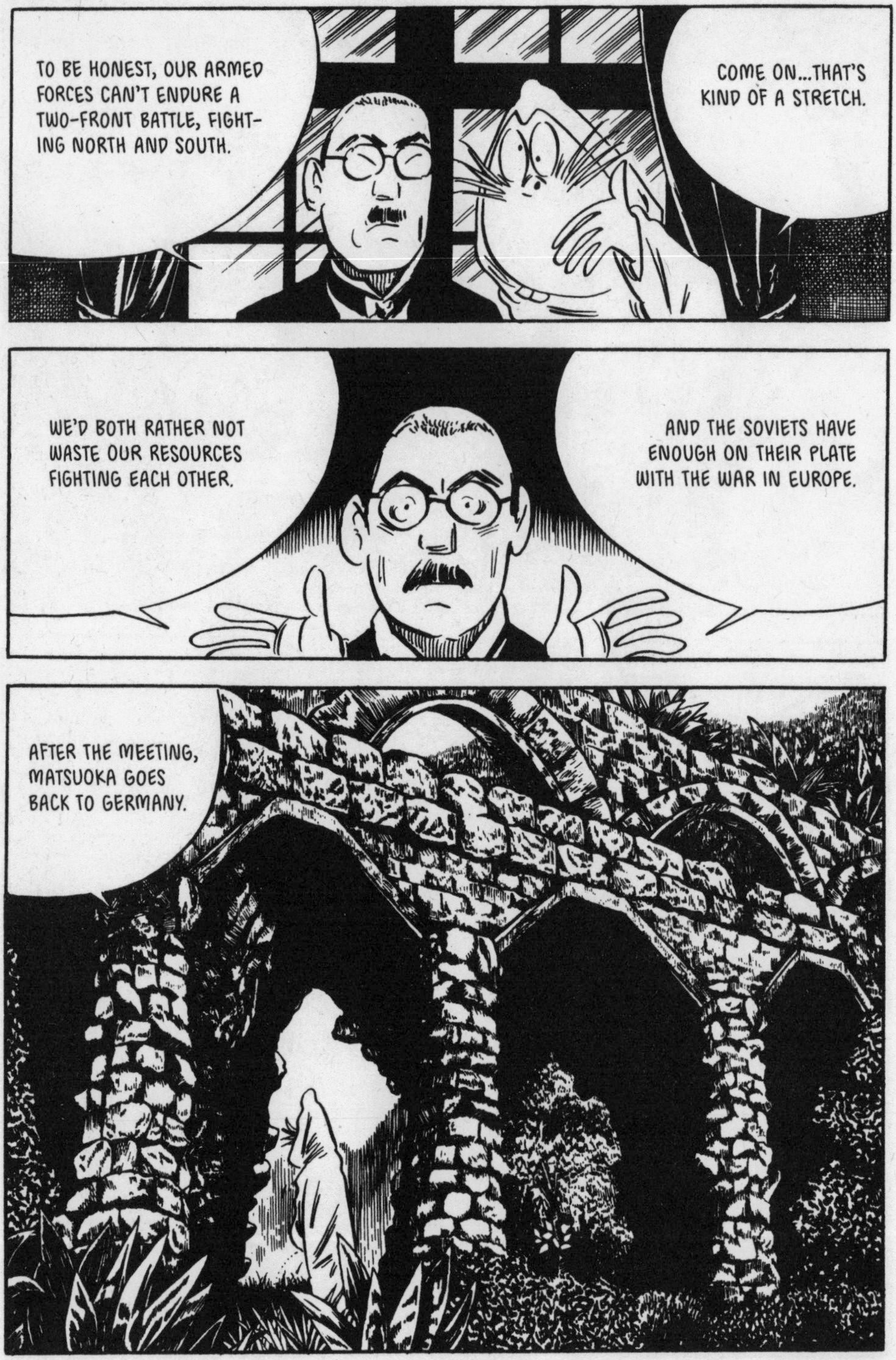
COME ON...THAT'S KIND OF A STRETCH.
TO BE HONEST, OUR ARMED FORCES CAN'T ENDURE A TWO-FRONT BATTLE, FIGHT-ING NORTH AND SOUTH.
AND THE SOVIETS HAVE ENOUGH ON THEIR PLATE WITH THE WAR IN EUROPE.
WE'D BOTH RATHER NOT WASTE OUR RESOURCES FIGHTING EACH OTHER.
AFTER THE MEETING, MATSUOKA GOES BACK TO GERMANY.

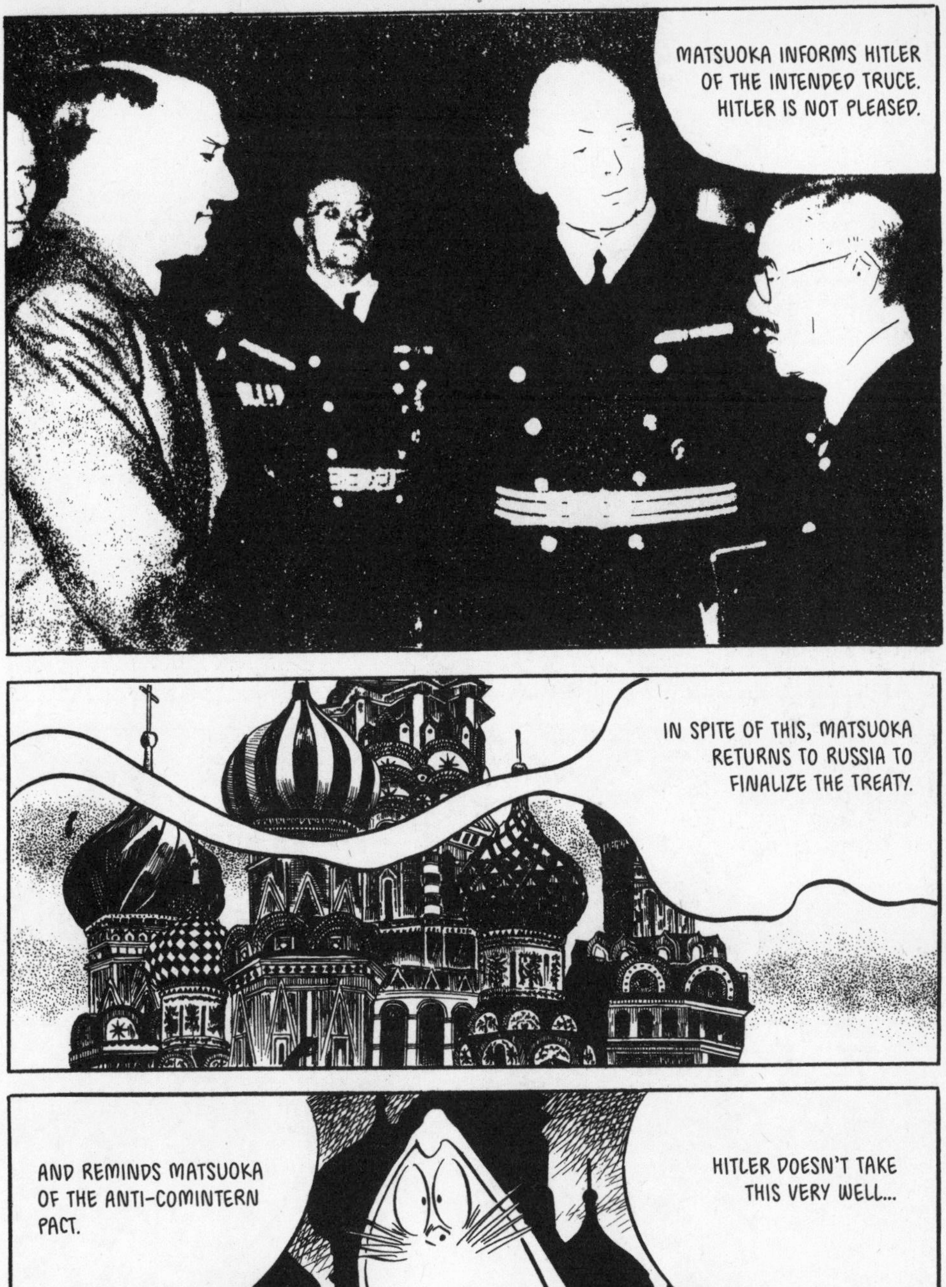
MATSUOKA INFORMS HITLER OF THE INTENDED TRUCE. HITLER IS NOT PLEASED.
IN SPITE OF THIS, MATSUOKA RETURNS TO RUSSIA TO FINALIZE THE TREATY.
HITLER DOESN'T TAKE THIS VERY WELL...
AND REMINDS MATSUOKA OF THE ANTI-COMINTERN PACT.

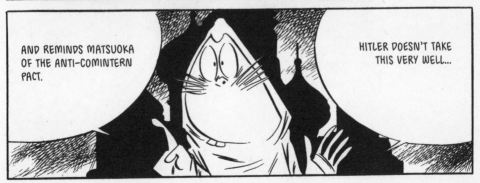

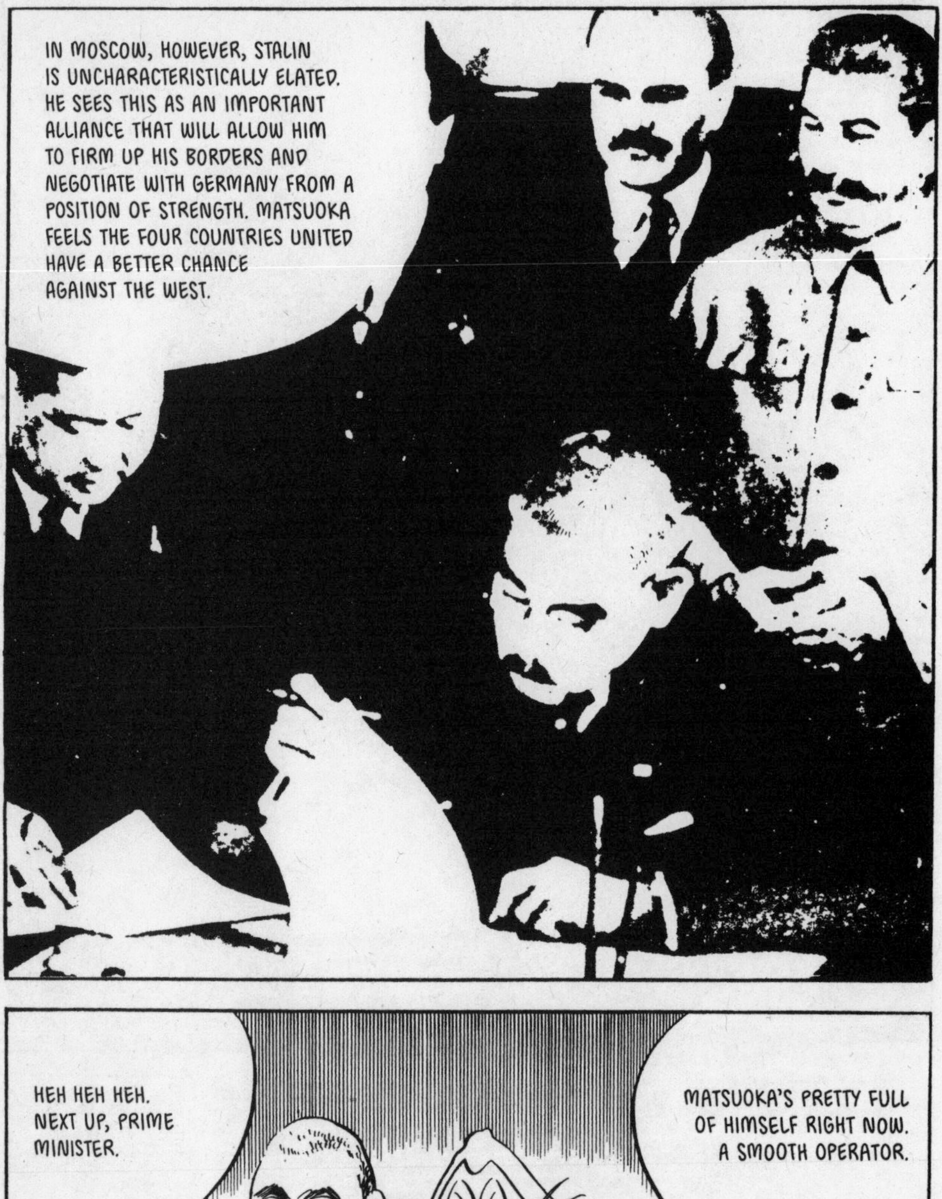
IN MOSCOW, HOWEVER, STALIN IS UNCHARACTERISTICALLY ELATED. HE SEES THIS AS AN IMPORTANT ALLIANCE THAT WILL ALLOW HIM TO FIRM UP HIS BORDERS AND NEGOTIATE WITH GERMANY FROM A POSITION OF STRENGTH. MATSUOKA FEELS THE FOUR COUNTRIES UNITED HAVE A BETTER CHANCE AGAINST THE WEST.

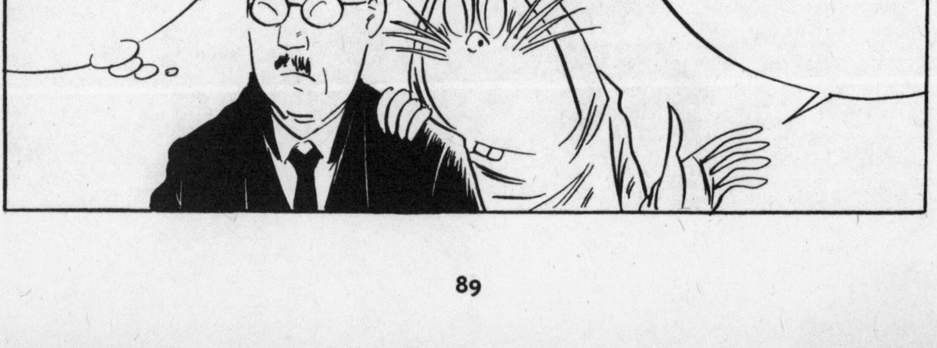
MATSUOKA'S PRETTY FULL OF HIMSELF RIGHT NOW. A SMOOTH OPERATOR.
HEH HEH HEH. NEXT UP, PRIME MINISTER.

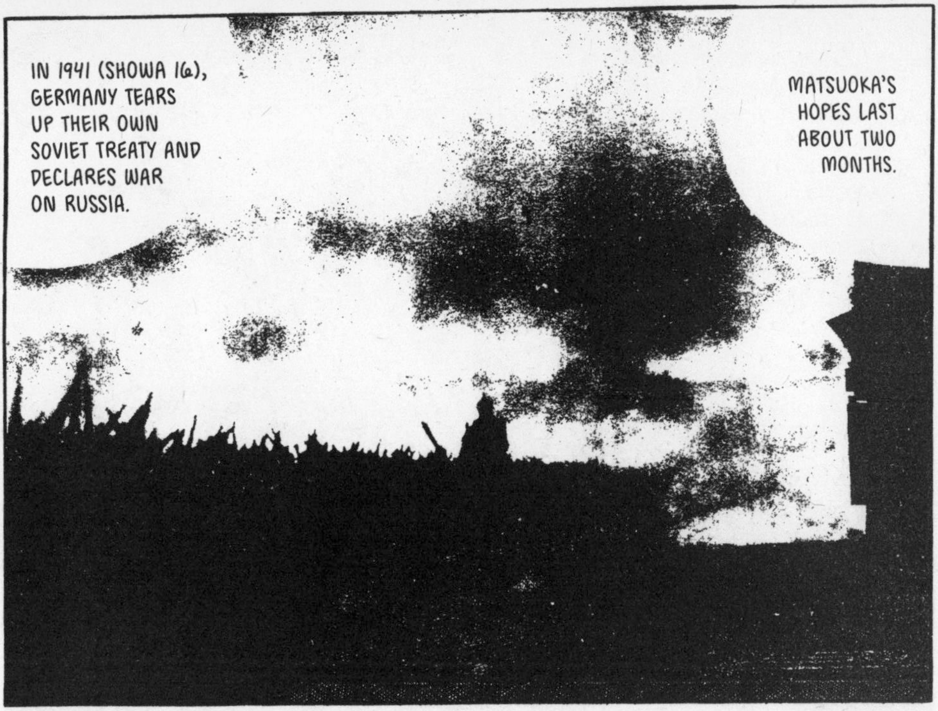
MATSUOKA'S HOPES LAST ABOUT TWO MONTHS.
IN 1941 (SHOWA 16), GERMANY TEARS UP THEIR OWN SOVIET TREATY AND DECLARES WAR ON RUSSIA.

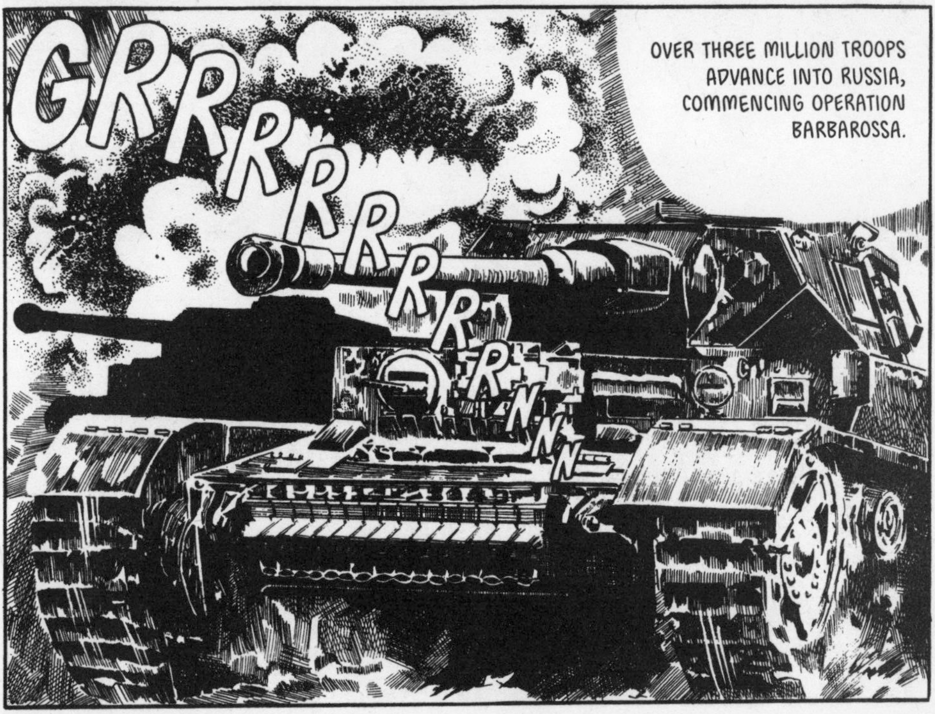
OVER THREE MILLION TROOPS ADVANCE INTO RUSSIA, COMMENCING OPERATION BARBAROSSA.
GRRRRRRRRRNNN

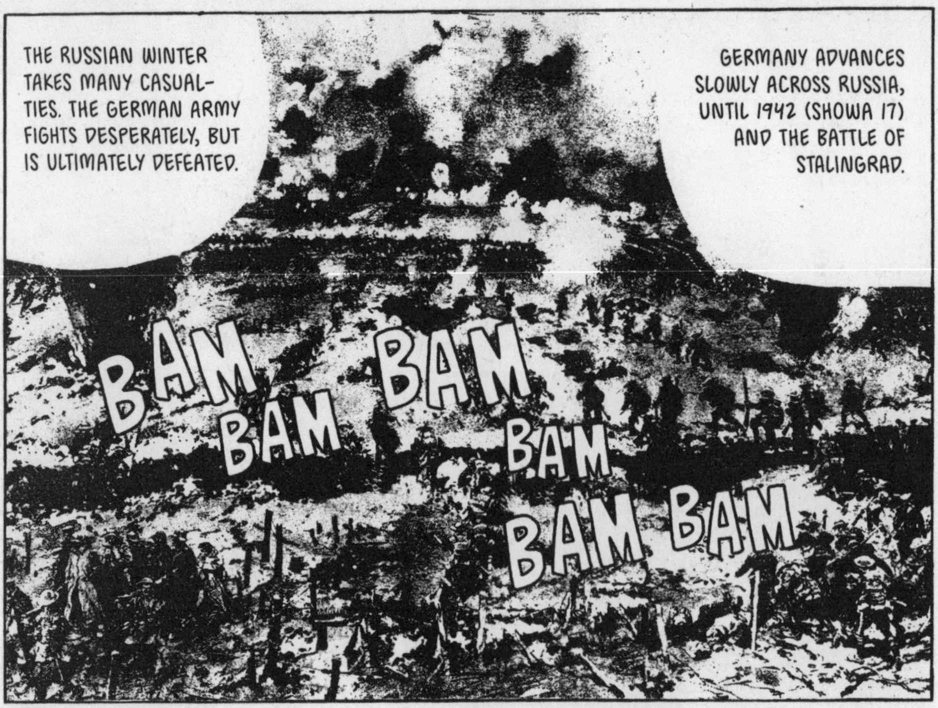
GERMANY ADVANCES SLOWLY ACROSS RUSSIA, UNTIL 1942 (SHOWA 17) AND THE BATTLE OF STALINGRAD.
THE RUSSIAN WINTER TAKES MANY CASUAL-TIES. THE GERMAN ARMY FIGHTS DESPERATELY, BUT IS ULTIMATELY DEFEATED.
BAM BAM BAM BAM BAM BAM

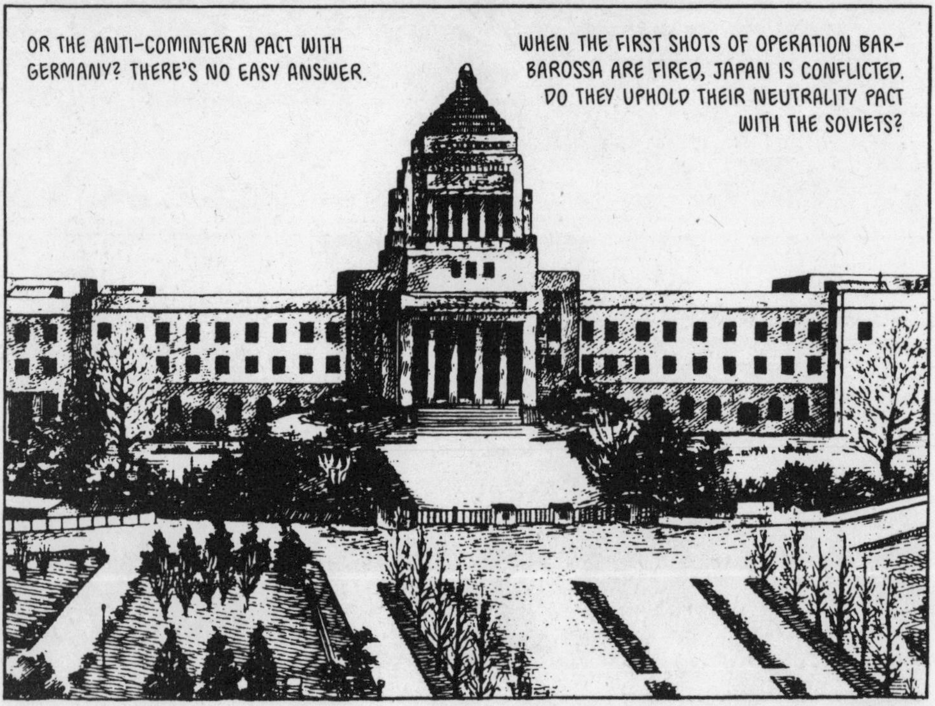
WHEN THE FIRST SHOTS OF OPERATION BAR-BAROSSA ARE FIRED, JAPAN IS CONFLICTED. DO THEY UPHOLD THEIR NEUTRALITY PACT WITH THE SOVIETS?
OR THE ANTI-COMINTERN PACT WITH GERMANY? THERE'S NO EASY ANSWER.

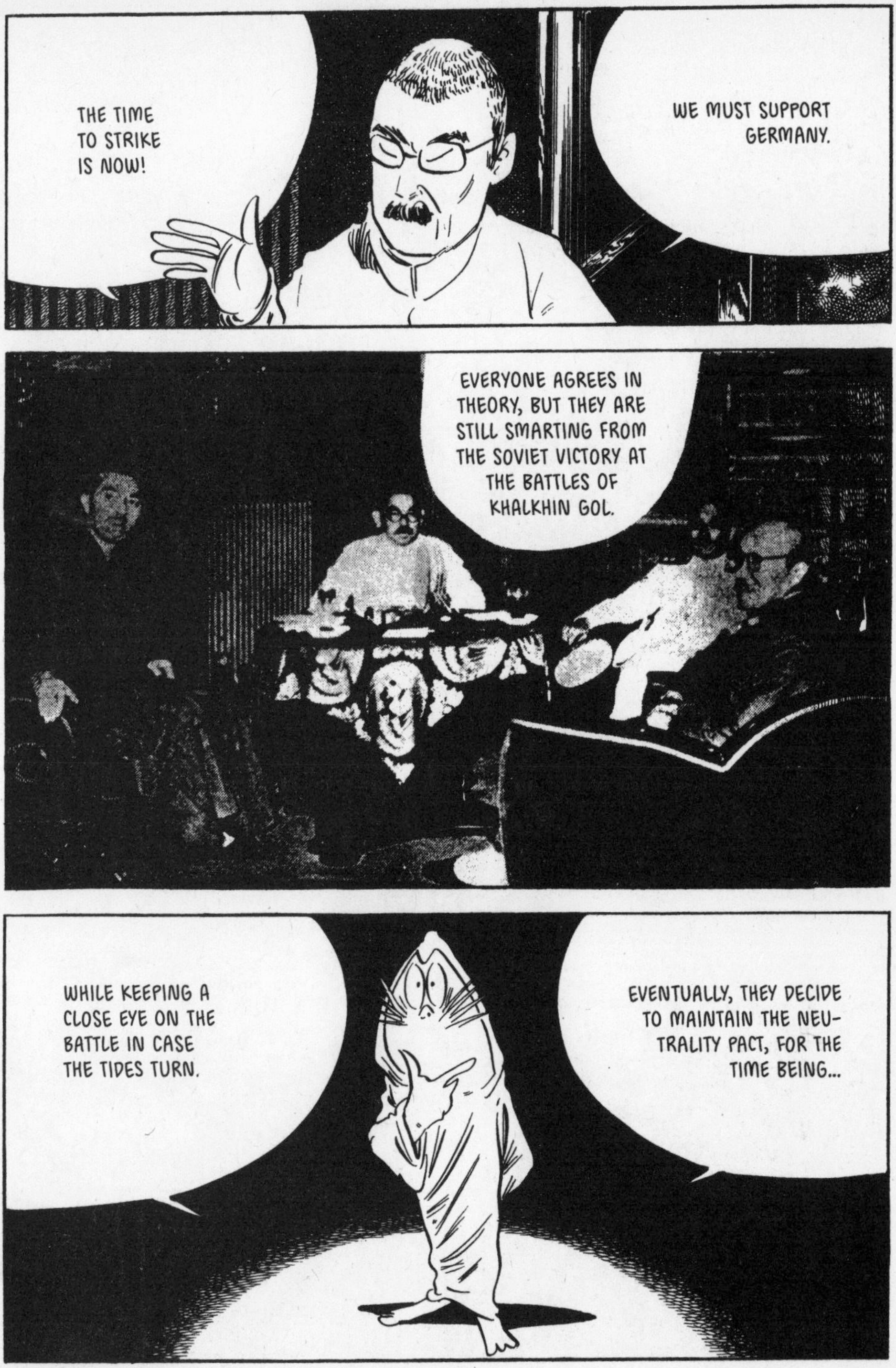
WE MUST SUPPORT GERMANY.
THE TIME TO STRIKE IS NOW!
EVERYONE AGREES IN THEORY, BUT THEY ARE STILL SMARTING FROM THE SOVIET VICTORY AT THE BATTLES OF KHALKHIN GOL.
EVENTUALLY, THEY DECIDE TO MAINTAIN THE NEU-TRALITY PACT, FOR THE TIME BEING...
WHILE KEEPING A CLOSE EYE ON THE BATTLE IN CASE THE TIDES TURN.

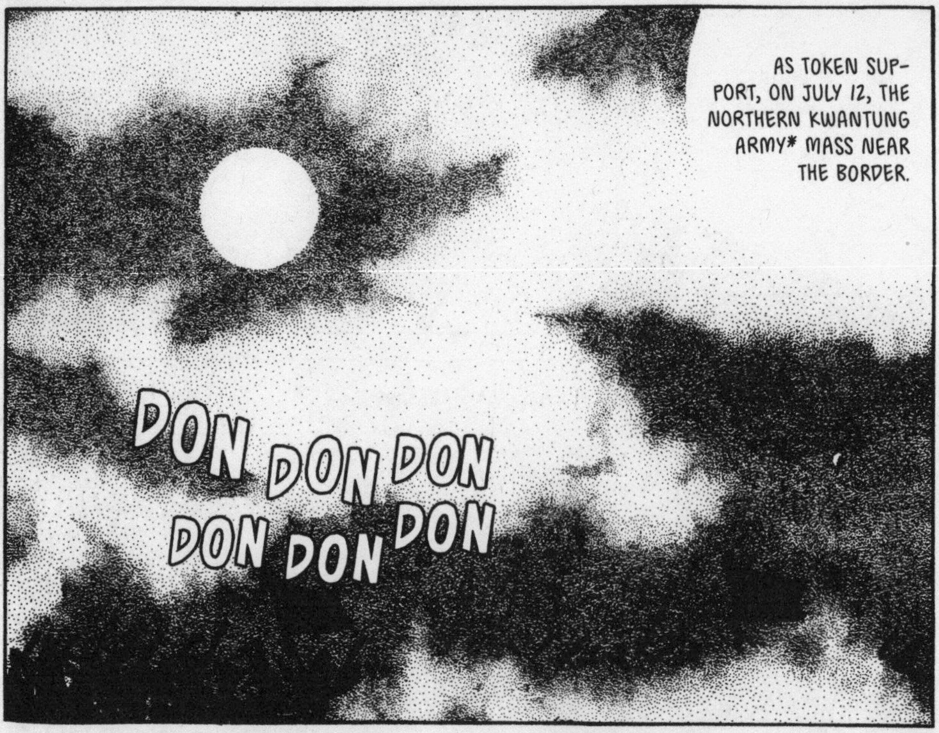
AS TOKEN SUPPORT, ON JULY 12, THE NORTHERN KWANTUNG ARMY* MASS NEAR THE BORDER.
DON DON DON
DON DON DON
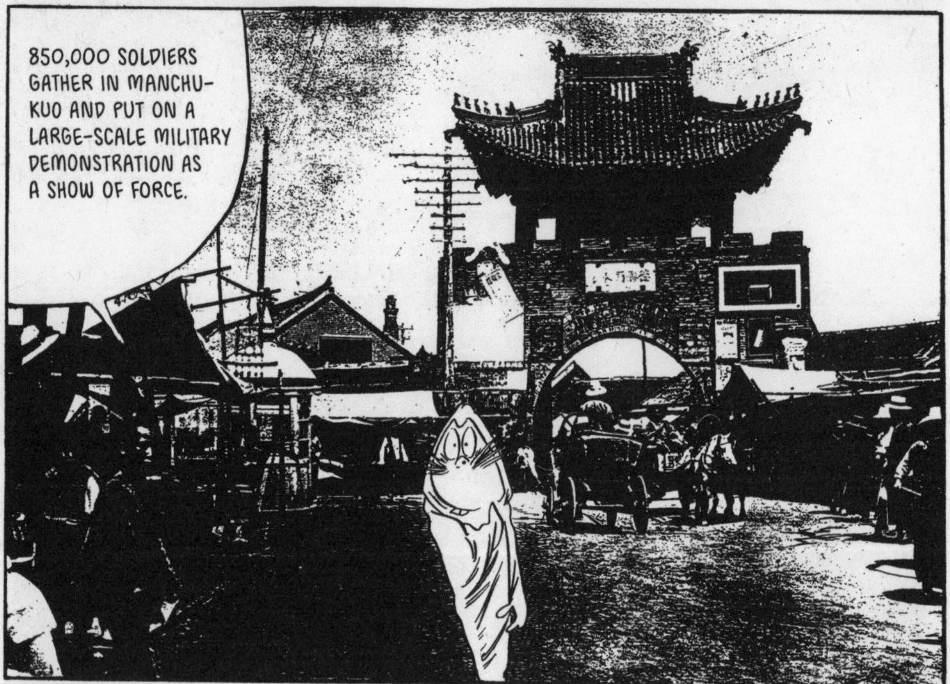
850,000 SOLDIERS GATHER IN MANCHUKUO AND PUT ON A LARGE-SCALE MILITARY DEMONSTRATION AS A SHOW OF FORCE.

*SEE NOTE ON PAGE 543.

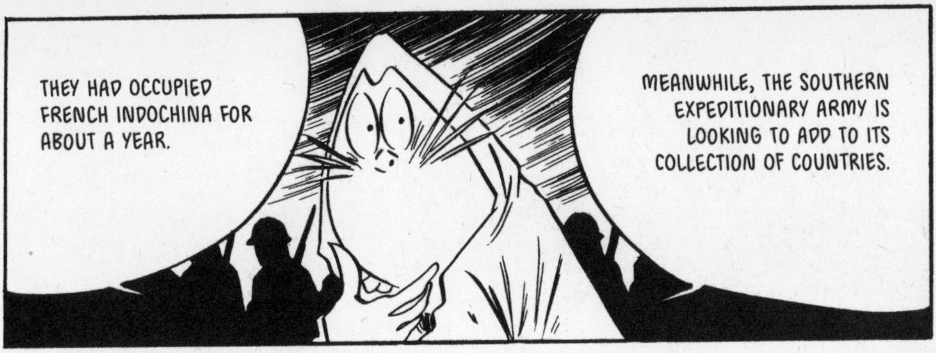
MEANWHILE, THE SOUTHERN EXPEDITIONARY ARMY IS LOOKING TO ADD TO ITS COLLECTION OF COUNTRIES.
THEY HAD OCCUPIED FRENCH INDOCHINA FOR ABOUT A YEAR.

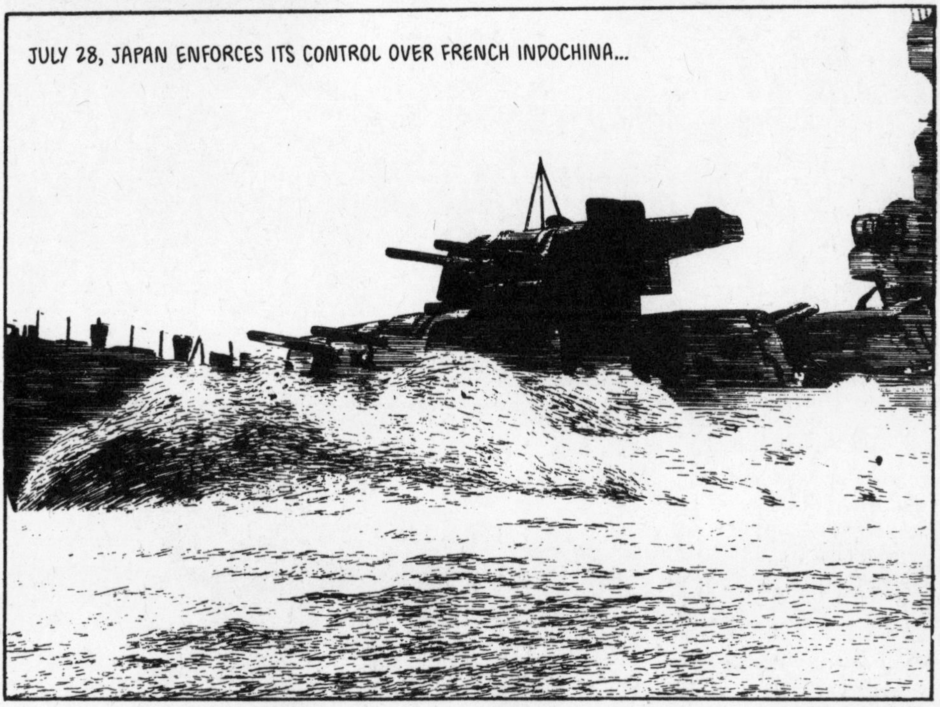
JULY 28, JAPAN ENFORCES ITS CONTROL OVER FRENCH INDOCHINA...

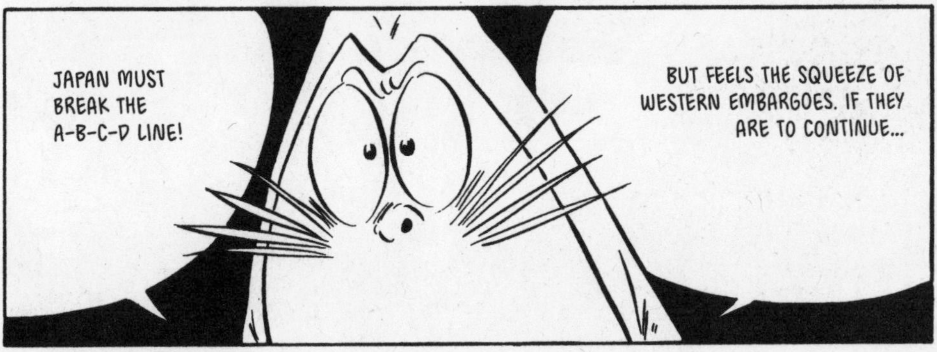
BUT FEELS THE SQUEEZE OF WESTERN EMBARGOES. IF THEY ARE TO CONTINUE...
JAPAN MUST BREAK THE A-B-C-D LINE!

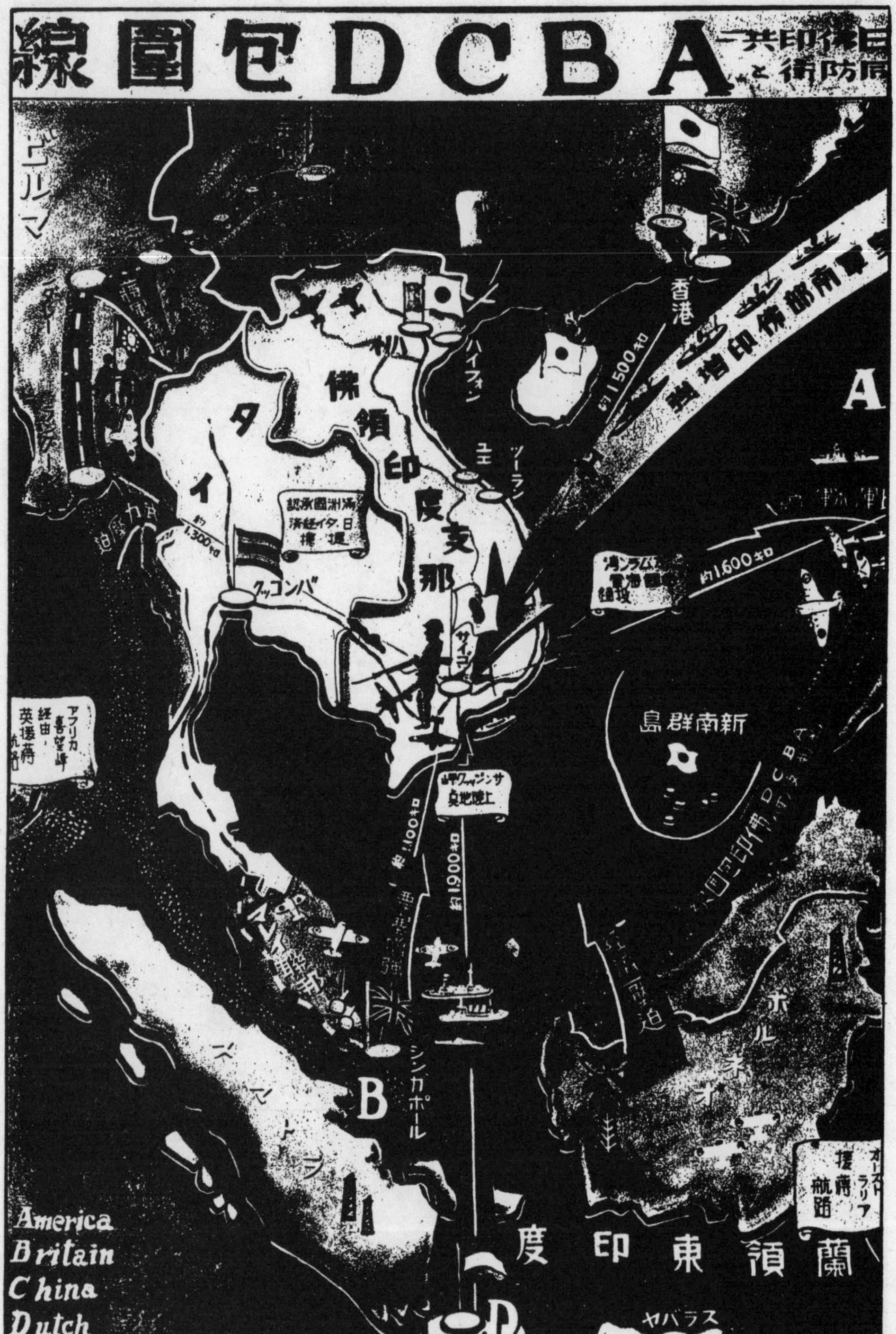
ABCD包圍線
タイ
佛領印度支那
香港
ハイフォン
ユエ
ツーラン
バンコック
サイゴン
新南群島
シンガポール
ボルネオ
蘭領東印度
スラバヤ
A
B
D
America
Britain
China
Dutch

SIGN: MAP OF THE A-B-C-D LINE.

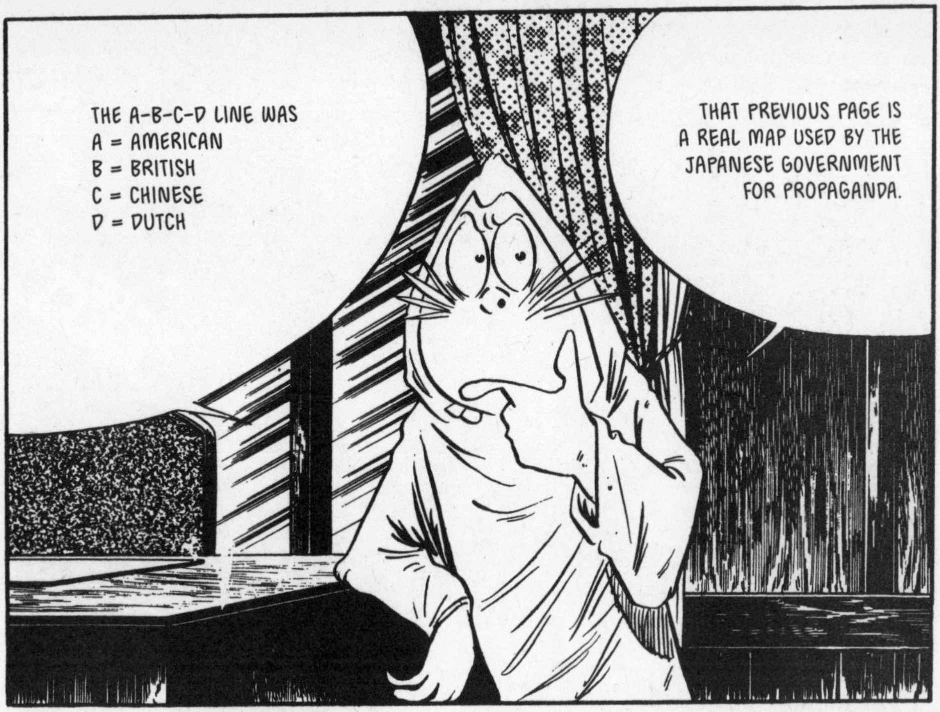
THAT PREVIOUS PAGE IS A REAL MAP USED BY THE JAPANESE GOVERNMENT FOR PROPAGANDA.
THE A-B-C-D LINE WAS
A = AMERICAN
B = BRITISH
C = CHINESE
D = DUTCH

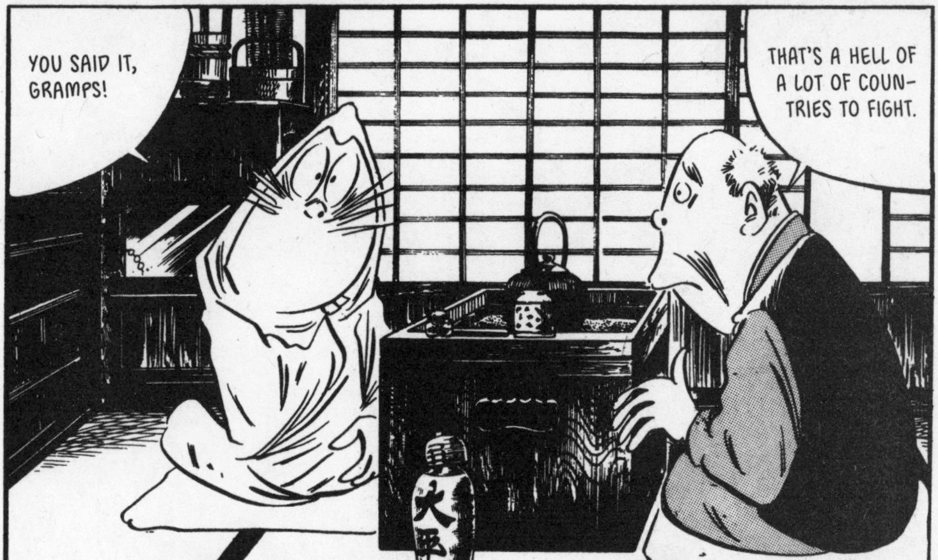
THAT'S A HELL OF A LOT OF COUN-TRIES TO FIGHT.
YOU SAID IT, GRAMPS!

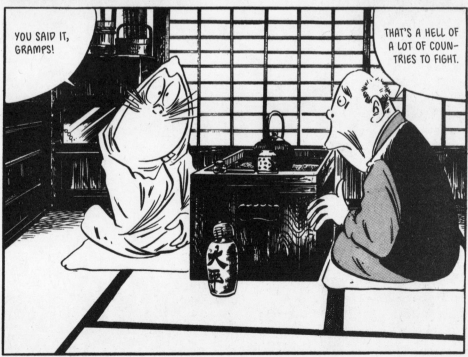

WAR AND PEACE

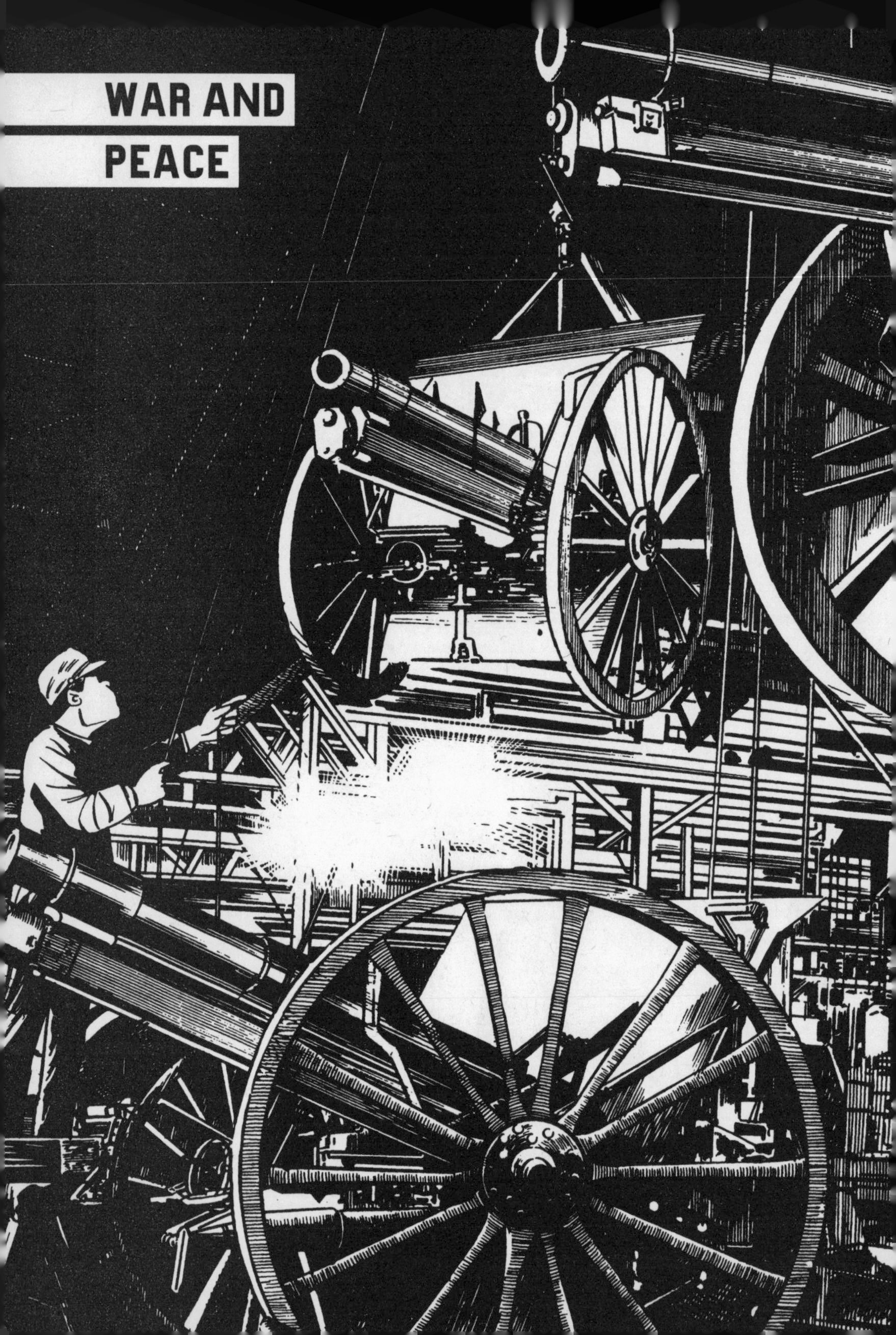

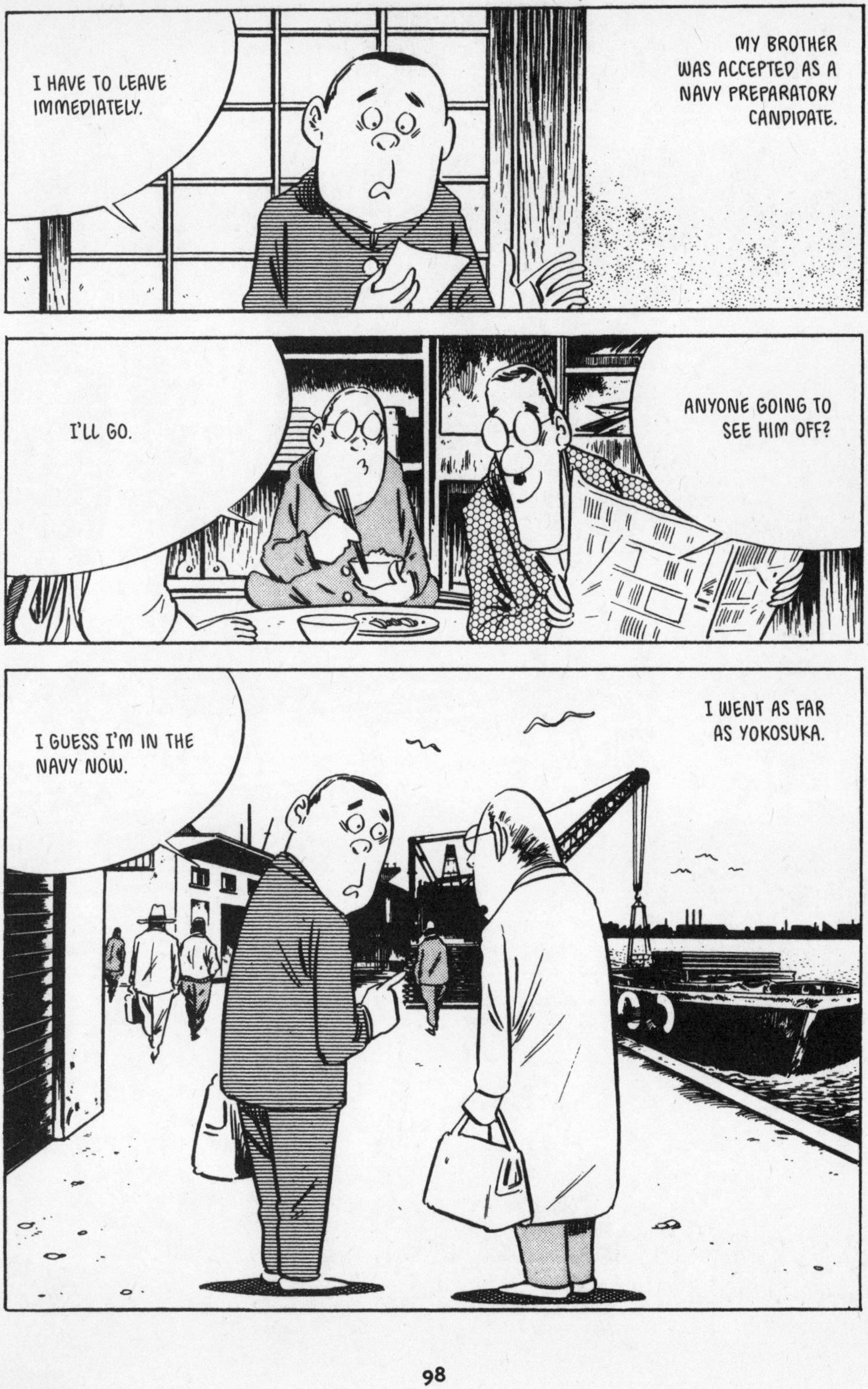
MY BROTHER WAS ACCEPTED AS A NAVY PREPARATORY CANDIDATE.
I HAVE TO LEAVE IMMEDIATELY.
ANYONE GOING TO SEE HIM OFF?
I'LL GO.
I WENT AS FAR AS YOKOSUKA.
I GUESS I'M IN THE NAVY NOW.

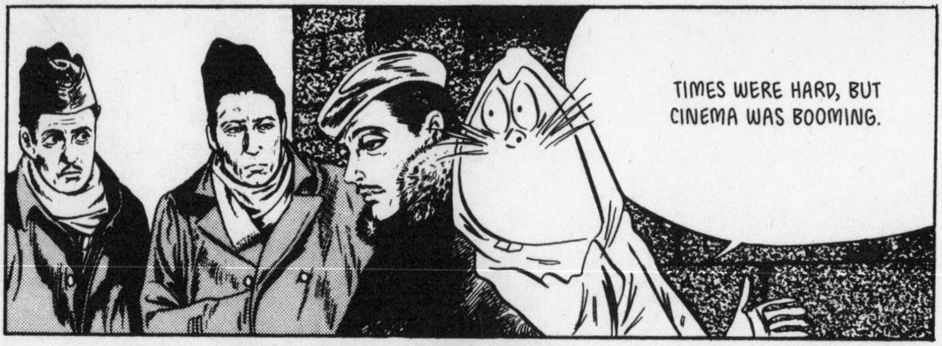
TIMES WERE HARD, BUT CINEMA WAS BOOMING.

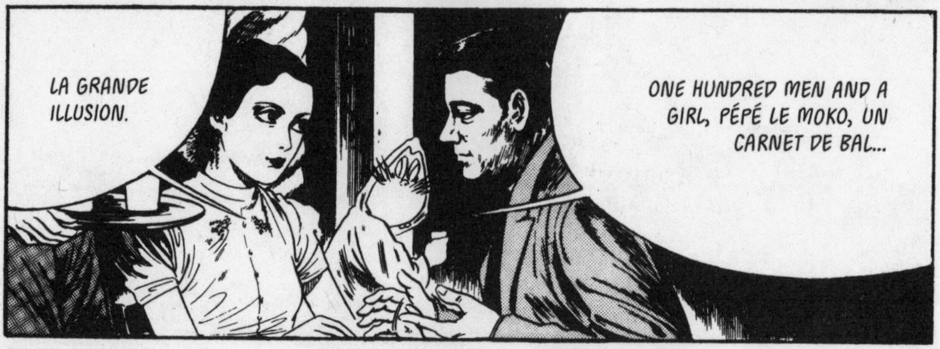
ONE HUNDRED MEN AND A GIRL, PÉPÉ LE MOKO, UN CARNET DE BAL...
LA GRANDE ILLUSION.

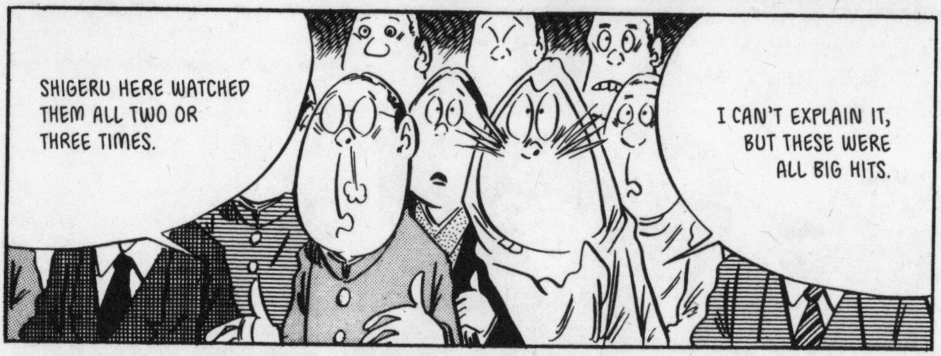
I CAN'T EXPLAIN IT, BUT THESE WERE ALL BIG HITS.
SHIGERU HERE WATCHED THEM ALL TWO OR THREE TIMES.

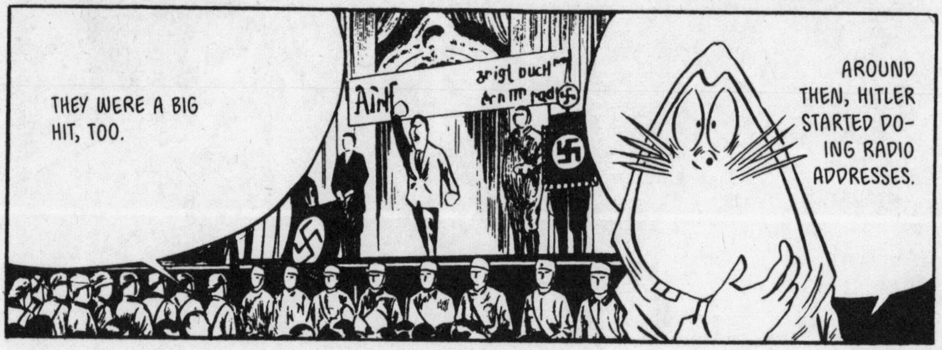
AROUND THEN, HITLER STARTED DO-ING RADIO ADDRESSES.
THEY WERE A BIG HIT, TOO.

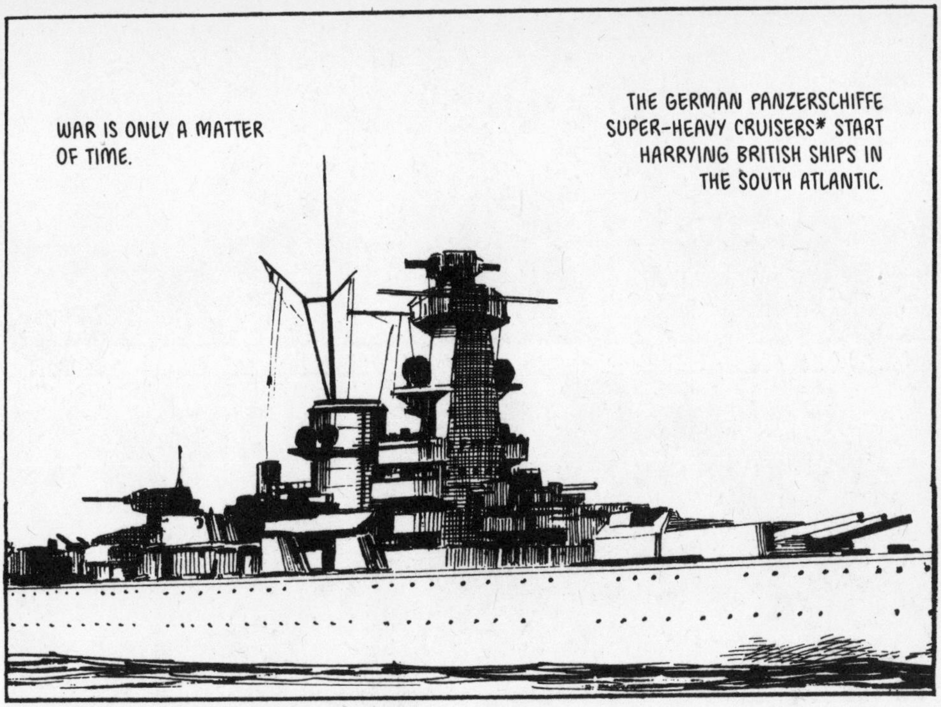
THE GERMAN PANZERSCHIFFE SUPER-HEAVY CRUISERS* START HARRYING BRITISH SHIPS IN THE SOUTH ATLANTIC.
WAR IS ONLY A MATTER OF TIME.

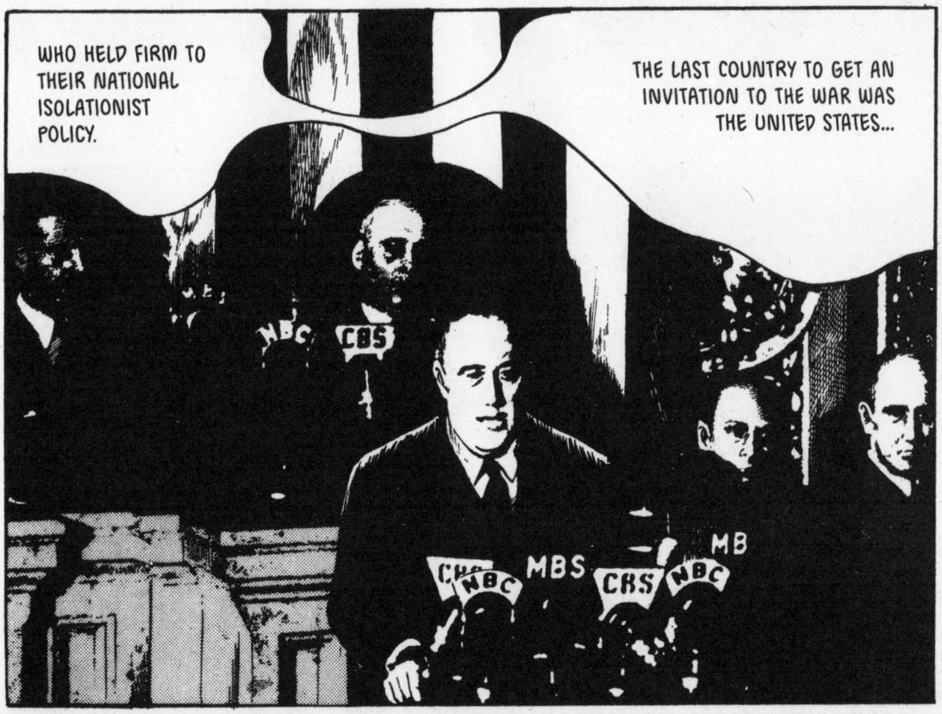
THE LAST COUNTRY TO GET AN INVITATION TO THE WAR WAS THE UNITED STATES...
WHO HELD FIRM TO THEIR NATIONAL ISOLATIONIST POLICY.
NBC
CBS
MB
MBS
CBS
NBC

*A TYPE OF NAVAL BATTLESHIP. TONNAGE AND ARMAMENT WAS RESTRICTED VIA THE LONDON NAVAL TREATY, WITH GUNS LIMITED TO 203MM CALIBER.

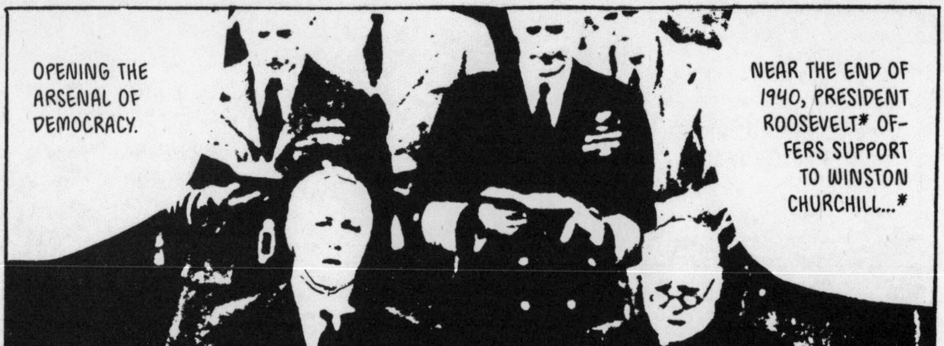
NEAR THE END OF 1940, PRESIDENT ROOSEVELT* OFFERS SUPPORT TO WINSTON CHURCHILL...*
OPENING THE ARSENAL OF DEMOCRACY.

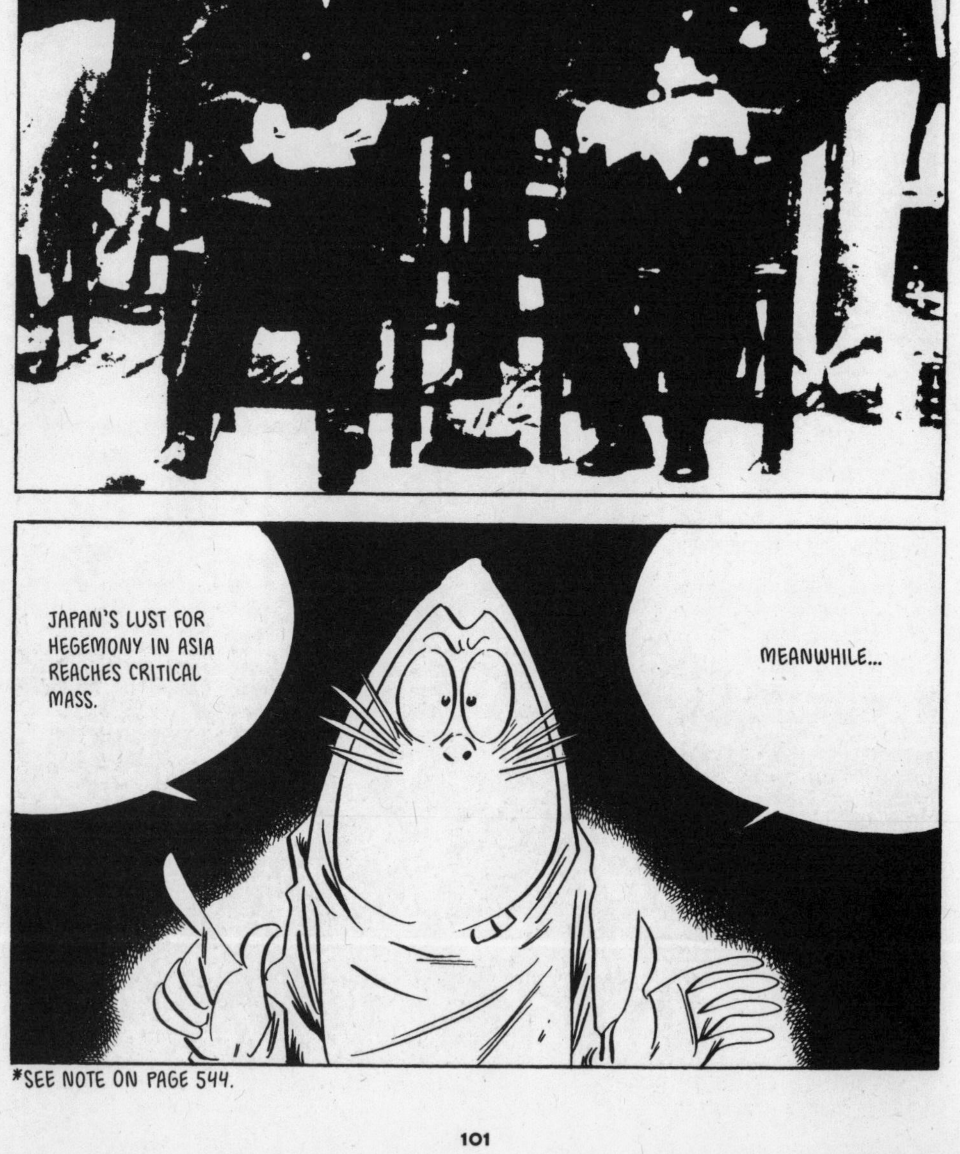
MEANWHILE...
JAPAN'S LUST FOR HEGEMONY IN ASIA REACHES CRITICAL MASS.

*SEE NOTE ON PAGE 544.

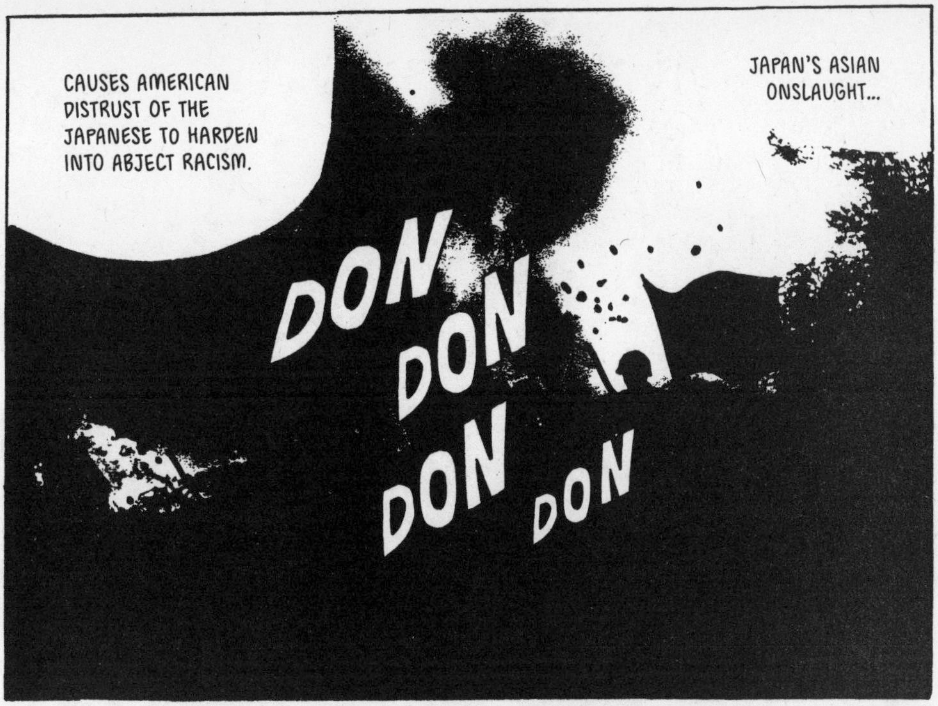
JAPAN'S ASIAN ONSLAUGHT...
CAUSES AMERICAN DISTRUST OF THE JAPANESE TO HARDEN INTO ABJECT RACISM.
DON DON DON DON

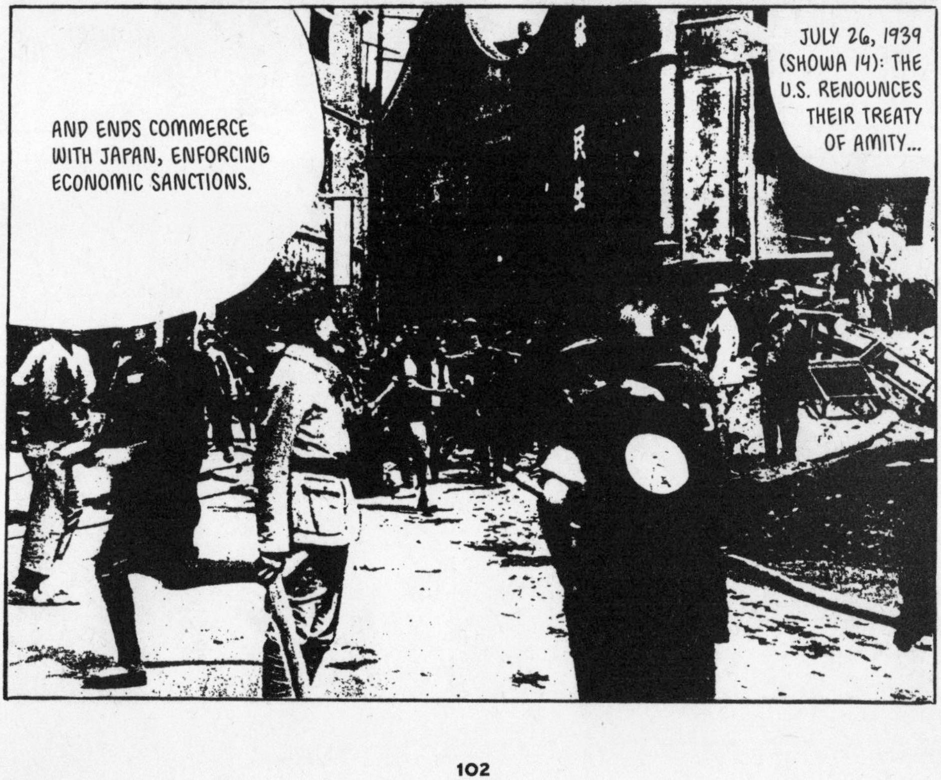
JULY 26, 1939 (SHOWA 14): THE U.S. RENOUNCES THEIR TREATY OF AMITY...
AND ENDS COMMERCE WITH JAPAN, ENFORCING ECONOMIC SANCTIONS.

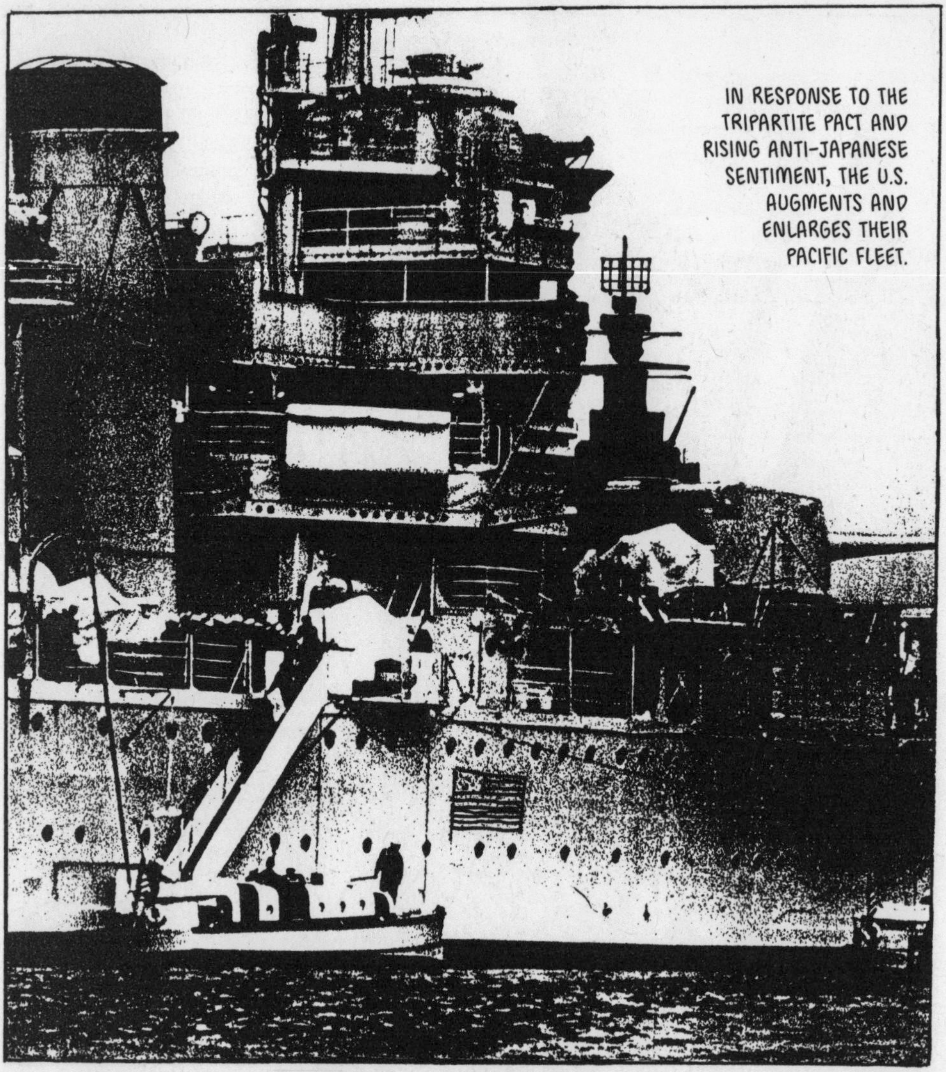
IN RESPONSE TO THE TRIPARTITE PACT AND RISING ANTI-JAPANESE SENTIMENT, THE U.S. AUGMENTS AND ENLARGES THEIR PACIFIC FLEET.

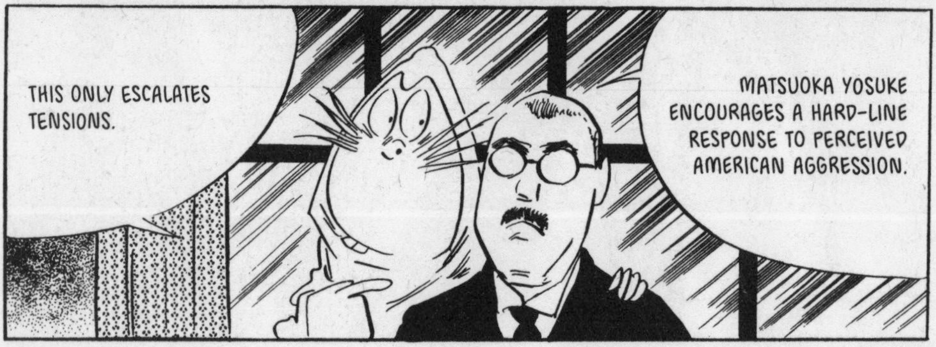
MATSUOKA YOSUKE ENCOURAGES A HARD-LINE RESPONSE TO PERCEIVED AMERICAN AGGRESSION.
THIS ONLY ESCALATES TENSIONS.

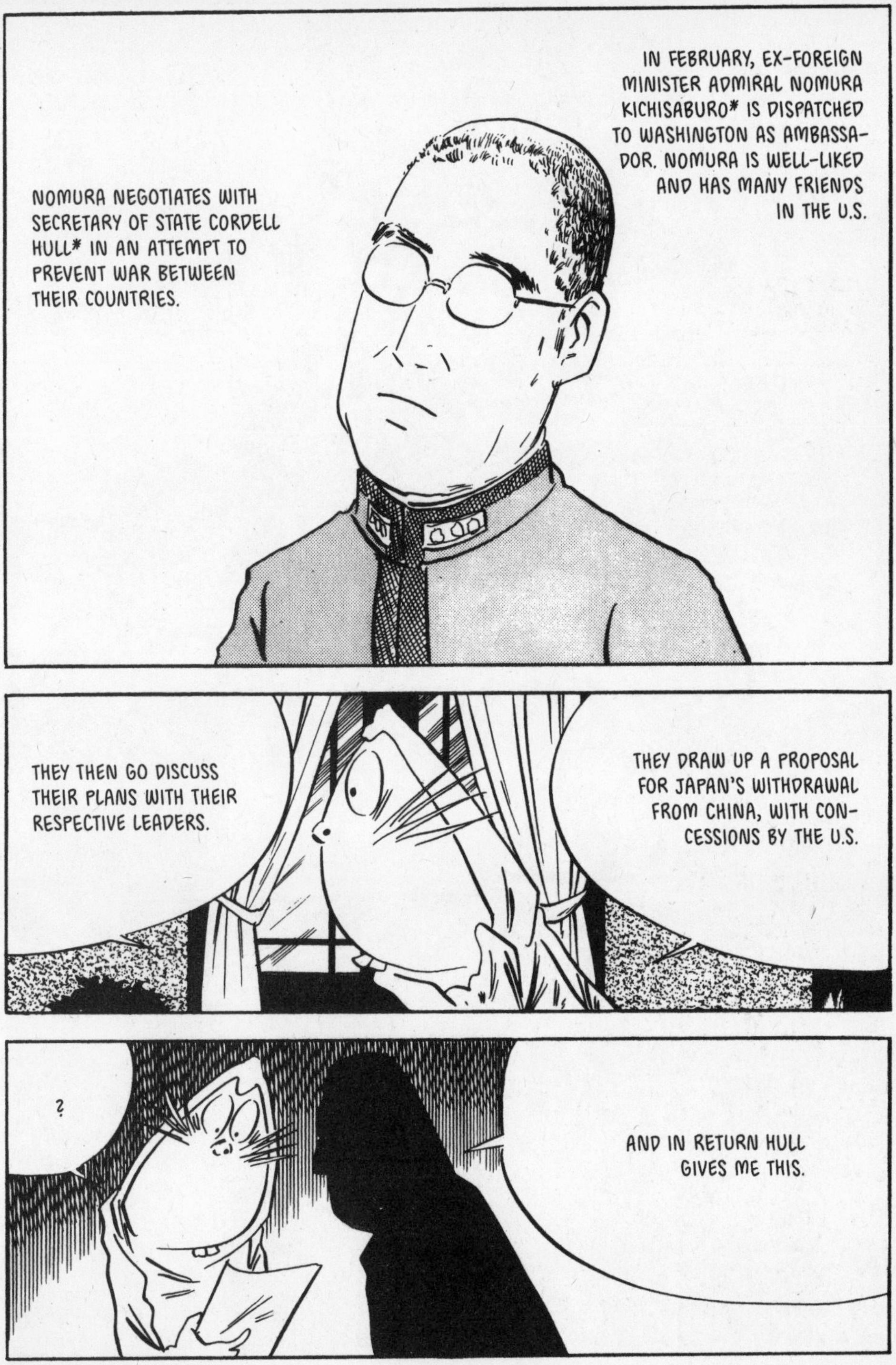

IN FEBRUARY, EX-FOREIGN MINISTER ADMIRAL NOMURA KICHISABURO* IS DISPATCHED TO WASHINGTON AS AMBASSADOR. NOMURA IS WELL-LIKED AND HAS MANY FRIENDS IN THE U.S.
NOMURA NEGOTIATES WITH SECRETARY OF STATE CORDELL HULL* IN AN ATTEMPT TO PREVENT WAR BETWEEN THEIR COUNTRIES.
THEY DRAW UP A PROPOSAL FOR JAPAN'S WITHDRAWAL FROM CHINA, WITH CONCESSIONS BY THE U.S.
THEY THEN GO DISCUSS THEIR PLANS WITH THEIR RESPECTIVE LEADERS.
AND IN RETURN HULL GIVES ME THIS.
?

*SEE NOTES ON PAGE 544.

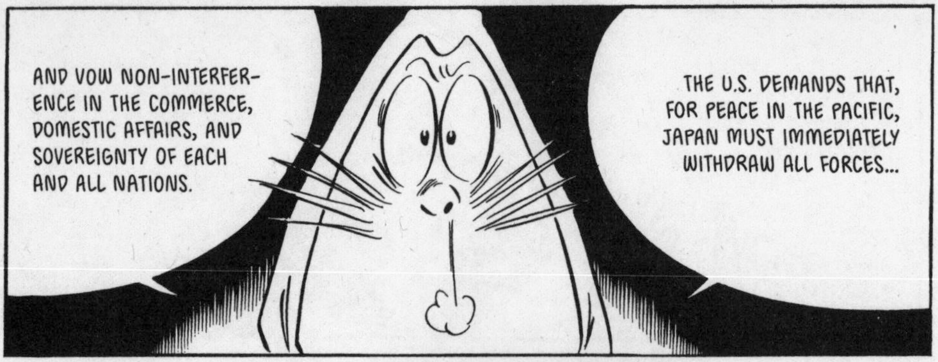
THE U.S. DEMANDS THAT, FOR PEACE IN THE PACIFIC, JAPAN MUST IMMEDIATELY WITHDRAW ALL FORCES...
AND VOW NON-INTERFERENCE IN THE COMMERCE, DOMESTIC AFFAIRS, AND SOVEREIGNTY OF EACH AND ALL NATIONS.

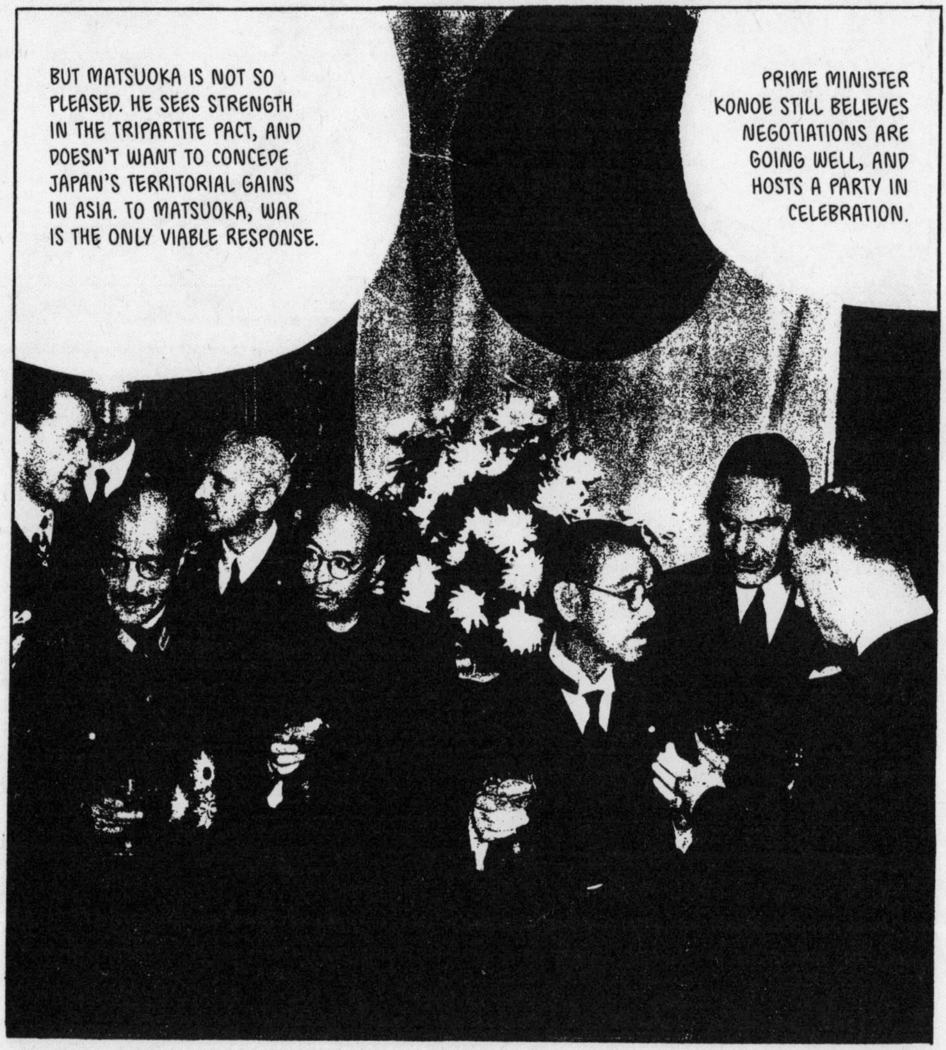
PRIME MINISTER KONOE STILL BELIEVES NEGOTIATIONS ARE GOING WELL, AND HOSTS A PARTY IN CELEBRATION.
BUT MATSUOKA IS NOT SO PLEASED. HE SEES STRENGTH IN THE TRIPARTITE PACT, AND DOESN'T WANT TO CONCEDE JAPAN'S TERRITORIAL GAINS IN ASIA. TO MATSUOKA, WAR IS THE ONLY VIABLE RESPONSE.

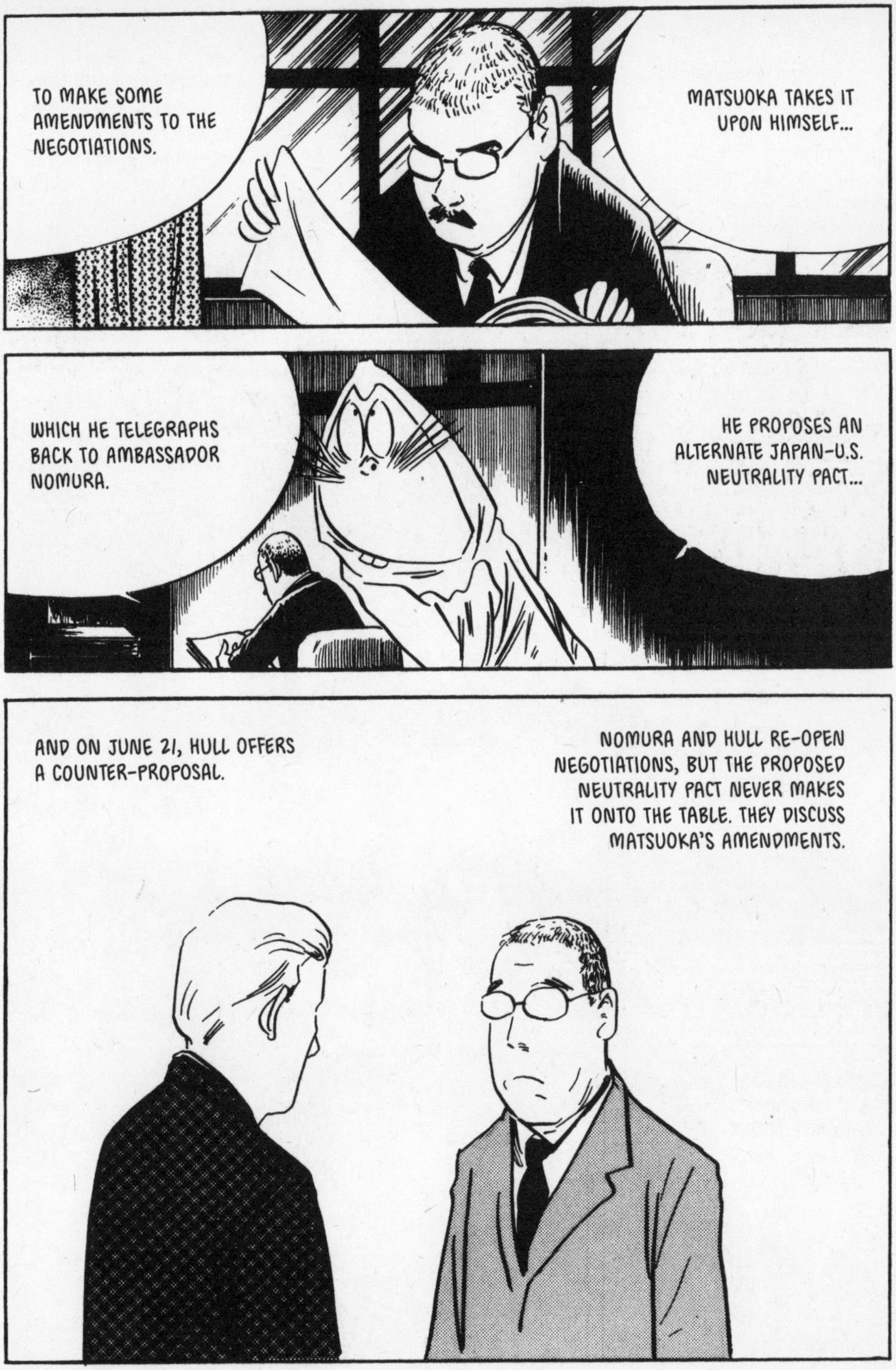
MATSUOKA TAKES IT UPON HIMSELF...
TO MAKE SOME AMENDMENTS TO THE NEGOTIATIONS.
HE PROPOSES AN ALTERNATE JAPAN-U.S. NEUTRALITY PACT...
WHICH HE TELEGRAPHS BACK TO AMBASSADOR NOMURA.
NOMURA AND HULL RE-OPEN NEGOTIATIONS, BUT THE PROPOSED NEUTRALITY PACT NEVER MAKES IT ONTO THE TABLE. THEY DISCUSS MATSUOKA'S AMENDMENTS.
AND ON JUNE 21, HULL OFFERS A COUNTER-PROPOSAL.

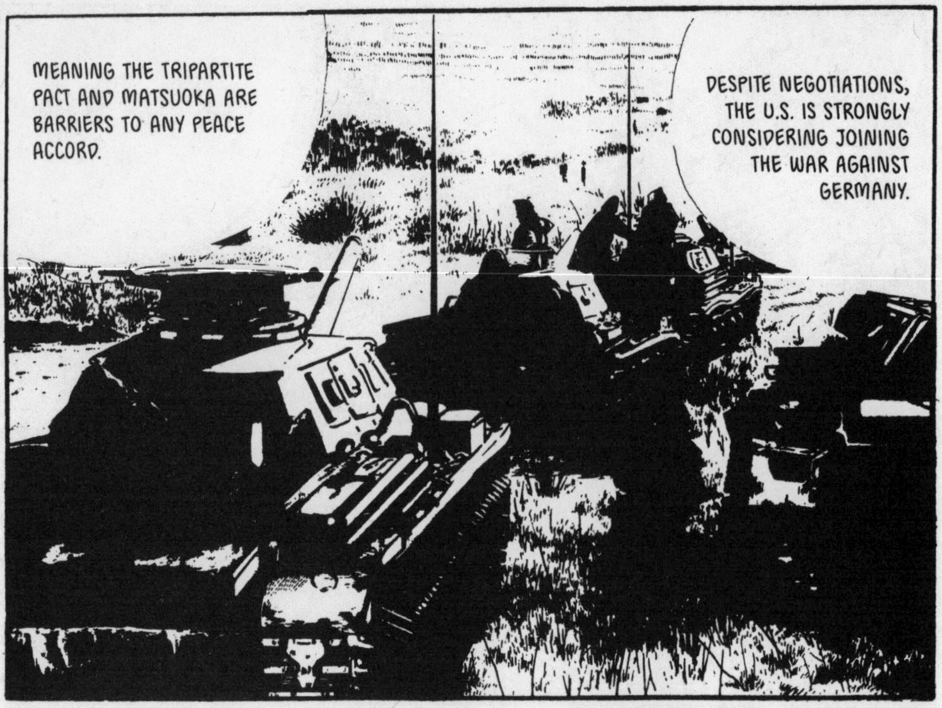
DESPITE NEGOTIATIONS, THE U.S. IS STRONGLY CONSIDERING JOINING THE WAR AGAINST GERMANY.
MEANING THE TRIPARTITE PACT AND MATSUOKA ARE BARRIERS TO ANY PEACE ACCORD.

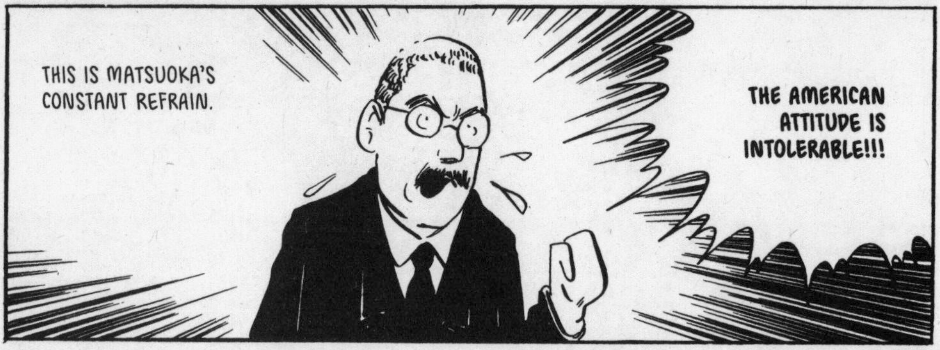
THE AMERICAN ATTITUDE IS INTOLERABLE!!!
THIS IS MATSUOKA'S CONSTANT REFRAIN.

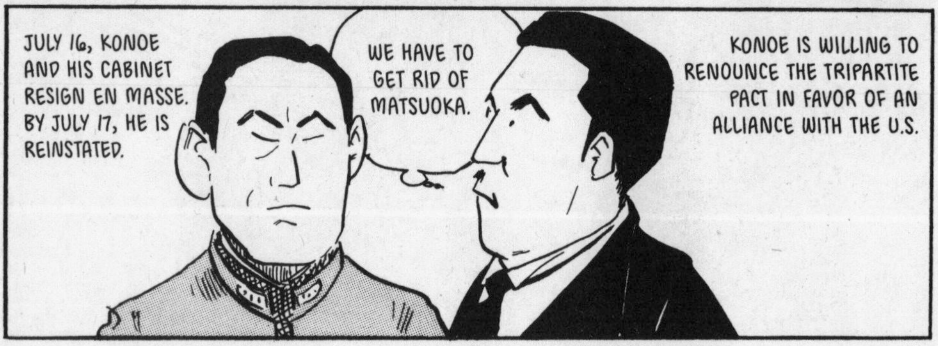
KONOE IS WILLING TO RENOUNCE THE TRIPARTITE PACT IN FAVOR OF AN ALLIANCE WITH THE U.S.
WE HAVE TO GET RID OF MATSUOKA.
JULY 16, KONOE AND HIS CABINET RESIGN EN MASSE. BY JULY 17, HE IS REINSTATED.

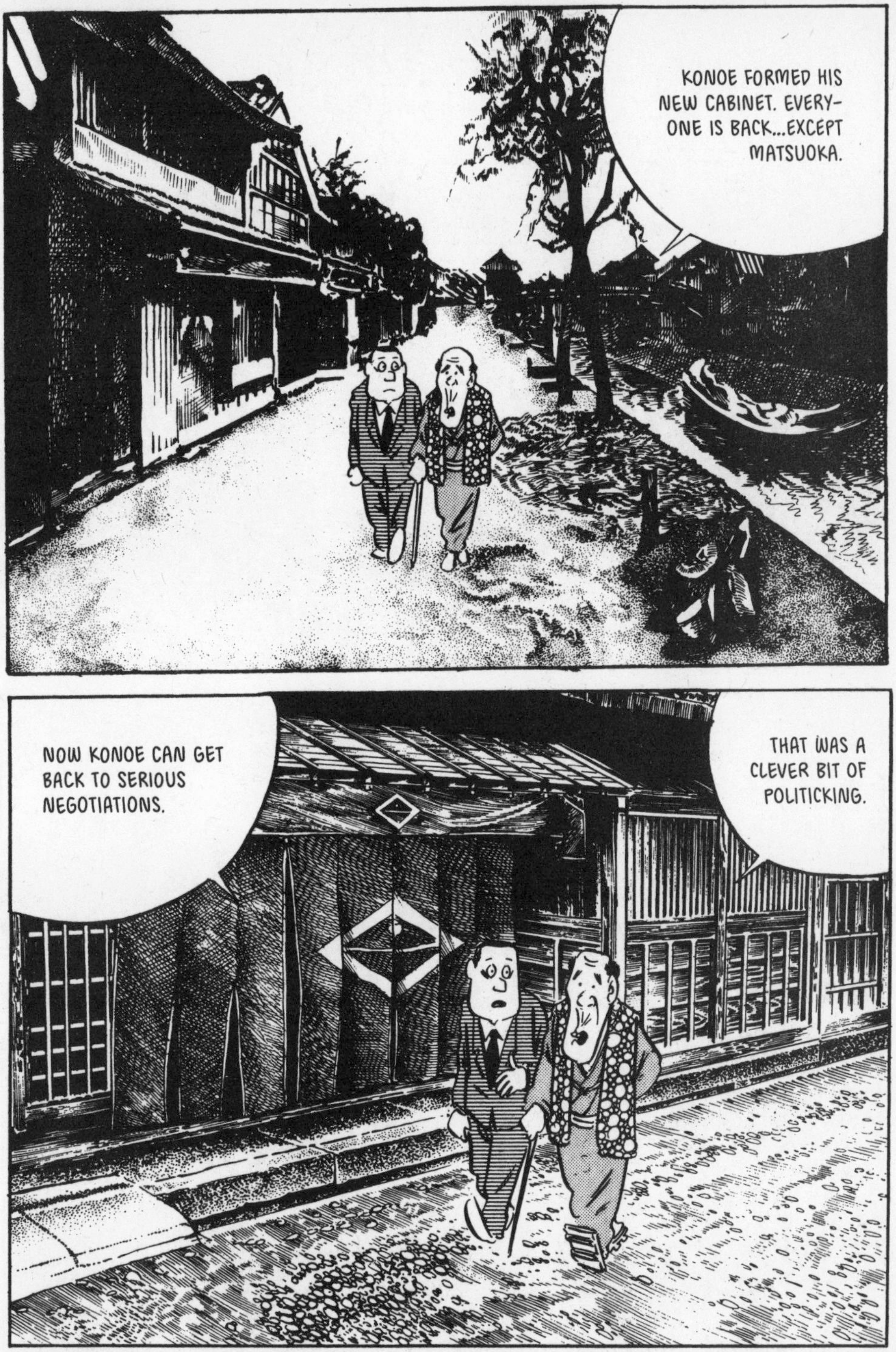
KONOE FORMED HIS NEW CABINET. EVERY-ONE IS BACK...EXCEPT MATSUOKA.
THAT WAS A CLEVER BIT OF POLITICKING.
NOW KONOE CAN GET BACK TO SERIOUS NEGOTIATIONS.

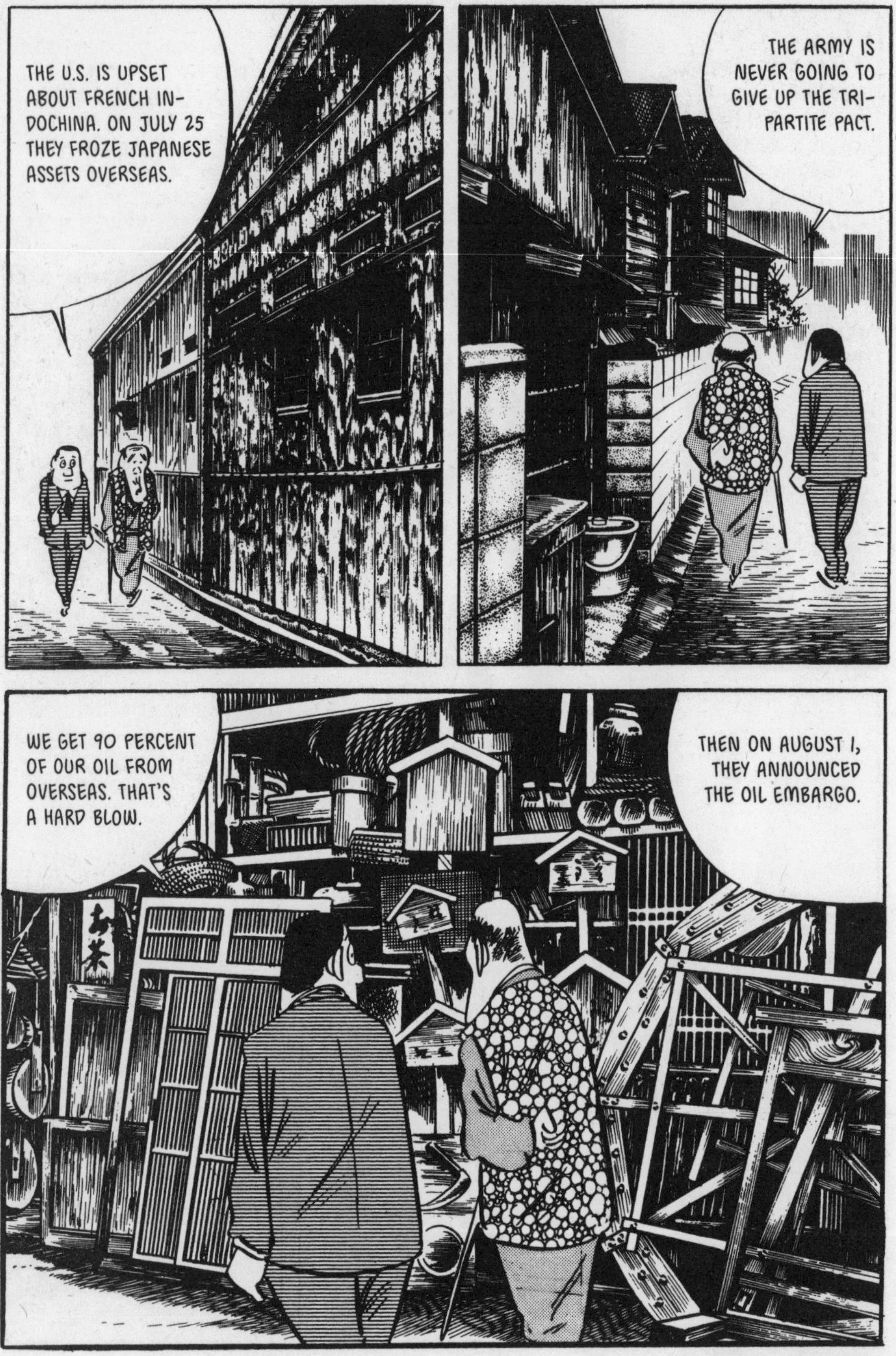
THE ARMY IS NEVER GOING TO GIVE UP THE TRI-PARTITE PACT.
THE U.S. IS UPSET ABOUT FRENCH IN-DOCHINA. ON JULY 25 THEY FROZE JAPANESE ASSETS OVERSEAS.
THEN ON AUGUST 1, THEY ANNOUNCED THE OIL EMBARGO.
WE GET 90 PERCENT OF OUR OIL FROM OVERSEAS. THAT'S A HARD BLOW.
お茶

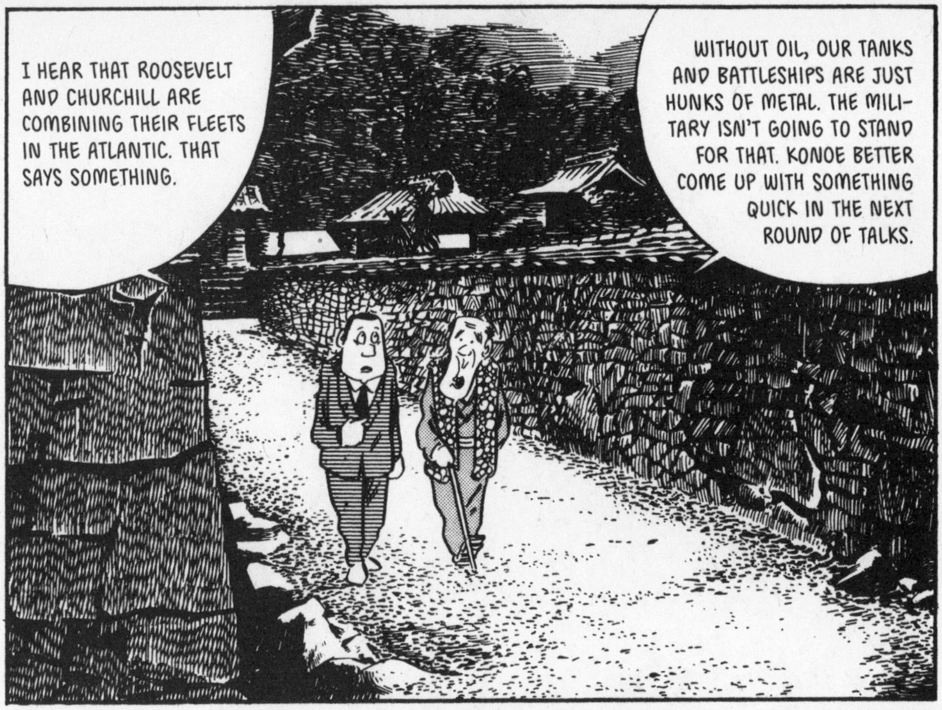
WITHOUT OIL, OUR TANKS AND BATTLESHIPS ARE JUST HUNKS OF METAL. THE MILITARY ISN'T GOING TO STAND FOR THAT. KONOE BETTER COME UP WITH SOMETHING QUICK IN THE NEXT ROUND OF TALKS.
I HEAR THAT ROOSEVELT AND CHURCHILL ARE COMBINING THEIR FLEETS IN THE ATLANTIC. THAT SAYS SOMETHING.

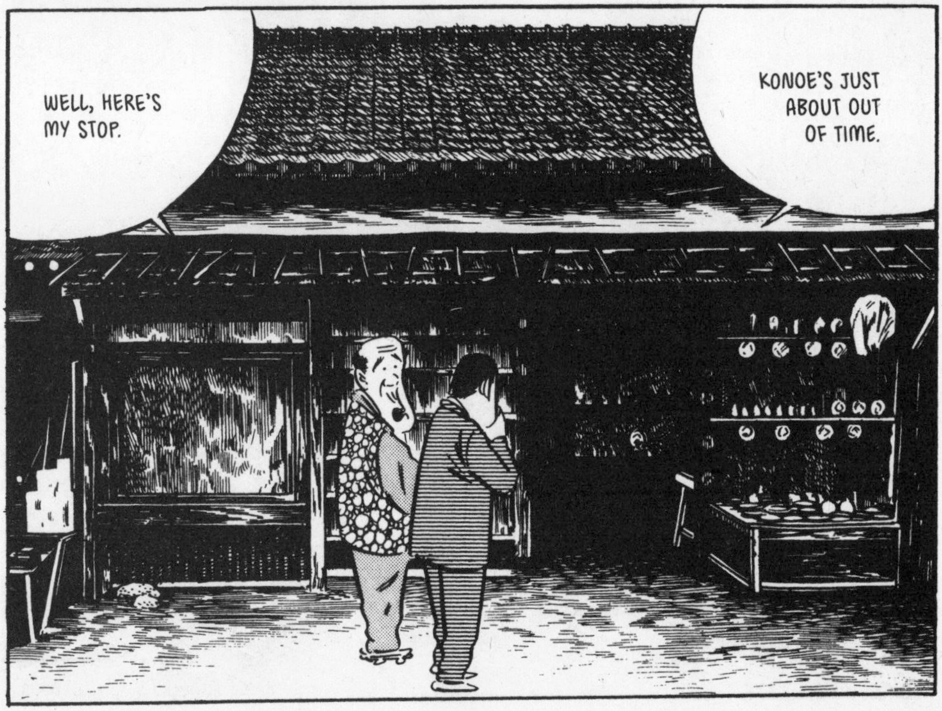
KONOE'S JUST ABOUT OUT OF TIME.
WELL, HERE'S MY STOP.

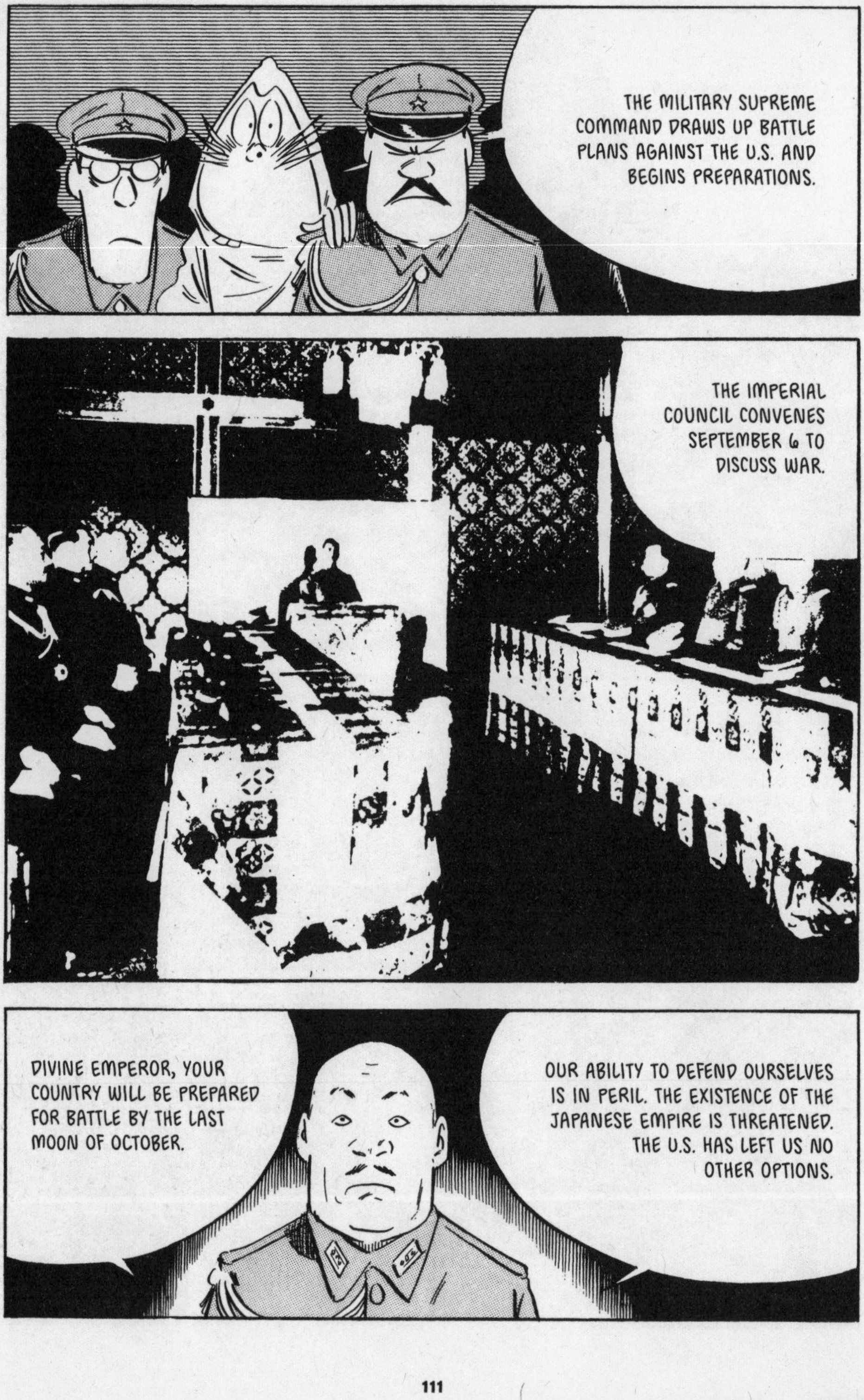
THE MILITARY SUPREME COMMAND DRAWS UP BATTLE PLANS AGAINST THE U.S. AND BEGINS PREPARATIONS.
THE IMPERIAL COUNCIL CONVENES SEPTEMBER 6 TO DISCUSS WAR.
OUR ABILITY TO DEFEND OURSELVES IS IN PERIL. THE EXISTENCE OF THE JAPANESE EMPIRE IS THREATENED. THE U.S. HAS LEFT US NO OTHER OPTIONS.
DIVINE EMPEROR, YOUR COUNTRY WILL BE PREPARED FOR BATTLE BY THE LAST MOON OF OCTOBER.

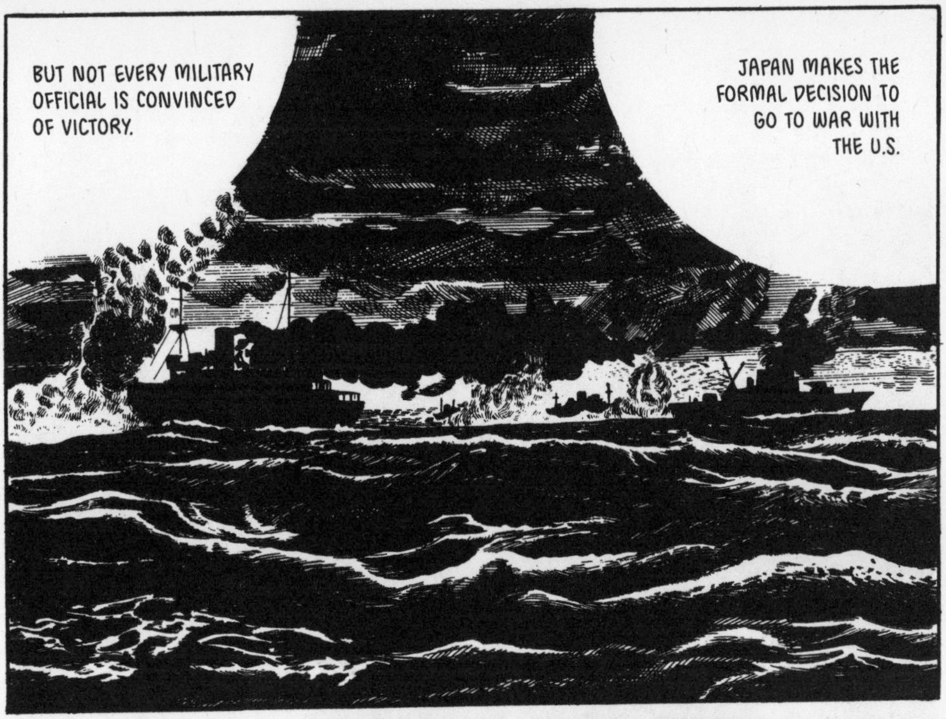
JAPAN MAKES THE FORMAL DECISION TO GO TO WAR WITH THE U.S.
BUT NOT EVERY MILITARY OFFICIAL IS CONVINCED OF VICTORY.

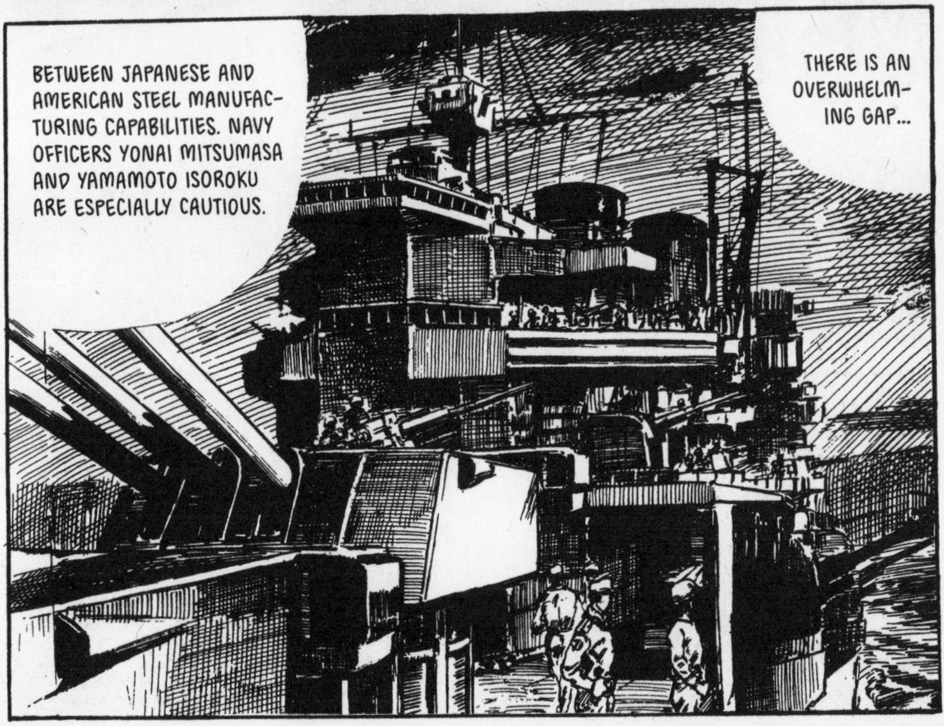
THERE IS AN OVERWHELM-ING GAP...
BETWEEN JAPANESE AND AMERICAN STEEL MANUFAC-TURING CAPABILITIES. NAVY OFFICERS YONAI MITSUMASA AND YAMAMOTO ISOROKU ARE ESPECIALLY CAUTIOUS.

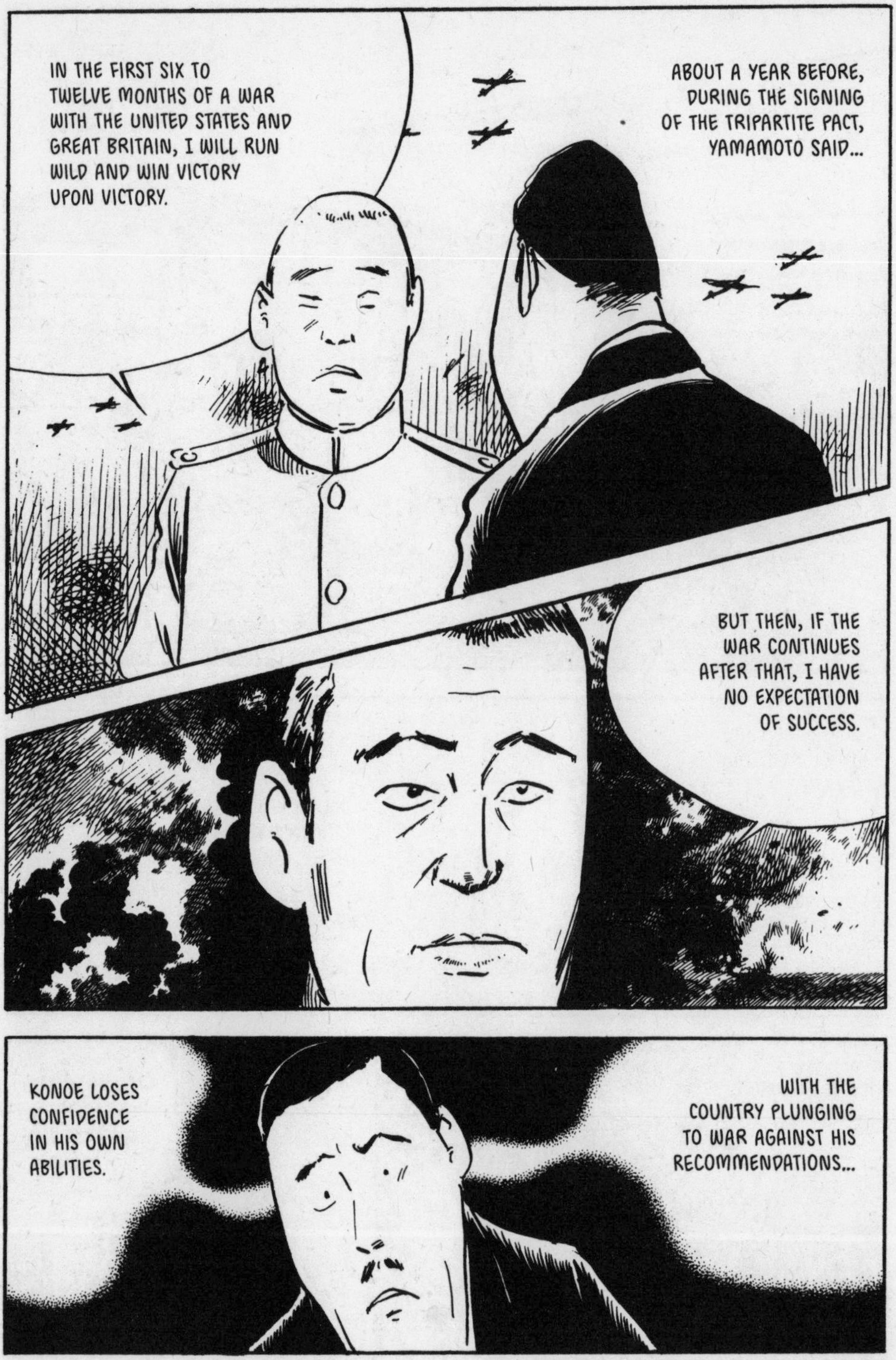
ABOUT A YEAR BEFORE, DURING THE SIGNING OF THE TRIPARTITE PACT, YAMAMOTO SAID...
IN THE FIRST SIX TO TWELVE MONTHS OF A WAR WITH THE UNITED STATES AND GREAT BRITAIN, I WILL RUN WILD AND WIN VICTORY UPON VICTORY.
BUT THEN, IF THE WAR CONTINUES AFTER THAT, I HAVE NO EXPECTATION OF SUCCESS.
WITH THE COUNTRY PLUNGING TO WAR AGAINST HIS RECOMMENDATIONS...
KONOE LOSES CONFIDENCE IN HIS OWN ABILITIES.

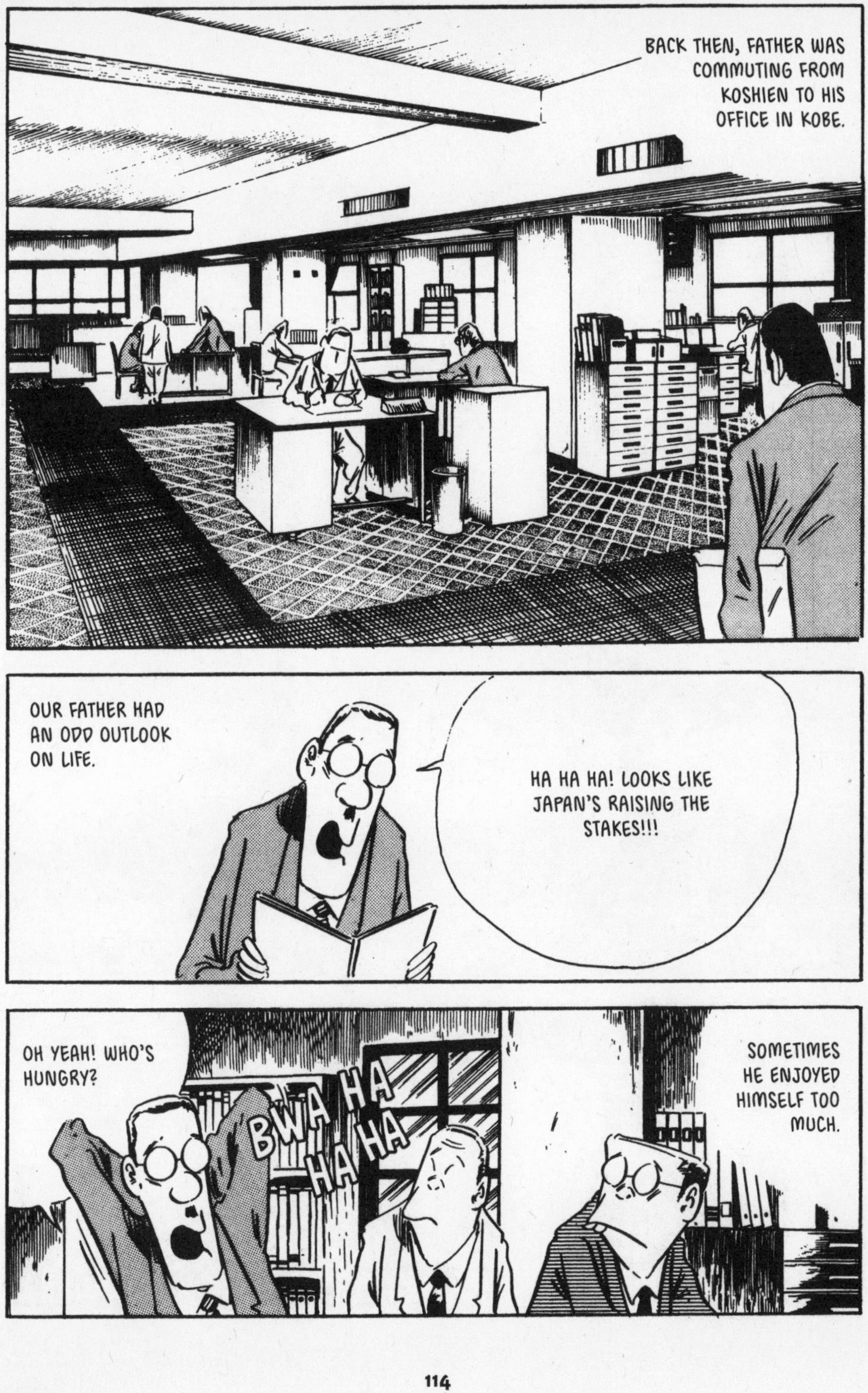
BACK THEN, FATHER WAS COMMUTING FROM KOSHIEN TO HIS OFFICE IN KOBE.
HA HA HA! LOOKS LIKE JAPAN'S RAISING THE STAKES!!!
OUR FATHER HAD AN ODD OUTLOOK ON LIFE.
SOMETIMES HE ENJOYED HIMSELF TOO MUCH.
OH YEAH! WHO'S HUNGRY?
BWA HA HA HA

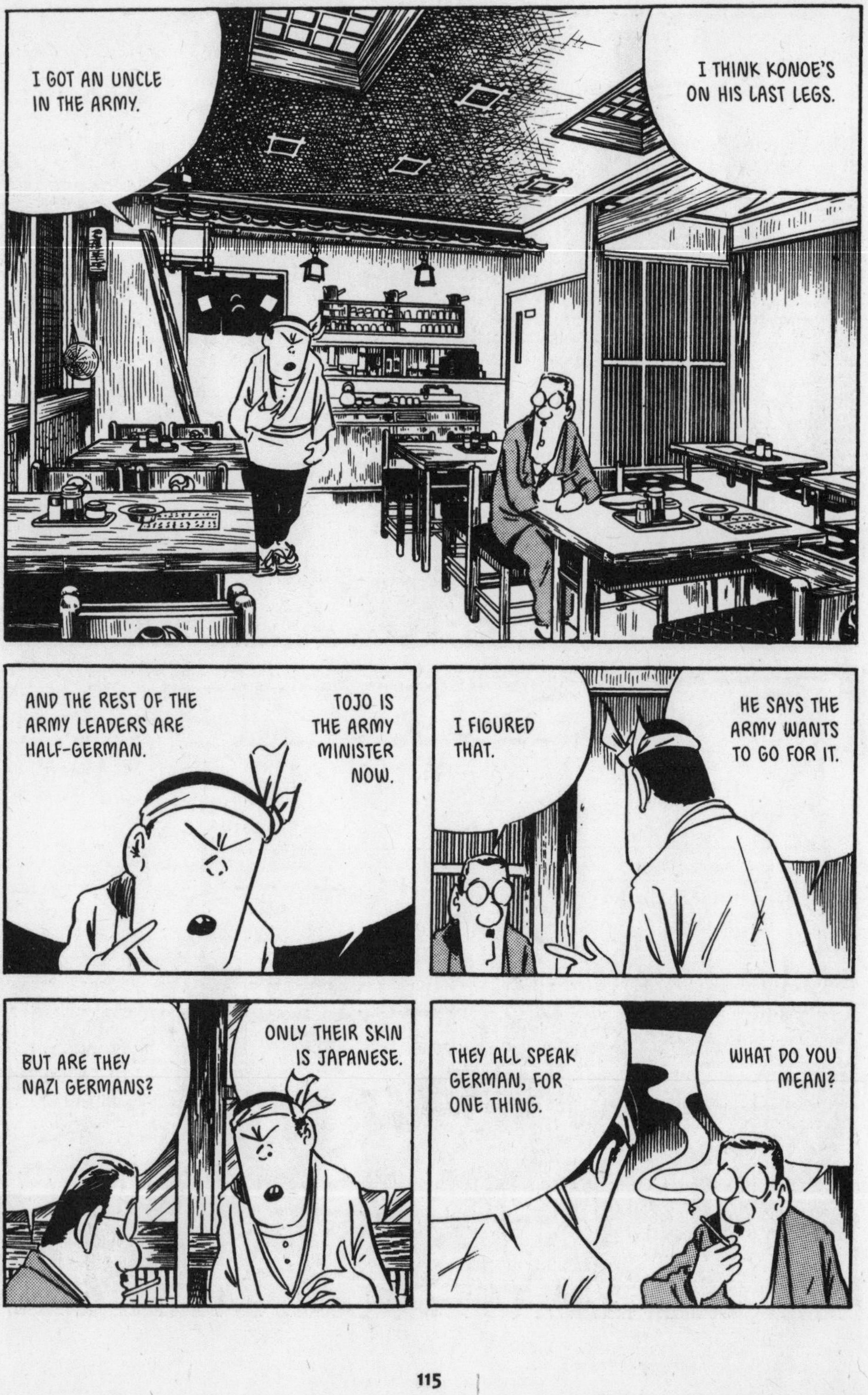
I THINK KONOE'S ON HIS LAST LEGS.
I GOT AN UNCLE IN THE ARMY.
HE SAYS THE ARMY WANTS TO GO FOR IT.
I FIGURED THAT.
TOJO IS THE ARMY MINISTER NOW.
AND THE REST OF THE ARMY LEADERS ARE HALF-GERMAN.
WHAT DO YOU MEAN?
THEY ALL SPEAK GERMAN, FOR ONE THING.
ONLY THEIR SKIN IS JAPANESE.
BUT ARE THEY NAZI GERMANS?

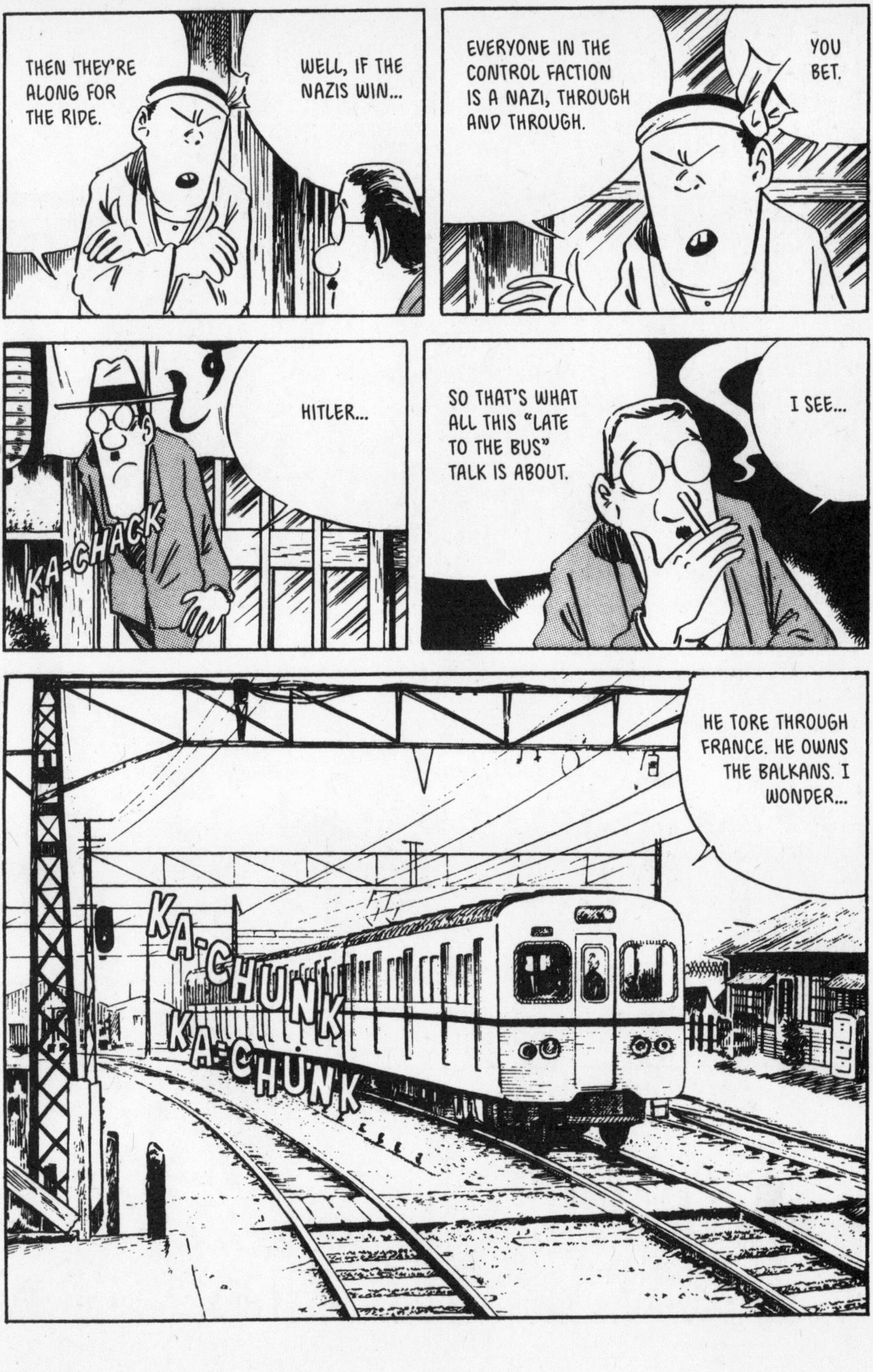
YOU BET.
EVERYONE IN THE CONTROL FACTION IS A NAZI, THROUGH AND THROUGH.
WELL, IF THE NAZIS WIN...
THEN THEY'RE ALONG FOR THE RIDE.
I SEE...
SO THAT'S WHAT ALL THIS "LATE TO THE BUS" TALK IS ABOUT.
HITLER...
KA-CHACK
HE TORE THROUGH FRANCE. HE OWNS THE BALKANS. I WONDER...
KA-CHUNK
KA-CHUNK

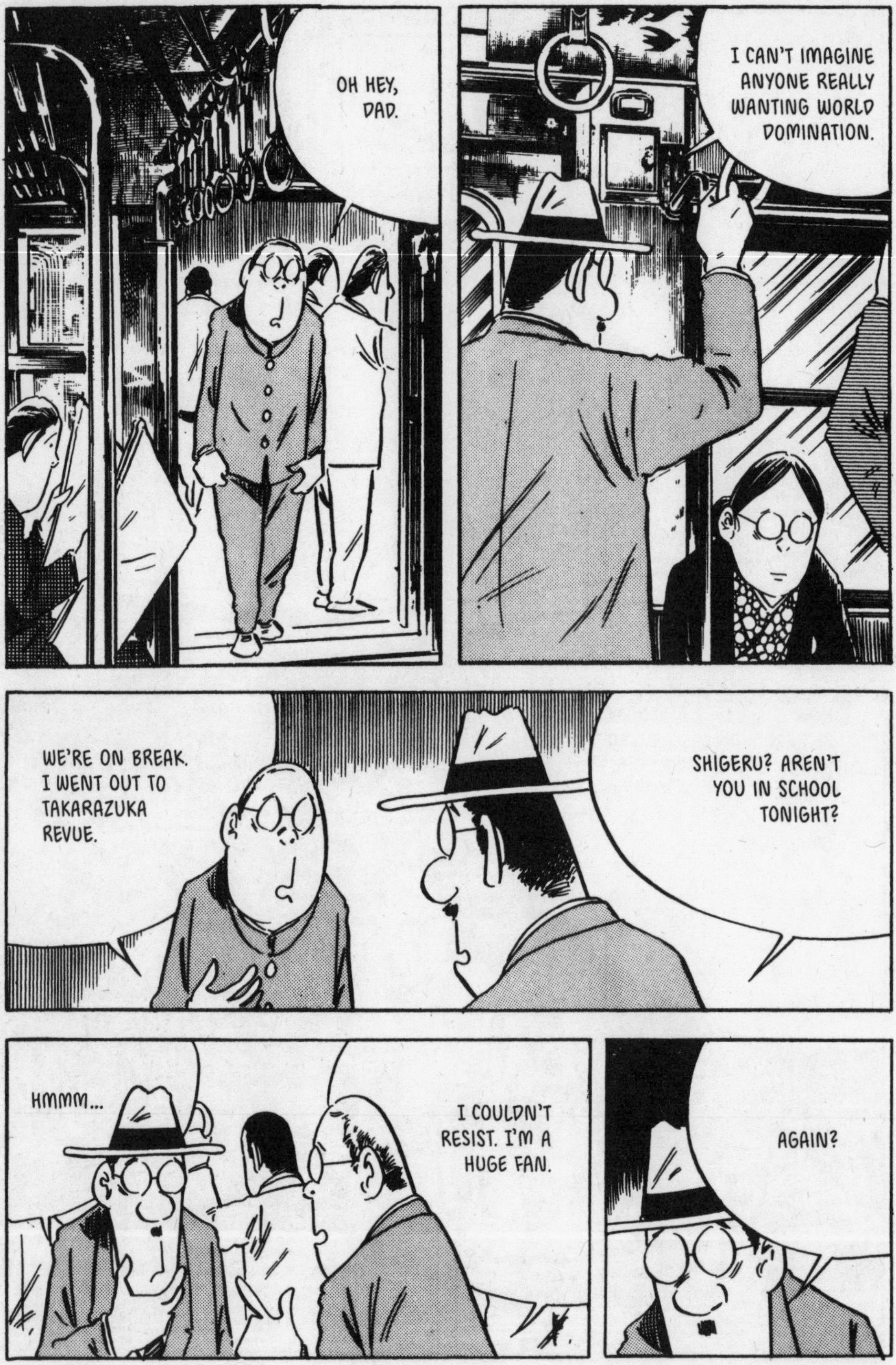
I CAN'T IMAGINE ANYONE REALLY WANTING WORLD DOMINATION.
OH HEY, DAD.
SHIGERU? AREN'T YOU IN SCHOOL TONIGHT?
WE'RE ON BREAK. I WENT OUT TO TAKARAZUKA REVUE.
AGAIN?
I COULDN'T RESIST. I'M A HUGE FAN.
HMMM...

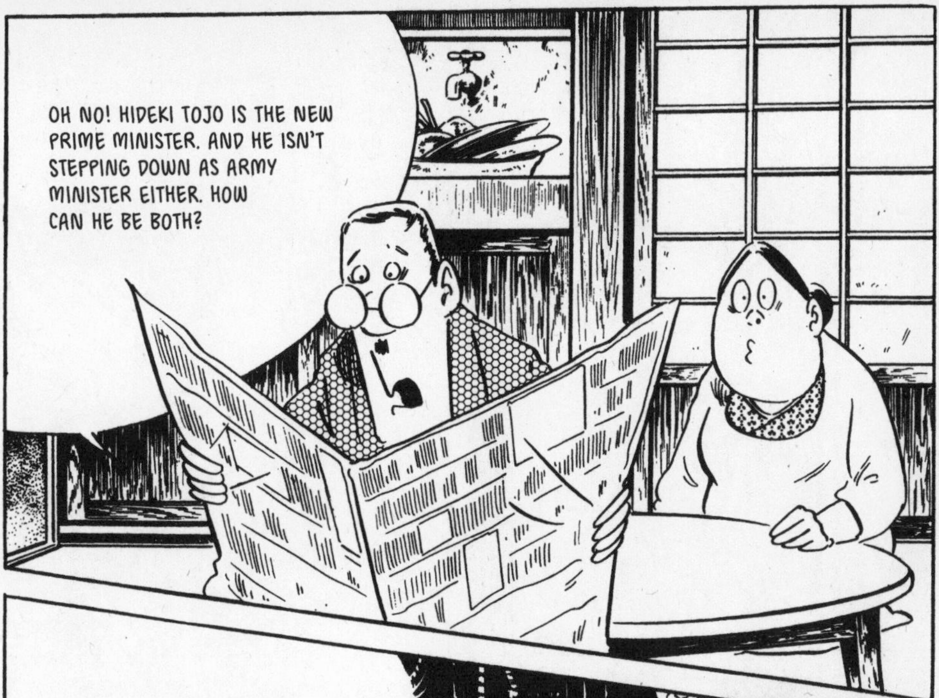
OH NO! HIDEKI TOJO IS THE NEW PRIME MINISTER. AND HE ISN'T STEPPING DOWN AS ARMY MINISTER EITHER. HOW CAN HE BE BOTH?

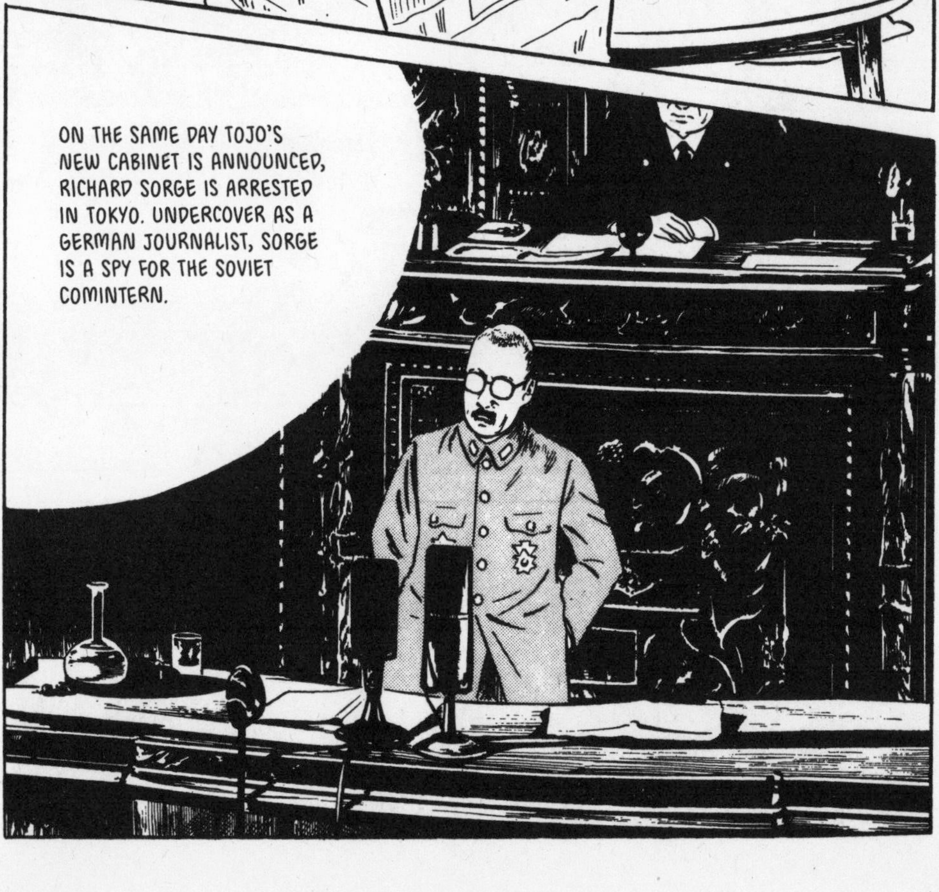
ON THE SAME DAY TOJO'S NEW CABINET IS ANNOUNCED, RICHARD SORGE IS ARRESTED IN TOKYO. UNDERCOVER AS A GERMAN JOURNALIST, SORGE IS A SPY FOR THE SOVIET COMINTERN.

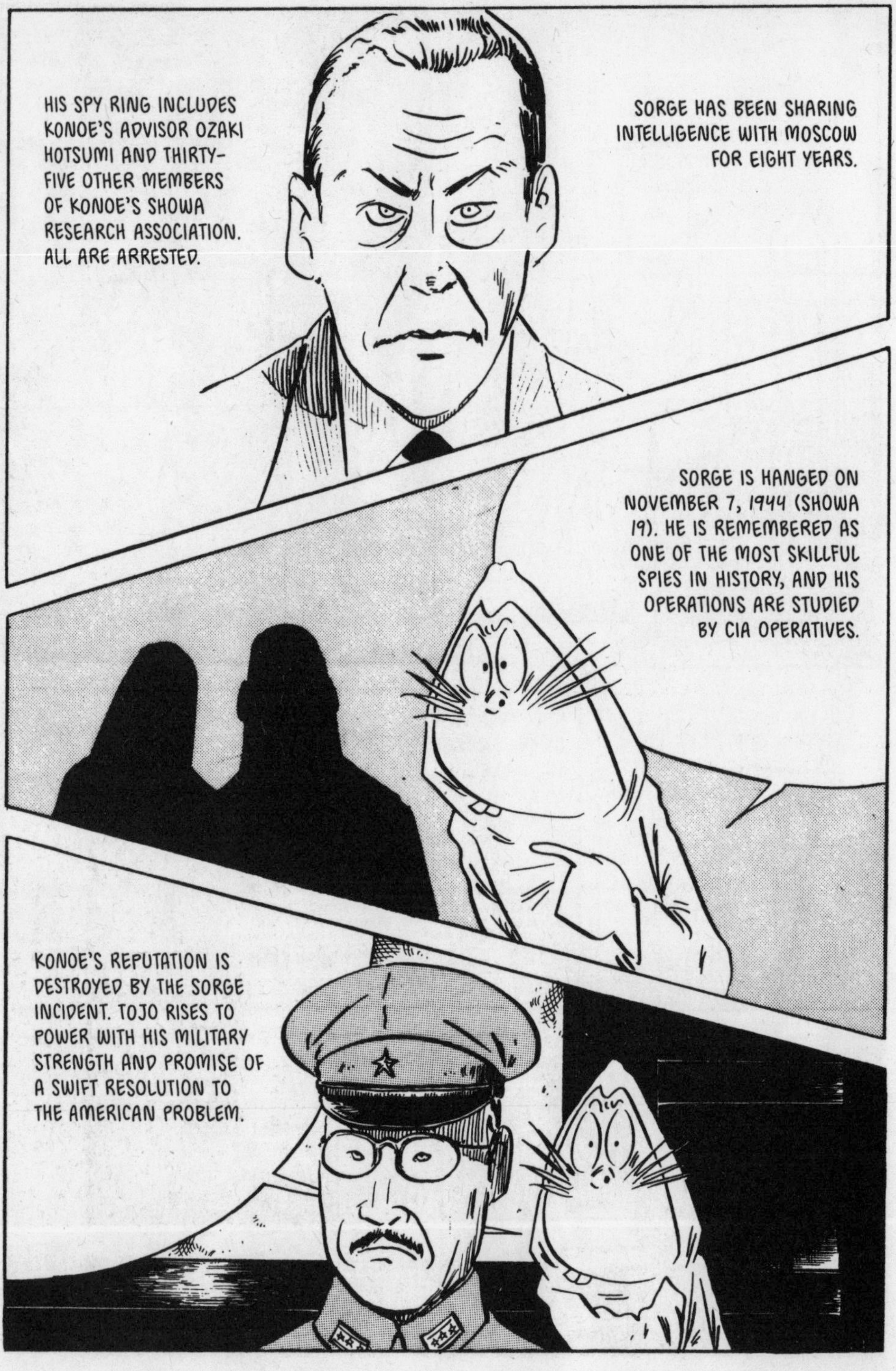
SORGE HAS BEEN SHARING INTELLIGENCE WITH MOSCOW FOR EIGHT YEARS.
HIS SPY RING INCLUDES KONOE'S ADVISOR OZAKI HOTSUMI AND THIRTY-FIVE OTHER MEMBERS OF KONOE'S SHOWA RESEARCH ASSOCIATION. ALL ARE ARRESTED.
SORGE IS HANGED ON NOVEMBER 7, 1944 (SHOWA 19). HE IS REMEMBERED AS ONE OF THE MOST SKILLFUL SPIES IN HISTORY, AND HIS OPERATIONS ARE STUDIED BY CIA OPERATIVES.
KONOE'S REPUTATION IS DESTROYED BY THE SORGE INCIDENT. TOJO RISES TO POWER WITH HIS MILITARY STRENGTH AND PROMISE OF A SWIFT RESOLUTION TO THE AMERICAN PROBLEM.

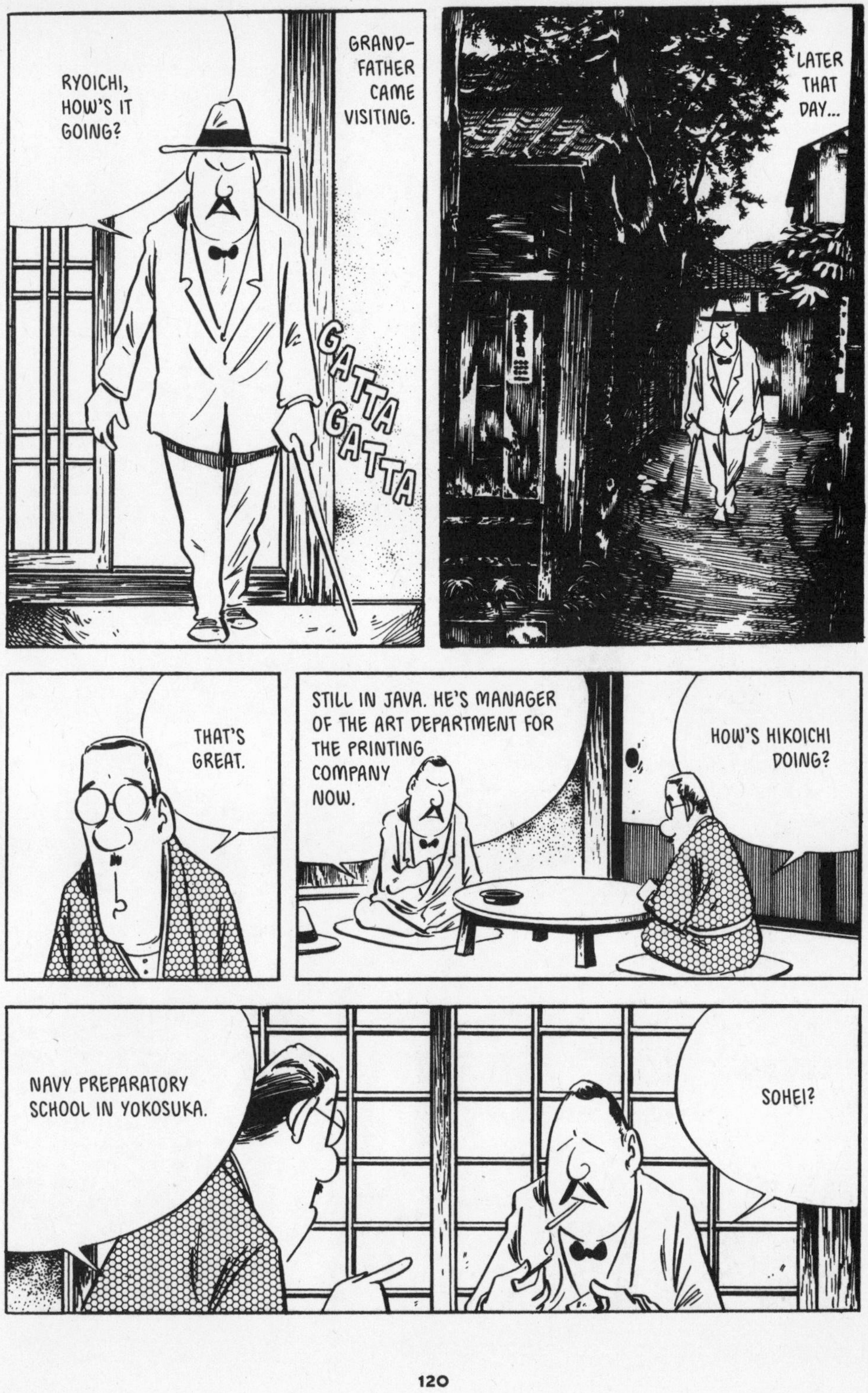
LATER THAT DAY...
GRAND-FATHER CAME VISITING.
RYOICHI, HOW'S IT GOING?
GATTA GATTA
HOW'S HIKOICHI DOING?
STILL IN JAVA. HE'S MANAGER OF THE ART DEPARTMENT FOR THE PRINTING COMPANY NOW.
THAT'S GREAT.
SOHEI?
NAVY PREPARATORY SCHOOL IN YOKOSUKA.

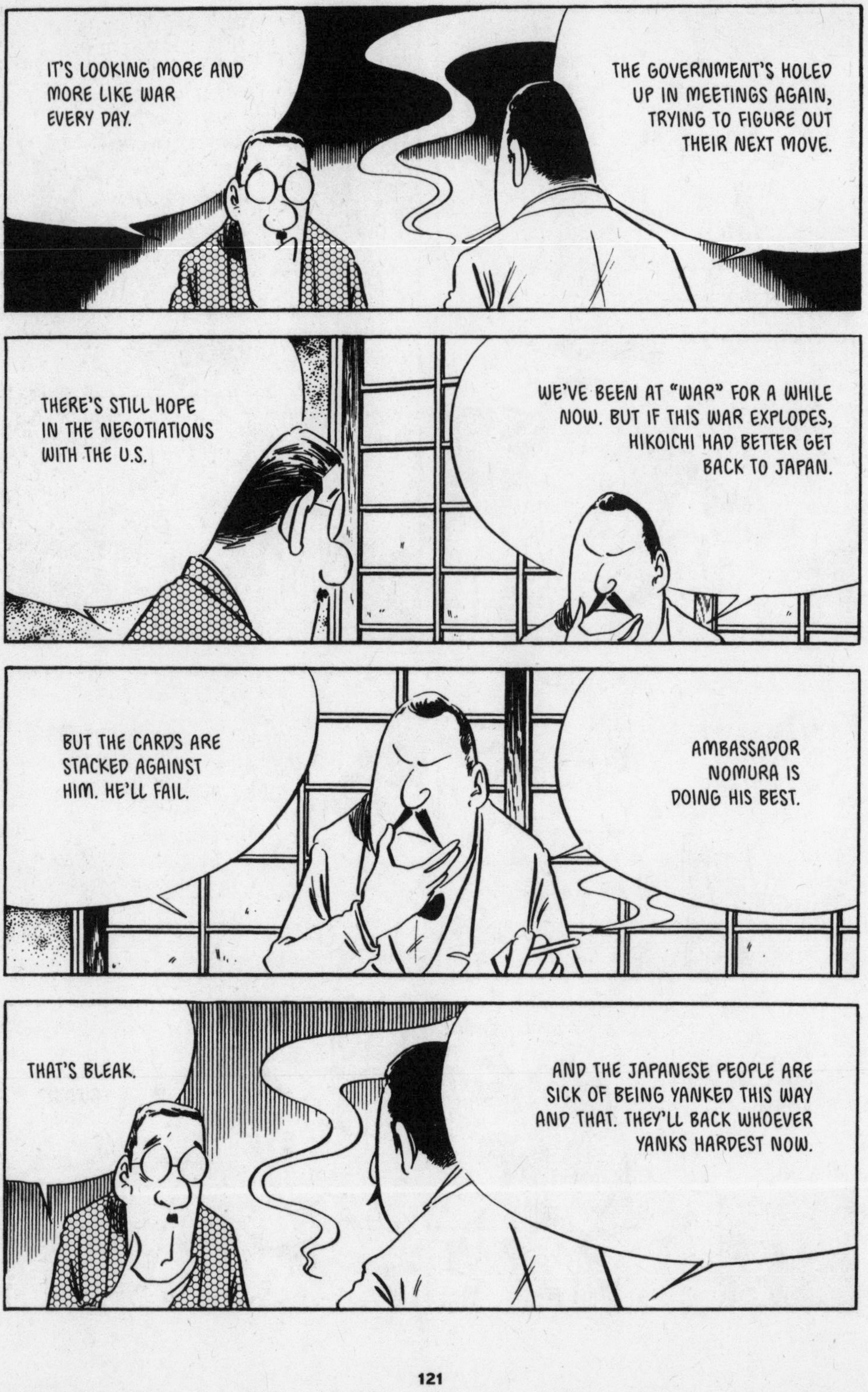
THE GOVERNMENT'S HOLED UP IN MEETINGS AGAIN, TRYING TO FIGURE OUT THEIR NEXT MOVE.
IT'S LOOKING MORE AND MORE LIKE WAR EVERY DAY.
WE'VE BEEN AT "WAR" FOR A WHILE NOW. BUT IF THIS WAR EXPLODES, HIKOICHI HAD BETTER GET BACK TO JAPAN.
THERE'S STILL HOPE IN THE NEGOTIATIONS WITH THE U.S.
AMBASSADOR NOMURA IS DOING HIS BEST.
BUT THE CARDS ARE STACKED AGAINST HIM. HE'LL FAIL.
AND THE JAPANESE PEOPLE ARE SICK OF BEING YANKED THIS WAY AND THAT. THEY'LL BACK WHOEVER YANKS HARDEST NOW.
THAT'S BLEAK.

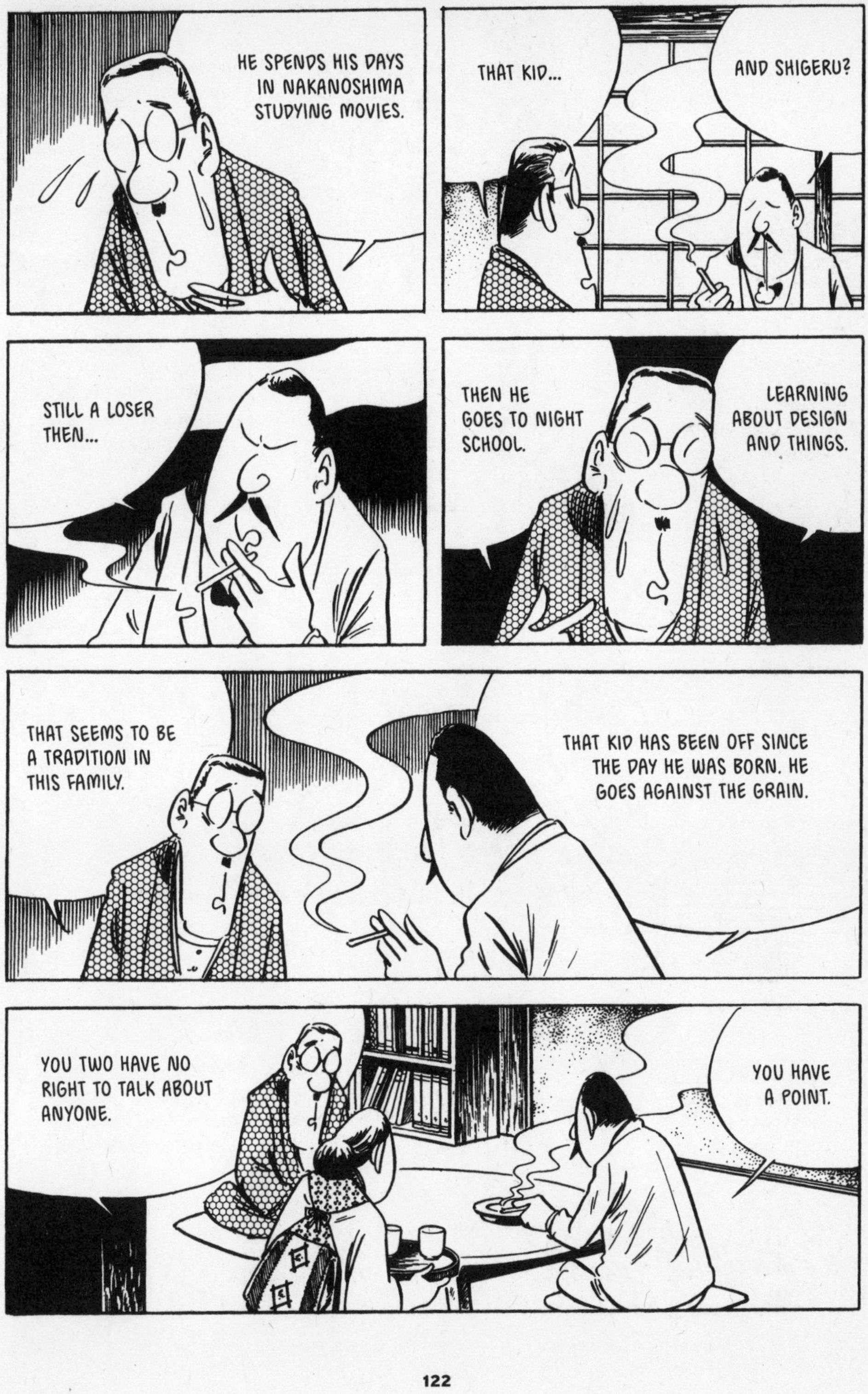
AND SHIGERU?
THAT KID...
HE SPENDS HIS DAYS IN NAKANOSHIMA STUDYING MOVIES.
LEARNING ABOUT DESIGN AND THINGS.
THEN HE GOES TO NIGHT SCHOOL.
STILL A LOSER THEN...
THAT KID HAS BEEN OFF SINCE THE DAY HE WAS BORN. HE GOES AGAINST THE GRAIN.
THAT SEEMS TO BE A TRADITION IN THIS FAMILY.
YOU HAVE A POINT.
YOU TWO HAVE NO RIGHT TO TALK ABOUT ANYONE.

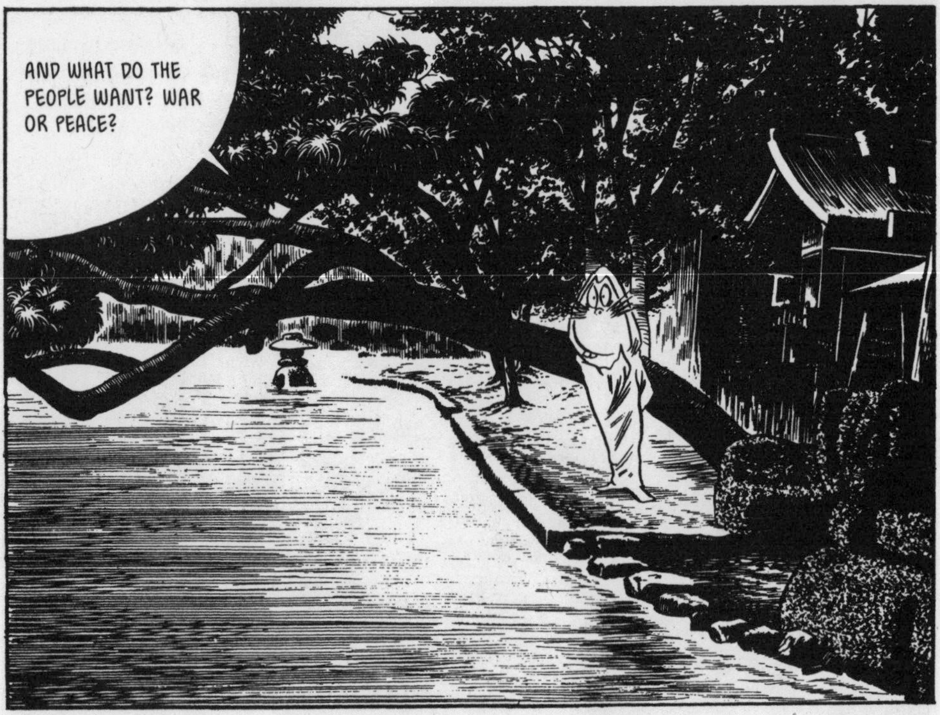
AND WHAT DO THE PEOPLE WANT? WAR OR PEACE?

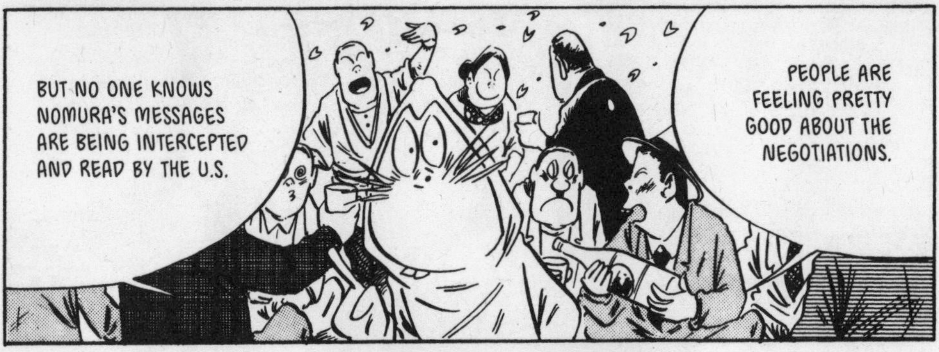
PEOPLE ARE FEELING PRETTY GOOD ABOUT THE NEGOTIATIONS.
BUT NO ONE KNOWS NOMURA'S MESSAGES ARE BEING INTERCEPTED AND READ BY THE U.S.

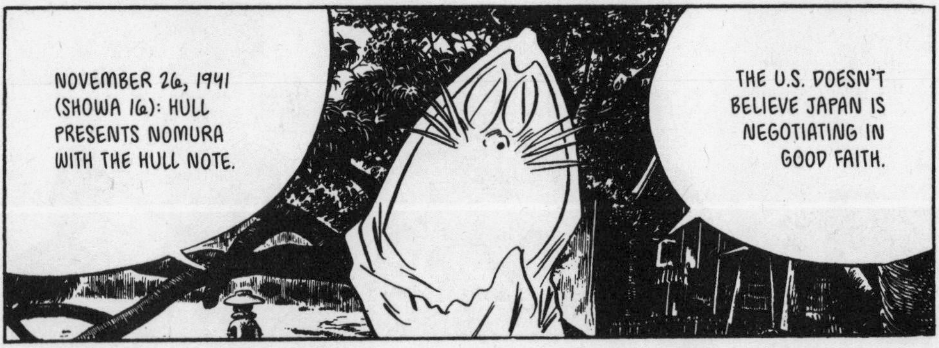
THE U.S. DOESN'T BELIEVE JAPAN IS NEGOTIATING IN GOOD FAITH.
NOVEMBER 26, 1941 (SHOWA 16): HULL PRESENTS NOMURA WITH THE HULL NOTE.

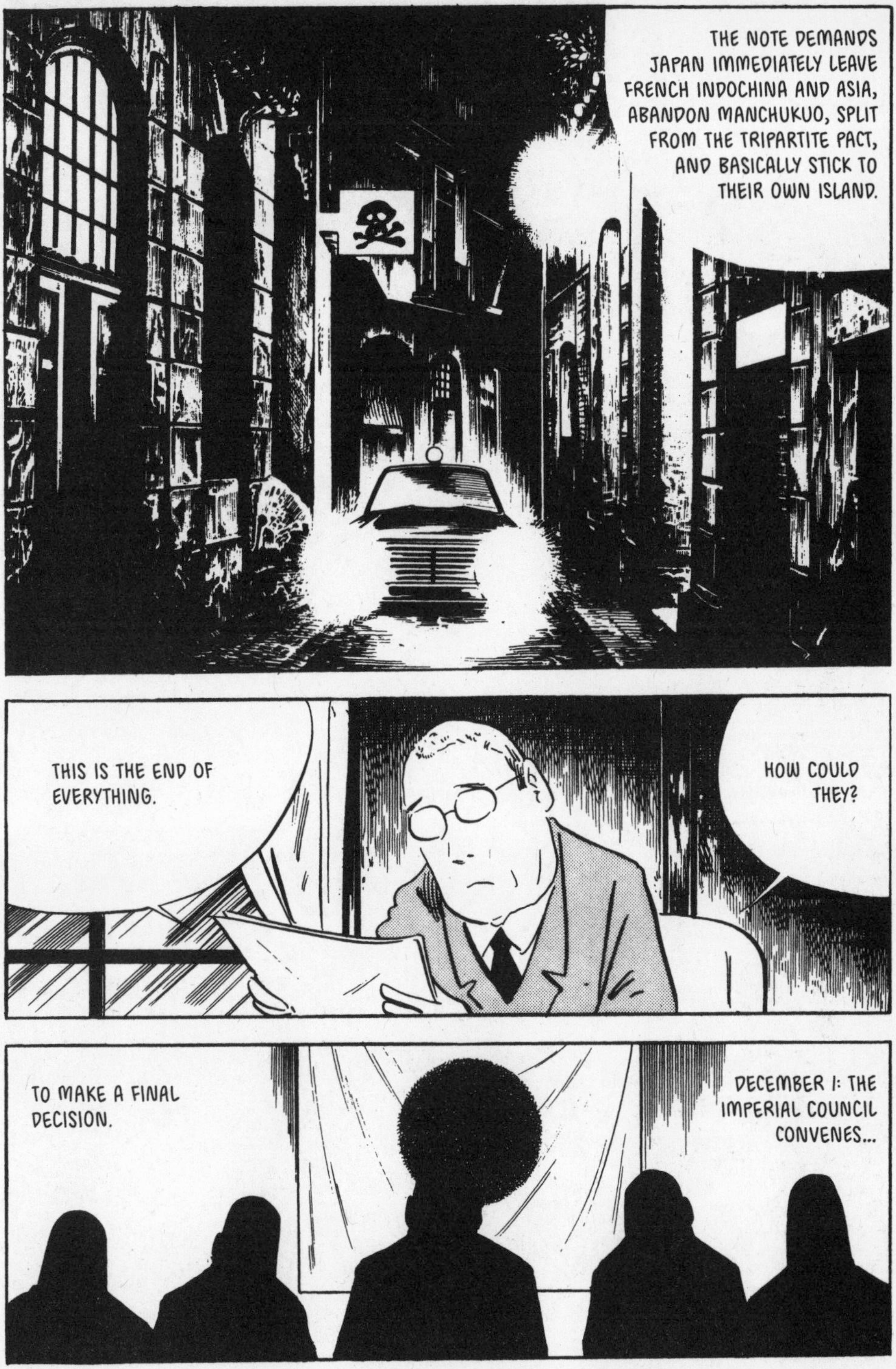
THE NOTE DEMANDS JAPAN IMMEDIATELY LEAVE FRENCH INDOCHINA AND ASIA, ABANDON MANCHUKUO, SPLIT FROM THE TRIPARTITE PACT, AND BASICALLY STICK TO THEIR OWN ISLAND.
HOW COULD THEY?
THIS IS THE END OF EVERYTHING.
DECEMBER 1: THE IMPERIAL COUNCIL CONVENES...
TO MAKE A FINAL DECISION.

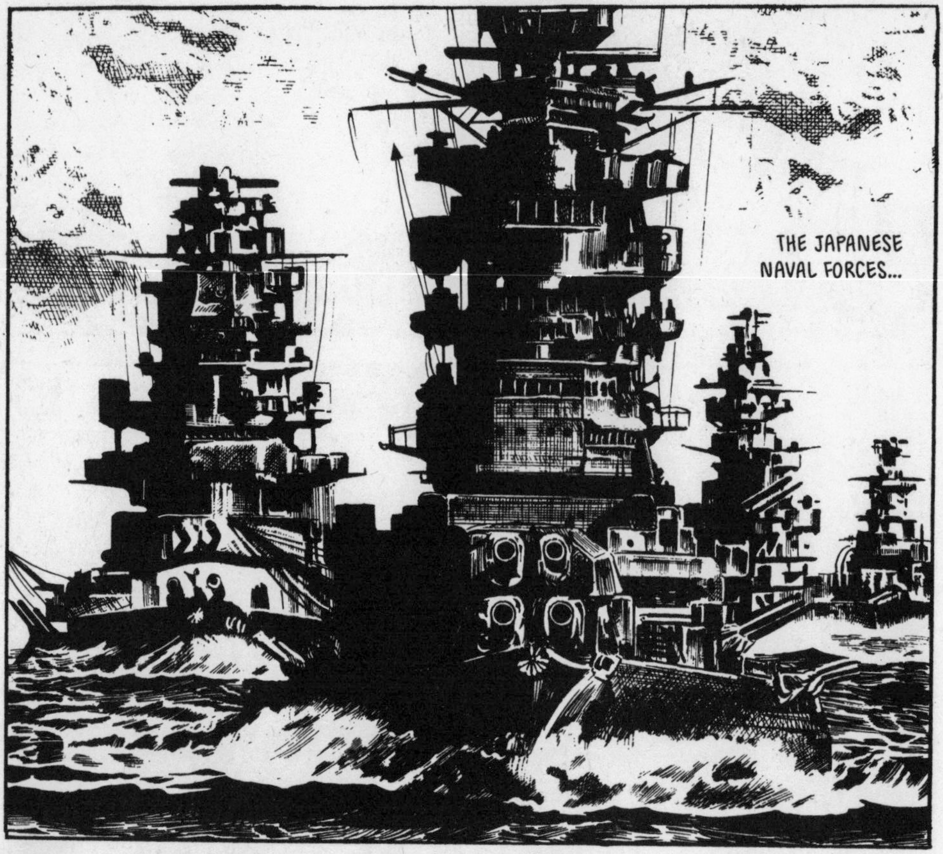
THE JAPANESE NAVAL FORCES...

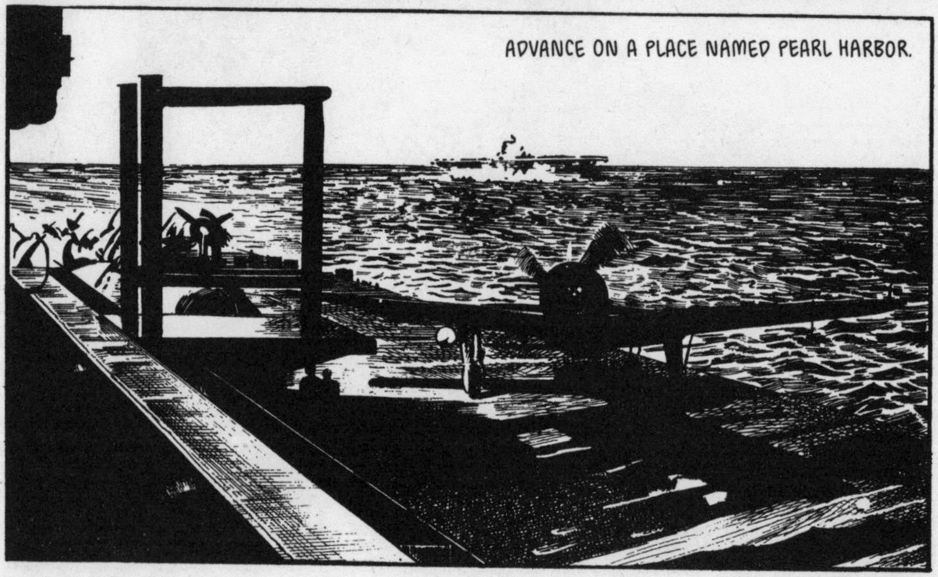
ADVANCE ON A PLACE NAMED PEARL HARBOR.

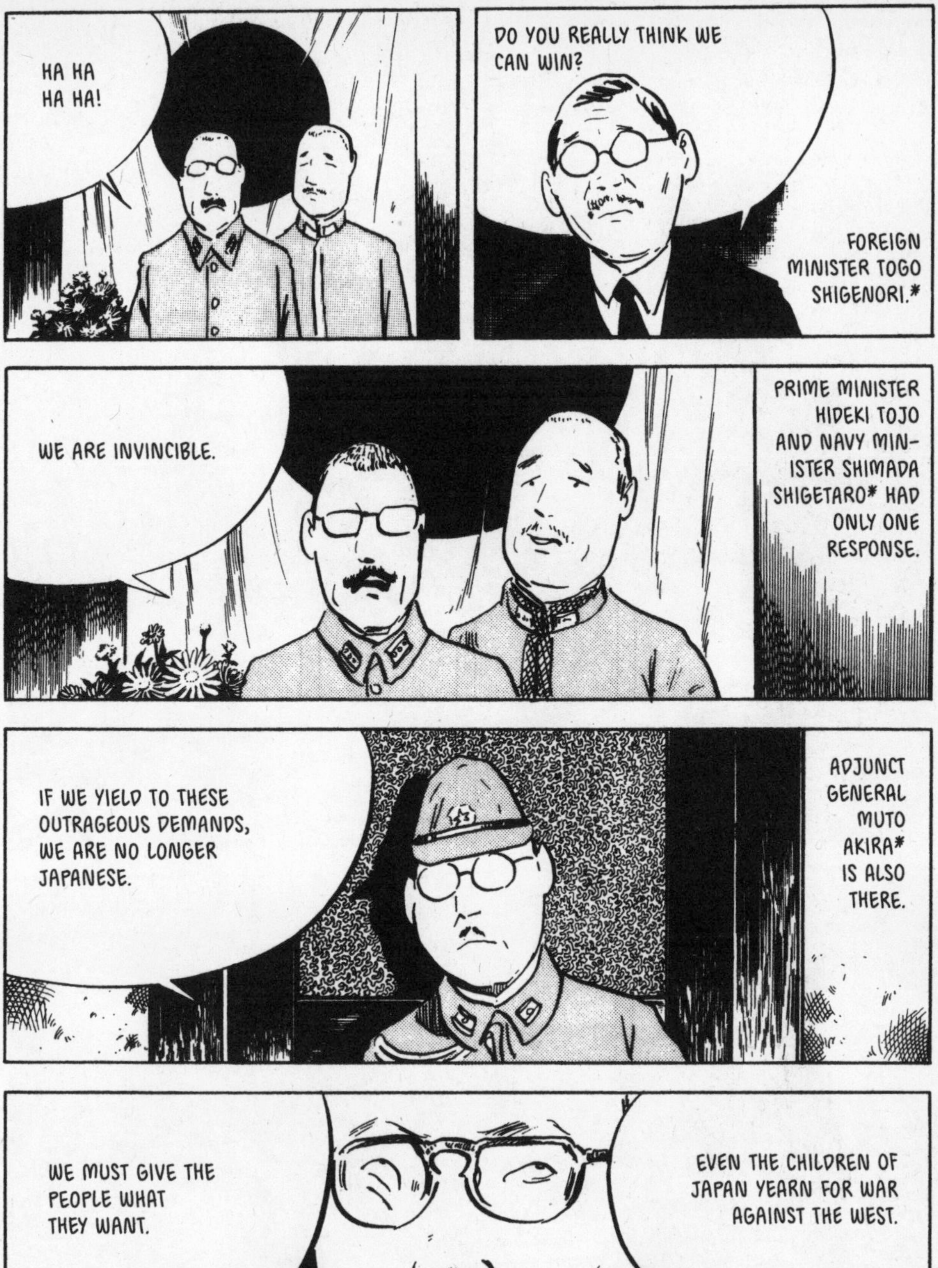
DO YOU REALLY THINK WE CAN WIN?
FOREIGN MINISTER TOGO SHIGENORI.*
HA HA HA HA!
PRIME MINISTER HIDEKI TOJO AND NAVY MIN-ISTER SHIMADA SHIGETARO* HAD ONLY ONE RESPONSE.
WE ARE INVINCIBLE.
ADJUNCT GENERAL MUTO AKIRA* IS ALSO THERE.
IF WE YIELD TO THESE OUTRAGEOUS DEMANDS, WE ARE NO LONGER JAPANESE.
EVEN THE CHILDREN OF JAPAN YEARN FOR WAR AGAINST THE WEST.
WE MUST GIVE THE PEOPLE WHAT THEY WANT.

*SEE NOTE ON PAGE 544.

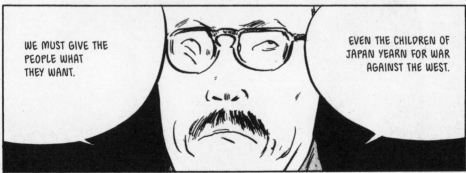

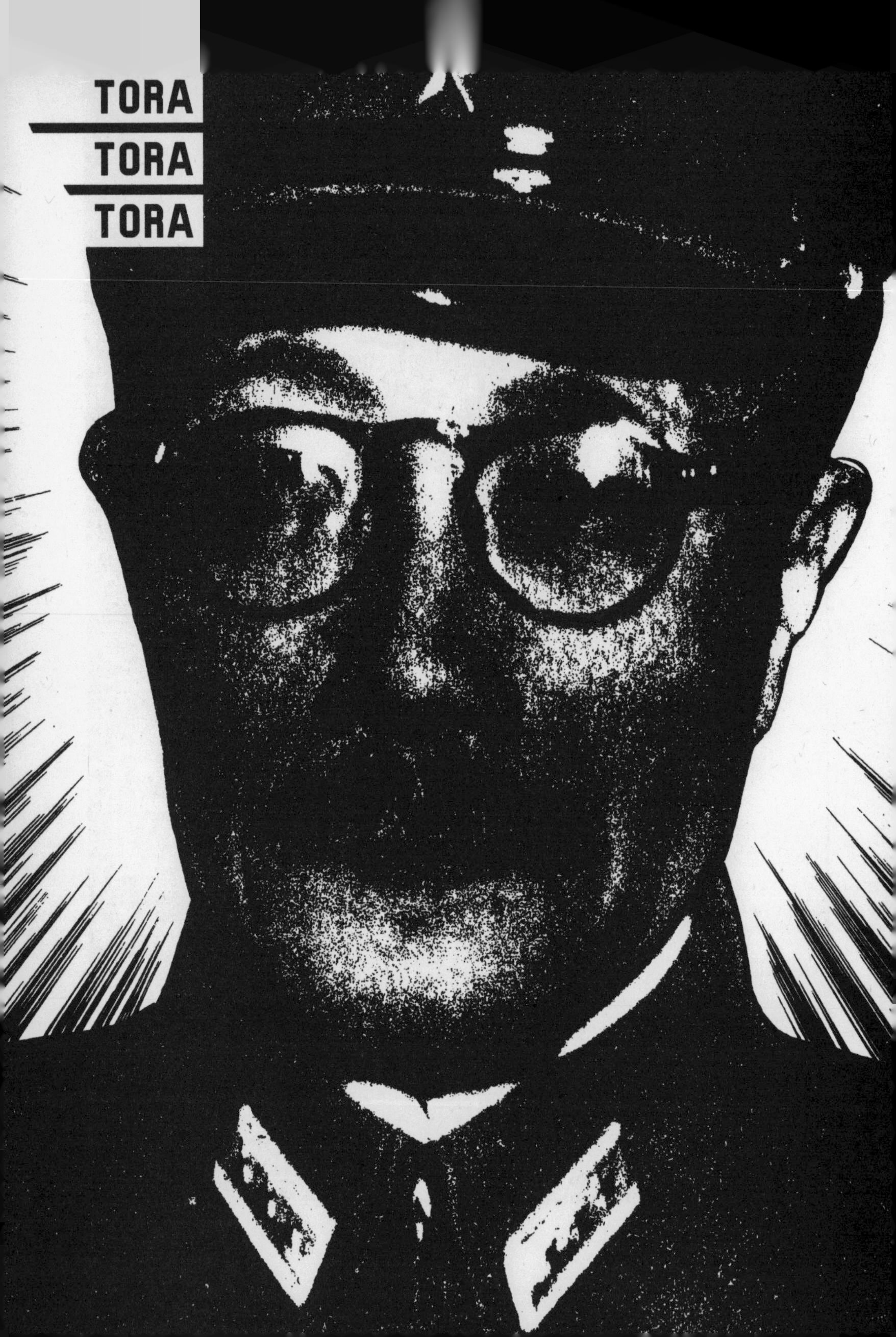
TORA
TORA
TORA

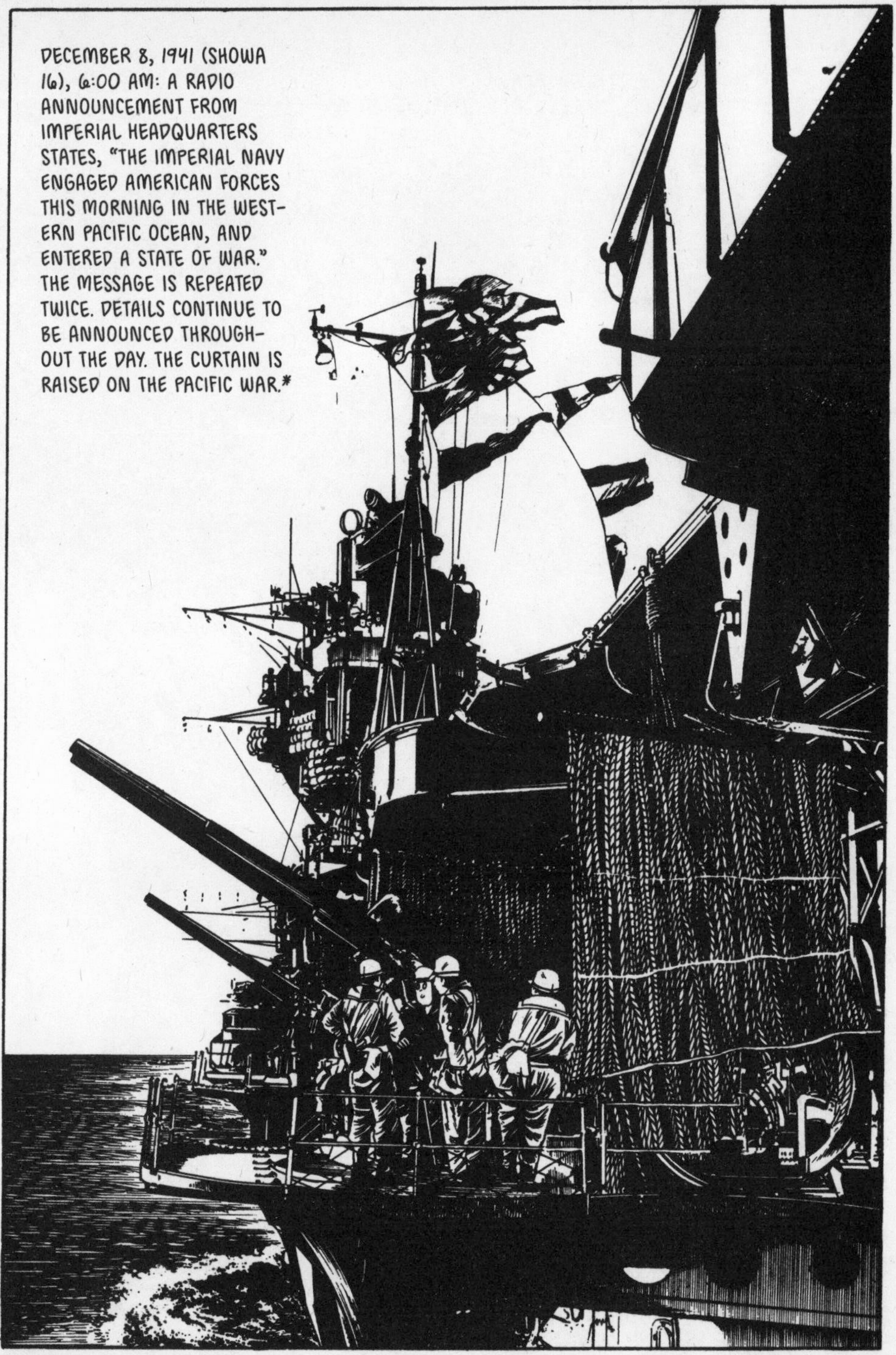
DECEMBER 8, 1941 (SHOWA 16), 6:00 AM: A RADIO ANNOUNCEMENT FROM IMPERIAL HEADQUARTERS STATES, "THE IMPERIAL NAVY ENGAGED AMERICAN FORCES THIS MORNING IN THE WESTERN PACIFIC OCEAN, AND ENTERED A STATE OF WAR." THE MESSAGE IS REPEATED TWICE. DETAILS CONTINUE TO BE ANNOUNCED THROUGHOUT THE DAY. THE CURTAIN IS RAISED ON THE PACIFIC WAR.*

*SEE NOTE ON PAGE 544.

海軍通信記録文用紙
軍極秘
暗號
緊急信
東京
聯合艦隊
聯合艦隊電令第十三號
皇國ノ興廢繫リテ此ノ征戰ニ在リ
粉骨碎身各員其ノ任ヲ完ウセヨ
本電十二月七日〇六〇〇一斉令

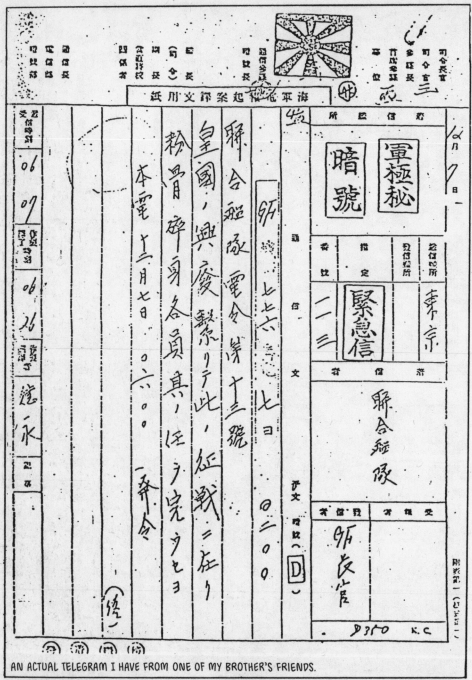

AN ACTUAL TELEGRAM I HAVE FROM ONE OF MY BROTHER'S FRIENDS.

*AN OFFICIAL MILITARY EMERGENCY TELEGRAM SENT FROM TOKYO ON DECEMBER 7. WRITTEN IN CODE, THE COMBINED FLEET ORDER #13 STATES: "THIS IS THE DECISIVE BATTLE THAT WILL DECIDE THE FUTURE OF THE JAPANESE EMPIRE. EACH MAN MUST DO THEIR DUTY TO THE FULLEST EXTENT OF THEIR ABILITIES, AND CARRY OUT THIS MISSION."

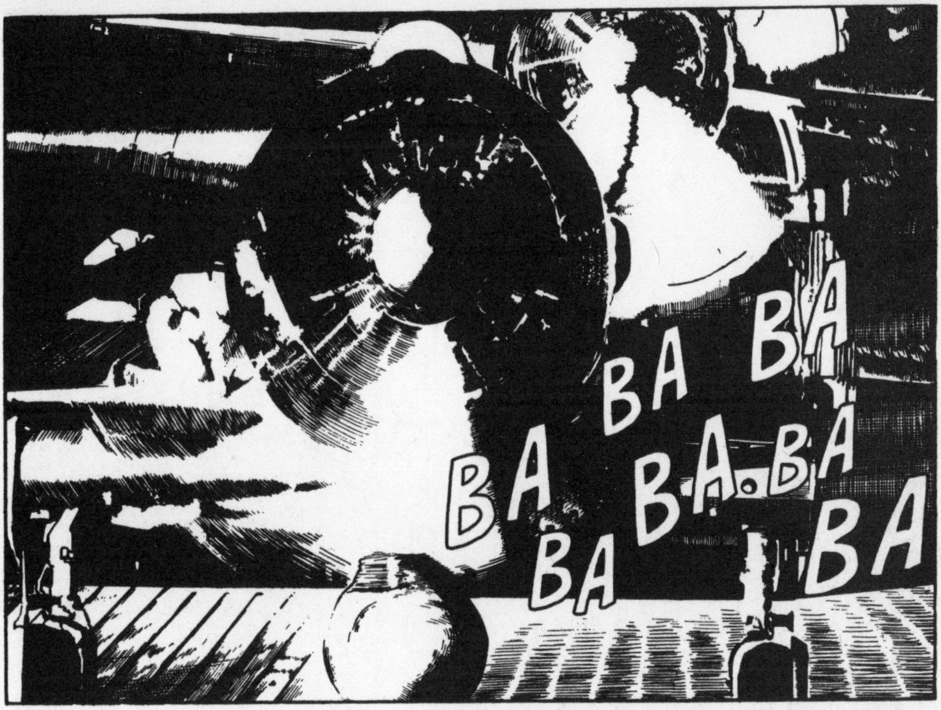
BA
BA
BA.BA.BA
BA
BA
BA
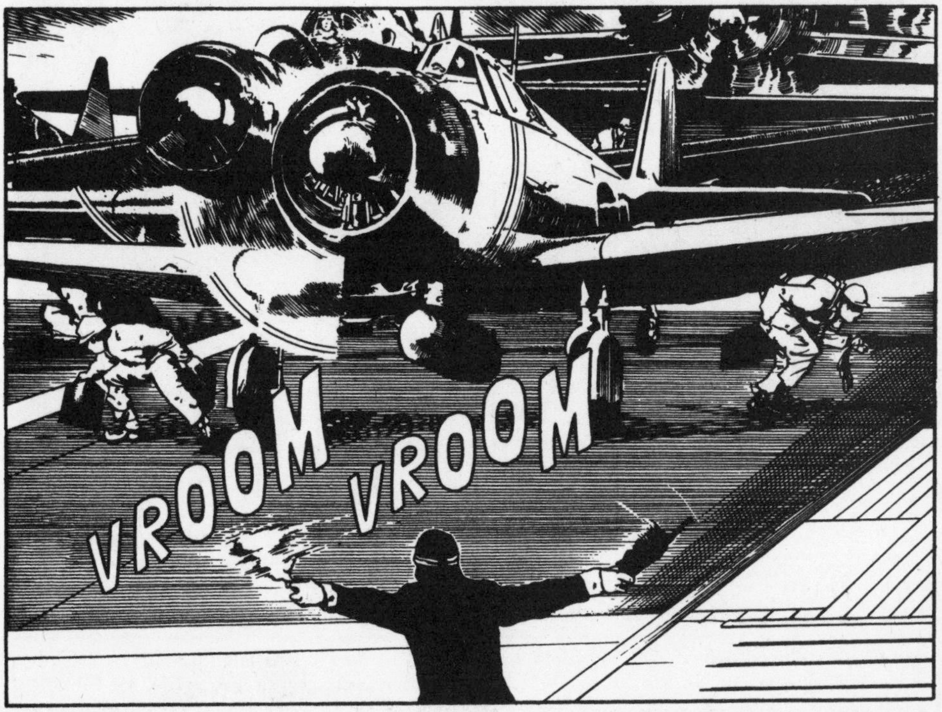
VROOM
VROOM

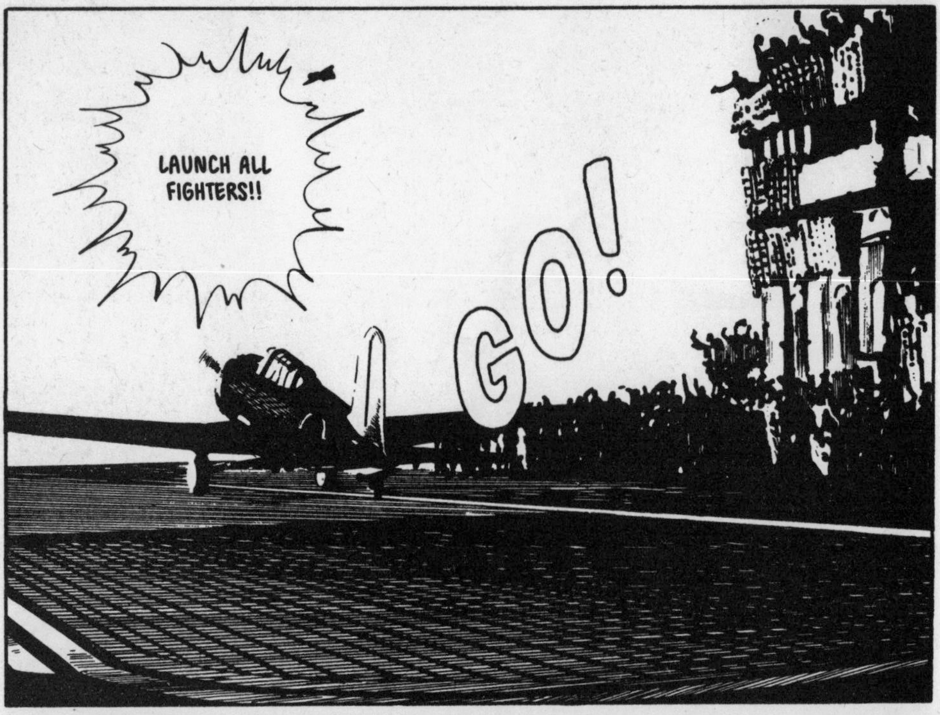
LAUNCH ALL FIGHTERS!!
GO!

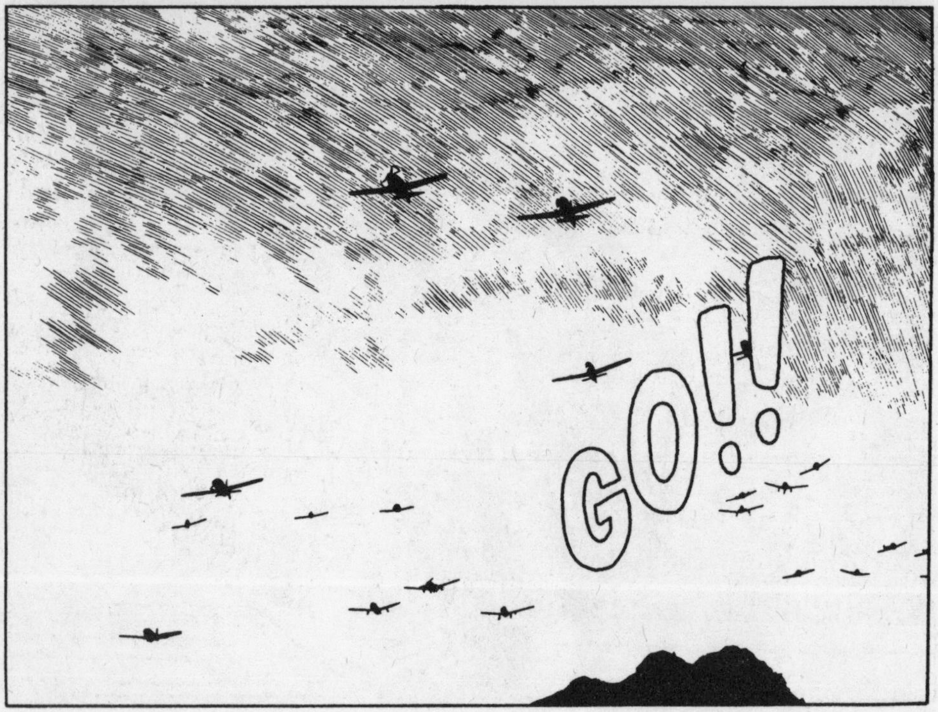
GO!!

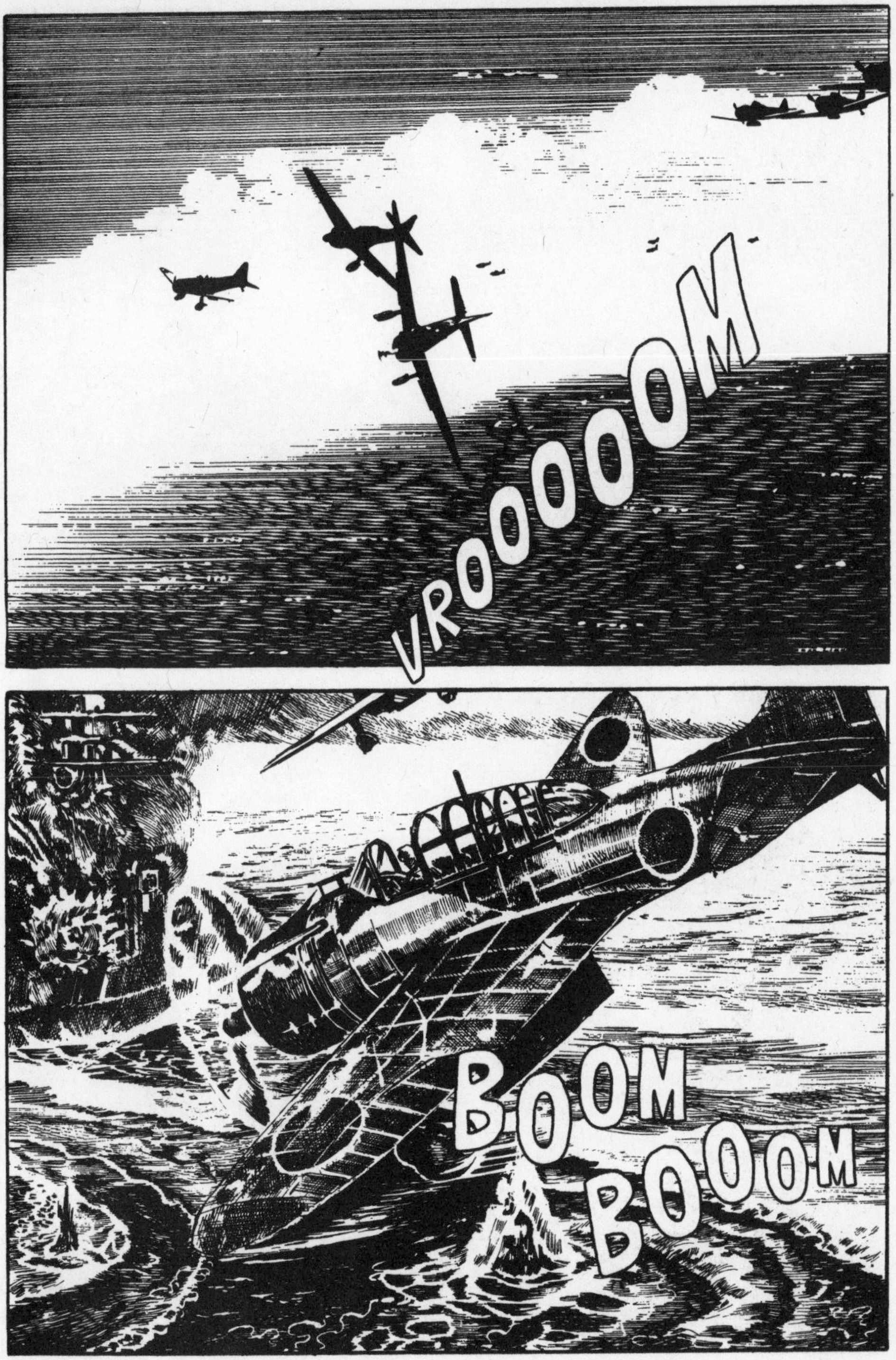
VROOOOOM
BOOM
BOOOM

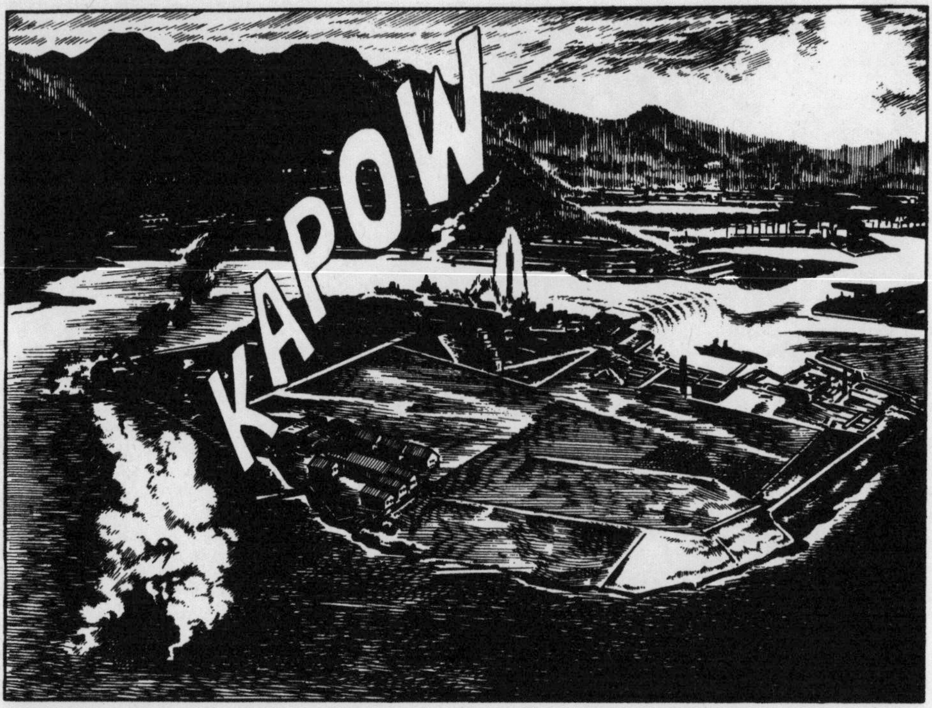
KAPOW
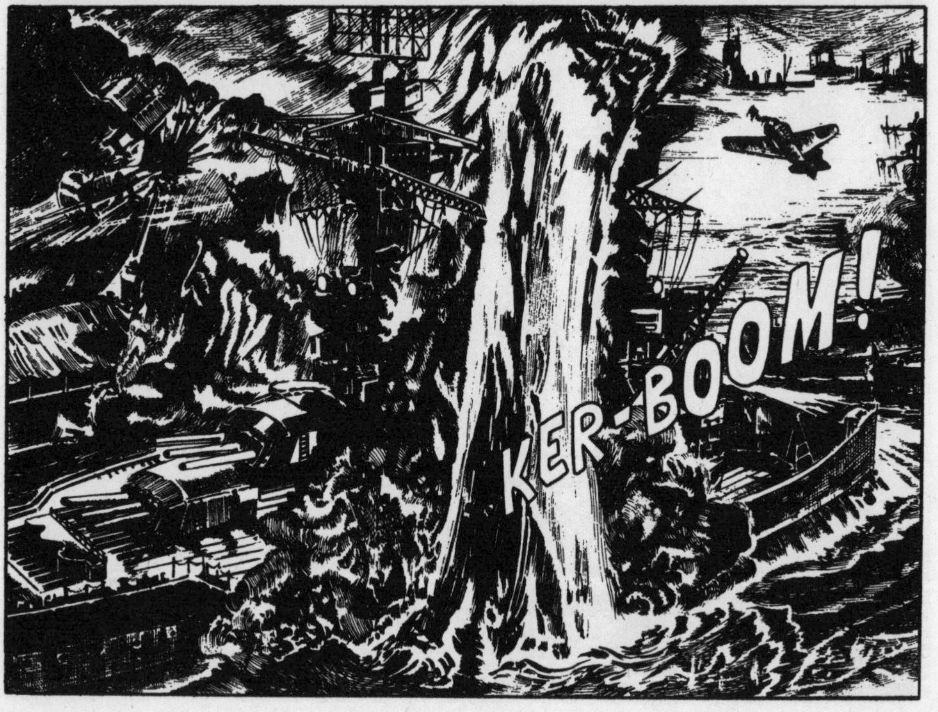
KER-BOOM!

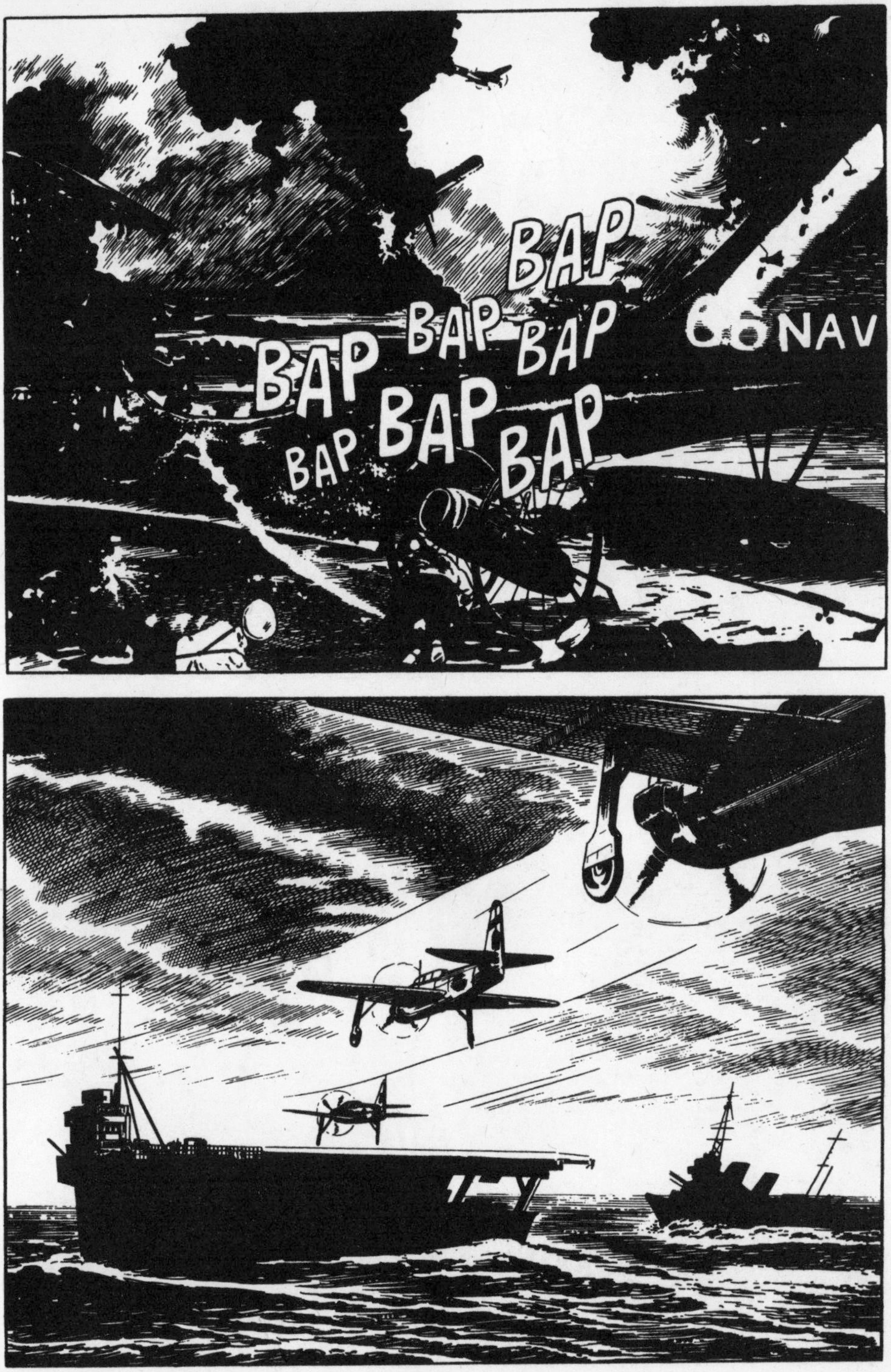
BAP
NAV
BAP
BAP
BAP
BAP
BAP
BAP
BAP

海軍電報起案譯文用紙
暗号略号 ト(・・－・・)ラ(・・・)トラトラ
艦橋届済
奇襲成功セリ
〇三二三
12月8日

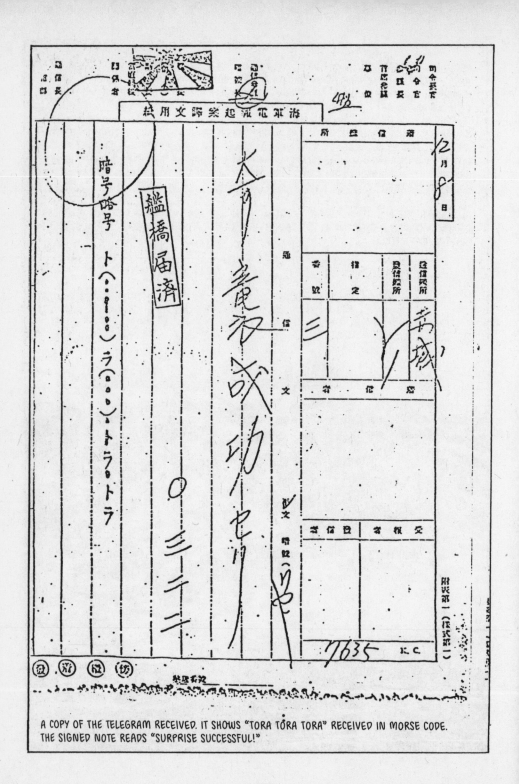

A COPY OF THE TELEGRAM RECEIVED. IT SHOWS "TORA TORA TORA" RECEIVED IN MORSE CODE. THE SIGNED NOTE READS "SURPRISE SUCCESSFUL!"

DECEMBER 2: FLEET COMMANDER VICE ADMIRAL NAGUMO CHUICHI,* ABOARD THE FLAGSHIP *AKAGI*, RECEIVES A TELEGRAM FROM COMBINED FLEET COMMANDER-IN-CHIEF ADMIRAL YAMAMOTO ISOROKU. THE MESSAGE INSTRUCTS NAGUMO TO "CLIMB MOUNT NITAKA." THOSE OMINOUS WORDS ARE HIS ORDERS TO LAUNCH THE SNEAK ATTACK ON HAWAII.

NAGUMO'S STRIKE FORCE FLEET NUMBERS TWENTY-THREE SHIPS AND THIRTY THOUSAND MEN. HE WAS SUPPORTED BY LIEUTENANT COMMANDER GENDA MINORU—ARCHITECT OF THE ATTACK PLAN—AND COMMANDER FUCHIDA MISUO WHO LED THE FIRST WAVE OF 183 AIRCRAFT. IN THE AIR OVER HAWAII, FUCHIDA TRANSMITS THE CODE "TORA TORA TORA," MEANING A COMPLETE SNEAK ATTACK HAD BEEN ACHIEVED.

ALONG WITH THE AIR ATTACK, FIVE MIDGET SUBMARINES ATTACK FROM UNDER THE WATER. THESE SMALL, TWO-MAN SUBS MANAGE TO FIRE THE FIRST SHOTS OF THE PACIFIC WAR, ALTHOUGH NONE RETURN TO THE FLEET.

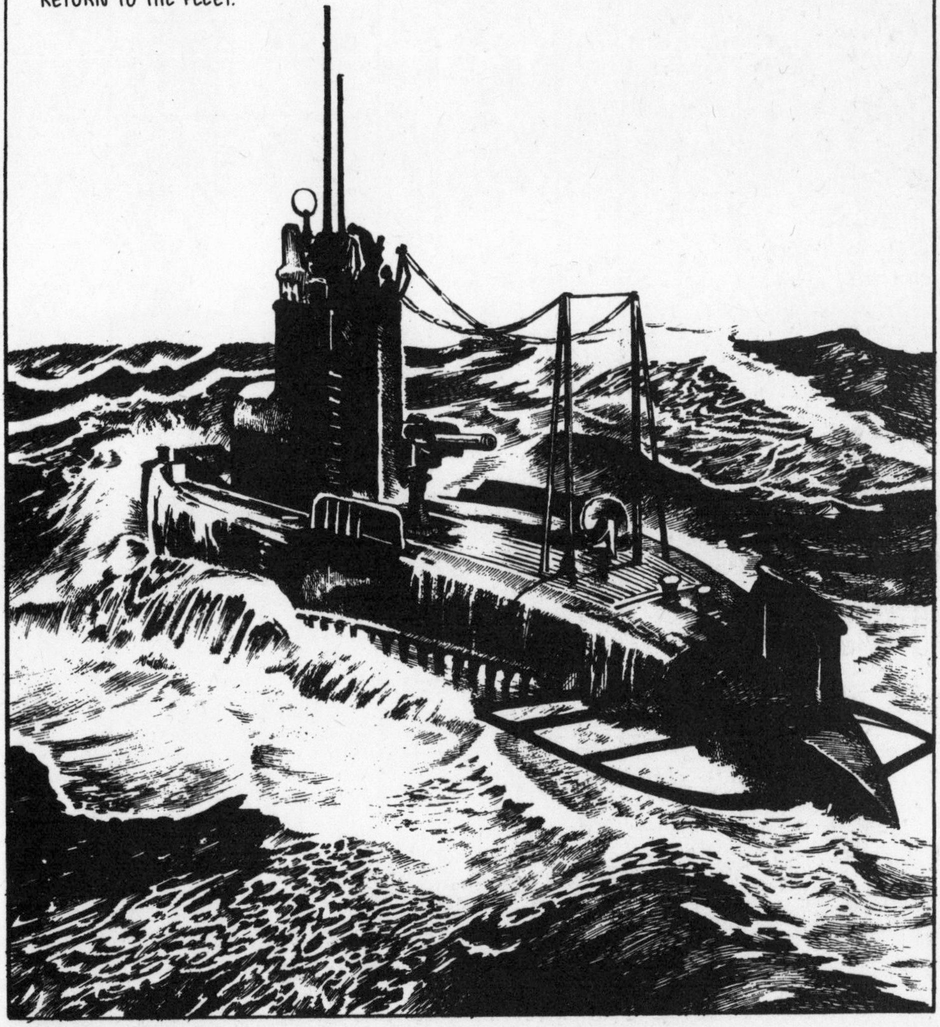

*SEE NOTE ON PAGE 544.

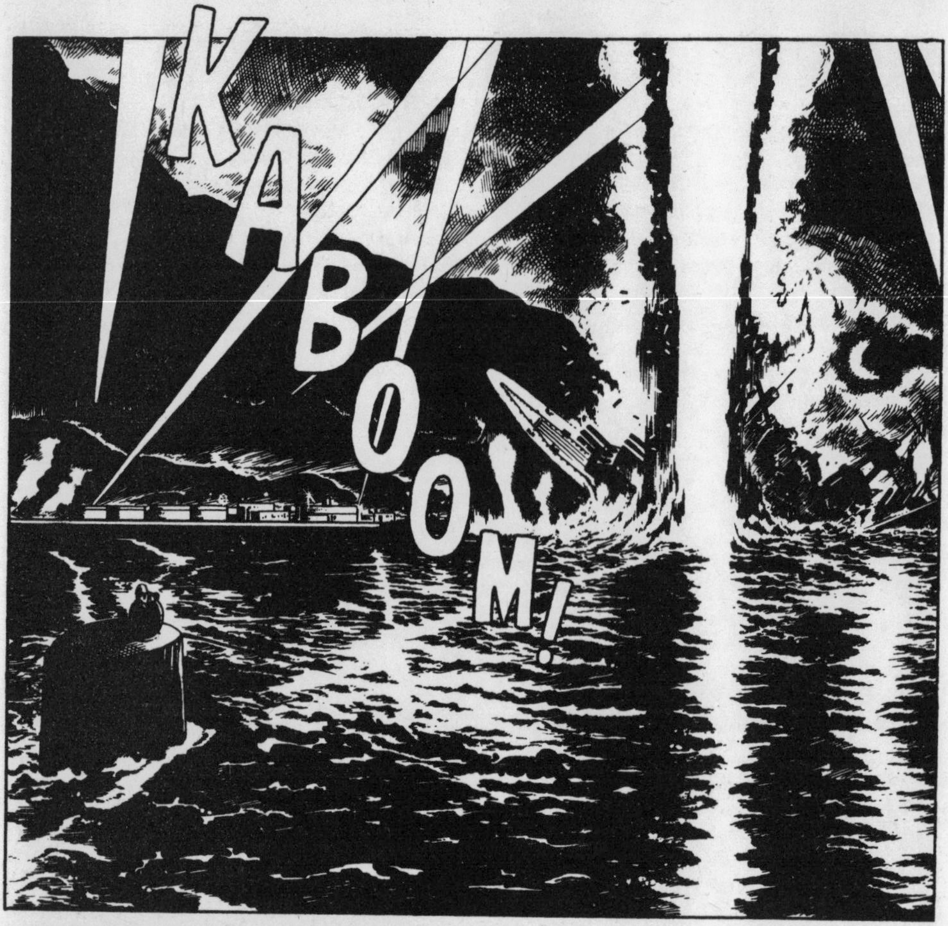
KABOOM!
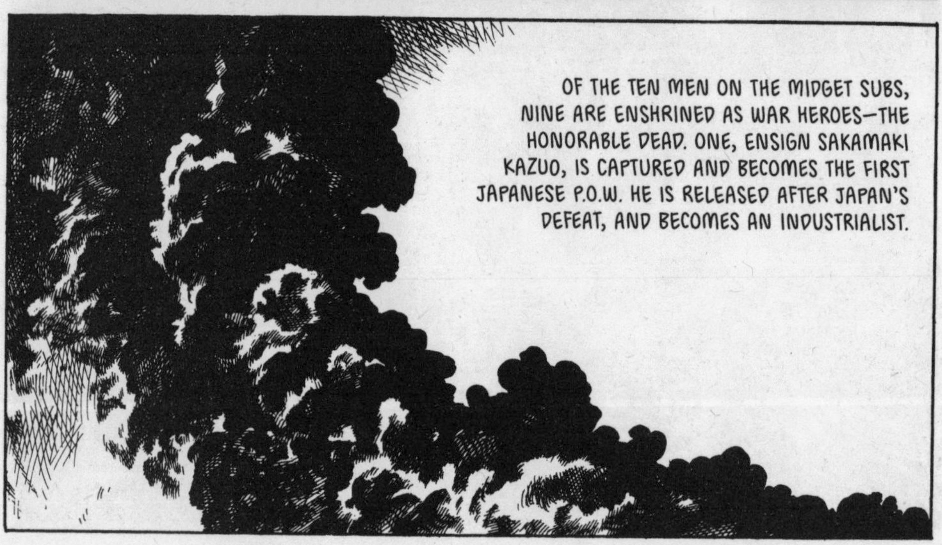
OF THE TEN MEN ON THE MIDGET SUBS, NINE ARE ENSHRINED AS WAR HEROES—THE HONORABLE DEAD. ONE, ENSIGN SAKAMAKI KAZUO, IS CAPTURED AND BECOMES THE FIRST JAPANESE P.O.W. HE IS RELEASED AFTER JAPAN'S DEFEAT, AND BECOMES AN INDUSTRIALIST.

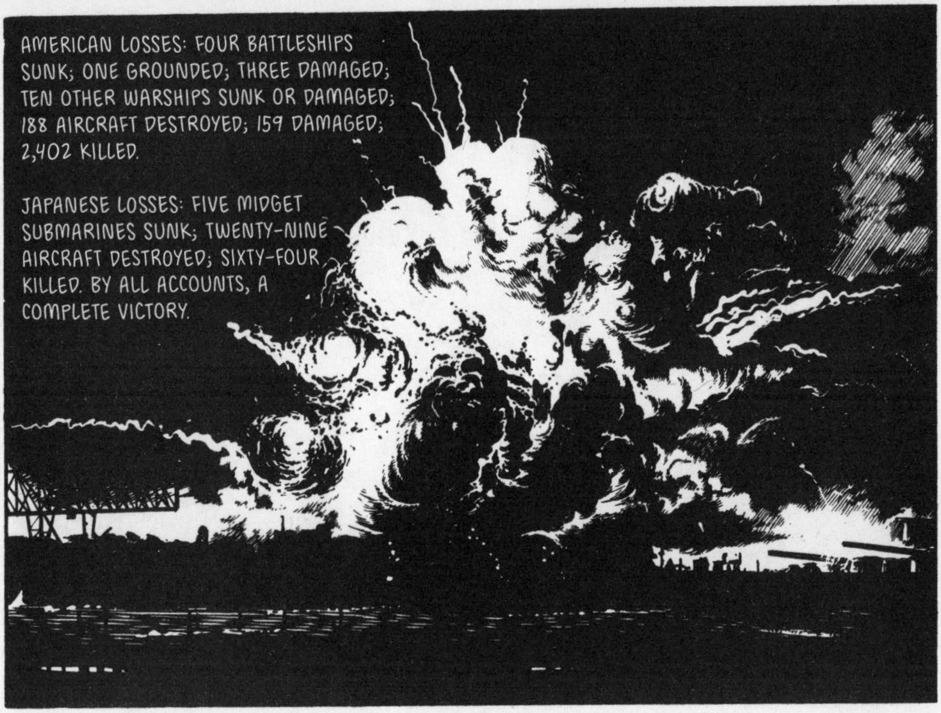
AMERICAN LOSSES: FOUR BATTLESHIPS SUNK; ONE GROUNDED; THREE DAMAGED; TEN OTHER WARSHIPS SUNK OR DAMAGED; 188 AIRCRAFT DESTROYED; 159 DAMAGED; 2,402 KILLED.
JAPANESE LOSSES: FIVE MIDGET SUBMARINES SUNK; TWENTY-NINE AIRCRAFT DESTROYED; SIXTY-FOUR KILLED. BY ALL ACCOUNTS, A COMPLETE VICTORY.

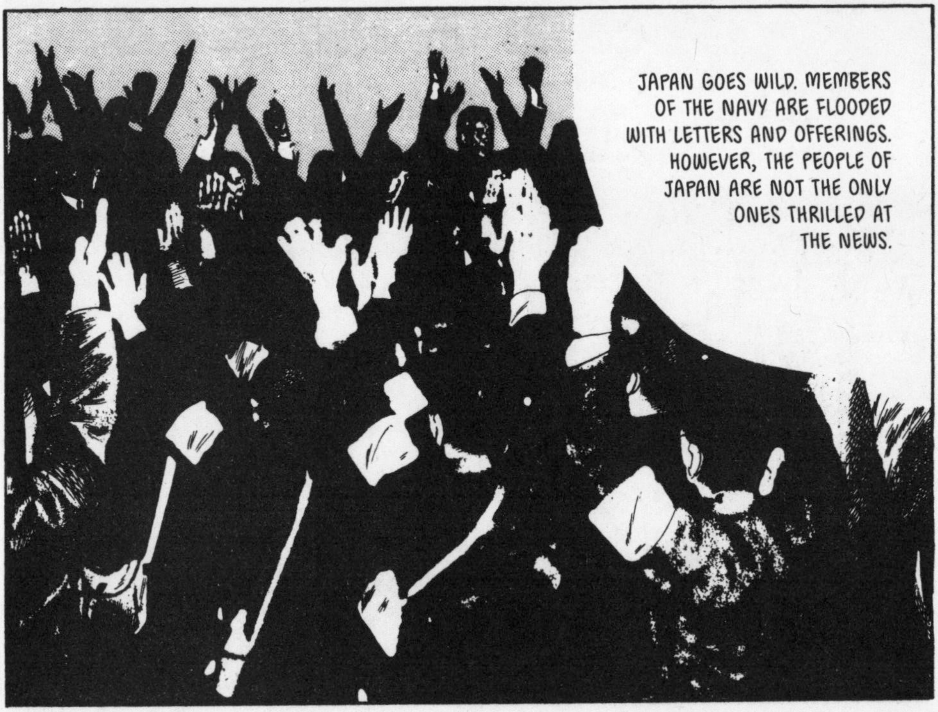
JAPAN GOES WILD. MEMBERS OF THE NAVY ARE FLOODED WITH LETTERS AND OFFERINGS. HOWEVER, THE PEOPLE OF JAPAN ARE NOT THE ONLY ONES THRILLED AT THE NEWS.

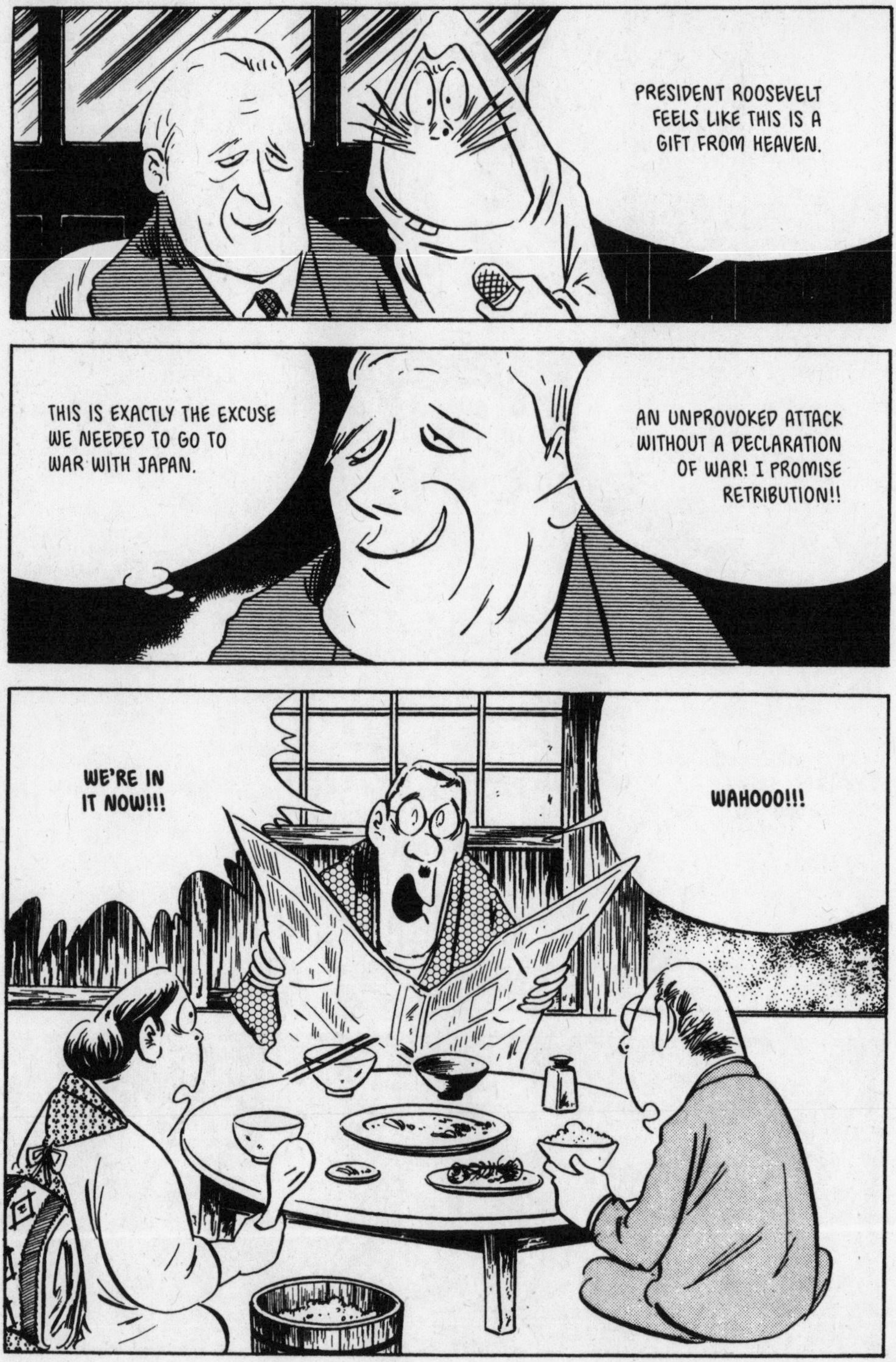
PRESIDENT ROOSEVELT FEELS LIKE THIS IS A GIFT FROM HEAVEN.
AN UNPROVOKED ATTACK WITHOUT A DECLARATION OF WAR! I PROMISE RETRIBUTION!!
THIS IS EXACTLY THE EXCUSE WE NEEDED TO GO TO WAR WITH JAPAN.
WAHOOO!!!
WE'RE IN IT NOW!!!

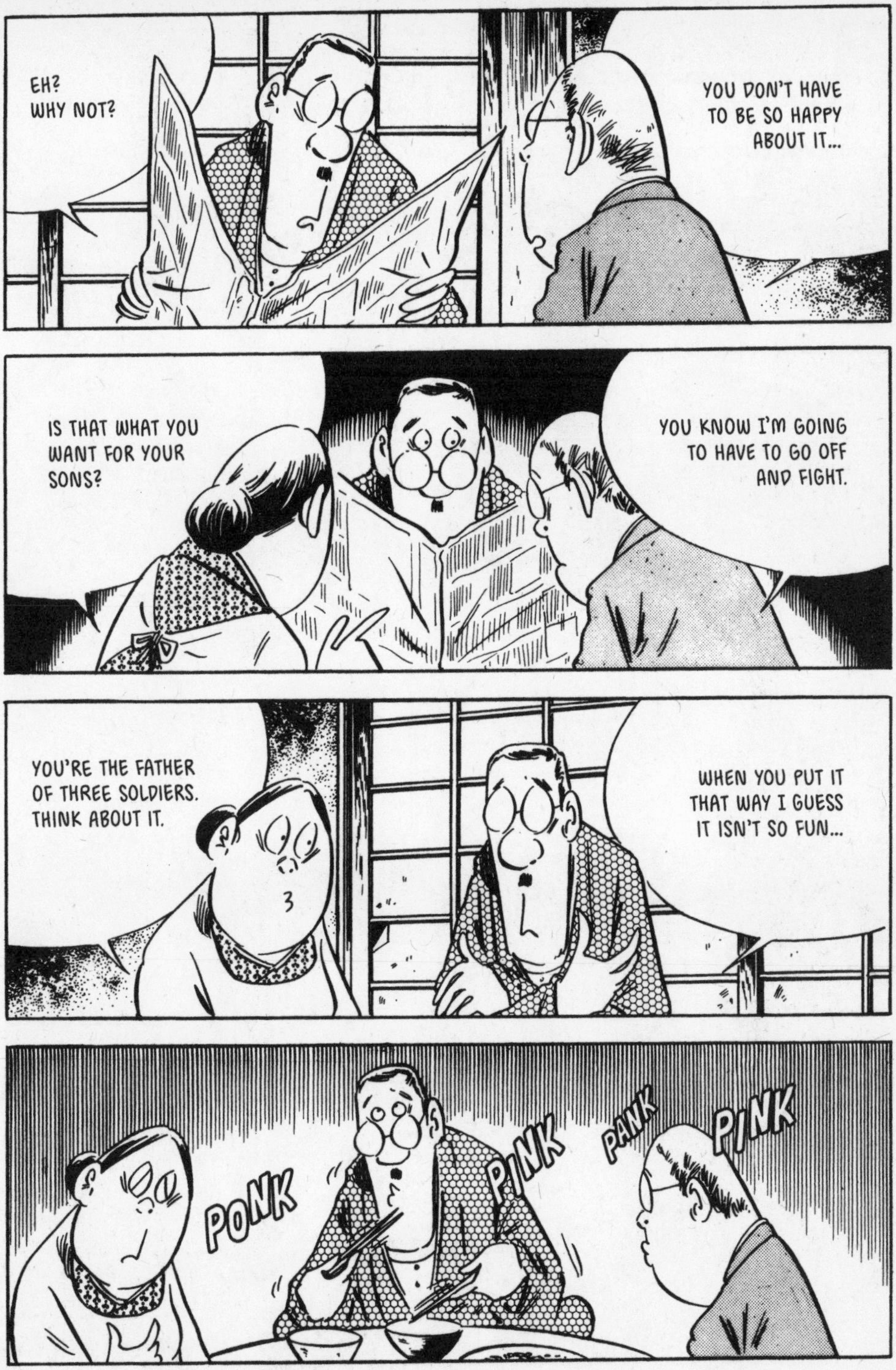
YOU DON'T HAVE TO BE SO HAPPY ABOUT IT...
EH? WHY NOT?
YOU KNOW I'M GOING TO HAVE TO GO OFF AND FIGHT.
IS THAT WHAT YOU WANT FOR YOUR SONS?
WHEN YOU PUT IT THAT WAY I GUESS IT ISN'T SO FUN...
YOU'RE THE FATHER OF THREE SOLDIERS. THINK ABOUT IT.
PINK
PANK
PINK
PONK

THE CAPTURE OF SINGAPORE AND MALAYA

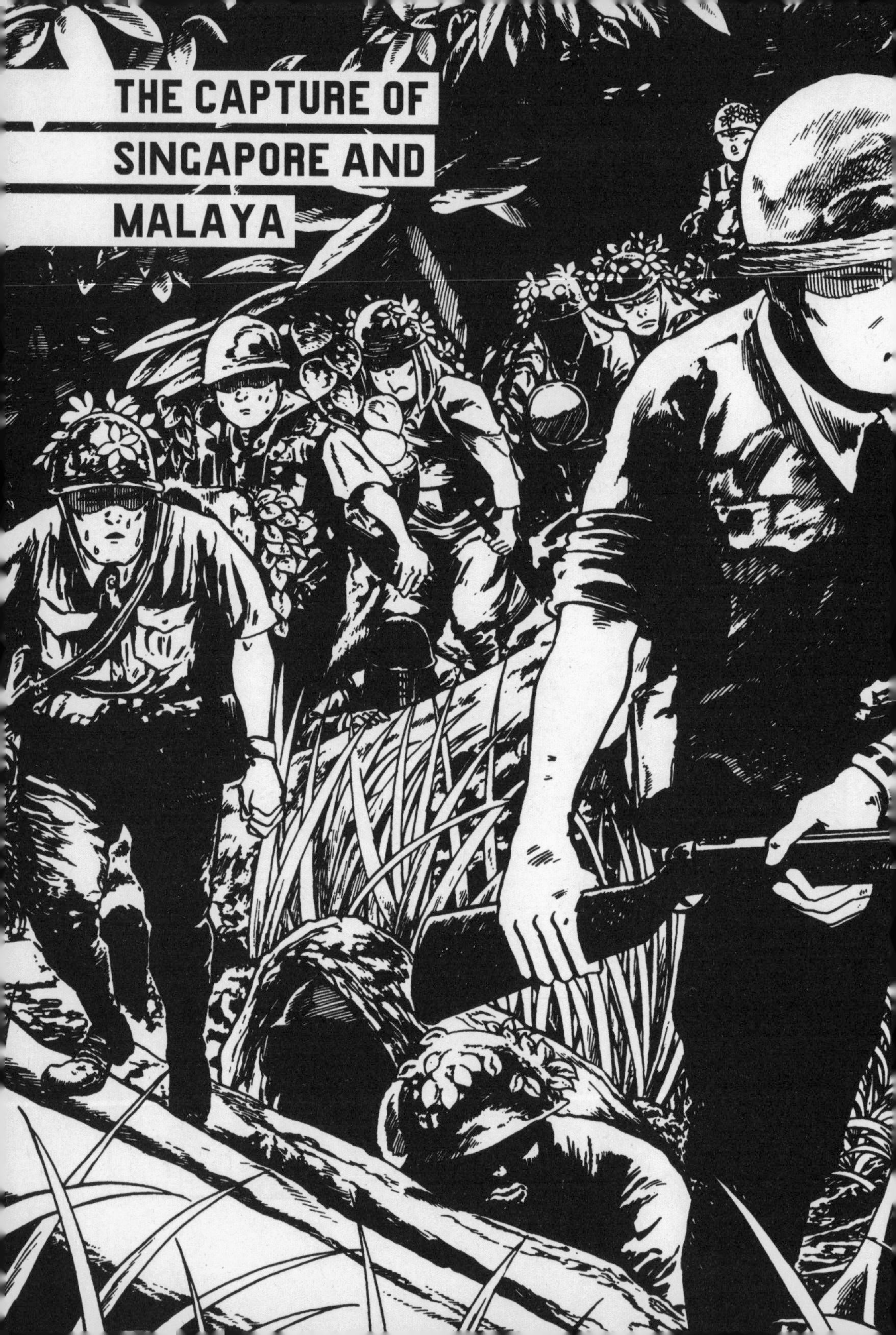

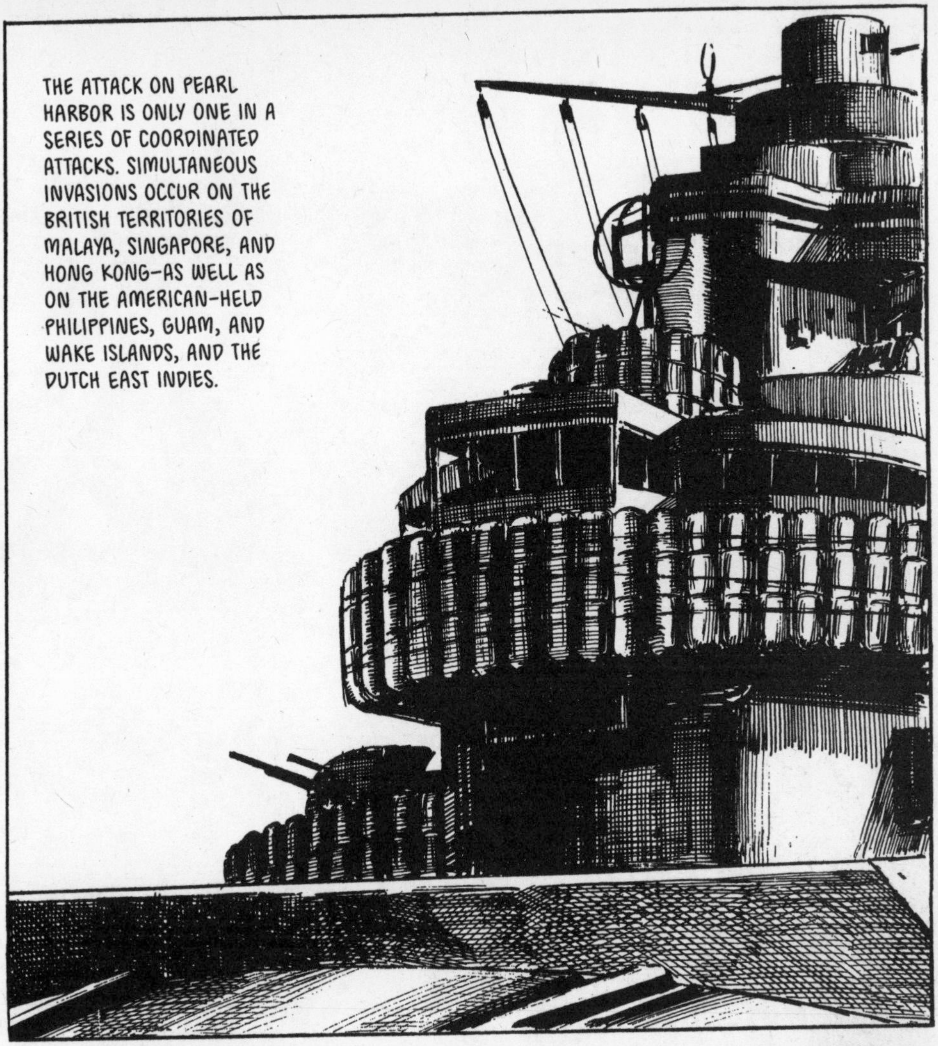
THE ATTACK ON PEARL HARBOR IS ONLY ONE IN A SERIES OF COORDINATED ATTACKS. SIMULTANEOUS INVASIONS OCCUR ON THE BRITISH TERRITORIES OF MALAYA, SINGAPORE, AND HONG KONG—AS WELL AS ON THE AMERICAN-HELD PHILIPPINES, GUAM, AND WAKE ISLANDS, AND THE DUTCH EAST INDIES.

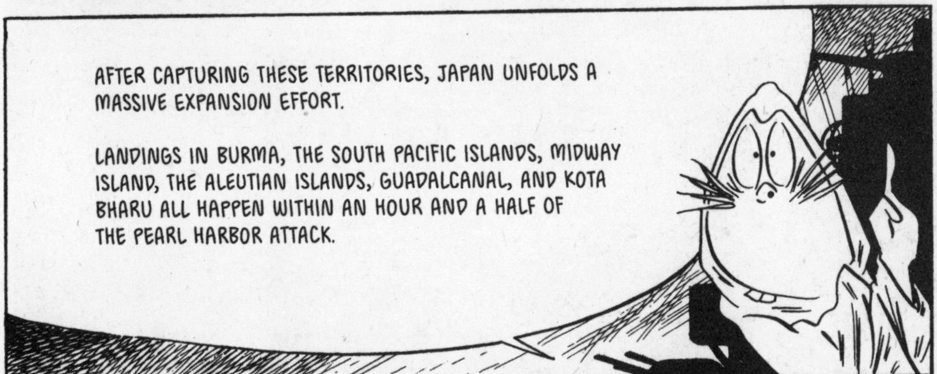
AFTER CAPTURING THESE TERRITORIES, JAPAN UNFOLDS A MASSIVE EXPANSION EFFORT.
LANDINGS IN BURMA, THE SOUTH PACIFIC ISLANDS, MIDWAY ISLAND, THE ALEUTIAN ISLANDS, GUADALCANAL, AND KOTA BHARU ALL HAPPEN WITHIN AN HOUR AND A HALF OF THE PEARL HARBOR ATTACK.

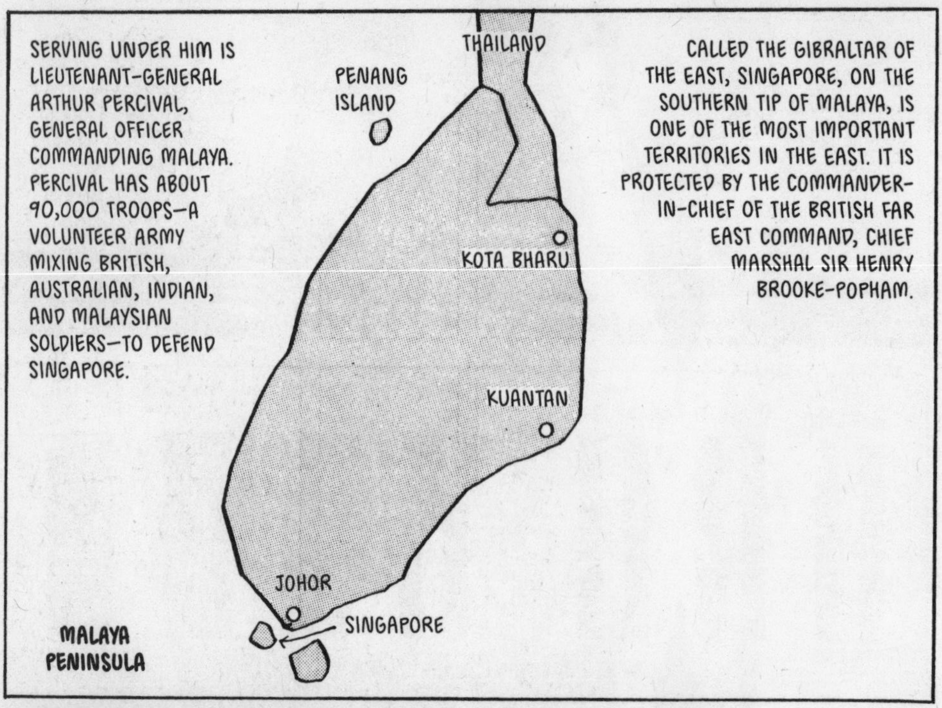
CALLED THE GIBRALTAR OF THE EAST, SINGAPORE, ON THE SOUTHERN TIP OF MALAYA, IS ONE OF THE MOST IMPORTANT TERRITORIES IN THE EAST. IT IS PROTECTED BY THE COMMANDER-IN-CHIEF OF THE BRITISH FAR EAST COMMAND, CHIEF MARSHAL SIR HENRY BROOKE-POPHAM.
THAILAND
PENANG ISLAND
SERVING UNDER HIM IS LIEUTENANT-GENERAL ARTHUR PERCIVAL, GENERAL OFFICER COMMANDING MALAYA. PERCIVAL HAS ABOUT 90,000 TROOPS—A VOLUNTEER ARMY MIXING BRITISH, AUSTRALIAN, INDIAN, AND MALAYSIAN SOLDIERS—TO DEFEND SINGAPORE.
KOTA BHARU
KUANTAN
JOHOR
SINGAPORE
MALAYA PENINSULA

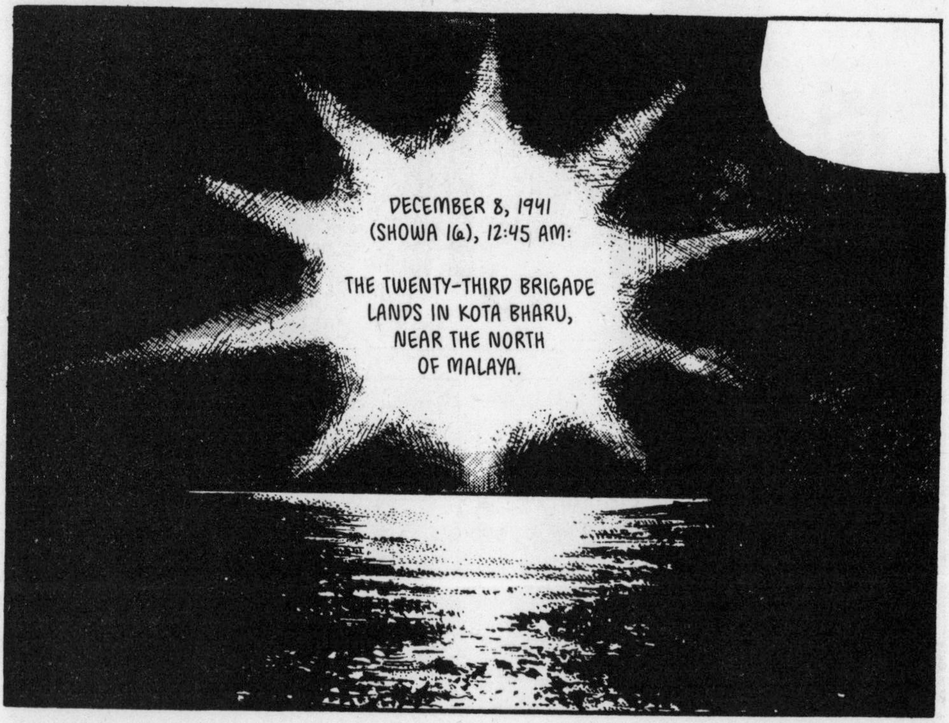
DECEMBER 8, 1941 (SHOWA 16), 12:45 AM:
THE TWENTY-THIRD BRIGADE LANDS IN KOTA BHARU, NEAR THE NORTH OF MALAYA.

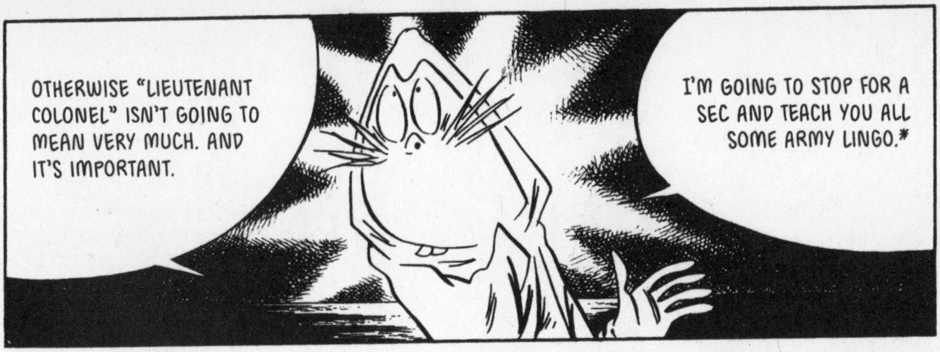
I'M GOING TO STOP FOR A SEC AND TEACH YOU ALL SOME ARMY LINGO.*
OTHERWISE "LIEUTENANT COLONEL" ISN'T GOING TO MEAN VERY MUCH. AND IT'S IMPORTANT.

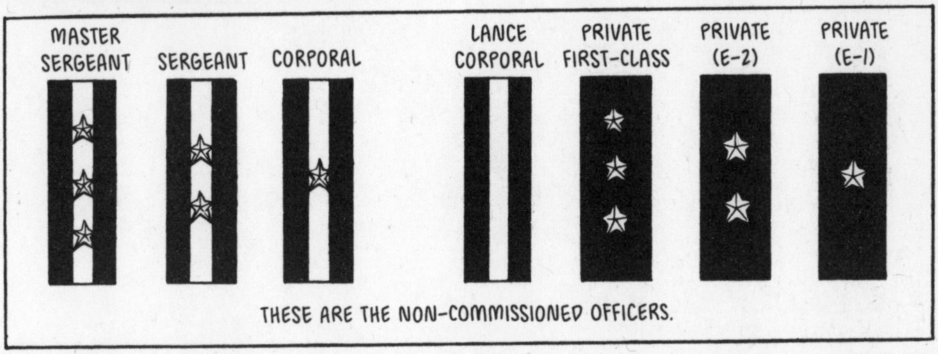
PRIVATE (E-1)
PRIVATE (E-2)
PRIVATE FIRST-CLASS
LANCE CORPORAL
CORPORAL
SERGEANT
MASTER SERGEANT
THESE ARE THE NON-COMMISSIONED OFFICERS.

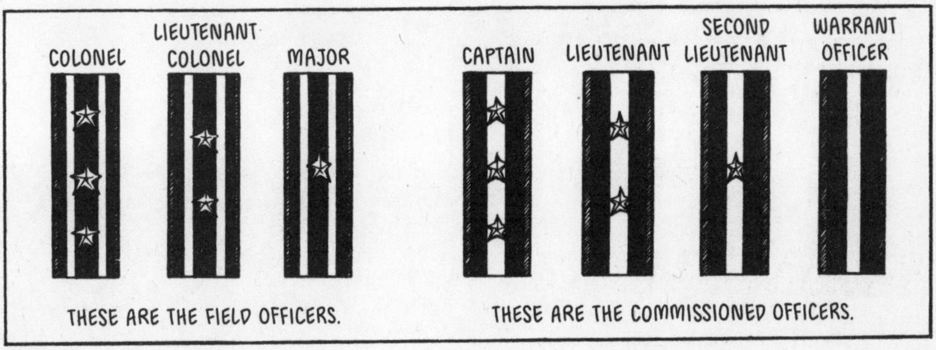
WARRANT OFFICER
SECOND LIEUTENANT
LIEUTENANT
CAPTAIN
THESE ARE THE COMMISSIONED OFFICERS.
MAJOR
LIEUTENANT COLONEL
COLONEL
THESE ARE THE FIELD OFFICERS.

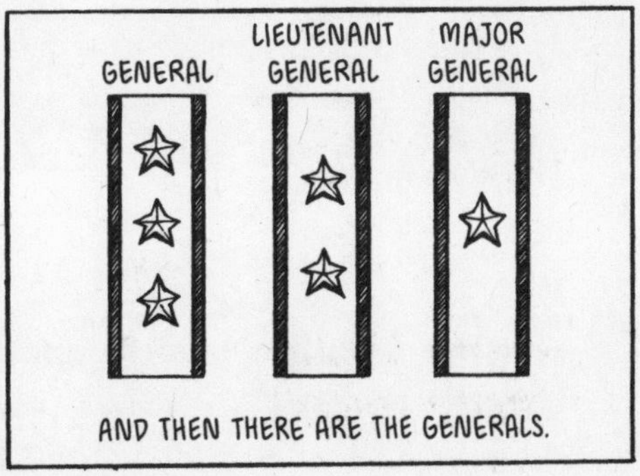
MAJOR GENERAL
LIEUTENANT GENERAL
GENERAL
AND THEN THERE ARE THE GENERALS.

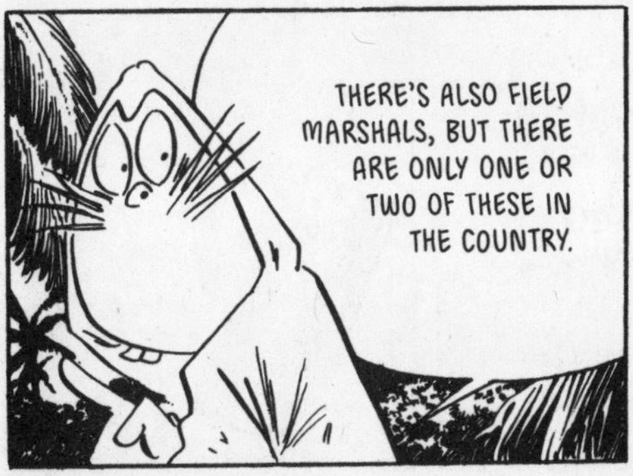
THERE'S ALSO FIELD MARSHALS, BUT THERE ARE ONLY ONE OR TWO OF THESE IN THE COUNTRY.

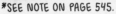

*SEE NOTE ON PAGE 545.

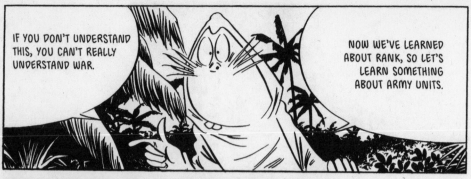

NOW WE'VE LEARNED ABOUT RANK, SO LET'S LEARN SOMETHING ABOUT ARMY UNITS.
IF YOU DON'T UNDERSTAND THIS, YOU CAN'T REALLY UNDERSTAND WAR.
PUT TEN SOLDIERS IN ONE GROUP, AND YOU HAVE A SQUAD.
THE MOST BASIC UNIT, SQUADS ARE LED BY A SQUAD LEADER. USUALLY A CORPORAL.
PUT TOGETHER FOUR SQUADS, AND YOU HAVE A PLATOON.
THAT'S FORTY MEN, LED BY A SECOND LIEUTENANT.
FOUR PLATOONS EQUALS A COMPANY.

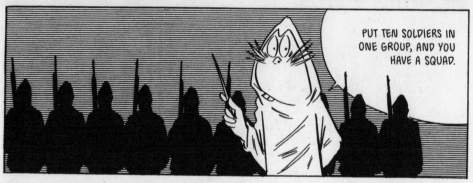

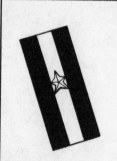

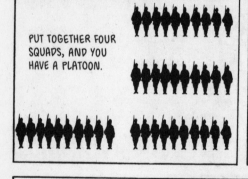

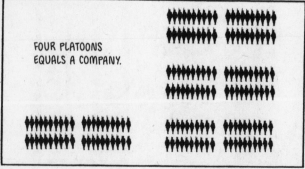

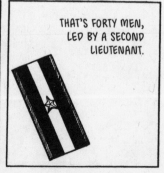

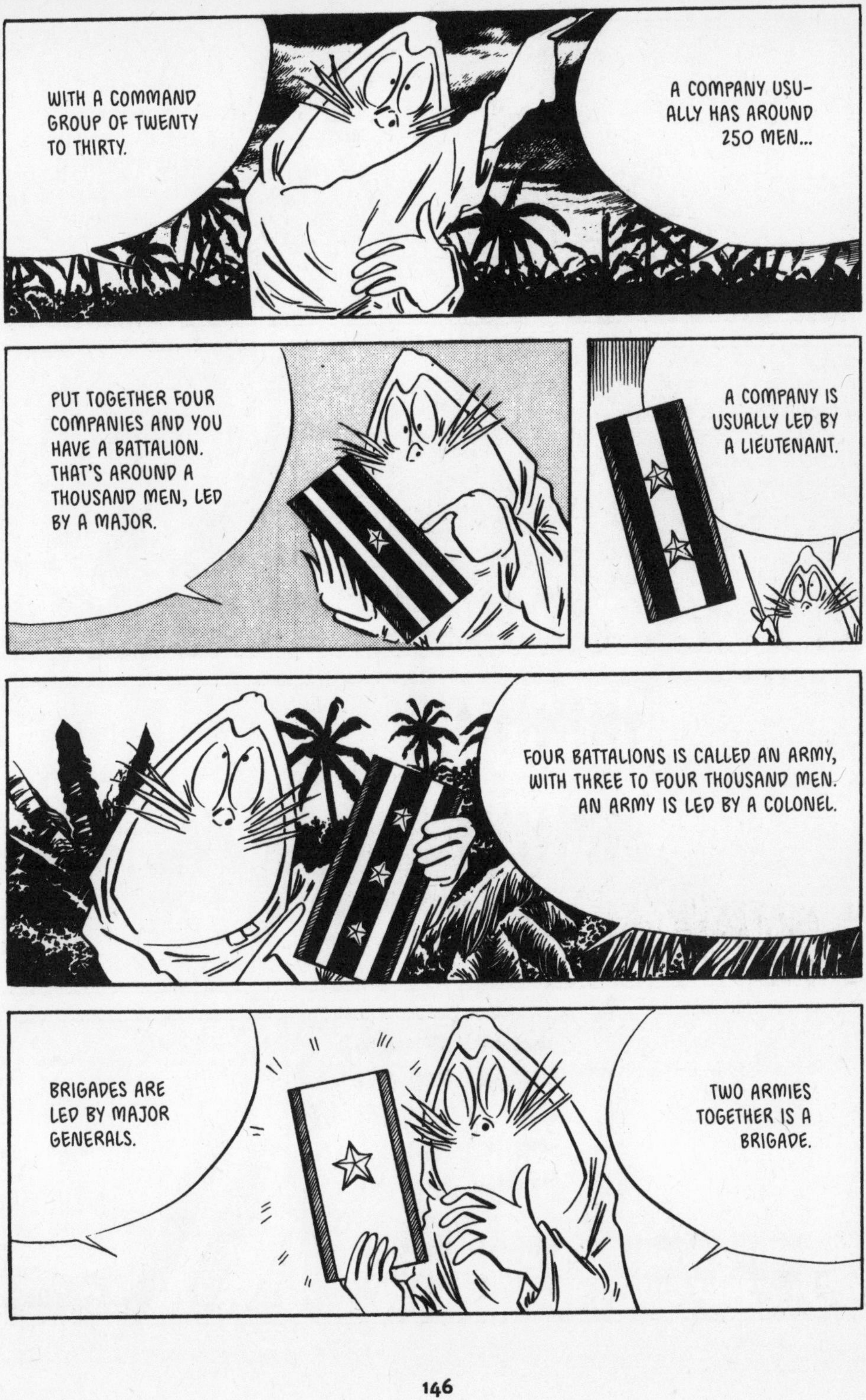
A COMPANY USU-ALLY HAS AROUND 250 MEN...
WITH A COMMAND GROUP OF TWENTY TO THIRTY.
A COMPANY IS USUALLY LED BY A LIEUTENANT.
PUT TOGETHER FOUR COMPANIES AND YOU HAVE A BATTALION. THAT'S AROUND A THOUSAND MEN, LED BY A MAJOR.
FOUR BATTALIONS IS CALLED AN ARMY, WITH THREE TO FOUR THOUSAND MEN. AN ARMY IS LED BY A COLONEL.
TWO ARMIES TOGETHER IS A BRIGADE.
BRIGADES ARE LED BY MAJOR GENERALS.

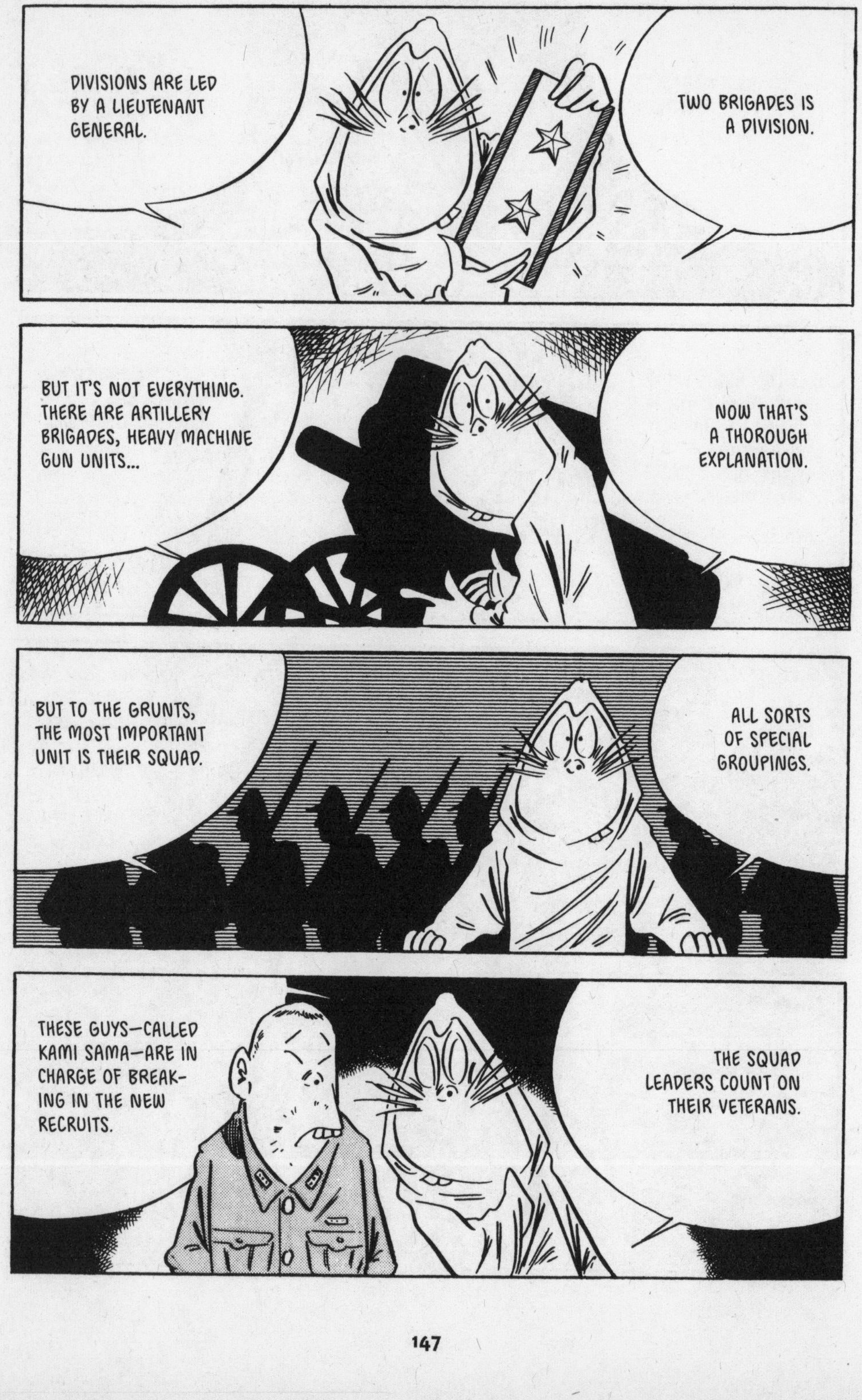
TWO BRIGADES IS A DIVISION.
DIVISIONS ARE LED BY A LIEUTENANT GENERAL.
NOW THAT'S A THOROUGH EXPLANATION.
BUT IT'S NOT EVERYTHING. THERE ARE ARTILLERY BRIGADES, HEAVY MACHINE GUN UNITS...
ALL SORTS OF SPECIAL GROUPINGS.
BUT TO THE GRUNTS, THE MOST IMPORTANT UNIT IS THEIR SQUAD.
THE SQUAD LEADERS COUNT ON THEIR VETERANS.
THESE GUYS—CALLED KAMI SAMA—ARE IN CHARGE OF BREAK-ING IN THE NEW RECRUITS.

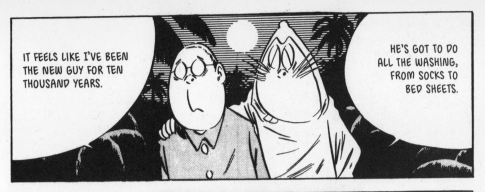

HE'S GOT TO DO ALL THE WASHING, FROM SOCKS TO BED SHEETS.
IT FEELS LIKE I'VE BEEN THE NEW GUY FOR TEN THOUSAND YEARS.
YOU'RE THE SQUAD PUNCHING BAG. YOU'VE GOT TO DO WHAT THEY SAY.
I KNEW THINGS WERE GOING TO BE HARD, BUT I NEVER DREAMED LIFE COULD BE THIS MISERABLE.
HUFF HUFF
NOW YOU CAN UNDERSTAND BETTER WHEN I TELL YOU THE TWENTY-THIRD BRIGADE LANDS ON KOTA BAHRU.
BAM
BAM
BAM
BAM
BAM
BAM

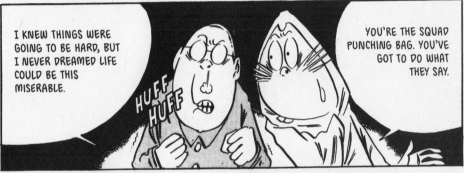

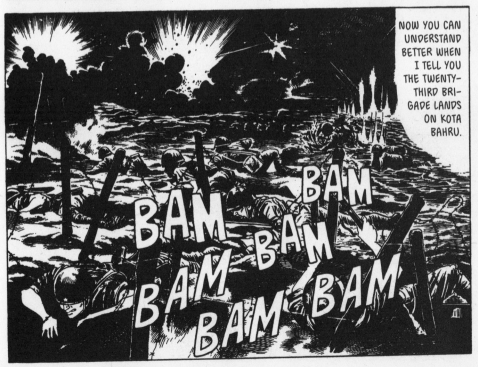

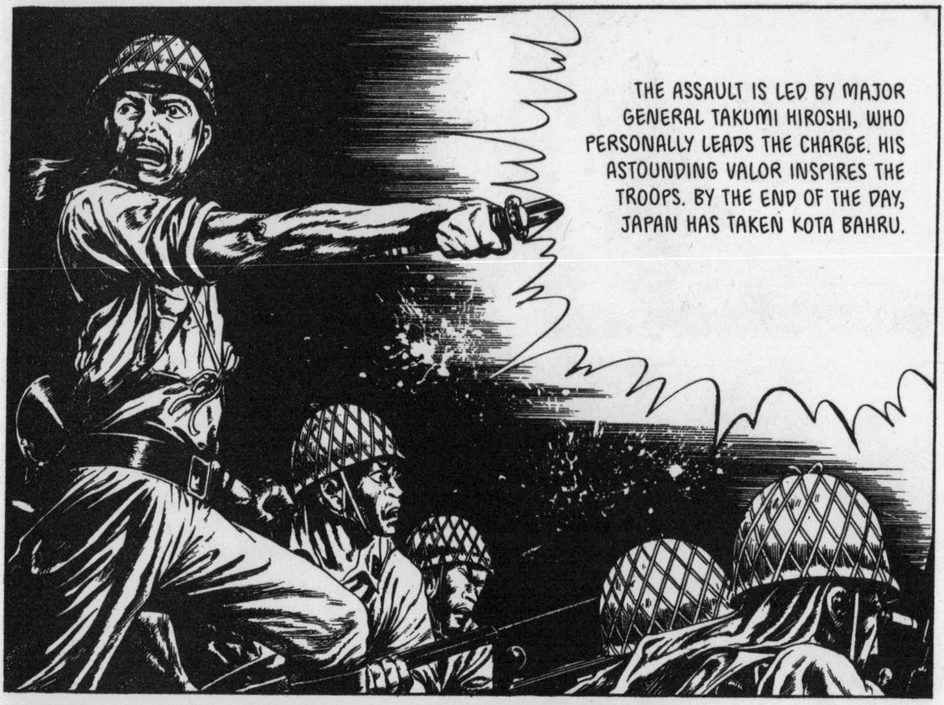
THE ASSAULT IS LED BY MAJOR GENERAL TAKUMI HIROSHI, WHO PERSONALLY LEADS THE CHARGE. HIS ASTOUNDING VALOR INSPIRES THE TROOPS. BY THE END OF THE DAY, JAPAN HAS TAKEN KOTA BAHRU.

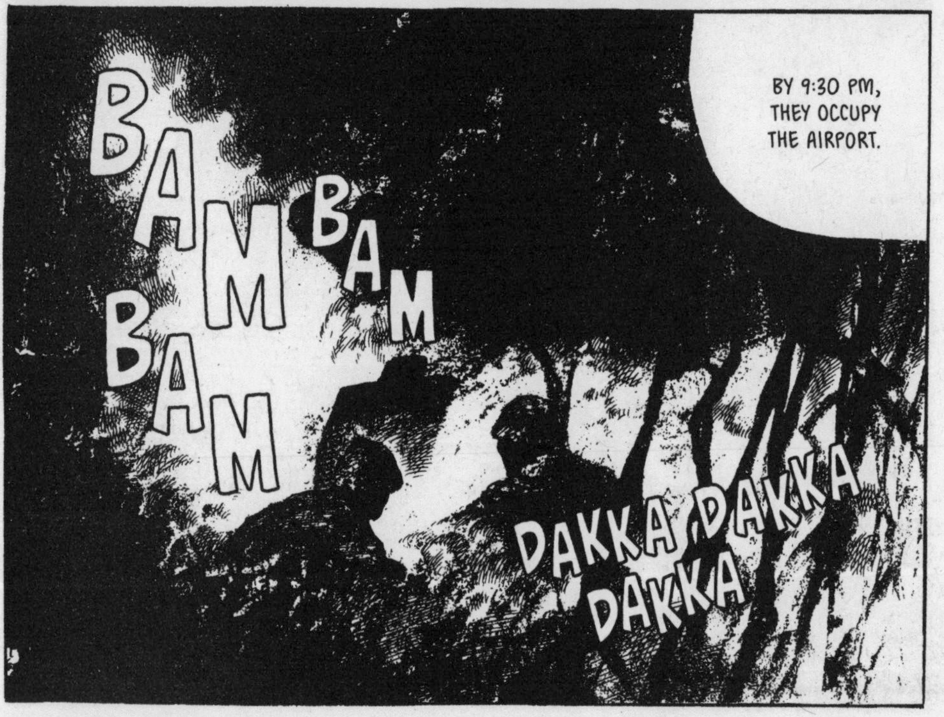
BY 9:30 PM, THEY OCCUPY THE AIRPORT.
BAM BAM
BAM BAM
DAKKA DAKKA DAKKA

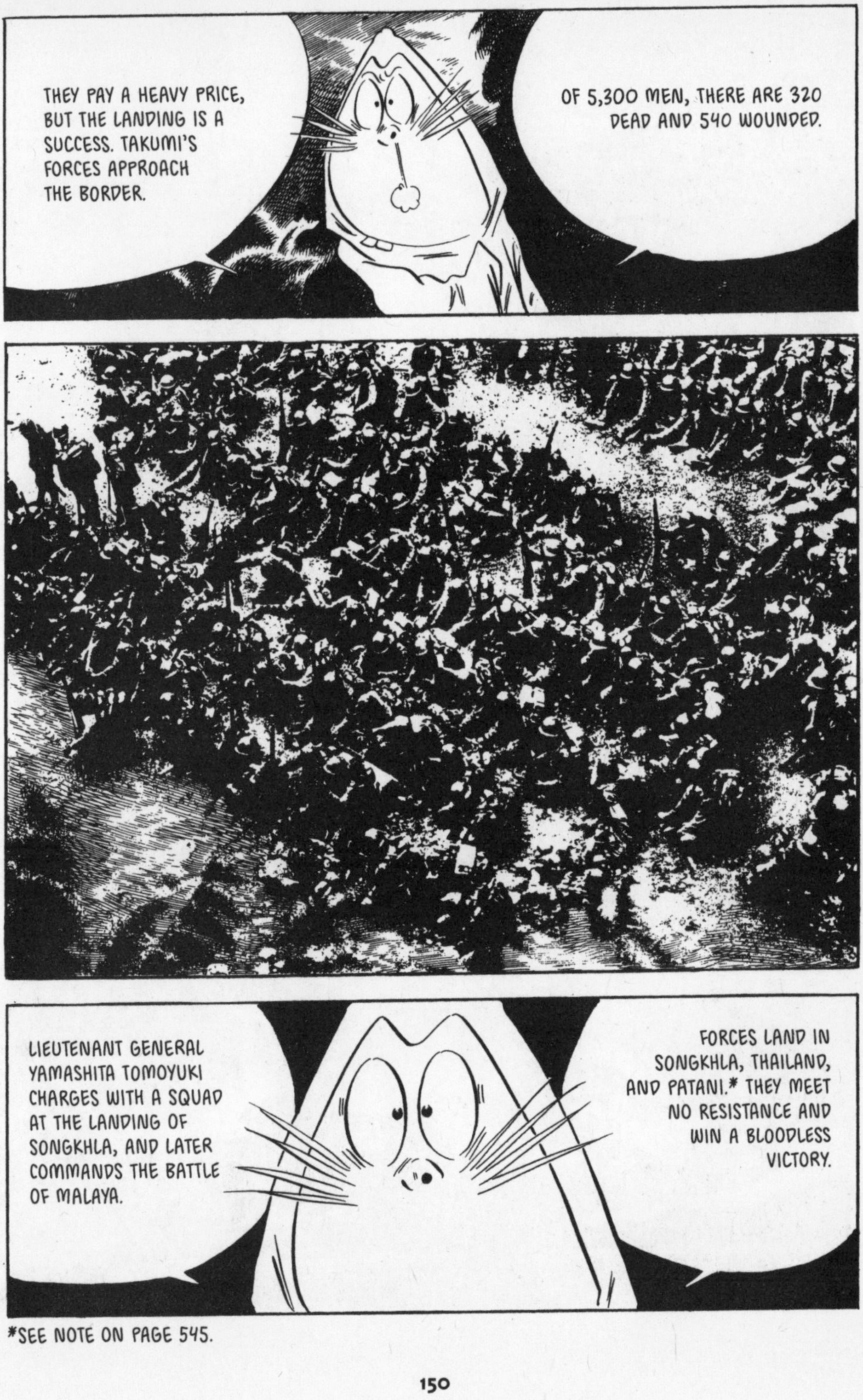
OF 5,300 MEN, THERE ARE 320 DEAD AND 540 WOUNDED.
THEY PAY A HEAVY PRICE, BUT THE LANDING IS A SUCCESS. TAKUMI'S FORCES APPROACH THE BORDER.
FORCES LAND IN SONGKHLA, THAILAND, AND PATANI.* THEY MEET NO RESISTANCE AND WIN A BLOODLESS VICTORY.
LIEUTENANT GENERAL YAMASHITA TOMOYUKI CHARGES WITH A SQUAD AT THE LANDING OF SONGKHLA, AND LATER COMMANDS THE BATTLE OF MALAYA.

*SEE NOTE ON PAGE 545.

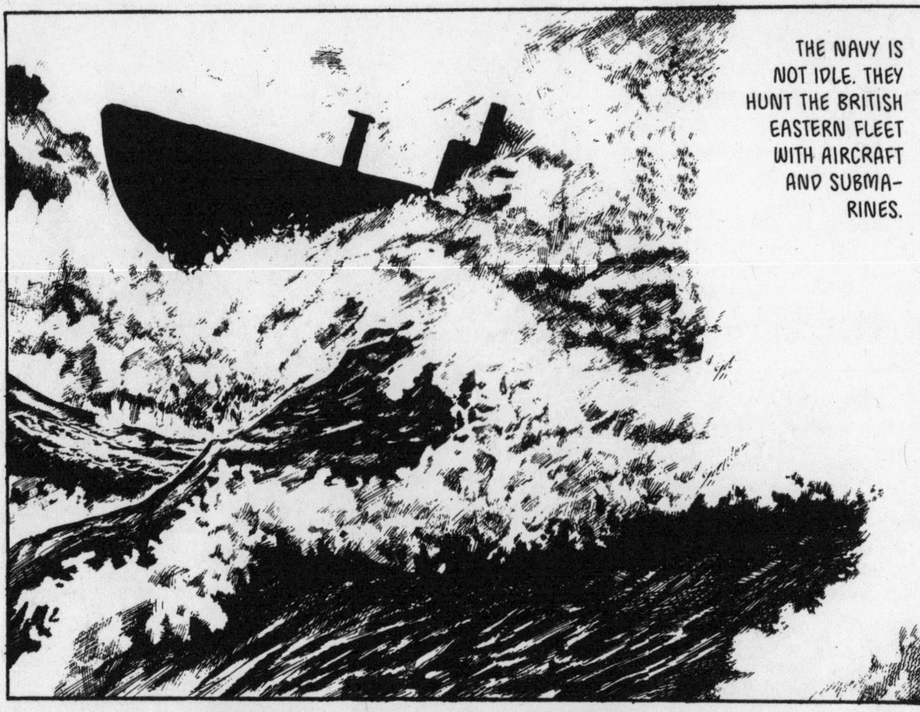
THE NAVY IS NOT IDLE. THEY HUNT THE BRITISH EASTERN FLEET WITH AIRCRAFT AND SUBMA-RINES.

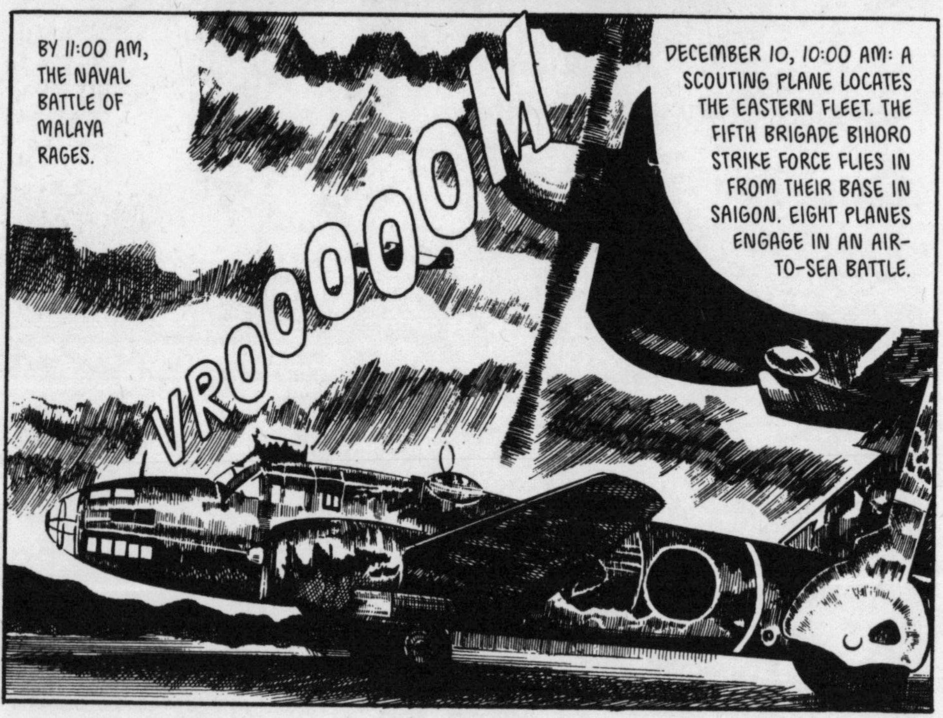
DECEMBER 10, 10:00 AM: A SCOUTING PLANE LOCATES THE EASTERN FLEET. THE FIFTH BRIGADE BIHORO STRIKE FORCE FLIES IN FROM THEIR BASE IN SAIGON. EIGHT PLANES ENGAGE IN AN AIR-TO-SEA BATTLE.
VROOOOOM
BY 11:00 AM, THE NAVAL BATTLE OF MALAYA RAGES.

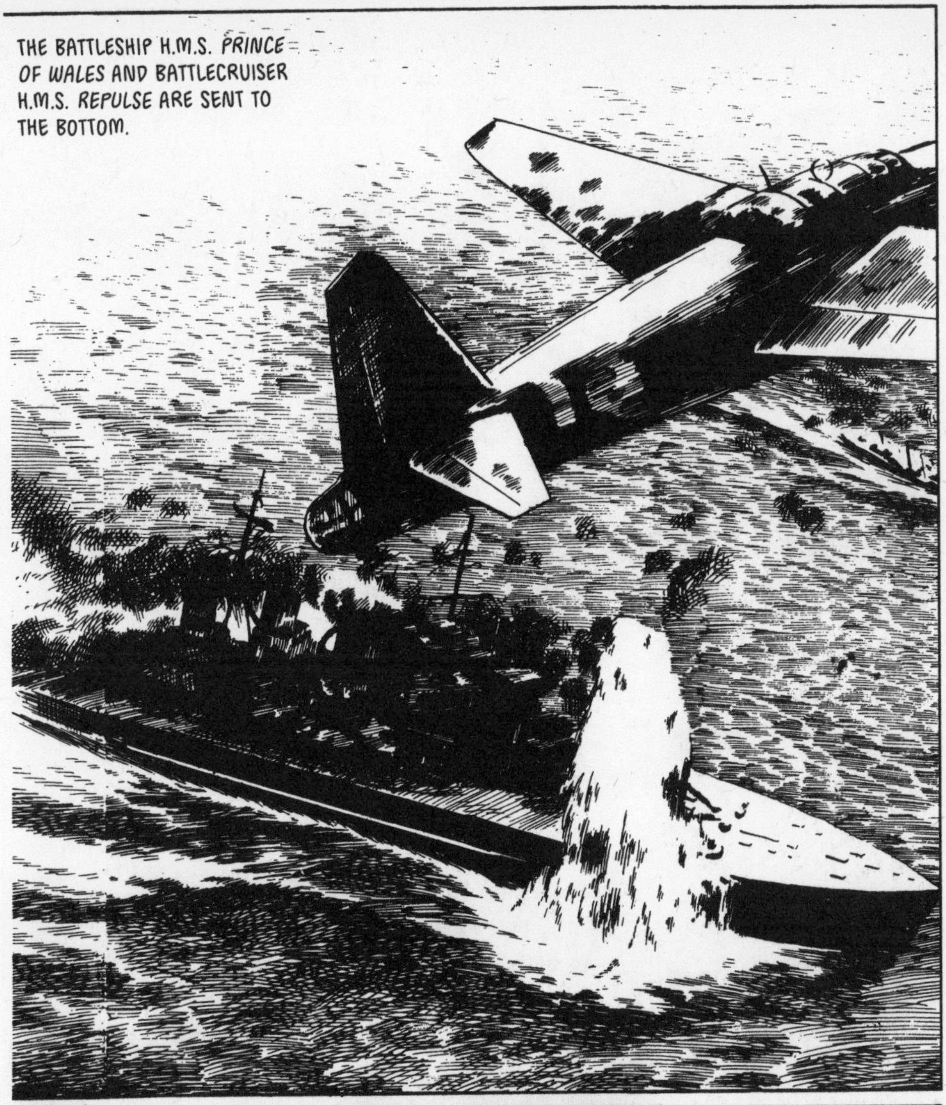
THE BATTLESHIP H.M.S. *PRINCE OF WALES* AND BATTLECRUISER H.M.S. *REPULSE* ARE SENT TO THE BOTTOM.
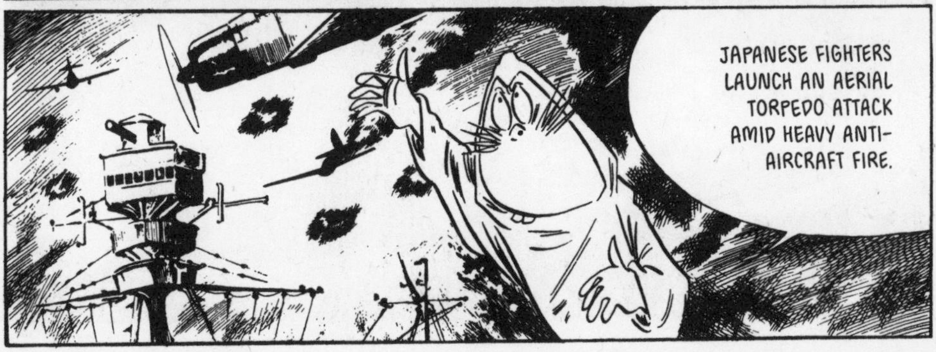
JAPANESE FIGHTERS LAUNCH AN AERIAL TORPEDO ATTACK AMID HEAVY ANTI-AIRCRAFT FIRE.

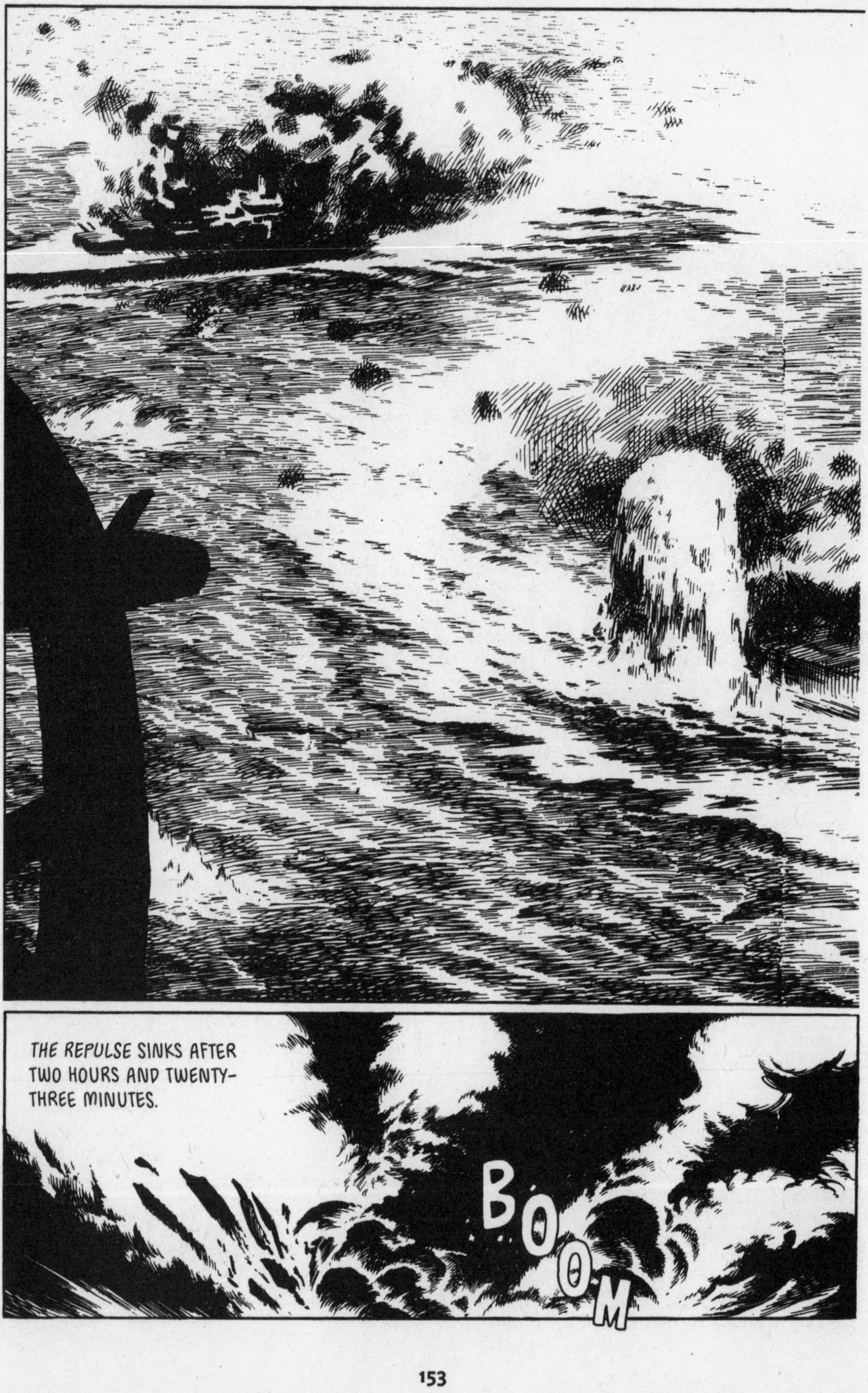
THE *REPULSE* SINKS AFTER TWO HOURS AND TWENTY-THREE MINUTES.
BOOM

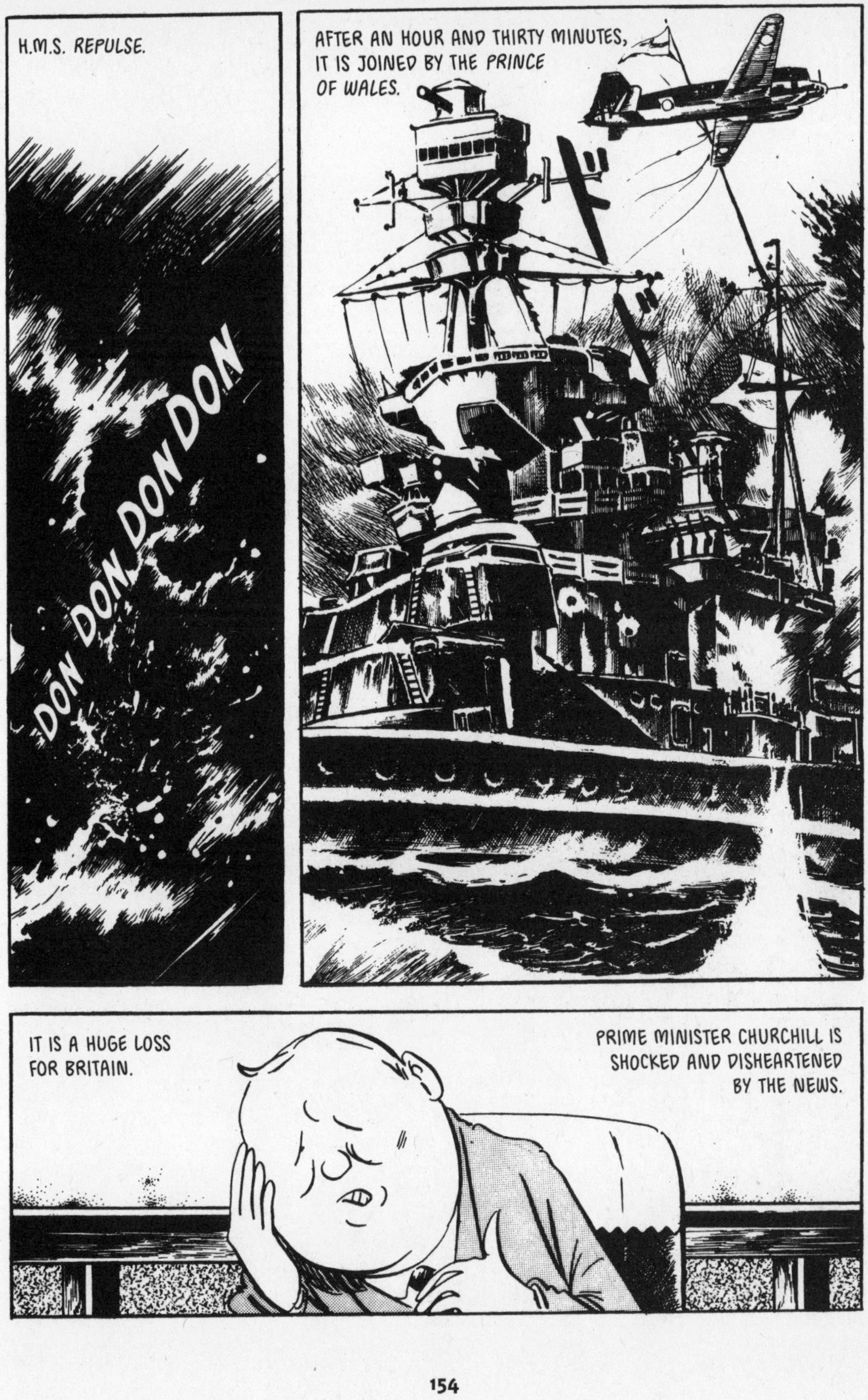
AFTER AN HOUR AND THIRTY MINUTES, IT IS JOINED BY THE *PRINCE OF WALES*.
H.M.S. *REPULSE*.
DON DON DON DON
PRIME MINISTER CHURCHILL IS SHOCKED AND DISHEARTENED BY THE NEWS.
IT IS A HUGE LOSS FOR BRITAIN.

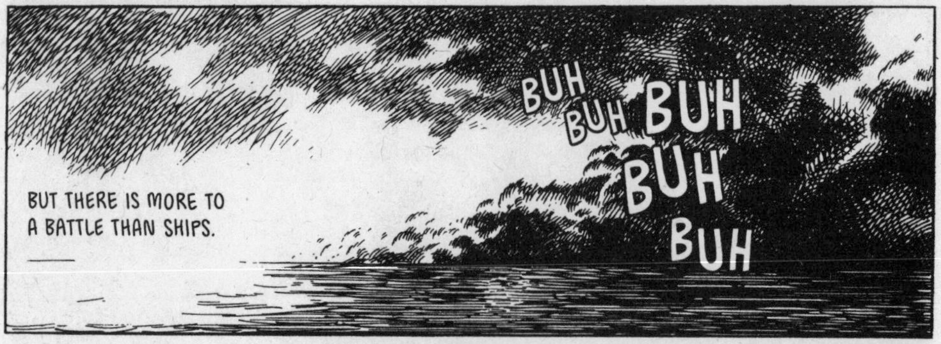
BUH BUH BUH BUH BUH
BUT THERE IS MORE TO A BATTLE THAN SHIPS.
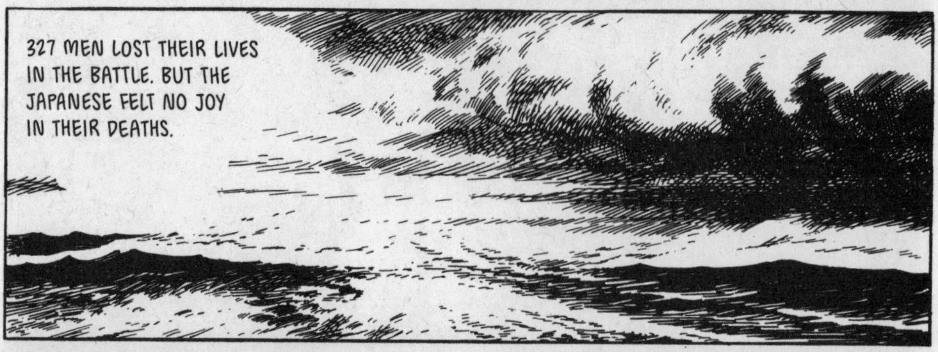
327 MEN LOST THEIR LIVES IN THE BATTLE. BUT THE JAPANESE FELT NO JOY IN THEIR DEATHS.
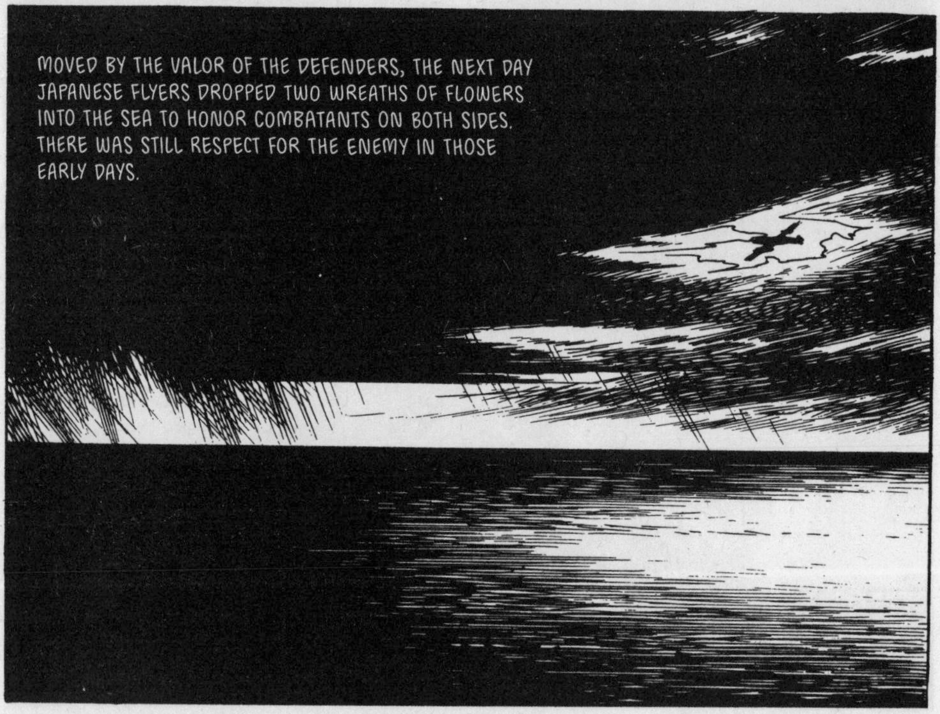
MOVED BY THE VALOR OF THE DEFENDERS, THE NEXT DAY JAPANESE FLYERS DROPPED TWO WREATHS OF FLOWERS INTO THE SEA TO HONOR COMBATANTS ON BOTH SIDES. THERE WAS STILL RESPECT FOR THE ENEMY IN THOSE EARLY DAYS.

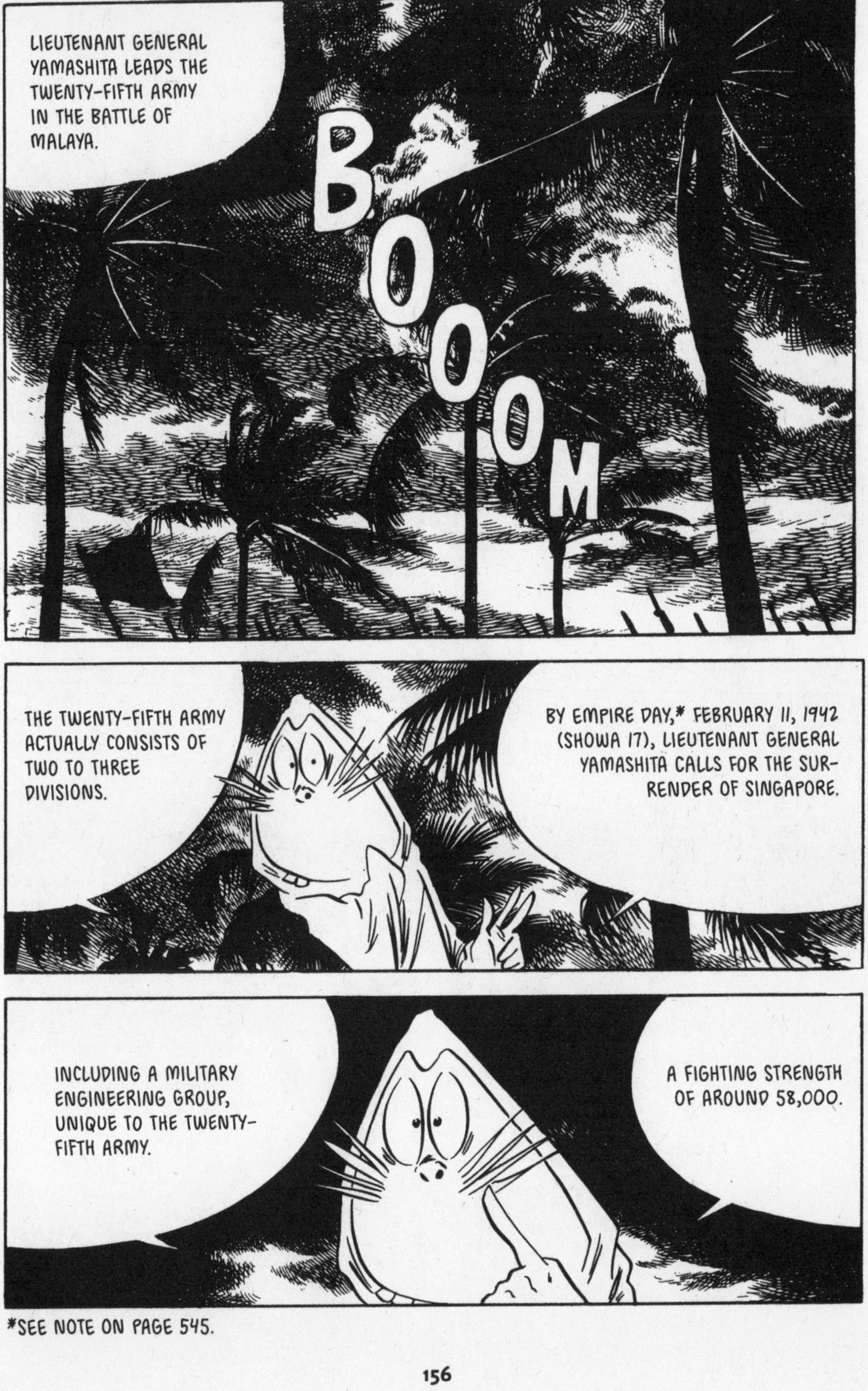
LIEUTENANT GENERAL YAMASHITA LEADS THE TWENTY-FIFTH ARMY IN THE BATTLE OF MALAYA.
BOOOOM
BY EMPIRE DAY,* FEBRUARY 11, 1942 (SHOWA 17), LIEUTENANT GENERAL YAMASHITA CALLS FOR THE SURRENDER OF SINGAPORE.
THE TWENTY-FIFTH ARMY ACTUALLY CONSISTS OF TWO TO THREE DIVISIONS.
A FIGHTING STRENGTH OF AROUND 58,000.
INCLUDING A MILITARY ENGINEERING GROUP, UNIQUE TO THE TWENTY-FIFTH ARMY.

*SEE NOTE ON PAGE 545.

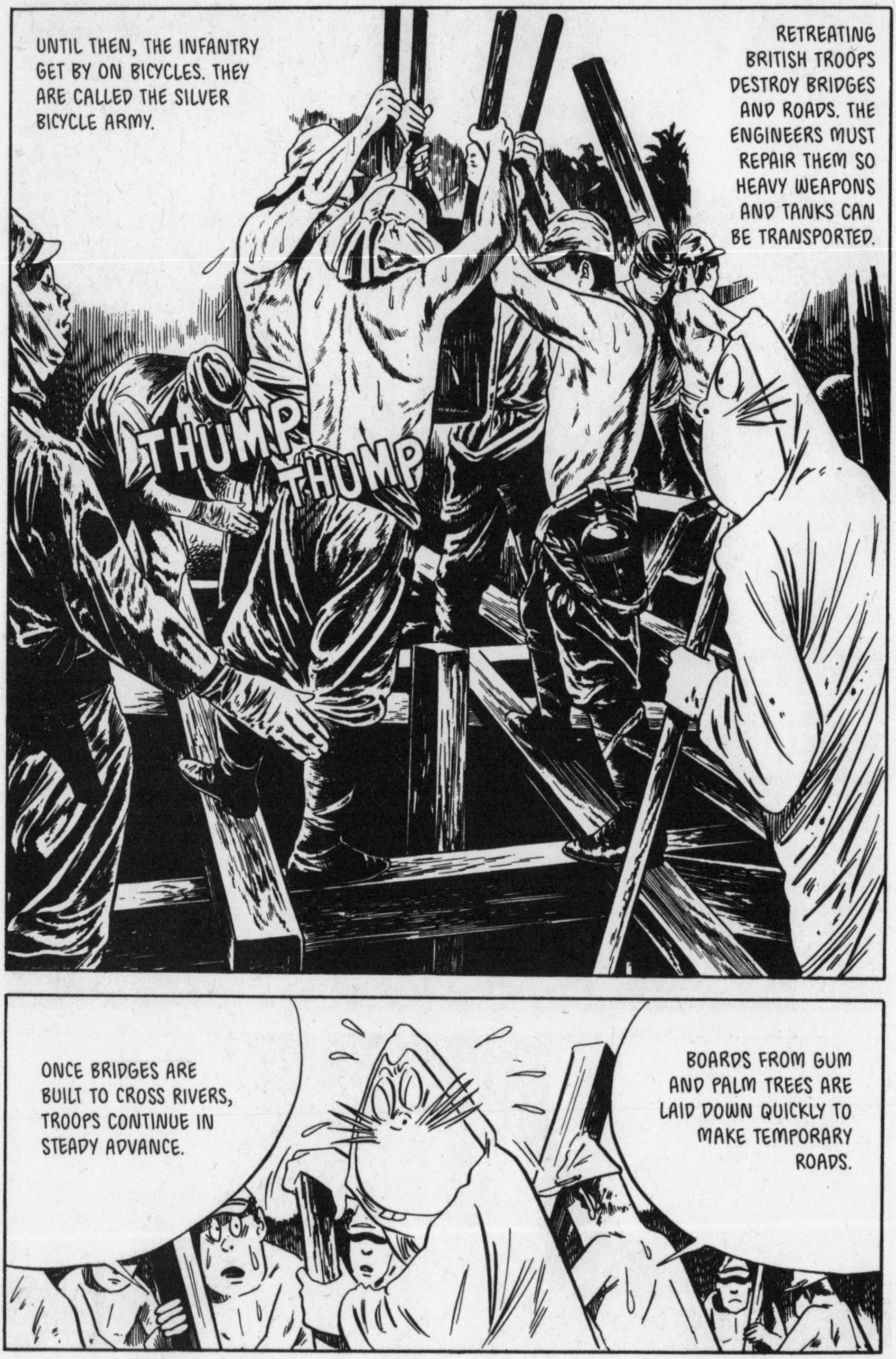
RETREATING BRITISH TROOPS DESTROY BRIDGES AND ROADS. THE ENGINEERS MUST REPAIR THEM SO HEAVY WEAPONS AND TANKS CAN BE TRANSPORTED.
UNTIL THEN, THE INFANTRY GET BY ON BICYCLES. THEY ARE CALLED THE SILVER BICYCLE ARMY.
THUMP
THUMP
BOARDS FROM GUM AND PALM TREES ARE LAID DOWN QUICKLY TO MAKE TEMPORARY ROADS.
ONCE BRIDGES ARE BUILT TO CROSS RIVERS, TROOPS CONTINUE IN STEADY ADVANCE.

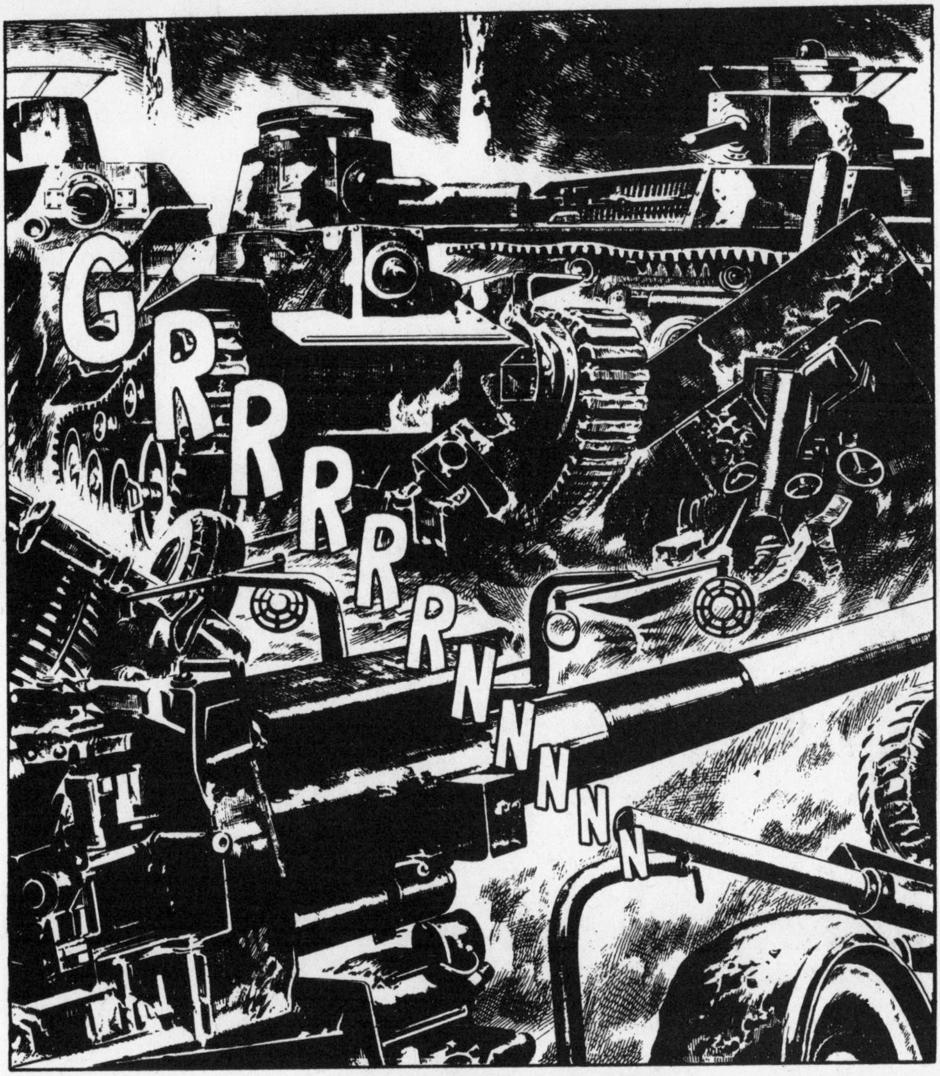
GRRRRRRNNNNN

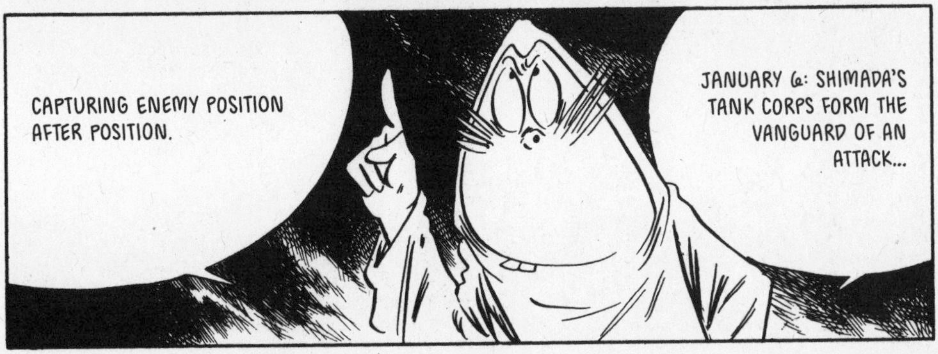
JANUARY 6: SHIMADA'S TANK CORPS FORM THE VANGUARD OF AN ATTACK...
CAPTURING ENEMY POSITION AFTER POSITION.

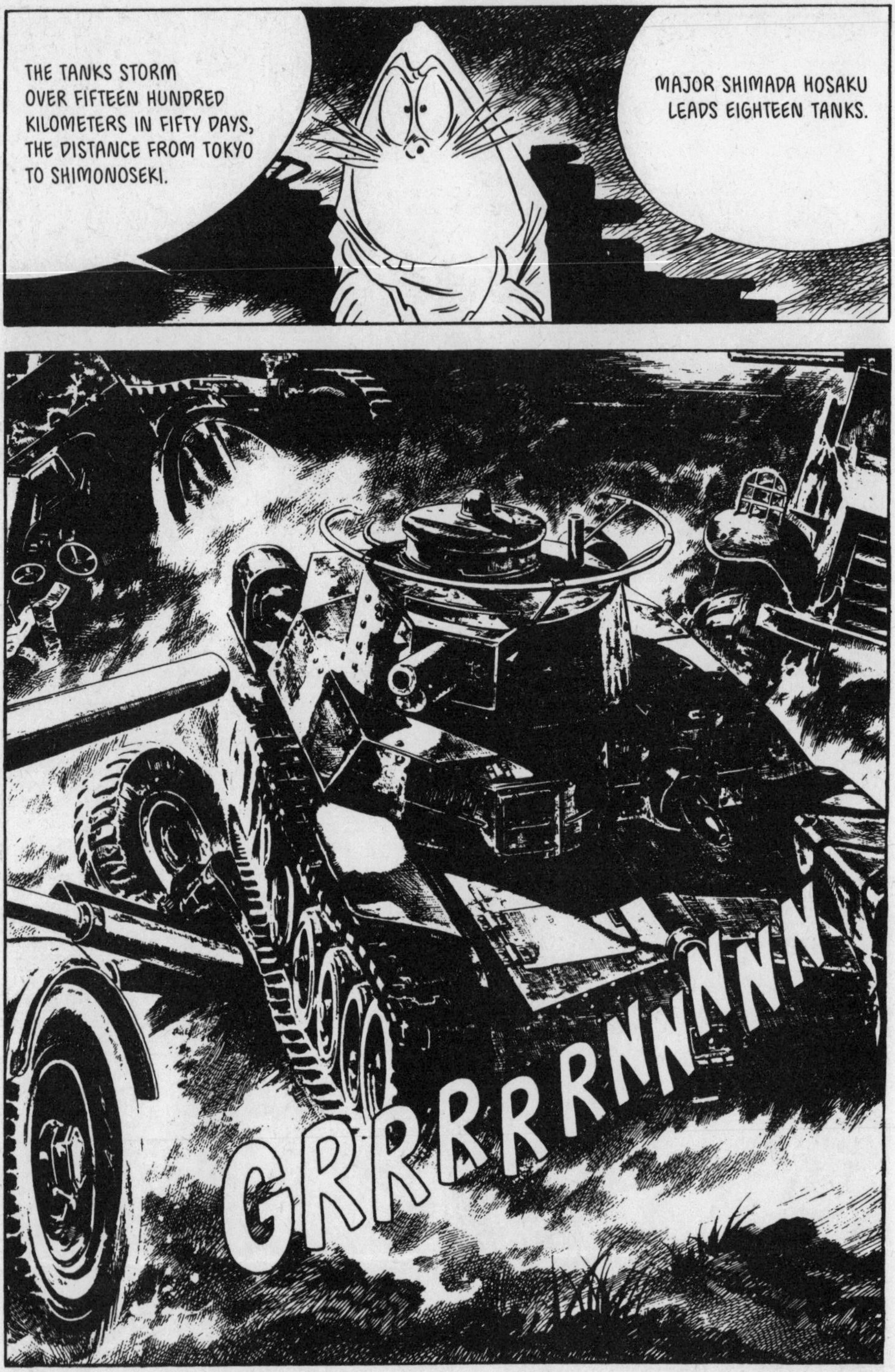
MAJOR SHIMADA HOSAKU LEADS EIGHTEEN TANKS.
THE TANKS STORM OVER FIFTEEN HUNDRED KILOMETERS IN FIFTY DAYS, THE DISTANCE FROM TOKYO TO SHIMONOSEKI.
GRRRRRNNNNNNN

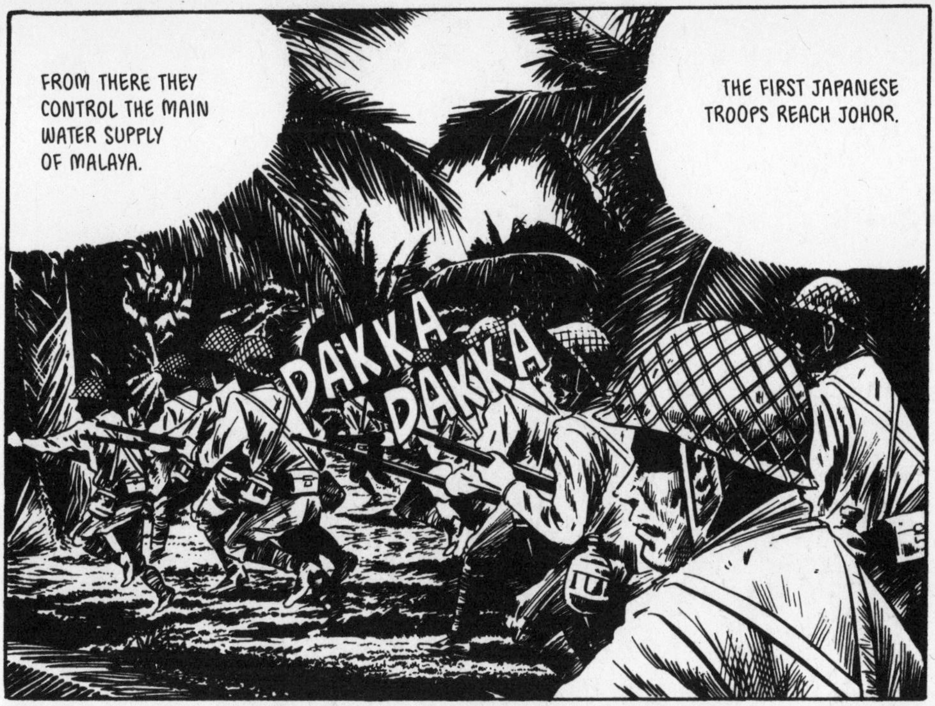
THE FIRST JAPANESE TROOPS REACH JOHOR.
FROM THERE THEY CONTROL THE MAIN WATER SUPPLY OF MALAYA.
DAKKA DAKKA

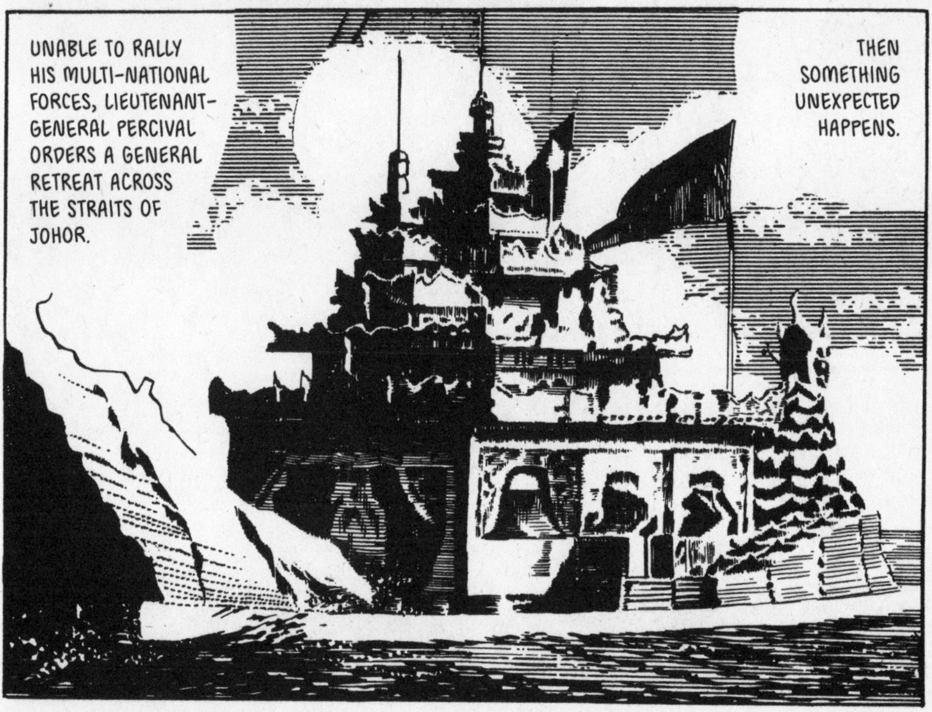
THEN SOMETHING UNEXPECTED HAPPENS.
UNABLE TO RALLY HIS MULTI-NATIONAL FORCES, LIEUTENANT-GENERAL PERCIVAL ORDERS A GENERAL RETREAT ACROSS THE STRAITS OF JOHOR.

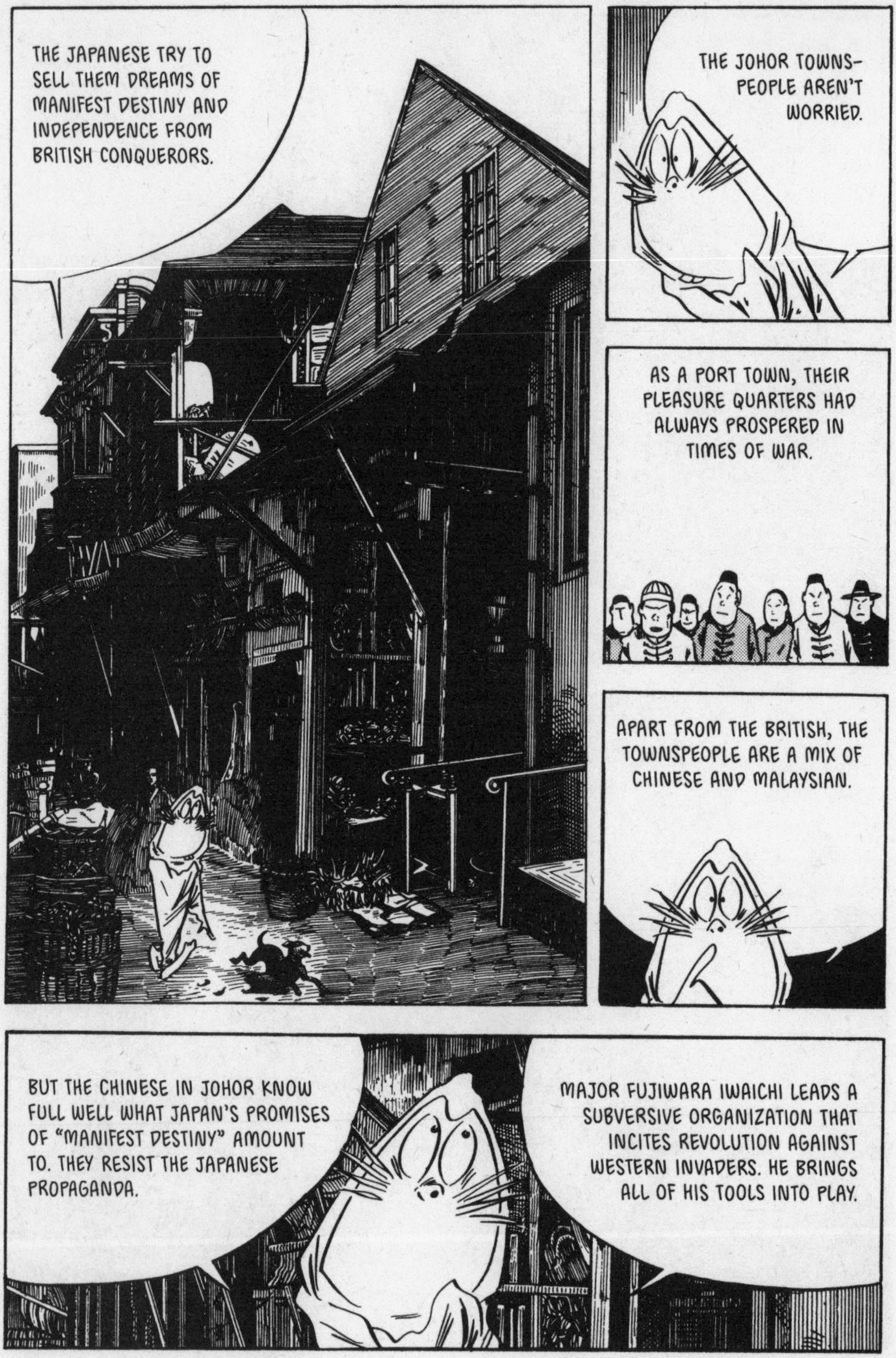
THE JOHOR TOWNSPEOPLE AREN'T WORRIED.
AS A PORT TOWN, THEIR PLEASURE QUARTERS HAD ALWAYS PROSPERED IN TIMES OF WAR.
APART FROM THE BRITISH, THE TOWNSPEOPLE ARE A MIX OF CHINESE AND MALAYSIAN.
THE JAPANESE TRY TO SELL THEM DREAMS OF MANIFEST DESTINY AND INDEPENDENCE FROM BRITISH CONQUERORS.
MAJOR FUJIWARA IWAICHI LEADS A SUBVERSIVE ORGANIZATION THAT INCITES REVOLUTION AGAINST WESTERN INVADERS. HE BRINGS ALL OF HIS TOOLS INTO PLAY.
BUT THE CHINESE IN JOHOR KNOW FULL WELL WHAT JAPAN'S PROMISES OF "MANIFEST DESTINY" AMOUNT TO. THEY RESIST THE JAPANESE PROPAGANDA.

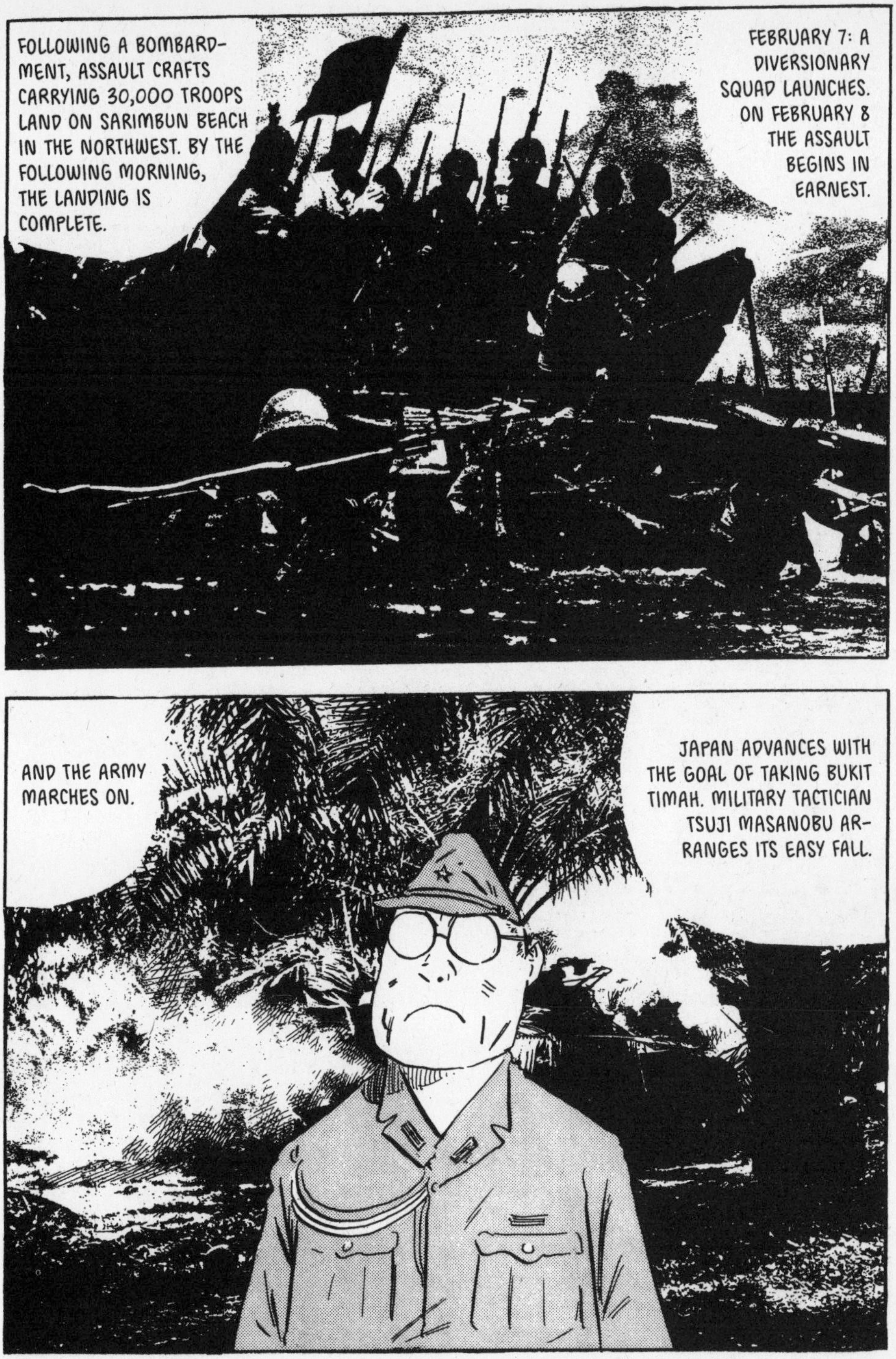
FEBRUARY 7: A DIVERSIONARY SQUAD LAUNCHES. ON FEBRUARY 8 THE ASSAULT BEGINS IN EARNEST.
FOLLOWING A BOMBARDMENT, ASSAULT CRAFTS CARRYING 30,000 TROOPS LAND ON SARIMBUN BEACH IN THE NORTHWEST. BY THE FOLLOWING MORNING, THE LANDING IS COMPLETE.
JAPAN ADVANCES WITH THE GOAL OF TAKING BUKIT TIMAH. MILITARY TACTICIAN TSUJI MASANOBU ARRANGES ITS EASY FALL.
AND THE ARMY MARCHES ON.

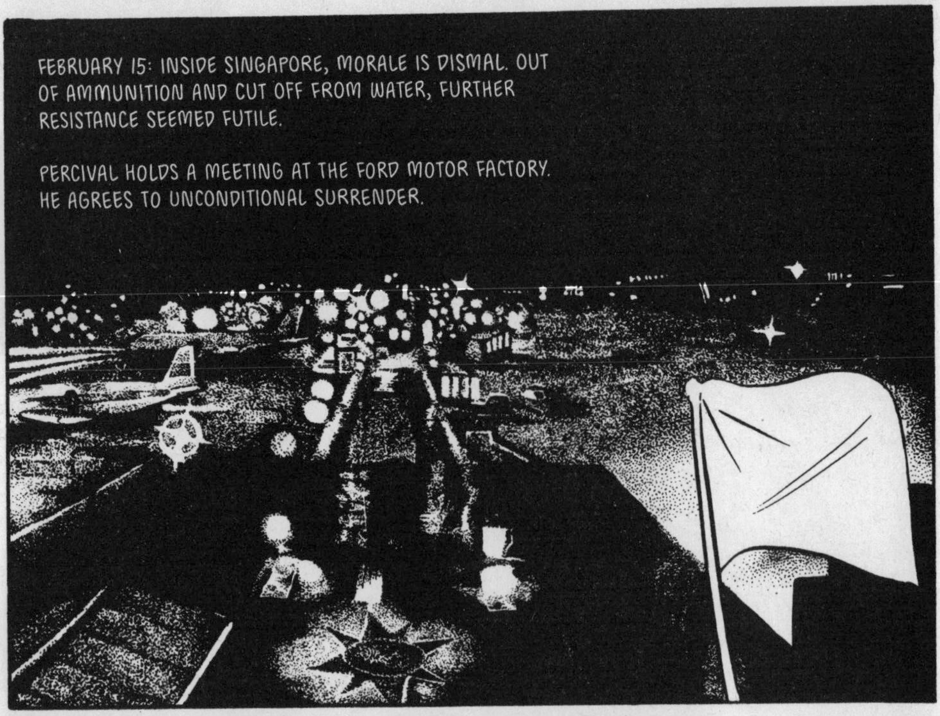
FEBRUARY 15: INSIDE SINGAPORE, MORALE IS DISMAL. OUT OF AMMUNITION AND CUT OFF FROM WATER, FURTHER RESISTANCE SEEMED FUTILE.
PERCIVAL HOLDS A MEETING AT THE FORD MOTOR FACTORY. HE AGREES TO UNCONDITIONAL SURRENDER.

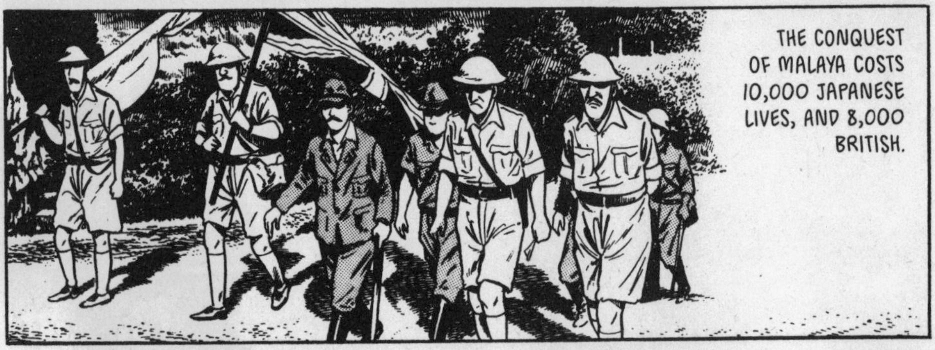
THE CONQUEST OF MALAYA COSTS 10,000 JAPANESE LIVES, AND 8,000 BRITISH.

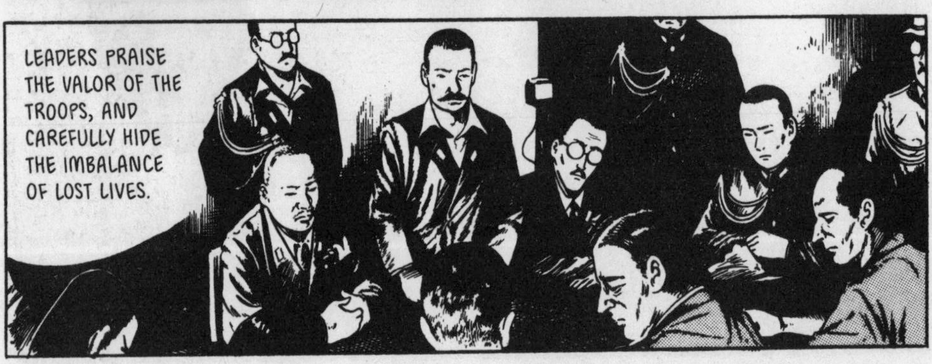
LEADERS PRAISE THE VALOR OF THE TROOPS, AND CAREFULLY HIDE THE IMBALANCE OF LOST LIVES.

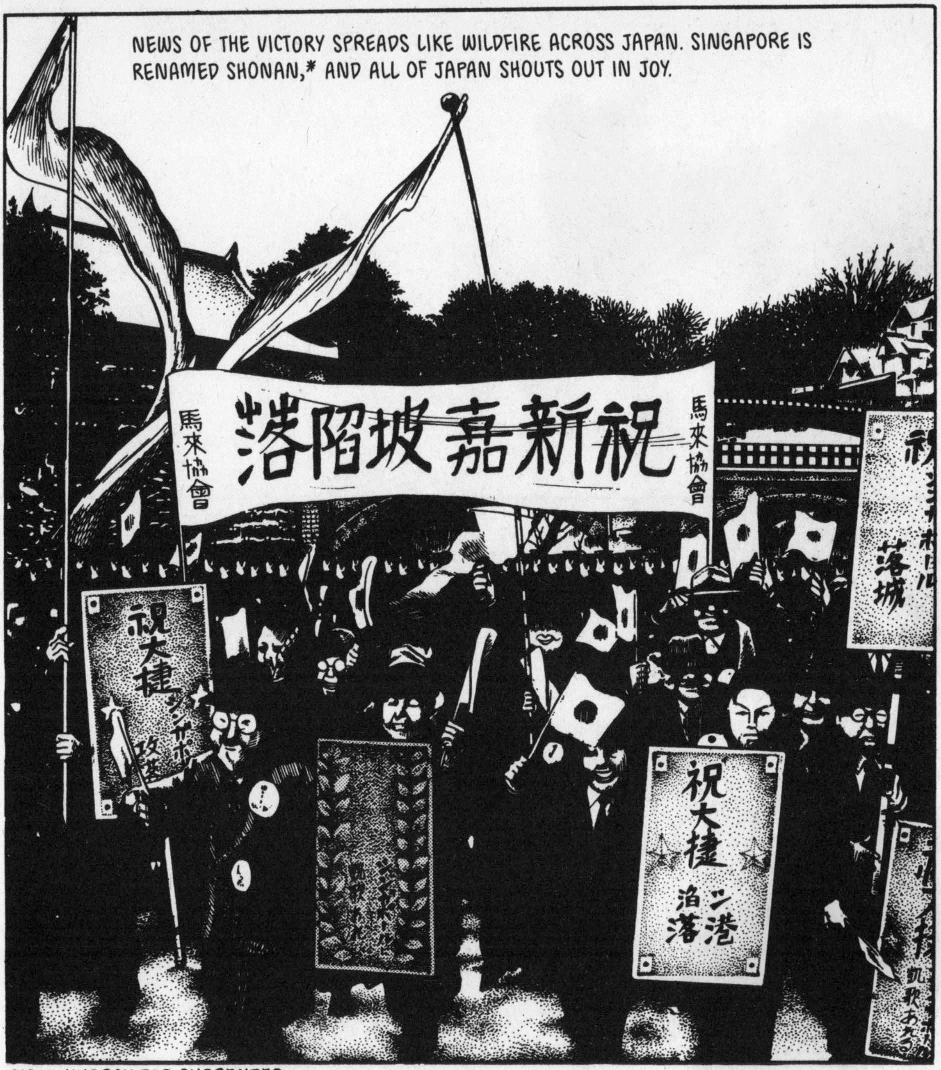
NEWS OF THE VICTORY SPREADS LIKE WILDFIRE ACROSS JAPAN. SINGAPORE IS RENAMED SHONAN,* AND ALL OF JAPAN SHOUTS OUT IN JOY.
馬來協會
祝新嘉坡陥落
馬來協會
祝大捷
祝大捷
SIGN: HURRAY FOR SURRENDER.

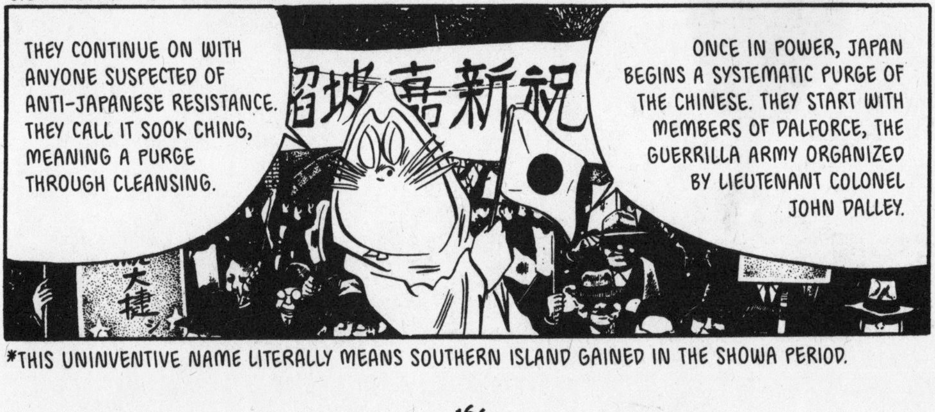
ONCE IN POWER, JAPAN BEGINS A SYSTEMATIC PURGE OF THE CHINESE. THEY START WITH MEMBERS OF DALFORCE, THE GUERRILLA ARMY ORGANIZED BY LIEUTENANT COLONEL JOHN DALLEY.
THEY CONTINUE ON WITH ANYONE SUSPECTED OF ANTI-JAPANESE RESISTANCE. THEY CALL IT SOOK CHING, MEANING A PURGE THROUGH CLEANSING.

*THIS UNINVENTIVE NAME LITERALLY MEANS SOUTHERN ISLAND GAINED IN THE SHOWA PERIOD.

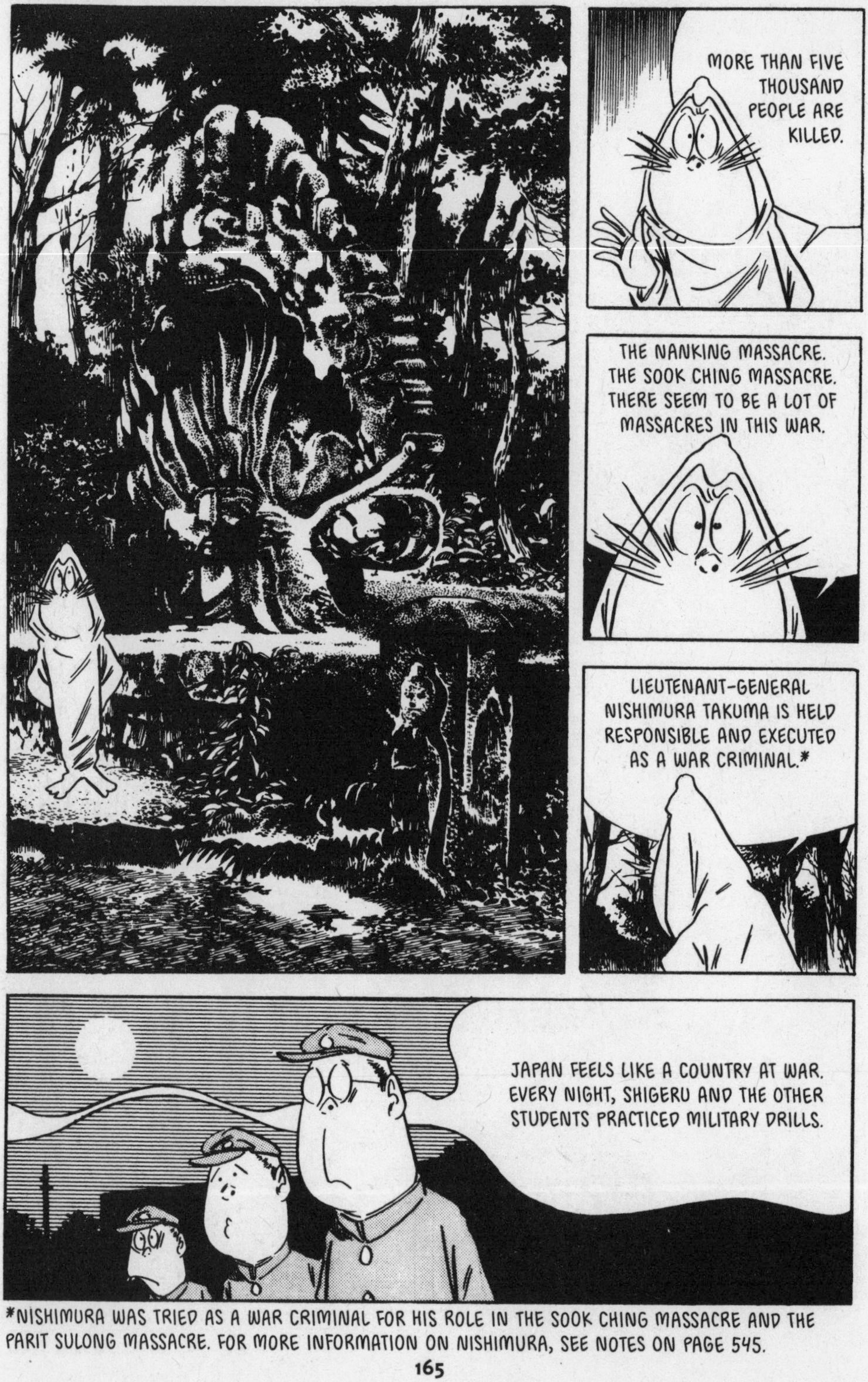

MORE THAN FIVE THOUSAND PEOPLE ARE KILLED.
THE NANKING MASSACRE. THE SOOK CHING MASSACRE. THERE SEEM TO BE A LOT OF MASSACRES IN THIS WAR.
LIEUTENANT-GENERAL NISHIMURA TAKUMA IS HELD RESPONSIBLE AND EXECUTED AS A WAR CRIMINAL.*
JAPAN FEELS LIKE A COUNTRY AT WAR. EVERY NIGHT, SHIGERU AND THE OTHER STUDENTS PRACTICED MILITARY DRILLS.

*NISHIMURA WAS TRIED AS A WAR CRIMINAL FOR HIS ROLE IN THE SOOK CHING MASSACRE AND THE PARIT SULONG MASSACRE. FOR MORE INFORMATION ON NISHIMURA, SEE NOTES ON PAGE 545.

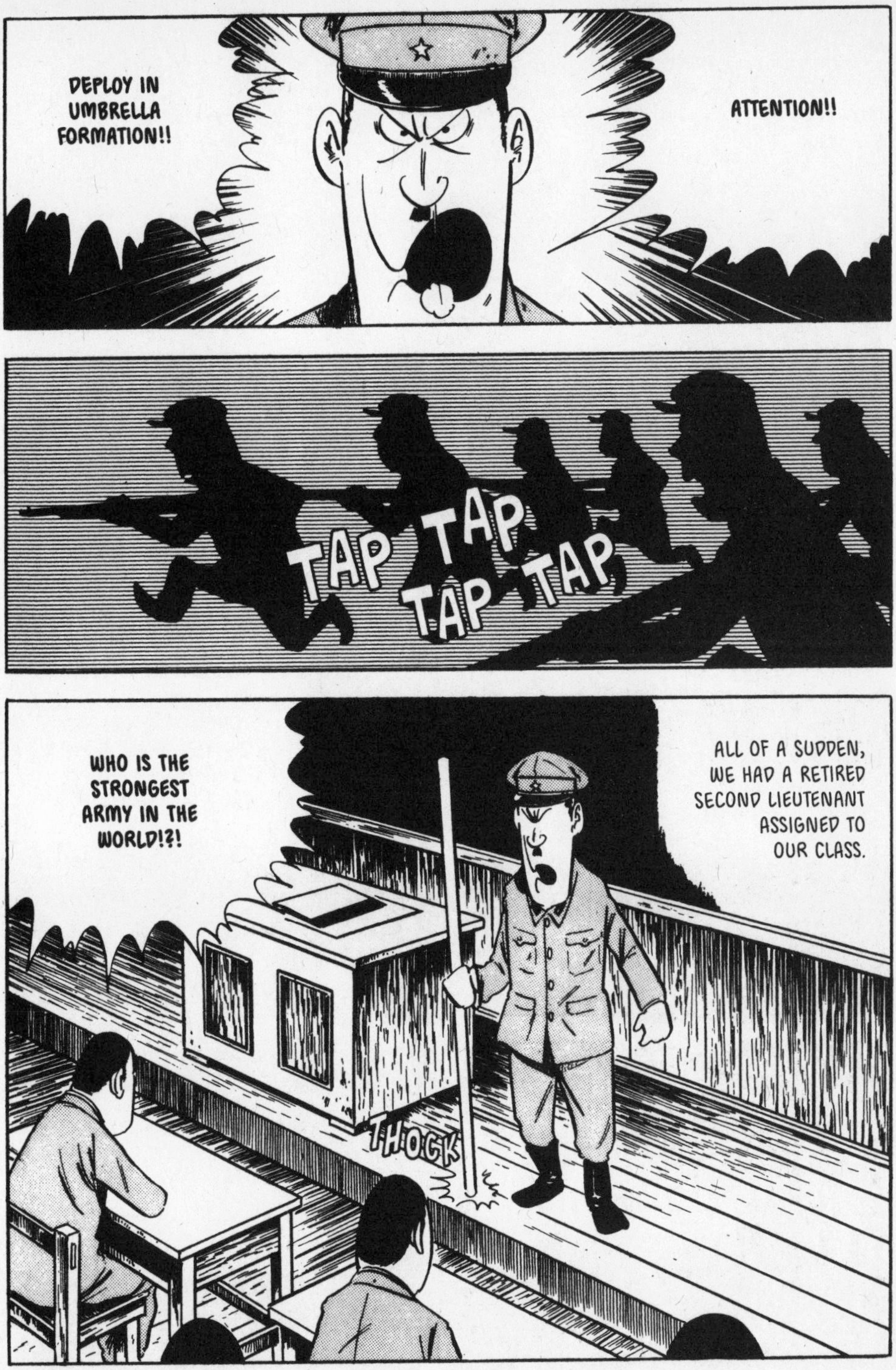
ATTENTION!!
DEPLOY IN UMBRELLA FORMATION!!
TAP TAP TAP TAP
ALL OF A SUDDEN, WE HAD A RETIRED SECOND LIEUTENANT ASSIGNED TO OUR CLASS.
WHO IS THE STRONGEST ARMY IN THE WORLD!?!
THOCK

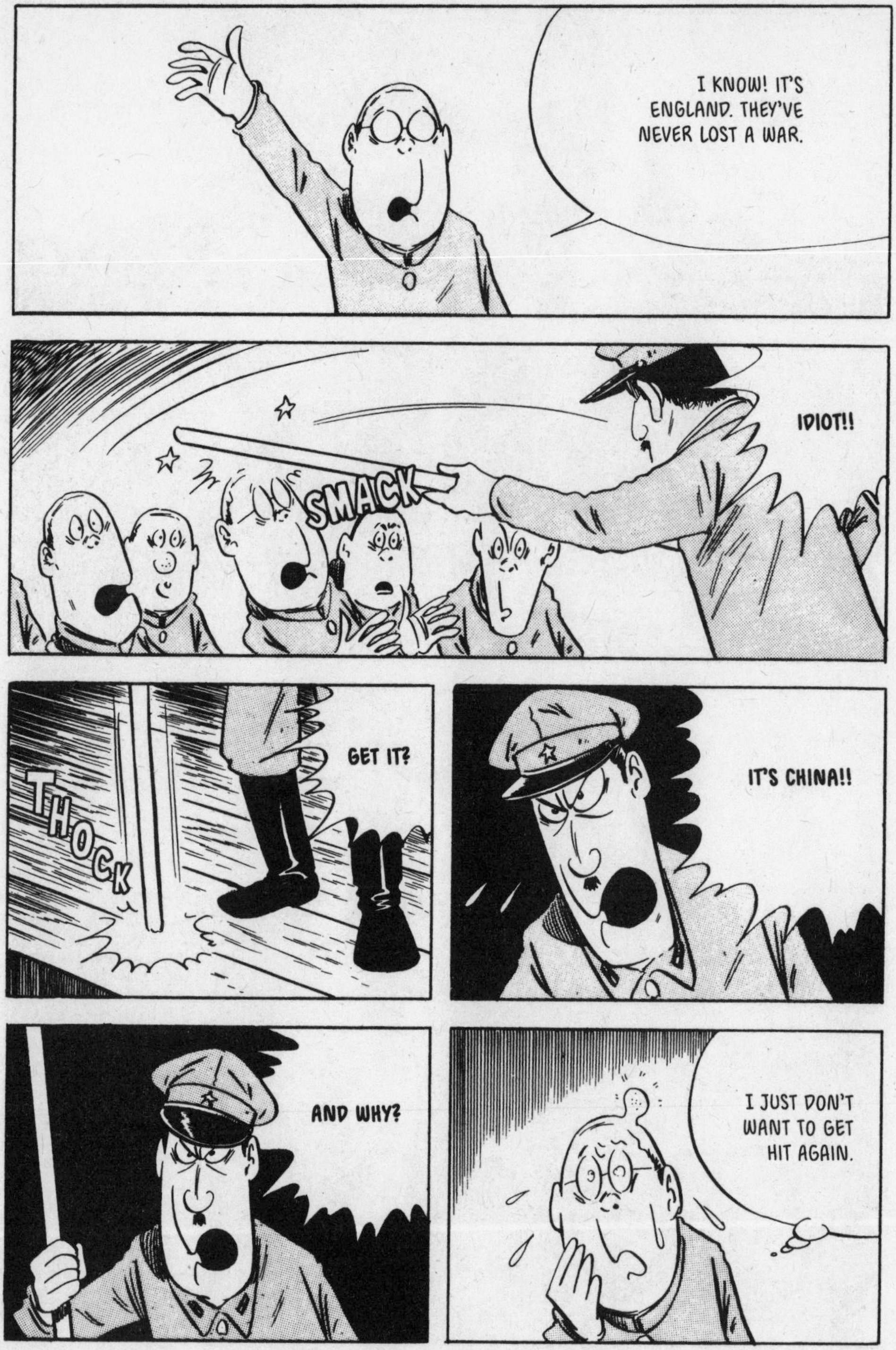

I KNOW! IT'S ENGLAND. THEY'VE NEVER LOST A WAR.
IDIOT!!
SMACK
GET IT?
THOCK
IT'S CHINA!!
AND WHY?
I JUST DON'T WANT TO GET HIT AGAIN.

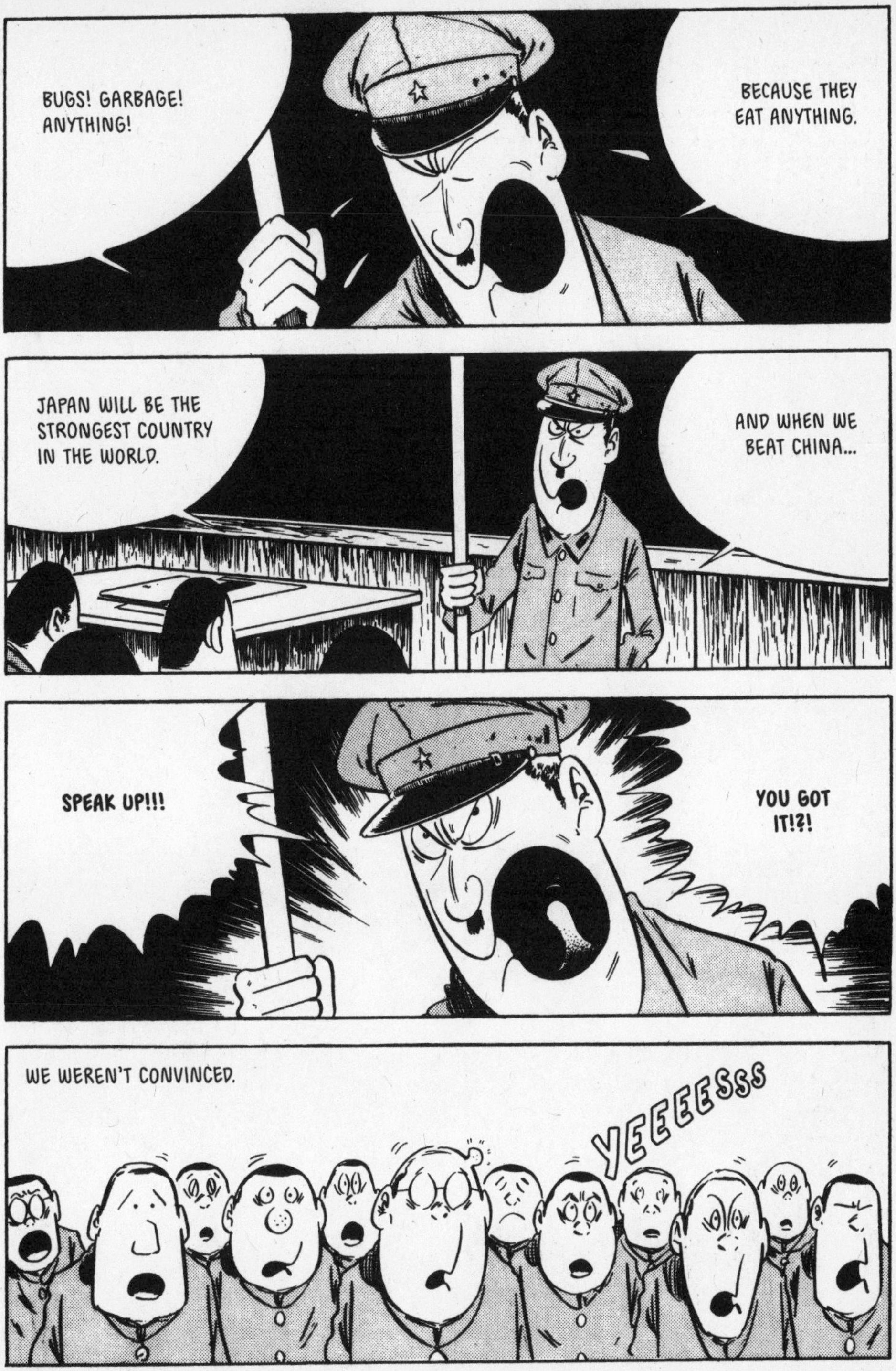
BECAUSE THEY EAT ANYTHING.
BUGS! GARBAGE! ANYTHING!
AND WHEN WE BEAT CHINA...
JAPAN WILL BE THE STRONGEST COUNTRY IN THE WORLD.
YOU GOT IT!?!
SPEAK UP!!!
YEEEESSS
WE WEREN'T CONVINCED.

THE CAPTURE OF HONG KONG AND THE PHILIPPINES

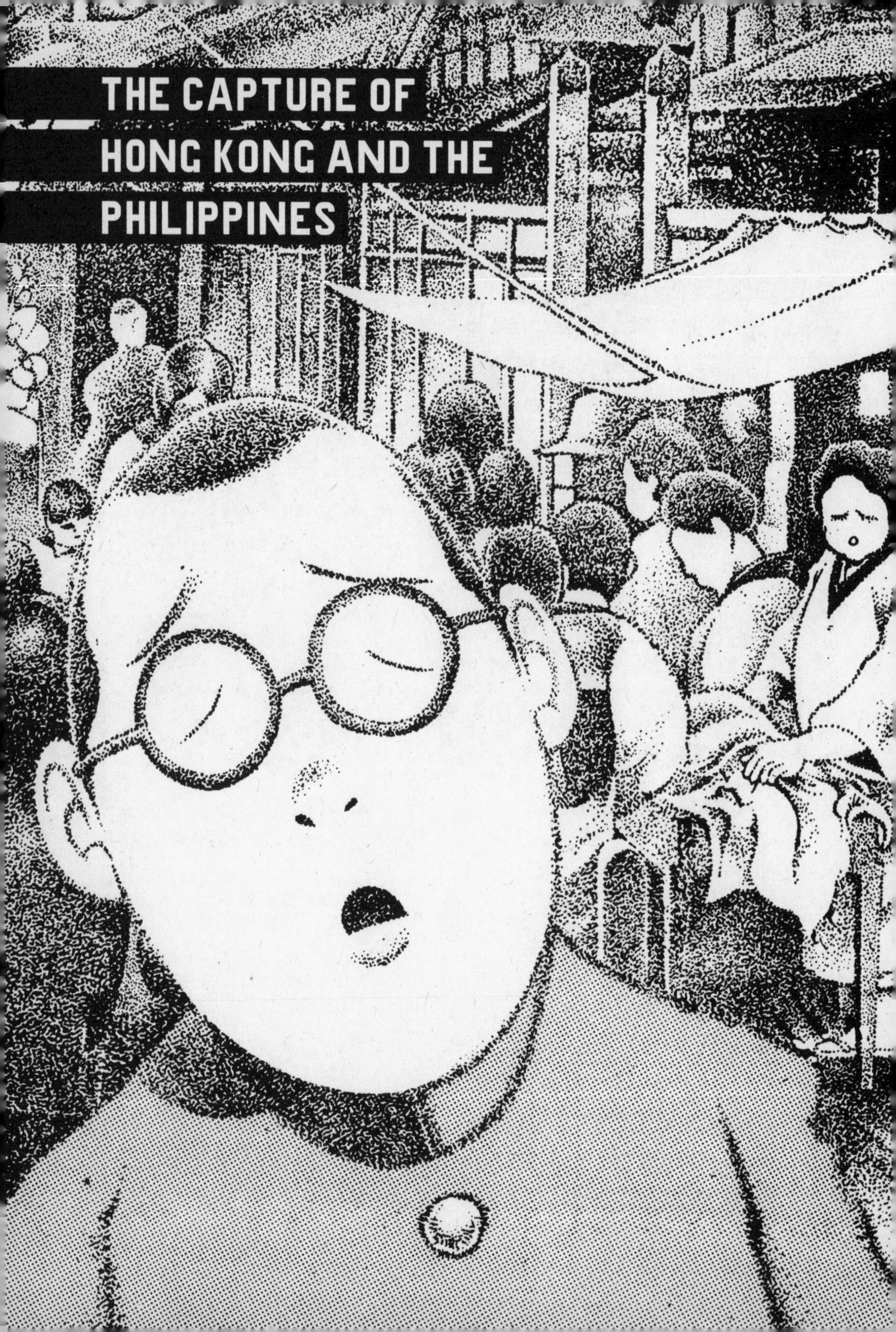

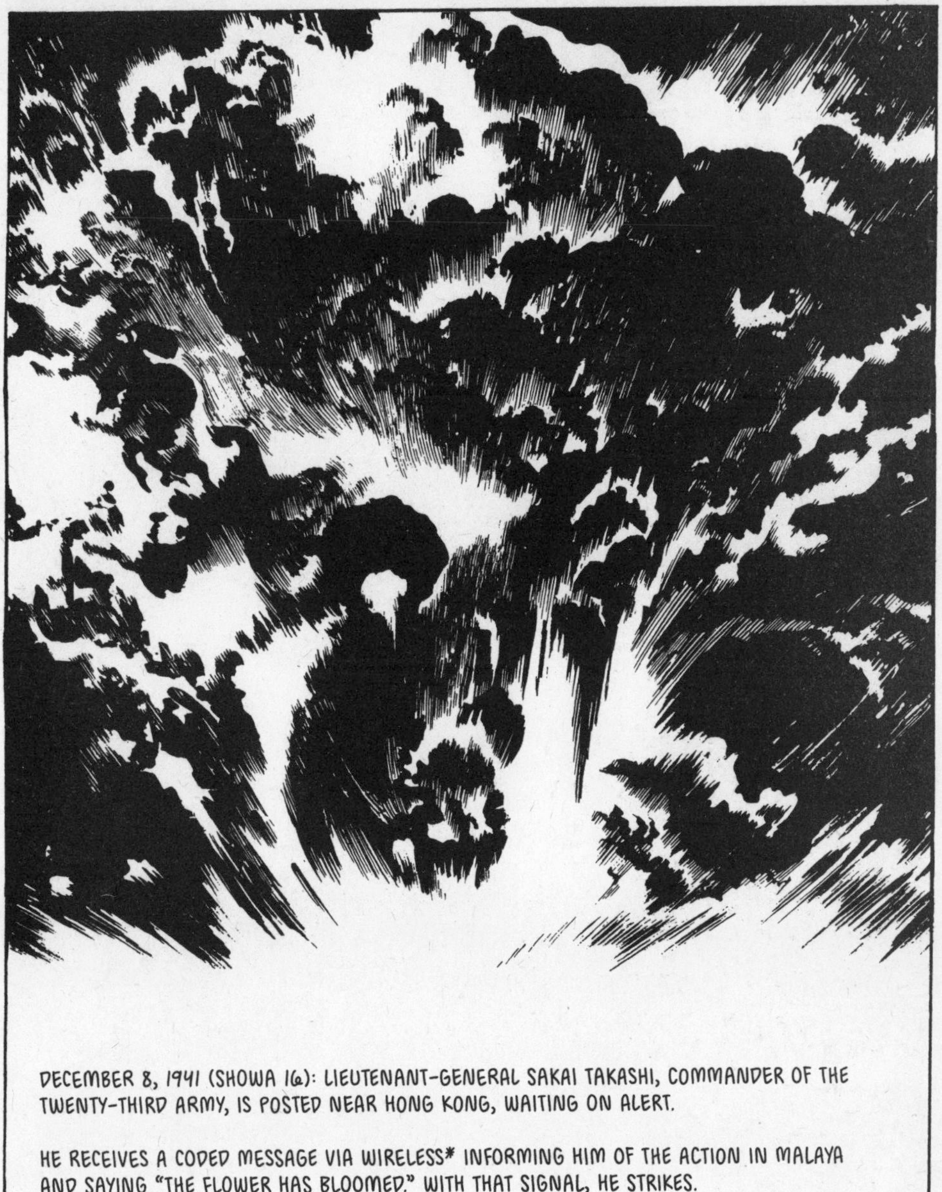

DECEMBER 8, 1941 (SHOWA 16): LIEUTENANT-GENERAL SAKAI TAKASHI, COMMANDER OF THE TWENTY-THIRD ARMY, IS POSTED NEAR HONG KONG, WAITING ON ALERT.

HE RECEIVES A CODED MESSAGE VIA WIRELESS* INFORMING HIM OF THE ACTION IN MALAYA AND SAYING "THE FLOWER HAS BLOOMED." WITH THAT SIGNAL, HE STRIKES.

HE SENDS IN HIS BOMBERS TO DESTROY KAI TAK AIRPORT. FIVE BRITISH WAR PLANES AND SEVERAL CIVILIAN AIRCRAFT ARE DESTROYED.

TWENTY THOUSAND JAPANESE SOLDIERS MARCH FORWARD TO BREAK THE SO-CALLED GIN DRINKER'S LINE. SAKAI ADVANCES CAUTIOUSLY, AND ON DECEMBER 9, HE SENDS LIEUTENANT WAKAMURA ON RECONNAISSANCE.

*A TERM USED DURING WWII FOR RADIO COMMUNICATION.

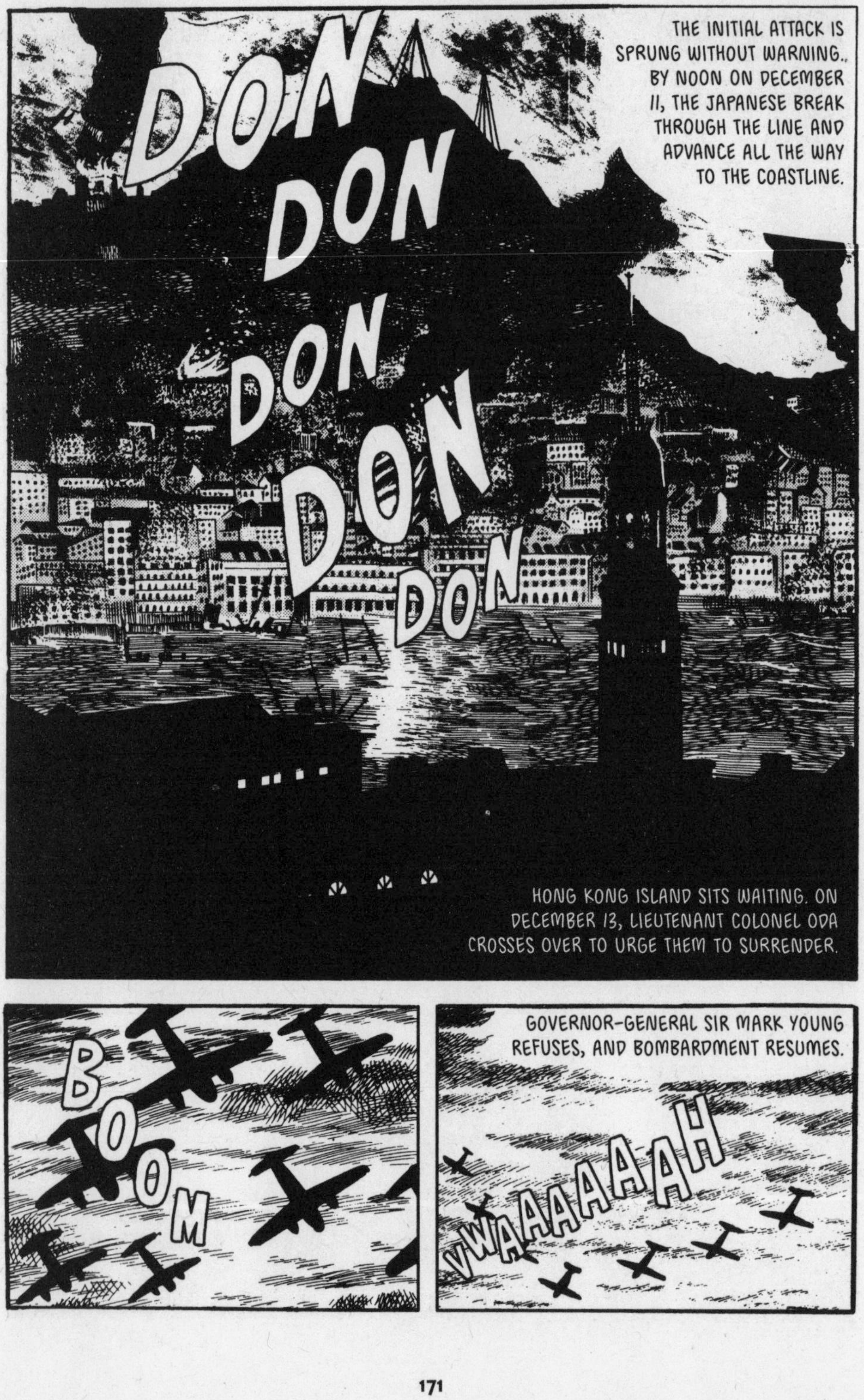
THE INITIAL ATTACK IS SPRUNG WITHOUT WARNING.. BY NOON ON DECEMBER 11, THE JAPANESE BREAK THROUGH THE LINE AND ADVANCE ALL THE WAY TO THE COASTLINE.
DON DON DON DON DON DON
HONG KONG ISLAND SITS WAITING. ON DECEMBER 13, LIEUTENANT COLONEL ODA CROSSES OVER TO URGE THEM TO SURRENDER.
GOVERNOR-GENERAL SIR MARK YOUNG REFUSES, AND BOMBARDMENT RESUMES.
VWAAAAAAH
BOOM

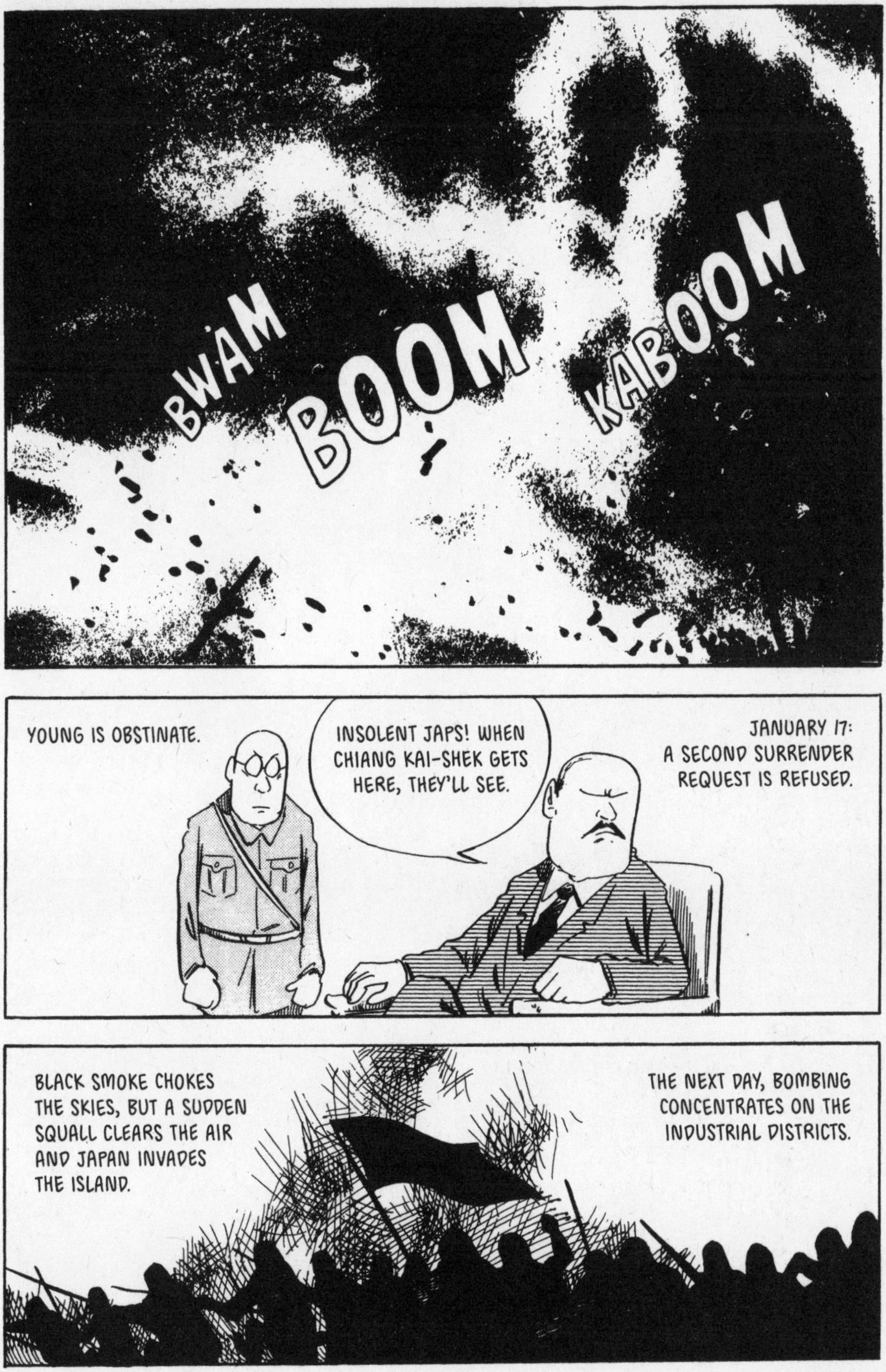
KABOOM
BOOM
BWAM
JANUARY 17: A SECOND SURRENDER REQUEST IS REFUSED.
INSOLENT JAPS! WHEN CHIANG KAI-SHEK GETS HERE, THEY'LL SEE.
YOUNG IS OBSTINATE.
THE NEXT DAY, BOMBING CONCENTRATES ON THE INDUSTRIAL DISTRICTS.
BLACK SMOKE CHOKES THE SKIES, BUT A SUDDEN SQUALL CLEARS THE AIR AND JAPAN INVADES THE ISLAND.

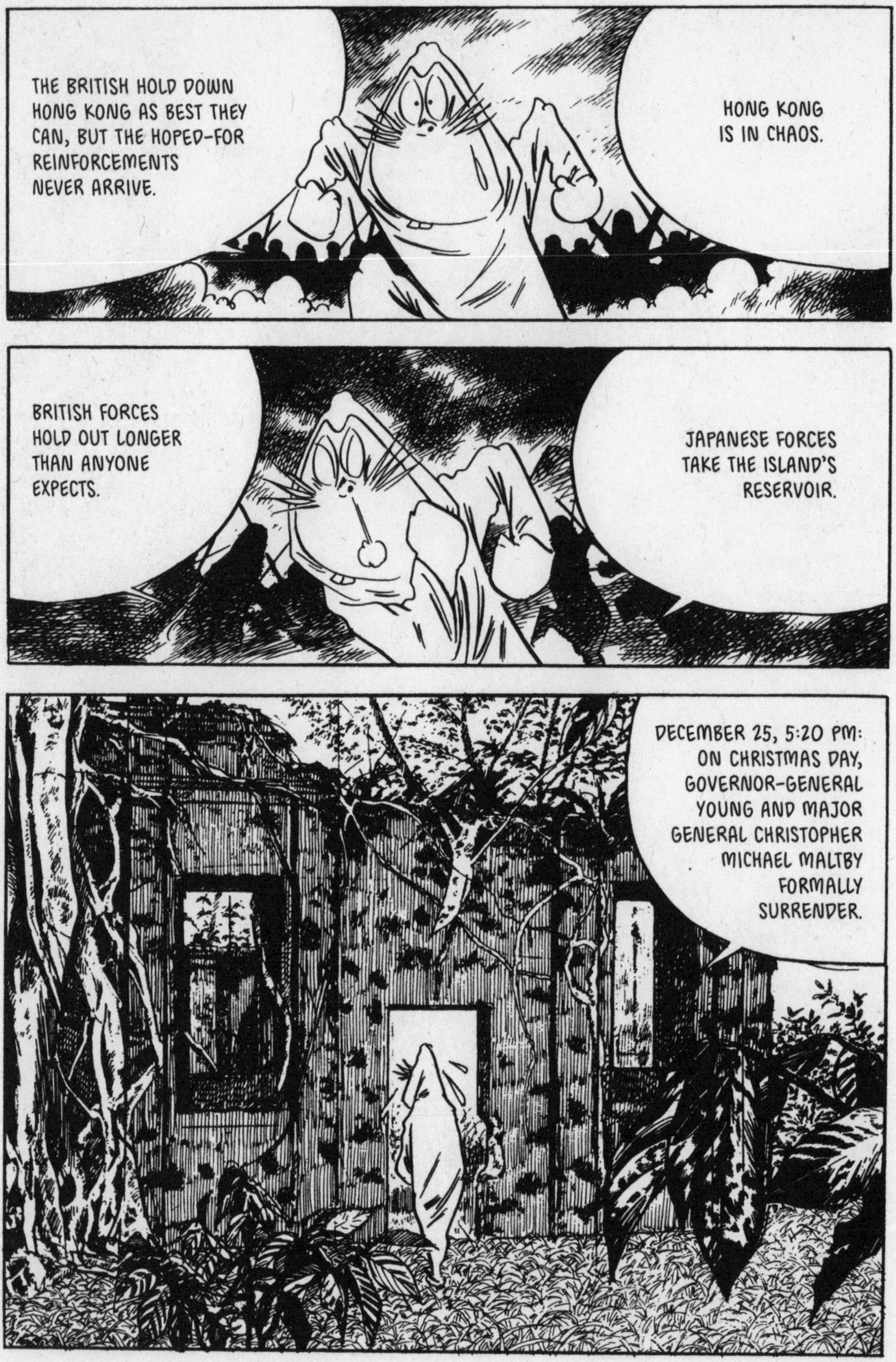
HONG KONG IS IN CHAOS.
THE BRITISH HOLD DOWN HONG KONG AS BEST THEY CAN, BUT THE HOPED-FOR REINFORCEMENTS NEVER ARRIVE.
JAPANESE FORCES TAKE THE ISLAND'S RESERVOIR.
BRITISH FORCES HOLD OUT LONGER THAN ANYONE EXPECTS.
DECEMBER 25, 5:20 PM: ON CHRISTMAS DAY, GOVERNOR-GENERAL YOUNG AND MAJOR GENERAL CHRISTOPHER MICHAEL MALTBY FORMALLY SURRENDER.

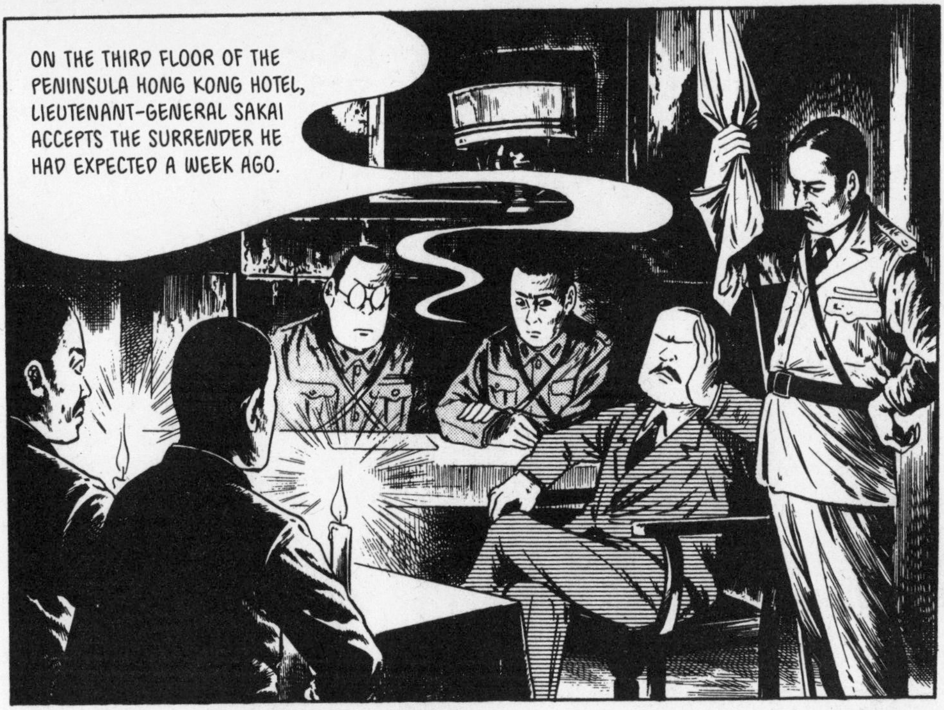
ON THE THIRD FLOOR OF THE PENINSULA HONG KONG HOTEL, LIEUTENANT-GENERAL SAKAI ACCEPTS THE SURRENDER HE HAD EXPECTED A WEEK AGO.

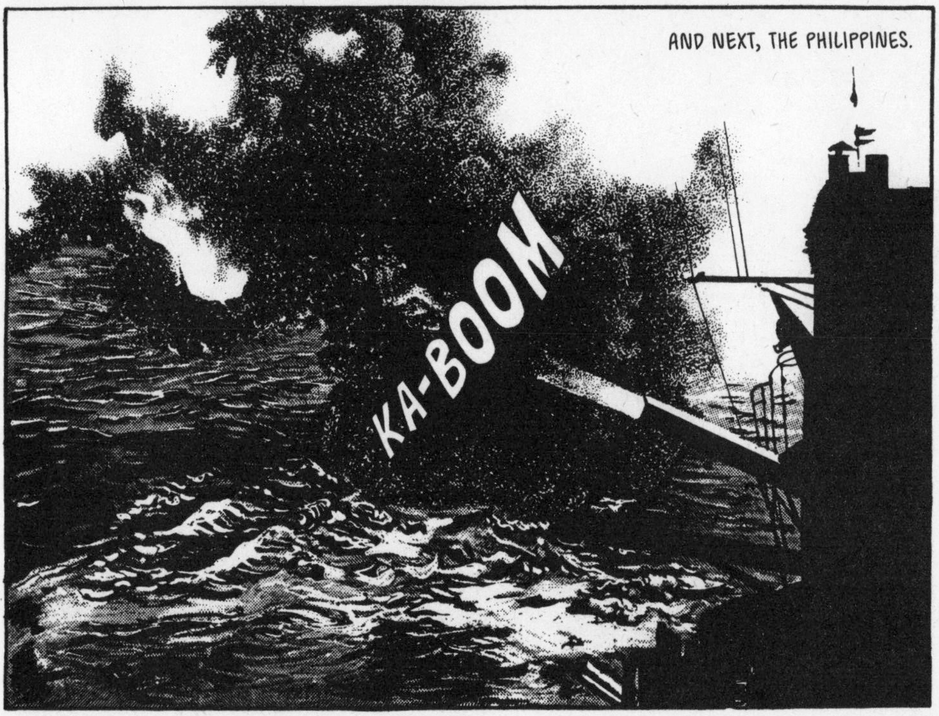
AND NEXT, THE PHILIPPINES.
KA-BOOM

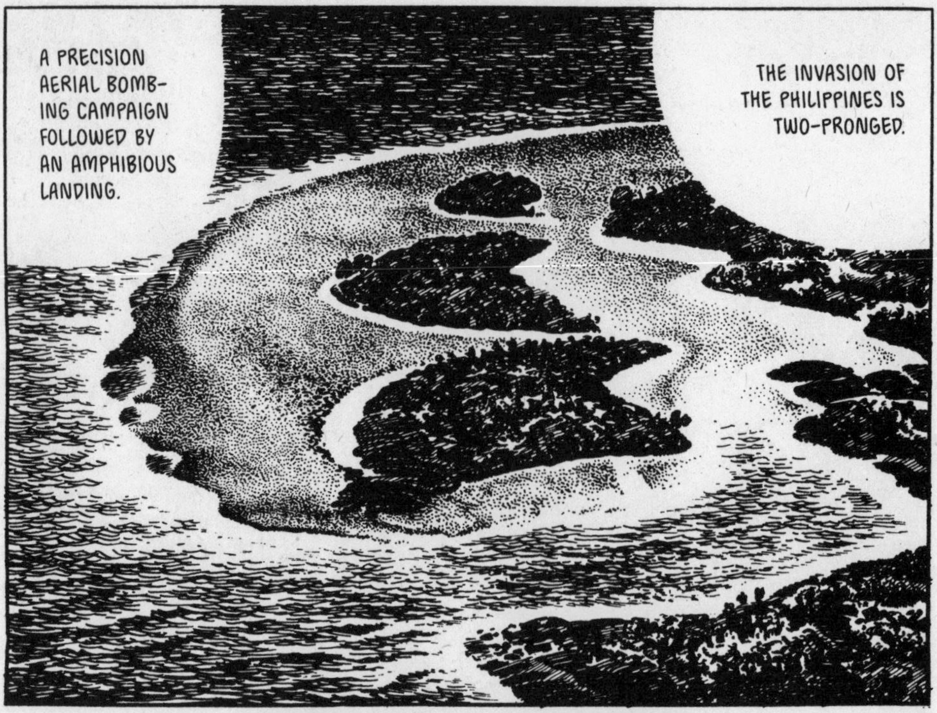
THE INVASION OF THE PHILIPPINES IS TWO-PRONGED.
A PRECISION AERIAL BOMB-ING CAMPAIGN FOLLOWED BY AN AMPHIBIOUS LANDING.

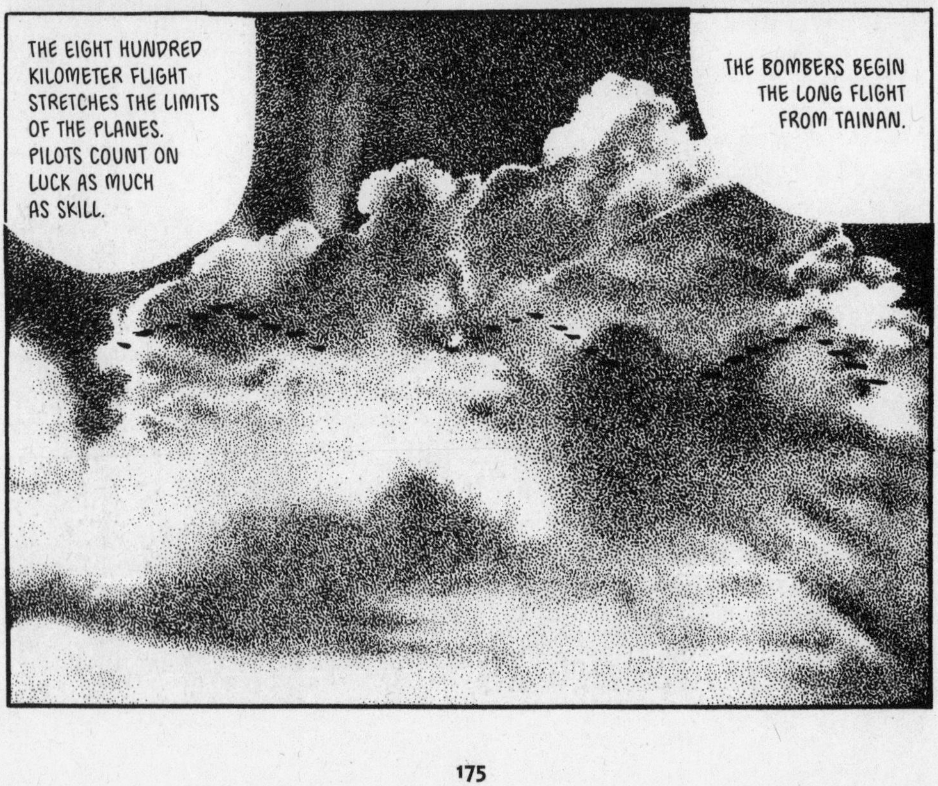
THE BOMBERS BEGIN THE LONG FLIGHT FROM TAINAN.
THE EIGHT HUNDRED KILOMETER FLIGHT STRETCHES THE LIMITS OF THE PLANES. PILOTS COUNT ON LUCK AS MUCH AS SKILL.

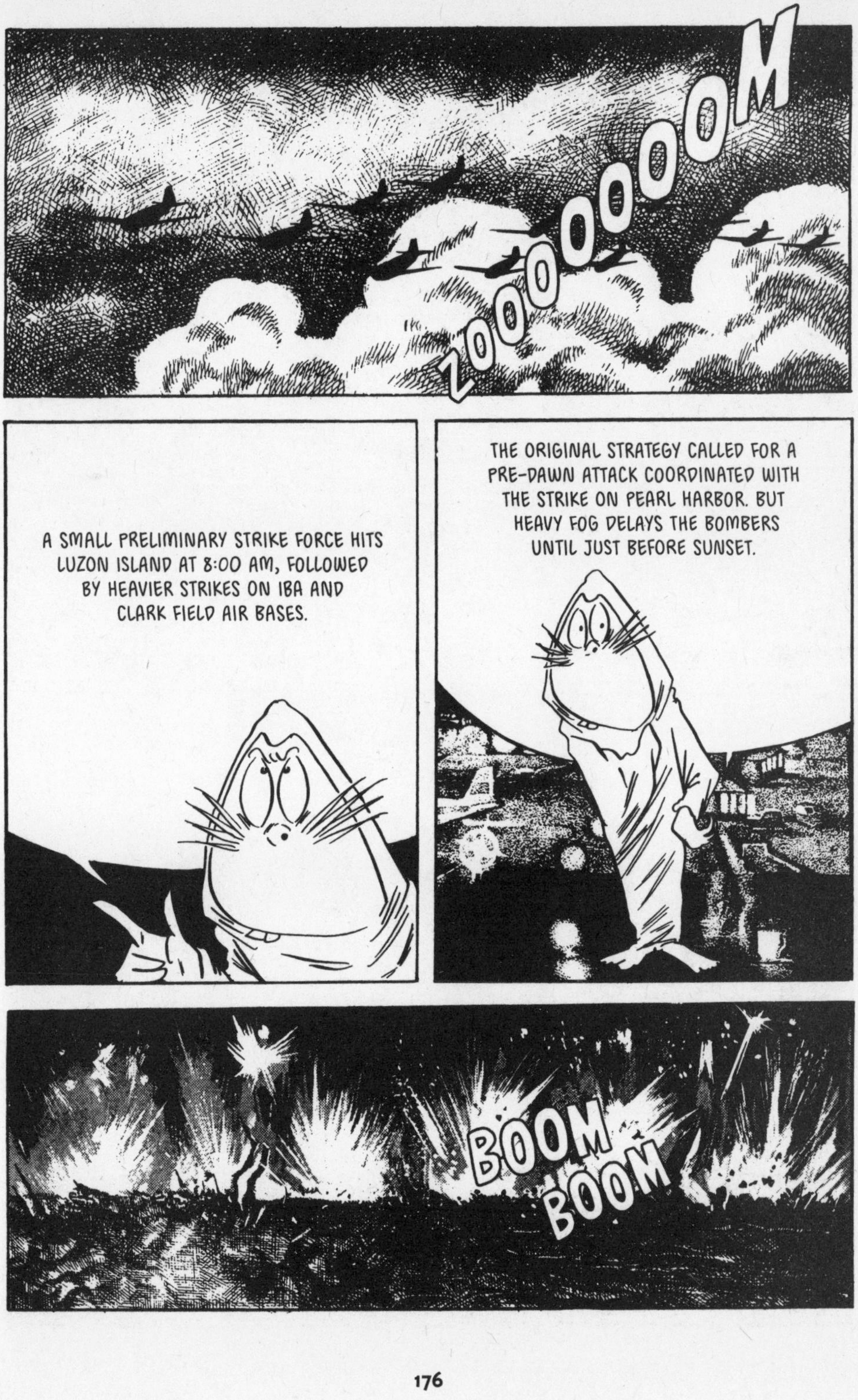
ZOOOOOOOOM
THE ORIGINAL STRATEGY CALLED FOR A PRE-DAWN ATTACK COORDINATED WITH THE STRIKE ON PEARL HARBOR. BUT HEAVY FOG DELAYS THE BOMBERS UNTIL JUST BEFORE SUNSET.
A SMALL PRELIMINARY STRIKE FORCE HITS LUZON ISLAND AT 8:00 AM, FOLLOWED BY HEAVIER STRIKES ON IBA AND CLARK FIELD AIR BASES.
BOOM
BOOM

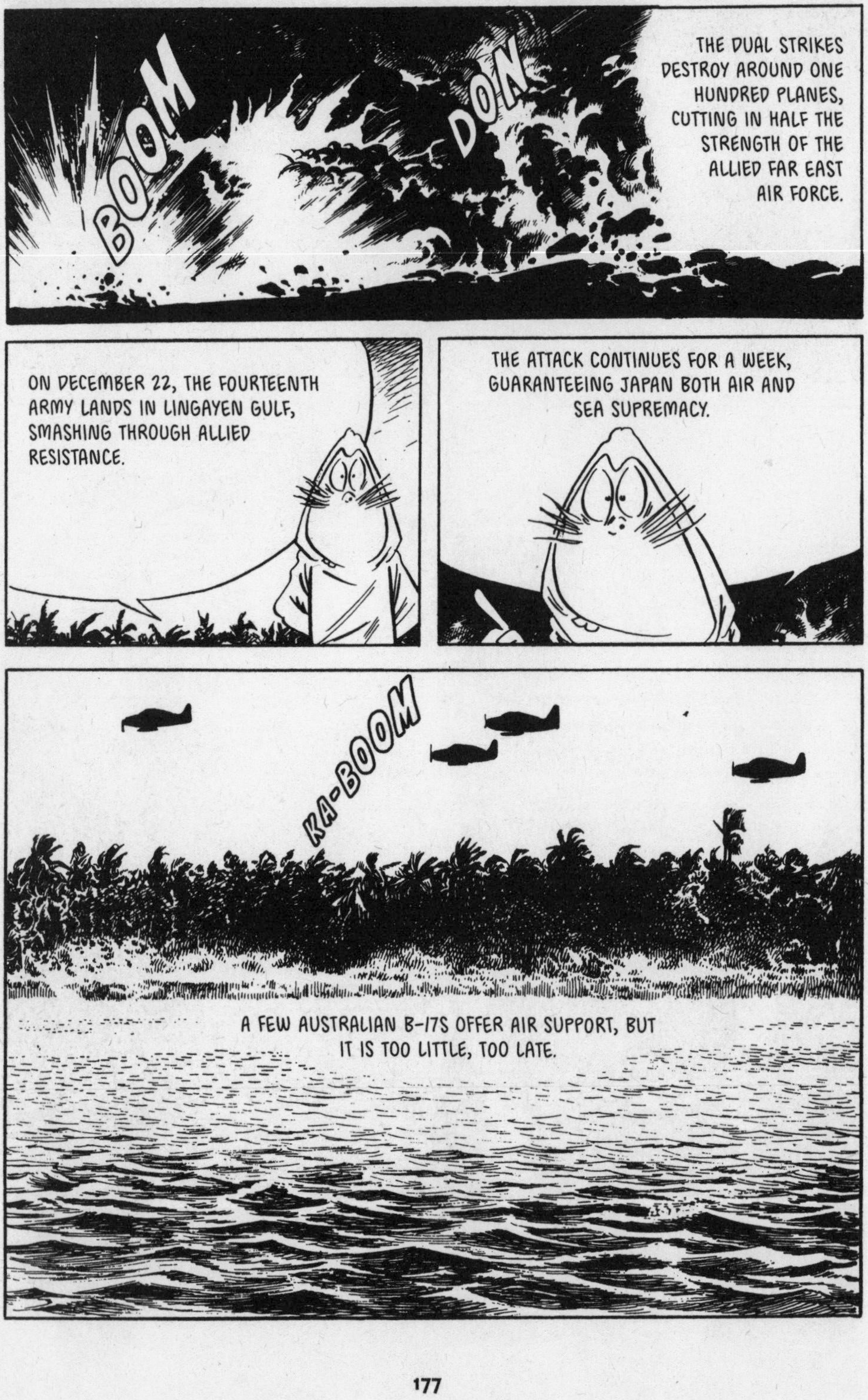
THE DUAL STRIKES DESTROY AROUND ONE HUNDRED PLANES, CUTTING IN HALF THE STRENGTH OF THE ALLIED FAR EAST AIR FORCE.
DON
BOOM
THE ATTACK CONTINUES FOR A WEEK, GUARANTEEING JAPAN BOTH AIR AND SEA SUPREMACY.
ON DECEMBER 22, THE FOURTEENTH ARMY LANDS IN LINGAYEN GULF, SMASHING THROUGH ALLIED RESISTANCE.
KA-BOOM
A FEW AUSTRALIAN B-17S OFFER AIR SUPPORT, BUT IT IS TOO LITTLE, TOO LATE.

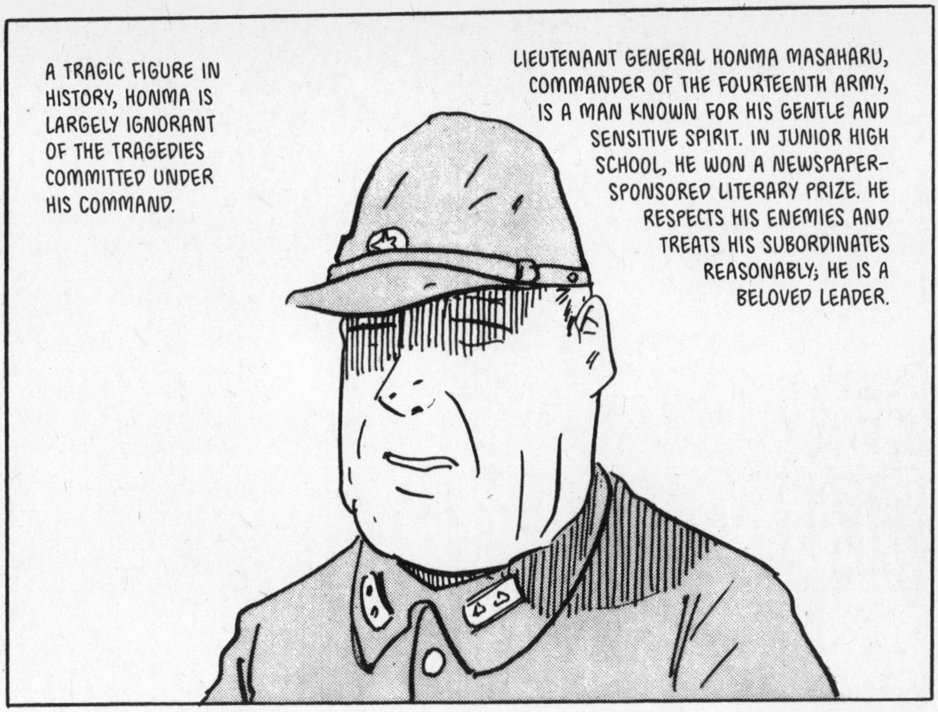
LIEUTENANT GENERAL HONMA MASAHARU, COMMANDER OF THE FOURTEENTH ARMY, IS A MAN KNOWN FOR HIS GENTLE AND SENSITIVE SPIRIT. IN JUNIOR HIGH SCHOOL, HE WON A NEWSPAPER-SPONSORED LITERARY PRIZE. HE RESPECTS HIS ENEMIES AND TREATS HIS SUBORDINATES REASONABLY; HE IS A BELOVED LEADER.
A TRAGIC FIGURE IN HISTORY, HONMA IS LARGELY IGNORANT OF THE TRAGEDIES COMMITTED UNDER HIS COMMAND.

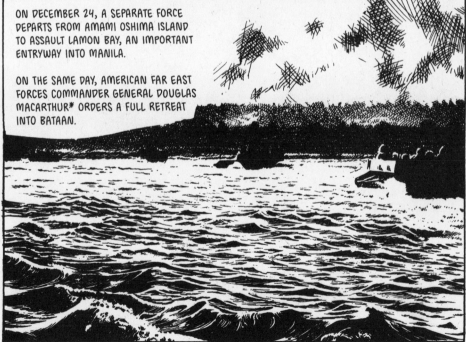

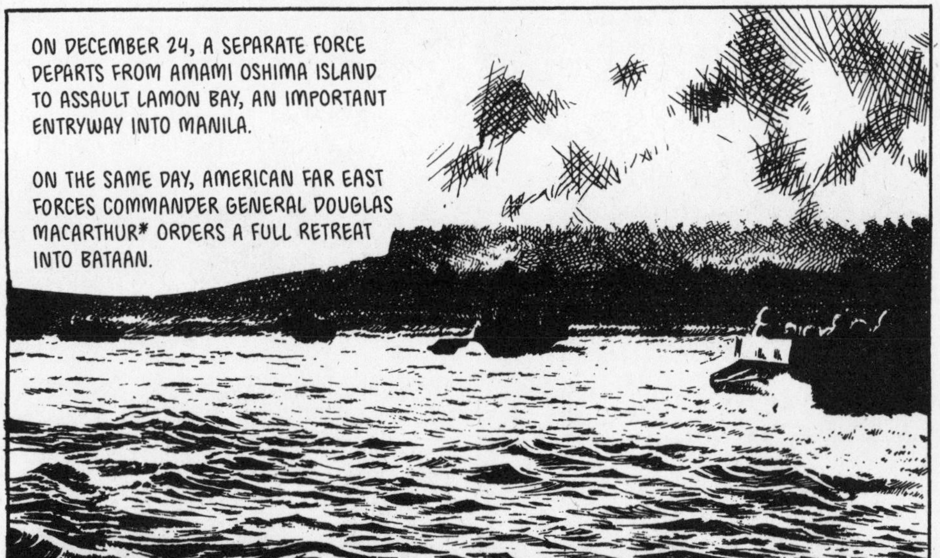
ON DECEMBER 24, A SEPARATE FORCE DEPARTS FROM AMAMI OSHIMA ISLAND TO ASSAULT LAMON BAY, AN IMPORTANT ENTRYWAY INTO MANILA.
ON THE SAME DAY, AMERICAN FAR EAST FORCES COMMANDER GENERAL DOUGLAS MACARTHUR* ORDERS A FULL RETREAT INTO BATAAN.

*SEE NOTE ON PAGE 545.

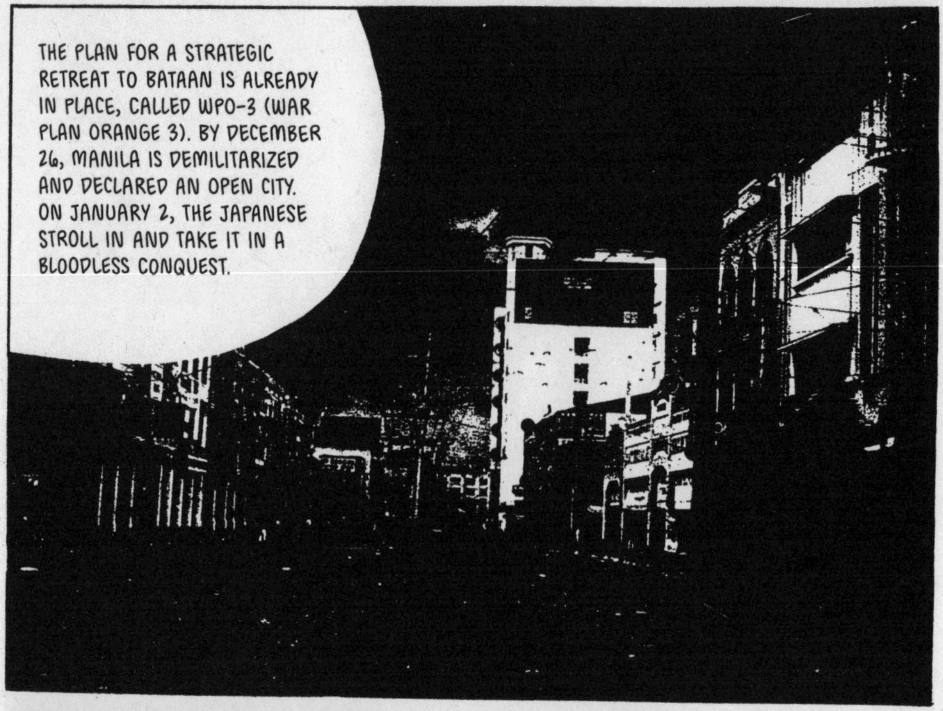
THE PLAN FOR A STRATEGIC RETREAT TO BATAAN IS ALREADY IN PLACE, CALLED WPO-3 (WAR PLAN ORANGE 3). BY DECEMBER 26, MANILA IS DEMILITARIZED AND DECLARED AN OPEN CITY. ON JANUARY 2, THE JAPANESE STROLL IN AND TAKE IT IN A BLOODLESS CONQUEST.

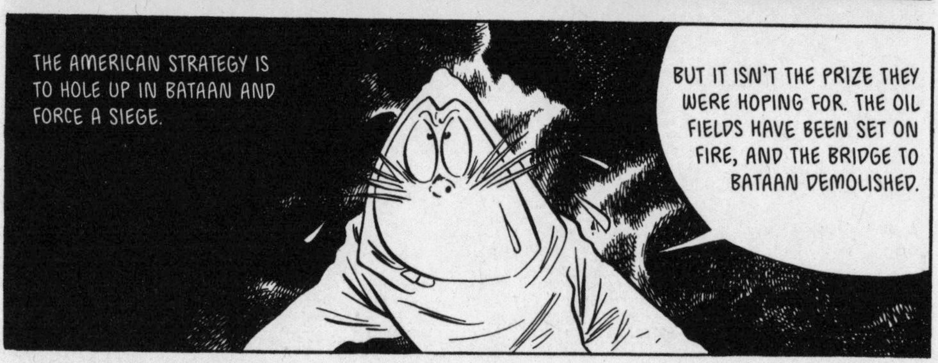
BUT IT ISN'T THE PRIZE THEY WERE HOPING FOR. THE OIL FIELDS HAVE BEEN SET ON FIRE, AND THE BRIDGE TO BATAAN DEMOLISHED.
THE AMERICAN STRATEGY IS TO HOLE UP IN BATAAN AND FORCE A SIEGE.

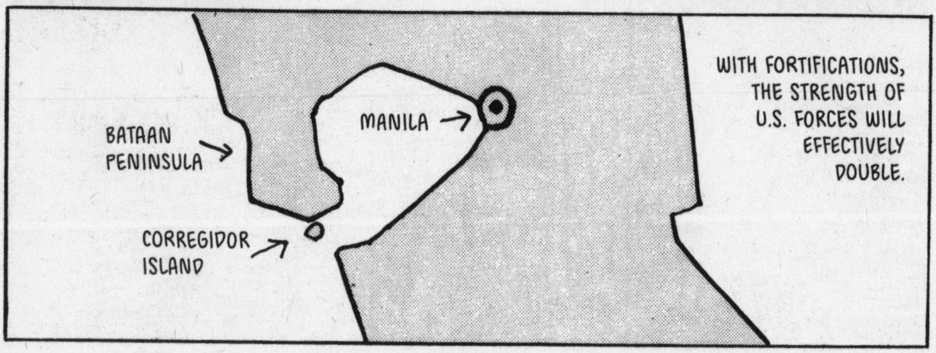
WITH FORTIFICATIONS, THE STRENGTH OF U.S. FORCES WILL EFFECTIVELY DOUBLE.
MANILA
BATAAN PENINSULA
CORREGIDOR ISLAND

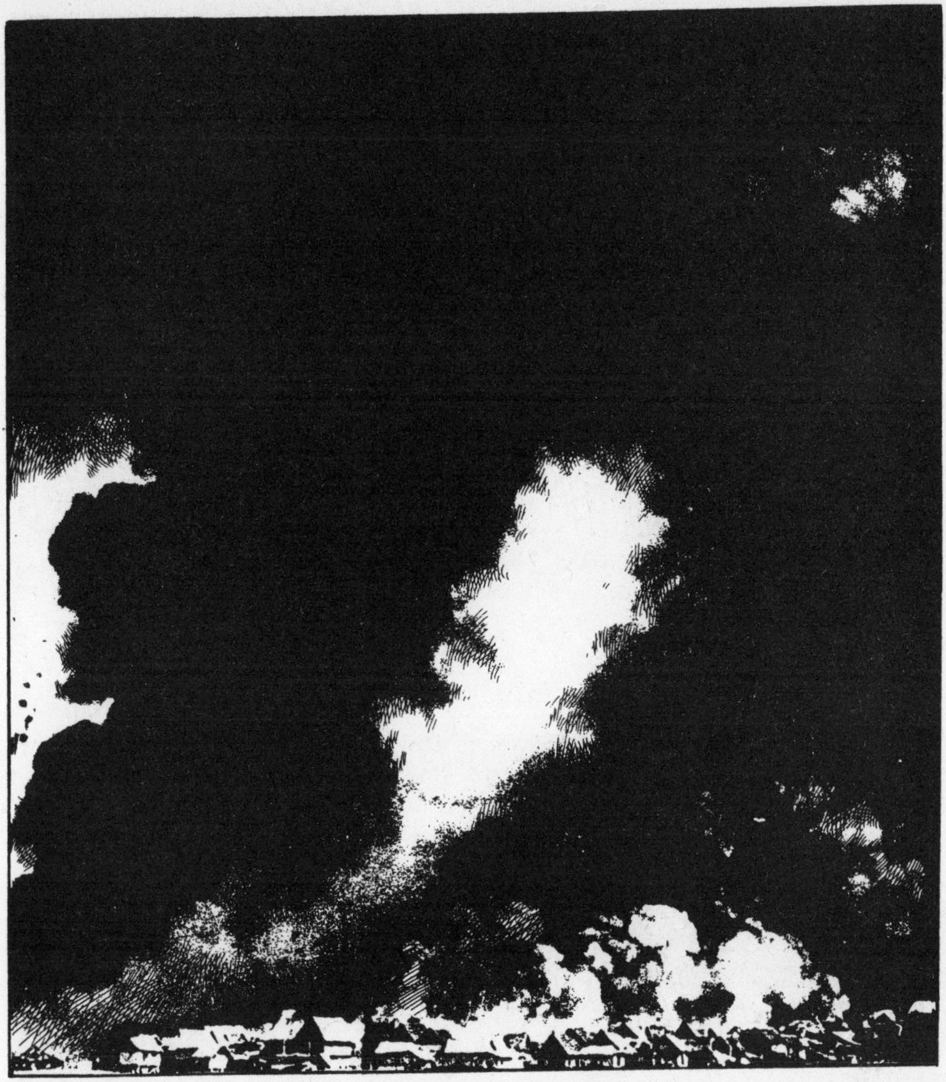

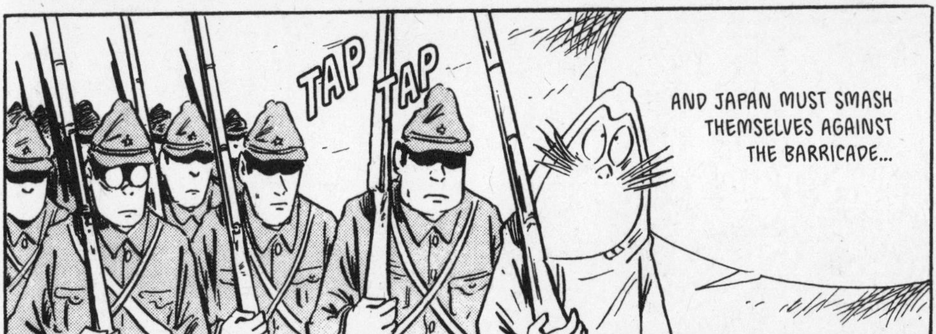
AND JAPAN MUST SMASH
THEMSELVES AGAINST
THE BARRICADE...
TAP TAP

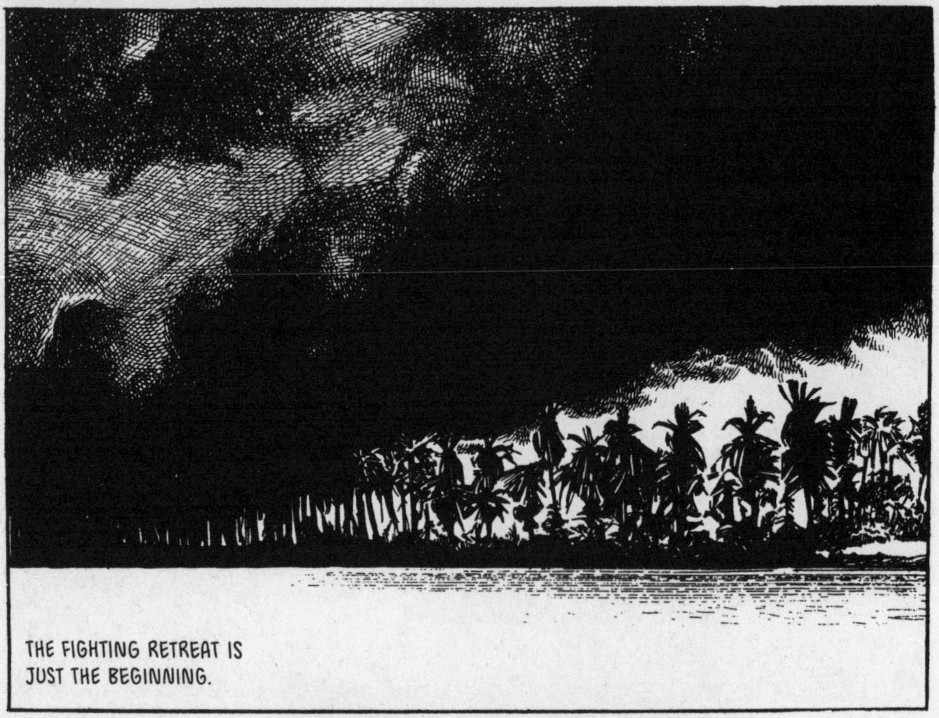
THE FIGHTING RETREAT IS JUST THE BEGINNING.

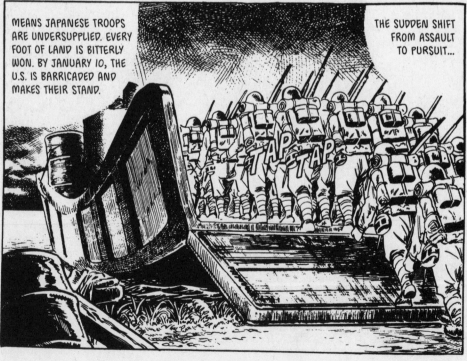

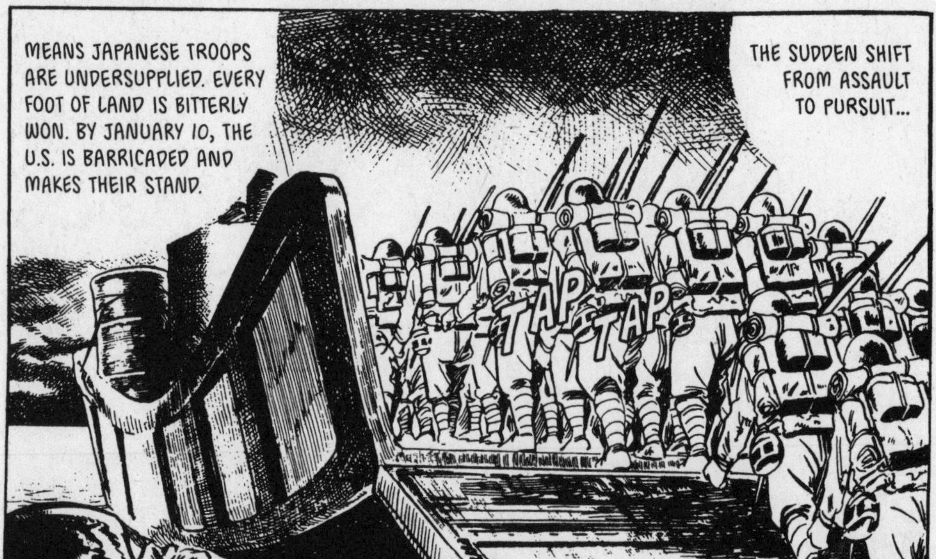
THE SUDDEN SHIFT FROM ASSAULT TO PURSUIT...
MEANS JAPANESE TROOPS ARE UNDERSUPPLIED. EVERY FOOT OF LAND IS BITTERLY WON. BY JANUARY 10, THE U.S. IS BARRICADED AND MAKES THEIR STAND.
TAP
TAP

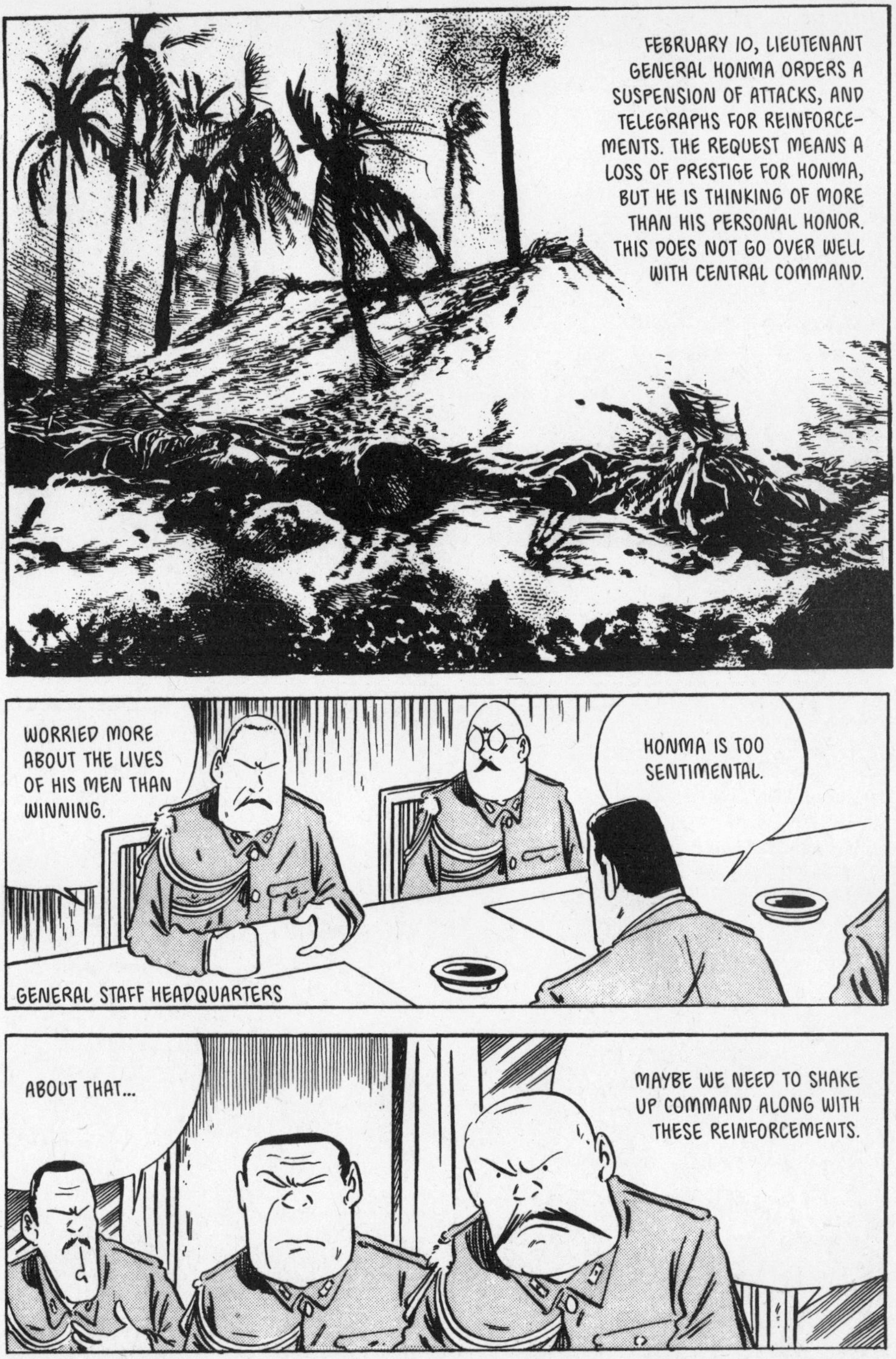
FEBRUARY 10, LIEUTENANT GENERAL HONMA ORDERS A SUSPENSION OF ATTACKS, AND TELEGRAPHS FOR REINFORCEMENTS. THE REQUEST MEANS A LOSS OF PRESTIGE FOR HONMA, BUT HE IS THINKING OF MORE THAN HIS PERSONAL HONOR. THIS DOES NOT GO OVER WELL WITH CENTRAL COMMAND.
HONMA IS TOO SENTIMENTAL.
WORRIED MORE ABOUT THE LIVES OF HIS MEN THAN WINNING.
GENERAL STAFF HEADQUARTERS
MAYBE WE NEED TO SHAKE UP COMMAND ALONG WITH THESE REINFORCEMENTS.
ABOUT THAT...

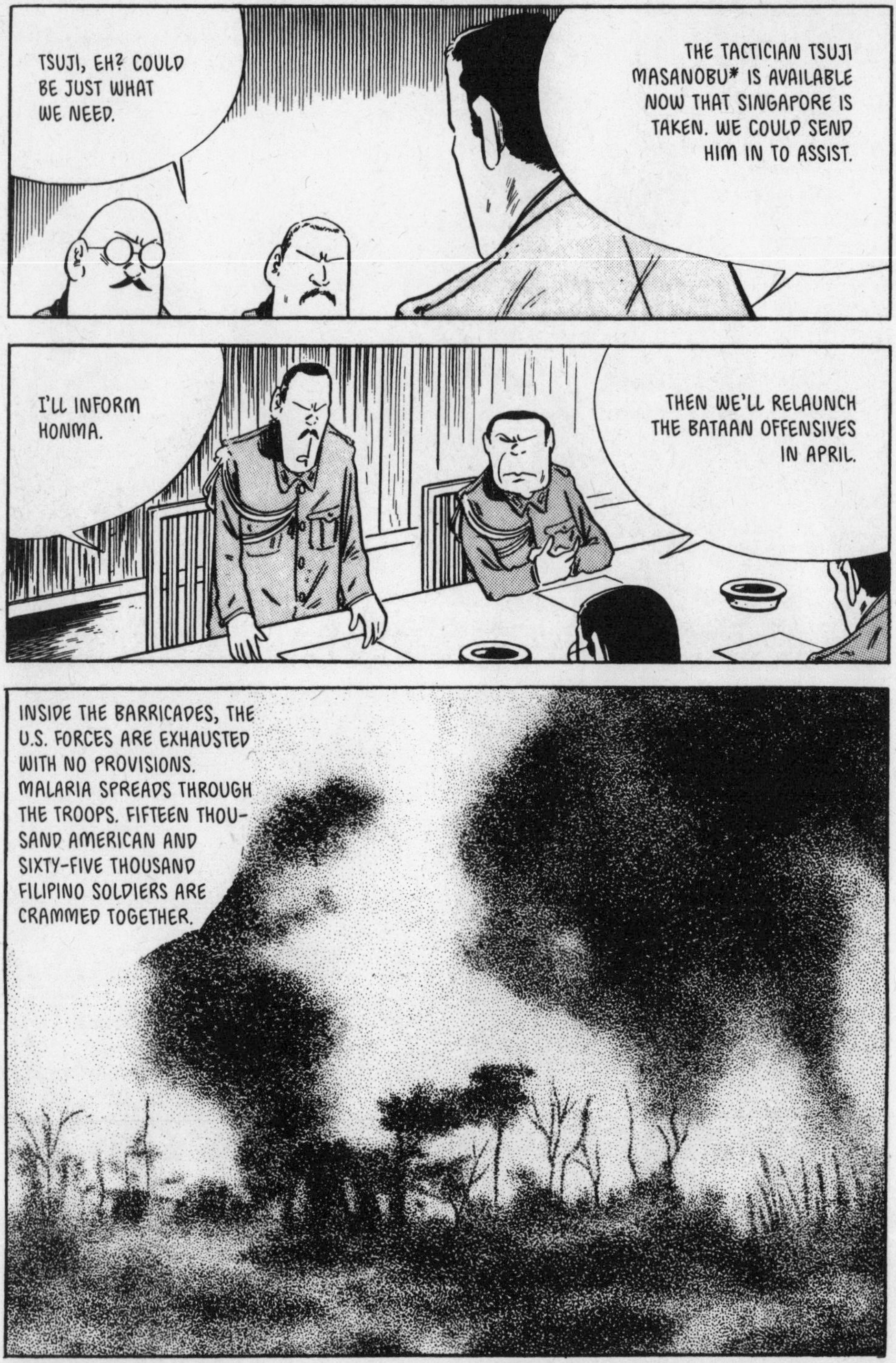
THE TACTICIAN TSUJI MASANOBU* IS AVAILABLE NOW THAT SINGAPORE IS TAKEN. WE COULD SEND HIM IN TO ASSIST.
TSUJI, EH? COULD BE JUST WHAT WE NEED.
THEN WE'LL RELAUNCH THE BATAAN OFFENSIVES IN APRIL.
I'LL INFORM HONMA.
INSIDE THE BARRICADES, THE U.S. FORCES ARE EXHAUSTED WITH NO PROVISIONS. MALARIA SPREADS THROUGH THE TROOPS. FIFTEEN THOUSAND AMERICAN AND SIXTY-FIVE THOUSAND FILIPINO SOLDIERS ARE CRAMMED TOGETHER.

*SEE NOTE ON PAGE 545.

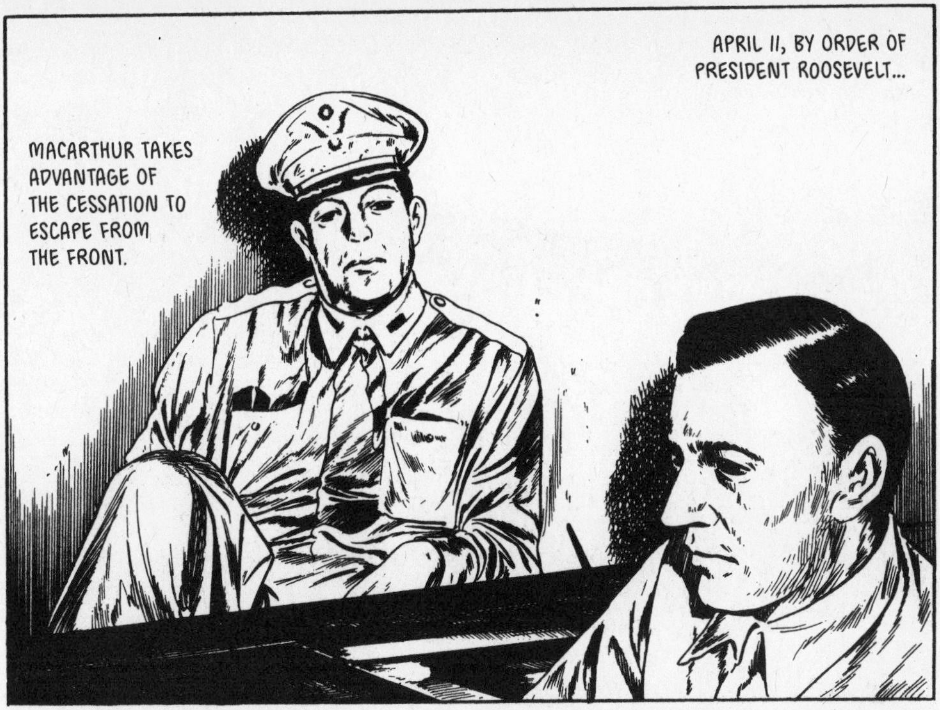
APRIL 11, BY ORDER OF PRESIDENT ROOSEVELT...
MACARTHUR TAKES ADVANTAGE OF THE CESSATION TO ESCAPE FROM THE FRONT.

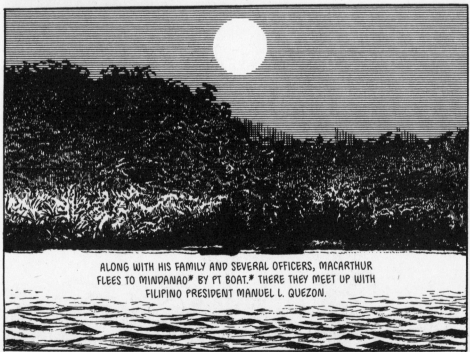

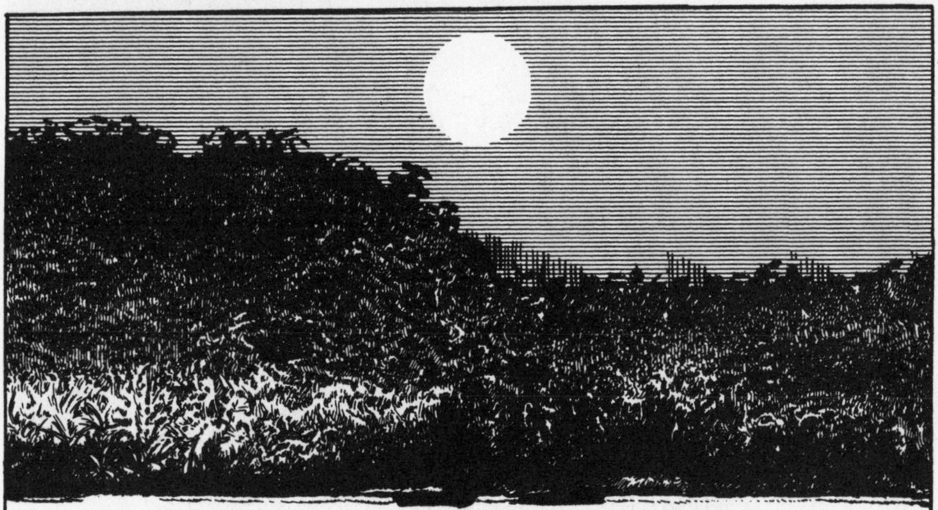
ALONG WITH HIS FAMILY AND SEVERAL OFFICERS, MACARTHUR FLEES TO MINDANAO* BY PT BOAT.* THERE THEY MEET UP WITH FILIPINO PRESIDENT MANUEL L. QUEZON.

*MINDANAO: SECOND LARGEST ISLAND OF THE PHILIPPINES, LOCATED IN THE SOUTH.

*PATROL TORPEDO BOAT: A FAST ATTACK VESSEL ARMED WITH TORPEDOS WHICH WAS COMMONLY USED BY THE U.S. NAVY DURING WWII.

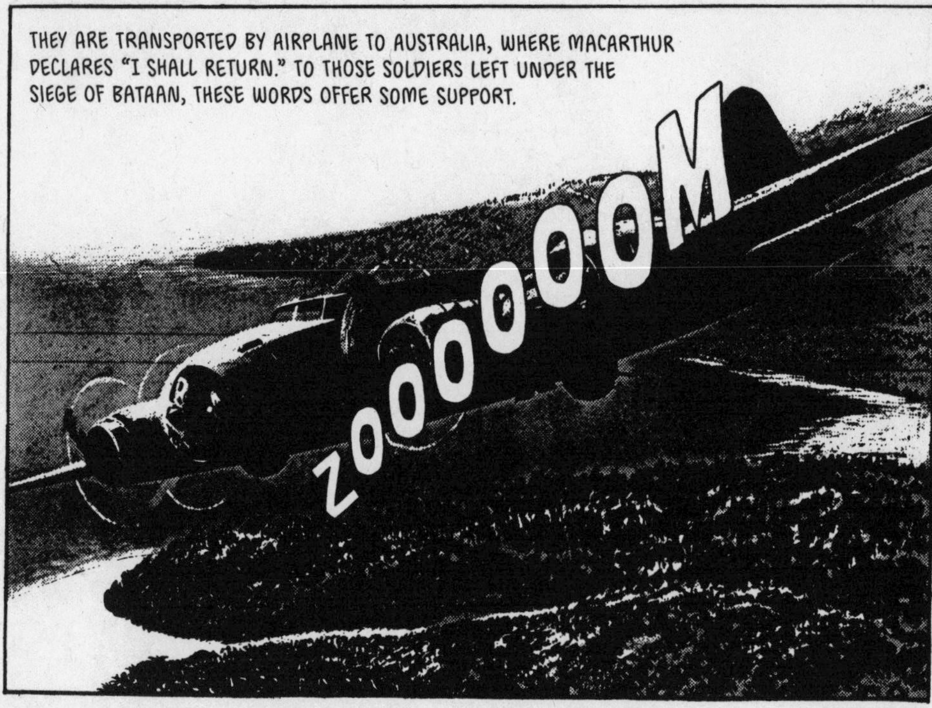
THEY ARE TRANSPORTED BY AIRPLANE TO AUSTRALIA, WHERE MACARTHUR DECLARES "I SHALL RETURN." TO THOSE SOLDIERS LEFT UNDER THE SIEGE OF BATAAN, THESE WORDS OFFER SOME SUPPORT.
ZOOOOOOOM

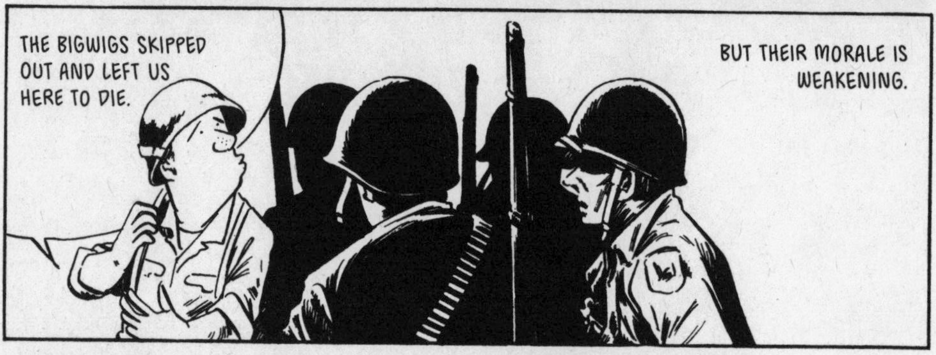
BUT THEIR MORALE IS WEAKENING.
THE BIGWIGS SKIPPED OUT AND LEFT US HERE TO DIE.

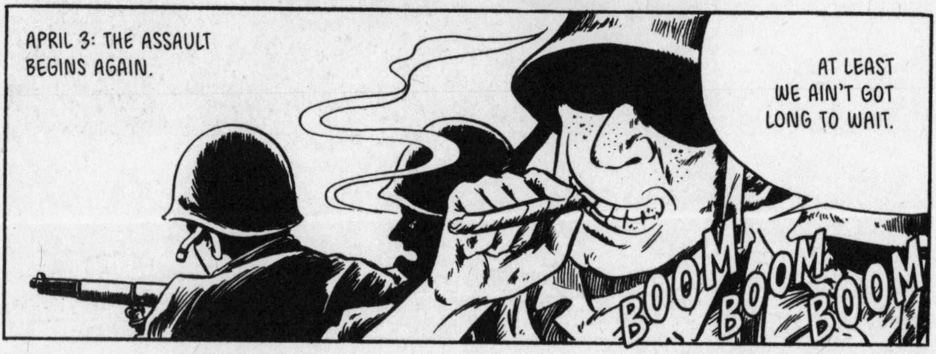
AT LEAST WE AIN'T GOT LONG TO WAIT.
APRIL 3: THE ASSAULT BEGINS AGAIN.
BOOM BOOM BOOM

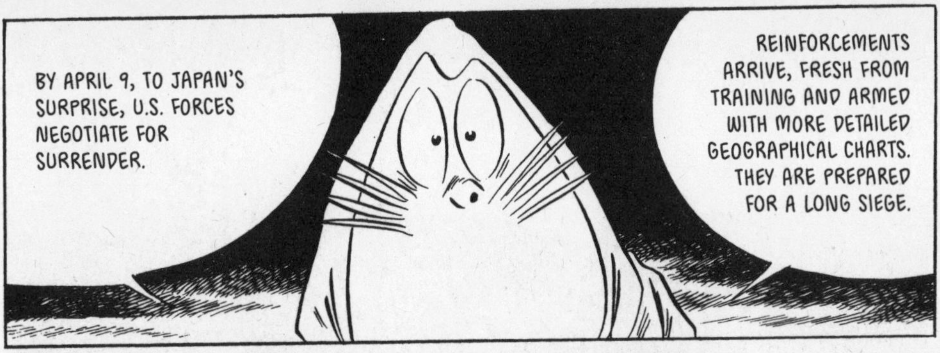
REINFORCEMENTS ARRIVE, FRESH FROM TRAINING AND ARMED WITH MORE DETAILED GEOGRAPHICAL CHARTS. THEY ARE PREPARED FOR A LONG SIEGE.
BY APRIL 9, TO JAPAN'S SURPRISE, U.S. FORCES NEGOTIATE FOR SURRENDER.

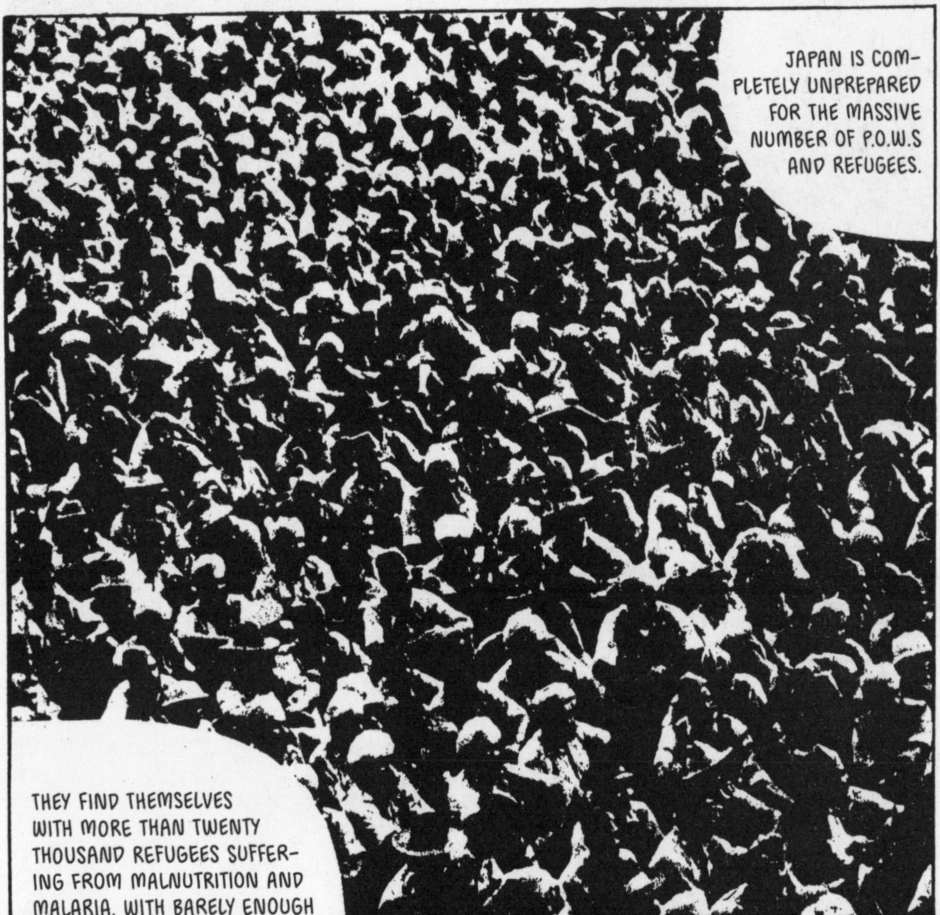
JAPAN IS COMPLETELY UNPREPARED FOR THE MASSIVE NUMBER OF P.O.W.S AND REFUGEES.
THEY FIND THEMSELVES WITH MORE THAN TWENTY THOUSAND REFUGEES SUFFERING FROM MALNUTRITION AND MALARIA. WITH BARELY ENOUGH SUPPLIES FOR THE JAPANESE, FAMINE IS RAMPANT. JAPAN MAKES PLANS TO MOVE THEIR PRISONERS.

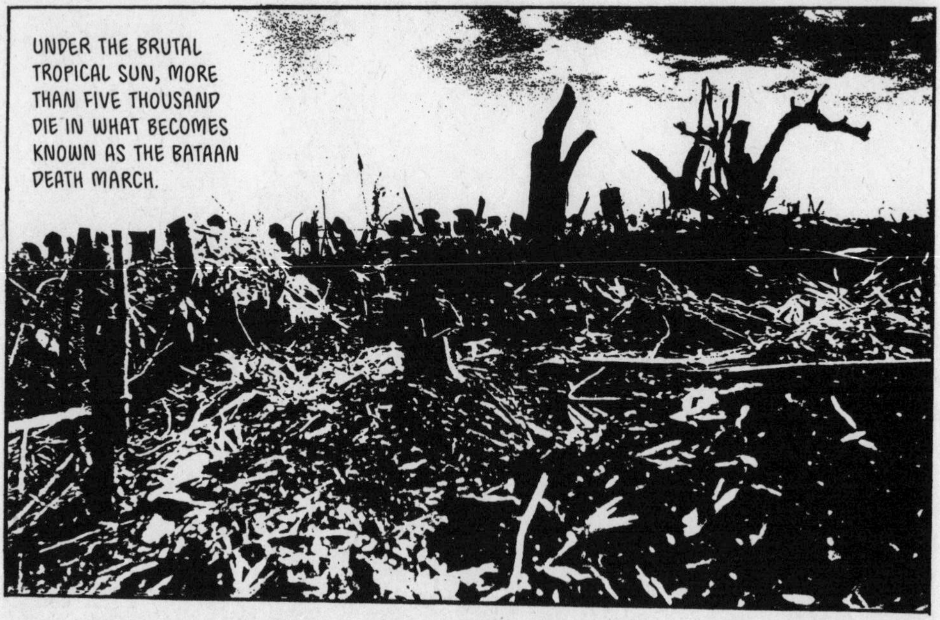
UNDER THE BRUTAL TROPICAL SUN, MORE THAN FIVE THOUSAND DIE IN WHAT BECOMES KNOWN AS THE BATAAN DEATH MARCH.

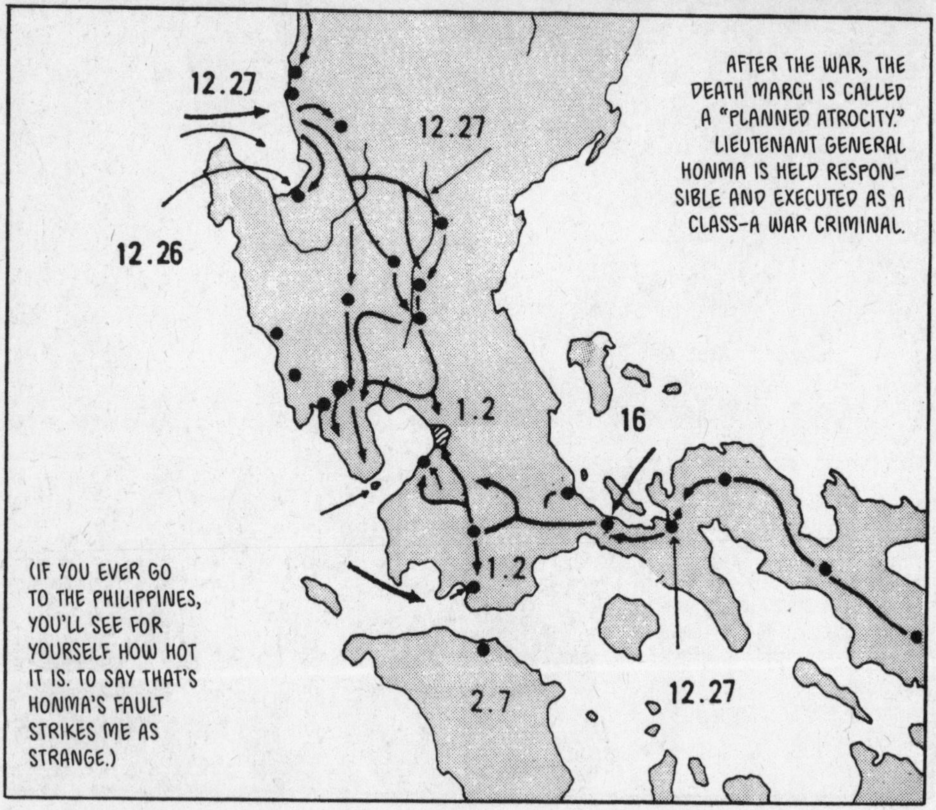
AFTER THE WAR, THE DEATH MARCH IS CALLED A "PLANNED ATROCITY." LIEUTENANT GENERAL HONMA IS HELD RESPONSIBLE AND EXECUTED AS A CLASS-A WAR CRIMINAL.
12.27
12.27
12.26
1.2
16
1.2
2.7
12.27
(IF YOU EVER GO TO THE PHILIPPINES, YOU'LL SEE FOR YOURSELF HOW HOT IT IS. TO SAY THAT'S HONMA'S FAULT STRIKES ME AS STRANGE.)

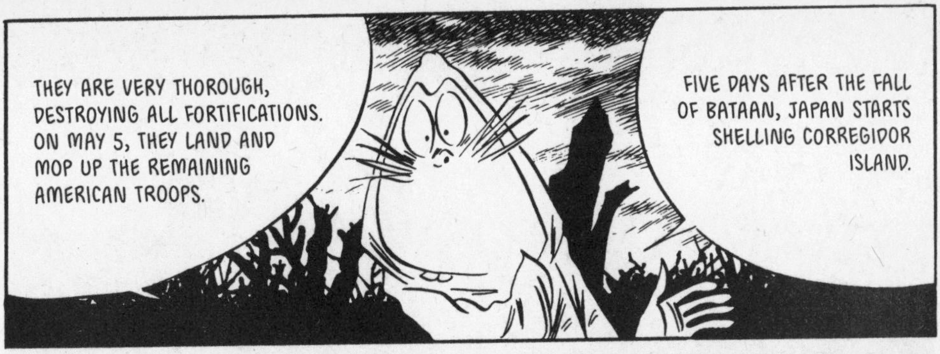
FIVE DAYS AFTER THE FALL OF BATAAN, JAPAN STARTS SHELLING CORREGIDOR ISLAND.
THEY ARE VERY THOROUGH, DESTROYING ALL FORTIFICATIONS. ON MAY 5, THEY LAND AND MOP UP THE REMAINING AMERICAN TROOPS.

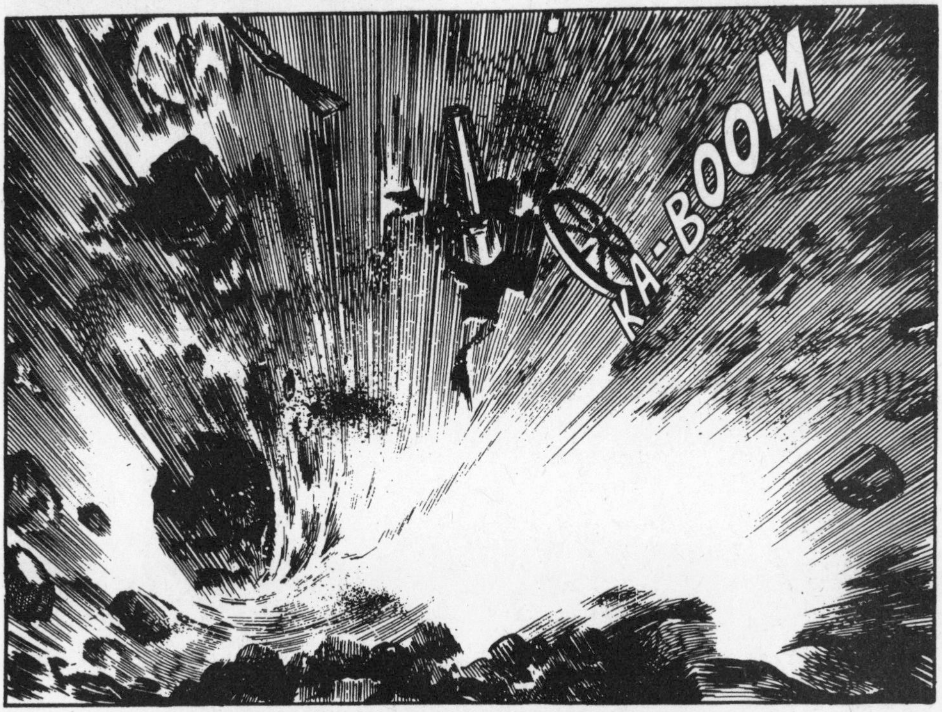
KA-BOOM

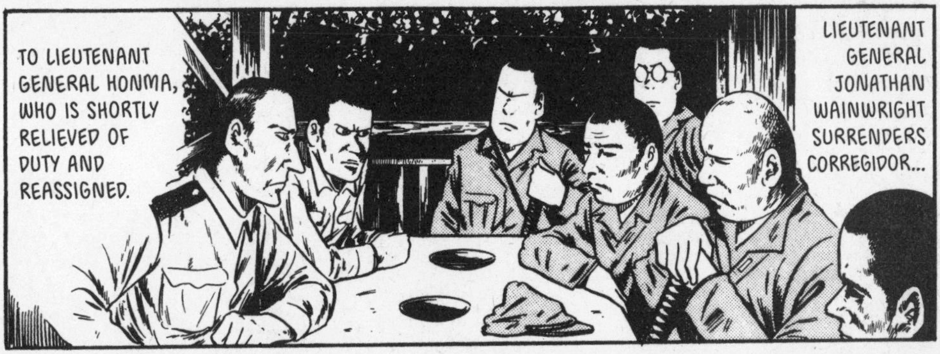
LIEUTENANT GENERAL JONATHAN WAINWRIGHT SURRENDERS CORREGIDOR...
TO LIEUTENANT GENERAL HONMA, WHO IS SHORTLY RELIEVED OF DUTY AND REASSIGNED.

THE CAPTURE OF GUAM AND WAKE ISLAND

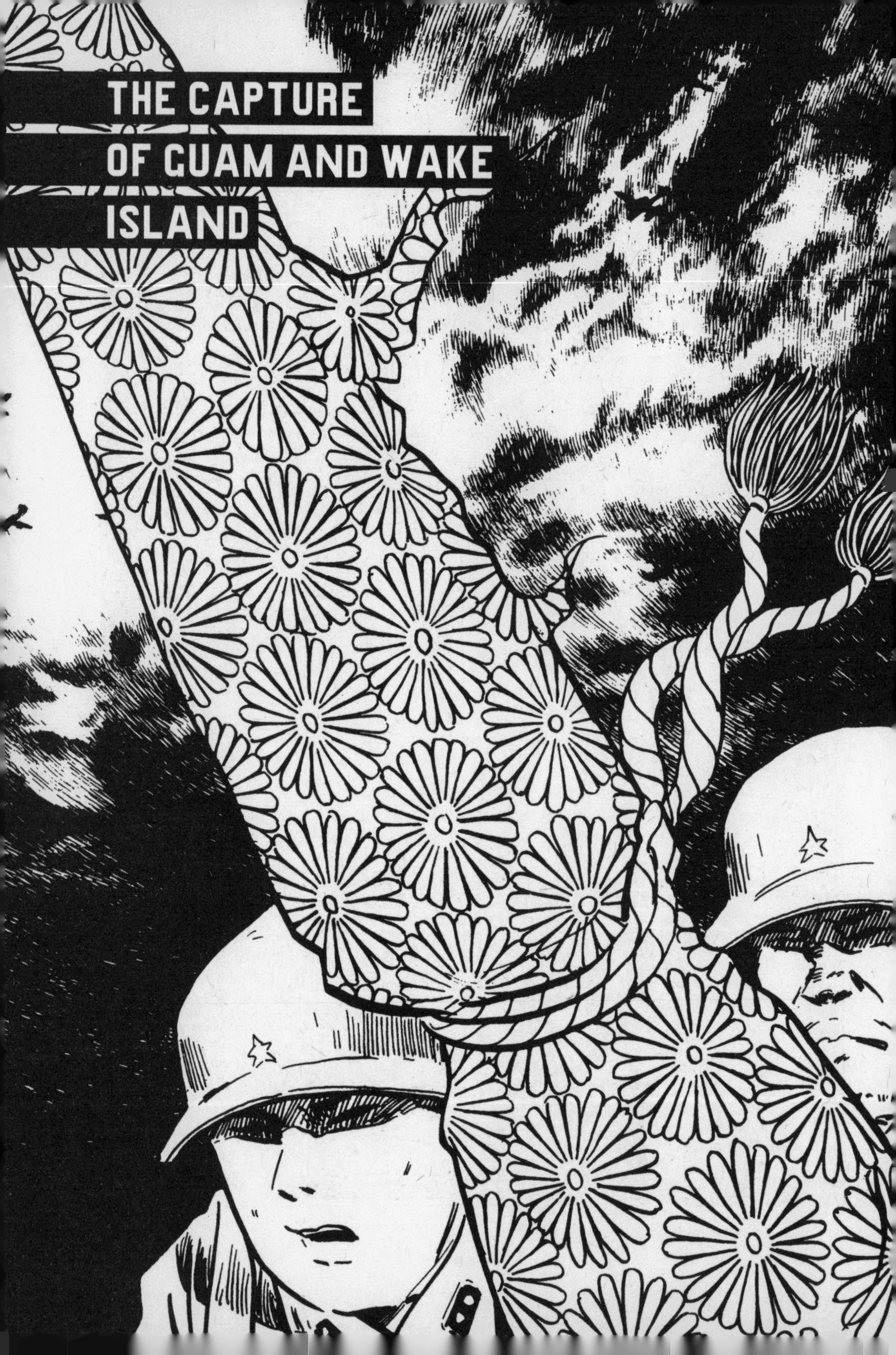

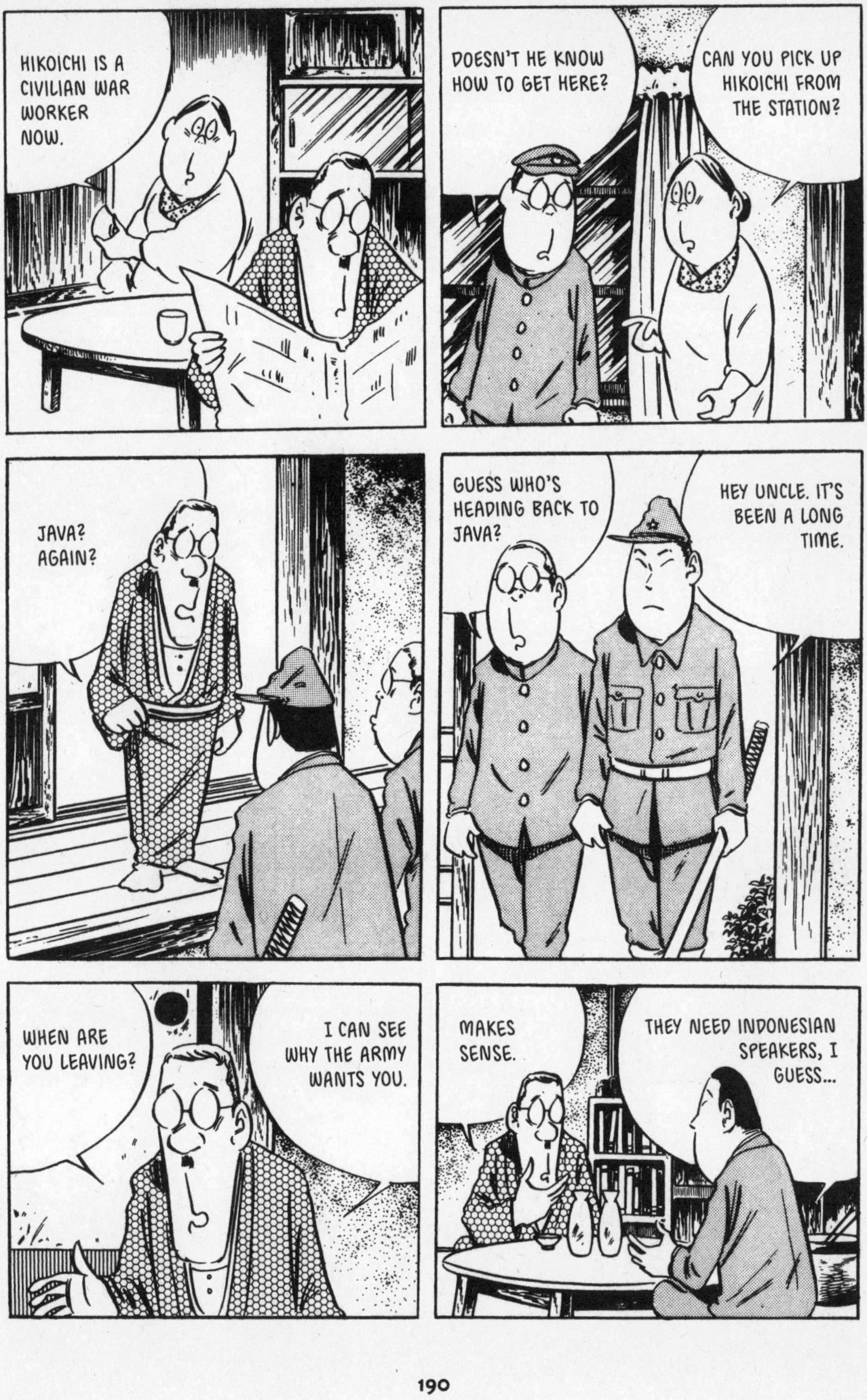
CAN YOU PICK UP HIKOICHI FROM THE STATION?
DOESN'T HE KNOW HOW TO GET HERE?
HIKOICHI IS A CIVILIAN WAR WORKER NOW.
HEY UNCLE. IT'S BEEN A LONG TIME.
GUESS WHO'S HEADING BACK TO JAVA?
JAVA? AGAIN?
THEY NEED INDONESIAN SPEAKERS, I GUESS...
MAKES SENSE.
I CAN SEE WHY THE ARMY WANTS YOU.
WHEN ARE YOU LEAVING?

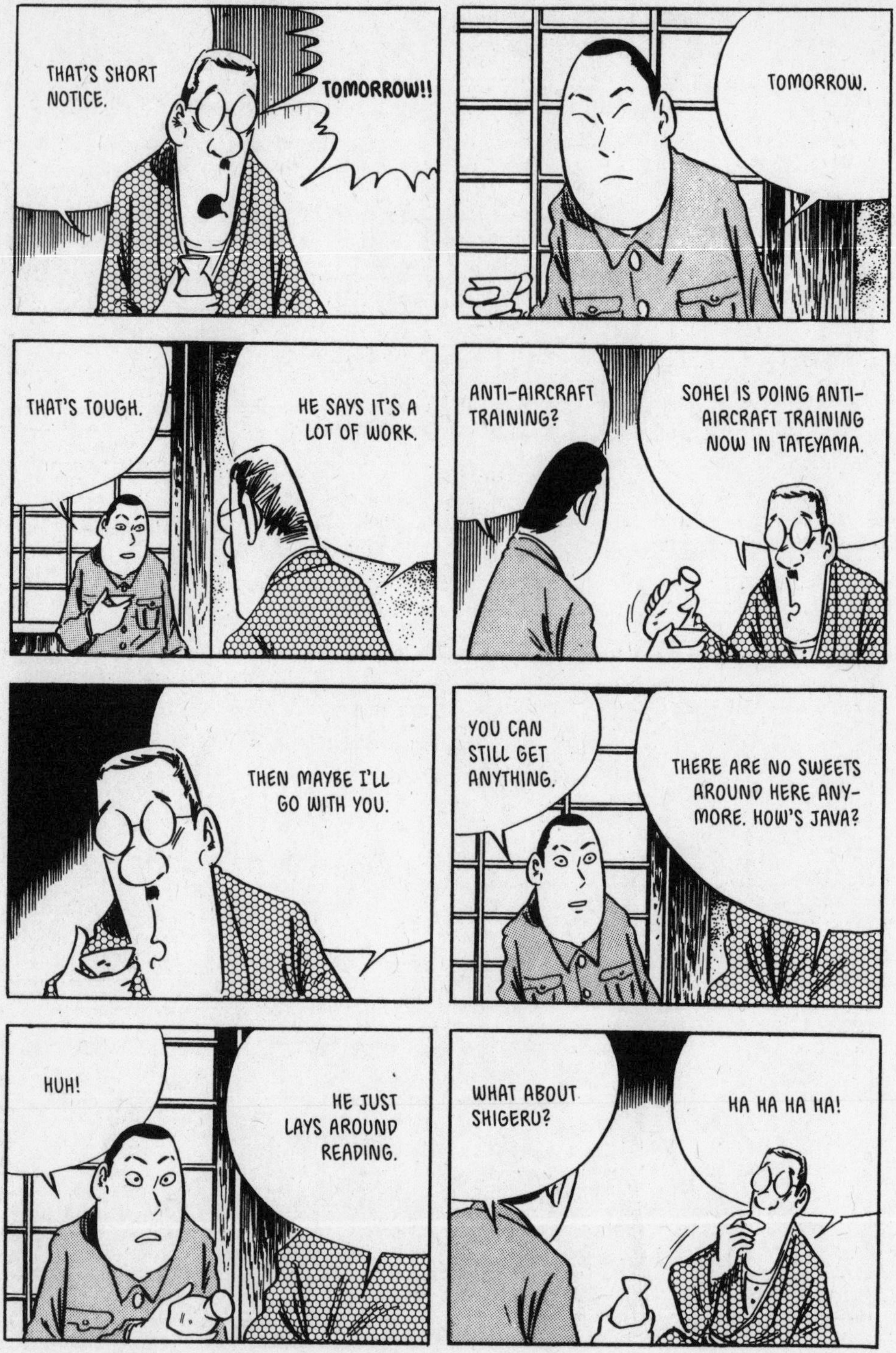
TOMORROW.
TOMORROW!!
THAT'S SHORT NOTICE.
SOHEI IS DOING ANTI-AIRCRAFT TRAINING NOW IN TATEYAMA.
ANTI-AIRCRAFT TRAINING?
HE SAYS IT'S A LOT OF WORK.
THAT'S TOUGH.
THERE ARE NO SWEETS AROUND HERE ANY-MORE. HOW'S JAVA?
YOU CAN STILL GET ANYTHING.
THEN MAYBE I'LL GO WITH YOU.
HA HA HA HA!
WHAT ABOUT SHIGERU?
HE JUST LAYS AROUND READING.
HUH!

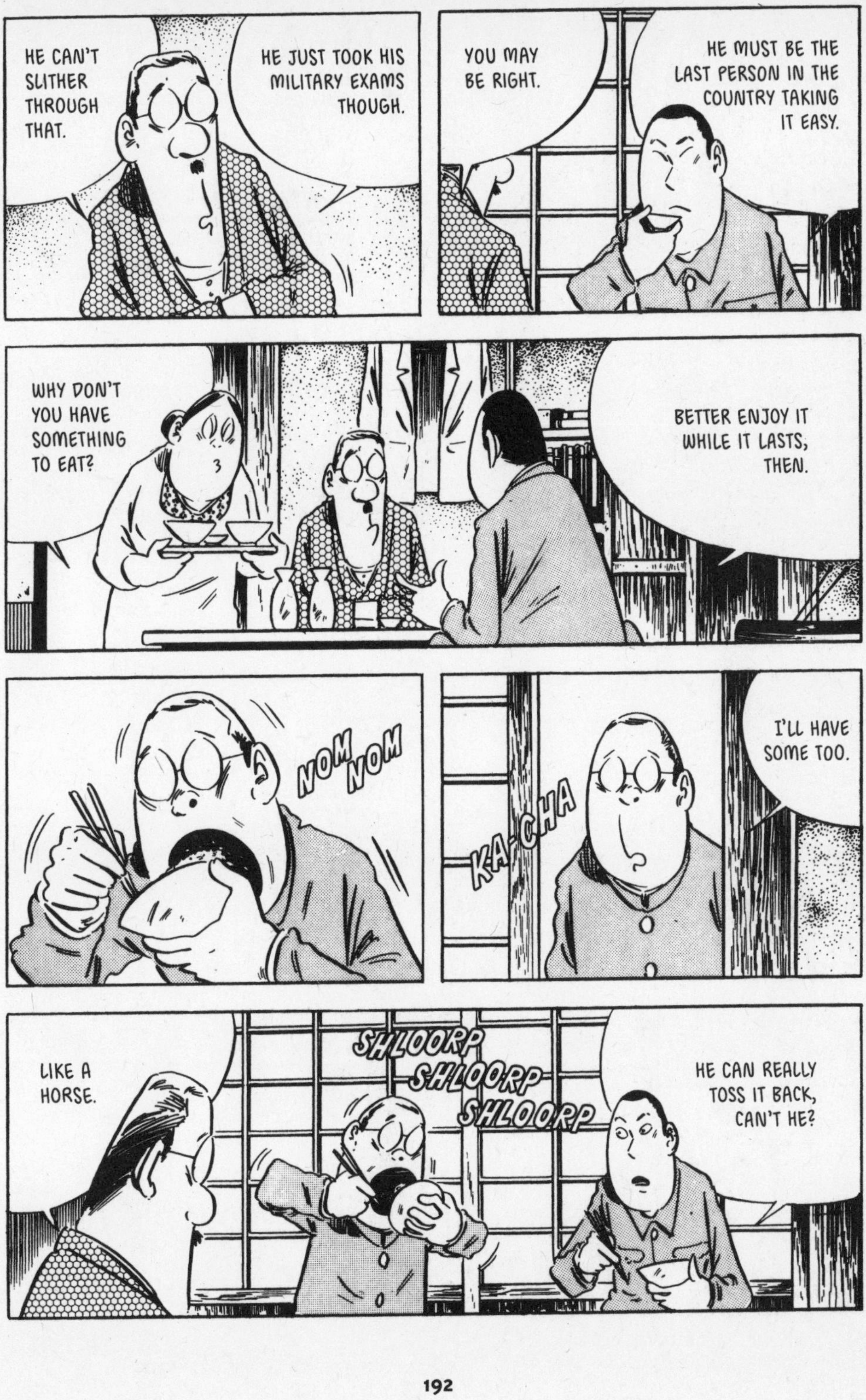
HE MUST BE THE LAST PERSON IN THE COUNTRY TAKING IT EASY.
YOU MAY BE RIGHT.
HE JUST TOOK HIS MILITARY EXAMS THOUGH.
HE CAN'T SLITHER THROUGH THAT.
BETTER ENJOY IT WHILE IT LASTS, THEN.
WHY DON'T YOU HAVE SOMETHING TO EAT?
I'LL HAVE SOME TOO.
KA-CHA
NOM NOM
HE CAN REALLY TOSS IT BACK, CAN'T HE?
SHLOORP SHLOORP SHLOORP
LIKE A HORSE.

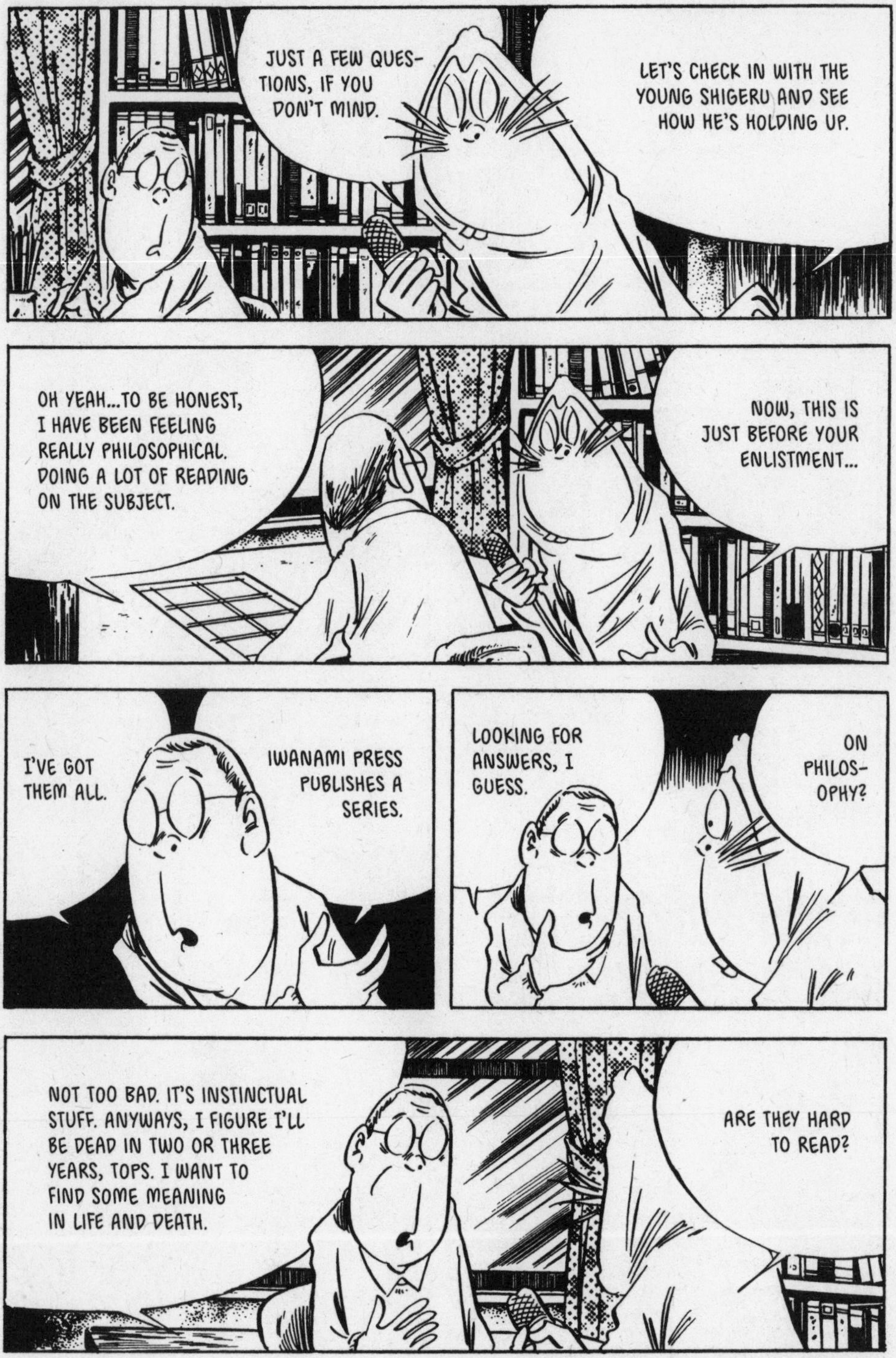
LET'S CHECK IN WITH THE YOUNG SHIGERU AND SEE HOW HE'S HOLDING UP.
JUST A FEW QUESTIONS, IF YOU DON'T MIND.
NOW, THIS IS JUST BEFORE YOUR ENLISTMENT...
OH YEAH...TO BE HONEST, I HAVE BEEN FEELING REALLY PHILOSOPHICAL. DOING A LOT OF READING ON THE SUBJECT.
ON PHILOSOPHY?
LOOKING FOR ANSWERS, I GUESS.
IWANAMI PRESS PUBLISHES A SERIES.
I'VE GOT THEM ALL.
ARE THEY HARD TO READ?
NOT TOO BAD. IT'S INSTINCTUAL STUFF. ANYWAYS, I FIGURE I'LL BE DEAD IN TWO OR THREE YEARS, TOPS. I WANT TO FIND SOME MEANING IN LIFE AND DEATH.

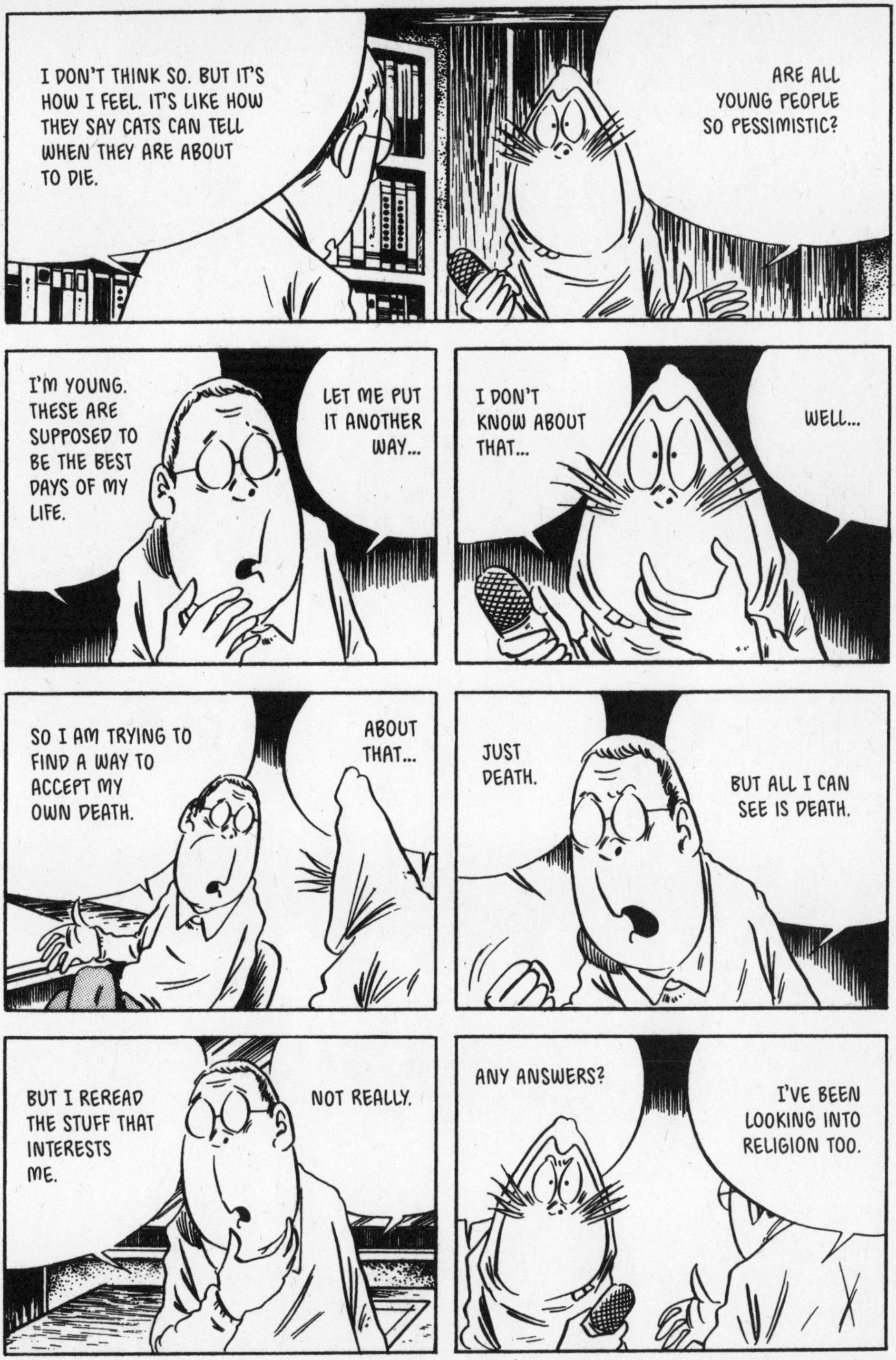
ARE ALL YOUNG PEOPLE SO PESSIMISTIC?
I DON'T THINK SO. BUT IT'S HOW I FEEL. IT'S LIKE HOW THEY SAY CATS CAN TELL WHEN THEY ARE ABOUT TO DIE.
WELL...
I DON'T KNOW ABOUT THAT...
LET ME PUT IT ANOTHER WAY...
I'M YOUNG. THESE ARE SUPPOSED TO BE THE BEST DAYS OF MY LIFE.
BUT ALL I CAN SEE IS DEATH.
JUST DEATH.
ABOUT THAT...
SO I AM TRYING TO FIND A WAY TO ACCEPT MY OWN DEATH.
I'VE BEEN LOOKING INTO RELIGION TOO.
ANY ANSWERS?
NOT REALLY.
BUT I REREAD THE STUFF THAT INTERESTS ME.

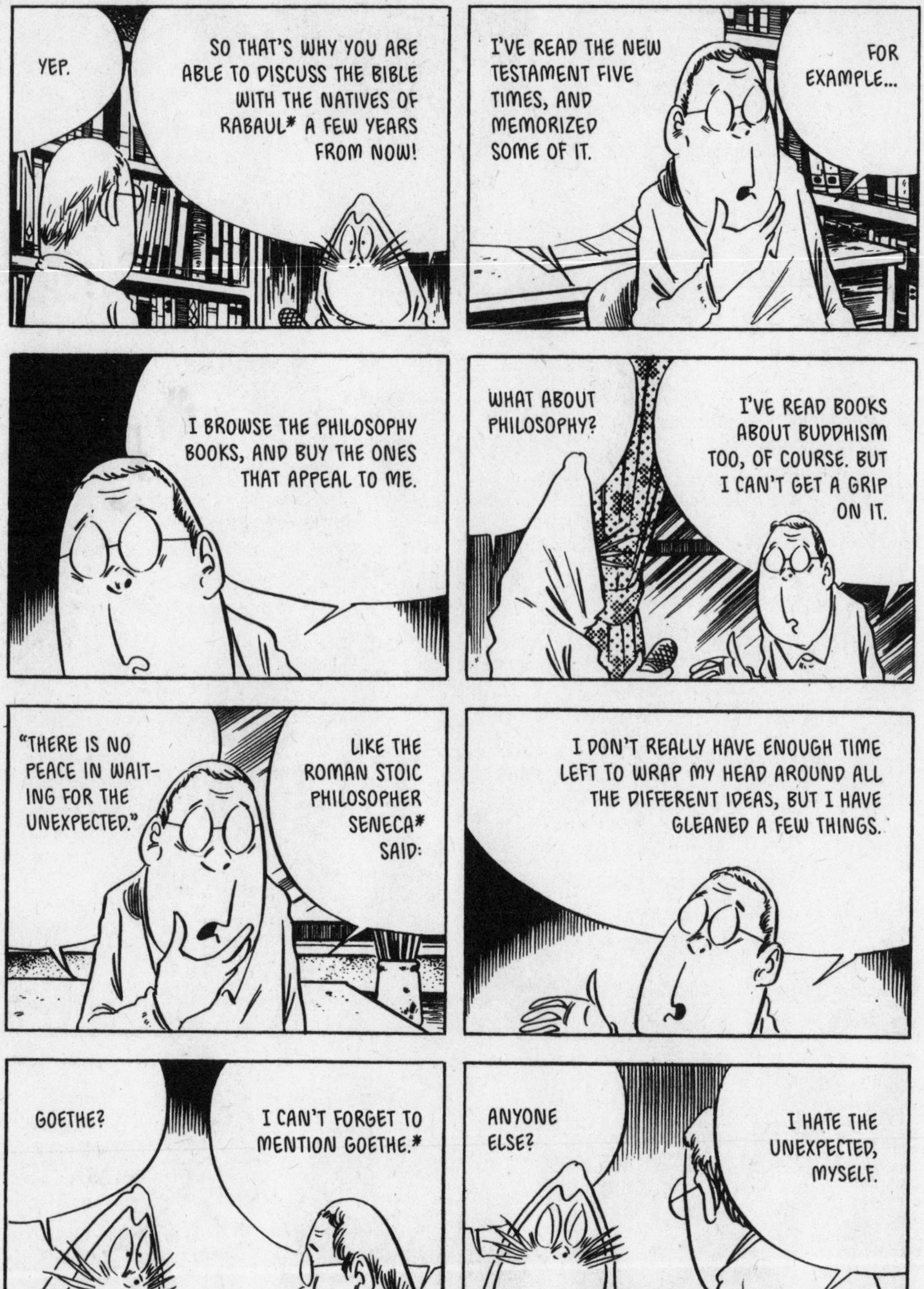
FOR EXAMPLE...
I'VE READ THE NEW TESTAMENT FIVE TIMES, AND MEMORIZED SOME OF IT.
SO THAT'S WHY YOU ARE ABLE TO DISCUSS THE BIBLE WITH THE NATIVES OF RABAUL* A FEW YEARS FROM NOW!
YEP.
I'VE READ BOOKS ABOUT BUDDHISM TOO, OF COURSE. BUT I CAN'T GET A GRIP ON IT.
WHAT ABOUT PHILOSOPHY?
I BROWSE THE PHILOSOPHY BOOKS, AND BUY THE ONES THAT APPEAL TO ME.
I DON'T REALLY HAVE ENOUGH TIME LEFT TO WRAP MY HEAD AROUND ALL THE DIFFERENT IDEAS, BUT I HAVE GLEANED A FEW THINGS.
LIKE THE ROMAN STOIC PHILOSOPHER SENECA* SAID:
"THERE IS NO PEACE IN WAIT-ING FOR THE UNEXPECTED."
I HATE THE UNEXPECTED, MYSELF.
ANYONE ELSE?
I CAN'T FORGET TO MENTION GOETHE.*
GOETHE?

*SEE NOTES ON PAGES 545–546.

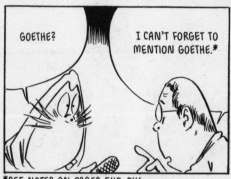

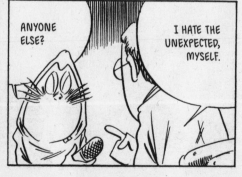

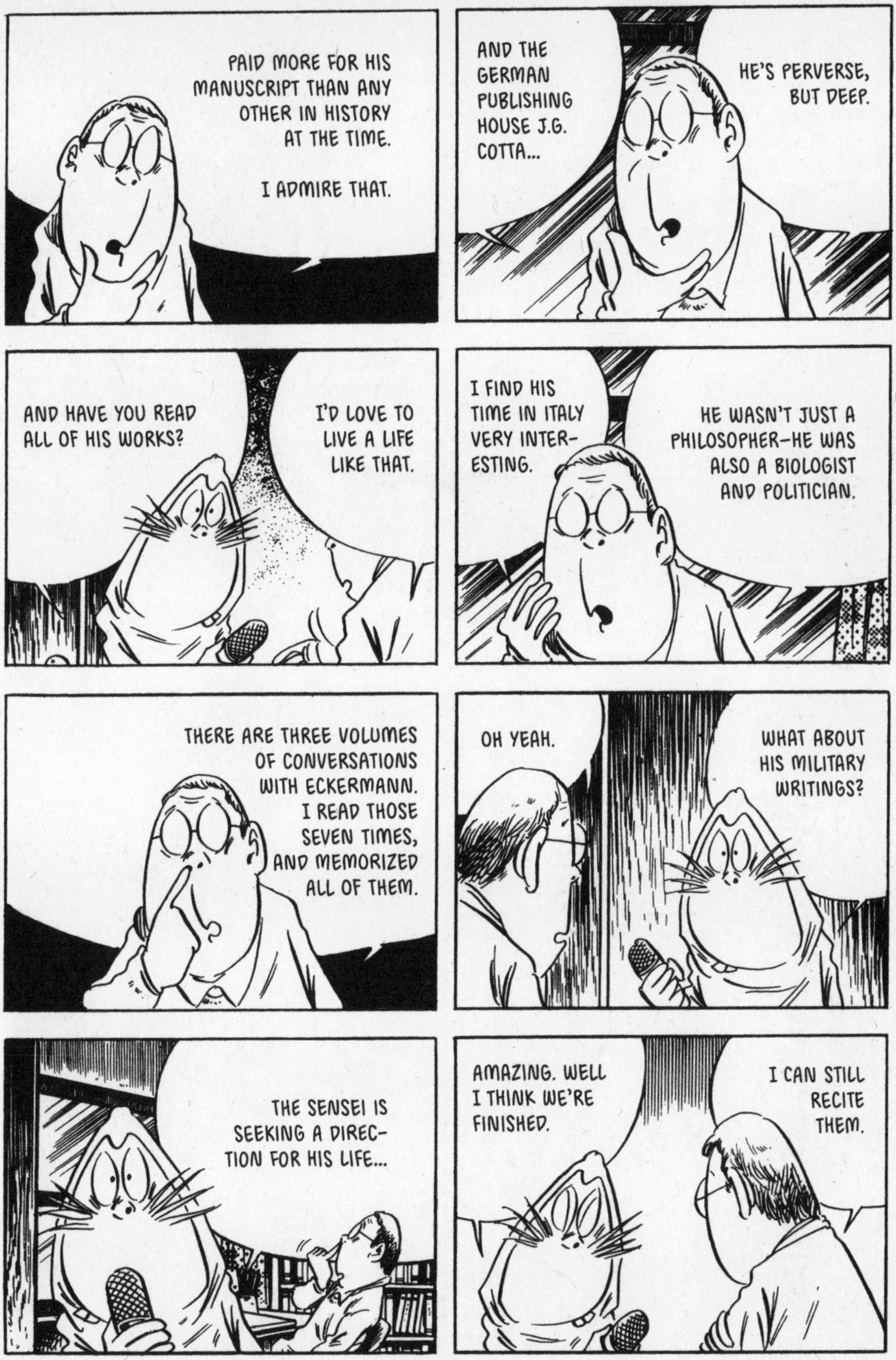
HE'S PERVERSE, BUT DEEP.
AND THE GERMAN PUBLISHING HOUSE J.G. COTTA...
PAID MORE FOR HIS MANUSCRIPT THAN ANY OTHER IN HISTORY AT THE TIME.
I ADMIRE THAT.
HE WASN'T JUST A PHILOSOPHER–HE WAS ALSO A BIOLOGIST AND POLITICIAN.
I FIND HIS TIME IN ITALY VERY INTER-ESTING.
I'D LOVE TO LIVE A LIFE LIKE THAT.
AND HAVE YOU READ ALL OF HIS WORKS?
WHAT ABOUT HIS MILITARY WRITINGS?
OH YEAH.
THERE ARE THREE VOLUMES OF CONVERSATIONS WITH ECKERMANN. I READ THOSE SEVEN TIMES, AND MEMORIZED ALL OF THEM.
I CAN STILL RECITE THEM.
AMAZING. WELL I THINK WE'RE FINISHED.
THE SENSEI IS SEEKING A DIREC-TION FOR HIS LIFE...

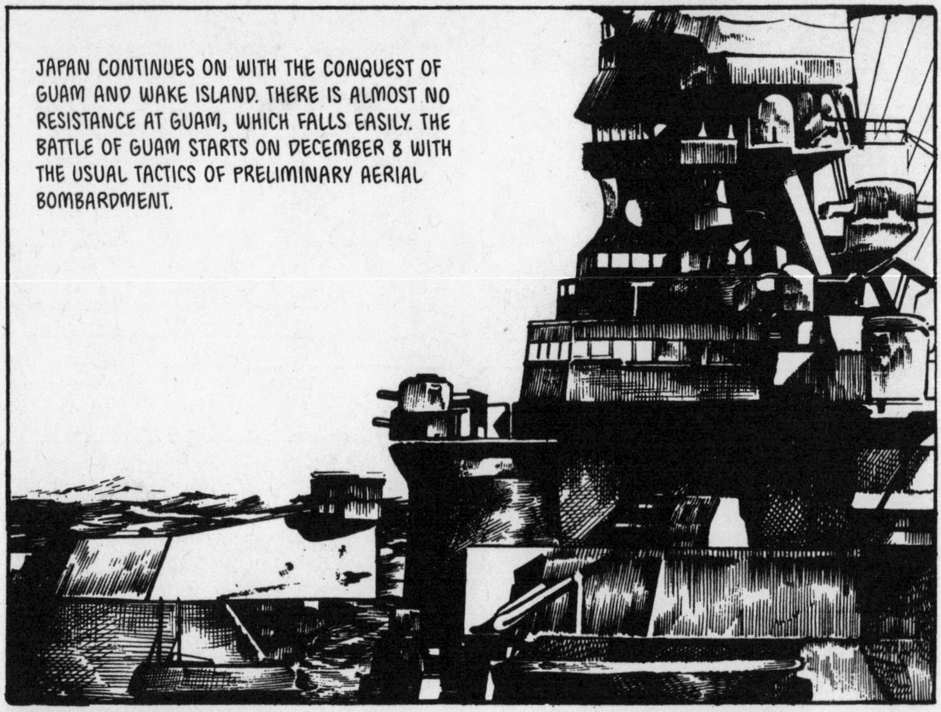
JAPAN CONTINUES ON WITH THE CONQUEST OF GUAM AND WAKE ISLAND. THERE IS ALMOST NO RESISTANCE AT GUAM, WHICH FALLS EASILY. THE BATTLE OF GUAM STARTS ON DECEMBER 8 WITH THE USUAL TACTICS OF PRELIMINARY AERIAL BOMBARDMENT.

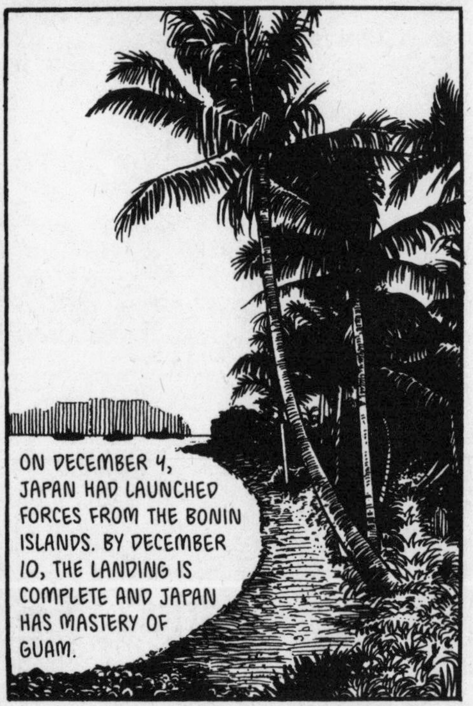
ON DECEMBER 4, JAPAN HAD LAUNCHED FORCES FROM THE BONIN ISLANDS. BY DECEMBER 10, THE LANDING IS COMPLETE AND JAPAN HAS MASTERY OF GUAM.

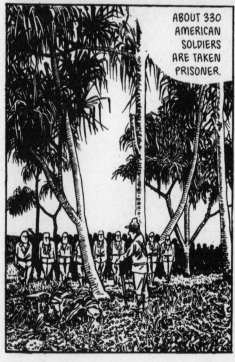

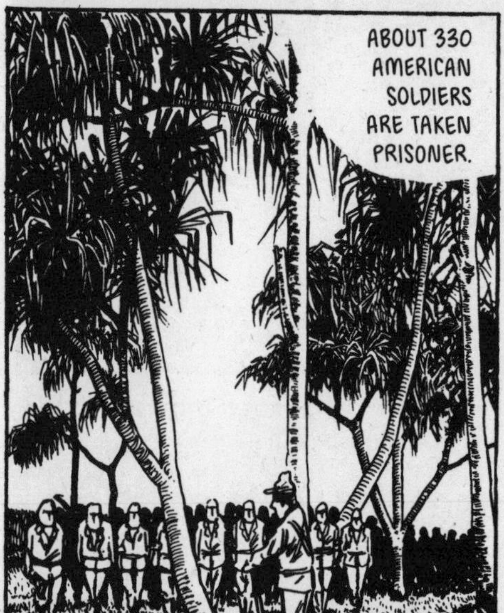
ABOUT 330 AMERICAN SOLDIERS ARE TAKEN PRISONER.

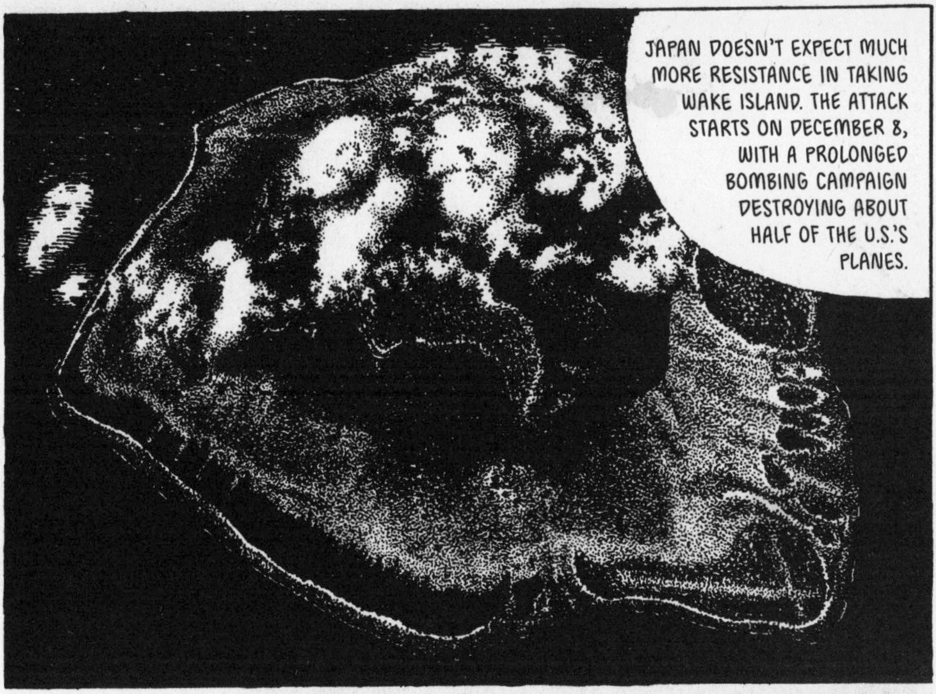
JAPAN DOESN'T EXPECT MUCH MORE RESISTANCE IN TAKING WAKE ISLAND. THE ATTACK STARTS ON DECEMBER 8, WITH A PROLONGED BOMBING CAMPAIGN DESTROYING ABOUT HALF OF THE U.S.'S PLANES.

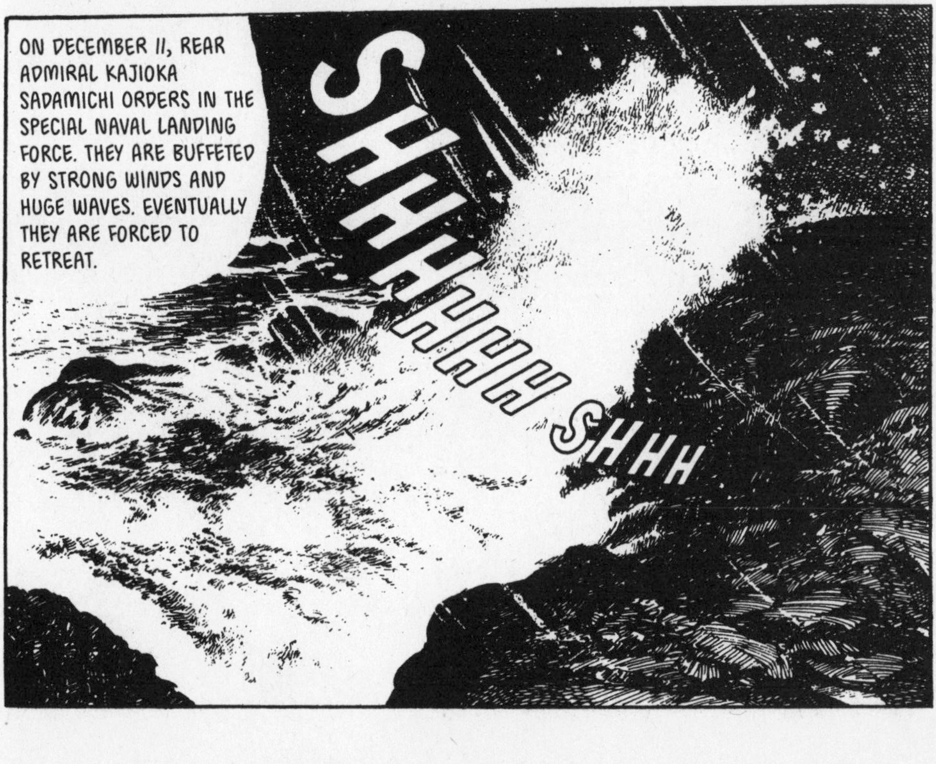
ON DECEMBER 11, REAR ADMIRAL KAJIOKA SADAMICHI ORDERS IN THE SPECIAL NAVAL LANDING FORCE. THEY ARE BUFFETED BY STRONG WINDS AND HUGE WAVES. EVENTUALLY THEY ARE FORCED TO RETREAT.
SHHHHHHHH
SHHH

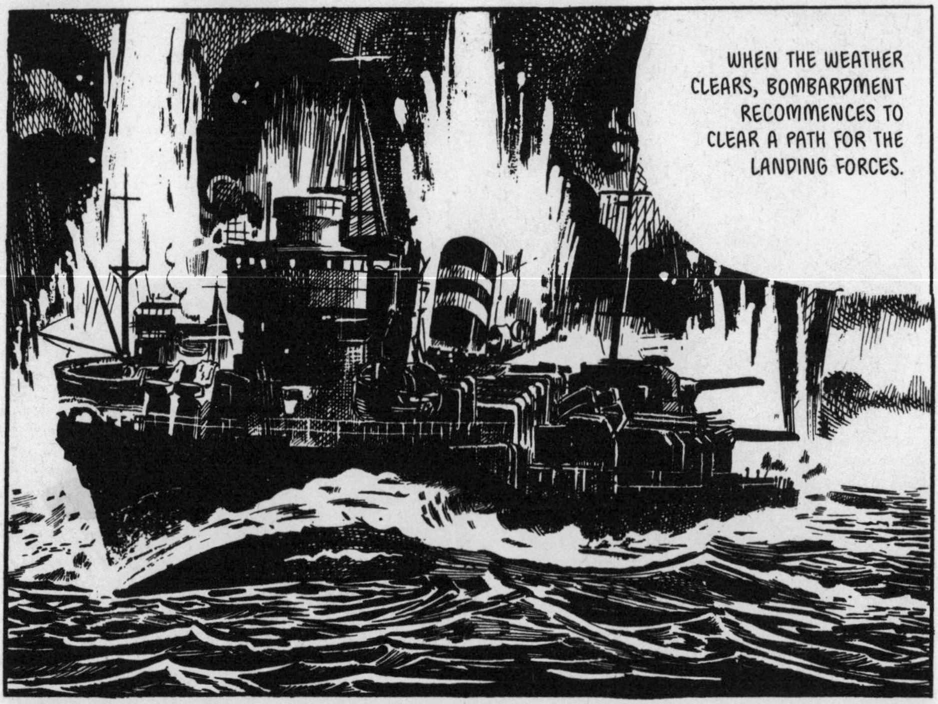
WHEN THE WEATHER CLEARS, BOMBARDMENT RECOMMENCES TO CLEAR A PATH FOR THE LANDING FORCES.

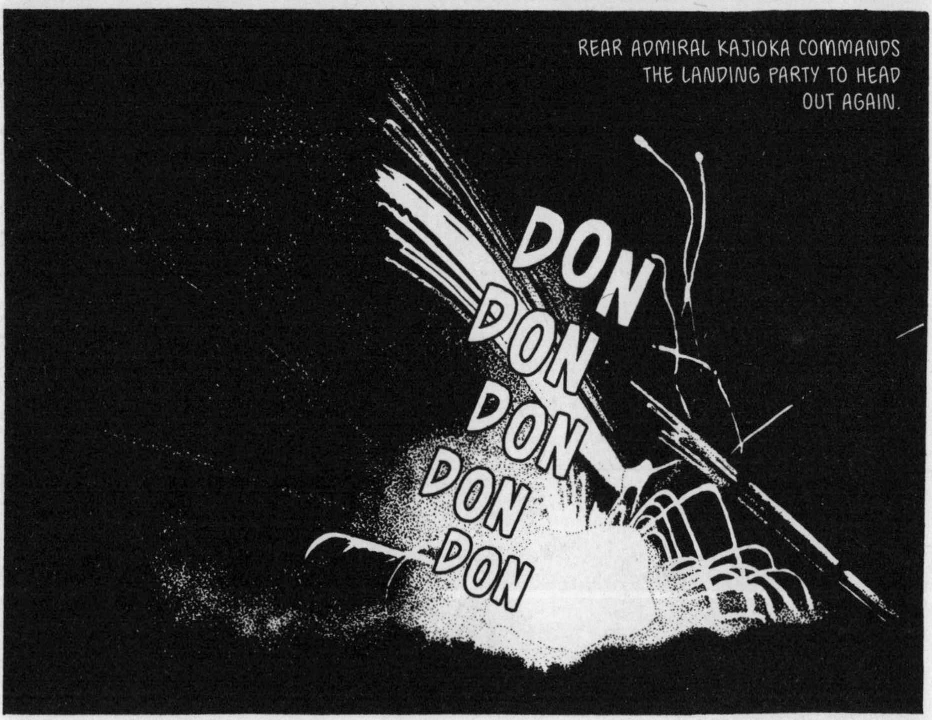
REAR ADMIRAL KAJIOKA COMMANDS THE LANDING PARTY TO HEAD OUT AGAIN.
DON DON DON DON DON DON

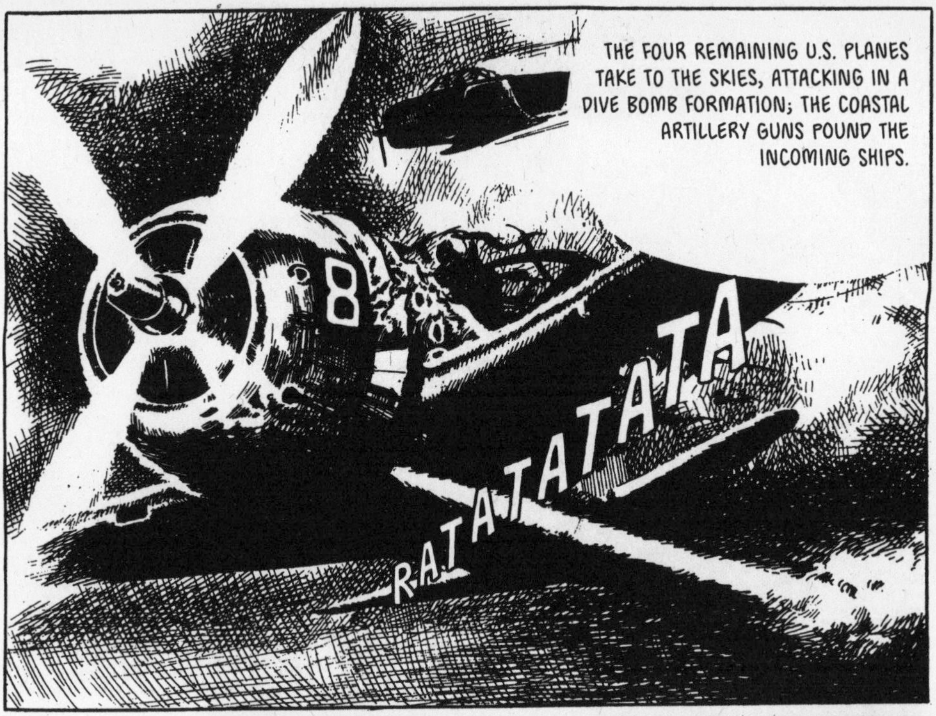
THE FOUR REMAINING U.S. PLANES TAKE TO THE SKIES, ATTACKING IN A DIVE BOMB FORMATION; THE COASTAL ARTILLERY GUNS POUND THE INCOMING SHIPS.
RATATATATA
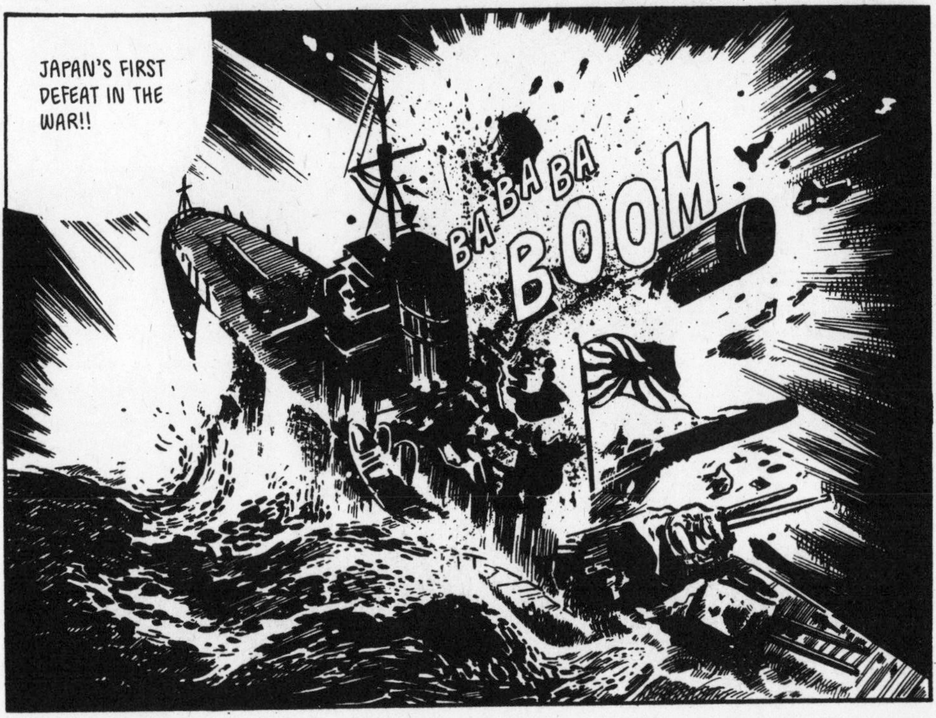
JAPAN'S FIRST DEFEAT IN THE WAR!!
BA BA BA BOOM

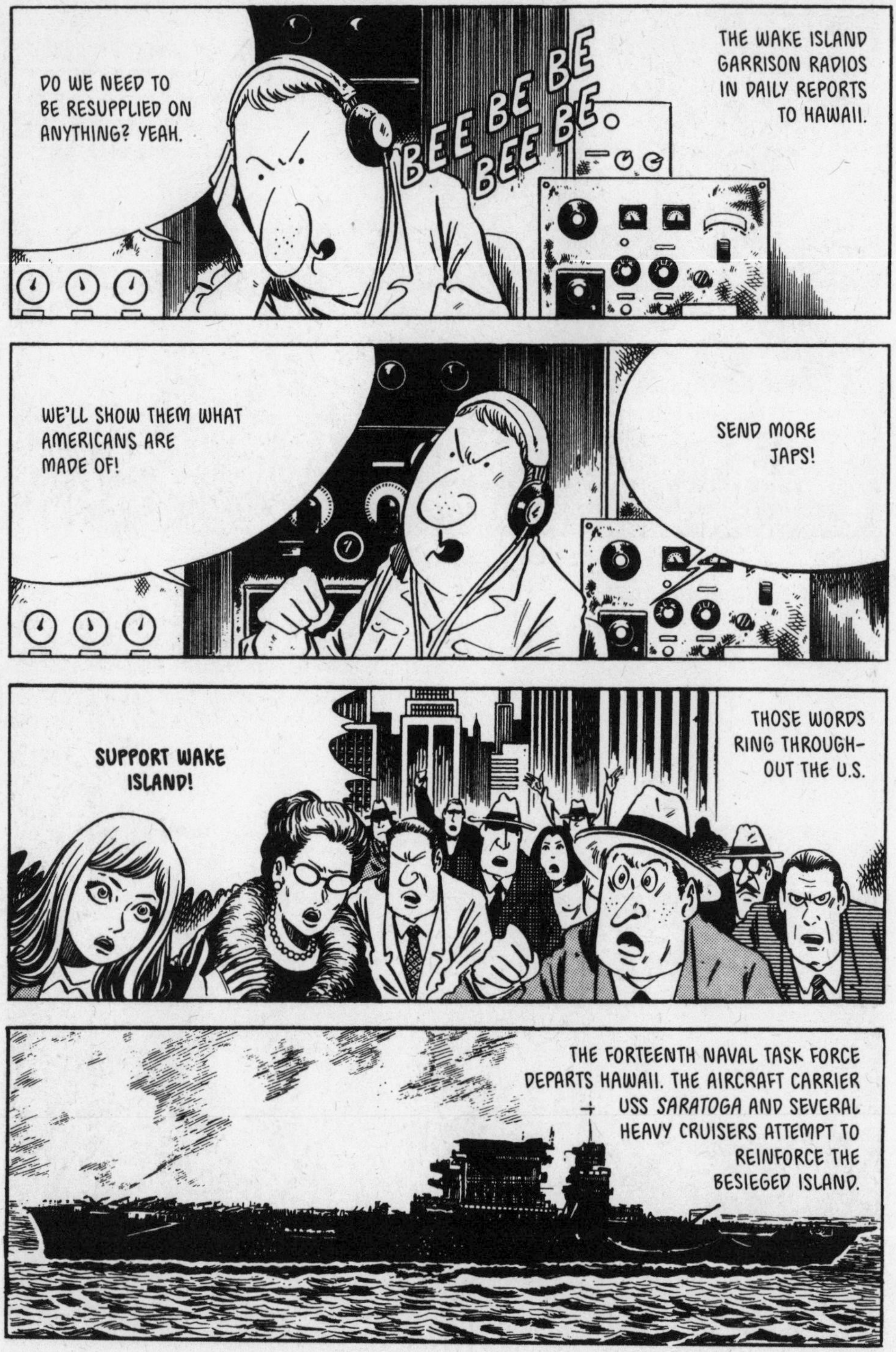
THE WAKE ISLAND GARRISON RADIOS IN DAILY REPORTS TO HAWAII.
BEE BE BE BEE BE
DO WE NEED TO BE RESUPPLIED ON ANYTHING? YEAH.
SEND MORE JAPS!
WE'LL SHOW THEM WHAT AMERICANS ARE MADE OF!
THOSE WORDS RING THROUGH-OUT THE U.S.
SUPPORT WAKE ISLAND!
THE FORTEENTH NAVAL TASK FORCE DEPARTS HAWAII. THE AIRCRAFT CARRIER USS *SARATOGA* AND SEVERAL HEAVY CRUISERS ATTEMPT TO REINFORCE THE BESIEGED ISLAND.

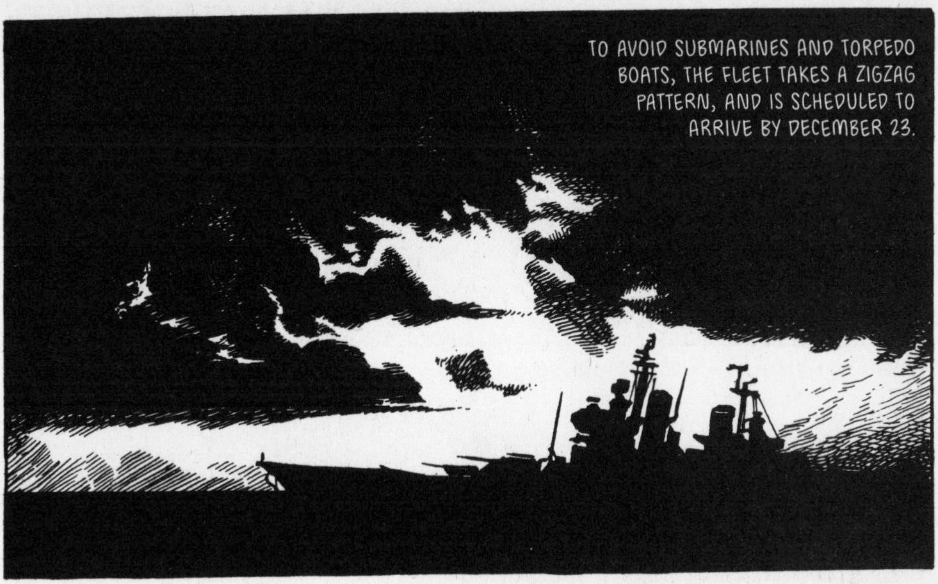
TO AVOID SUBMARINES AND TORPEDO BOATS, THE FLEET TAKES A ZIGZAG PATTERN, AND IS SCHEDULED TO ARRIVE BY DECEMBER 23.

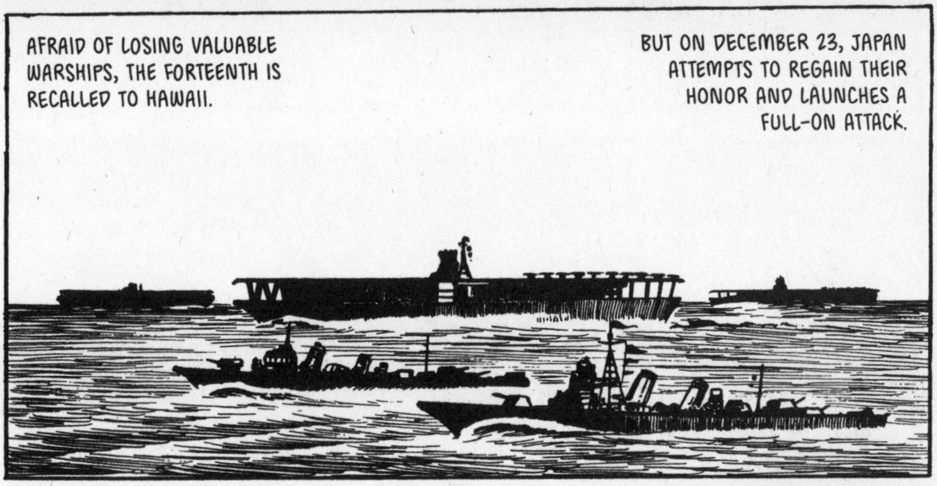
AFRAID OF LOSING VALUABLE WARSHIPS, THE FORTEENTH IS RECALLED TO HAWAII.
BUT ON DECEMBER 23, JAPAN ATTEMPTS TO REGAIN THEIR HONOR AND LAUNCHES A FULL-ON ATTACK.

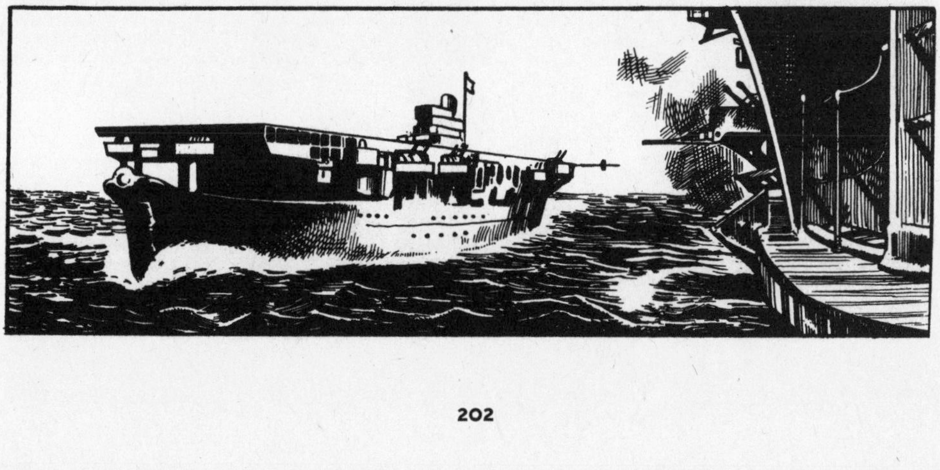

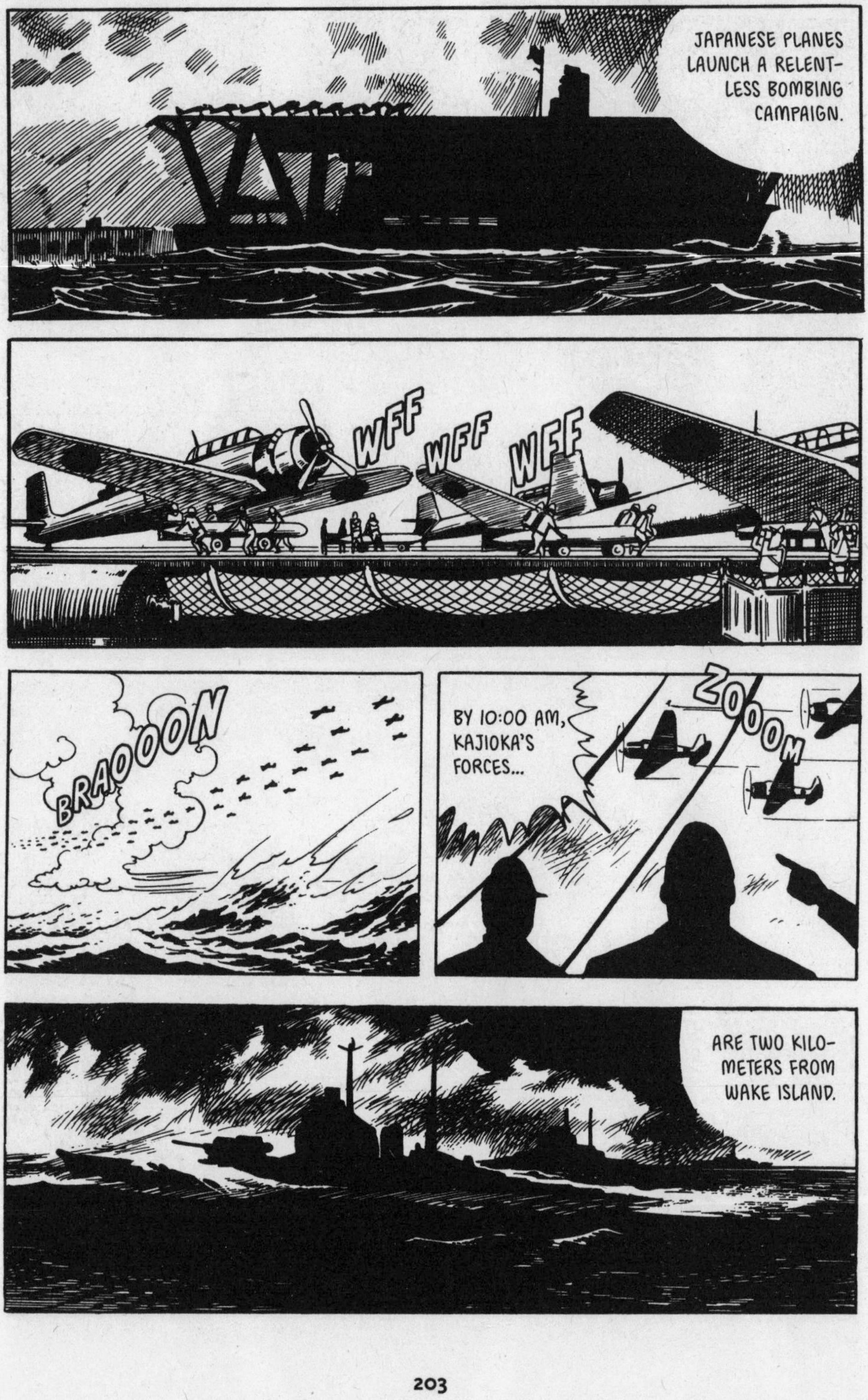
JAPANESE PLANES LAUNCH A RELENT-LESS BOMBING CAMPAIGN.
WFF
WFF
WFF
ZOOOM
BY 10:00 AM, KAJIOKA'S FORCES...
BRAOOON
ARE TWO KILO-METERS FROM WAKE ISLAND.

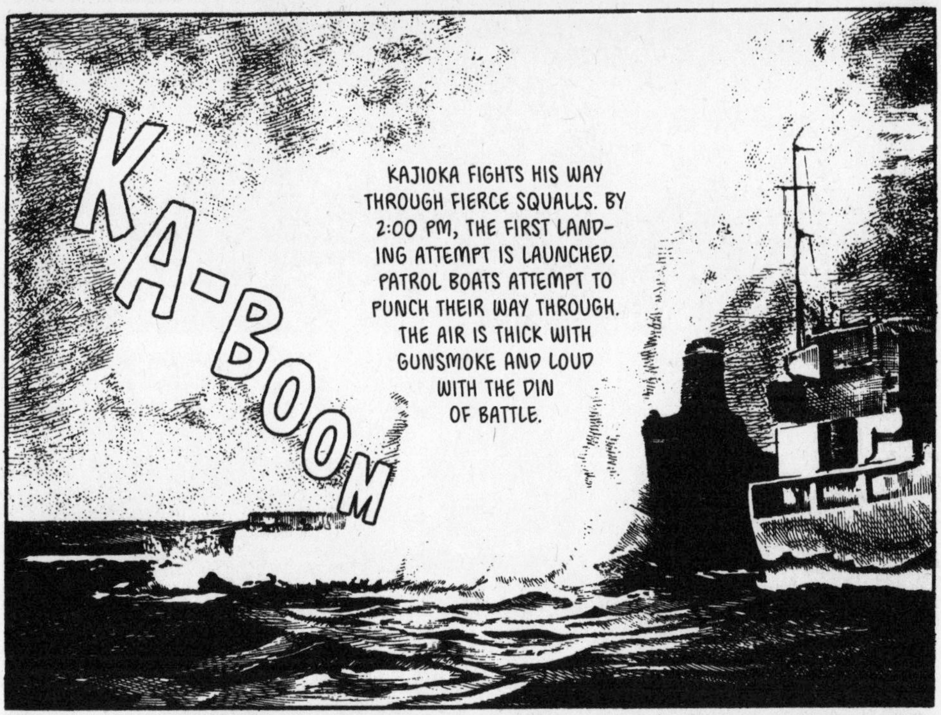
KAJIOKA FIGHTS HIS WAY THROUGH FIERCE SQUALLS. BY 2:00 PM, THE FIRST LANDING ATTEMPT IS LAUNCHED. PATROL BOATS ATTEMPT TO PUNCH THEIR WAY THROUGH. THE AIR IS THICK WITH GUNSMOKE AND LOUD WITH THE DIN OF BATTLE.
KA-BOOM

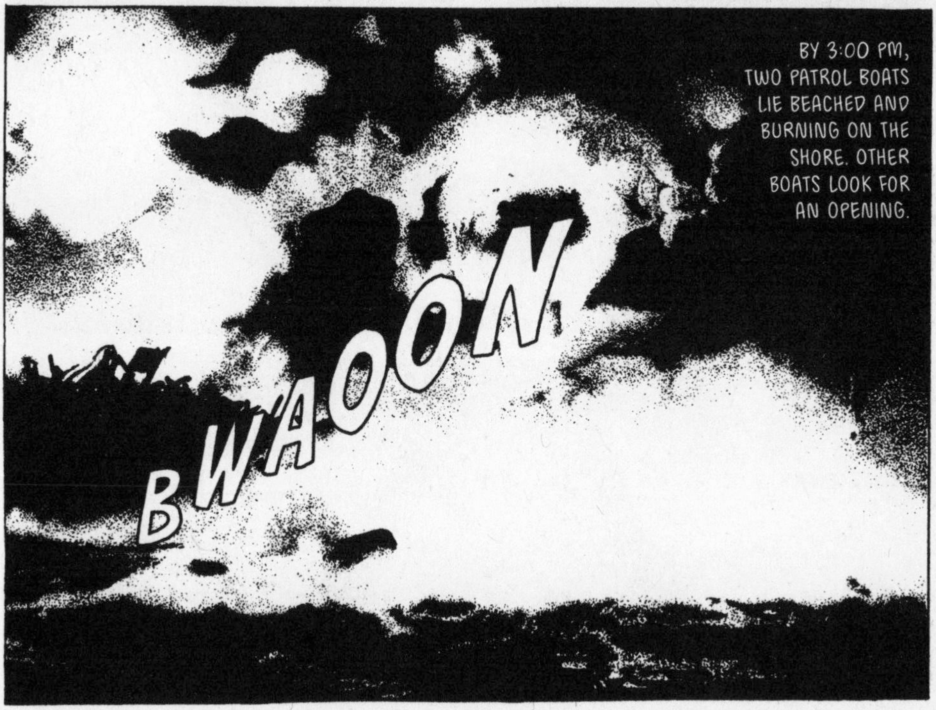
BY 3:00 PM, TWO PATROL BOATS LIE BEACHED AND BURNING ON THE SHORE. OTHER BOATS LOOK FOR AN OPENING.
BWAOON

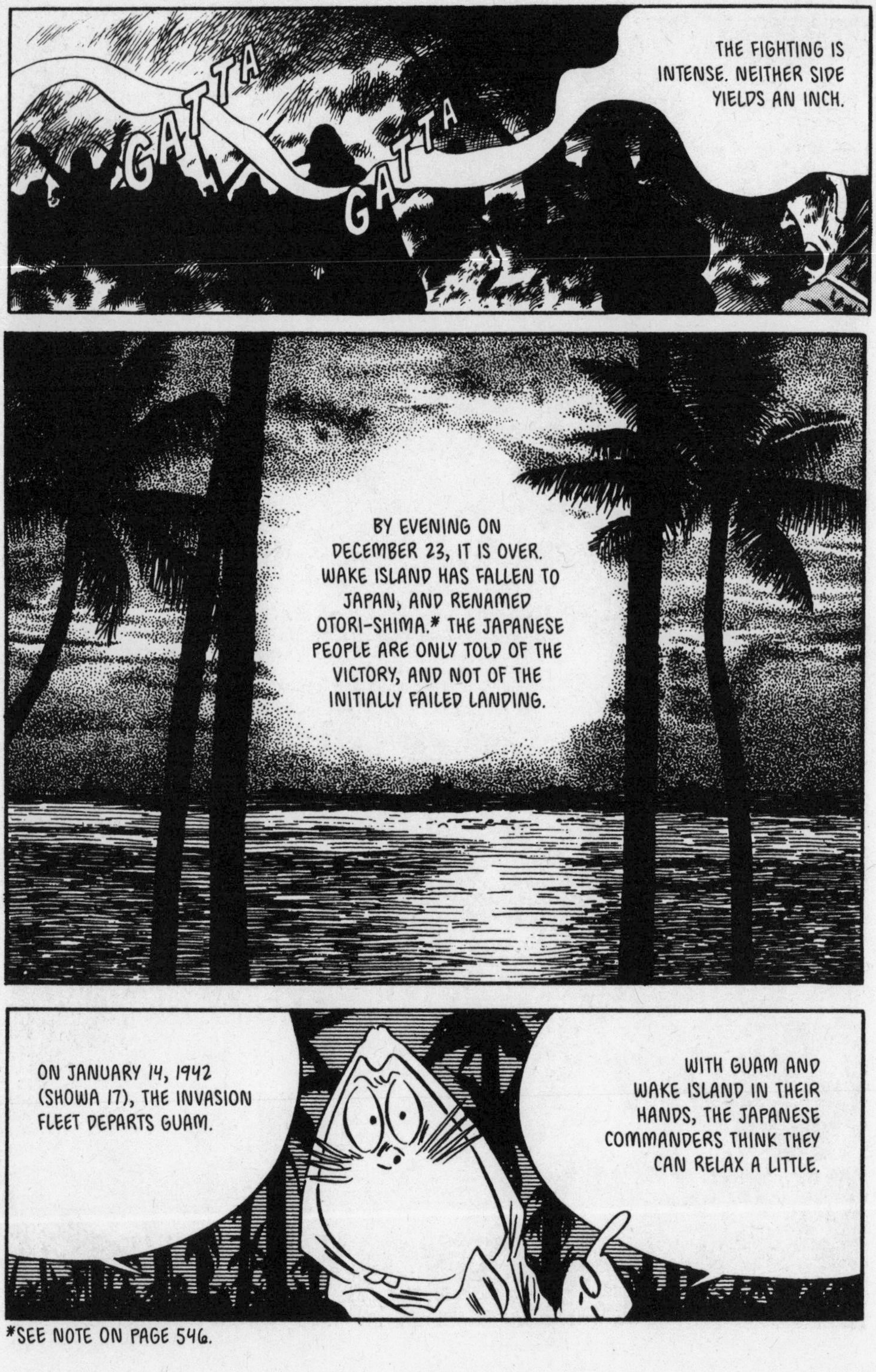
THE FIGHTING IS INTENSE. NEITHER SIDE YIELDS AN INCH.
GATTA
GATTA
BY EVENING ON DECEMBER 23, IT IS OVER. WAKE ISLAND HAS FALLEN TO JAPAN, AND RENAMED OTORI-SHIMA.* THE JAPANESE PEOPLE ARE ONLY TOLD OF THE VICTORY, AND NOT OF THE INITIALLY FAILED LANDING.
WITH GUAM AND WAKE ISLAND IN THEIR HANDS, THE JAPANESE COMMANDERS THINK THEY CAN RELAX A LITTLE.
ON JANUARY 14, 1942 (SHOWA 17), THE INVASION FLEET DEPARTS GUAM.

*SEE NOTE ON PAGE 546.

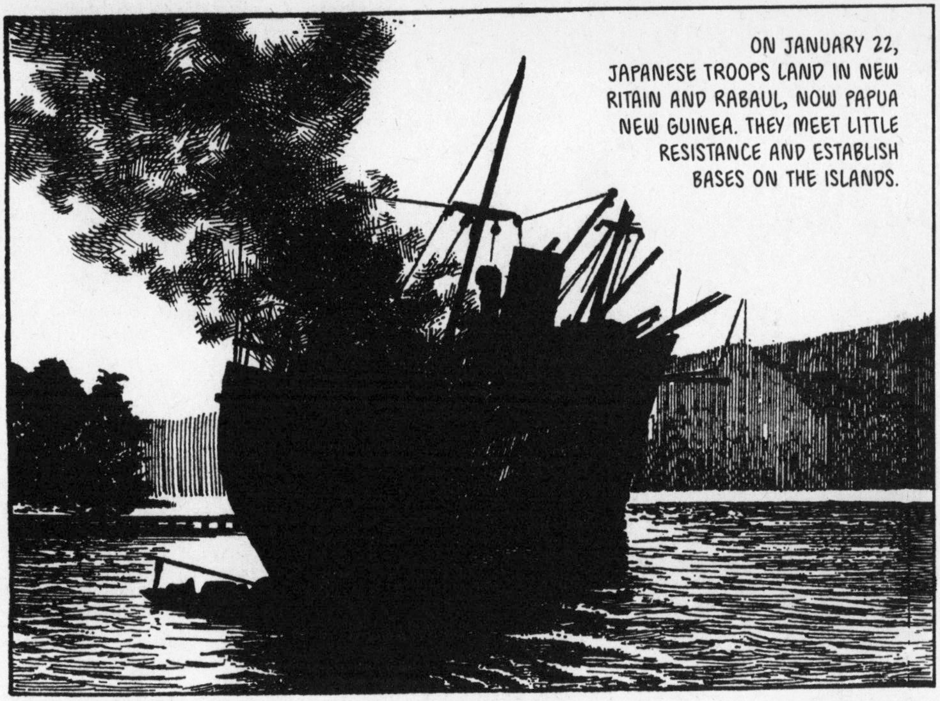
ON JANUARY 22, JAPANESE TROOPS LAND IN NEW RITAIN AND RABAUL, NOW PAPUA NEW GUINEA. THEY MEET LITTLE RESISTANCE AND ESTABLISH BASES ON THE ISLANDS.

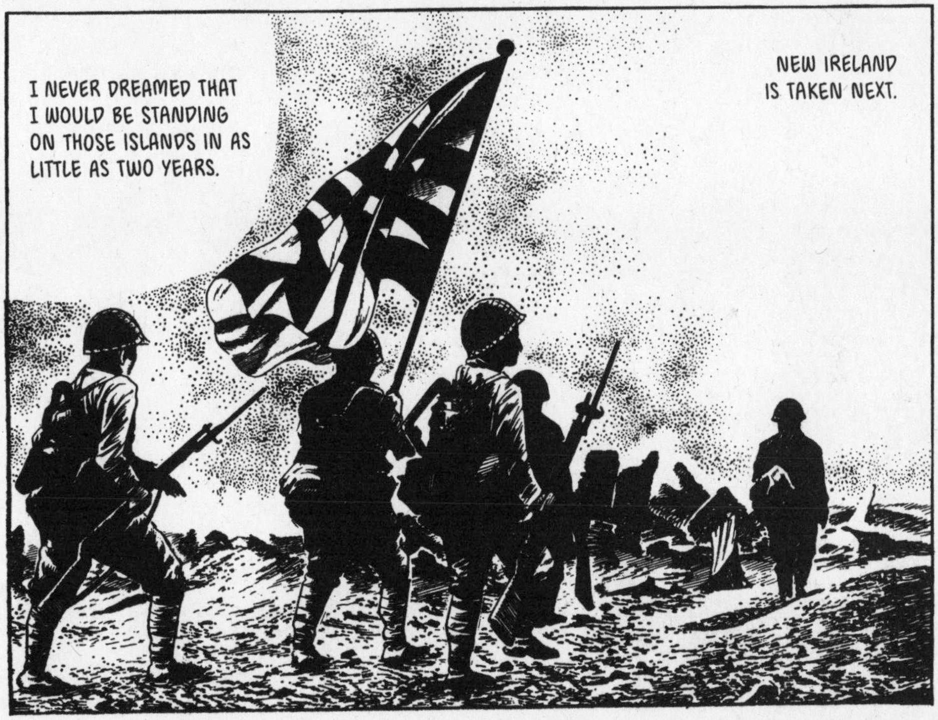
NEW IRELAND IS TAKEN NEXT.
I NEVER DREAMED THAT I WOULD BE STANDING ON THOSE ISLANDS IN AS LITTLE AS TWO YEARS.

THE CAPTURE OF THE DUTCH EAST INDIES

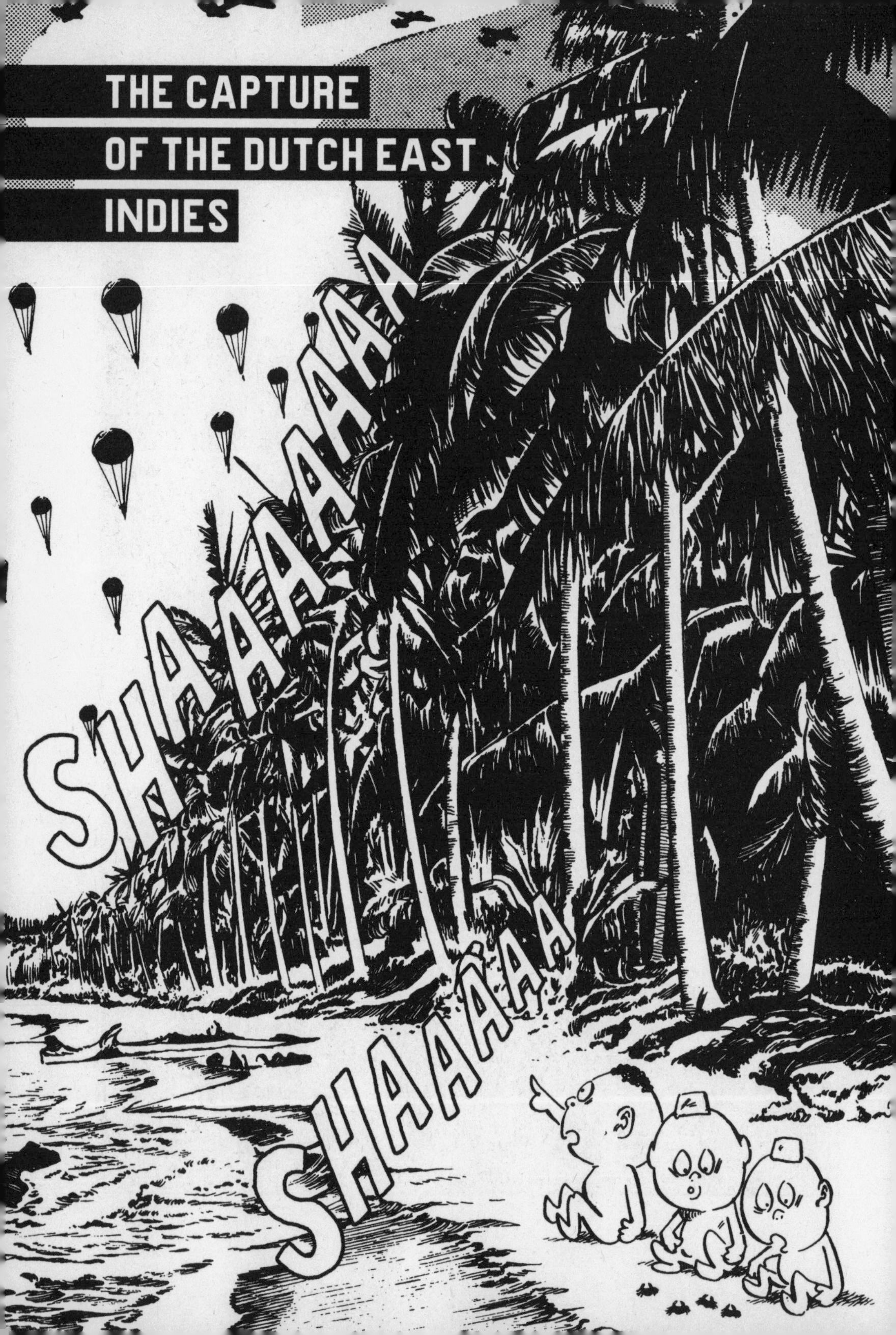
SHAAAAAAAA
SHAAAAAAA

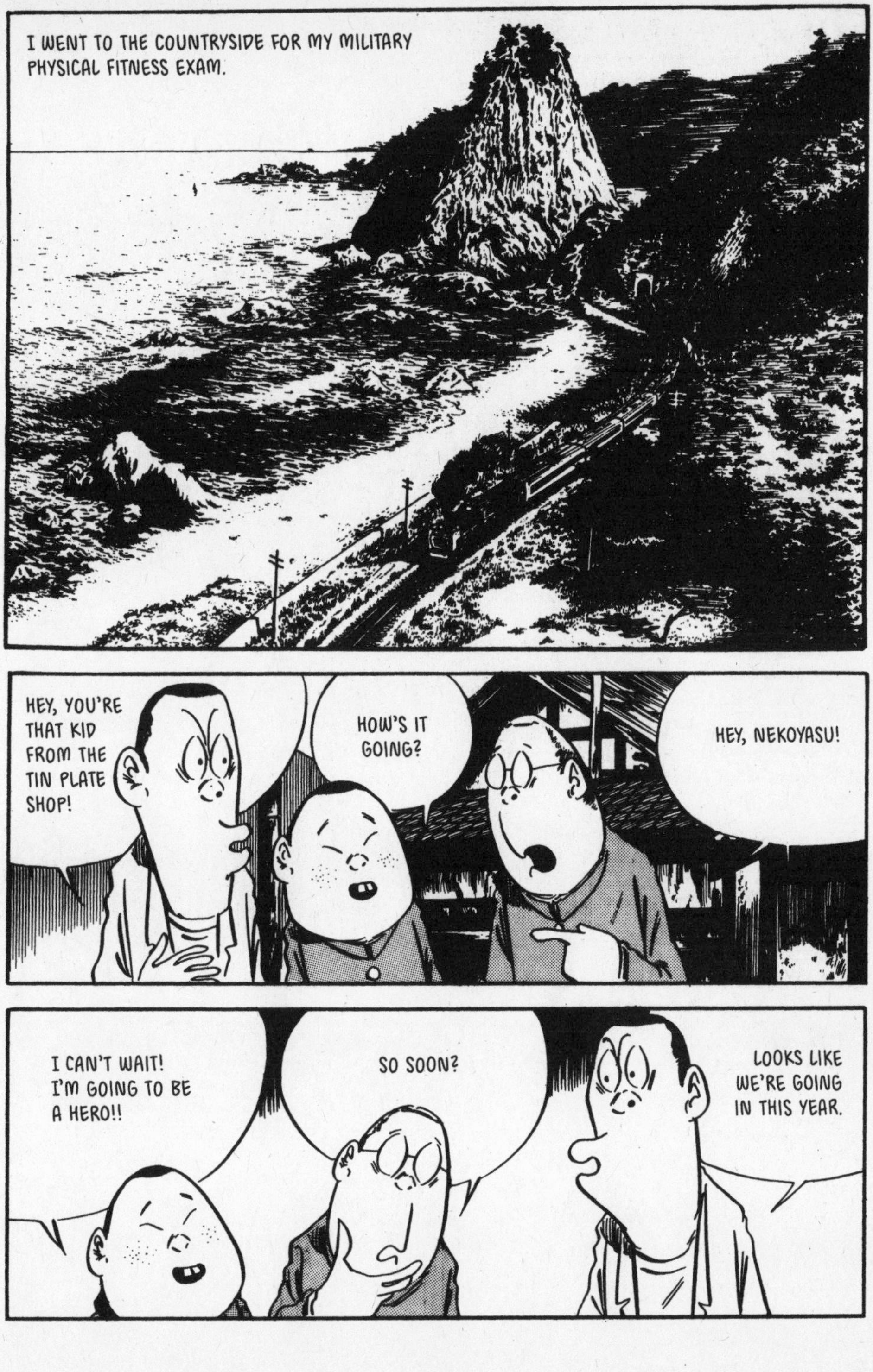
I WENT TO THE COUNTRYSIDE FOR MY MILITARY PHYSICAL FITNESS EXAM.
HEY, NEKOYASU!
HOW'S IT GOING?
HEY, YOU'RE THAT KID FROM THE TIN PLATE SHOP!
LOOKS LIKE WE'RE GOING IN THIS YEAR.
SO SOON?
I CAN'T WAIT! I'M GOING TO BE A HERO!!

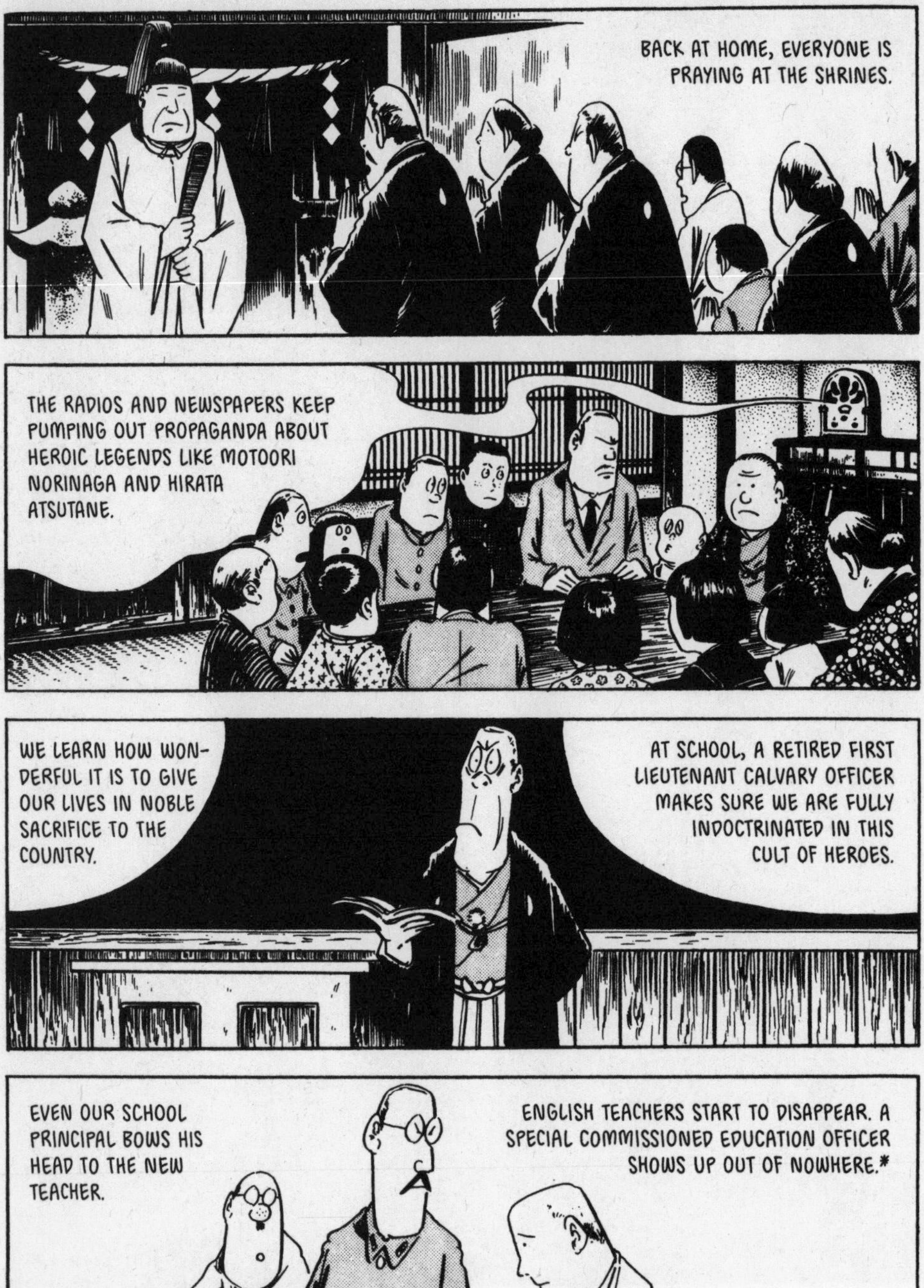
BACK AT HOME, EVERYONE IS PRAYING AT THE SHRINES.
THE RADIOS AND NEWSPAPERS KEEP PUMPING OUT PROPAGANDA ABOUT HEROIC LEGENDS LIKE MOTOORI NORINAGA AND HIRATA ATSUTANE.
AT SCHOOL, A RETIRED FIRST LIEUTENANT CALVARY OFFICER MAKES SURE WE ARE FULLY INDOCTRINATED IN THIS CULT OF HEROES.
WE LEARN HOW WON-DERFUL IT IS TO GIVE OUR LIVES IN NOBLE SACRIFICE TO THE COUNTRY.
ENGLISH TEACHERS START TO DISAPPEAR. A SPECIAL COMMISSIONED EDUCATION OFFICER SHOWS UP OUT OF NOWHERE.*
EVEN OUR SCHOOL PRINCIPAL BOWS HIS HEAD TO THE NEW TEACHER.

*SEE NOTE ON PAGE 546.

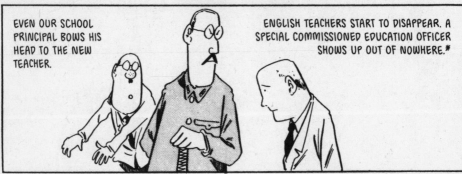

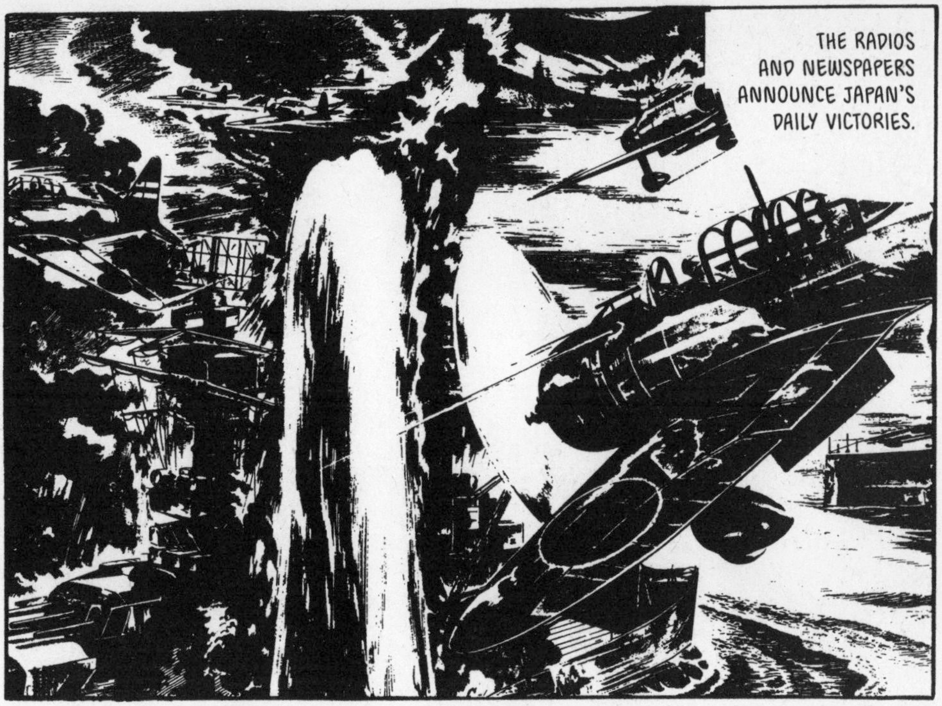
THE RADIOS AND NEWSPAPERS ANNOUNCE JAPAN'S DAILY VICTORIES.

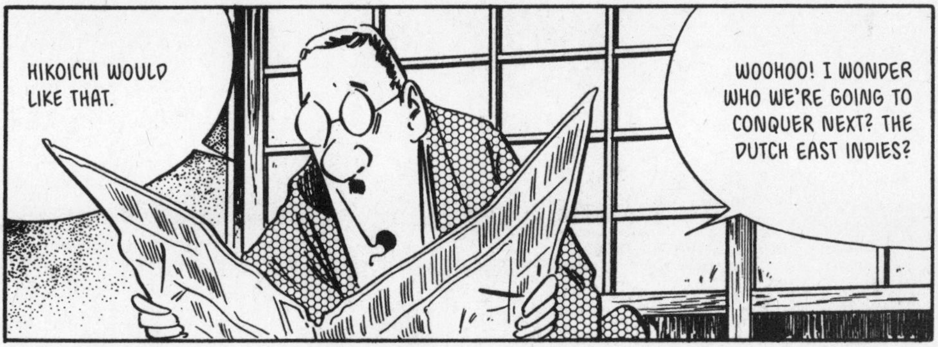
WOOHOO! I WONDER WHO WE'RE GOING TO CONQUER NEXT? THE DUTCH EAST INDIES?
HIKOICHI WOULD LIKE THAT.

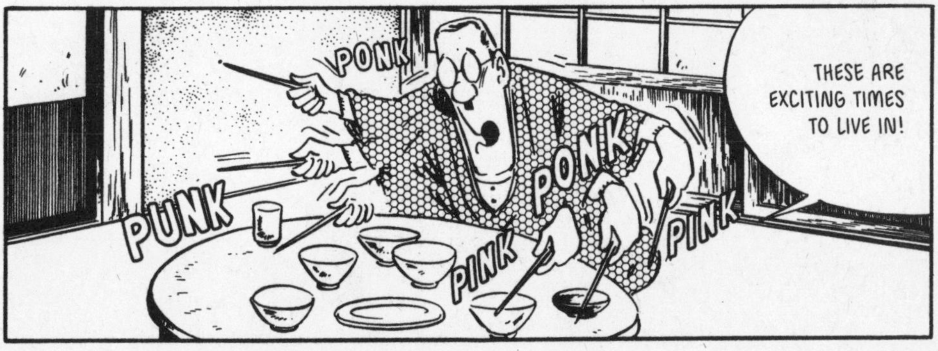
THESE ARE EXCITING TIMES TO LIVE IN!
PONK
PONK
PINK
PUNK
PINK

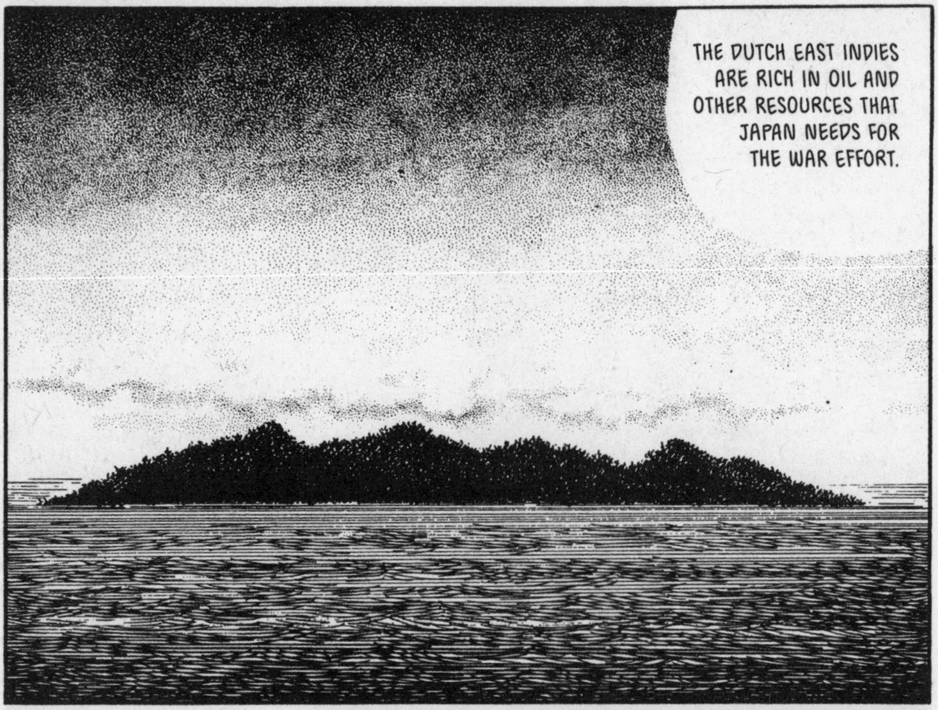
THE DUTCH EAST INDIES ARE RICH IN OIL AND OTHER RESOURCES THAT JAPAN NEEDS FOR THE WAR EFFORT.

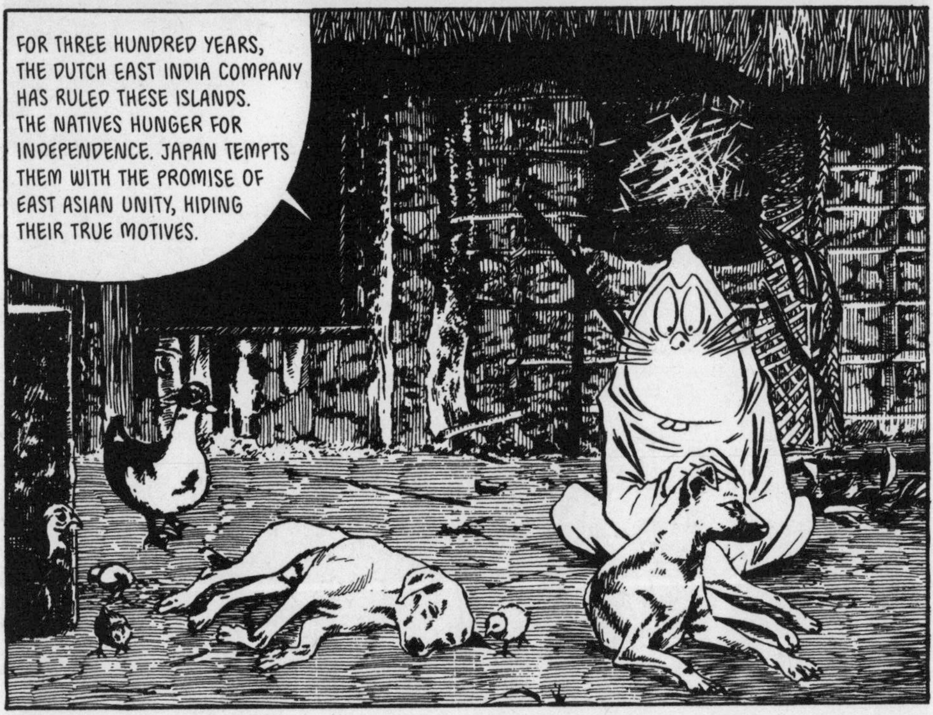
FOR THREE HUNDRED YEARS, THE DUTCH EAST INDIA COMPANY HAS RULED THESE ISLANDS. THE NATIVES HUNGER FOR INDEPENDENCE. JAPAN TEMPTS THEM WITH THE PROMISE OF EAST ASIAN UNITY, HIDING THEIR TRUE MOTIVES.

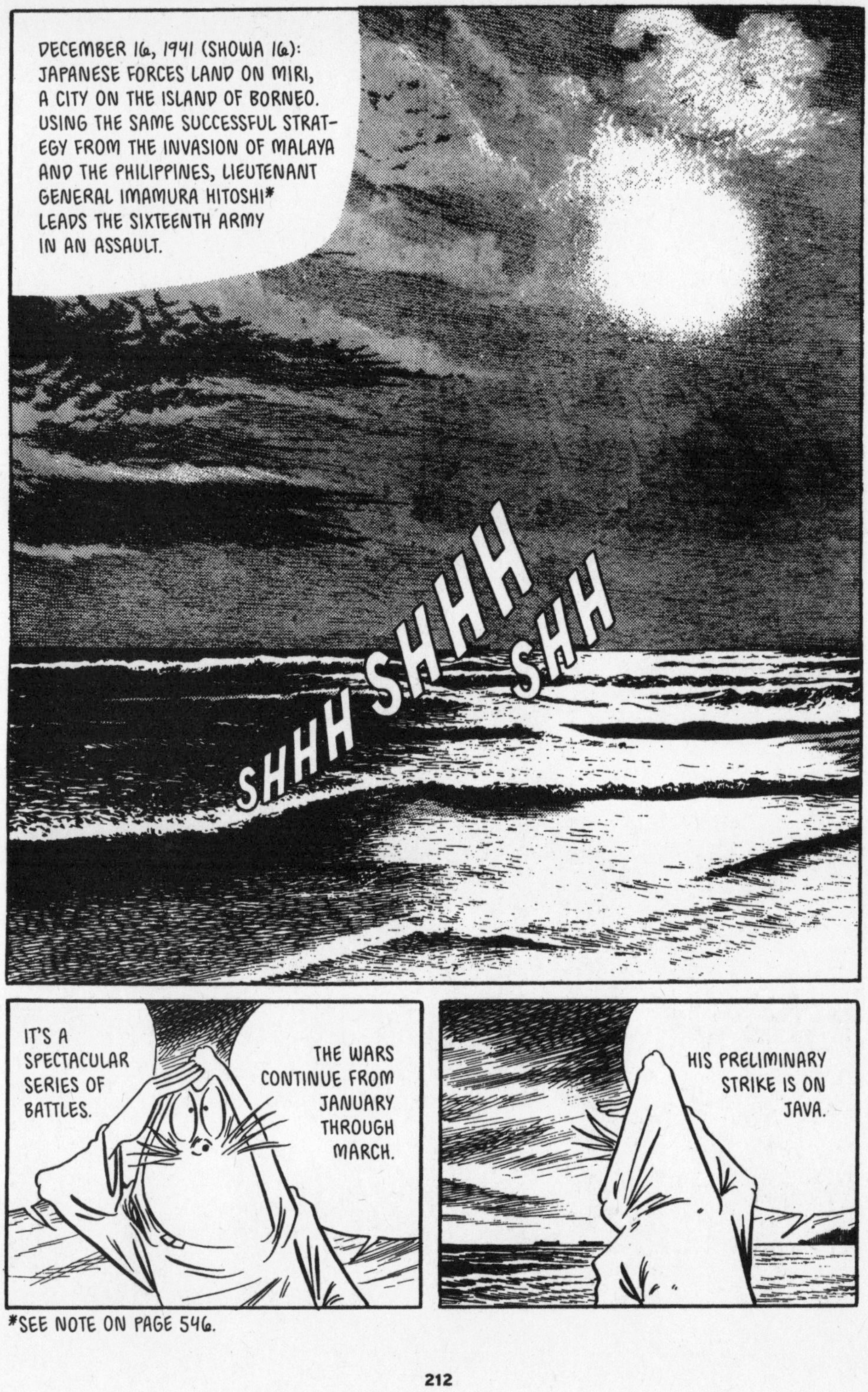
DECEMBER 16, 1941 (SHOWA 16): JAPANESE FORCES LAND ON MIRI, A CITY ON THE ISLAND OF BORNEO. USING THE SAME SUCCESSFUL STRATEGY FROM THE INVASION OF MALAYA AND THE PHILIPPINES, LIEUTENANT GENERAL IMAMURA HITOSHI* LEADS THE SIXTEENTH ARMY IN AN ASSAULT.
SHH
SHHH
SHHH
HIS PRELIMINARY STRIKE IS ON JAVA.
THE WARS CONTINUE FROM JANUARY THROUGH MARCH.
IT'S A SPECTACULAR SERIES OF BATTLES.

*SEE NOTE ON PAGE 546.

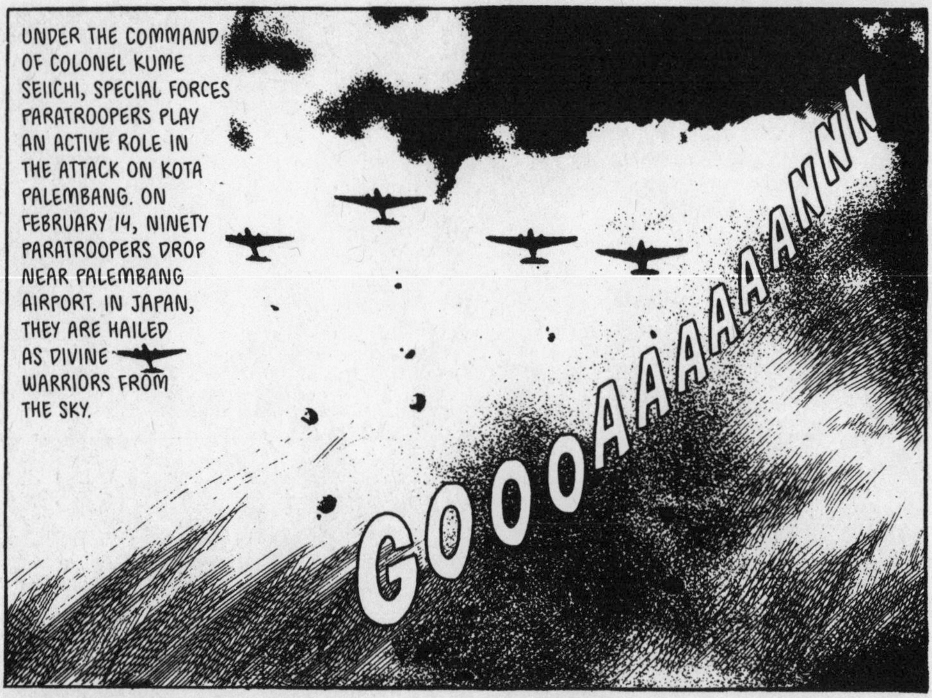
UNDER THE COMMAND OF COLONEL KUME SEIICHI, SPECIAL FORCES PARATROOPERS PLAY AN ACTIVE ROLE IN THE ATTACK ON KOTA PALEMBANG. ON FEBRUARY 14, NINETY PARATROOPERS DROP NEAR PALEMBANG AIRPORT. IN JAPAN, THEY ARE HAILED AS DIVINE WARRIORS FROM THE SKY.
GOOOAAAAAAANNN

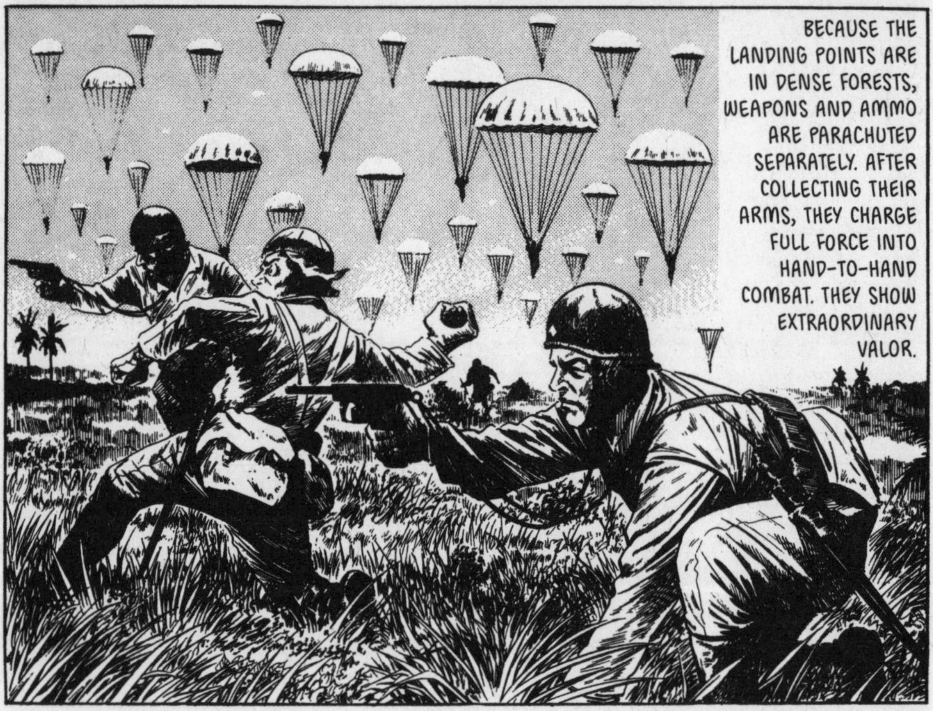
BECAUSE THE LANDING POINTS ARE IN DENSE FORESTS, WEAPONS AND AMMO ARE PARACHUTED SEPARATELY. AFTER COLLECTING THEIR ARMS, THEY CHARGE FULL FORCE INTO HAND-TO-HAND COMBAT. THEY SHOW EXTRAORDINARY VALOR.

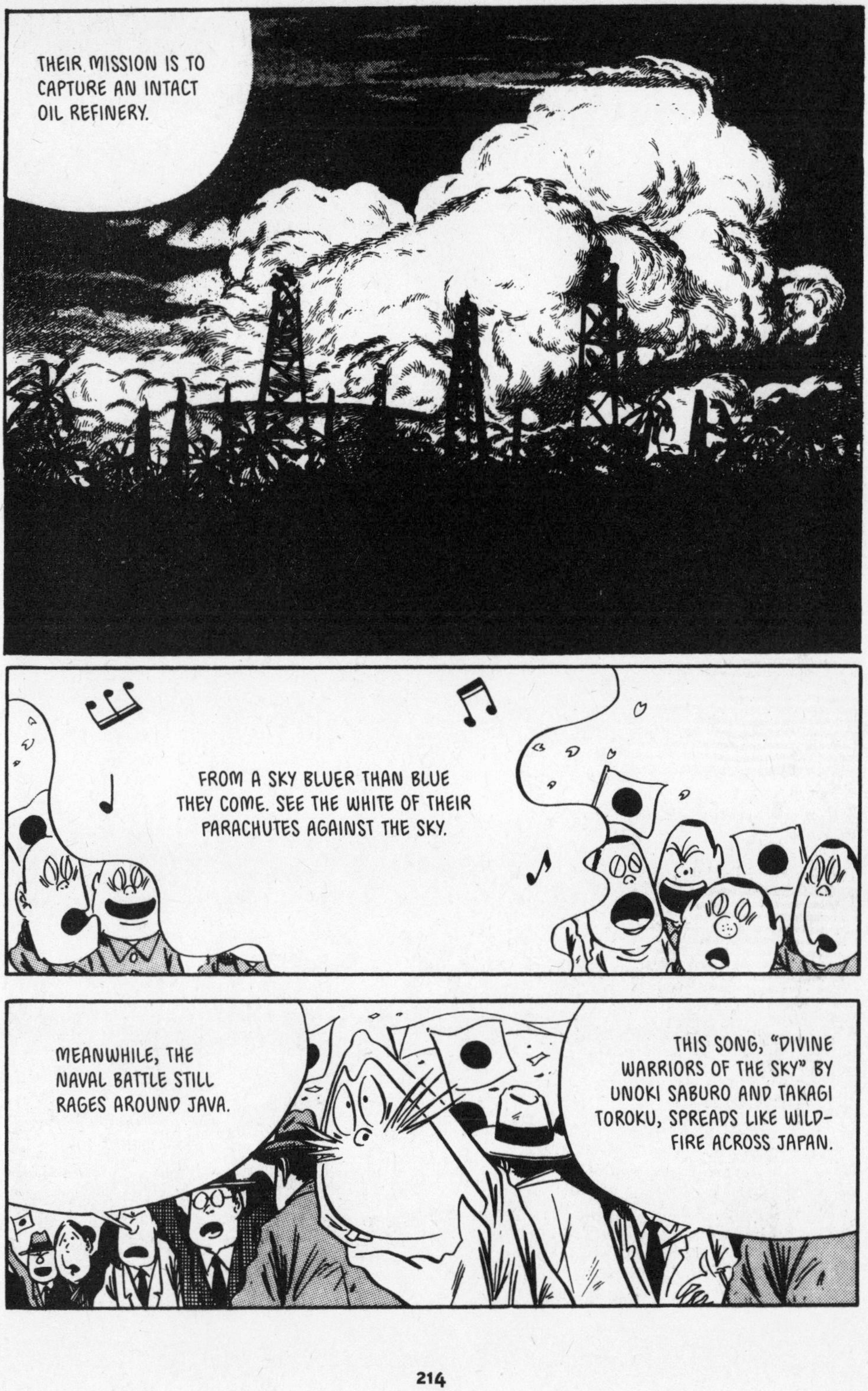
THEIR MISSION IS TO CAPTURE AN INTACT OIL REFINERY.
FROM A SKY BLUER THAN BLUE THEY COME. SEE THE WHITE OF THEIR PARACHUTES AGAINST THE SKY.
THIS SONG, "DIVINE WARRIORS OF THE SKY" BY UNOKI SABURO AND TAKAGI TOROKU, SPREADS LIKE WILD-FIRE ACROSS JAPAN.
MEANWHILE, THE NAVAL BATTLE STILL RAGES AROUND JAVA.

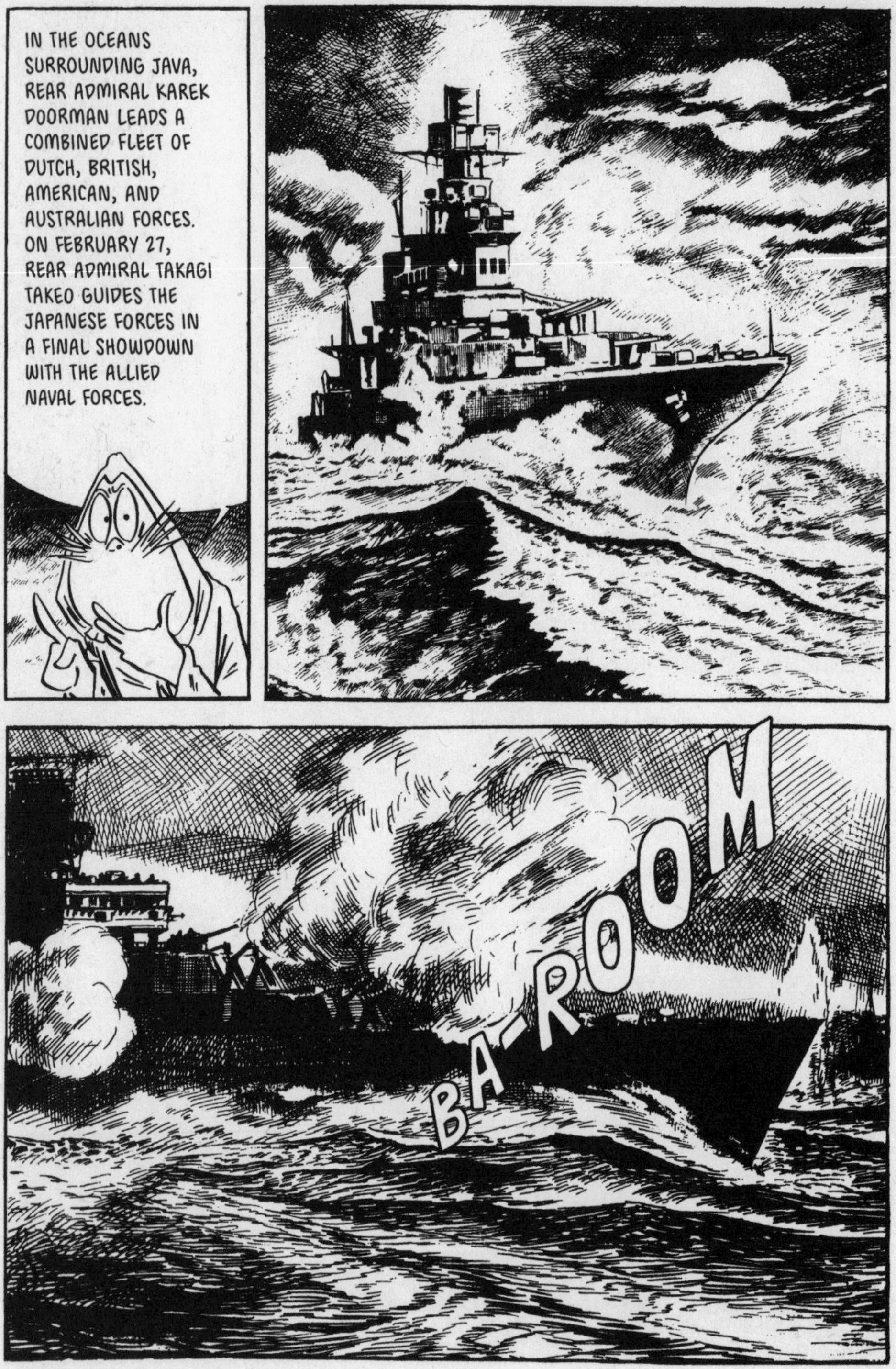
IN THE OCEANS SURROUNDING JAVA, REAR ADMIRAL KAREK DOORMAN LEADS A COMBINED FLEET OF DUTCH, BRITISH, AMERICAN, AND AUSTRALIAN FORCES. ON FEBRUARY 27, REAR ADMIRAL TAKAGI TAKEO GUIDES THE JAPANESE FORCES IN A FINAL SHOWDOWN WITH THE ALLIED NAVAL FORCES.
BA-ROOM

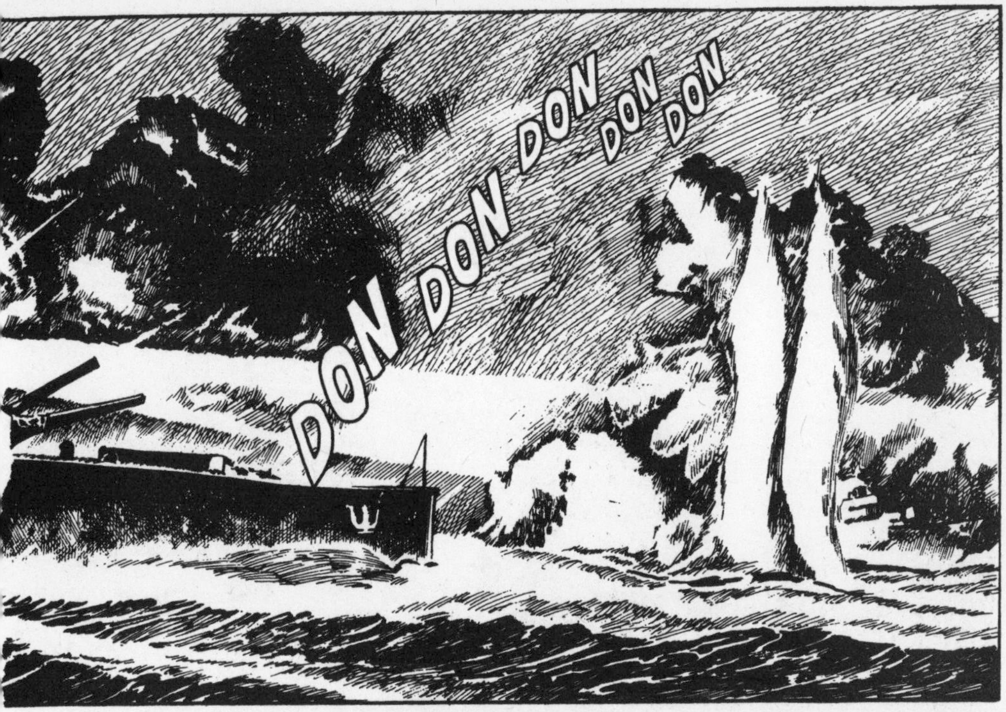
DON DON DON DON DON DON

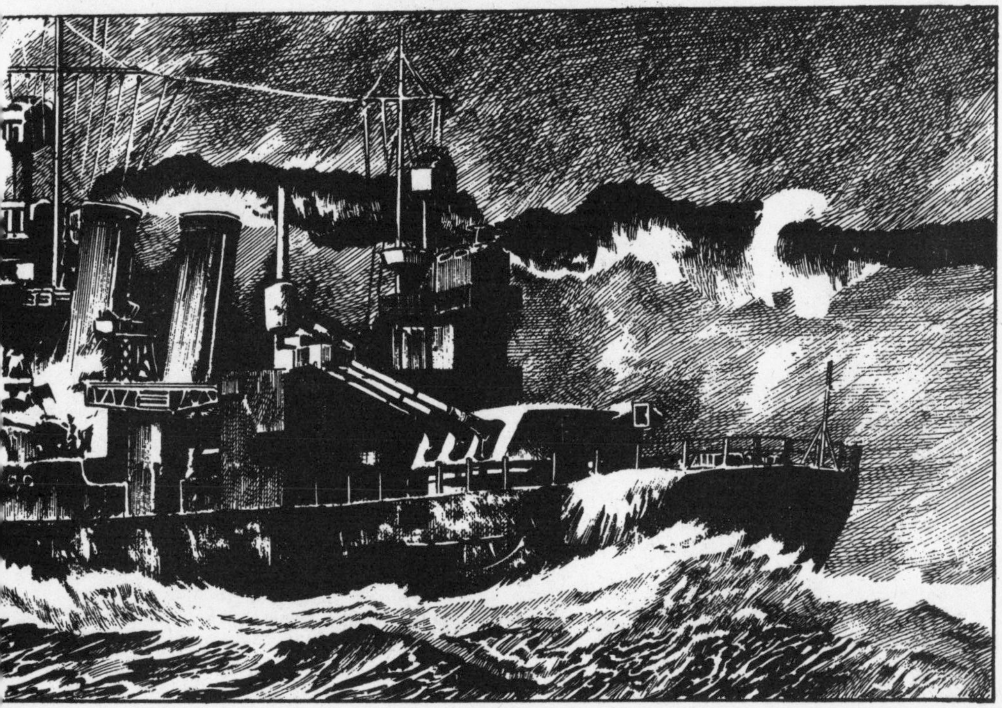

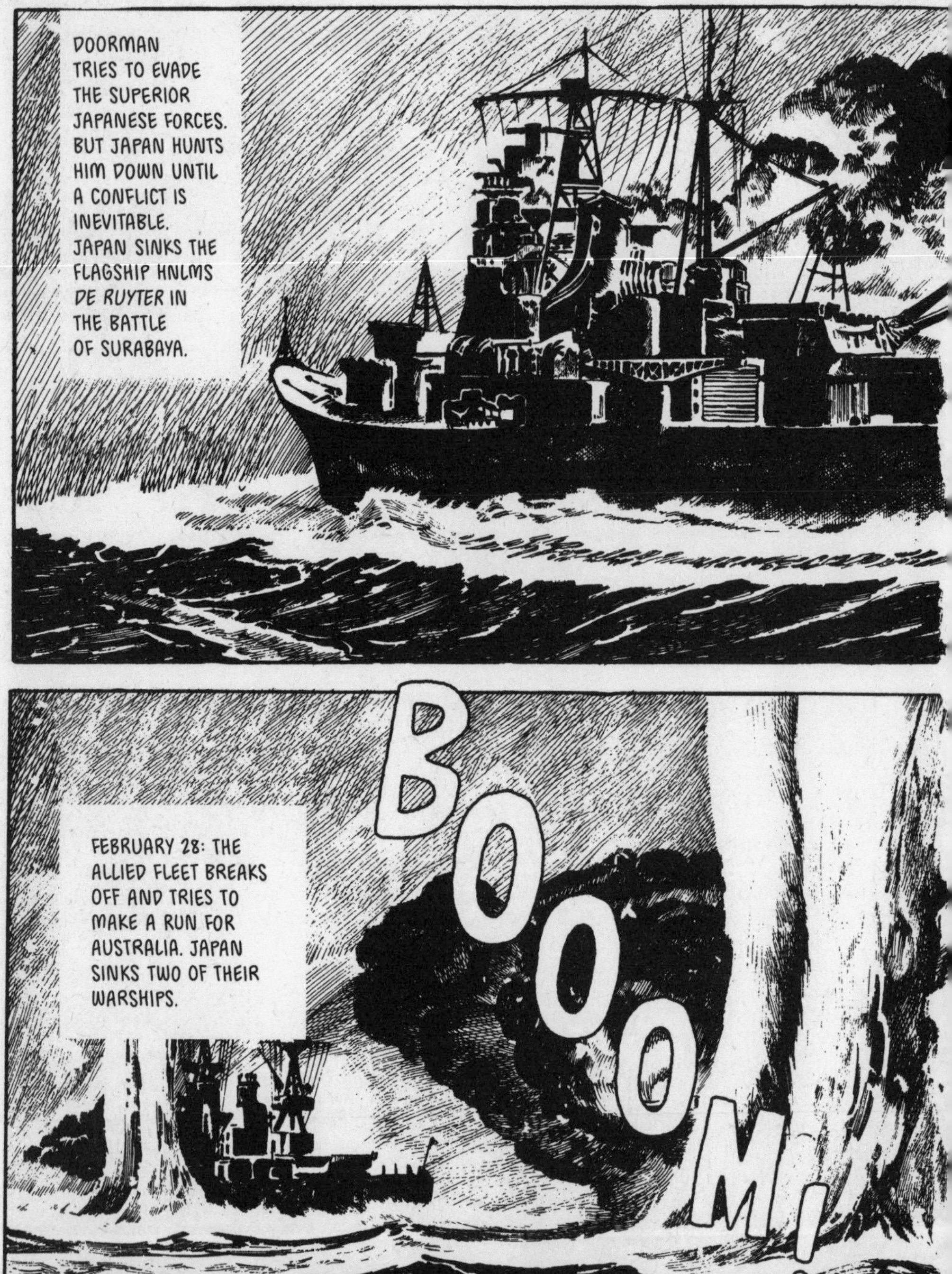
DOORMAN TRIES TO EVADE THE SUPERIOR JAPANESE FORCES. BUT JAPAN HUNTS HIM DOWN UNTIL A CONFLICT IS INEVITABLE. JAPAN SINKS THE FLAGSHIP HNLMS *DE RUYTER* IN THE BATTLE OF SURABAYA.
FEBRUARY 28: THE ALLIED FLEET BREAKS OFF AND TRIES TO MAKE A RUN FOR AUSTRALIA. JAPAN SINKS TWO OF THEIR WARSHIPS.
BOOOOM!

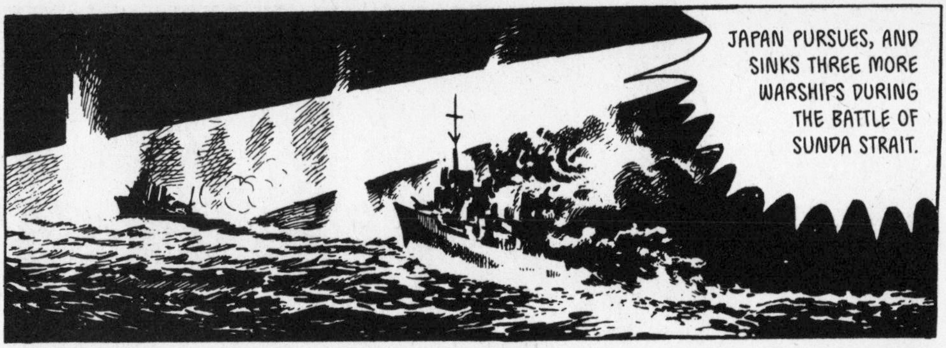
JAPAN PURSUES, AND SINKS THREE MORE WARSHIPS DURING THE BATTLE OF SUNDA STRAIT.

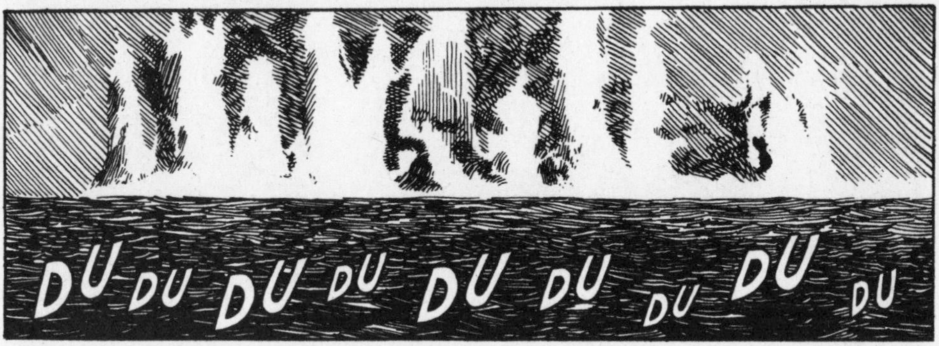
DU DU DU DU DU DU DU DU DU

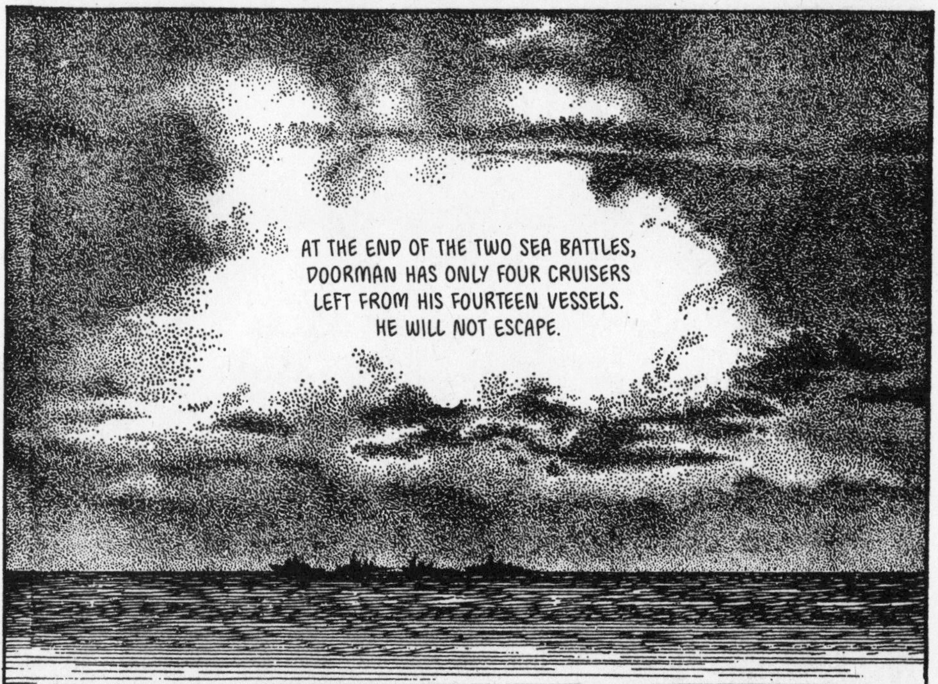
AT THE END OF THE TWO SEA BATTLES, DOORMAN HAS ONLY FOUR CRUISERS LEFT FROM HIS FOURTEEN VESSELS. HE WILL NOT ESCAPE.

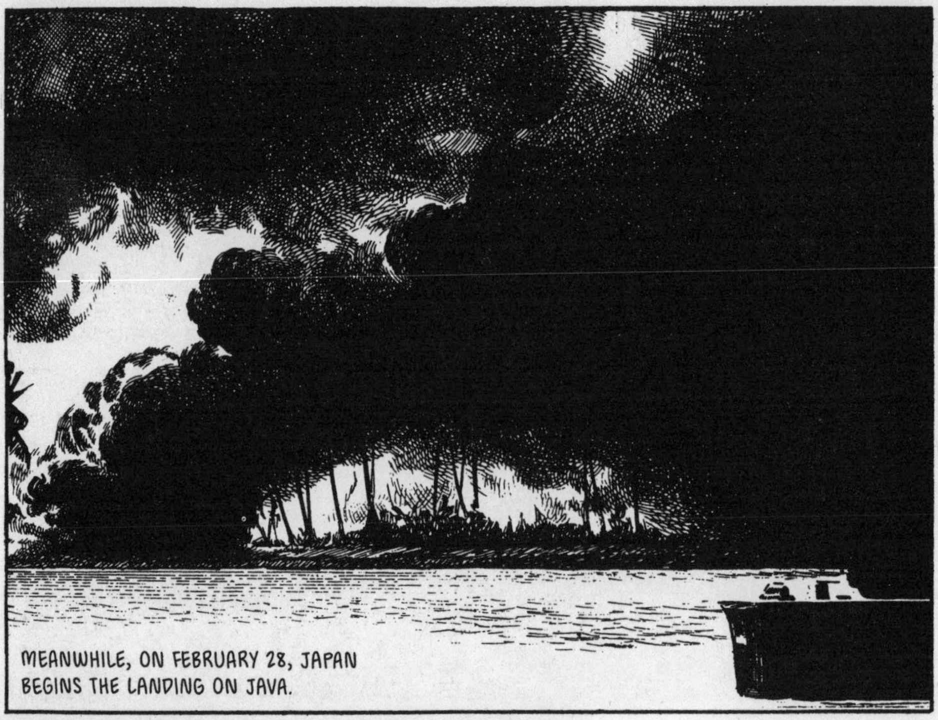
MEANWHILE, ON FEBRUARY 28, JAPAN BEGINS THE LANDING ON JAVA.

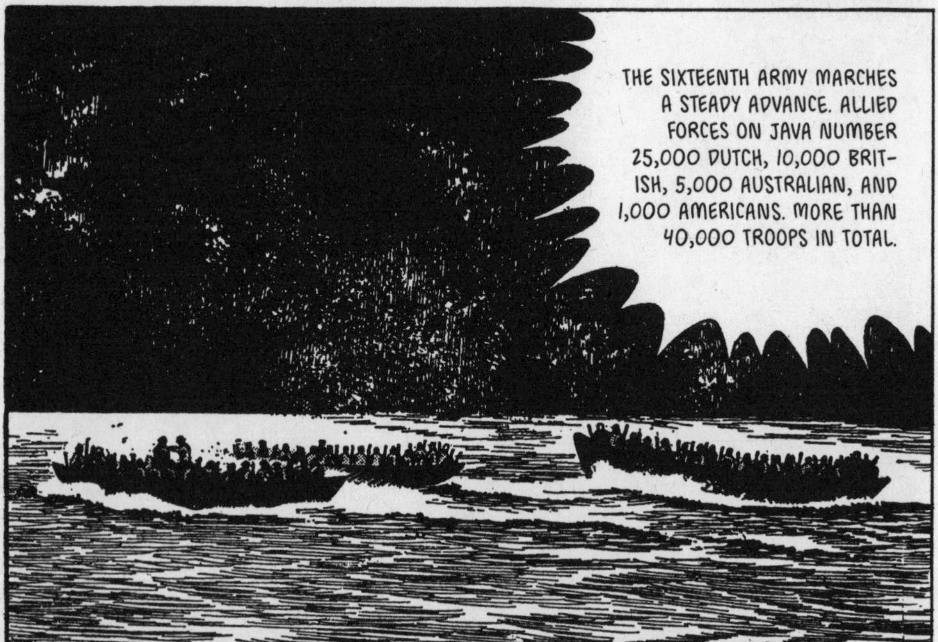
THE SIXTEENTH ARMY MARCHES A STEADY ADVANCE. ALLIED FORCES ON JAVA NUMBER 25,000 DUTCH, 10,000 BRITISH, 5,000 AUSTRALIAN, AND 1,000 AMERICANS. MORE THAN 40,000 TROOPS IN TOTAL.

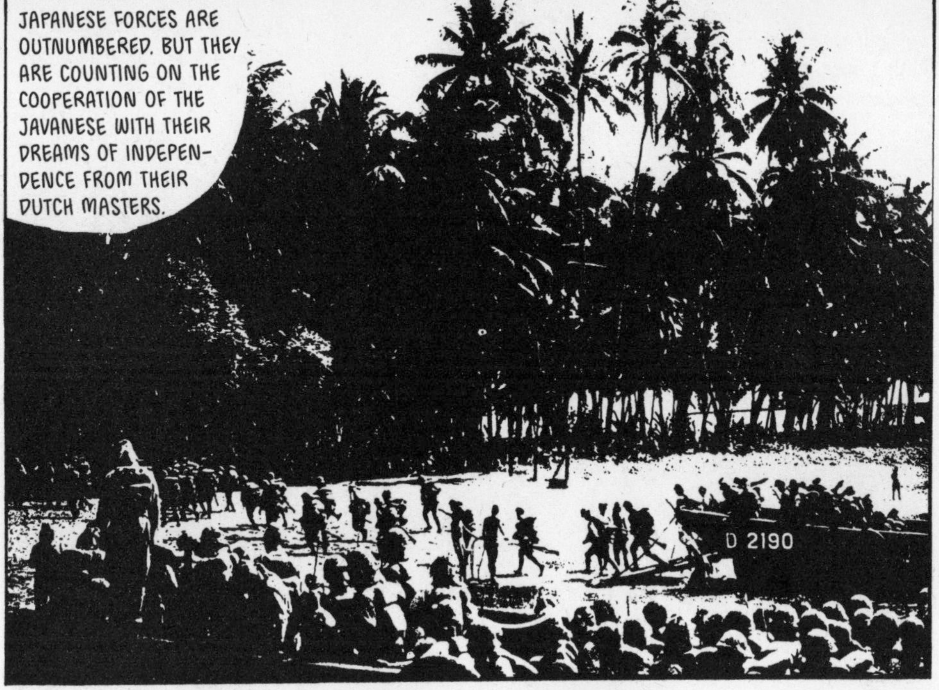
JAPANESE FORCES ARE OUTNUMBERED. BUT THEY ARE COUNTING ON THE COOPERATION OF THE JAVANESE WITH THEIR DREAMS OF INDEPENDENCE FROM THEIR DUTCH MASTERS.
D 2190

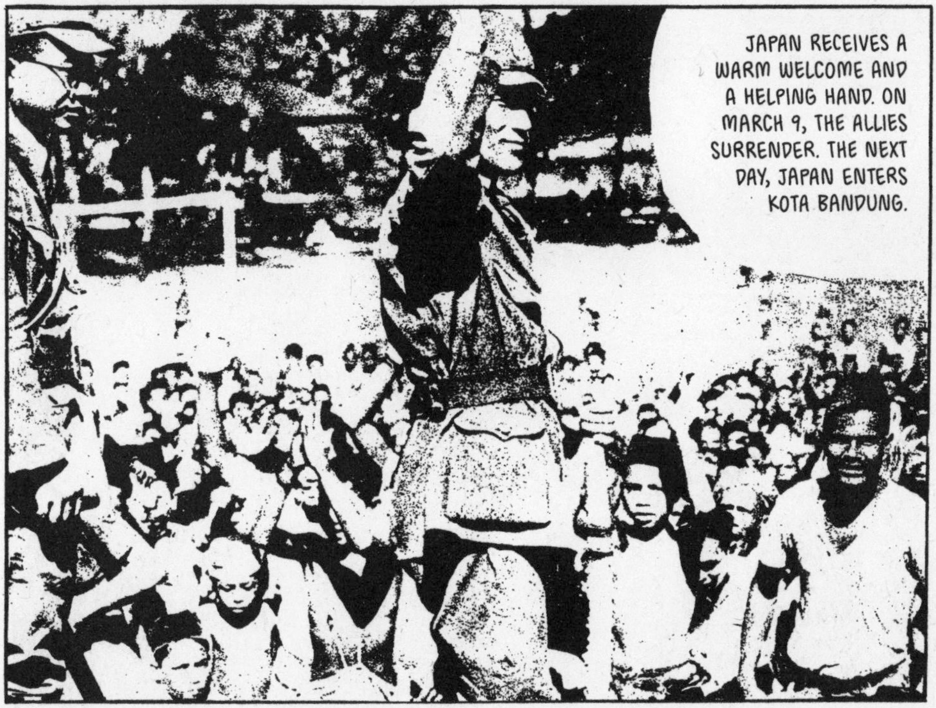
JAPAN RECEIVES A WARM WELCOME AND A HELPING HAND. ON MARCH 9, THE ALLIES SURRENDER. THE NEXT DAY, JAPAN ENTERS KOTA BANDUNG.

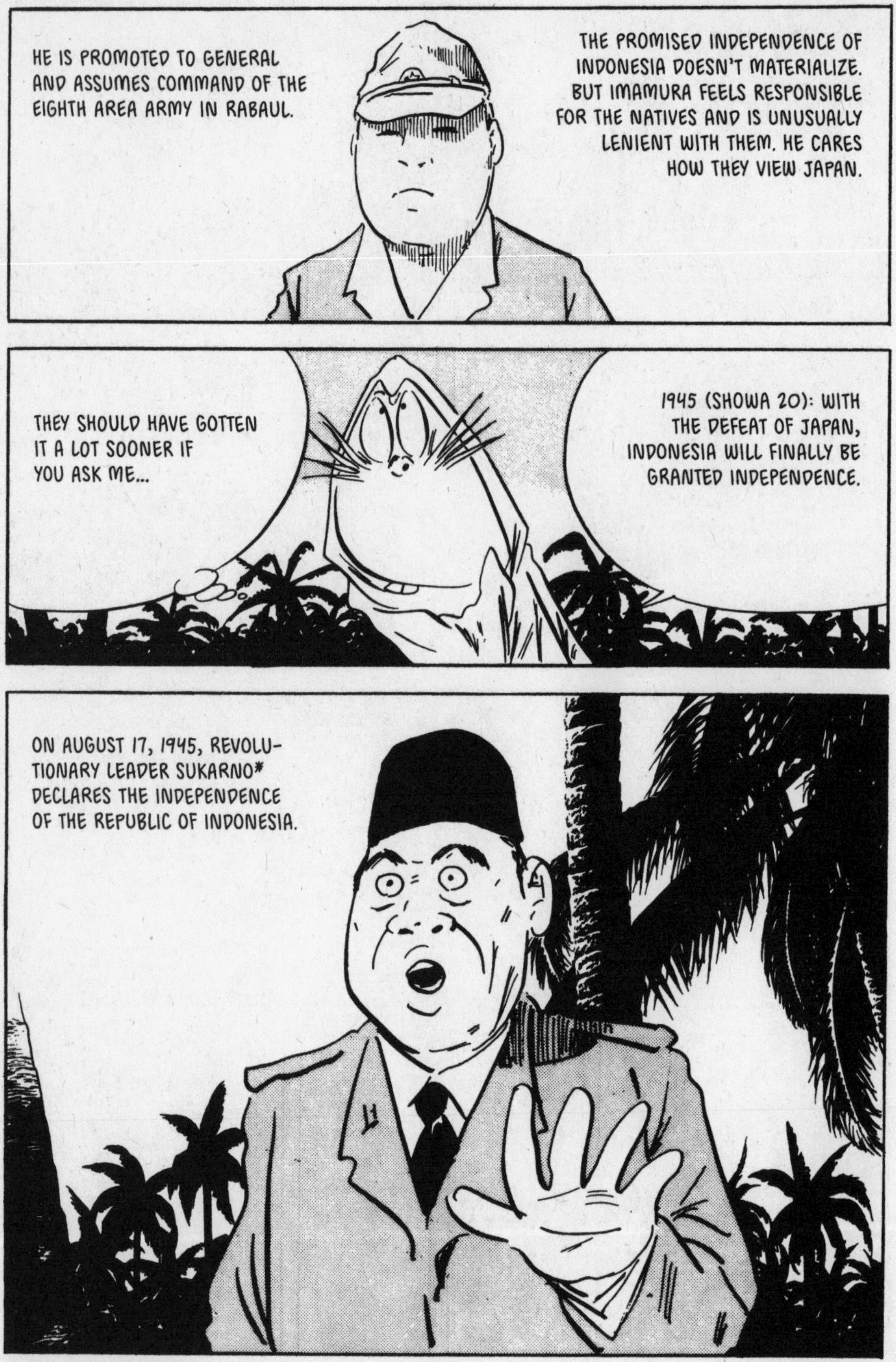
THE PROMISED INDEPENDENCE OF INDONESIA DOESN'T MATERIALIZE. BUT IMAMURA FEELS RESPONSIBLE FOR THE NATIVES AND IS UNUSUALLY LENIENT WITH THEM. HE CARES HOW THEY VIEW JAPAN.
HE IS PROMOTED TO GENERAL AND ASSUMES COMMAND OF THE EIGHTH AREA ARMY IN RABAUL.
1945 (SHOWA 20): WITH THE DEFEAT OF JAPAN, INDONESIA WILL FINALLY BE GRANTED INDEPENDENCE.
THEY SHOULD HAVE GOTTEN IT A LOT SOONER IF YOU ASK ME...
ON AUGUST 17, 1945, REVOLUTIONARY LEADER SUKARNO* DECLARES THE INDEPENDENCE OF THE REPUBLIC OF INDONESIA.

*SEE NOTE ON PAGE 546.

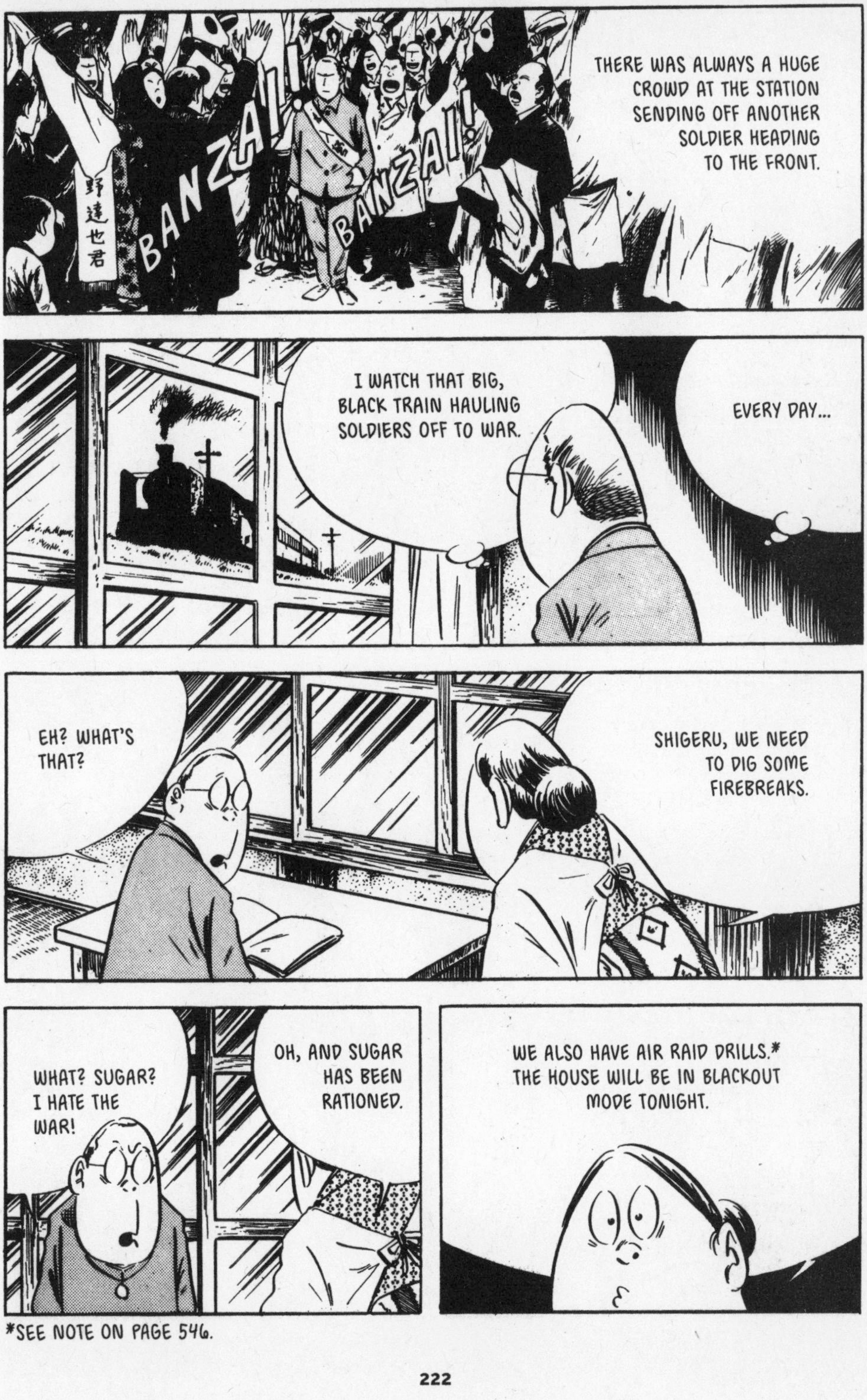
THERE WAS ALWAYS A HUGE CROWD AT THE STATION SENDING OFF ANOTHER SOLDIER HEADING TO THE FRONT.
BANZAI!
BANZAI!
野達也君
EVERY DAY...
I WATCH THAT BIG, BLACK TRAIN HAULING SOLDIERS OFF TO WAR.
SHIGERU, WE NEED TO DIG SOME FIREBREAKS.
EH? WHAT'S THAT?
WE ALSO HAVE AIR RAID DRILLS.* THE HOUSE WILL BE IN BLACKOUT MODE TONIGHT.
OH, AND SUGAR HAS BEEN RATIONED.
WHAT? SUGAR? I HATE THE WAR!

*SEE NOTE ON PAGE 546.

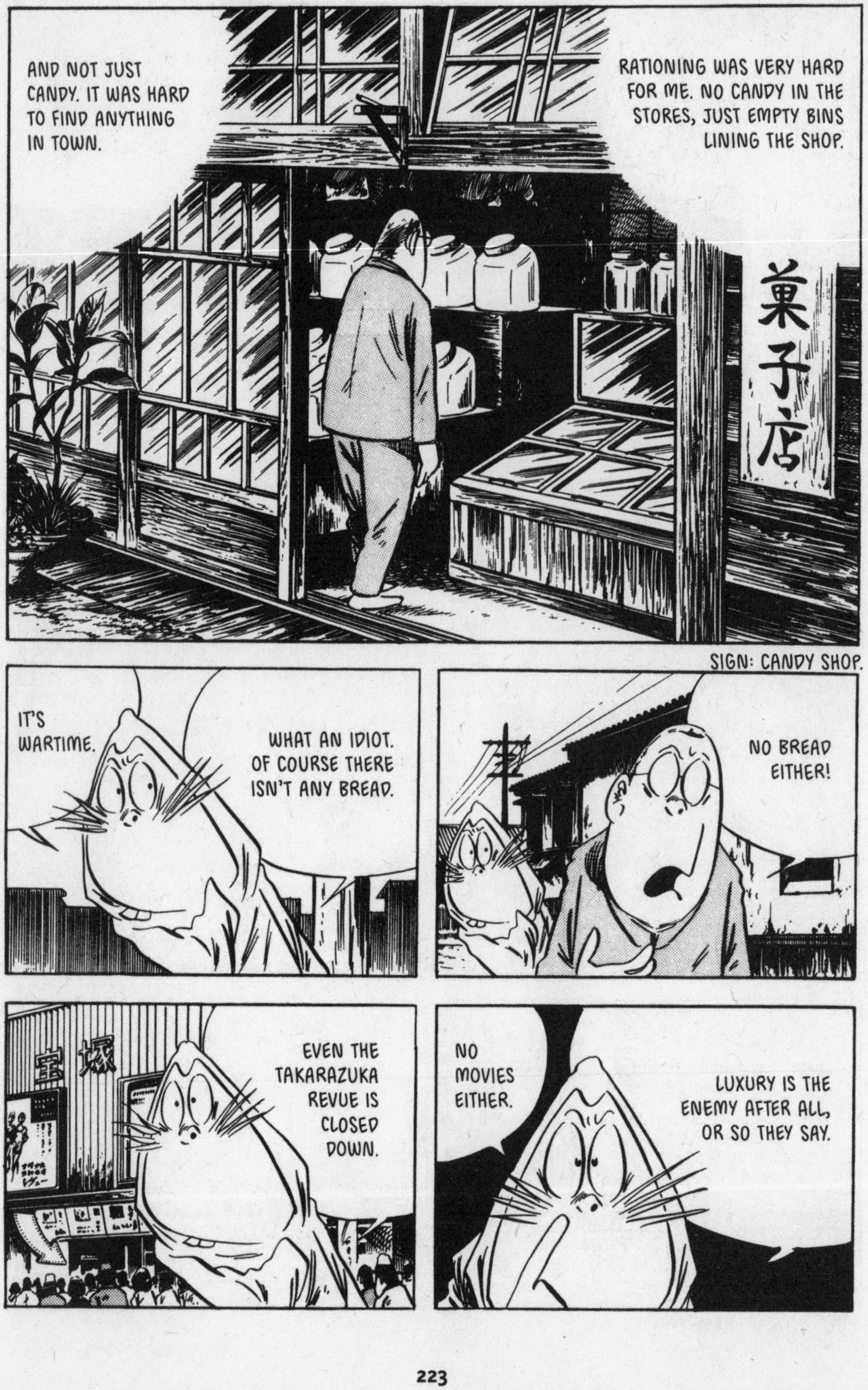
RATIONING WAS VERY HARD FOR ME. NO CANDY IN THE STORES, JUST EMPTY BINS LINING THE SHOP.
AND NOT JUST CANDY. IT WAS HARD TO FIND ANYTHING IN TOWN.
菓子店
SIGN: CANDY SHOP.
NO BREAD EITHER!
WHAT AN IDIOT. OF COURSE THERE ISN'T ANY BREAD.
IT'S WARTIME.
LUXURY IS THE ENEMY AFTER ALL, OR SO THEY SAY.
NO MOVIES EITHER.
EVEN THE TAKARAZUKA REVUE IS CLOSED DOWN.
宝塚

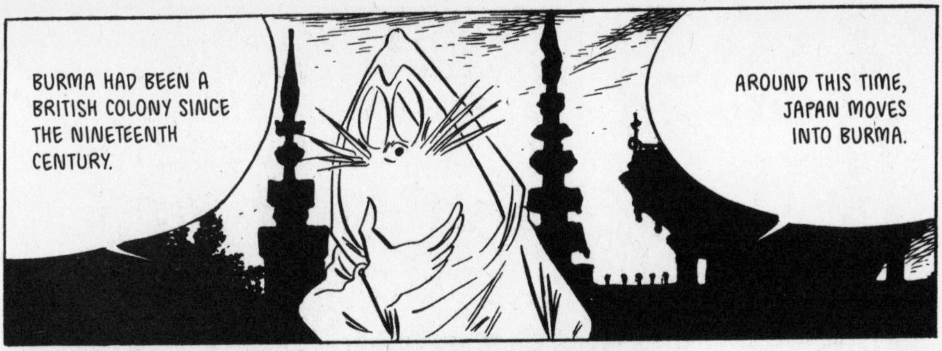
AROUND THIS TIME, JAPAN MOVES INTO BURMA.
BURMA HAD BEEN A BRITISH COLONY SINCE THE NINETEENTH CENTURY.

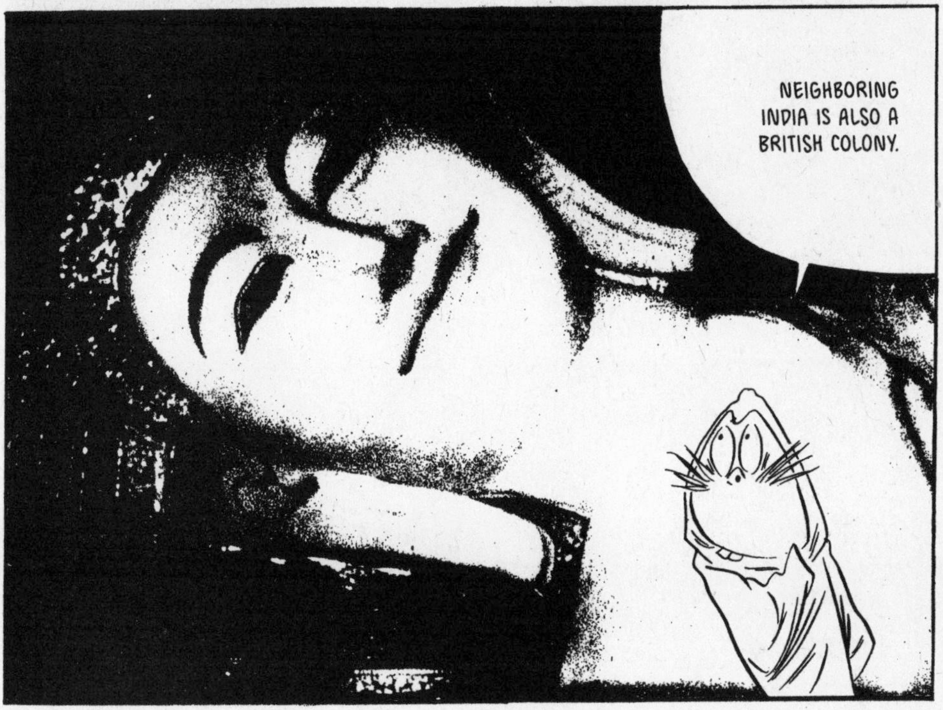
NEIGHBORING INDIA IS ALSO A BRITISH COLONY.

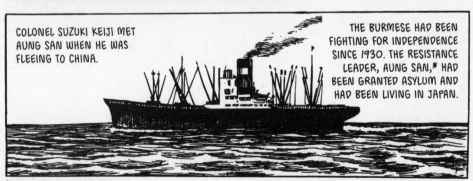

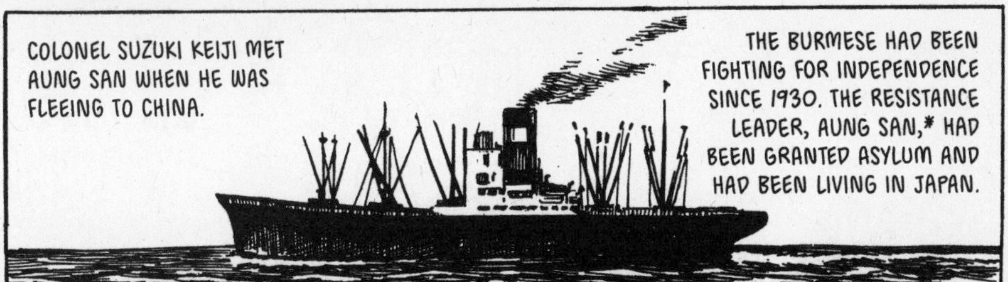
THE BURMESE HAD BEEN FIGHTING FOR INDEPENDENCE SINCE 1930. THE RESISTANCE LEADER, AUNG SAN,* HAD BEEN GRANTED ASYLUM AND HAD BEEN LIVING IN JAPAN.
COLONEL SUZUKI KEIJI MET AUNG SAN WHEN HE WAS FLEEING TO CHINA.

*SEE NOTE ON PAGE 546.

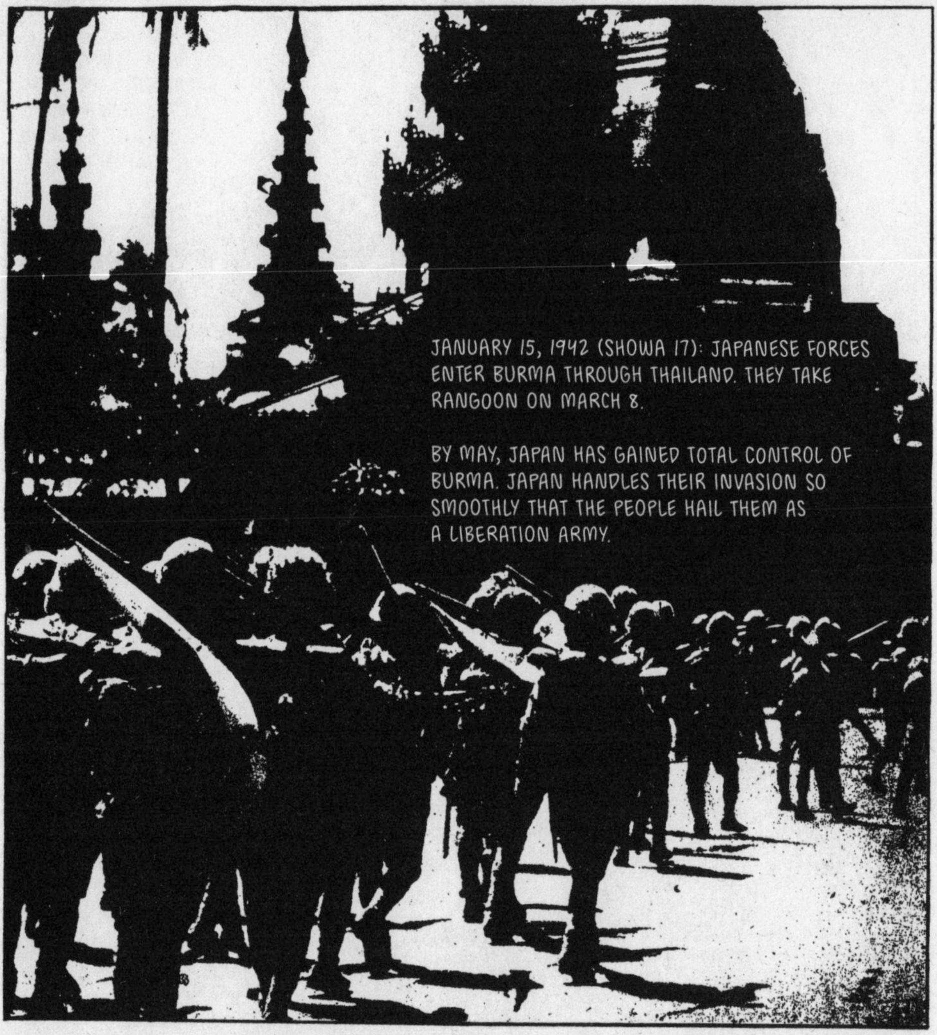
JANUARY 15, 1942 (SHOWA 17): JAPANESE FORCES ENTER BURMA THROUGH THAILAND. THEY TAKE RANGOON ON MARCH 8.
BY MAY, JAPAN HAS GAINED TOTAL CONTROL OF BURMA. JAPAN HANDLES THEIR INVASION SO SMOOTHLY THAT THE PEOPLE HAIL THEM AS A LIBERATION ARMY.

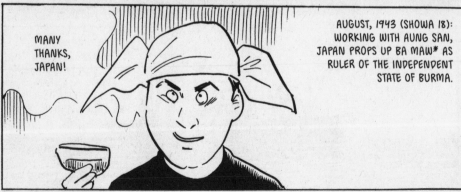

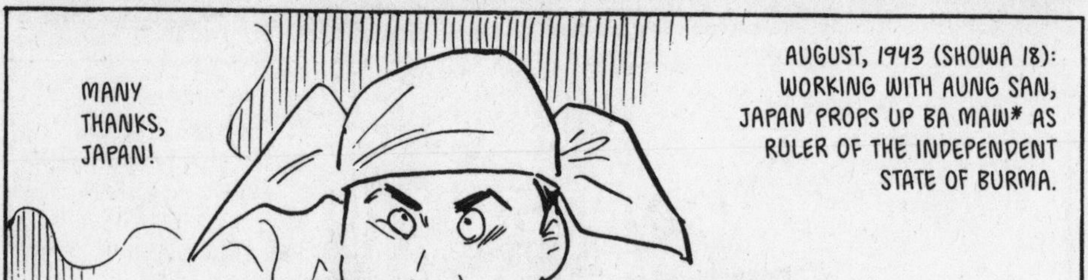
AUGUST, 1943 (SHOWA 18): WORKING WITH AUNG SAN, JAPAN PROPS UP BA MAW* AS RULER OF THE INDEPENDENT STATE OF BURMA.
MANY THANKS, JAPAN!

*SEE NOTE ON PAGE 546.

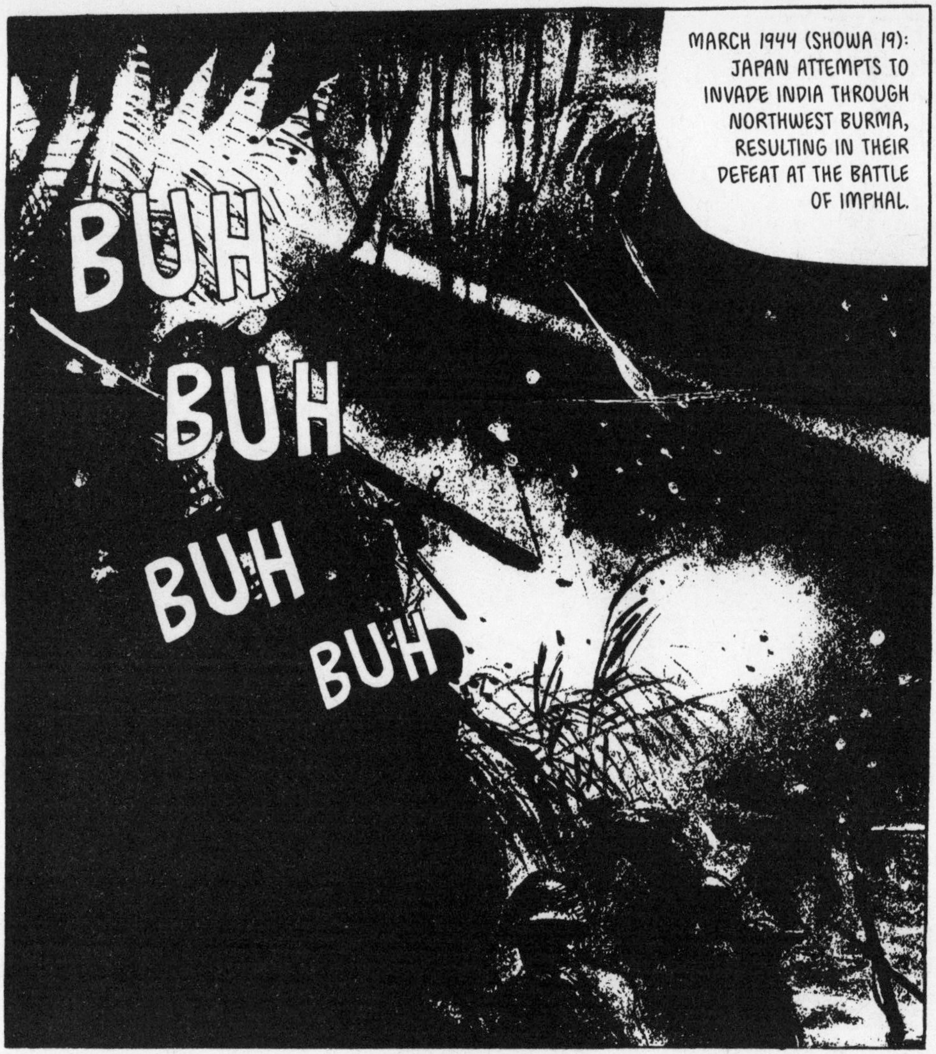
MARCH 1944 (SHOWA 19): JAPAN ATTEMPTS TO INVADE INDIA THROUGH NORTHWEST BURMA, RESULTING IN THEIR DEFEAT AT THE BATTLE OF IMPHAL.
BUH
BUH
BUH
BUH

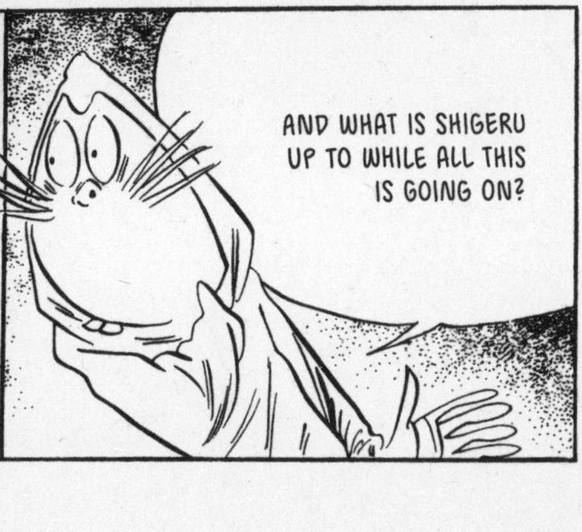
AND WHAT IS SHIGERU UP TO WHILE ALL THIS IS GOING ON?

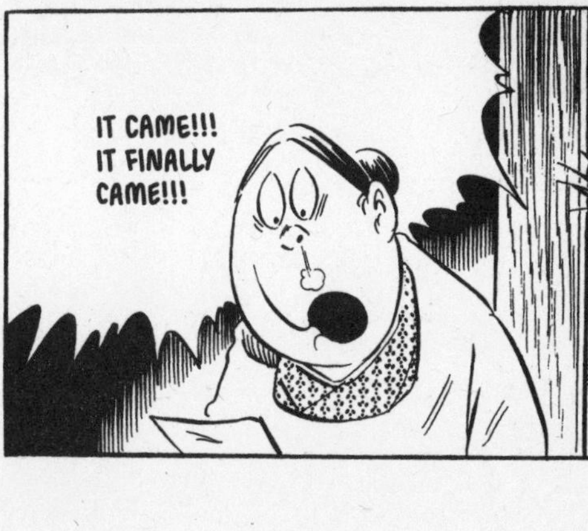
IT CAME!!! IT FINALLY CAME!!!

DRAFT PAPERS

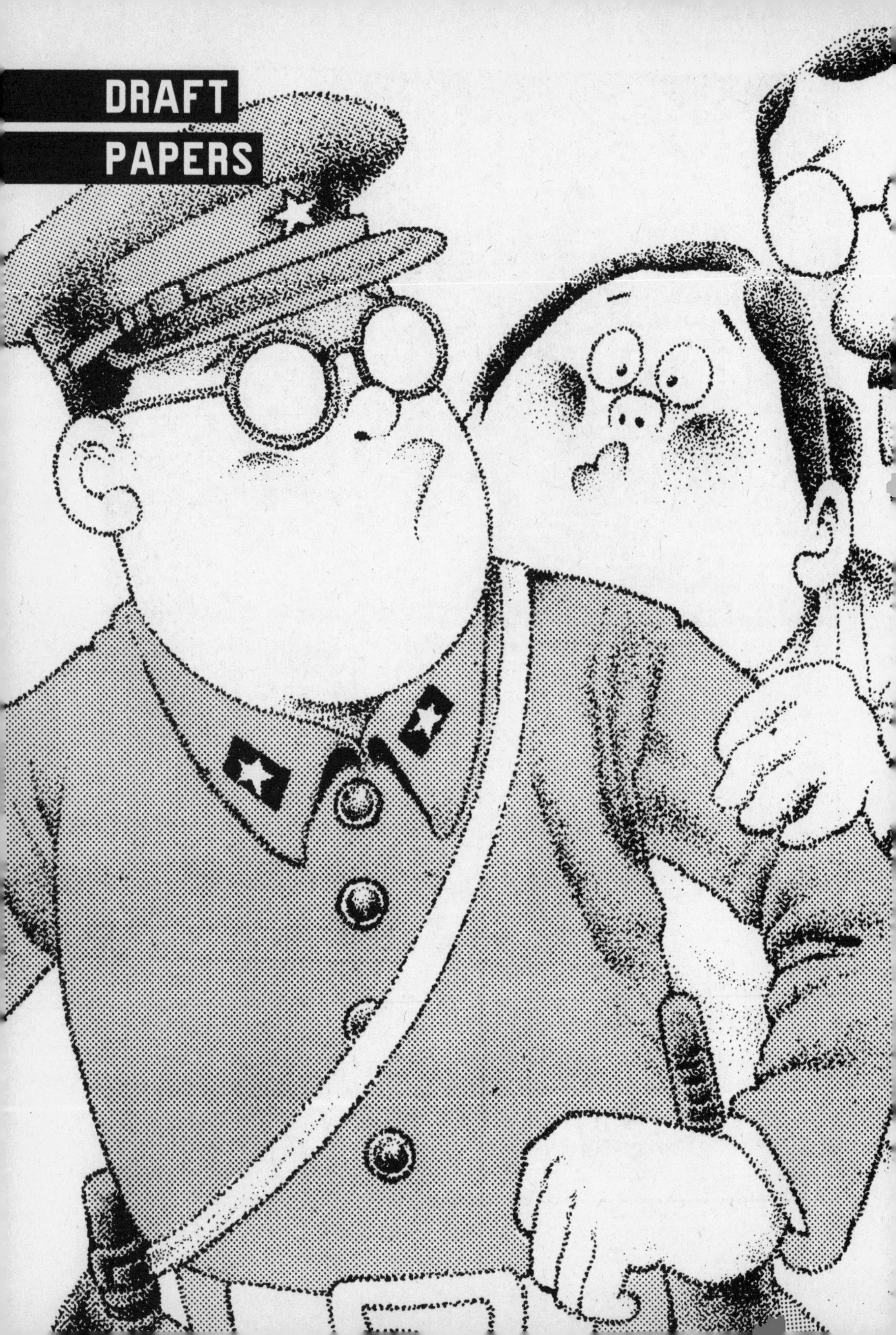

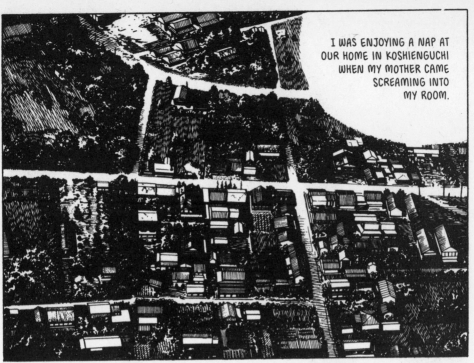

I WAS ENJOYING A NAP AT OUR HOME IN KOSHIENGUCHI WHEN MY MOTHER CAME SCREAMING INTO MY ROOM.

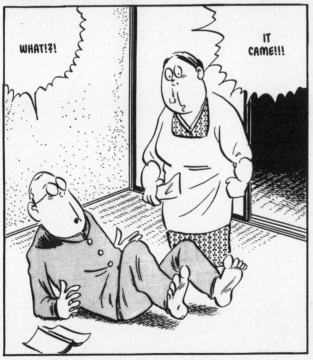

WHAT!?!

IT CAME!!!

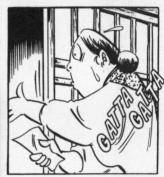

GATTA GATTA

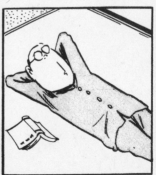

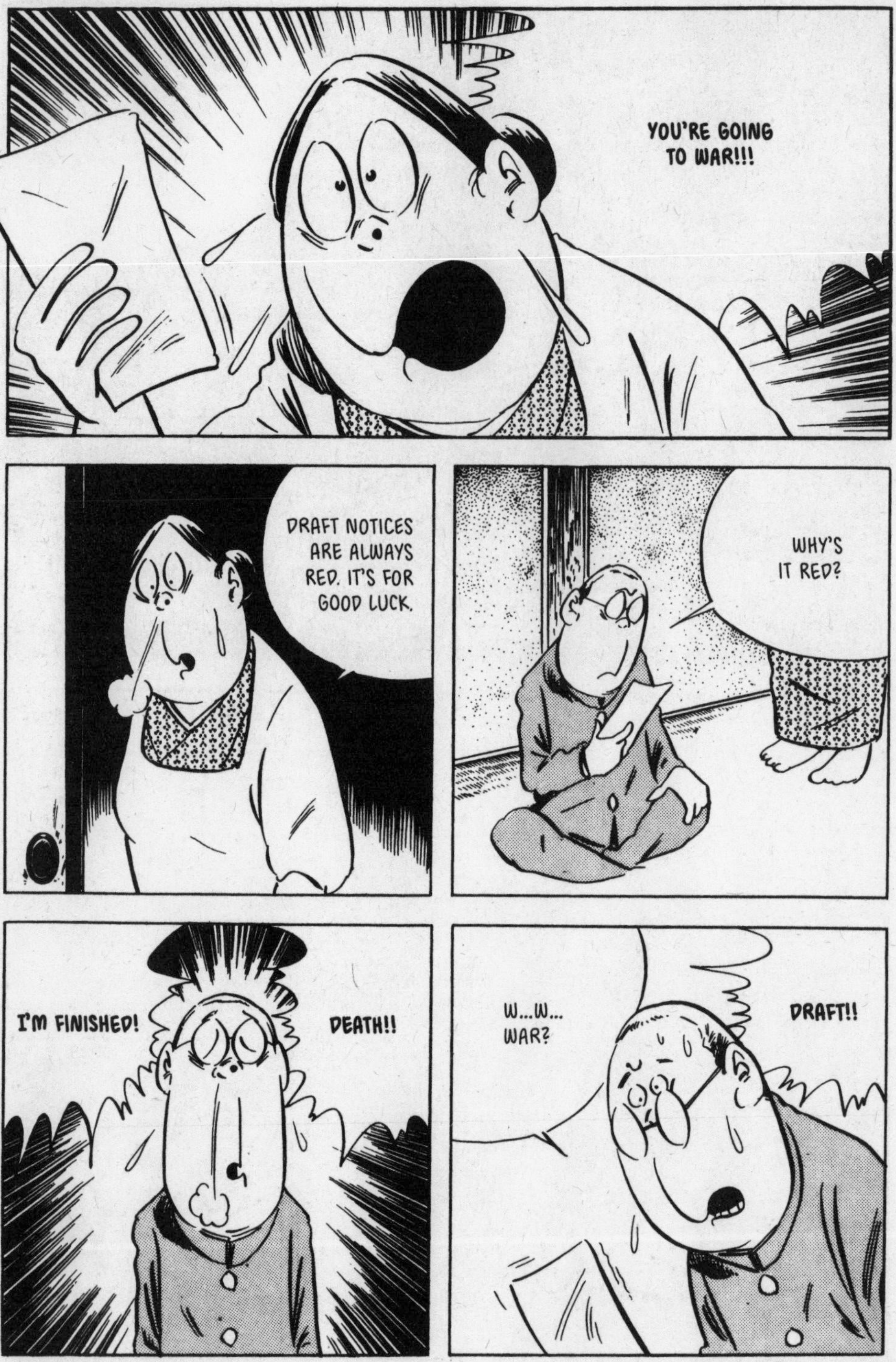
YOU'RE GOING TO WAR!!!
WHY'S IT RED?
DRAFT NOTICES ARE ALWAYS RED. IT'S FOR GOOD LUCK.
DRAFT!!
W...W... WAR?
DEATH!!
I'M FINISHED!

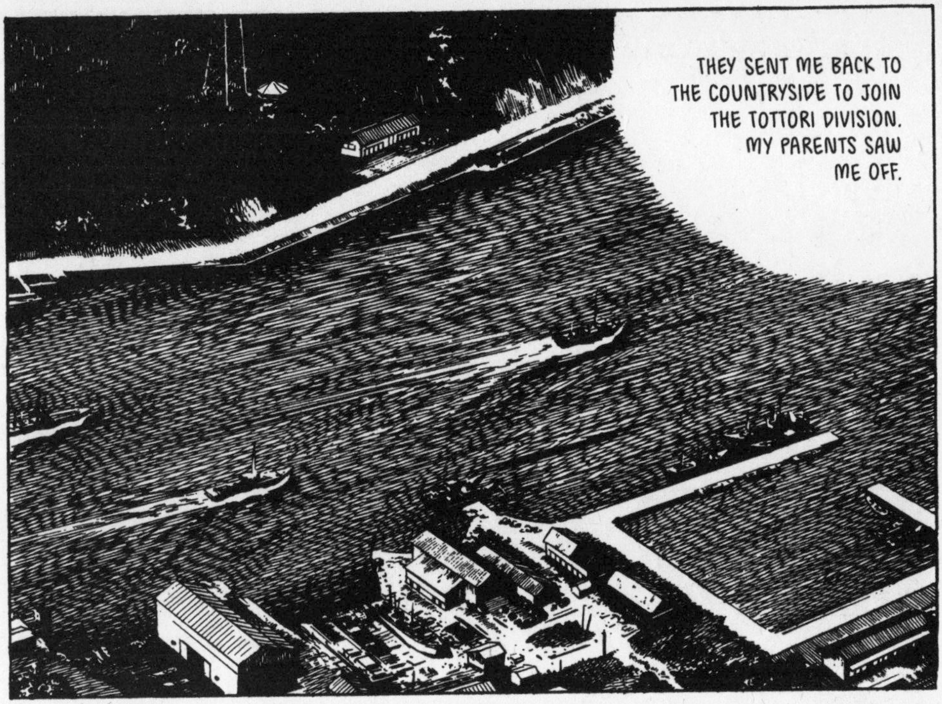
THEY SENT ME BACK TO THE COUNTRYSIDE TO JOIN THE TOTTORI DIVISION. MY PARENTS SAW ME OFF.

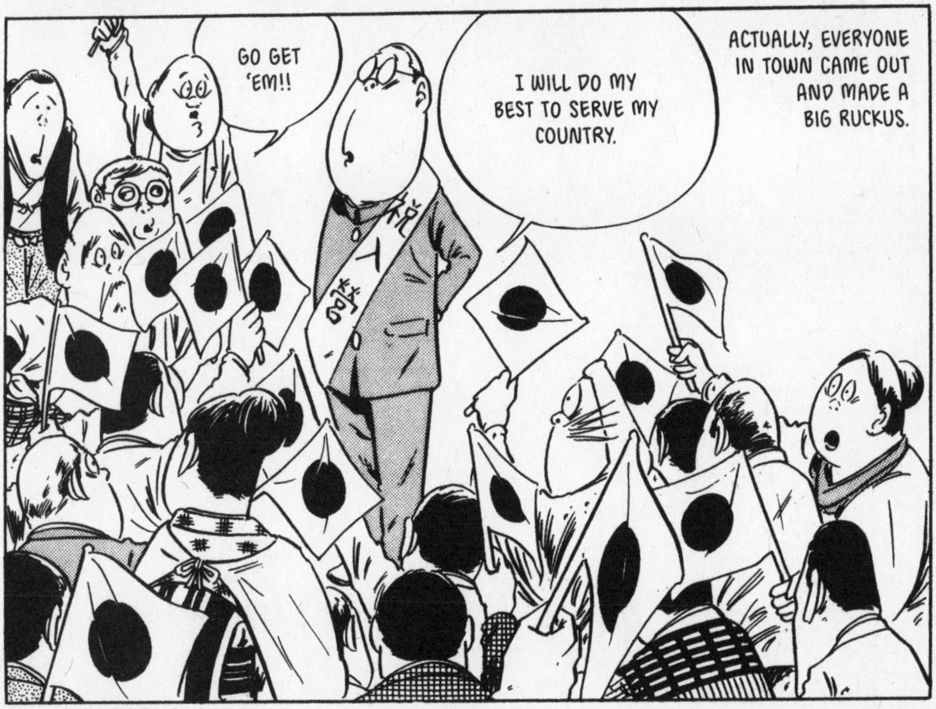
ACTUALLY, EVERYONE IN TOWN CAME OUT AND MADE A BIG RUCKUS.
I WILL DO MY BEST TO SERVE MY COUNTRY.
GO GET 'EM!!

SASH: NEW RECRUIT.

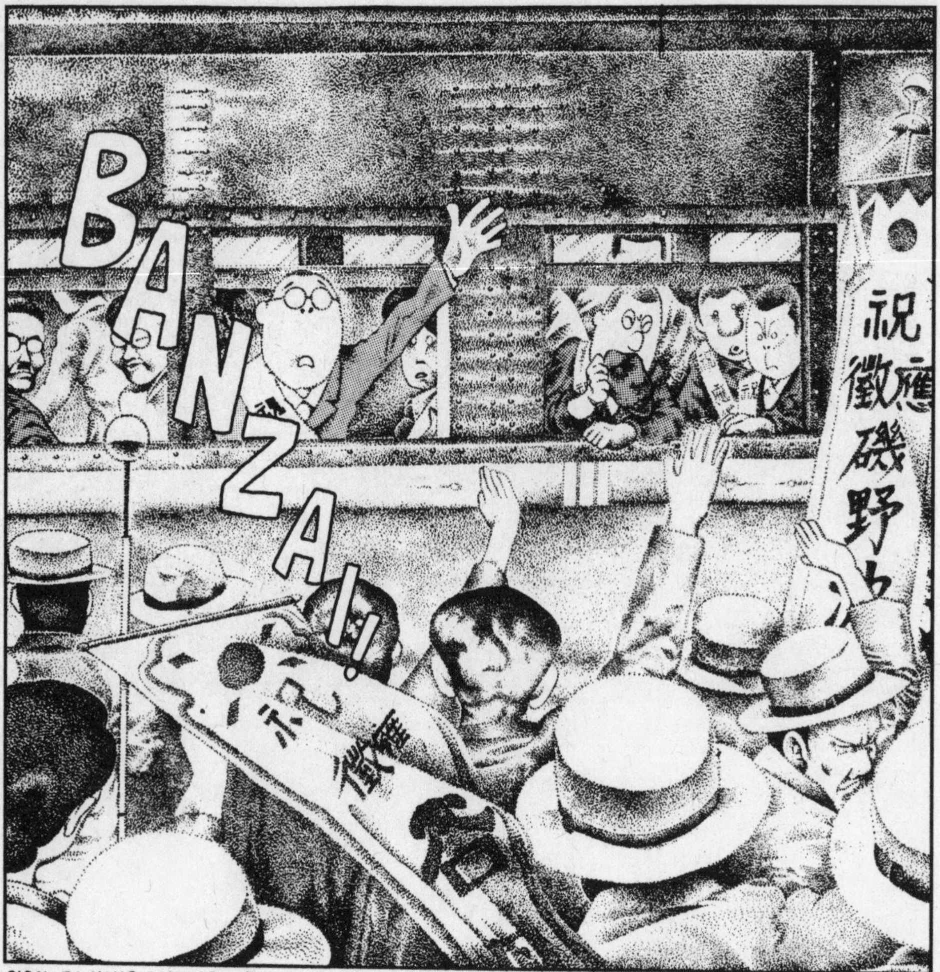
BANZAI!
祝應徵磯野
SIGN: DO YOUR BEST ISONO!

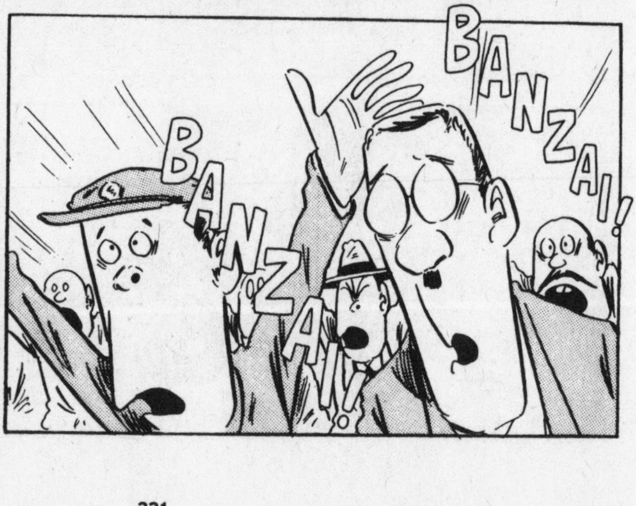
BANZAI!
BANZAI!

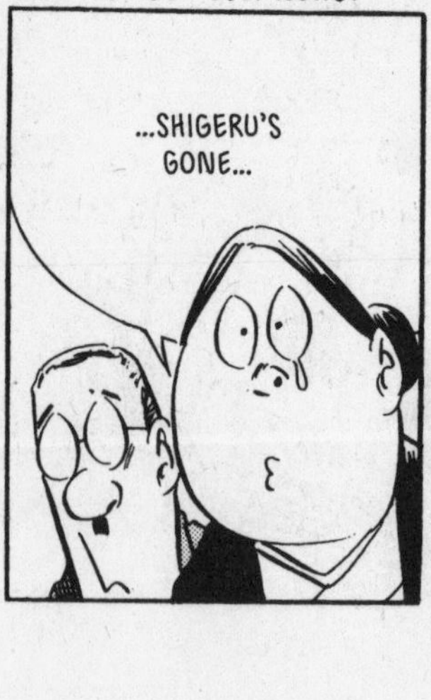
...SHIGERU'S GONE...

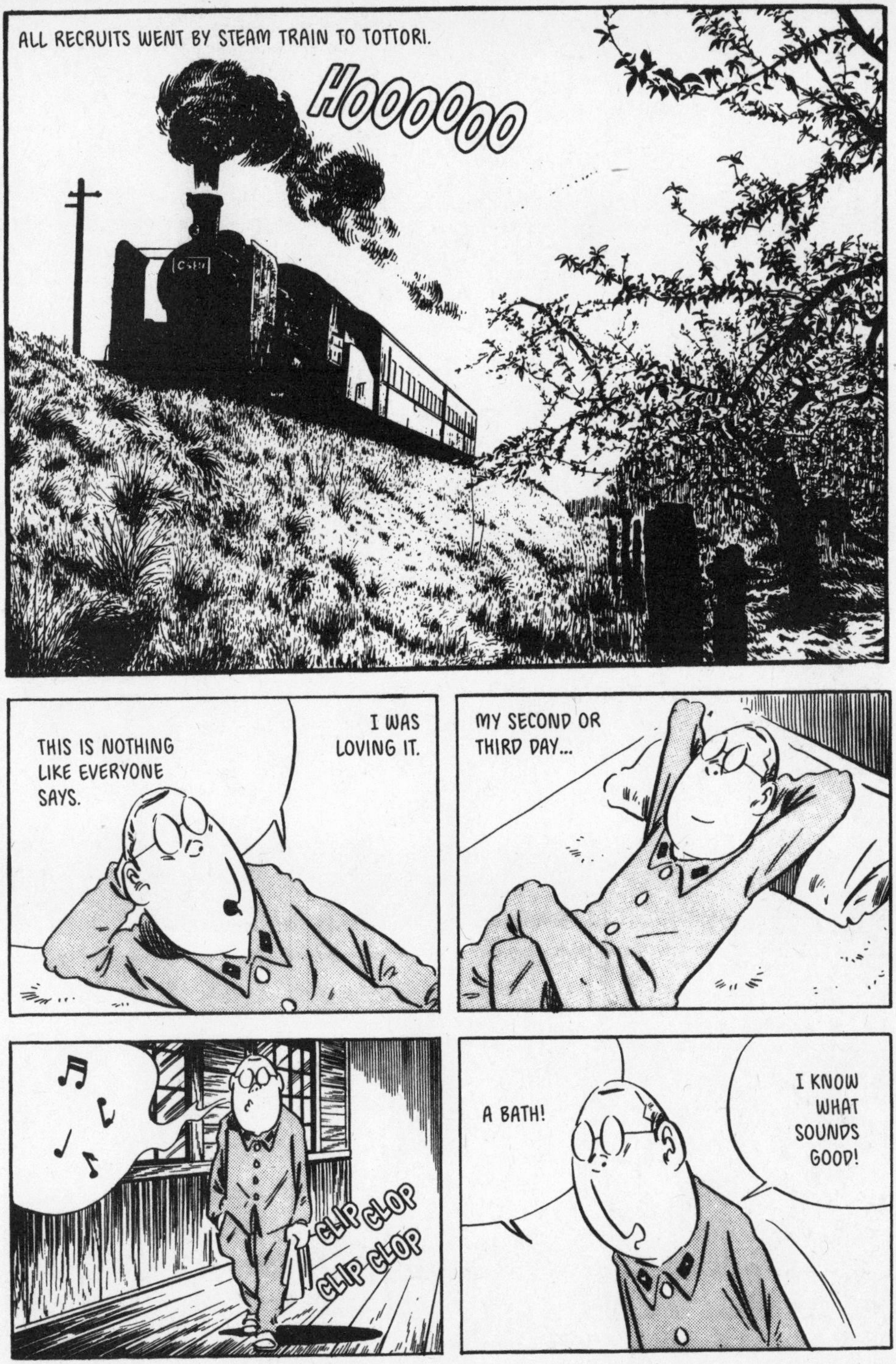
ALL RECRUITS WENT BY STEAM TRAIN TO TOTTORI.
HOOOOOO
MY SECOND OR THIRD DAY...
I WAS LOVING IT.
THIS IS NOTHING LIKE EVERYONE SAYS.
I KNOW WHAT SOUNDS GOOD!
A BATH!
CLIP CLOP
CLIP CLOP

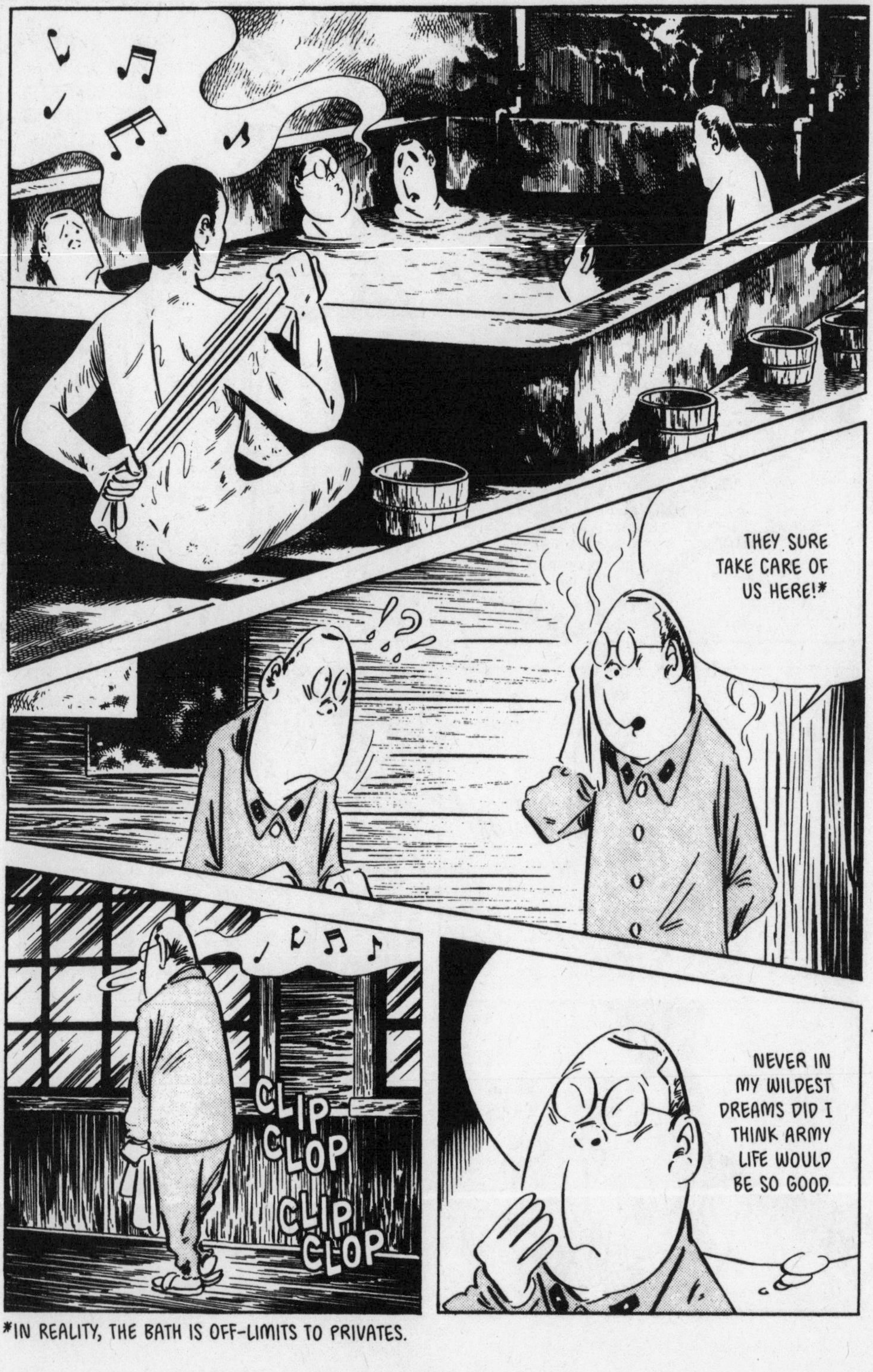
THEY SURE TAKE CARE OF US HERE!*
NEVER IN MY WILDEST DREAMS DID I THINK ARMY LIFE WOULD BE SO GOOD.
CLIP CLOP
CLIP CLOP

*IN REALITY, THE BATH IS OFF-LIMITS TO PRIVATES.

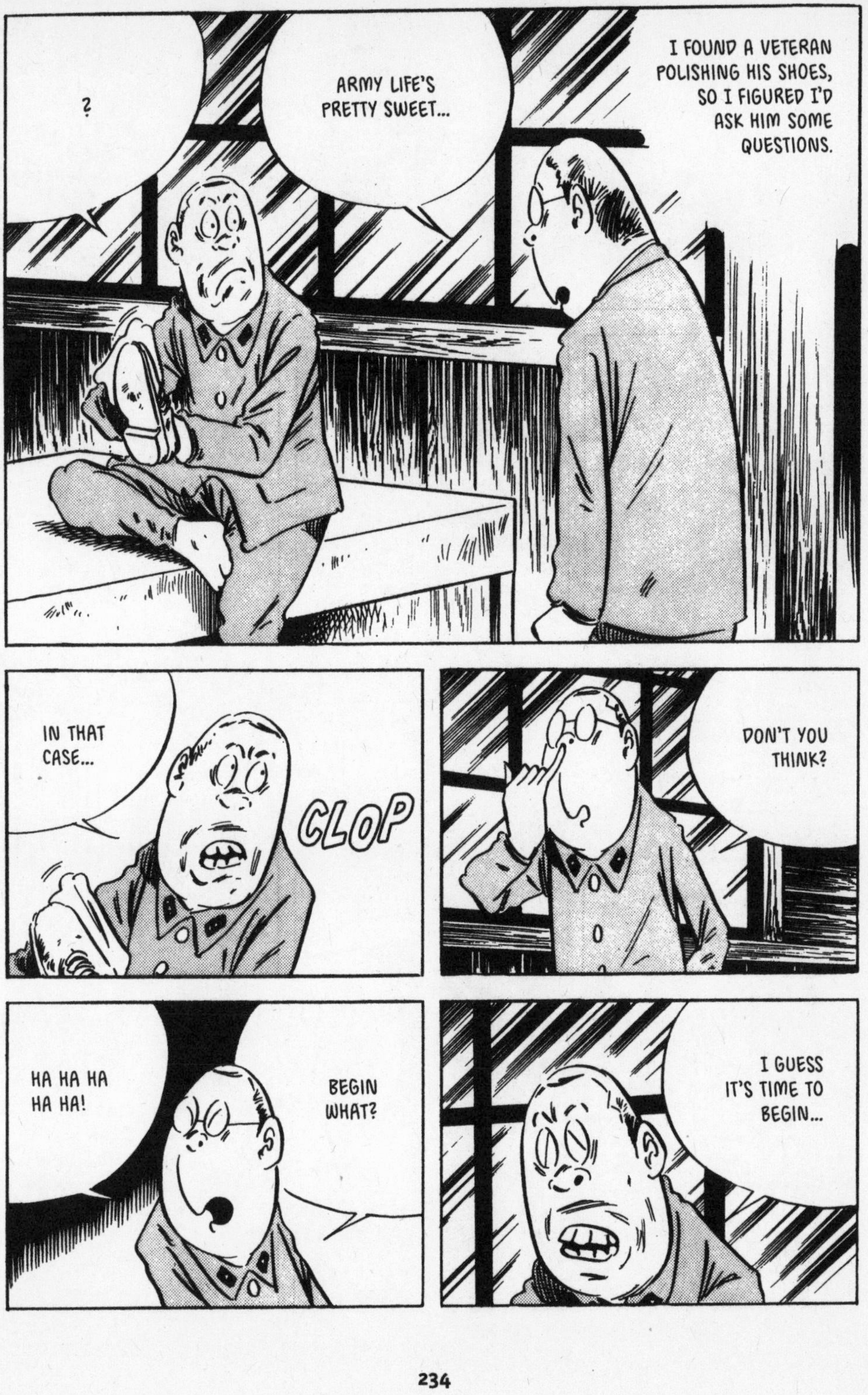
I FOUND A VETERAN POLISHING HIS SHOES, SO I FIGURED I'D ASK HIM SOME QUESTIONS.
ARMY LIFE'S PRETTY SWEET...
?
DON'T YOU THINK?
IN THAT CASE...
CLOP
I GUESS IT'S TIME TO BEGIN...
BEGIN WHAT?
HA HA HA HA HA!

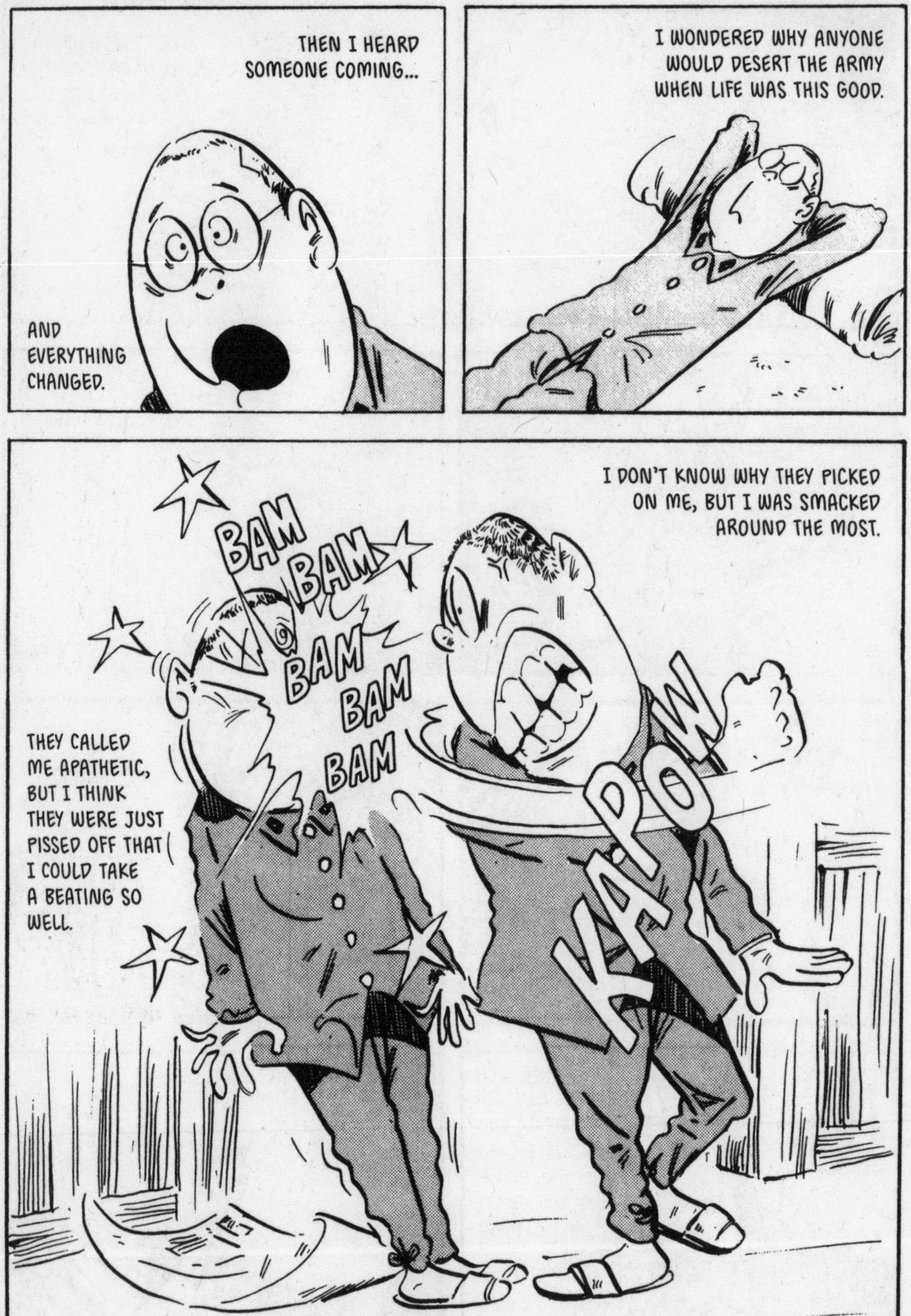
I WONDERED WHY ANYONE WOULD DESERT THE ARMY WHEN LIFE WAS THIS GOOD.
THEN I HEARD SOMEONE COMING...
AND EVERYTHING CHANGED.
I DON'T KNOW WHY THEY PICKED ON ME, BUT I WAS SMACKED AROUND THE MOST.
KAPOW
BAM BAM BAM BAM BAM
THEY CALLED ME APATHETIC, BUT I THINK THEY WERE JUST PISSED OFF THAT I COULD TAKE A BEATING SO WELL.

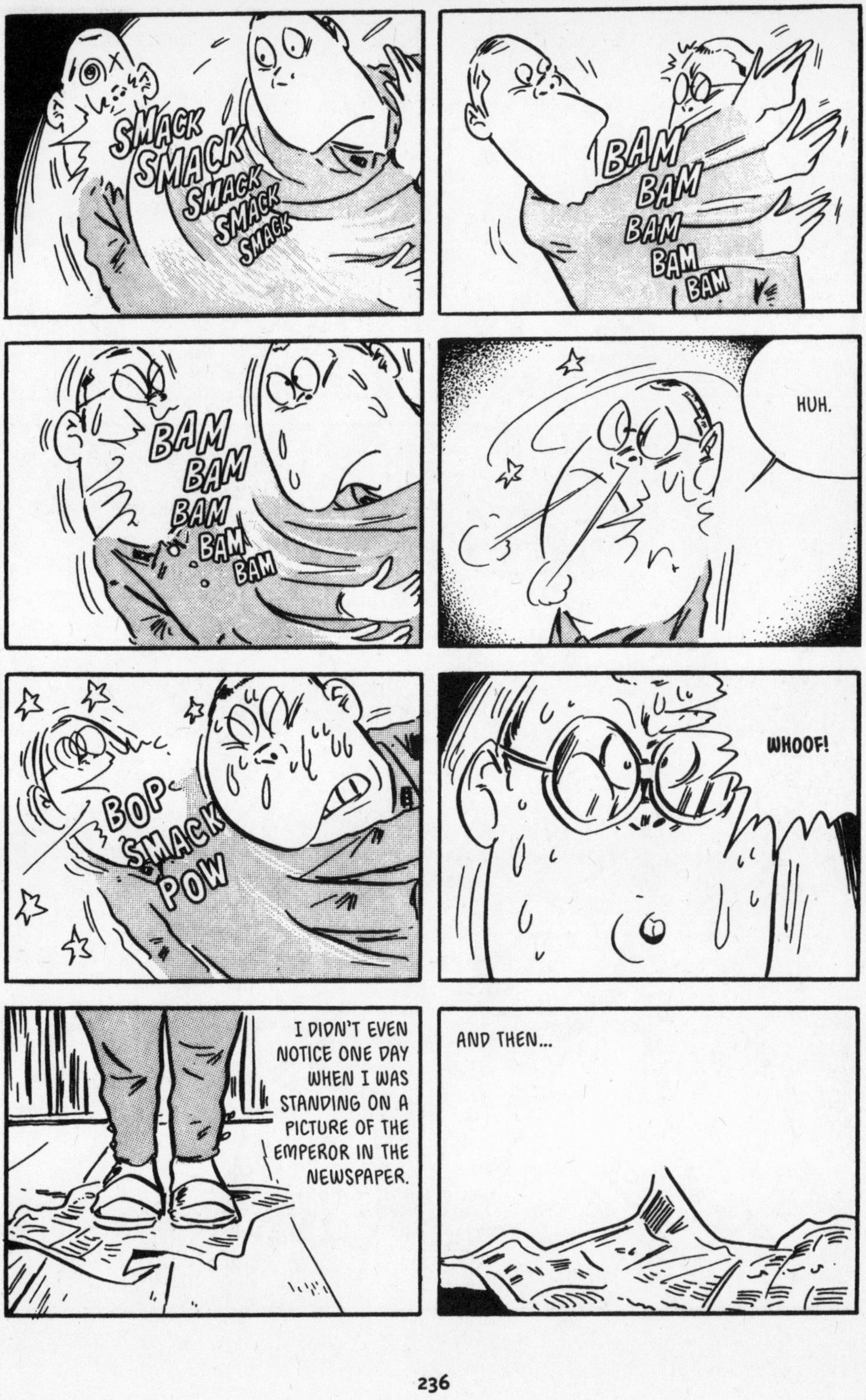
SMACK
SMACK
SMACK
SMACK
SMACK
BAM
BAM
BAM
BAM
BAM
BAM
BAM
BAM
BAM
BAM
HUH.
BOP
SMACK
POW
WHOOF!
I DIDN'T EVEN NOTICE ONE DAY WHEN I WAS STANDING ON A PICTURE OF THE EMPEROR IN THE NEWSPAPER.
AND THEN...

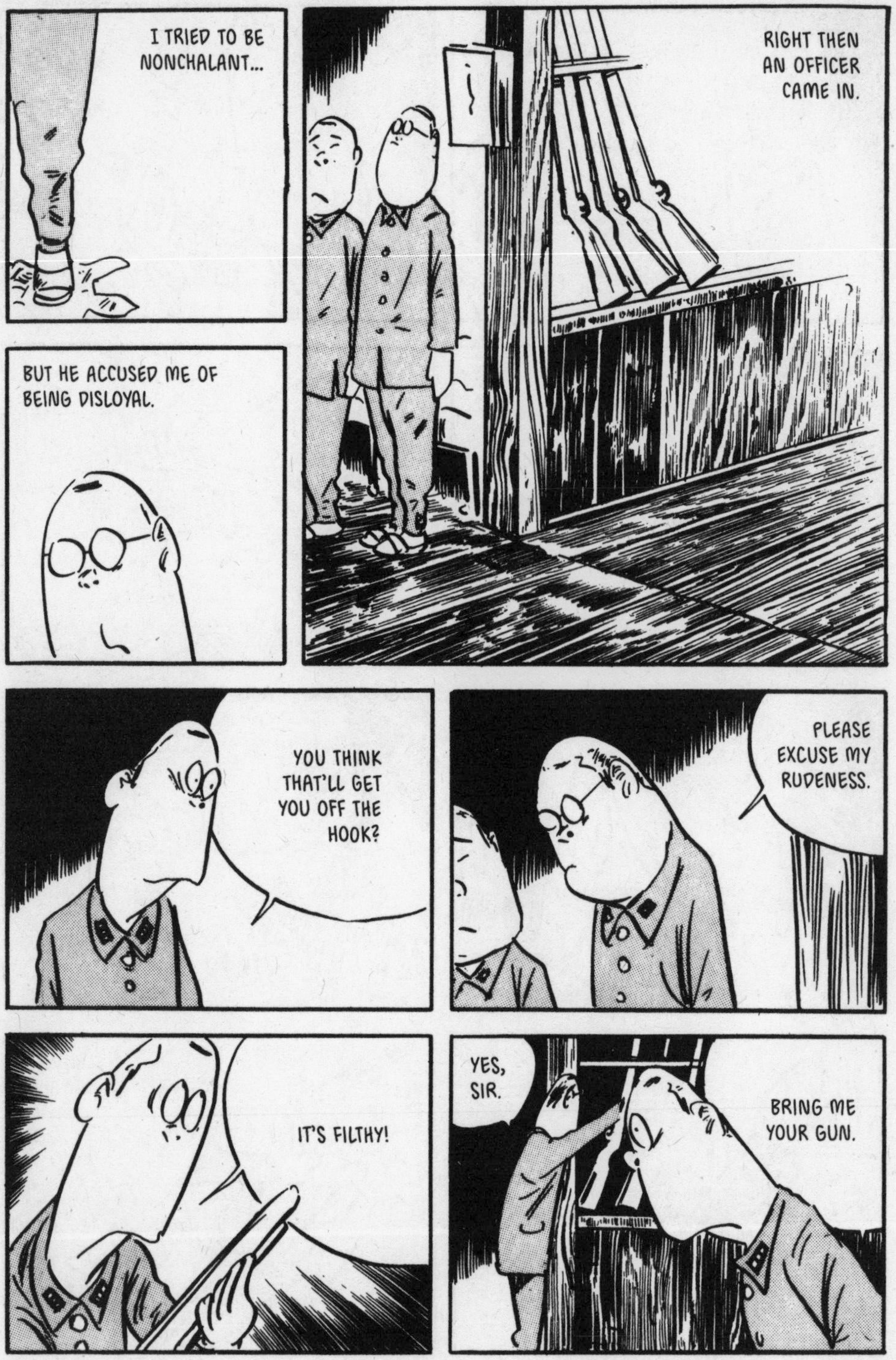
RIGHT THEN AN OFFICER CAME IN.
I TRIED TO BE NONCHALANT...
BUT HE ACCUSED ME OF BEING DISLOYAL.
PLEASE EXCUSE MY RUDENESS.
YOU THINK THAT'LL GET YOU OFF THE HOOK?
BRING ME YOUR GUN.
YES, SIR.
IT'S FILTHY!

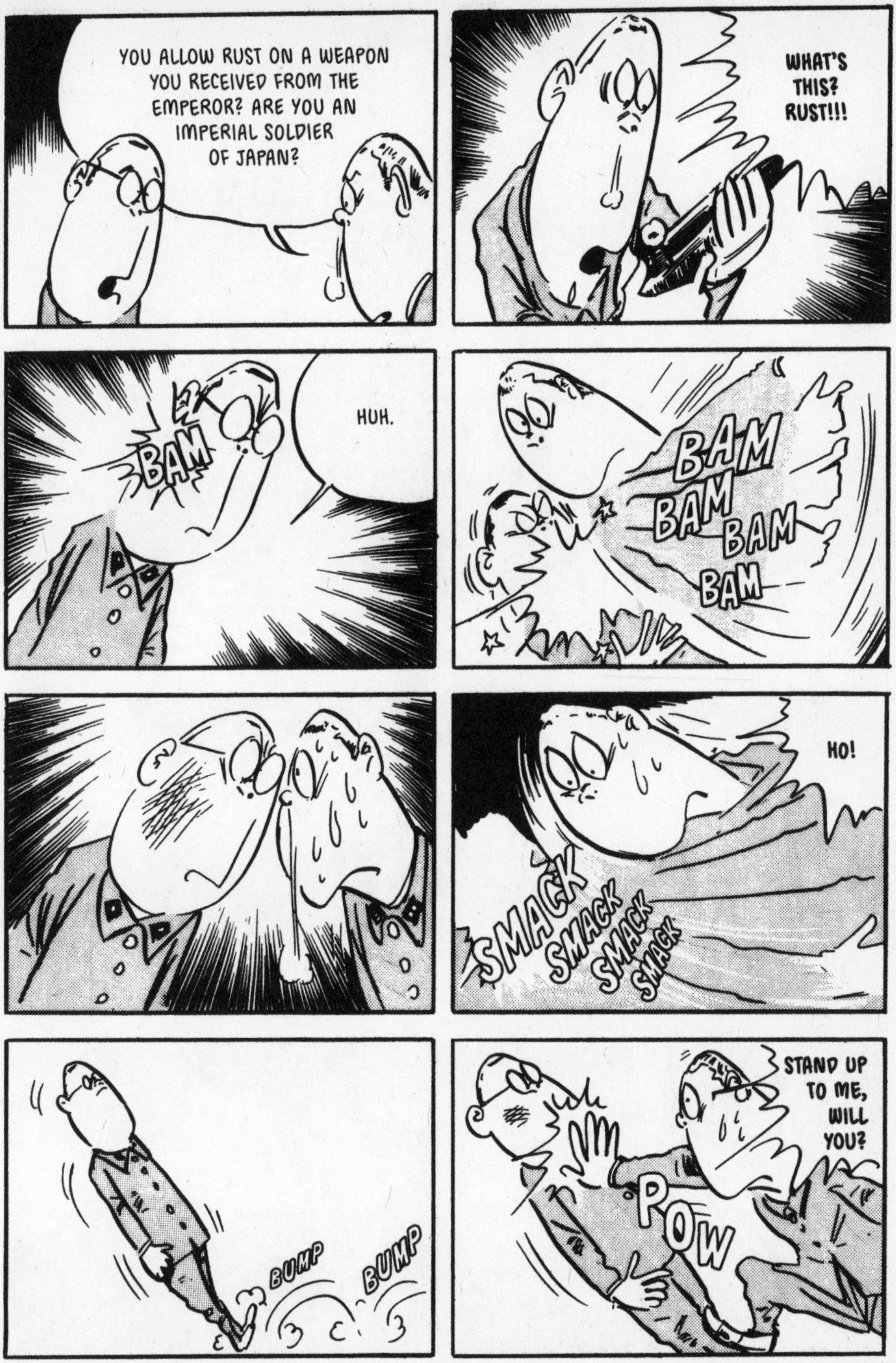
WHAT'S THIS? RUST!!!
YOU ALLOW RUST ON A WEAPON YOU RECEIVED FROM THE EMPEROR? ARE YOU AN IMPERIAL SOLDIER OF JAPAN?
BAM BAM BAM BAM
HUH.
BAM
HO!
SMACK SMACK SMACK SMACK
STAND UP TO ME, WILL YOU?
POW
BUMP
BUMP

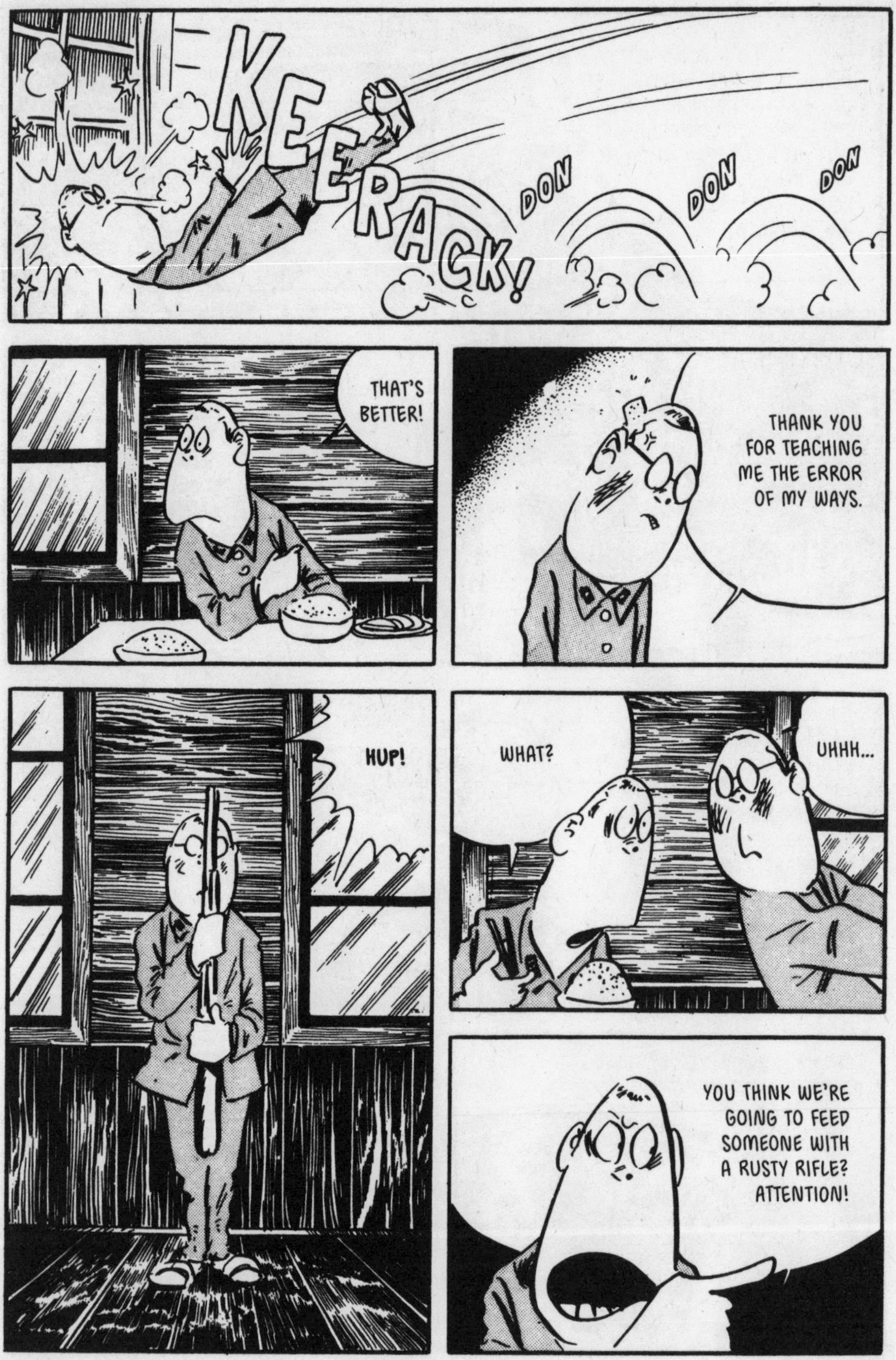
KEERACK!
DON
DON
DON
THANK YOU FOR TEACHING ME THE ERROR OF MY WAYS.
THAT'S BETTER!
UHHH...
WHAT?
YOU THINK WE'RE GOING TO FEED SOMEONE WITH A RUSTY RIFLE? ATTENTION!
HUP!

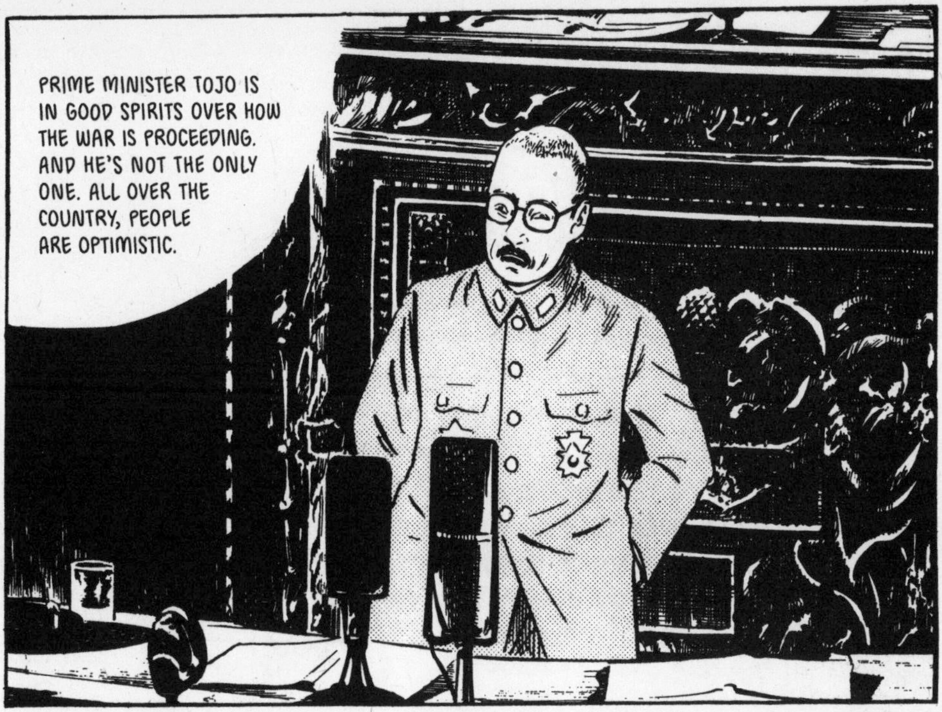
PRIME MINISTER TOJO IS IN GOOD SPIRITS OVER HOW THE WAR IS PROCEEDING. AND HE'S NOT THE ONLY ONE. ALL OVER THE COUNTRY, PEOPLE ARE OPTIMISTIC.

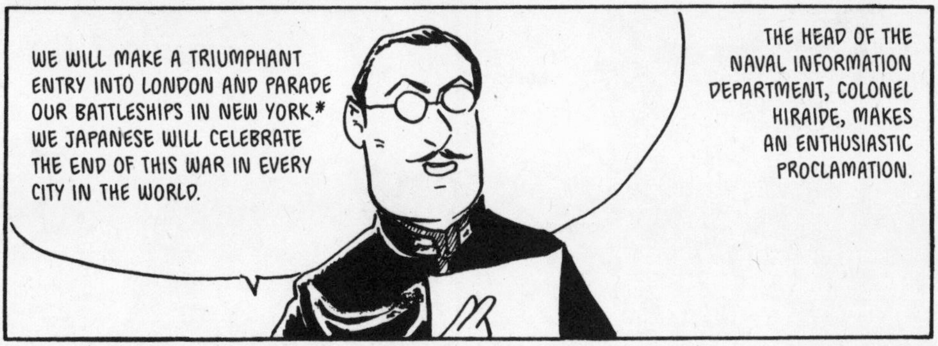
THE HEAD OF THE NAVAL INFORMATION DEPARTMENT, COLONEL HIRAIDE, MAKES AN ENTHUSIASTIC PROCLAMATION.
WE WILL MAKE A TRIUMPHANT ENTRY INTO LONDON AND PARADE OUR BATTLESHIPS IN NEW YORK.* WE JAPANESE WILL CELEBRATE THE END OF THIS WAR IN EVERY CITY IN THE WORLD.

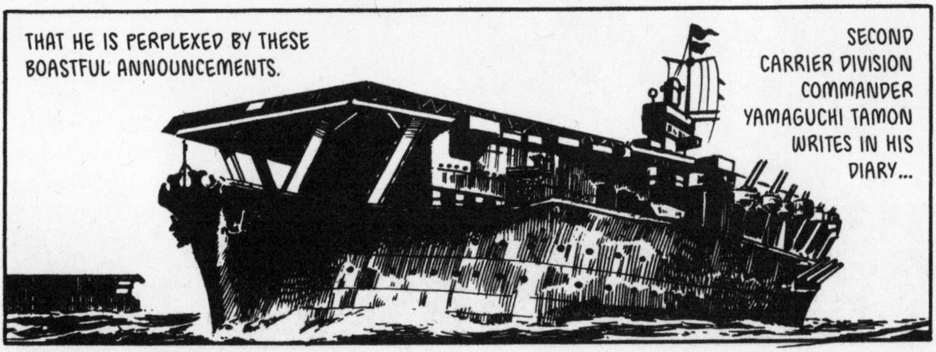
SECOND CARRIER DIVISION COMMANDER YAMAGUCHI TAMON WRITES IN HIS DIARY...
THAT HE IS PERPLEXED BY THESE BOASTFUL ANNOUNCEMENTS.

*SEE NOTE ON PAGE 546.

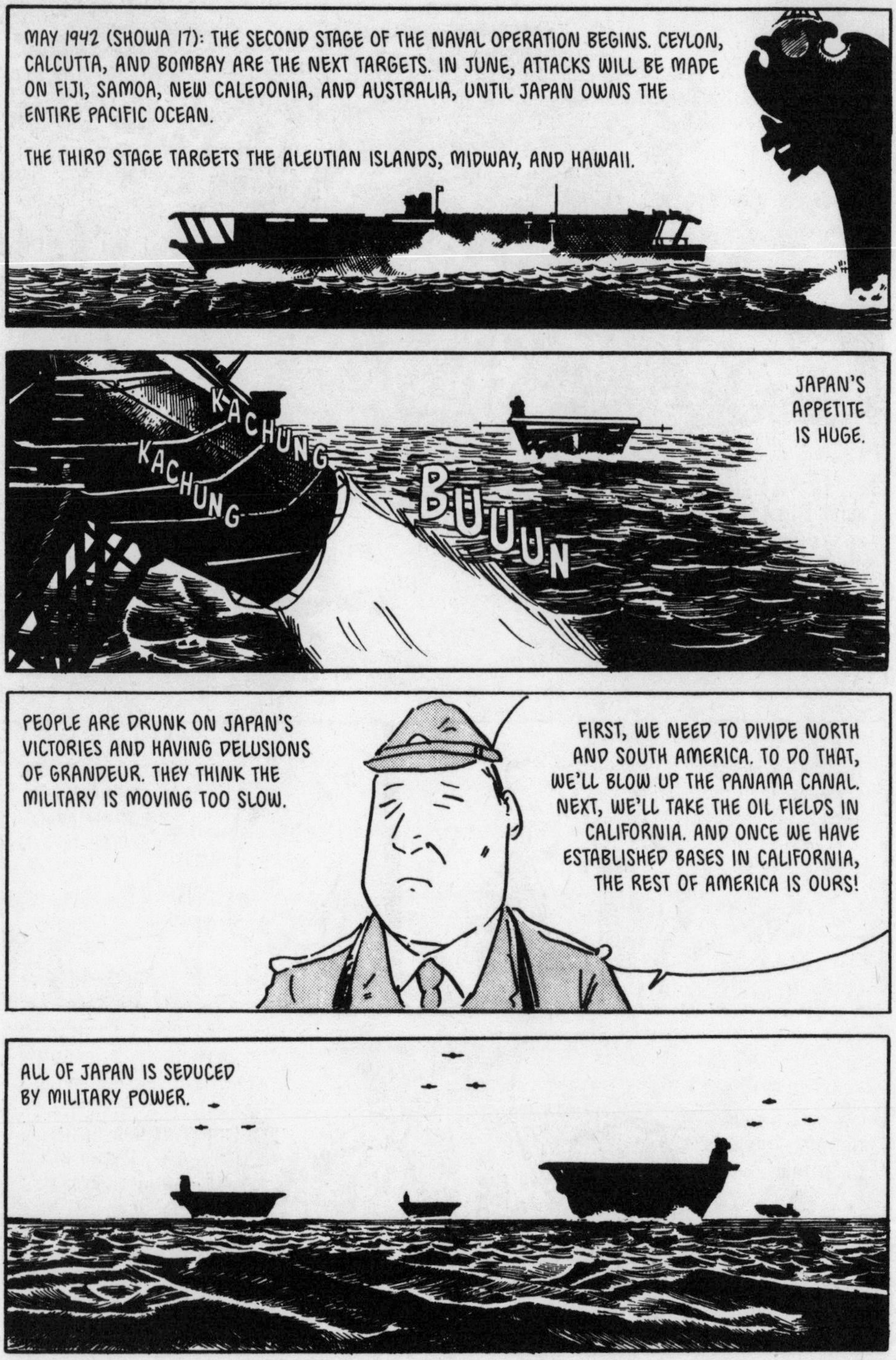
MAY 1942 (SHOWA 17): THE SECOND STAGE OF THE NAVAL OPERATION BEGINS. CEYLON, CALCUTTA, AND BOMBAY ARE THE NEXT TARGETS. IN JUNE, ATTACKS WILL BE MADE ON FIJI, SAMOA, NEW CALEDONIA, AND AUSTRALIA, UNTIL JAPAN OWNS THE ENTIRE PACIFIC OCEAN.
THE THIRD STAGE TARGETS THE ALEUTIAN ISLANDS, MIDWAY, AND HAWAII.
JAPAN'S APPETITE IS HUGE.
BUUUN
KACHUNG
KACHUNG
FIRST, WE NEED TO DIVIDE NORTH AND SOUTH AMERICA. TO DO THAT, WE'LL BLOW UP THE PANAMA CANAL. NEXT, WE'LL TAKE THE OIL FIELDS IN CALIFORNIA. AND ONCE WE HAVE ESTABLISHED BASES IN CALIFORNIA, THE REST OF AMERICA IS OURS!
PEOPLE ARE DRUNK ON JAPAN'S VICTORIES AND HAVING DELUSIONS OF GRANDEUR. THEY THINK THE MILITARY IS MOVING TOO SLOW.
ALL OF JAPAN IS SEDUCED BY MILITARY POWER.

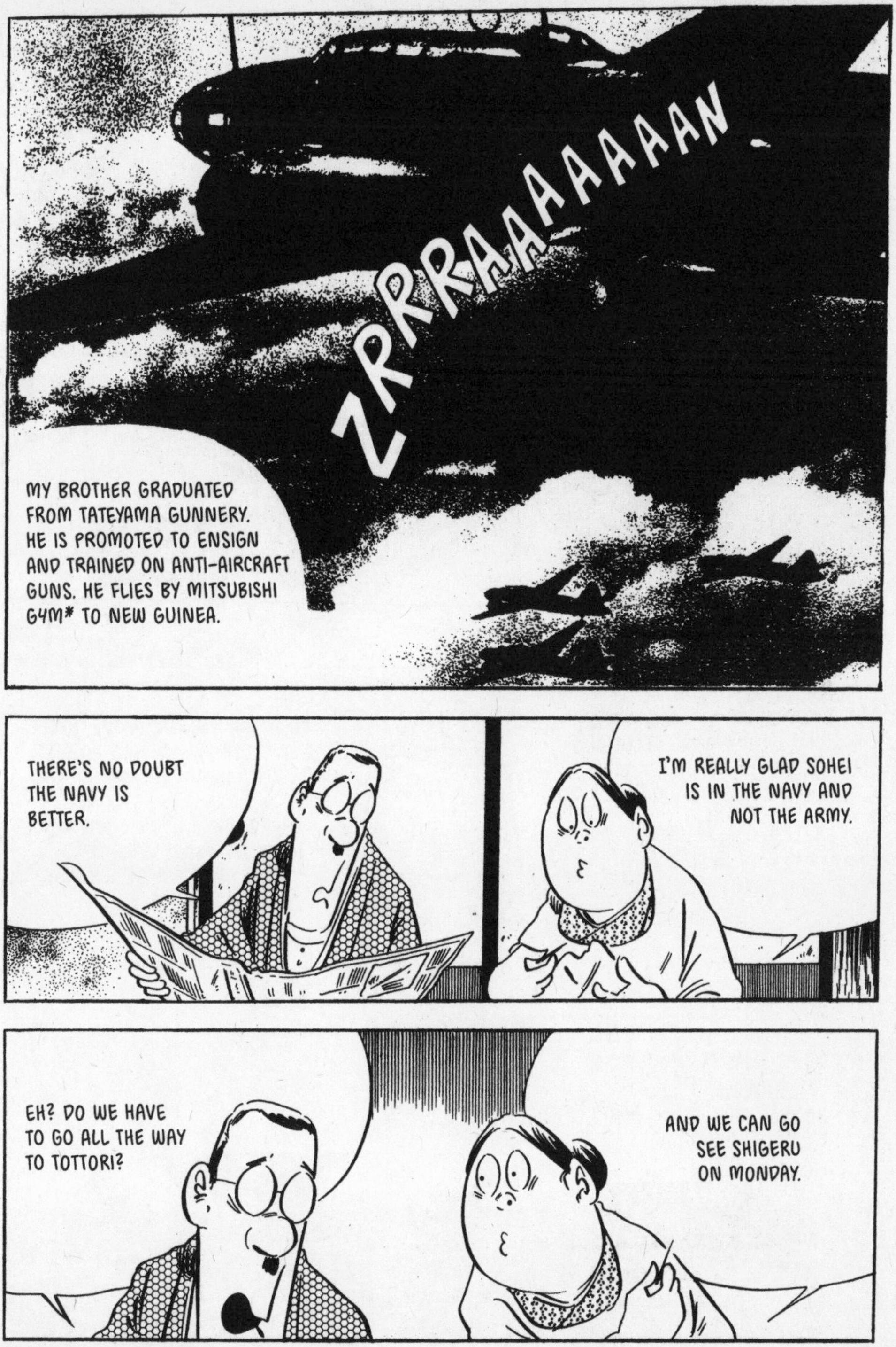
ZRRRAAAAAAAN
MY BROTHER GRADUATED FROM TATEYAMA GUNNERY. HE IS PROMOTED TO ENSIGN AND TRAINED ON ANTI-AIRCRAFT GUNS. HE FLIES BY MITSUBISHI G4M* TO NEW GUINEA.
I'M REALLY GLAD SOHEI IS IN THE NAVY AND NOT THE ARMY.
THERE'S NO DOUBT THE NAVY IS BETTER.
AND WE CAN GO SEE SHIGERU ON MONDAY.
EH? DO WE HAVE TO GO ALL THE WAY TO TOTTORI?

*SEE NOTE ON PAGE 546.

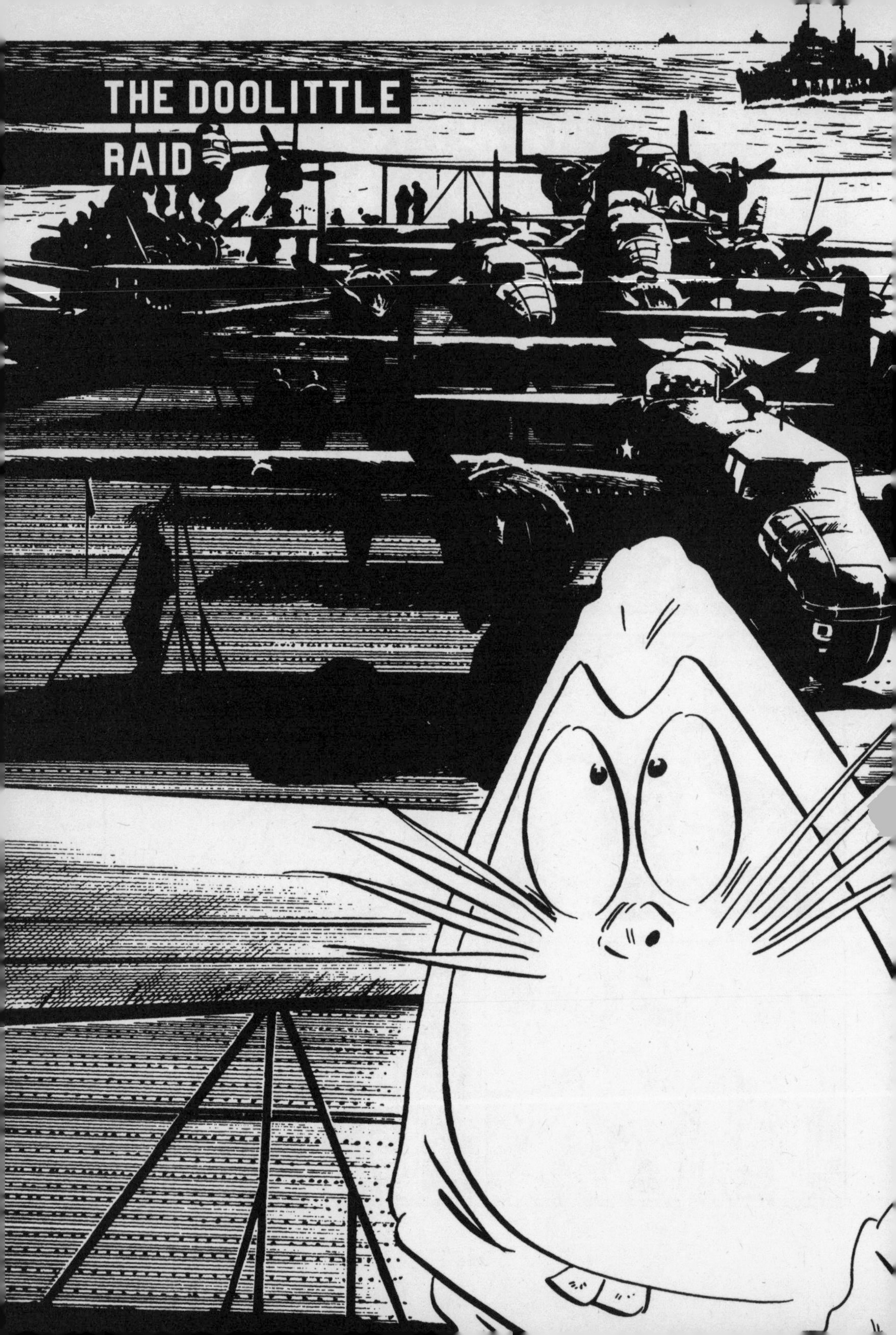
THE DOOLITTLE RAID

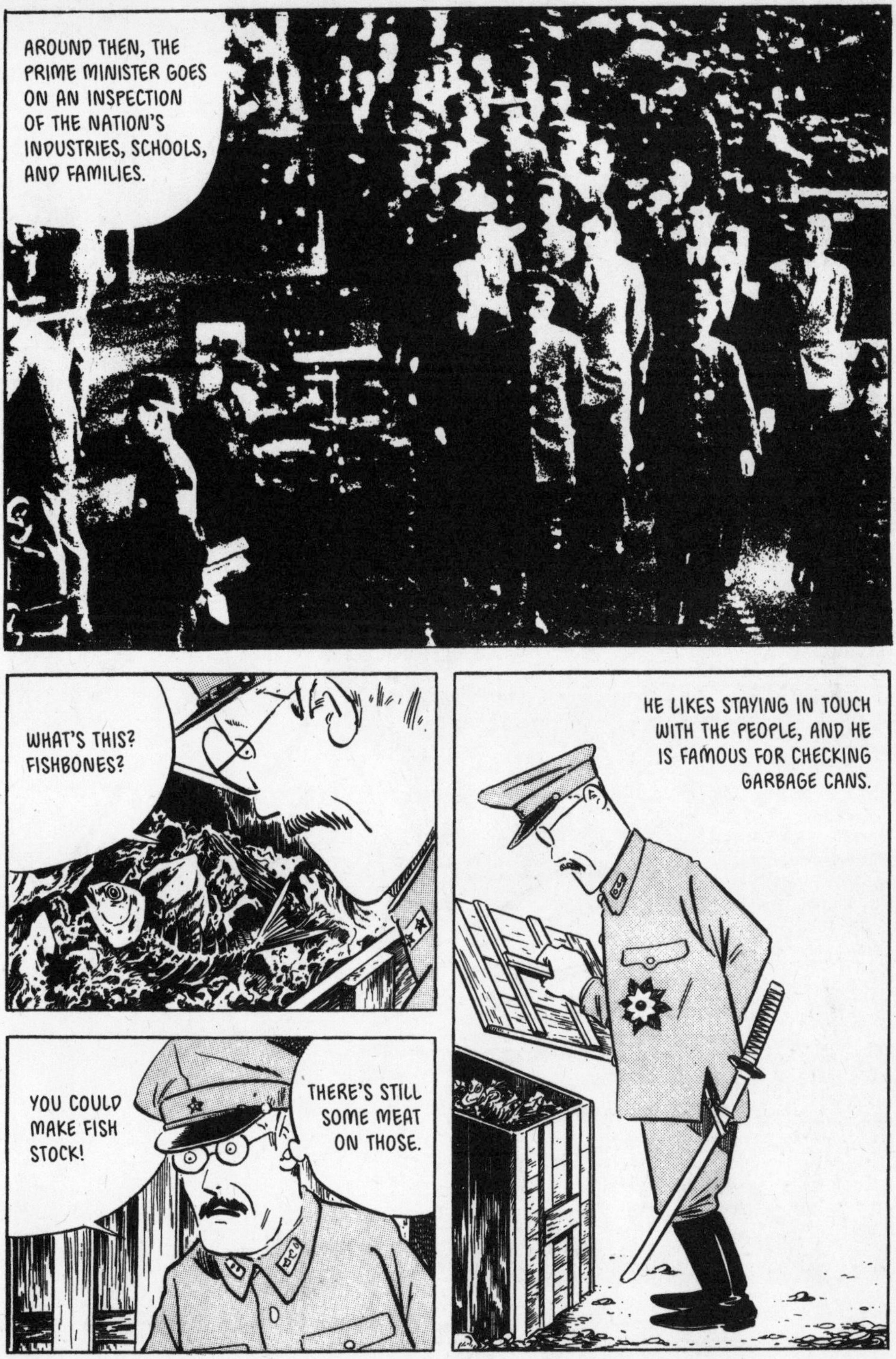
AROUND THEN, THE PRIME MINISTER GOES ON AN INSPECTION OF THE NATION'S INDUSTRIES, SCHOOLS, AND FAMILIES.
HE LIKES STAYING IN TOUCH WITH THE PEOPLE, AND HE IS FAMOUS FOR CHECKING GARBAGE CANS.
WHAT'S THIS? FISHBONES?
THERE'S STILL SOME MEAT ON THOSE.
YOU COULD MAKE FISH STOCK!

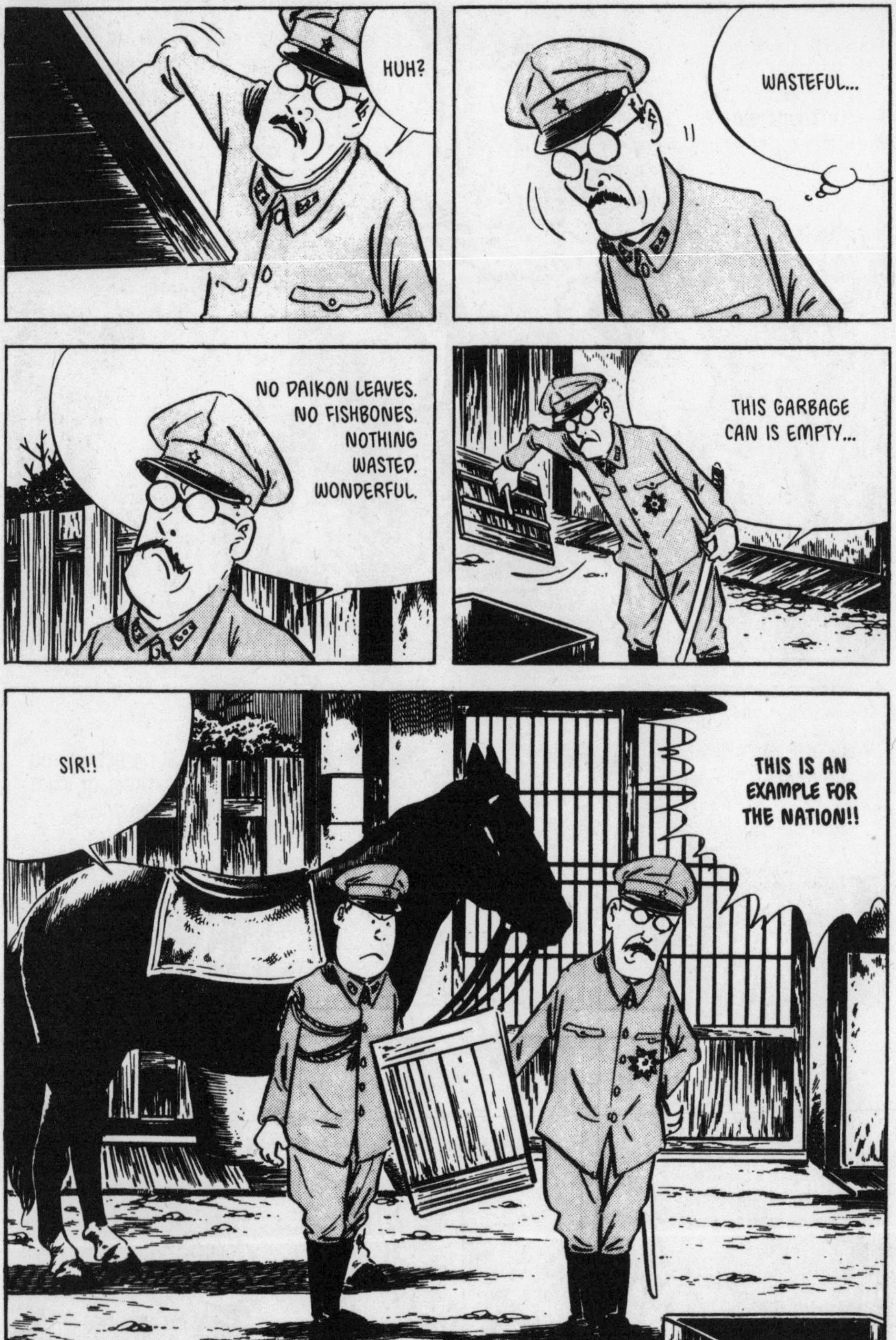
WASTEFUL...
HUH?
THIS GARBAGE CAN IS EMPTY...
NO DAIKON LEAVES. NO FISHBONES. NOTHING WASTED. WONDERFUL.
THIS IS AN EXAMPLE FOR THE NATION!!
SIR!!

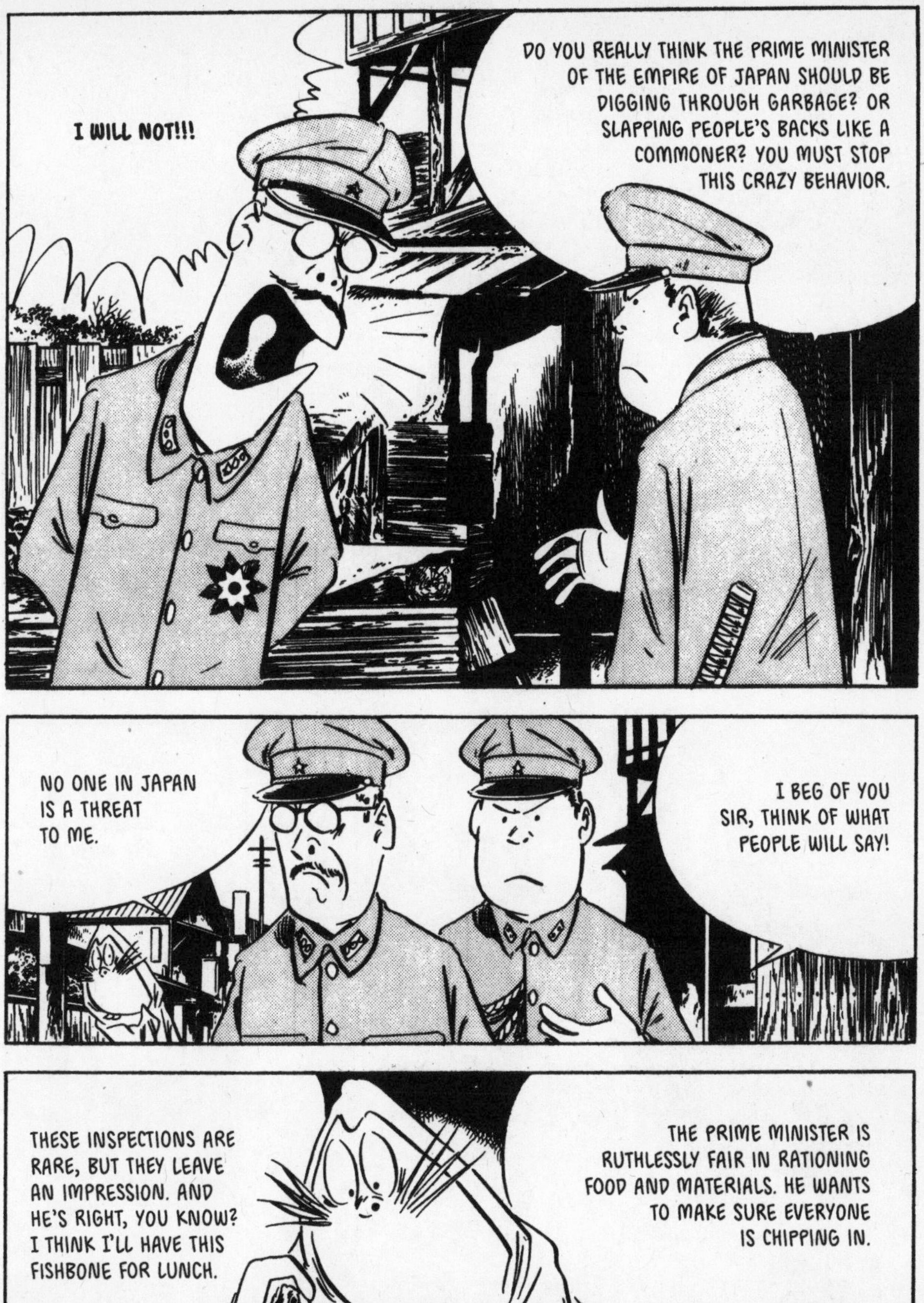
DO YOU REALLY THINK THE PRIME MINISTER OF THE EMPIRE OF JAPAN SHOULD BE DIGGING THROUGH GARBAGE? OR SLAPPING PEOPLE'S BACKS LIKE A COMMONER? YOU MUST STOP THIS CRAZY BEHAVIOR.
I WILL NOT!!!
I BEG OF YOU SIR, THINK OF WHAT PEOPLE WILL SAY!
NO ONE IN JAPAN IS A THREAT TO ME.
THE PRIME MINISTER IS RUTHLESSLY FAIR IN RATIONING FOOD AND MATERIALS. HE WANTS TO MAKE SURE EVERYONE IS CHIPPING IN.
THESE INSPECTIONS ARE RARE, BUT THEY LEAVE AN IMPRESSION. AND HE'S RIGHT, YOU KNOW? I THINK I'LL HAVE THIS FISHBONE FOR LUNCH.

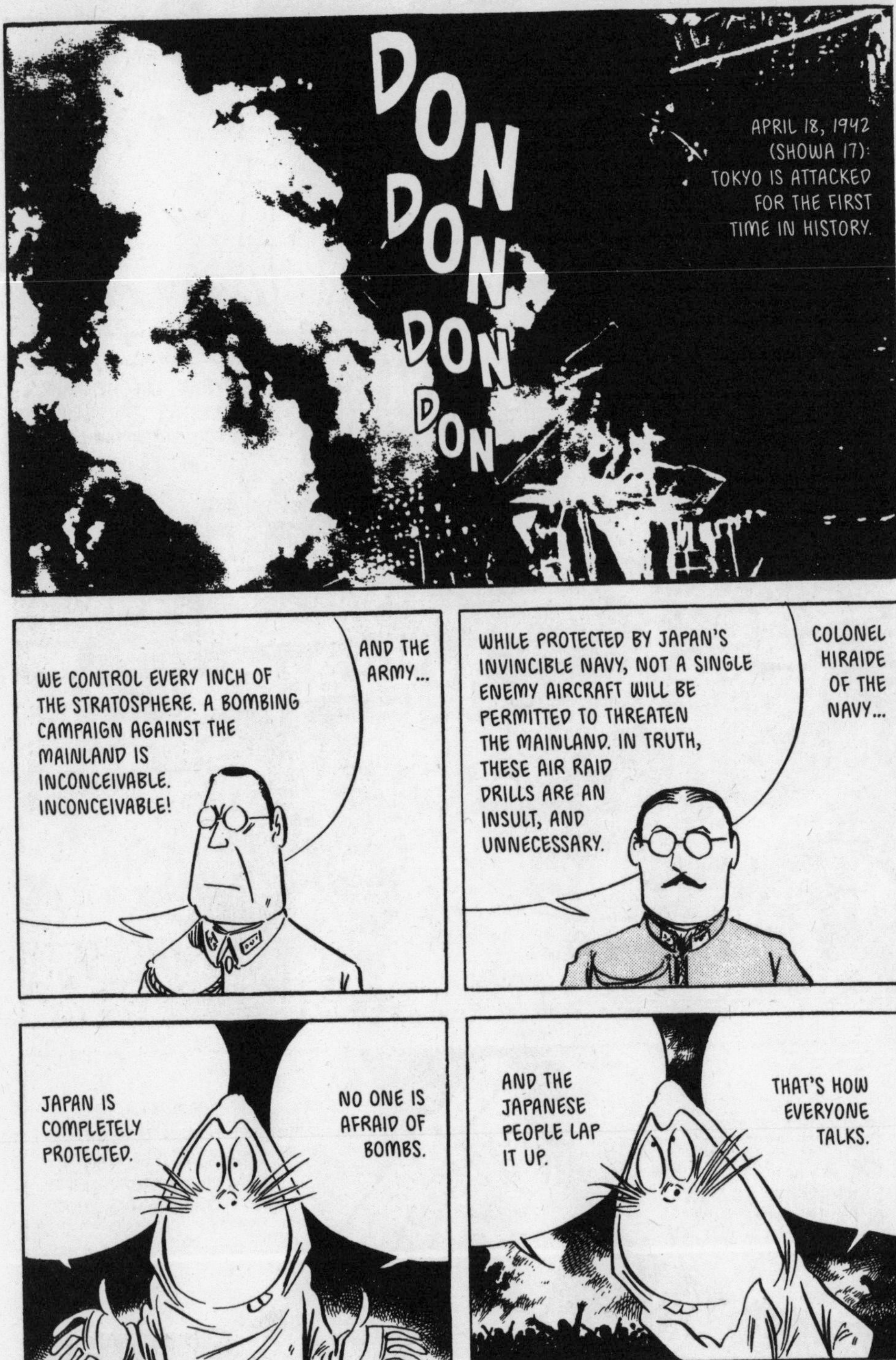
APRIL 18, 1942 (SHOWA 17): TOKYO IS ATTACKED FOR THE FIRST TIME IN HISTORY.
DON DON DON DON DON DON
COLONEL HIRAIDE OF THE NAVY...
WHILE PROTECTED BY JAPAN'S INVINCIBLE NAVY, NOT A SINGLE ENEMY AIRCRAFT WILL BE PERMITTED TO THREATEN THE MAINLAND. IN TRUTH, THESE AIR RAID DRILLS ARE AN INSULT, AND UNNECESSARY.
AND THE ARMY...
WE CONTROL EVERY INCH OF THE STRATOSPHERE. A BOMBING CAMPAIGN AGAINST THE MAINLAND IS INCONCEIVABLE. INCONCEIVABLE!
THAT'S HOW EVERYONE TALKS.
AND THE JAPANESE PEOPLE LAP IT UP.
NO ONE IS AFRAID OF BOMBS.
JAPAN IS COMPLETELY PROTECTED.

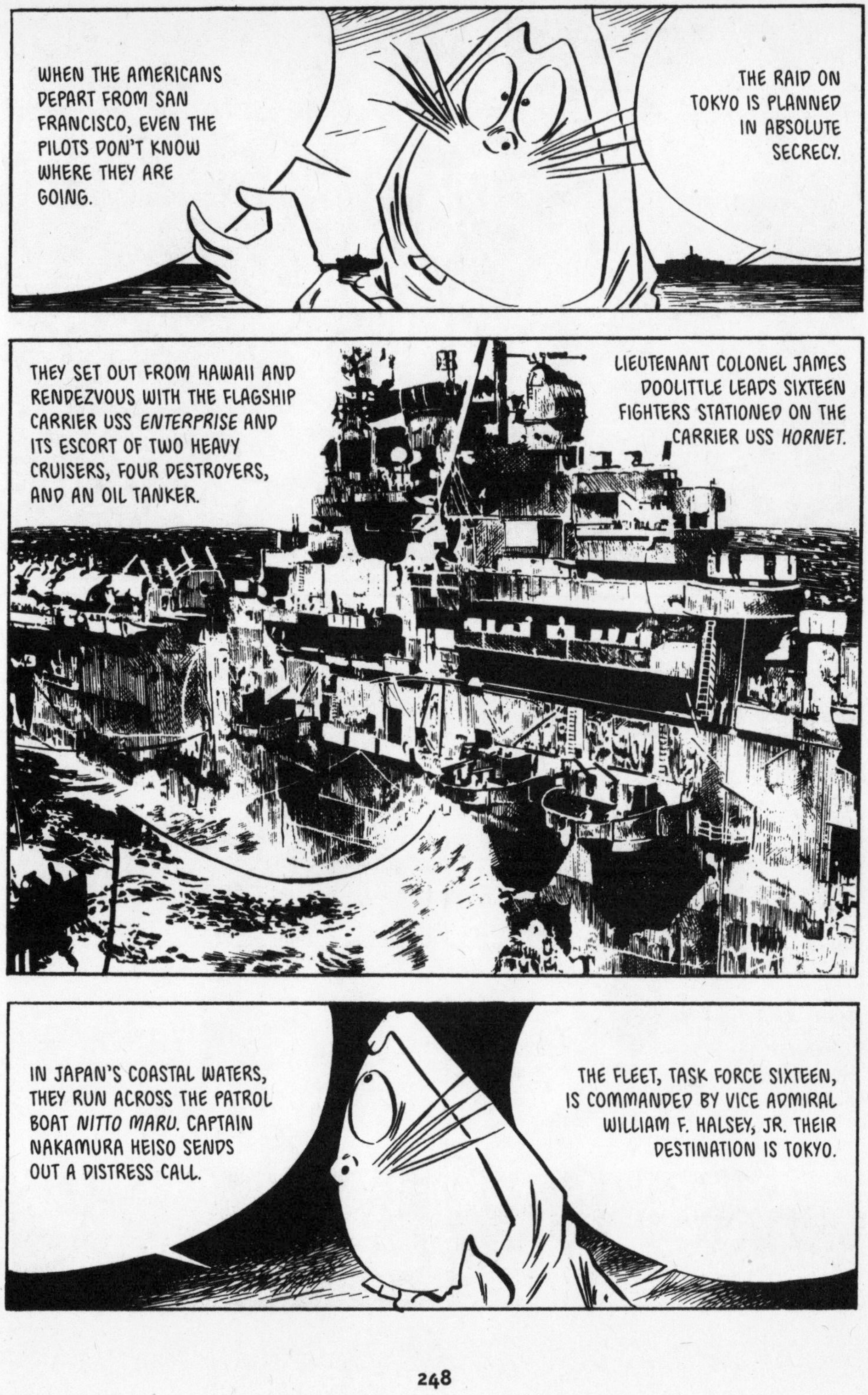
THE RAID ON TOKYO IS PLANNED IN ABSOLUTE SECRECY.
WHEN THE AMERICANS DEPART FROM SAN FRANCISCO, EVEN THE PILOTS DON'T KNOW WHERE THEY ARE GOING.
LIEUTENANT COLONEL JAMES DOOLITTLE LEADS SIXTEEN FIGHTERS STATIONED ON THE CARRIER USS *HORNET*.
THEY SET OUT FROM HAWAII AND RENDEZVOUS WITH THE FLAGSHIP CARRIER USS *ENTERPRISE* AND ITS ESCORT OF TWO HEAVY CRUISERS, FOUR DESTROYERS, AND AN OIL TANKER.
THE FLEET, TASK FORCE SIXTEEN, IS COMMANDED BY VICE ADMIRAL WILLIAM F. HALSEY, JR. THEIR DESTINATION IS TOKYO.
IN JAPAN'S COASTAL WATERS, THEY RUN ACROSS THE PATROL BOAT *NITTO MARU*. CAPTAIN NAKAMURA HEISO SENDS OUT A DISTRESS CALL.

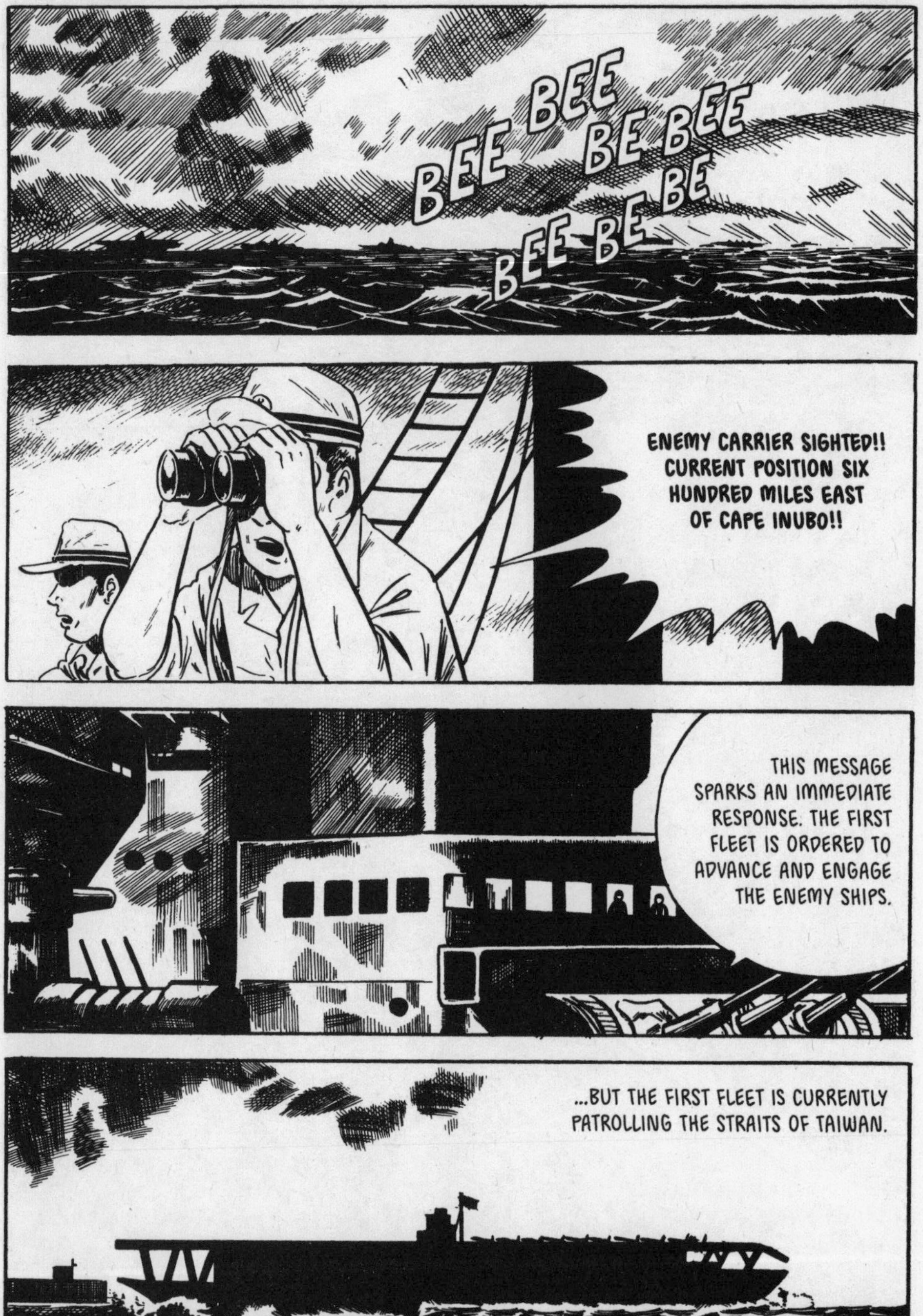
BEE BEE
BE BEE
BEE BE BE
ENEMY CARRIER SIGHTED!! CURRENT POSITION SIX HUNDRED MILES EAST OF CAPE INUBO!!
THIS MESSAGE SPARKS AN IMMEDIATE RESPONSE. THE FIRST FLEET IS ORDERED TO ADVANCE AND ENGAGE THE ENEMY SHIPS.
...BUT THE FIRST FLEET IS CURRENTLY PATROLLING THE STRAITS OF TAIWAN.

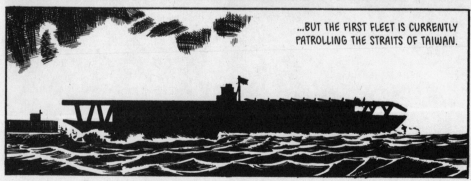

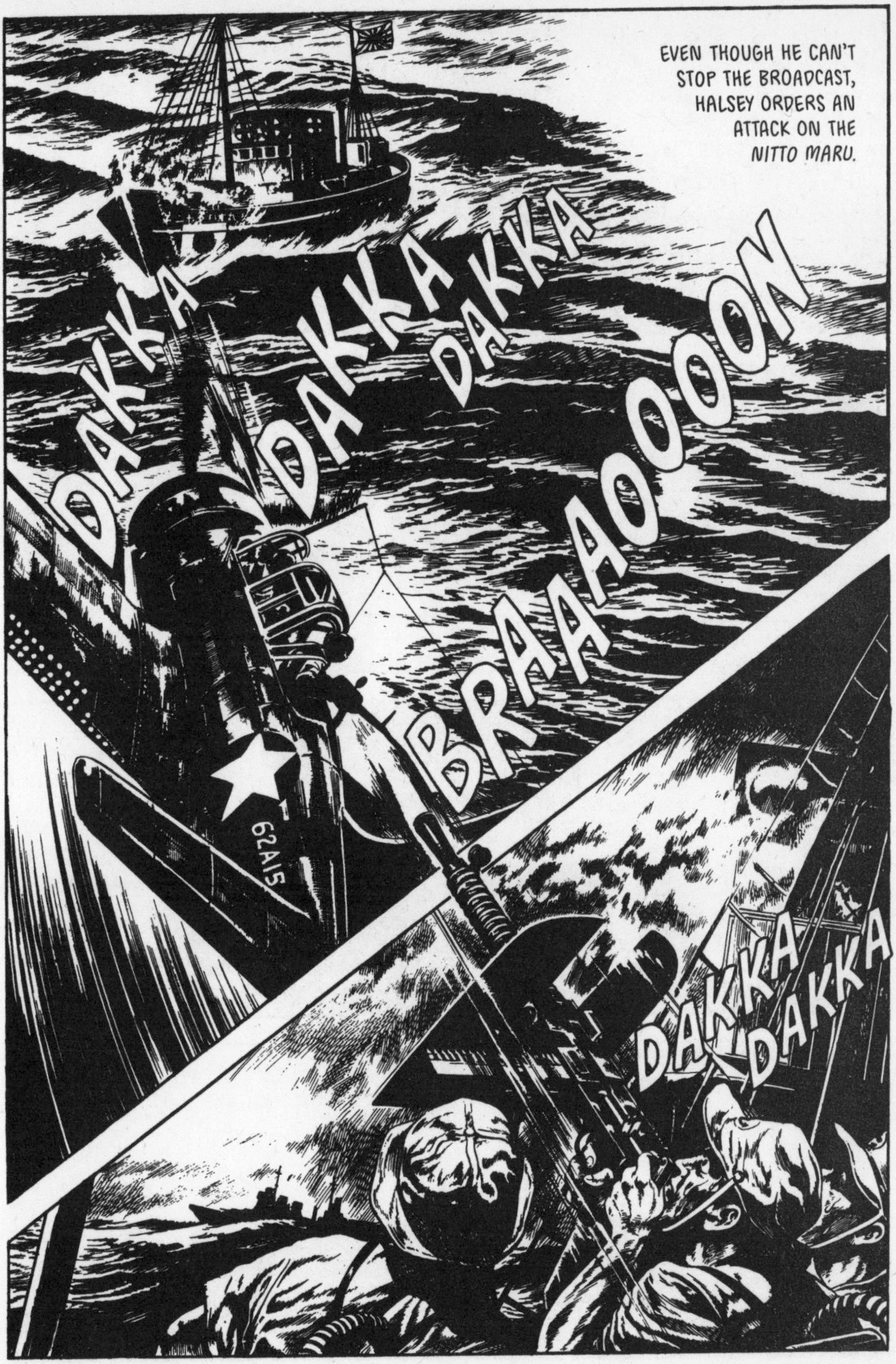
EVEN THOUGH HE CAN'T STOP THE BROADCAST, HALSEY ORDERS AN ATTACK ON THE *NITTO MARU.*
DAKKA DAKKA DAKKA DAKKA
BRAAAOOOON
DAKKA DAKKA

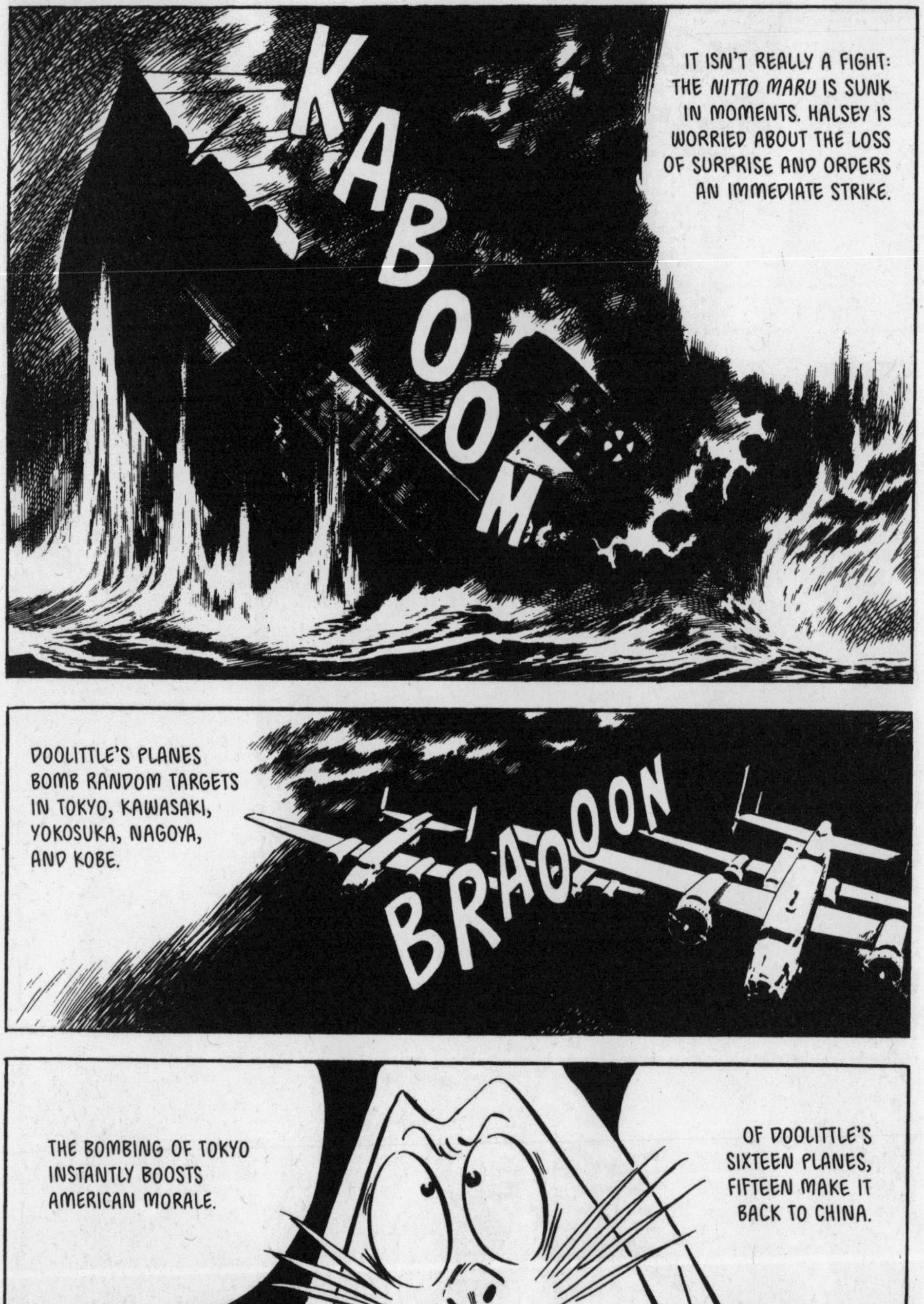
IT ISN'T REALLY A FIGHT: THE *NITTO MARU* IS SUNK IN MOMENTS. HALSEY IS WORRIED ABOUT THE LOSS OF SURPRISE AND ORDERS AN IMMEDIATE STRIKE.
KABOOM
BRAOOON
DOOLITTLE'S PLANES BOMB RANDOM TARGETS IN TOKYO, KAWASAKI, YOKOSUKA, NAGOYA, AND KOBE.
OF DOOLITTLE'S SIXTEEN PLANES, FIFTEEN MAKE IT BACK TO CHINA.
THE BOMBING OF TOKYO INSTANTLY BOOSTS AMERICAN MORALE.

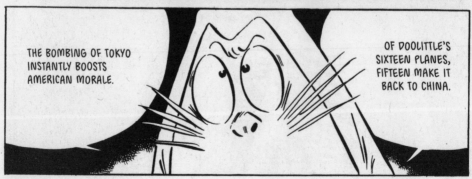

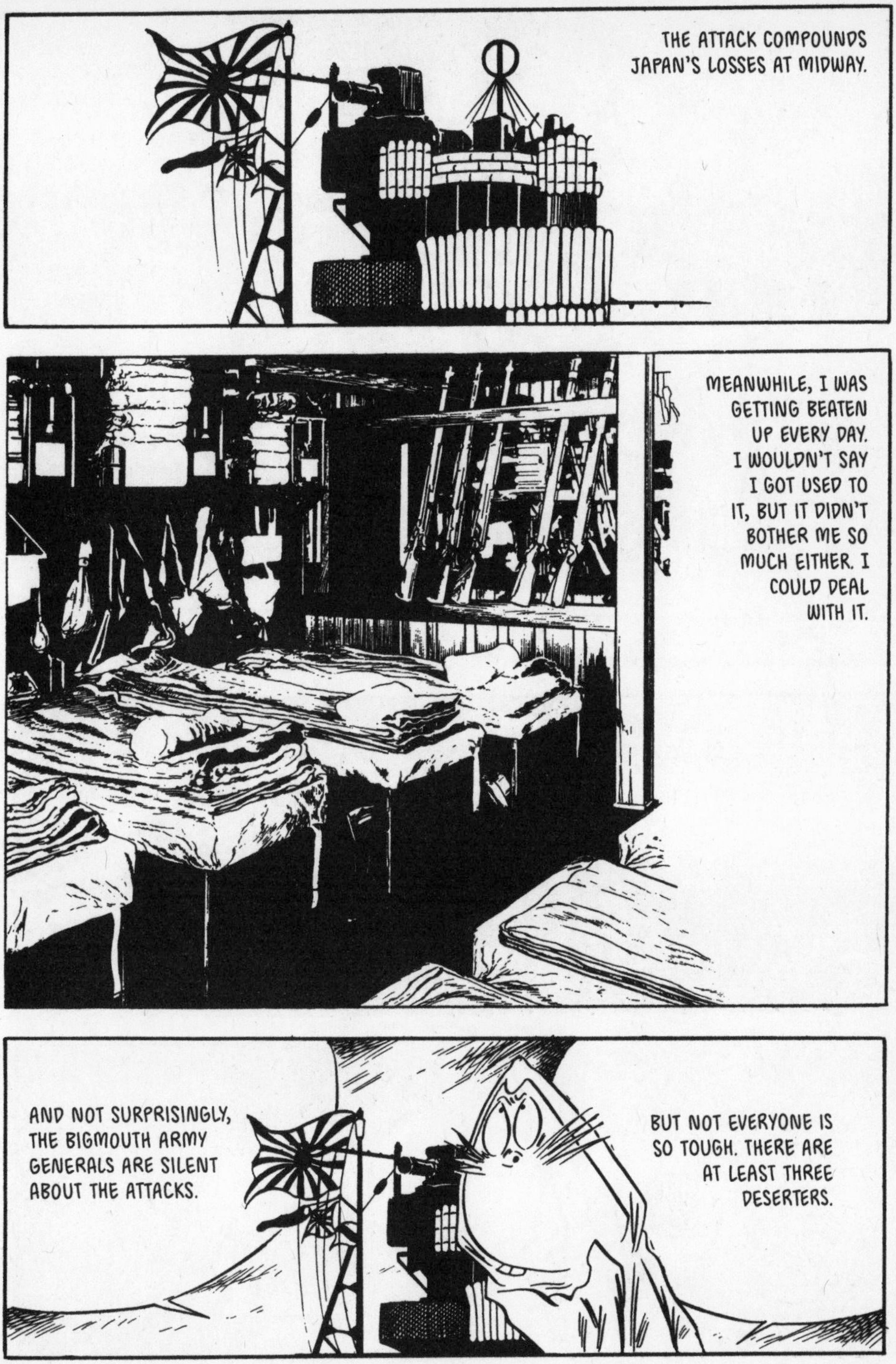
THE ATTACK COMPOUNDS JAPAN'S LOSSES AT MIDWAY.
MEANWHILE, I WAS GETTING BEATEN UP EVERY DAY. I WOULDN'T SAY I GOT USED TO IT, BUT IT DIDN'T BOTHER ME SO MUCH EITHER. I COULD DEAL WITH IT.
BUT NOT EVERYONE IS SO TOUGH. THERE ARE AT LEAST THREE DESERTERS.
AND NOT SURPRISINGLY, THE BIGMOUTH ARMY GENERALS ARE SILENT ABOUT THE ATTACKS.

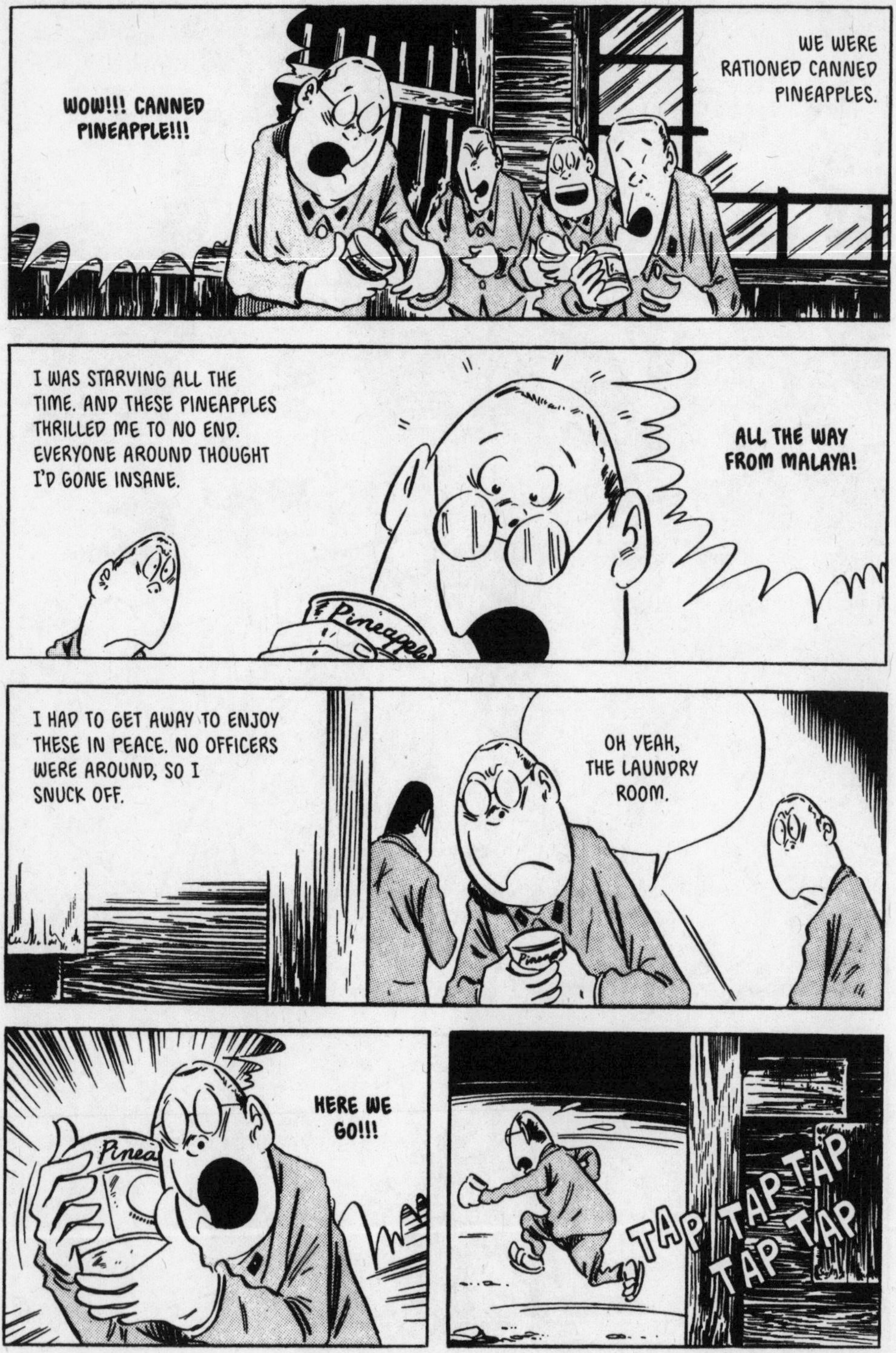
WE WERE RATIONED CANNED PINEAPPLES.
WOW!!! CANNED PINEAPPLE!!!
ALL THE WAY FROM MALAYA!
I WAS STARVING ALL THE TIME. AND THESE PINEAPPLES THRILLED ME TO NO END. EVERYONE AROUND THOUGHT I'D GONE INSANE.
OH YEAH, THE LAUNDRY ROOM.
I HAD TO GET AWAY TO ENJOY THESE IN PEACE. NO OFFICERS WERE AROUND, SO I SNUCK OFF.
TAP TAP TAP TAP TAP
HERE WE GO!!!

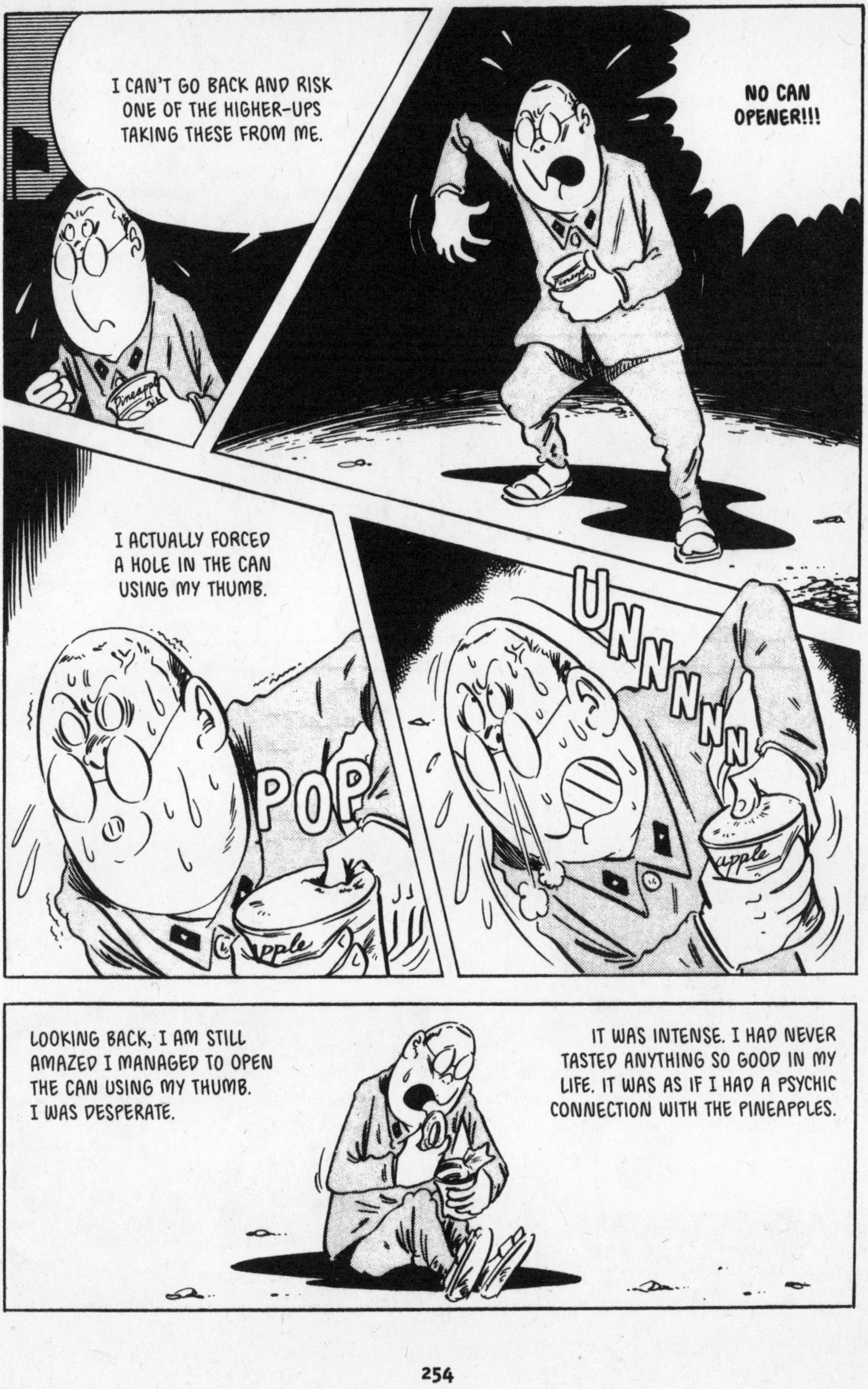
NO CAN OPENER!!!
I CAN'T GO BACK AND RISK ONE OF THE HIGHER-UPS TAKING THESE FROM ME.
Pineapple
UNNNNNN
apple
I ACTUALLY FORCED A HOLE IN THE CAN USING MY THUMB.
POP
apple
IT WAS INTENSE. I HAD NEVER TASTED ANYTHING SO GOOD IN MY LIFE. IT WAS AS IF I HAD A PSYCHIC CONNECTION WITH THE PINEAPPLES.
LOOKING BACK, I AM STILL AMAZED I MANAGED TO OPEN THE CAN USING MY THUMB. I WAS DESPERATE.

THE BATTLE OF THE CORAL SEA

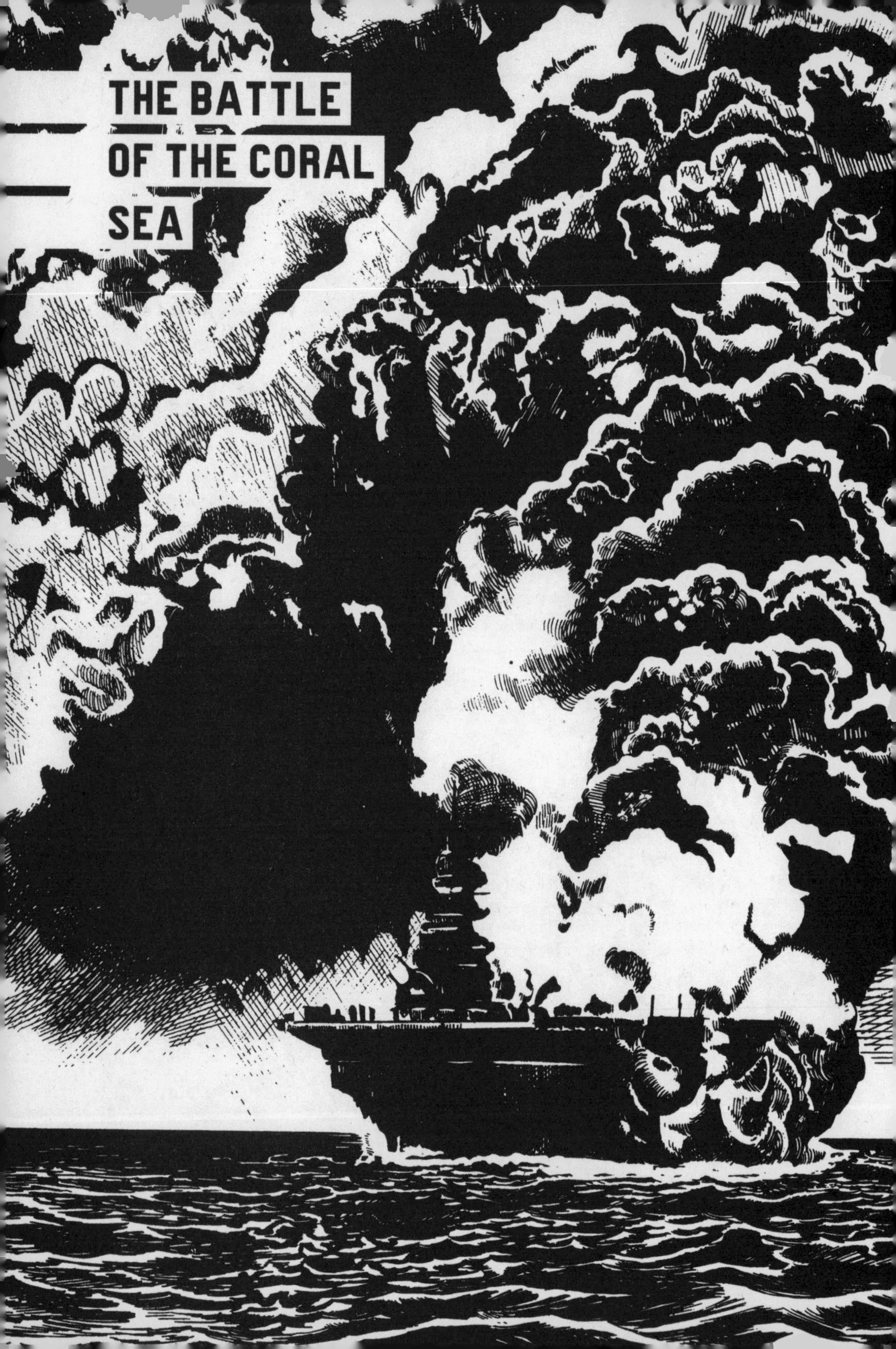

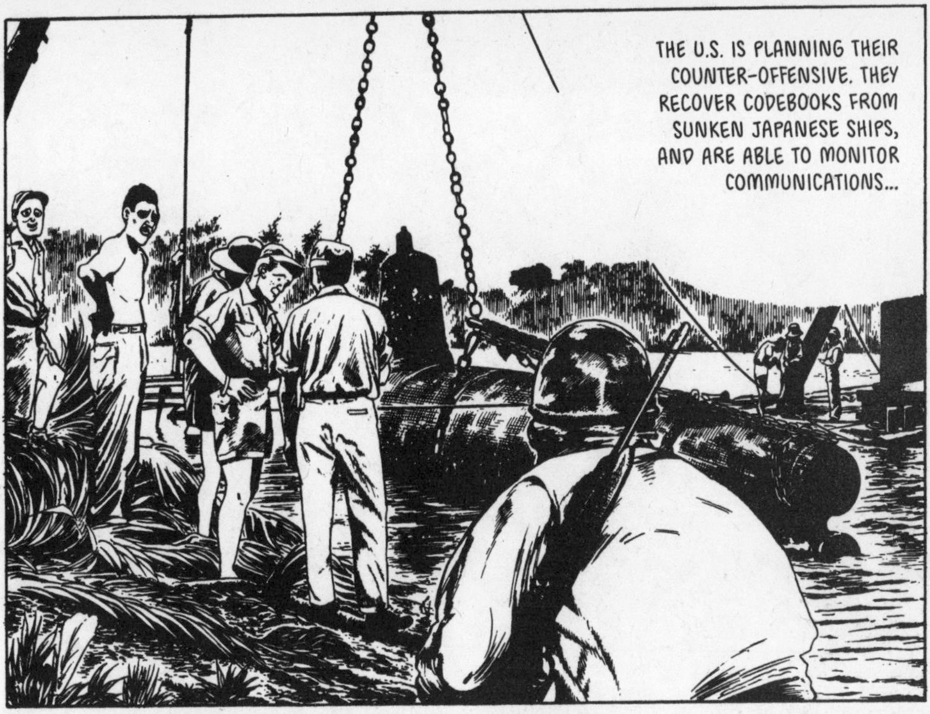
THE U.S. IS PLANNING THEIR COUNTER-OFFENSIVE. THEY RECOVER CODEBOOKS FROM SUNKEN JAPANESE SHIPS, AND ARE ABLE TO MONITOR COMMUNICATIONS...
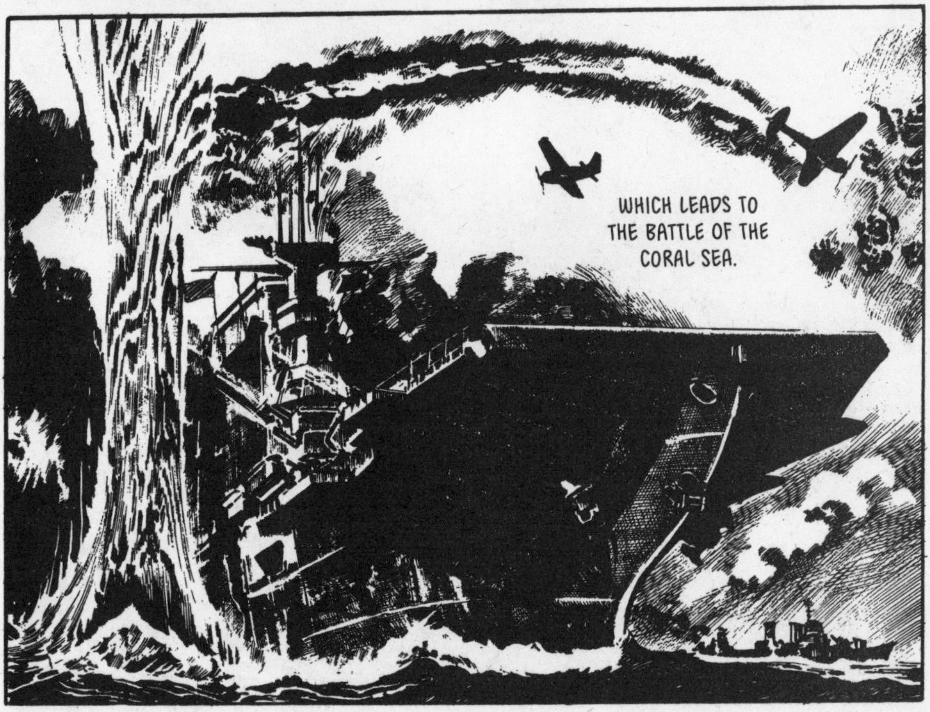
WHICH LEADS TO THE BATTLE OF THE CORAL SEA.

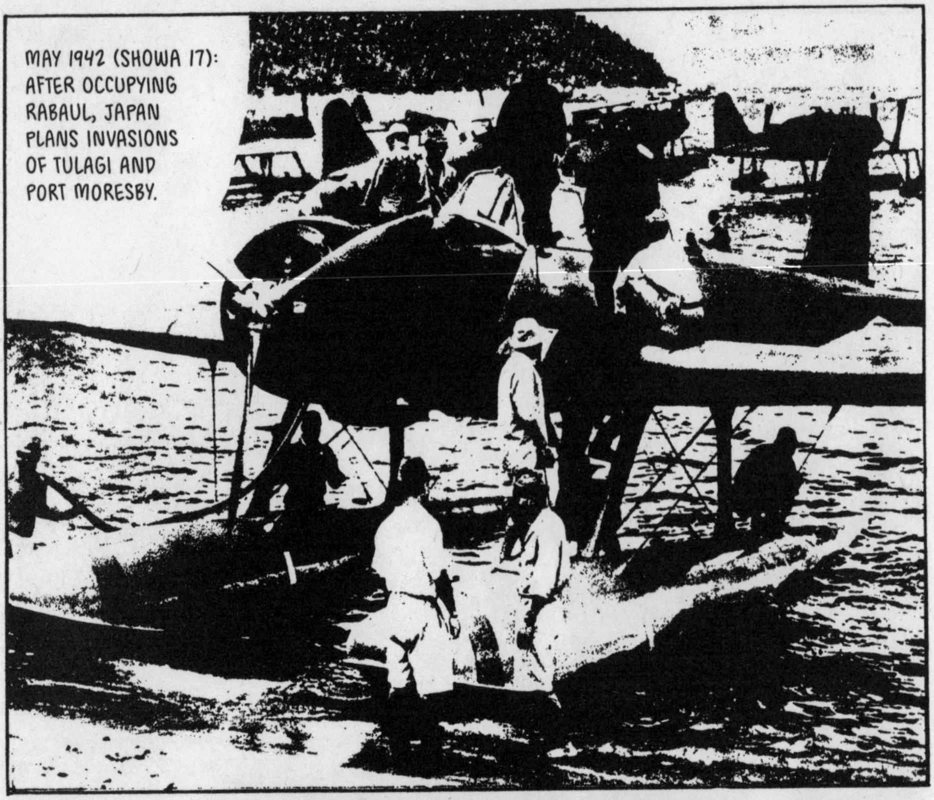
MAY 1942 (SHOWA 17): AFTER OCCUPYING RABAUL, JAPAN PLANS INVASIONS OF TULAGI AND PORT MORESBY.

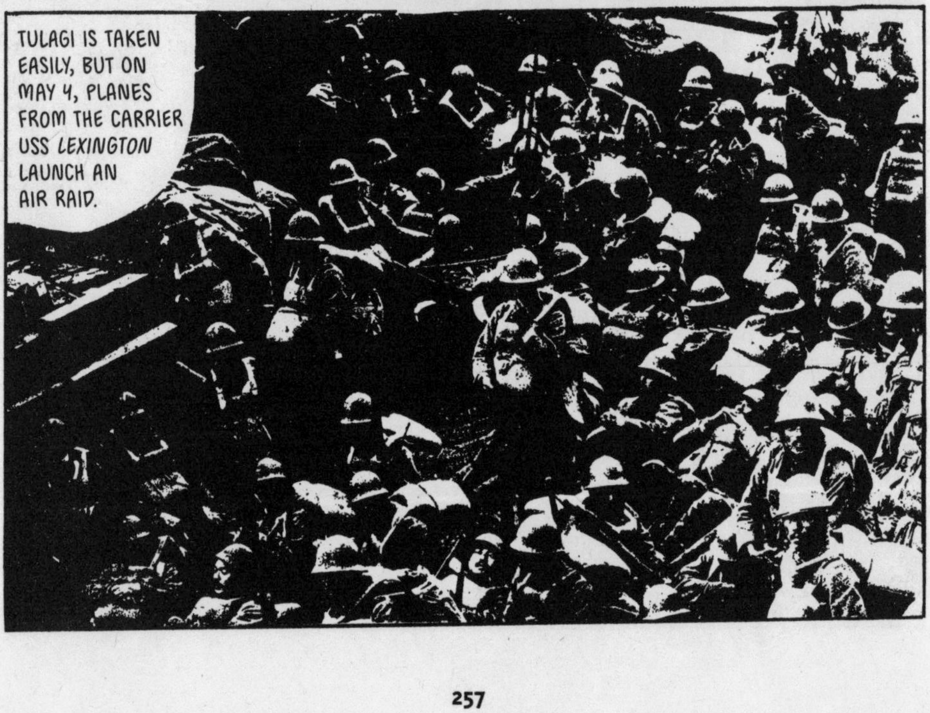
TULAGI IS TAKEN EASILY, BUT ON MAY 4, PLANES FROM THE CARRIER USS *LEXINGTON* LAUNCH AN AIR RAID.

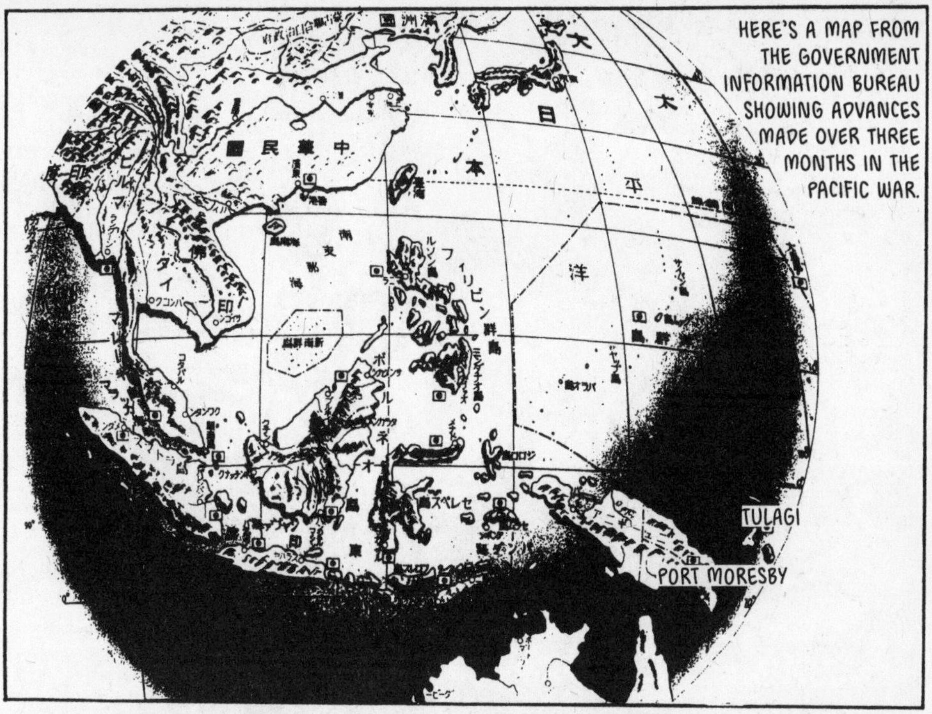
HERE'S A MAP FROM THE GOVERNMENT INFORMATION BUREAU SHOWING ADVANCES MADE OVER THREE MONTHS IN THE PACIFIC WAR.
TULAGI
PORT MORESBY

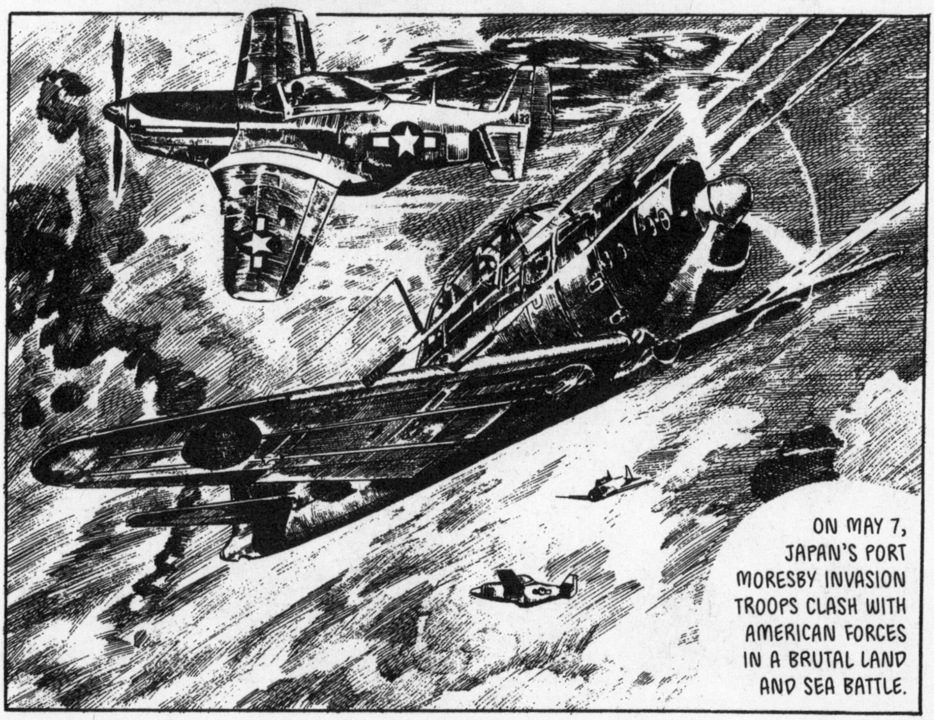
ON MAY 7, JAPAN'S PORT MORESBY INVASION TROOPS CLASH WITH AMERICAN FORCES IN A BRUTAL LAND AND SEA BATTLE.

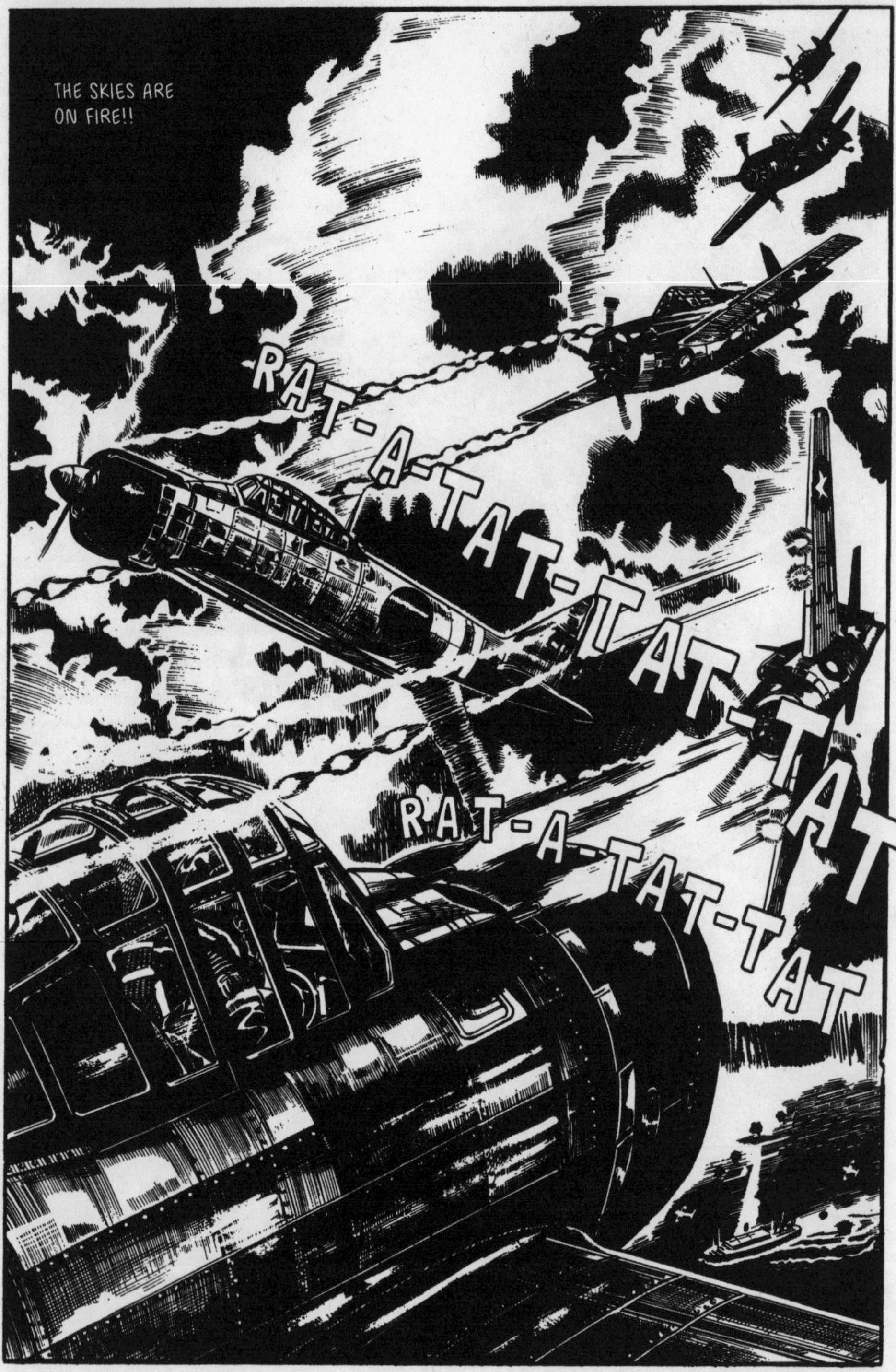
THE SKIES ARE ON FIRE!!
RAT-A-TAT-TAT-TAT-TAT-TAT
RAT-A-TAT-TAT-TAT

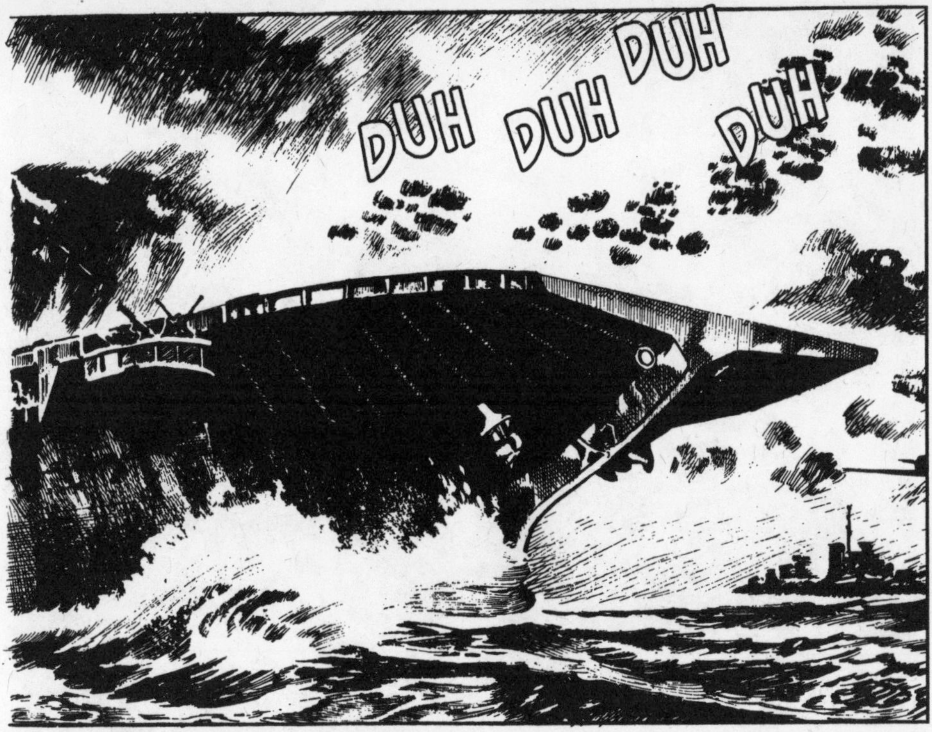
DUH DUH DUH DUH

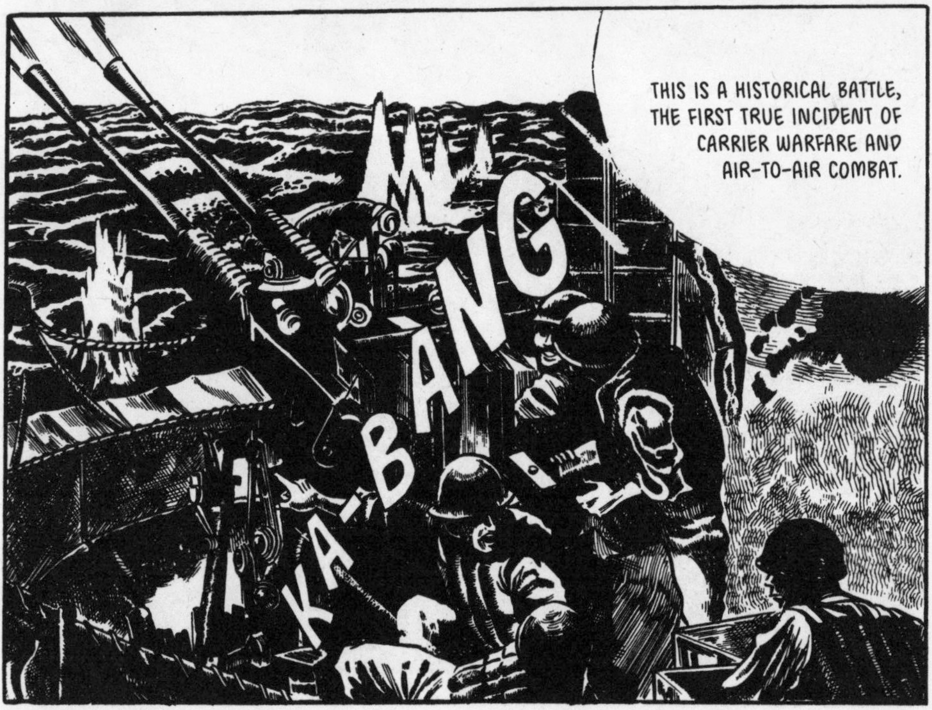
THIS IS A HISTORICAL BATTLE, THE FIRST TRUE INCIDENT OF CARRIER WARFARE AND AIR-TO-AIR COMBAT.
KA-BANG

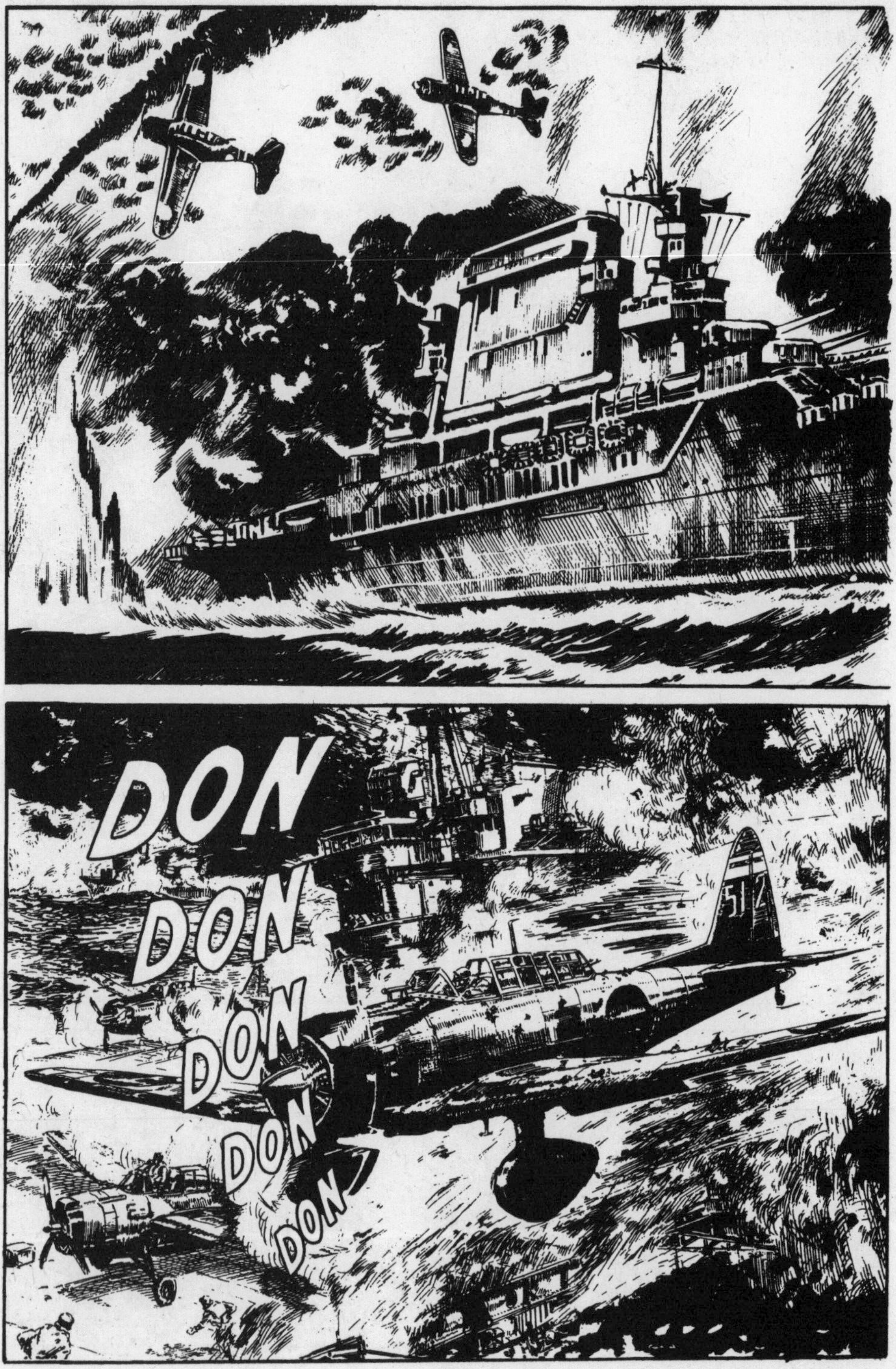
DON
DON
DON
DON
DON
DON

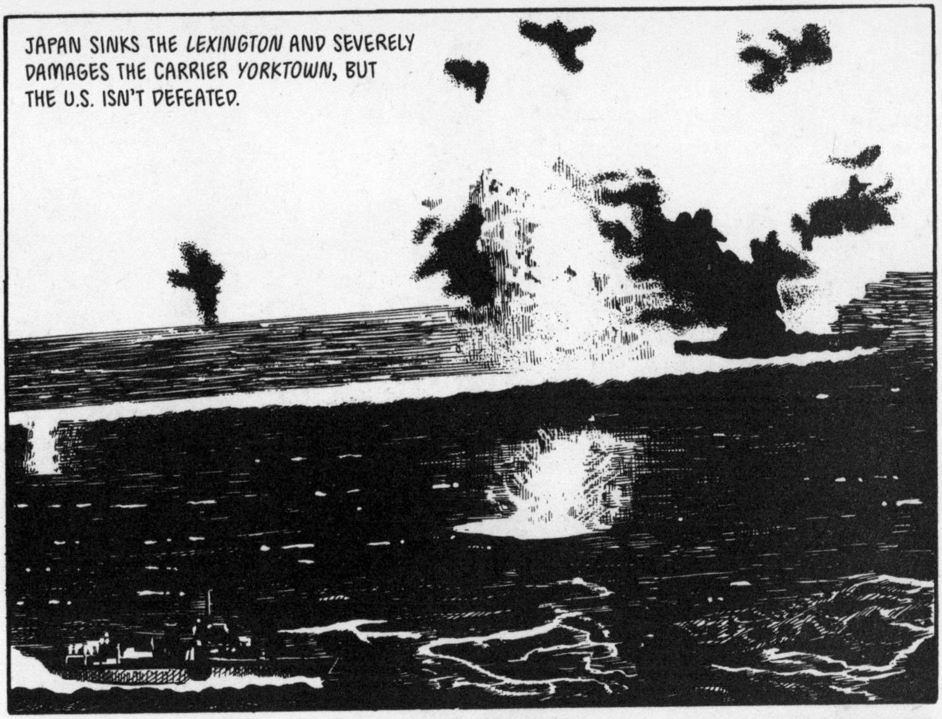
JAPAN SINKS THE *LEXINGTON* AND SEVERELY DAMAGES THE CARRIER *YORKTOWN*, BUT THE U.S. ISN'T DEFEATED.

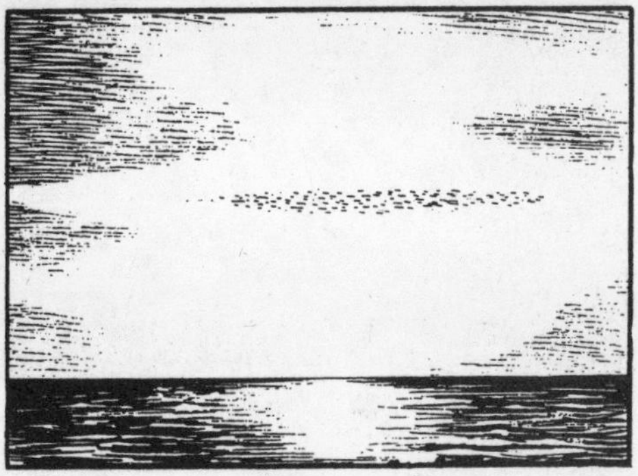

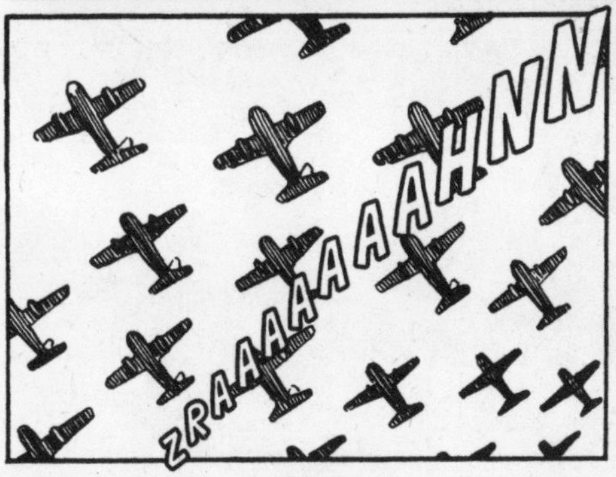
ZRAAAAAAAHNN

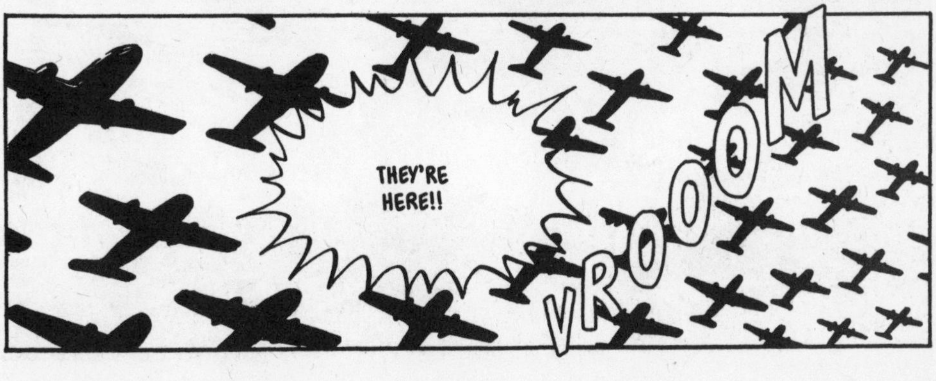
VROOOM
THEY'RE HERE!!

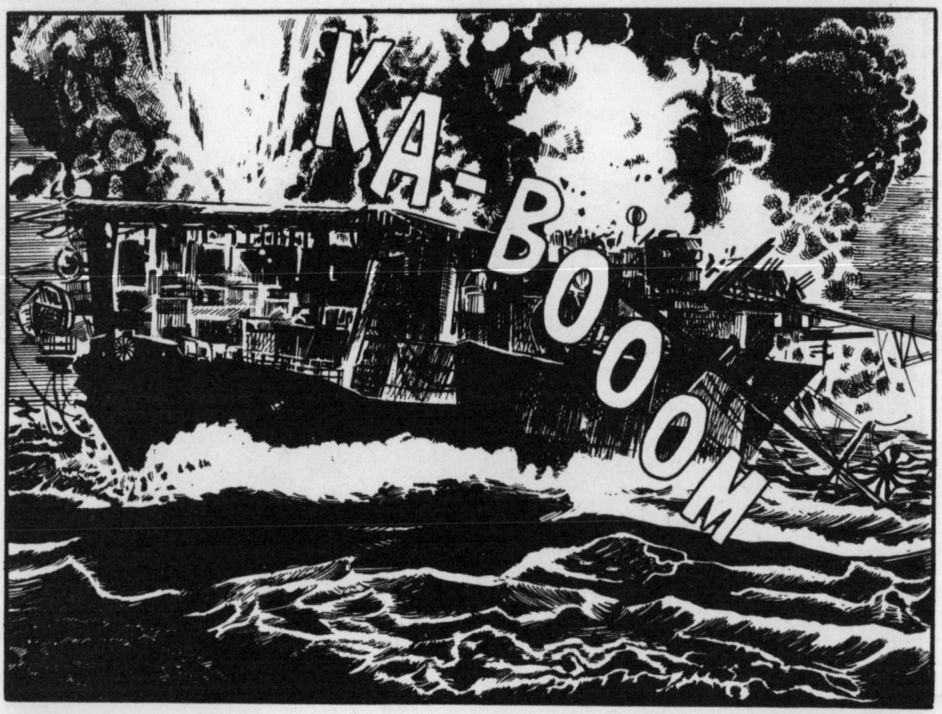
KA-BOOOOM

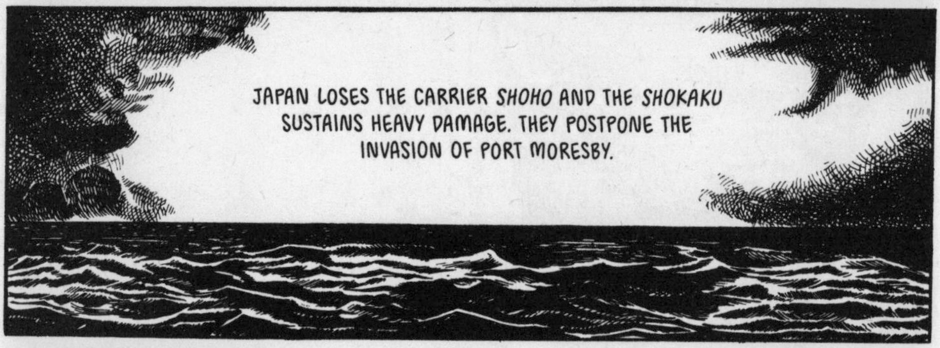
JAPAN LOSES THE CARRIER *SHOHO* AND THE *SHOKAKU* SUSTAINS HEAVY DAMAGE. THEY POSTPONE THE INVASION OF PORT MORESBY.

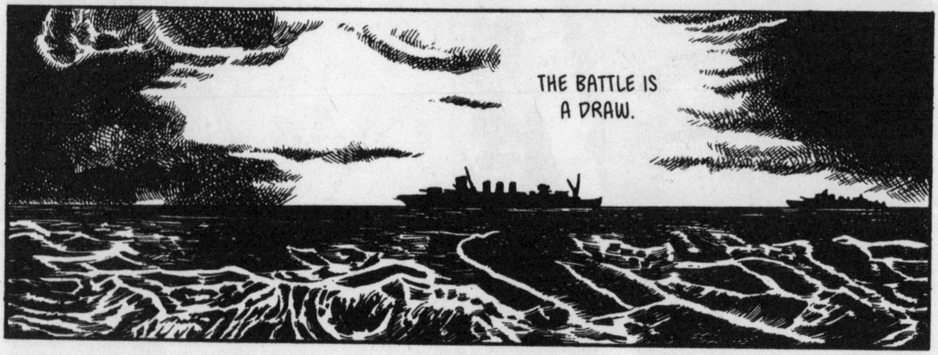
THE BATTLE IS A DRAW.

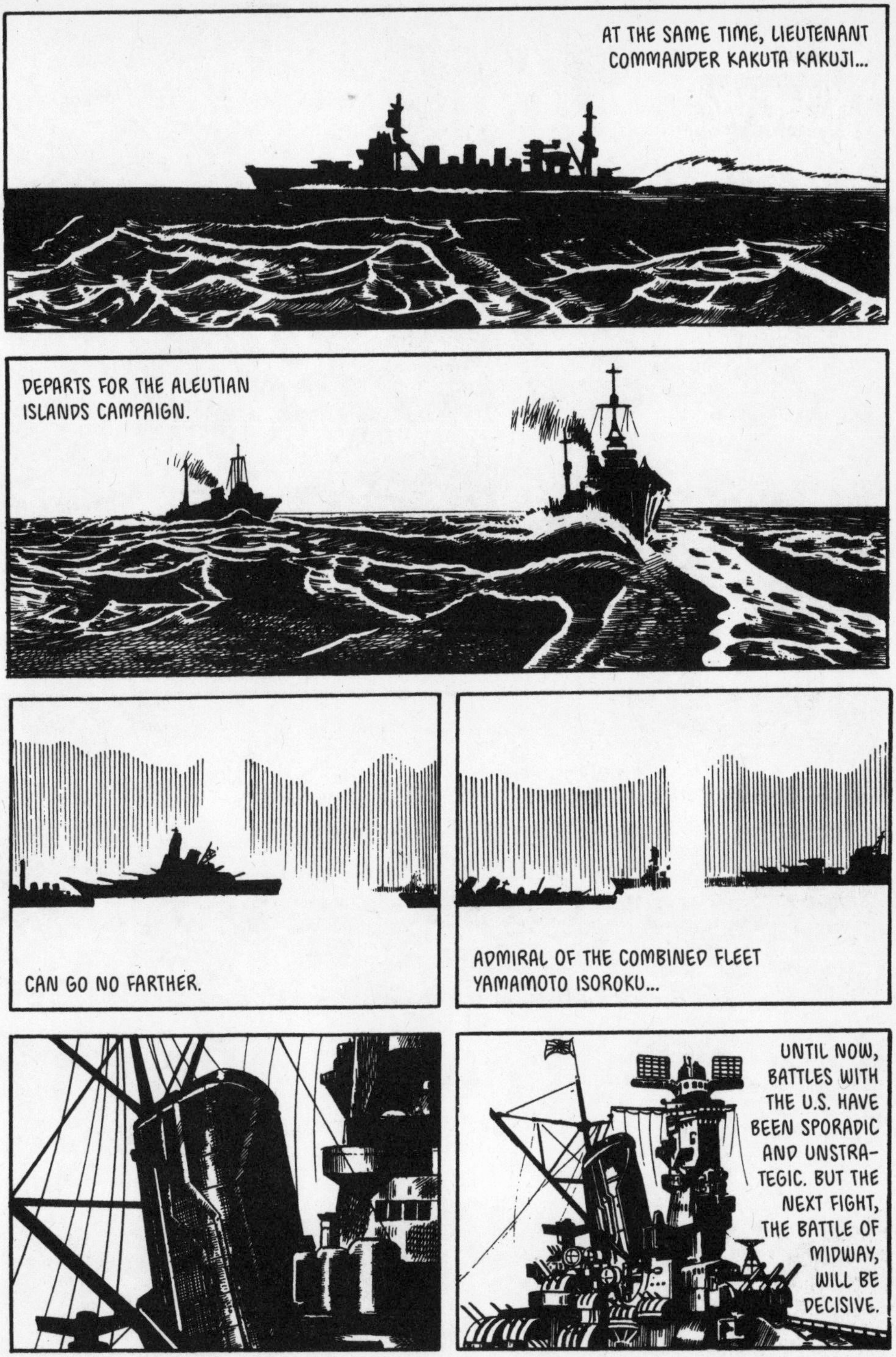
AT THE SAME TIME, LIEUTENANT COMMANDER KAKUTA KAKUJI...
DEPARTS FOR THE ALEUTIAN ISLANDS CAMPAIGN.
ADMIRAL OF THE COMBINED FLEET YAMAMOTO ISOROKU...
CAN GO NO FARTHER.
UNTIL NOW, BATTLES WITH THE U.S. HAVE BEEN SPORADIC AND UNSTRA-TEGIC. BUT THE NEXT FIGHT, THE BATTLE OF MIDWAY, WILL BE DECISIVE.

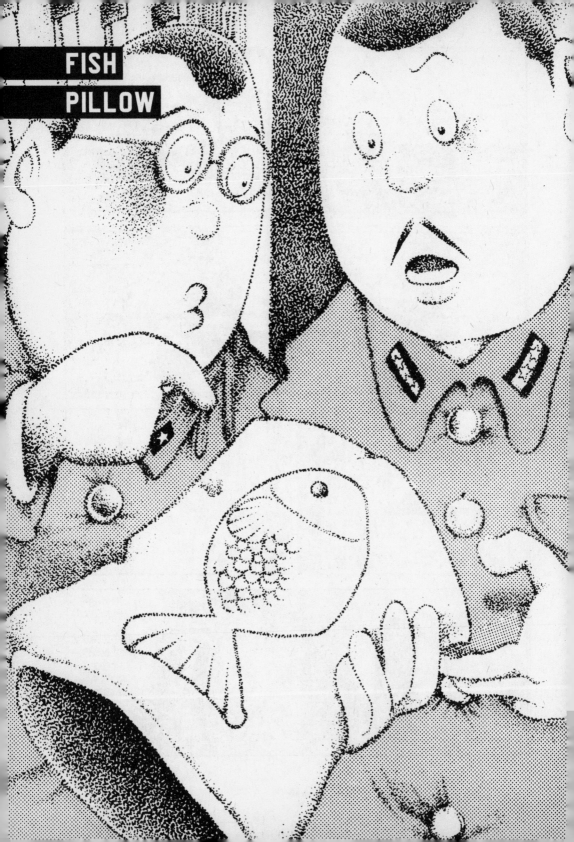

FISH
PILLOW

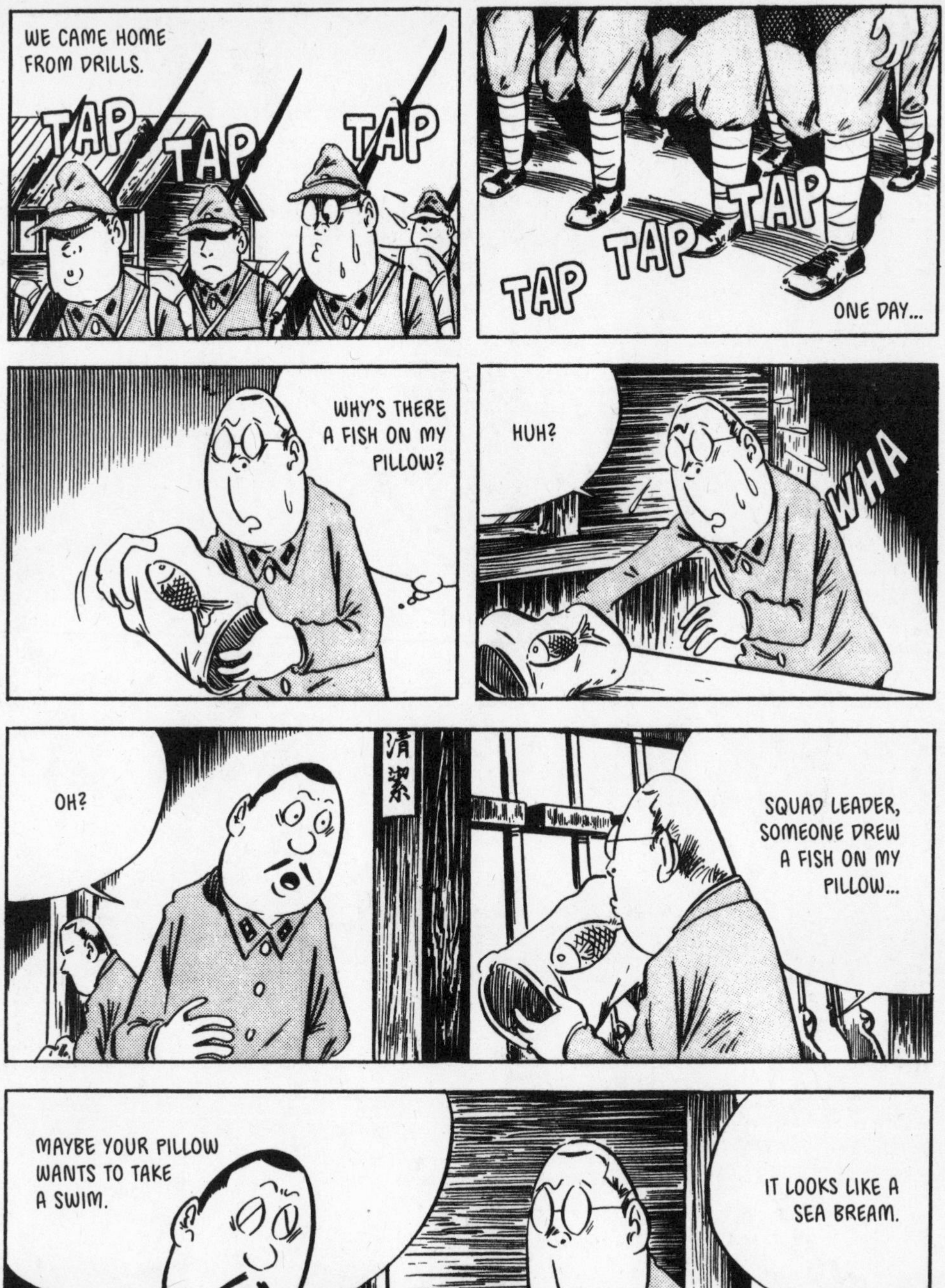
ONE DAY...
TAP TAP TAP TAP
WE CAME HOME FROM DRILLS.
TAP TAP TAP
HUH?
WHA
WHY'S THERE A FISH ON MY PILLOW?
SQUAD LEADER, SOMEONE DREW A FISH ON MY PILLOW...
OH?
IT LOOKS LIKE A SEA BREAM.
MAYBE YOUR PILLOW WANTS TO TAKE A SWIM.

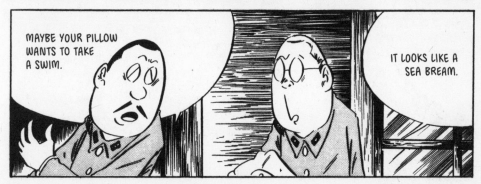

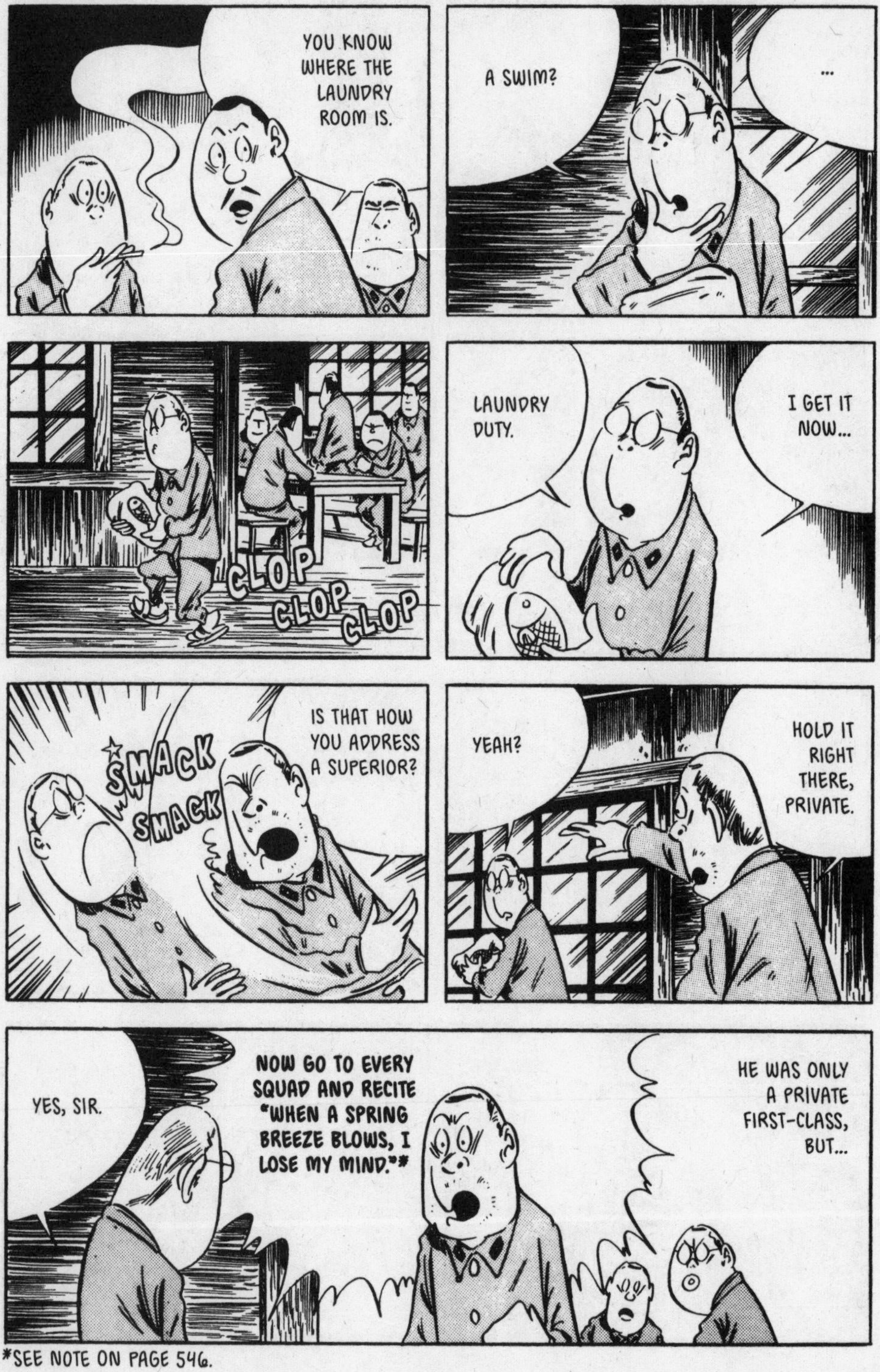
...
A SWIM?
YOU KNOW WHERE THE LAUNDRY ROOM IS.
I GET IT NOW...
LAUNDRY DUTY.
CLOP
CLOP
CLOP
HOLD IT RIGHT THERE, PRIVATE.
YEAH?
IS THAT HOW YOU ADDRESS A SUPERIOR?
SMACK
SMACK
HE WAS ONLY A PRIVATE FIRST-CLASS, BUT...
NOW GO TO EVERY SQUAD AND RECITE "WHEN A SPRING BREEZE BLOWS, I LOSE MY MIND."*
YES, SIR.

*SEE NOTE ON PAGE 546.

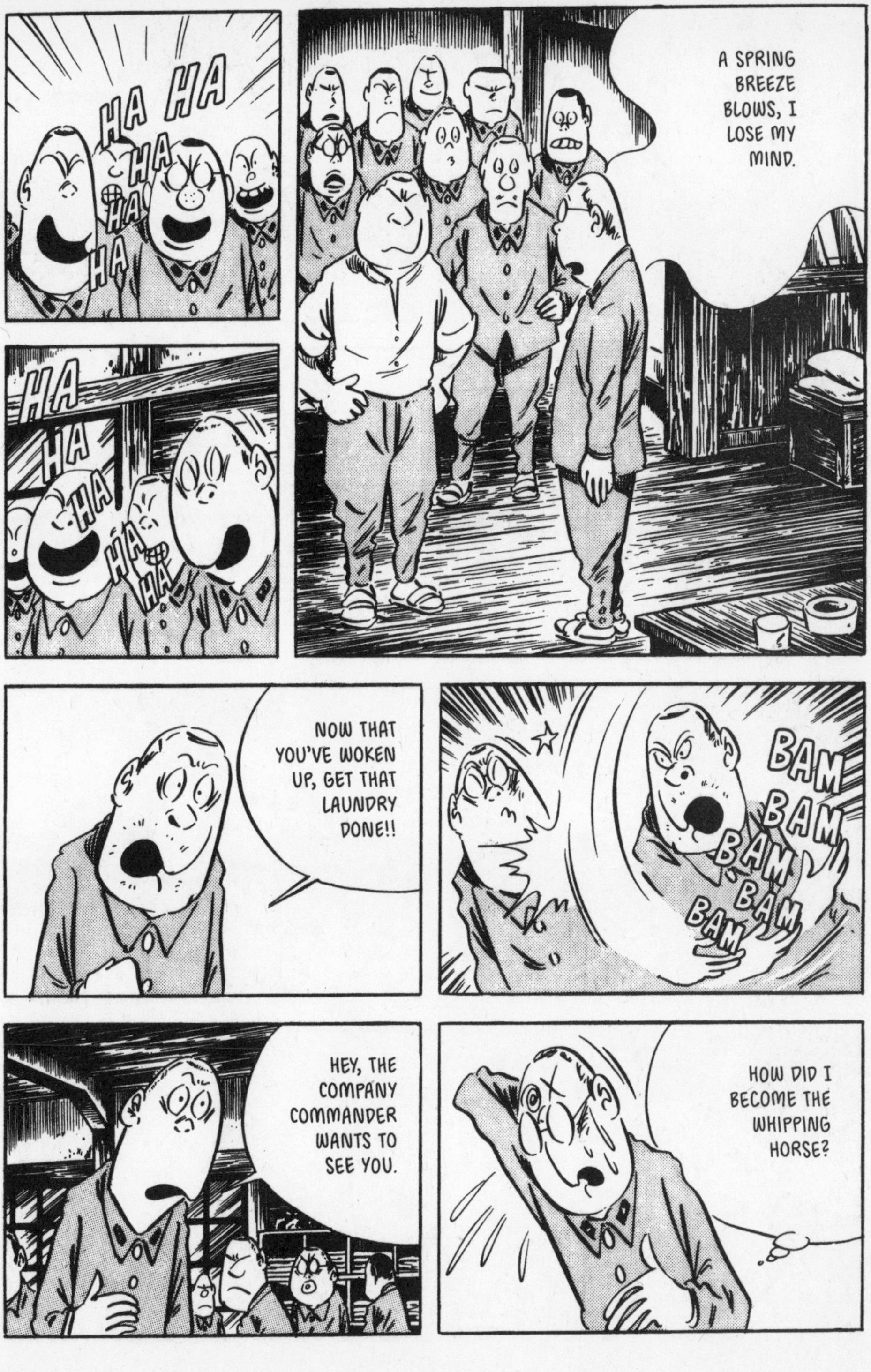
A SPRING BREEZE BLOWS, I LOSE MY MIND.
HA HA HA HA HA
HA HA HA HA HA
BAM BAM BAM BAM BAM
NOW THAT YOU'VE WOKEN UP, GET THAT LAUNDRY DONE!!
HOW DID I BECOME THE WHIPPING HORSE?
HEY, THE COMPANY COMMANDER WANTS TO SEE YOU.

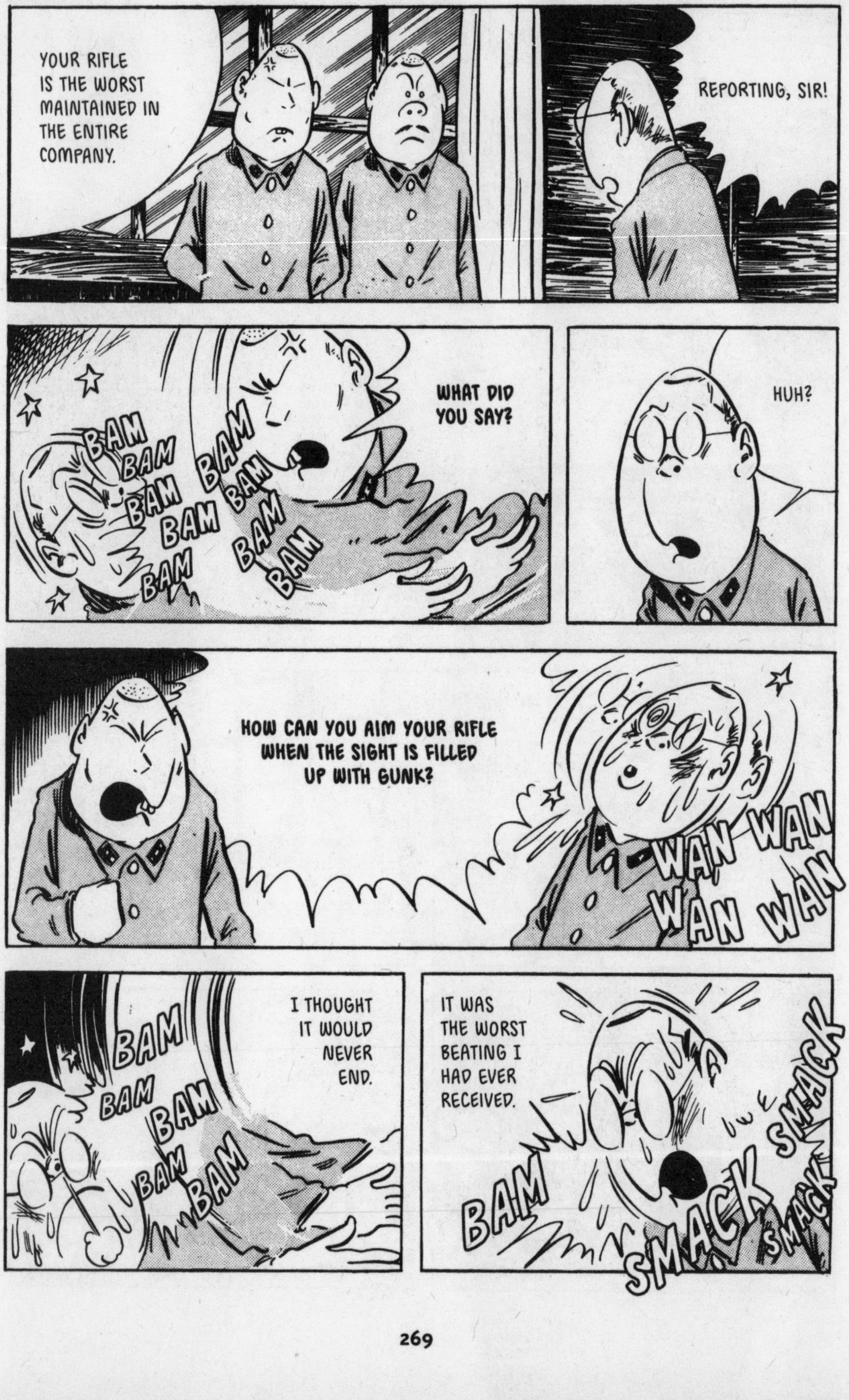
REPORTING, SIR!
YOUR RIFLE IS THE WORST MAINTAINED IN THE ENTIRE COMPANY.
HUH?
WHAT DID YOU SAY?
BAM BAM BAM BAM BAM BAM BAM BAM BAM BAM
HOW CAN YOU AIM YOUR RIFLE WHEN THE SIGHT IS FILLED UP WITH GUNK?
WAN WAN WAN WAN
IT WAS THE WORST BEATING I HAD EVER RECEIVED.
SMACK SMACK SMACK SMACK
BAM
I THOUGHT IT WOULD NEVER END.
BAM BAM BAM BAM BAM

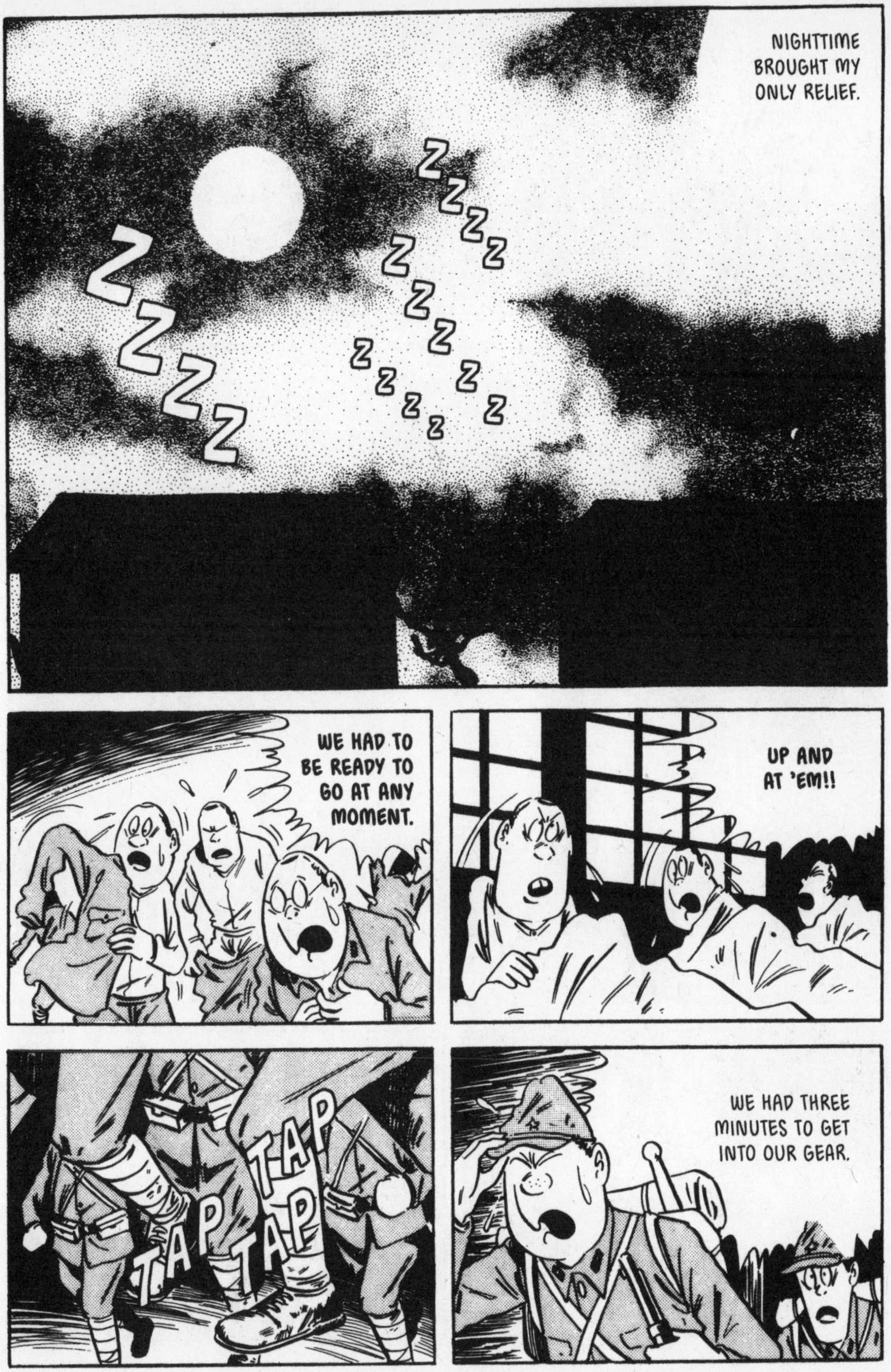
NIGHTTIME BROUGHT MY ONLY RELIEF.
ZZZZ
ZZZZ
ZZZZZ
ZZZZ
UP AND AT 'EM!!
WE HAD TO BE READY TO GO AT ANY MOMENT.
WE HAD THREE MINUTES TO GET INTO OUR GEAR.
TAP TAP
TAP TAP

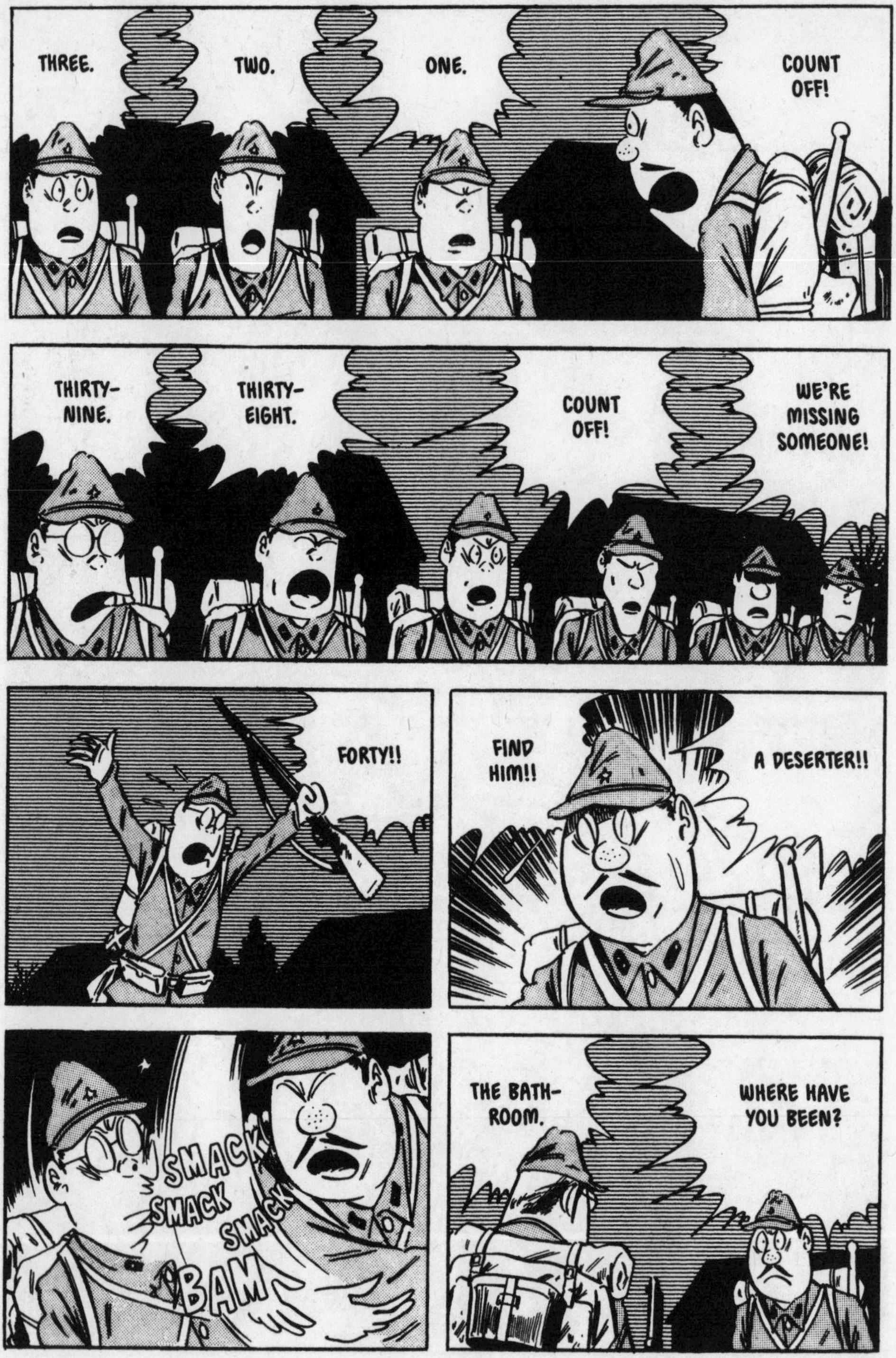
COUNT OFF!
ONE.
TWO.
THREE.
WE'RE MISSING SOMEONE!
COUNT OFF!
THIRTY-EIGHT.
THIRTY-NINE.
A DESERTER!!
FIND HIM!!
FORTY!!
WHERE HAVE YOU BEEN?
THE BATH-ROOM.
SMACK
SMACK
SMACK
BAM

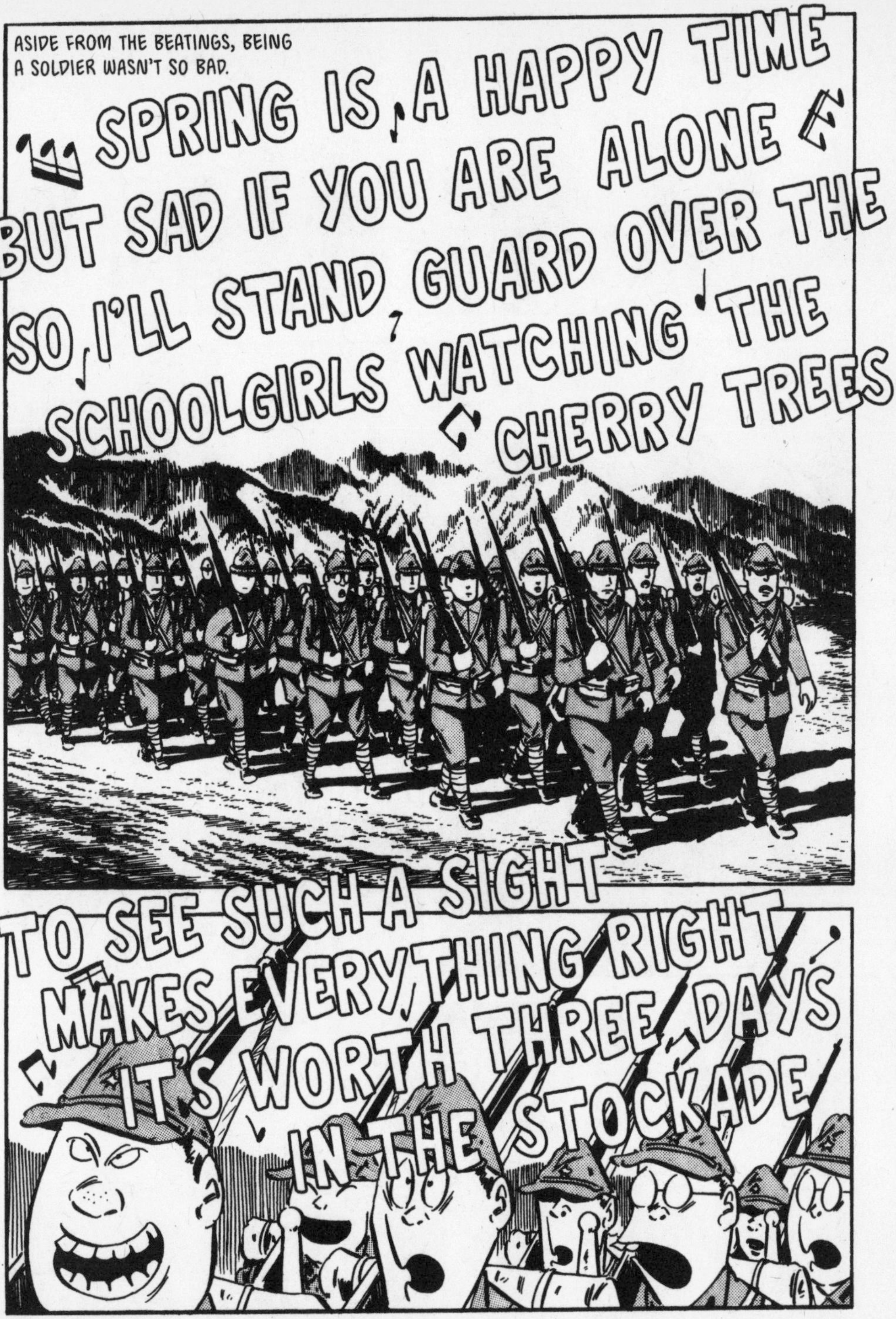
ASIDE FROM THE BEATINGS, BEING A SOLDIER WASN'T SO BAD.
SPRING IS A HAPPY TIME
BUT SAD IF YOU ARE ALONE
SO I'LL STAND GUARD OVER THE
SCHOOLGIRLS WATCHING THE
CHERRY TREES
TO SEE SUCH A SIGHT
MAKES EVERYTHING RIGHT
IT'S WORTH THREE DAYS
IN THE STOCKADE

*SEE NOTE ON PAGE 546.

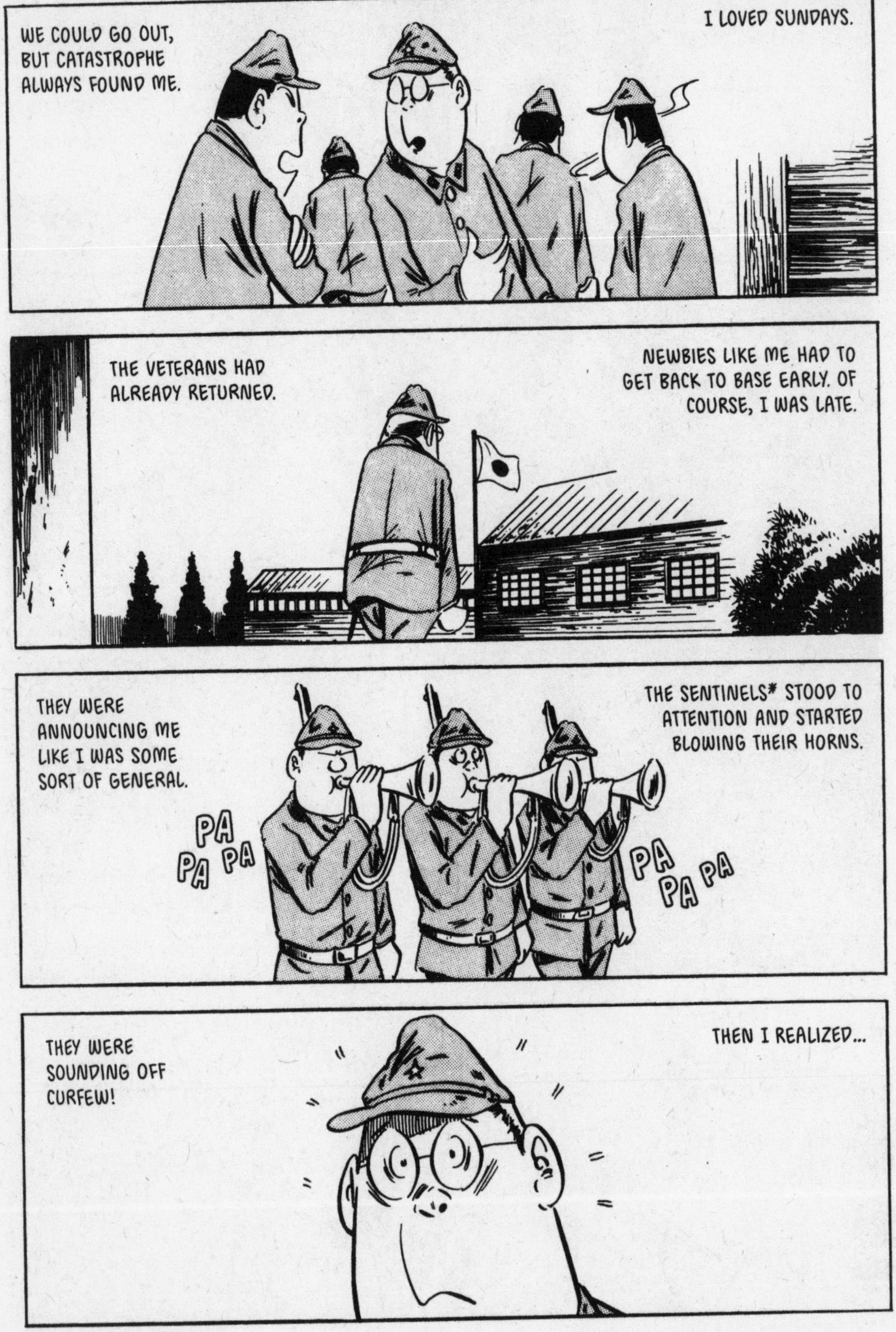
I LOVED SUNDAYS.
WE COULD GO OUT, BUT CATASTROPHE ALWAYS FOUND ME.
NEWBIES LIKE ME HAD TO GET BACK TO BASE EARLY. OF COURSE, I WAS LATE.
THE VETERANS HAD ALREADY RETURNED.
THE SENTINELS* STOOD TO ATTENTION AND STARTED BLOWING THEIR HORNS.
THEY WERE ANNOUNCING ME LIKE I WAS SOME SORT OF GENERAL.
PA PA PA
PA PA PA
THEN I REALIZED...
THEY WERE SOUNDING OFF CURFEW!

*SEE NOTE ON PAGE 546.

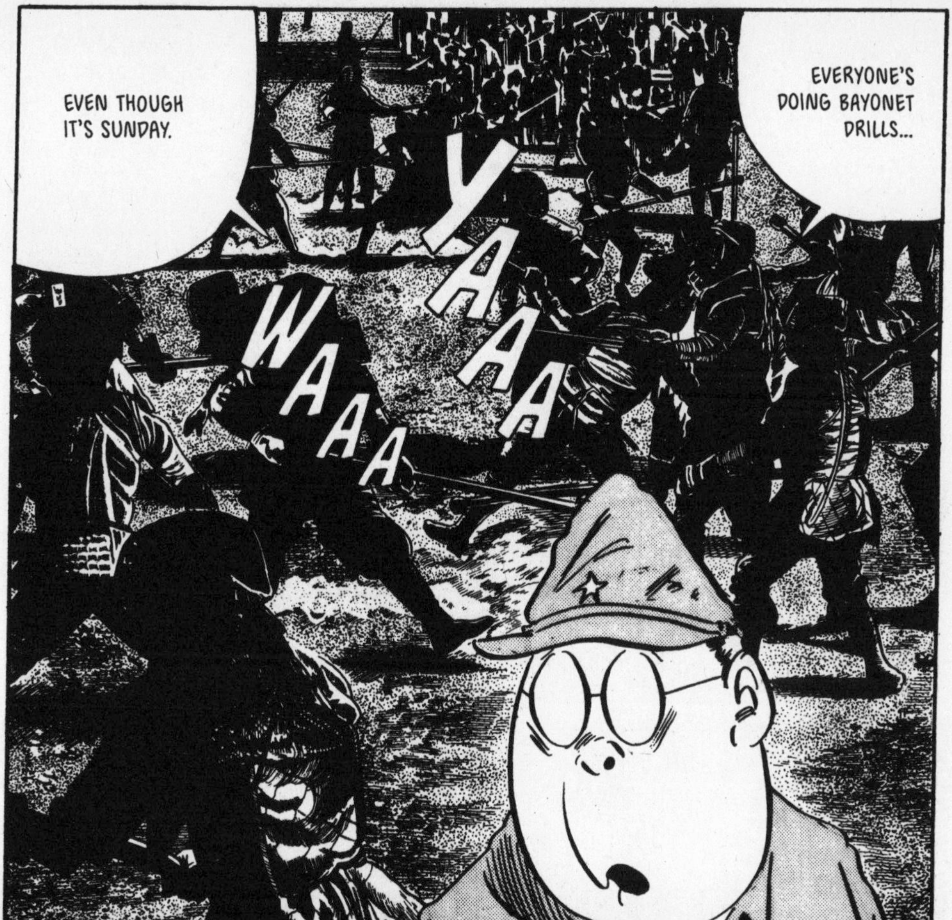
EVERYONE'S DOING BAYONET DRILLS...
EVEN THOUGH IT'S SUNDAY.
YAAAA
WAAAA

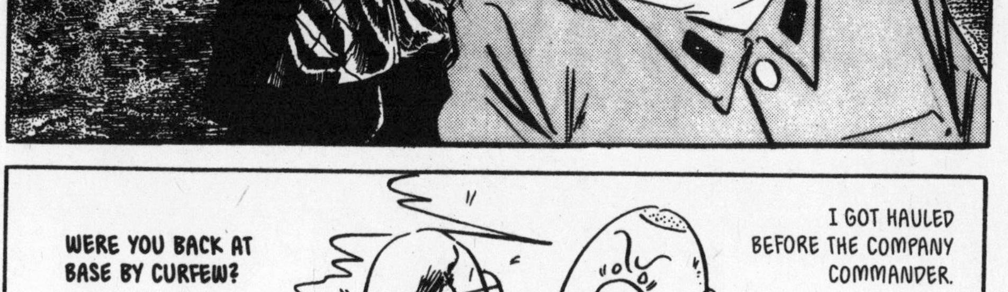
I GOT HAULED BEFORE THE COMPANY COMMANDER.
WERE YOU BACK AT BASE BY CURFEW?
HMM? ANSWER ME!

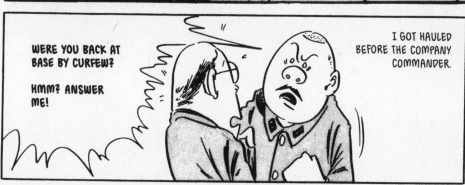

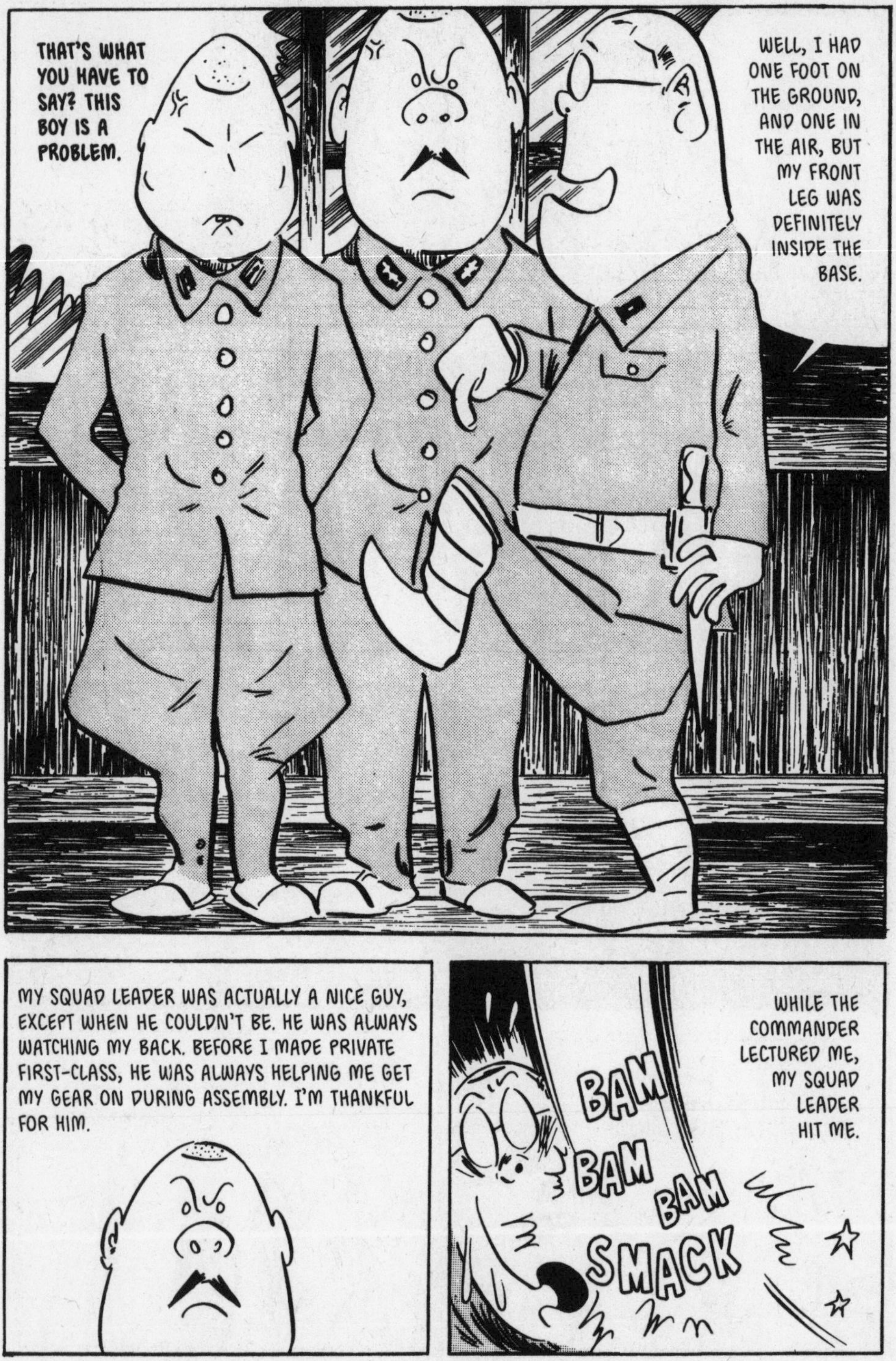
WELL, I HAD ONE FOOT ON THE GROUND, AND ONE IN THE AIR, BUT MY FRONT LEG WAS DEFINITELY INSIDE THE BASE.
THAT'S WHAT YOU HAVE TO SAY? THIS BOY IS A PROBLEM.
WHILE THE COMMANDER LECTURED ME, MY SQUAD LEADER HIT ME.
BAM
BAM
BAM
SMACK
MY SQUAD LEADER WAS ACTUALLY A NICE GUY, EXCEPT WHEN HE COULDN'T BE. HE WAS ALWAYS WATCHING MY BACK. BEFORE I MADE PRIVATE FIRST-CLASS, HE WAS ALWAYS HELPING ME GET MY GEAR ON DURING ASSEMBLY. I'M THANKFUL FOR HIM.

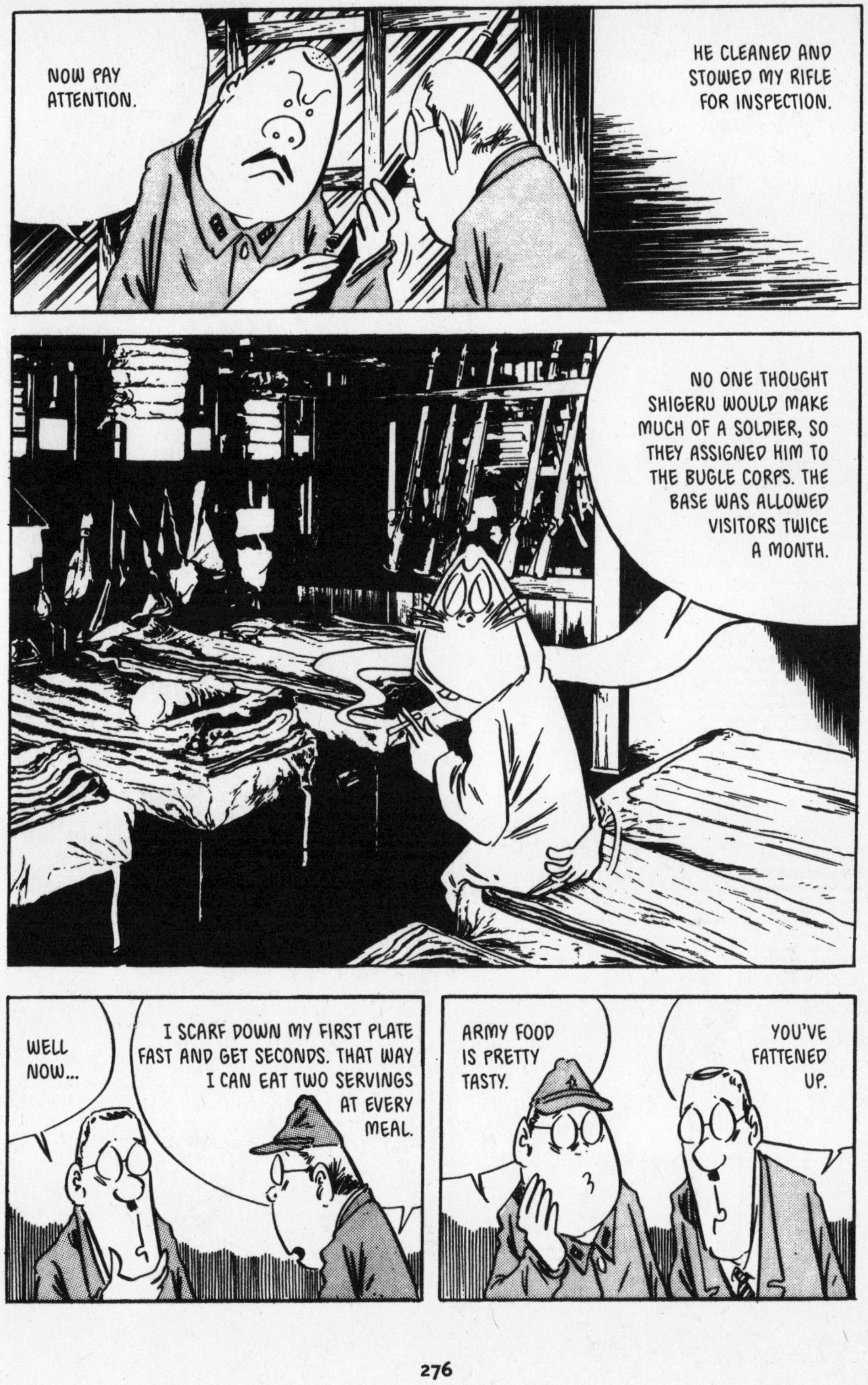
HE CLEANED AND STOWED MY RIFLE FOR INSPECTION.
NOW PAY ATTENTION.
NO ONE THOUGHT SHIGERU WOULD MAKE MUCH OF A SOLDIER, SO THEY ASSIGNED HIM TO THE BUGLE CORPS. THE BASE WAS ALLOWED VISITORS TWICE A MONTH.
YOU'VE FATTENED UP.
ARMY FOOD IS PRETTY TASTY.
I SCARF DOWN MY FIRST PLATE FAST AND GET SECONDS. THAT WAY I CAN EAT TWO SERVINGS AT EVERY MEAL.
WELL NOW...

THE BUGLE CORPS

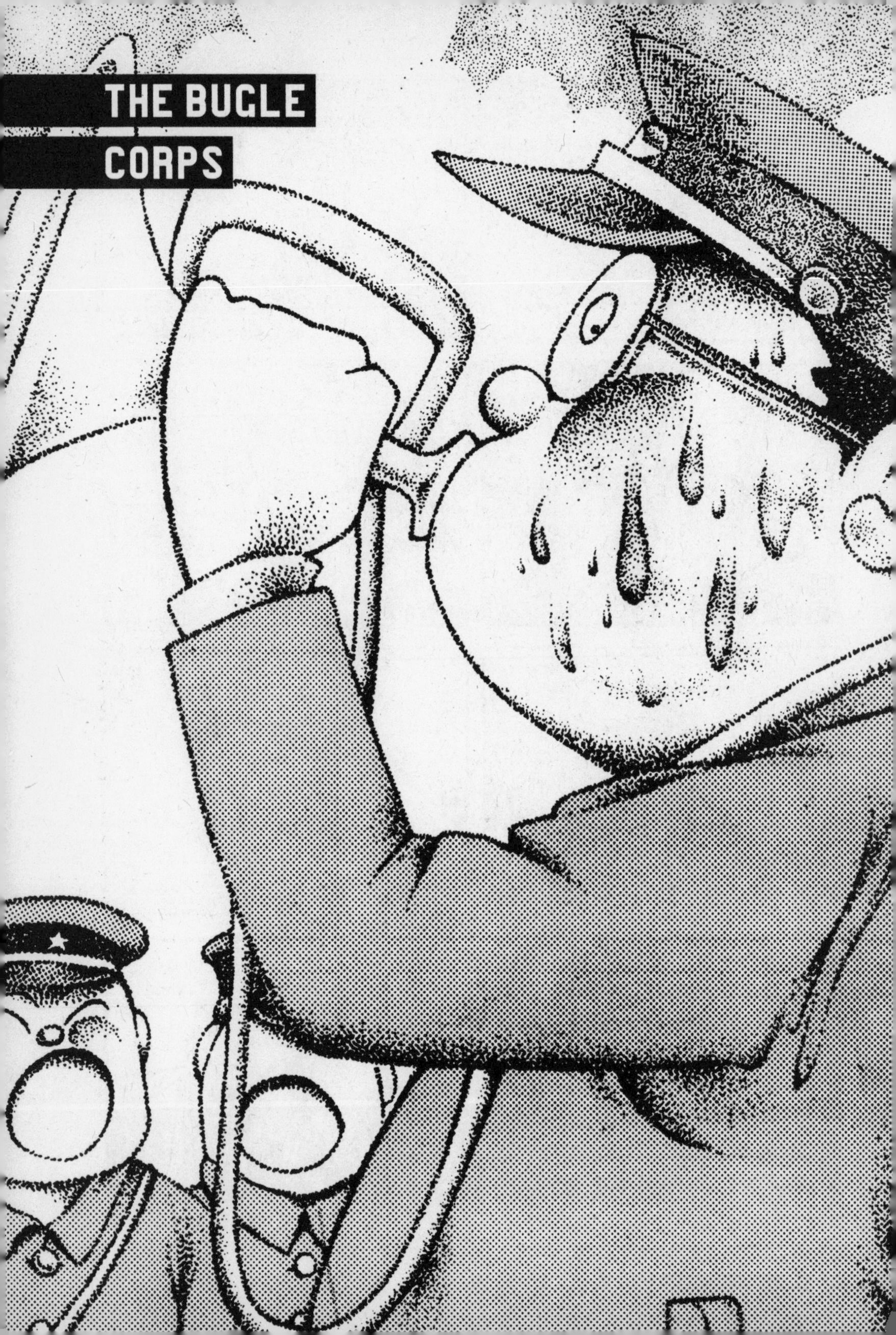

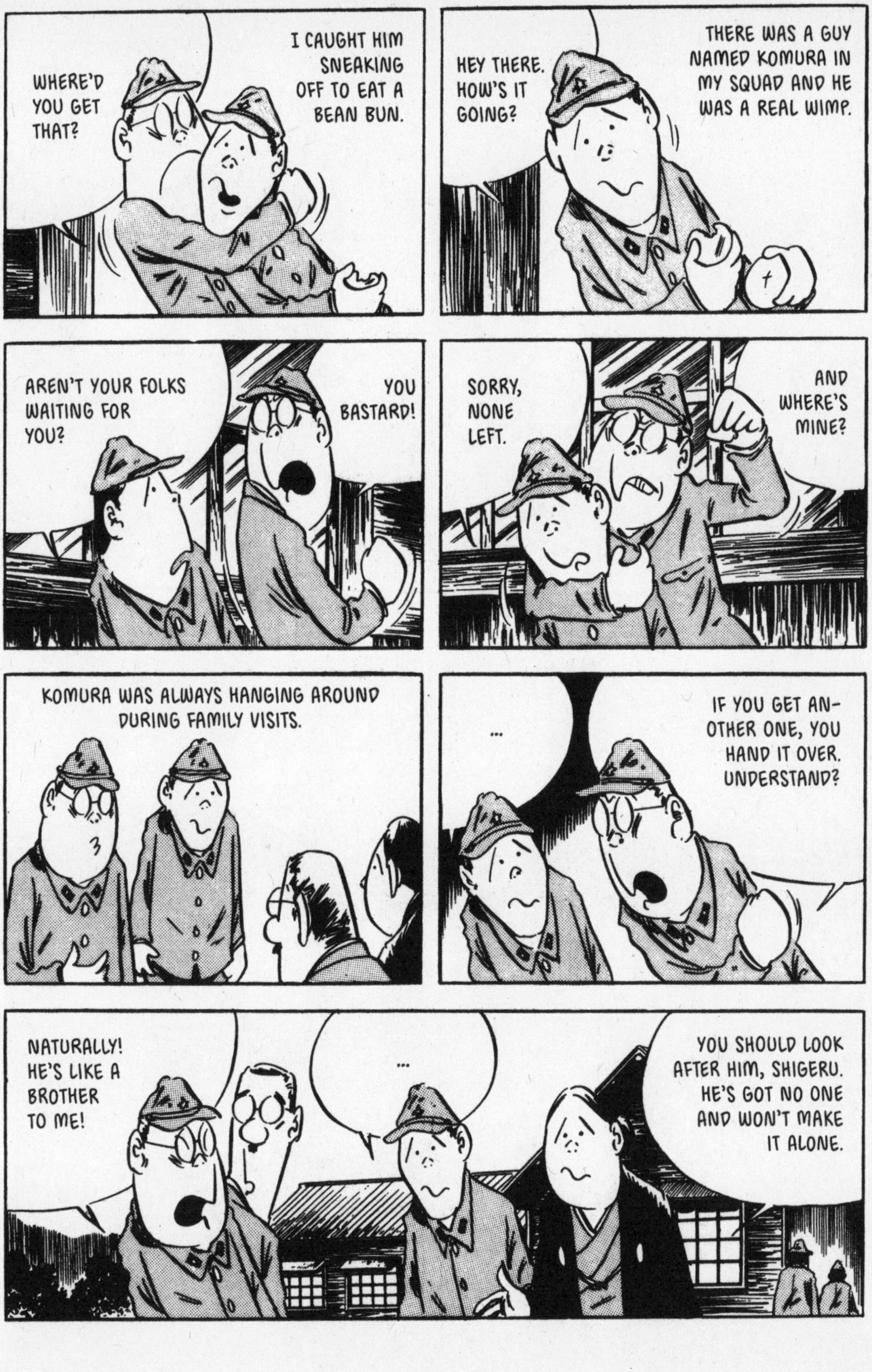
THERE WAS A GUY NAMED KOMURA IN MY SQUAD AND HE WAS A REAL WIMP.
HEY THERE. HOW'S IT GOING?
I CAUGHT HIM SNEAKING OFF TO EAT A BEAN BUN.
WHERE'D YOU GET THAT?
AND WHERE'S MINE?
SORRY, NONE LEFT.
YOU BASTARD!
AREN'T YOUR FOLKS WAITING FOR YOU?
IF YOU GET AN-OTHER ONE, YOU HAND IT OVER. UNDERSTAND?
...
KOMURA WAS ALWAYS HANGING AROUND DURING FAMILY VISITS.
YOU SHOULD LOOK AFTER HIM, SHIGERU. HE'S GOT NO ONE AND WON'T MAKE IT ALONE.
...
NATURALLY! HE'S LIKE A BROTHER TO ME!

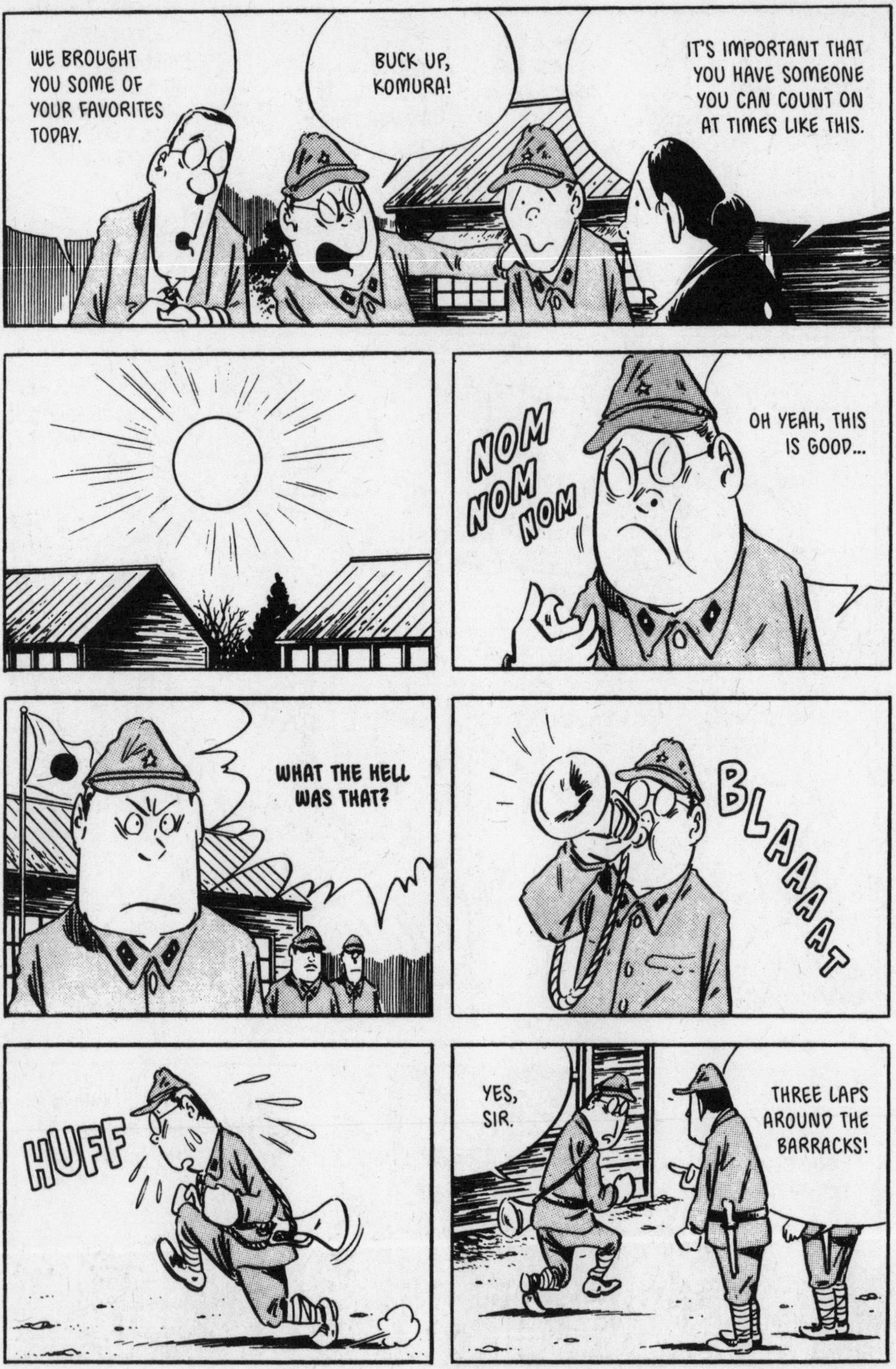
IT'S IMPORTANT THAT YOU HAVE SOMEONE YOU CAN COUNT ON AT TIMES LIKE THIS.
BUCK UP, KOMURA!
WE BROUGHT YOU SOME OF YOUR FAVORITES TODAY.
OH YEAH, THIS IS GOOD...
NOM NOM NOM
BLAAAAT
WHAT THE HELL WAS THAT?
THREE LAPS AROUND THE BARRACKS!
YES, SIR.
HUFF

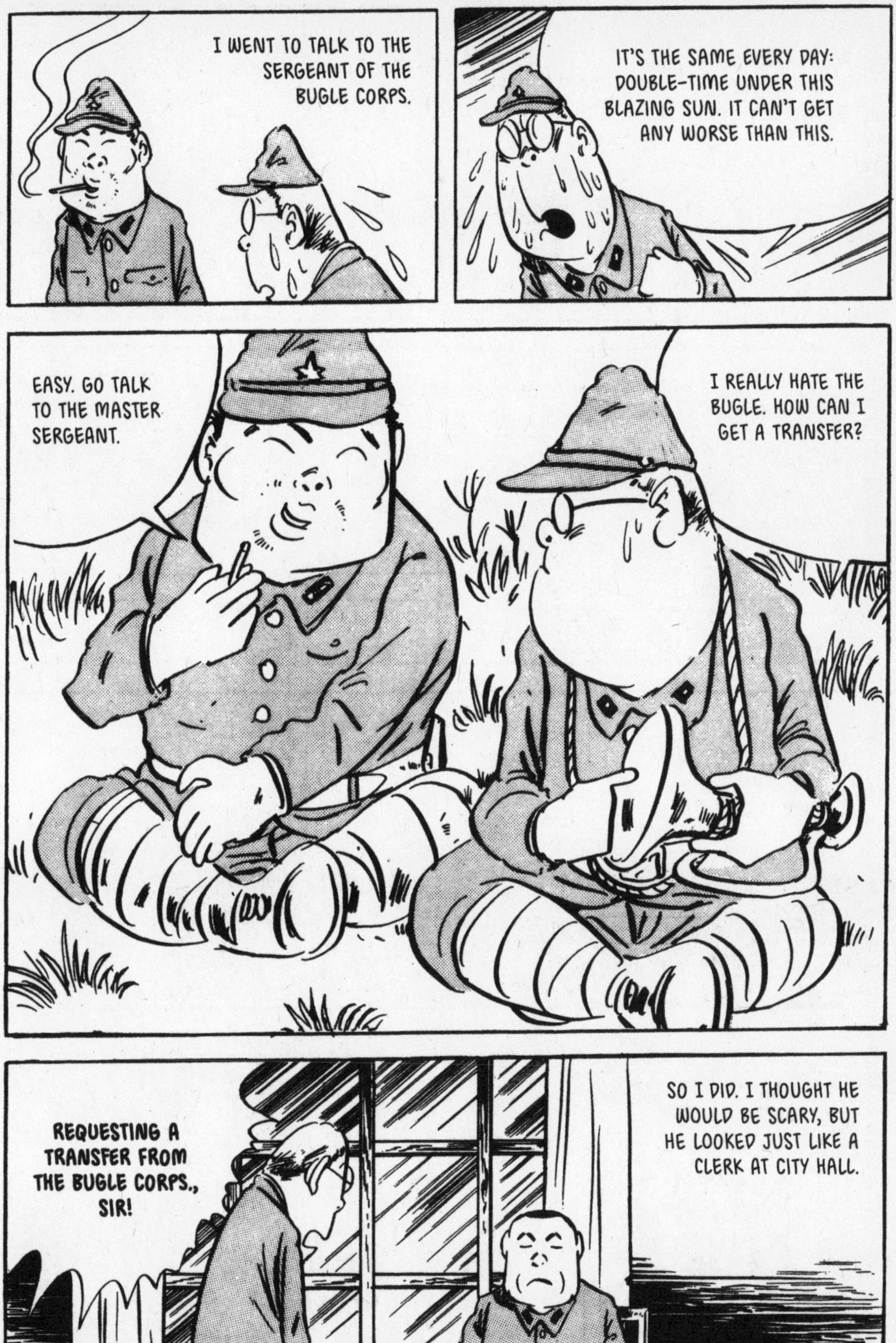
IT'S THE SAME EVERY DAY: DOUBLE-TIME UNDER THIS BLAZING SUN. IT CAN'T GET ANY WORSE THAN THIS.
I WENT TO TALK TO THE SERGEANT OF THE BUGLE CORPS.
I REALLY HATE THE BUGLE. HOW CAN I GET A TRANSFER?
EASY. GO TALK TO THE MASTER SERGEANT.
SO I DID. I THOUGHT HE WOULD BE SCARY, BUT HE LOOKED JUST LIKE A CLERK AT CITY HALL.
REQUESTING A TRANSFER FROM THE BUGLE CORPS., SIR!

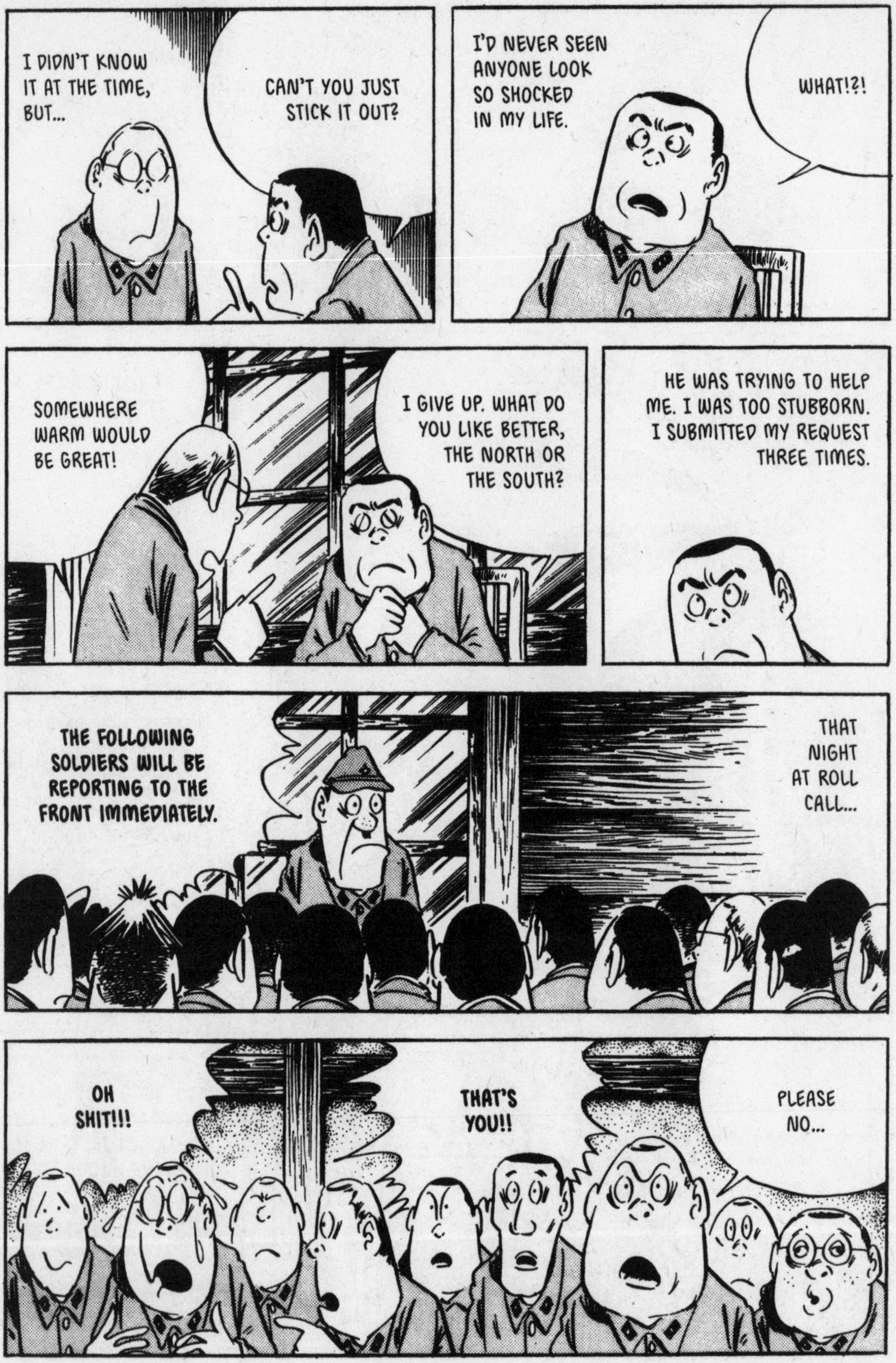
WHAT!?!
I'D NEVER SEEN ANYONE LOOK SO SHOCKED IN MY LIFE.
CAN'T YOU JUST STICK IT OUT?
I DIDN'T KNOW IT AT THE TIME, BUT...
HE WAS TRYING TO HELP ME. I WAS TOO STUBBORN. I SUBMITTED MY REQUEST THREE TIMES.
I GIVE UP. WHAT DO YOU LIKE BETTER, THE NORTH OR THE SOUTH?
SOMEWHERE WARM WOULD BE GREAT!
THAT NIGHT AT ROLL CALL...
THE FOLLOWING SOLDIERS WILL BE REPORTING TO THE FRONT IMMEDIATELY.
PLEASE NO...
THAT'S YOU!!
OH SHIT!!!

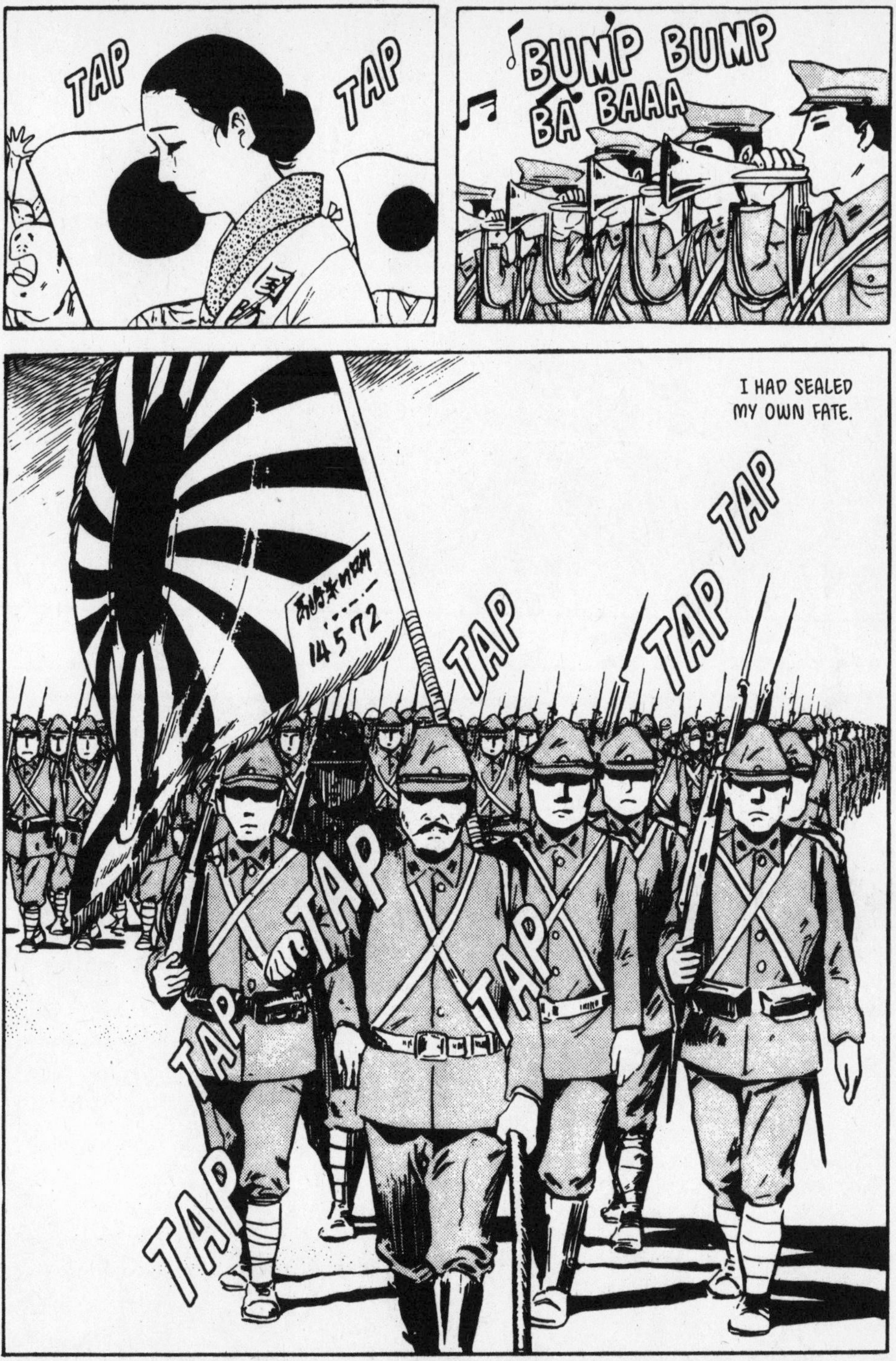
BUMP BUMP
BA BAAA
TAP
TAP
I HAD SEALED MY OWN FATE.
TAP
TAP
TAP
14572
TAP
TAP
TAP
TAP

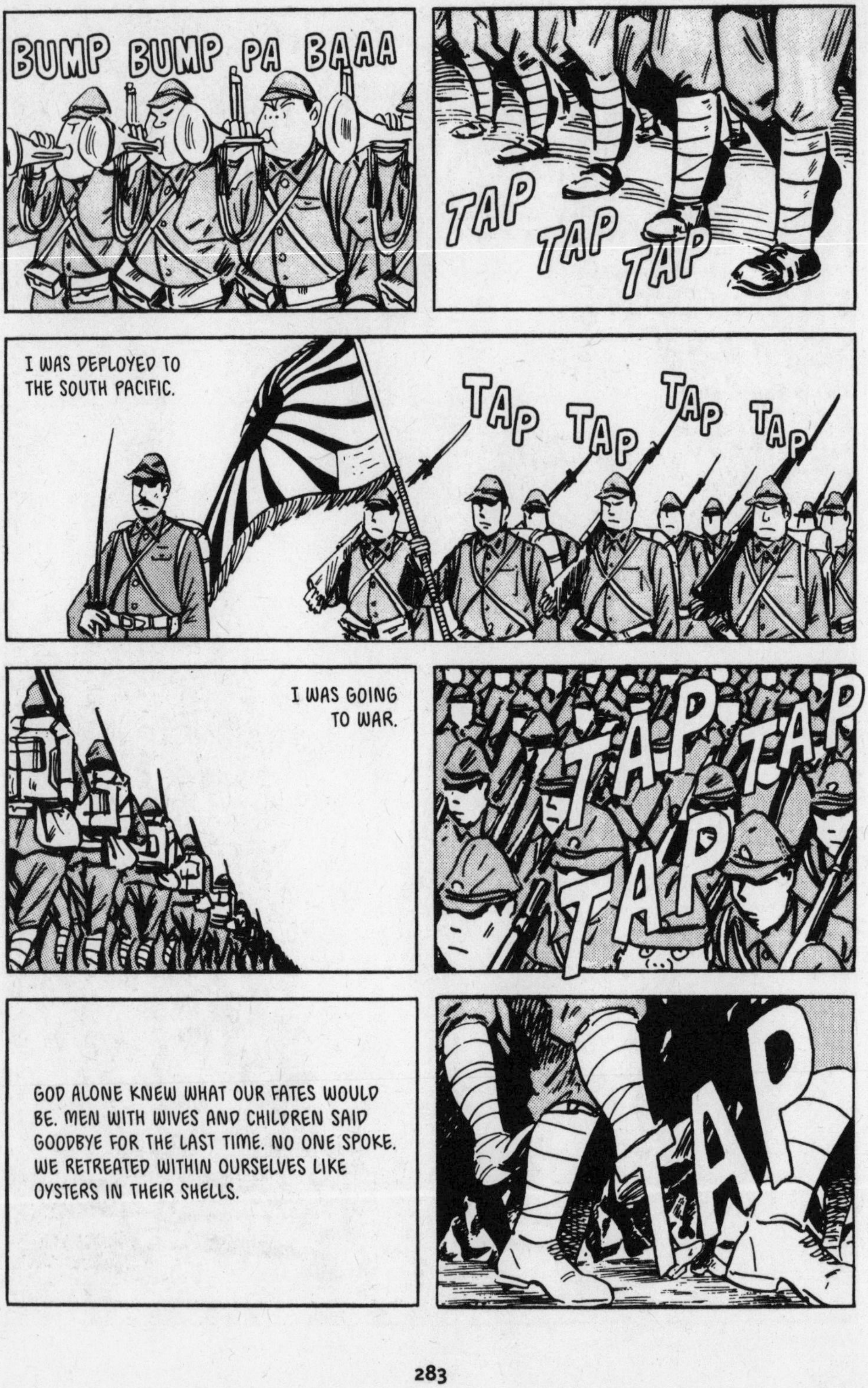
TAP
TAP
TAP
BUMP BUMP PA BAAA
I WAS DEPLOYED TO THE SOUTH PACIFIC.
TAP TAP TAP TAP
TAP
TAP
TAP
TAP
I WAS GOING TO WAR.
TAP
GOD ALONE KNEW WHAT OUR FATES WOULD BE. MEN WITH WIVES AND CHILDREN SAID GOODBYE FOR THE LAST TIME. NO ONE SPOKE. WE RETREATED WITHIN OURSELVES LIKE OYSTERS IN THEIR SHELLS.

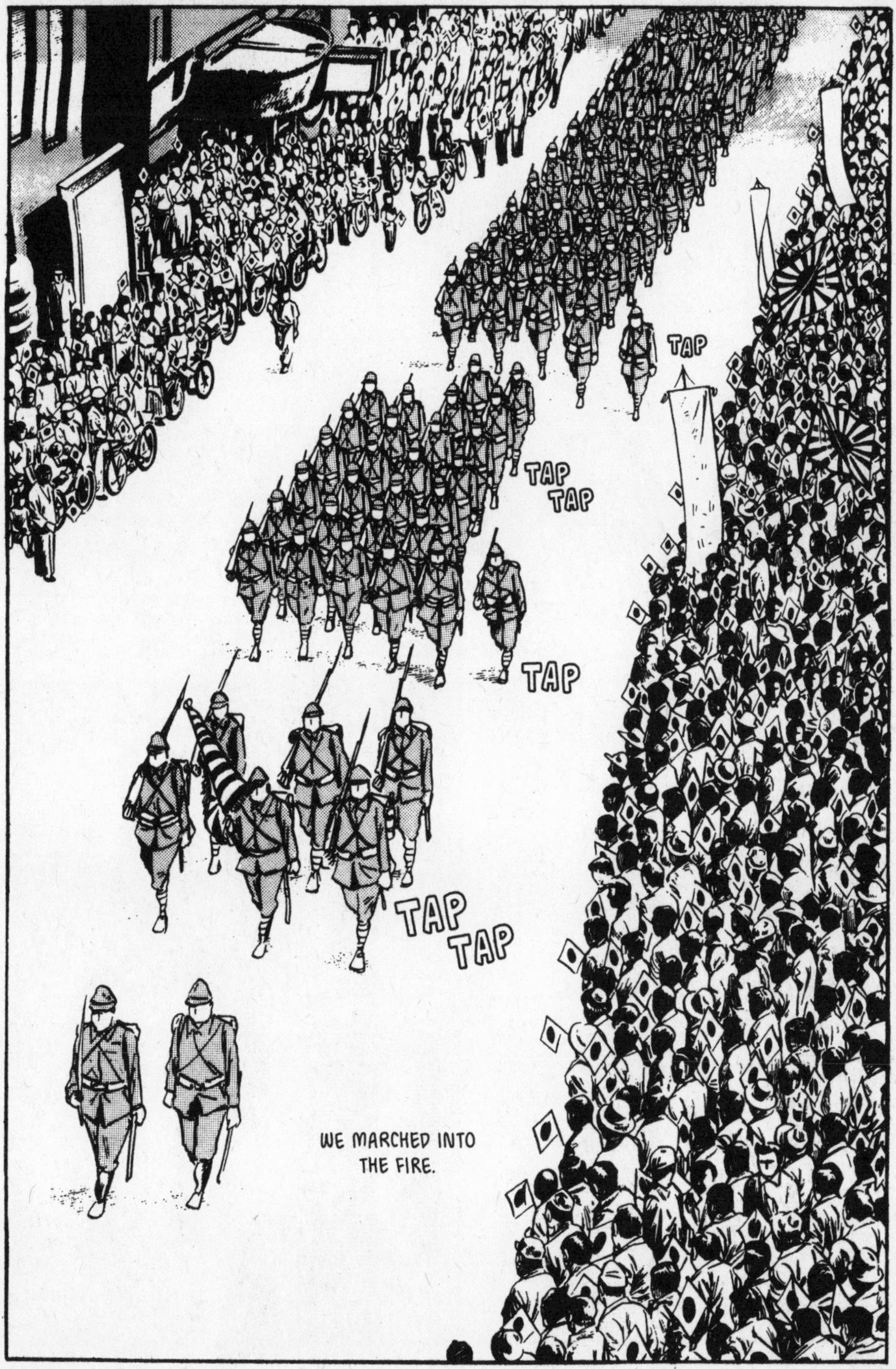
TAP
TAP TAP
TAP
TAP TAP
WE MARCHED INTO THE FIRE.

THE BATTLE OF MIDWAY

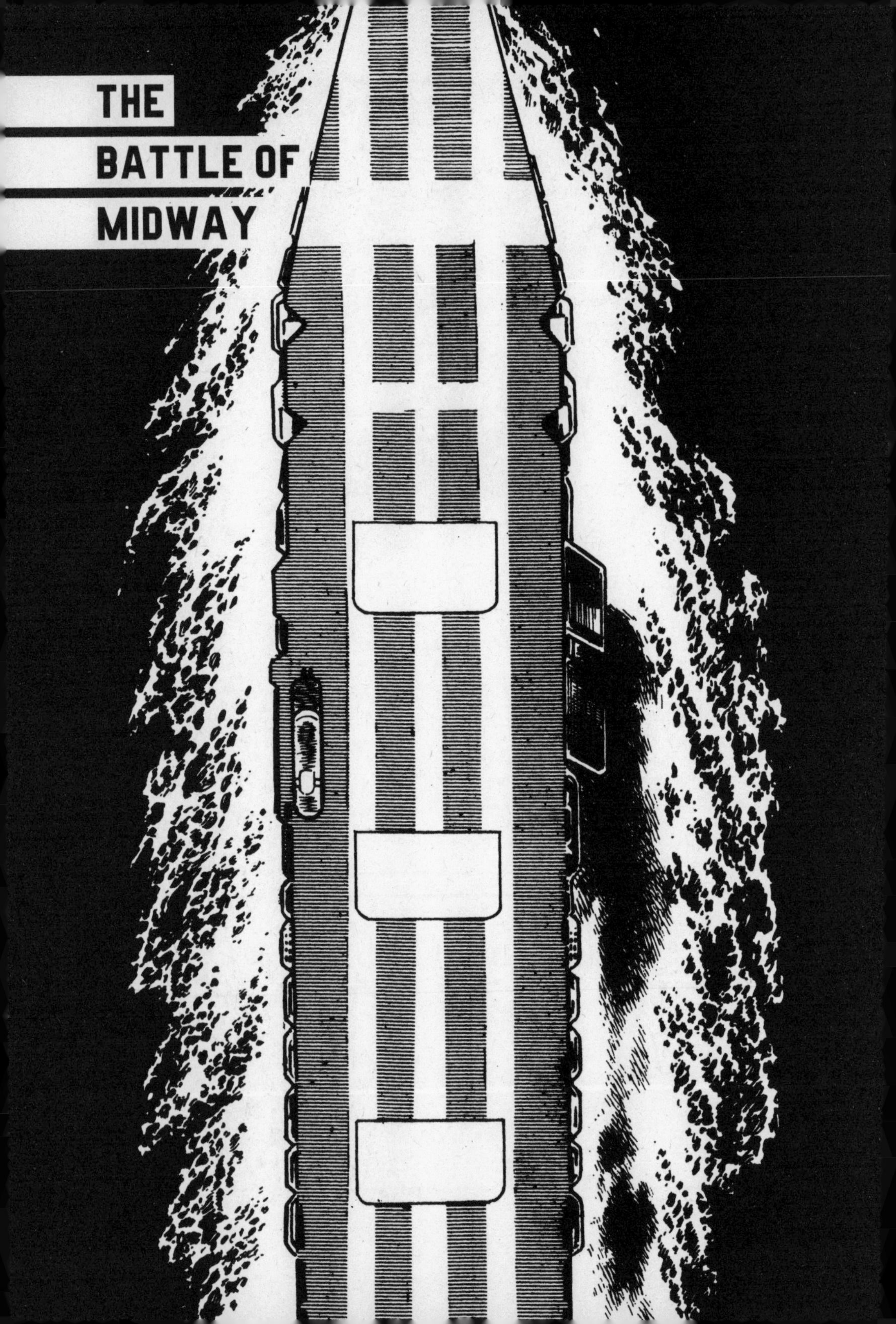

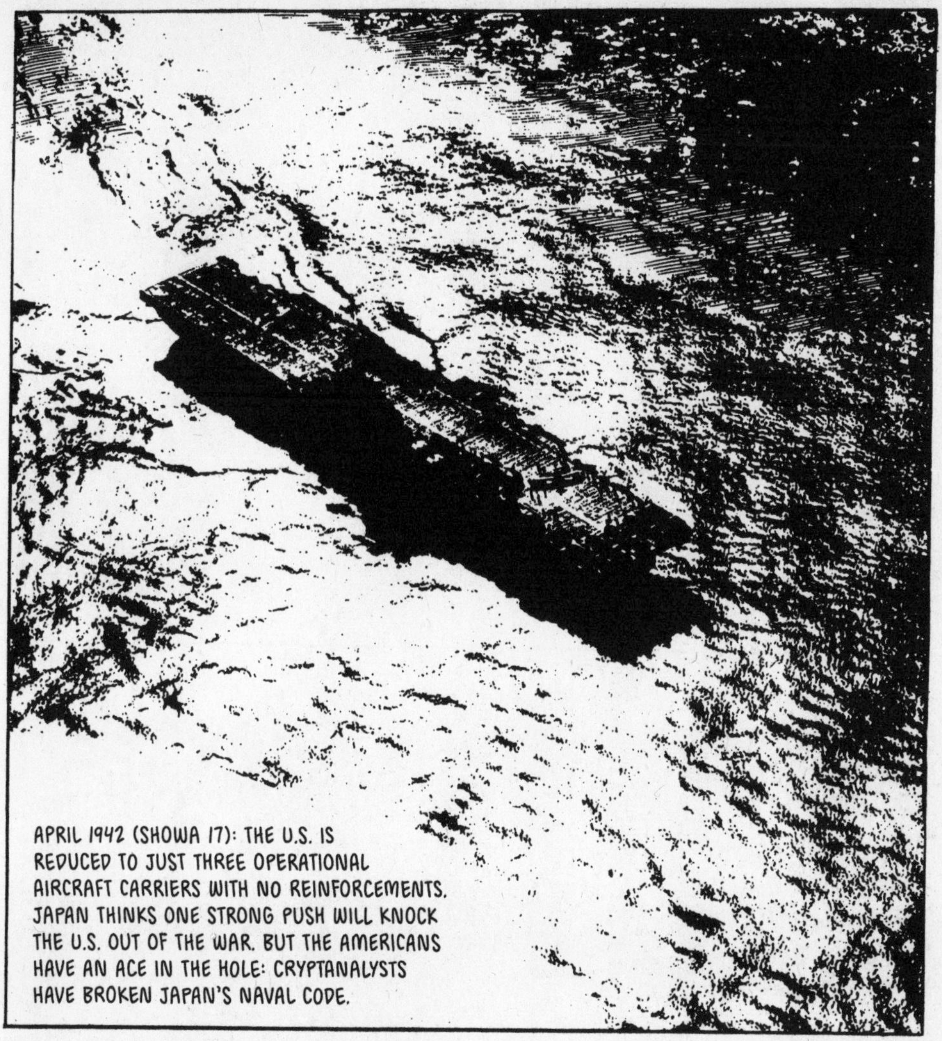
APRIL 1942 (SHOWA 17): THE U.S. IS REDUCED TO JUST THREE OPERATIONAL AIRCRAFT CARRIERS WITH NO REINFORCEMENTS. JAPAN THINKS ONE STRONG PUSH WILL KNOCK THE U.S. OUT OF THE WAR. BUT THE AMERICANS HAVE AN ACE IN THE HOLE: CRYPTANALYSTS HAVE BROKEN JAPAN'S NAVAL CODE.

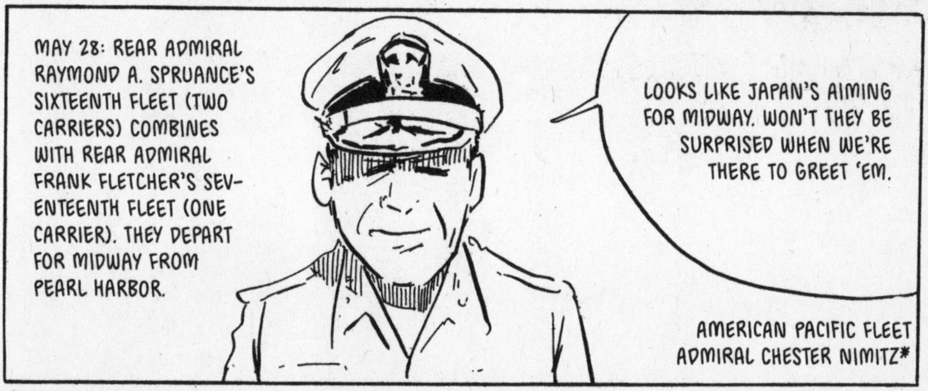
LOOKS LIKE JAPAN'S AIMING FOR MIDWAY. WON'T THEY BE SURPRISED WHEN WE'RE THERE TO GREET 'EM.
MAY 28: REAR ADMIRAL RAYMOND A. SPRUANCE'S SIXTEENTH FLEET (TWO CARRIERS) COMBINES WITH REAR ADMIRAL FRANK FLETCHER'S SEVENTEENTH FLEET (ONE CARRIER). THEY DEPART FOR MIDWAY FROM PEARL HARBOR.
AMERICAN PACIFIC FLEET ADMIRAL CHESTER NIMITZ*

*SEE NOTE ON PAGE 547.

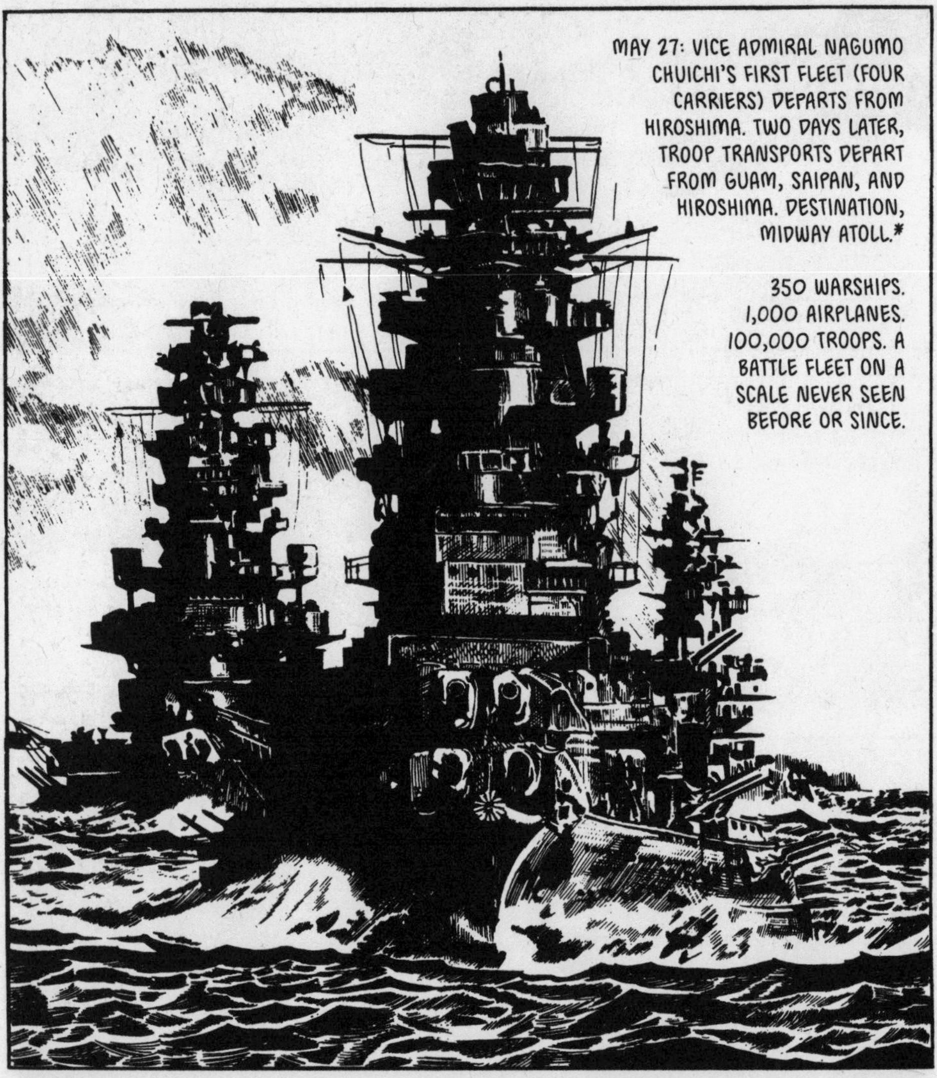
MAY 27: VICE ADMIRAL NAGUMO CHUICHI'S FIRST FLEET (FOUR CARRIERS) DEPARTS FROM HIROSHIMA. TWO DAYS LATER, TROOP TRANSPORTS DEPART FROM GUAM, SAIPAN, AND HIROSHIMA. DESTINATION, MIDWAY ATOLL.*
350 WARSHIPS. 1,000 AIRPLANES. 100,000 TROOPS. A BATTLE FLEET ON A SCALE NEVER SEEN BEFORE OR SINCE.

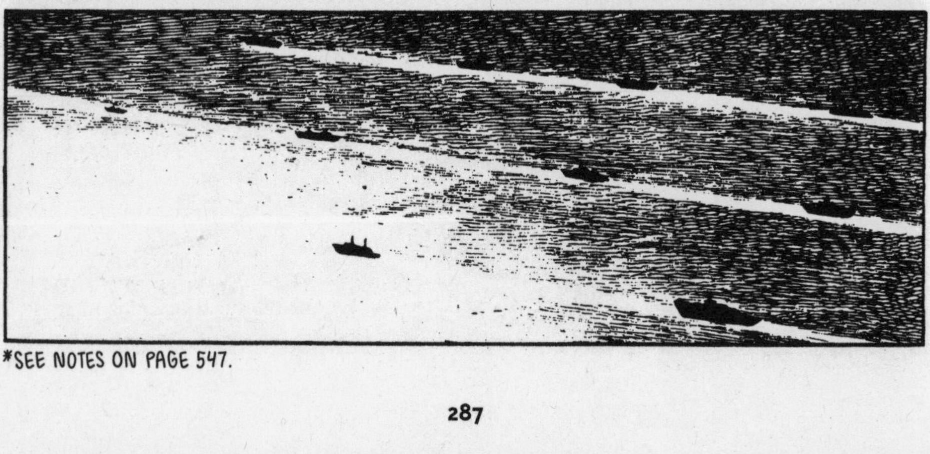

*SEE NOTES ON PAGE 547.

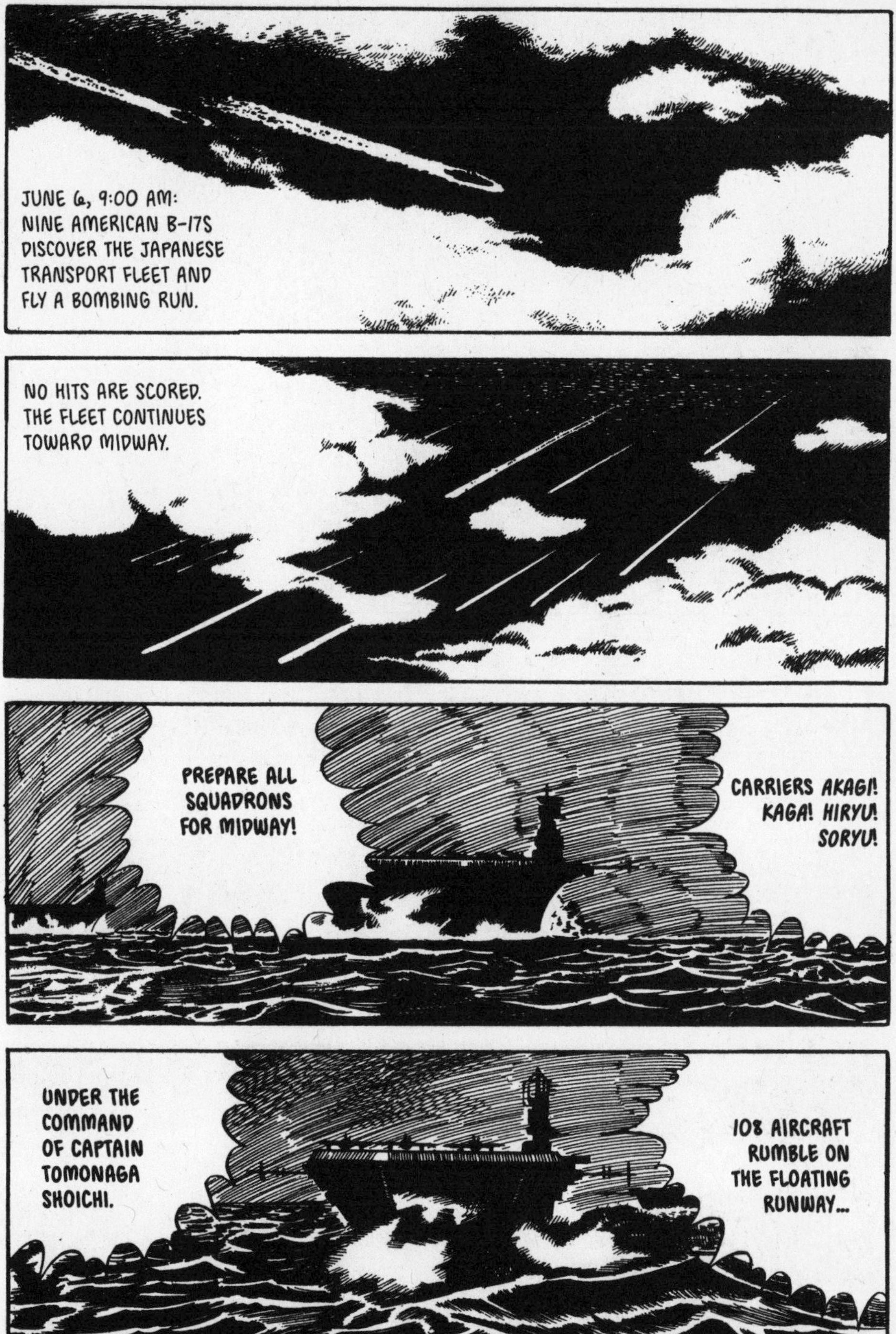
JUNE 6, 9:00 AM: NINE AMERICAN B-17S DISCOVER THE JAPANESE TRANSPORT FLEET AND FLY A BOMBING RUN.
NO HITS ARE SCORED. THE FLEET CONTINUES TOWARD MIDWAY.
CARRIERS AKAGI! KAGA! HIRYU! SORYU!
PREPARE ALL SQUADRONS FOR MIDWAY!
108 AIRCRAFT RUMBLE ON THE FLOATING RUNWAY...
UNDER THE COMMAND OF CAPTAIN TOMONAGA SHOICHI.

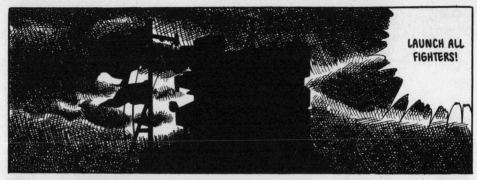

LAUNCH ALL FIGHTERS!

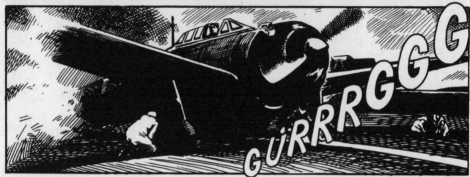

GURRRGGG

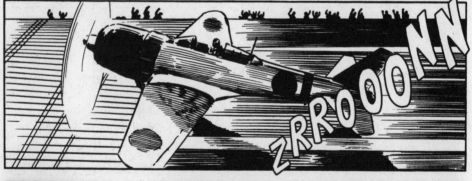

ZRROOONN

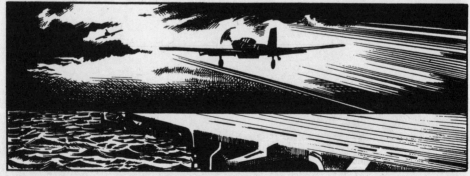

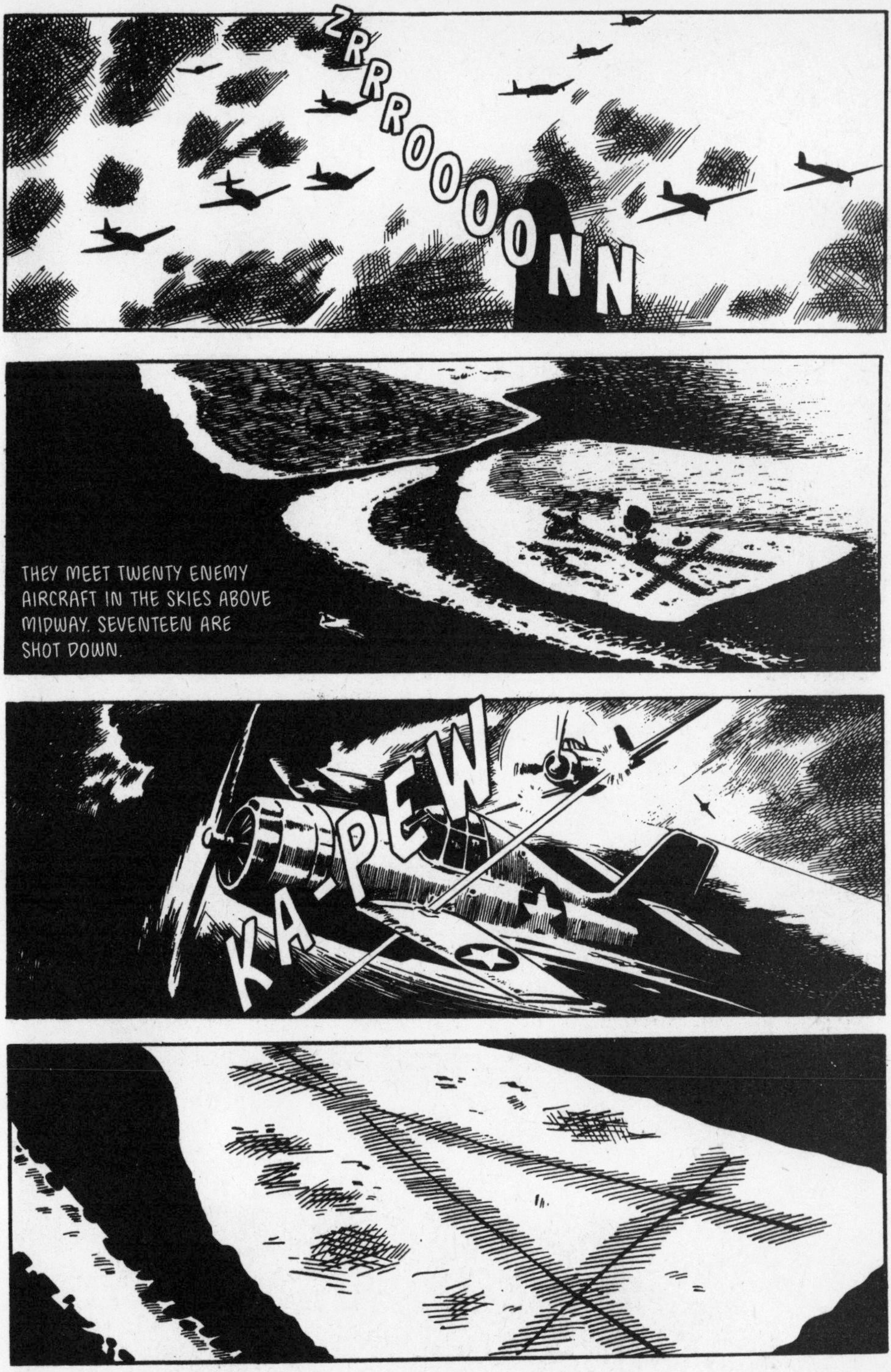
ZRRROOOOONN
THEY MEET TWENTY ENEMY AIRCRAFT IN THE SKIES ABOVE MIDWAY. SEVENTEEN ARE SHOT DOWN.
KA-PEW

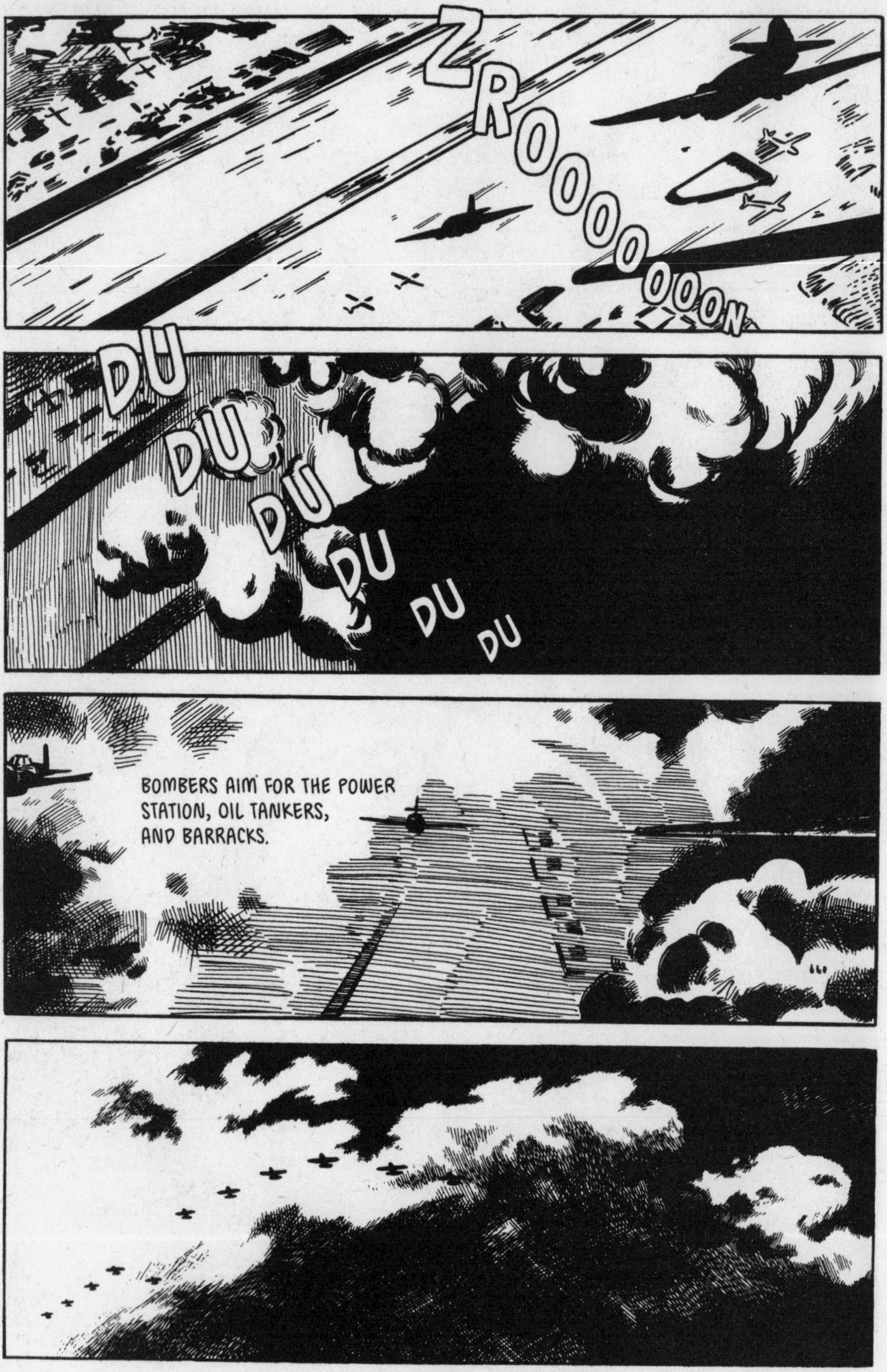
ZROOOOOOOON
DU
DU
DU
DU
DU
DU
BOMBERS AIM FOR THE POWER STATION, OIL TANKERS, AND BARRACKS.

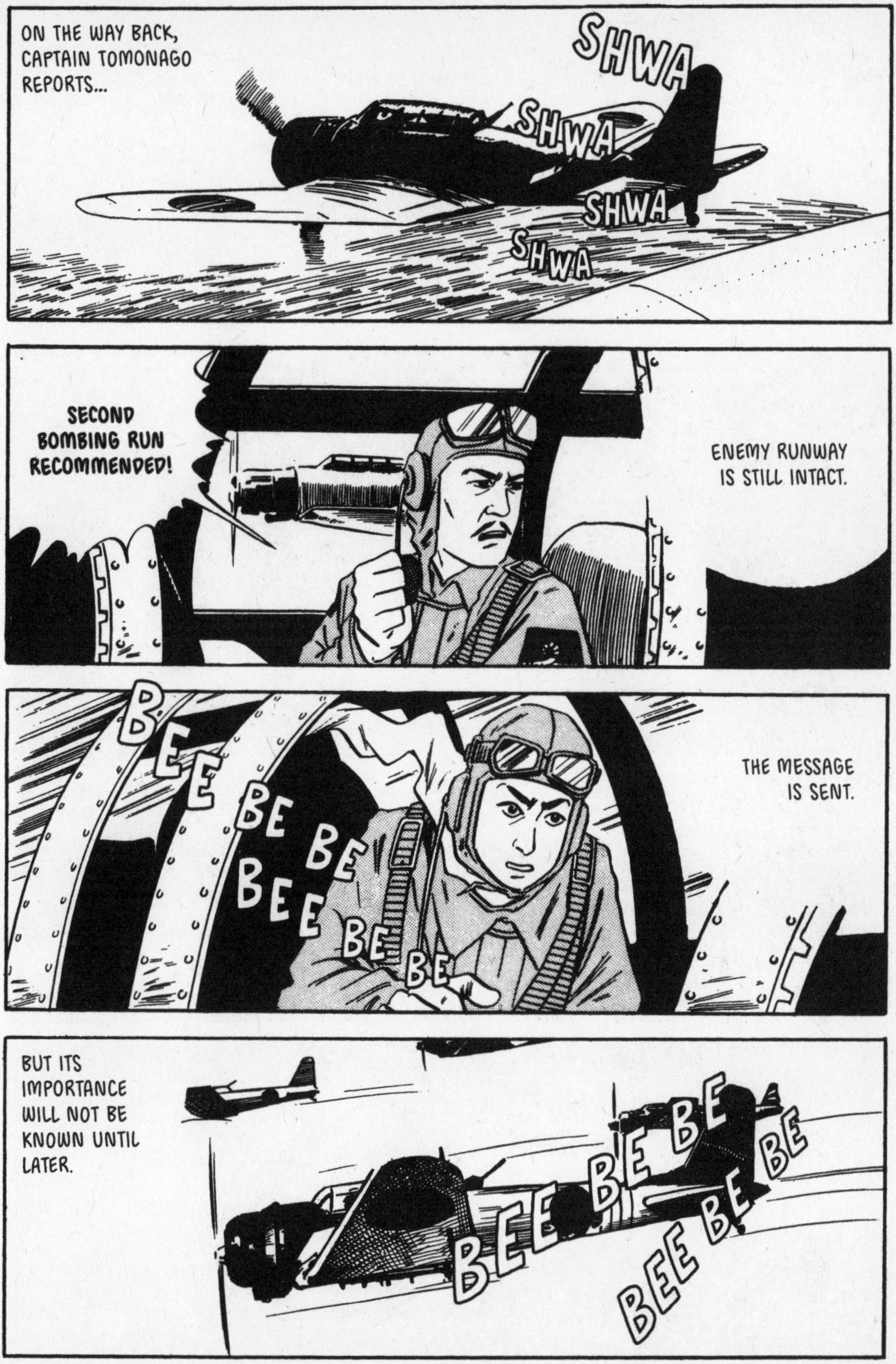
SHWA
SHWA
SHWA
SHWA
ON THE WAY BACK, CAPTAIN TOMONAGO REPORTS...
ENEMY RUNWAY IS STILL INTACT.
SECOND BOMBING RUN RECOMMENDED!
THE MESSAGE IS SENT.
BEE BE BE BEE BE BE
BEE BE BE
BEE BE BE
BUT ITS IMPORTANCE WILL NOT BE KNOWN UNTIL LATER.

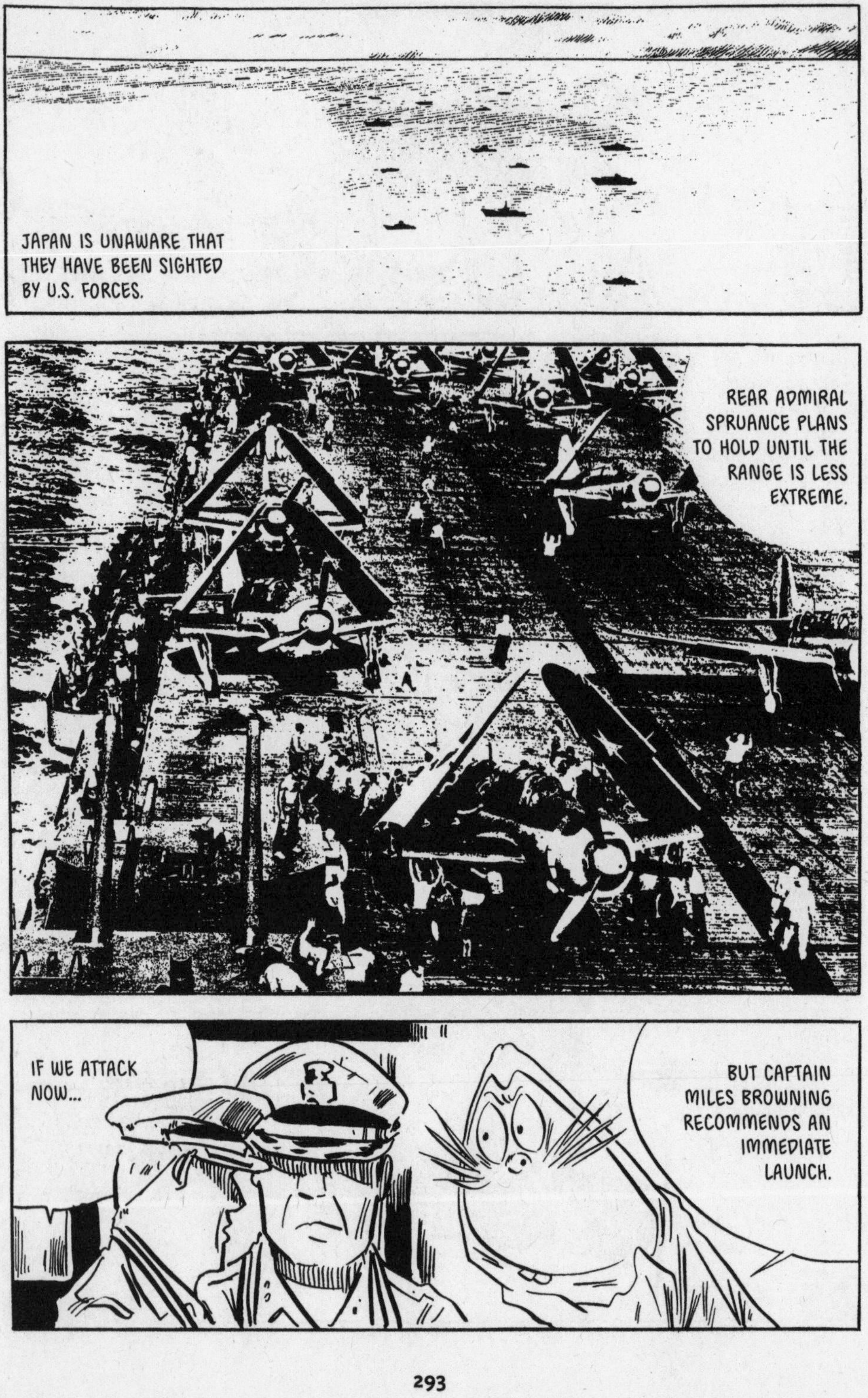
JAPAN IS UNAWARE THAT THEY HAVE BEEN SIGHTED BY U.S. FORCES.
REAR ADMIRAL SPRUANCE PLANS TO HOLD UNTIL THE RANGE IS LESS EXTREME.
BUT CAPTAIN MILES BROWNING RECOMMENDS AN IMMEDIATE LAUNCH.
IF WE ATTACK NOW...

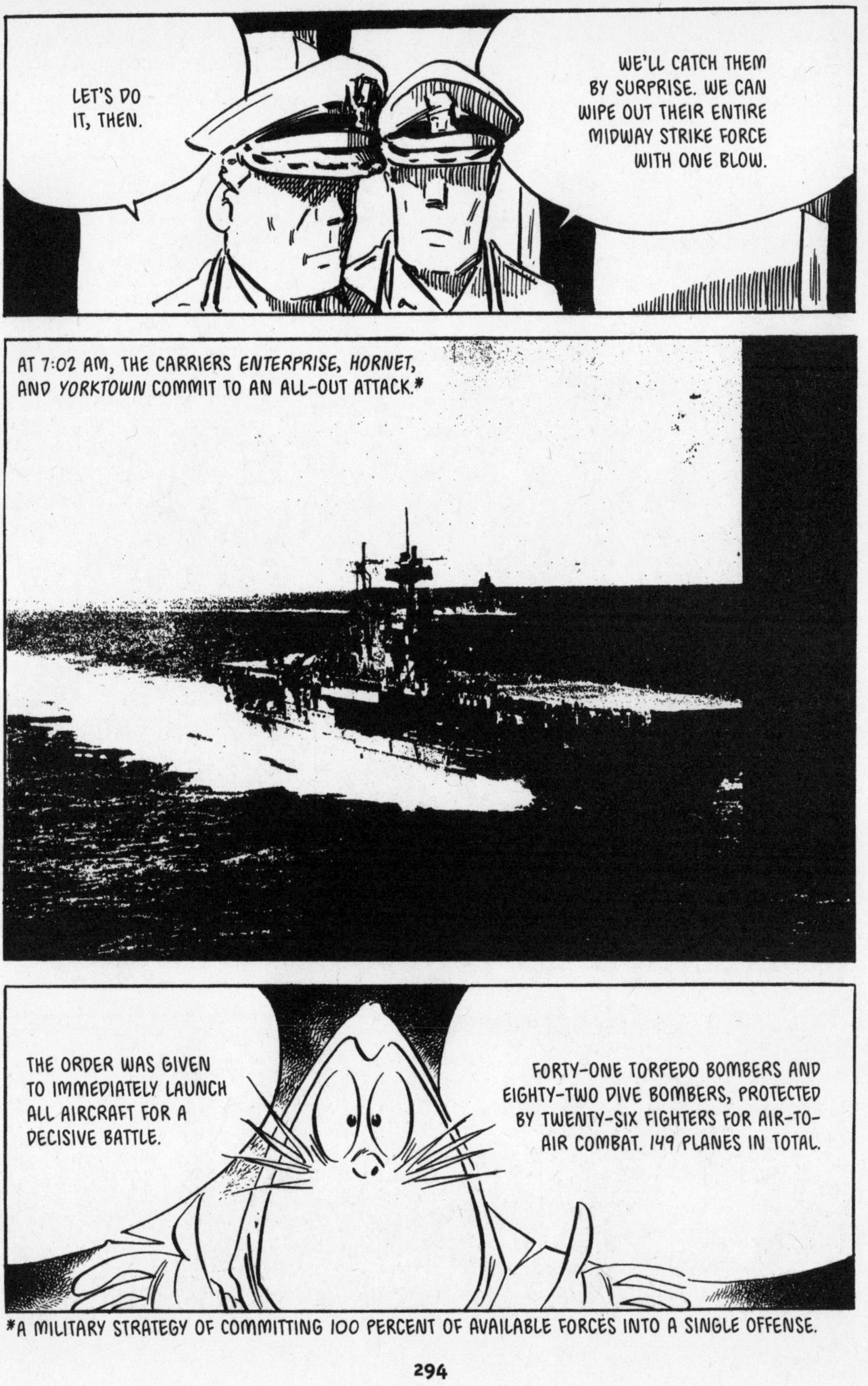
WE'LL CATCH THEM BY SURPRISE. WE CAN WIPE OUT THEIR ENTIRE MIDWAY STRIKE FORCE WITH ONE BLOW.
LET'S DO IT, THEN.
AT 7:02 AM, THE CARRIERS *ENTERPRISE*, *HORNET*, AND *YORKTOWN* COMMIT TO AN ALL-OUT ATTACK.*
FORTY-ONE TORPEDO BOMBERS AND EIGHTY-TWO DIVE BOMBERS, PROTECTED BY TWENTY-SIX FIGHTERS FOR AIR-TO-AIR COMBAT. 149 PLANES IN TOTAL.
THE ORDER WAS GIVEN TO IMMEDIATELY LAUNCH ALL AIRCRAFT FOR A DECISIVE BATTLE.

*A MILITARY STRATEGY OF COMMITTING 100 PERCENT OF AVAILABLE FORCES INTO A SINGLE OFFENSE.

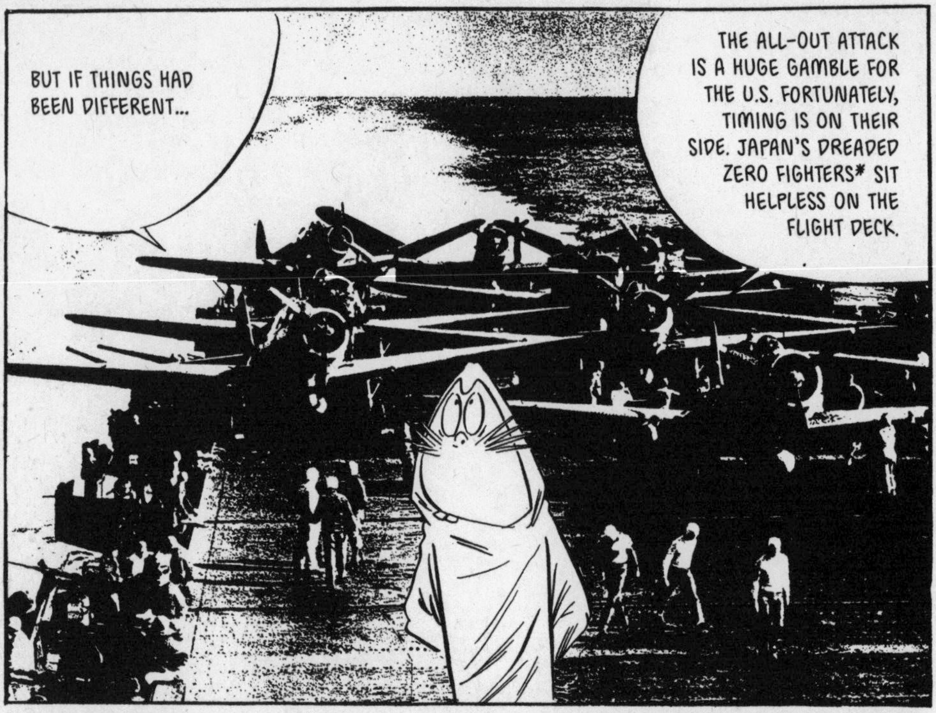
THE ALL-OUT ATTACK IS A HUGE GAMBLE FOR THE U.S. FORTUNATELY, TIMING IS ON THEIR SIDE. JAPAN'S DREADED ZERO FIGHTERS* SIT HELPLESS ON THE FLIGHT DECK.
BUT IF THINGS HAD BEEN DIFFERENT...

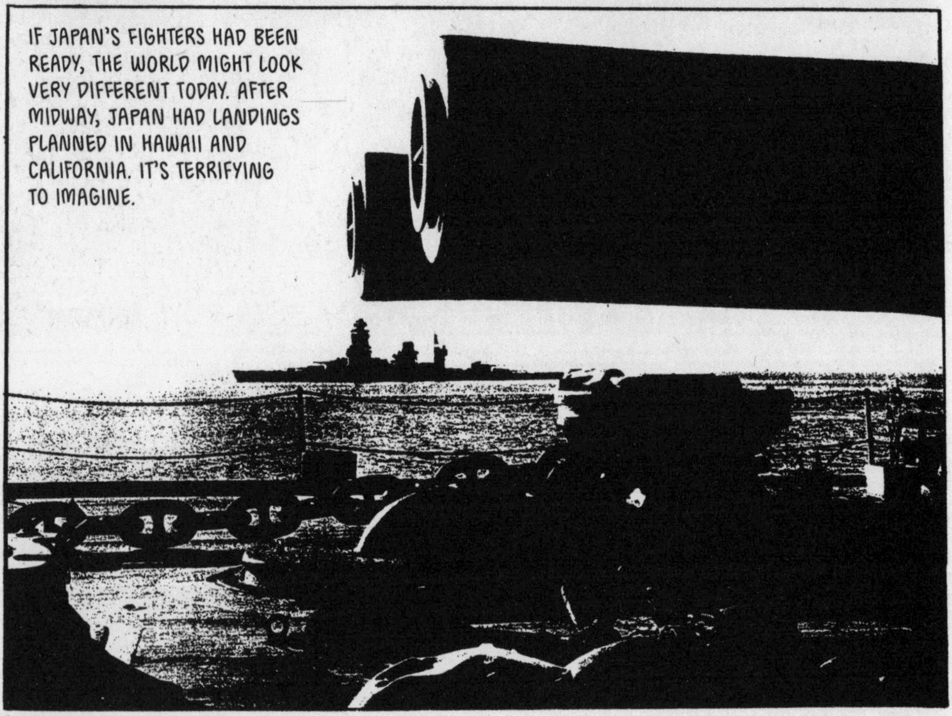
IF JAPAN'S FIGHTERS HAD BEEN READY, THE WORLD MIGHT LOOK VERY DIFFERENT TODAY. AFTER MIDWAY, JAPAN HAD LANDINGS PLANNED IN HAWAII AND CALIFORNIA. IT'S TERRIFYING TO IMAGINE.

*SEE NOTES ON PAGE 547.

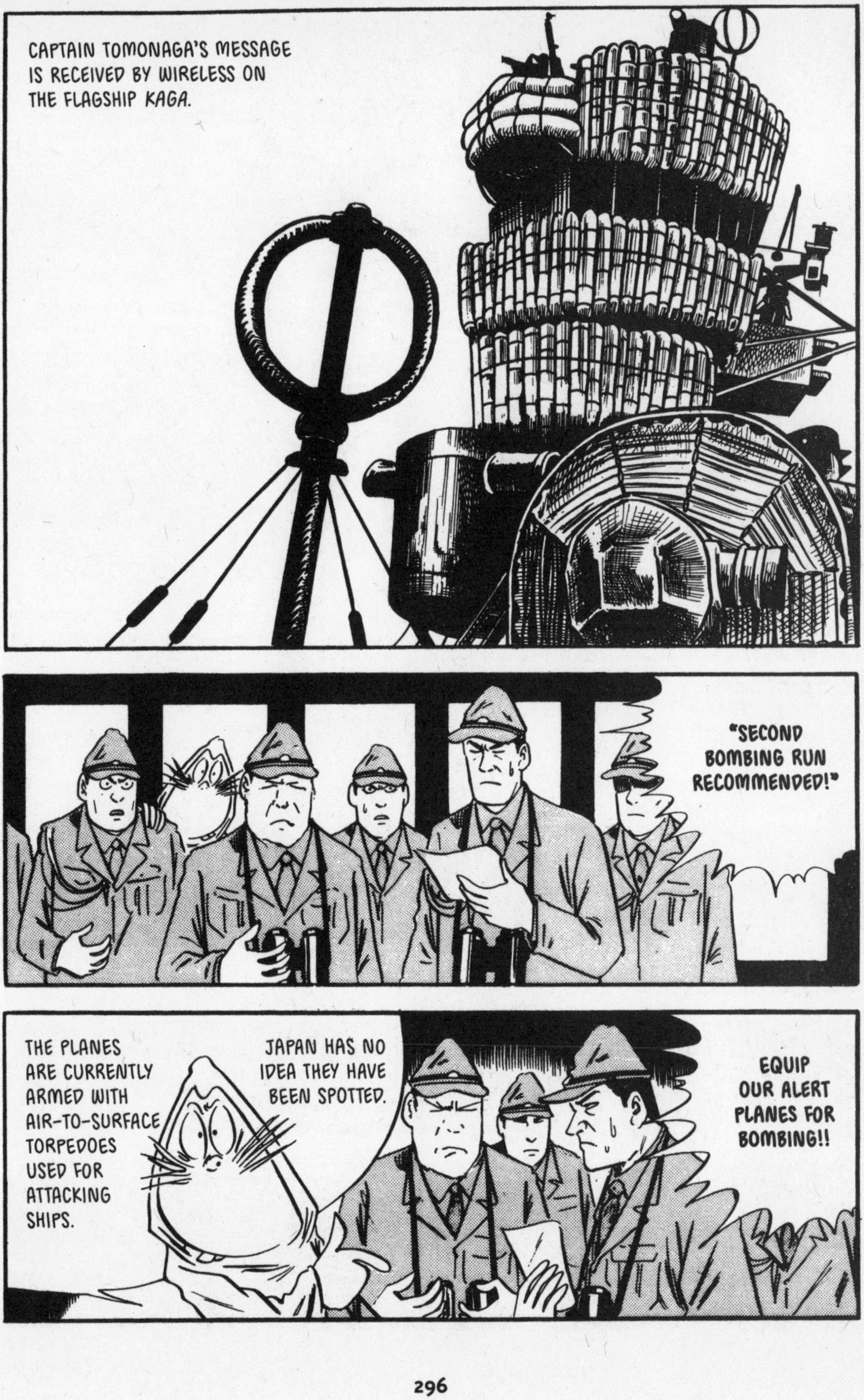
CAPTAIN TOMONAGA'S MESSAGE IS RECEIVED BY WIRELESS ON THE FLAGSHIP *KAGA*.
"SECOND BOMBING RUN RECOMMENDED!"
EQUIP OUR ALERT PLANES FOR BOMBING!!
JAPAN HAS NO IDEA THEY HAVE BEEN SPOTTED.
THE PLANES ARE CURRENTLY ARMED WITH AIR-TO-SURFACE TORPEDOES USED FOR ATTACKING SHIPS.

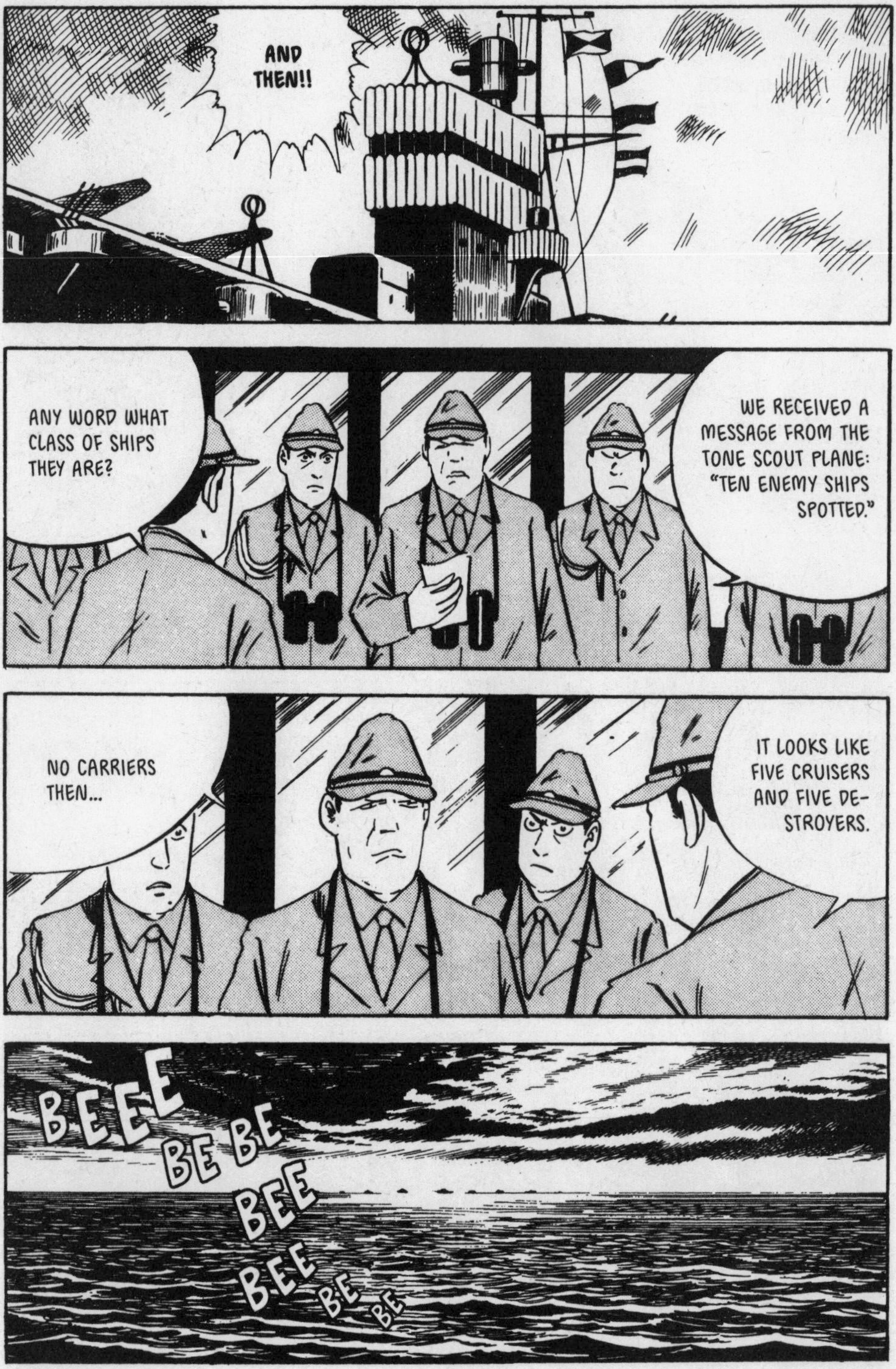
AND THEN!!
WE RECEIVED A MESSAGE FROM THE TONE SCOUT PLANE: "TEN ENEMY SHIPS SPOTTED."
ANY WORD WHAT CLASS OF SHIPS THEY ARE?
IT LOOKS LIKE FIVE CRUISERS AND FIVE DE-STROYERS.
NO CARRIERS THEN...
BEEE BE BE BEE BEE BE BE

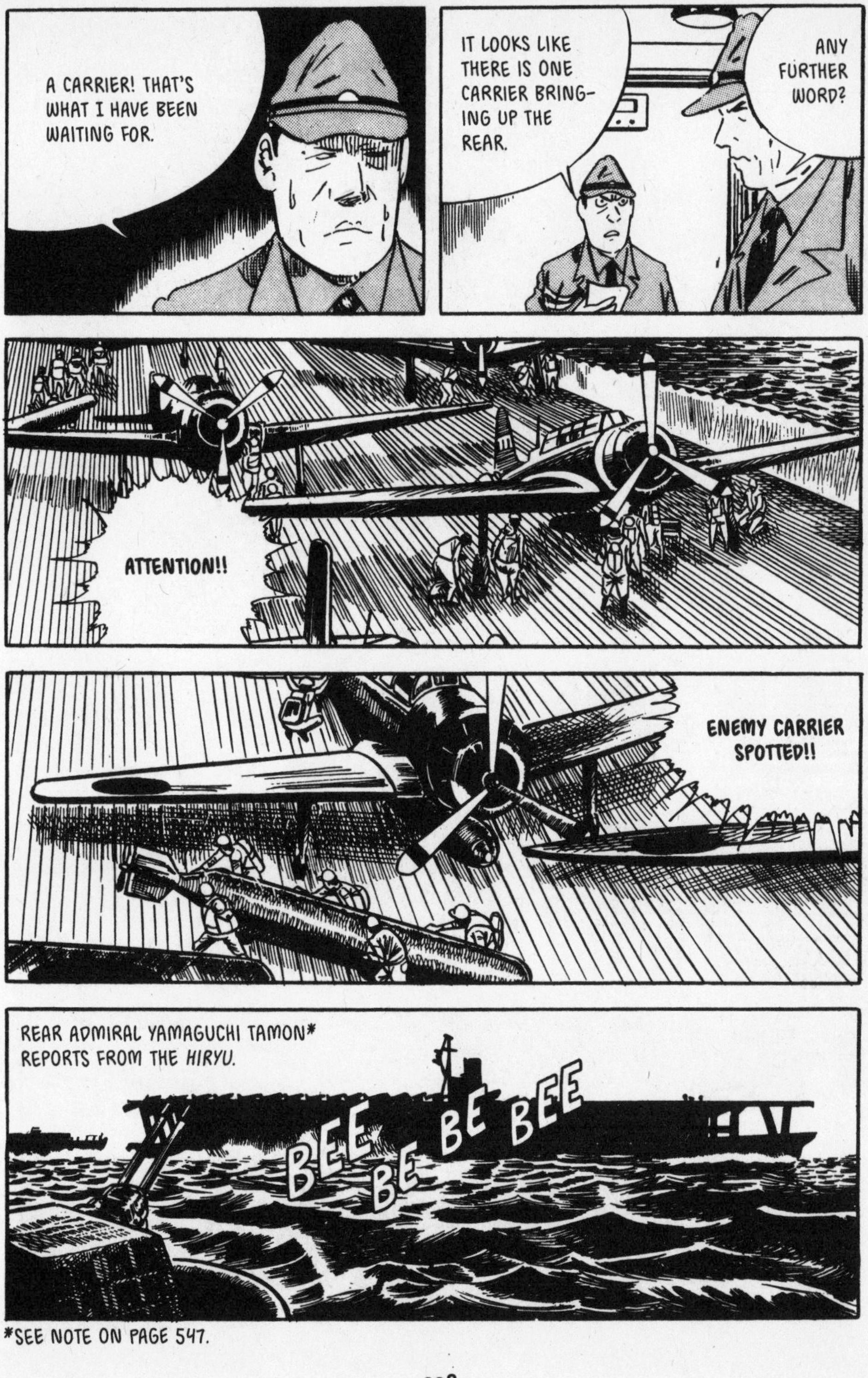
ANY FURTHER WORD?
IT LOOKS LIKE THERE IS ONE CARRIER BRING-ING UP THE REAR.
A CARRIER! THAT'S WHAT I HAVE BEEN WAITING FOR.
ATTENTION!!
ENEMY CARRIER SPOTTED!!
REAR ADMIRAL YAMAGUCHI TAMON* REPORTS FROM THE *HIRYU*.
BEE BE BE BEE

*SEE NOTE ON PAGE 547.

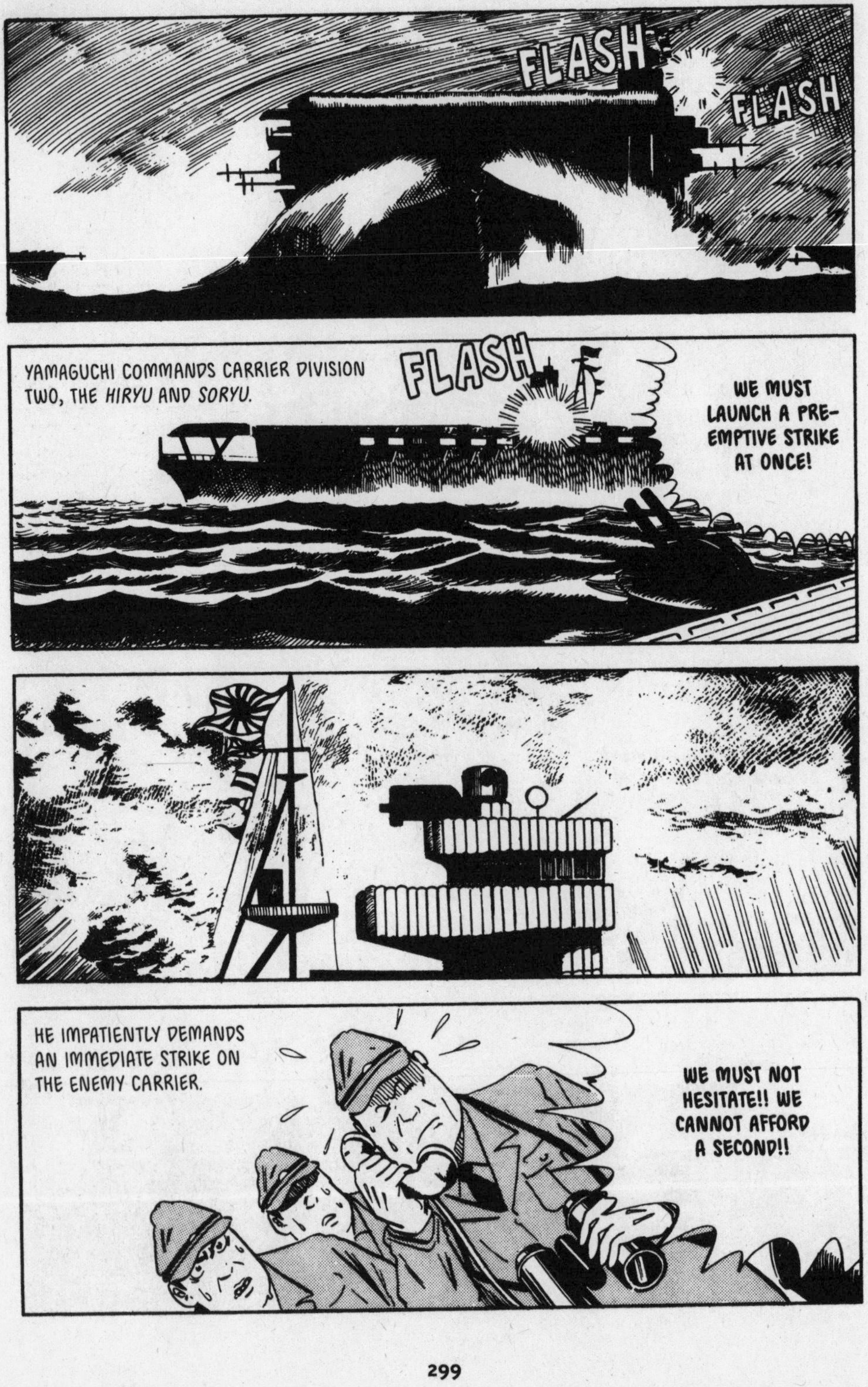
FLASH
FLASH
WE MUST LAUNCH A PRE-EMPTIVE STRIKE AT ONCE!
FLASH
YAMAGUCHI COMMANDS CARRIER DIVISION TWO, THE *HIRYU* AND *SORYU*.
WE MUST NOT HESITATE!! WE CANNOT AFFORD A SECOND!!
HE IMPATIENTLY DEMANDS AN IMMEDIATE STRIKE ON THE ENEMY CARRIER.

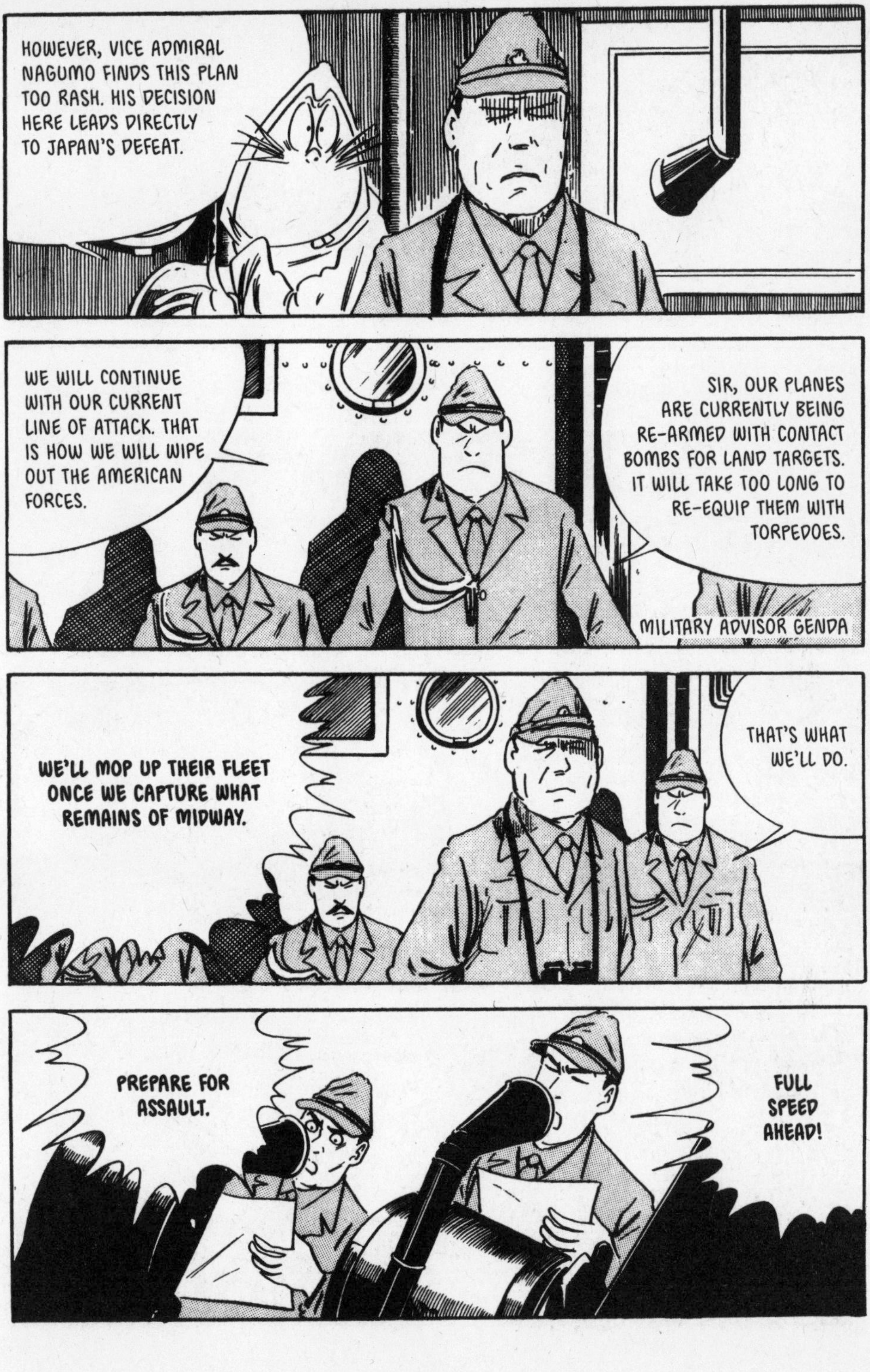
HOWEVER, VICE ADMIRAL NAGUMO FINDS THIS PLAN TOO RASH. HIS DECISION HERE LEADS DIRECTLY TO JAPAN'S DEFEAT.
SIR, OUR PLANES ARE CURRENTLY BEING RE-ARMED WITH CONTACT BOMBS FOR LAND TARGETS. IT WILL TAKE TOO LONG TO RE-EQUIP THEM WITH TORPEDOES.
MILITARY ADVISOR GENDA
WE WILL CONTINUE WITH OUR CURRENT LINE OF ATTACK. THAT IS HOW WE WILL WIPE OUT THE AMERICAN FORCES.
THAT'S WHAT WE'LL DO.
WE'LL MOP UP THEIR FLEET ONCE WE CAPTURE WHAT REMAINS OF MIDWAY.
FULL SPEED AHEAD!
PREPARE FOR ASSAULT.

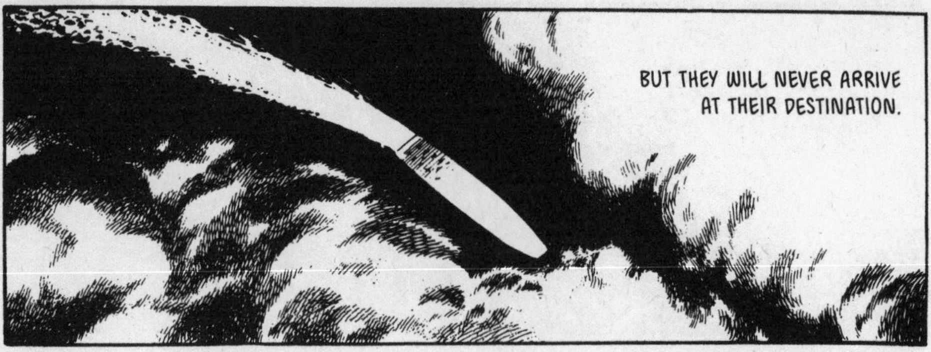
BUT THEY WILL NEVER ARRIVE AT THEIR DESTINATION.

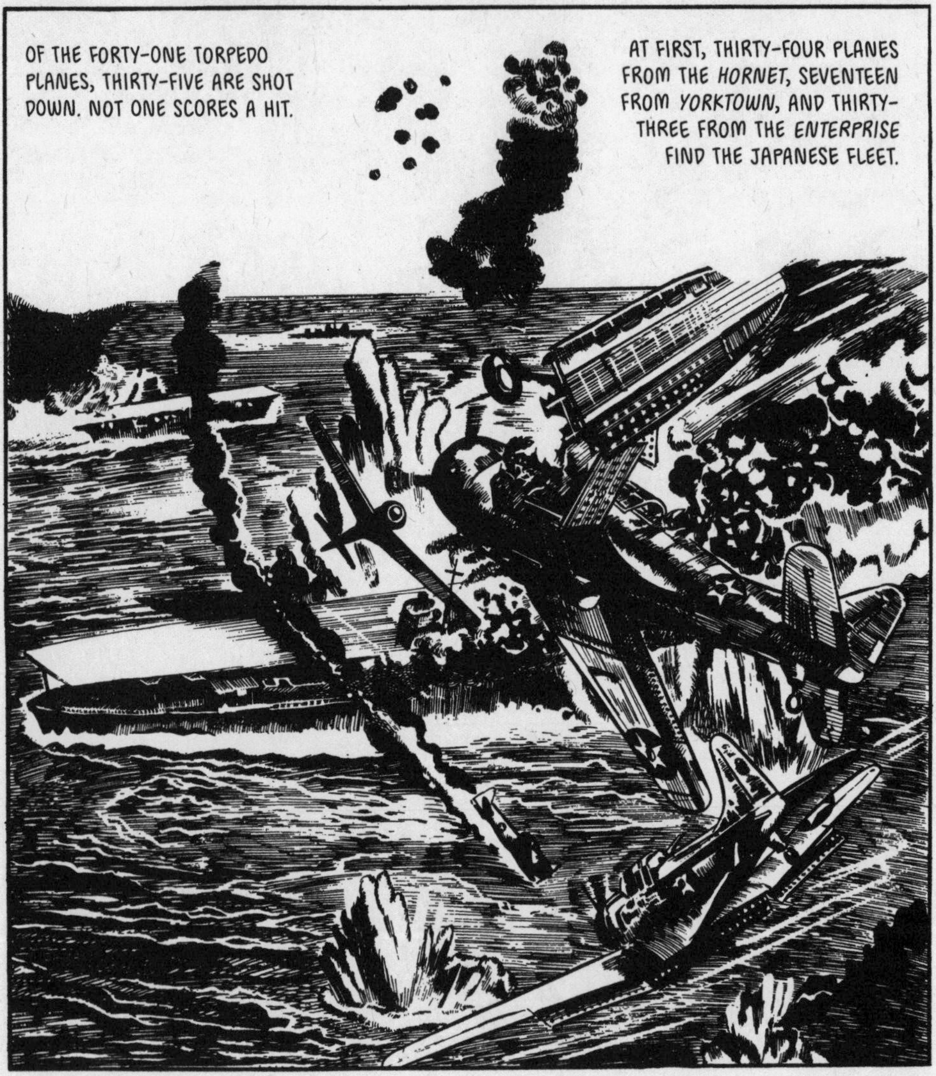
AT FIRST, THIRTY-FOUR PLANES FROM THE *HORNET*, SEVENTEEN FROM *YORKTOWN*, AND THIRTY-THREE FROM THE *ENTERPRISE* FIND THE JAPANESE FLEET.
OF THE FORTY-ONE TORPEDO PLANES, THIRTY-FIVE ARE SHOT DOWN. NOT ONE SCORES A HIT.

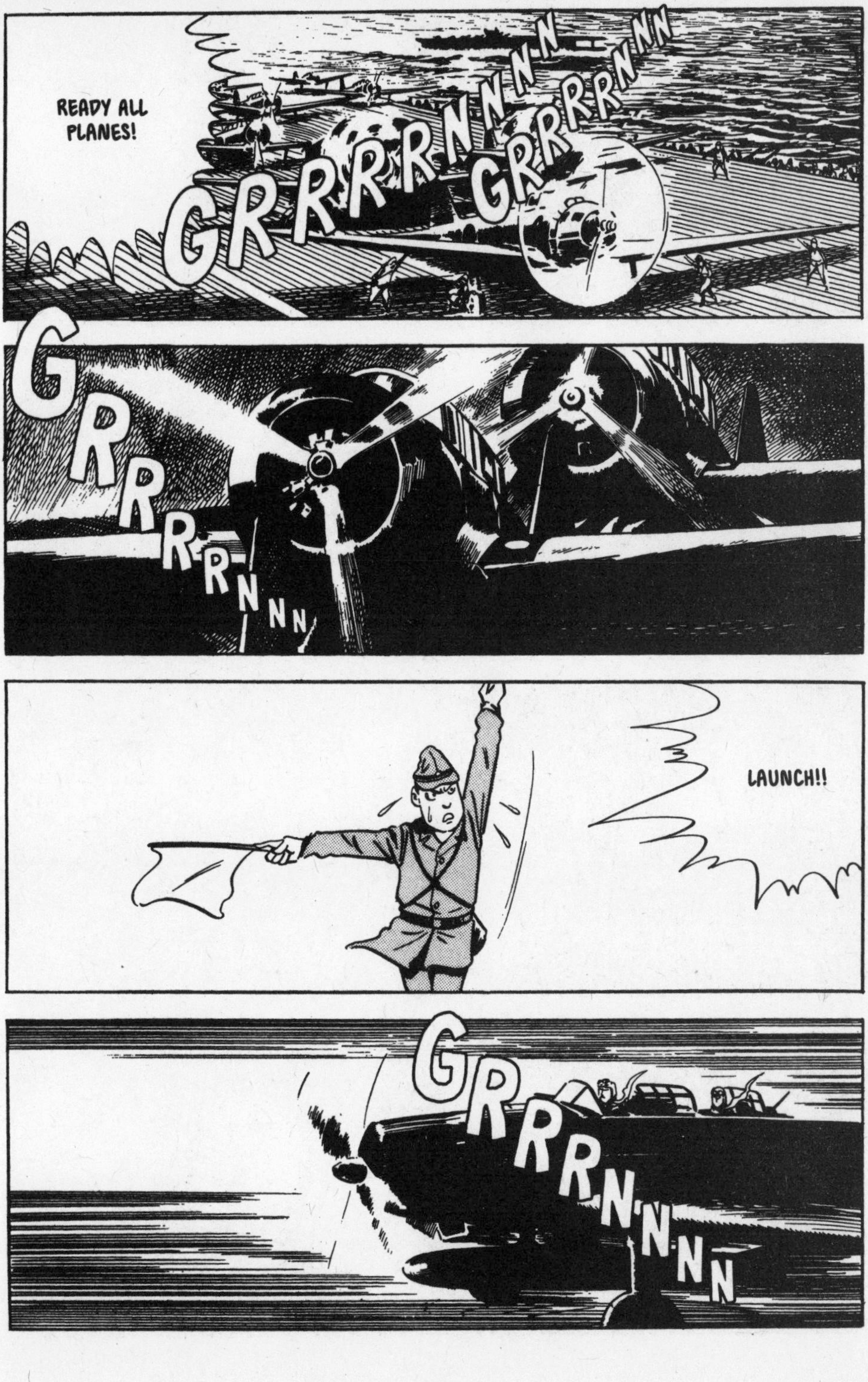
GRRRRRNNN
GRRRRNNNNN
READY ALL PLANES!
GRRRRNNN
LAUNCH!!
GRRRRNNNNN

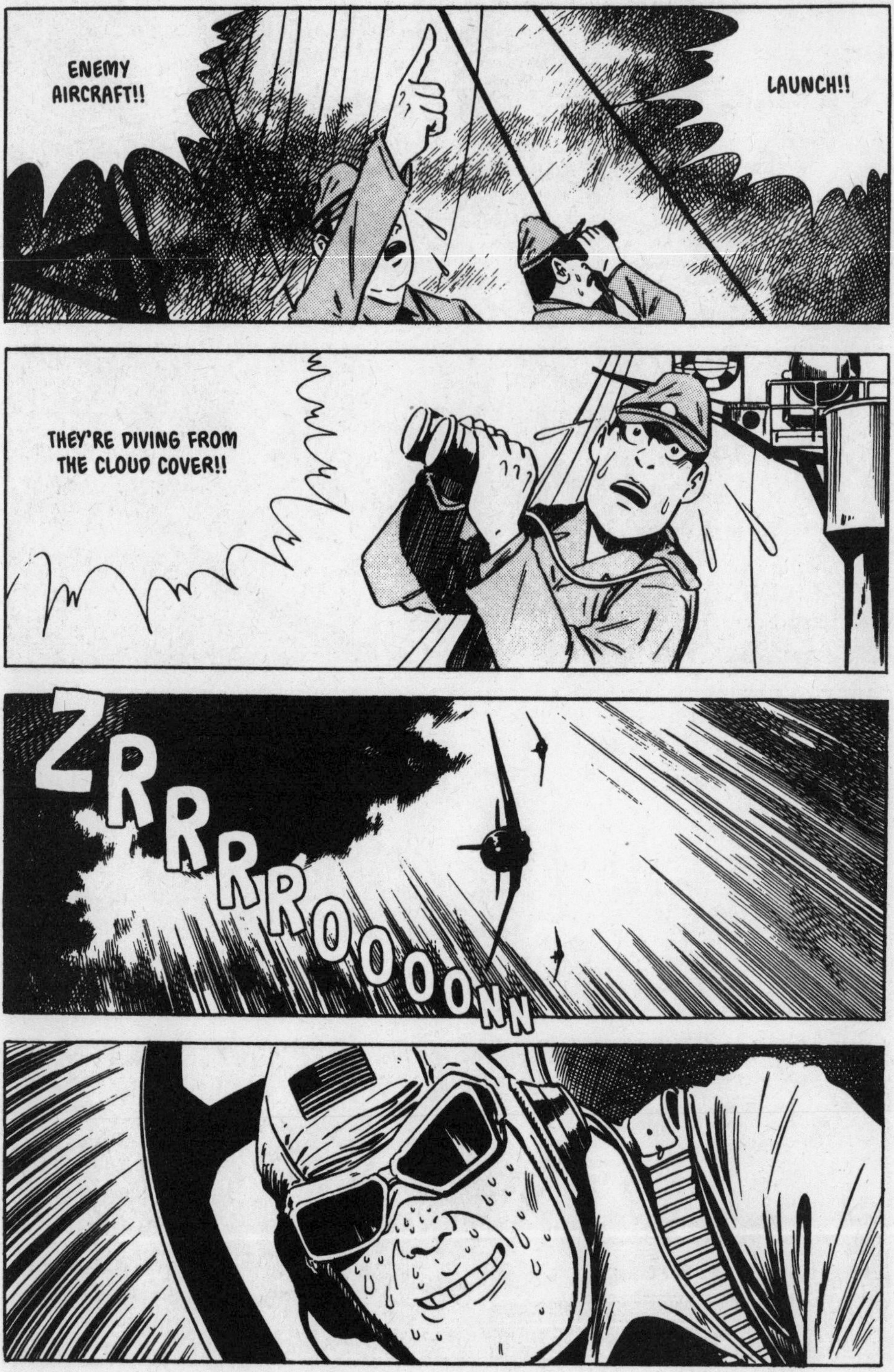
LAUNCH!!
ENEMY AIRCRAFT!!
THEY'RE DIVING FROM THE CLOUD COVER!!
ZRRRROOOOONN

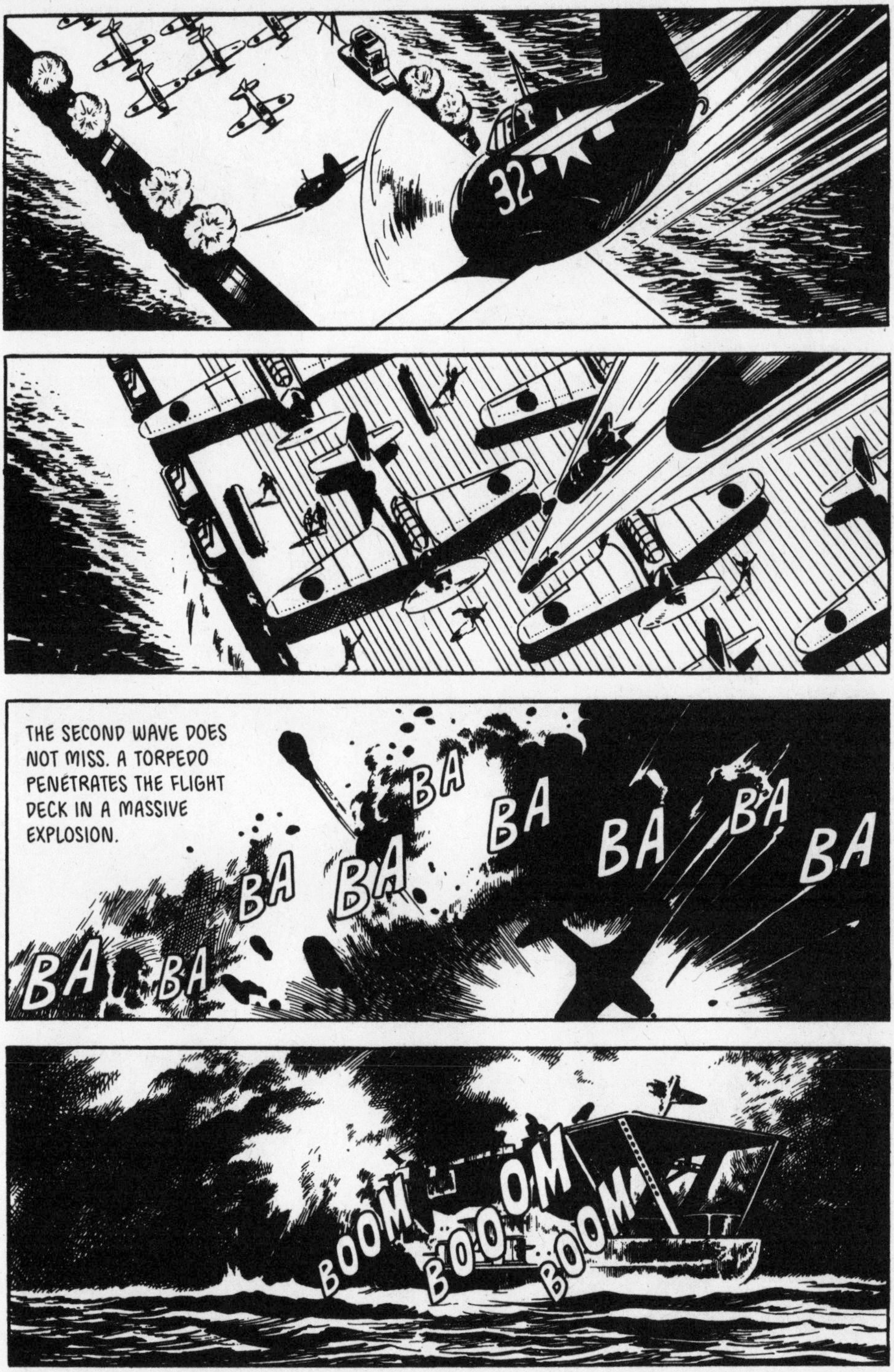
THE SECOND WAVE DOES NOT MISS. A TORPEDO PENETRATES THE FLIGHT DECK IN A MASSIVE EXPLOSION.
BA BA BA BA BA BA BA BA BA BA
BOOM BOOOM BOOM

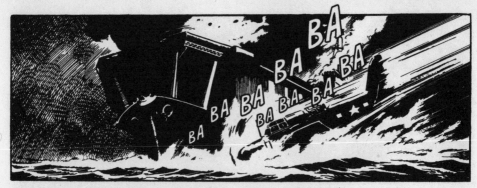

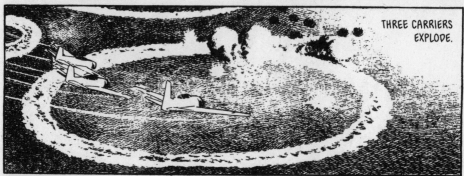

THREE CARRIERS EXPLODE.

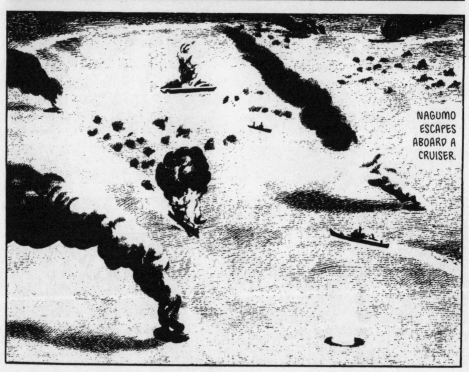

NAGUMO ESCAPES ABOARD A CRUISER.

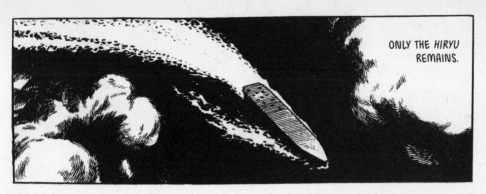

ONLY THE *HIRYU* REMAINS.

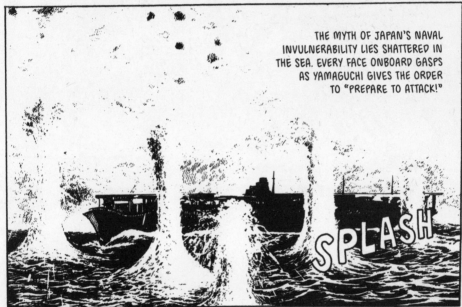

THE MYTH OF JAPAN'S NAVAL INVULNERABILITY LIES SHATTERED IN THE SEA. EVERY FACE ONBOARD GASPS AS YAMAGUCHI GIVES THE ORDER TO "PREPARE TO ATTACK!"

SPLASH

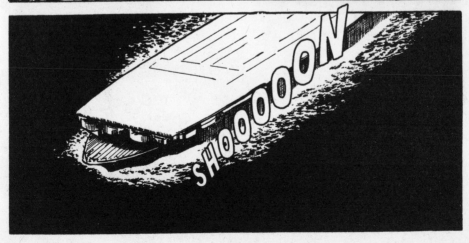

SHOOOOON

ATTACK OF THE *HIRYU*

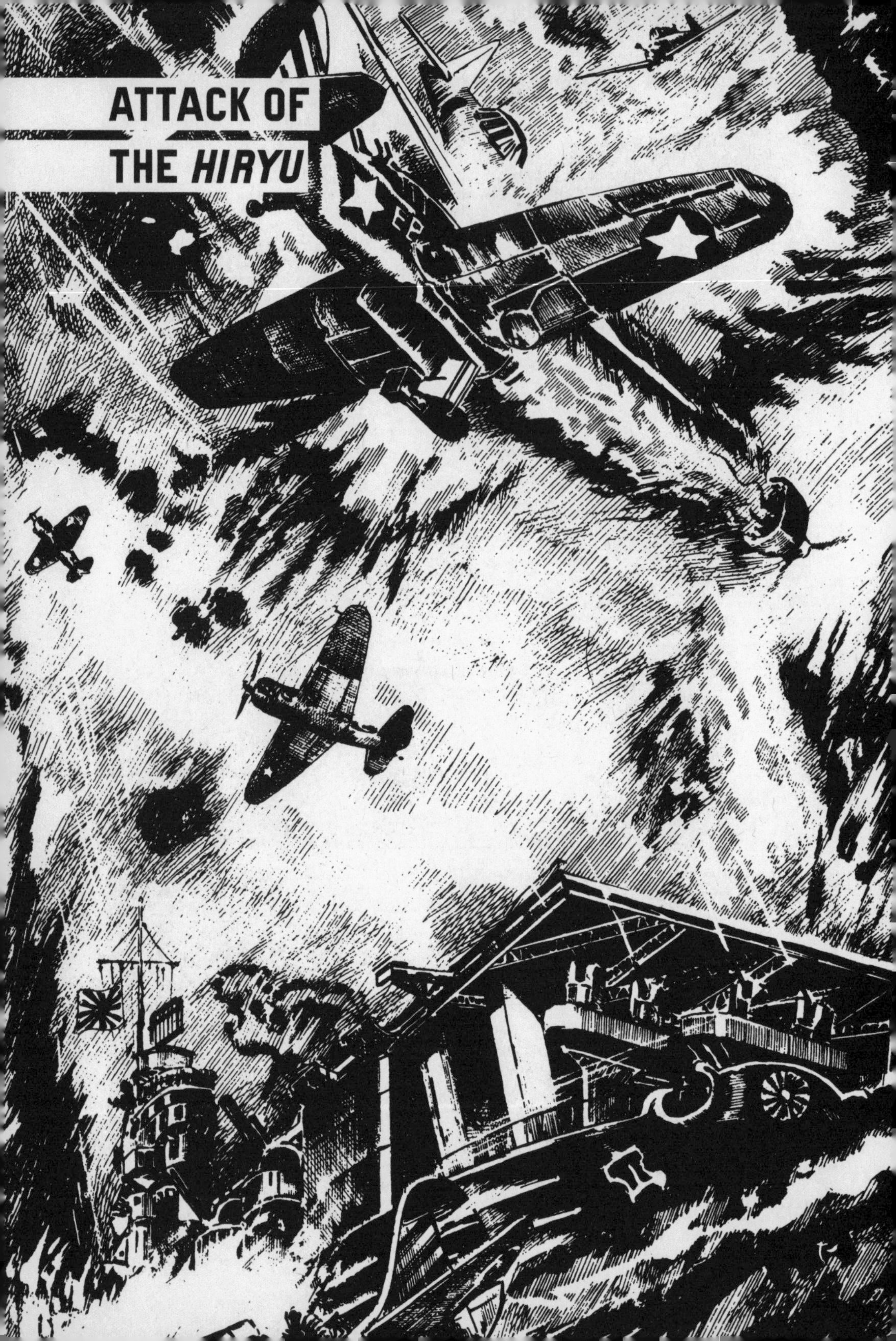

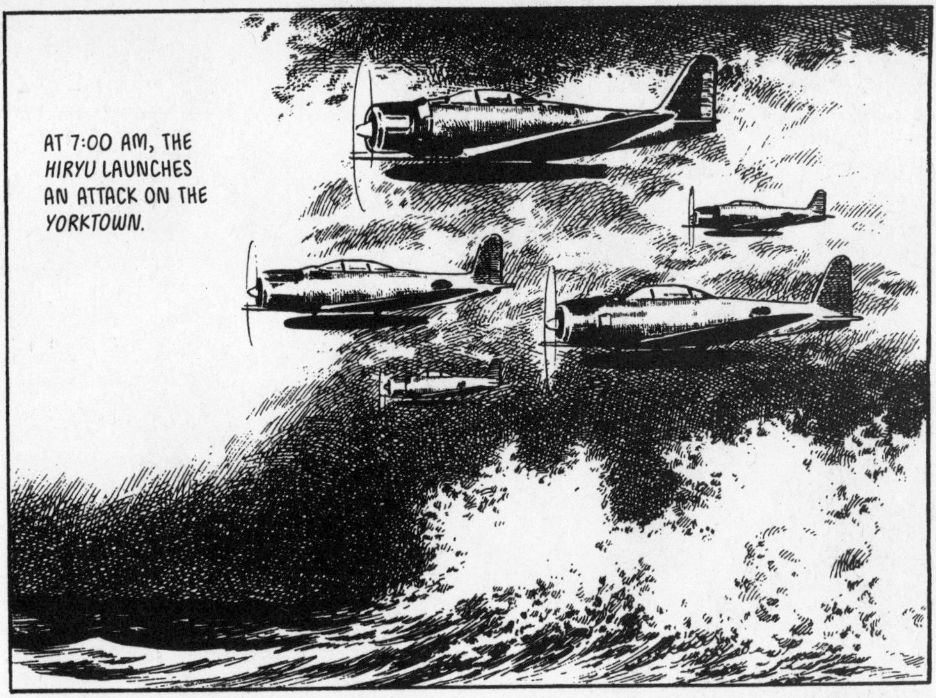
AT 7:00 AM, THE *HIRYU* LAUNCHES AN ATTACK ON THE *YORKTOWN*.

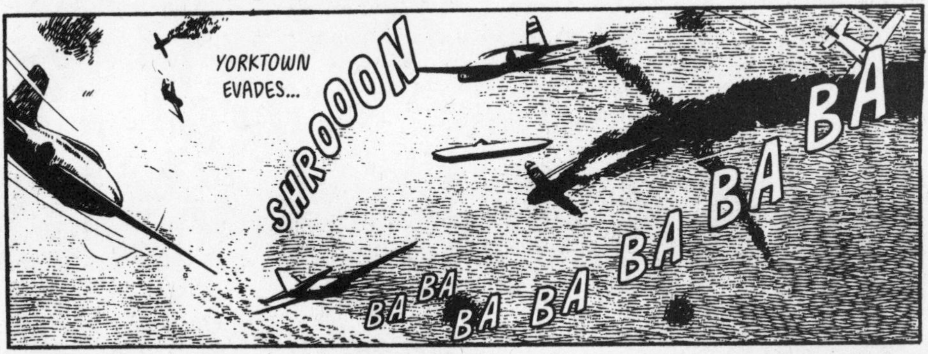
YORKTOWN EVADES...
SHROOON
BA BA BA BA BA BA BA BA

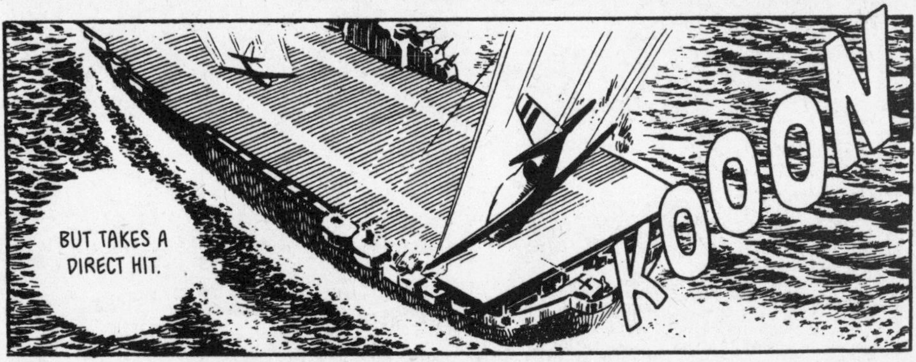
KOOOON
BUT TAKES A DIRECT HIT.

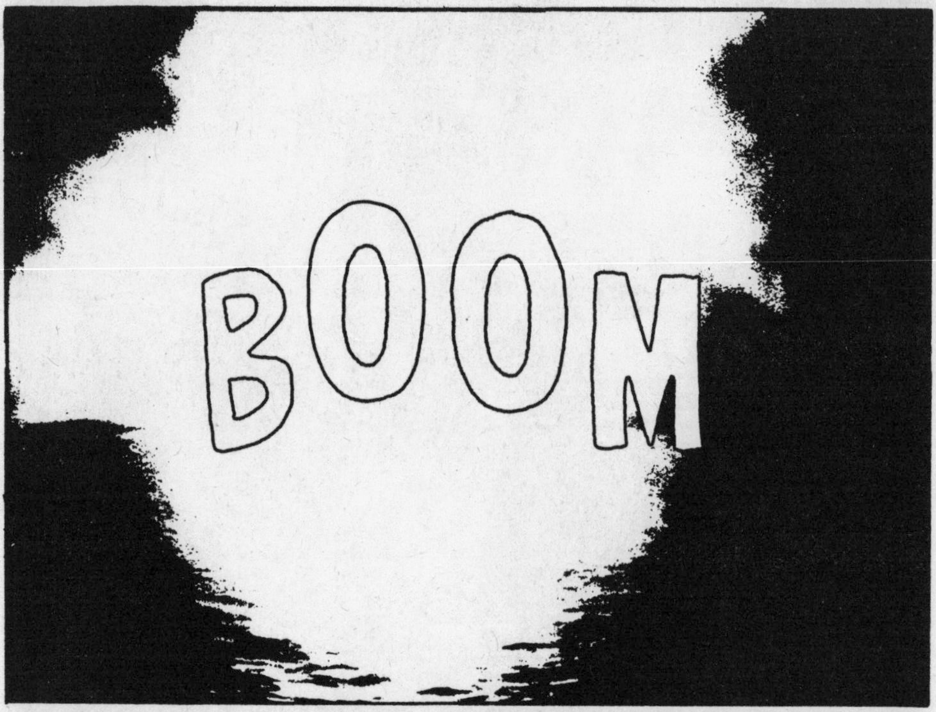
BOOM

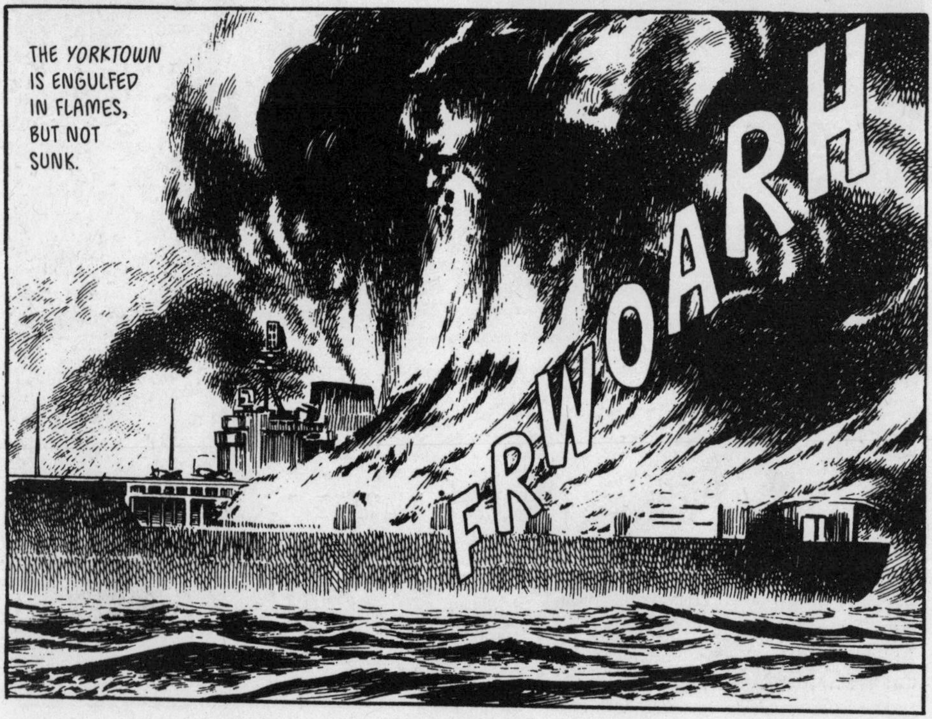
THE *YORKTOWN* IS ENGULFED IN FLAMES, BUT NOT SUNK.
FRWOARH

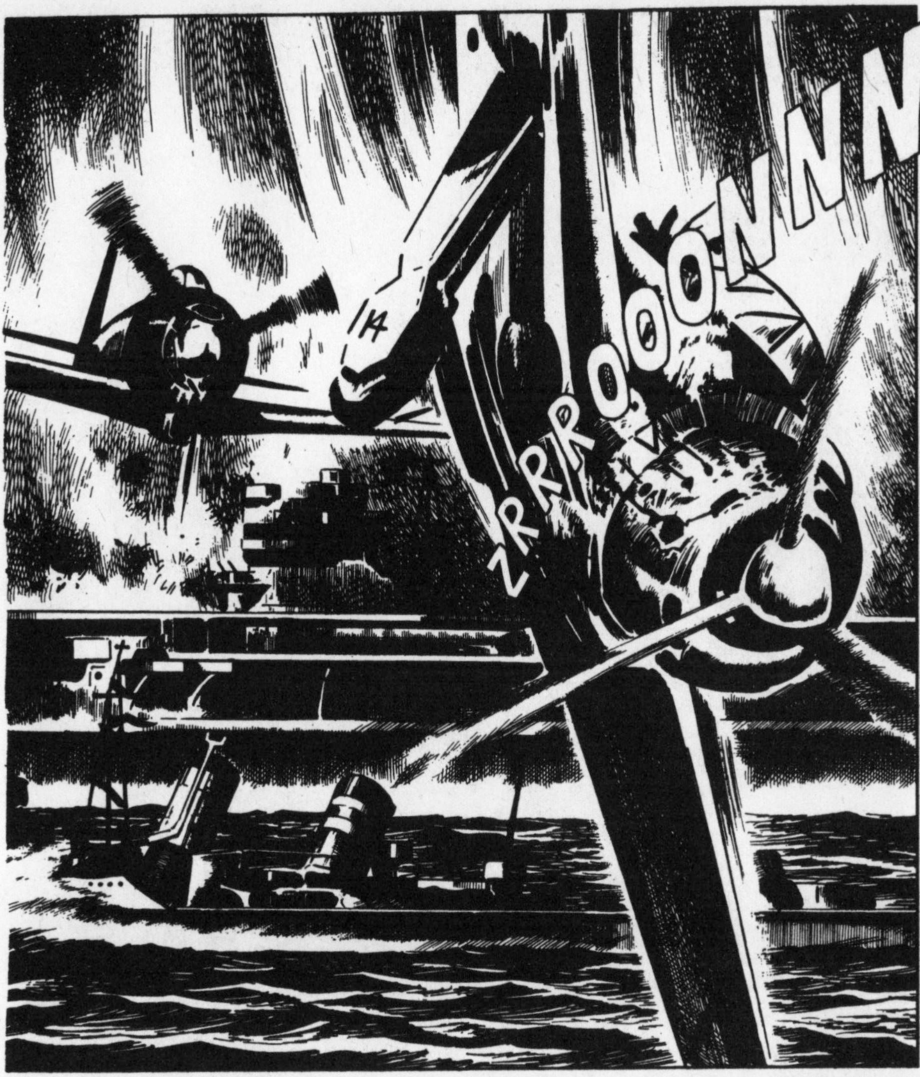
ZRRROOOONNN

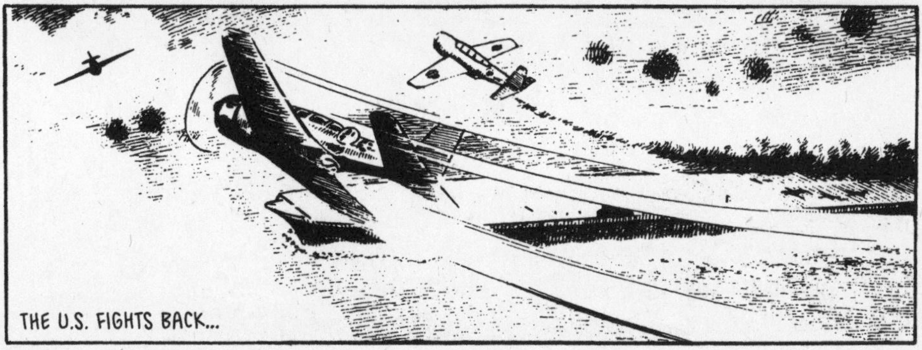
THE U.S. FIGHTS BACK...

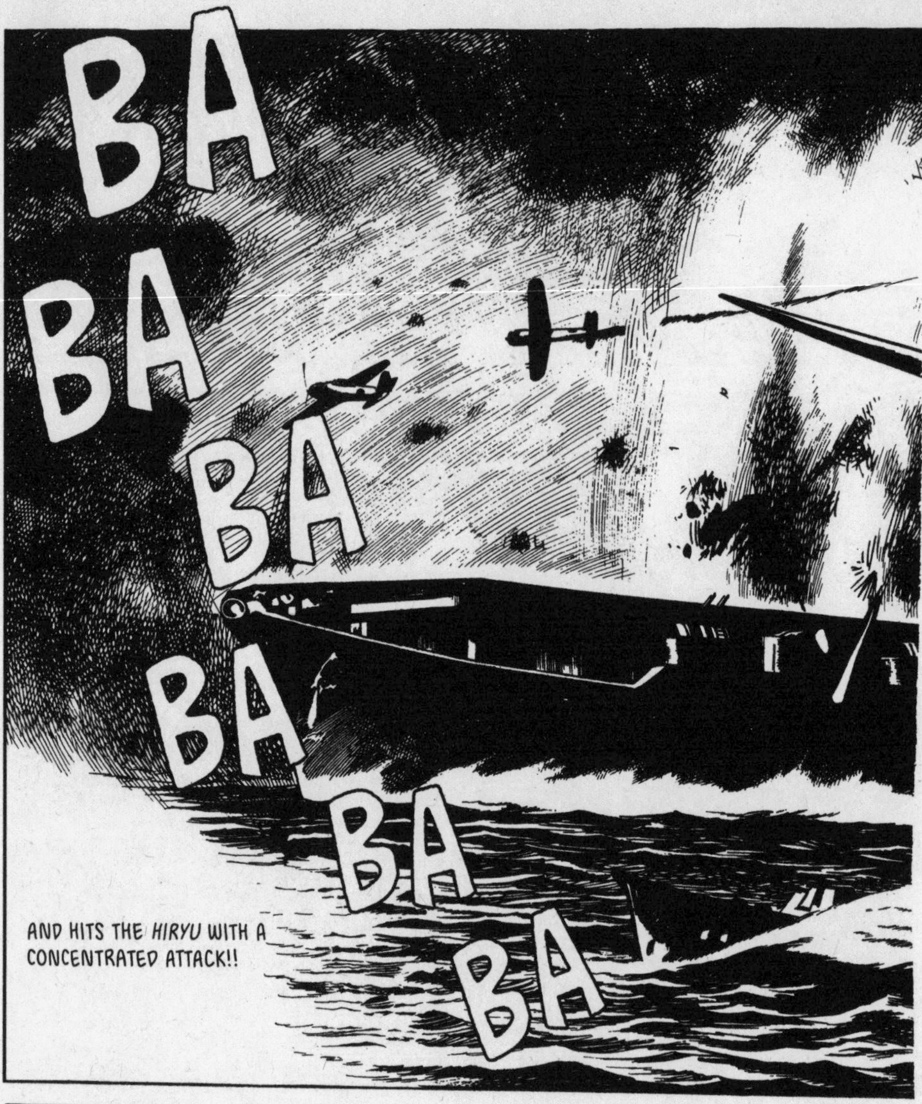
BA
BA
BA
BA
BA
BA
AND HITS THE *HIRYU* WITH A CONCENTRATED ATTACK!!

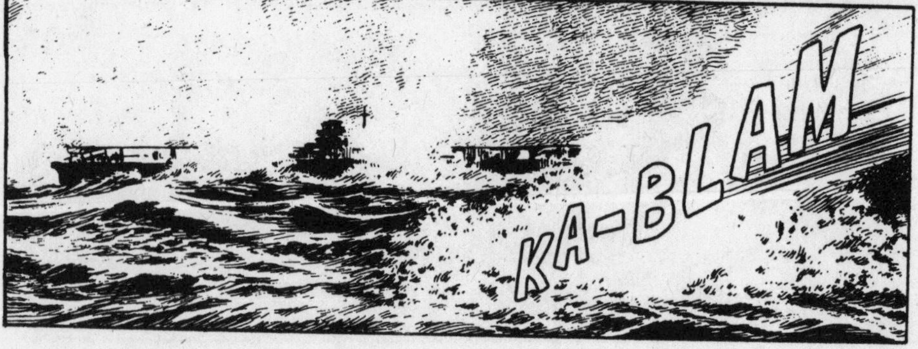
KA-BLAM

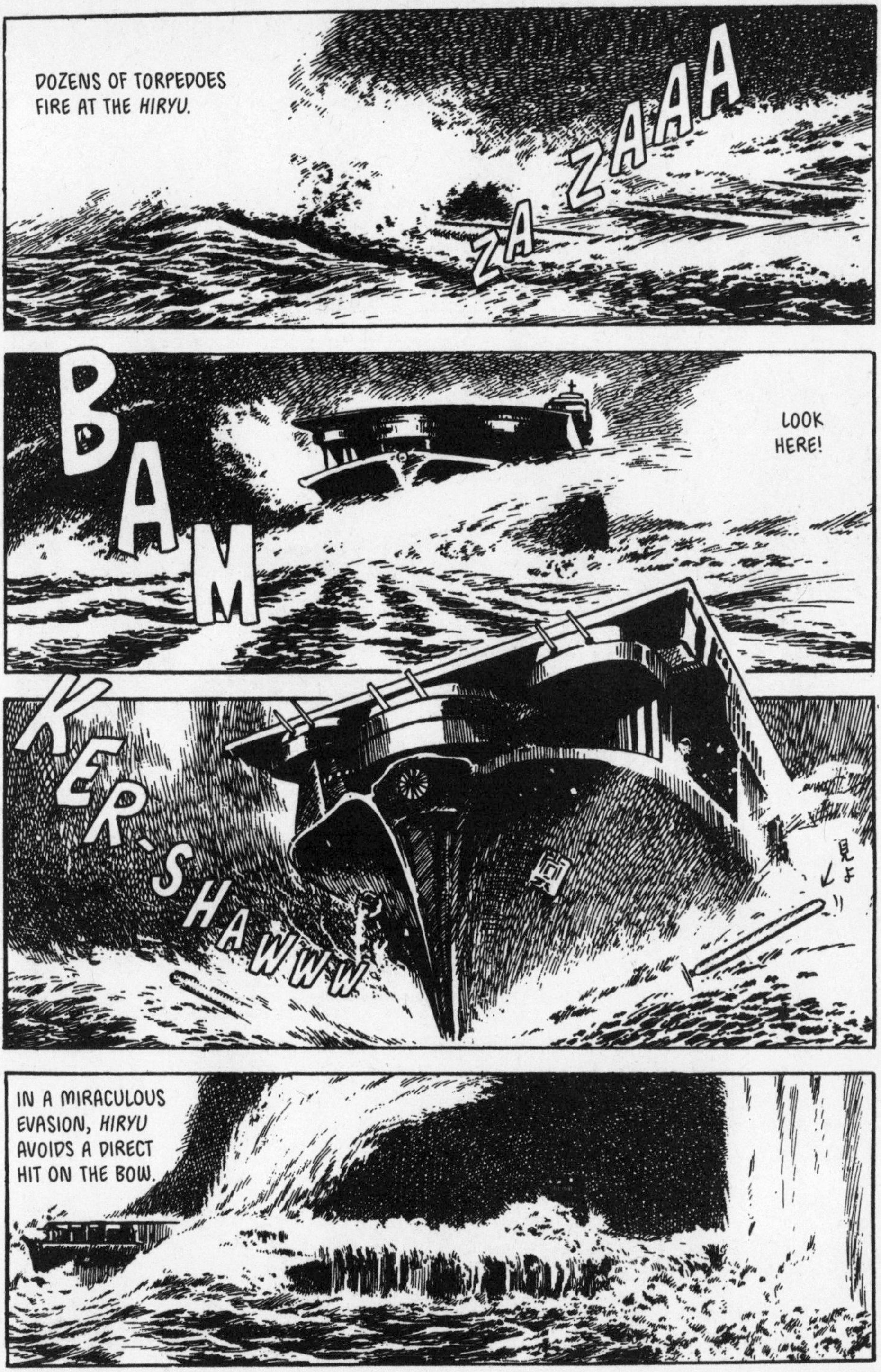
DOZENS OF TORPEDOES FIRE AT THE *HIRYU*.
ZA ZA ZAAAA
LOOK HERE!
BAM
KER-SHAWWW
見よ
IN A MIRACULOUS EVASION, *HIRYU* AVOIDS A DIRECT HIT ON THE BOW.

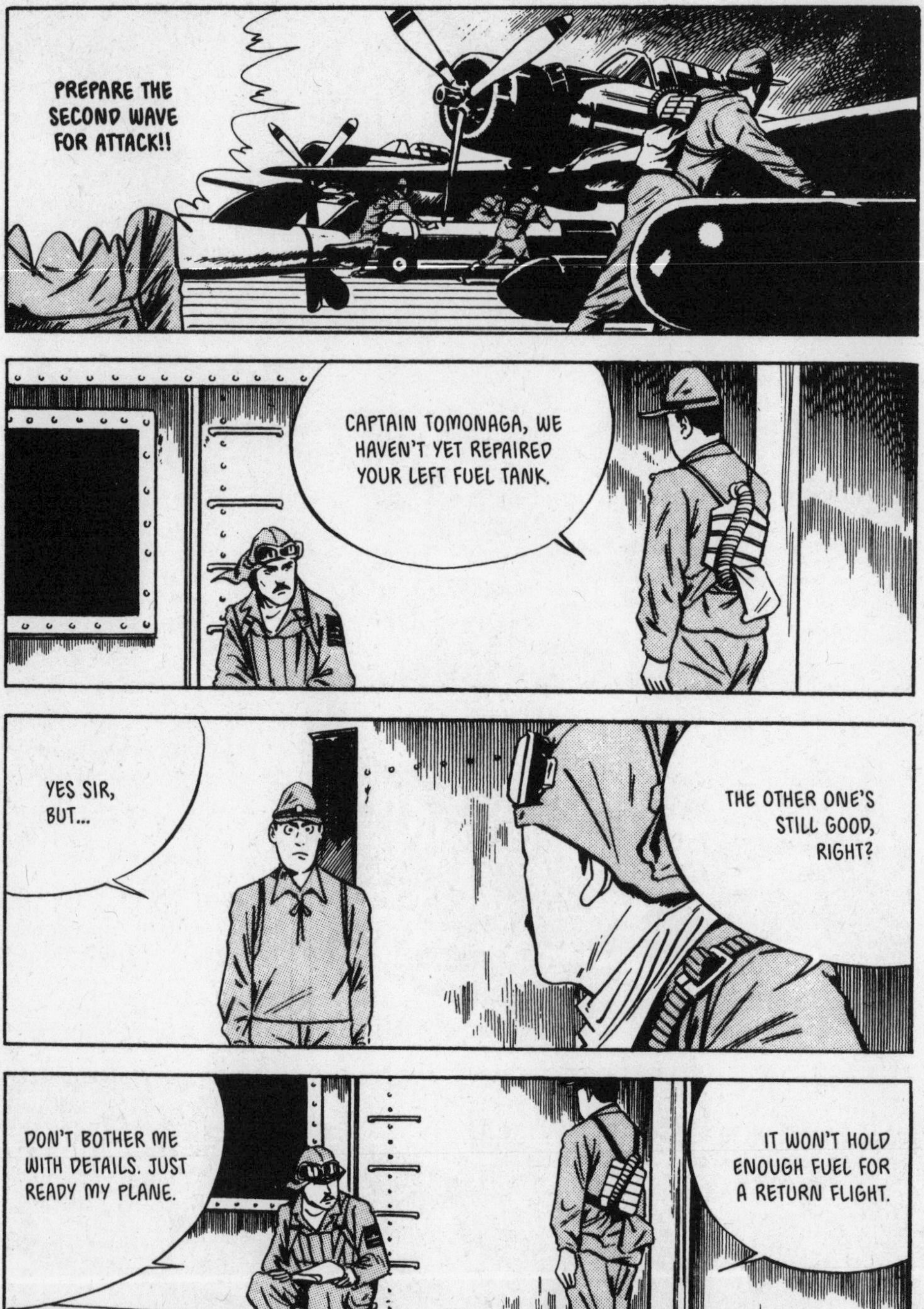
PREPARE THE SECOND WAVE FOR ATTACK!!
CAPTAIN TOMONAGA, WE HAVEN'T YET REPAIRED YOUR LEFT FUEL TANK.
THE OTHER ONE'S STILL GOOD, RIGHT?
YES SIR, BUT...
IT WON'T HOLD ENOUGH FUEL FOR A RETURN FLIGHT.
DON'T BOTHER ME WITH DETAILS. JUST READY MY PLANE.

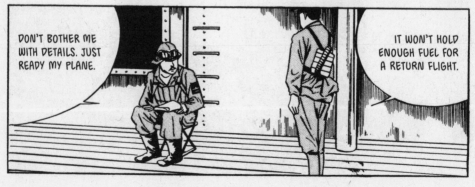

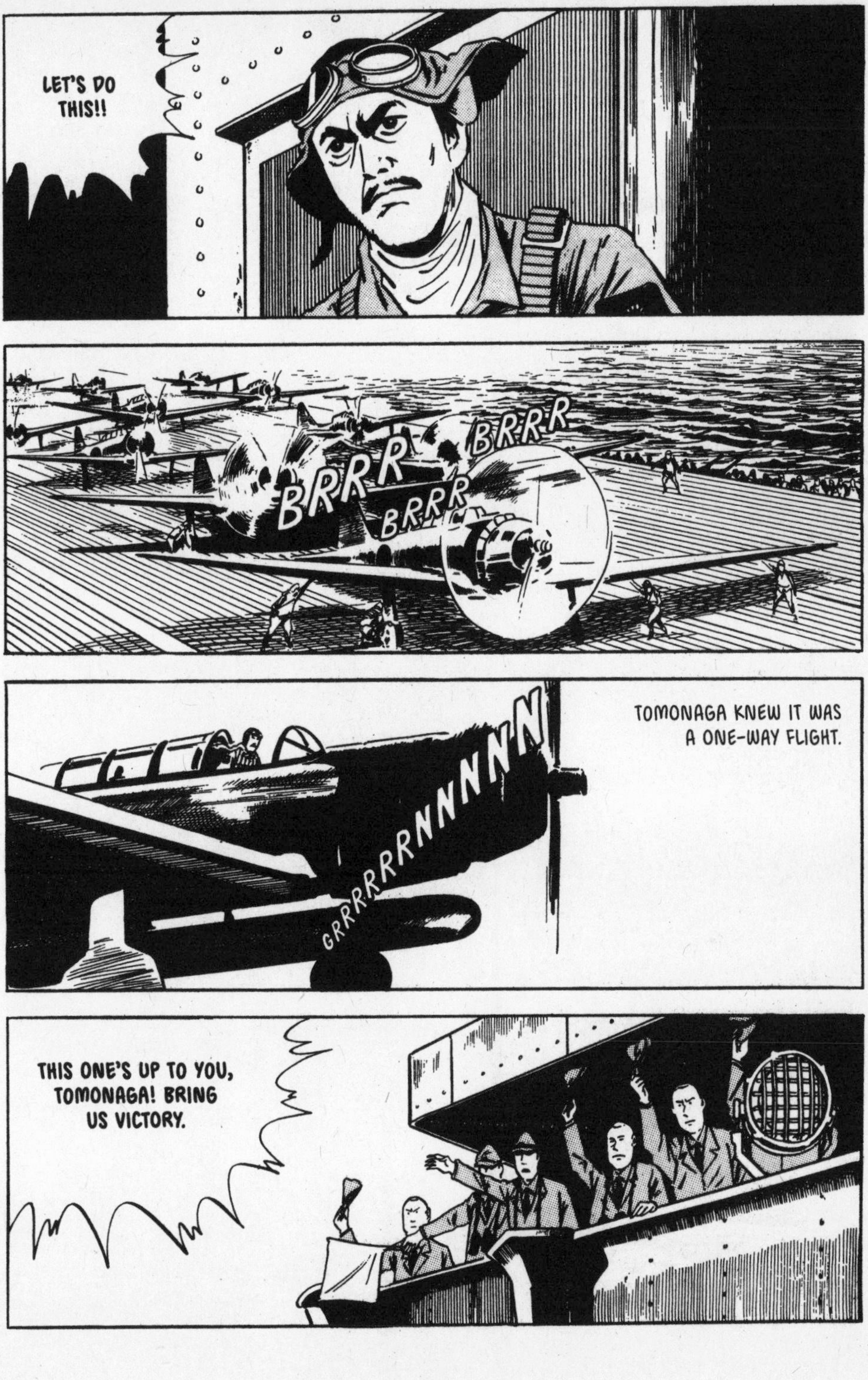
LET'S DO THIS!!
BRRR
BRRR
BRRR
BRRR
TOMONAGA KNEW IT WAS A ONE-WAY FLIGHT.
GRRRRRRNNNNNN
THIS ONE'S UP TO YOU, TOMONAGA! BRING US VICTORY.

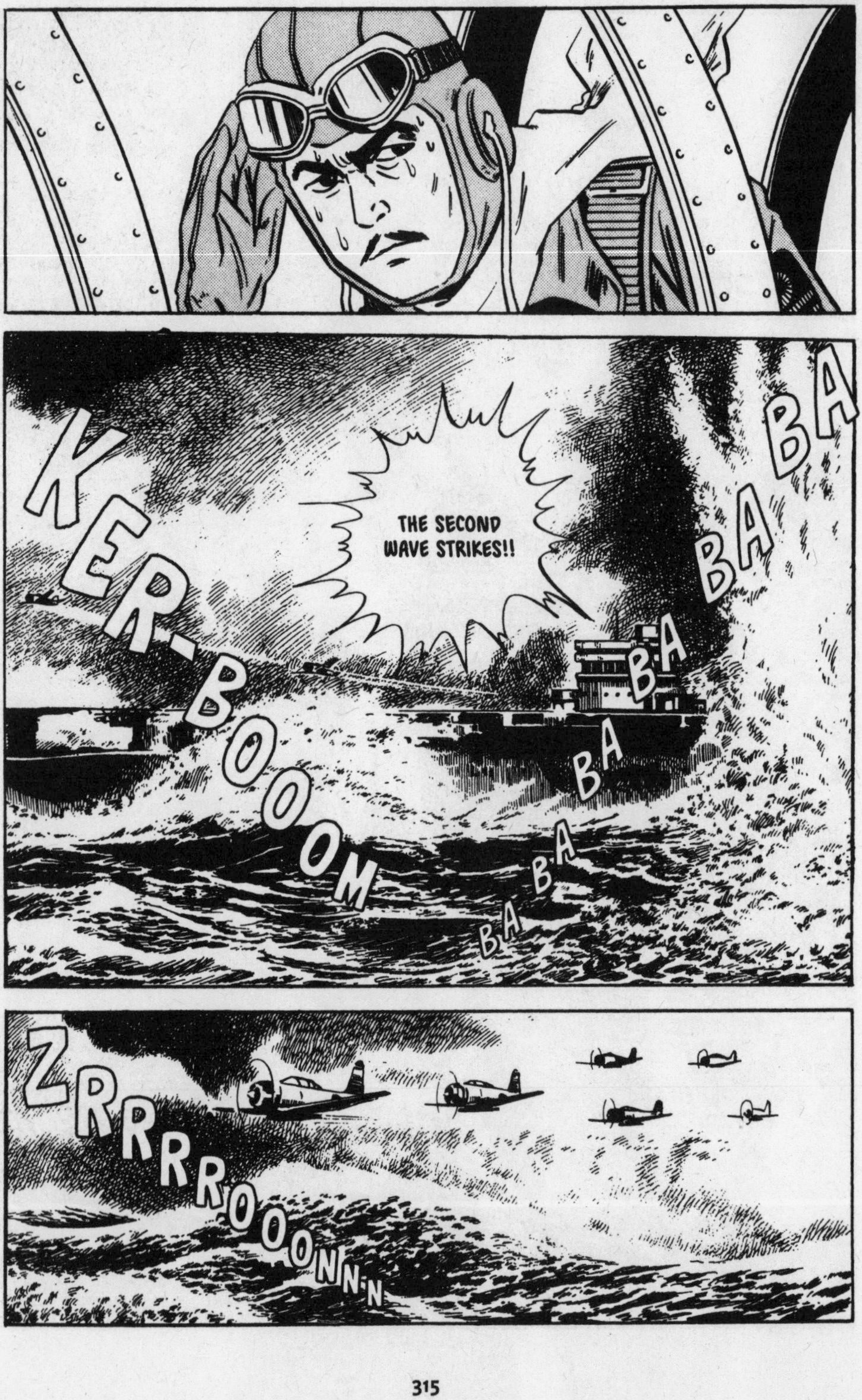
THE SECOND WAVE STRIKES!!
KER-BOOOOM
BA BA BA BA BA BA BA
ZRRRRROOOONNN-N

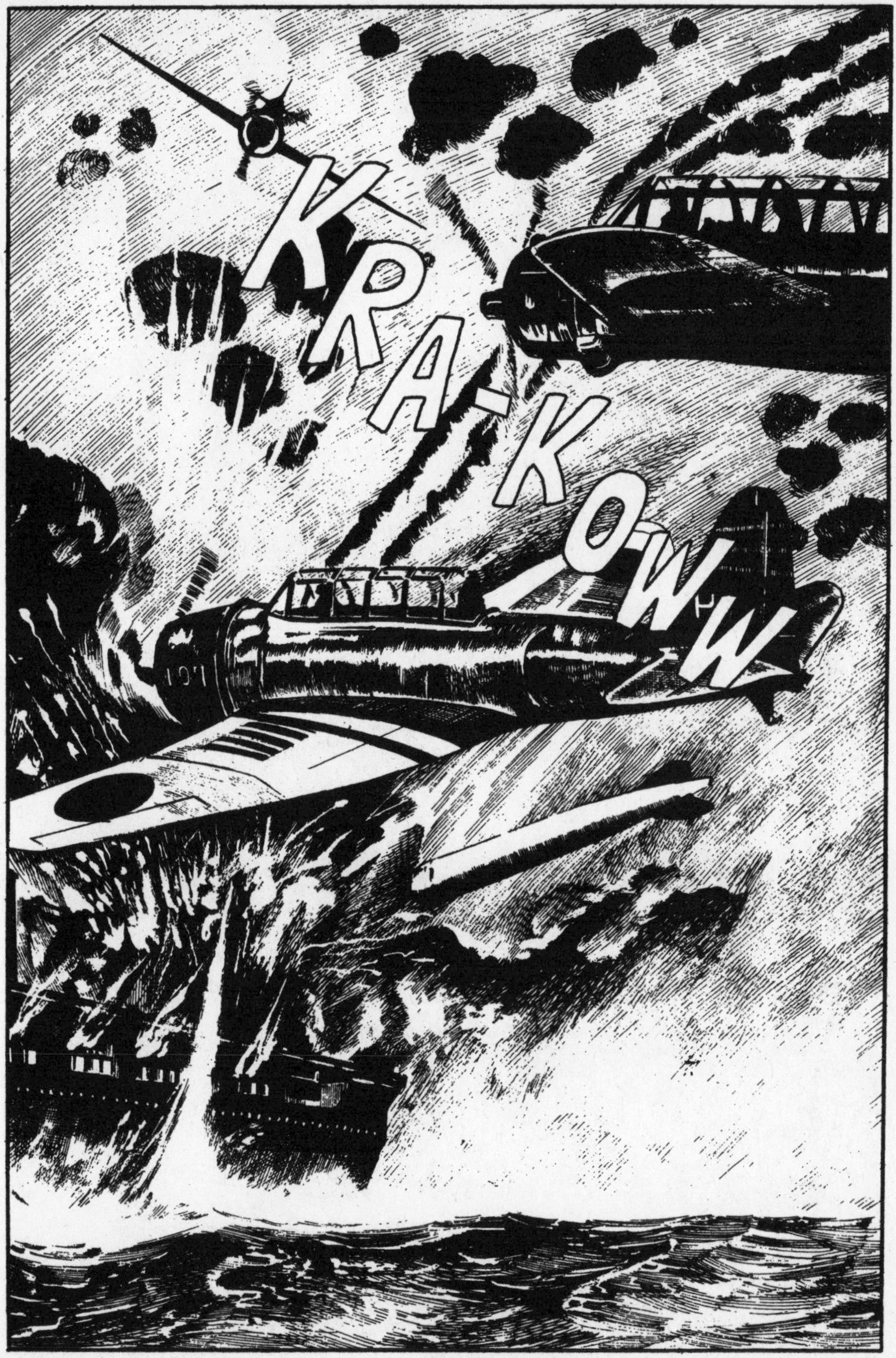
KRA-KOWW

BAM
DON
DON
DON
DON

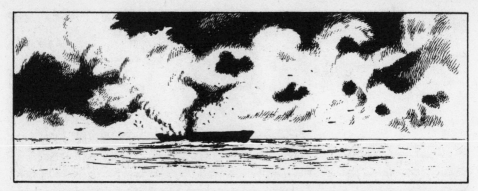

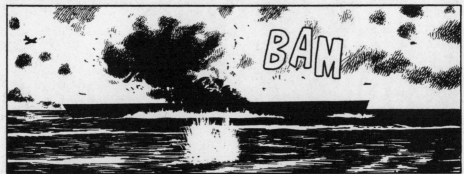

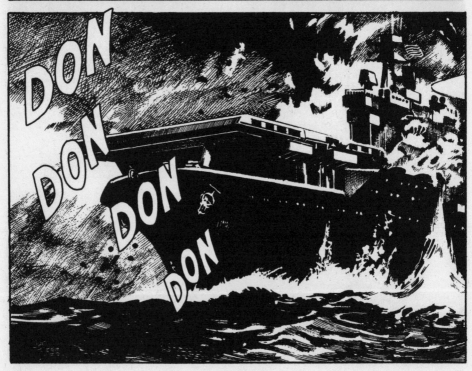

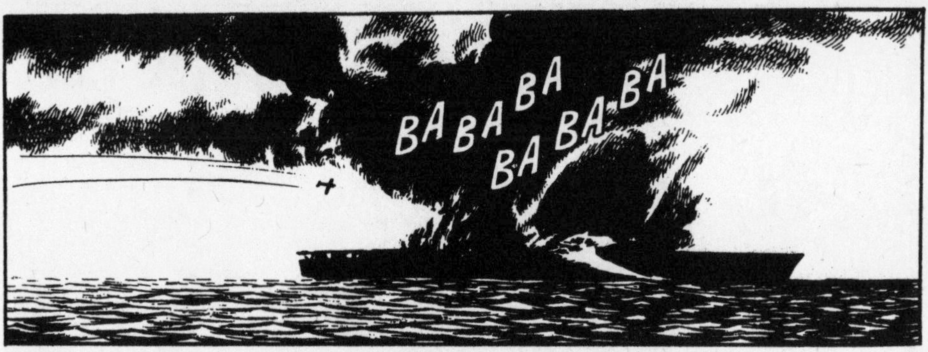
BA BA BA
BA BA BA

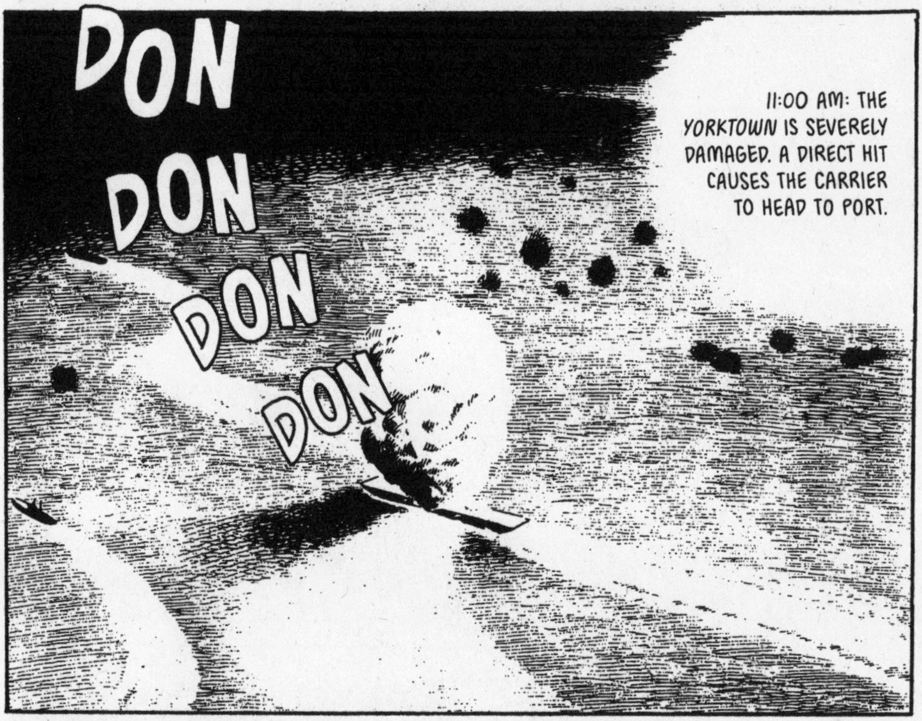
DON
DON
DON
DON
11:00 AM: THE *YORKTOWN* IS SEVERELY DAMAGED. A DIRECT HIT CAUSES THE CARRIER TO HEAD TO PORT.

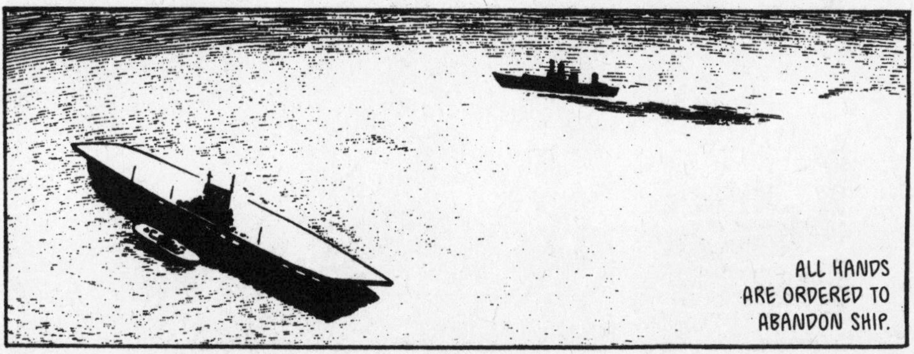
ALL HANDS ARE ORDERED TO ABANDON SHIP.

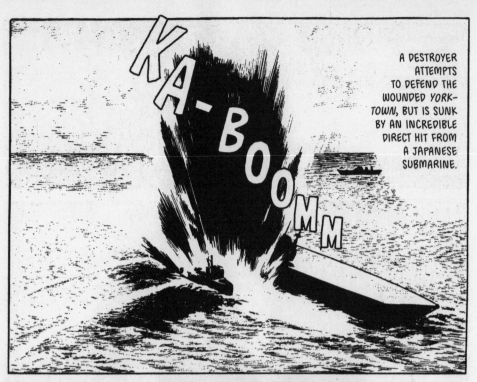

KA-BOOMM
A DESTROYER ATTEMPTS TO DEFEND THE WOUNDED *YORKTOWN*, BUT IS SUNK BY AN INCREDIBLE DIRECT HIT FROM A JAPANESE SUBMARINE.
A SECOND SUBMARINE STRIKE SENDS THE *YORKTOWN* TO THE BOTTOM OF THE OCEAN.
MEANWHILE, THE *HIRYU* IS UNDER HEAVY ATTACK. SHE TAKES A DIRECT HIT ON HER DECK.
BOOM

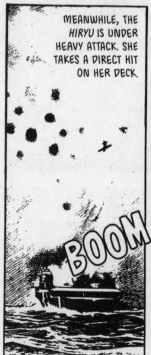

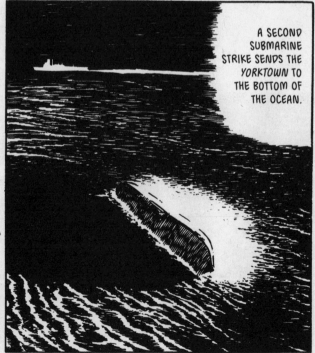

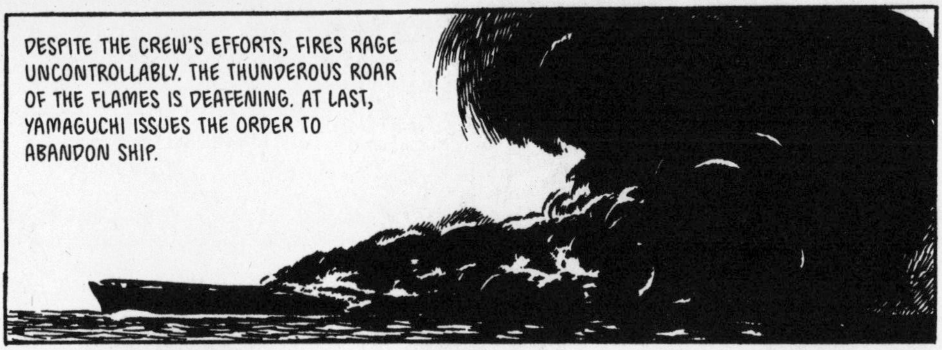
DESPITE THE CREW'S EFFORTS, FIRES RAGE UNCONTROLLABLY. THE THUNDEROUS ROAR OF THE FLAMES IS DEAFENING. AT LAST, YAMAGUCHI ISSUES THE ORDER TO ABANDON SHIP.

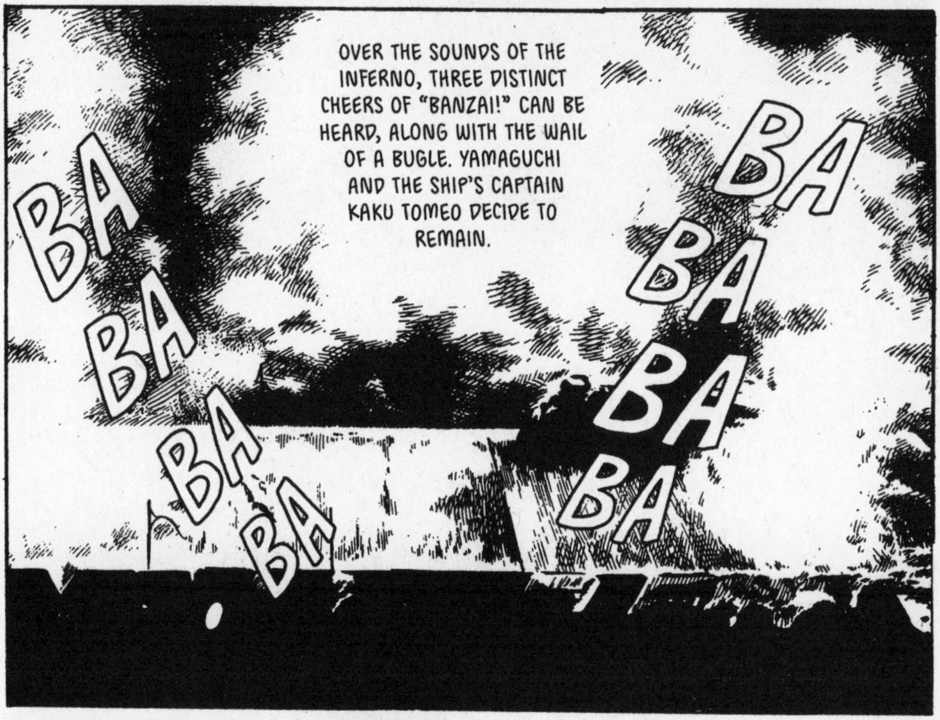
OVER THE SOUNDS OF THE INFERNO, THREE DISTINCT CHEERS OF "BANZAI!" CAN BE HEARD, ALONG WITH THE WAIL OF A BUGLE. YAMAGUCHI AND THE SHIP'S CAPTAIN KAKU TOMEO DECIDE TO REMAIN.
BA BA BA BA BA
BA BA BA BA

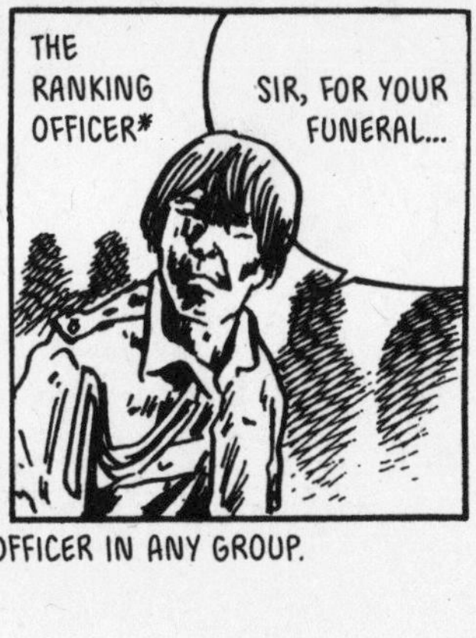
SIR, FOR YOUR FUNERAL...
THE RANKING OFFICER*

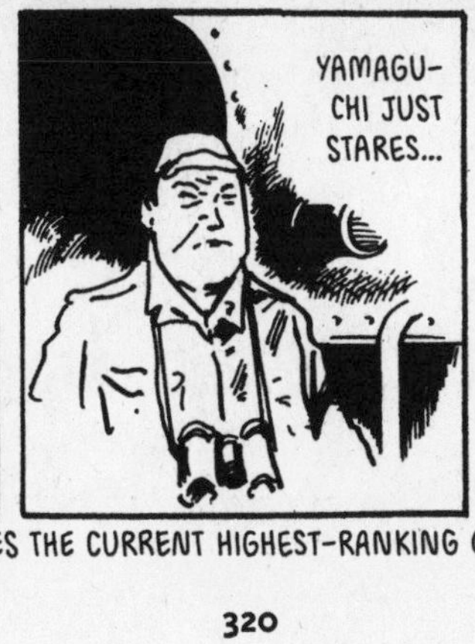
YAMAGU-CHI JUST STARES...

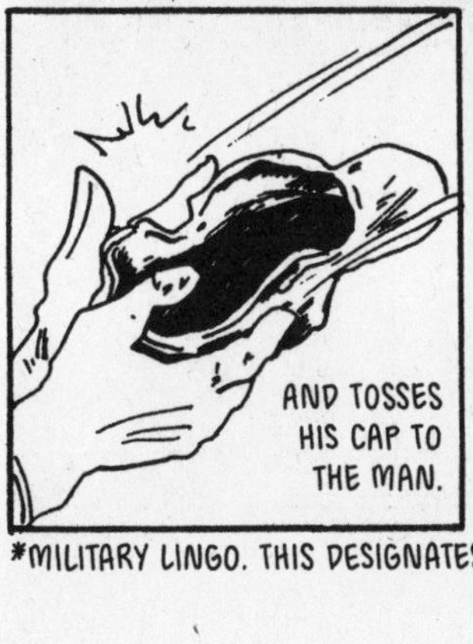
AND TOSSES HIS CAP TO THE MAN.

*MILITARY LINGO. THIS DESIGNATES THE CURRENT HIGHEST-RANKING OFFICER IN ANY GROUP.

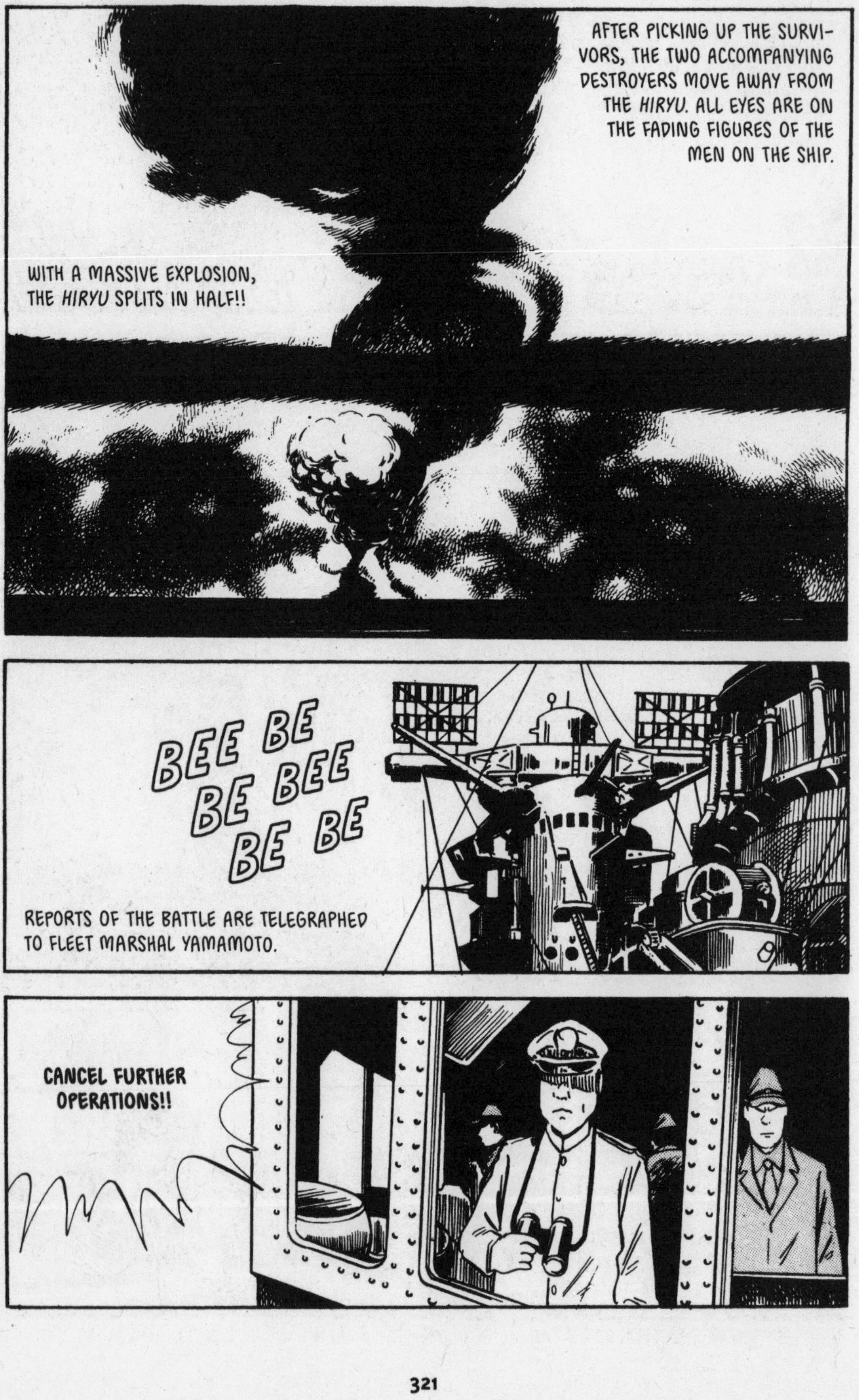
AFTER PICKING UP THE SURVIVORS, THE TWO ACCOMPANYING DESTROYERS MOVE AWAY FROM THE *HIRYU*. ALL EYES ARE ON THE FADING FIGURES OF THE MEN ON THE SHIP.
WITH A MASSIVE EXPLOSION, THE *HIRYU* SPLITS IN HALF!!
BEE BE BE BEE BE BE
REPORTS OF THE BATTLE ARE TELEGRAPHED TO FLEET MARSHAL YAMAMOTO.
CANCEL FURTHER OPERATIONS!!

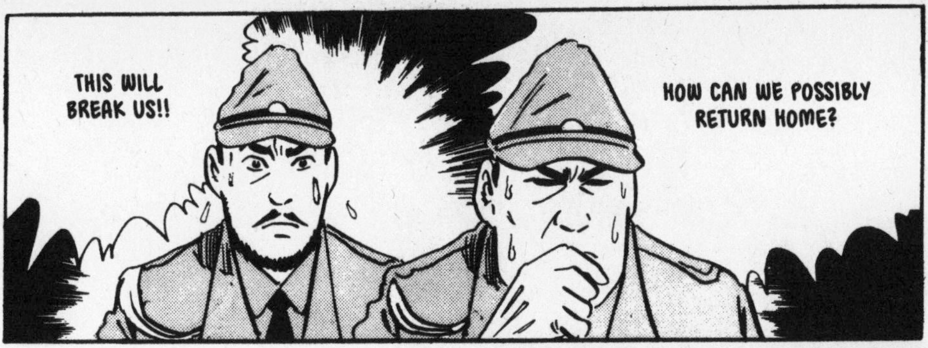
HOW CAN WE POSSIBLY RETURN HOME?
THIS WILL BREAK US!!

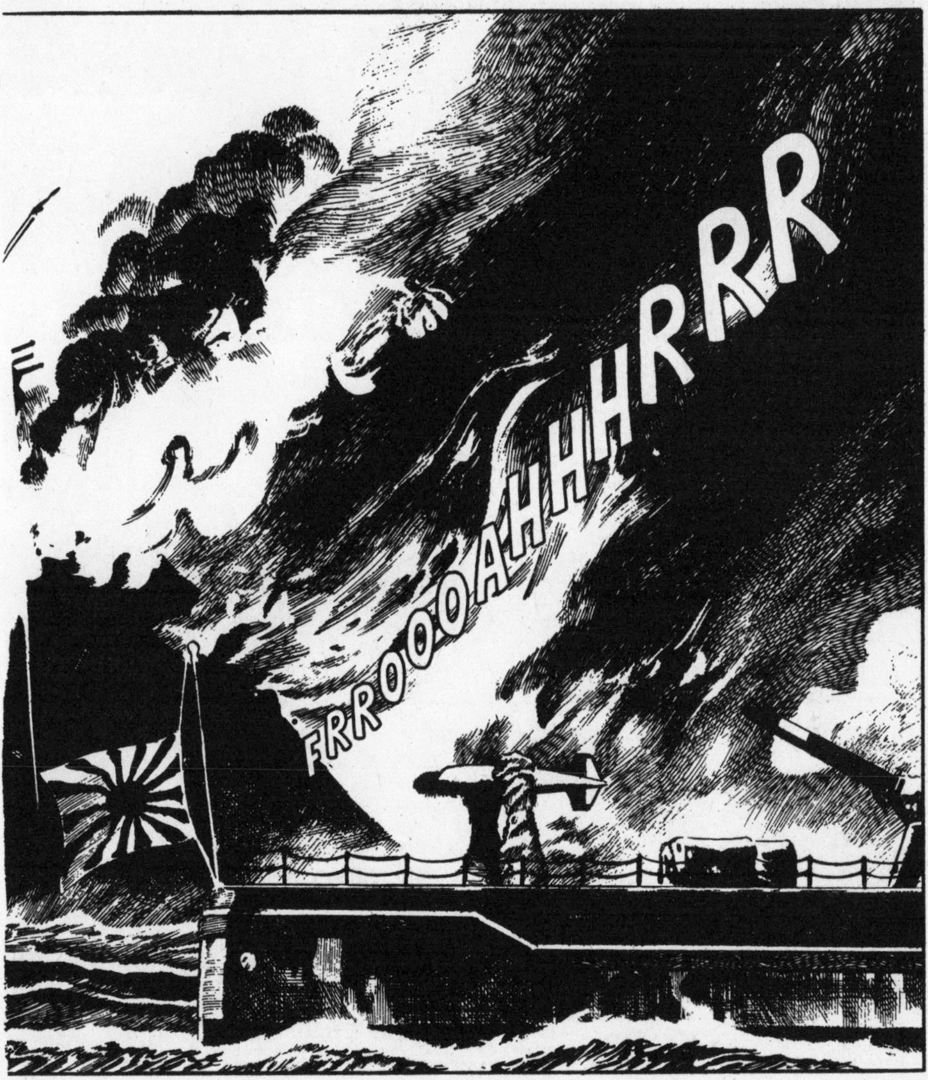
FRROOOOAHHHRRRR

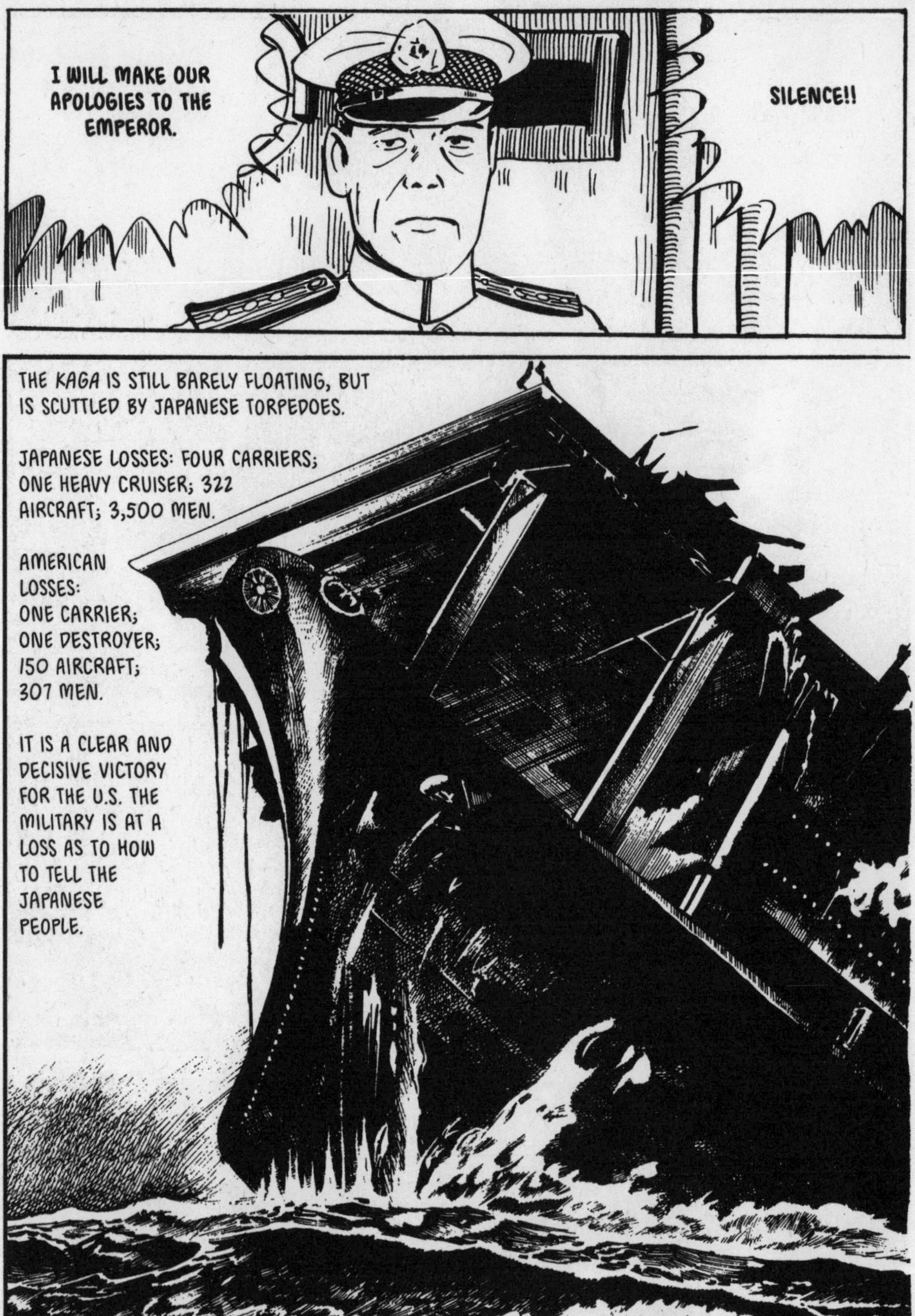
SILENCE!!
I WILL MAKE OUR APOLOGIES TO THE EMPEROR.
THE *KAGA* IS STILL BARELY FLOATING, BUT IS SCUTTLED BY JAPANESE TORPEDOES.
JAPANESE LOSSES: FOUR CARRIERS; ONE HEAVY CRUISER; 322 AIRCRAFT; 3,500 MEN.
AMERICAN LOSSES: ONE CARRIER; ONE DESTROYER; 150 AIRCRAFT; 307 MEN.
IT IS A CLEAR AND DECISIVE VICTORY FOR THE U.S. THE MILITARY IS AT A LOSS AS TO HOW TO TELL THE JAPANESE PEOPLE.

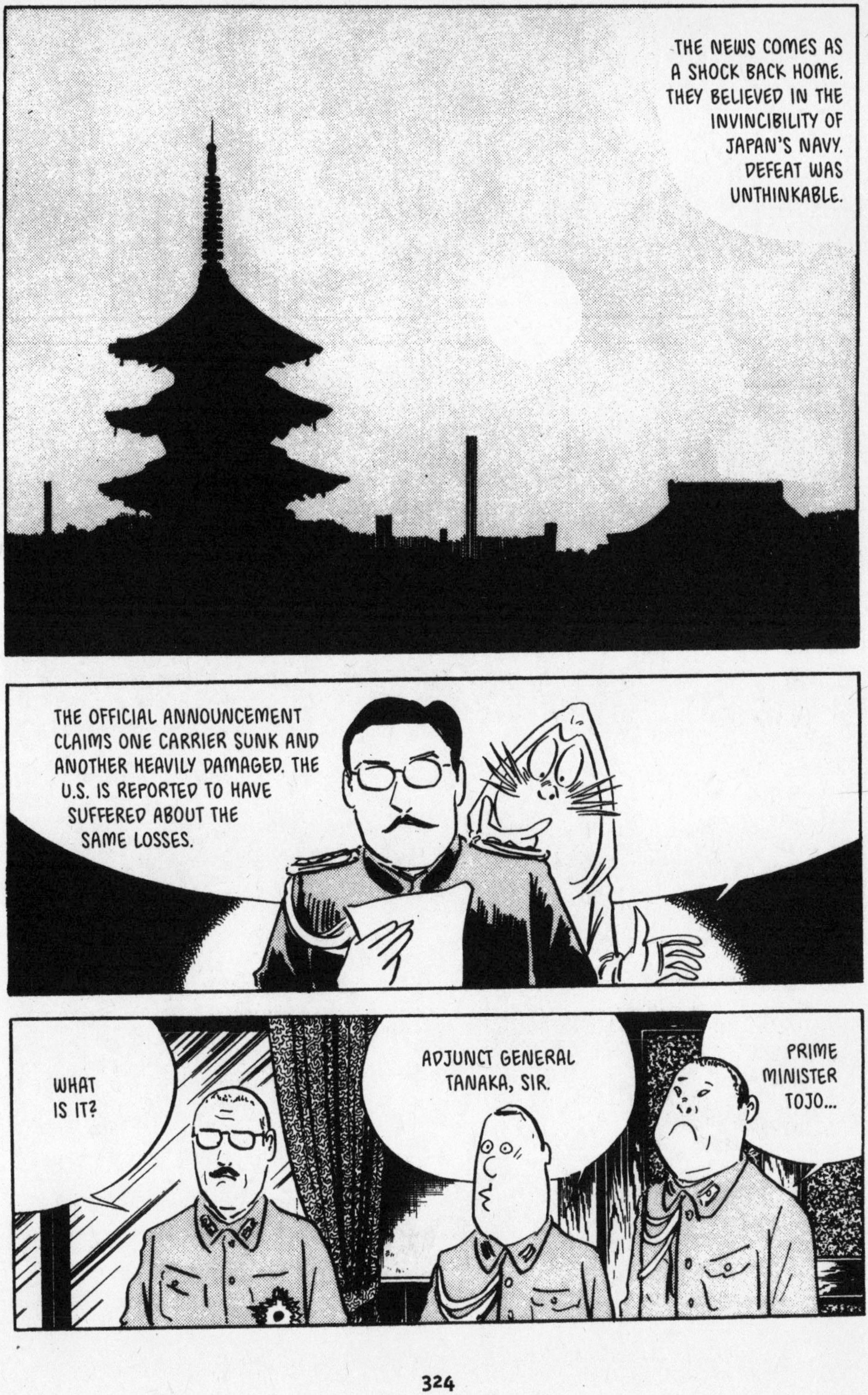
THE NEWS COMES AS A SHOCK BACK HOME. THEY BELIEVED IN THE INVINCIBILITY OF JAPAN'S NAVY. DEFEAT WAS UNTHINKABLE.
THE OFFICIAL ANNOUNCEMENT CLAIMS ONE CARRIER SUNK AND ANOTHER HEAVILY DAMAGED. THE U.S. IS REPORTED TO HAVE SUFFERED ABOUT THE SAME LOSSES.
PRIME MINISTER TOJO...
ADJUNCT GENERAL TANAKA, SIR.
WHAT IS IT?

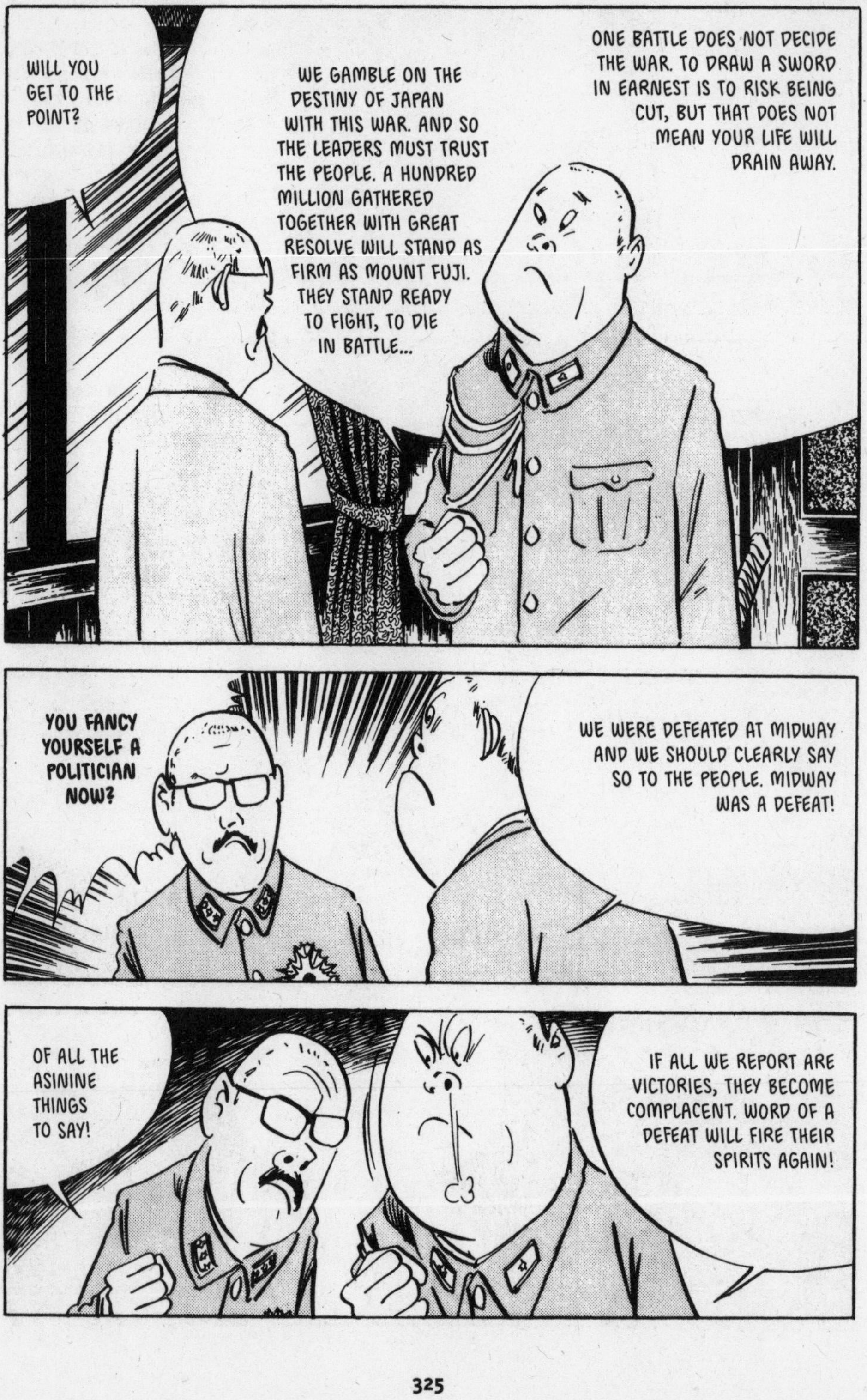
ONE BATTLE DOES NOT DECIDE THE WAR. TO DRAW A SWORD IN EARNEST IS TO RISK BEING CUT, BUT THAT DOES NOT MEAN YOUR LIFE WILL DRAIN AWAY.
WE GAMBLE ON THE DESTINY OF JAPAN WITH THIS WAR. AND SO THE LEADERS MUST TRUST THE PEOPLE. A HUNDRED MILLION GATHERED TOGETHER WITH GREAT RESOLVE WILL STAND AS FIRM AS MOUNT FUJI. THEY STAND READY TO FIGHT, TO DIE IN BATTLE...
WILL YOU GET TO THE POINT?
WE WERE DEFEATED AT MIDWAY AND WE SHOULD CLEARLY SAY SO TO THE PEOPLE. MIDWAY WAS A DEFEAT!
YOU FANCY YOURSELF A POLITICIAN NOW?
IF ALL WE REPORT ARE VICTORIES, THEY BECOME COMPLACENT. WORD OF A DEFEAT WILL FIRE THEIR SPIRITS AGAIN!
OF ALL THE ASININE THINGS TO SAY!

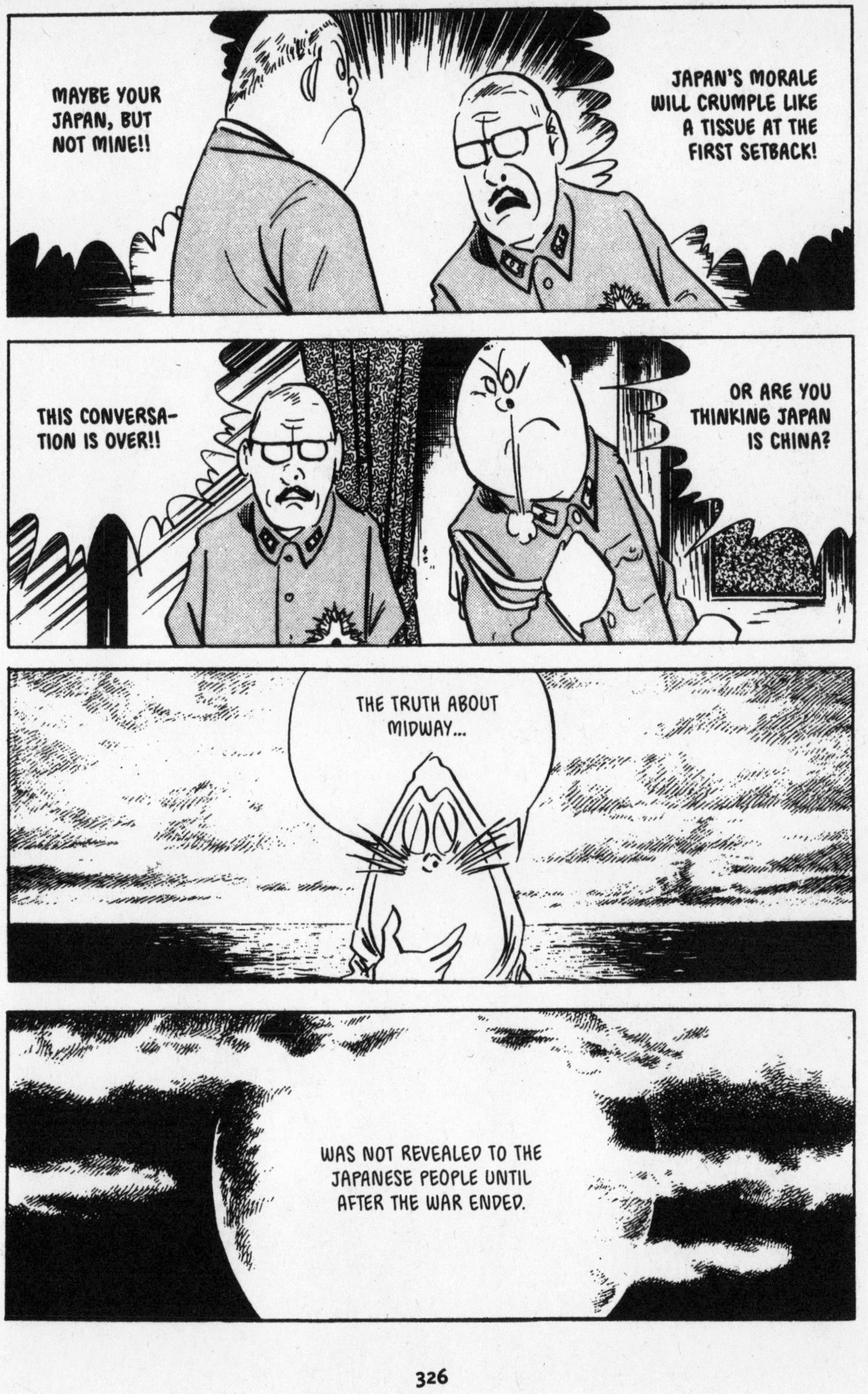
JAPAN'S MORALE WILL CRUMPLE LIKE A TISSUE AT THE FIRST SETBACK!
MAYBE YOUR JAPAN, BUT NOT MINE!!
OR ARE YOU THINKING JAPAN IS CHINA?
THIS CONVERSATION IS OVER!!
THE TRUTH ABOUT MIDWAY...
WAS NOT REVEALED TO THE JAPANESE PEOPLE UNTIL AFTER THE WAR ENDED.

MOVING UP

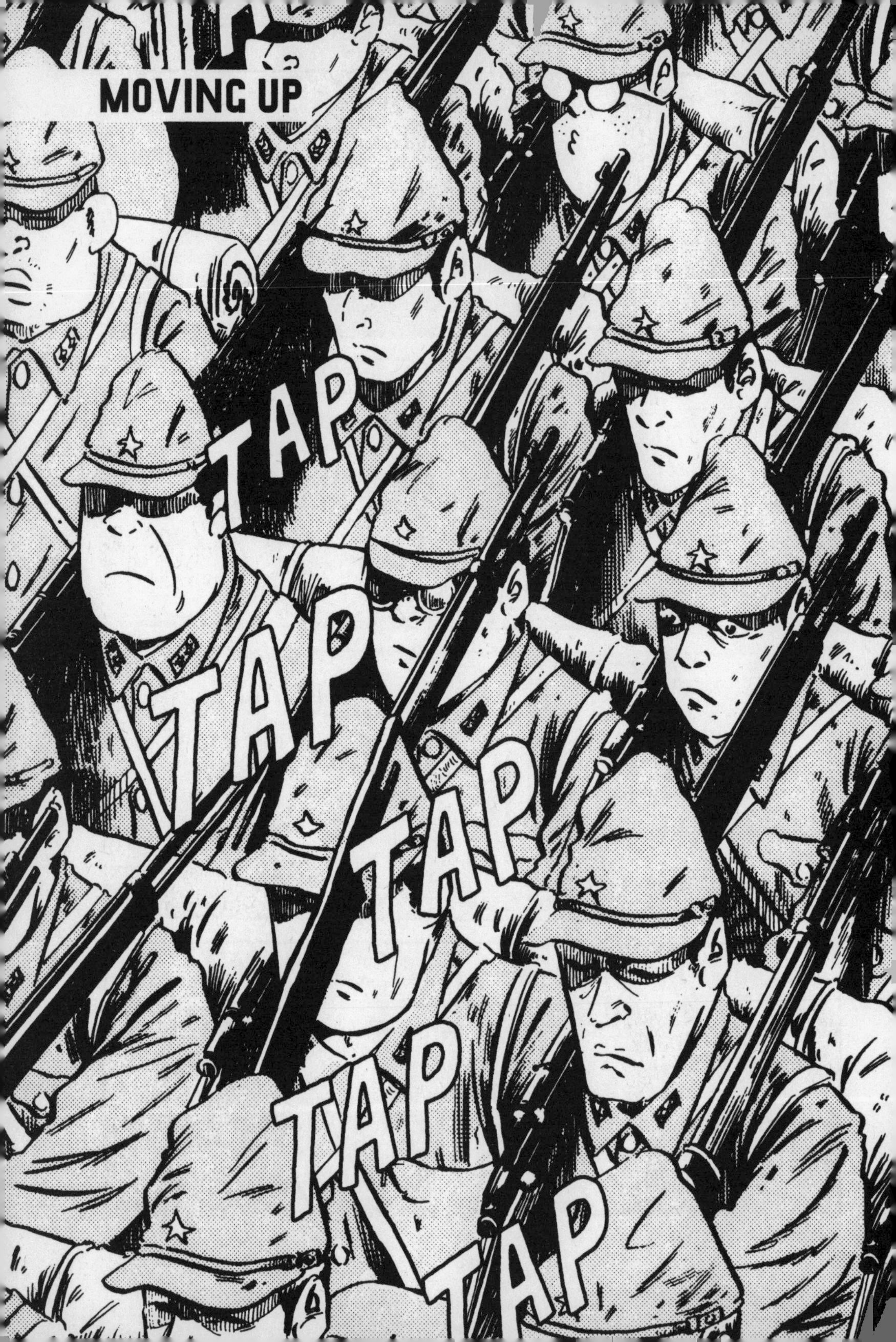
TAP
TAP
TAP
TAP
TAP
TAP

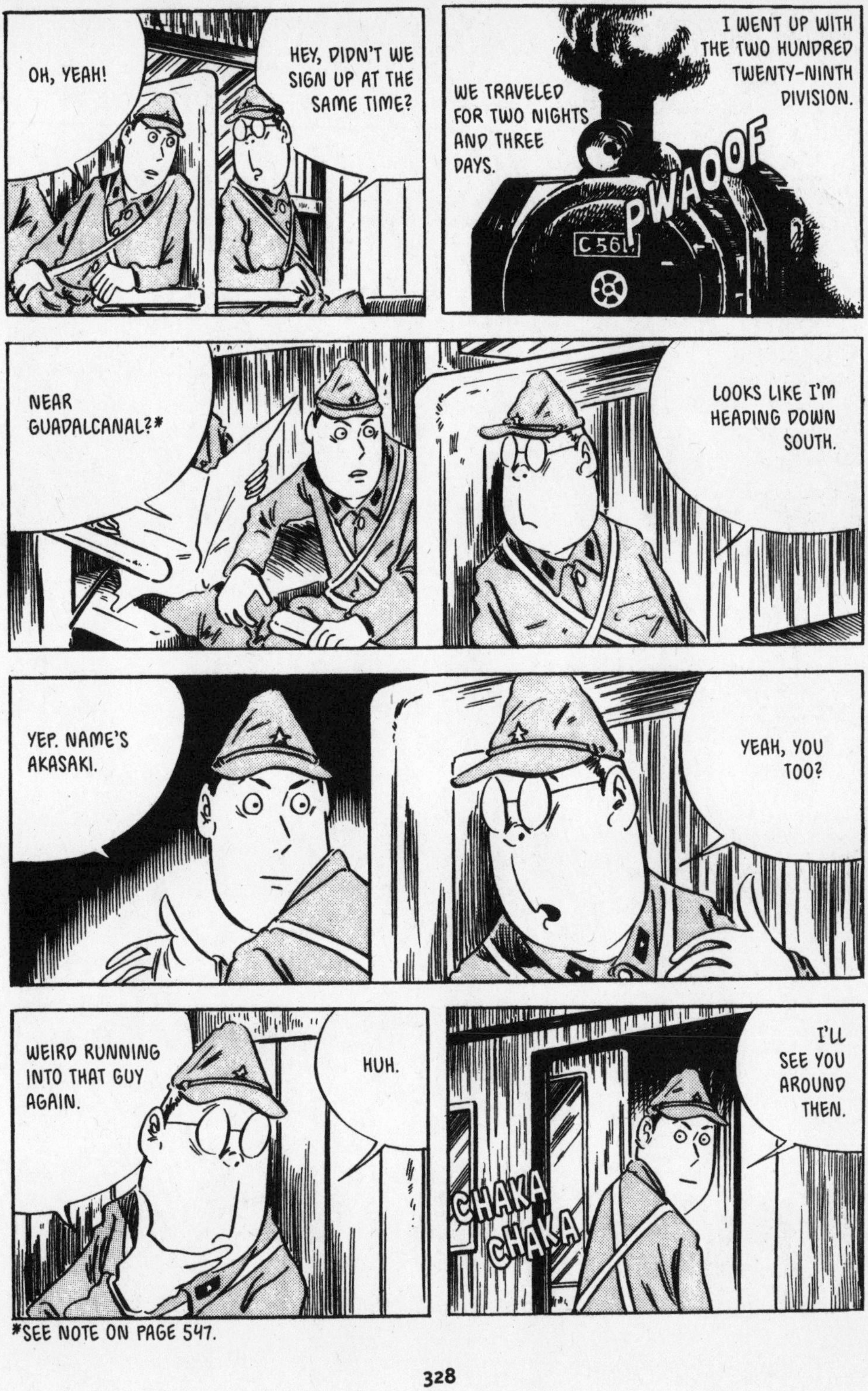
I WENT UP WITH THE TWO HUNDRED TWENTY-NINTH DIVISION.
WE TRAVELED FOR TWO NIGHTS AND THREE DAYS.
PWAOOF
C561
HEY, DIDN'T WE SIGN UP AT THE SAME TIME?
OH, YEAH!
LOOKS LIKE I'M HEADING DOWN SOUTH.
NEAR GUADALCANAL?*
YEAH, YOU TOO?
YEP. NAME'S AKASAKI.
I'LL SEE YOU AROUND THEN.
CHAKA CHAKA
HUH.
WEIRD RUNNING INTO THAT GUY AGAIN.

*SEE NOTE ON PAGE 547.

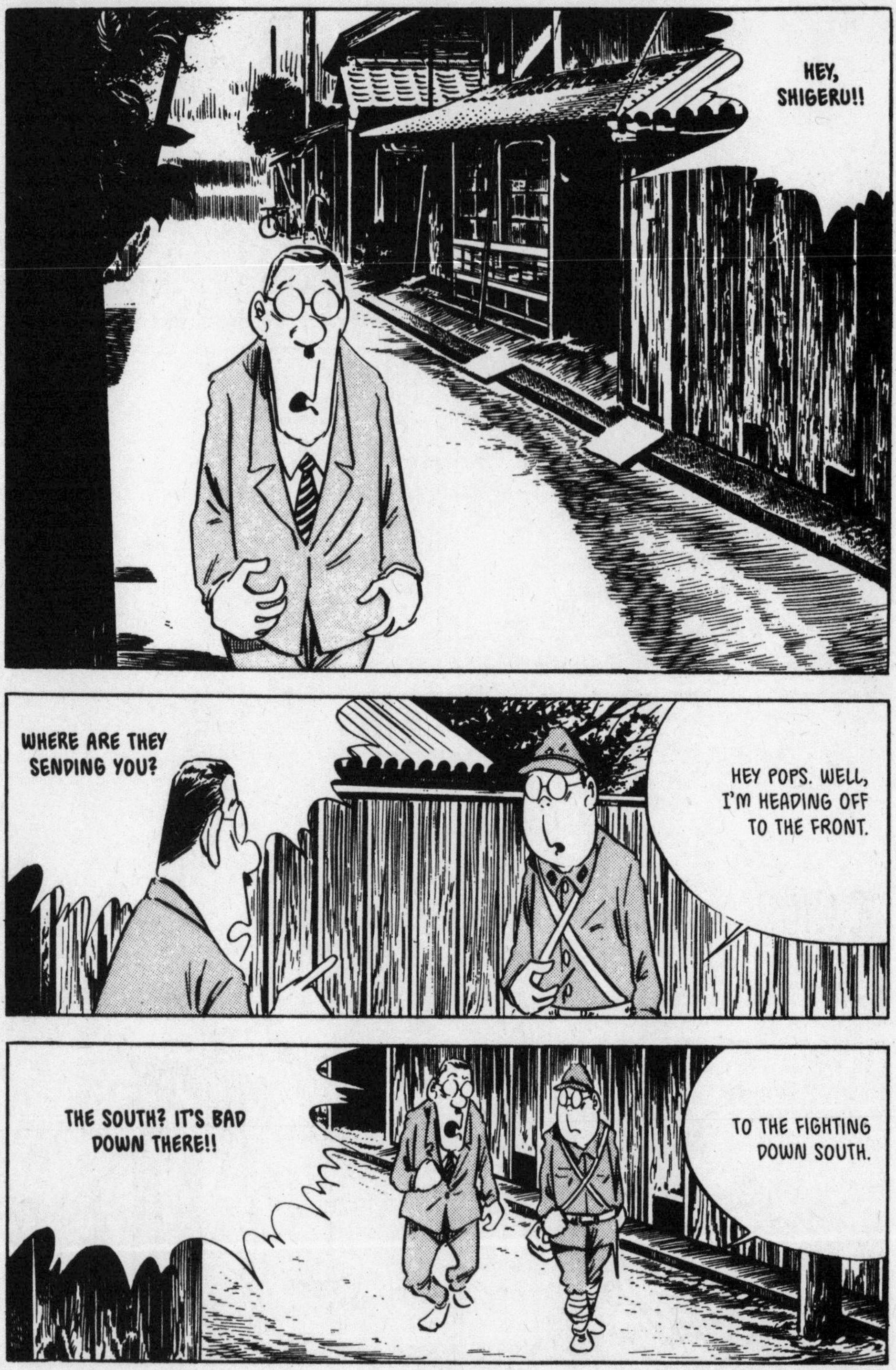
HEY, SHIGERU!!
HEY POPS. WELL, I'M HEADING OFF TO THE FRONT.
WHERE ARE THEY SENDING YOU?
TO THE FIGHTING DOWN SOUTH.
THE SOUTH? IT'S BAD DOWN THERE!!

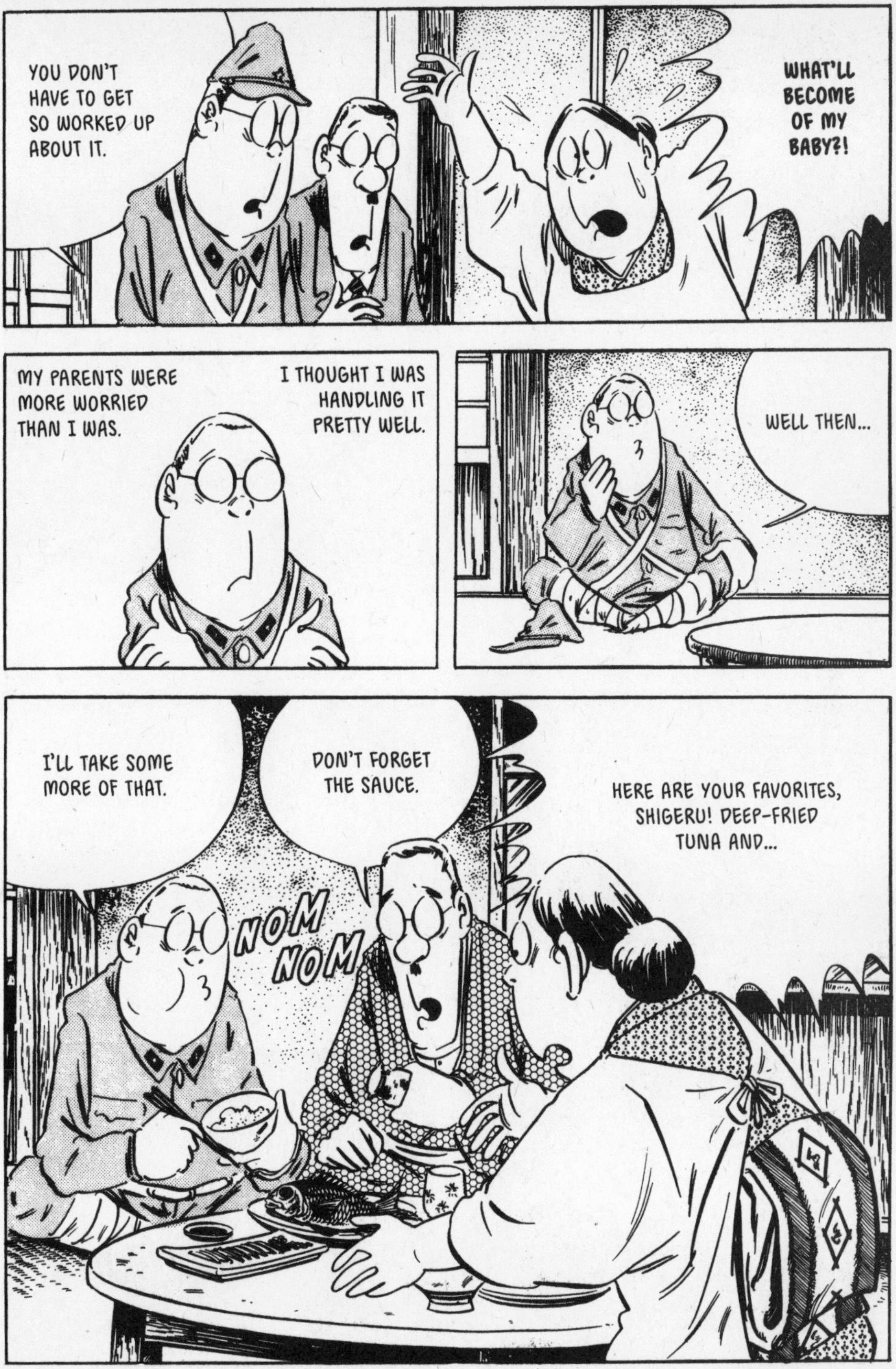
WHAT'LL BECOME OF MY BABY?!
YOU DON'T HAVE TO GET SO WORKED UP ABOUT IT.
WELL THEN...
I THOUGHT I WAS HANDLING IT PRETTY WELL.
MY PARENTS WERE MORE WORRIED THAN I WAS.
HERE ARE YOUR FAVORITES, SHIGERU! DEEP-FRIED TUNA AND...
DON'T FORGET THE SAUCE.
NOM NOM
I'LL TAKE SOME MORE OF THAT.

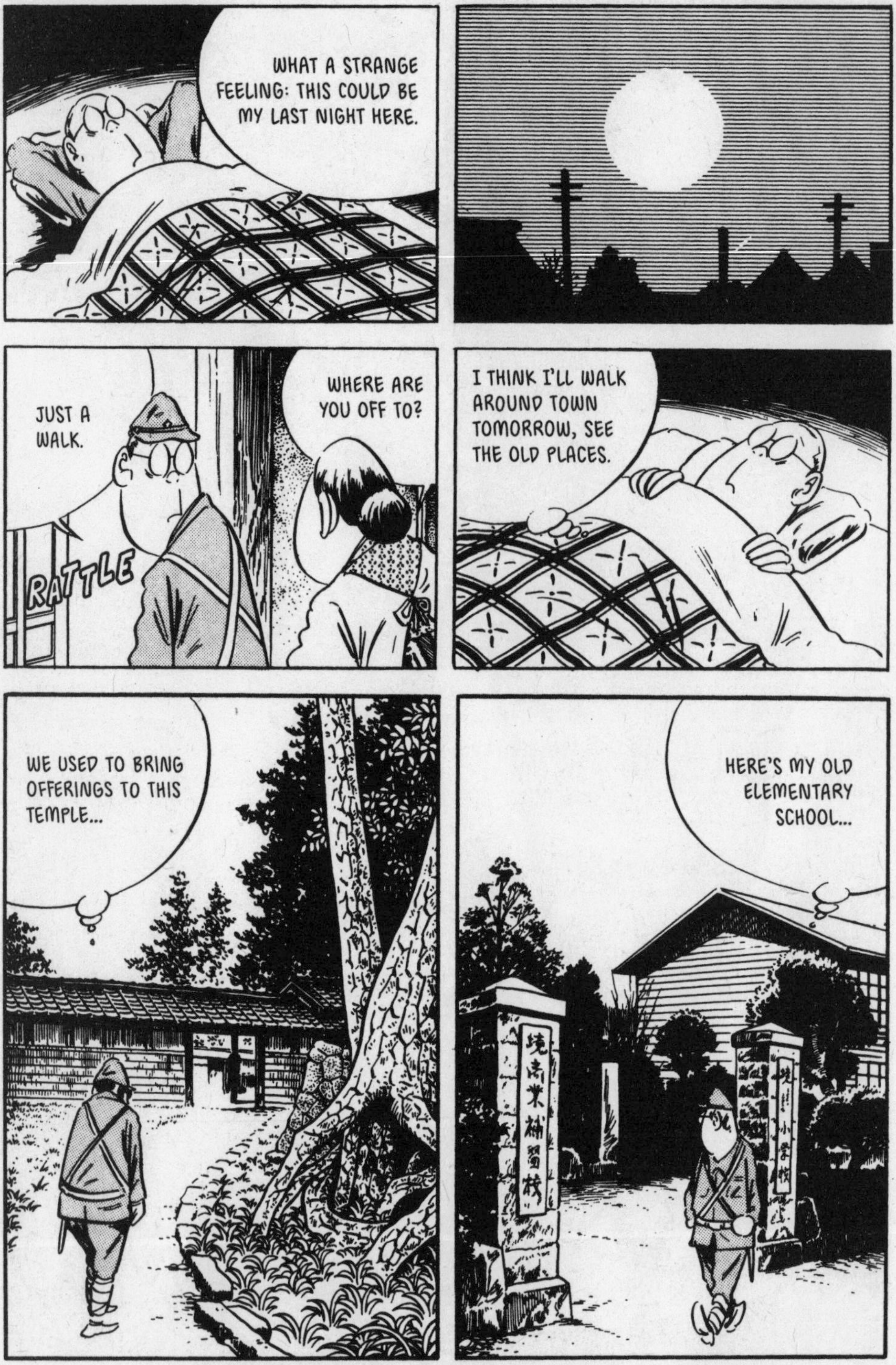
WHAT A STRANGE FEELING: THIS COULD BE MY LAST NIGHT HERE.
I THINK I'LL WALK AROUND TOWN TOMORROW, SEE THE OLD PLACES.
WHERE ARE YOU OFF TO?
JUST A WALK.
RATTLE
HERE'S MY OLD ELEMENTARY SCHOOL...
WE USED TO BRING OFFERINGS TO THIS TEMPLE...

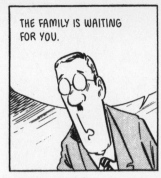

WHAT ARE YOU DOING, SHIGERU?
OH, HI DAD.
THE FAMILY IS WAITING FOR YOU.
OH YEAH, THE PARTY.
BLAH BLAH
SHIGERU MY BOY, YOU GOTTA GET OUT THERE AND FIGHT.
LIKE ME! I GOT SHOT IN THE ASS CHARGING THE 203RD HILL!*
HA HA HA HA!
I WISH THEY'D SHOT HIM SOMEWHERE ELSE.

*IN CHINA, NEAR PORT ARTHUR. A BATTLE SITE DURING THE RUSSO-JAPANESE WAR.

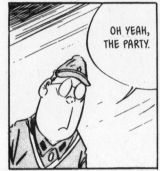

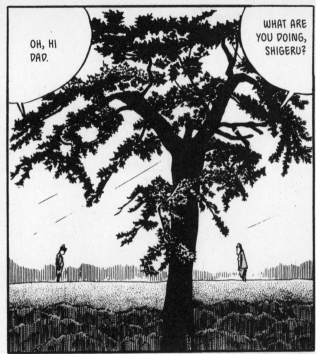

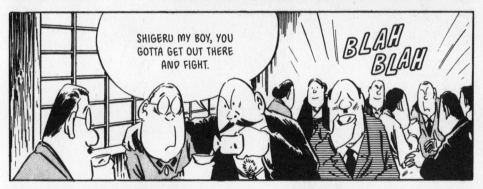

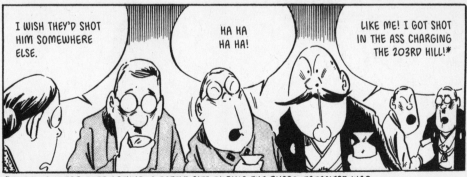

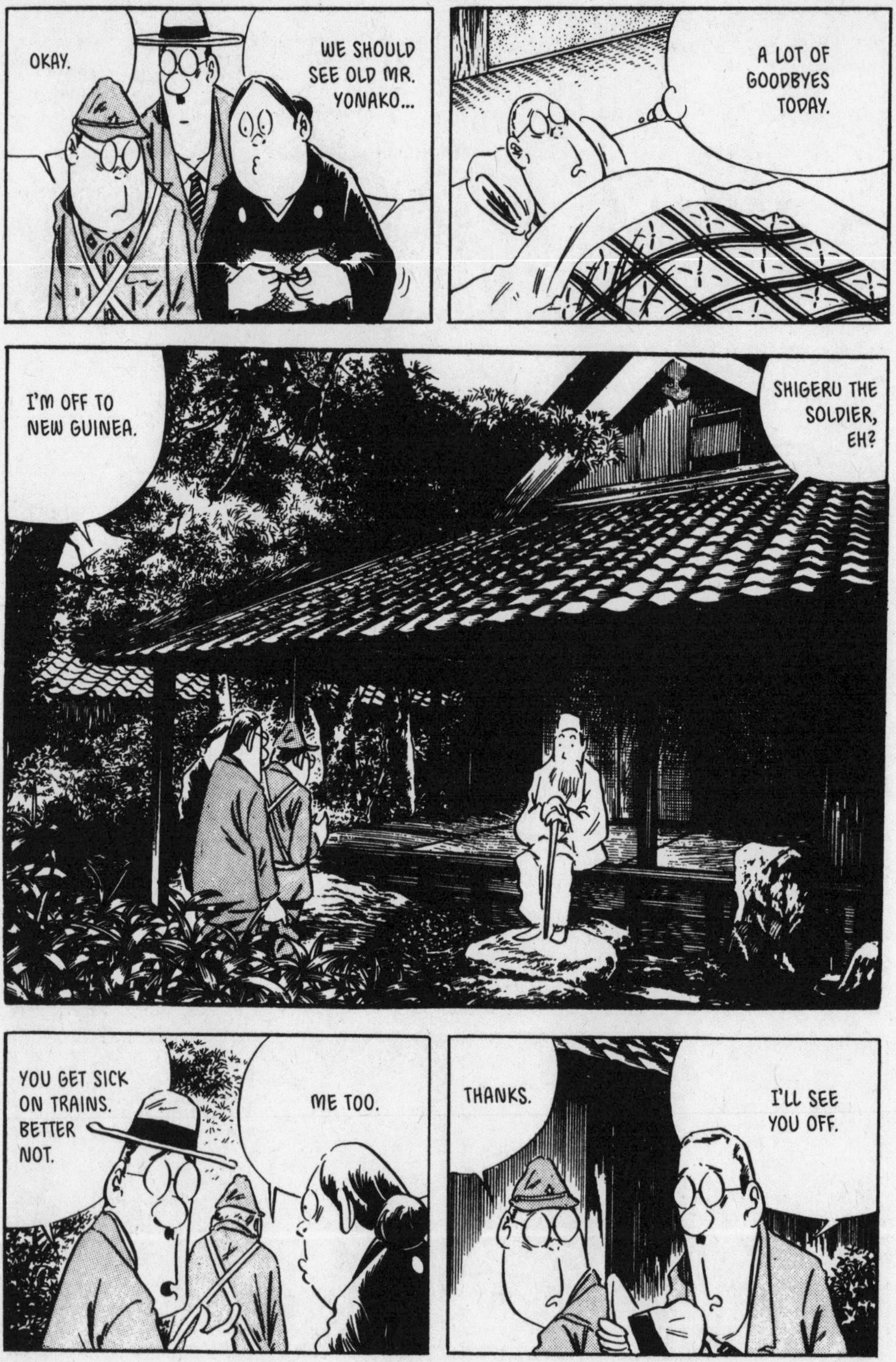
A LOT OF GOODBYES TODAY.
WE SHOULD SEE OLD MR. YONAKO...
OKAY.
SHIGERU THE SOLDIER, EH?
I'M OFF TO NEW GUINEA.
I'LL SEE YOU OFF.
THANKS.
ME TOO.
YOU GET SICK ON TRAINS. BETTER NOT.

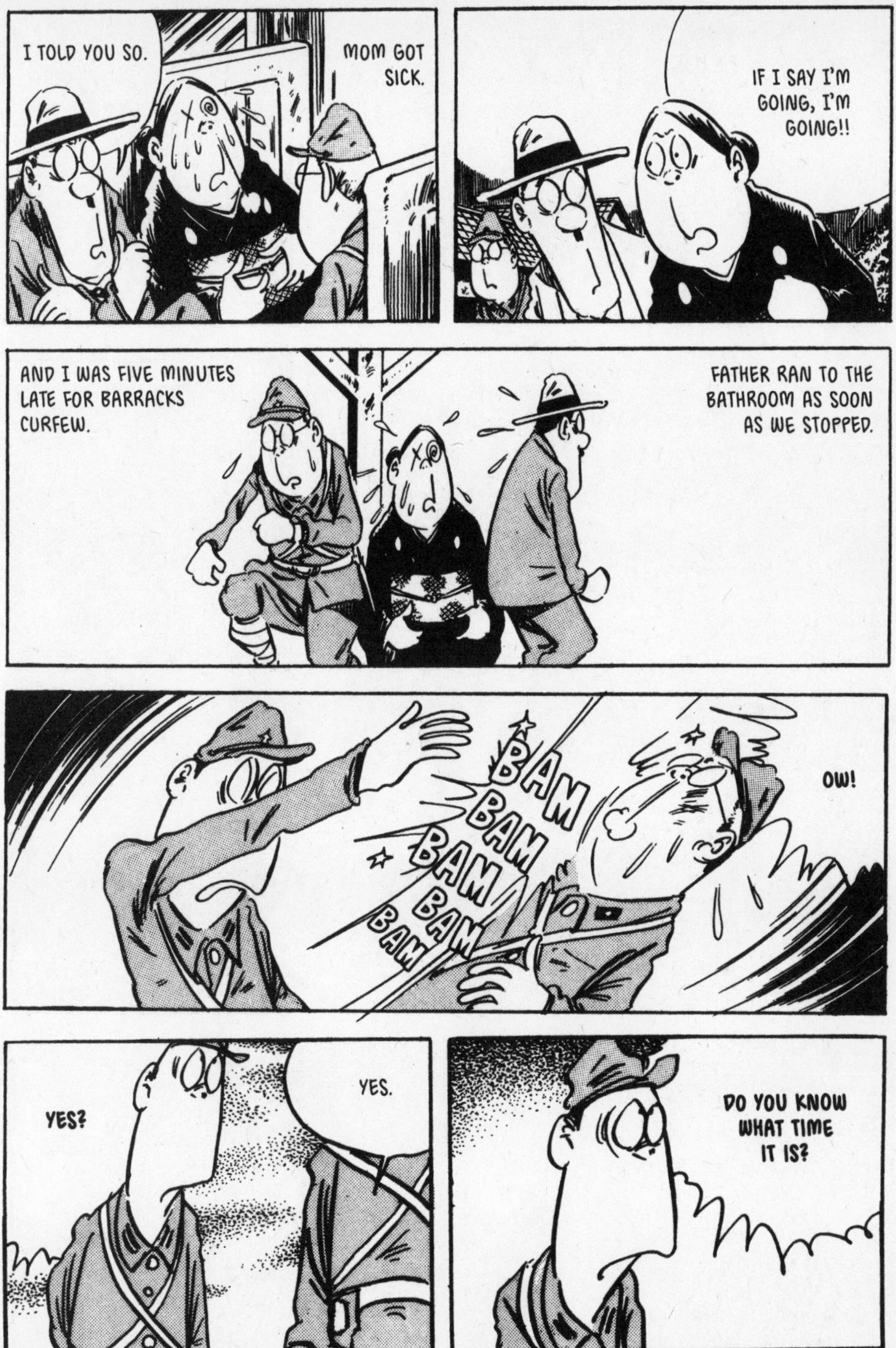

IF I SAY I'M GOING, I'M GOING!!
MOM GOT SICK.
I TOLD YOU SO.
FATHER RAN TO THE BATHROOM AS SOON AS WE STOPPED.
AND I WAS FIVE MINUTES LATE FOR BARRACKS CURFEW.
OW!
BAM BAM BAM BAM BAM
DO YOU KNOW WHAT TIME IT IS?
YES.
YES?

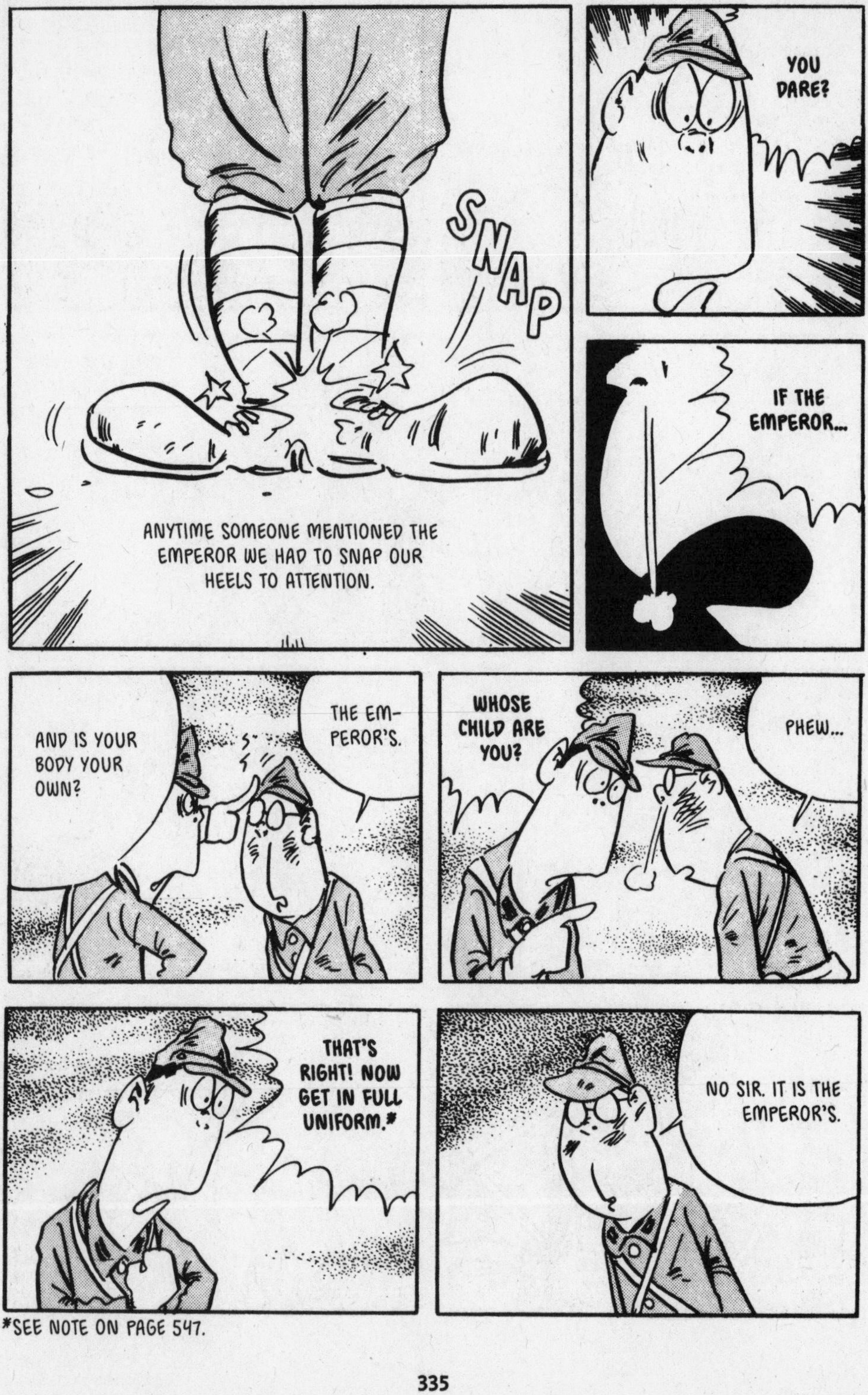
YOU DARE?
IF THE EMPEROR...
SNAP
ANYTIME SOMEONE MENTIONED THE EMPEROR WE HAD TO SNAP OUR HEELS TO ATTENTION.
WHOSE CHILD ARE YOU?
PHEW...
THE EM-PEROR'S.
AND IS YOUR BODY YOUR OWN?
NO SIR. IT IS THE EMPEROR'S.
THAT'S RIGHT! NOW GET IN FULL UNIFORM.*

*SEE NOTE ON PAGE 547.

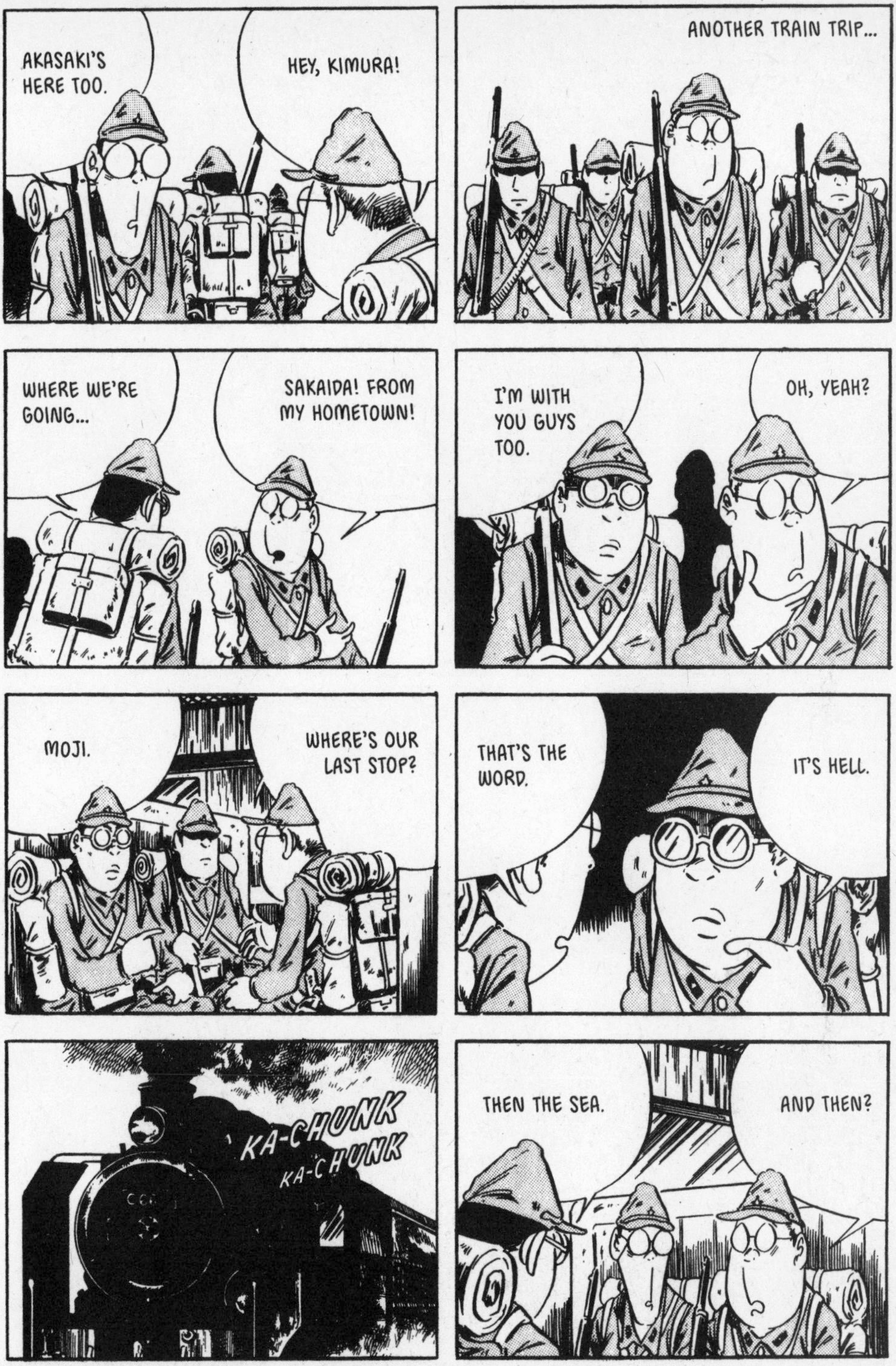
ANOTHER TRAIN TRIP...
HEY, KIMURA!
AKASAKI'S HERE TOO.
OH, YEAH?
I'M WITH YOU GUYS TOO.
SAKAIDA! FROM MY HOMETOWN!
WHERE WE'RE GOING...
IT'S HELL.
THAT'S THE WORD.
WHERE'S OUR LAST STOP?
MOJI.
AND THEN?
THEN THE SEA.
KA-CHUNK
KA-CHUNK

THE SOLOMON ISLANDS CAMPAIGN

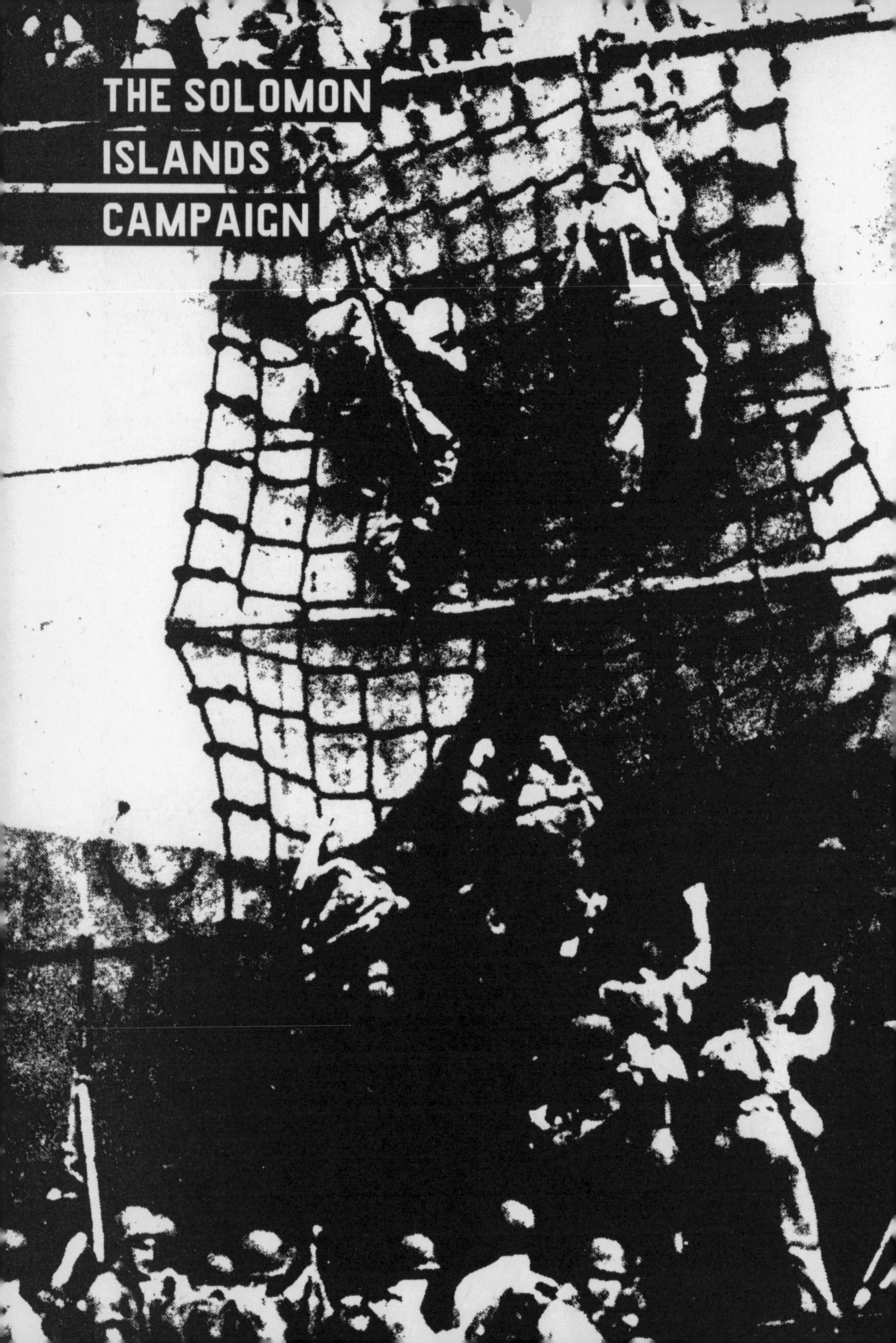

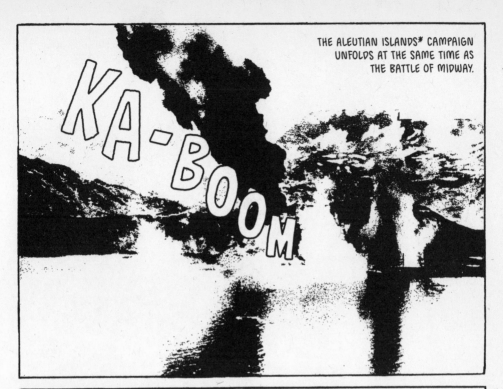

THE ALEUTIAN ISLANDS* CAMPAIGN UNFOLDS AT THE SAME TIME AS THE BATTLE OF MIDWAY.

KA-BOOM

THE U.S. DOESN'T ATTACH MUCH IMPORTANCE TO THE ALEUTIANS. ON JUNE 7, 1942 (SHOWA 17), JAPAN EASILY TAKES KISKA AND ATTU ISLANDS.

THE SOLOMON ISLANDS CAMPAIGN IS A DIFFERENT STORY.

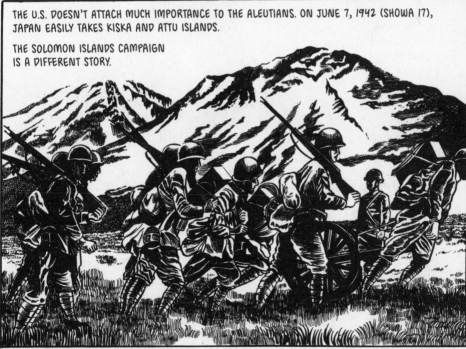

*SEE NOTE ON PAGE 547.

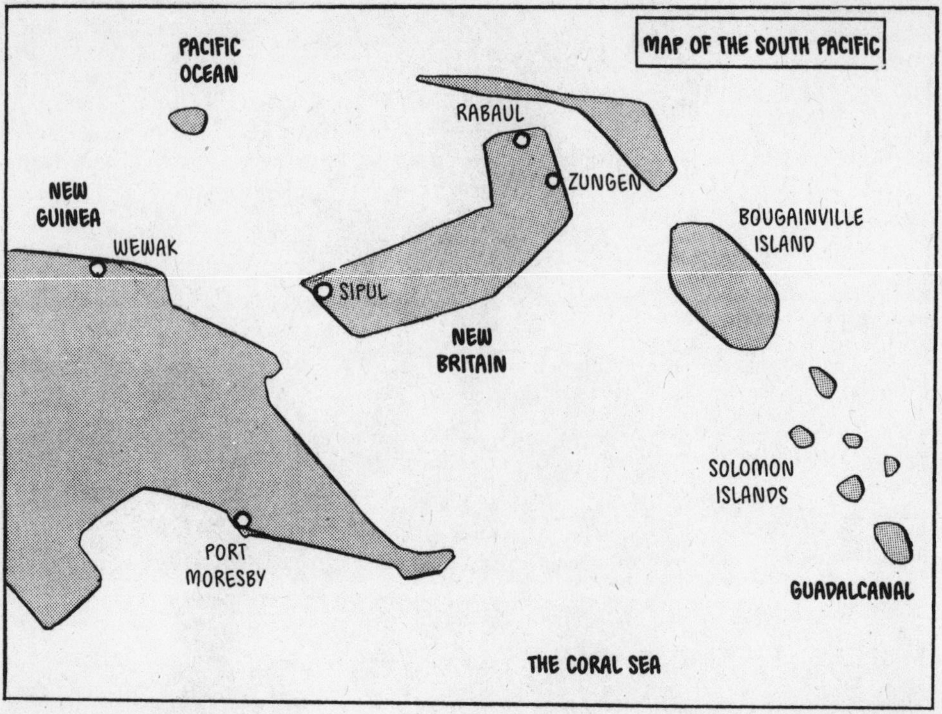
MAP OF THE SOUTH PACIFIC
PACIFIC OCEAN
RABAUL
ZUNGEN
NEW GUINEA
WEWAK
SIPUL
BOUGAINVILLE ISLAND
NEW BRITAIN
SOLOMON ISLANDS
PORT MORESBY
GUADALCANAL
THE CORAL SEA

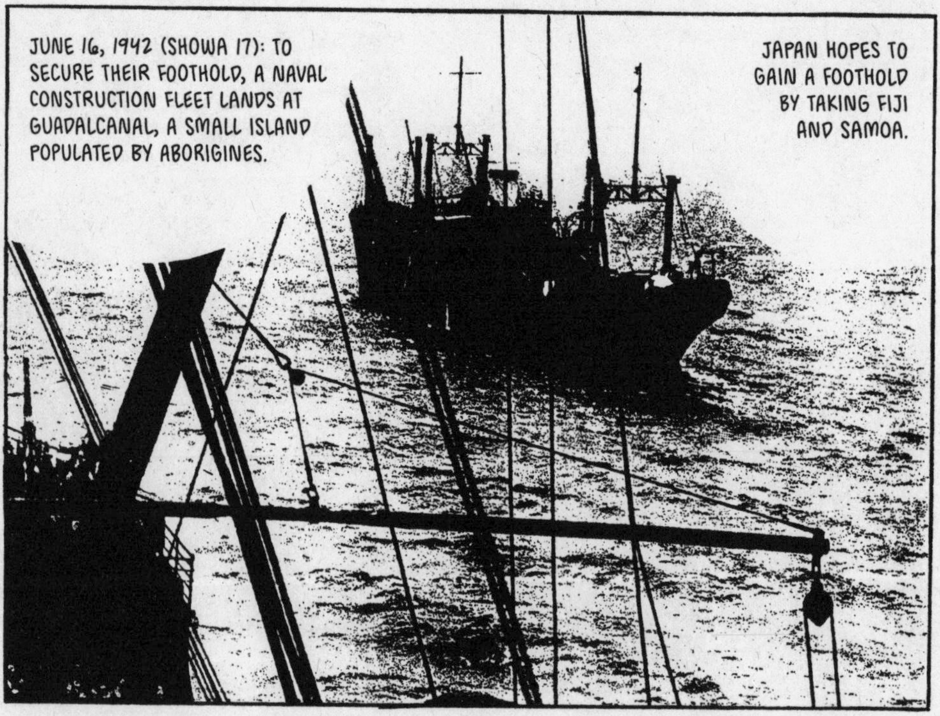
JAPAN HOPES TO GAIN A FOOTHOLD BY TAKING FIJI AND SAMOA.
JUNE 16, 1942 (SHOWA 17): TO SECURE THEIR FOOTHOLD, A NAVAL CONSTRUCTION FLEET LANDS AT GUADALCANAL, A SMALL ISLAND POPULATED BY ABORIGINES.

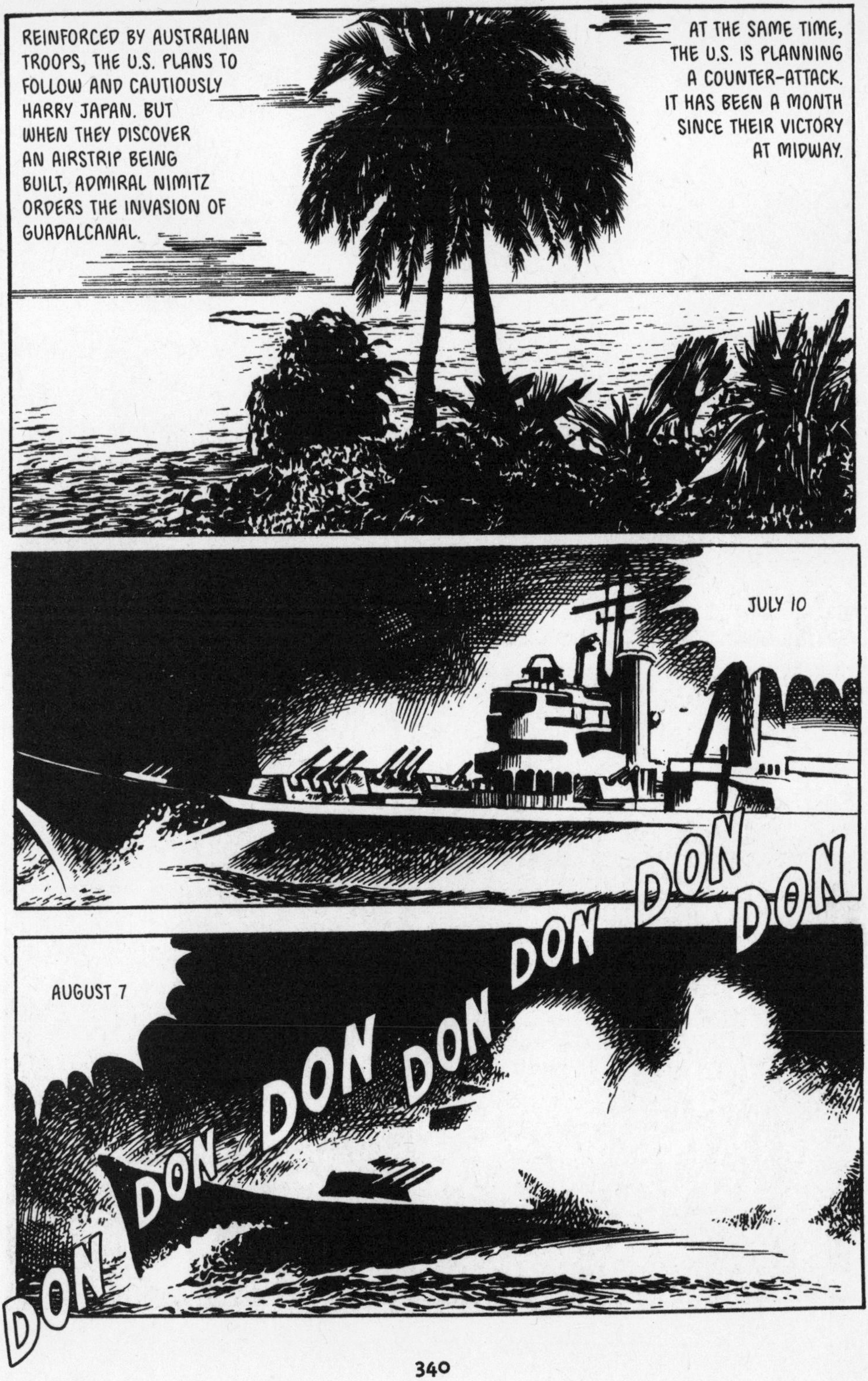
AT THE SAME TIME, THE U.S. IS PLANNING A COUNTER-ATTACK. IT HAS BEEN A MONTH SINCE THEIR VICTORY AT MIDWAY.
REINFORCED BY AUSTRALIAN TROOPS, THE U.S. PLANS TO FOLLOW AND CAUTIOUSLY HARRY JAPAN. BUT WHEN THEY DISCOVER AN AIRSTRIP BEING BUILT, ADMIRAL NIMITZ ORDERS THE INVASION OF GUADALCANAL.
JULY 10
AUGUST 7
DON DON DON DON DON DON DON

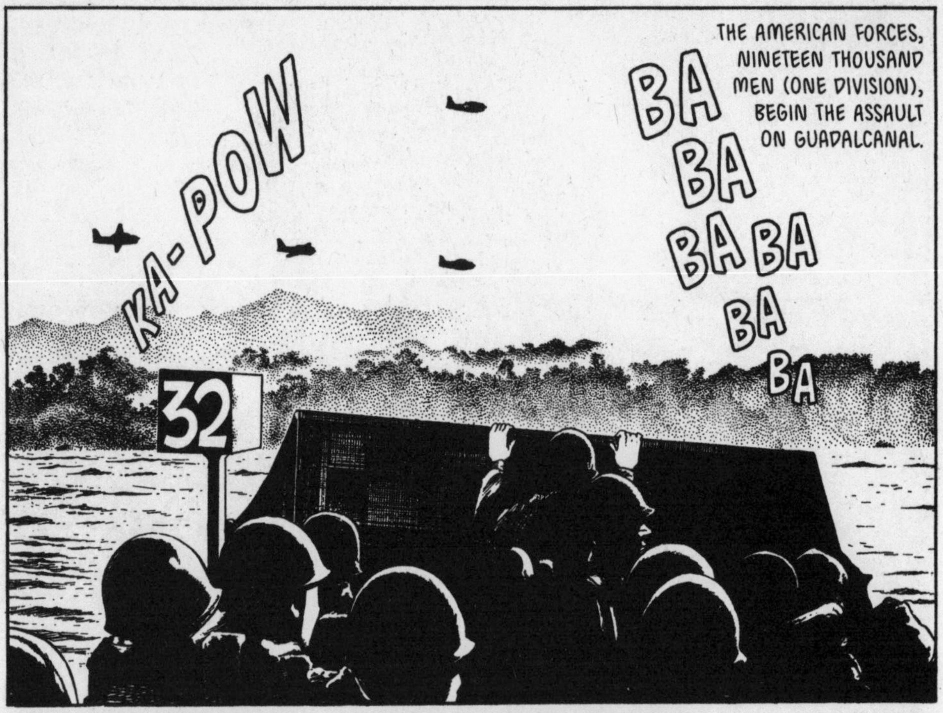
THE AMERICAN FORCES, NINETEEN THOUSAND MEN (ONE DIVISION), BEGIN THE ASSAULT ON GUADALCANAL.
BA BA BA BA BA BA
KA-POW
32

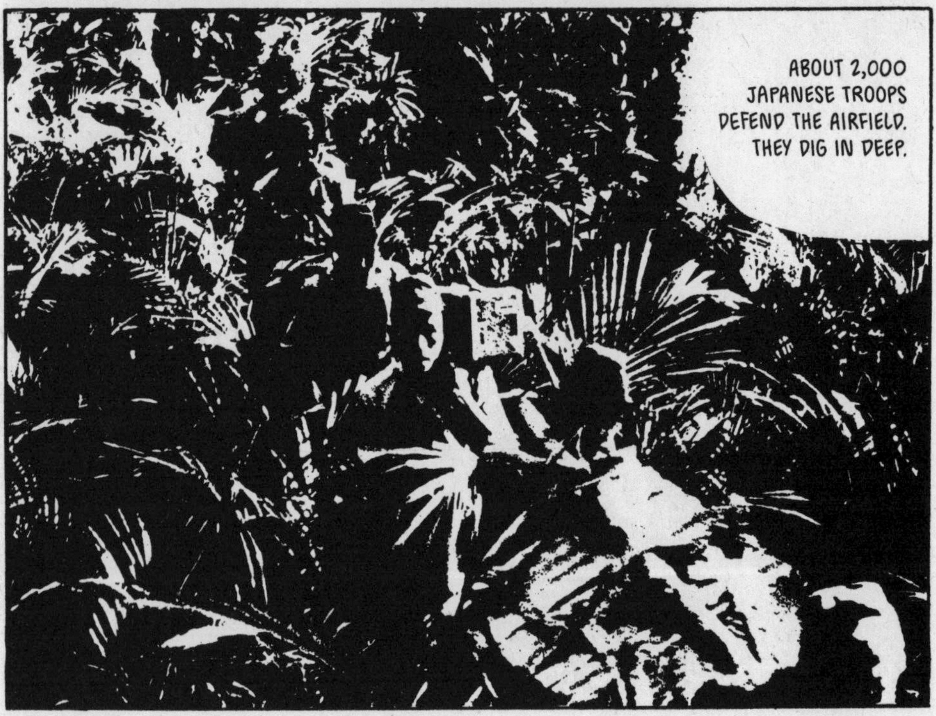
ABOUT 2,000 JAPANESE TROOPS DEFEND THE AIRFIELD. THEY DIG IN DEEP.

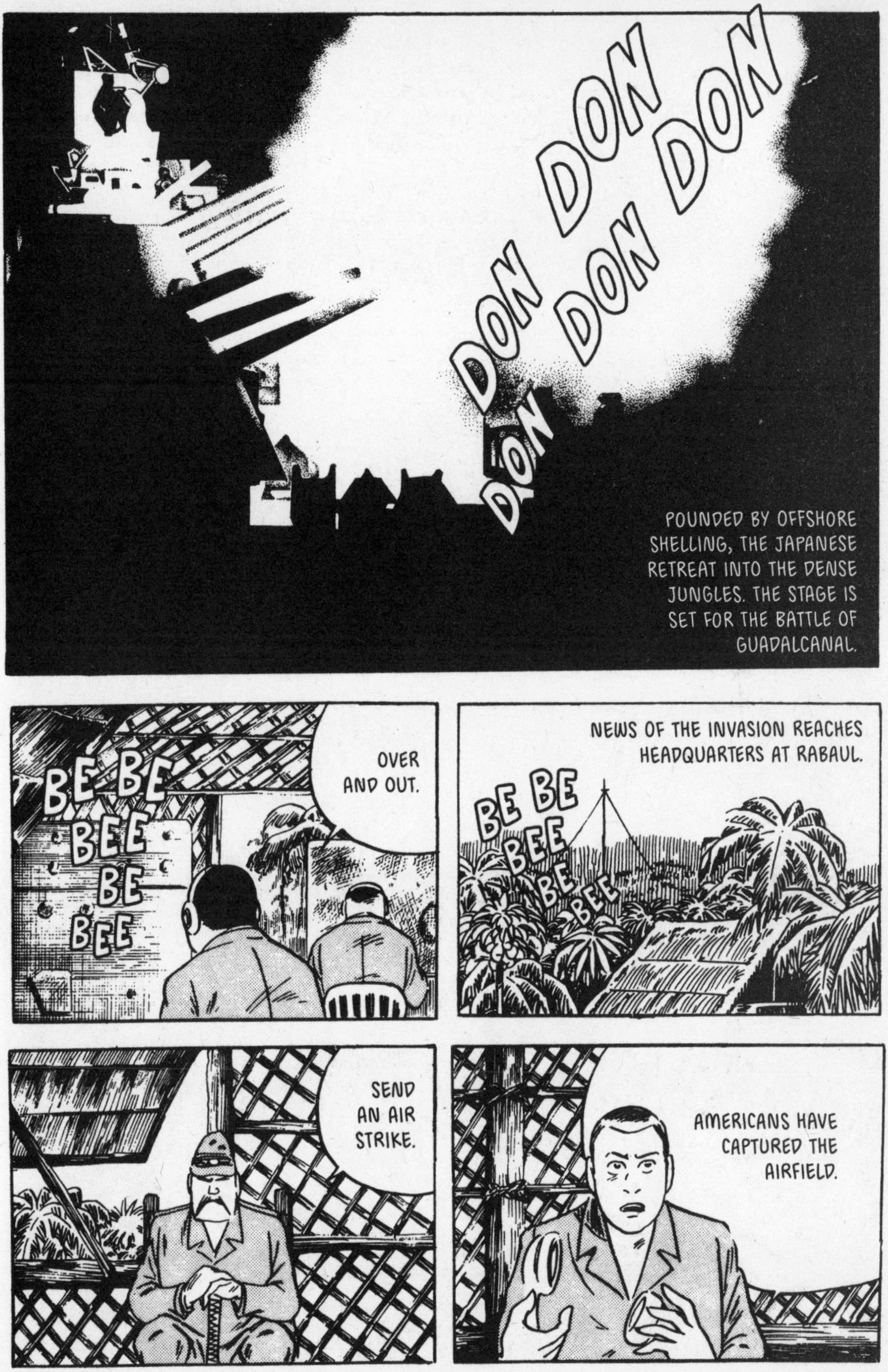
DON DON DON
DON DON DON
POUNDED BY OFFSHORE SHELLING, THE JAPANESE RETREAT INTO THE DENSE JUNGLES. THE STAGE IS SET FOR THE BATTLE OF GUADALCANAL.
NEWS OF THE INVASION REACHES HEADQUARTERS AT RABAUL.
BE BE BEE BE BEE
OVER AND OUT.
BE BE BEE BE BEE
AMERICANS HAVE CAPTURED THE AIRFIELD.
SEND AN AIR STRIKE.

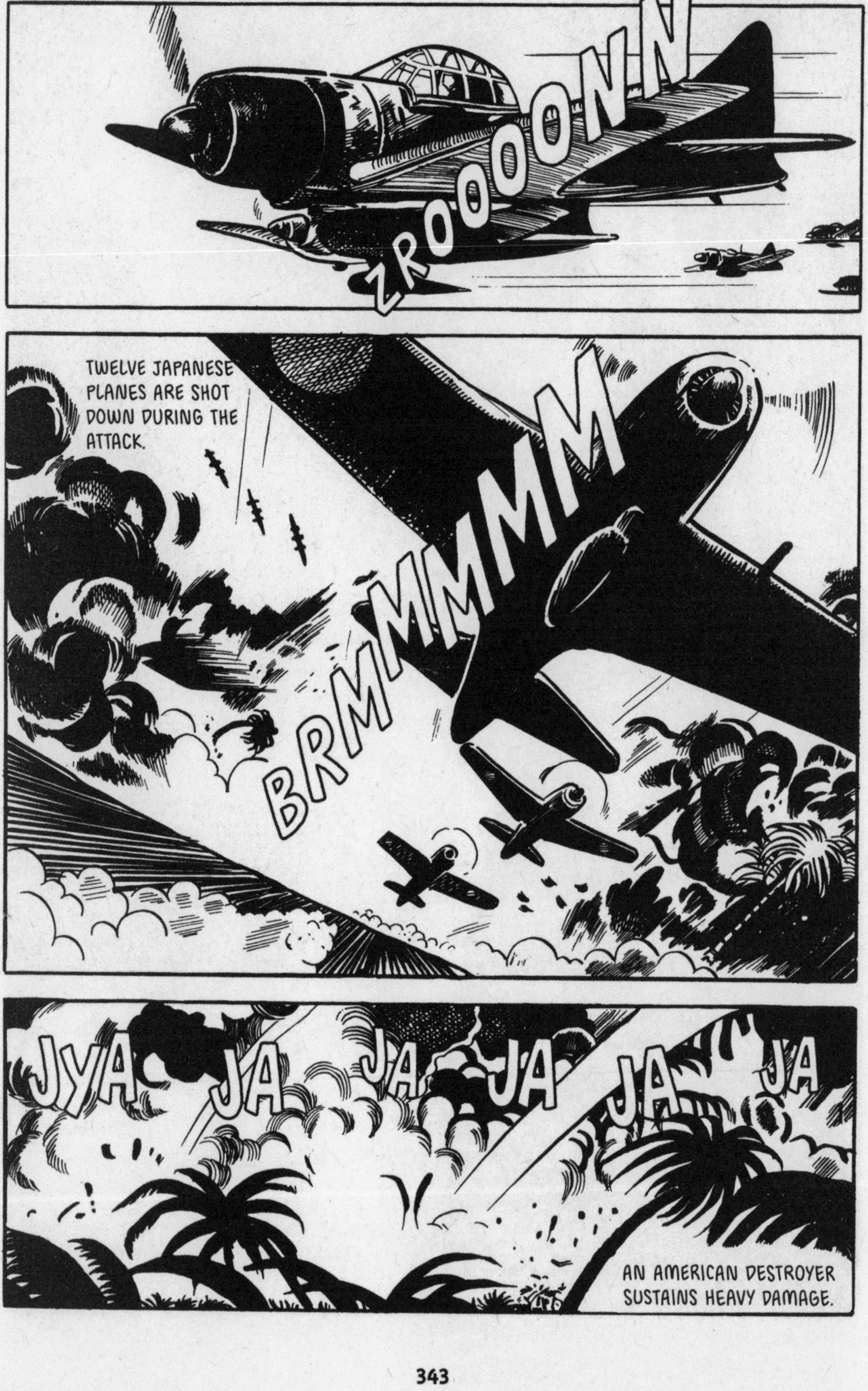
ZROOOONN
TWELVE JAPANESE PLANES ARE SHOT DOWN DURING THE ATTACK.
BRMMMMMM
JYA JA JA JA JA JA
AN AMERICAN DESTROYER SUSTAINS HEAVY DAMAGE.

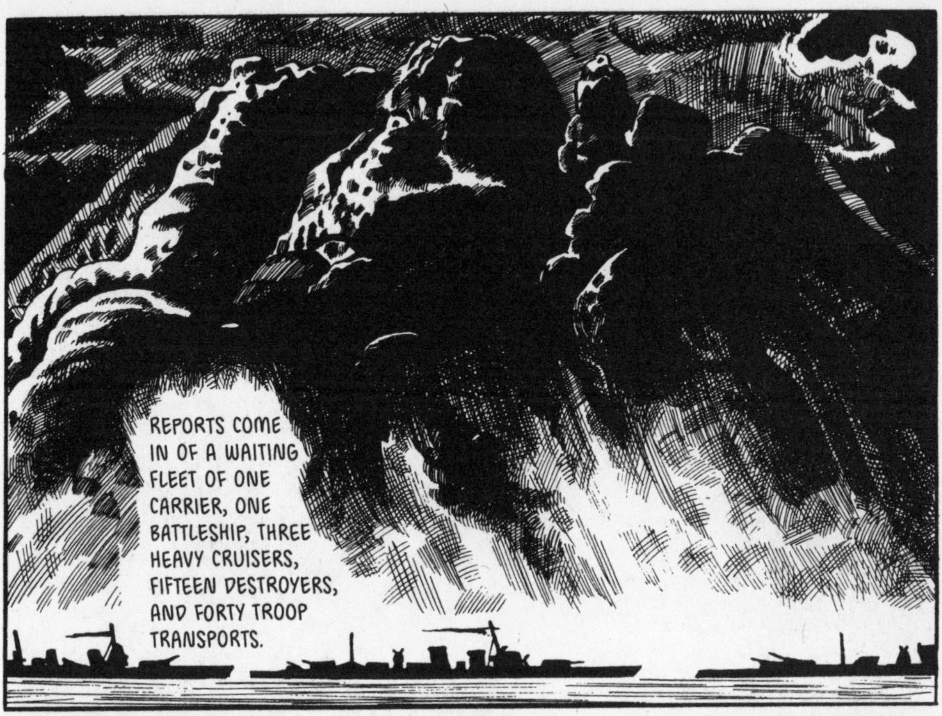
REPORTS COME IN OF A WAITING FLEET OF ONE CARRIER, ONE BATTLESHIP, THREE HEAVY CRUISERS, FIFTEEN DESTROYERS, AND FORTY TROOP TRANSPORTS.

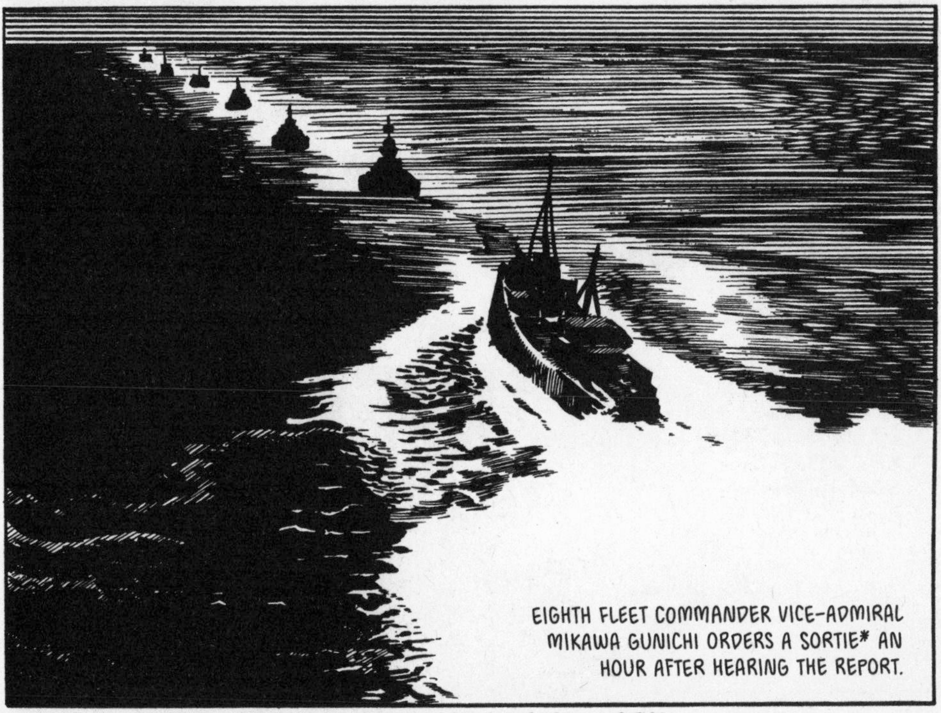
EIGHTH FLEET COMMANDER VICE-ADMIRAL MIKAWA GUNICHI ORDERS A SORTIE* AN HOUR AFTER HEARING THE REPORT.

*A QUICK MOVEMENT OF AIRCRAFT OR TROOPS FROM A BESIEGED POSITION.

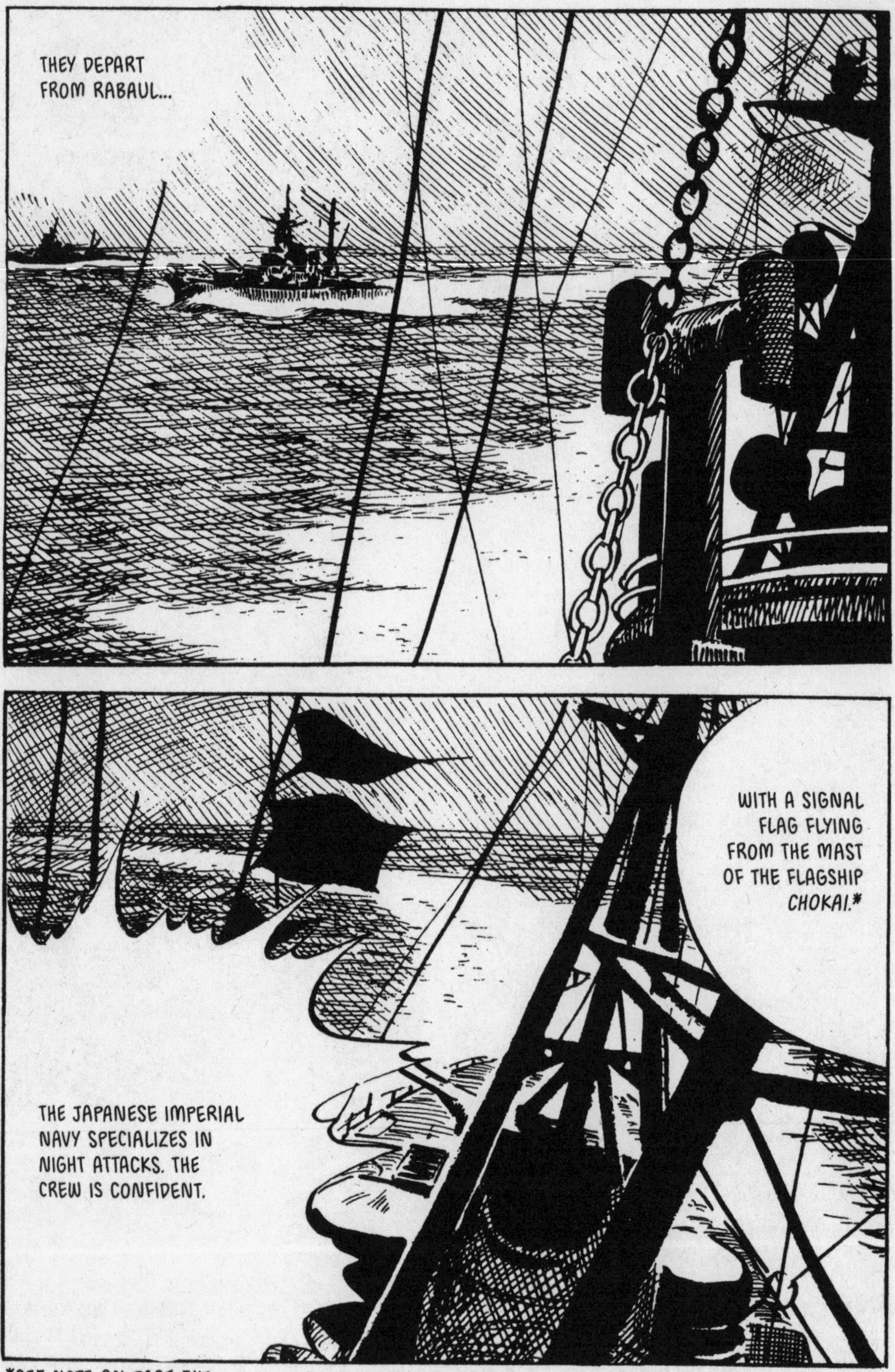
THEY DEPART FROM RABAUL...
WITH A SIGNAL FLAG FLYING FROM THE MAST OF THE FLAGSHIP *CHOKAI.**
THE JAPANESE IMPERIAL NAVY SPECIALIZES IN NIGHT ATTACKS. THE CREW IS CONFIDENT.

*SEE NOTE ON PAGE 547.

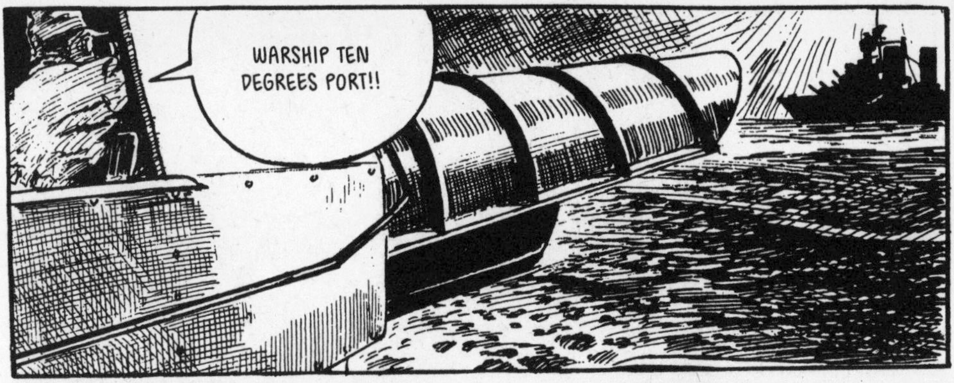
WARSHIP TEN DEGREES PORT!!
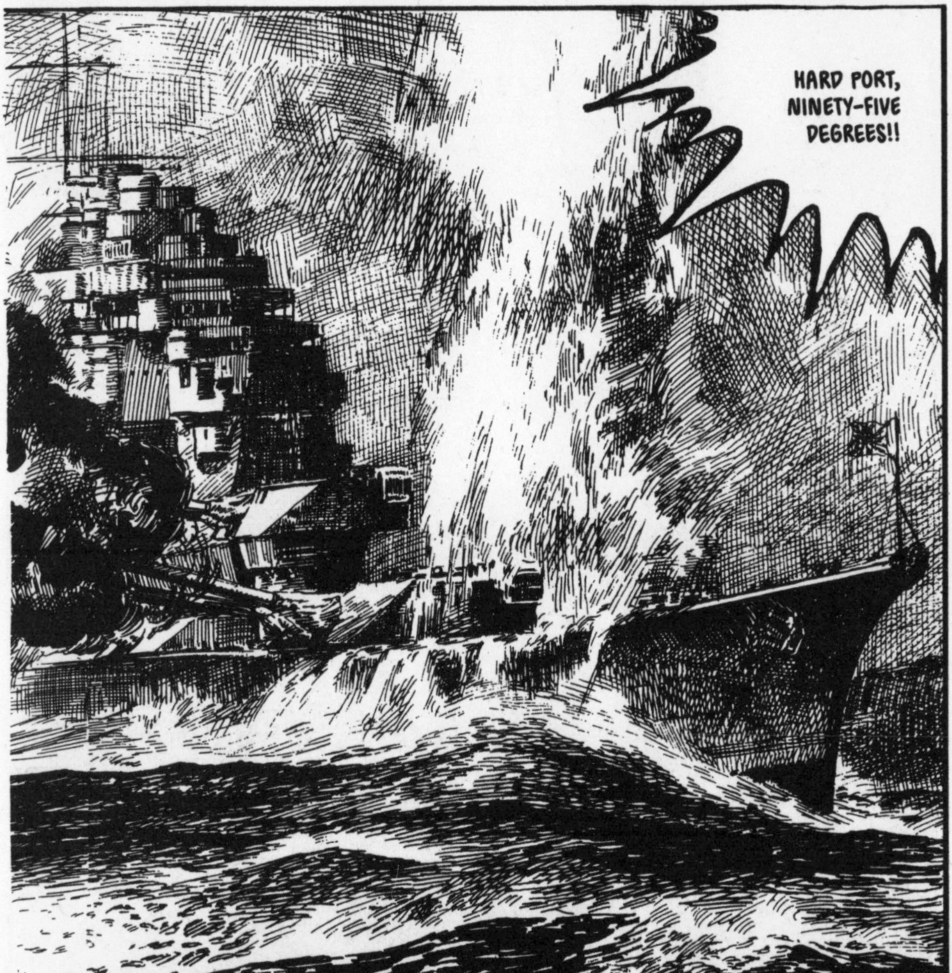
HARD PORT, NINETY-FIVE DEGREES!!

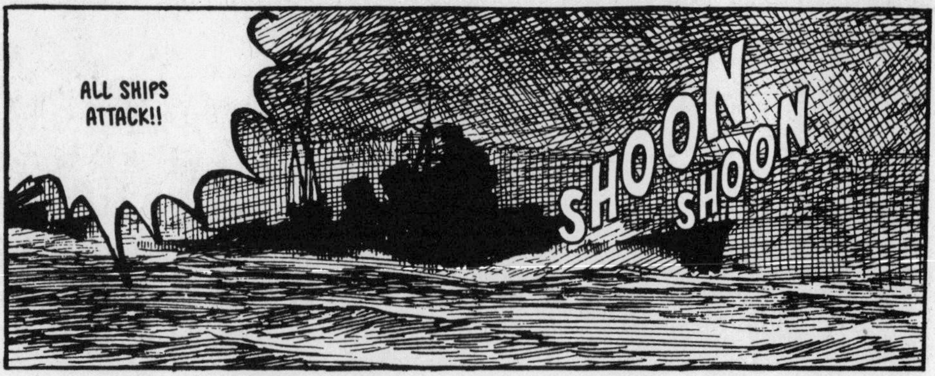
ALL SHIPS ATTACK!!
SHOON
SHOON

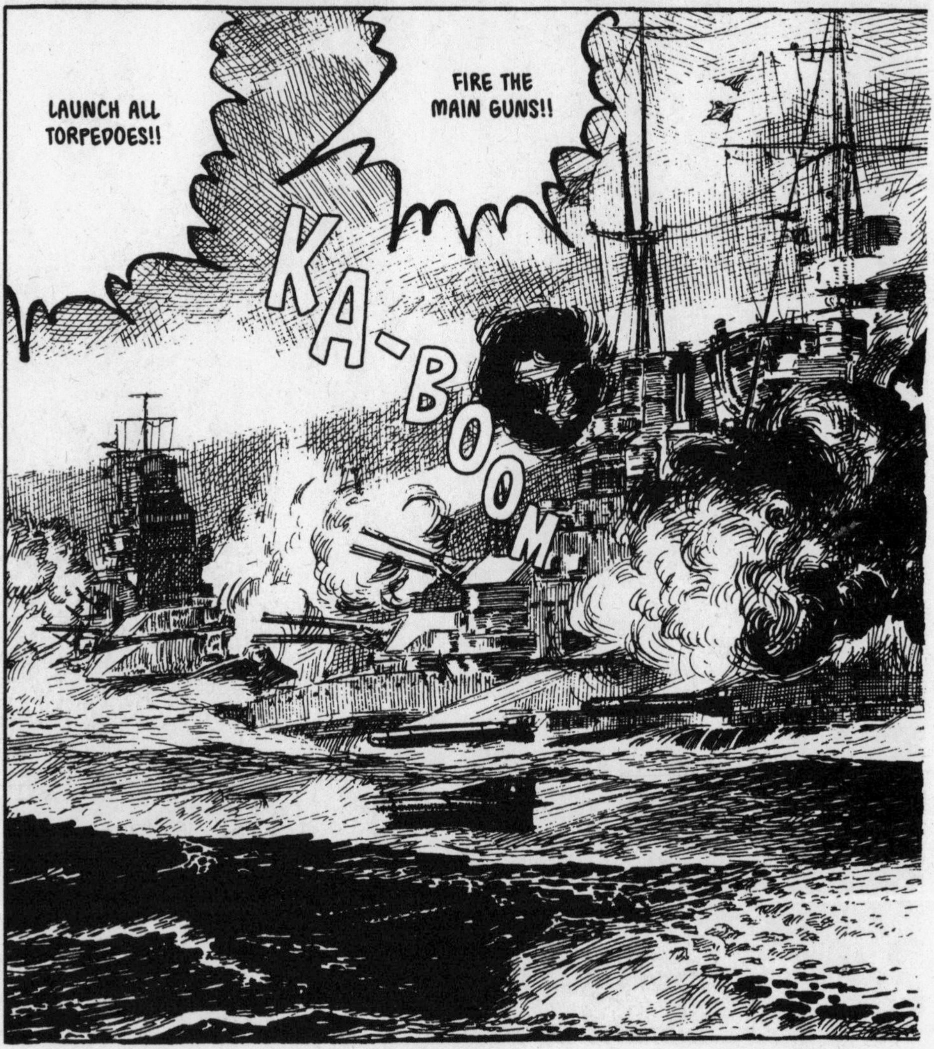
FIRE THE MAIN GUNS!!
LAUNCH ALL TORPEDOES!!
KA-BOOM

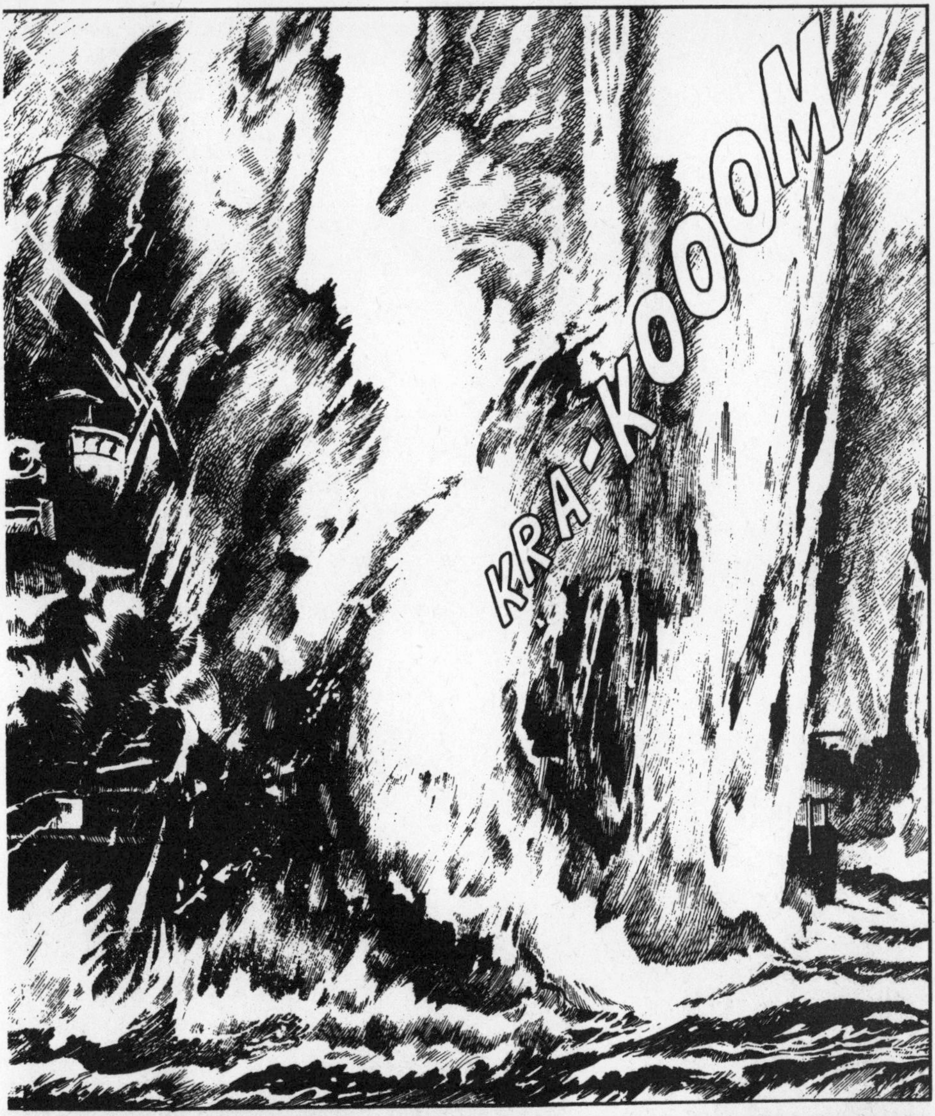
KRA-KOOOM
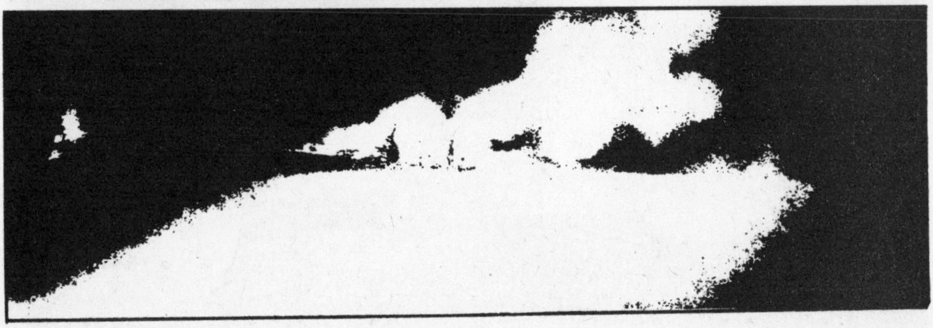

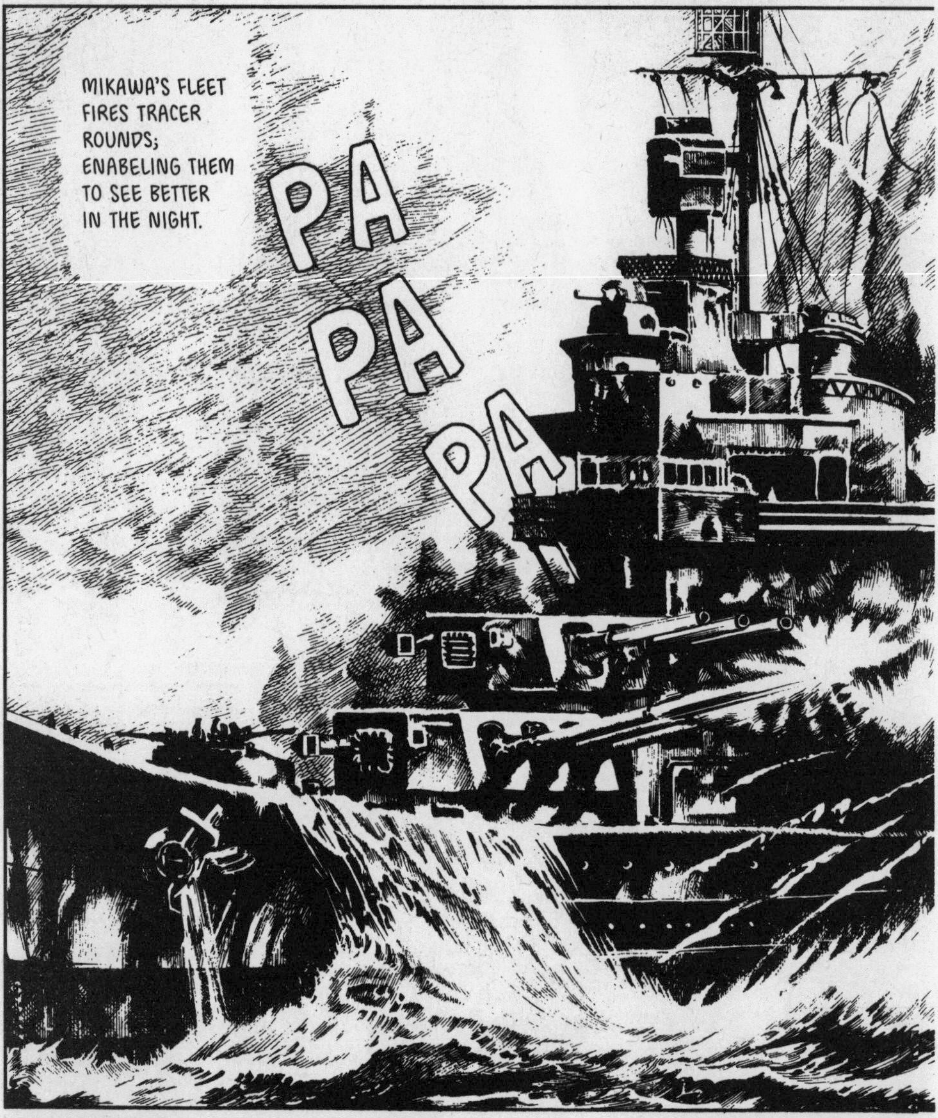
MIKAWA'S FLEET FIRES TRACER ROUNDS; ENABELING THEM TO SEE BETTER IN THE NIGHT.
PA
PA
PA

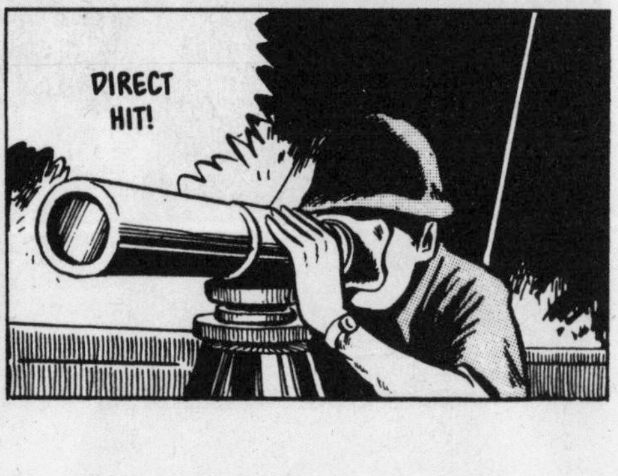
DIRECT HIT!

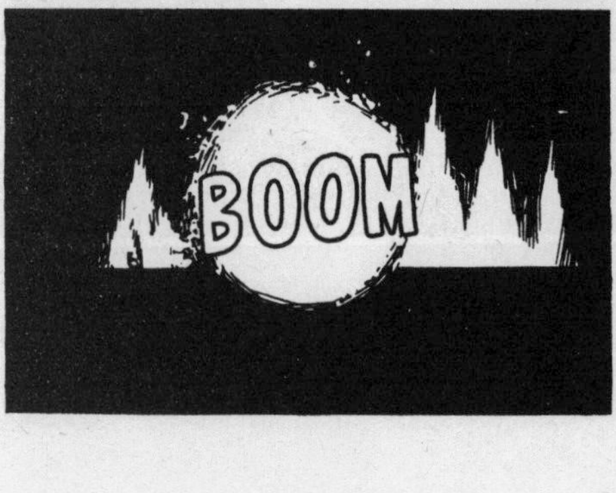
BOOM

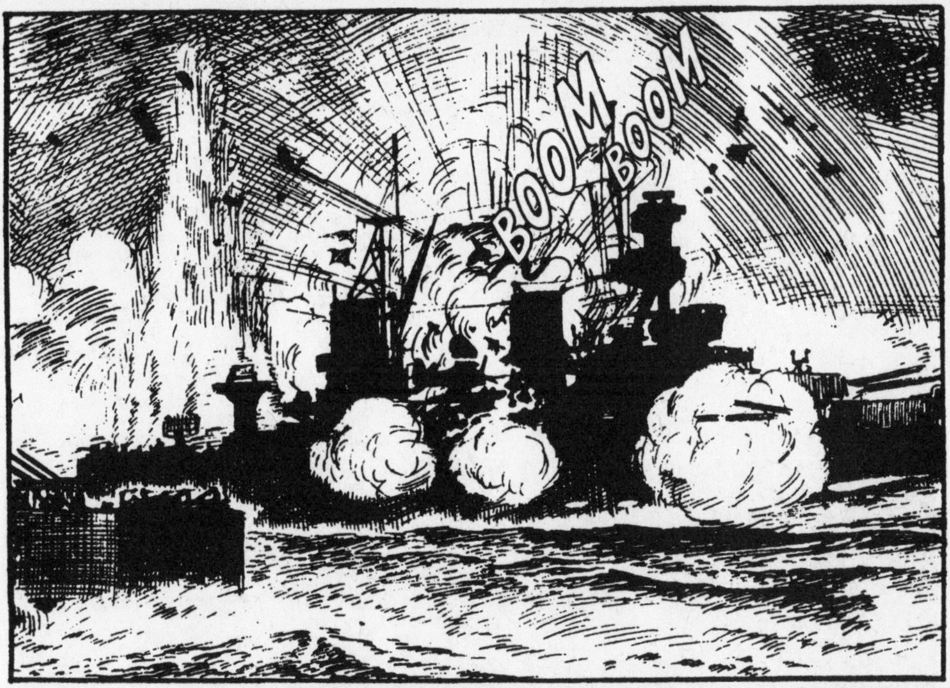
BOOM BOOM BOOM

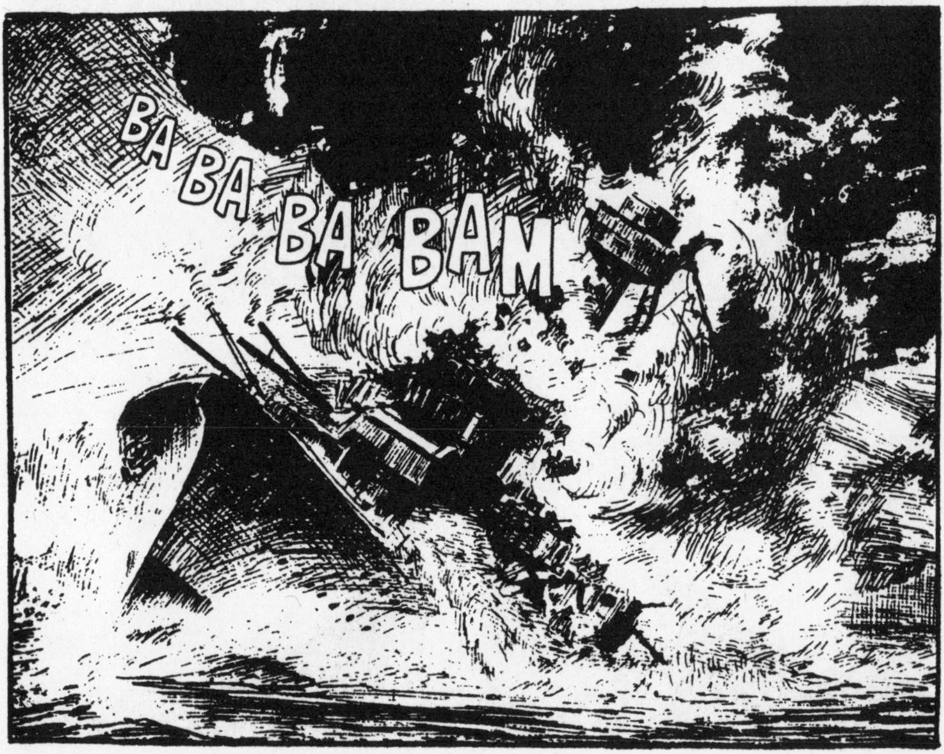
BA BA BA BAM

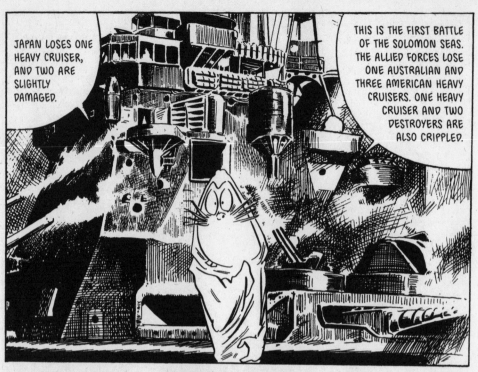

THIS IS THE FIRST BATTLE OF THE SOLOMON SEAS. THE ALLIED FORCES LOSE ONE AUSTRALIAN AND THREE AMERICAN HEAVY CRUISERS. ONE HEAVY CRUISER AND TWO DESTROYERS ARE ALSO CRIPPLED.
JAPAN LOSES ONE HEAVY CRUISER, AND TWO ARE SLIGHTLY DAMAGED.
LIKE KOJIRO AND MUSASHI'S DUEL AT GANRYU ISLAND, THE BATTLE IS QUICKLY DECIDED.* IT IS OVER IN SIXTEEN MINUTES.
MANY THOUGHT JAPAN SHOULD PRESS ITS ADVANTAGE AND ATTACK THE TROOP TRANSPORTS.
MIKAWA HAS ONE SHIP, THE *TENRYU*, FLOATING POWERLESS AFTER A DIRECT HIT.
HE FEELS RESPONSIBLE FOR THE LIVES HE BROUGHT ALONG ON THIS VENTURE.

*SEE NOTE ON PAGE 547.

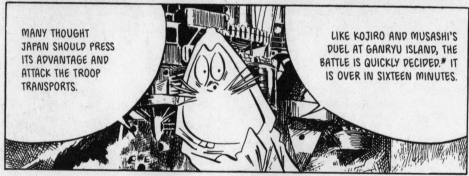

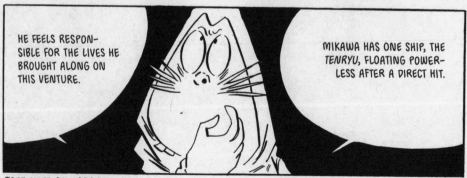

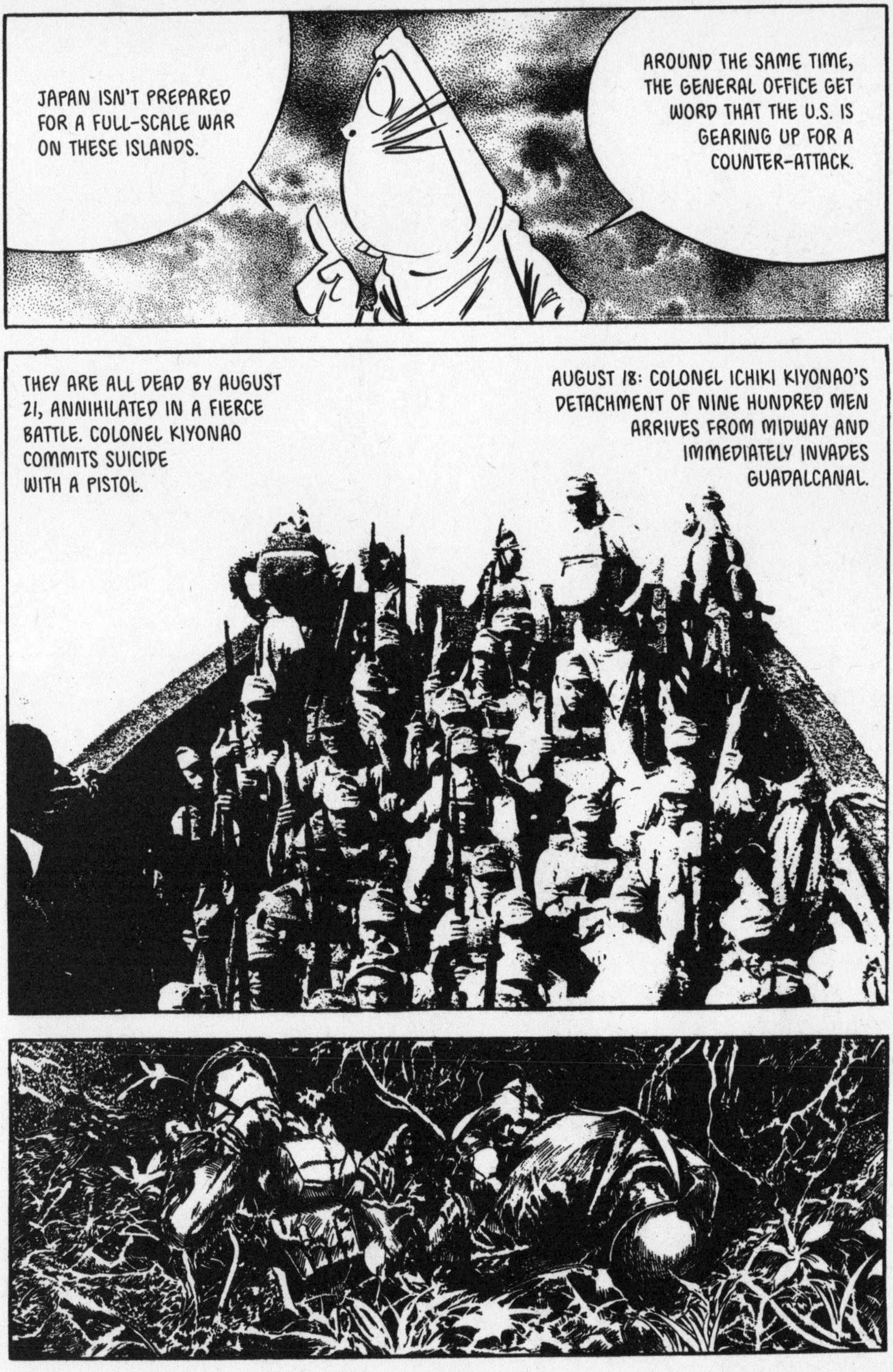
AROUND THE SAME TIME, THE GENERAL OFFICE GET WORD THAT THE U.S. IS GEARING UP FOR A COUNTER-ATTACK.
JAPAN ISN'T PREPARED FOR A FULL-SCALE WAR ON THESE ISLANDS.
AUGUST 18: COLONEL ICHIKI KIYONAO'S DETACHMENT OF NINE HUNDRED MEN ARRIVES FROM MIDWAY AND IMMEDIATELY INVADES GUADALCANAL.
THEY ARE ALL DEAD BY AUGUST 21, ANNIHILATED IN A FIERCE BATTLE. COLONEL KIYONAO COMMITS SUICIDE WITH A PISTOL.

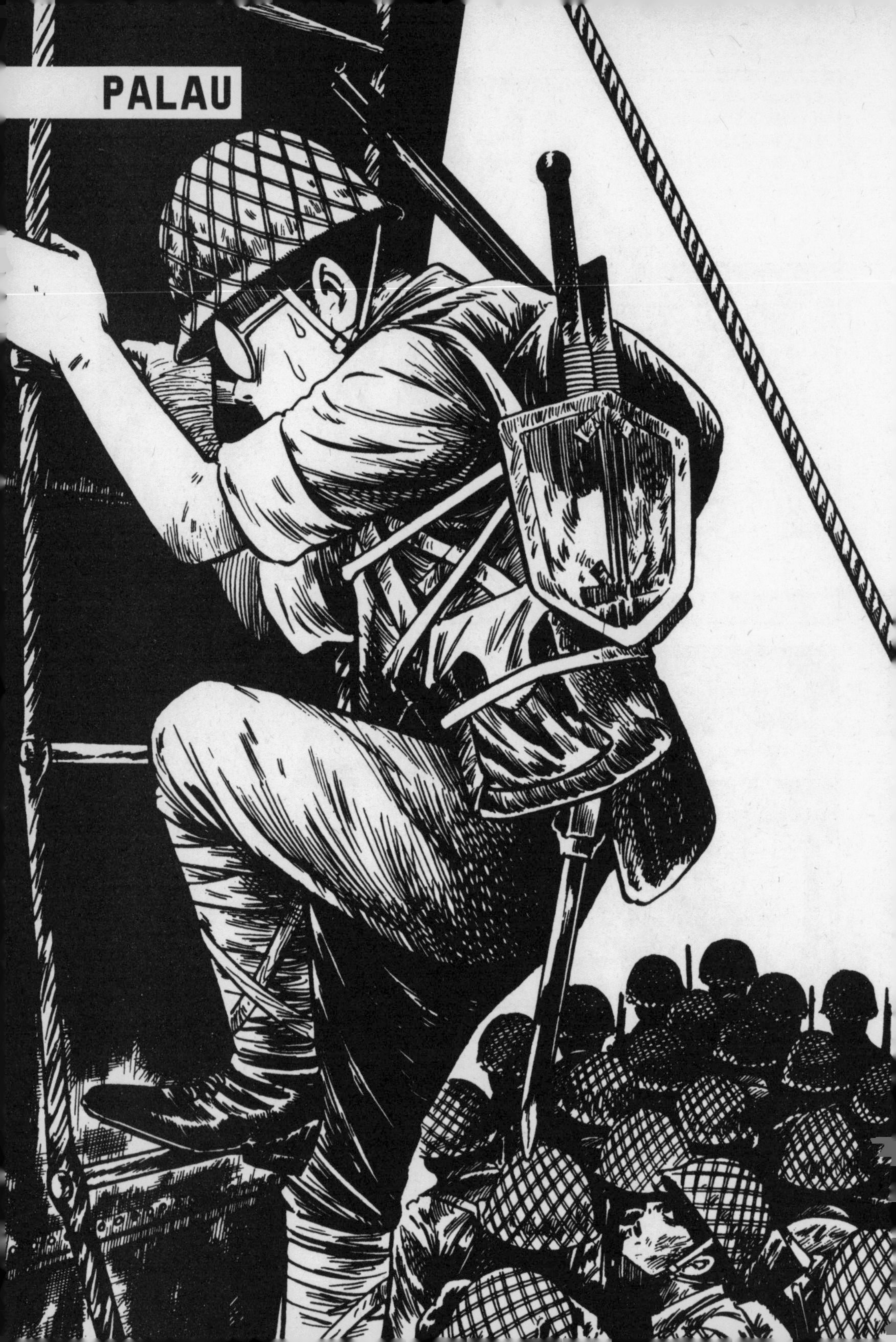
PALAU

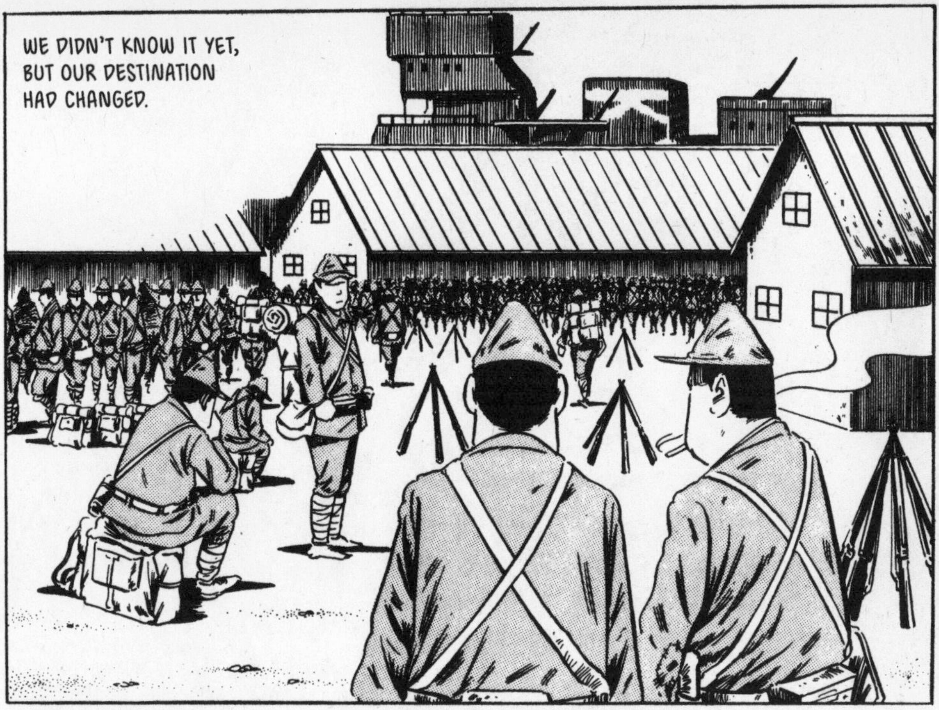
WE DIDN'T KNOW IT YET, BUT OUR DESTINATION HAD CHANGED.

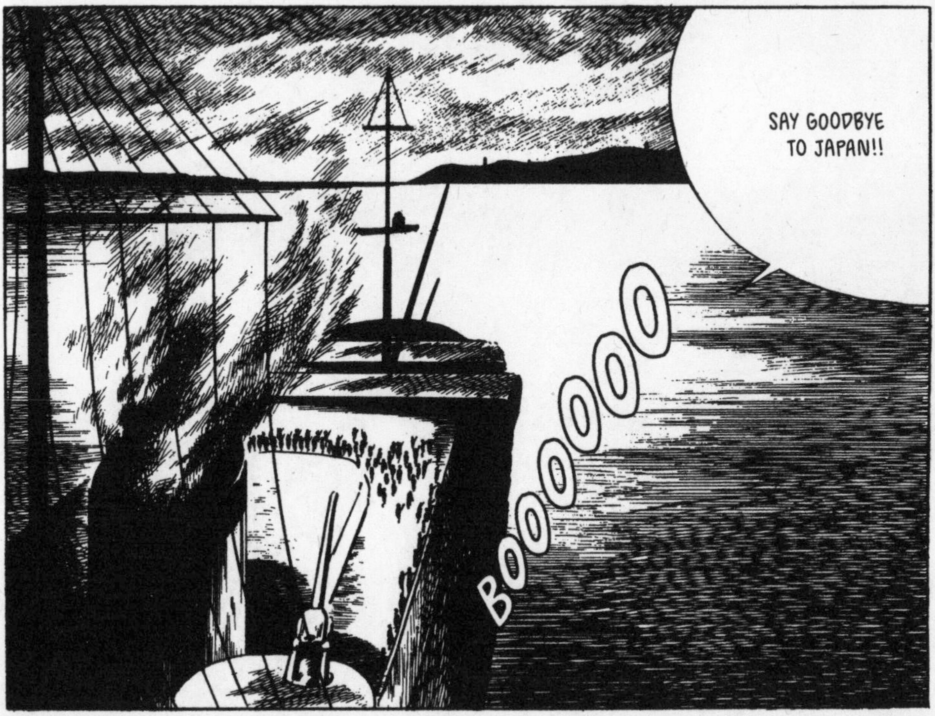
SAY GOODBYE TO JAPAN!!
BOOOOOO

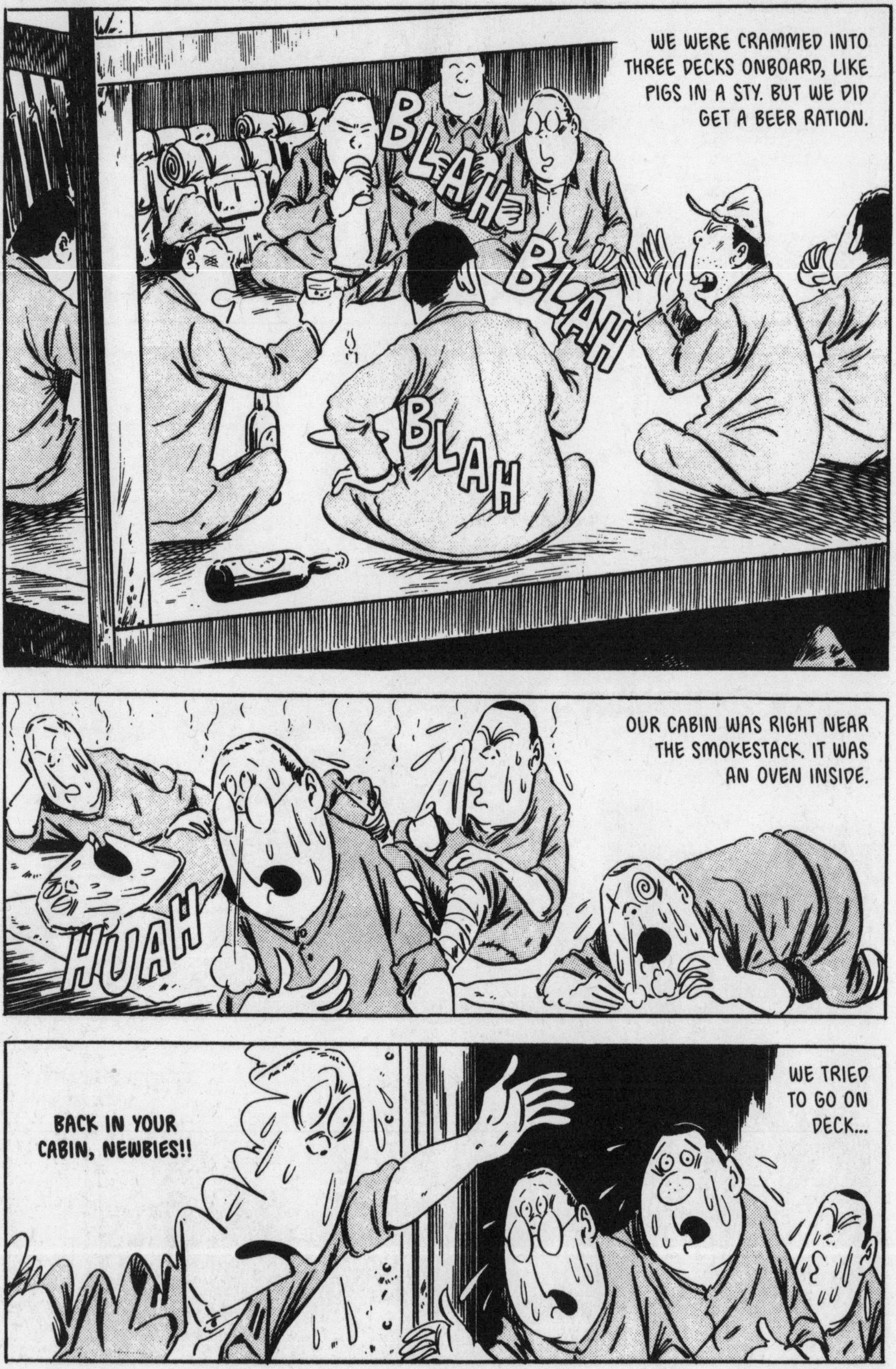
WE WERE CRAMMED INTO THREE DECKS ONBOARD, LIKE PIGS IN A STY. BUT WE DID GET A BEER RATION.
BLAH
BLAH
BLAH
OUR CABIN WAS RIGHT NEAR THE SMOKESTACK. IT WAS AN OVEN INSIDE.
HUAH
WE TRIED TO GO ON DECK...
BACK IN YOUR CABIN, NEWBIES!!

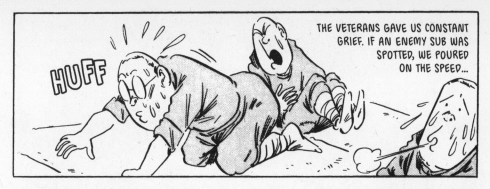

THE VETERANS GAVE US CONSTANT GRIEF. IF AN ENEMY SUB WAS SPOTTED, WE POURED ON THE SPEED...

HUFF

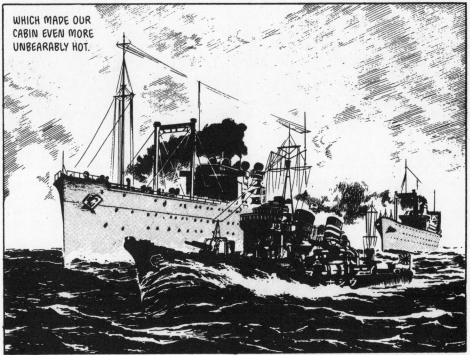

WHICH MADE OUR CABIN EVEN MORE UNBEARABLY HOT.

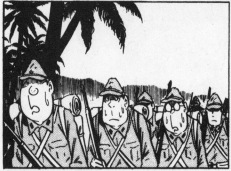

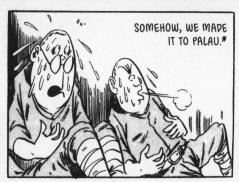

SOMEHOW, WE MADE IT TO PALAU.*

*SEE NOTE ON PAGE 547.

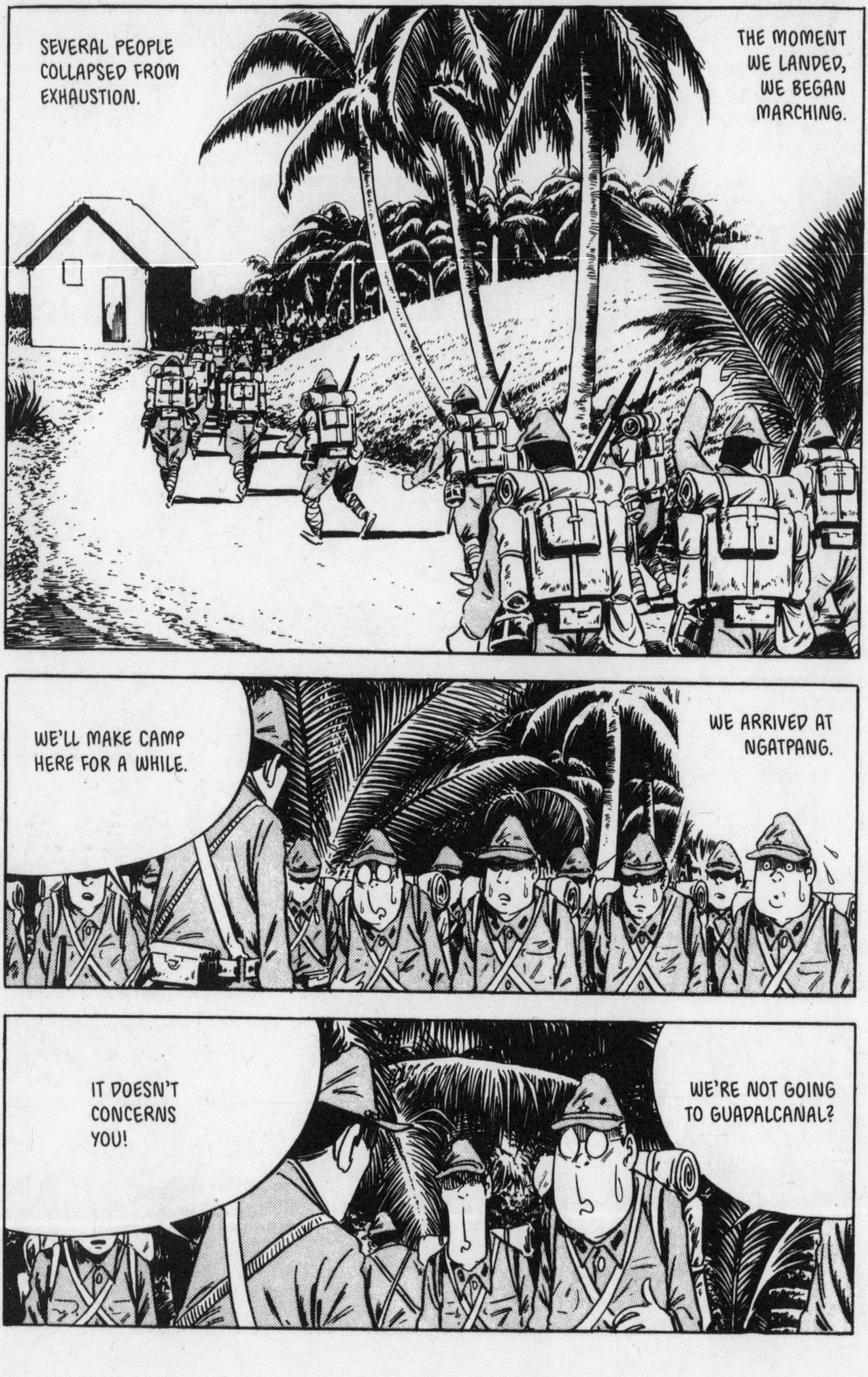
THE MOMENT WE LANDED, WE BEGAN MARCHING.
SEVERAL PEOPLE COLLAPSED FROM EXHAUSTION.
WE ARRIVED AT NGATPANG.
WE'LL MAKE CAMP HERE FOR A WHILE.
WE'RE NOT GOING TO GUADALCANAL?
IT DOESN'T CONCERNS YOU!

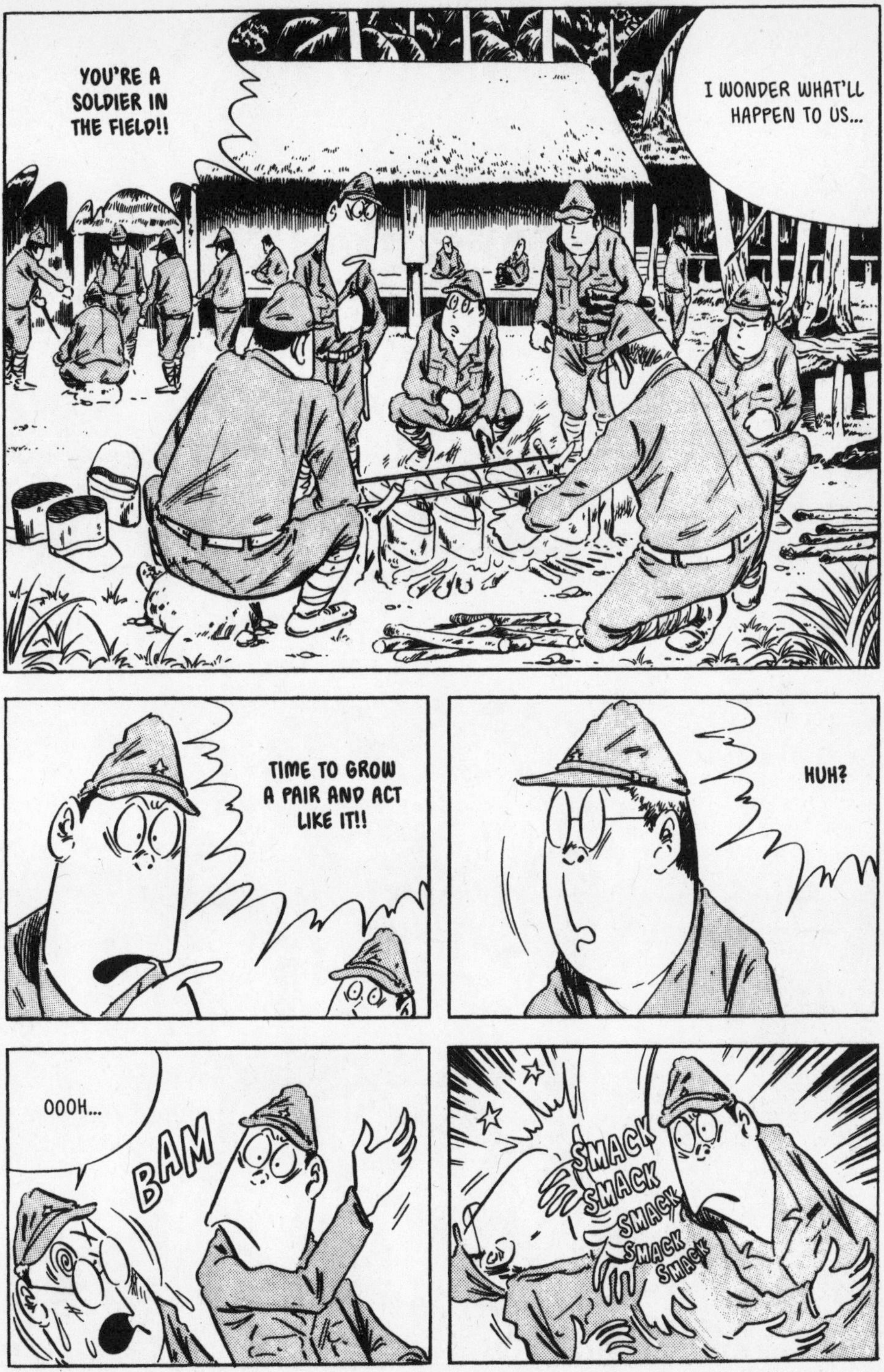
I WONDER WHAT'LL HAPPEN TO US...
YOU'RE A SOLDIER IN THE FIELD!!
HUH?
TIME TO GROW A PAIR AND ACT LIKE IT!!
SMACK
SMACK
SMACK
SMACK
SMACK
BAM
OOOH...

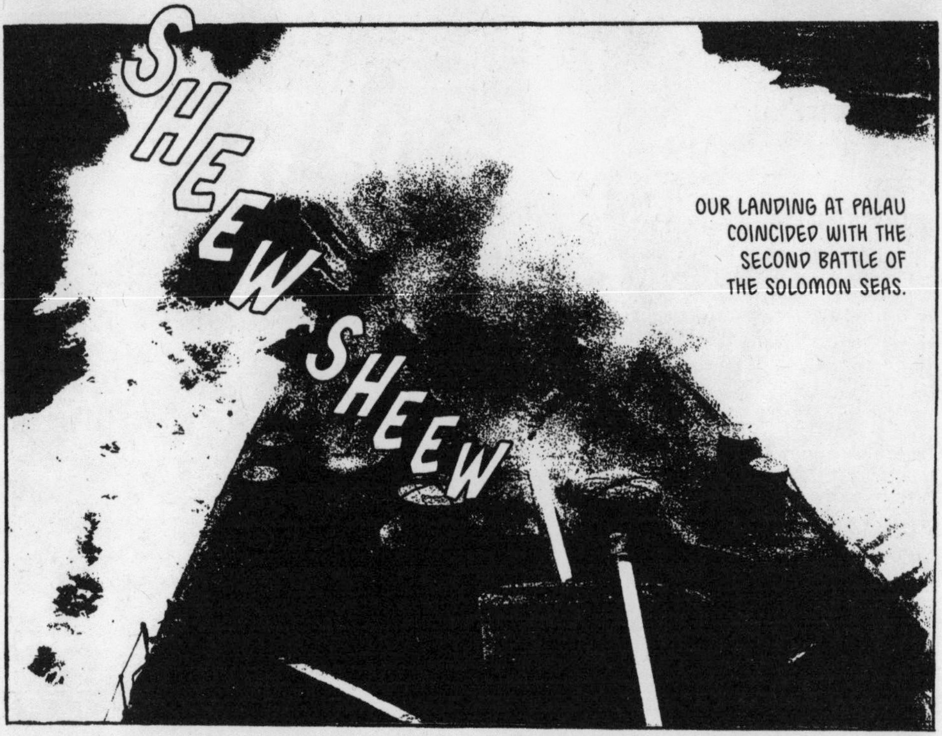
SHEEW SHEEW
OUR LANDING AT PALAU COINCIDED WITH THE SECOND BATTLE OF THE SOLOMON SEAS.

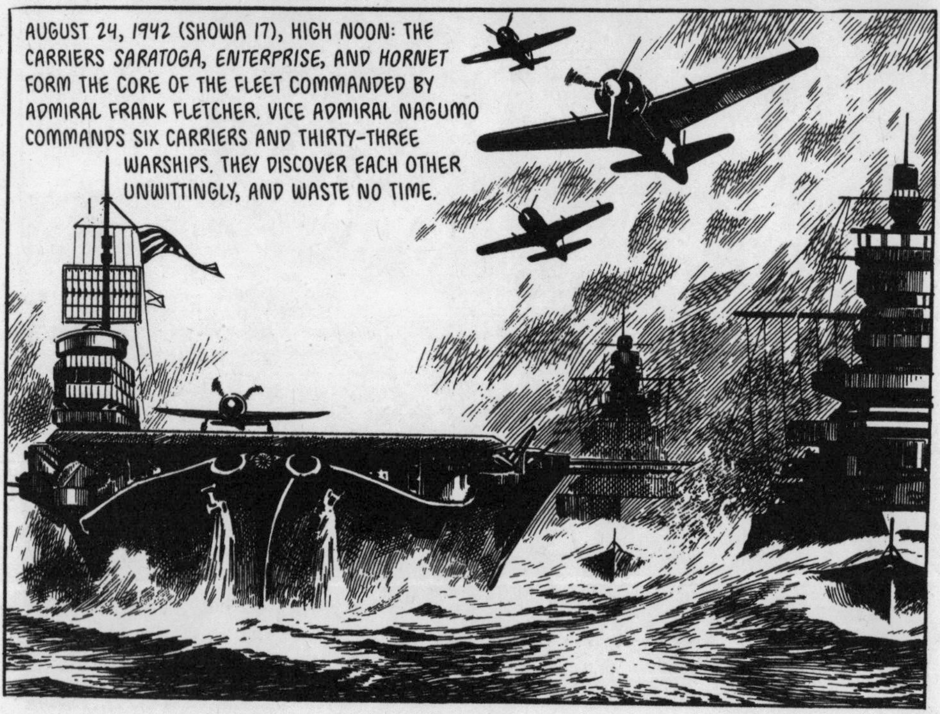
AUGUST 24, 1942 (SHOWA 17), HIGH NOON: THE CARRIERS *SARATOGA*, *ENTERPRISE*, AND *HORNET* FORM THE CORE OF THE FLEET COMMANDED BY ADMIRAL FRANK FLETCHER. VICE ADMIRAL NAGUMO COMMANDS SIX CARRIERS AND THIRTY-THREE WARSHIPS. THEY DISCOVER EACH OTHER UNWITTINGLY, AND WASTE NO TIME.

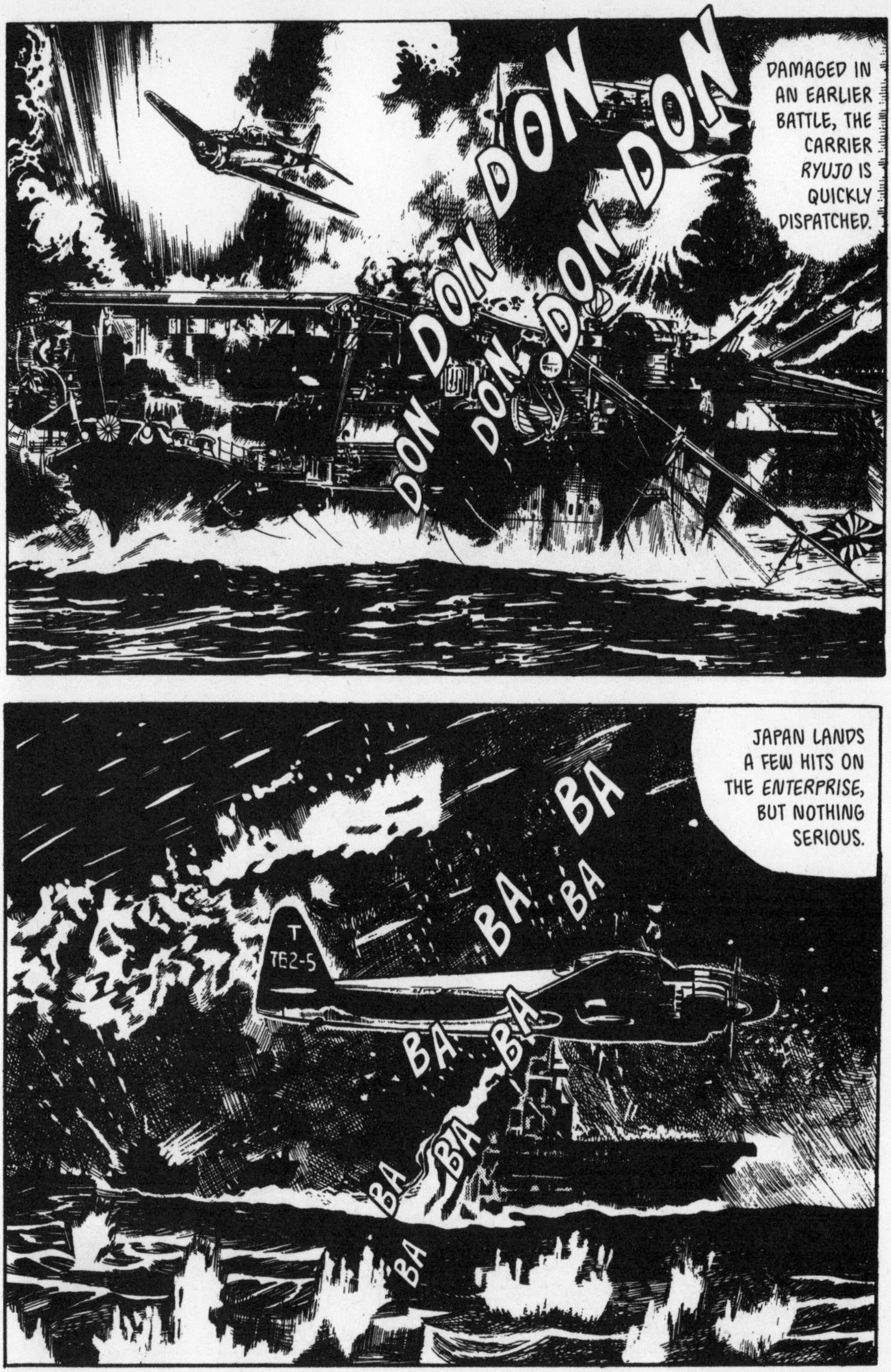
DAMAGED IN AN EARLIER BATTLE, THE CARRIER *RYUJO* IS QUICKLY DISPATCHED.
DON DON DON
DON DON DON
JAPAN LANDS A FEW HITS ON THE *ENTERPRISE*, BUT NOTHING SERIOUS.
BA BA BA BA
BA BA BA
BA BA BA

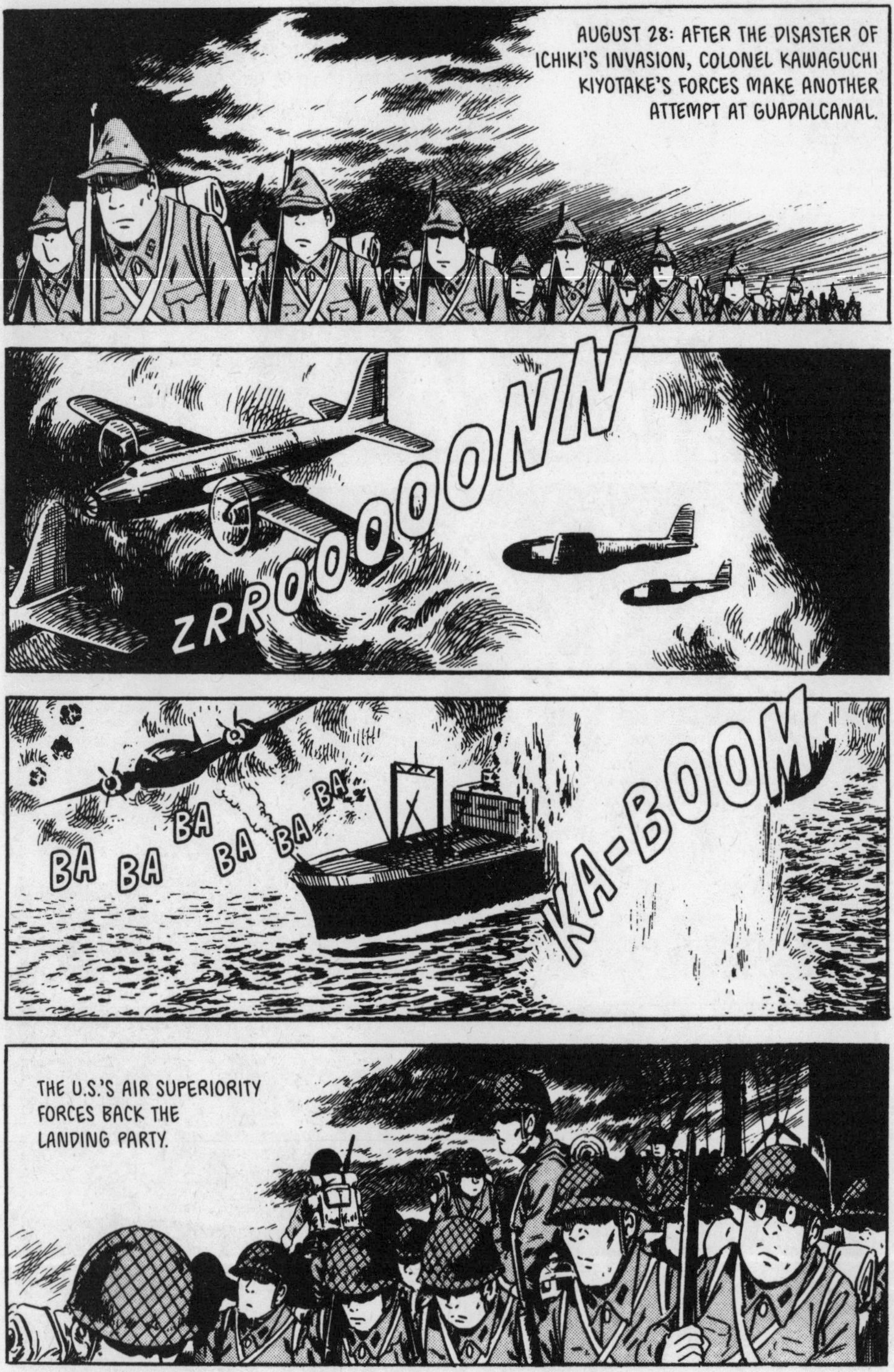
AUGUST 28: AFTER THE DISASTER OF ICHIKI'S INVASION, COLONEL KAWAGUCHI KIYOTAKE'S FORCES MAKE ANOTHER ATTEMPT AT GUADALCANAL.
ZRROOOOOONN
KA-BOOM
BA BA BA BA BA BA
THE U.S.'S AIR SUPERIORITY FORCES BACK THE LANDING PARTY.

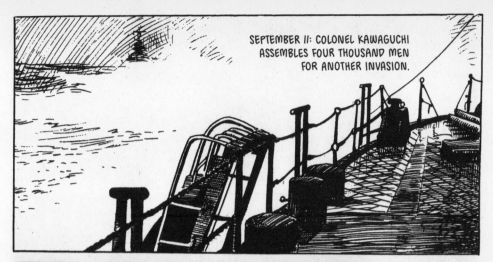

SEPTEMBER 11: COLONEL KAWAGUCHI ASSEMBLES FOUR THOUSAND MEN FOR ANOTHER INVASION.

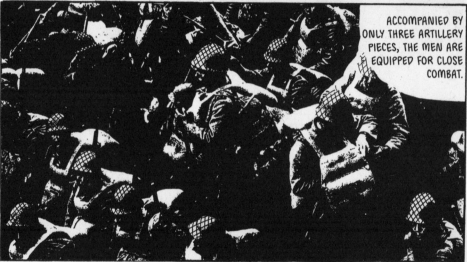

ACCOMPANIED BY ONLY THREE ARTILLERY PIECES, THE MEN ARE EQUIPPED FOR CLOSE COMBAT.

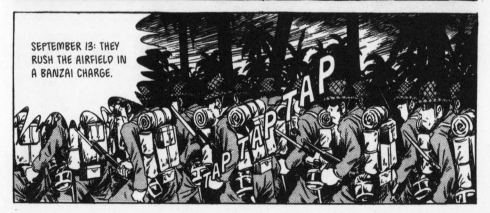

SEPTEMBER 13: THEY RUSH THE AIRFIELD IN A BANZAI CHARGE.

TAP TAP TAP TAP

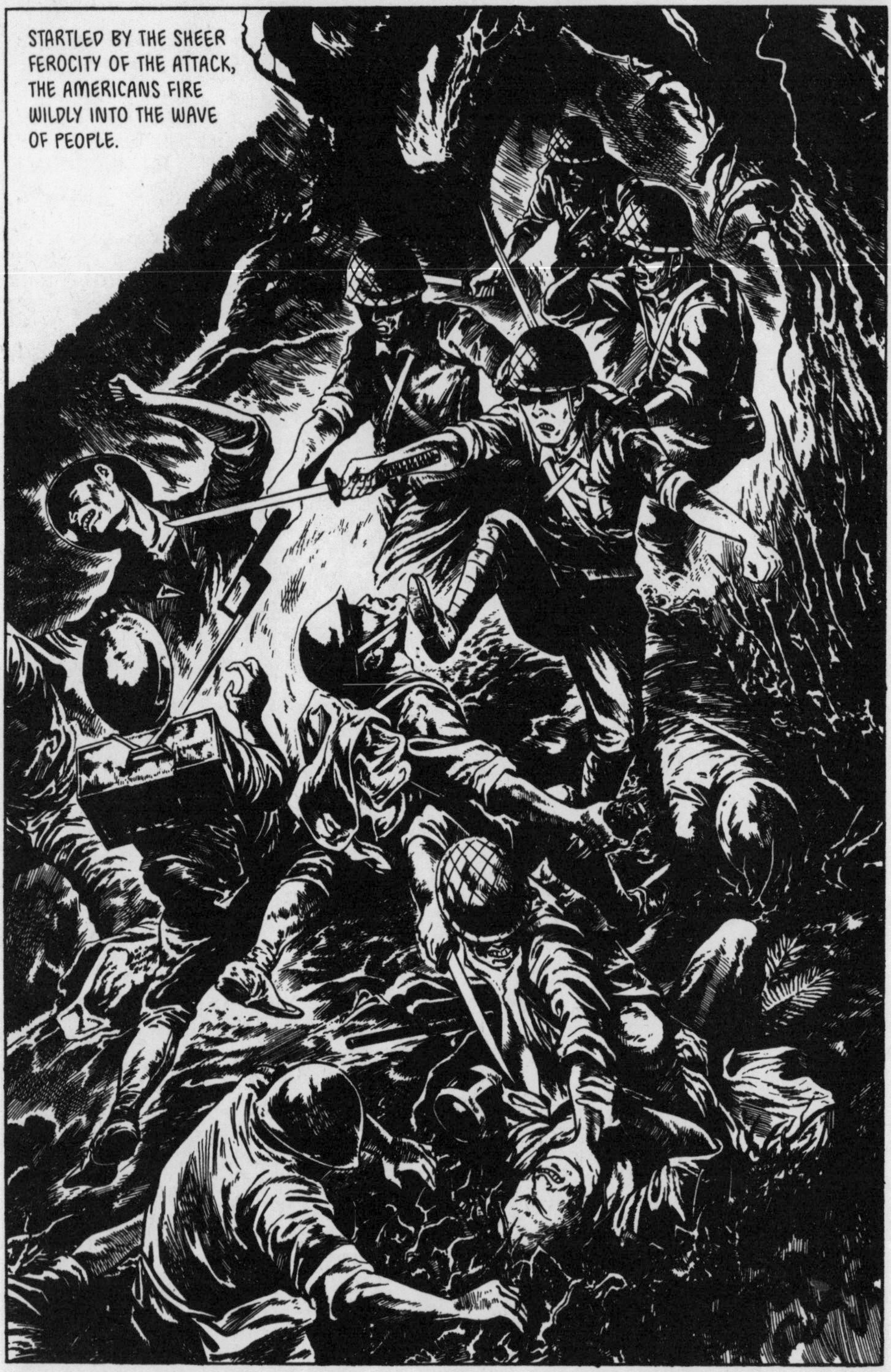
STARTLED BY THE SHEER FEROCITY OF THE ATTACK, THE AMERICANS FIRE WILDLY INTO THE WAVE OF PEOPLE.

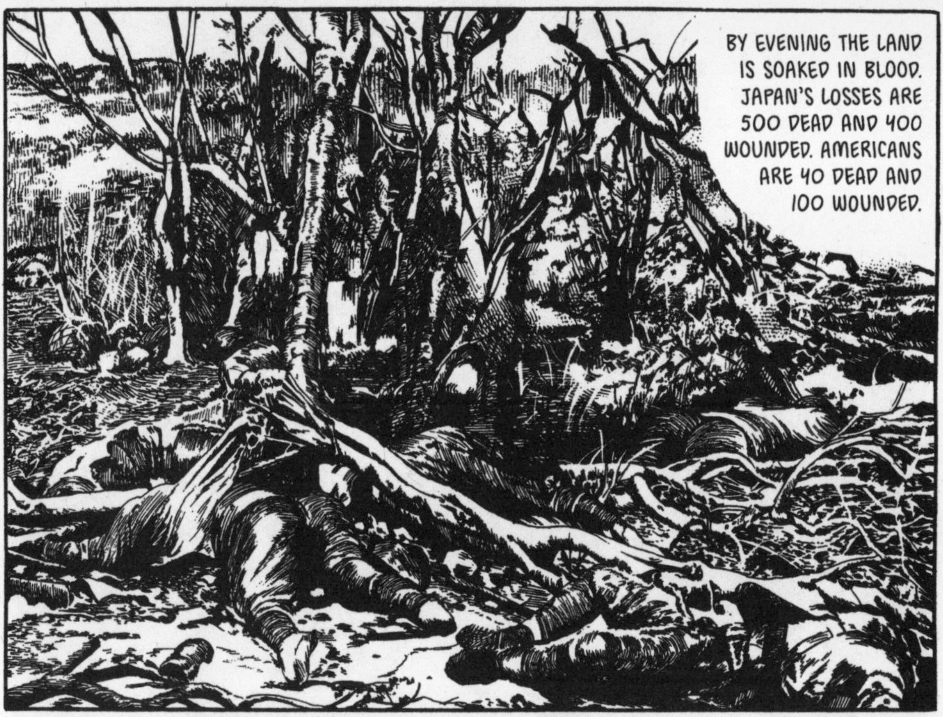
BY EVENING THE LAND IS SOAKED IN BLOOD. JAPAN'S LOSSES ARE 500 DEAD AND 400 WOUNDED. AMERICANS ARE 40 DEAD AND 100 WOUNDED.

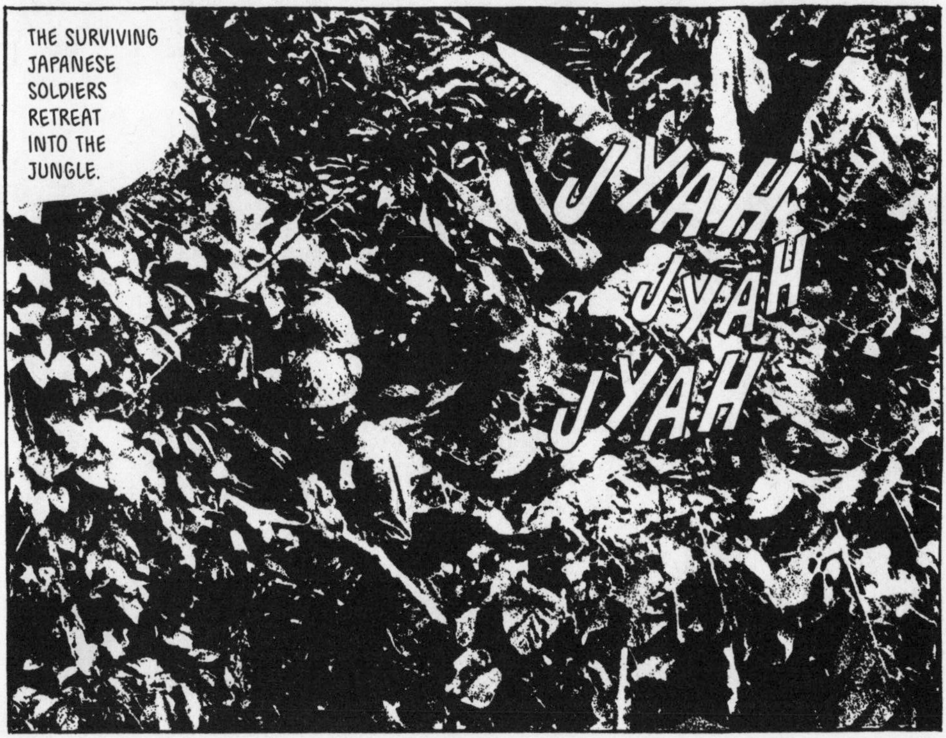
THE SURVIVING JAPANESE SOLDIERS RETREAT INTO THE JUNGLE.
JYAH
JYAH
JYAH

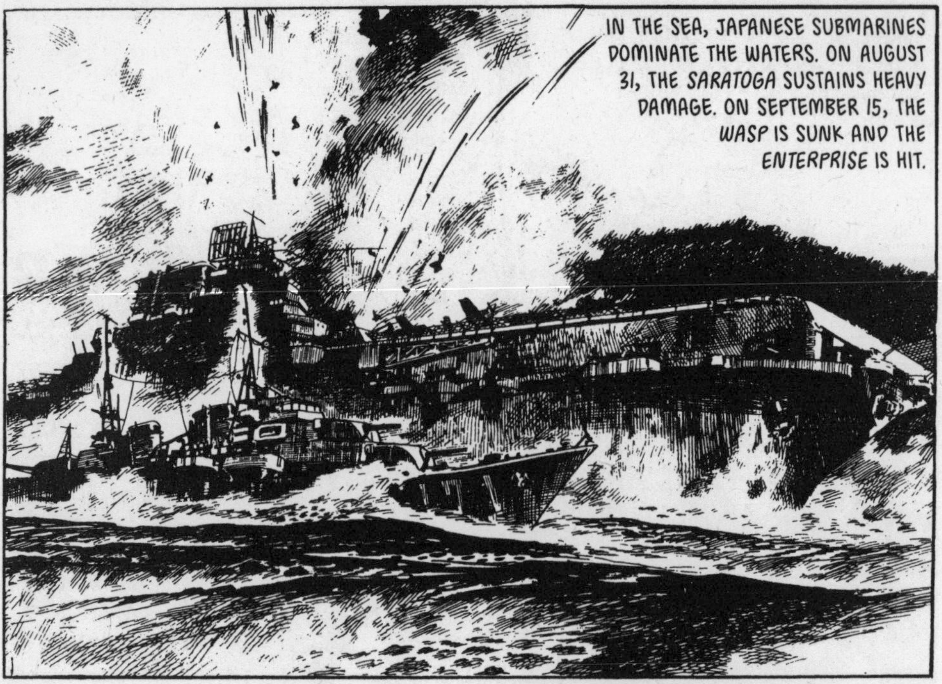
IN THE SEA, JAPANESE SUBMARINES DOMINATE THE WATERS. ON AUGUST 31, THE *SARATOGA* SUSTAINS HEAVY DAMAGE. ON SEPTEMBER 15, THE *WASP* IS SUNK AND THE *ENTERPRISE* IS HIT.

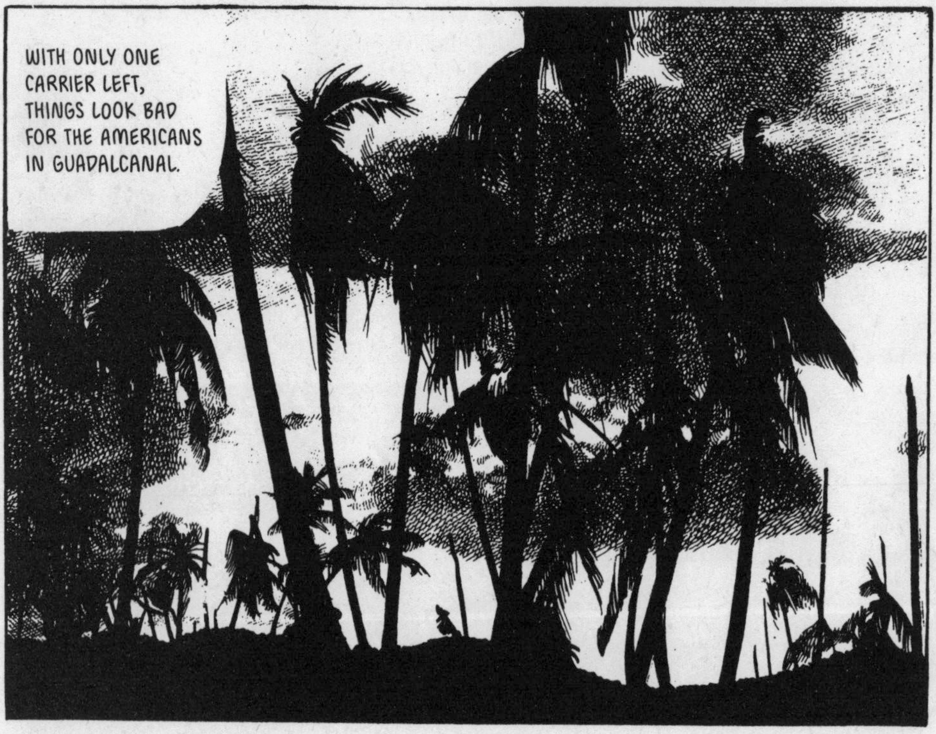
WITH ONLY ONE CARRIER LEFT, THINGS LOOK BAD FOR THE AMERICANS IN GUADALCANAL.

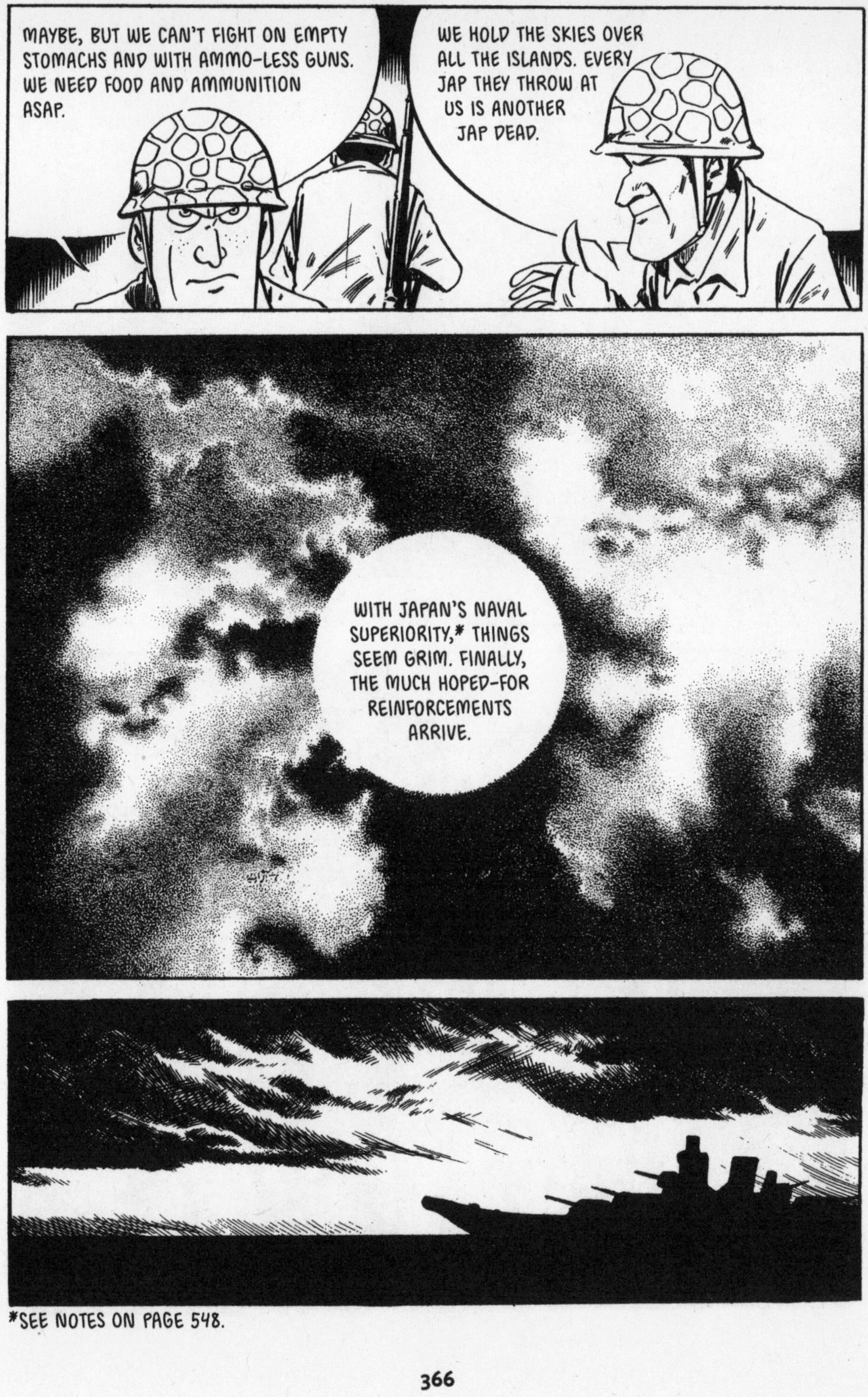
WE HOLD THE SKIES OVER ALL THE ISLANDS. EVERY JAP THEY THROW AT US IS ANOTHER JAP DEAD.
MAYBE, BUT WE CAN'T FIGHT ON EMPTY STOMACHS AND WITH AMMO-LESS GUNS. WE NEED FOOD AND AMMUNITION ASAP.
WITH JAPAN'S NAVAL SUPERIORITY,* THINGS SEEM GRIM. FINALLY, THE MUCH HOPED-FOR REINFORCEMENTS ARRIVE.

*SEE NOTES ON PAGE 548.

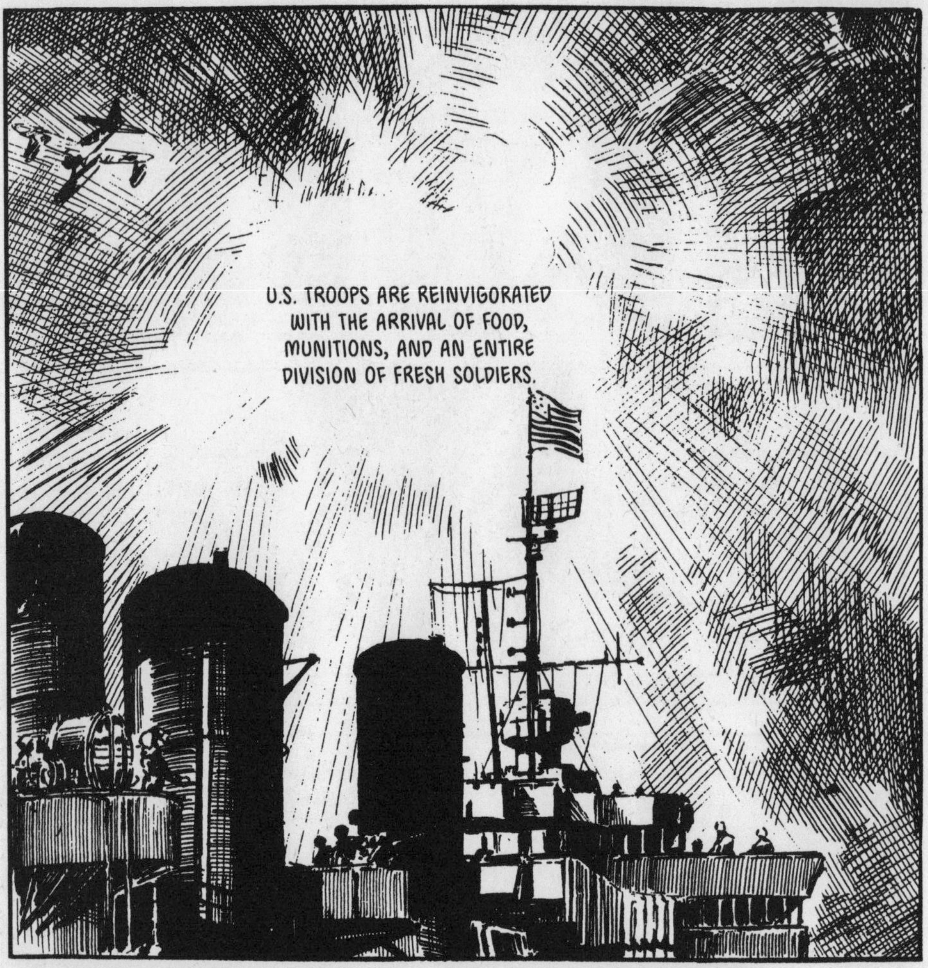
U.S. TROOPS ARE REINVIGORATED WITH THE ARRIVAL OF FOOD, MUNITIONS, AND AN ENTIRE DIVISION OF FRESH SOLDIERS.

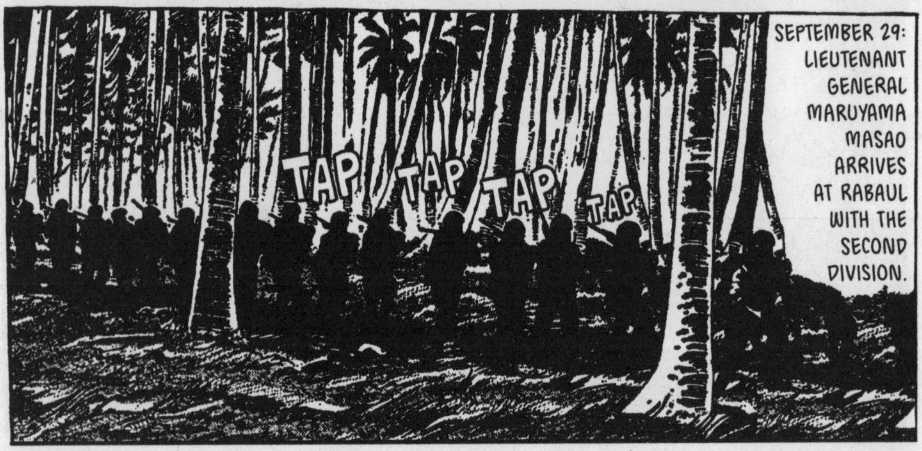
SEPTEMBER 29: LIEUTENANT GENERAL MARUYAMA MASAO ARRIVES AT RABAUL WITH THE SECOND DIVISION.
TAP
TAP
TAP
TAP

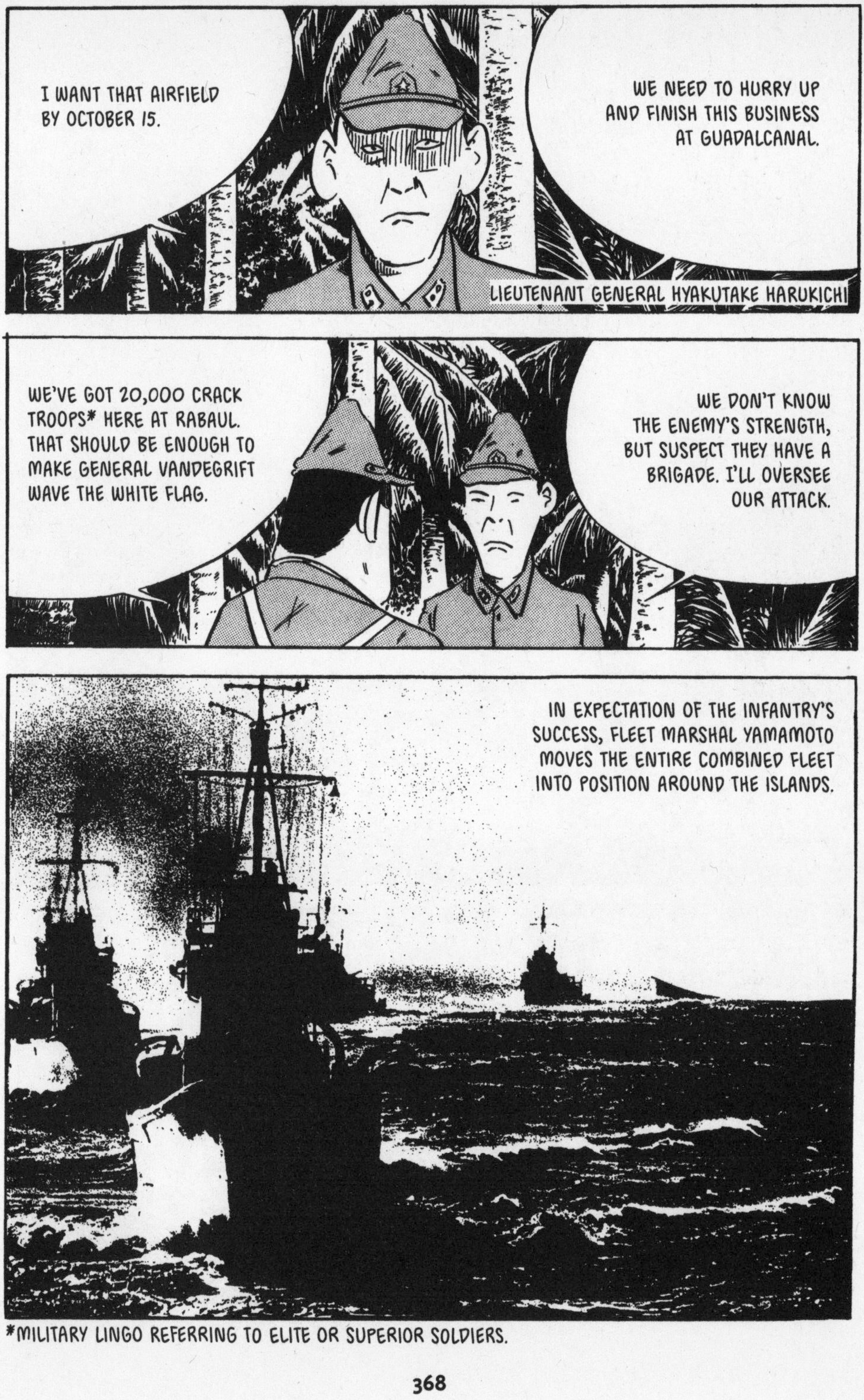
WE NEED TO HURRY UP AND FINISH THIS BUSINESS AT GUADALCANAL.
I WANT THAT AIRFIELD BY OCTOBER 15.
LIEUTENANT GENERAL HYAKUTAKE HARUKICHI
WE DON'T KNOW THE ENEMY'S STRENGTH, BUT SUSPECT THEY HAVE A BRIGADE. I'LL OVERSEE OUR ATTACK.
WE'VE GOT 20,000 CRACK TROOPS* HERE AT RABAUL. THAT SHOULD BE ENOUGH TO MAKE GENERAL VANDEGRIFT WAVE THE WHITE FLAG.
IN EXPECTATION OF THE INFANTRY'S SUCCESS, FLEET MARSHAL YAMAMOTO MOVES THE ENTIRE COMBINED FLEET INTO POSITION AROUND THE ISLANDS.

*MILITARY LINGO REFERRING TO ELITE OR SUPERIOR SOLDIERS.

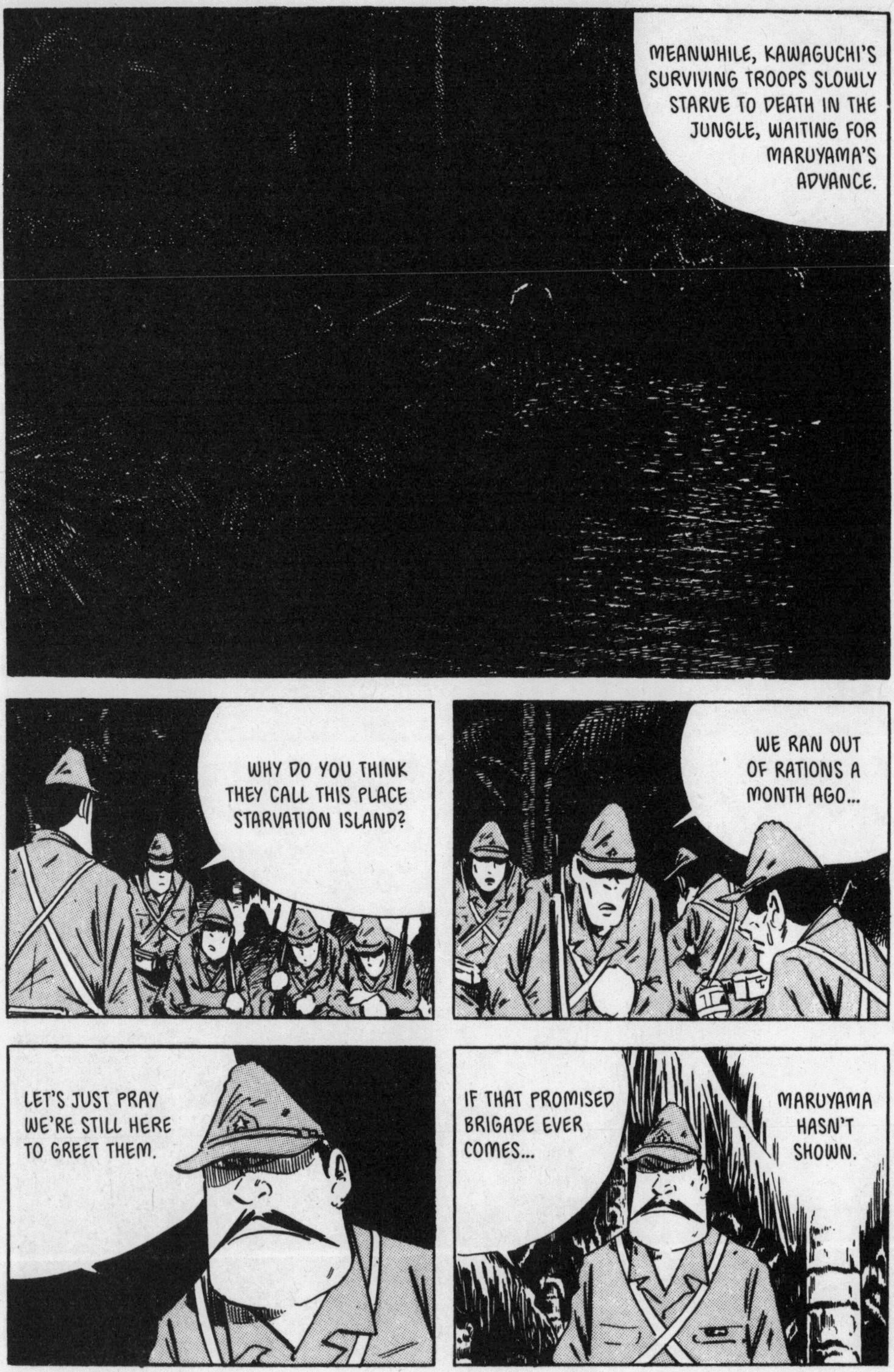
MEANWHILE, KAWAGUCHI'S SURVIVING TROOPS SLOWLY STARVE TO DEATH IN THE JUNGLE, WAITING FOR MARUYAMA'S ADVANCE.
WE RAN OUT OF RATIONS A MONTH AGO...
WHY DO YOU THINK THEY CALL THIS PLACE STARVATION ISLAND?
MARUYAMA HASN'T SHOWN.
IF THAT PROMISED BRIGADE EVER COMES...
LET'S JUST PRAY WE'RE STILL HERE TO GREET THEM.

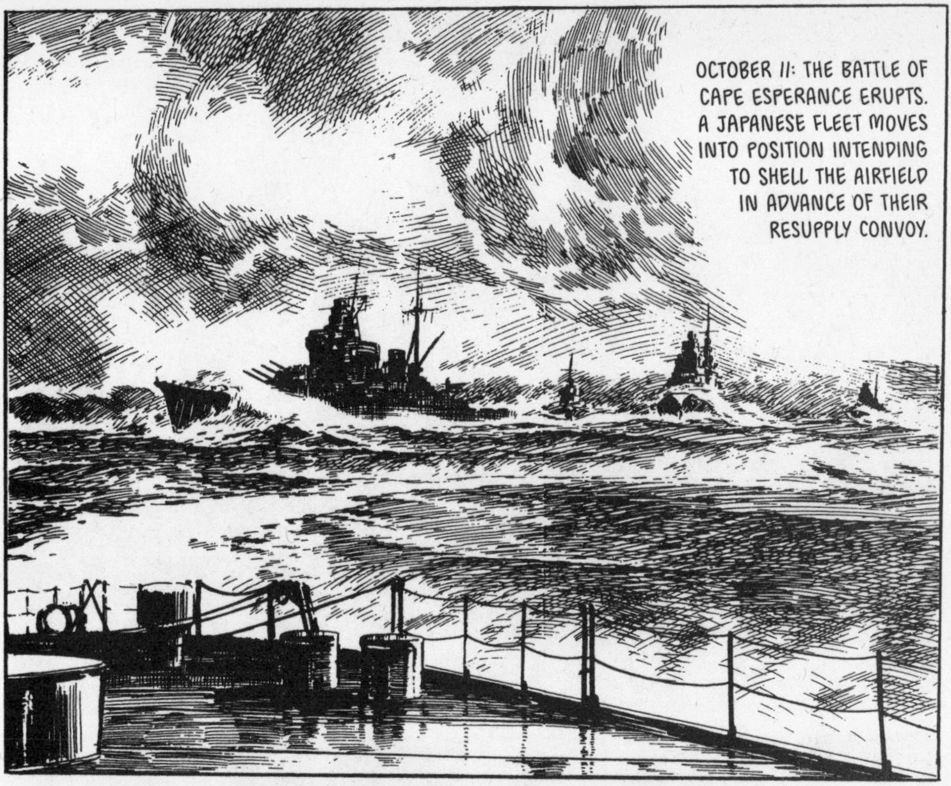
OCTOBER 11: THE BATTLE OF CAPE ESPERANCE ERUPTS. A JAPANESE FLEET MOVES INTO POSITION INTENDING TO SHELL THE AIRFIELD IN ADVANCE OF THEIR RESUPPLY CONVOY.

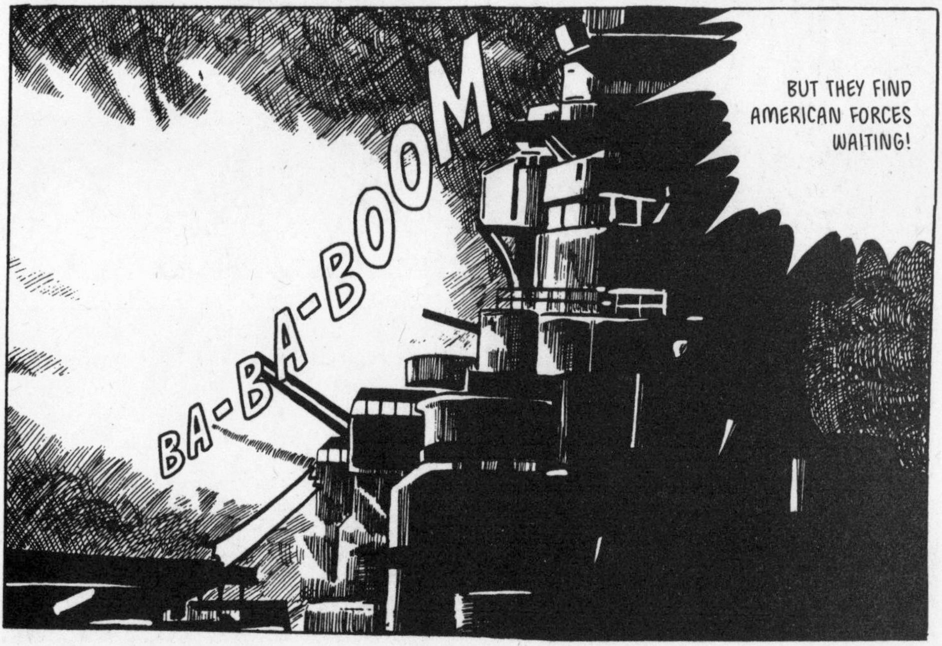
BUT THEY FIND AMERICAN FORCES WAITING!
BA-BA-BOOOM

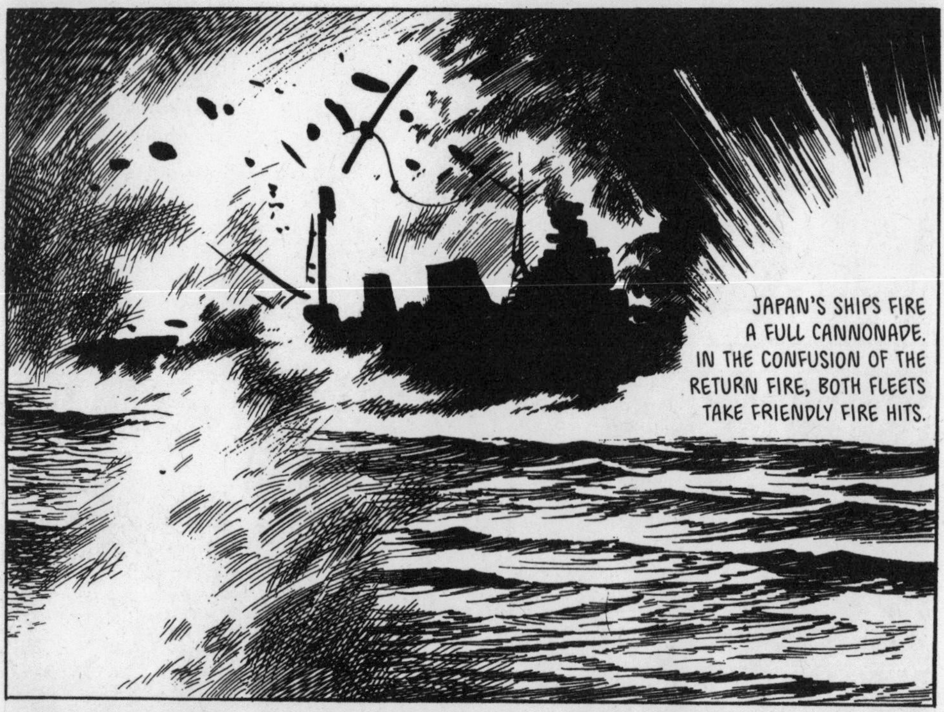
JAPAN'S SHIPS FIRE A FULL CANNONADE. IN THE CONFUSION OF THE RETURN FIRE, BOTH FLEETS TAKE FRIENDLY FIRE HITS.

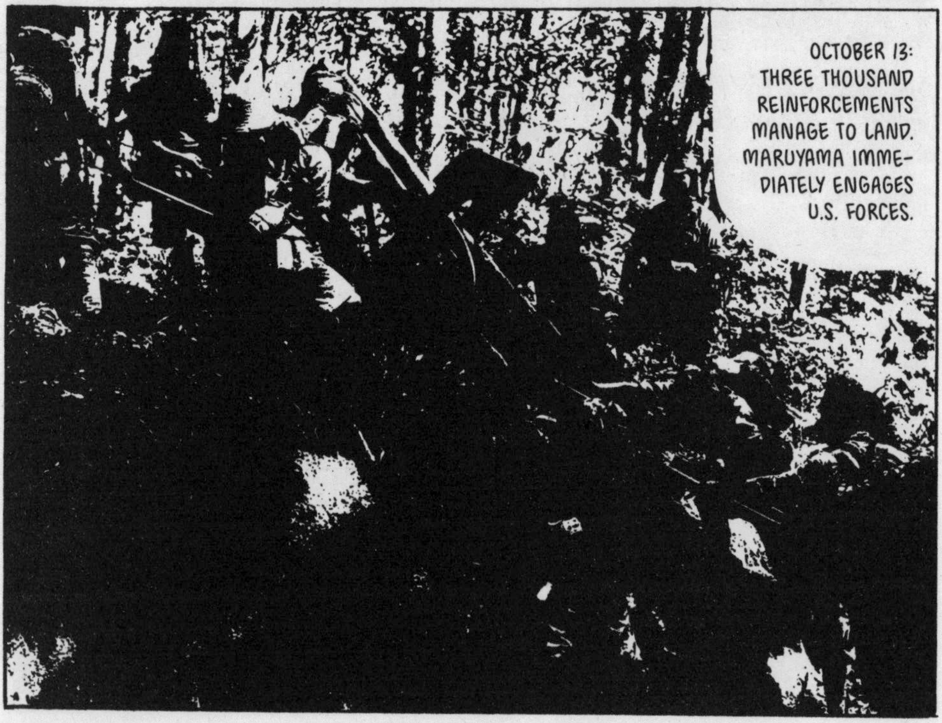
OCTOBER 13: THREE THOUSAND REINFORCEMENTS MANAGE TO LAND. MARUYAMA IMMEDIATELY ENGAGES U.S. FORCES.

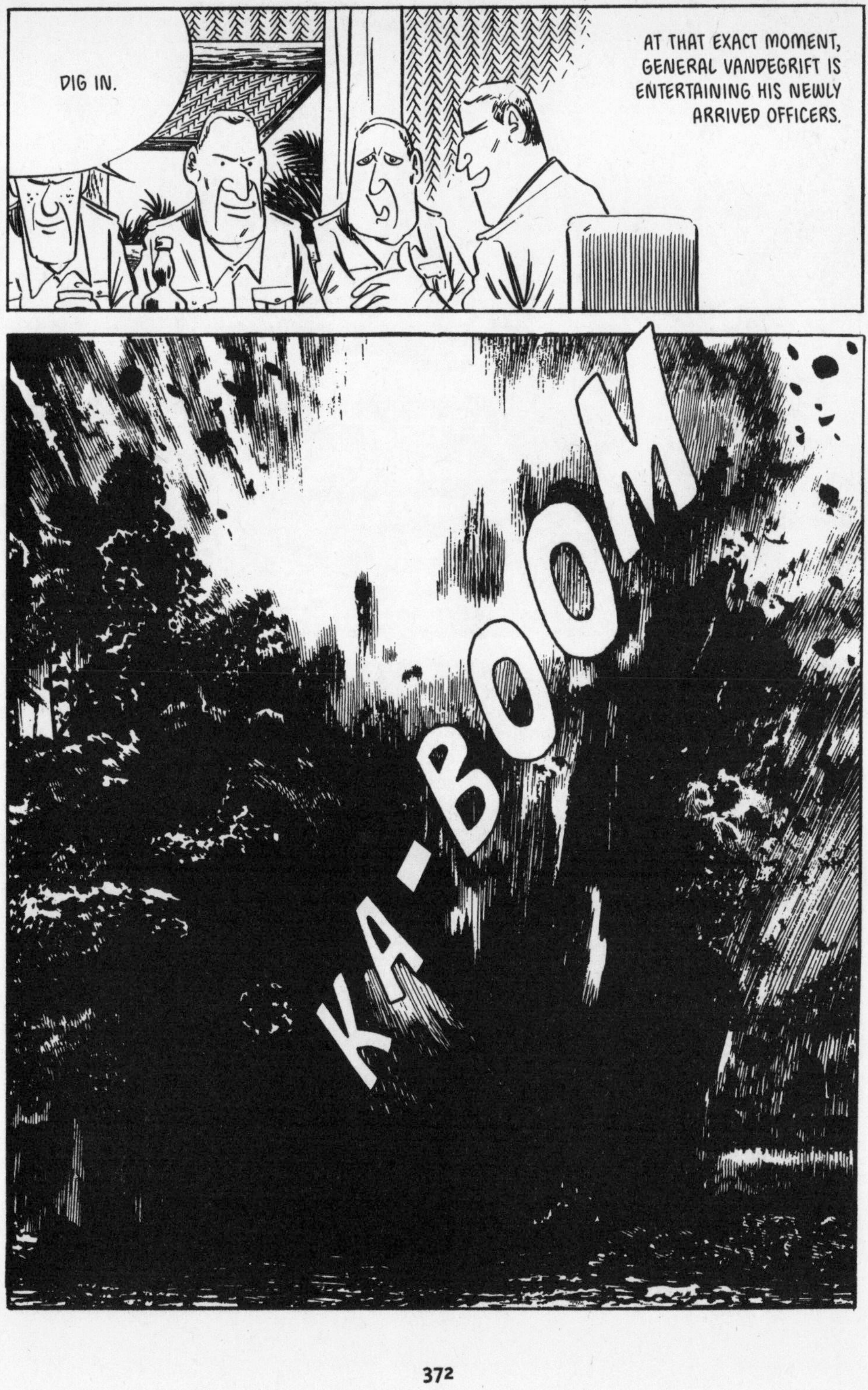
AT THAT EXACT MOMENT, GENERAL VANDEGRIFT IS ENTERTAINING HIS NEWLY ARRIVED OFFICERS.
DIG IN.
KA-BOOM

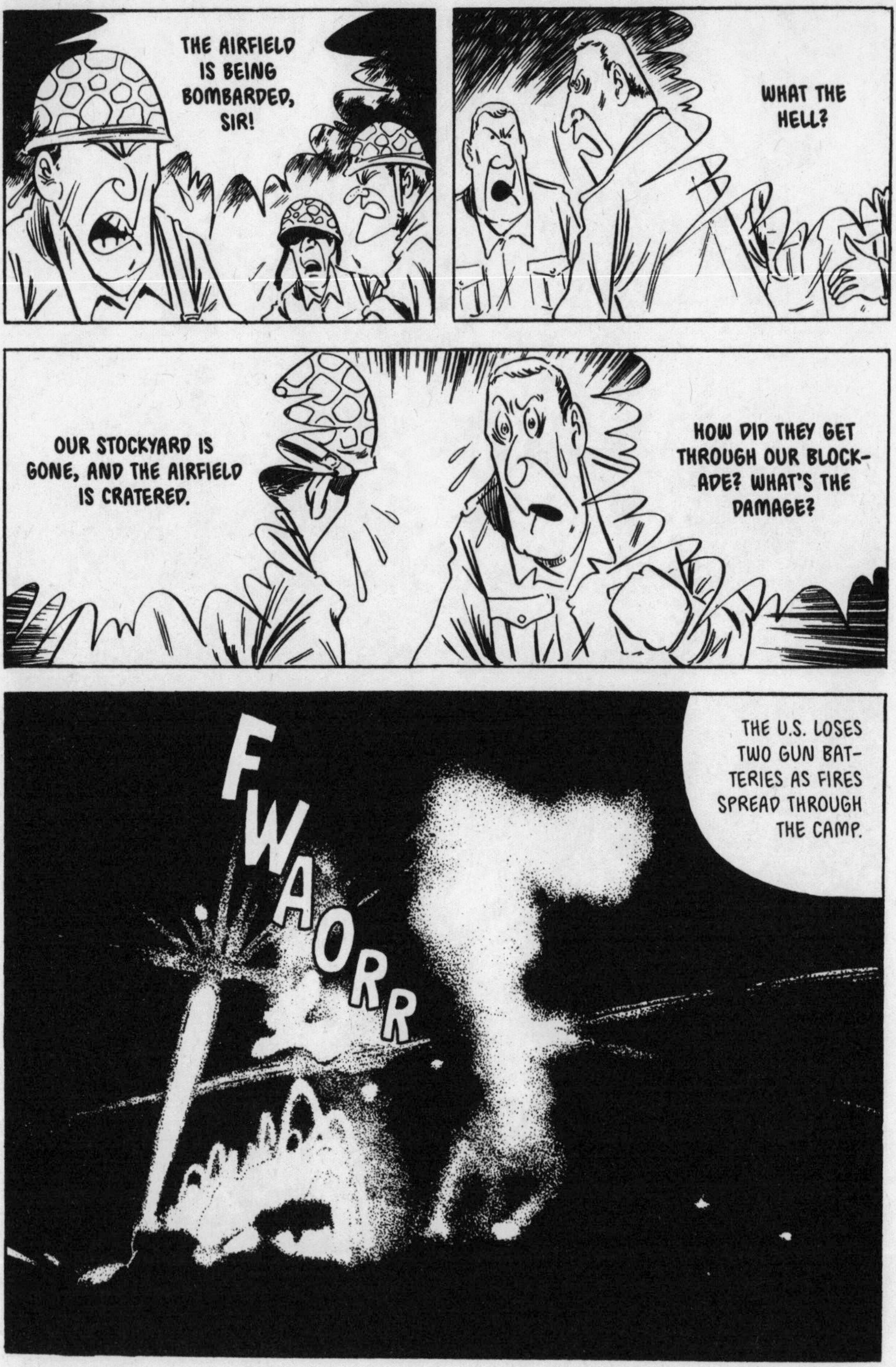
WHAT THE HELL?
THE AIRFIELD IS BEING BOMBARDED, SIR!
HOW DID THEY GET THROUGH OUR BLOCK-ADE? WHAT'S THE DAMAGE?
OUR STOCKYARD IS GONE, AND THE AIRFIELD IS CRATERED.
THE U.S. LOSES TWO GUN BAT-TERIES AS FIRES SPREAD THROUGH THE CAMP.
FWAORR

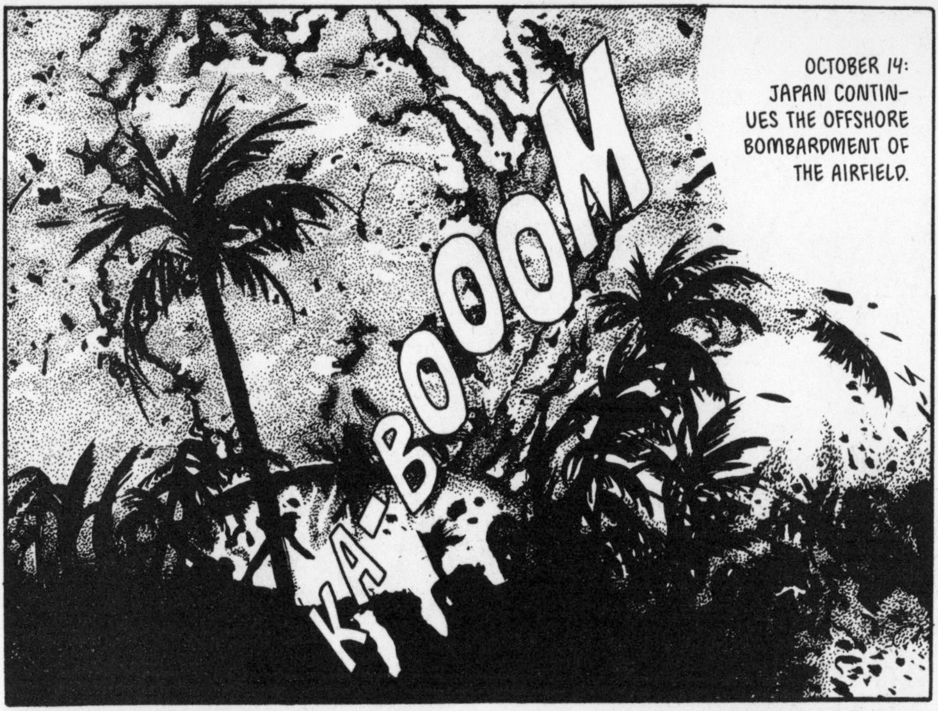
OCTOBER 14: JAPAN CONTINUES THE OFFSHORE BOMBARDMENT OF THE AIRFIELD.
KA-BOOOM
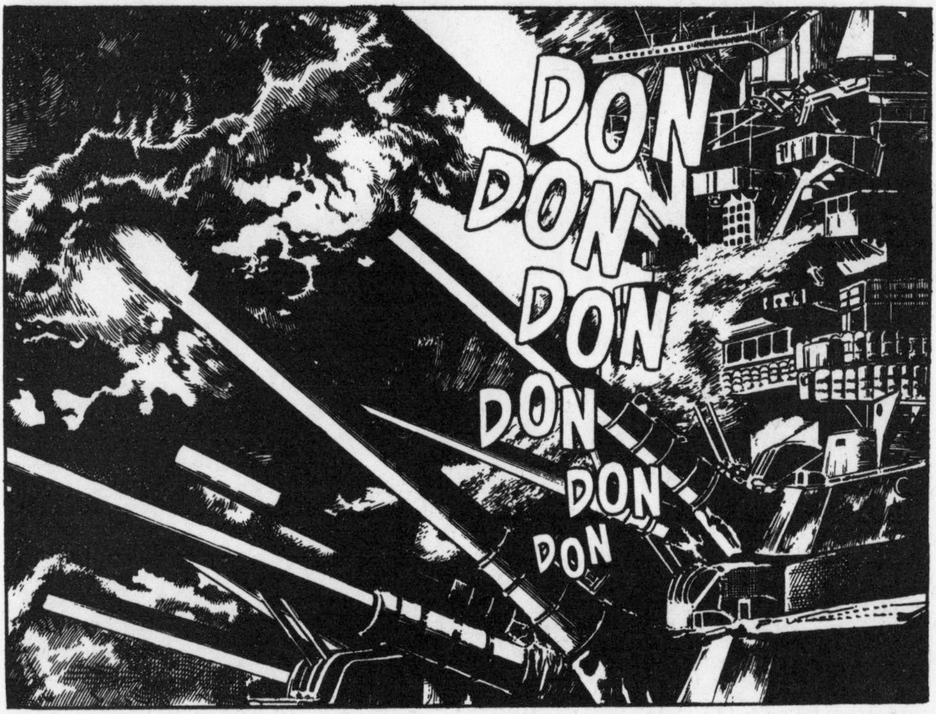
DON DON DON DON DON DON

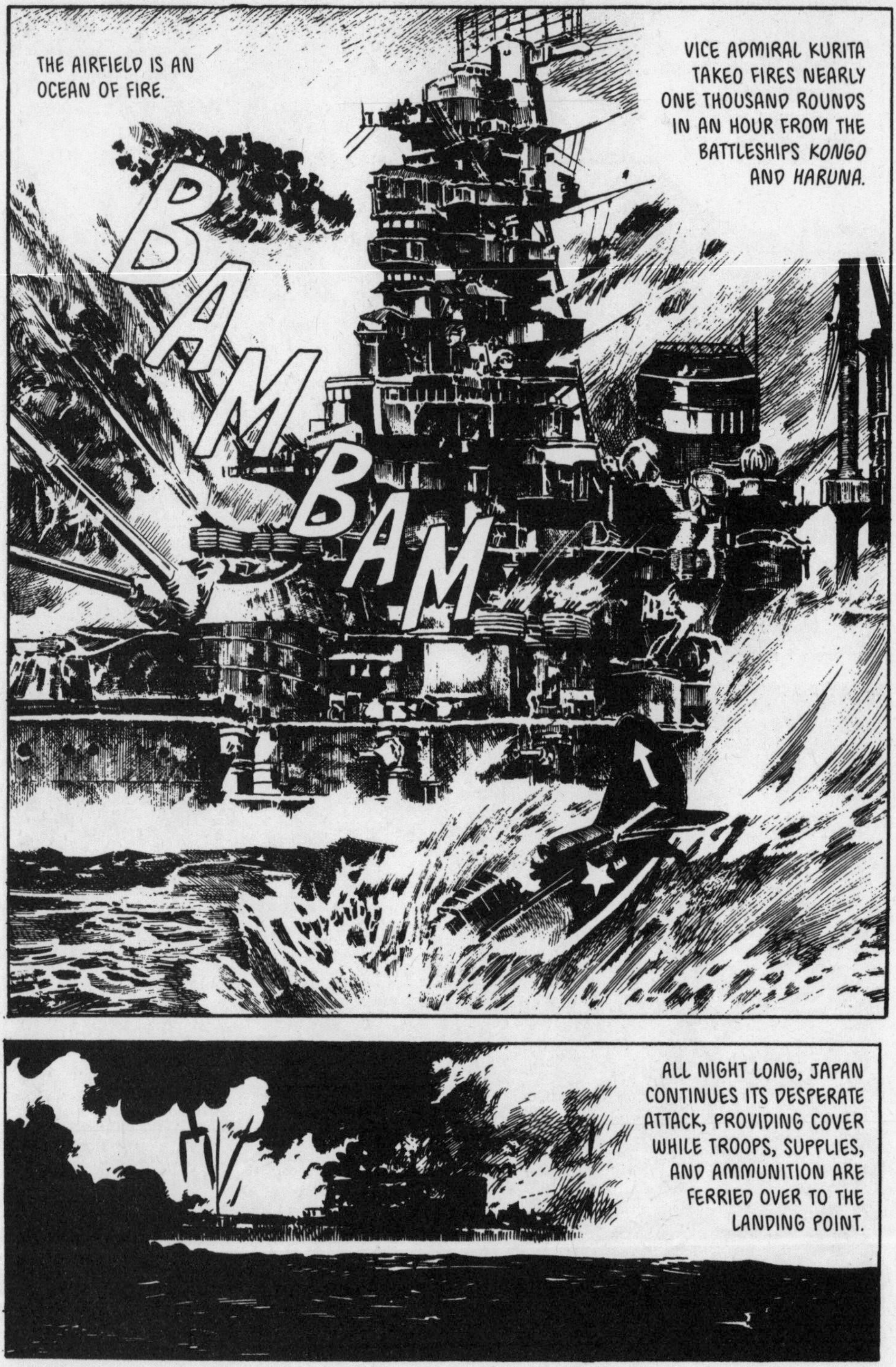
VICE ADMIRAL KURITA TAKEO FIRES NEARLY ONE THOUSAND ROUNDS IN AN HOUR FROM THE BATTLESHIPS *KONGO* AND *HARUNA*.
THE AIRFIELD IS AN OCEAN OF FIRE.
BAM BAM BAM BAM
ALL NIGHT LONG, JAPAN CONTINUES ITS DESPERATE ATTACK, PROVIDING COVER WHILE TROOPS, SUPPLIES, AND AMMUNITION ARE FERRIED OVER TO THE LANDING POINT.

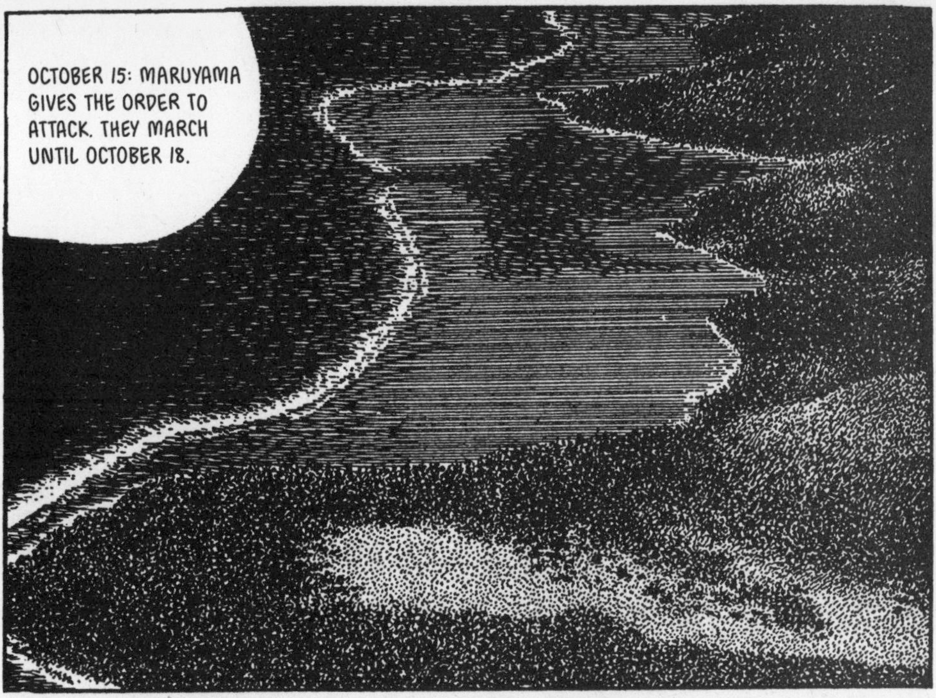
OCTOBER 15: MARUYAMA GIVES THE ORDER TO ATTACK. THEY MARCH UNTIL OCTOBER 18.
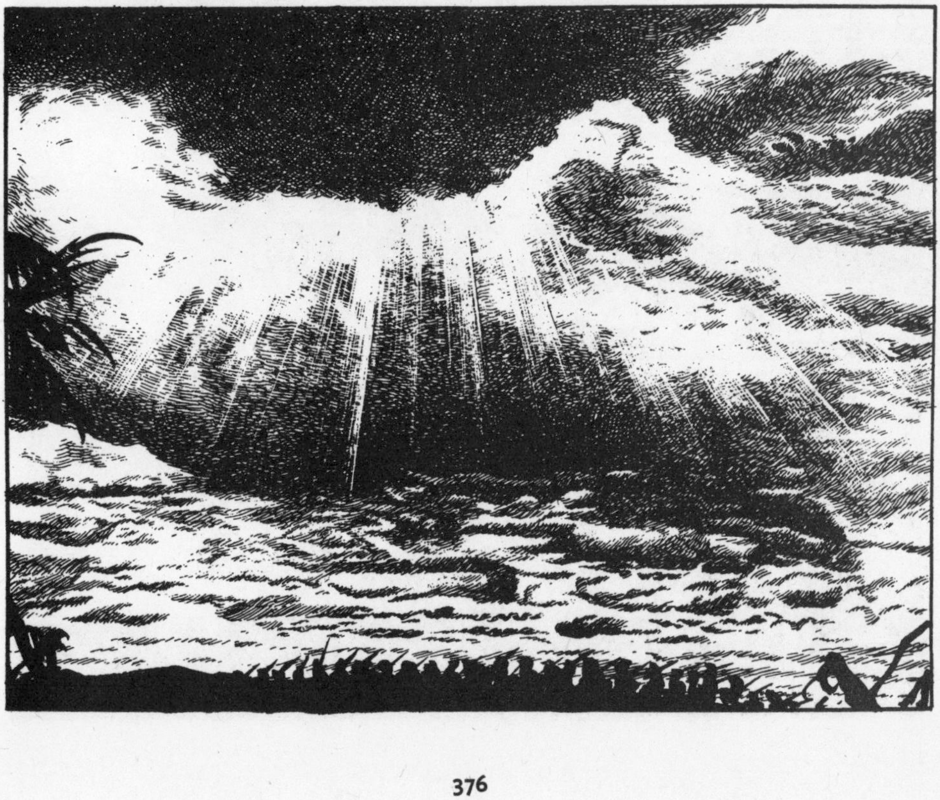

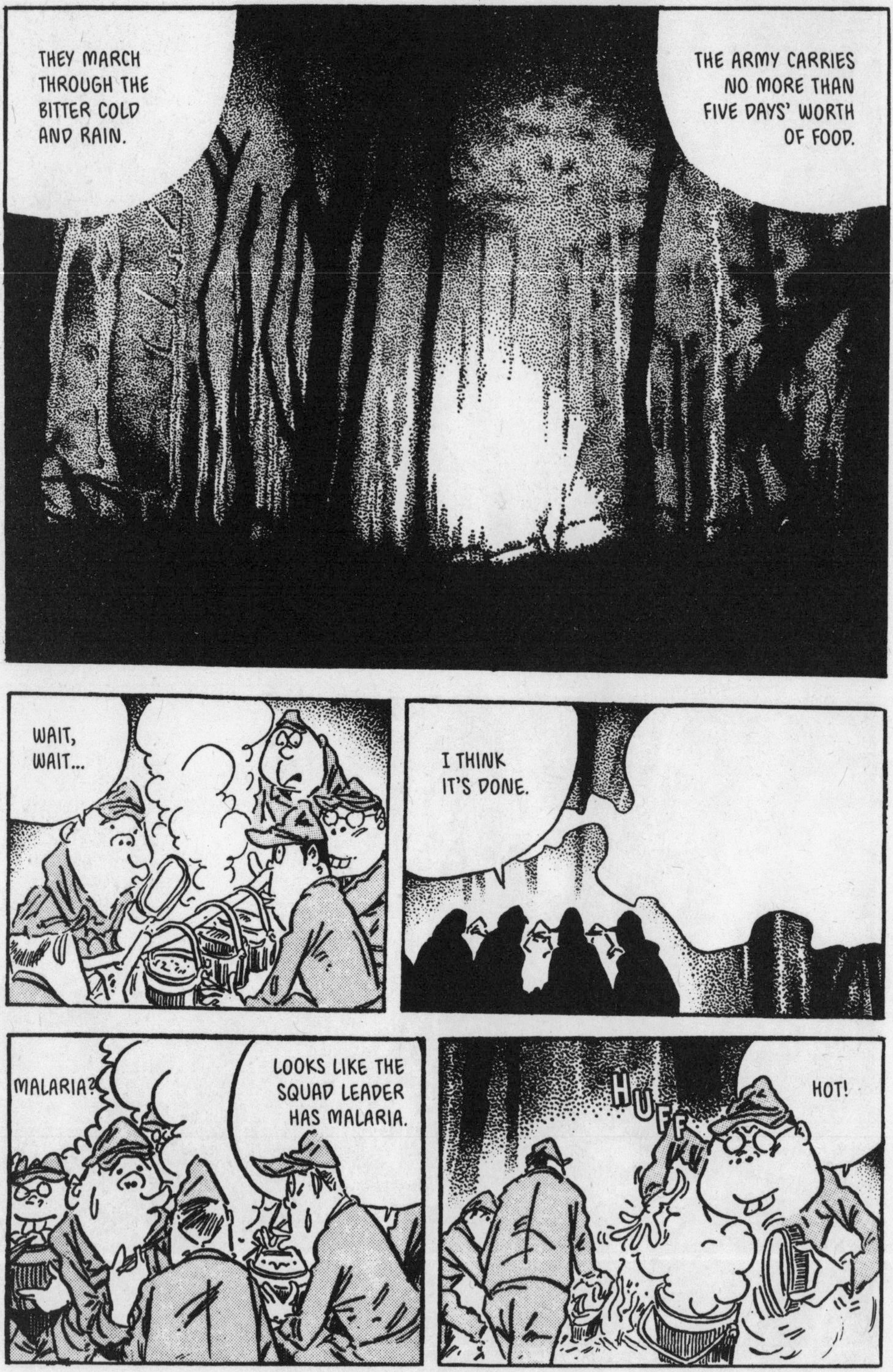
THE ARMY CARRIES NO MORE THAN FIVE DAYS' WORTH OF FOOD.
THEY MARCH THROUGH THE BITTER COLD AND RAIN.
I THINK IT'S DONE.
WAIT, WAIT...
HOT!
HUFF
LOOKS LIKE THE SQUAD LEADER HAS MALARIA.
MALARIA?

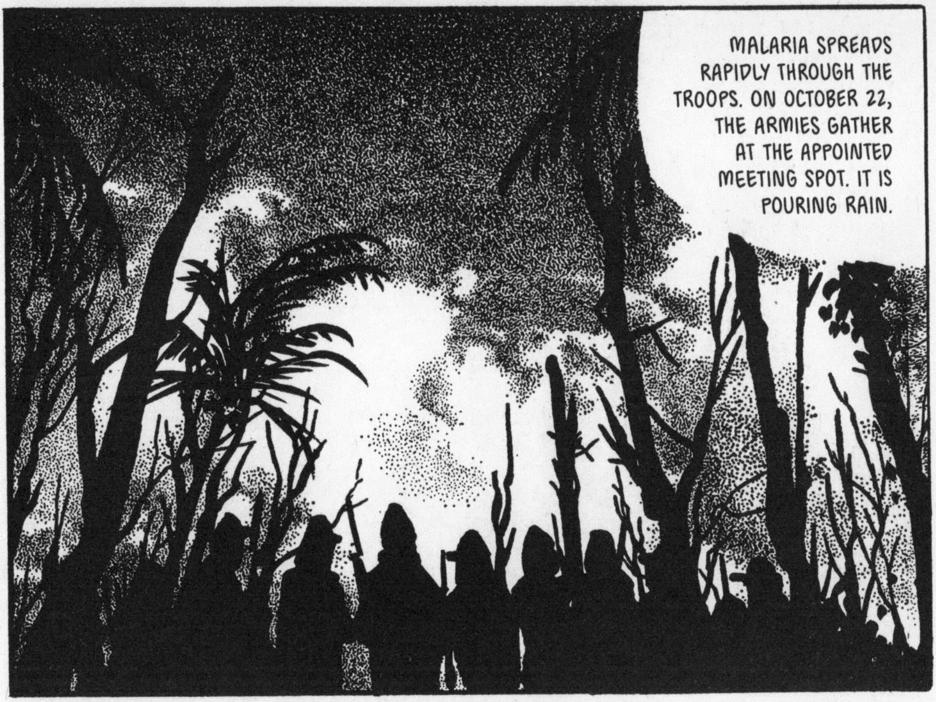
MALARIA SPREADS RAPIDLY THROUGH THE TROOPS. ON OCTOBER 22, THE ARMIES GATHER AT THE APPOINTED MEETING SPOT. IT IS POURING RAIN.

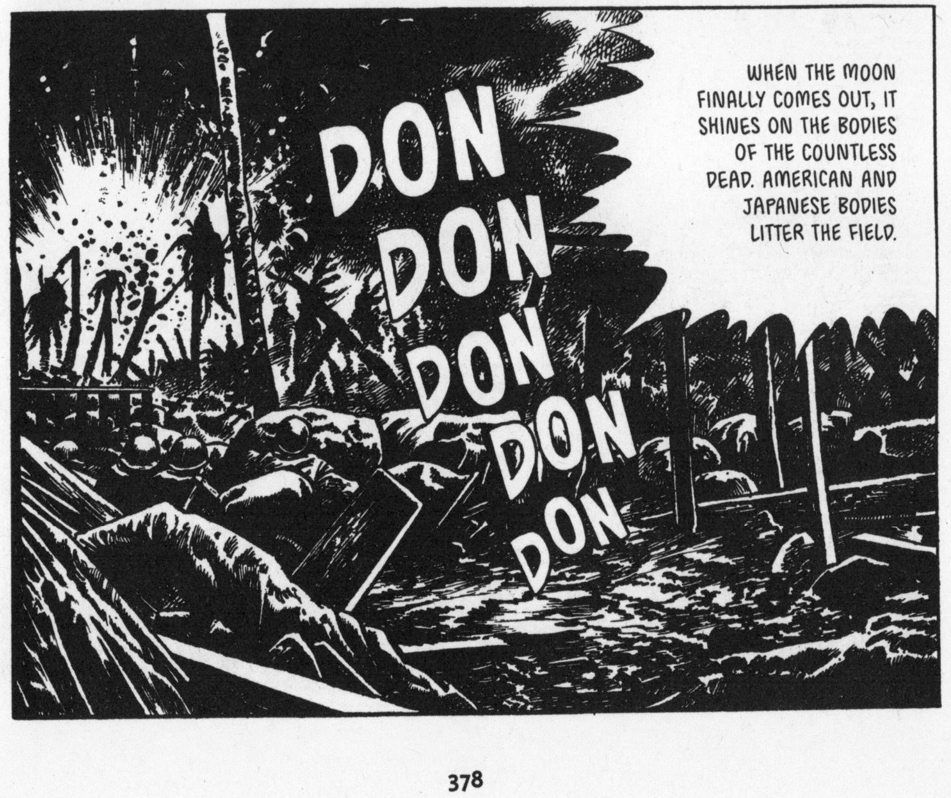
WHEN THE MOON FINALLY COMES OUT, IT SHINES ON THE BODIES OF THE COUNTLESS DEAD. AMERICAN AND JAPANESE BODIES LITTER THE FIELD.
DON
DON
DON
DON
DON
DON

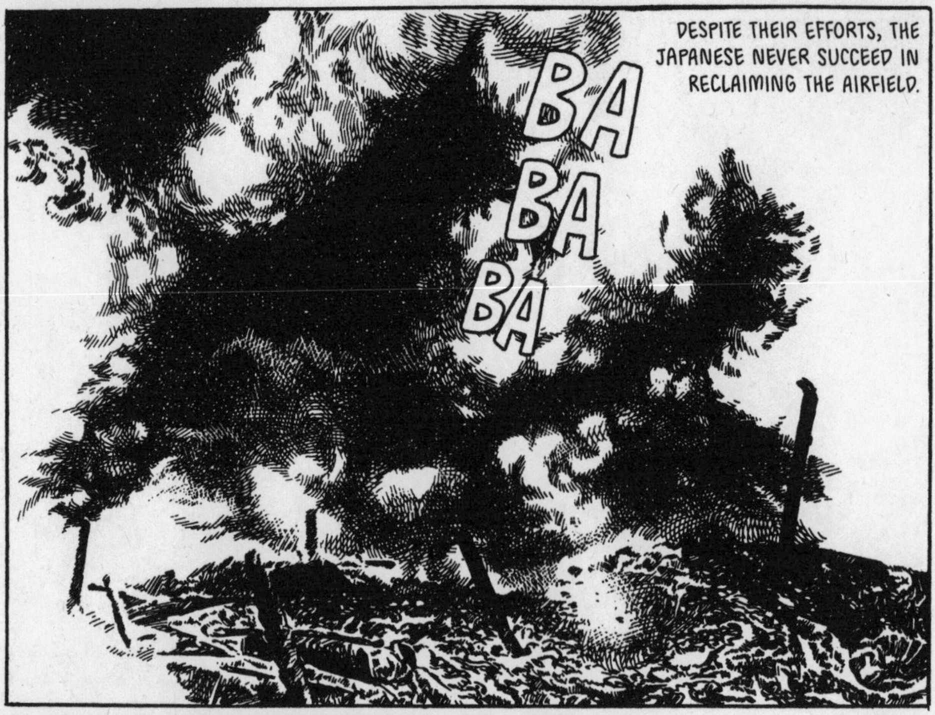
DESPITE THEIR EFFORTS, THE JAPANESE NEVER SUCCEED IN RECLAIMING THE AIRFIELD.
BA BA BA

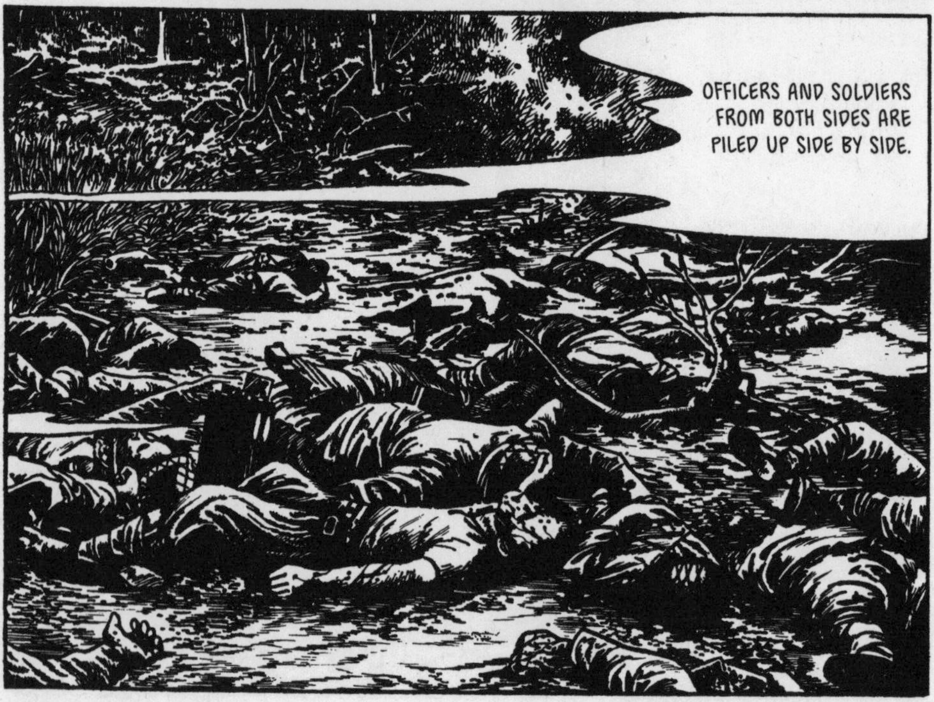
OFFICERS AND SOLDIERS FROM BOTH SIDES ARE PILED UP SIDE BY SIDE.

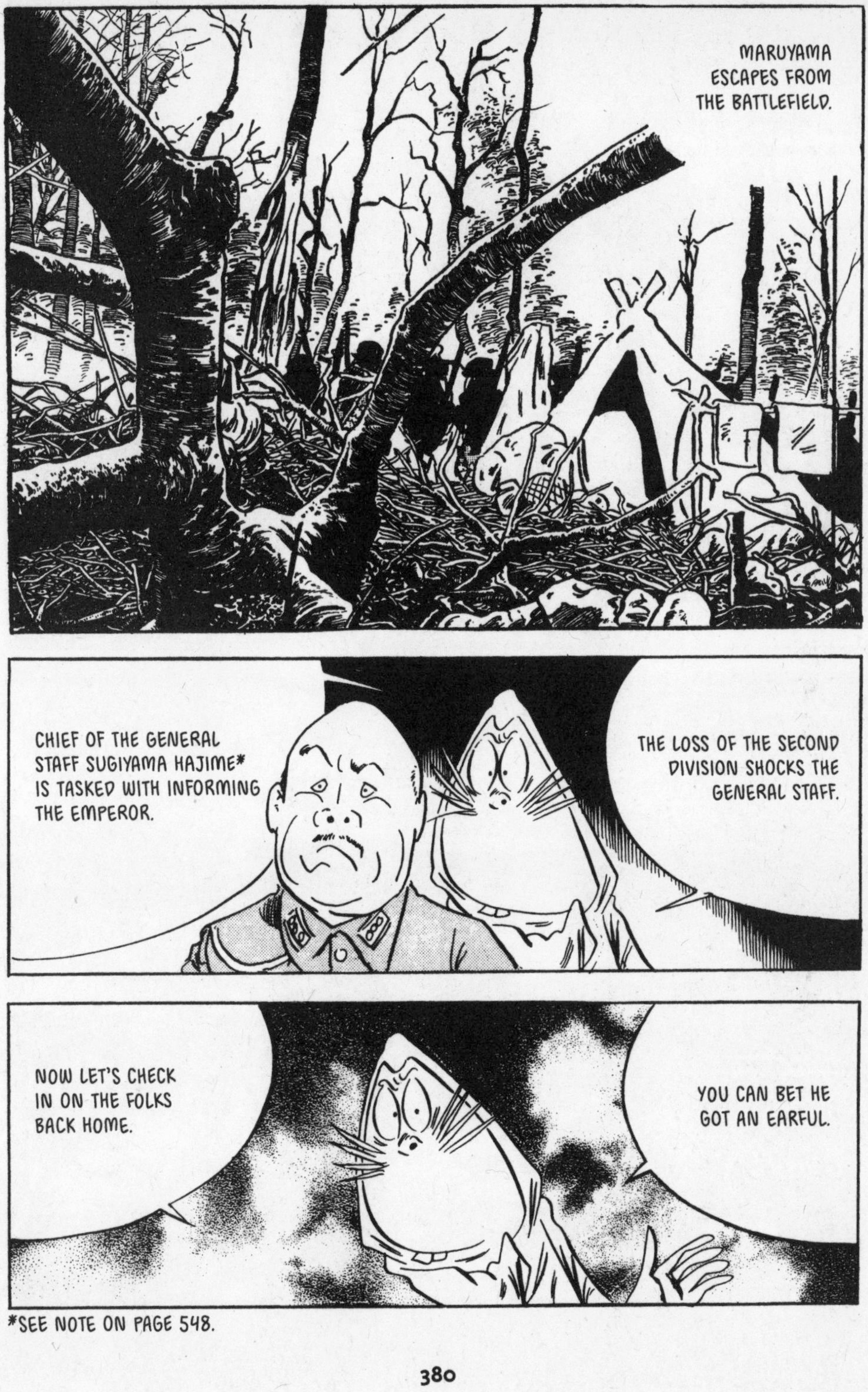
MARUYAMA ESCAPES FROM THE BATTLEFIELD.
THE LOSS OF THE SECOND DIVISION SHOCKS THE GENERAL STAFF.
CHIEF OF THE GENERAL STAFF SUGIYAMA HAJIME* IS TASKED WITH INFORMING THE EMPEROR.
YOU CAN BET HE GOT AN EARFUL.
NOW LET'S CHECK IN ON THE FOLKS BACK HOME.

*SEE NOTE ON PAGE 548.

DON'T WANT UNTIL WE WIN

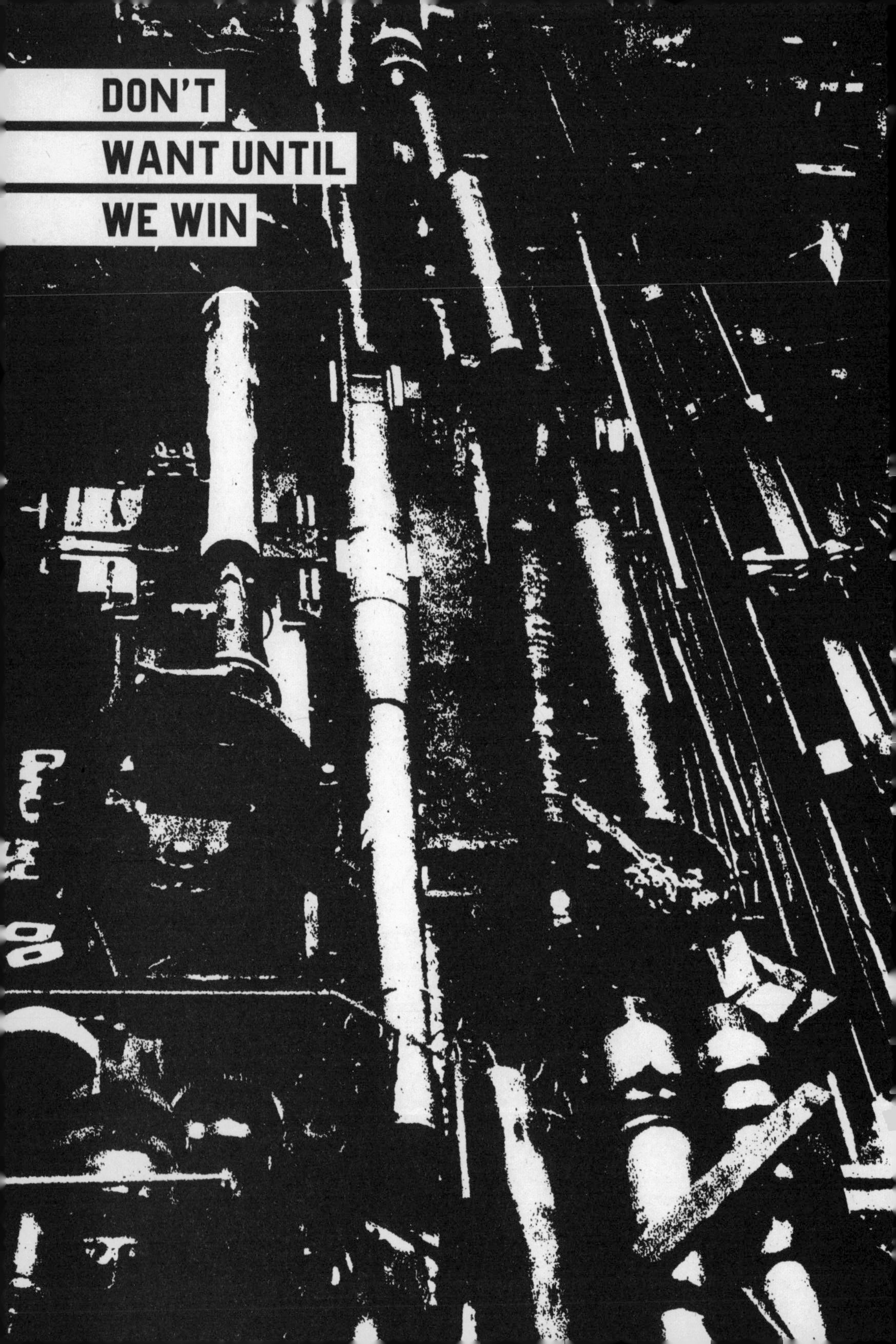

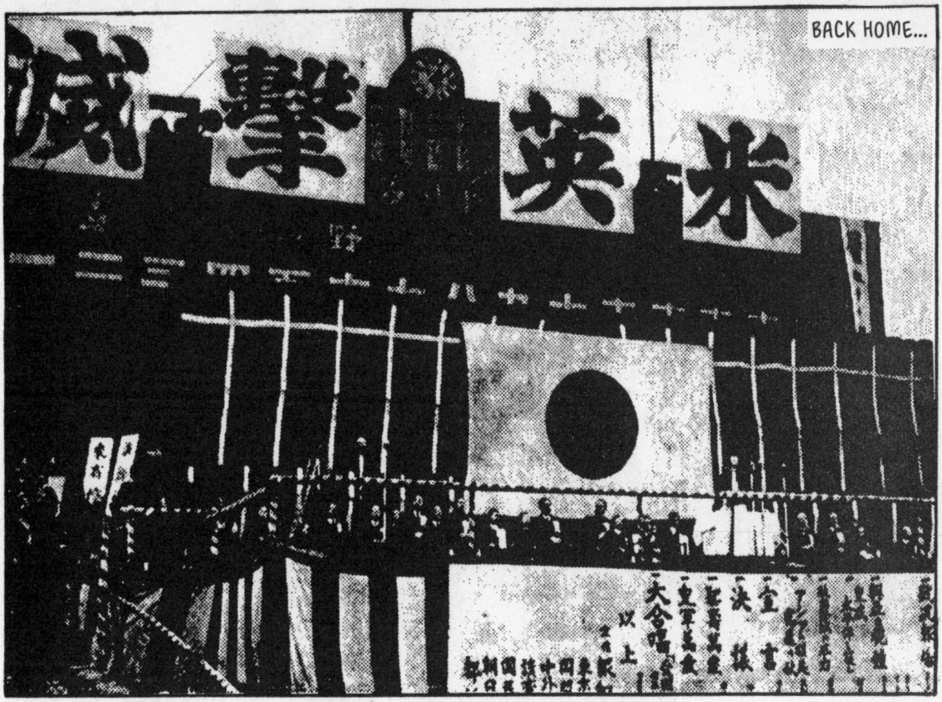
BACK HOME...
米英撃滅

SIGNS: WIPE OUT BRITAIN AND THE U.S.A.!

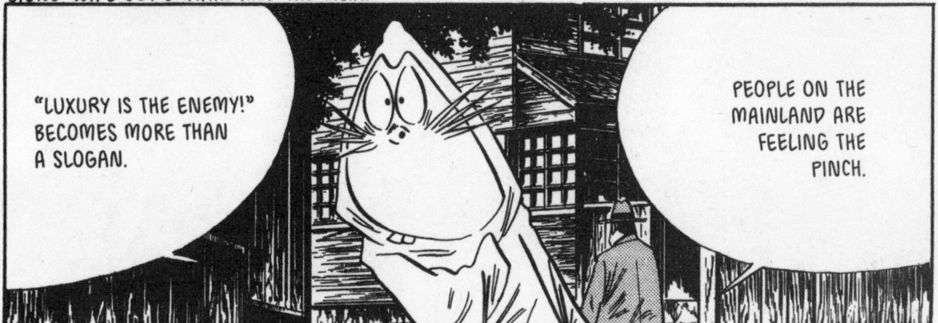
PEOPLE ON THE MAINLAND ARE FEELING THE PINCH.
"LUXURY IS THE ENEMY!" BECOMES MORE THAN A SLOGAN.

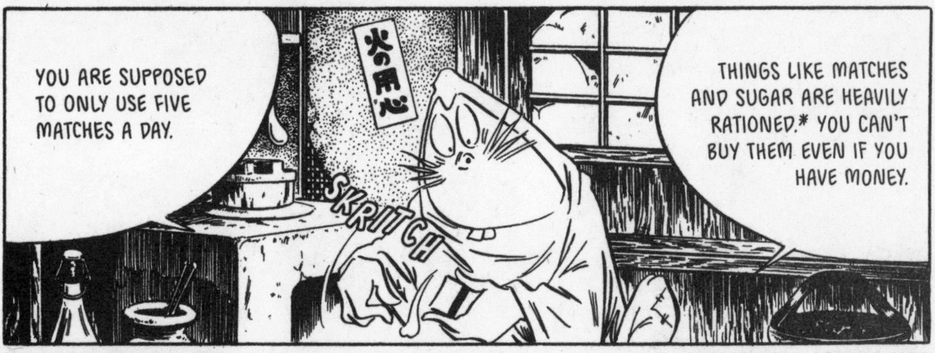
THINGS LIKE MATCHES AND SUGAR ARE HEAVILY RATIONED.* YOU CAN'T BUY THEM EVEN IF YOU HAVE MONEY.
火の用心
YOU ARE SUPPOSED TO ONLY USE FIVE MATCHES A DAY.
SKRITCH

*SEE NOTE ON PAGE 548.

SIGN: BE CAREFUL AROUND FIRE.

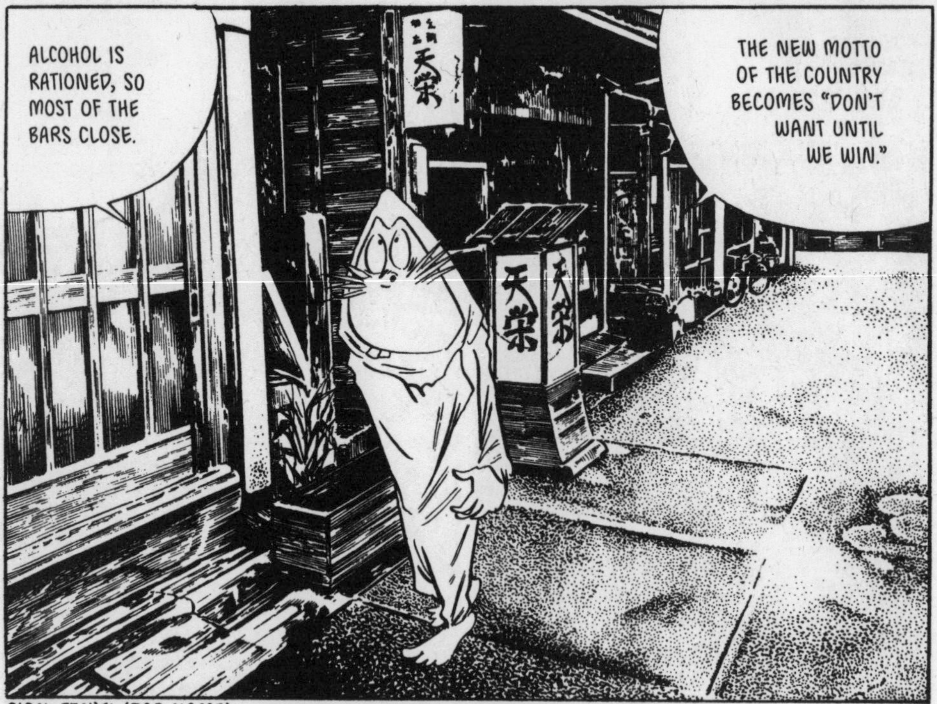
THE NEW MOTTO OF THE COUNTRY BECOMES "DON'T WANT UNTIL WE WIN."
ALCOHOL IS RATIONED, SO MOST OF THE BARS CLOSE.
天栄

SIGN: TEN'EI (BAR NAME).

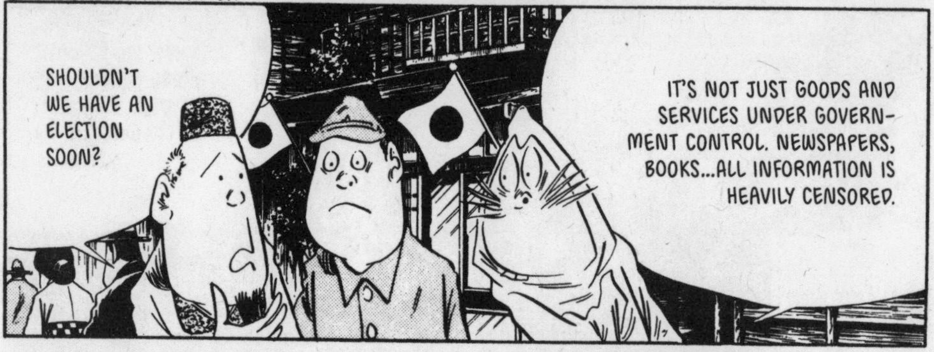
IT'S NOT JUST GOODS AND SERVICES UNDER GOVERNMENT CONTROL. NEWSPAPERS, BOOKS...ALL INFORMATION IS HEAVILY CENSORED.
SHOULDN'T WE HAVE AN ELECTION SOON?

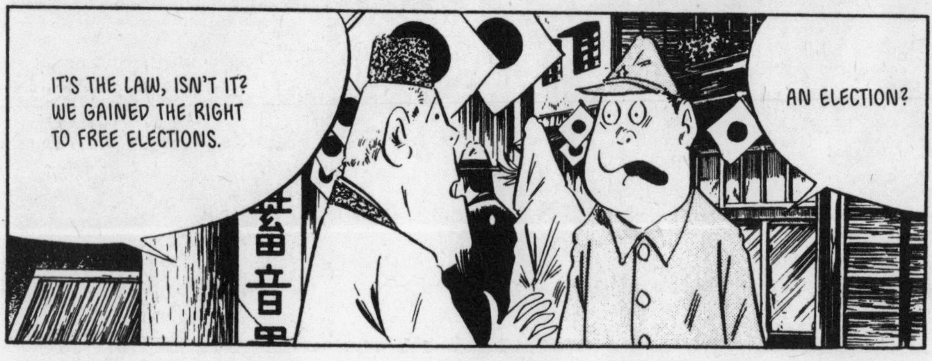
AN ELECTION?
IT'S THE LAW, ISN'T IT? WE GAINED THE RIGHT TO FREE ELECTIONS.

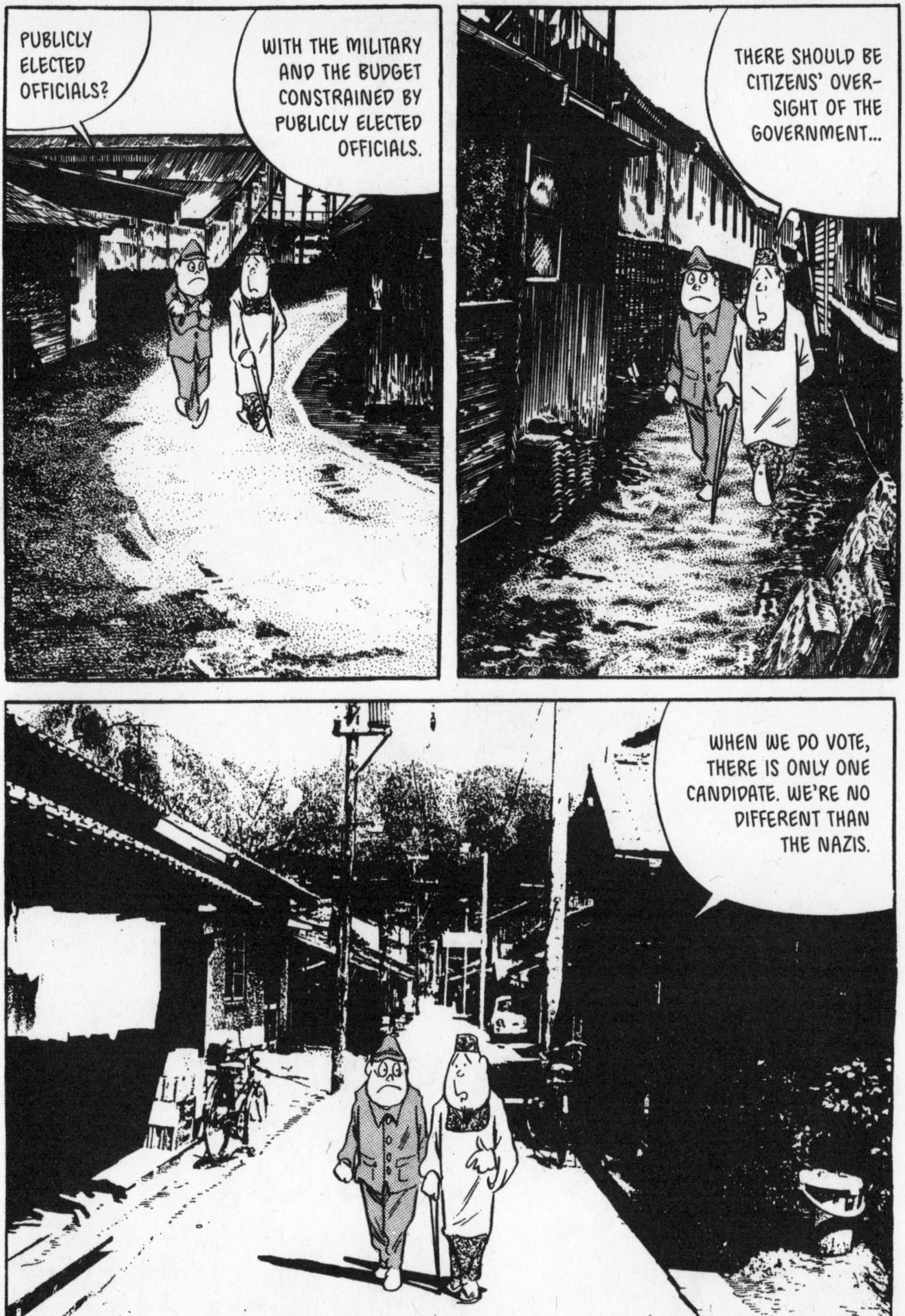
THERE SHOULD BE CITIZENS' OVER-SIGHT OF THE GOVERNMENT...
WITH THE MILITARY AND THE BUDGET CONSTRAINED BY PUBLICLY ELECTED OFFICIALS.
PUBLICLY ELECTED OFFICIALS?
WHEN WE DO VOTE, THERE IS ONLY ONE CANDIDATE. WE'RE NO DIFFERENT THAN THE NAZIS.

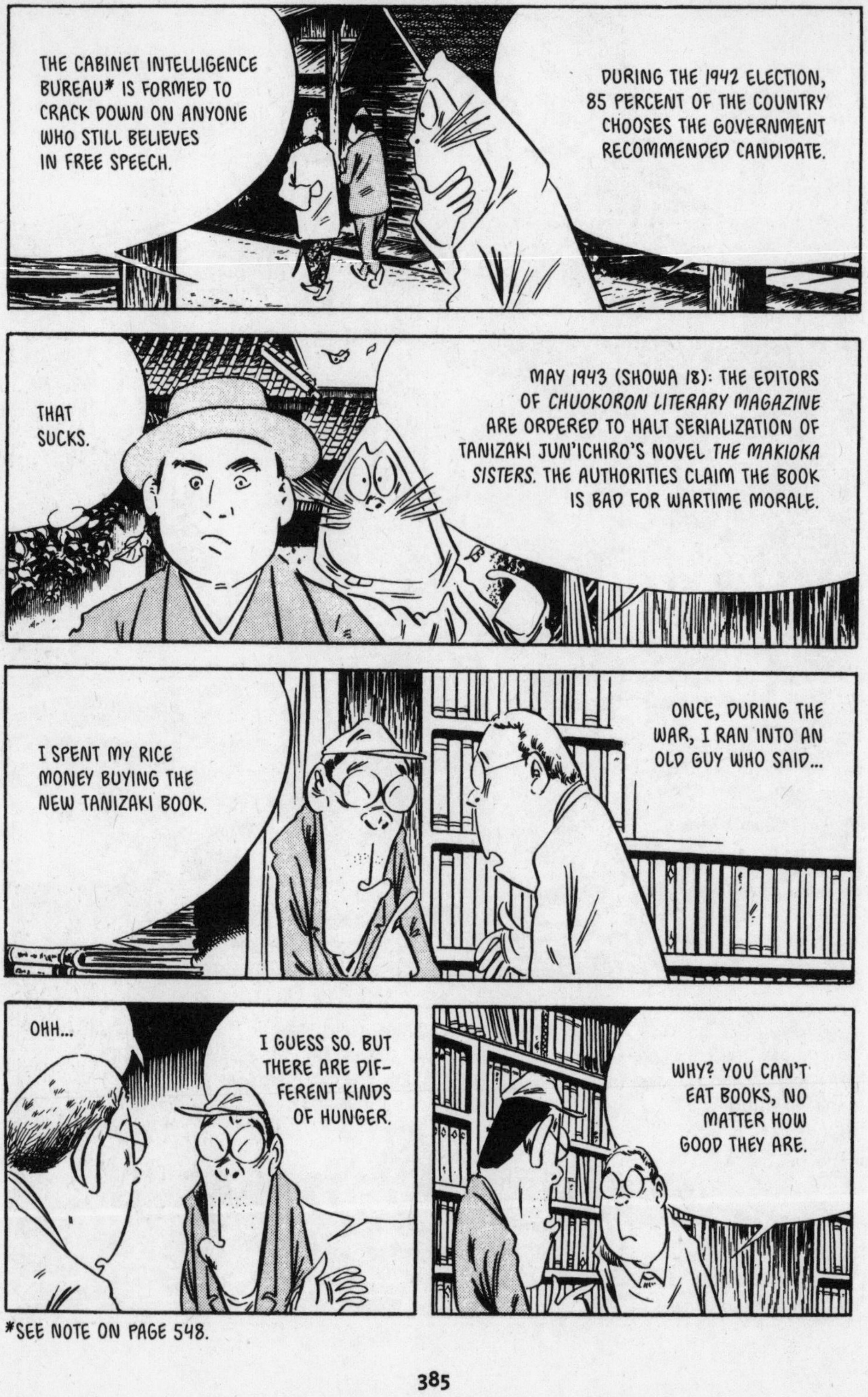
DURING THE 1942 ELECTION, 85 PERCENT OF THE COUNTRY CHOOSES THE GOVERNMENT RECOMMENDED CANDIDATE.
THE CABINET INTELLIGENCE BUREAU* IS FORMED TO CRACK DOWN ON ANYONE WHO STILL BELIEVES IN FREE SPEECH.
MAY 1943 (SHOWA 18): THE EDITORS OF *CHUOKORON LITERARY MAGAZINE* ARE ORDERED TO HALT SERIALIZATION OF TANIZAKI JUN'ICHIRO'S NOVEL *THE MAKIOKA SISTERS*. THE AUTHORITIES CLAIM THE BOOK IS BAD FOR WARTIME MORALE.
THAT SUCKS.
ONCE, DURING THE WAR, I RAN INTO AN OLD GUY WHO SAID...
I SPENT MY RICE MONEY BUYING THE NEW TANIZAKI BOOK.
WHY? YOU CAN'T EAT BOOKS, NO MATTER HOW GOOD THEY ARE.
I GUESS SO. BUT THERE ARE DIF-FERENT KINDS OF HUNGER.
OHH...

*SEE NOTE ON PAGE 548.

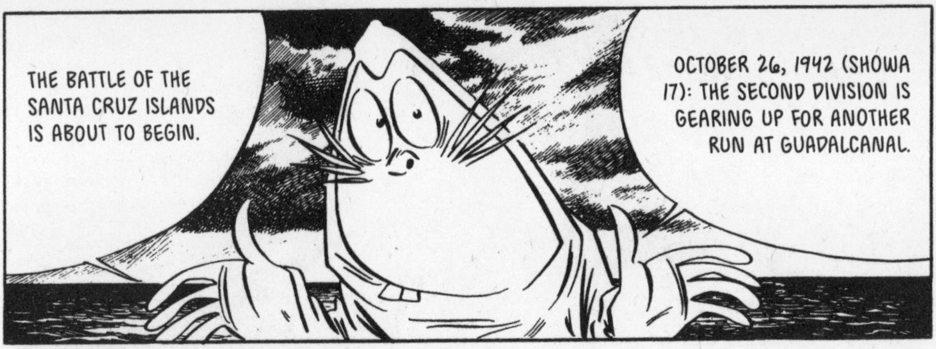
OCTOBER 26, 1942 (SHOWA 17): THE SECOND DIVISION IS GEARING UP FOR ANOTHER RUN AT GUADALCANAL.
THE BATTLE OF THE SANTA CRUZ ISLANDS IS ABOUT TO BEGIN.

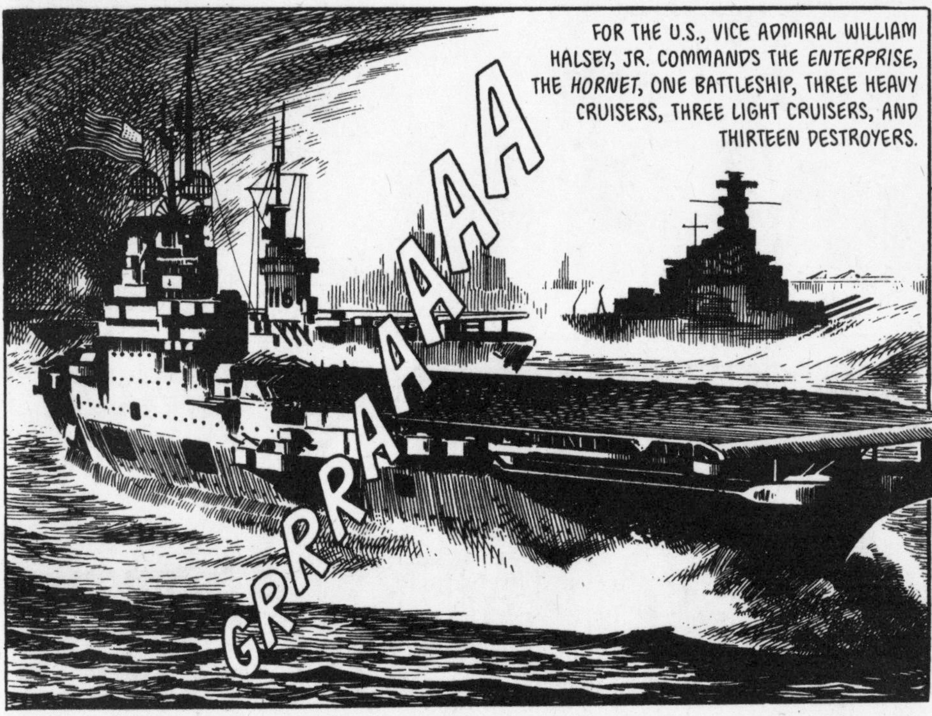
FOR THE U.S., VICE ADMIRAL WILLIAM HALSEY, JR. COMMANDS THE *ENTERPRISE*, THE *HORNET*, ONE BATTLESHIP, THREE HEAVY CRUISERS, THREE LIGHT CRUISERS, AND THIRTEEN DESTROYERS.
GRRRAAAAAA

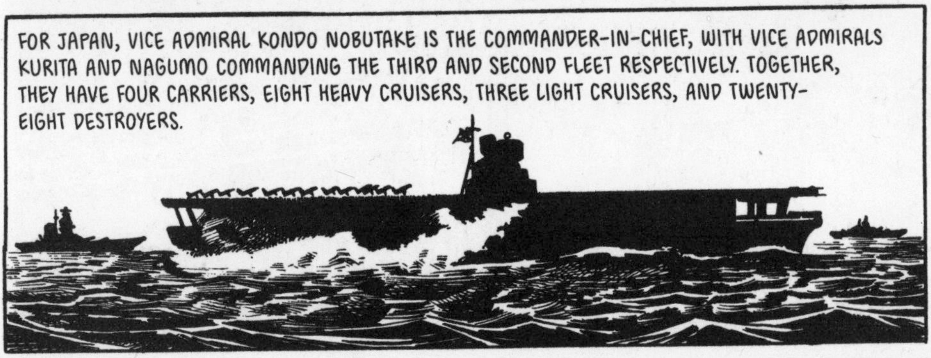
FOR JAPAN, VICE ADMIRAL KONDO NOBUTAKE IS THE COMMANDER-IN-CHIEF, WITH VICE ADMIRALS KURITA AND NAGUMO COMMANDING THE THIRD AND SECOND FLEET RESPECTIVELY. TOGETHER, THEY HAVE FOUR CARRIERS, EIGHT HEAVY CRUISERS, THREE LIGHT CRUISERS, AND TWENTY-EIGHT DESTROYERS.

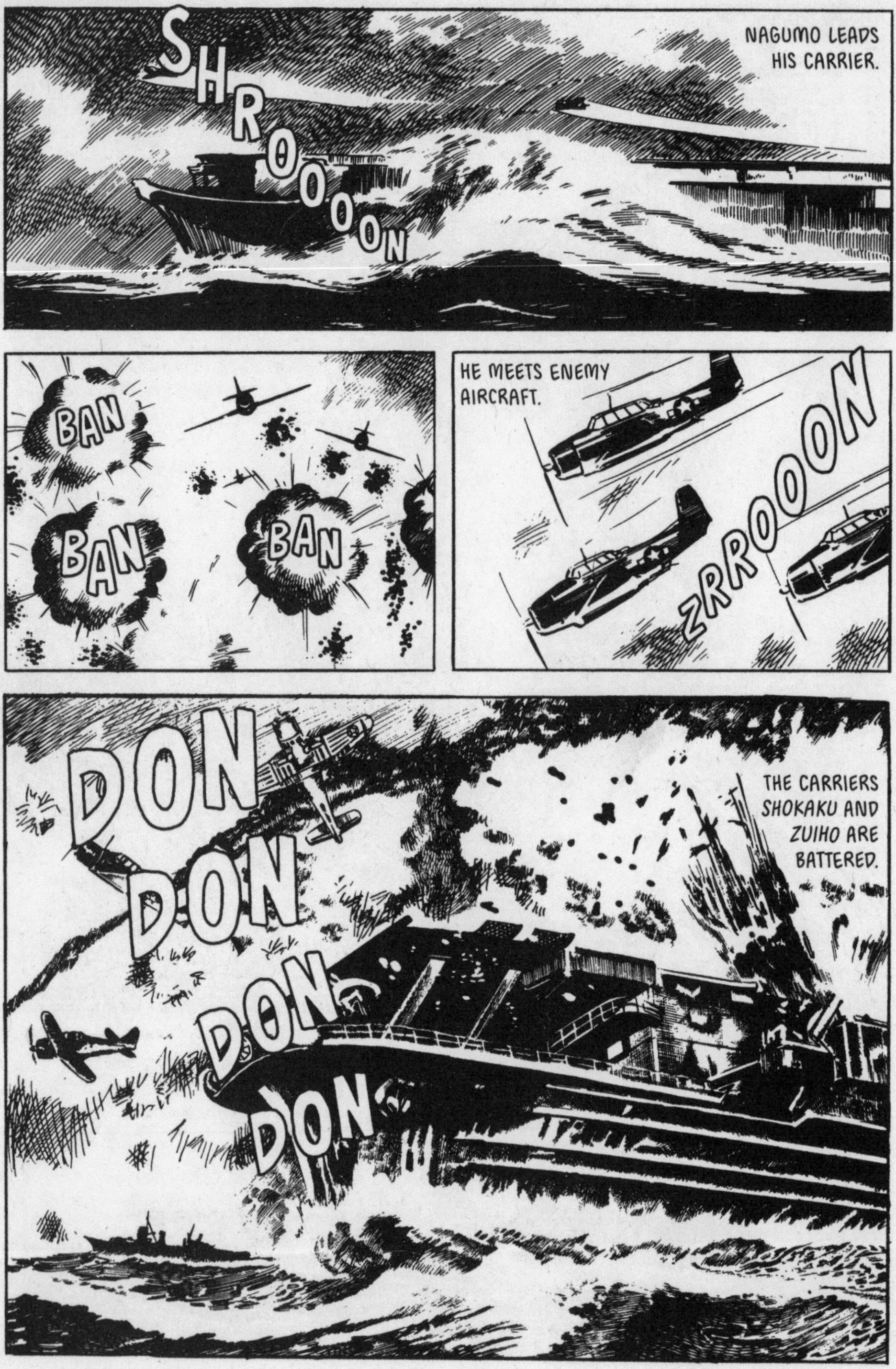
NAGUMO LEADS HIS CARRIER.
SHROOOOON
HE MEETS ENEMY AIRCRAFT.
ZRROOON
BAN
BAN
BAN
THE CARRIERS SHOKAKU AND ZUIHO ARE BATTERED.
DON
DON
DON
DON

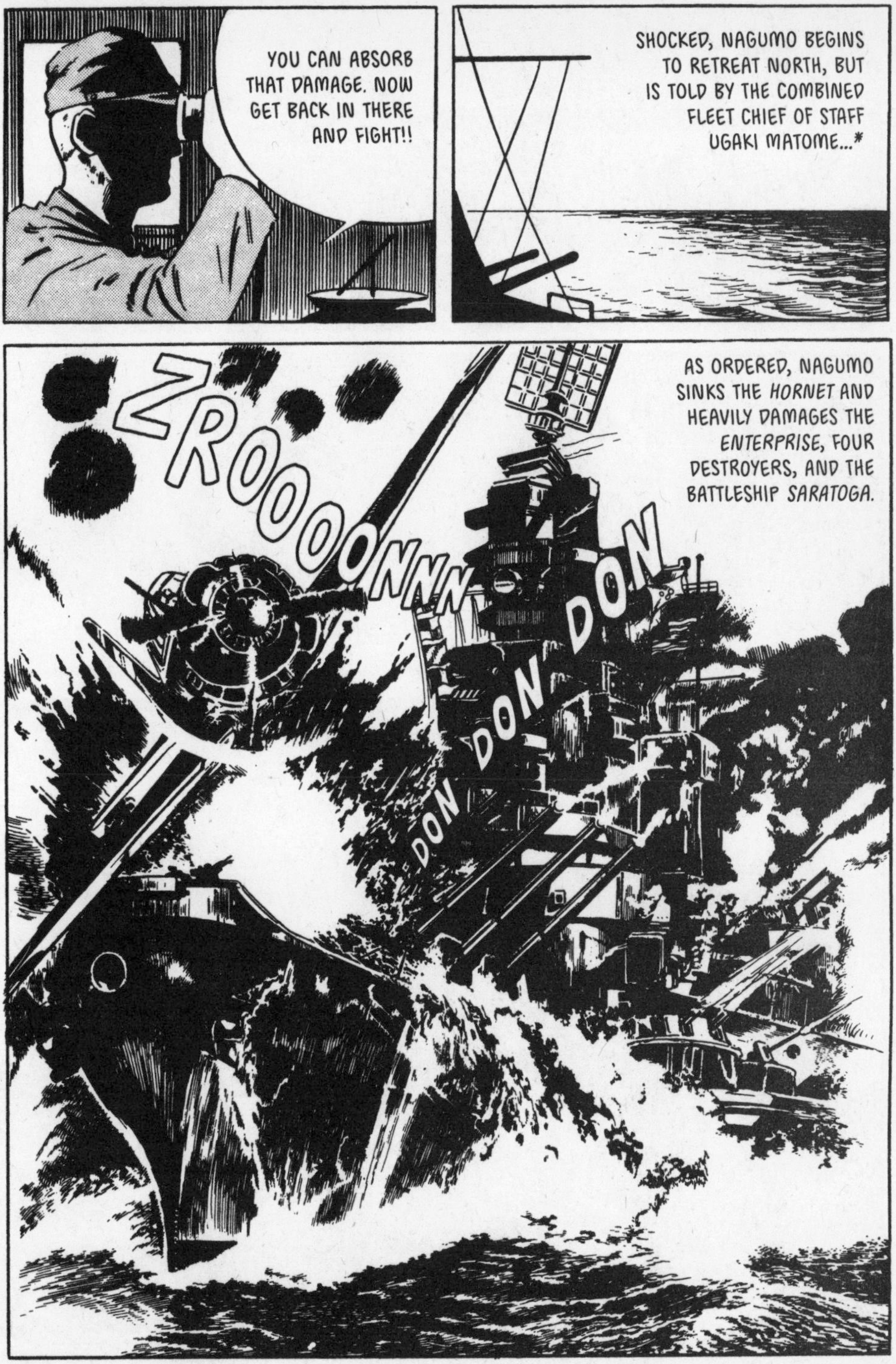
SHOCKED, NAGUMO BEGINS TO RETREAT NORTH, BUT IS TOLD BY THE COMBINED FLEET CHIEF OF STAFF UGAKI MATOME...*
YOU CAN ABSORB THAT DAMAGE. NOW GET BACK IN THERE AND FIGHT!!
AS ORDERED, NAGUMO SINKS THE HORNET AND HEAVILY DAMAGES THE ENTERPRISE, FOUR DESTROYERS, AND THE BATTLESHIP SARATOGA.
ZROOOONNN
DON DON DON DON

*SEE NOTE ON PAGE 548.

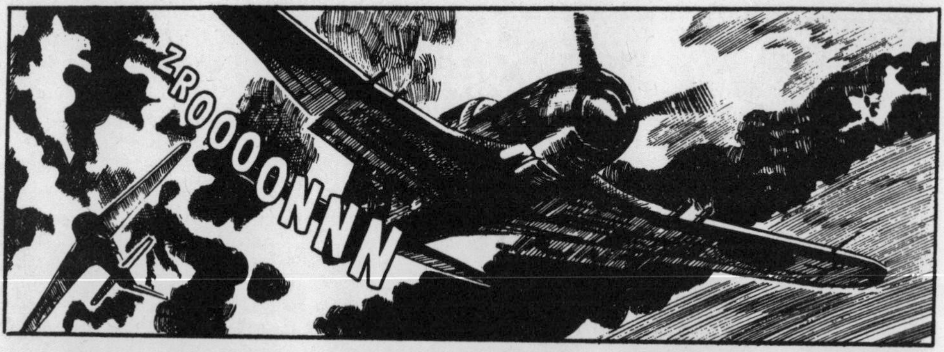
ZROOOONNNN

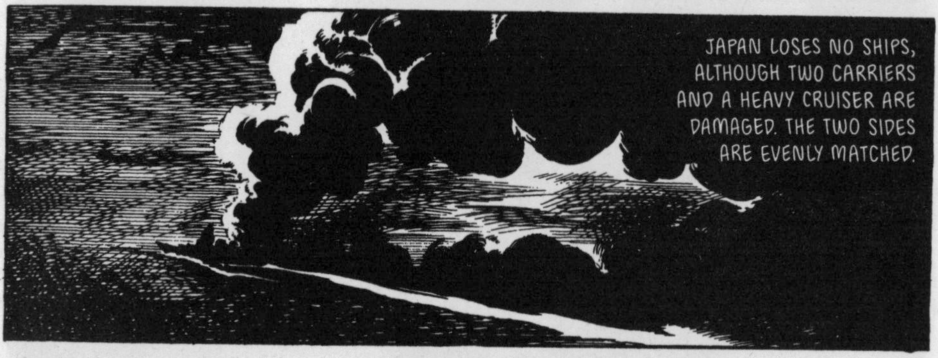
JAPAN LOSES NO SHIPS, ALTHOUGH TWO CARRIERS AND A HEAVY CRUISER ARE DAMAGED. THE TWO SIDES ARE EVENLY MATCHED.

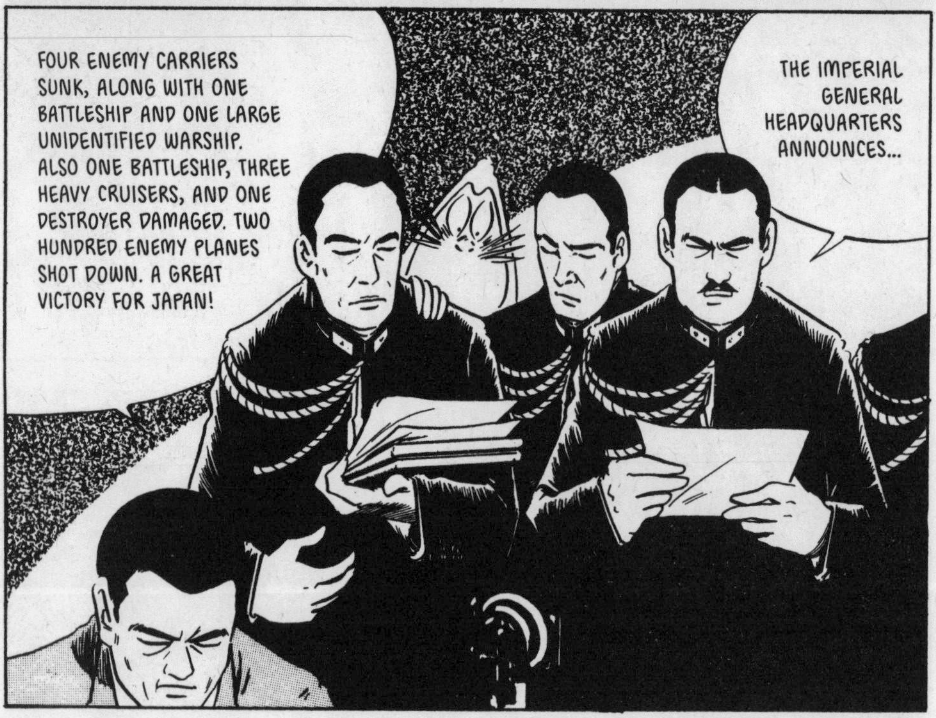
THE IMPERIAL GENERAL HEADQUARTERS ANNOUNCES...
FOUR ENEMY CARRIERS SUNK, ALONG WITH ONE BATTLESHIP AND ONE LARGE UNIDENTIFIED WARSHIP. ALSO ONE BATTLESHIP, THREE HEAVY CRUISERS, AND ONE DESTROYER DAMAGED. TWO HUNDRED ENEMY PLANES SHOT DOWN. A GREAT VICTORY FOR JAPAN!

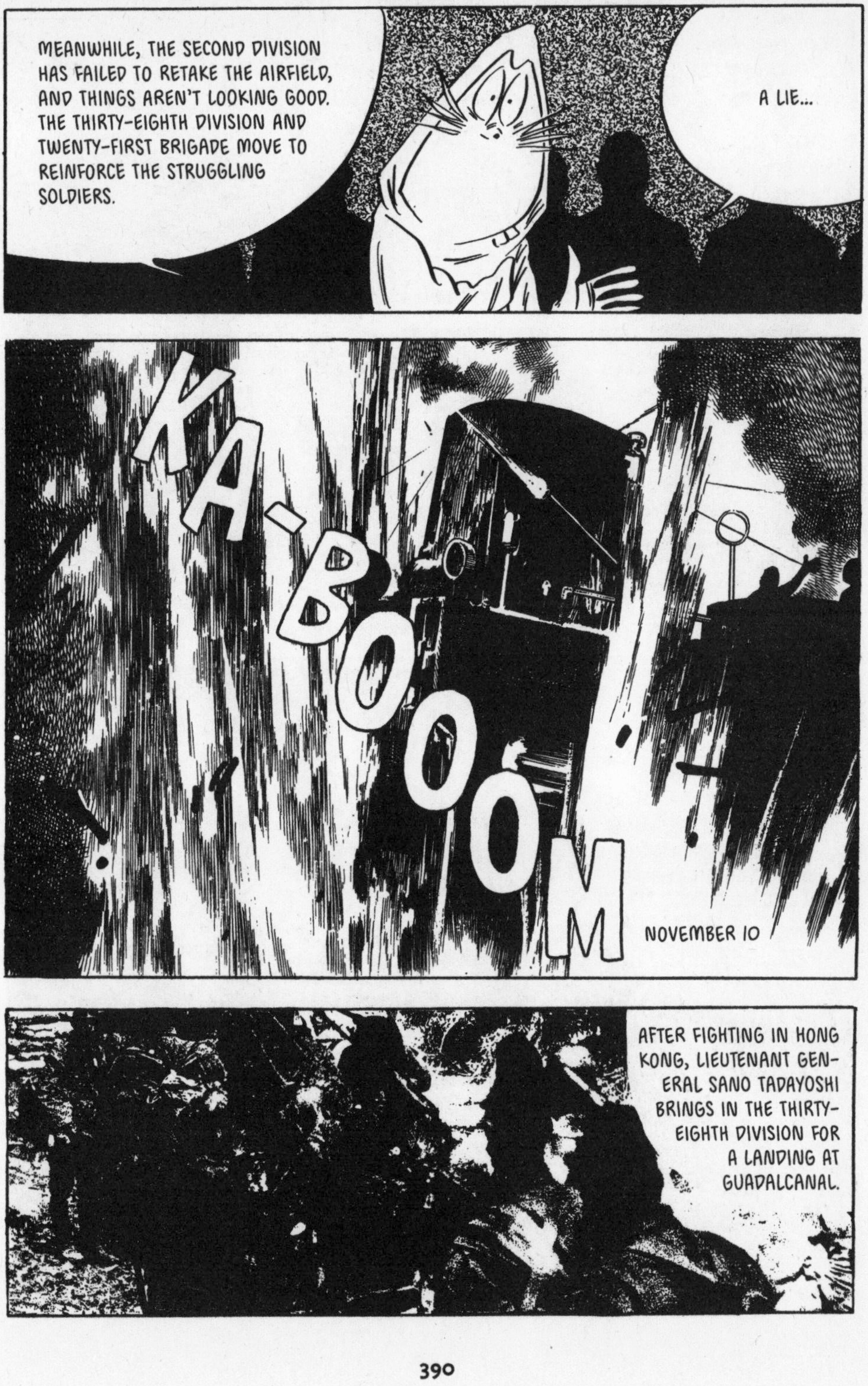
A LIE...
MEANWHILE, THE SECOND DIVISION HAS FAILED TO RETAKE THE AIRFIELD, AND THINGS AREN'T LOOKING GOOD. THE THIRTY-EIGHTH DIVISION AND TWENTY-FIRST BRIGADE MOVE TO REINFORCE THE STRUGGLING SOLDIERS.
KA-BOOOOM
NOVEMBER 10
AFTER FIGHTING IN HONG KONG, LIEUTENANT GENERAL SANO TADAYOSHI BRINGS IN THE THIRTY-EIGHTH DIVISION FOR A LANDING AT GUADALCANAL.

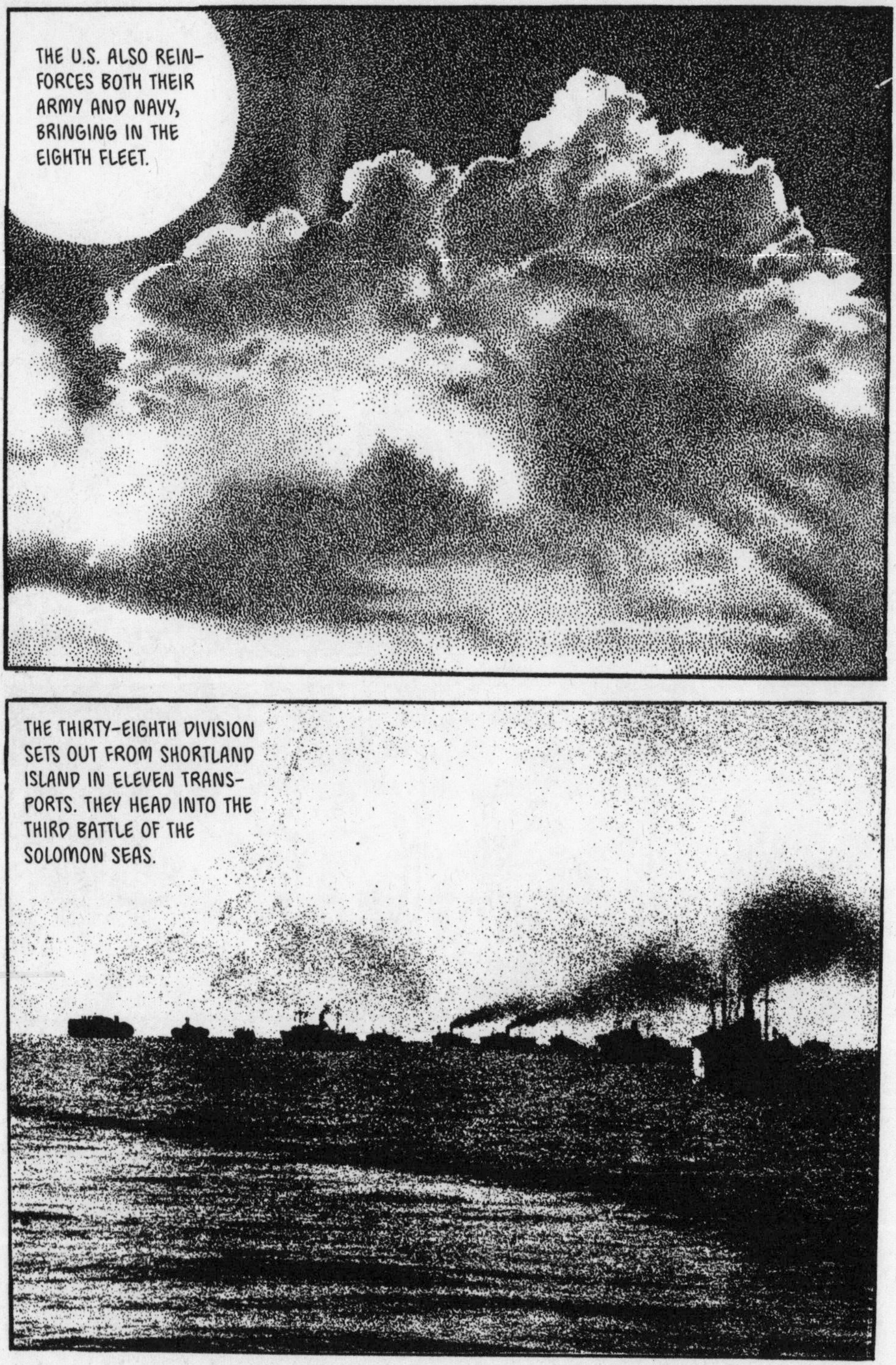
THE U.S. ALSO REIN-FORCES BOTH THEIR ARMY AND NAVY, BRINGING IN THE EIGHTH FLEET.
THE THIRTY-EIGHTH DIVISION SETS OUT FROM SHORTLAND ISLAND IN ELEVEN TRANS-PORTS. THEY HEAD INTO THE THIRD BATTLE OF THE SOLOMON SEAS.

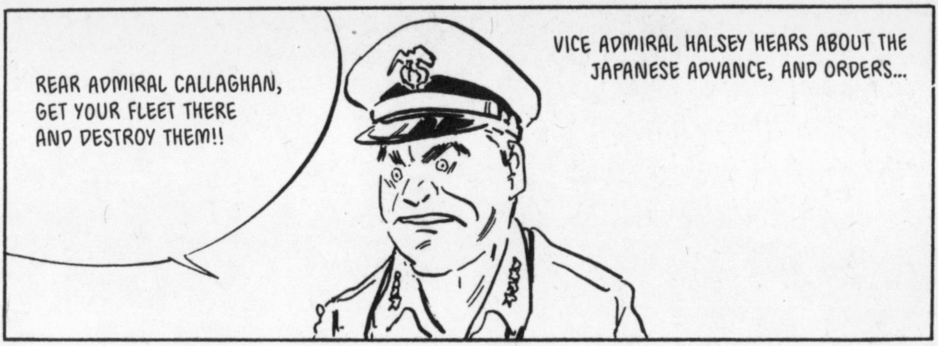
VICE ADMIRAL HALSEY HEARS ABOUT THE JAPANESE ADVANCE, AND ORDERS...
REAR ADMIRAL CALLAGHAN, GET YOUR FLEET THERE AND DESTROY THEM!!

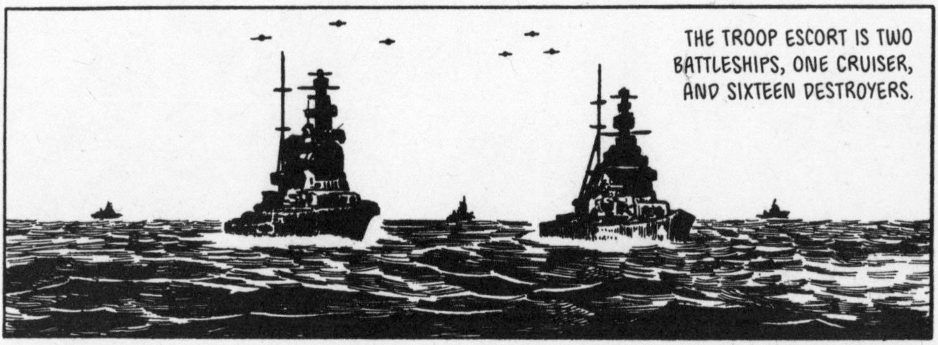
THE TROOP ESCORT IS TWO BATTLESHIPS, ONE CRUISER, AND SIXTEEN DESTROYERS.

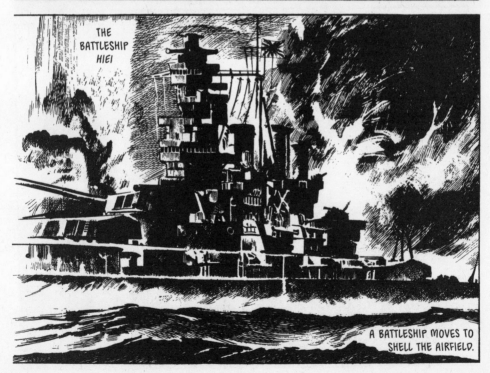

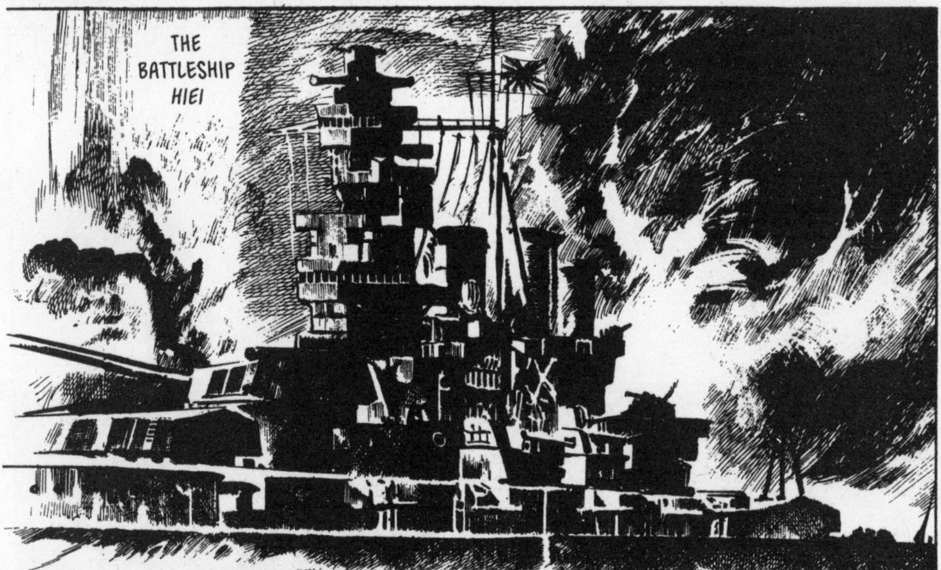
THE BATTLESHIP HIEI
A BATTLESHIP MOVES TO SHELL THE AIRFIELD.

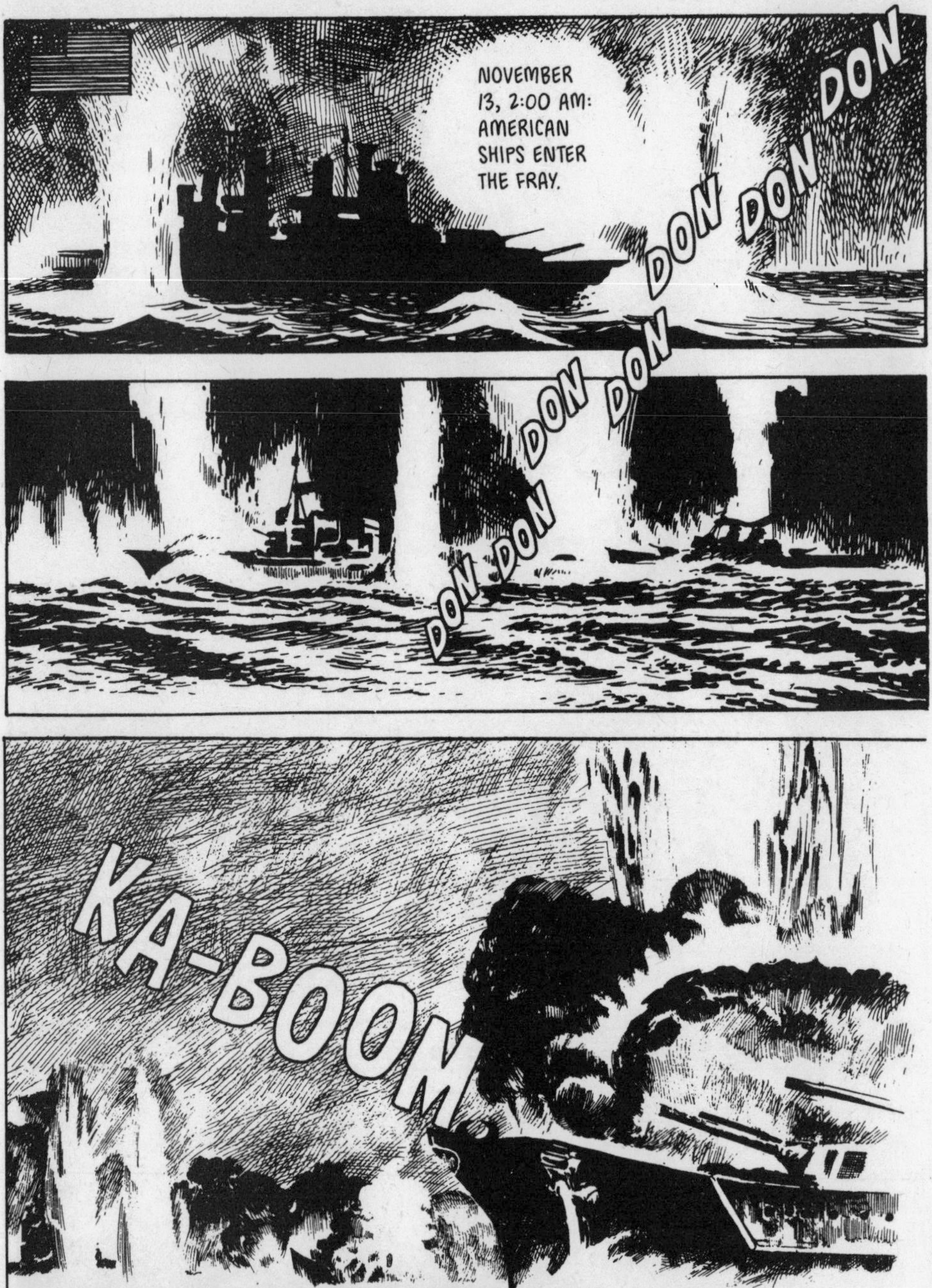
NOVEMBER 13, 2:00 AM: AMERICAN SHIPS ENTER THE FRAY.
DON DON DON DON DON DON DON DON
KA-BOOM

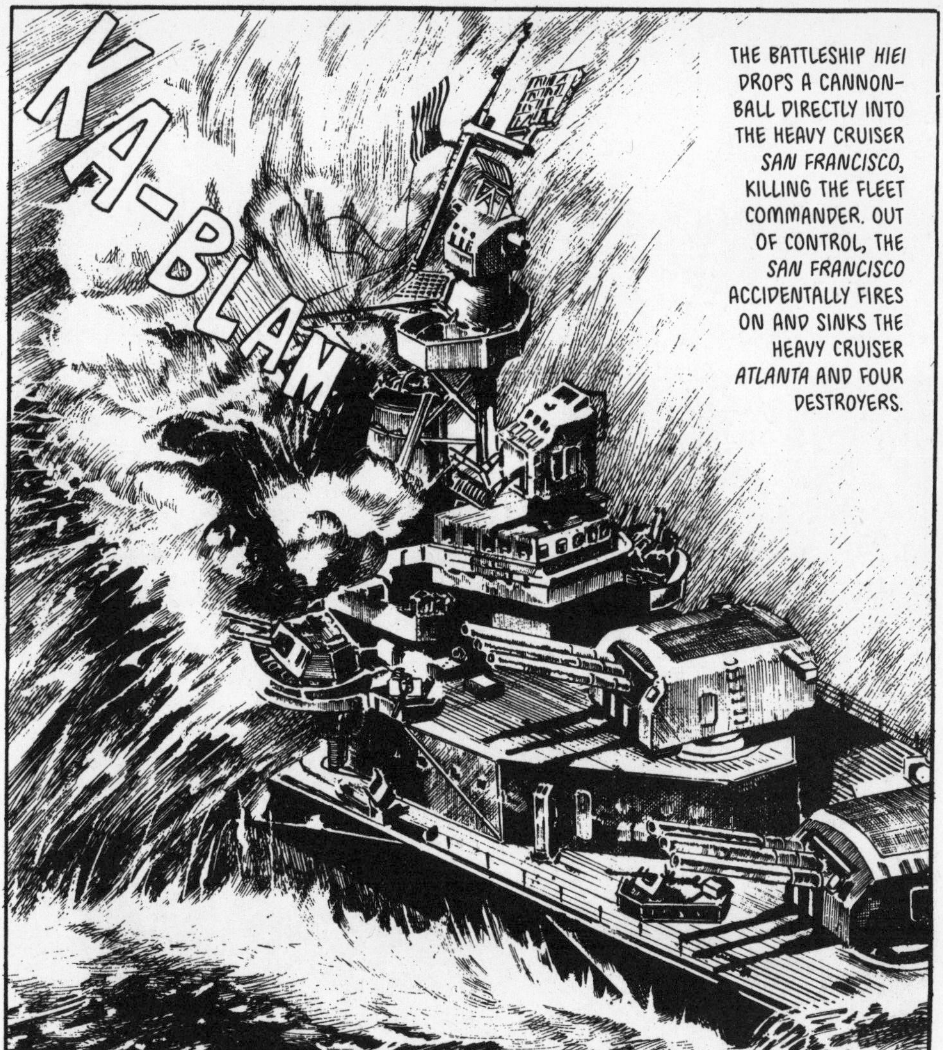
KA-BLAM
THE BATTLESHIP *HIEI* DROPS A CANNONBALL DIRECTLY INTO THE HEAVY CRUISER *SAN FRANCISCO*, KILLING THE FLEET COMMANDER. OUT OF CONTROL, THE *SAN FRANCISCO* ACCIDENTALLY FIRES ON AND SINKS THE HEAVY CRUISER *ATLANTA* AND FOUR DESTROYERS.
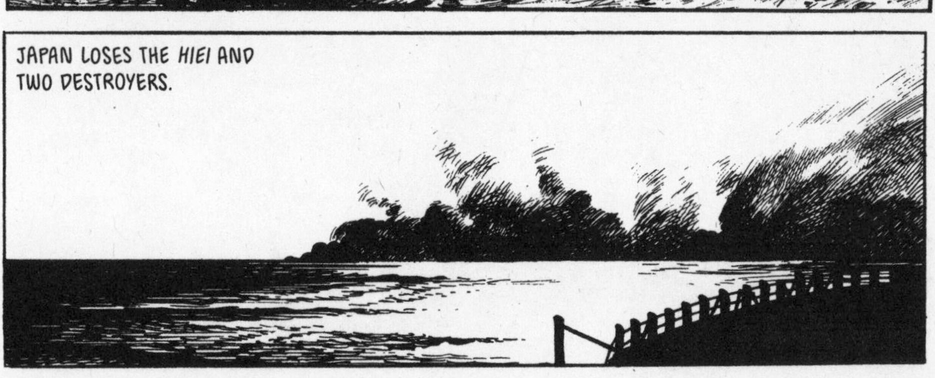
JAPAN LOSES THE *HIEI* AND TWO DESTROYERS.

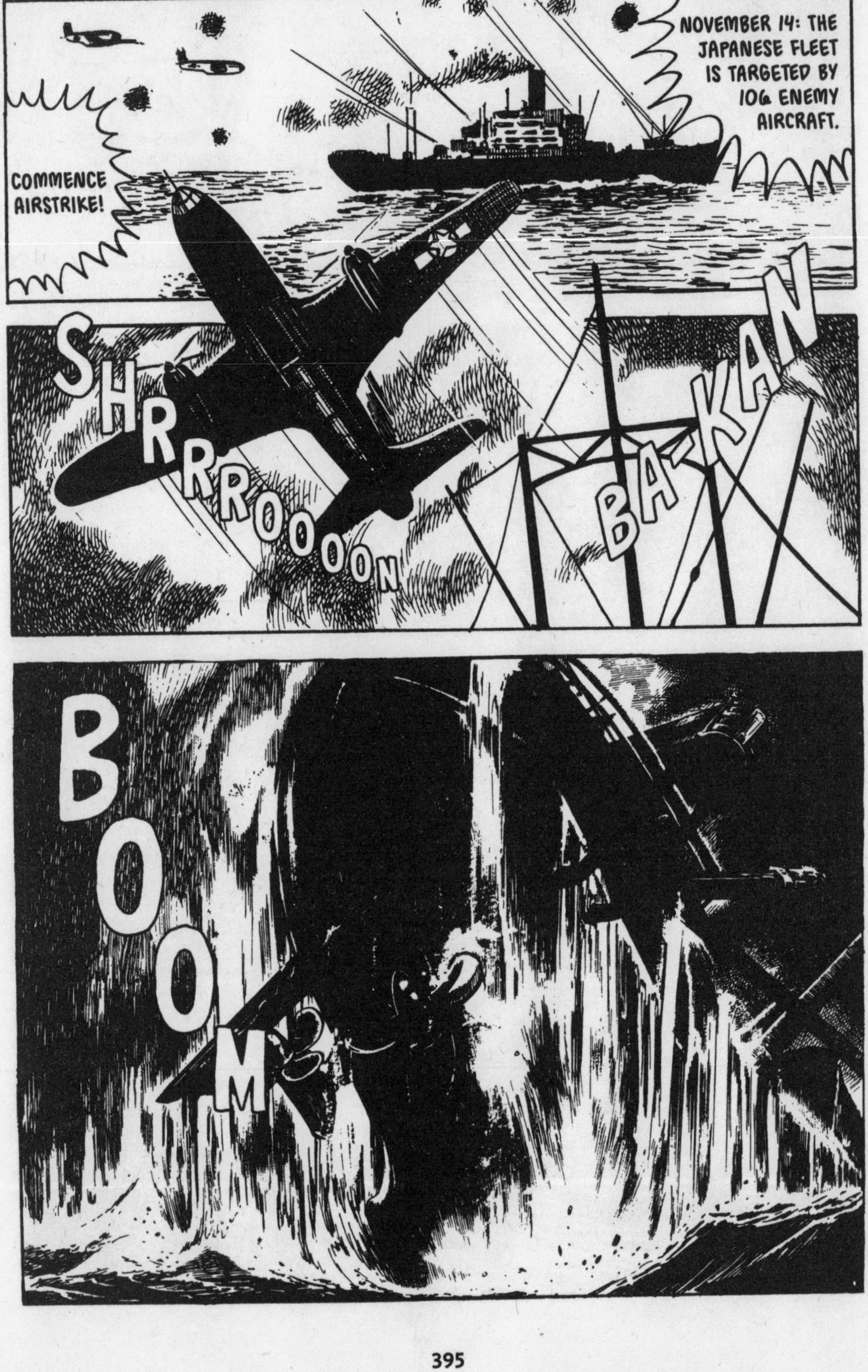

NOVEMBER 14: THE JAPANESE FLEET IS TARGETED BY 106 ENEMY AIRCRAFT.
COMMENCE AIRSTRIKE!
BA-KAN
SHRRROOOOON
BOOM

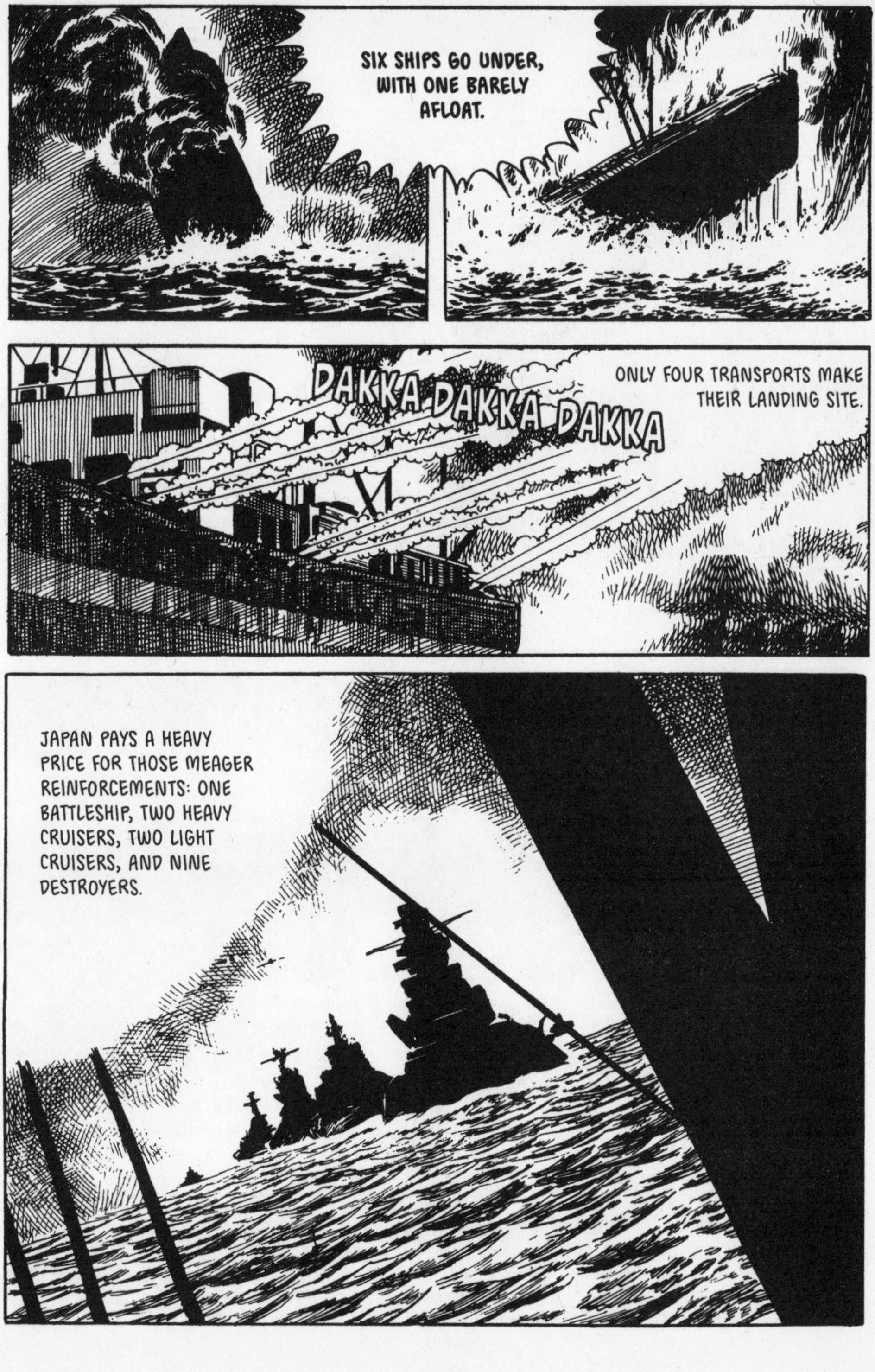
SIX SHIPS GO UNDER, WITH ONE BARELY AFLOAT.
ONLY FOUR TRANSPORTS MAKE THEIR LANDING SITE.
DAKKA DAKKA DAKKA DAKKA
JAPAN PAYS A HEAVY PRICE FOR THOSE MEAGER REINFORCEMENTS: ONE BATTLESHIP, TWO HEAVY CRUISERS, TWO LIGHT CRUISERS, AND NINE DESTROYERS.

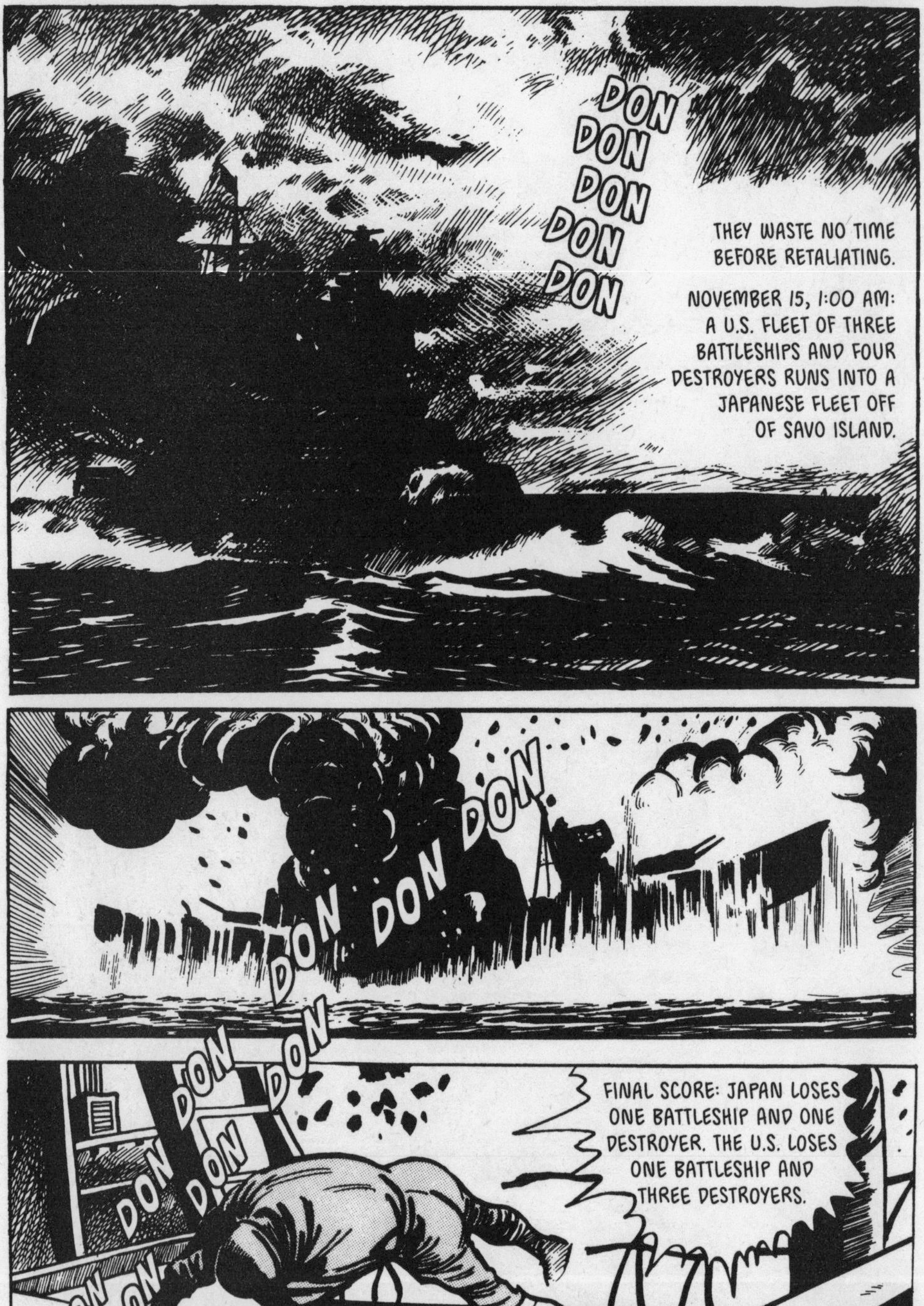
DON DON DON DON DON
THEY WASTE NO TIME BEFORE RETALIATING.
NOVEMBER 15, 1:00 AM: A U.S. FLEET OF THREE BATTLESHIPS AND FOUR DESTROYERS RUNS INTO A JAPANESE FLEET OFF OF SAVO ISLAND.
DON DON DON DON
FINAL SCORE: JAPAN LOSES ONE BATTLESHIP AND ONE DESTROYER. THE U.S. LOSES ONE BATTLESHIP AND THREE DESTROYERS.
DON DON DON DON
DON DON DON DON

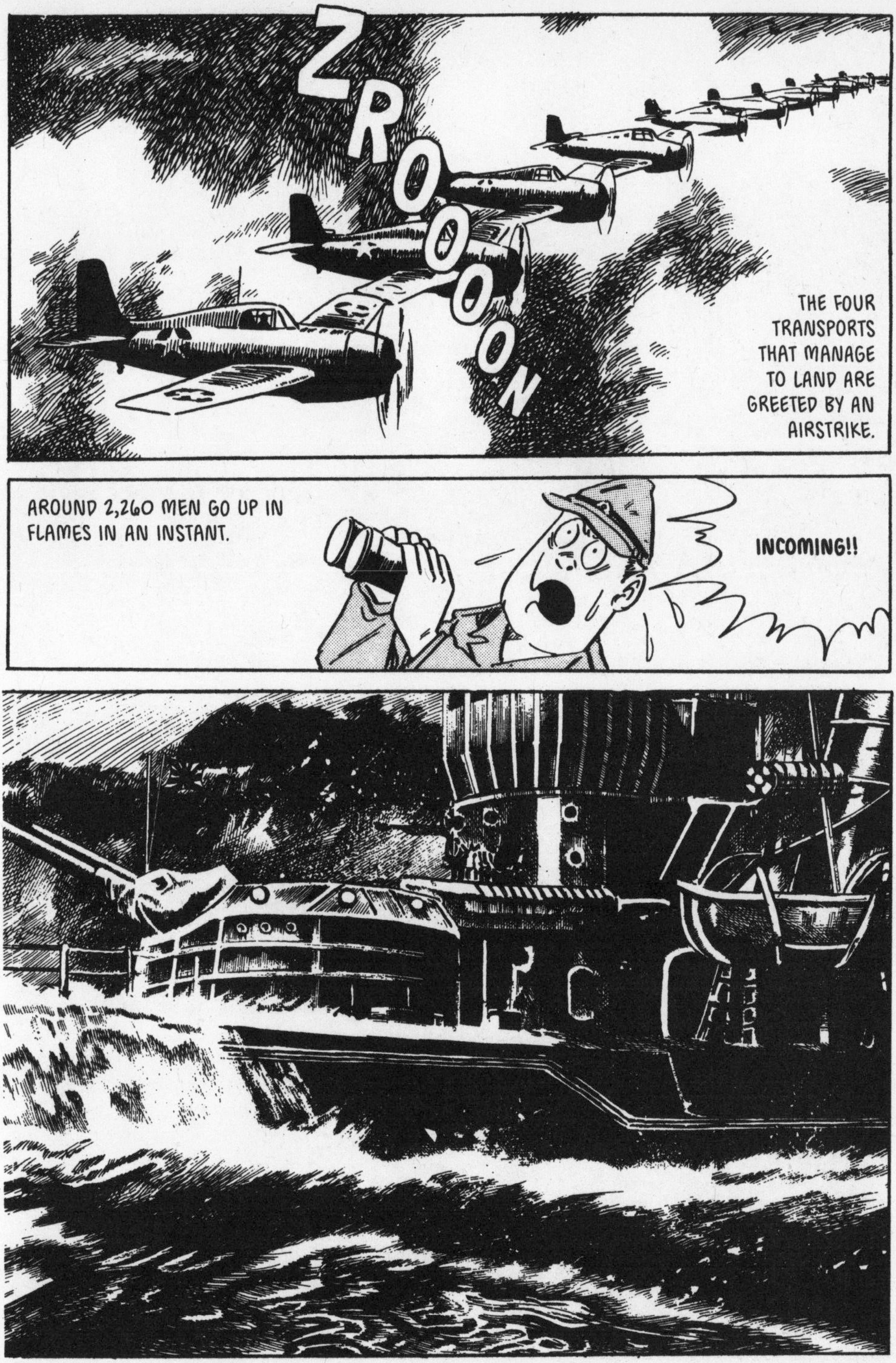
THE FOUR TRANSPORTS THAT MANAGE TO LAND ARE GREETED BY AN AIRSTRIKE.
ZROOOOON
INCOMING!!
AROUND 2,260 MEN GO UP IN FLAMES IN AN INSTANT.

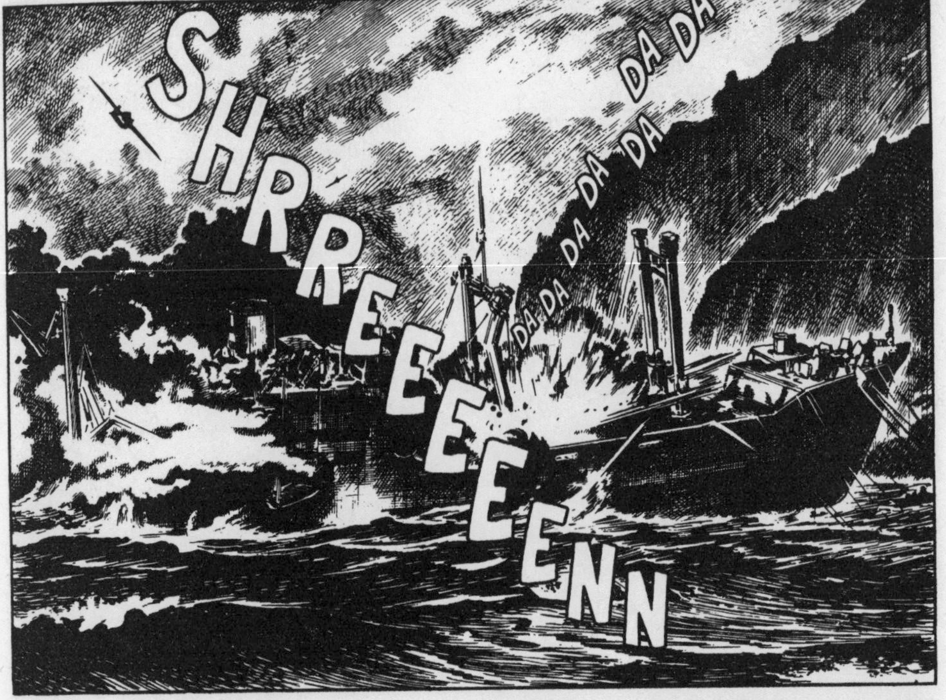
SHRREEEEENN
DA DA DA DA DA DA DA

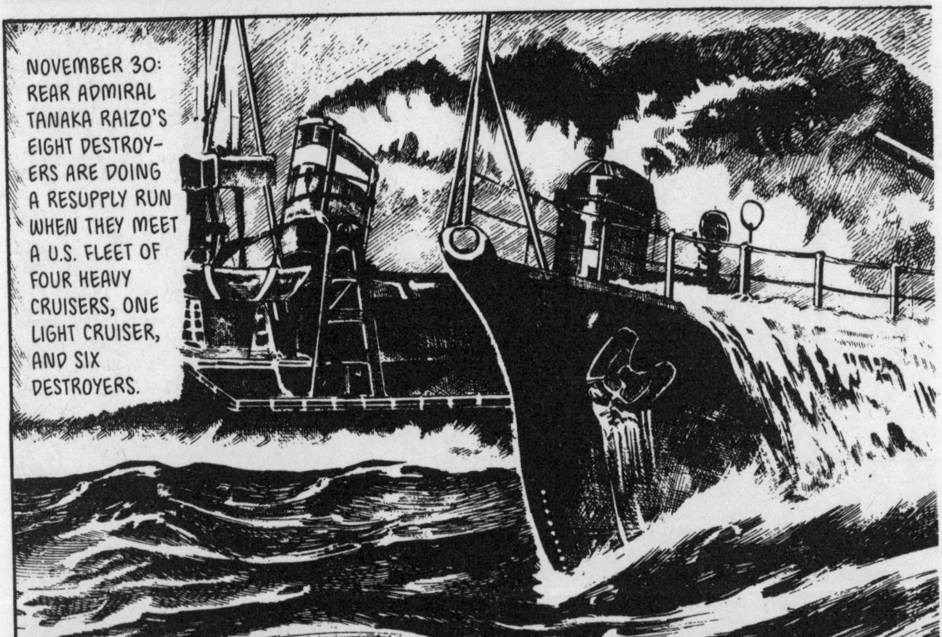
NOVEMBER 30: REAR ADMIRAL TANAKA RAIZO'S EIGHT DESTROYERS ARE DOING A RESUPPLY RUN WHEN THEY MEET A U.S. FLEET OF FOUR HEAVY CRUISERS, ONE LIGHT CRUISER, AND SIX DESTROYERS.

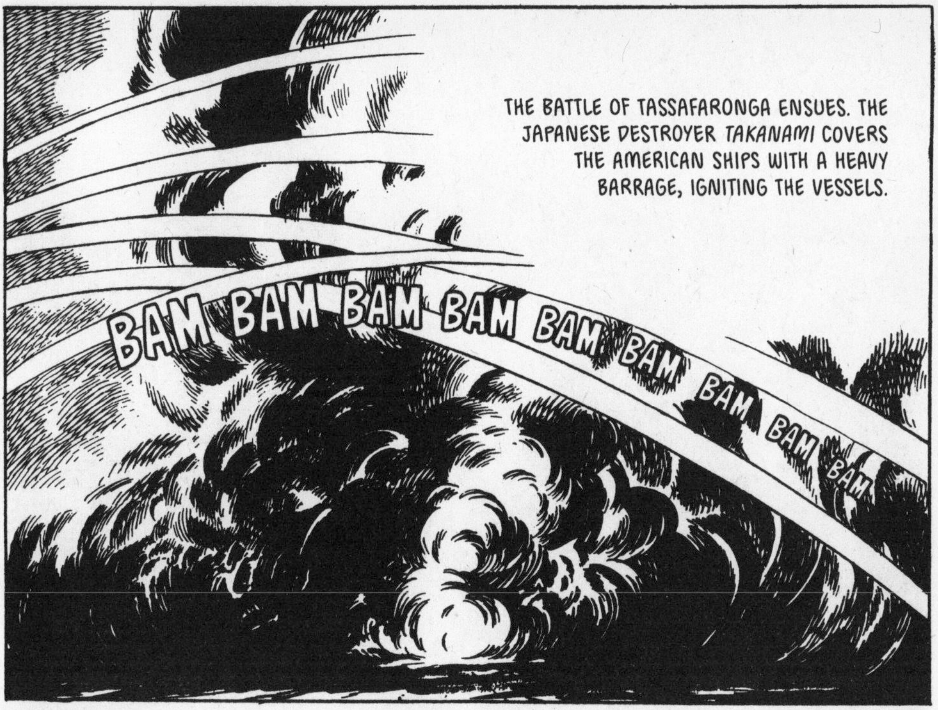
THE BATTLE OF TASSAFARONGA ENSUES. THE JAPANESE DESTROYER *TAKANAMI* COVERS THE AMERICAN SHIPS WITH A HEAVY BARRAGE, IGNITING THE VESSELS.
BAM BAM BAM BAM BAM BAM BAM BAM BAM

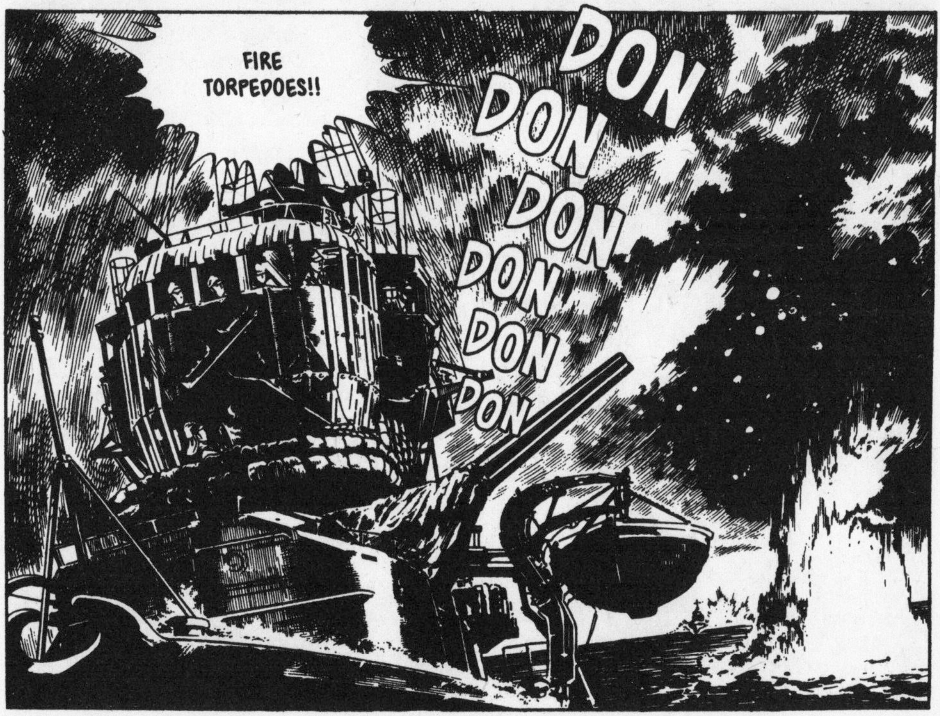
DON DON DON DON DON DON
FIRE TORPEDOES!!

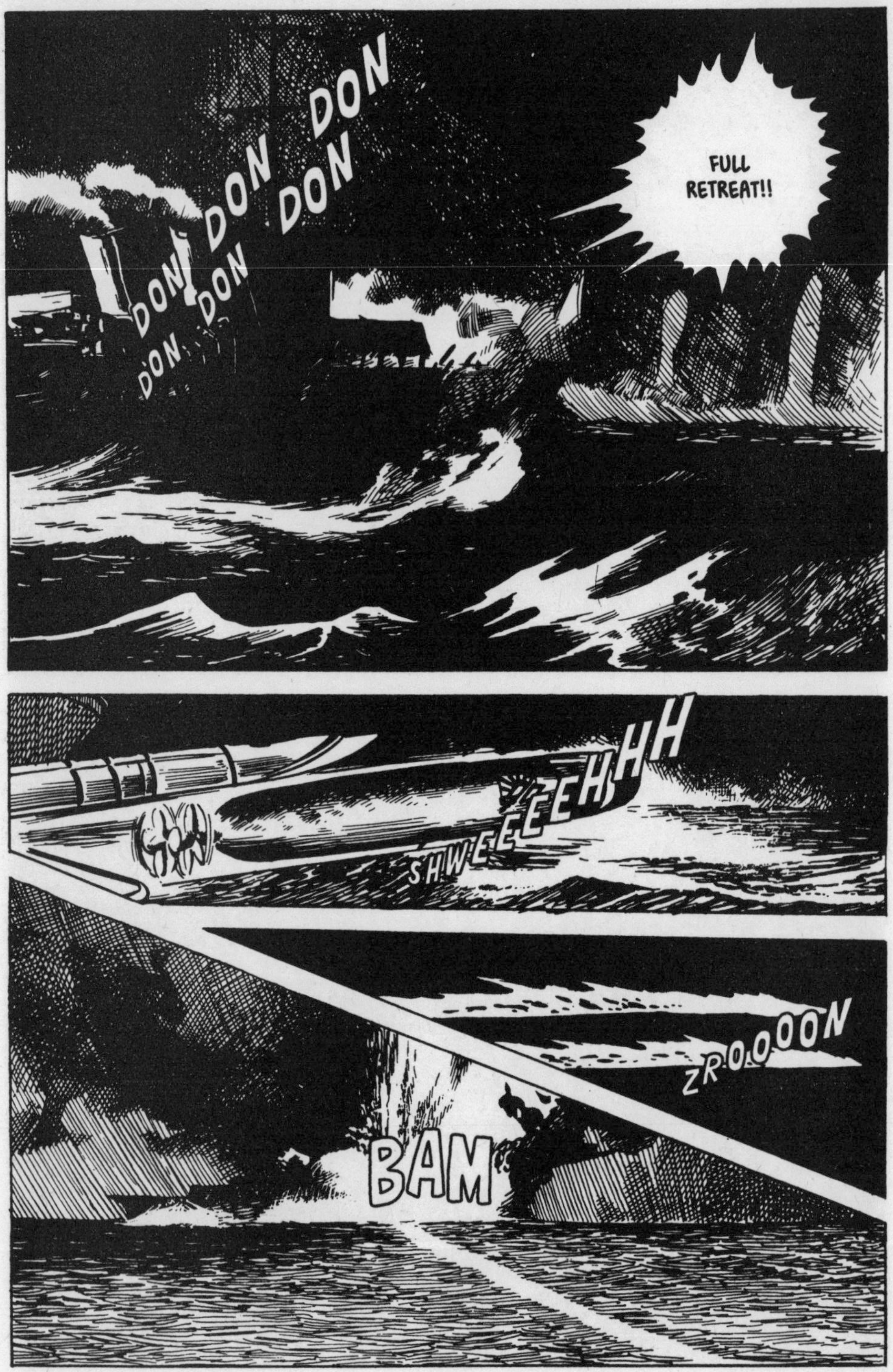
FULL RETREAT!!
DON DON DON
DON DON DON
SHWEEEEEHHH
ZROOOON
BAM

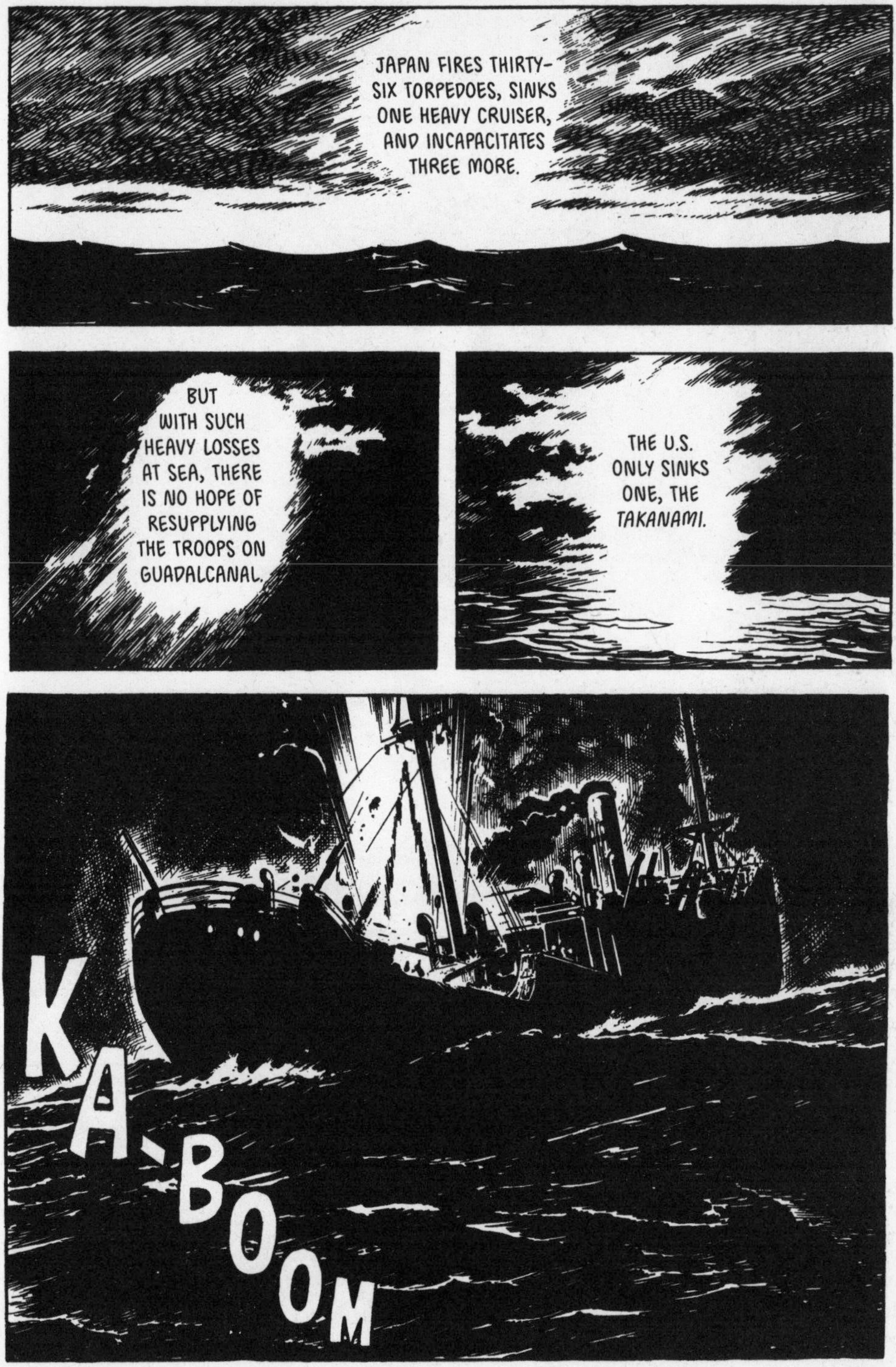
JAPAN FIRES THIRTY-SIX TORPEDOES, SINKS ONE HEAVY CRUISER, AND INCAPACITATES THREE MORE.
THE U.S. ONLY SINKS ONE, THE *TAKANAMI*.
BUT WITH SUCH HEAVY LOSSES AT SEA, THERE IS NO HOPE OF RESUPPLYING THE TROOPS ON GUADALCANAL.
KA-BOOM

THE TURNING OF THE TIDE

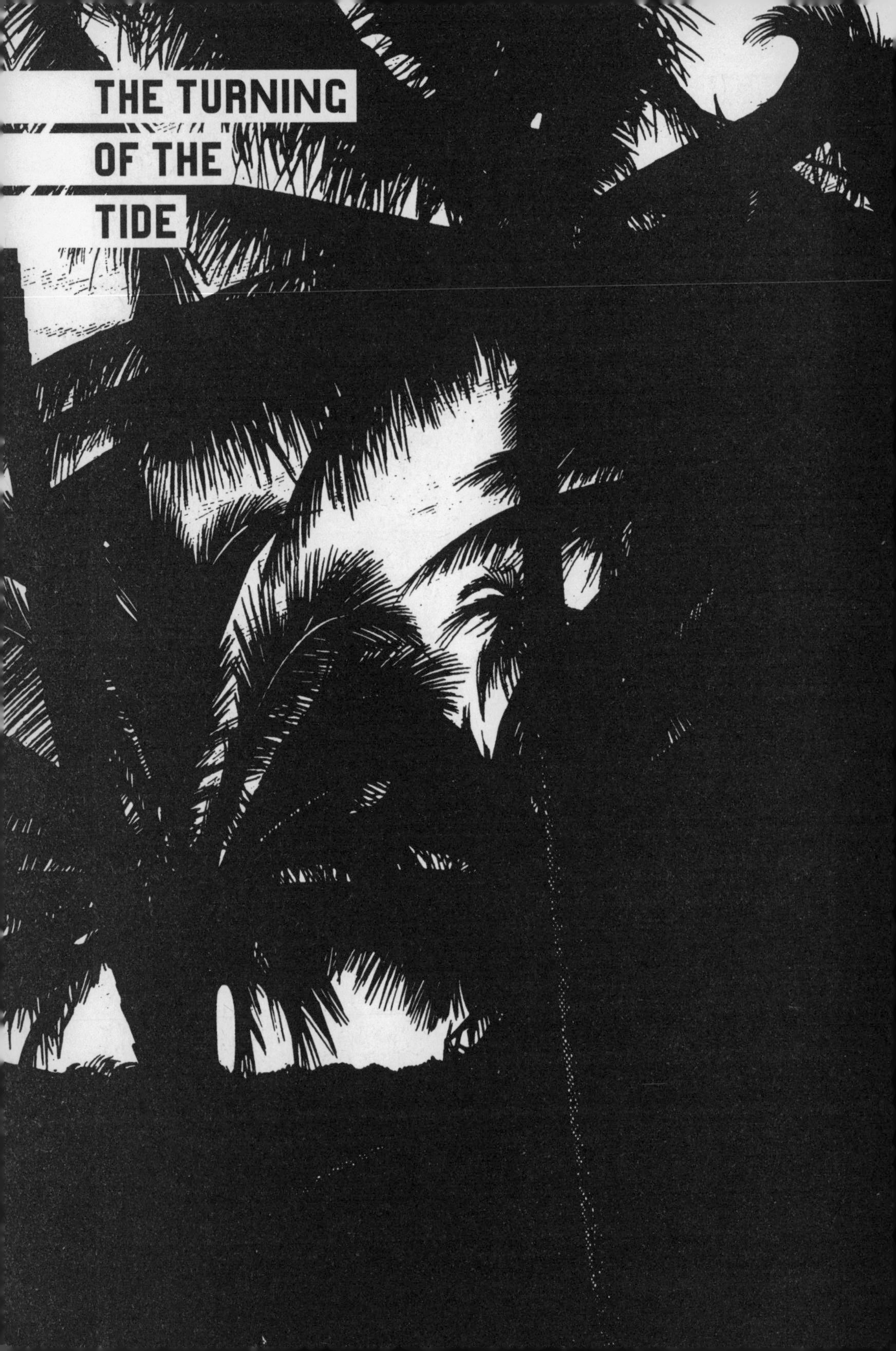

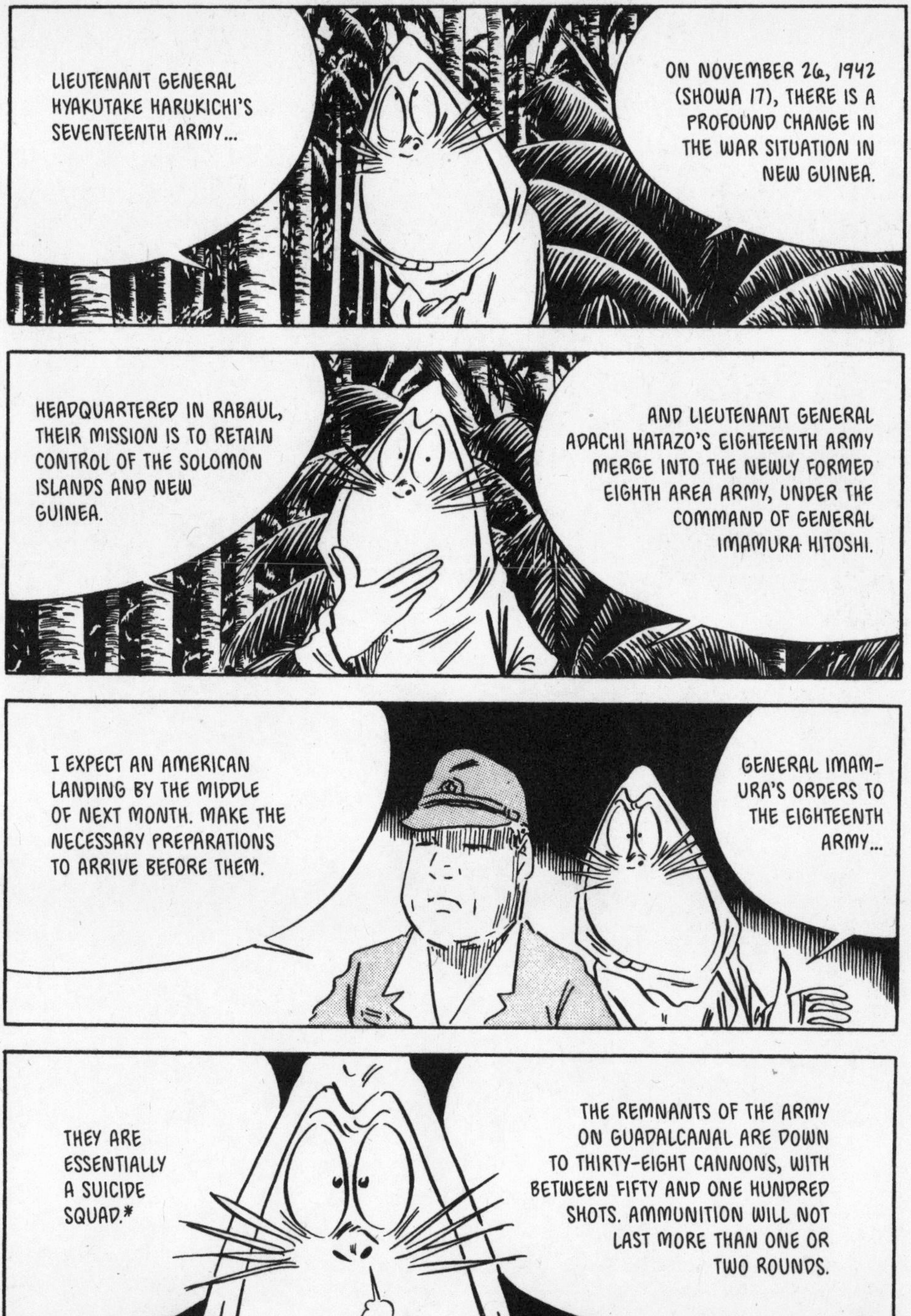
ON NOVEMBER 26, 1942 (SHOWA 17), THERE IS A PROFOUND CHANGE IN THE WAR SITUATION IN NEW GUINEA.
LIEUTENANT GENERAL HYAKUTAKE HARUKICHI'S SEVENTEENTH ARMY...
AND LIEUTENANT GENERAL ADACHI HATAZO'S EIGHTEENTH ARMY MERGE INTO THE NEWLY FORMED EIGHTH AREA ARMY, UNDER THE COMMAND OF GENERAL IMAMURA HITOSHI.
HEADQUARTERED IN RABAUL, THEIR MISSION IS TO RETAIN CONTROL OF THE SOLOMON ISLANDS AND NEW GUINEA.
GENERAL IMAMURA'S ORDERS TO THE EIGHTEENTH ARMY...
I EXPECT AN AMERICAN LANDING BY THE MIDDLE OF NEXT MONTH. MAKE THE NECESSARY PREPARATIONS TO ARRIVE BEFORE THEM.
THE REMNANTS OF THE ARMY ON GUADALCANAL ARE DOWN TO THIRTY-EIGHT CANNONS, WITH BETWEEN FIFTY AND ONE HUNDRED SHOTS. AMMUNITION WILL NOT LAST MORE THAN ONE OR TWO ROUNDS.
THEY ARE ESSENTIALLY A SUICIDE SQUAD.*

*SEE NOTE ON PAGE 548.

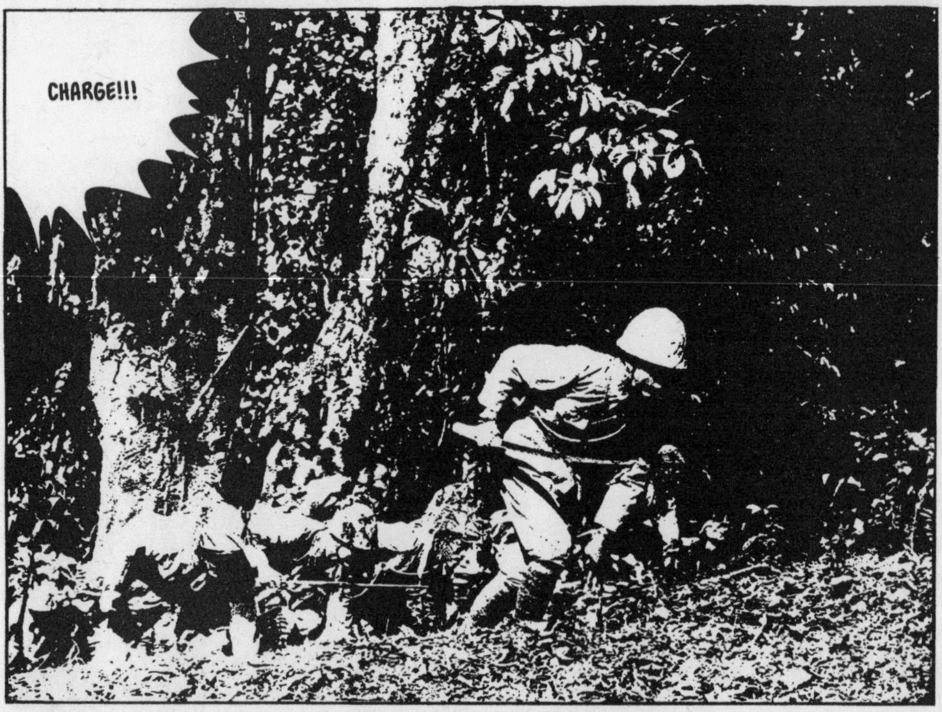
CHARGE!!!

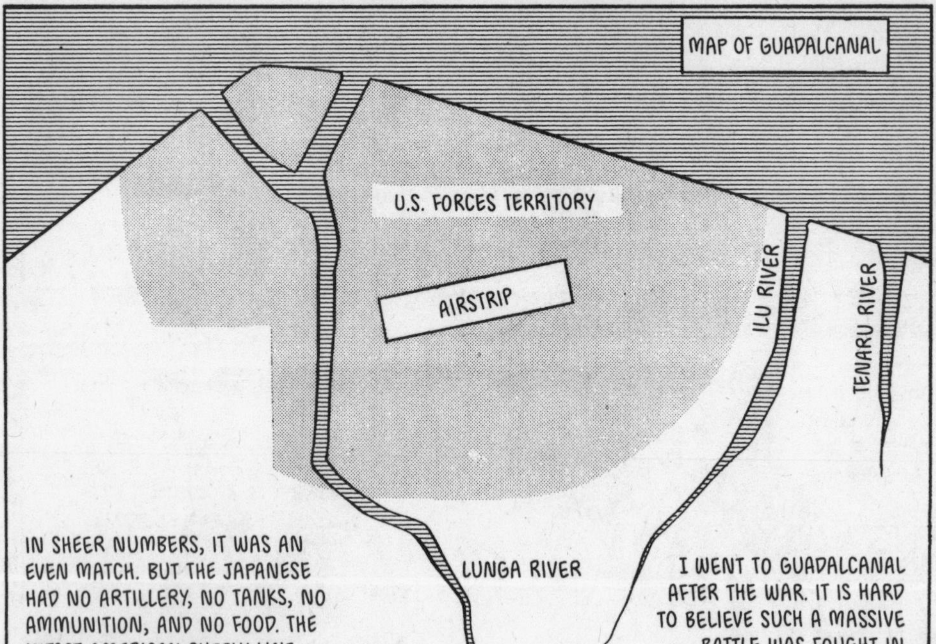
MAP OF GUADALCANAL
U.S. FORCES TERRITORY
AIRSTRIP
TENARU RIVER
ILU RIVER
I WENT TO GUADALCANAL AFTER THE WAR. IT IS HARD TO BELIEVE SUCH A MASSIVE BATTLE WAS FOUGHT IN SUCH A SMALL PLACE.
LUNGA RIVER
IN SHEER NUMBERS, IT WAS AN EVEN MATCH. BUT THE JAPANESE HAD NO ARTILLERY, NO TANKS, NO AMMUNITION, AND NO FOOD. THE INTACT AMERICAN SUPPLY LINE MADE ALL THE DIFFERENCE.

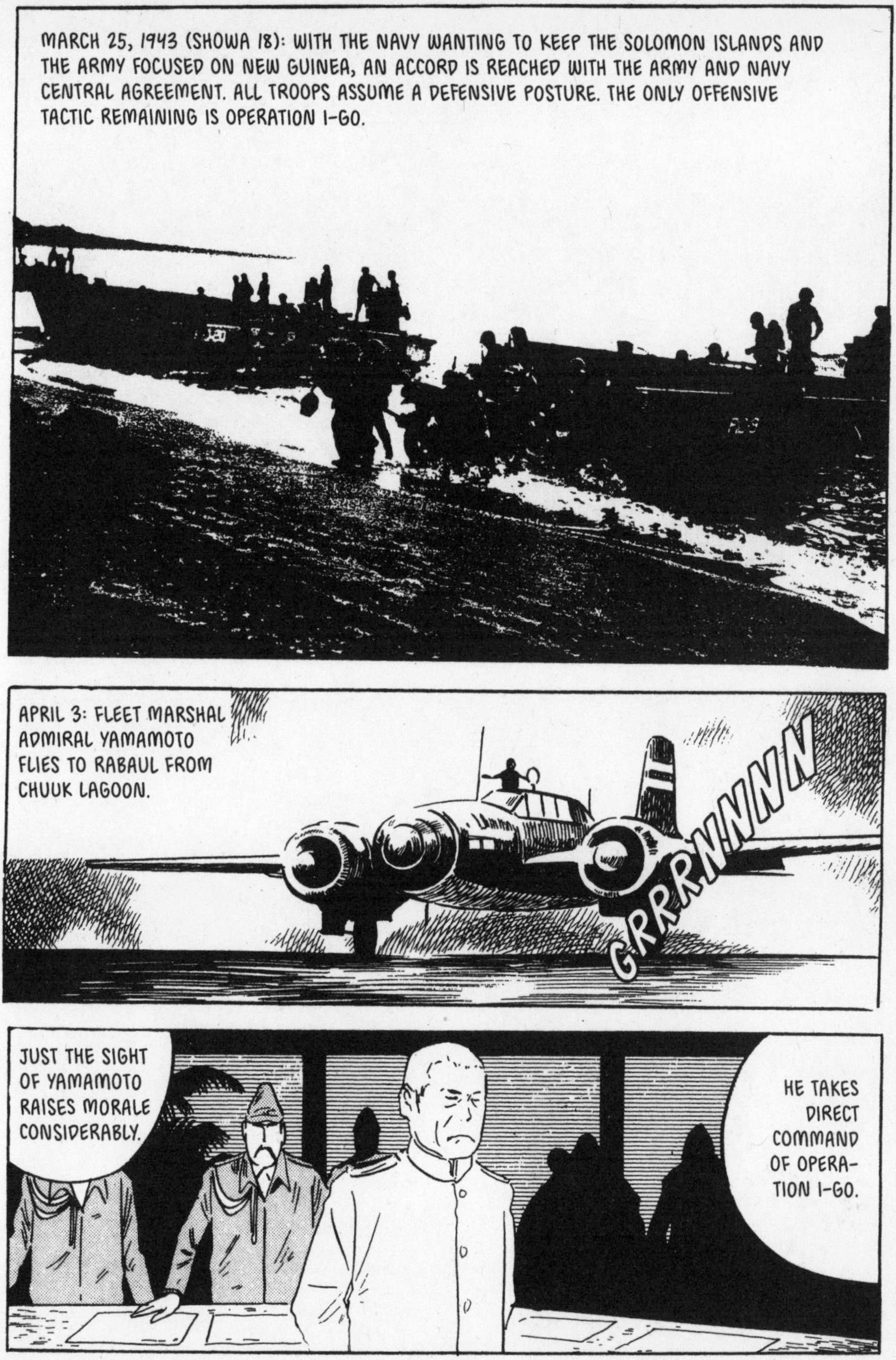
MARCH 25, 1943 (SHOWA 18): WITH THE NAVY WANTING TO KEEP THE SOLOMON ISLANDS AND THE ARMY FOCUSED ON NEW GUINEA, AN ACCORD IS REACHED WITH THE ARMY AND NAVY CENTRAL AGREEMENT. ALL TROOPS ASSUME A DEFENSIVE POSTURE. THE ONLY OFFENSIVE TACTIC REMAINING IS OPERATION I-GO.
APRIL 3: FLEET MARSHAL ADMIRAL YAMAMOTO FLIES TO RABAUL FROM CHUUK LAGOON.
GRRRNNNNN
HE TAKES DIRECT COMMAND OF OPERATION I-GO.
JUST THE SIGHT OF YAMAMOTO RAISES MORALE CONSIDERABLY.

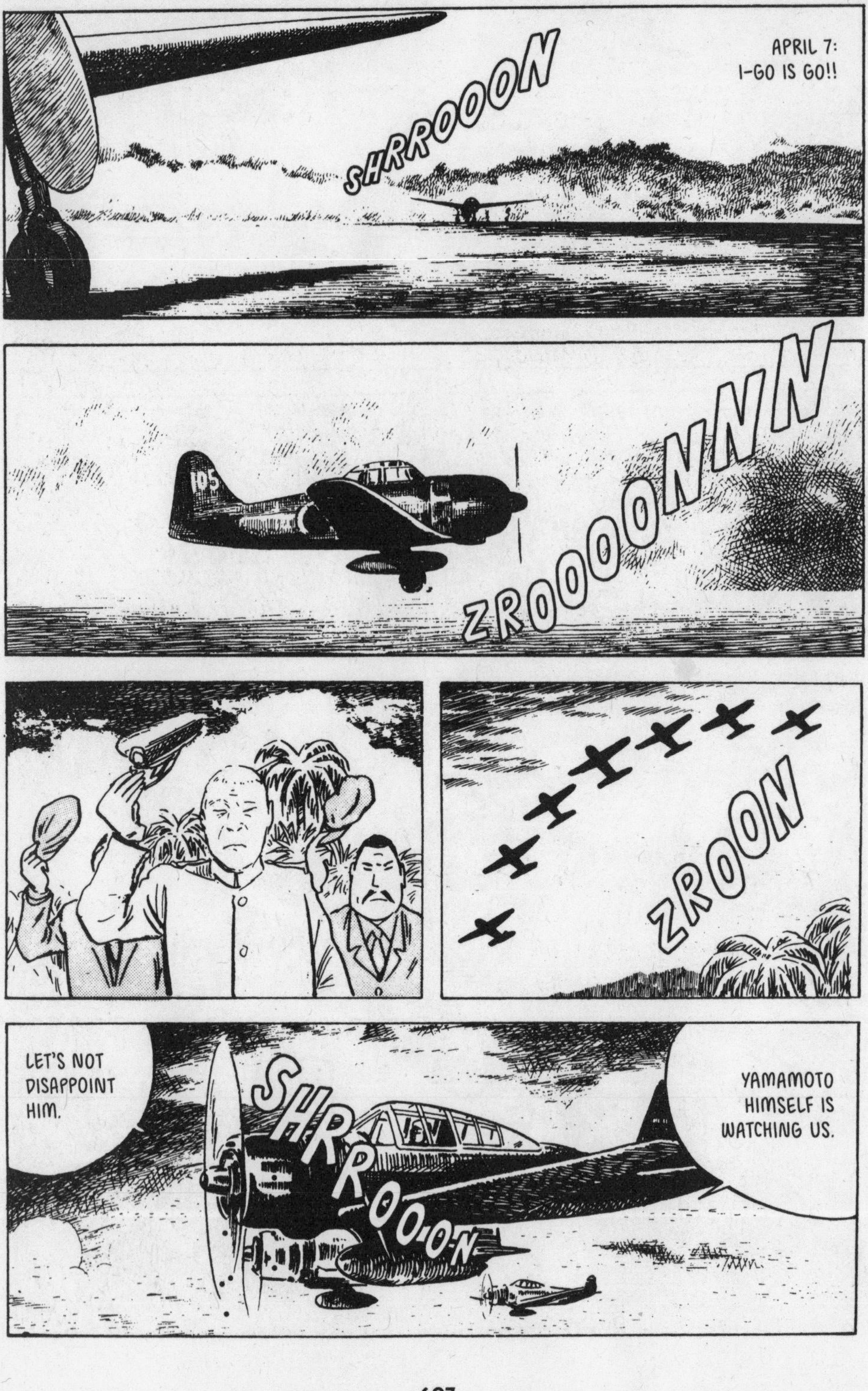
APRIL 7:
I-GO IS GO!!
SHRROOON
ZROOOOONNN
ZROON
YAMAMOTO HIMSELF IS WATCHING US.
LET'S NOT DISAPPOINT HIM.
SHRROOON

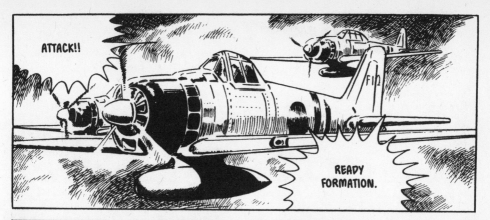

ATTACK!!

READY FORMATION.

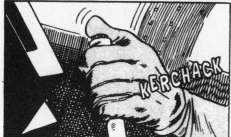

KERCHACK

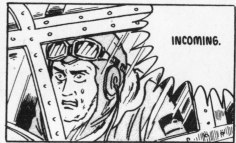

INCOMING.

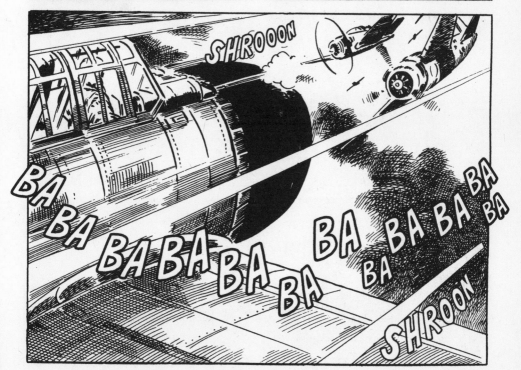

SHROOON

BA BA BA BA BA BA BA BA BA BA

SHROON

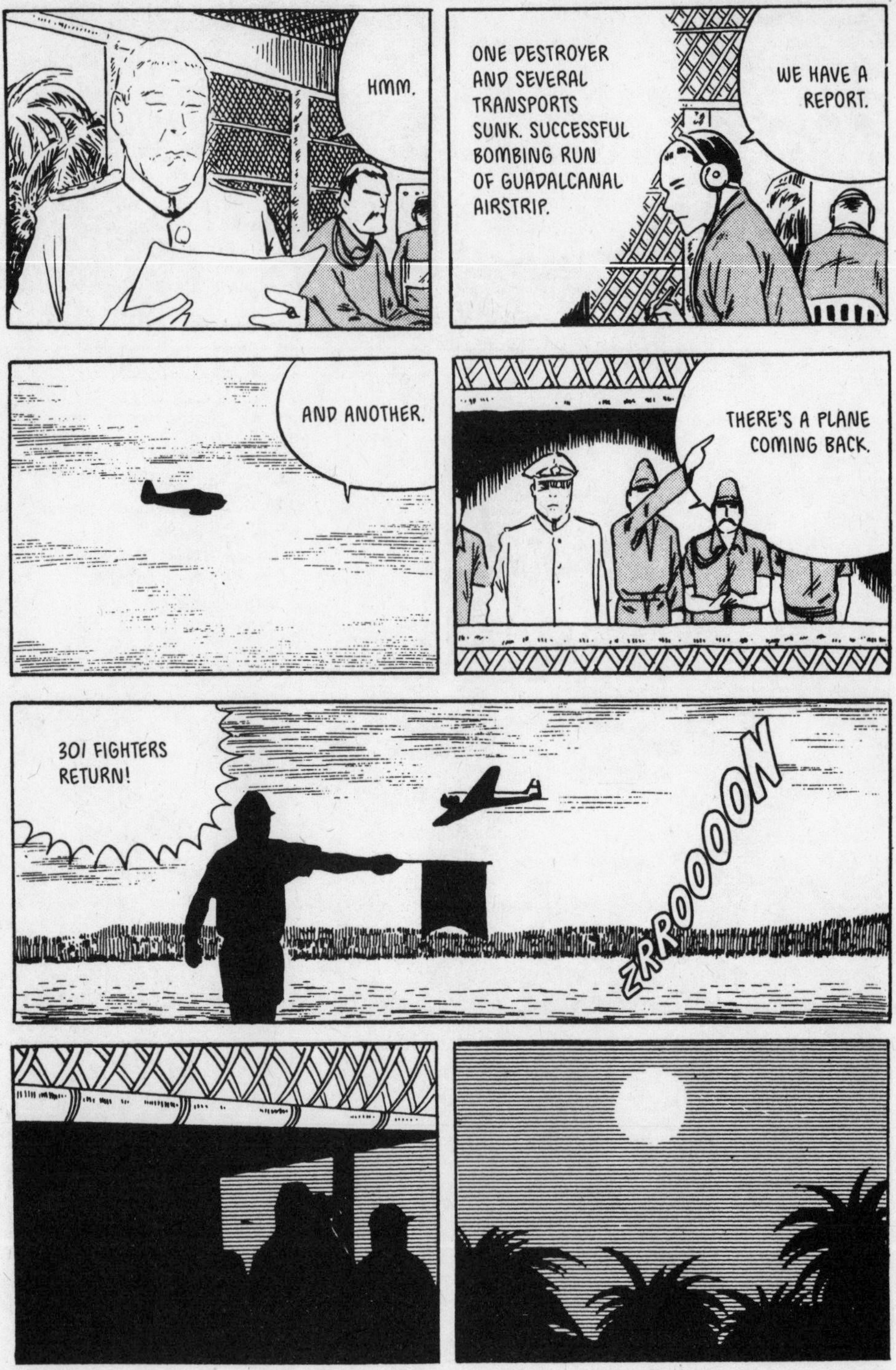
WE HAVE A REPORT.
ONE DESTROYER AND SEVERAL TRANSPORTS SUNK. SUCCESSFUL BOMBING RUN OF GUADALCANAL AIRSTRIP.
HMM.
THERE'S A PLANE COMING BACK.
AND ANOTHER.
301 FIGHTERS RETURN!
ZRROOOOON

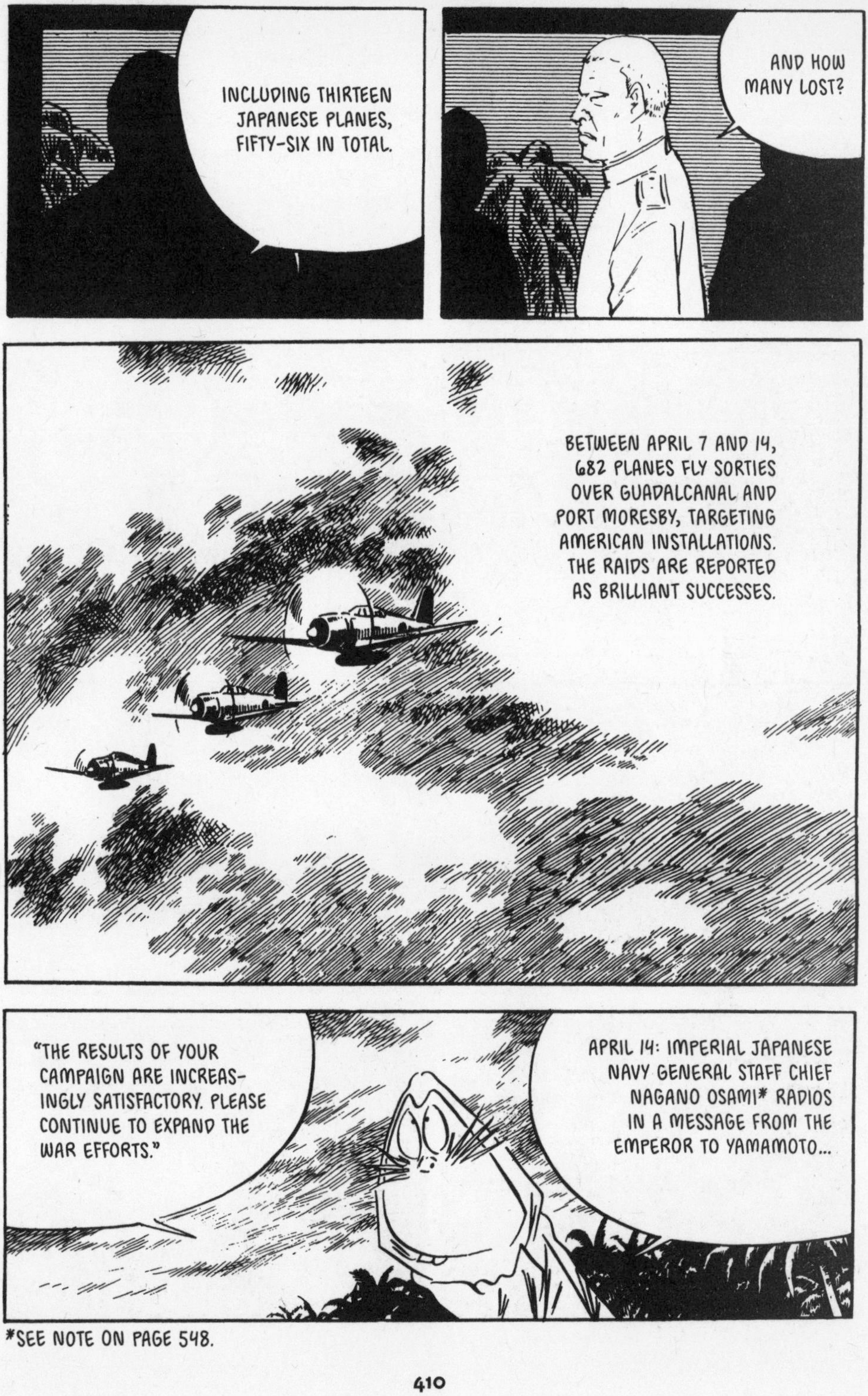
AND HOW MANY LOST?
INCLUDING THIRTEEN JAPANESE PLANES, FIFTY-SIX IN TOTAL.
BETWEEN APRIL 7 AND 14, 682 PLANES FLY SORTIES OVER GUADALCANAL AND PORT MORESBY, TARGETING AMERICAN INSTALLATIONS. THE RAIDS ARE REPORTED AS BRILLIANT SUCCESSES.
APRIL 14: IMPERIAL JAPANESE NAVY GENERAL STAFF CHIEF NAGANO OSAMI* RADIOS IN A MESSAGE FROM THE EMPEROR TO YAMAMOTO...
"THE RESULTS OF YOUR CAMPAIGN ARE INCREASINGLY SATISFACTORY. PLEASE CONTINUE TO EXPAND THE WAR EFFORTS."

*SEE NOTE ON PAGE 548.

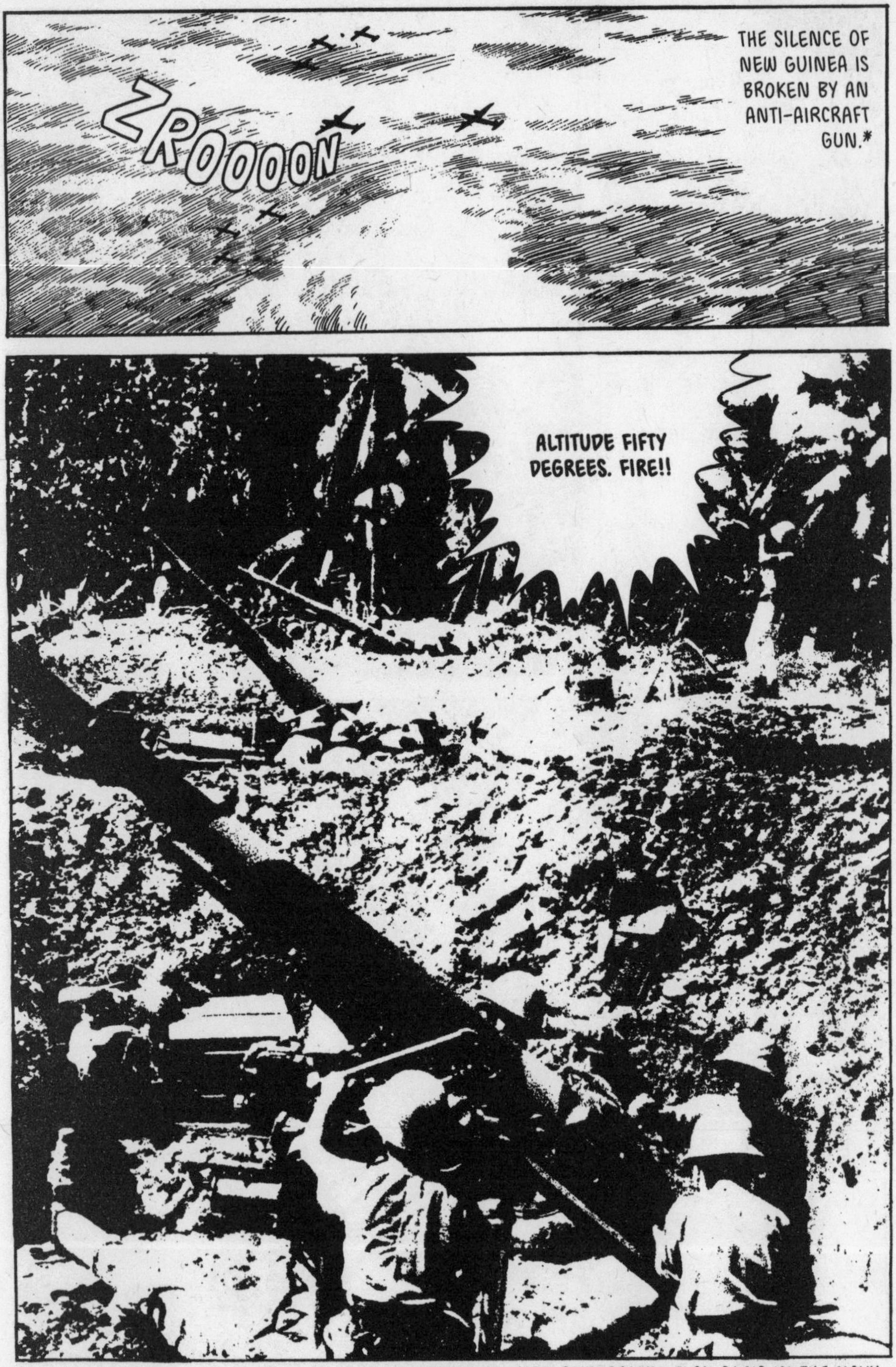
THE SILENCE OF NEW GUINEA IS BROKEN BY AN ANTI-AIRCRAFT GUN.*
ZROOOON
ALTITUDE FIFTY DEGREES. FIRE!!

*A LARGE MOUNTED GUN CAPABLE OF SHOOTING DOWN AN AIRPLANE. CALLED FLAK GUNS IN THE NAVY.

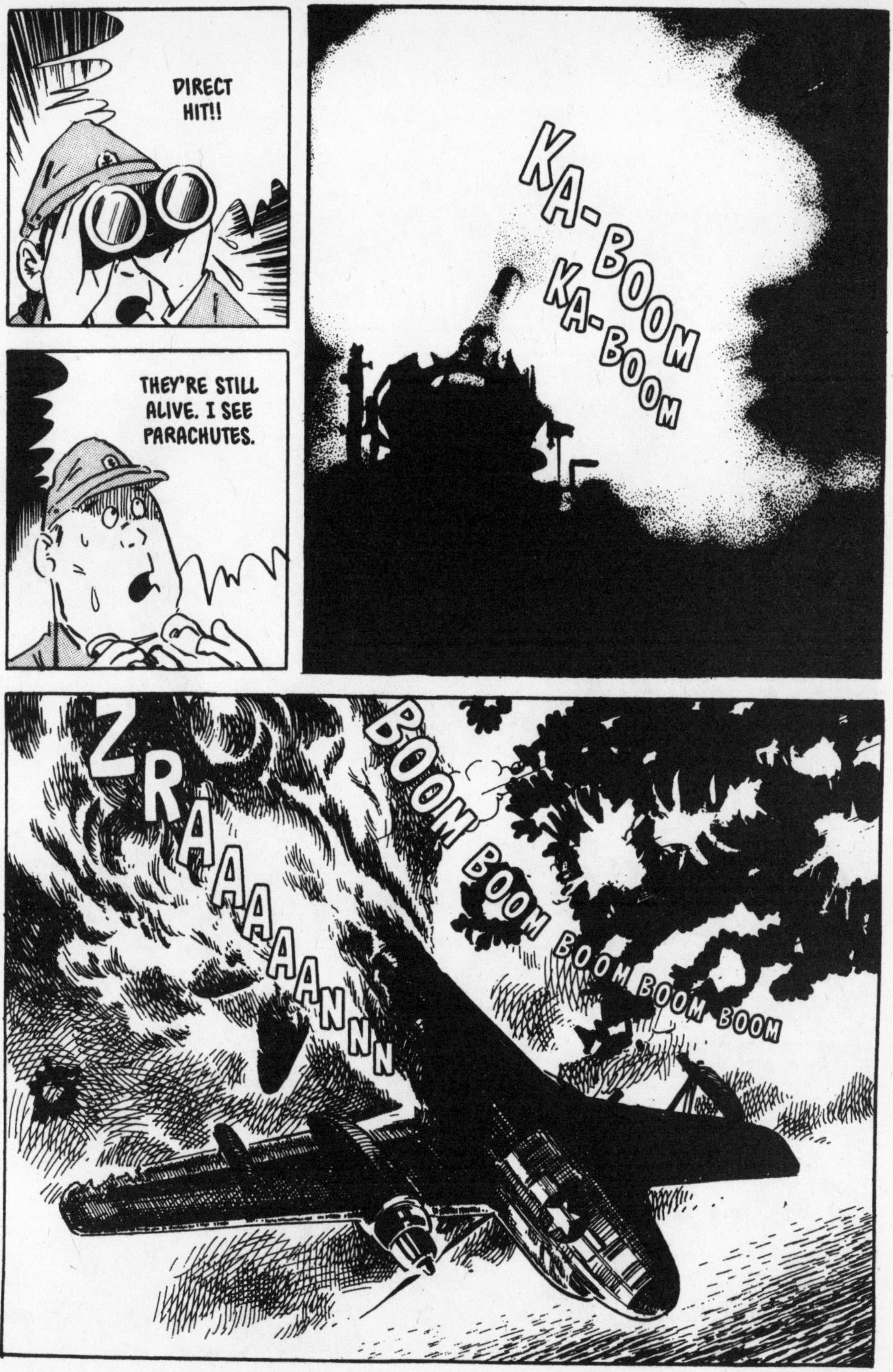
KA-BOOM
KA-BOOM
DIRECT HIT!!
THEY'RE STILL ALIVE. I SEE PARACHUTES.
BOOM BOOM BOOM BOOM BOOM
ZRAAAAAANNN

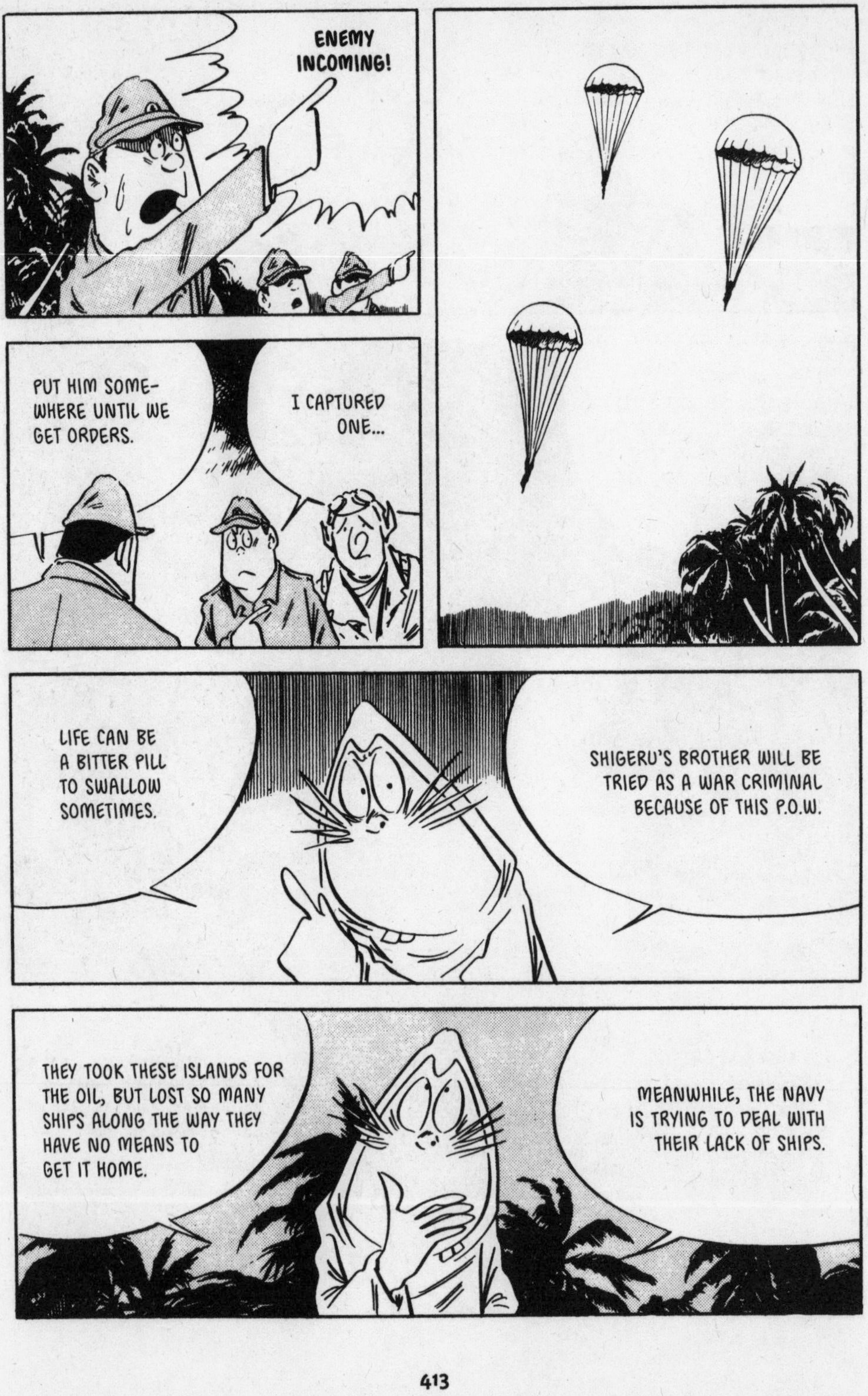
ENEMY INCOMING!
I CAPTURED ONE...
PUT HIM SOME-WHERE UNTIL WE GET ORDERS.
SHIGERU'S BROTHER WILL BE TRIED AS A WAR CRIMINAL BECAUSE OF THIS P.O.W.
LIFE CAN BE A BITTER PILL TO SWALLOW SOMETIMES.
MEANWHILE, THE NAVY IS TRYING TO DEAL WITH THEIR LACK OF SHIPS.
THEY TOOK THESE ISLANDS FOR THE OIL, BUT LOST SO MANY SHIPS ALONG THE WAY THEY HAVE NO MEANS TO GET IT HOME.

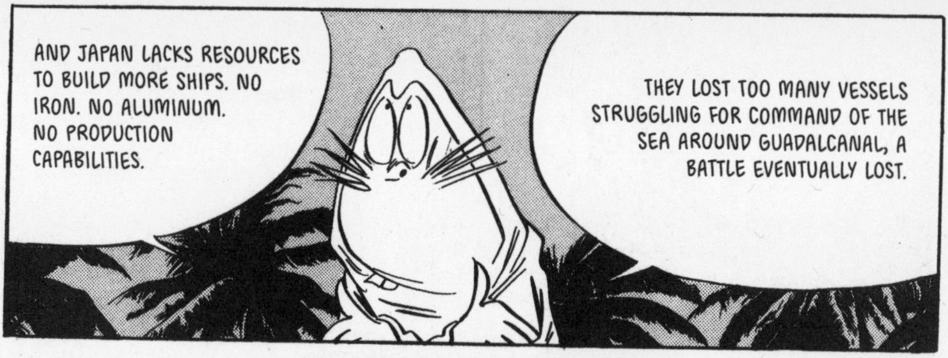
THEY LOST TOO MANY VESSELS STRUGGLING FOR COMMAND OF THE SEA AROUND GUADALCANAL, A BATTLE EVENTUALLY LOST.
AND JAPAN LACKS RESOURCES TO BUILD MORE SHIPS. NO IRON. NO ALUMINUM. NO PRODUCTION CAPABILITIES.

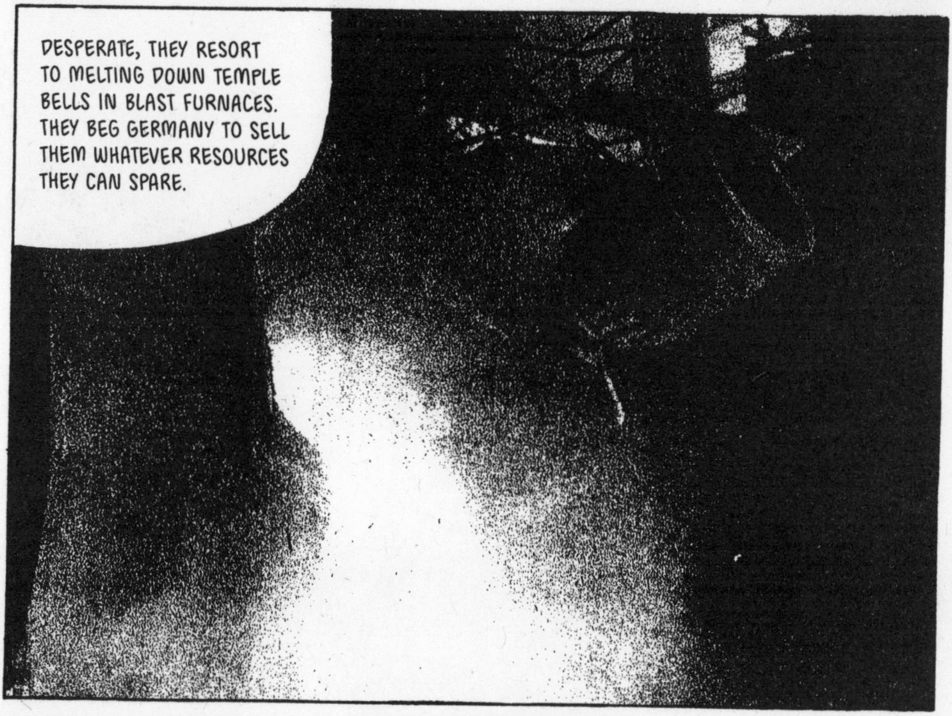
DESPERATE, THEY RESORT TO MELTING DOWN TEMPLE BELLS IN BLAST FURNACES. THEY BEG GERMANY TO SELL THEM WHATEVER RESOURCES THEY CAN SPARE.

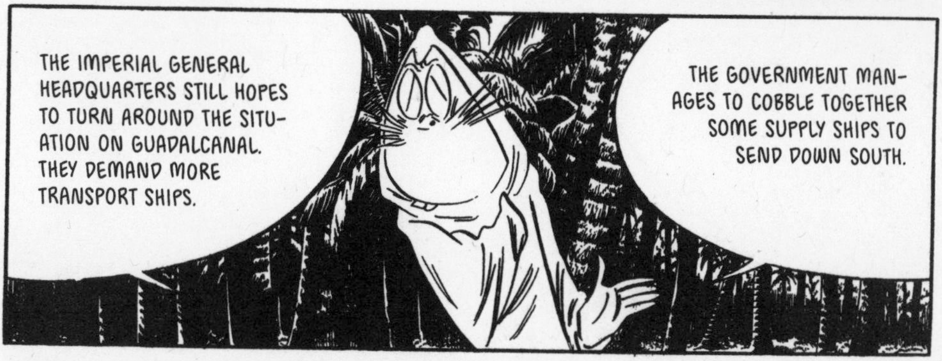
THE GOVERNMENT MAN-AGES TO COBBLE TOGETHER SOME SUPPLY SHIPS TO SEND DOWN SOUTH.
THE IMPERIAL GENERAL HEADQUARTERS STILL HOPES TO TURN AROUND THE SITU-ATION ON GUADALCANAL. THEY DEMAND MORE TRANSPORT SHIPS.

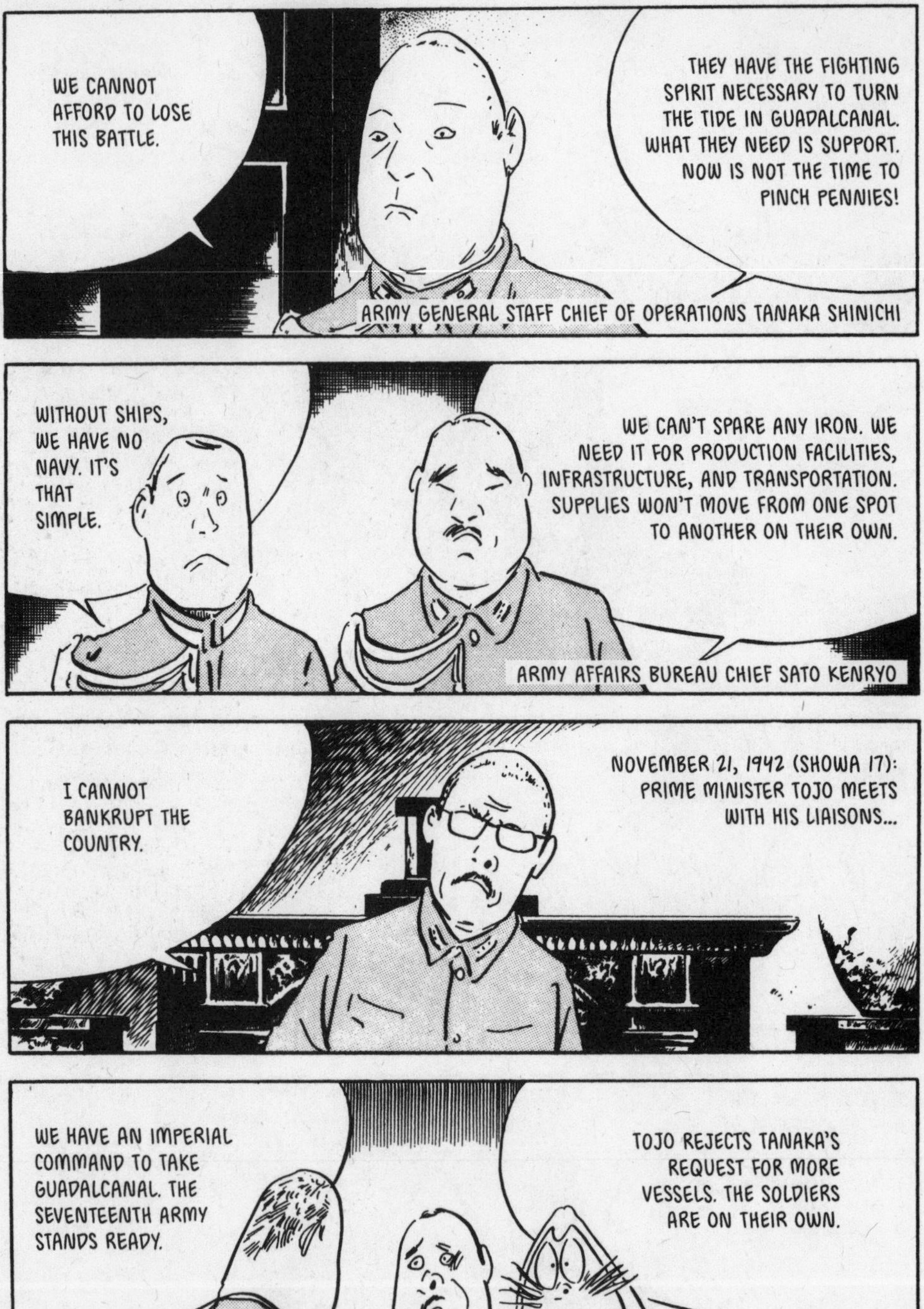
THEY HAVE THE FIGHTING SPIRIT NECESSARY TO TURN THE TIDE IN GUADALCANAL. WHAT THEY NEED IS SUPPORT. NOW IS NOT THE TIME TO PINCH PENNIES!
WE CANNOT AFFORD TO LOSE THIS BATTLE.
ARMY GENERAL STAFF CHIEF OF OPERATIONS TANAKA SHINICHI
WE CAN'T SPARE ANY IRON. WE NEED IT FOR PRODUCTION FACILITIES, INFRASTRUCTURE, AND TRANSPORTATION. SUPPLIES WON'T MOVE FROM ONE SPOT TO ANOTHER ON THEIR OWN.
WITHOUT SHIPS, WE HAVE NO NAVY. IT'S THAT SIMPLE.
ARMY AFFAIRS BUREAU CHIEF SATO KENRYO
NOVEMBER 21, 1942 (SHOWA 17): PRIME MINISTER TOJO MEETS WITH HIS LIAISONS...
I CANNOT BANKRUPT THE COUNTRY.
TOJO REJECTS TANAKA'S REQUEST FOR MORE VESSELS. THE SOLDIERS ARE ON THEIR OWN.
WE HAVE AN IMPERIAL COMMAND TO TAKE GUADALCANAL. THE SEVENTEENTH ARMY STANDS READY.

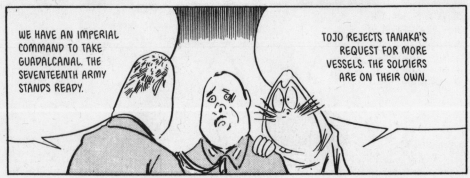

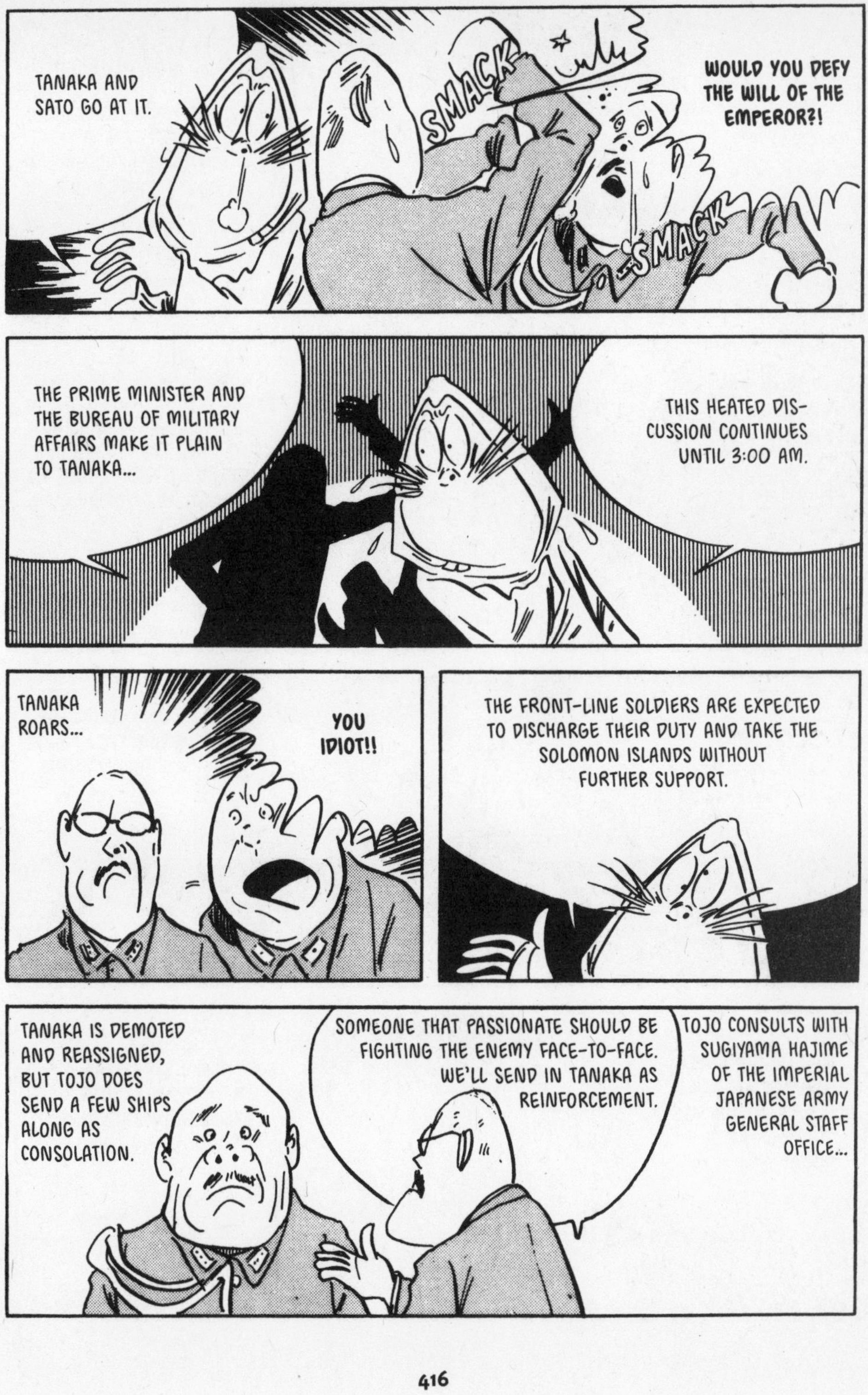
WOULD YOU DEFY THE WILL OF THE EMPEROR?!
SMACK
SMACK
TANAKA AND SATO GO AT IT.
THIS HEATED DISCUSSION CONTINUES UNTIL 3:00 AM.
THE PRIME MINISTER AND THE BUREAU OF MILITARY AFFAIRS MAKE IT PLAIN TO TANAKA...
THE FRONT-LINE SOLDIERS ARE EXPECTED TO DISCHARGE THEIR DUTY AND TAKE THE SOLOMON ISLANDS WITHOUT FURTHER SUPPORT.
YOU IDIOT!!
TANAKA ROARS...
TOJO CONSULTS WITH SUGIYAMA HAJIME OF THE IMPERIAL JAPANESE ARMY GENERAL STAFF OFFICE...
SOMEONE THAT PASSIONATE SHOULD BE FIGHTING THE ENEMY FACE-TO-FACE. WE'LL SEND IN TANAKA AS REINFORCEMENT.
TANAKA IS DEMOTED AND REASSIGNED, BUT TOJO DOES SEND A FEW SHIPS ALONG AS CONSOLATION.

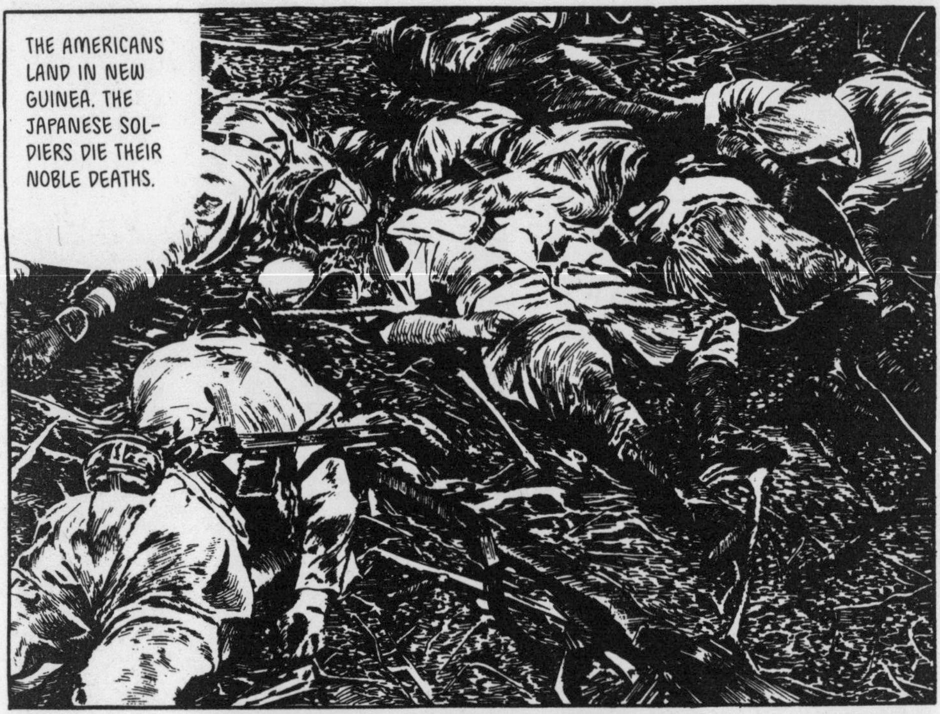
THE AMERICANS LAND IN NEW GUINEA. THE JAPANESE SOL-DIERS DIE THEIR NOBLE DEATHS.

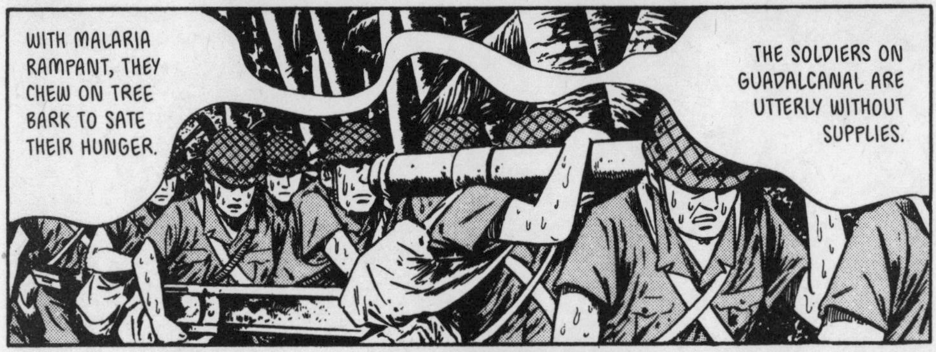
THE SOLDIERS ON GUADALCANAL ARE UTTERLY WITHOUT SUPPLIES.
WITH MALARIA RAMPANT, THEY CHEW ON TREE BARK TO SATE THEIR HUNGER.

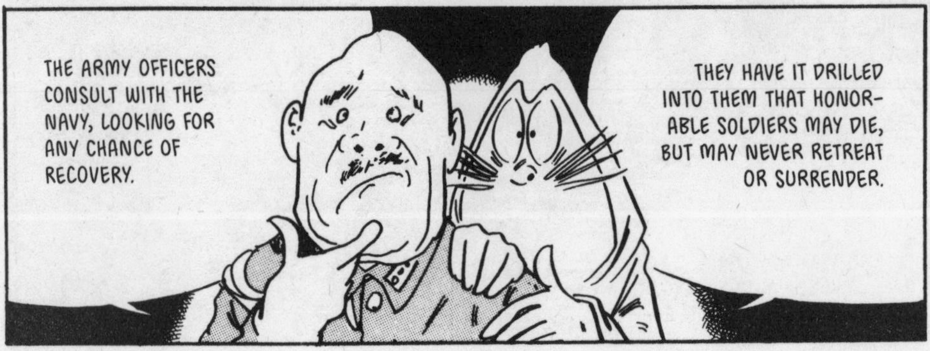
THEY HAVE IT DRILLED INTO THEM THAT HONOR-ABLE SOLDIERS MAY DIE, BUT MAY NEVER RETREAT OR SURRENDER.
THE ARMY OFFICERS CONSULT WITH THE NAVY, LOOKING FOR ANY CHANCE OF RECOVERY.

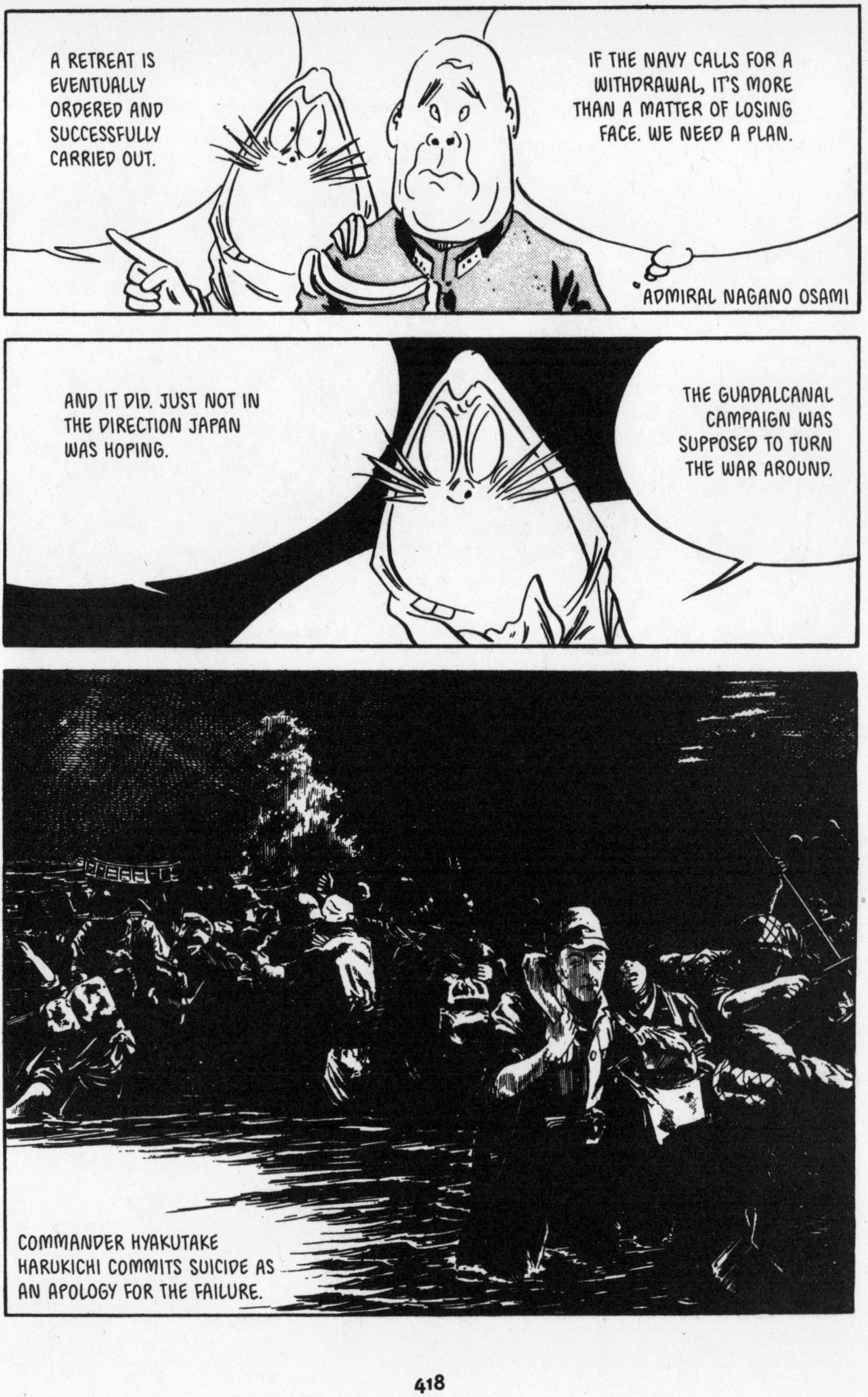
IF THE NAVY CALLS FOR A WITHDRAWAL, IT'S MORE THAN A MATTER OF LOSING FACE. WE NEED A PLAN.
A RETREAT IS EVENTUALLY ORDERED AND SUCCESSFULLY CARRIED OUT.
ADMIRAL NAGANO OSAMI
THE GUADALCANAL CAMPAIGN WAS SUPPOSED TO TURN THE WAR AROUND.
AND IT DID. JUST NOT IN THE DIRECTION JAPAN WAS HOPING.
COMMANDER HYAKUTAKE HARUKICHI COMMITS SUICIDE AS AN APOLOGY FOR THE FAILURE.

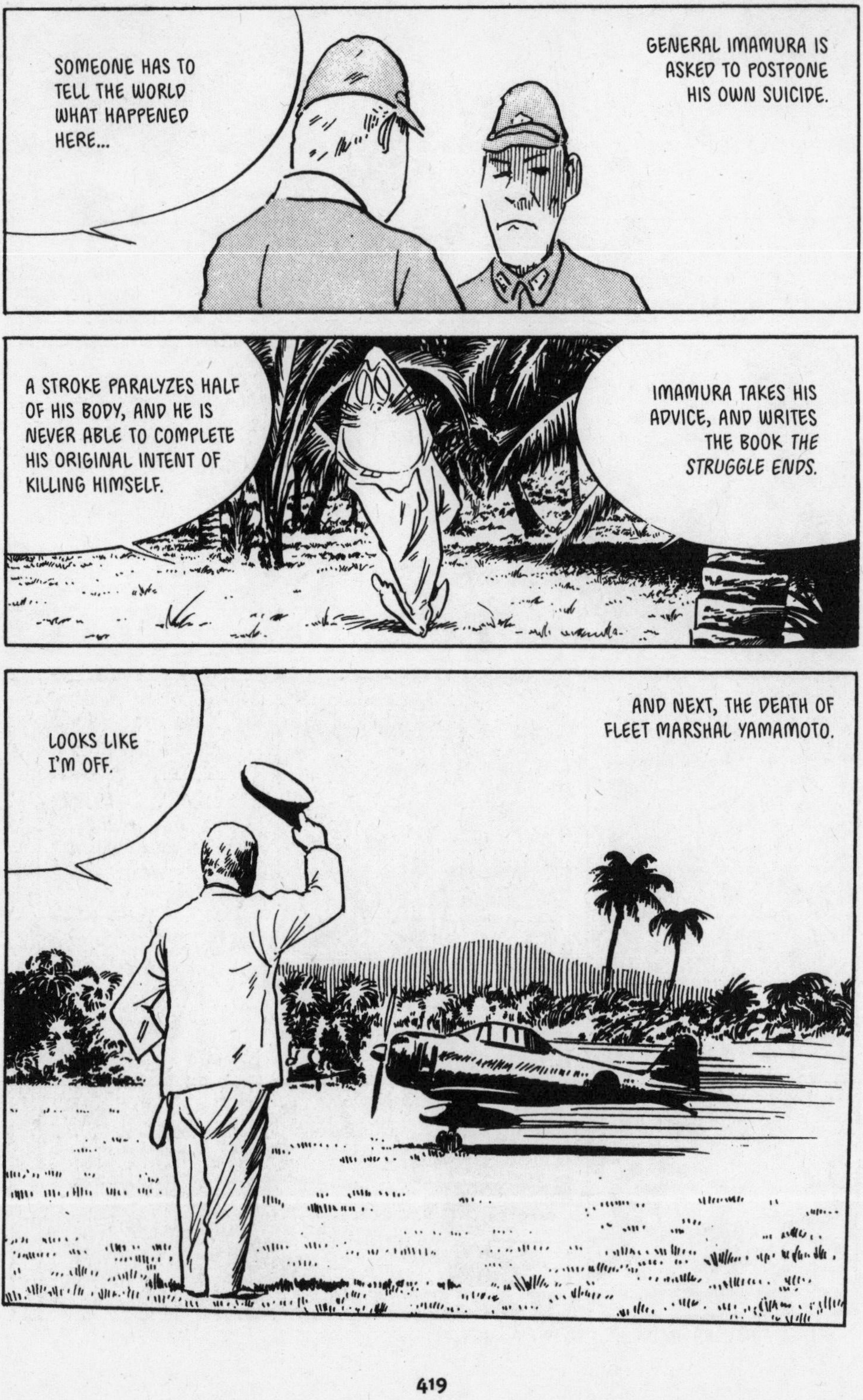
GENERAL IMAMURA IS ASKED TO POSTPONE HIS OWN SUICIDE.
SOMEONE HAS TO TELL THE WORLD WHAT HAPPENED HERE...
IMAMURA TAKES HIS ADVICE, AND WRITES THE BOOK *THE STRUGGLE ENDS.*
A STROKE PARALYZES HALF OF HIS BODY, AND HE IS NEVER ABLE TO COMPLETE HIS ORIGINAL INTENT OF KILLING HIMSELF.
AND NEXT, THE DEATH OF FLEET MARSHAL YAMAMOTO.
LOOKS LIKE I'M OFF.

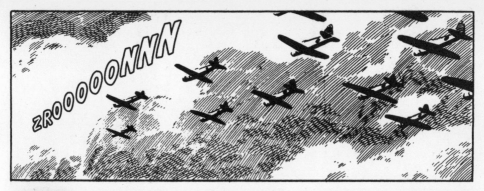

ZROOOOONNN
THE AMERICANS HAVE AMASSED ONE HUNDRED PLANES. I REQUESTED ONE HUNDRED PLANES TO MEET THEM.
I WAS TOLD I COULDN'T EVEN GET TWO OR THREE.
I HOPE THE LIAISON GETS HERE SOON.
I REGRET TO INFORM YOU THAT WE CANNOT RE-SUPPLY YOU WITH A SINGLE PLANE. YOU WILL HAVE TO MAKE DO WITH YOUR AVAILABLE UNITS.
THE LIAISON FROM THE GENERAL STAFF HEADQUARTERS
DO YOU REALLY EXPECT US TO FIGHT A WAR WITHOUT AIRPLANES?
WE WILL CONCENTRATE THE AVAILABLE AIRCRAFT. THAT SHOULD GIVE YOU ONE CARRIER'S FULL.*

*AVERAGE CARRIERS HELD ABOUT FIFTY AIRCRAFT.

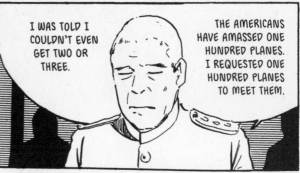

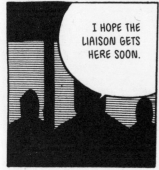

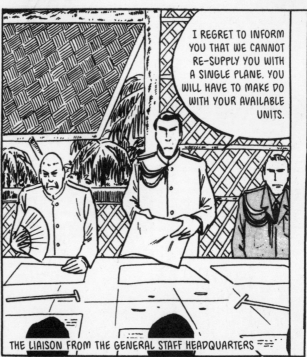

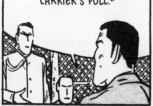

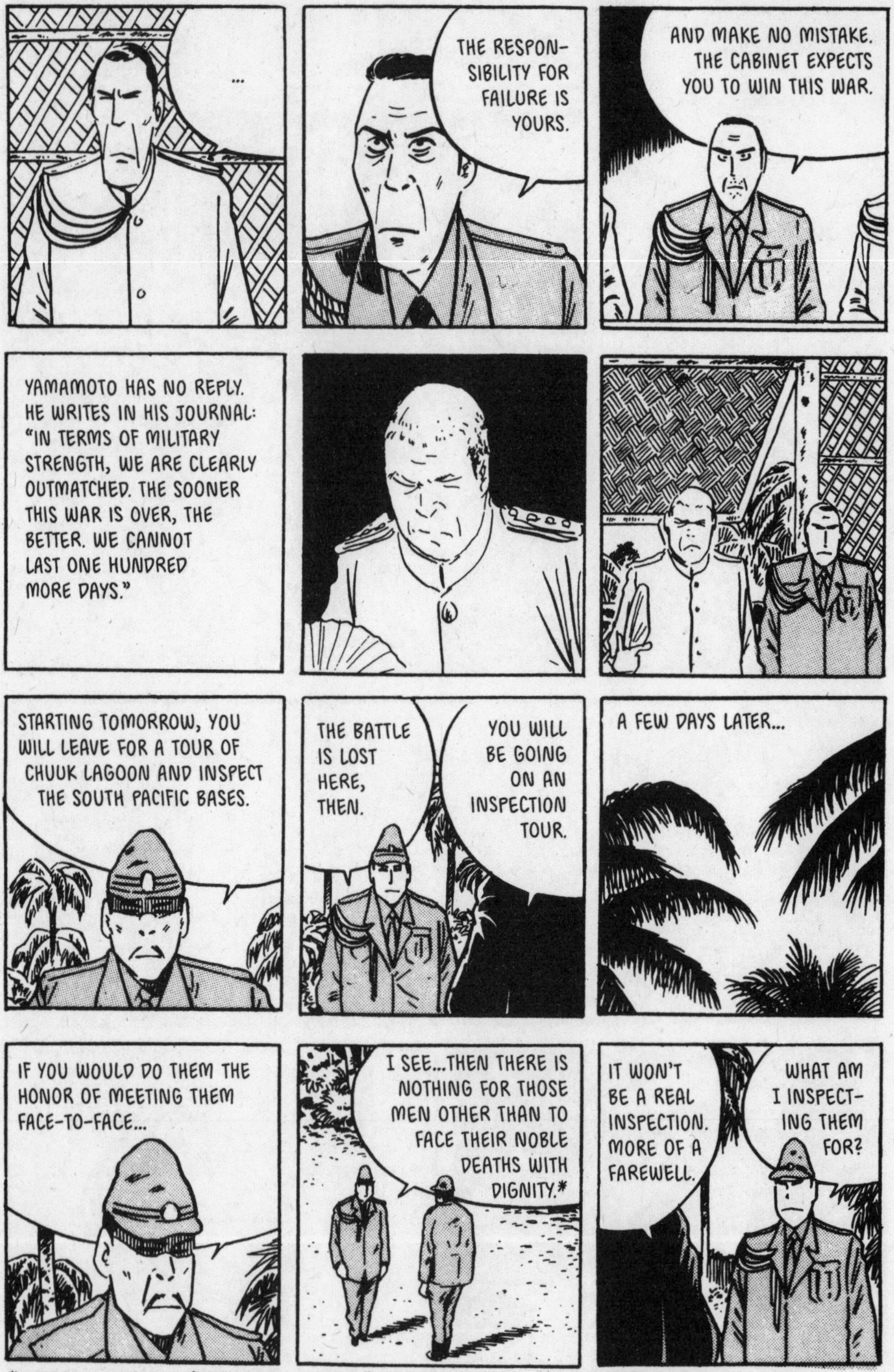
AND MAKE NO MISTAKE. THE CABINET EXPECTS YOU TO WIN THIS WAR.
THE RESPONSIBILITY FOR FAILURE IS YOURS.
...
YAMAMOTO HAS NO REPLY. HE WRITES IN HIS JOURNAL: "IN TERMS OF MILITARY STRENGTH, WE ARE CLEARLY OUTMATCHED. THE SOONER THIS WAR IS OVER, THE BETTER. WE CANNOT LAST ONE HUNDRED MORE DAYS."
A FEW DAYS LATER...
YOU WILL BE GOING ON AN INSPECTION TOUR.
THE BATTLE IS LOST HERE, THEN.
STARTING TOMORROW, YOU WILL LEAVE FOR A TOUR OF CHUUK LAGOON AND INSPECT THE SOUTH PACIFIC BASES.
WHAT AM I INSPECTING THEM FOR?
IT WON'T BE A REAL INSPECTION. MORE OF A FAREWELL.
I SEE...THEN THERE IS NOTHING FOR THOSE MEN OTHER THAN TO FACE THEIR NOBLE DEATHS WITH DIGNITY.*
IF YOU WOULD DO THEM THE HONOR OF MEETING THEM FACE-TO-FACE...

*LITERALLY MEANING "SHATTERED JEWELS," THIS IS THE TERM FOR SOLDIERS WHO DIE IN BATTLE.

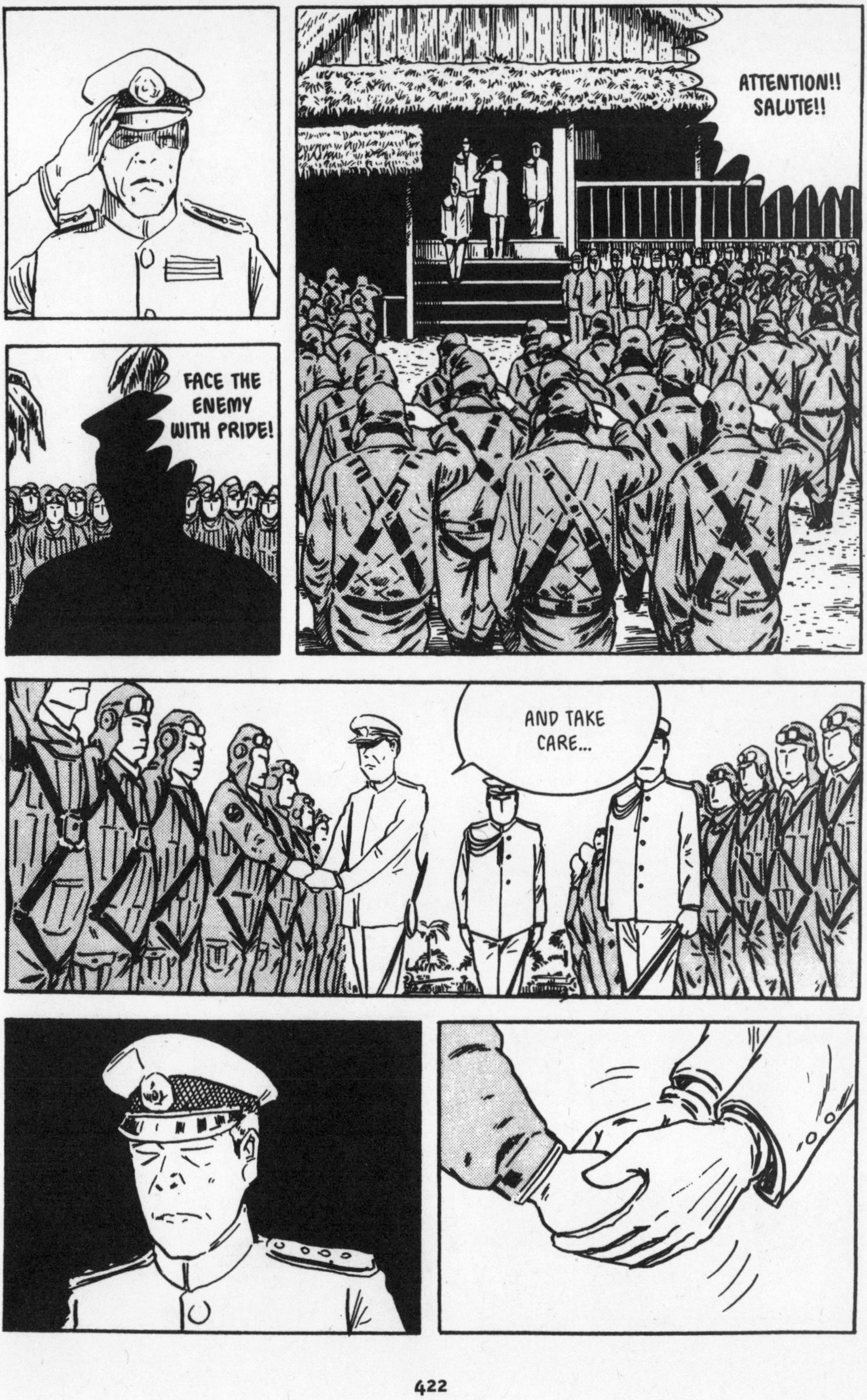
ATTENTION!!
SALUTE!!
FACE THE ENEMY WITH PRIDE!
AND TAKE CARE...

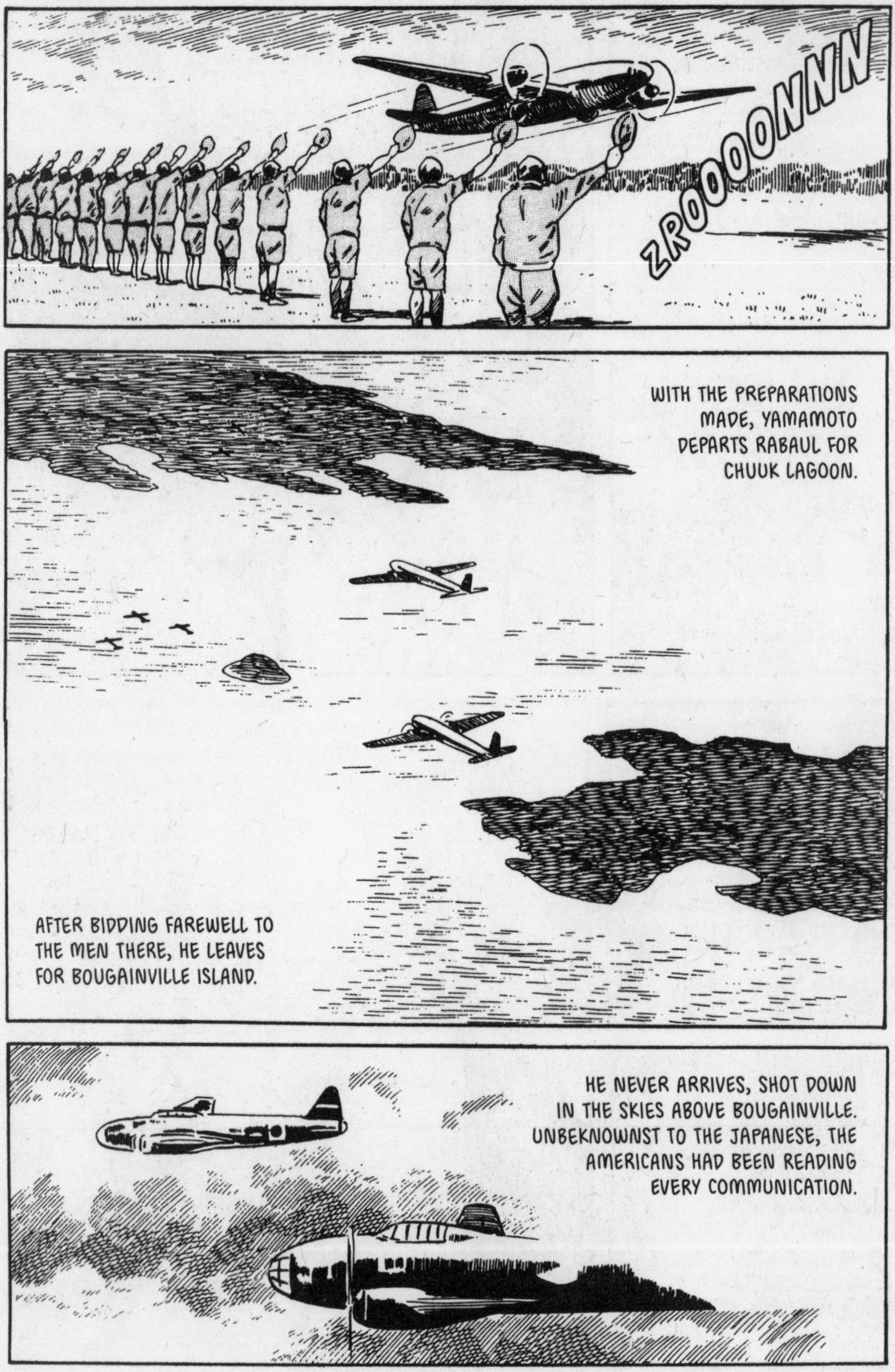
ZROOOONNN
WITH THE PREPARATIONS MADE, YAMAMOTO DEPARTS RABAUL FOR CHUUK LAGOON.
AFTER BIDDING FAREWELL TO THE MEN THERE, HE LEAVES FOR BOUGAINVILLE ISLAND.
HE NEVER ARRIVES, SHOT DOWN IN THE SKIES ABOVE BOUGAINVILLE. UNBEKNOWNST TO THE JAPANESE, THE AMERICANS HAD BEEN READING EVERY COMMUNICATION.

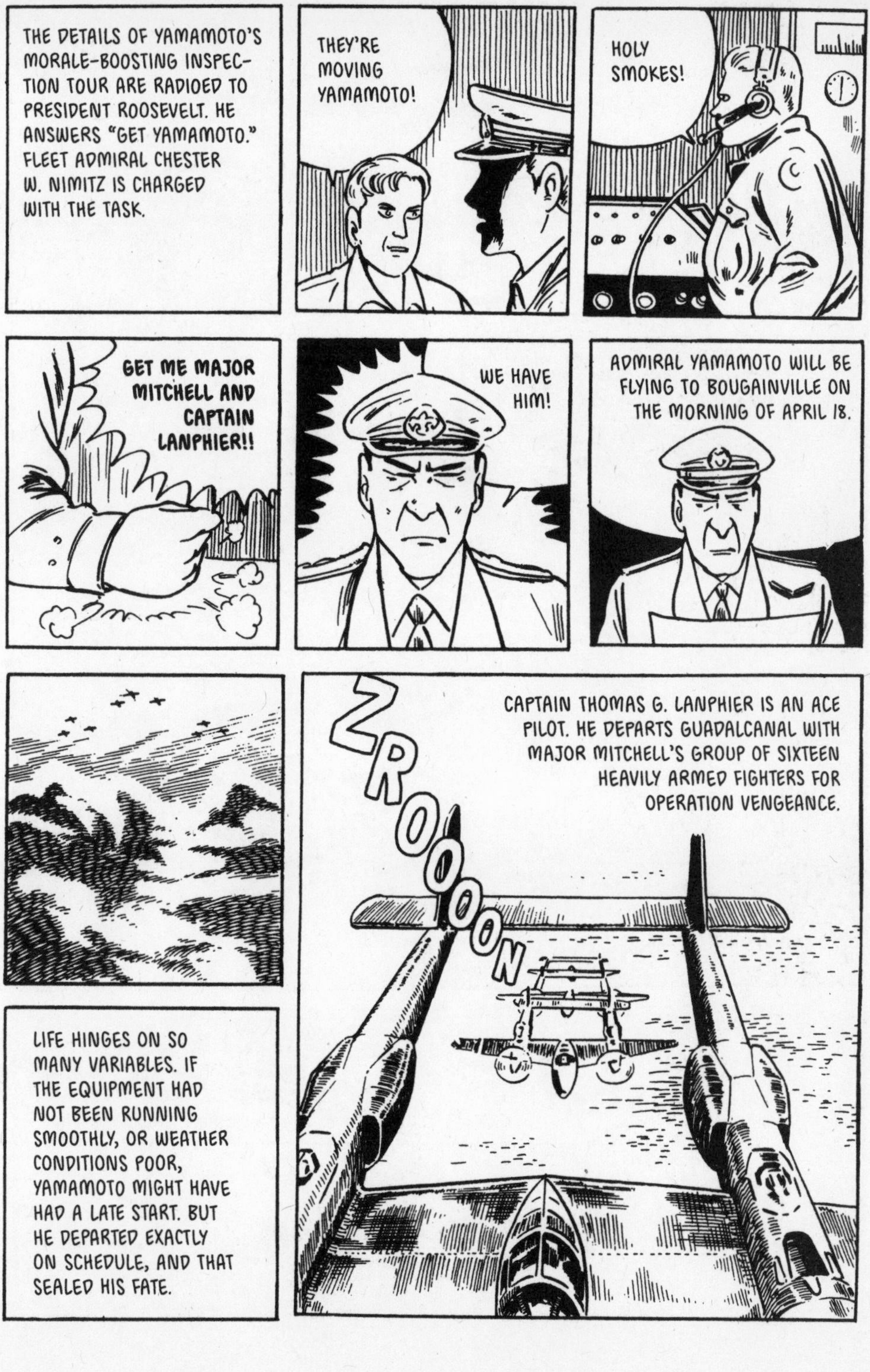
HOLY SMOKES!
THEY'RE MOVING YAMAMOTO!
THE DETAILS OF YAMAMOTO'S MORALE-BOOSTING INSPECTION TOUR ARE RADIOED TO PRESIDENT ROOSEVELT. HE ANSWERS "GET YAMAMOTO." FLEET ADMIRAL CHESTER W. NIMITZ IS CHARGED WITH THE TASK.
ADMIRAL YAMAMOTO WILL BE FLYING TO BOUGAINVILLE ON THE MORNING OF APRIL 18.
WE HAVE HIM!
GET ME MAJOR MITCHELL AND CAPTAIN LANPHIER!!
CAPTAIN THOMAS G. LANPHIER IS AN ACE PILOT. HE DEPARTS GUADALCANAL WITH MAJOR MITCHELL'S GROUP OF SIXTEEN HEAVILY ARMED FIGHTERS FOR OPERATION VENGEANCE.
ZROOOON
LIFE HINGES ON SO MANY VARIABLES. IF THE EQUIPMENT HAD NOT BEEN RUNNING SMOOTHLY, OR WEATHER CONDITIONS POOR, YAMAMOTO MIGHT HAVE HAD A LATE START. BUT HE DEPARTED EXACTLY ON SCHEDULE, AND THAT SEALED HIS FATE.

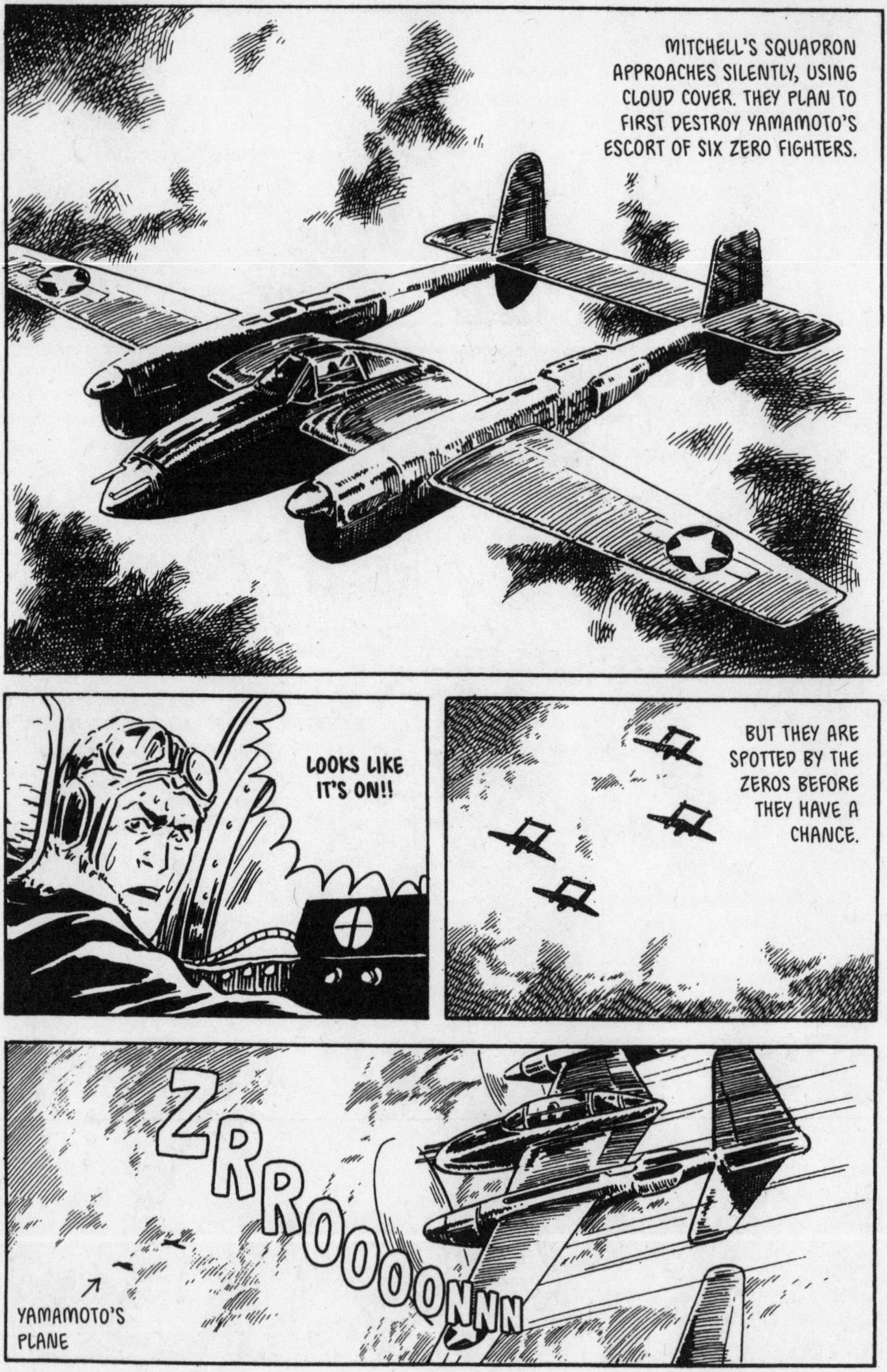
MITCHELL'S SQUADRON APPROACHES SILENTLY, USING CLOUD COVER. THEY PLAN TO FIRST DESTROY YAMAMOTO'S ESCORT OF SIX ZERO FIGHTERS.
BUT THEY ARE SPOTTED BY THE ZEROS BEFORE THEY HAVE A CHANCE.
LOOKS LIKE IT'S ON!!
ZRROOOOONNN
YAMAMOTO'S PLANE

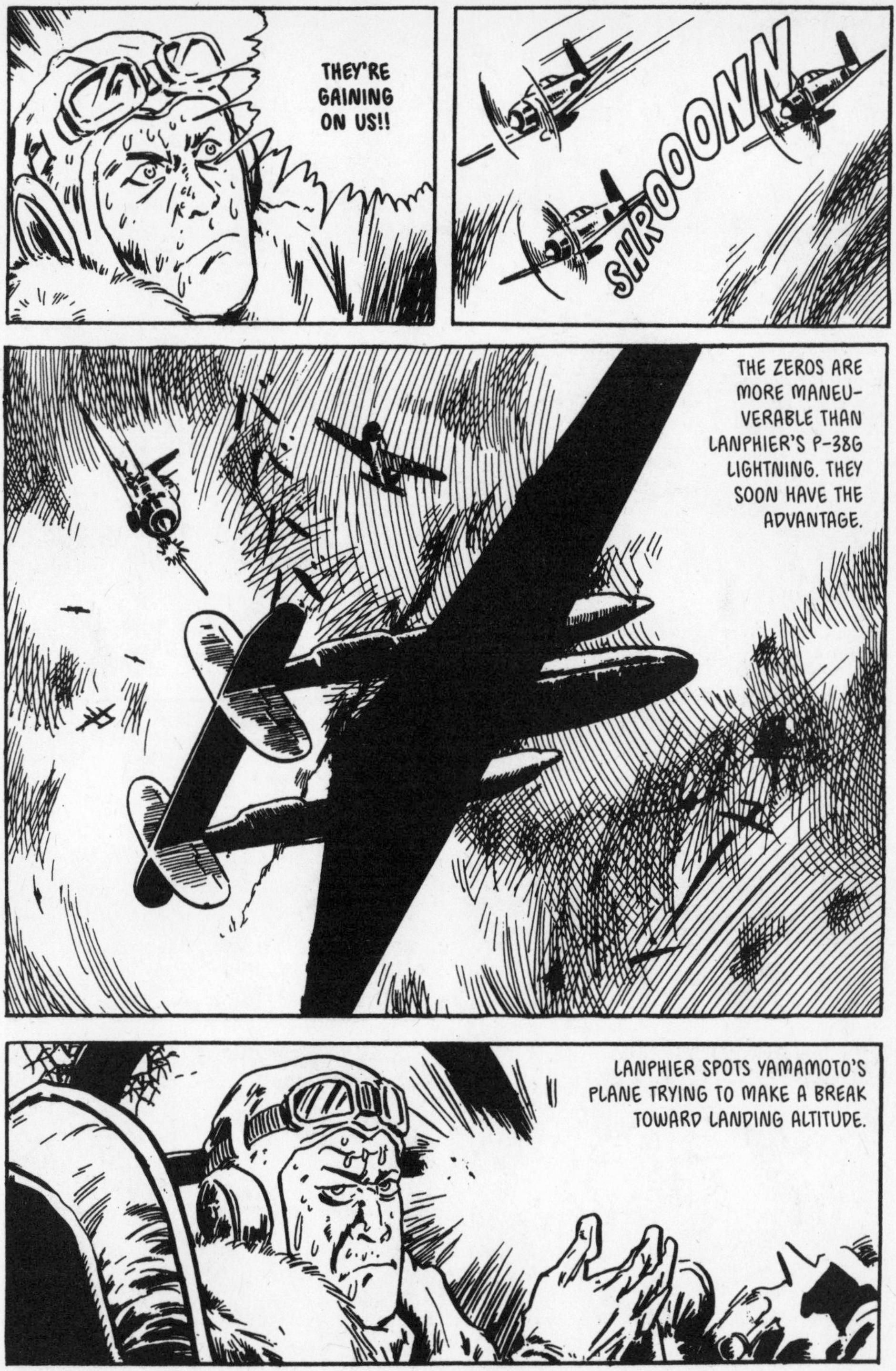
SHROOONN
THEY'RE GAINING ON US!!
THE ZEROS ARE MORE MANEU- VERABLE THAN LANPHIER'S P-38G LIGHTNING. THEY SOON HAVE THE ADVANTAGE.
LANPHIER SPOTS YAMAMOTO'S PLANE TRYING TO MAKE A BREAK TOWARD LANDING ALTITUDE.

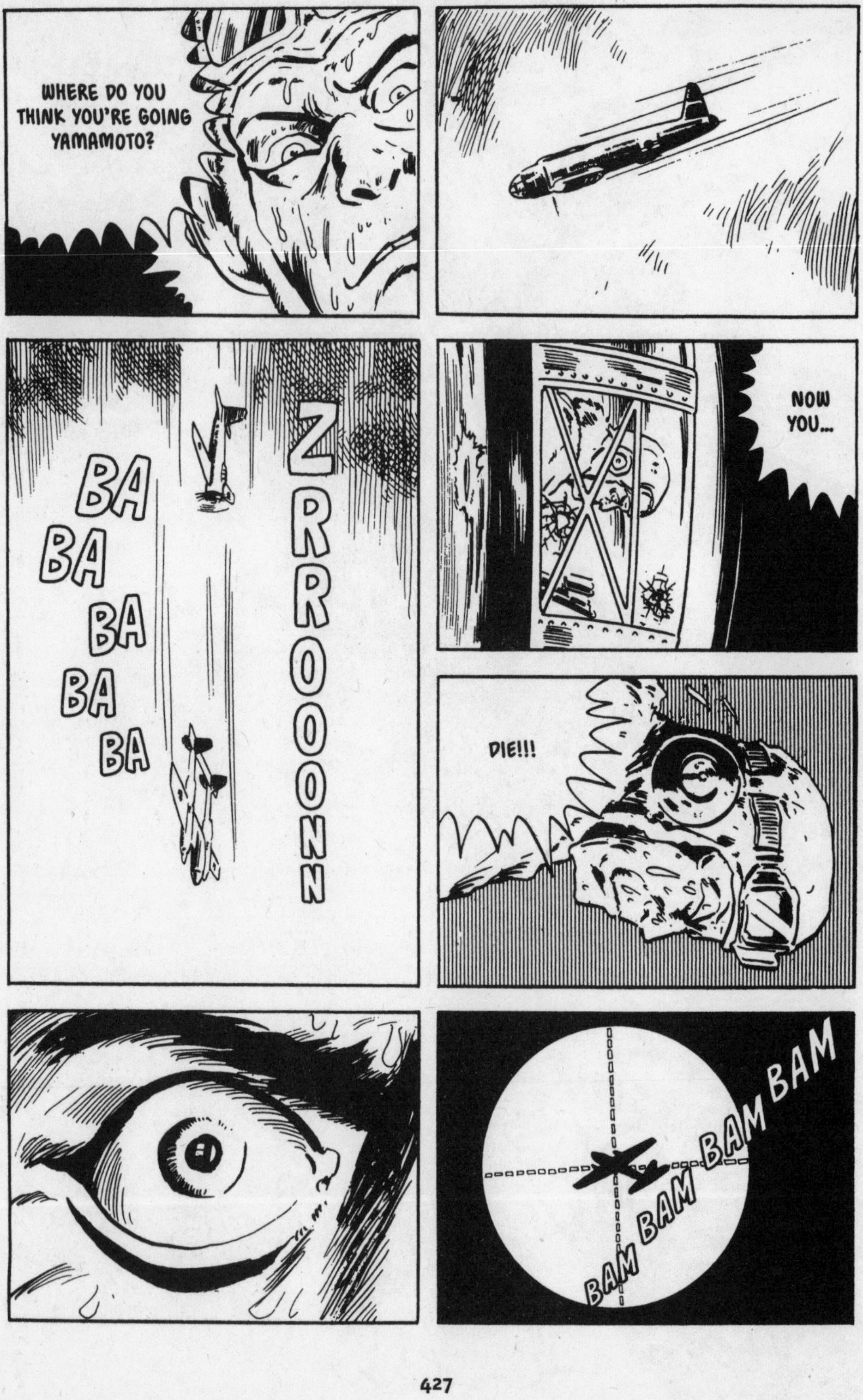

WHERE DO YOU THINK YOU'RE GOING YAMAMOTO?
NOW YOU...
DIE!!!
ZRROOOONN
BA BA BA BA BA
BAM BAM BAM BAM BAM

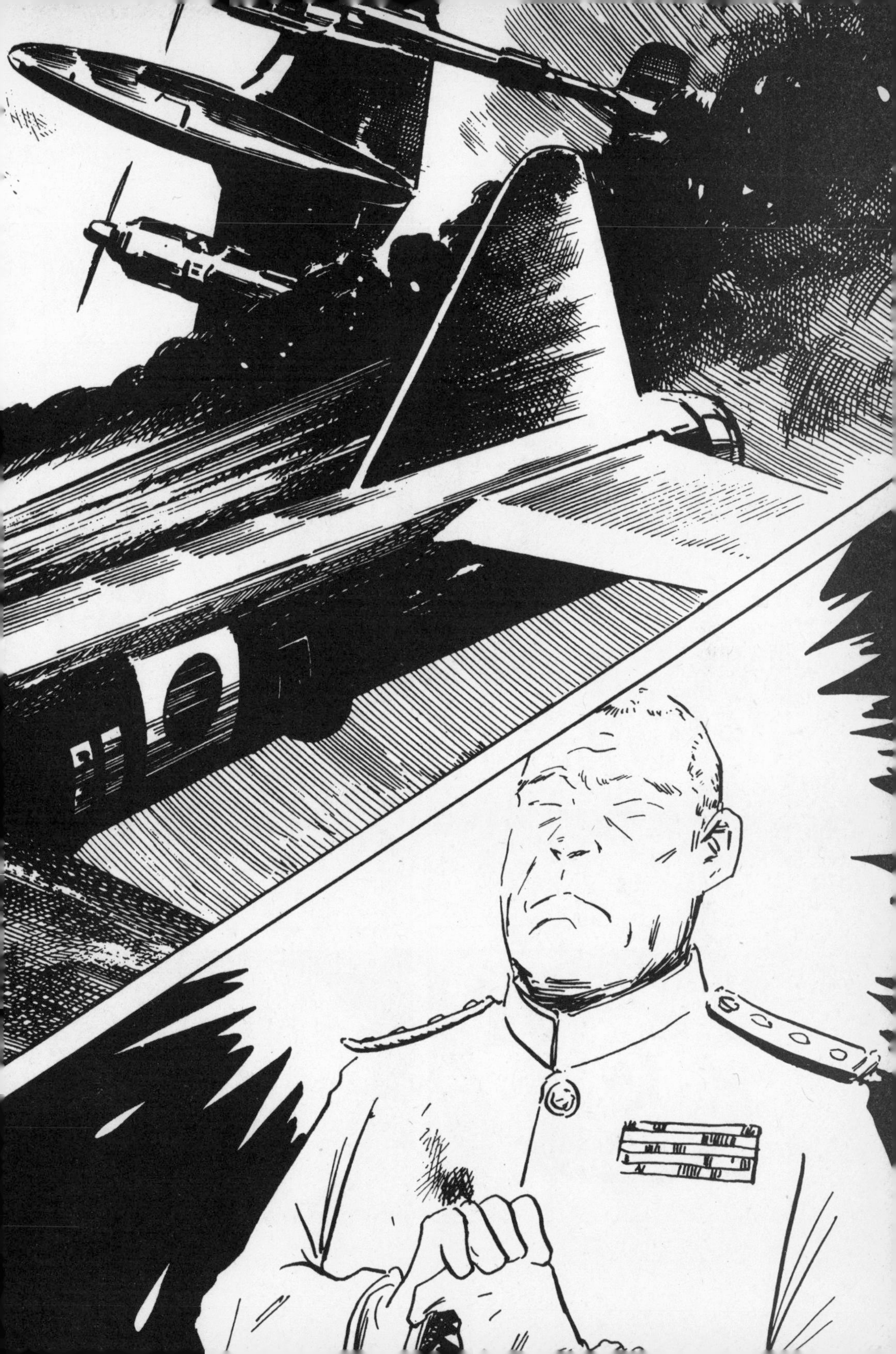

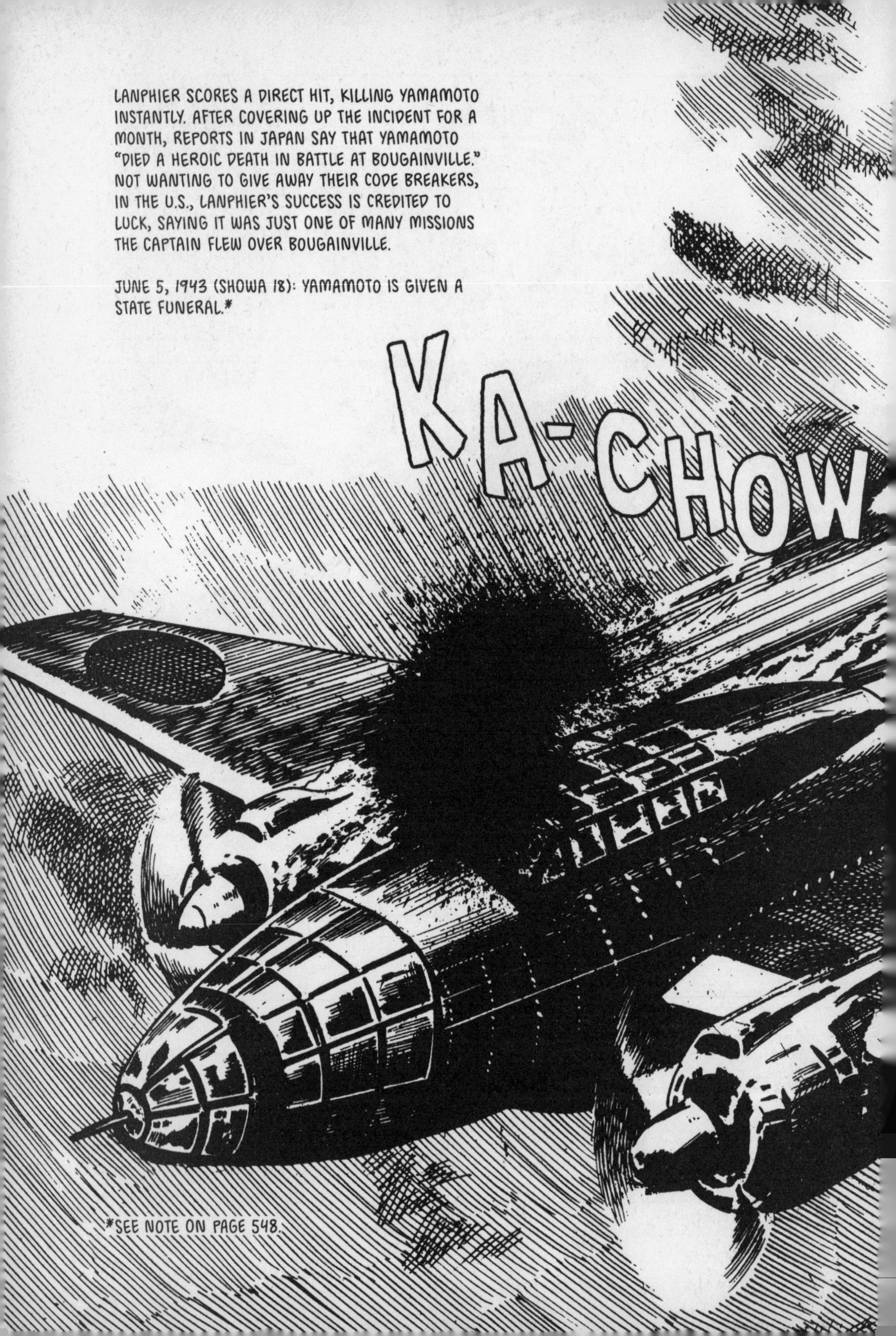
LANPHIER SCORES A DIRECT HIT, KILLING YAMAMOTO INSTANTLY. AFTER COVERING UP THE INCIDENT FOR A MONTH, REPORTS IN JAPAN SAY THAT YAMAMOTO "DIED A HEROIC DEATH IN BATTLE AT BOUGAINVILLE." NOT WANTING TO GIVE AWAY THEIR CODE BREAKERS, IN THE U.S., LANPHIER'S SUCCESS IS CREDITED TO LUCK, SAYING IT WAS JUST ONE OF MANY MISSIONS THE CAPTAIN FLEW OVER BOUGAINVILLE.
JUNE 5, 1943 (SHOWA 18): YAMAMOTO IS GIVEN A STATE FUNERAL.*
KA-CHOW
*SEE NOTE ON PAGE 548.

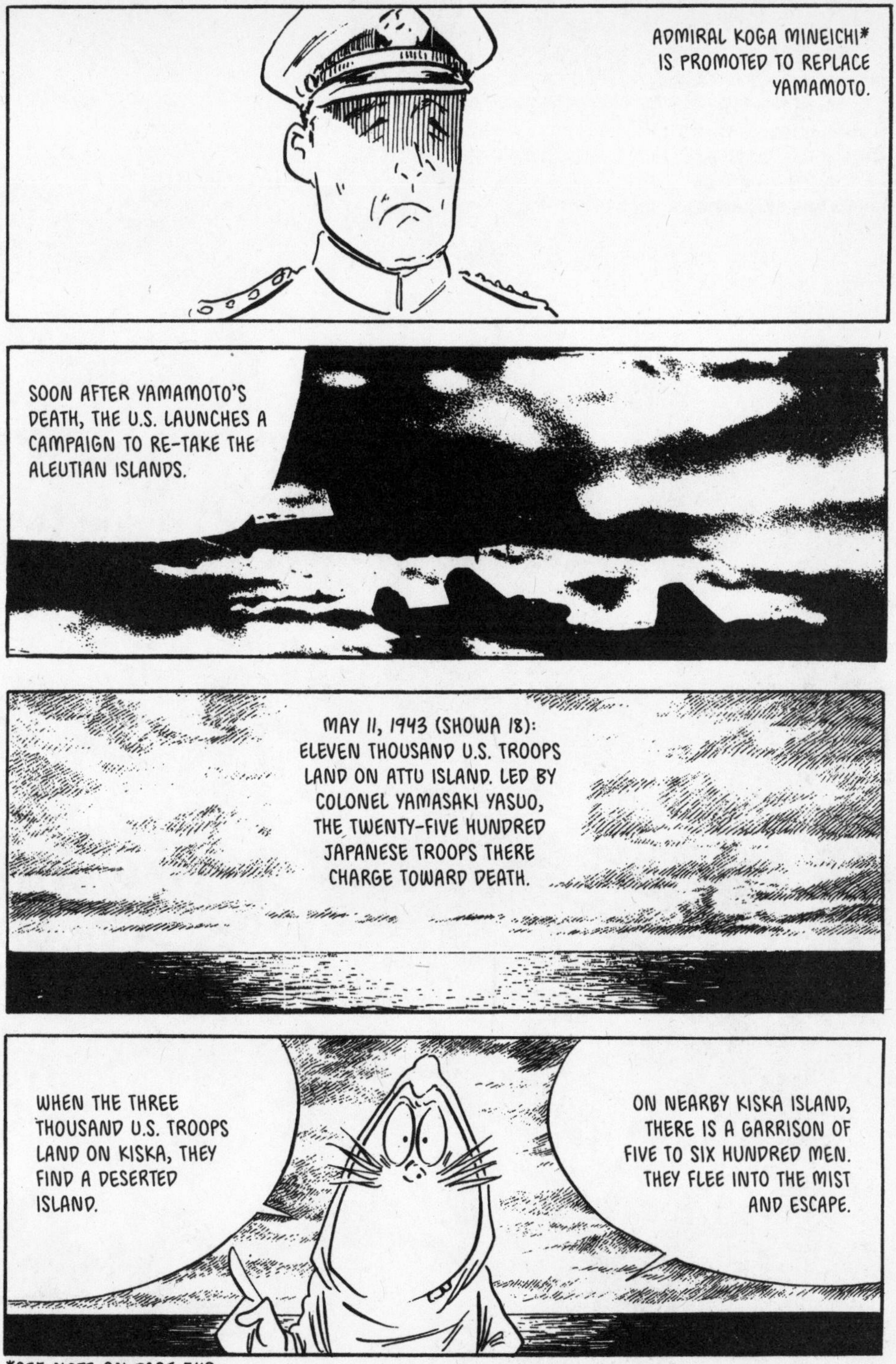
ADMIRAL KOGA MINEICHI* IS PROMOTED TO REPLACE YAMAMOTO.
SOON AFTER YAMAMOTO'S DEATH, THE U.S. LAUNCHES A CAMPAIGN TO RE-TAKE THE ALEUTIAN ISLANDS.
MAY 11, 1943 (SHOWA 18): ELEVEN THOUSAND U.S. TROOPS LAND ON ATTU ISLAND. LED BY COLONEL YAMASAKI YASUO, THE TWENTY-FIVE HUNDRED JAPANESE TROOPS THERE CHARGE TOWARD DEATH.
ON NEARBY KISKA ISLAND, THERE IS A GARRISON OF FIVE TO SIX HUNDRED MEN. THEY FLEE INTO THE MIST AND ESCAPE.
WHEN THE THREE THOUSAND U.S. TROOPS LAND ON KISKA, THEY FIND A DESERTED ISLAND.

*SEE NOTE ON PAGE 548.

FROM PALAU TO RABAUL

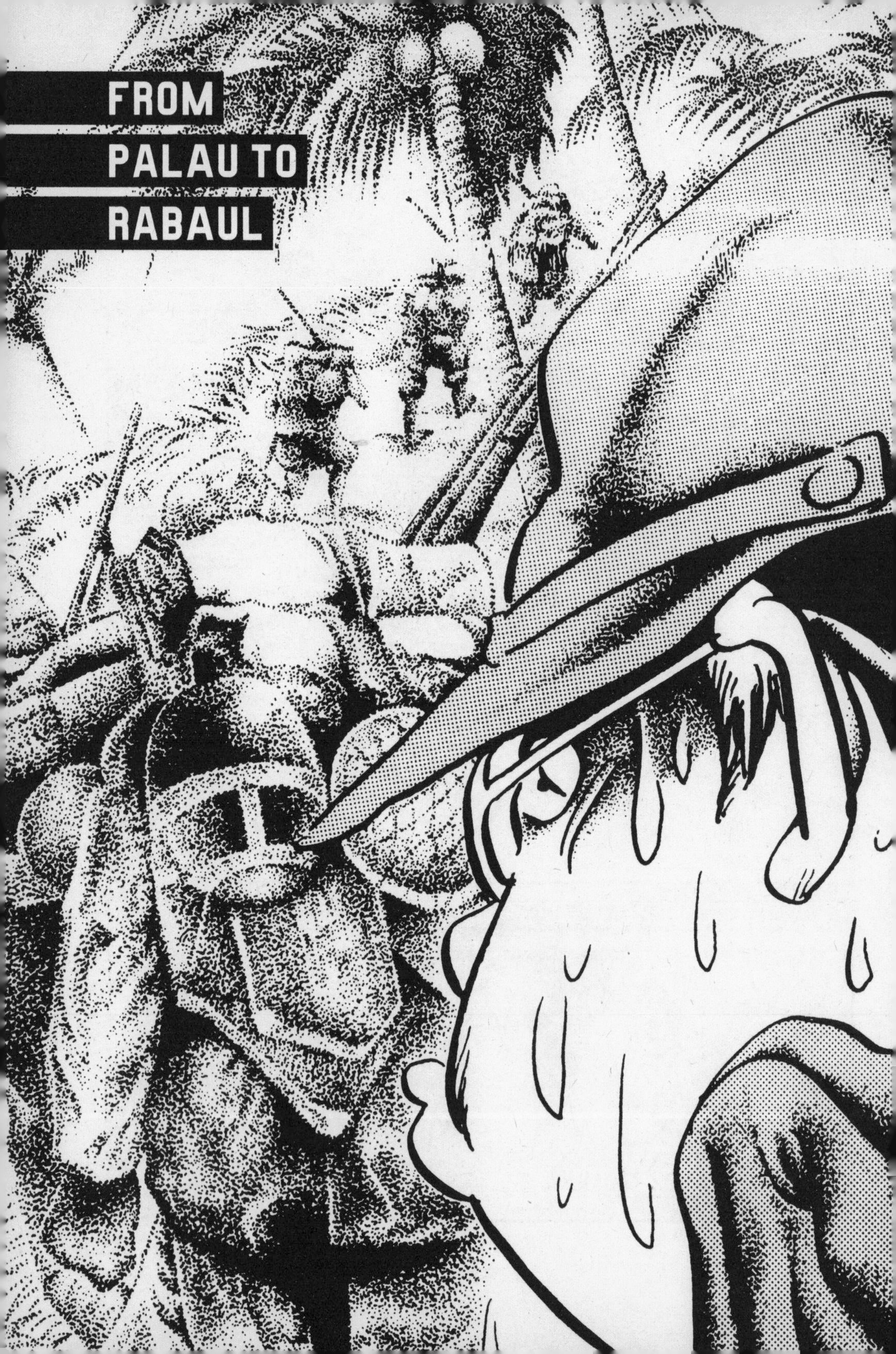

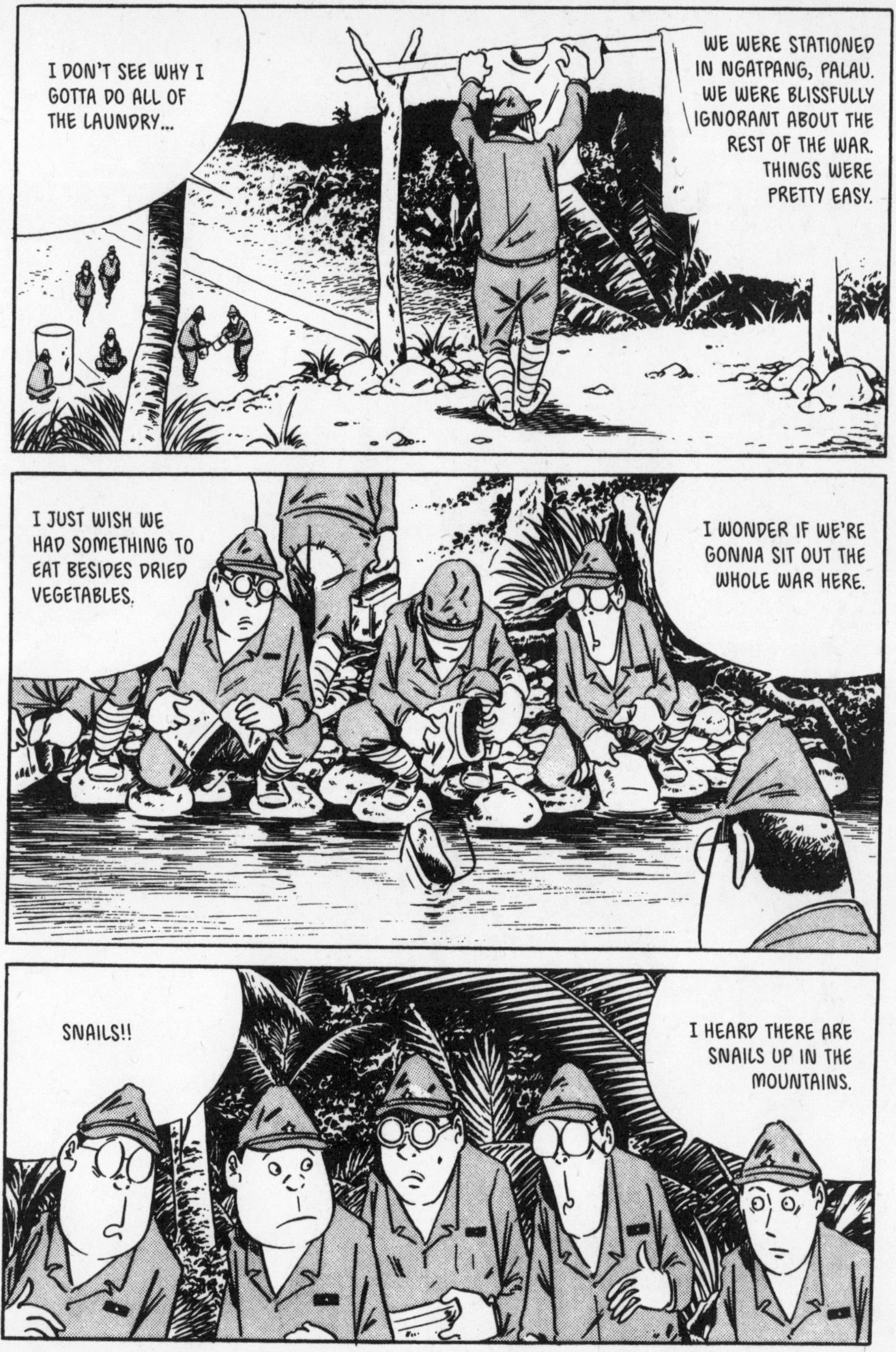
WE WERE STATIONED IN NGATPANG, PALAU. WE WERE BLISSFULLY IGNORANT ABOUT THE REST OF THE WAR. THINGS WERE PRETTY EASY.
I DON'T SEE WHY I GOTTA DO ALL OF THE LAUNDRY...
I WONDER IF WE'RE GONNA SIT OUT THE WHOLE WAR HERE.
I JUST WISH WE HAD SOMETHING TO EAT BESIDES DRIED VEGETABLES.
I HEARD THERE ARE SNAILS UP IN THE MOUNTAINS.
SNAILS!!

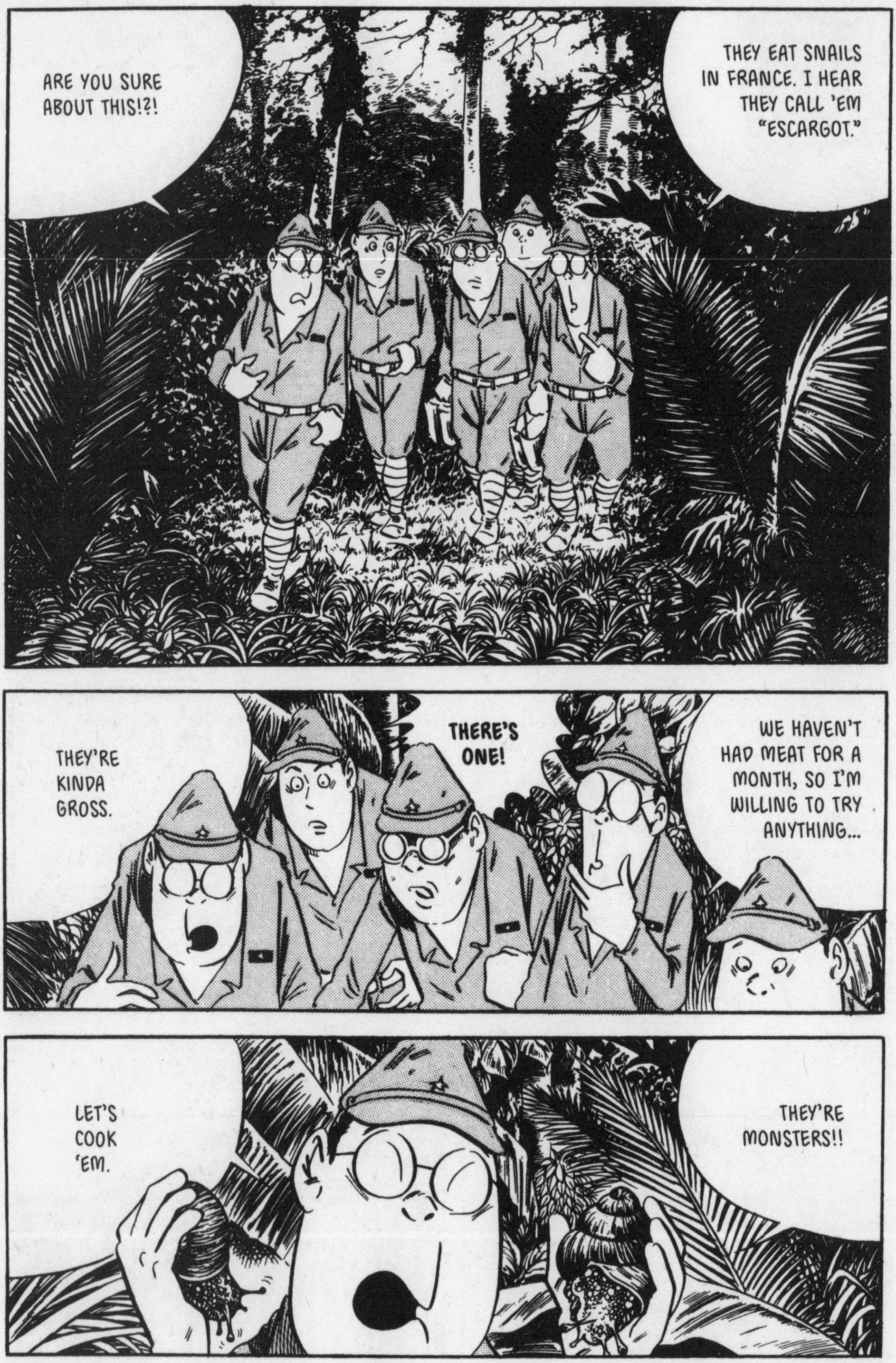
THEY EAT SNAILS IN FRANCE. I HEAR THEY CALL 'EM "ESCARGOT."
ARE YOU SURE ABOUT THIS!?!
WE HAVEN'T HAD MEAT FOR A MONTH, SO I'M WILLING TO TRY ANYTHING...
THERE'S ONE!
THEY'RE KINDA GROSS.
THEY'RE MONSTERS!!
LET'S COOK 'EM.

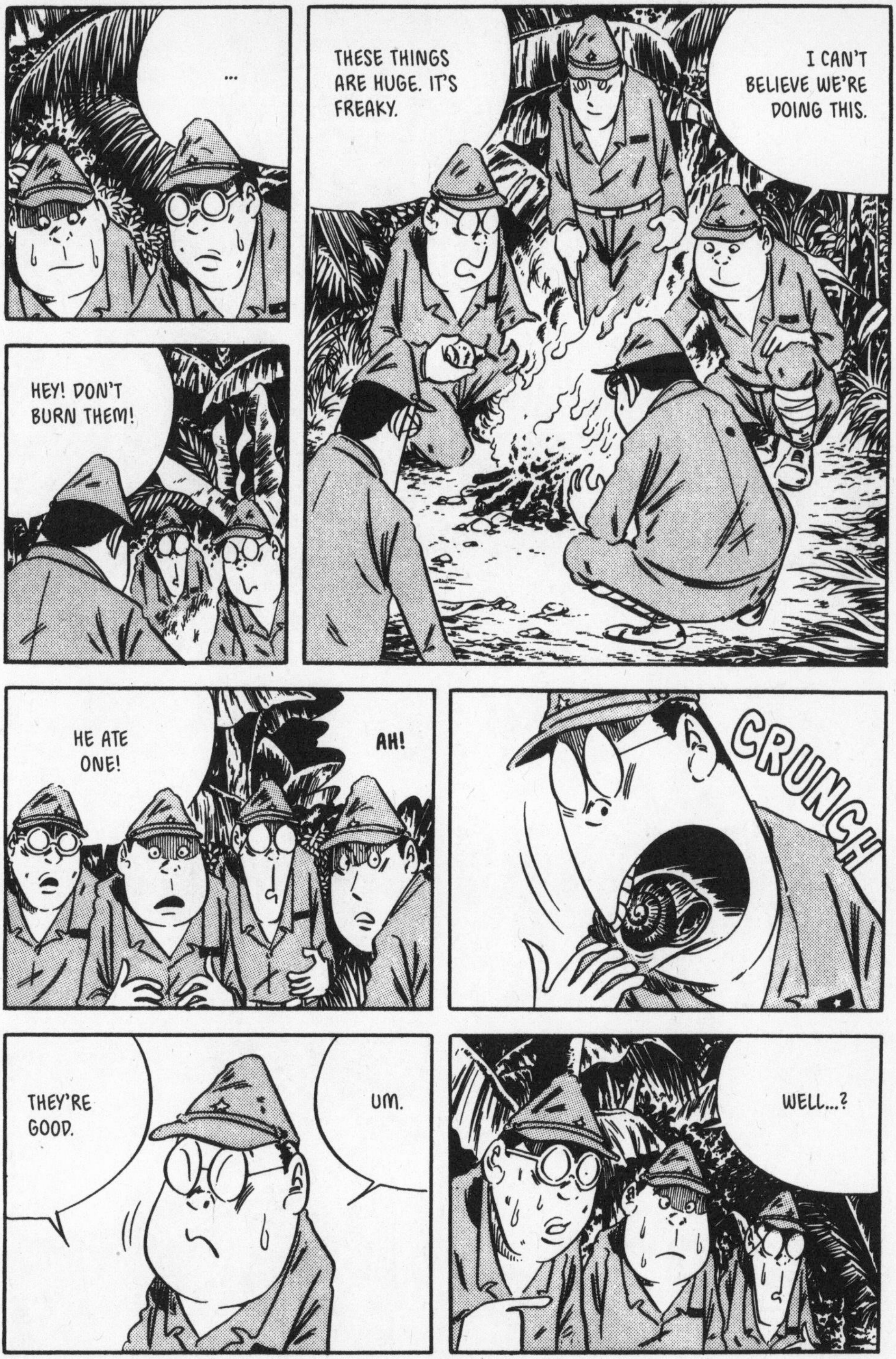
I CAN'T BELIEVE WE'RE DOING THIS.
THESE THINGS ARE HUGE. IT'S FREAKY.
...
HEY! DON'T BURN THEM!
CRUNCH
AH!
HE ATE ONE!
WELL...?
UM.
THEY'RE GOOD.

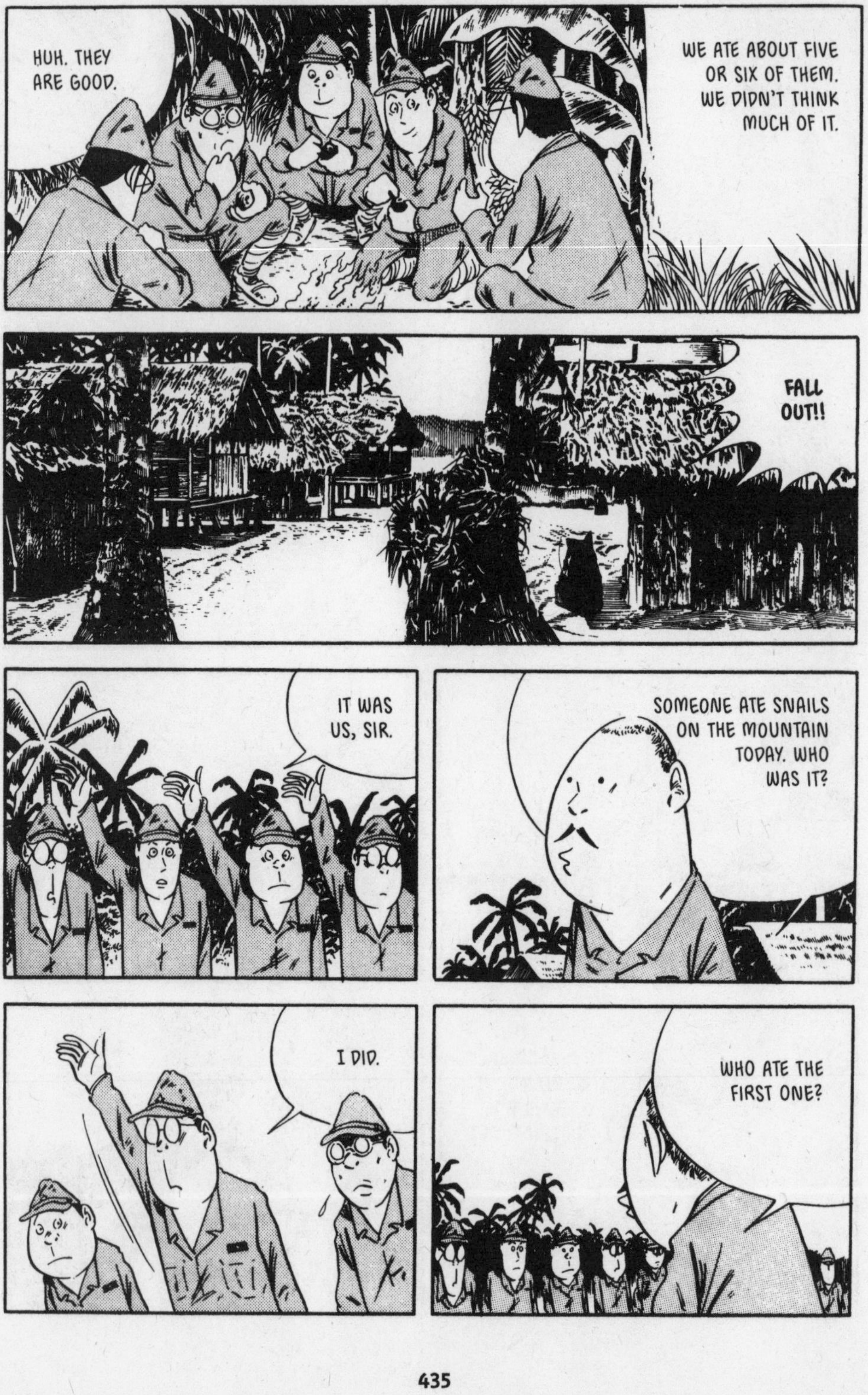

WE ATE ABOUT FIVE OR SIX OF THEM. WE DIDN'T THINK MUCH OF IT.
HUH. THEY ARE GOOD.
FALL OUT!!
SOMEONE ATE SNAILS ON THE MOUNTAIN TODAY. WHO WAS IT?
IT WAS US, SIR.
WHO ATE THE FIRST ONE?
I DID.

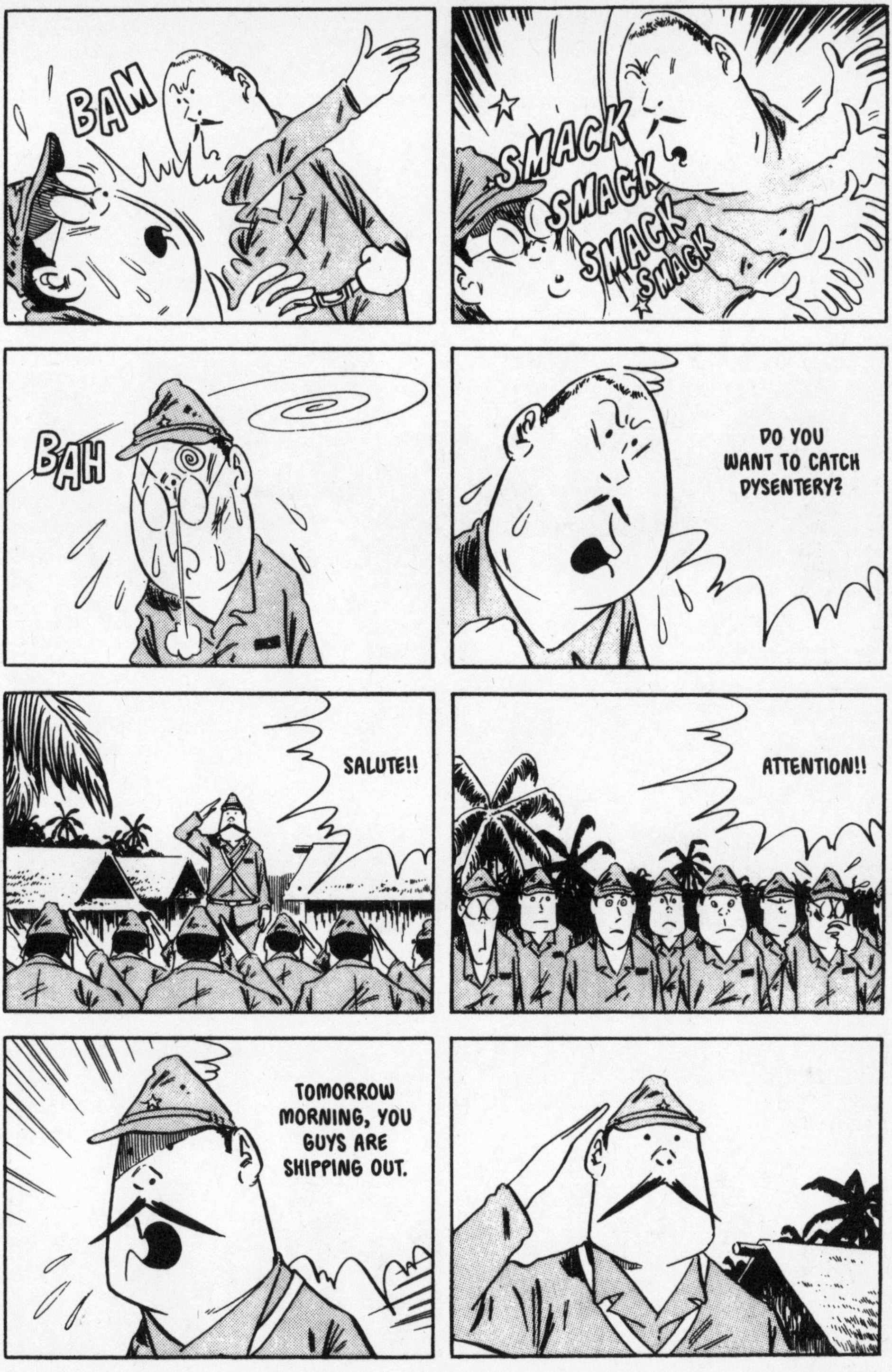
SMACK
SMACK
SMACK
SMACK
BAM
DO YOU WANT TO CATCH DYSENTERY?
BAH
ATTENTION!!
SALUTE!!
TOMORROW MORNING, YOU GUYS ARE SHIPPING OUT.

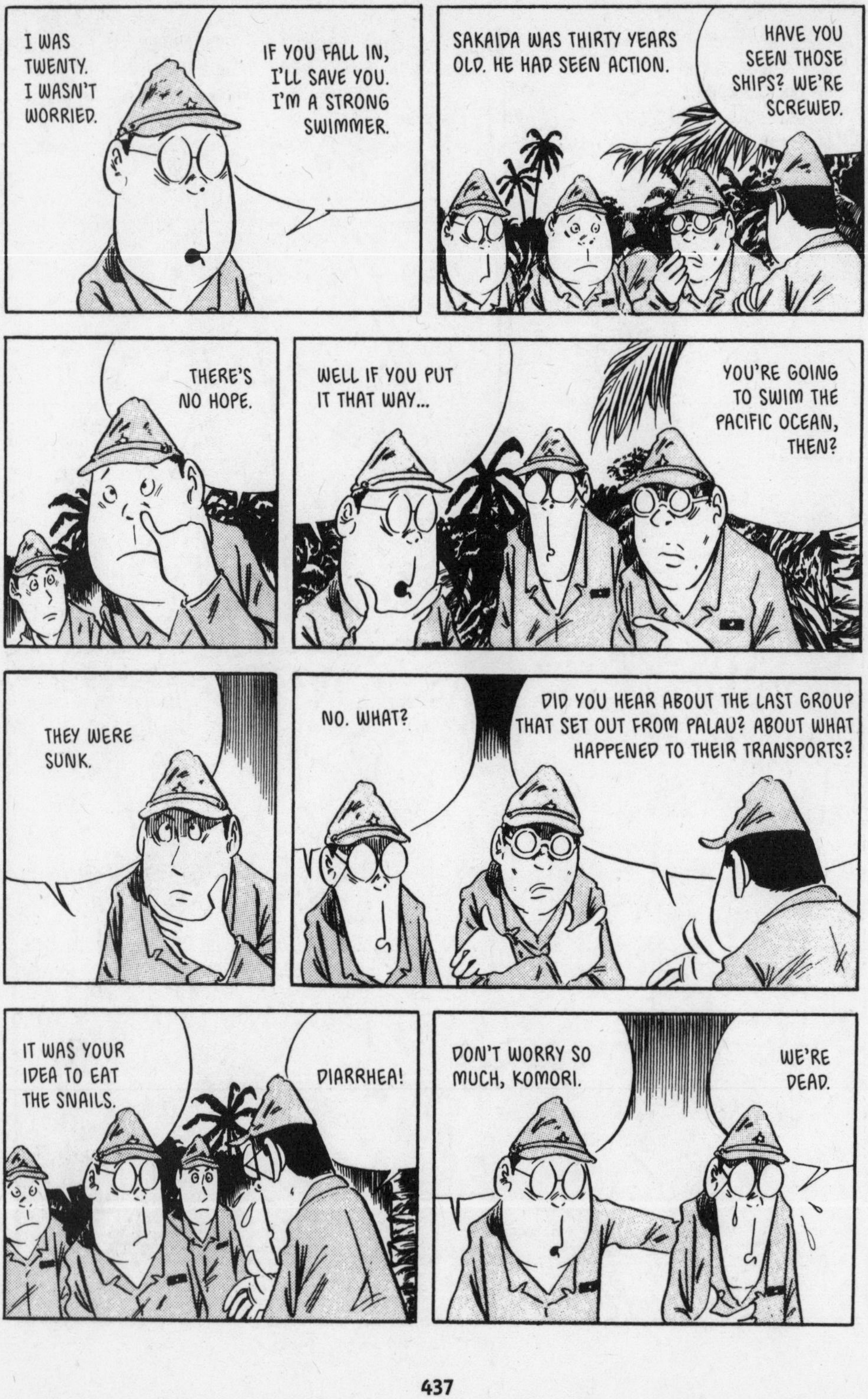
HAVE YOU SEEN THOSE SHIPS? WE'RE SCREWED.
SAKAIDA WAS THIRTY YEARS OLD. HE HAD SEEN ACTION.
IF YOU FALL IN, I'LL SAVE YOU. I'M A STRONG SWIMMER.
I WAS TWENTY. I WASN'T WORRIED.
YOU'RE GOING TO SWIM THE PACIFIC OCEAN, THEN?
WELL IF YOU PUT IT THAT WAY...
THERE'S NO HOPE.
DID YOU HEAR ABOUT THE LAST GROUP THAT SET OUT FROM PALAU? ABOUT WHAT HAPPENED TO THEIR TRANSPORTS?
NO. WHAT?
THEY WERE SUNK.
WE'RE DEAD.
DON'T WORRY SO MUCH, KOMORI.
DIARRHEA!
IT WAS YOUR IDEA TO EAT THE SNAILS.

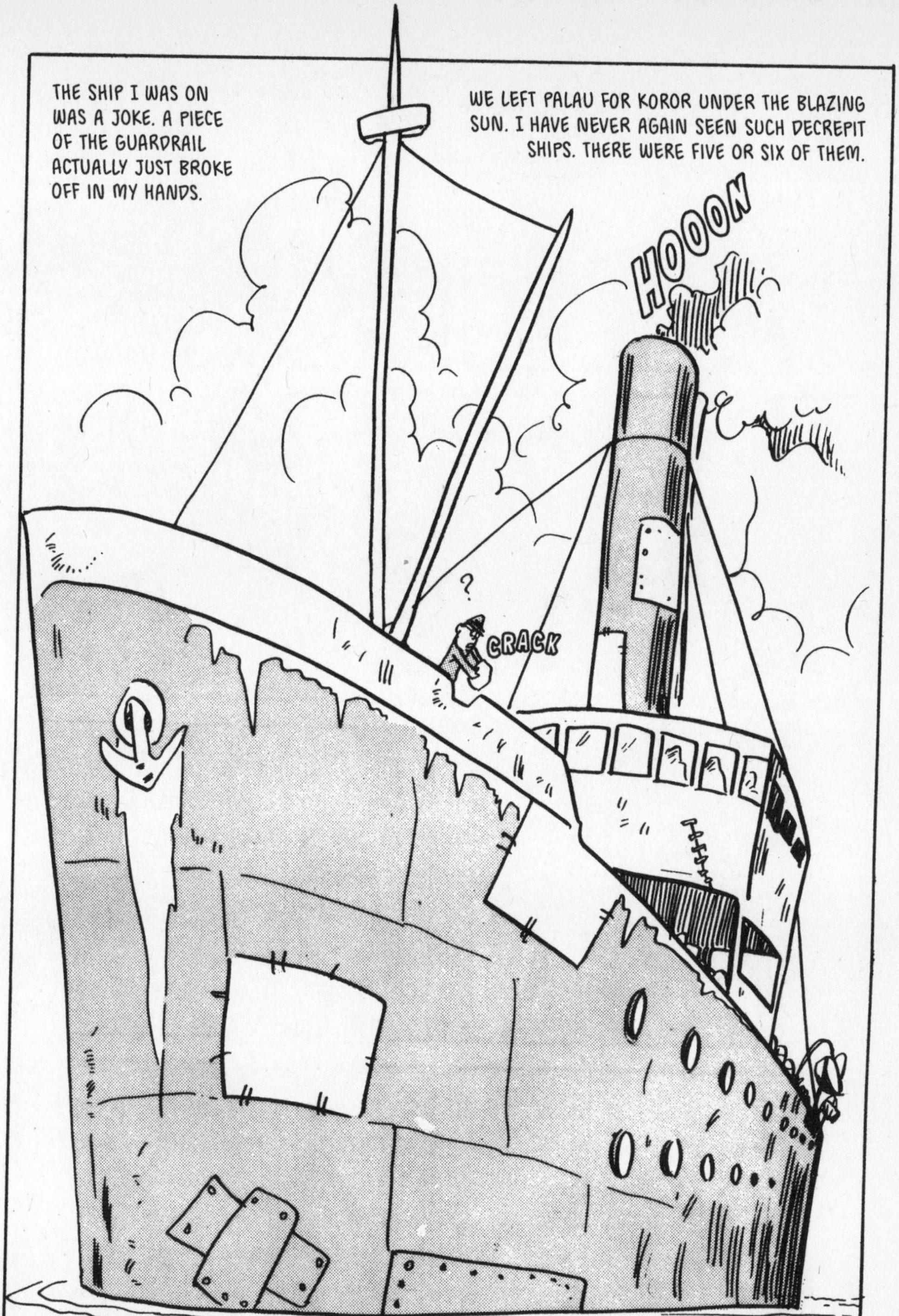
WE LEFT PALAU FOR KOROR UNDER THE BLAZING SUN. I HAVE NEVER AGAIN SEEN SUCH DECREPIT SHIPS. THERE WERE FIVE OR SIX OF THEM.
THE SHIP I WAS ON WAS A JOKE. A PIECE OF THE GUARDRAIL ACTUALLY JUST BROKE OFF IN MY HANDS.
HOOON
?
CRACK

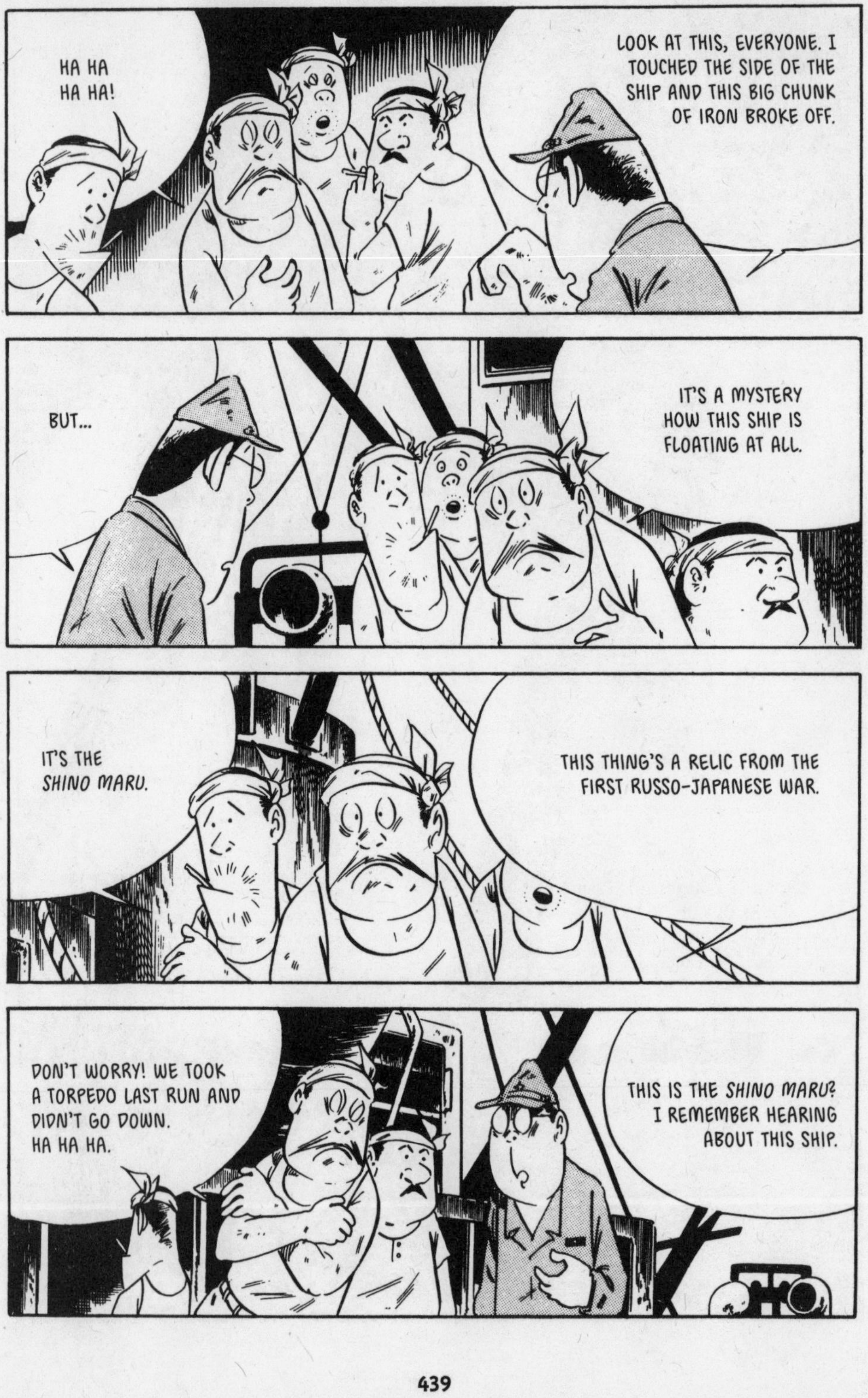
LOOK AT THIS, EVERYONE. I TOUCHED THE SIDE OF THE SHIP AND THIS BIG CHUNK OF IRON BROKE OFF.
HA HA HA HA!
IT'S A MYSTERY HOW THIS SHIP IS FLOATING AT ALL.
BUT...
THIS THING'S A RELIC FROM THE FIRST RUSSO-JAPANESE WAR.
IT'S THE *SHINO MARU.*
THIS IS THE *SHINO MARU?* I REMEMBER HEARING ABOUT THIS SHIP.
DON'T WORRY! WE TOOK A TORPEDO LAST RUN AND DIDN'T GO DOWN. HA HA HA.

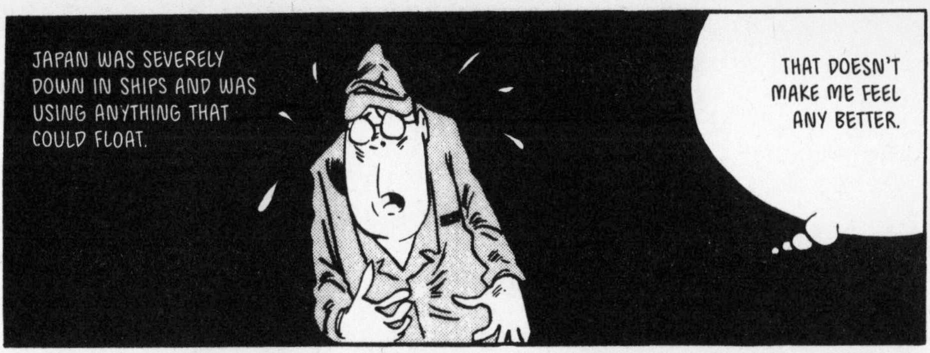
THAT DOESN'T MAKE ME FEEL ANY BETTER.
JAPAN WAS SEVERELY DOWN IN SHIPS AND WAS USING ANYTHING THAT COULD FLOAT.

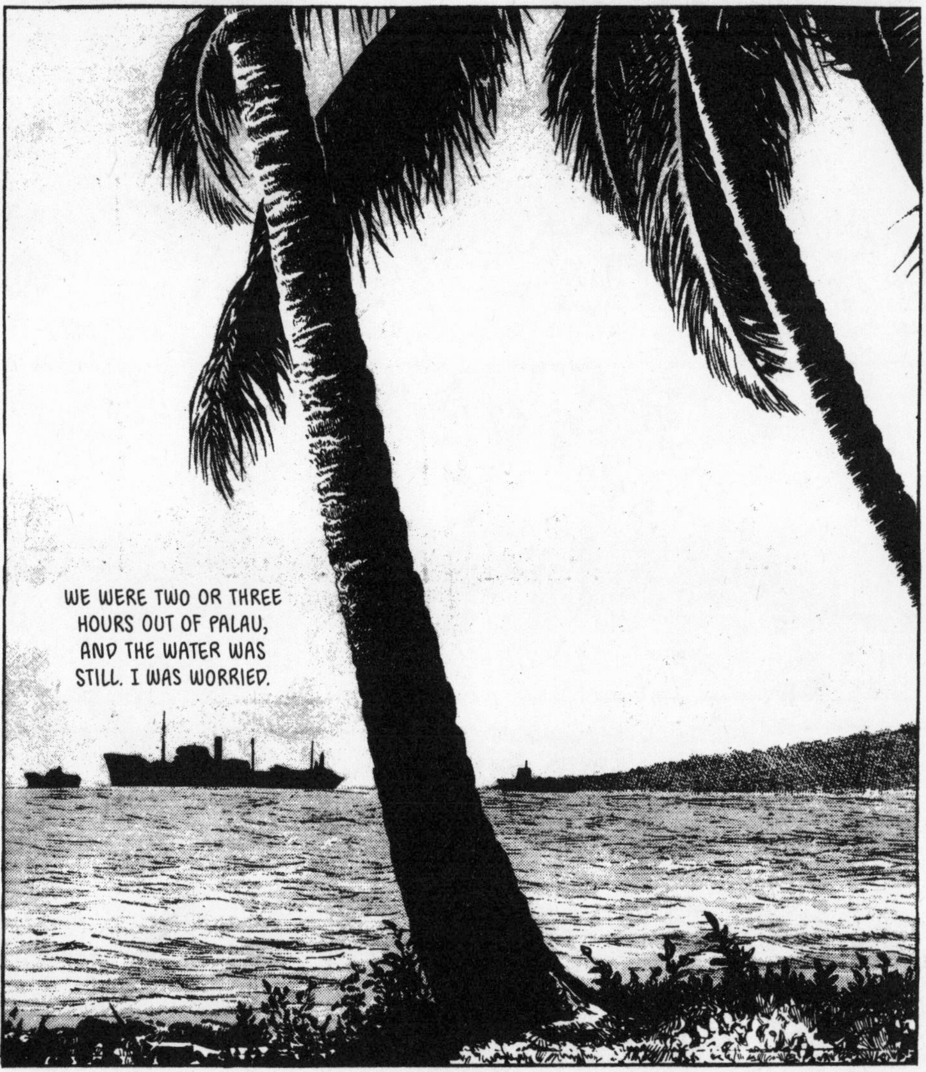
WE WERE TWO OR THREE HOURS OUT OF PALAU, AND THE WATER WAS STILL. I WAS WORRIED.

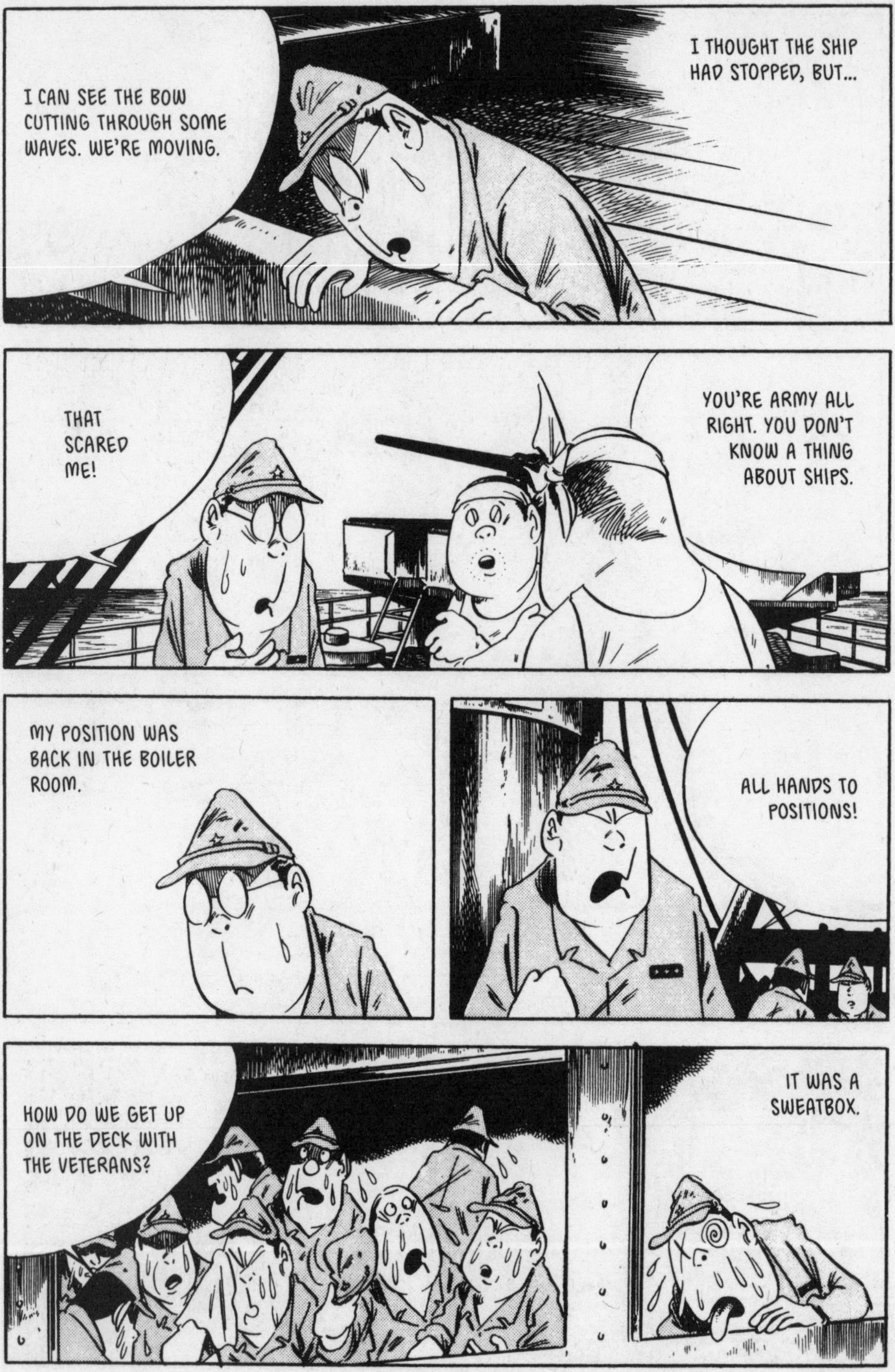
I THOUGHT THE SHIP HAD STOPPED, BUT...
I CAN SEE THE BOW CUTTING THROUGH SOME WAVES. WE'RE MOVING.
YOU'RE ARMY ALL RIGHT. YOU DON'T KNOW A THING ABOUT SHIPS.
THAT SCARED ME!
ALL HANDS TO POSITIONS!
MY POSITION WAS BACK IN THE BOILER ROOM.
IT WAS A SWEATBOX.
HOW DO WE GET UP ON THE DECK WITH THE VETERANS?

LET'S JUST GO UP THERE.
WE'LL DIE IN HERE.
CHOW TIME!!
GET A MOVE ON.
CARROTS AGAIN?
THAT'S ALL WE HAVE FOR RATIONS.
WE'RE NOT THE CAVALRY, YOU KNOW. WE DON'T HAVE HORSES.
ANY MORE COMPLAINTS?!
SMACK SMACK SMACK SMACK

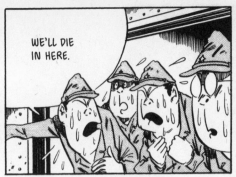

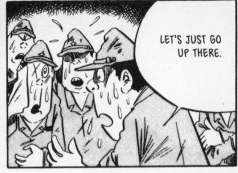

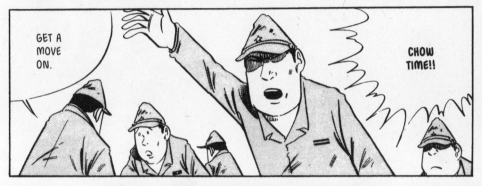

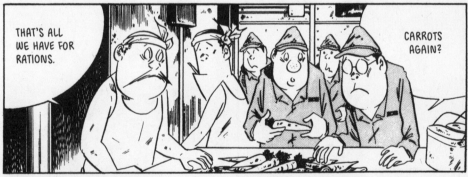

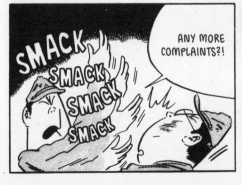

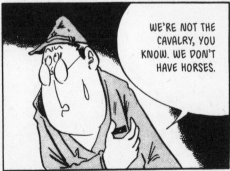

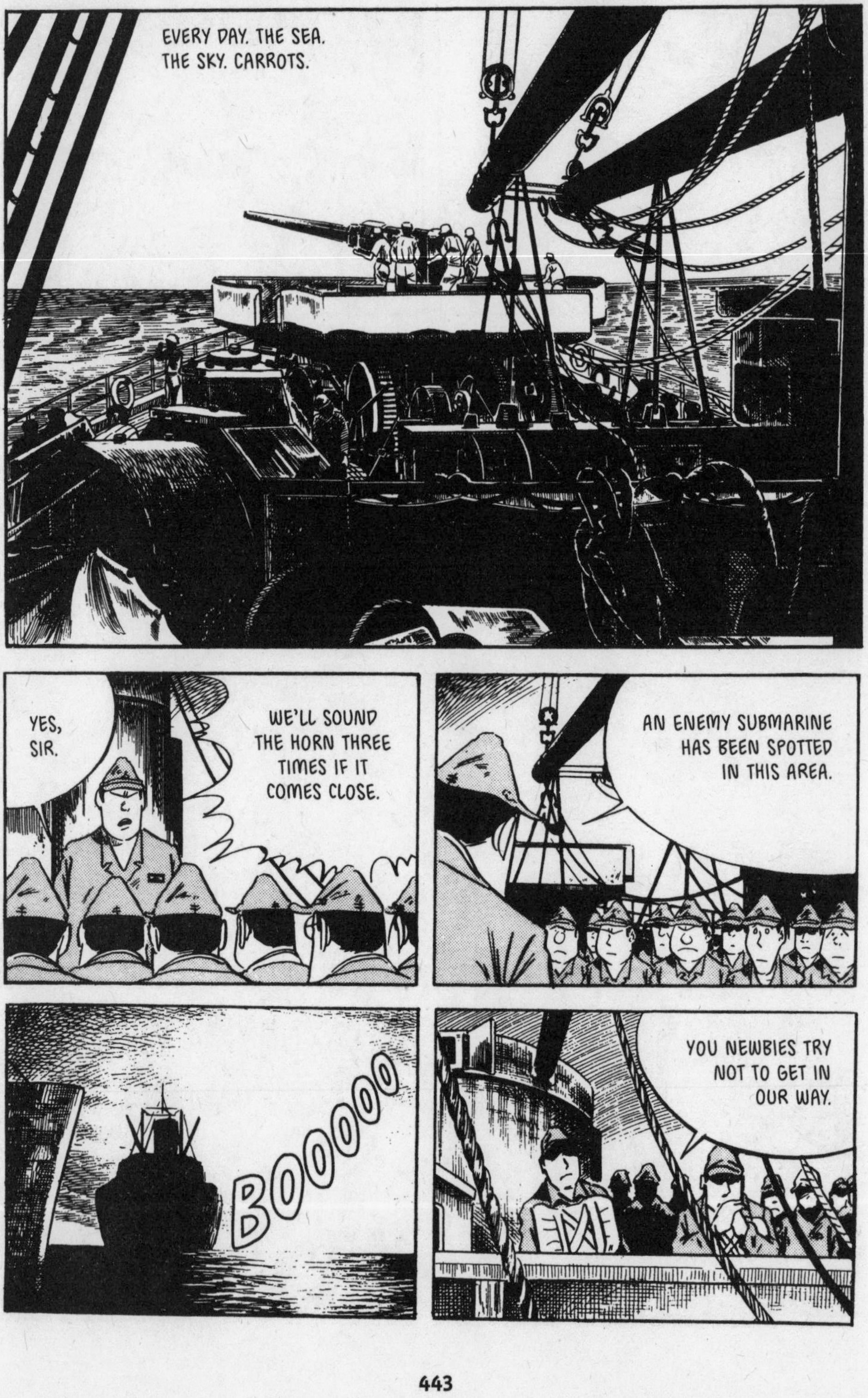

EVERY DAY. THE SEA. THE SKY. CARROTS.
AN ENEMY SUBMARINE HAS BEEN SPOTTED IN THIS AREA.
WE'LL SOUND THE HORN THREE TIMES IF IT COMES CLOSE.
YES, SIR.
YOU NEWBIES TRY NOT TO GET IN OUR WAY.
BOOOOO

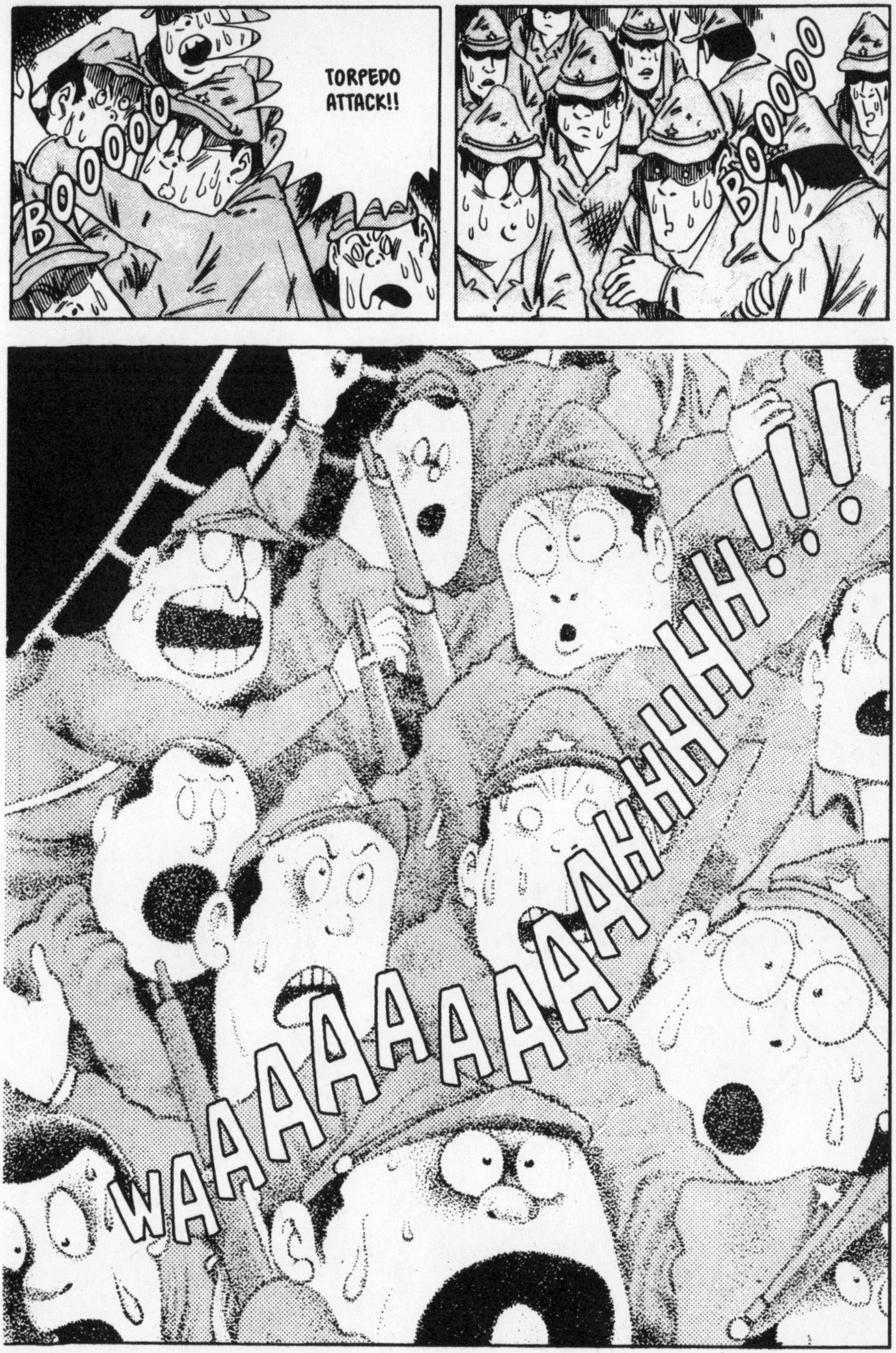
BOOOOO
TORPEDO ATTACK!!
BOOOOO
WAAAAAAAAAHHHHH!!!

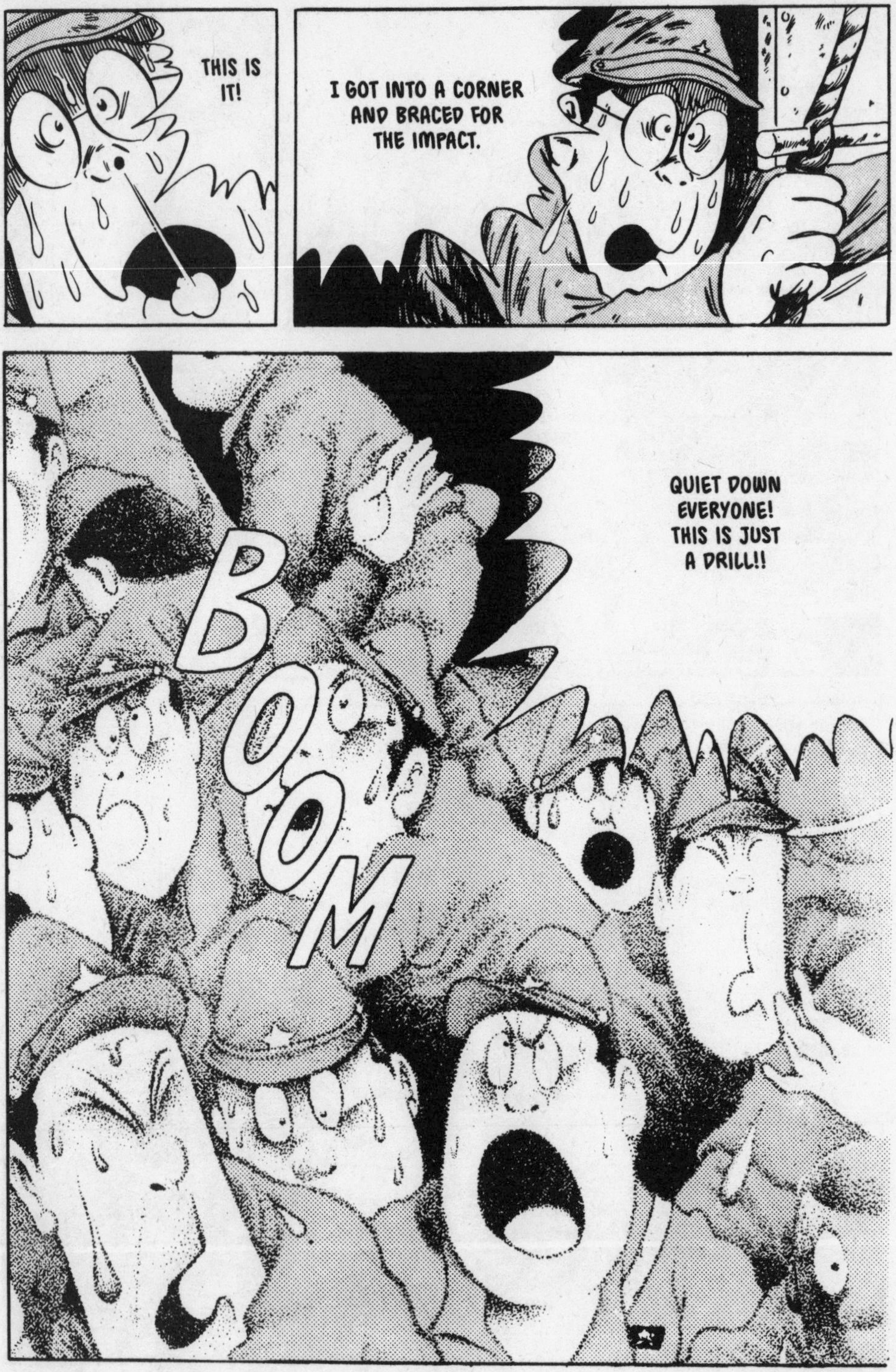
I GOT INTO A CORNER AND BRACED FOR THE IMPACT.
THIS IS IT!
QUIET DOWN EVERYONE! THIS IS JUST A DRILL!!
BOOM

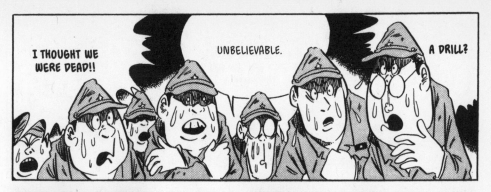

A DRILL?
UNBELIEVABLE.
I THOUGHT WE WERE DEAD!!
WHAT DO WE NEED DRILLS FOR ON THIS HUNK OF JUNK?
THEY'RE JUST TOYING WITH US!
IT WAS NICE ON THE DECK, WITH THE COOL BREEZE.

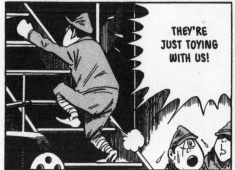

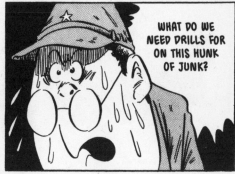

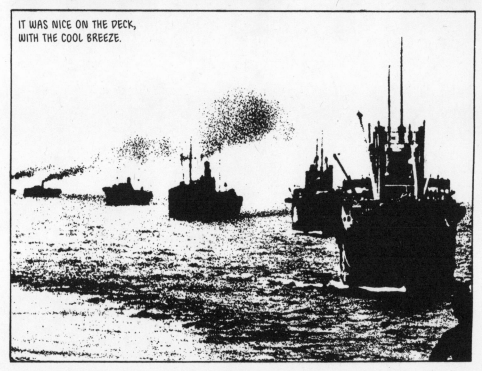

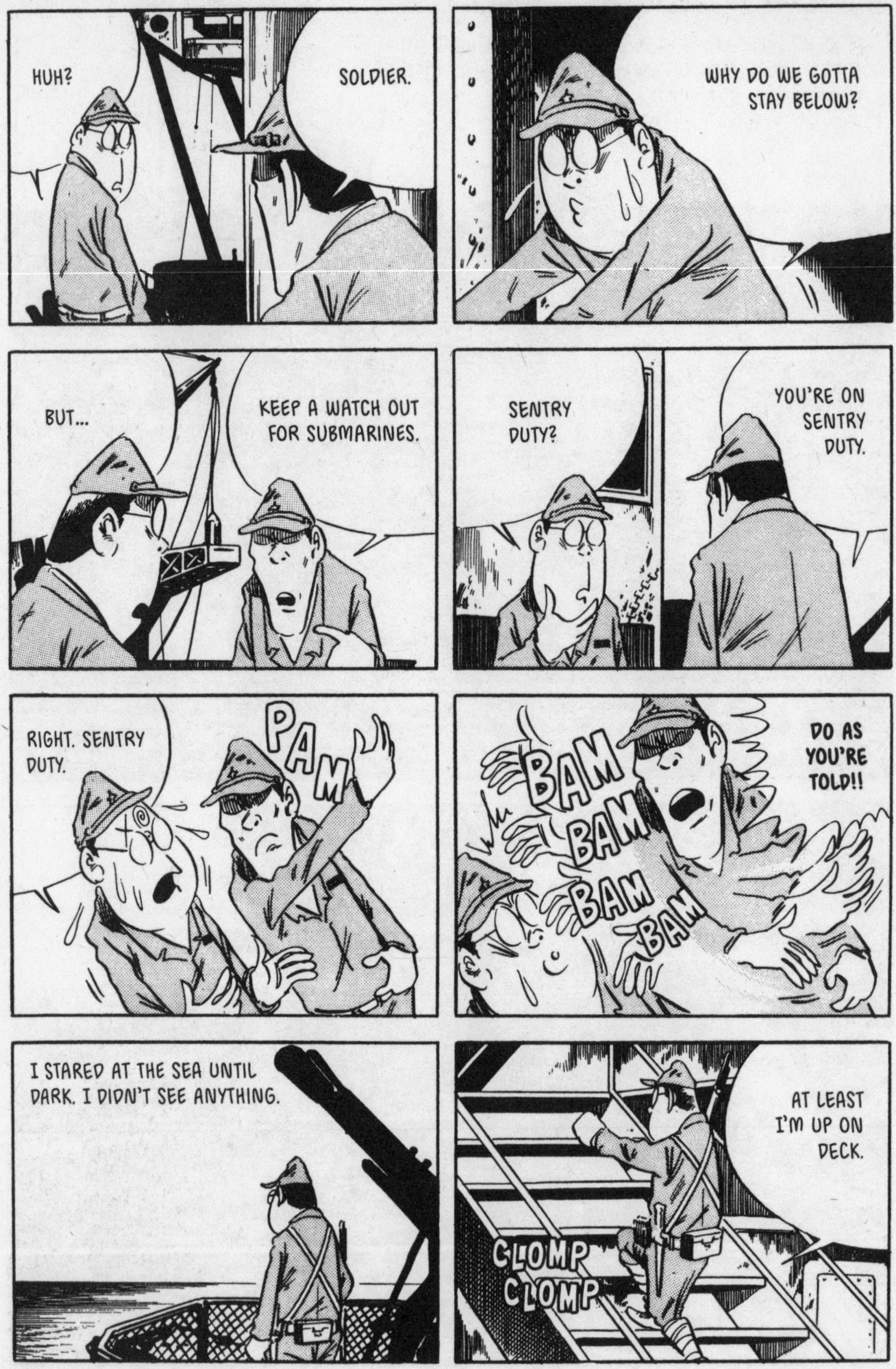
WHY DO WE GOTTA STAY BELOW?
SOLDIER.
HUH?
YOU'RE ON SENTRY DUTY.
SENTRY DUTY?
KEEP A WATCH OUT FOR SUBMARINES.
BUT...
DO AS YOU'RE TOLD!!
BAM BAM BAM BAM
PAM
RIGHT. SENTRY DUTY.
AT LEAST I'M UP ON DECK.
CLOMP CLOMP
I STARED AT THE SEA UNTIL DARK. I DIDN'T SEE ANYTHING.

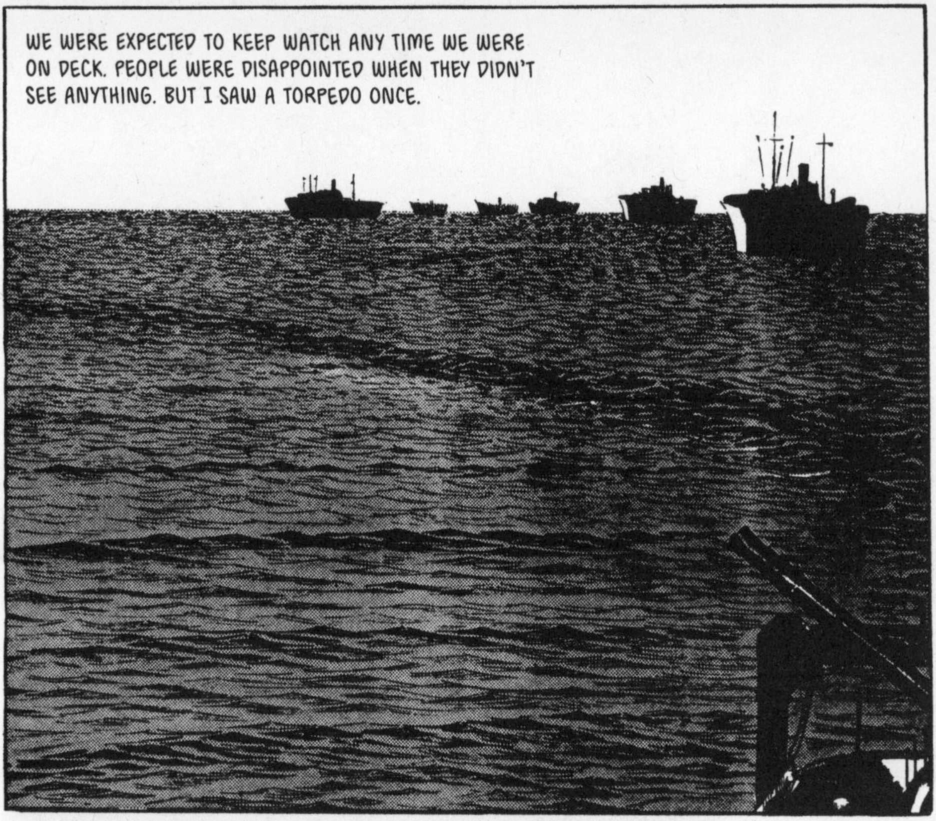
WE WERE EXPECTED TO KEEP WATCH ANY TIME WE WERE ON DECK. PEOPLE WERE DISAPPOINTED WHEN THEY DIDN'T SEE ANYTHING. BUT I SAW A TORPEDO ONCE.

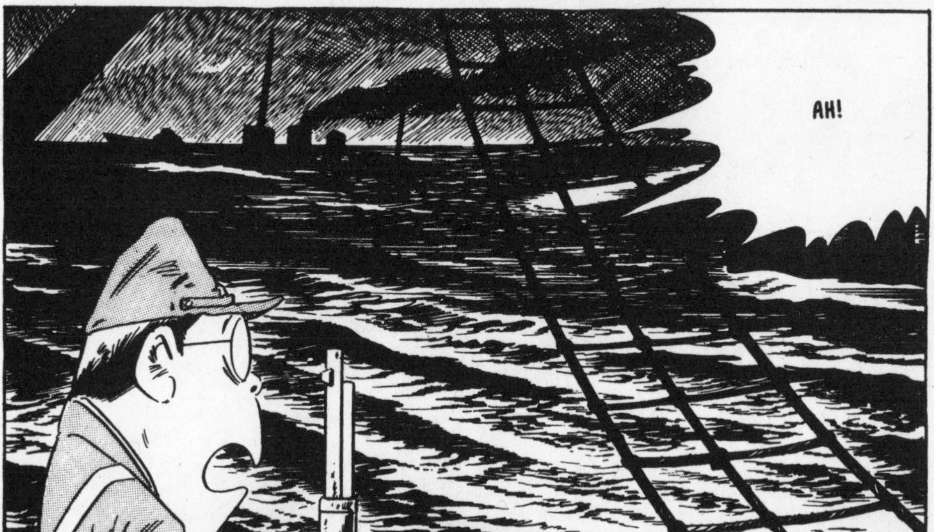
AH!

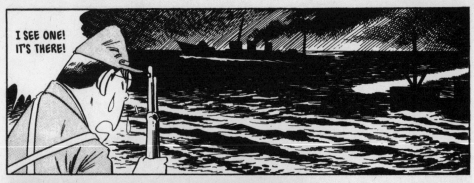

I SEE ONE! IT'S THERE!

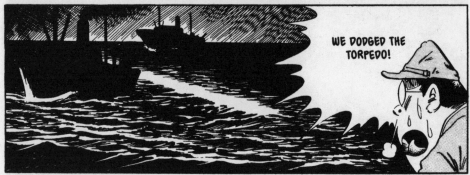

WE DODGED THE TORPEDO!

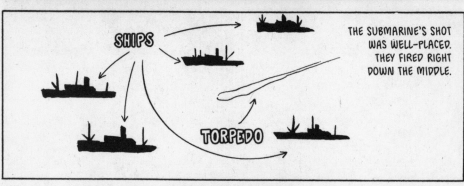

SHIPS

TORPEDO

THE SUBMARINE'S SHOT WAS WELL-PLACED. THEY FIRED RIGHT DOWN THE MIDDLE.

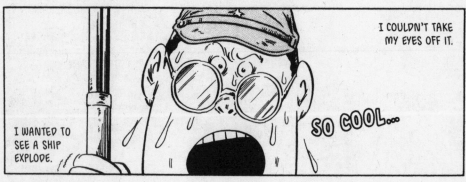

I COULDN'T TAKE MY EYES OFF IT.

SO COOL...

I WANTED TO SEE A SHIP EXPLODE.

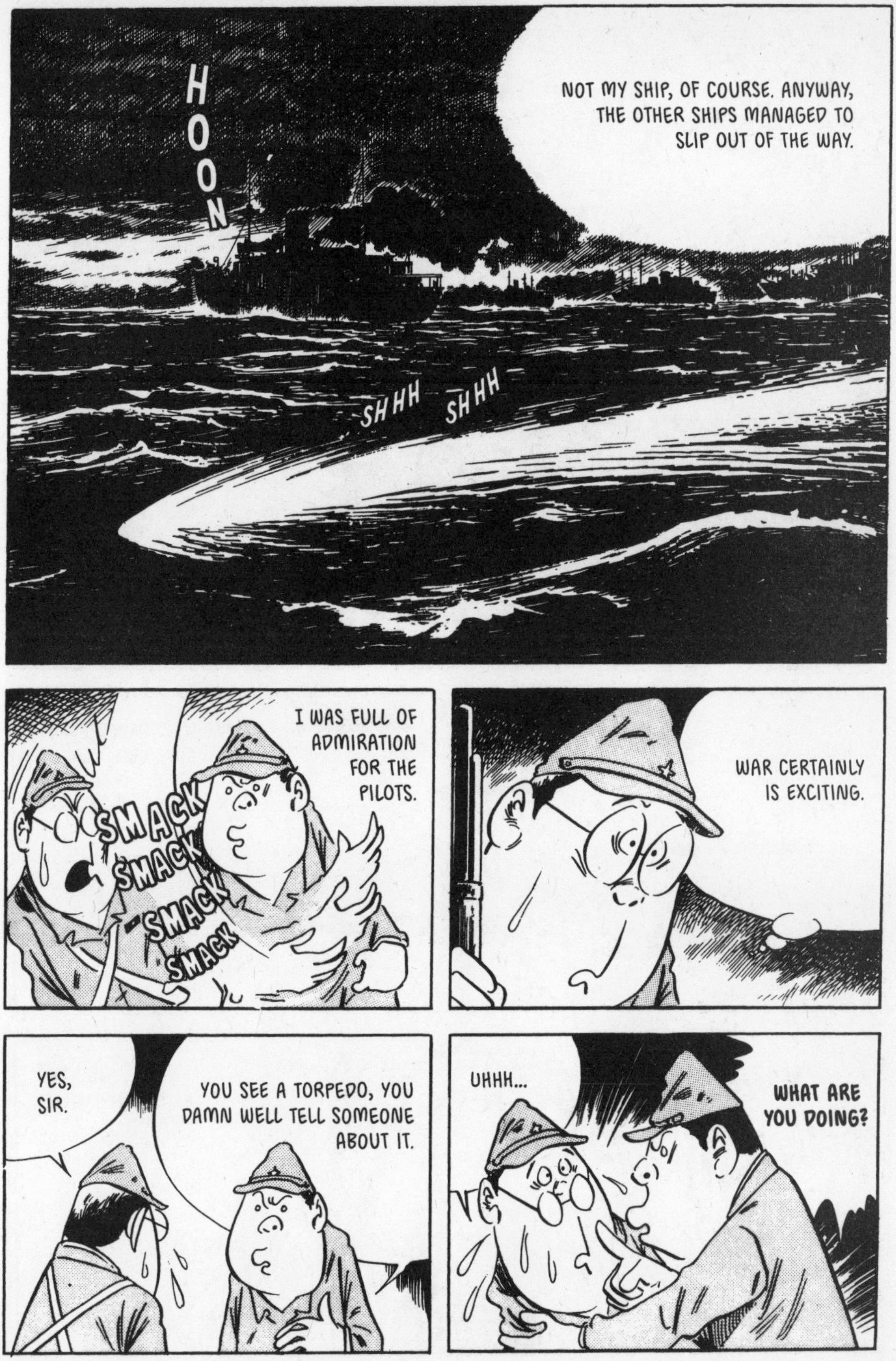
NOT MY SHIP, OF COURSE. ANYWAY, THE OTHER SHIPS MANAGED TO SLIP OUT OF THE WAY.
HOON
SHHH SHHH
WAR CERTAINLY IS EXCITING.
I WAS FULL OF ADMIRATION FOR THE PILOTS.
SMACK SMACK SMACK SMACK
WHAT ARE YOU DOING?
UHHH...
YOU SEE A TORPEDO, YOU DAMN WELL TELL SOMEONE ABOUT IT.
YES, SIR.

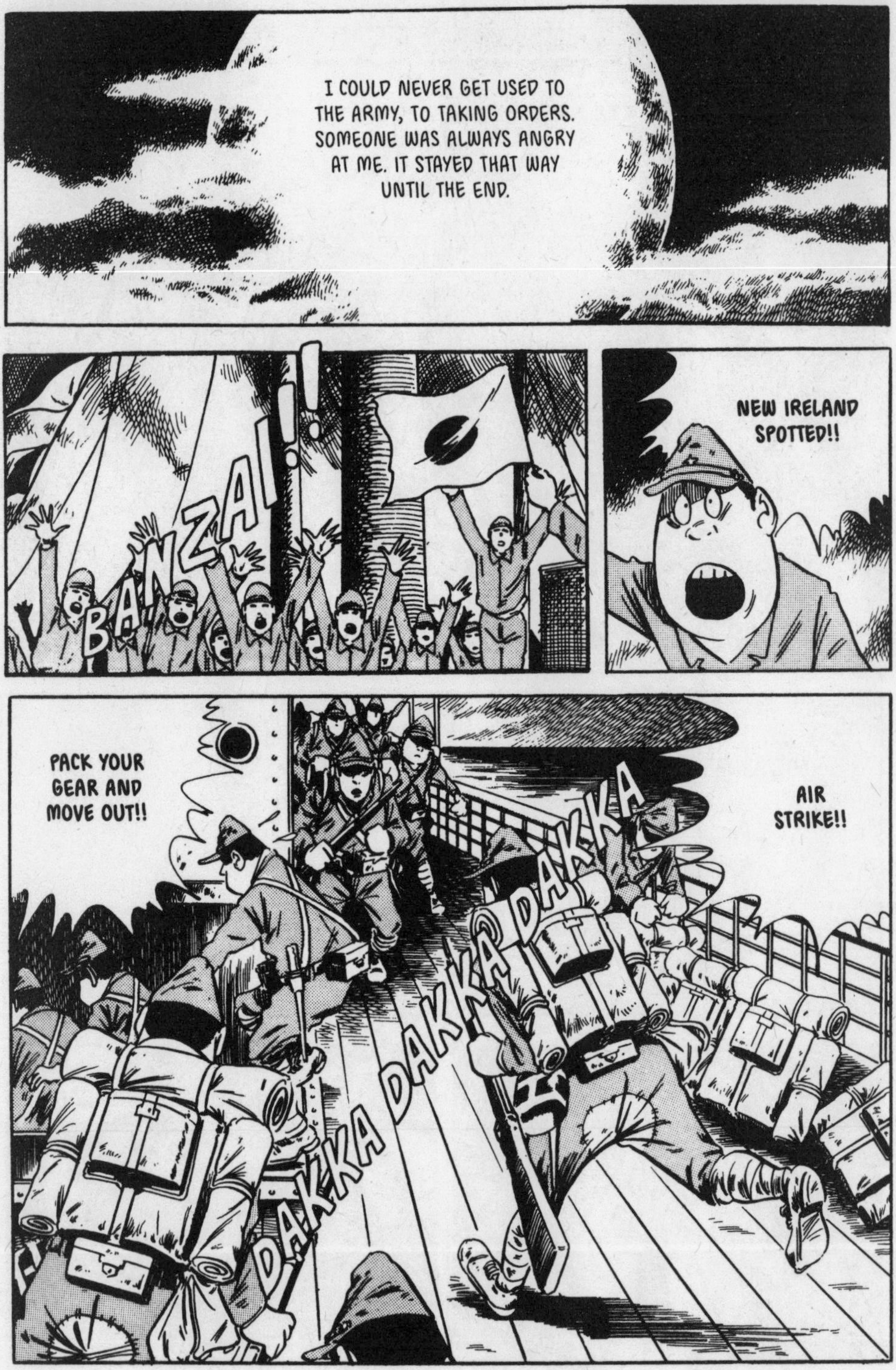
I COULD NEVER GET USED TO THE ARMY, TO TAKING ORDERS. SOMEONE WAS ALWAYS ANGRY AT ME. IT STAYED THAT WAY UNTIL THE END.
NEW IRELAND SPOTTED!!
BANZAI!!
AIR STRIKE!!
DAKKA DAKKA DAKKA DAKKA
PACK YOUR GEAR AND MOVE OUT!!

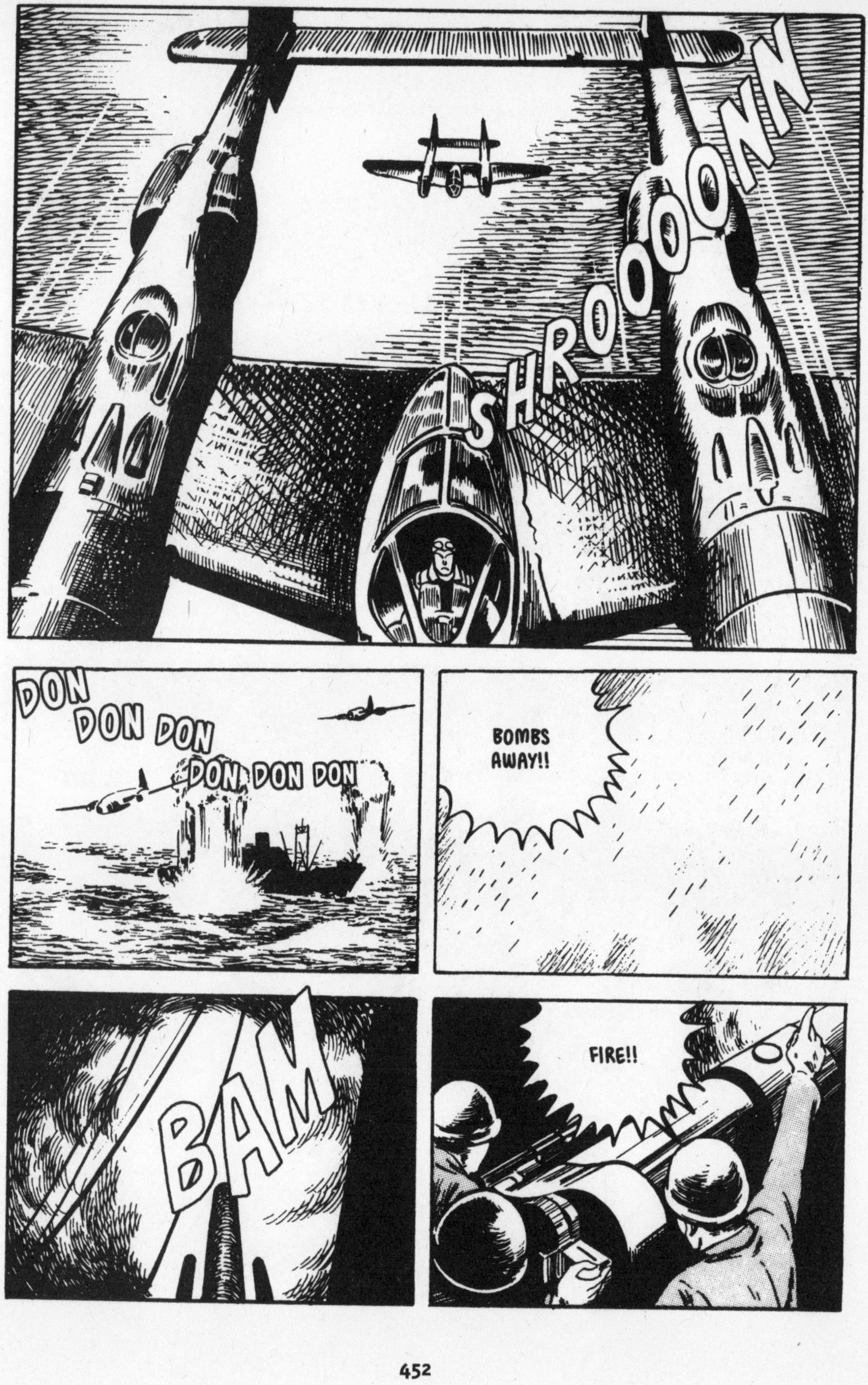
SHROOOOONN
BOMBS AWAY!!
DON DON DON DON DON DON
FIRE!!
BAM

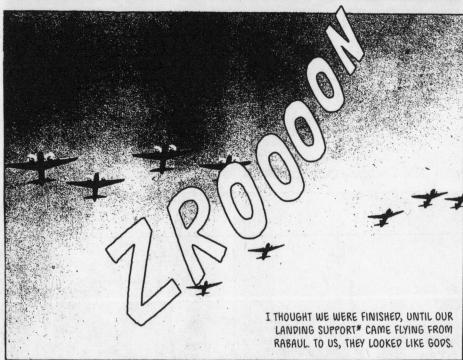

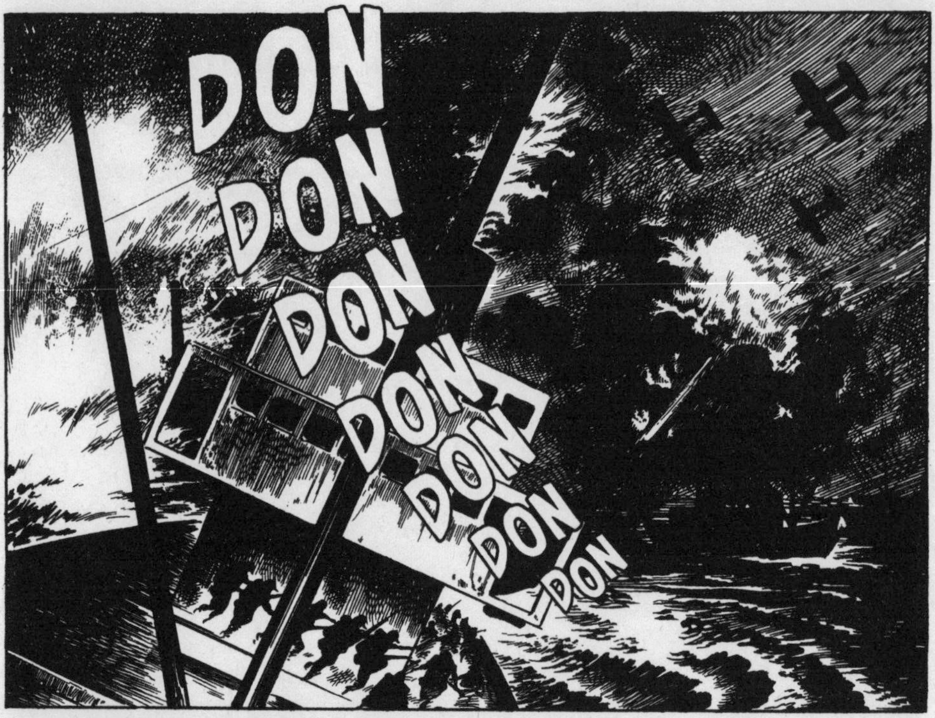
DON
DON
DON
DON
DON
DON
DON

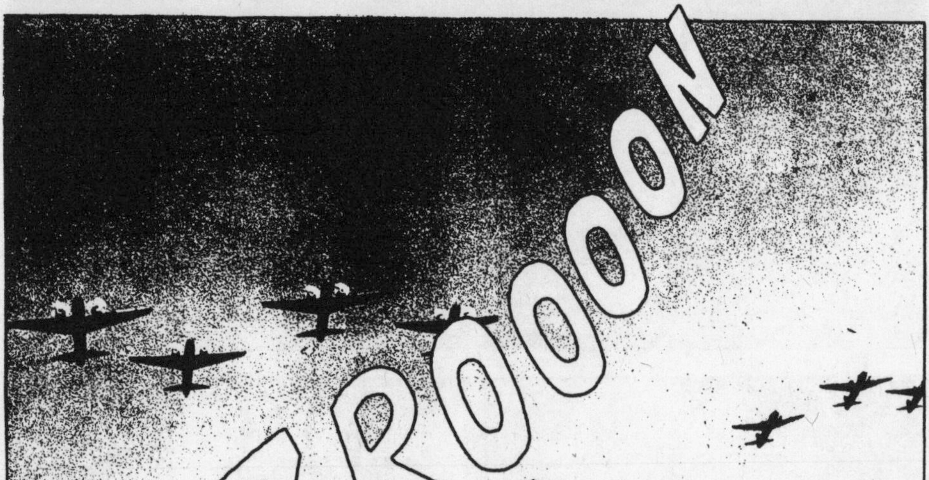
ZROOOOON
I THOUGHT WE WERE FINISHED, UNTIL OUR LANDING SUPPORT* CAME FLYING FROM RABAUL. TO US, THEY LOOKED LIKE GODS.

*AIRCRAFT SENT TO PROVIDE COVER FOR A LANDING. USUALLY NAVAL FLYERS.

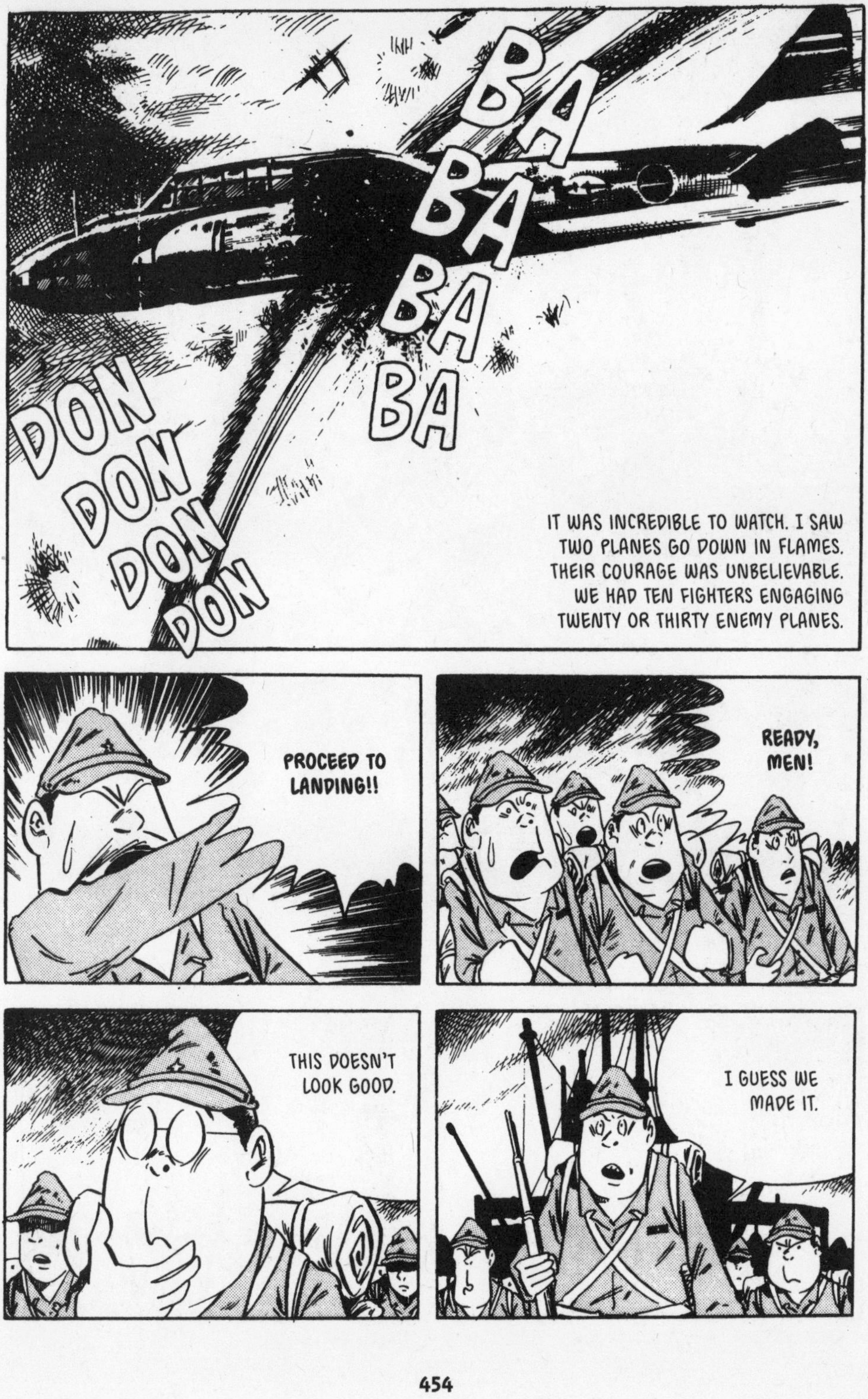
BA BA BA BA BA
DON DON DON DON DON
IT WAS INCREDIBLE TO WATCH. I SAW TWO PLANES GO DOWN IN FLAMES. THEIR COURAGE WAS UNBELIEVABLE. WE HAD TEN FIGHTERS ENGAGING TWENTY OR THIRTY ENEMY PLANES.
READY, MEN!
PROCEED TO LANDING!!
I GUESS WE MADE IT.
THIS DOESN'T LOOK GOOD.

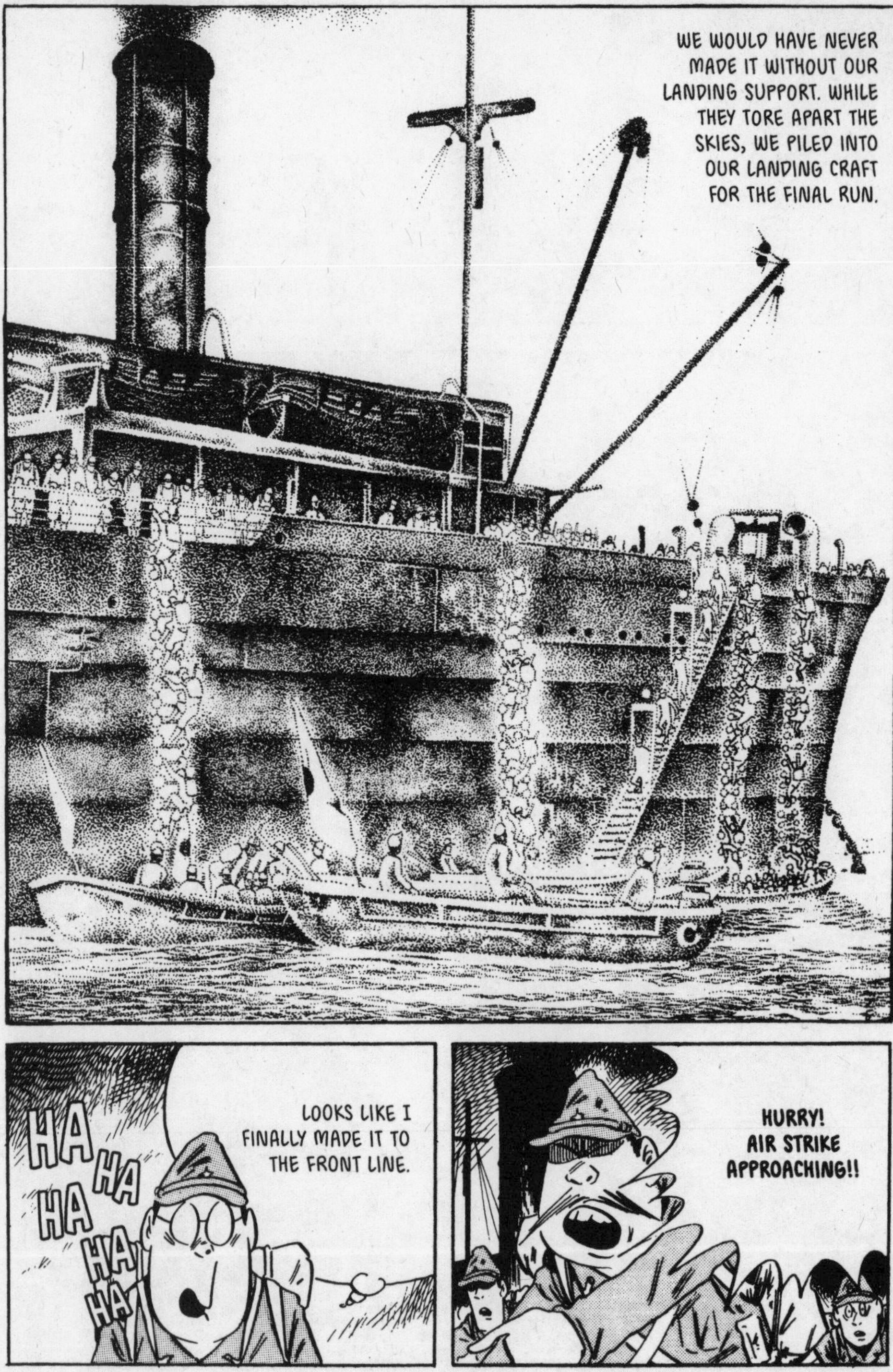
WE WOULD HAVE NEVER MADE IT WITHOUT OUR LANDING SUPPORT. WHILE THEY TORE APART THE SKIES, WE PILED INTO OUR LANDING CRAFT FOR THE FINAL RUN.
HURRY! AIR STRIKE APPROACHING!!
HA HA HA HA HA HA
LOOKS LIKE I FINALLY MADE IT TO THE FRONT LINE.

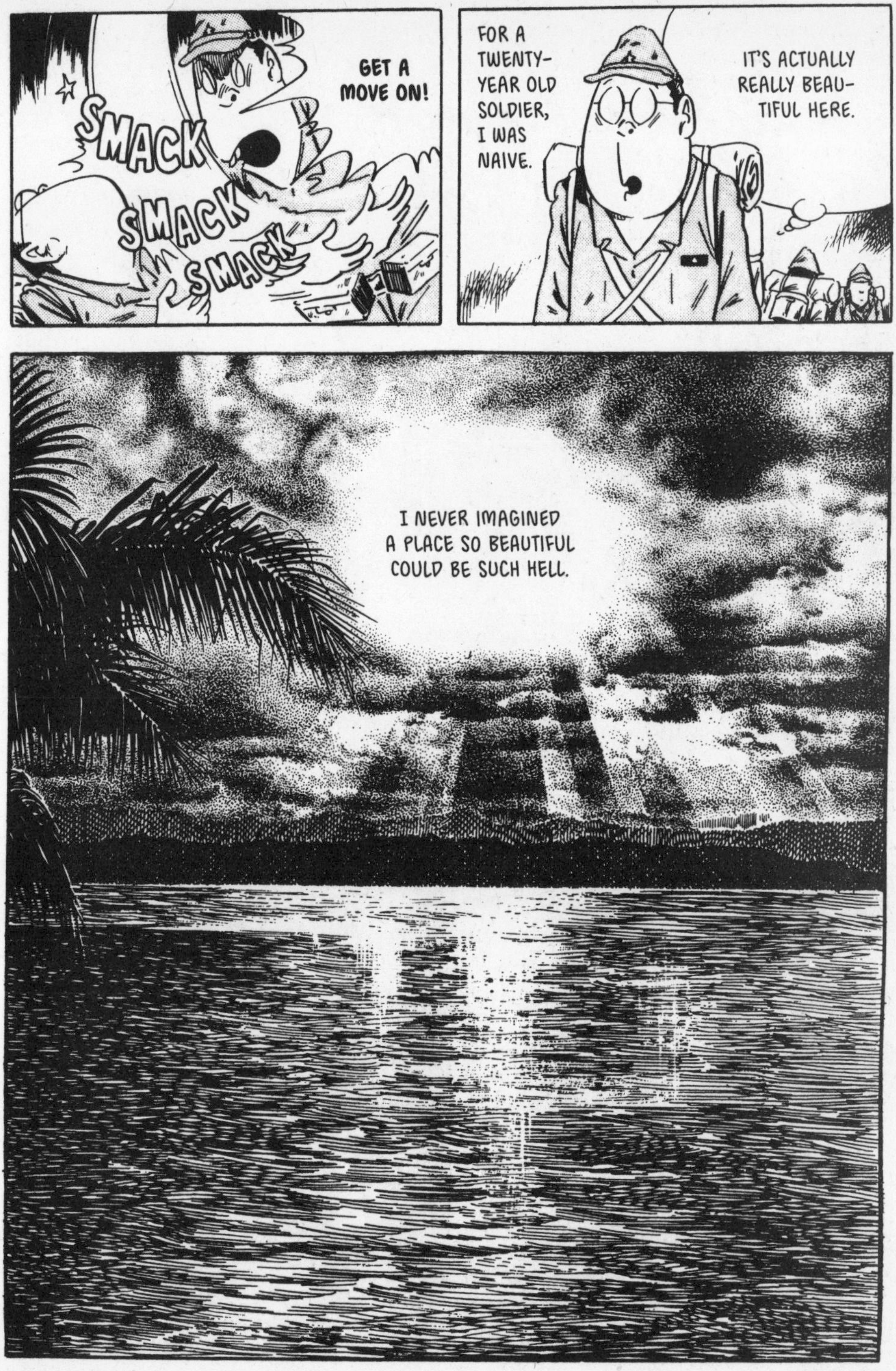

IT'S ACTUALLY REALLY BEAU-TIFUL HERE.
FOR A TWENTY-YEAR OLD SOLDIER, I WAS NAIVE.
GET A MOVE ON!
SMACK
SMACK
SMACK
I NEVER IMAGINED A PLACE SO BEAUTIFUL COULD BE SUCH HELL.

BATTLES IN THE CENTRAL PACIFIC

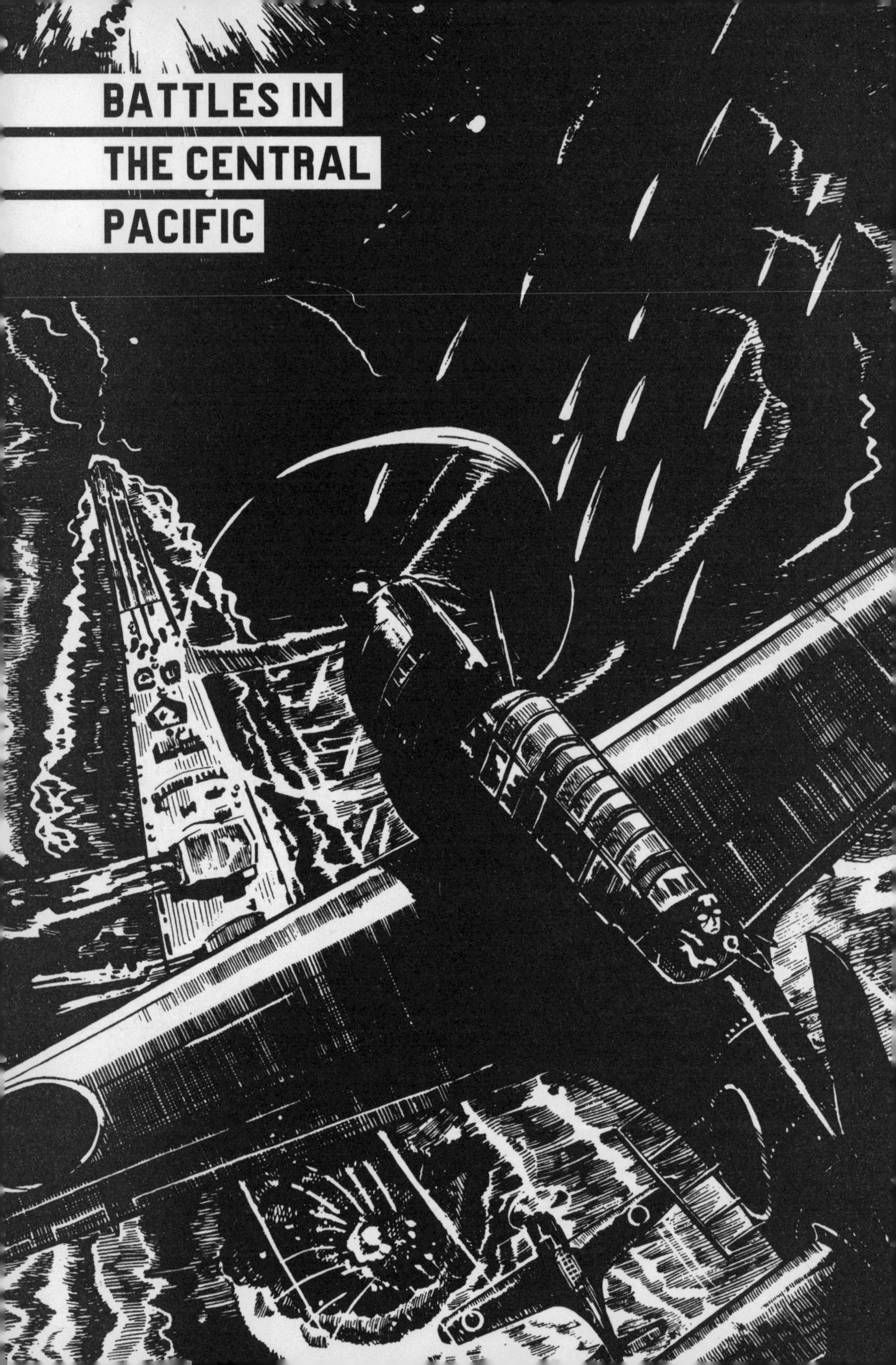

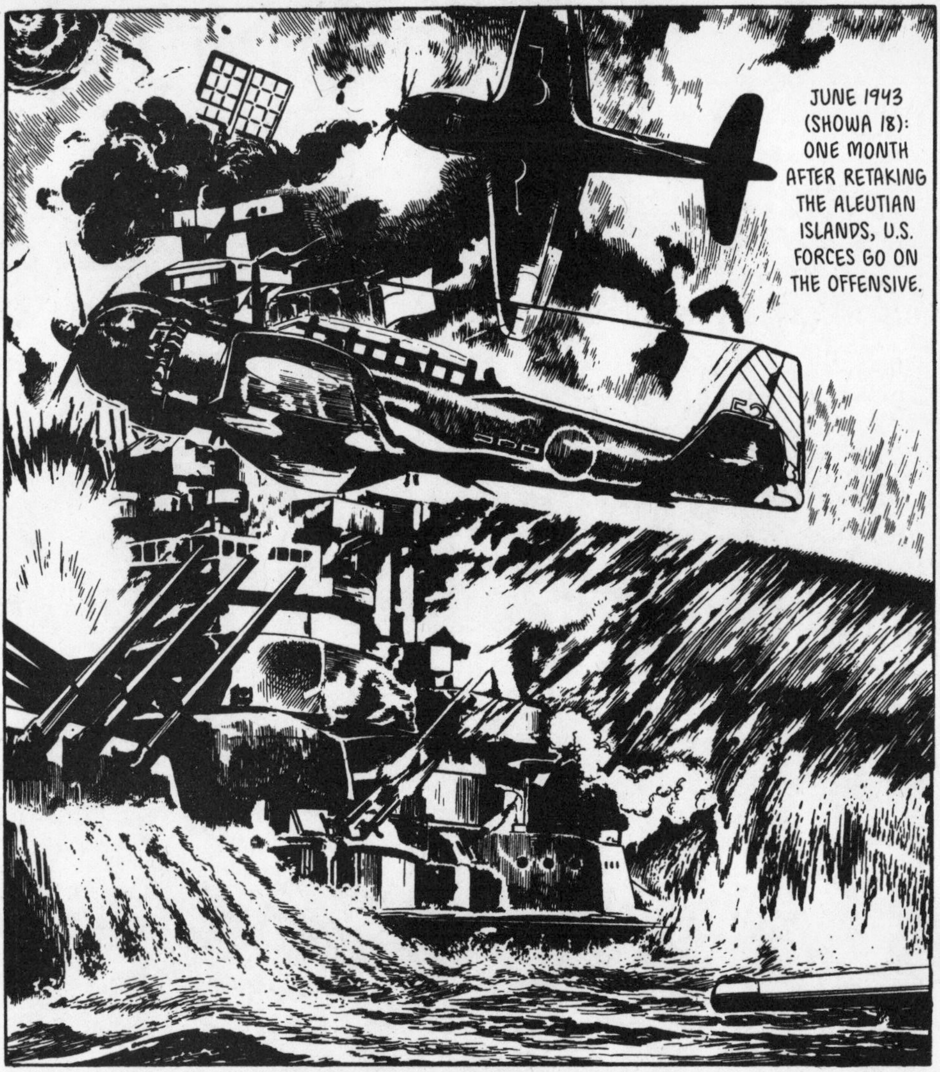
JUNE 1943 (SHOWA 18): ONE MONTH AFTER RETAKING THE ALEUTIAN ISLANDS, U.S. FORCES GO ON THE OFFENSIVE.

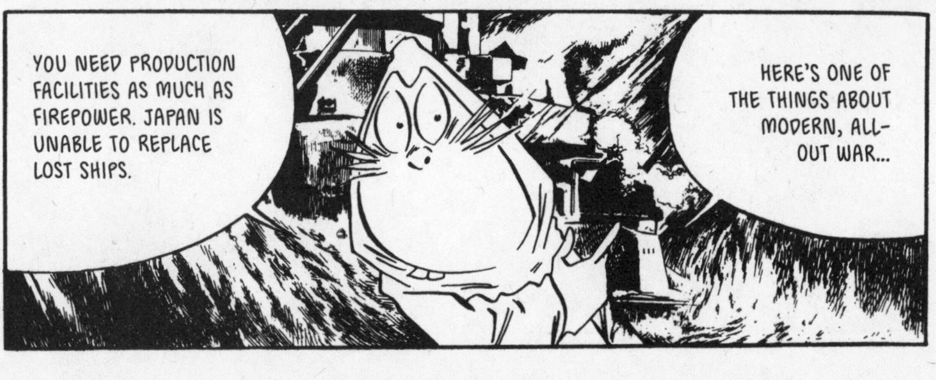
HERE'S ONE OF THE THINGS ABOUT MODERN, ALL-OUT WAR...
YOU NEED PRODUCTION FACILITIES AS MUCH AS FIREPOWER. JAPAN IS UNABLE TO REPLACE LOST SHIPS.

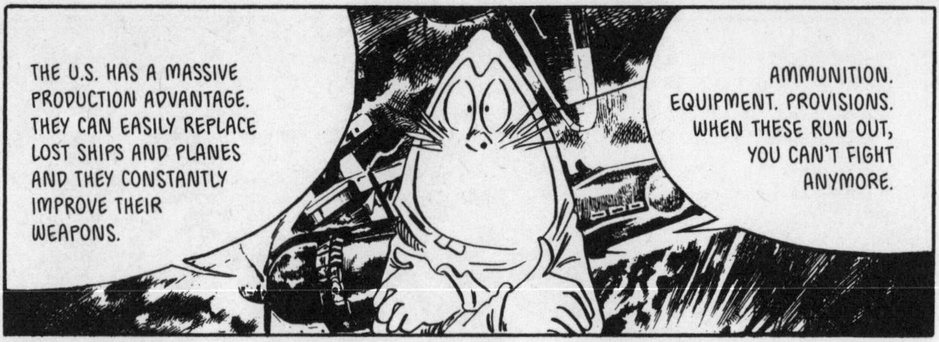
AMMUNITION. EQUIPMENT. PROVISIONS. WHEN THESE RUN OUT, YOU CAN'T FIGHT ANYMORE.
THE U.S. HAS A MASSIVE PRODUCTION ADVANTAGE. THEY CAN EASILY REPLACE LOST SHIPS AND PLANES AND THEY CONSTANTLY IMPROVE THEIR WEAPONS.

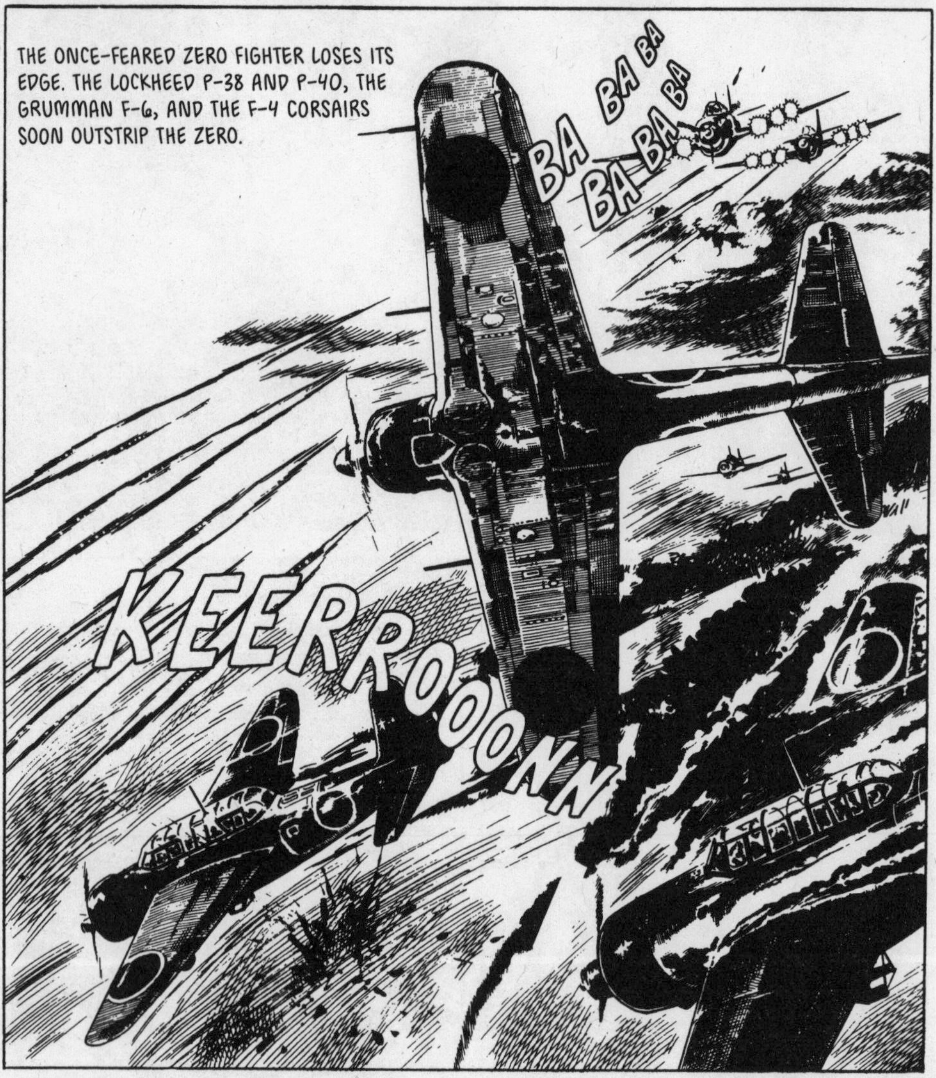
BA BA BA BA BA BA
THE ONCE-FEARED ZERO FIGHTER LOSES ITS EDGE. THE LOCKHEED P-38 AND P-40, THE GRUMMAN F-6, AND THE F-4 CORSAIRS SOON OUTSTRIP THE ZERO.
KEERROOONN

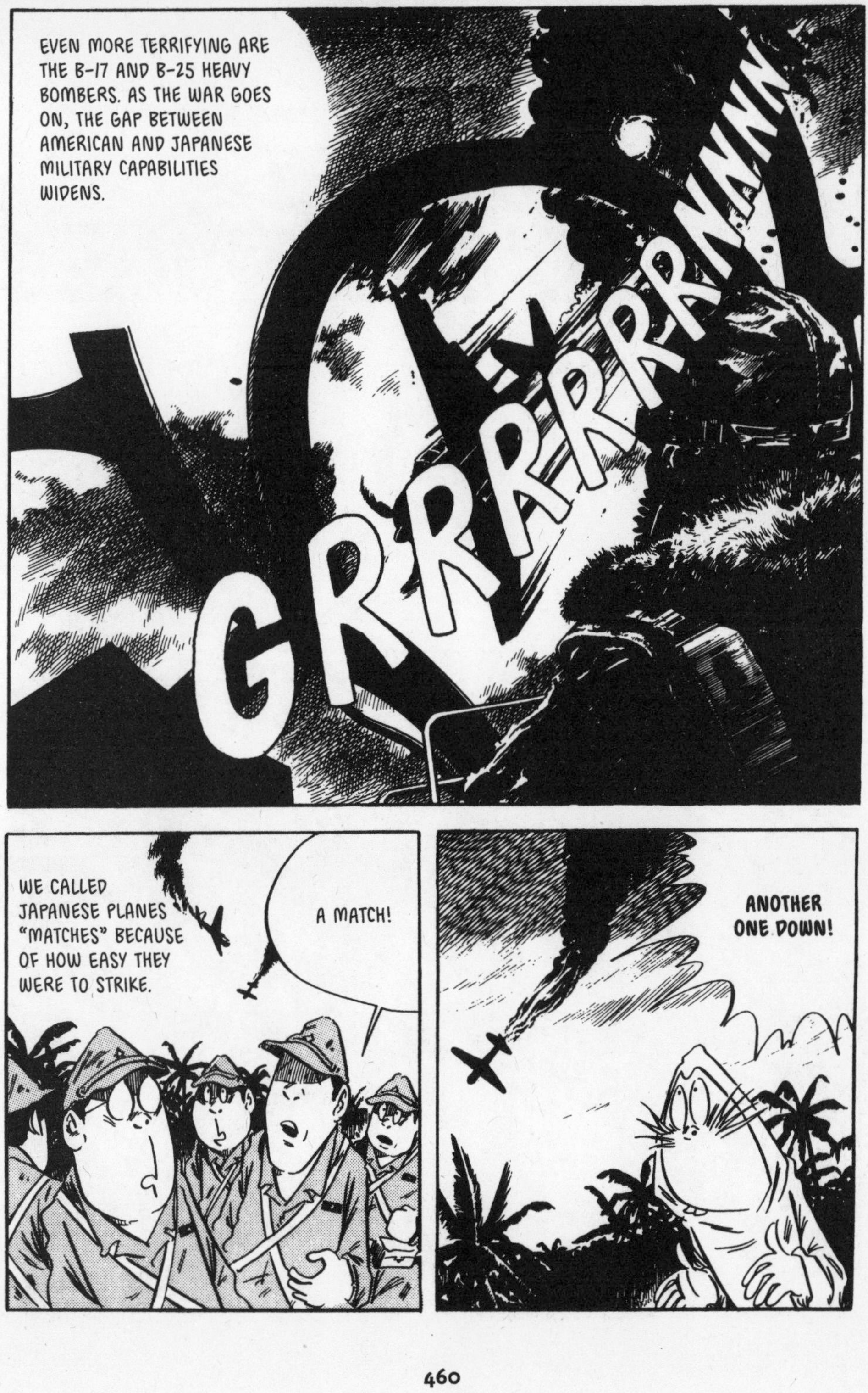

EVEN MORE TERRIFYING ARE THE B-17 AND B-25 HEAVY BOMBERS. AS THE WAR GOES ON, THE GAP BETWEEN AMERICAN AND JAPANESE MILITARY CAPABILITIES WIDENS.
GRRRRRRRNNNN
ANOTHER ONE DOWN!
A MATCH!
WE CALLED JAPANESE PLANES "MATCHES" BECAUSE OF HOW EASY THEY WERE TO STRIKE.

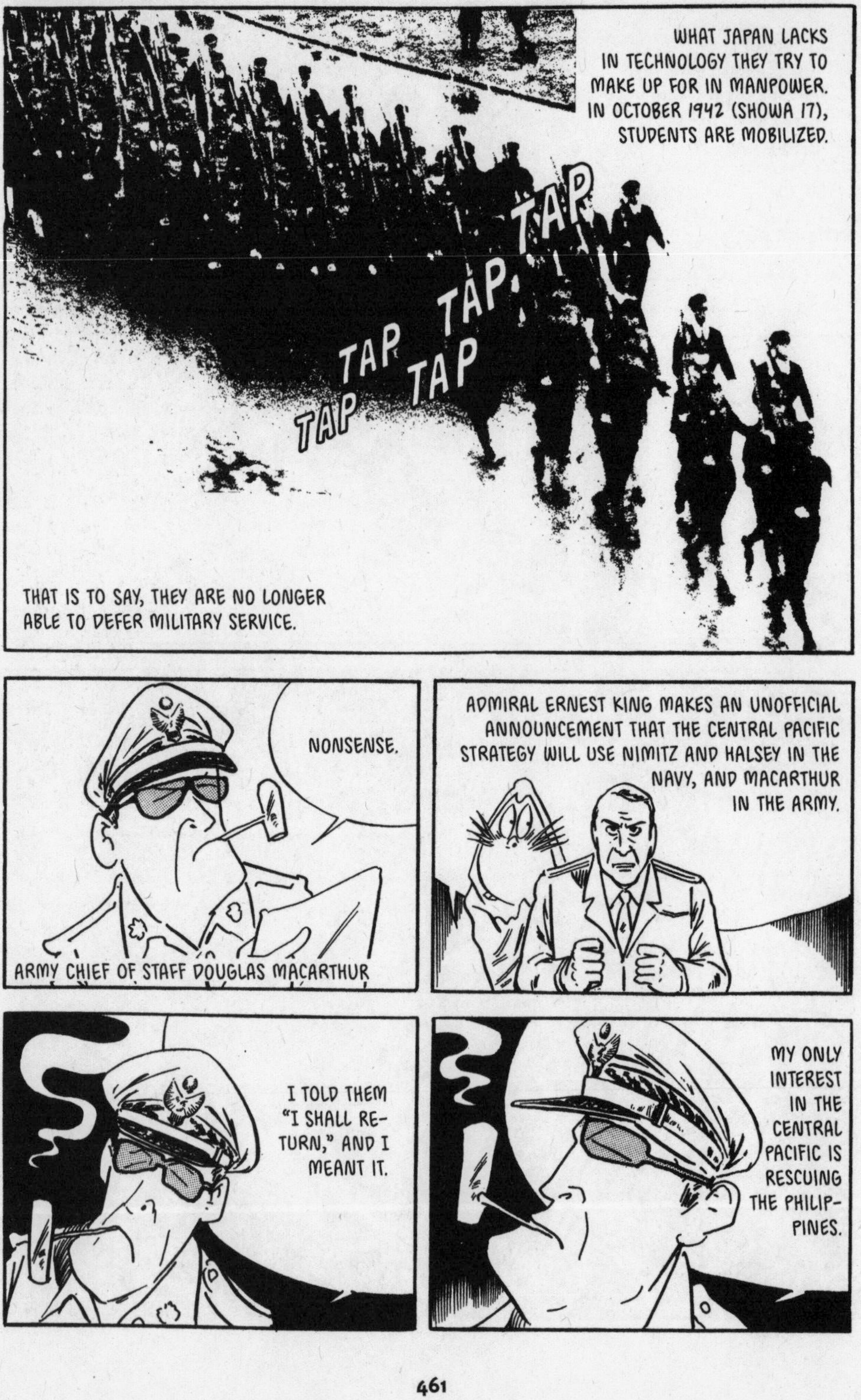
WHAT JAPAN LACKS IN TECHNOLOGY THEY TRY TO MAKE UP FOR IN MANPOWER. IN OCTOBER 1942 (SHOWA 17), STUDENTS ARE MOBILIZED.
TAP TAP TAP TAP TAP
THAT IS TO SAY, THEY ARE NO LONGER ABLE TO DEFER MILITARY SERVICE.
ADMIRAL ERNEST KING MAKES AN UNOFFICIAL ANNOUNCEMENT THAT THE CENTRAL PACIFIC STRATEGY WILL USE NIMITZ AND HALSEY IN THE NAVY, AND MACARTHUR IN THE ARMY.
NONSENSE.
ARMY CHIEF OF STAFF DOUGLAS MACARTHUR
MY ONLY INTEREST IN THE CENTRAL PACIFIC IS RESCUING THE PHILIP-PINES.
I TOLD THEM "I SHALL RE-TURN," AND I MEANT IT.

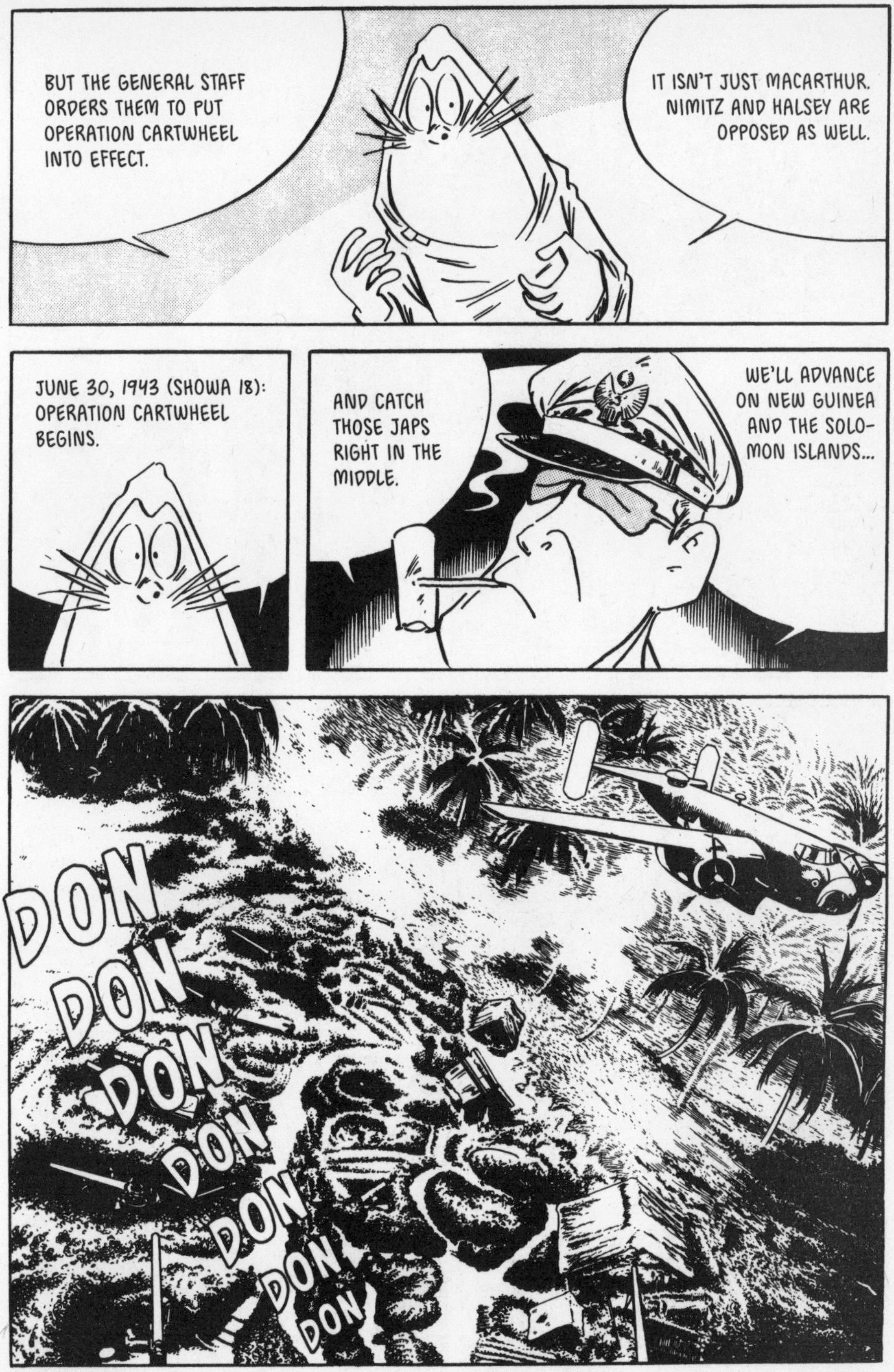
IT ISN'T JUST MACARTHUR. NIMITZ AND HALSEY ARE OPPOSED AS WELL.
BUT THE GENERAL STAFF ORDERS THEM TO PUT OPERATION CARTWHEEL INTO EFFECT.
WE'LL ADVANCE ON NEW GUINEA AND THE SOLOMON ISLANDS...
AND CATCH THOSE JAPS RIGHT IN THE MIDDLE.
JUNE 30, 1943 (SHOWA 18): OPERATION CARTWHEEL BEGINS.
DON DON DON DON DON DON DON

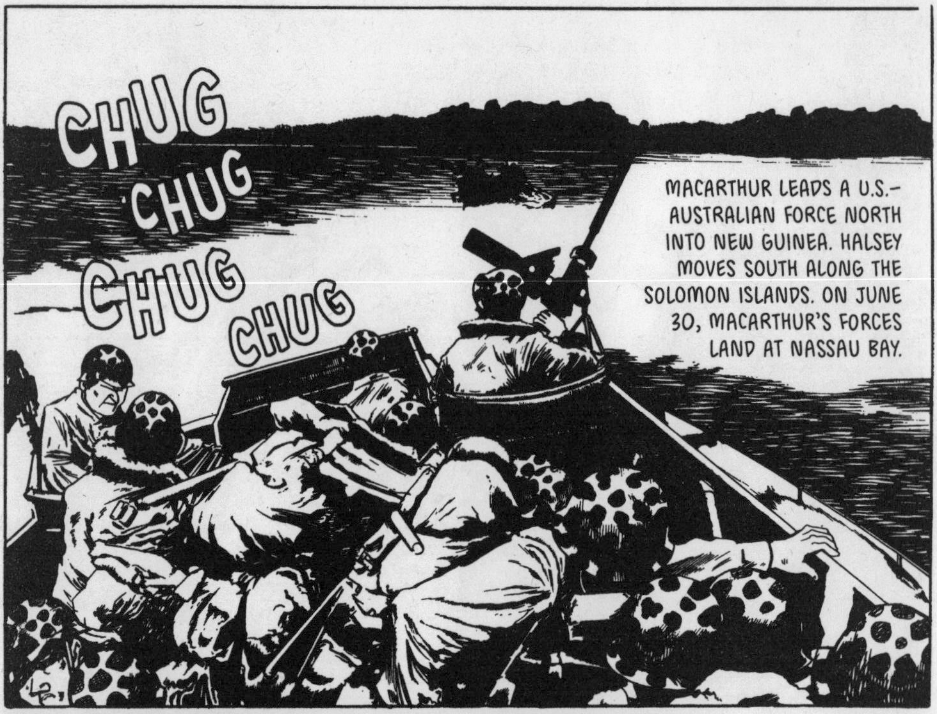
CHUG
CHUG
CHUG
CHUG
MACARTHUR LEADS A U.S.–AUSTRALIAN FORCE NORTH INTO NEW GUINEA. HALSEY MOVES SOUTH ALONG THE SOLOMON ISLANDS. ON JUNE 30, MACARTHUR'S FORCES LAND AT NASSAU BAY.
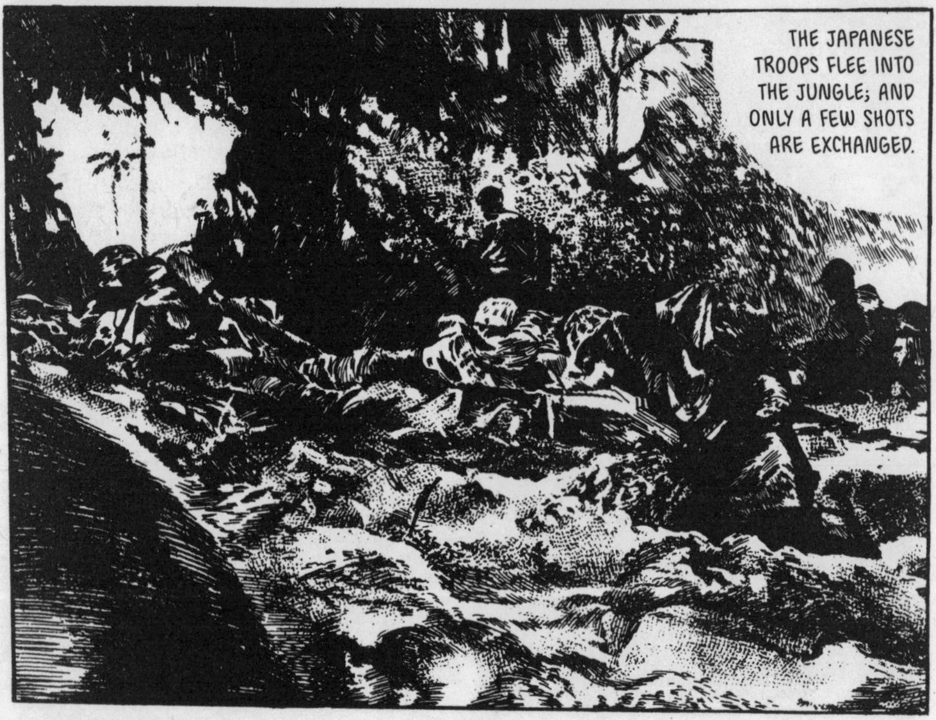
THE JAPANESE TROOPS FLEE INTO THE JUNGLE; AND ONLY A FEW SHOTS ARE EXCHANGED.

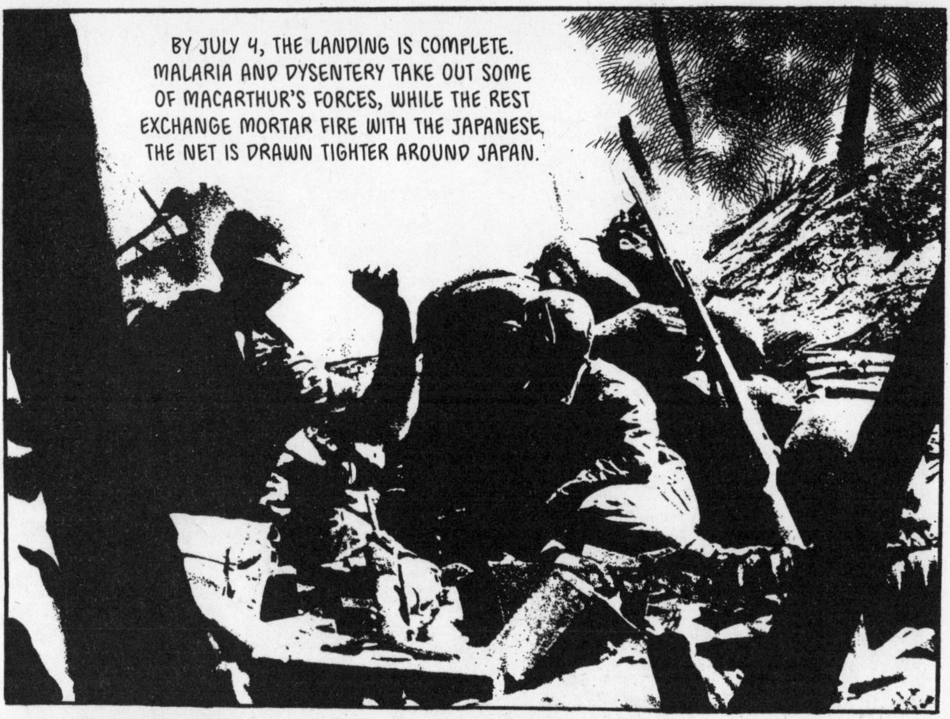
BY JULY 4, THE LANDING IS COMPLETE. MALARIA AND DYSENTERY TAKE OUT SOME OF MACARTHUR'S FORCES, WHILE THE REST EXCHANGE MORTAR FIRE WITH THE JAPANESE. THE NET IS DRAWN TIGHTER AROUND JAPAN.

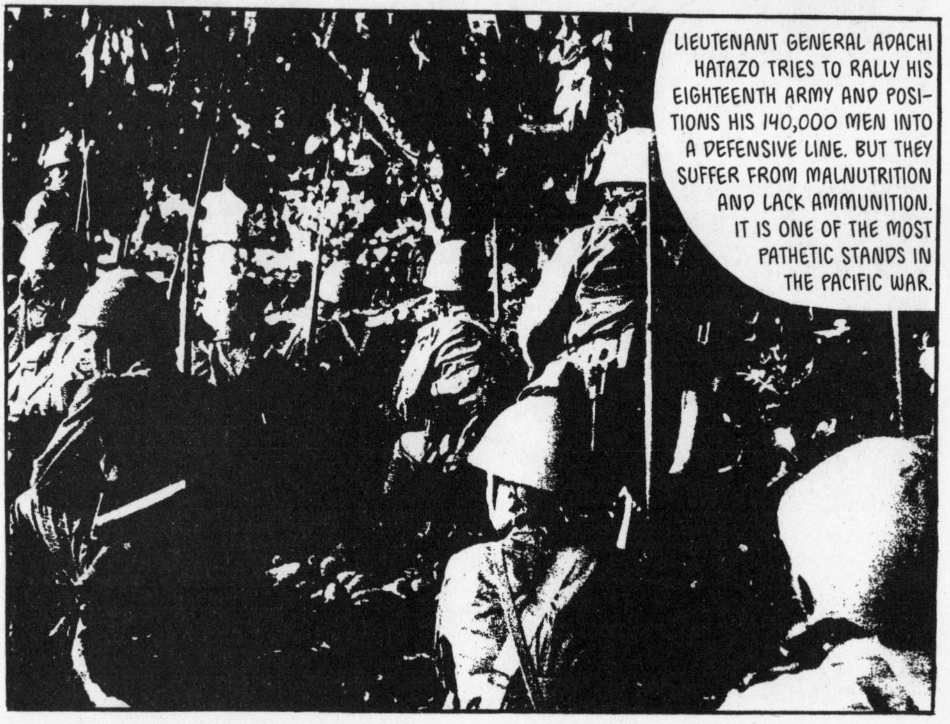
LIEUTENANT GENERAL ADACHI HATAZO TRIES TO RALLY HIS EIGHTEENTH ARMY AND POSITIONS HIS 140,000 MEN INTO A DEFENSIVE LINE. BUT THEY SUFFER FROM MALNUTRITION AND LACK AMMUNITION. IT IS ONE OF THE MOST PATHETIC STANDS IN THE PACIFIC WAR.

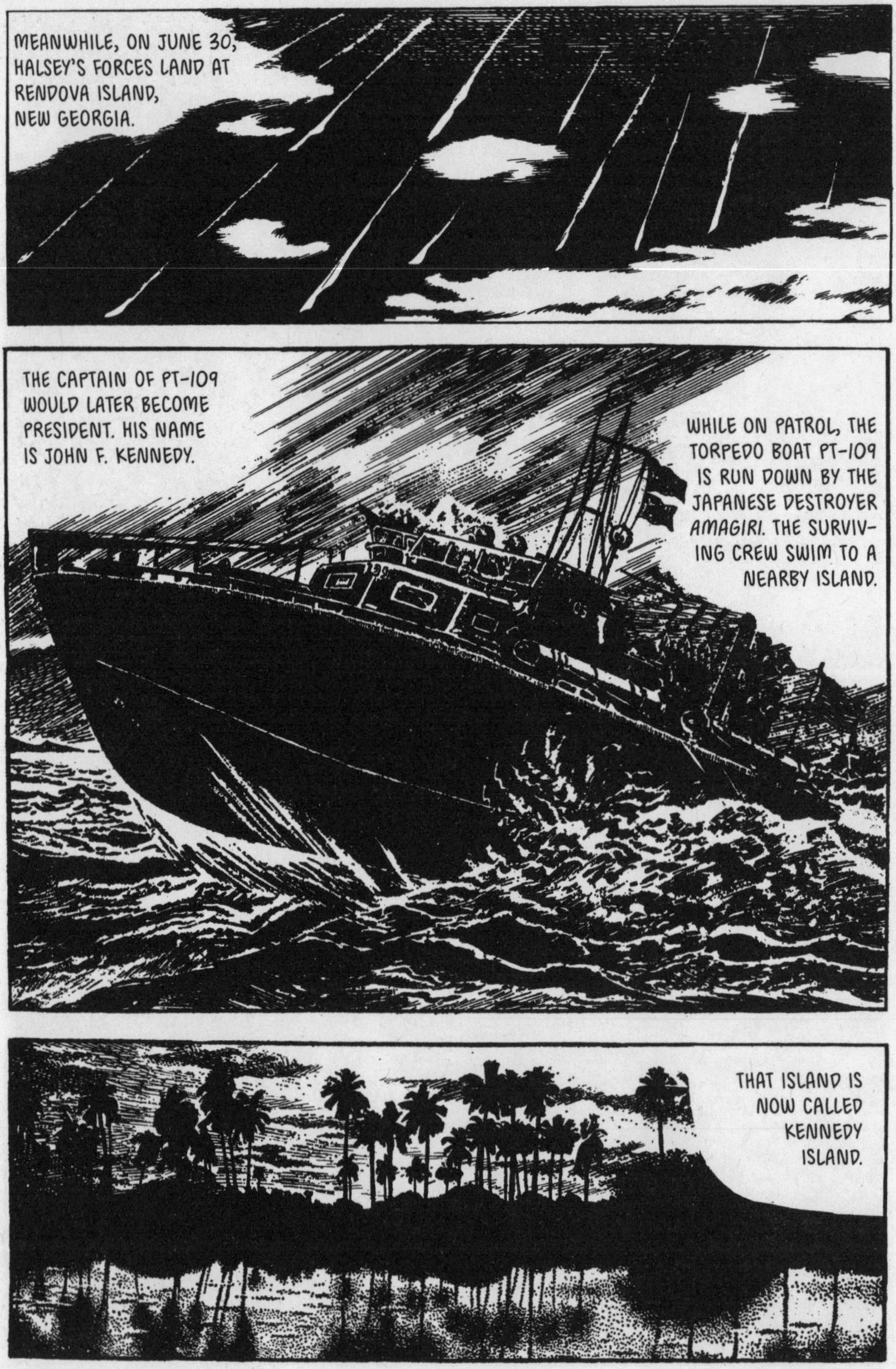
MEANWHILE, ON JUNE 30, HALSEY'S FORCES LAND AT RENDOVA ISLAND, NEW GEORGIA.
WHILE ON PATROL, THE TORPEDO BOAT PT-109 IS RUN DOWN BY THE JAPANESE DESTROYER *AMAGIRI*. THE SURVIVING CREW SWIM TO A NEARBY ISLAND.
THE CAPTAIN OF PT-109 WOULD LATER BECOME PRESIDENT. HIS NAME IS JOHN F. KENNEDY.
THAT ISLAND IS NOW CALLED KENNEDY ISLAND.

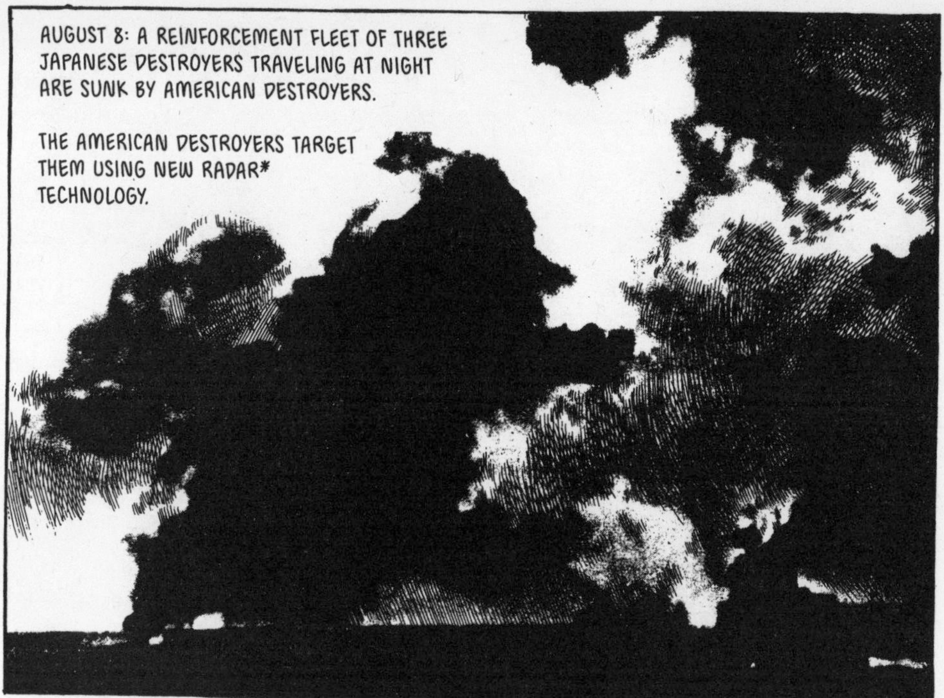
AUGUST 8: A REINFORCEMENT FLEET OF THREE JAPANESE DESTROYERS TRAVELING AT NIGHT ARE SUNK BY AMERICAN DESTROYERS.
THE AMERICAN DESTROYERS TARGET THEM USING NEW RADAR* TECHNOLOGY.

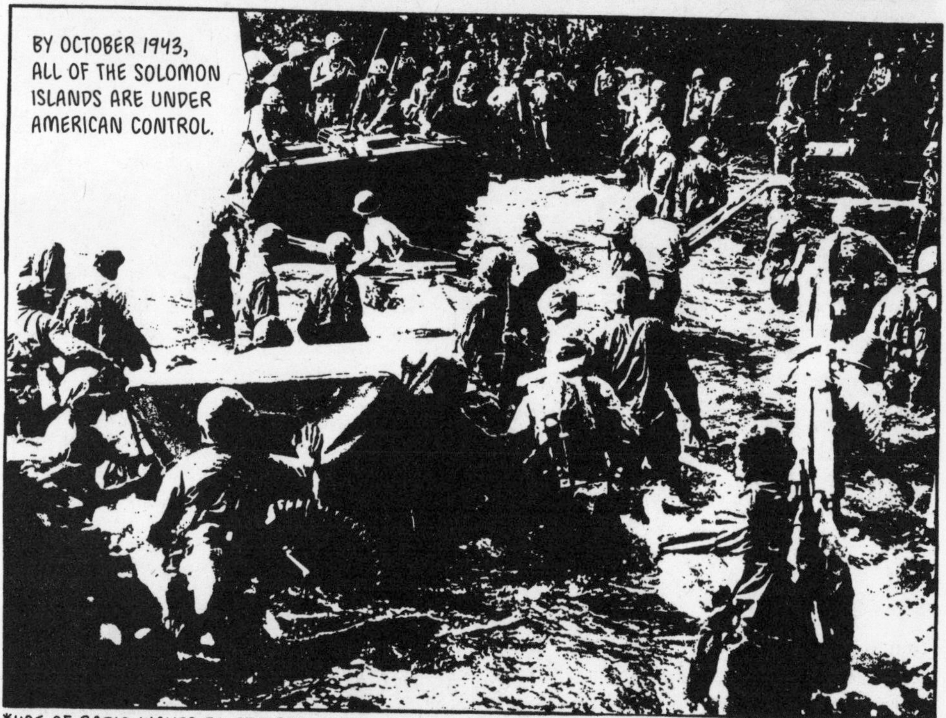
BY OCTOBER 1943, ALL OF THE SOLOMON ISLANDS ARE UNDER AMERICAN CONTROL.

*USE OF RADIO WAVES TO DETERMINE THE POSITION OF SHIPS AND AIRCRAFT.

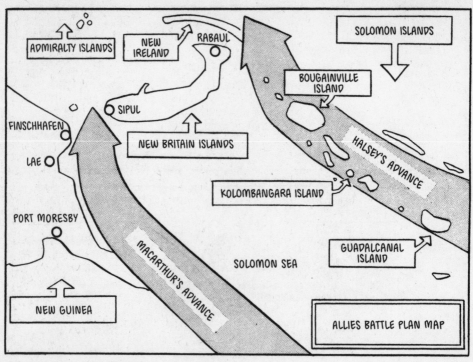

SOLOMON ISLANDS
RABAUL
NEW IRELAND
ADMIRALTY ISLANDS
BOUGAINVILLE ISLAND
SIPUL
NEW BRITAIN ISLANDS
FINSCHHAFEN
HALSEY'S ADVANCE
LAE
KOLOMBANGARA ISLAND
PORT MORESBY
GUADALCANAL ISLAND
MACARTHUR'S ADVANCE
SOLOMON SEA
NEW GUINEA
ALLIES BATTLE PLAN MAP
NOVEMBER 30, 1943 (SHOWA 18): A MEETING OF THE IMPERIAL COUNCIL. THE TOPIC IS JAPAN'S DEFENSE.
HIS IMPERIAL MAJESTY
PRIME MINISTER TOJO
NAVY GENERAL STAFF CHIEF NAGANO
ARMY GENERAL STAFF CHIEF SUGIYAMA
THE KURIL ISLANDS, THE SOUTH SEA ISLANDS, NEW GUINEA, THE SUNDA ISLANDS, BURMA...THEY ARE ALL CONNECTED.
WE MUST HOLD FAST TO OUR DEFENSE LINE!

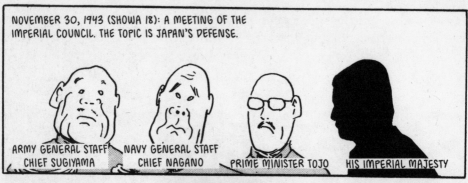

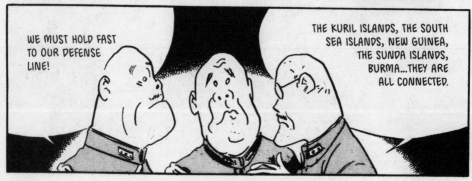

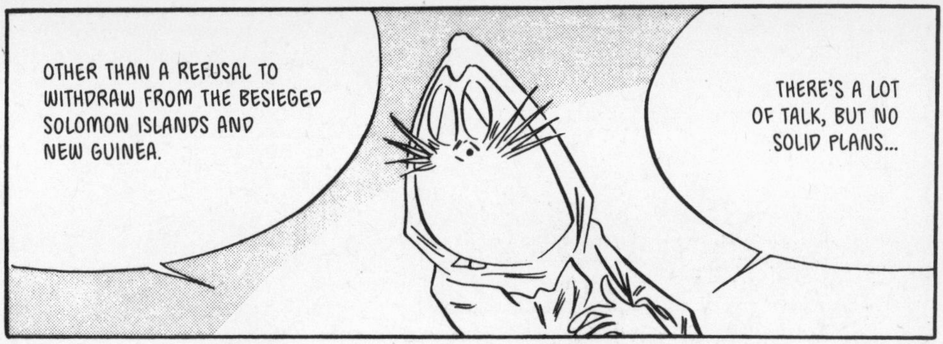
THERE'S A LOT OF TALK, BUT NO SOLID PLANS...
OTHER THAN A REFUSAL TO WITHDRAW FROM THE BESIEGED SOLOMON ISLANDS AND NEW GUINEA.

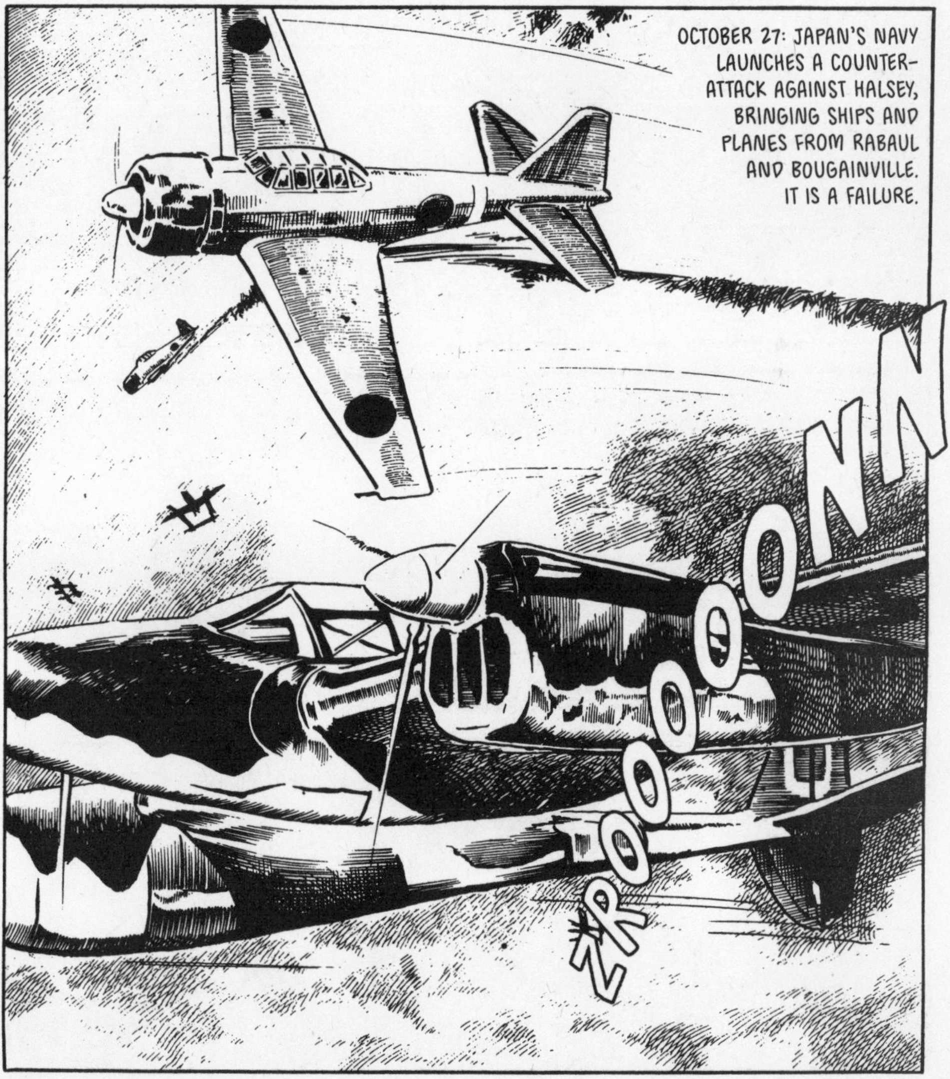
OCTOBER 27: JAPAN'S NAVY LAUNCHES A COUNTER-ATTACK AGAINST HALSEY, BRINGING SHIPS AND PLANES FROM RABAUL AND BOUGAINVILLE. IT IS A FAILURE.
ZROOOOOOONN

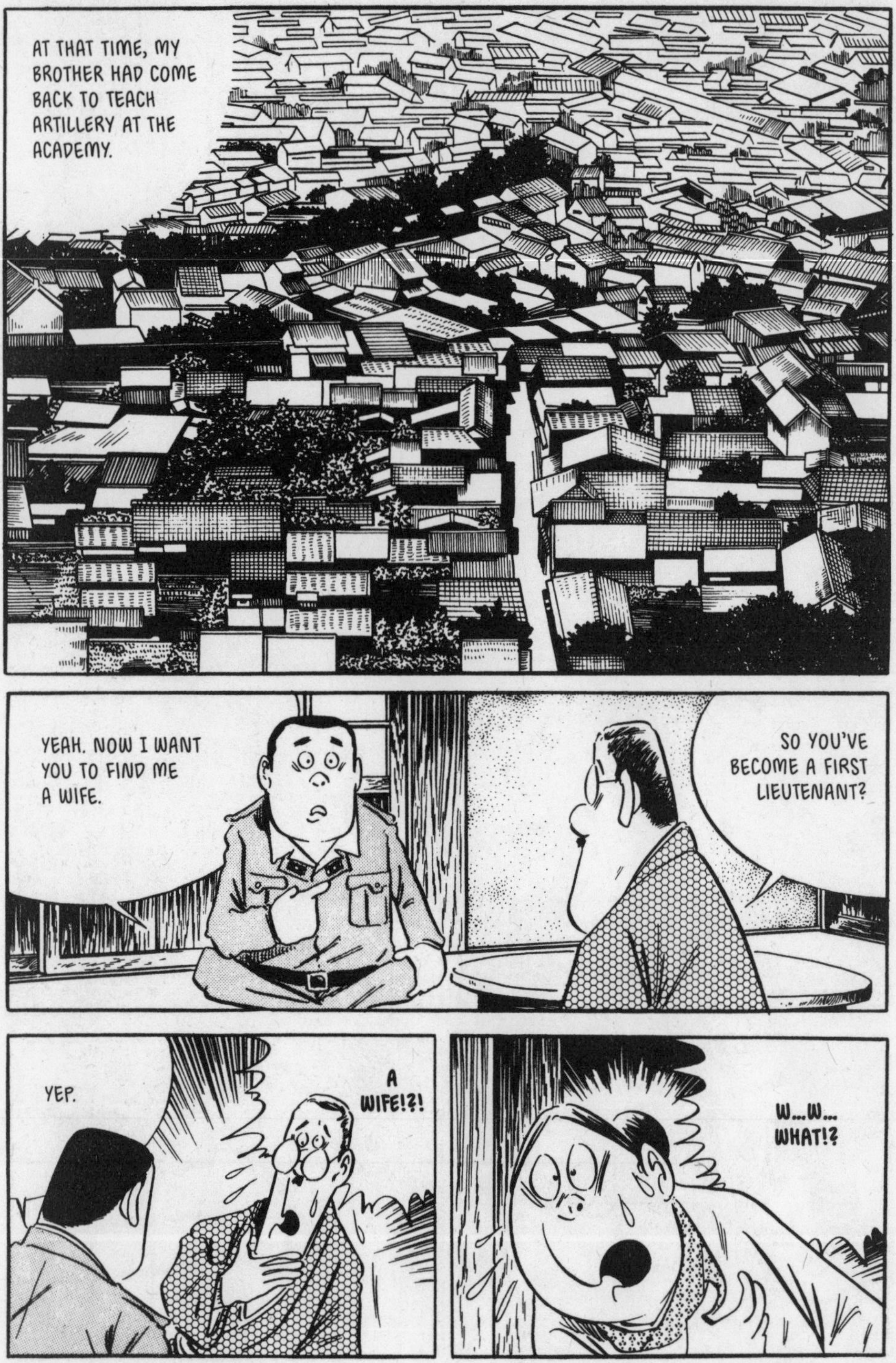
AT THAT TIME, MY BROTHER HAD COME BACK TO TEACH ARTILLERY AT THE ACADEMY.
SO YOU'VE BECOME A FIRST LIEUTENANT?
YEAH. NOW I WANT YOU TO FIND ME A WIFE.
W...W... WHAT!?
A WIFE!?!
YEP.

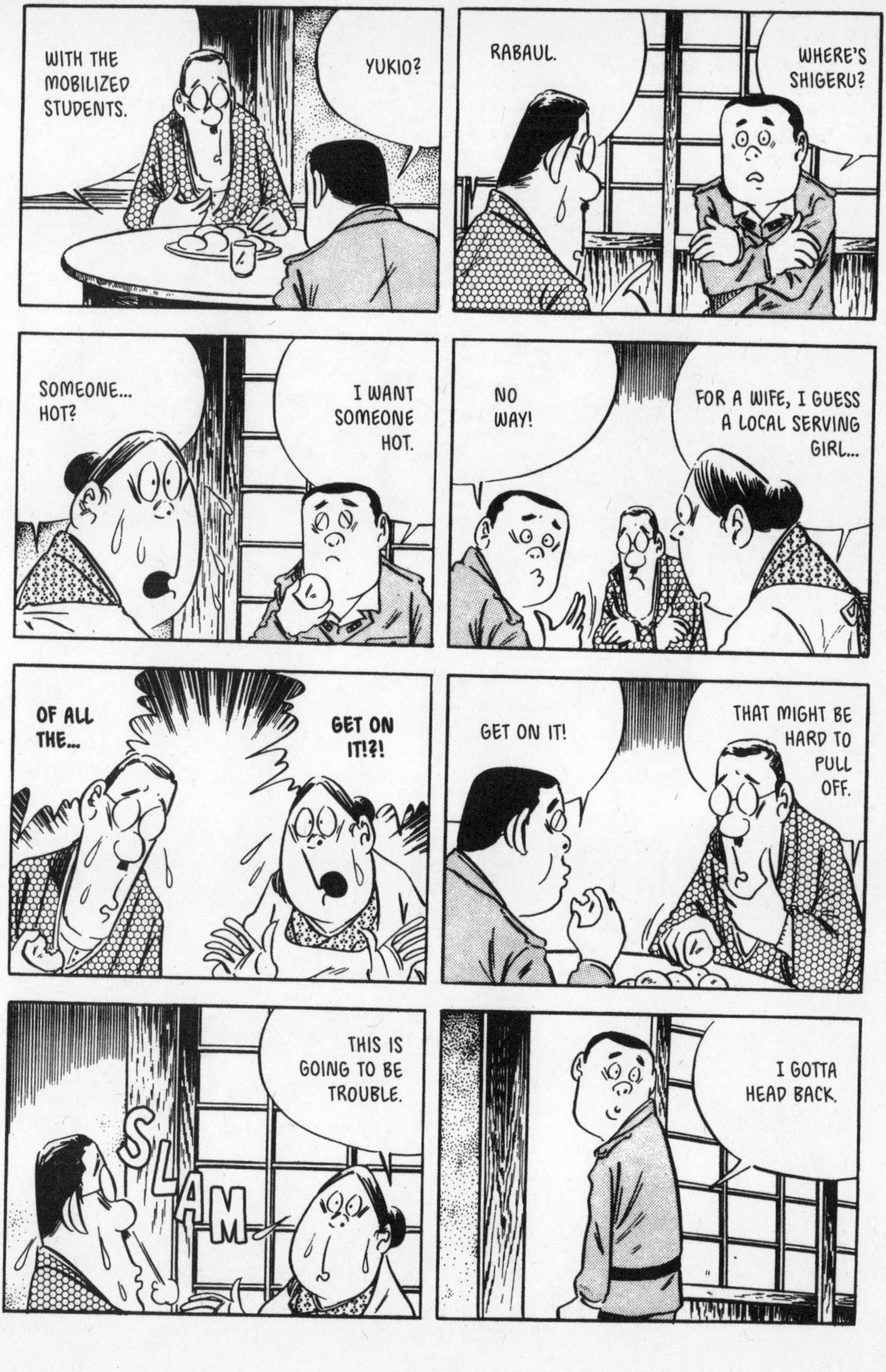
WHERE'S SHIGERU?
RABAUL.
YUKIO?
WITH THE MOBILIZED STUDENTS.
FOR A WIFE, I GUESS A LOCAL SERVING GIRL...
NO WAY!
I WANT SOMEONE HOT.
SOMEONE... HOT?
THAT MIGHT BE HARD TO PULL OFF.
GET ON IT!
GET ON IT!?!
OF ALL THE...
I GOTTA HEAD BACK.
THIS IS GOING TO BE TROUBLE.
SLAM

THE ENEMY LANDING AT NEW BRITAIN

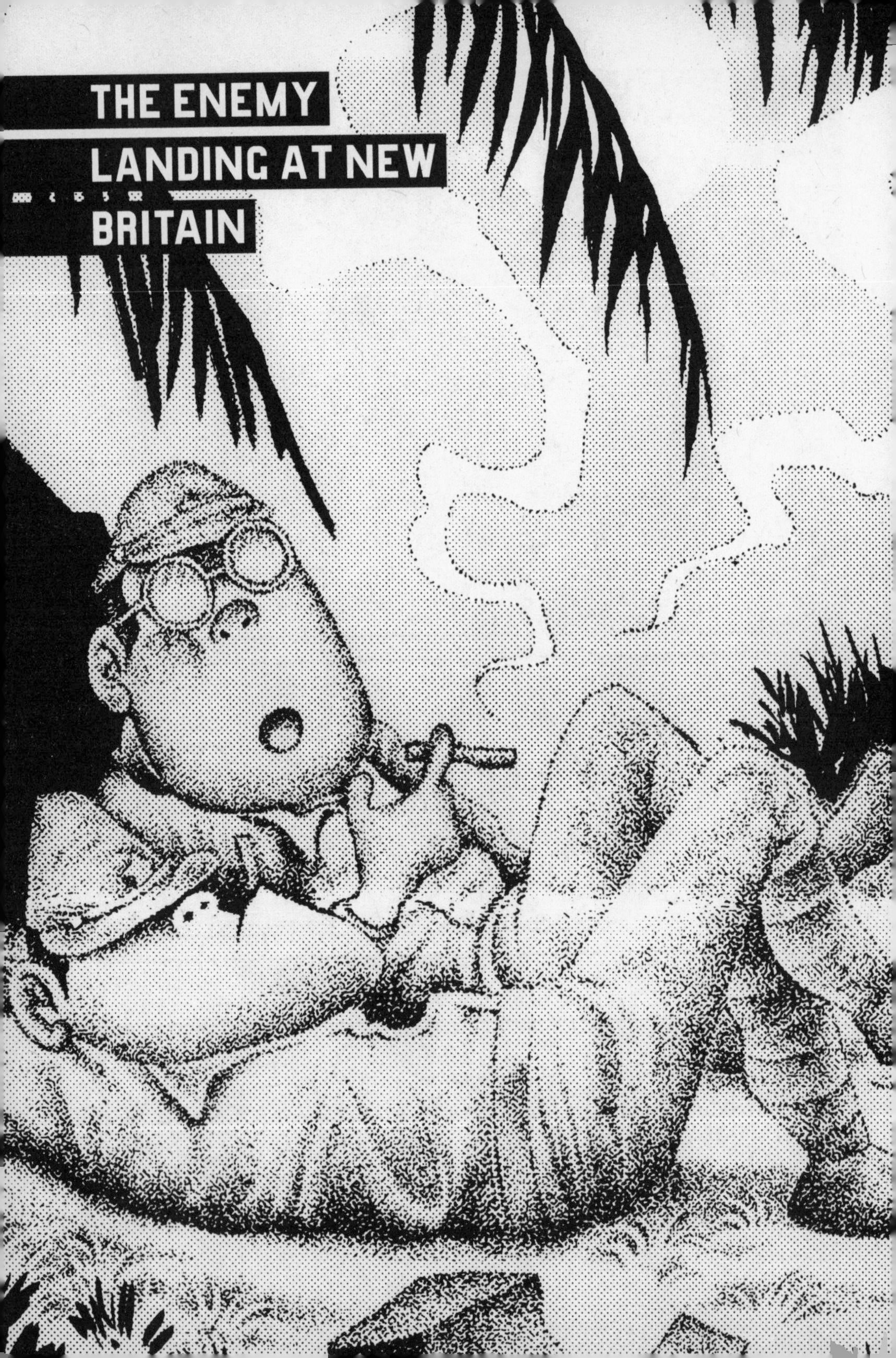

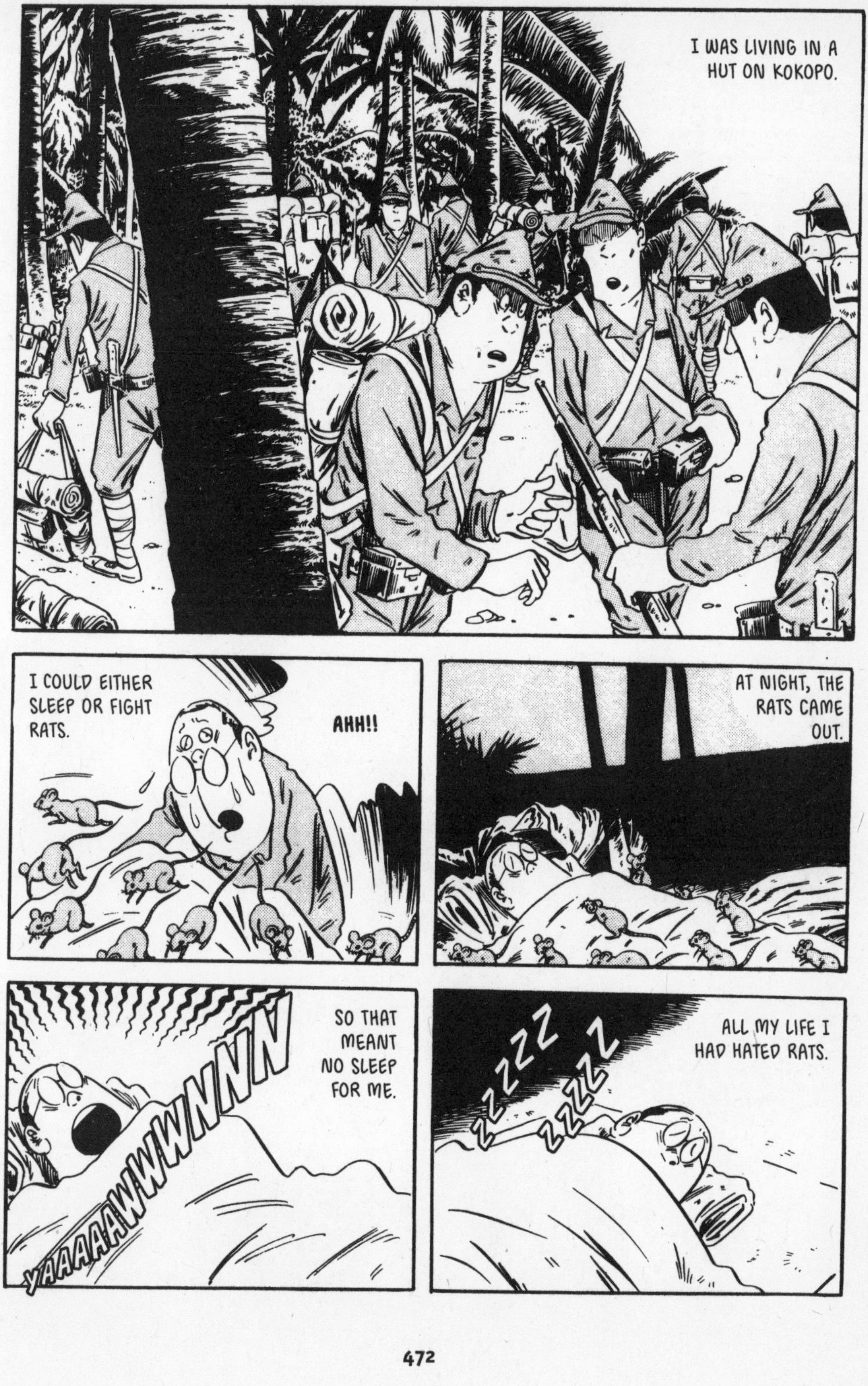

I WAS LIVING IN A HUT ON KOKOPO.
AT NIGHT, THE RATS CAME OUT.
I COULD EITHER SLEEP OR FIGHT RATS.
AHH!!
ALL MY LIFE I HAD HATED RATS.
ZZZZZ
ZZZZZ
SO THAT MEANT NO SLEEP FOR ME.
YAAAAAWWWNNNN

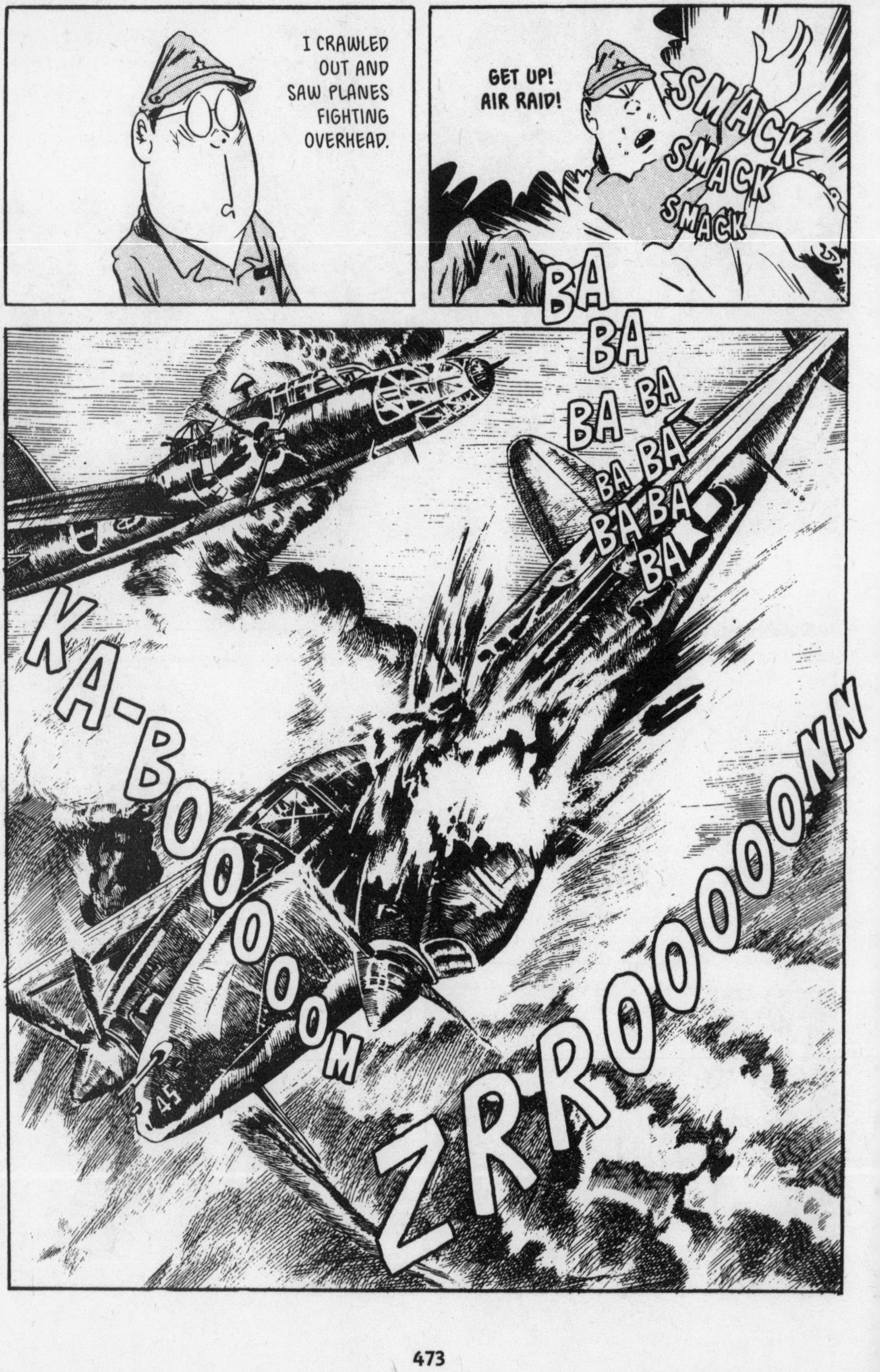
GET UP! AIR RAID!
SMACK
SMACK
SMACK
I CRAWLED OUT AND SAW PLANES FIGHTING OVERHEAD.
BA BA BA BA BA BA BA BA BA
KA-BOOOOOOM
ZRROOOOOONN

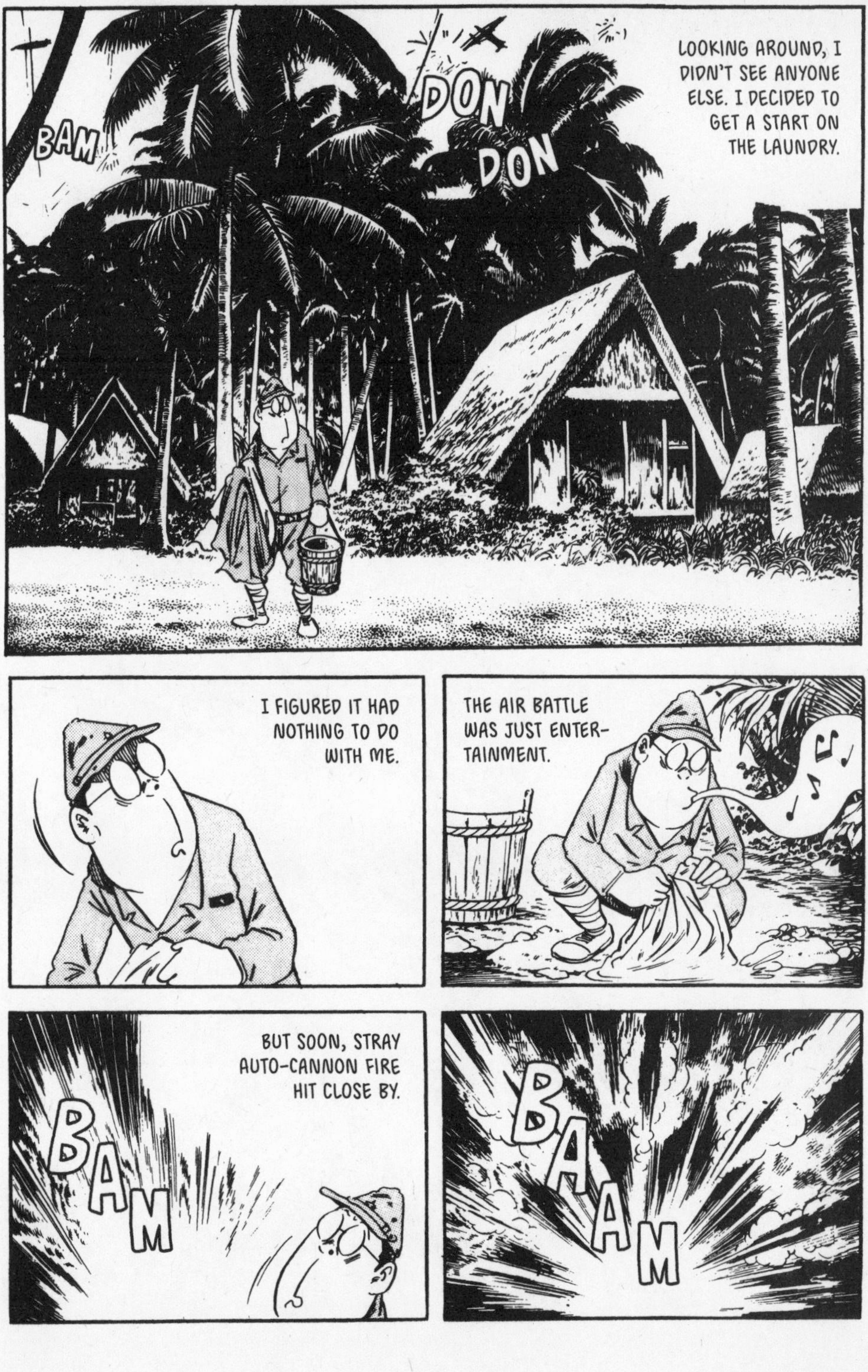
LOOKING AROUND, I DIDN'T SEE ANYONE ELSE. I DECIDED TO GET A START ON THE LAUNDRY.
DON
DON
BAM
THE AIR BATTLE WAS JUST ENTERTAINMENT.
I FIGURED IT HAD NOTHING TO DO WITH ME.
BAAAM
BUT SOON, STRAY AUTO-CANNON FIRE HIT CLOSE BY.
BAM

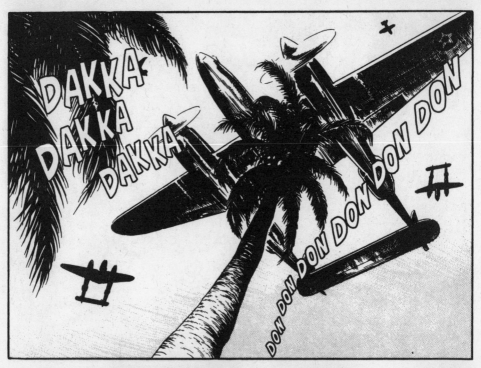

DAKKA
DAKKA
DAKKA
DON DON DON DON DON DON DON
EVERYONE'S IN THE SHELTER!!*
BAM
WHAT'S THAT IDIOT DOING?
GET INSIDE! YOU GOTTA DEATH WISH?
AIR RAIDS ARE DANGEROUS AFTER ALL.

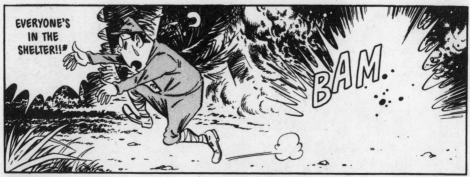

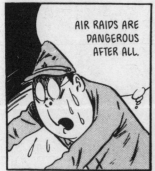

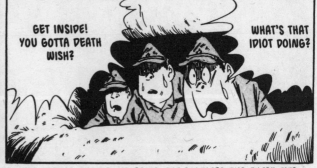

*A PROTECTIVE BUNKER TO SAVE GROUND TROOPS DURING AIR RAIDS. THE SOLDIERS DUG THESE PITS THEMSELVES.

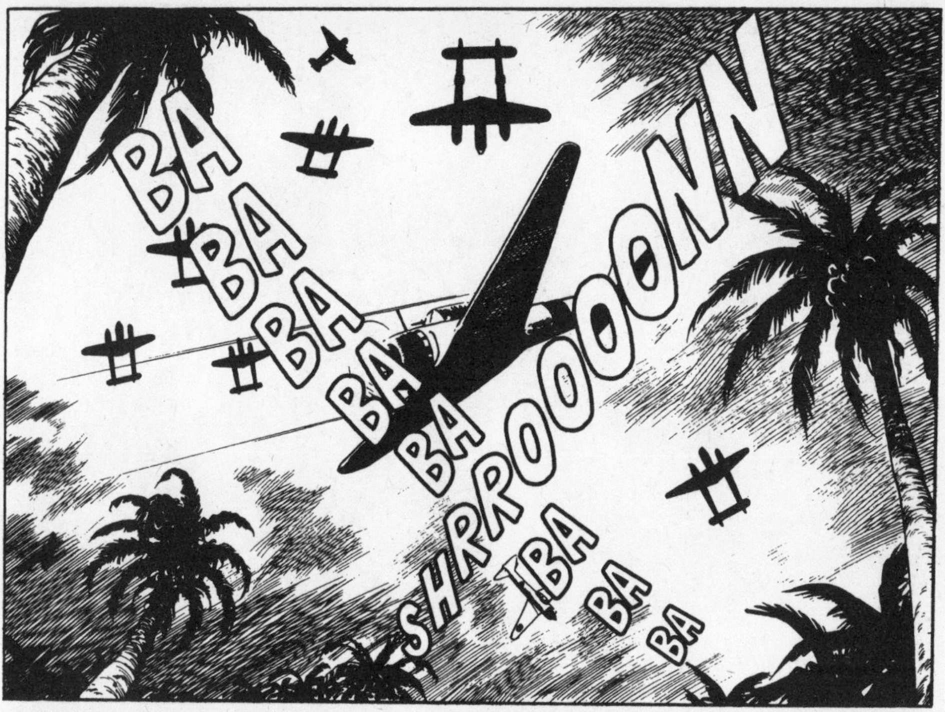
BA BA BA BA BA
BRROOOONN
SHRRBA BA BA

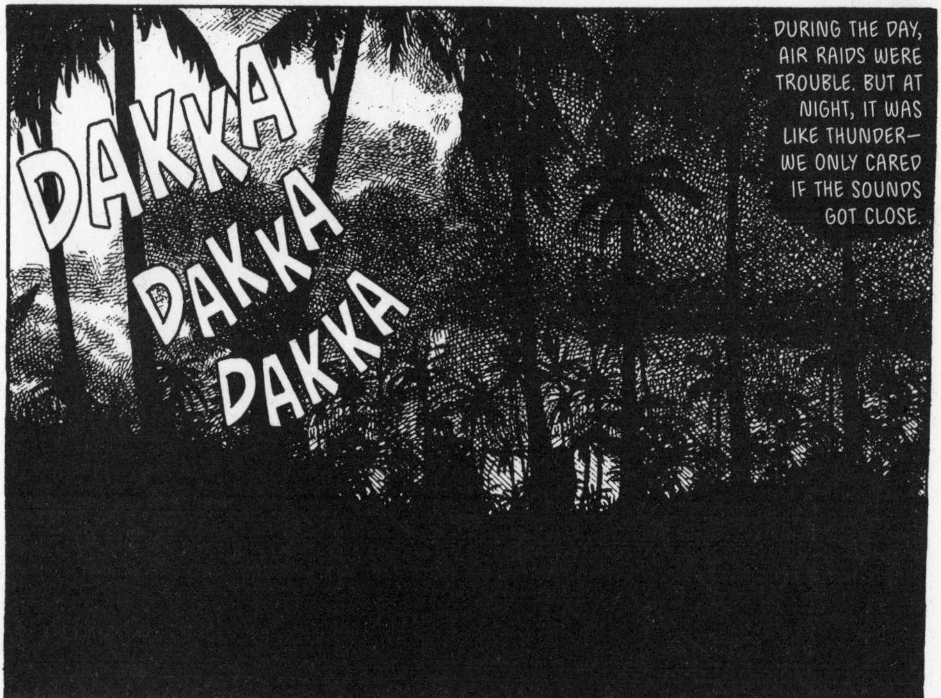
DURING THE DAY, AIR RAIDS WERE TROUBLE. BUT AT NIGHT, IT WAS LIKE THUNDER— WE ONLY CARED IF THE SOUNDS GOT CLOSE.
DAKKA DAKKA DAKKA DAKKA

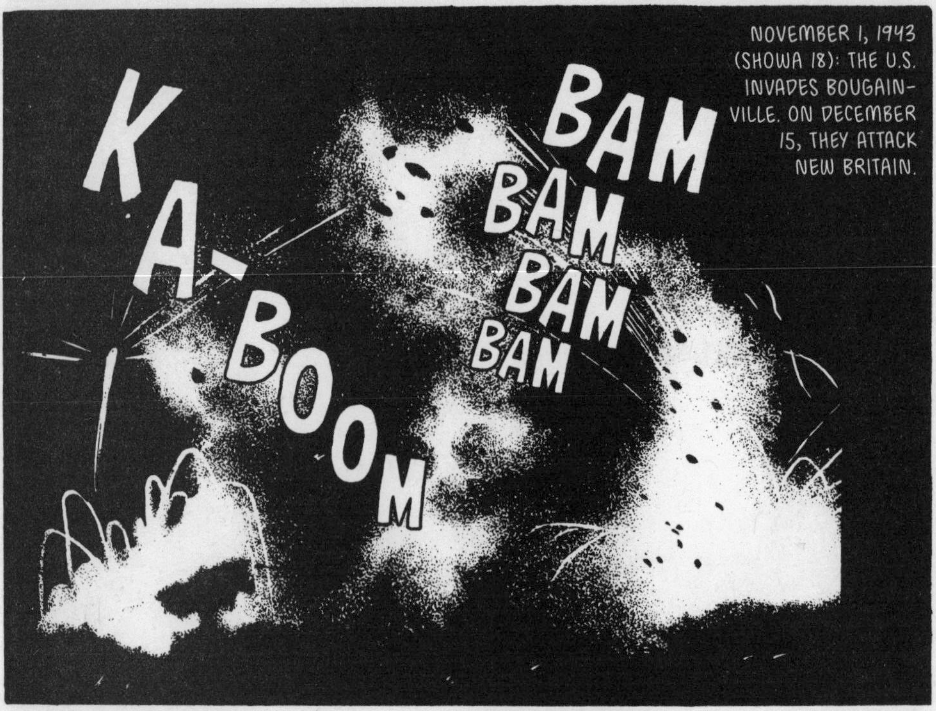
NOVEMBER 1, 1943 (SHOWA 18): THE U.S. INVADES BOUGAINVILLE. ON DECEMBER 15, THEY ATTACK NEW BRITAIN.
BAM
BAM
BAM
BAM
KA-BOOM

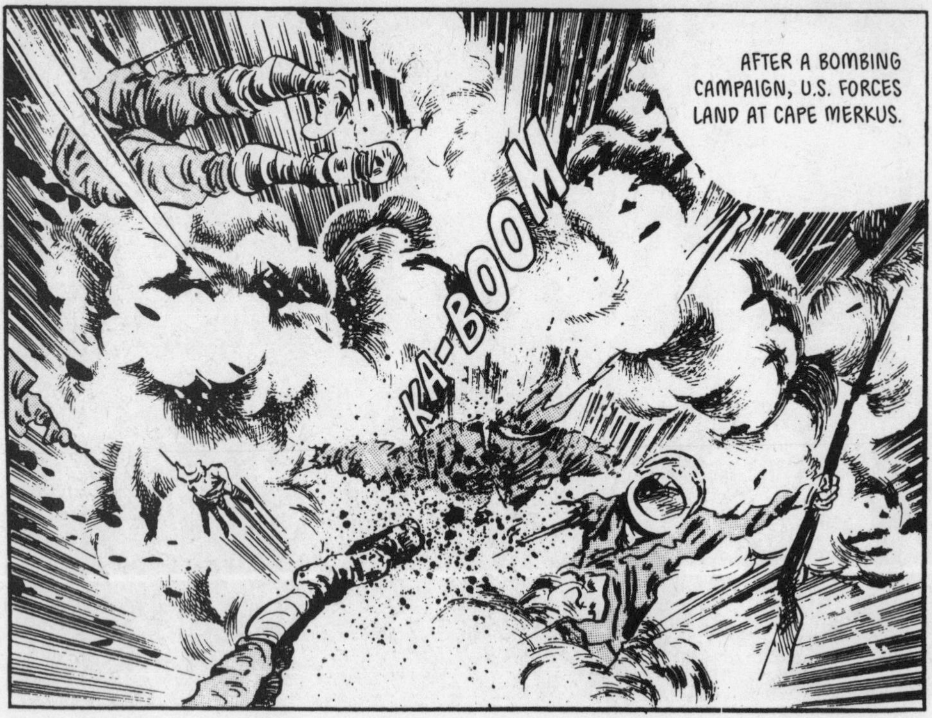
AFTER A BOMBING CAMPAIGN, U.S. FORCES LAND AT CAPE MERKUS.
KA-BOOM

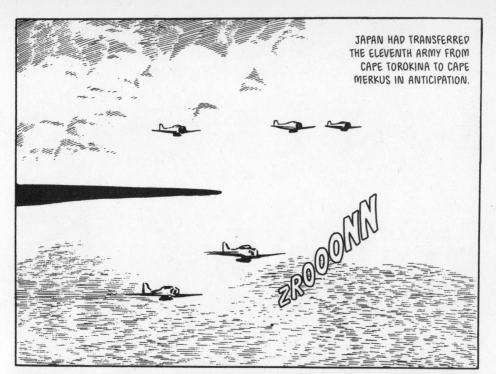

JAPAN HAD TRANSFERRED THE ELEVENTH ARMY FROM CAPE TOROKINA TO CAPE MERKUS IN ANTICIPATION.

ZROOOONN

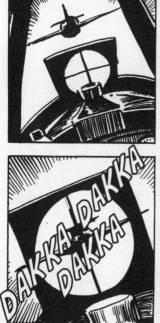

DAKKA DAKKA DAKKA

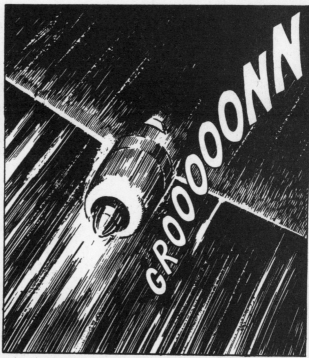

GROOOOONN

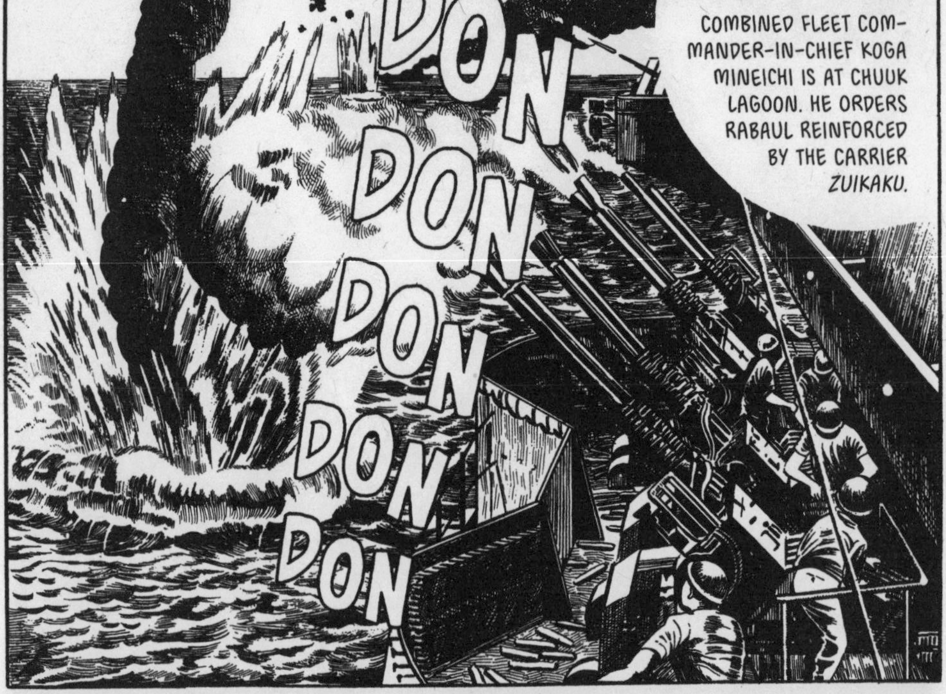
COMBINED FLEET COMMANDER-IN-CHIEF KOGA MINEICHI IS AT CHUUK LAGOON. HE ORDERS RABAUL REINFORCED BY THE CARRIER *ZUIKAKU*.
DON
DON
DON
DON
DON

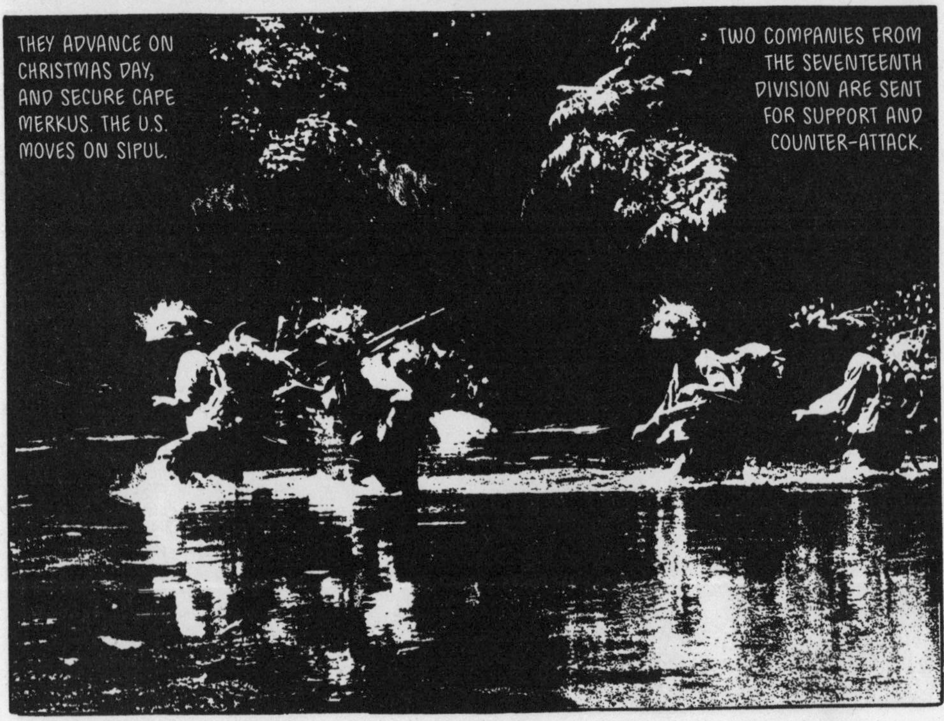
TWO COMPANIES FROM THE SEVENTEENTH DIVISION ARE SENT FOR SUPPORT AND COUNTER-ATTACK.
THEY ADVANCE ON CHRISTMAS DAY, AND SECURE CAPE MERKUS. THE U.S. MOVES ON SIPUL.

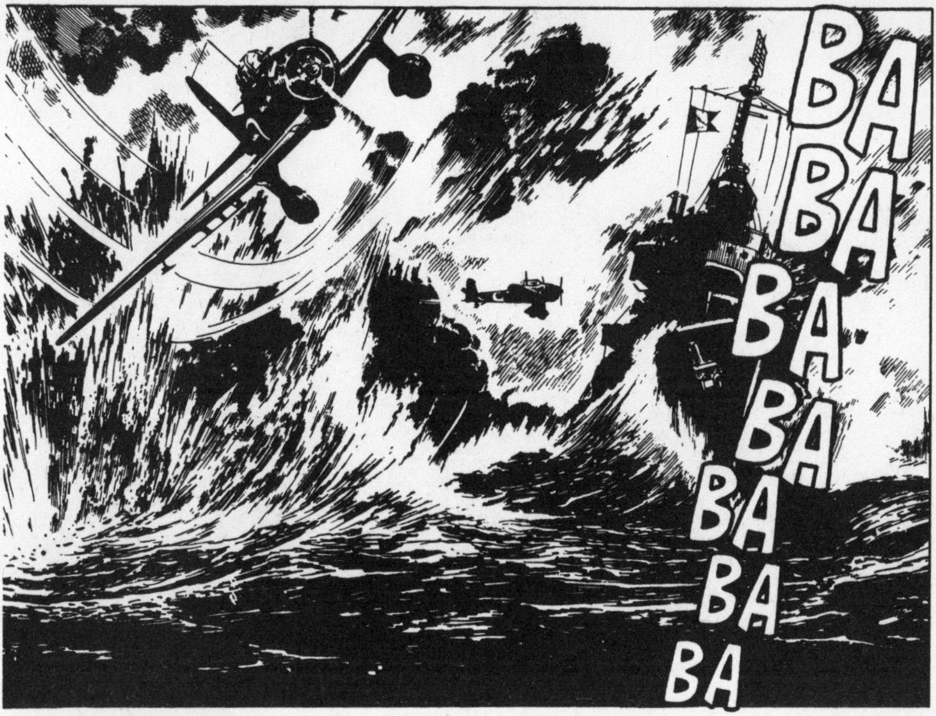
BA BA BA BA BA BA BA BA BA BA BA BA BA BA

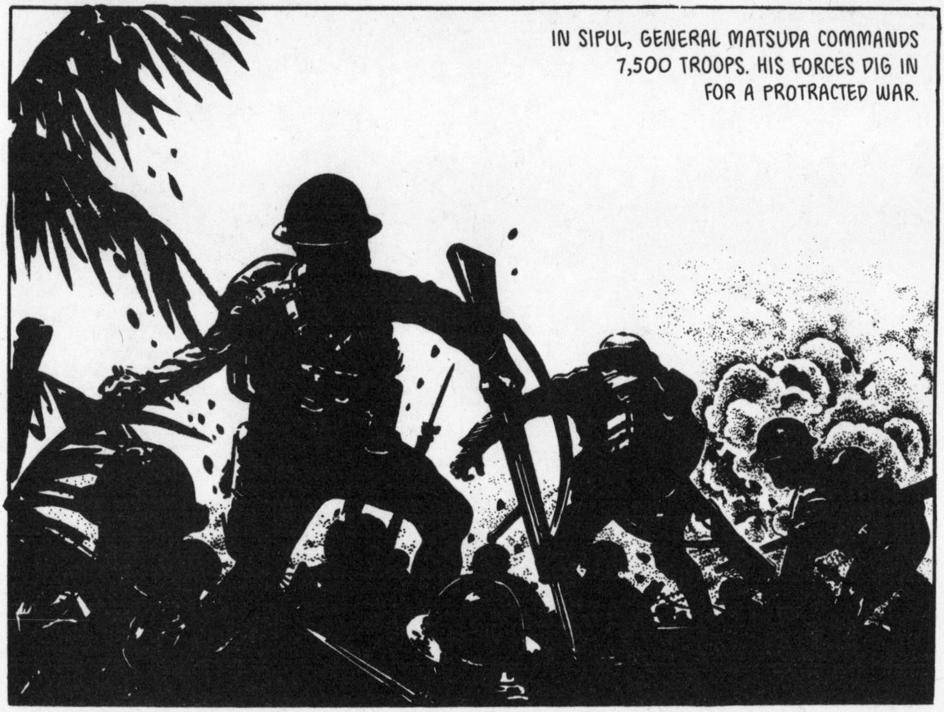
IN SIPUL, GENERAL MATSUDA COMMANDS 7,500 TROOPS. HIS FORCES DIG IN FOR A PROTRACTED WAR.

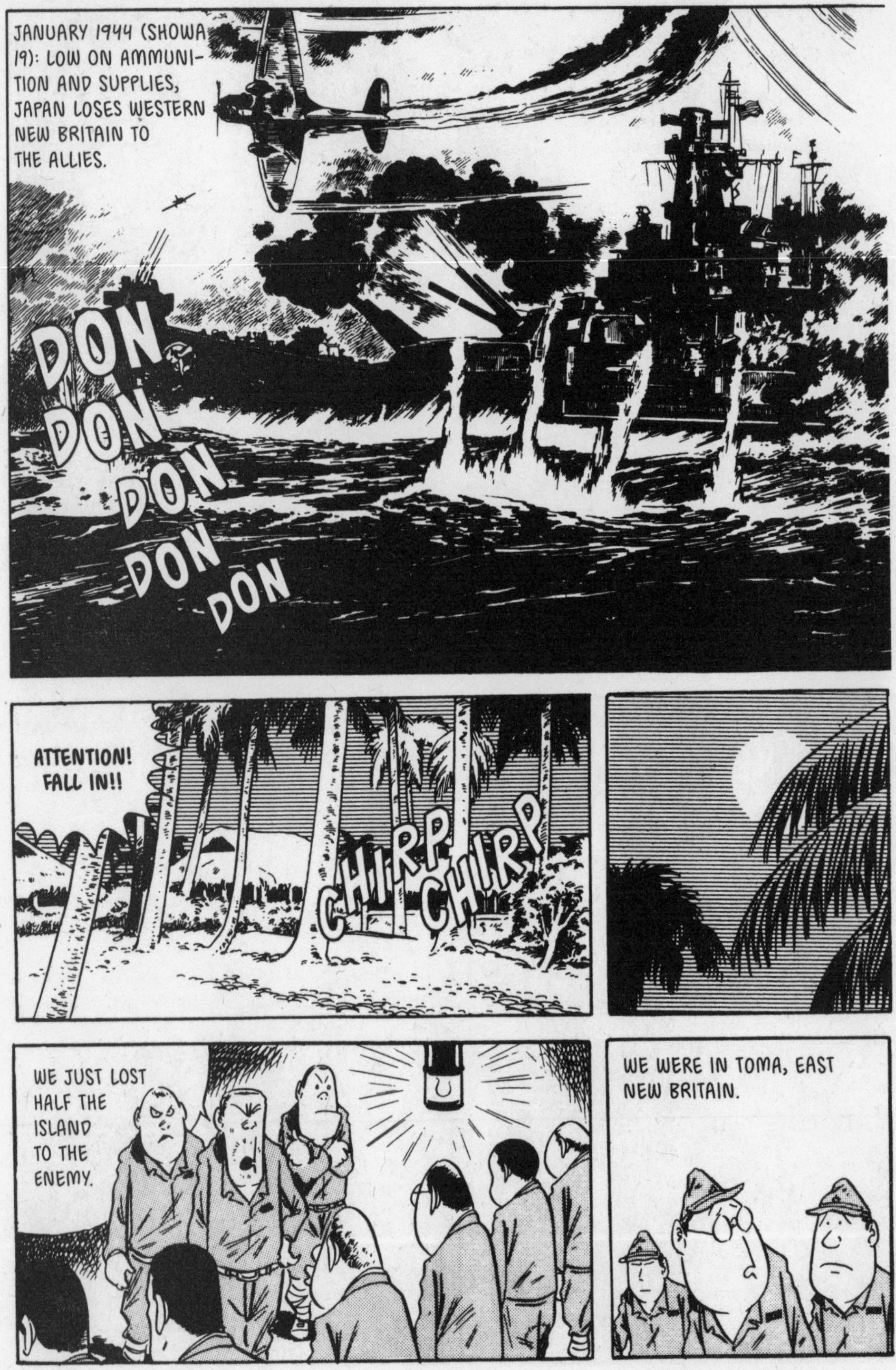
JANUARY 1944 (SHOWA 19): LOW ON AMMUNITION AND SUPPLIES, JAPAN LOSES WESTERN NEW BRITAIN TO THE ALLIES.
DON DON DON DON DON
ATTENTION! FALL IN!!
CHIRP CHIRP
WE WERE IN TOMA, EAST NEW BRITAIN.
WE JUST LOST HALF THE ISLAND TO THE ENEMY.

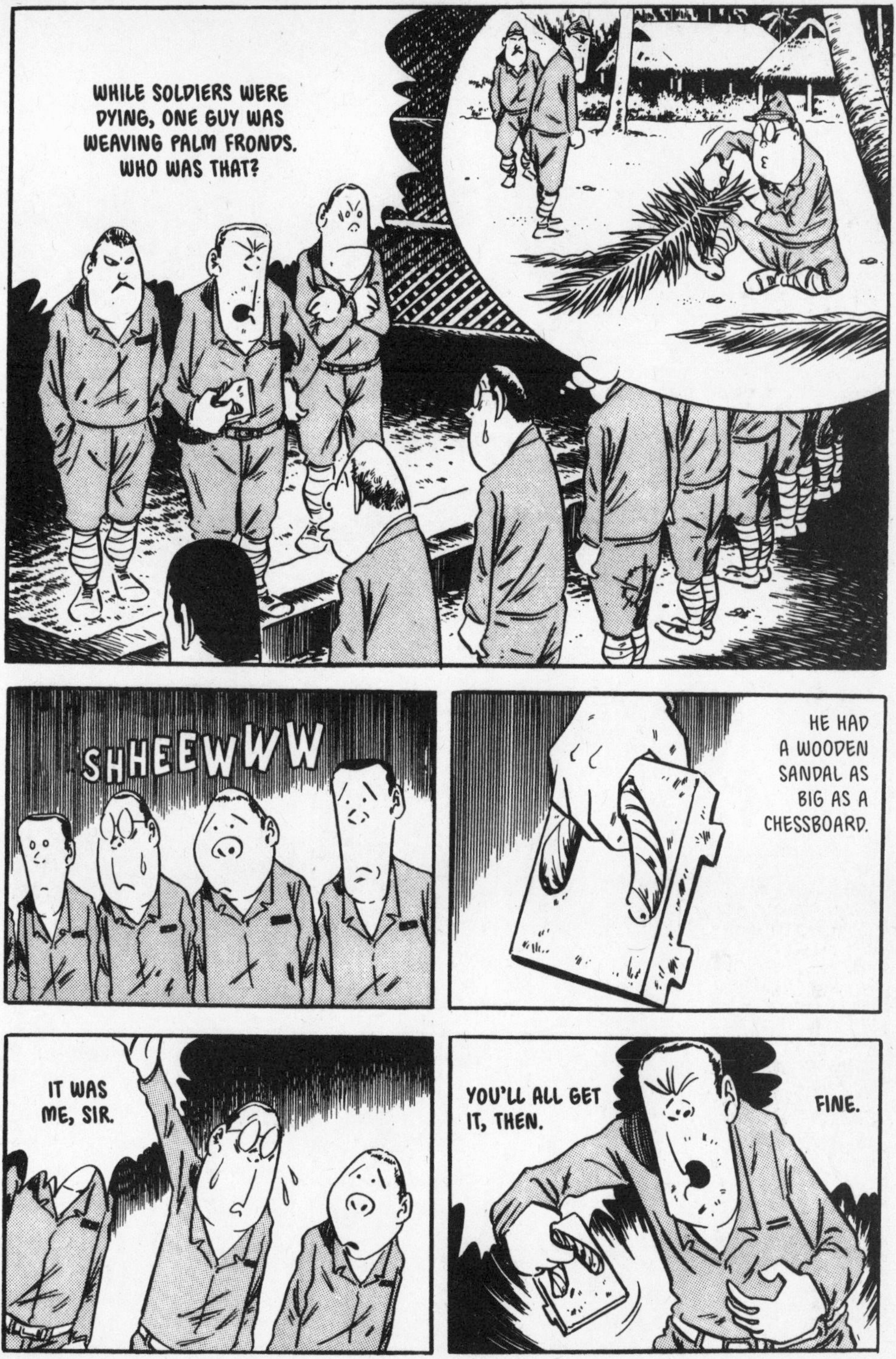
WHILE SOLDIERS WERE DYING, ONE GUY WAS WEAVING PALM FRONDS. WHO WAS THAT?
HE HAD A WOODEN SANDAL AS BIG AS A CHESSBOARD.
SHHEEWWW
FINE.
YOU'LL ALL GET IT, THEN.
IT WAS ME, SIR.

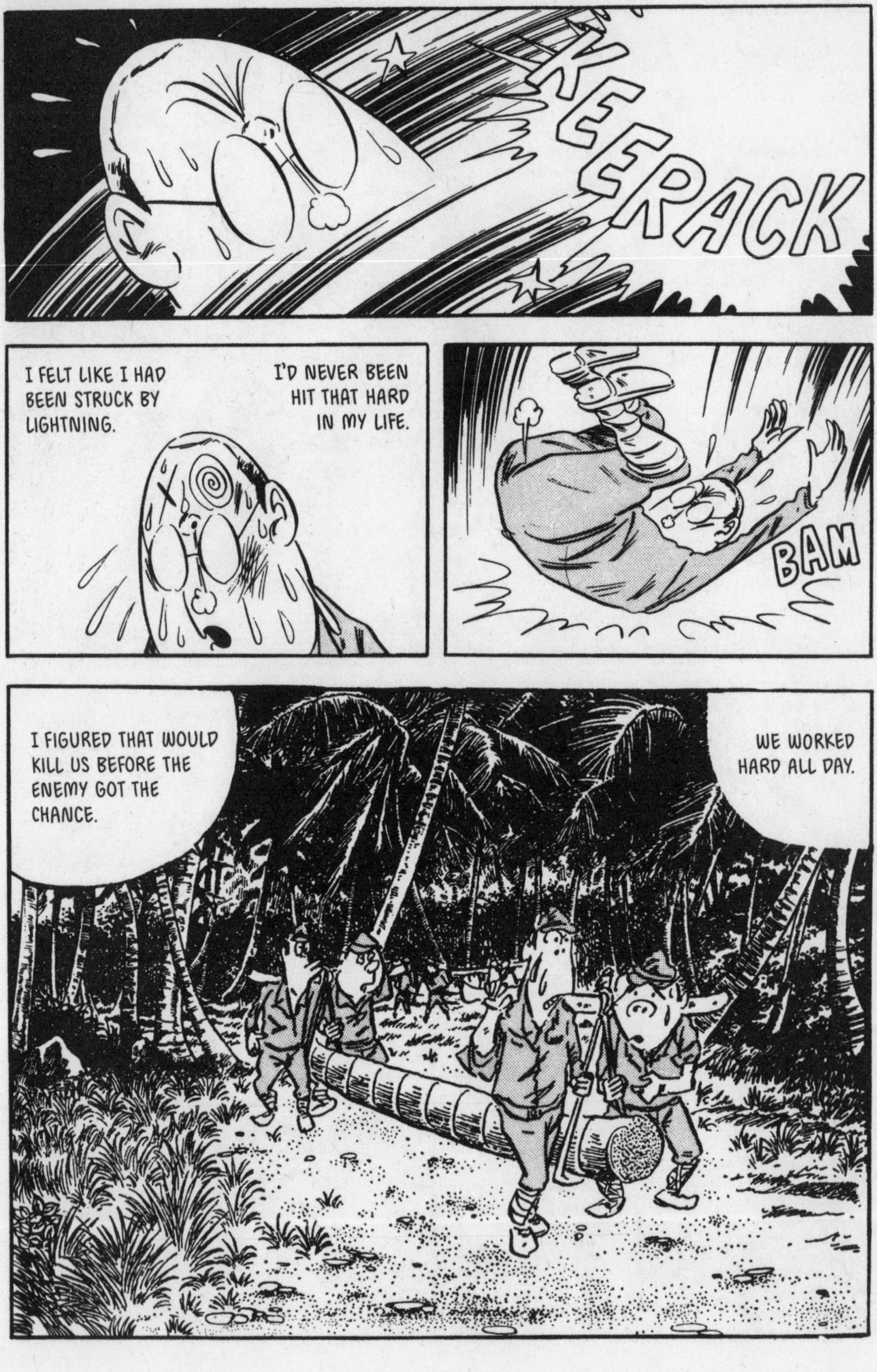
KEERACK
BAM
I'D NEVER BEEN HIT THAT HARD IN MY LIFE.
I FELT LIKE I HAD BEEN STRUCK BY LIGHTNING.
WE WORKED HARD ALL DAY.
I FIGURED THAT WOULD KILL US BEFORE THE ENEMY GOT THE CHANCE.

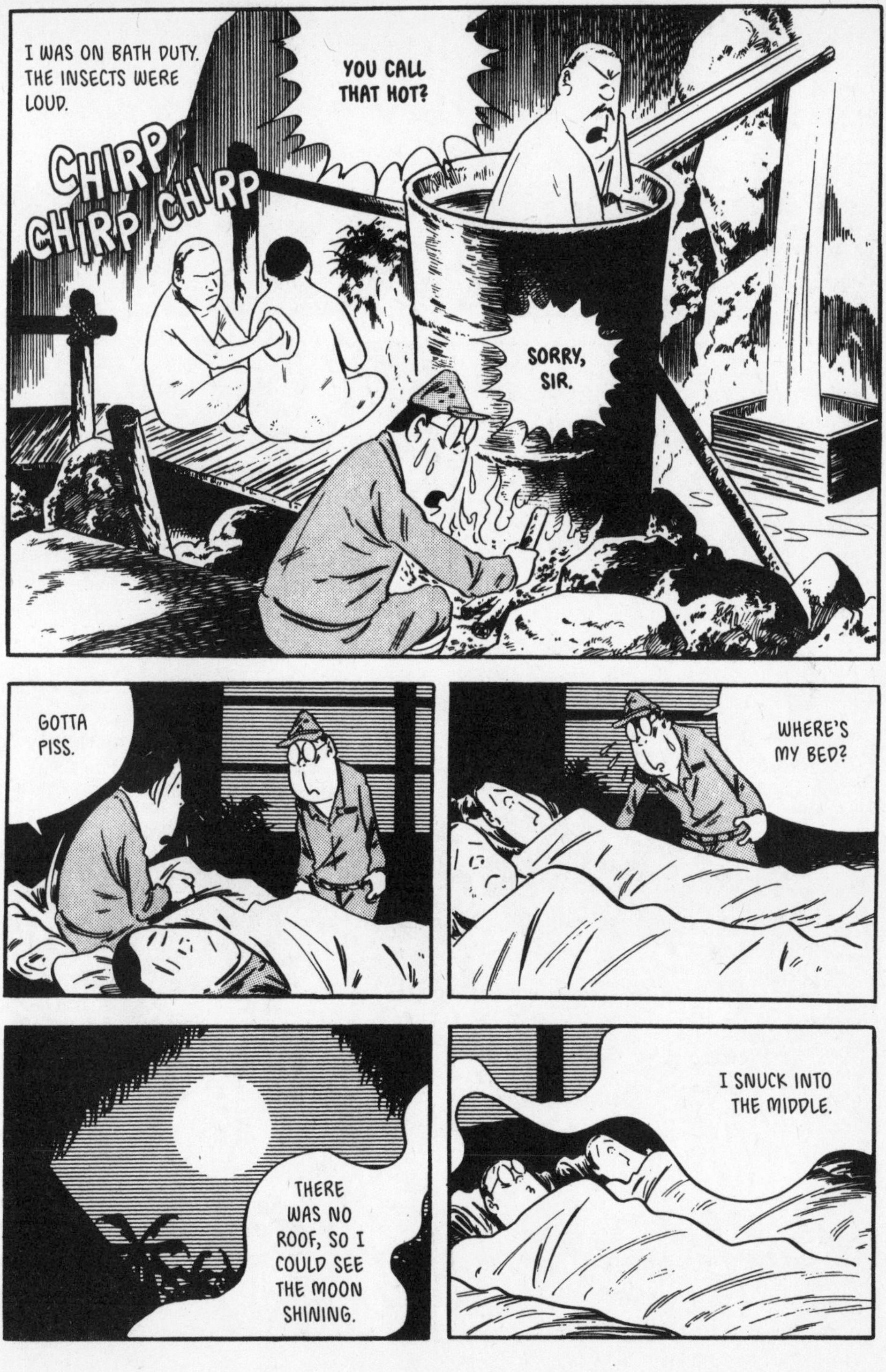
YOU CALL THAT HOT?
I WAS ON BATH DUTY. THE INSECTS WERE LOUD.
CHIRP CHIRP CHIRP CHIRP
SORRY, SIR.
WHERE'S MY BED?
GOTTA PISS.
I SNUCK INTO THE MIDDLE.
THERE WAS NO ROOF, SO I COULD SEE THE MOON SHINING.

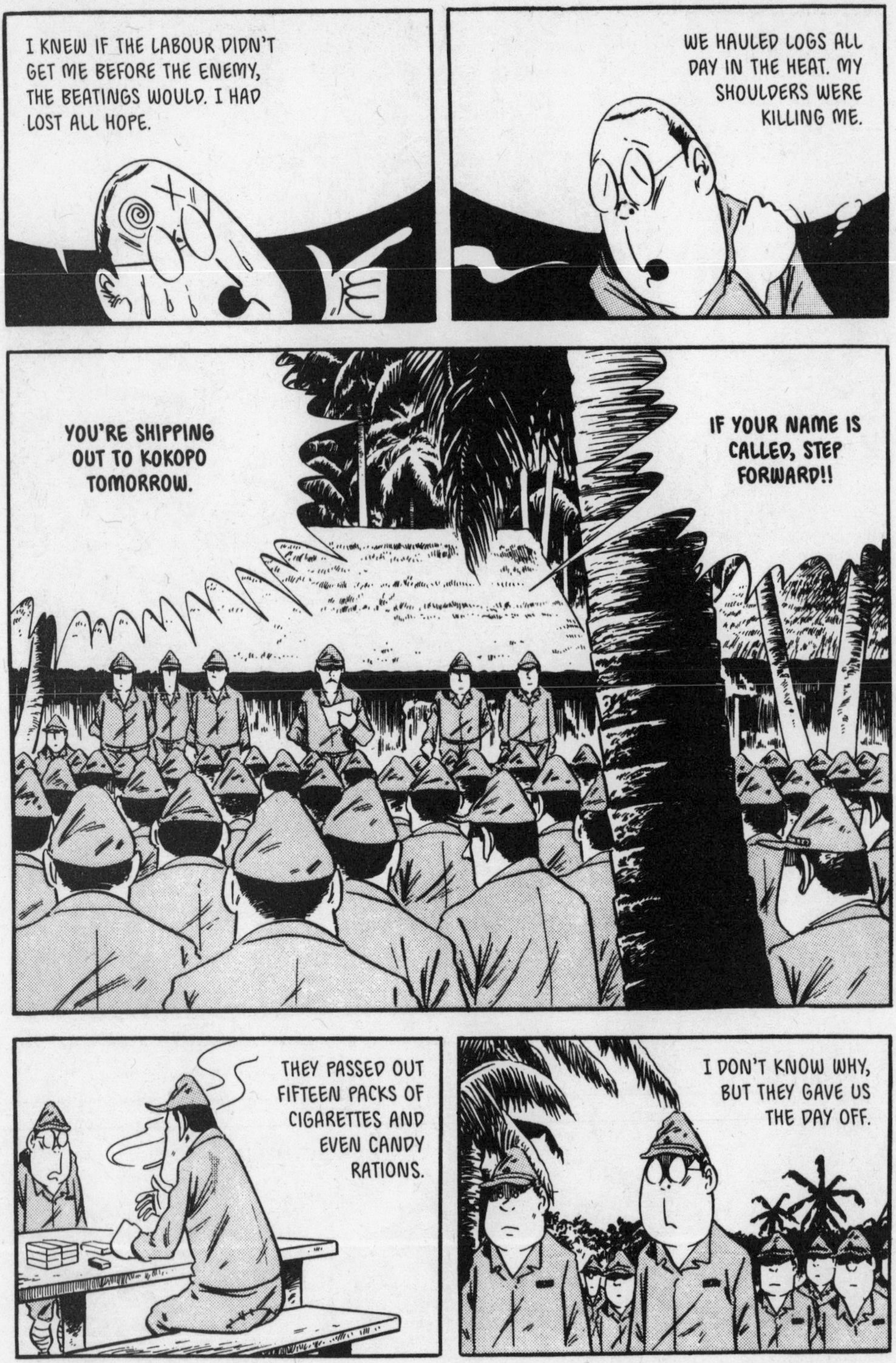
WE HAULED LOGS ALL DAY IN THE HEAT. MY SHOULDERS WERE KILLING ME.
I KNEW IF THE LABOUR DIDN'T GET ME BEFORE THE ENEMY, THE BEATINGS WOULD. I HAD LOST ALL HOPE.
IF YOUR NAME IS CALLED, STEP FORWARD!!
YOU'RE SHIPPING OUT TO KOKOPO TOMORROW.
I DON'T KNOW WHY, BUT THEY GAVE US THE DAY OFF.
THEY PASSED OUT FIFTEEN PACKS OF CIGARETTES AND EVEN CANDY RATIONS.

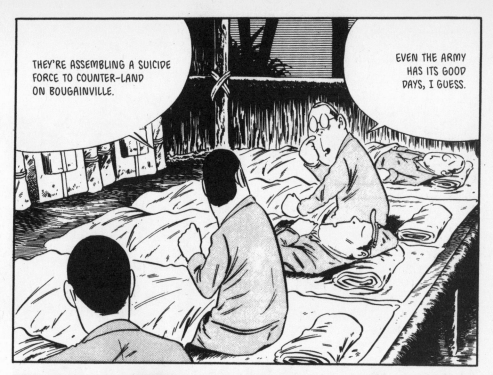

EVEN THE ARMY HAS ITS GOOD DAYS, I GUESS.
THEY'RE ASSEMBLING A SUICIDE FORCE TO COUNTER-LAND ON BOUGAINVILLE.
COUNTER-LAND?
TO TAKE BACK OUR TERRITORY.
OH!
THEY'LL GO BY DESTROYER.
WE HAVE TO DO SOMETHING. THE ENEMY HOLDS ABOUT TWO-THIRDS OF THE ISLAND NOW.
I SMOKED ABOUT THIRTY CIGARETTES THAT NIGHT.
PUFF
PUFF PUFF

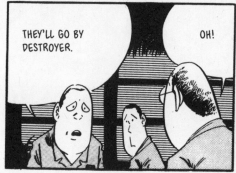

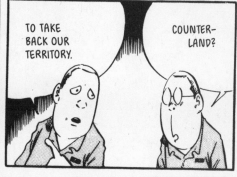

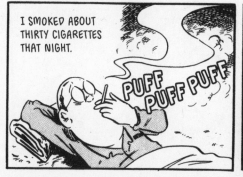

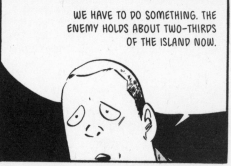

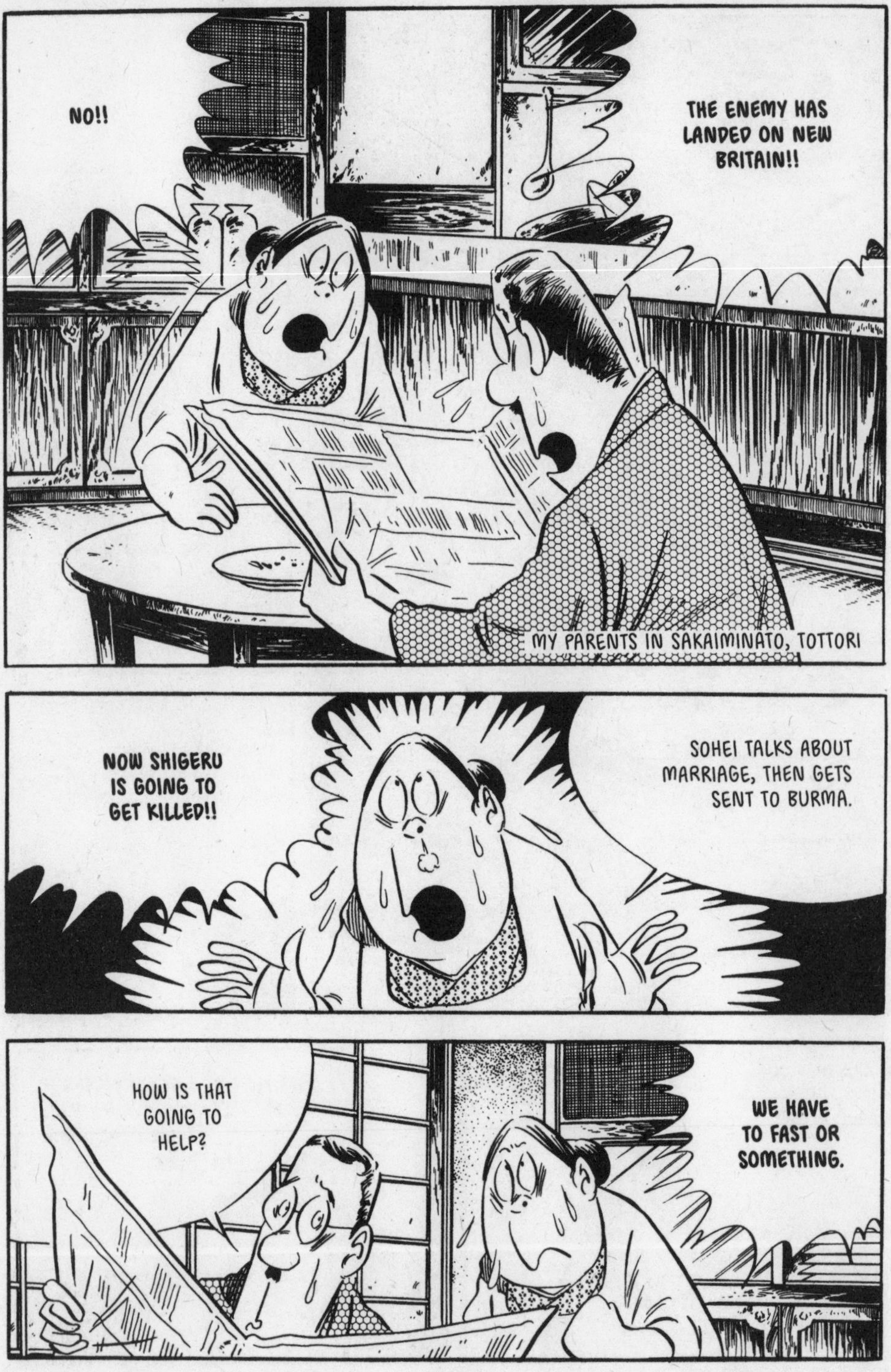
THE ENEMY HAS LANDED ON NEW BRITAIN!!
NO!!
MY PARENTS IN SAKAIMINATO, TOTTORI
SOHEI TALKS ABOUT MARRIAGE, THEN GETS SENT TO BURMA.
NOW SHIGERU IS GOING TO GET KILLED!!
WE HAVE TO FAST OR SOMETHING.
HOW IS THAT GOING TO HELP?

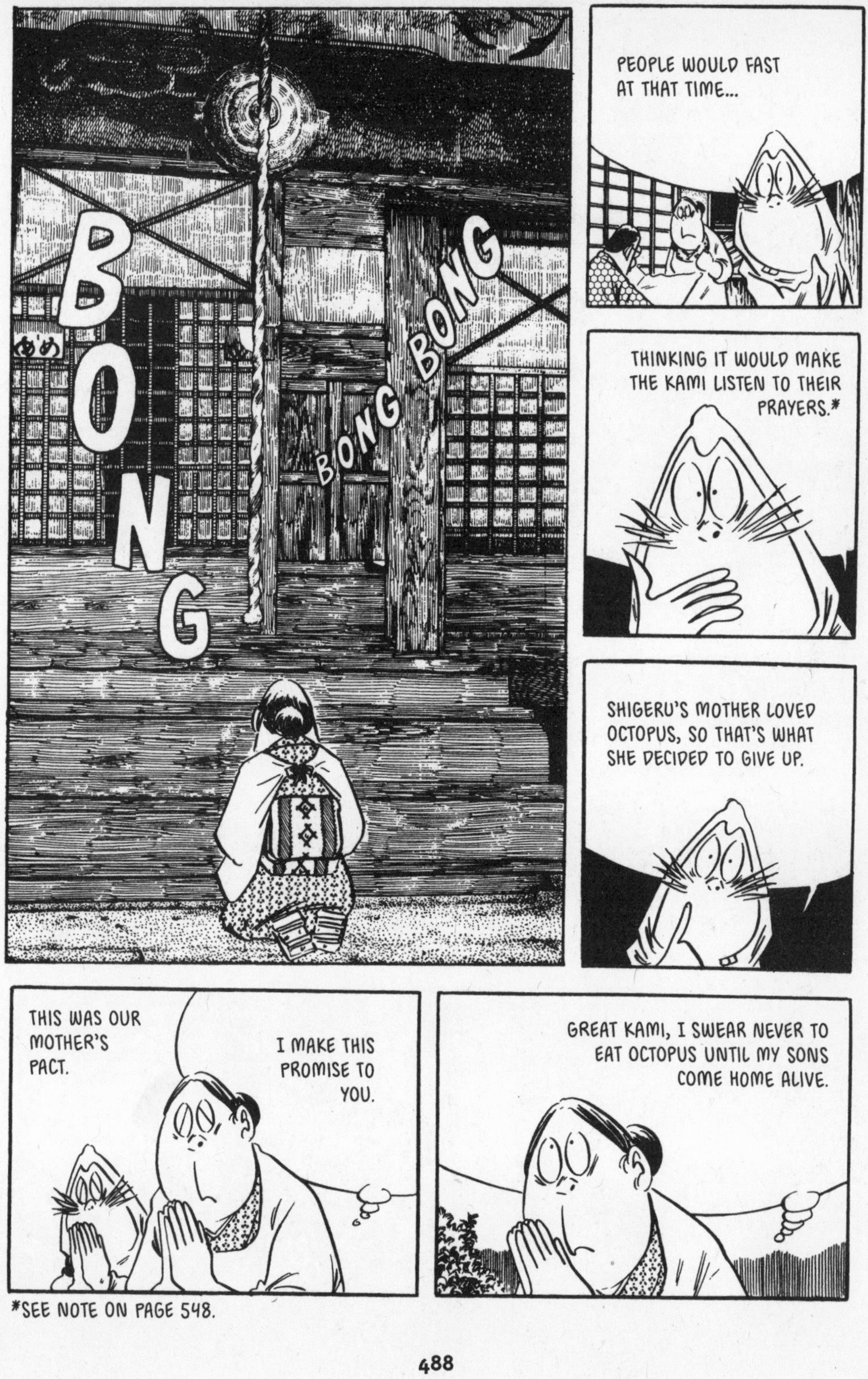
PEOPLE WOULD FAST AT THAT TIME...
THINKING IT WOULD MAKE THE KAMI LISTEN TO THEIR PRAYERS.*
SHIGERU'S MOTHER LOVED OCTOPUS, SO THAT'S WHAT SHE DECIDED TO GIVE UP.
BONG BONG
BONG
GREAT KAMI, I SWEAR NEVER TO EAT OCTOPUS UNTIL MY SONS COME HOME ALIVE.
I MAKE THIS PROMISE TO YOU.
THIS WAS OUR MOTHER'S PACT.

*SEE NOTE ON PAGE 548.

THE BATTLES OF TARAWA AND MAKIN

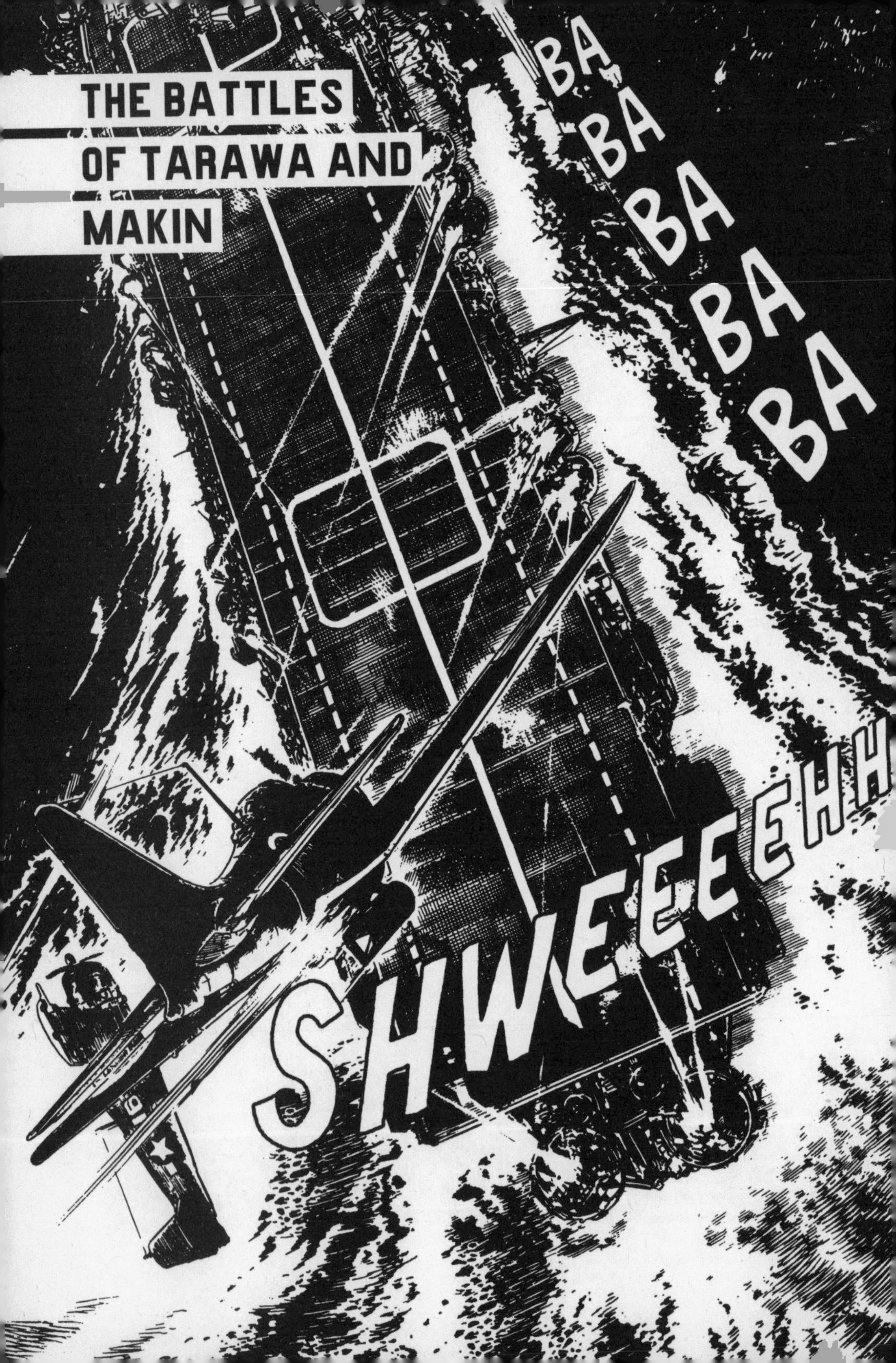
BA BA BA BA BA
SHWEEEEEHH

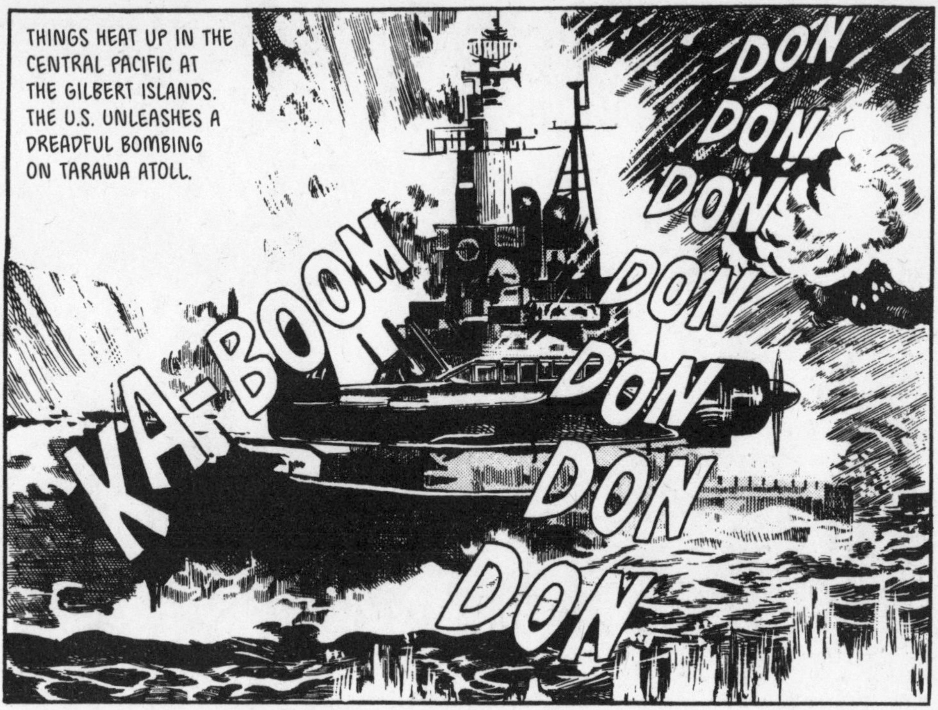
THINGS HEAT UP IN THE CENTRAL PACIFIC AT THE GILBERT ISLANDS. THE U.S. UNLEASHES A DREADFUL BOMBING ON TARAWA ATOLL.
DON
DON
DON
DON
DON
DON
DON
KA-BOOM

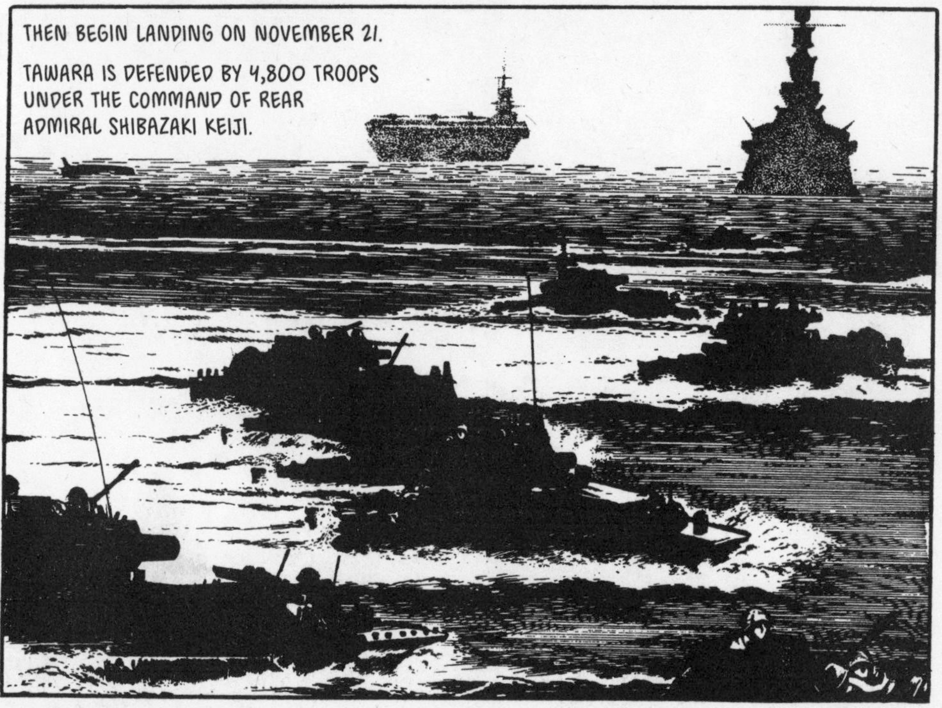
THEN BEGIN LANDING ON NOVEMBER 21.
TAWARA IS DEFENDED BY 4,800 TROOPS UNDER THE COMMAND OF REAR ADMIRAL SHIBAZAKI KEIJI.

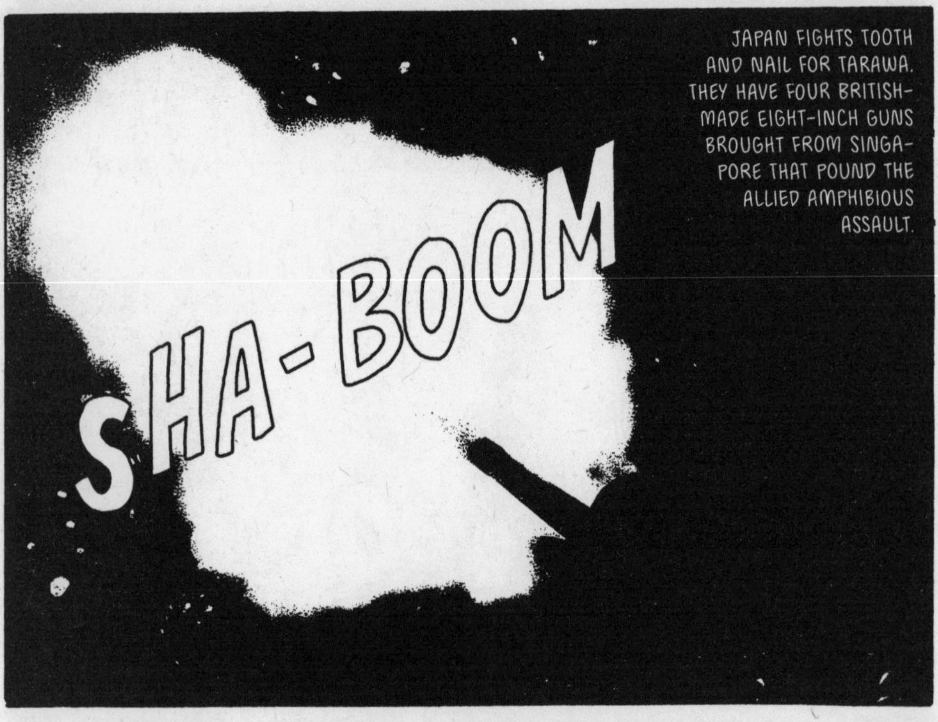
JAPAN FIGHTS TOOTH AND NAIL FOR TARAWA. THEY HAVE FOUR BRITISH-MADE EIGHT-INCH GUNS BROUGHT FROM SINGAPORE THAT POUND THE ALLIED AMPHIBIOUS ASSAULT.
SHA-BOOM

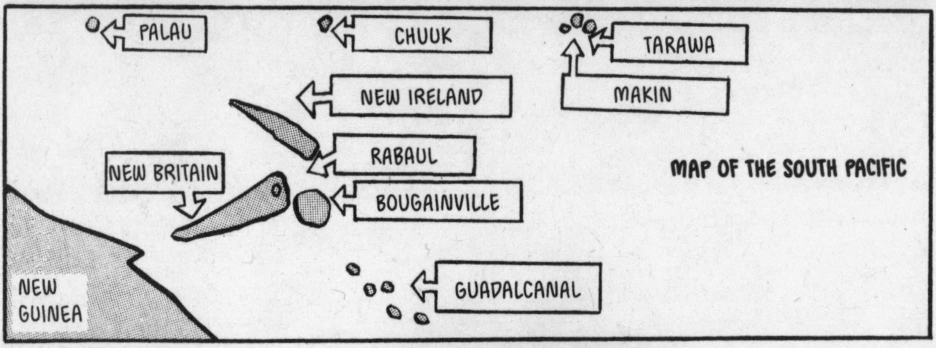
TARAWA
CHUUK
PALAU
MAKIN
NEW IRELAND
RABAUL
MAP OF THE SOUTH PACIFIC
NEW BRITAIN
BOUGAINVILLE
GUADALCANAL
NEW GUINEA

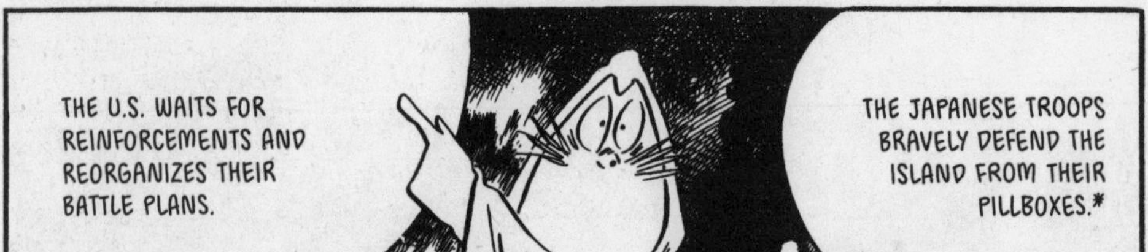
THE JAPANESE TROOPS BRAVELY DEFEND THE ISLAND FROM THEIR PILLBOXES.*
THE U.S. WAITS FOR REINFORCEMENTS AND REORGANIZES THEIR BATTLE PLANS.

*A SMALL CONCRETE STRUCTURE USED AS A GUARD POST AND EQUIPPED WITH HOLES TO FIRE WEAPONS.

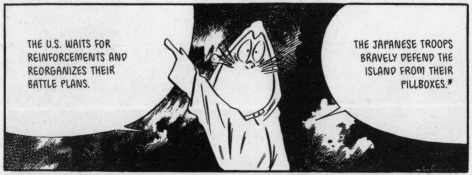

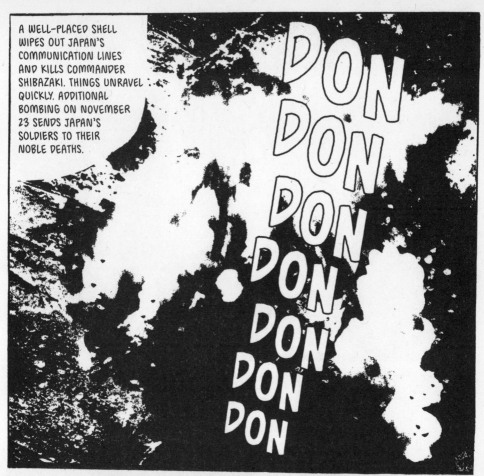

DON DON DON DON DON DON DON
A WELL-PLACED SHELL WIPES OUT JAPAN'S COMMUNICATION LINES AND KILLS COMMANDER SHIBAZAKI. THINGS UNRAVEL QUICKLY. ADDITIONAL BOMBING ON NOVEMBER 23 SENDS JAPAN'S SOLDIERS TO THEIR NOBLE DEATHS.

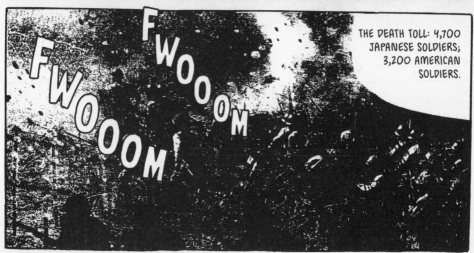

THE DEATH TOLL: 4,700 JAPANESE SOLDIERS; 3,200 AMERICAN SOLDIERS.
FWOOOM
FWOOOM

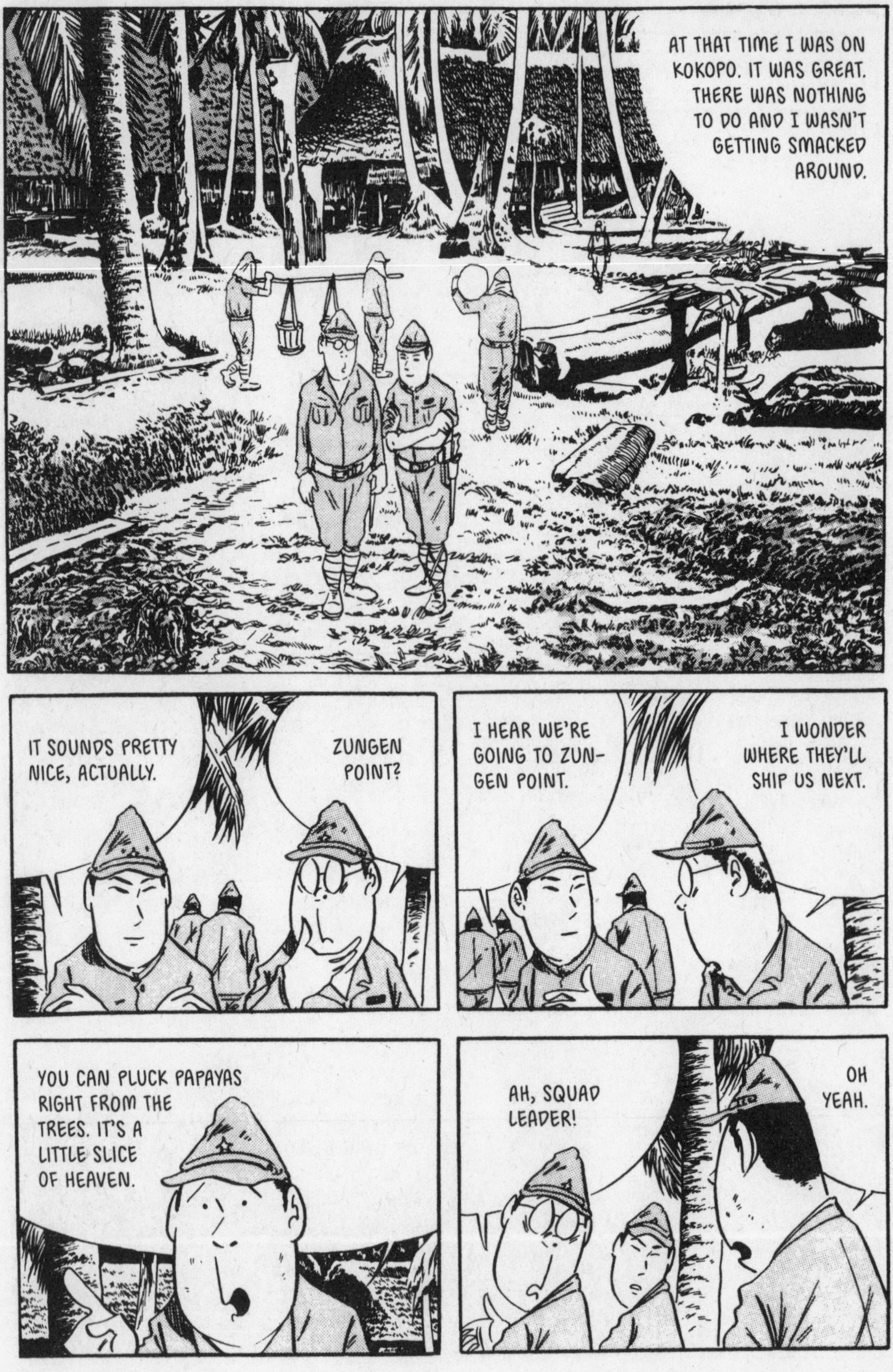
AT THAT TIME I WAS ON KOKOPO. IT WAS GREAT. THERE WAS NOTHING TO DO AND I WASN'T GETTING SMACKED AROUND.
I WONDER WHERE THEY'LL SHIP US NEXT.
I HEAR WE'RE GOING TO ZUN-GEN POINT.
ZUNGEN POINT?
IT SOUNDS PRETTY NICE, ACTUALLY.
OH YEAH.
AH, SQUAD LEADER!
YOU CAN PLUCK PAPAYAS RIGHT FROM THE TREES. IT'S A LITTLE SLICE OF HEAVEN.

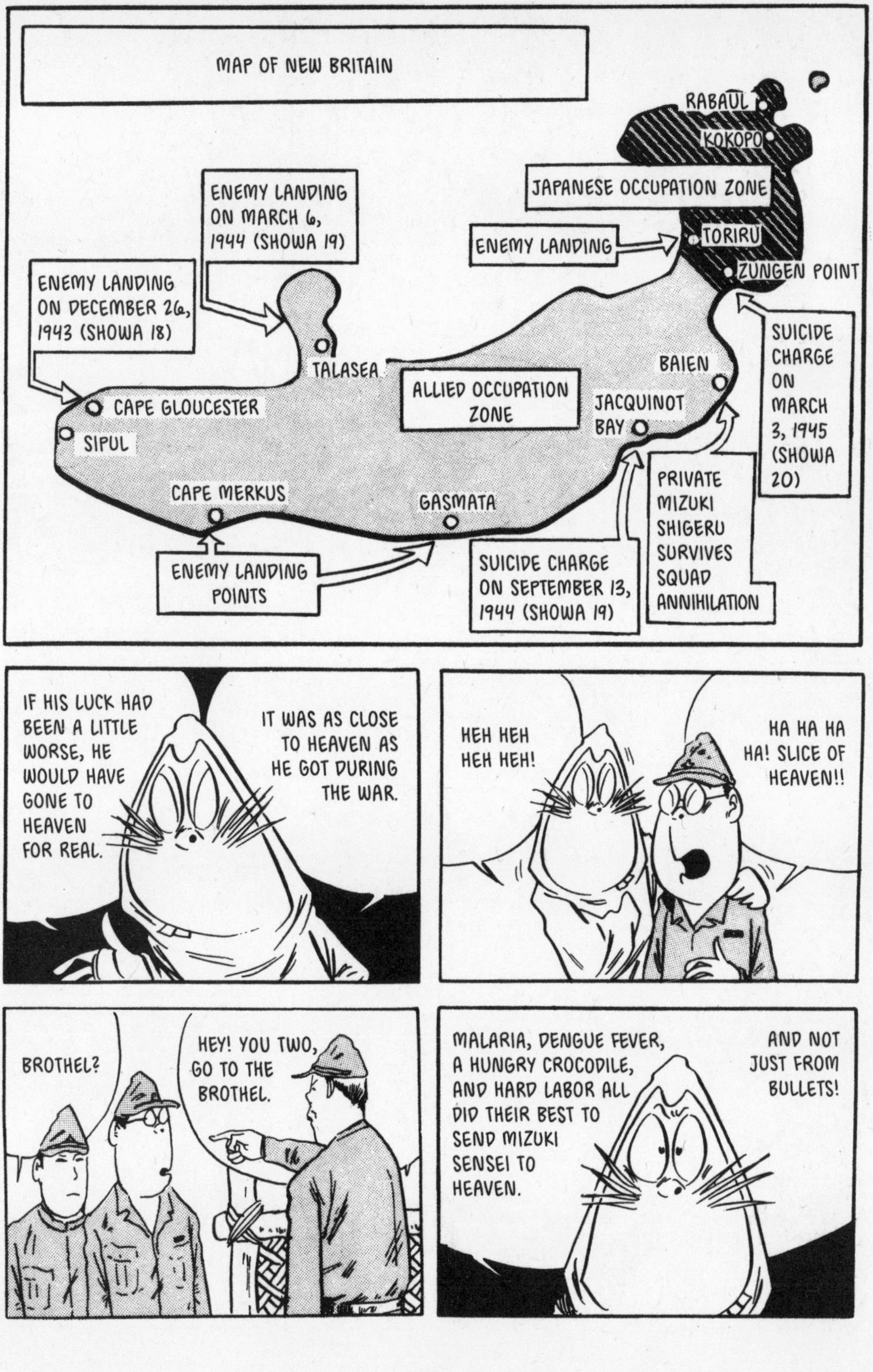
MAP OF NEW BRITAIN
RABAUL
KOKOPO
JAPANESE OCCUPATION ZONE
TORIRU
ENEMY LANDING
ZUNGEN POINT
ENEMY LANDING ON MARCH 6, 1944 (SHOWA 19)
ENEMY LANDING ON DECEMBER 26, 1943 (SHOWA 18)
SUICIDE CHARGE ON MARCH 3, 1945 (SHOWA 20)
BAIEN
JACQUINOT BAY
ALLIED OCCUPATION ZONE
TALASEA
CAPE GLOUCESTER
SIPUL
PRIVATE MIZUKI SHIGERU SURVIVES SQUAD ANNIHILATION
GASMATA
CAPE MERKUS
SUICIDE CHARGE ON SEPTEMBER 13, 1944 (SHOWA 19)
ENEMY LANDING POINTS
HA HA HA HA! SLICE OF HEAVEN!!
HEH HEH HEH HEH!
IT WAS AS CLOSE TO HEAVEN AS HE GOT DURING THE WAR.
IF HIS LUCK HAD BEEN A LITTLE WORSE, HE WOULD HAVE GONE TO HEAVEN FOR REAL.
AND NOT JUST FROM BULLETS!
MALARIA, DENGUE FEVER, A HUNGRY CROCODILE, AND HARD LABOR ALL DID THEIR BEST TO SEND MIZUKI SENSEI TO HEAVEN.
HEY! YOU TWO, GO TO THE BROTHEL.
BROTHEL?

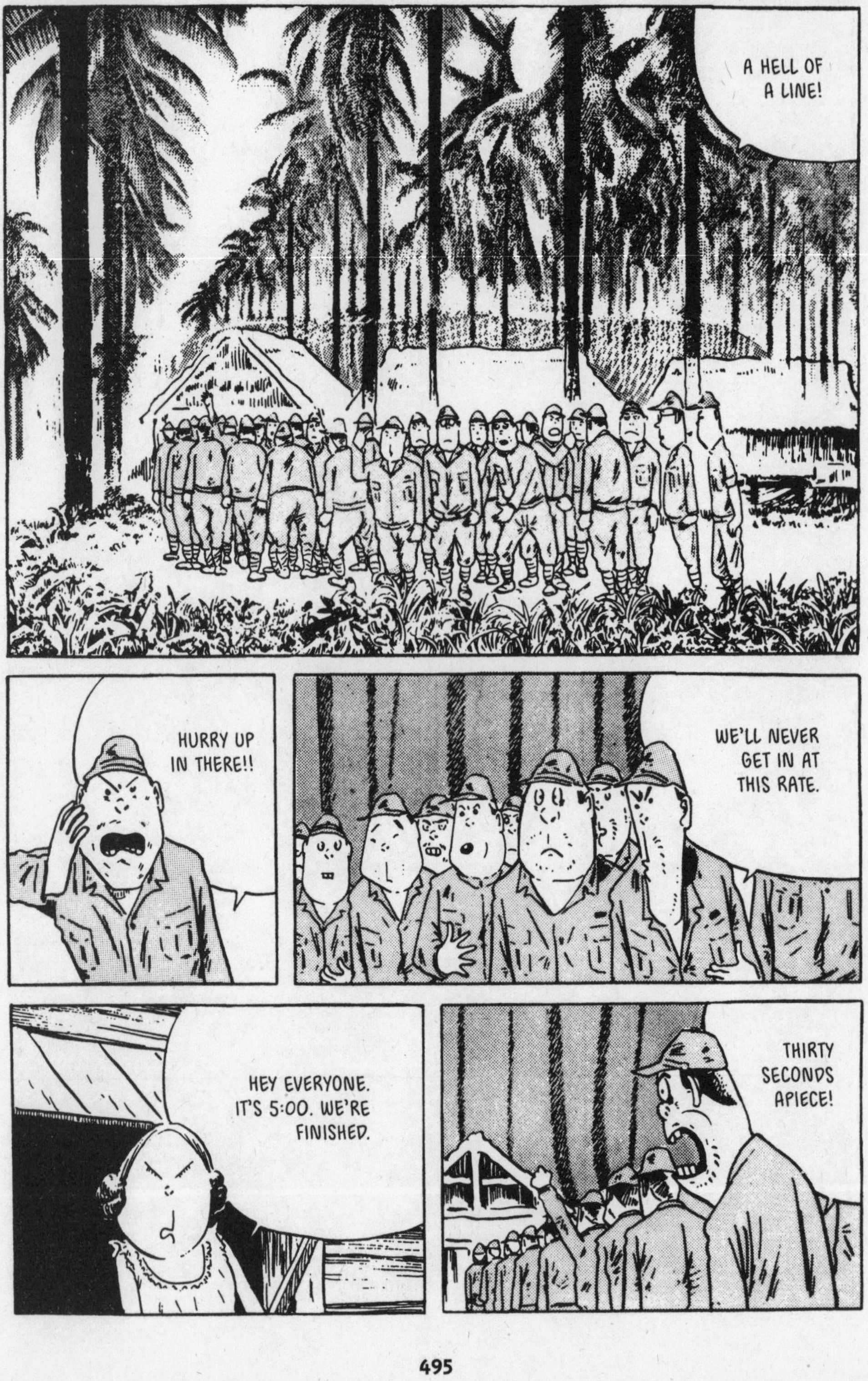
A HELL OF A LINE!
WE'LL NEVER GET IN AT THIS RATE.
HURRY UP IN THERE!!
THIRTY SECONDS APIECE!
HEY EVERYONE. IT'S 5:00. WE'RE FINISHED.

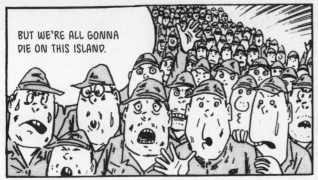

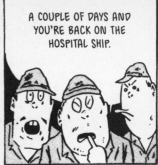

A COUPLE OF DAYS AND YOU'RE BACK ON THE HOSPITAL SHIP.
BUT WE'RE ALL GONNA DIE ON THIS ISLAND.
THEY GOT THAT RIGHT. MOST OF THESE GUYS WOULD NEVER SEE JAPAN AGAIN. THIS WAS A LITTLE SOMETHING TO LET THEM DIE HAPPIER.
BUT THESE WOMEN DOING THEIR "SACRED DUTY" WEREN'T ANY LUCKIER.
THE HOSPITAL SHIP IS SUNK BY A SUBMARINE RIGHT OUT OF PORT. EVERYONE DIES.
SHASHA
SHA

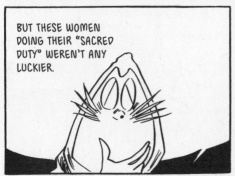

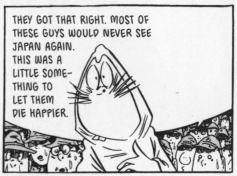

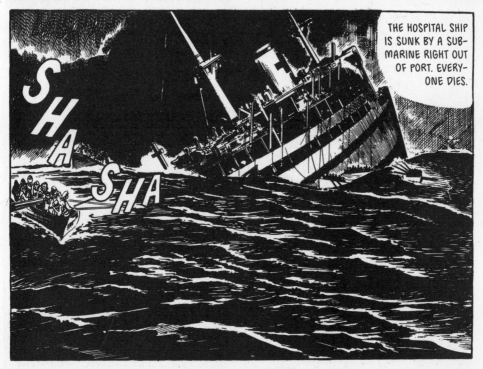

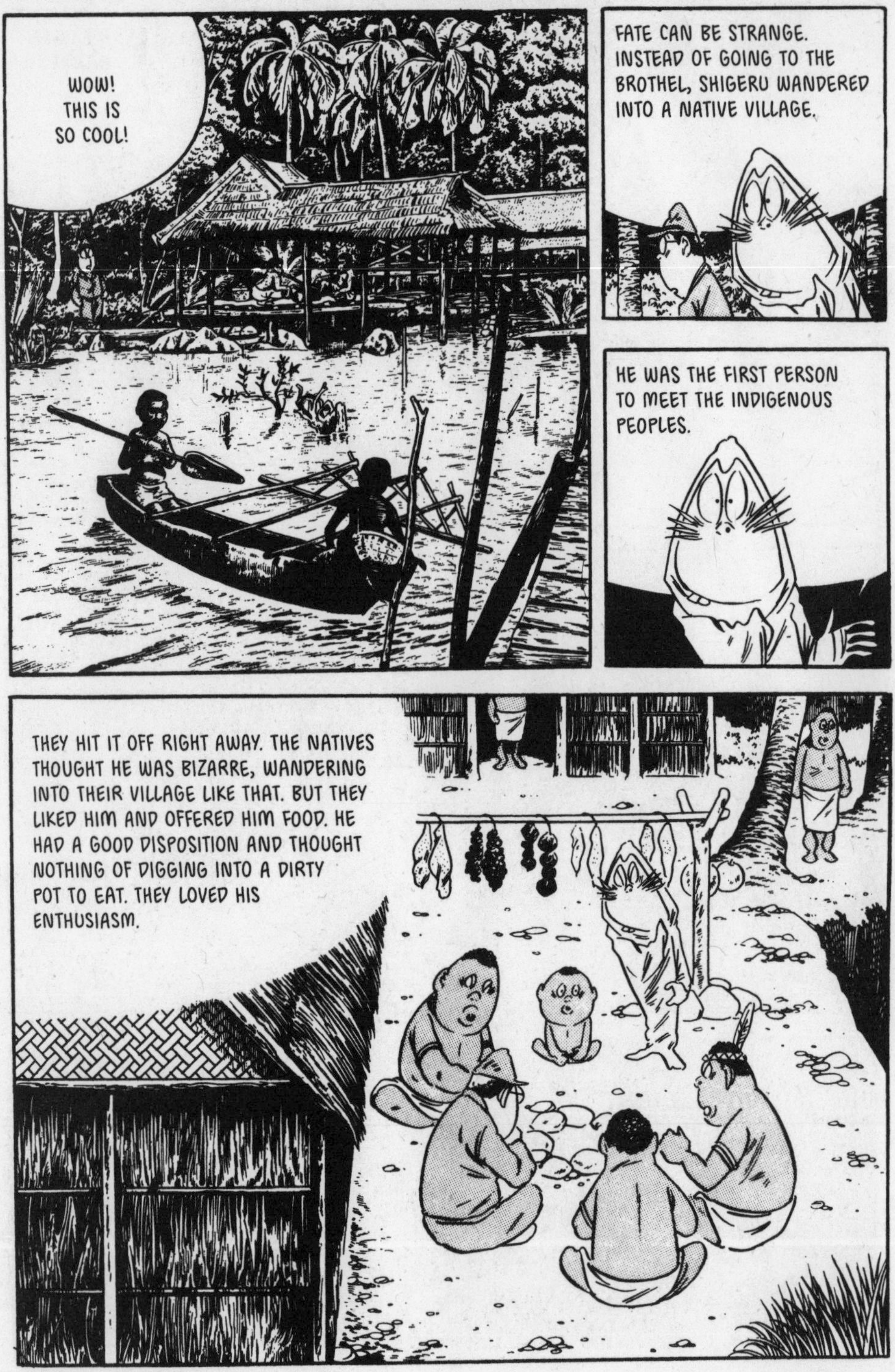
FATE CAN BE STRANGE. INSTEAD OF GOING TO THE BROTHEL, SHIGERU WANDERED INTO A NATIVE VILLAGE.
HE WAS THE FIRST PERSON TO MEET THE INDIGENOUS PEOPLES.
WOW! THIS IS SO COOL!
THEY HIT IT OFF RIGHT AWAY. THE NATIVES THOUGHT HE WAS BIZARRE, WANDERING INTO THEIR VILLAGE LIKE THAT. BUT THEY LIKED HIM AND OFFERED HIM FOOD. HE HAD A GOOD DISPOSITION AND THOUGHT NOTHING OF DIGGING INTO A DIRTY POT TO EAT. THEY LOVED HIS ENTHUSIASM.

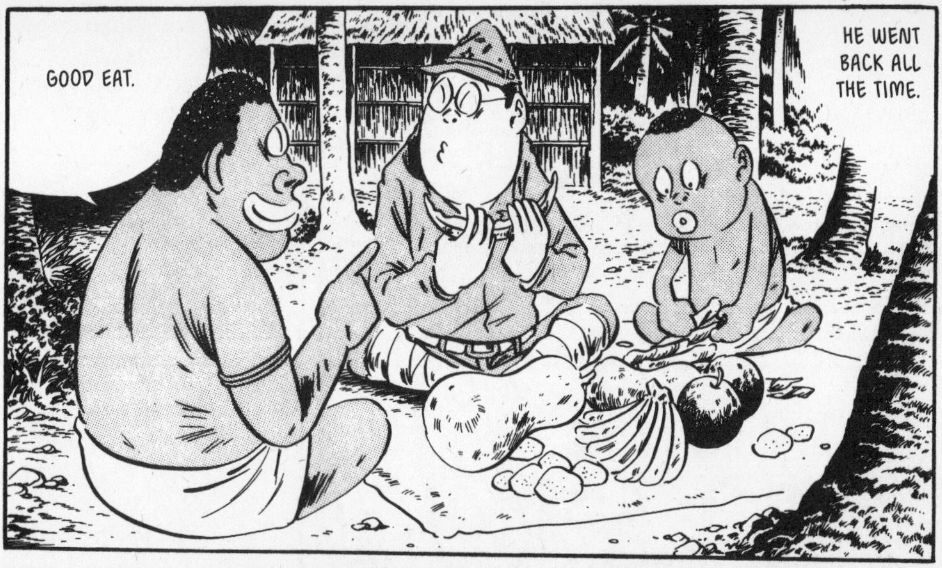
HE WENT BACK ALL THE TIME.
GOOD EAT.

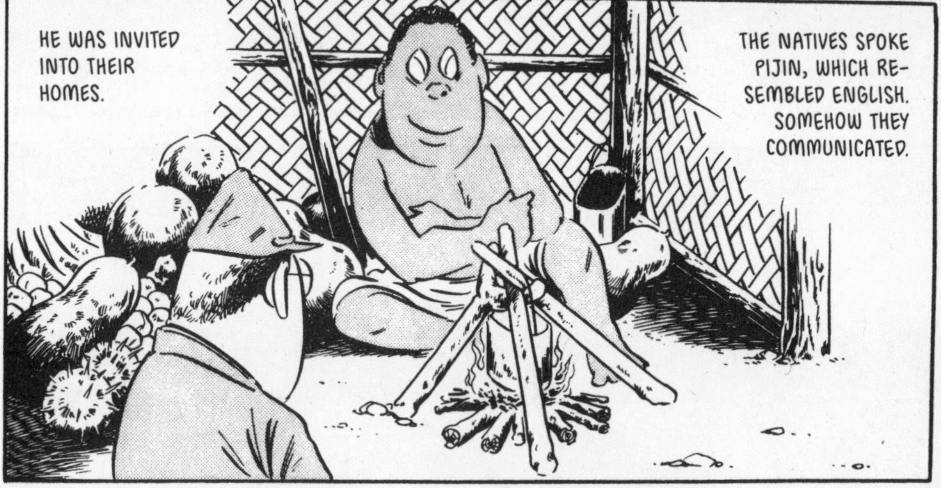
THE NATIVES SPOKE PIJIN, WHICH RE-SEMBLED ENGLISH. SOMEHOW THEY COMMUNICATED.
HE WAS INVITED INTO THEIR HOMES.

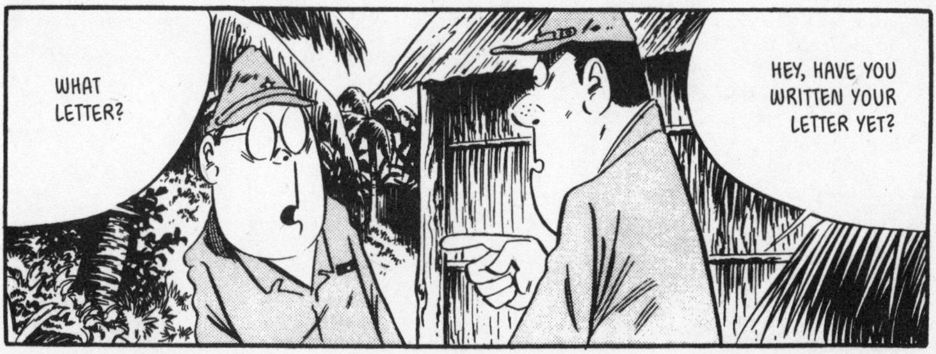
HEY, HAVE YOU WRITTEN YOUR LETTER YET?
WHAT LETTER?

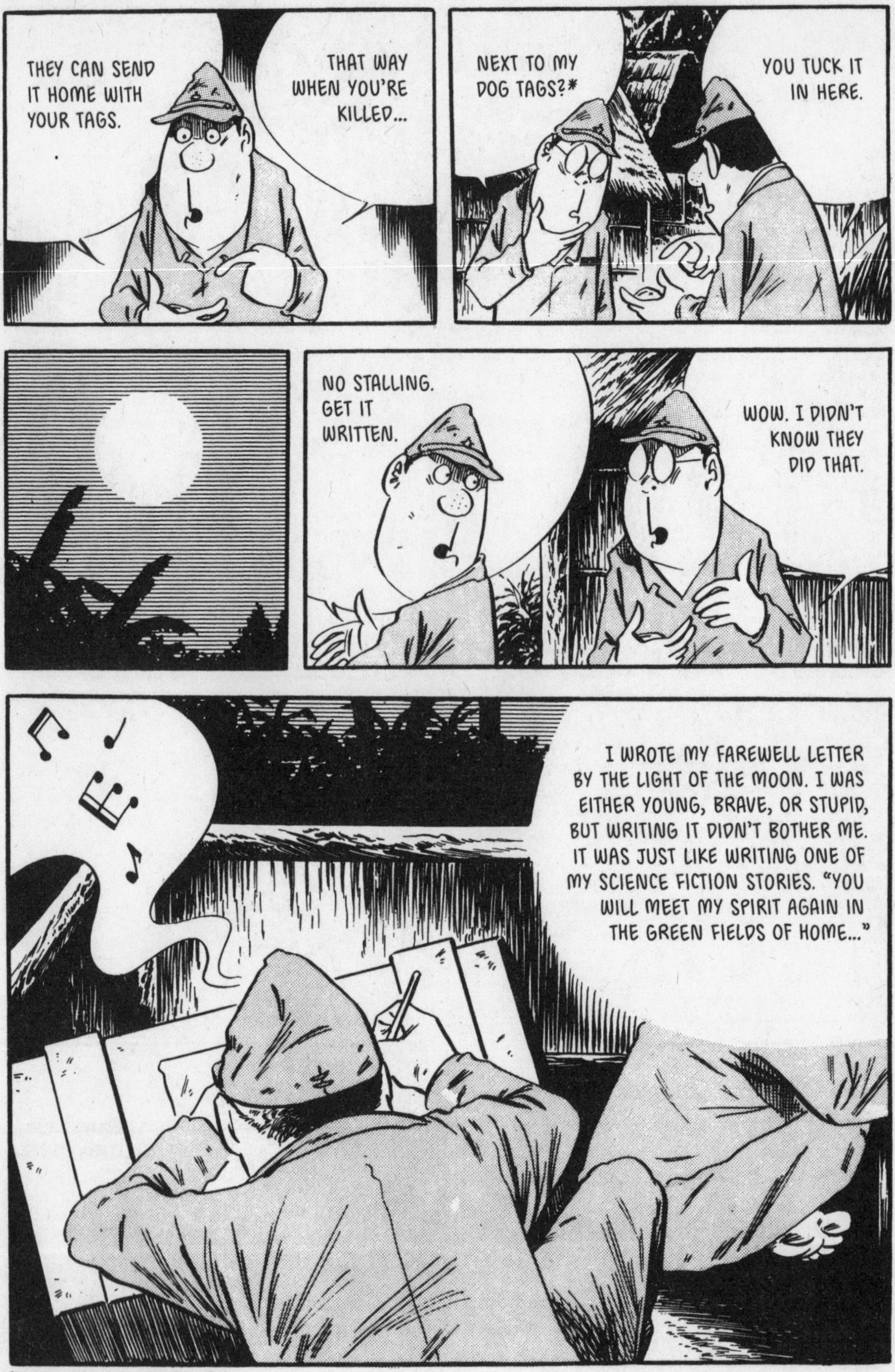
YOU TUCK IT IN HERE.
NEXT TO MY DOG TAGS?*
THAT WAY WHEN YOU'RE KILLED...
THEY CAN SEND IT HOME WITH YOUR TAGS.
WOW. I DIDN'T KNOW THEY DID THAT.
NO STALLING. GET IT WRITTEN.
I WROTE MY FAREWELL LETTER BY THE LIGHT OF THE MOON. I WAS EITHER YOUNG, BRAVE, OR STUPID, BUT WRITING IT DIDN'T BOTHER ME. IT WAS JUST LIKE WRITING ONE OF MY SCIENCE FICTION STORIES. "YOU WILL MEET MY SPIRIT AGAIN IN THE GREEN FIELDS OF HOME..."

*SEE NOTE ON PAGE 548.

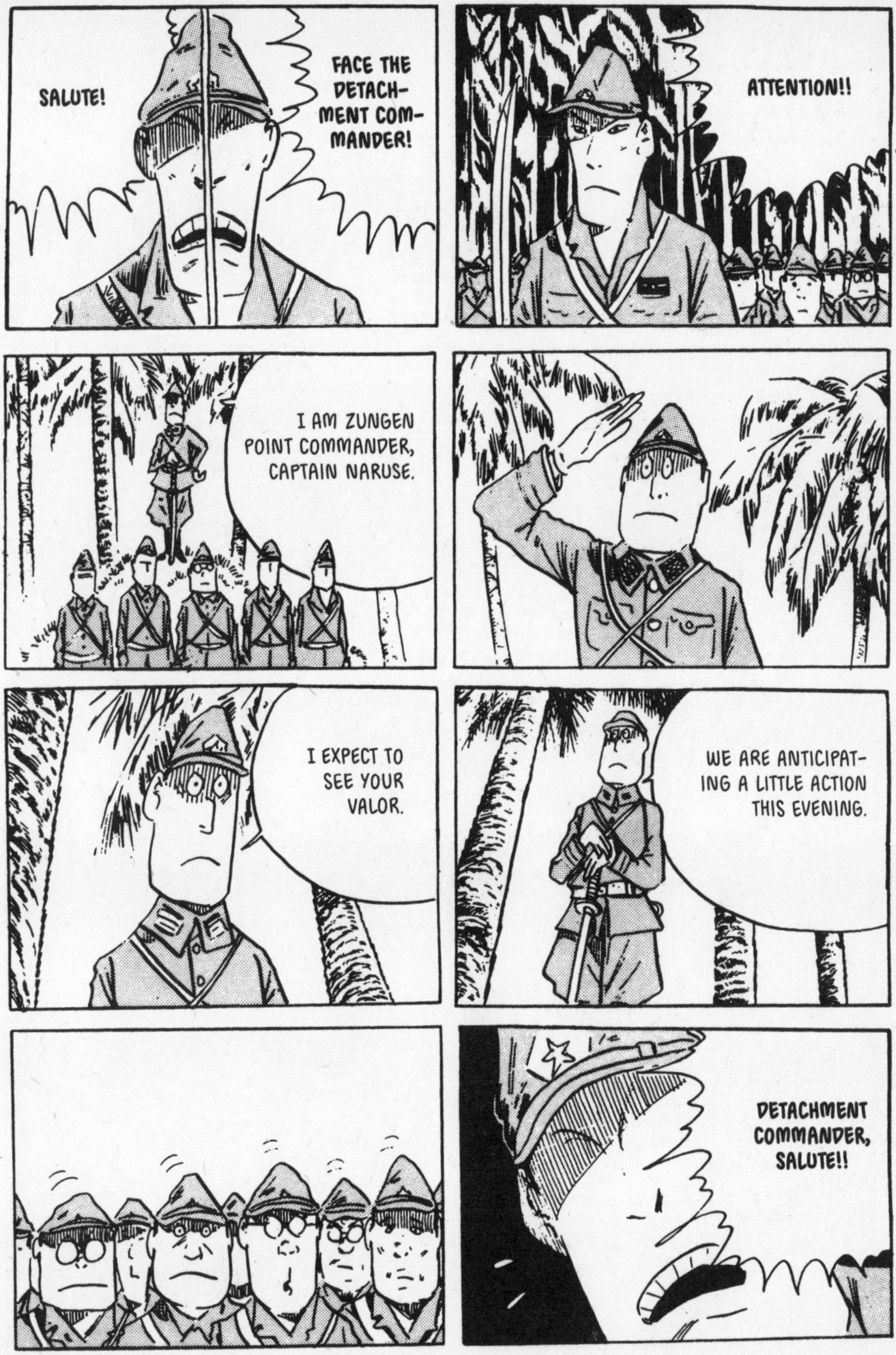
ATTENTION!!
FACE THE DETACHMENT COMMANDER!
SALUTE!
I AM ZUNGEN POINT COMMANDER, CAPTAIN NARUSE.
WE ARE ANTICIPATING A LITTLE ACTION THIS EVENING.
I EXPECT TO SEE YOUR VALOR.
DETACHMENT COMMANDER, SALUTE!!

SUICIDE SQUAD

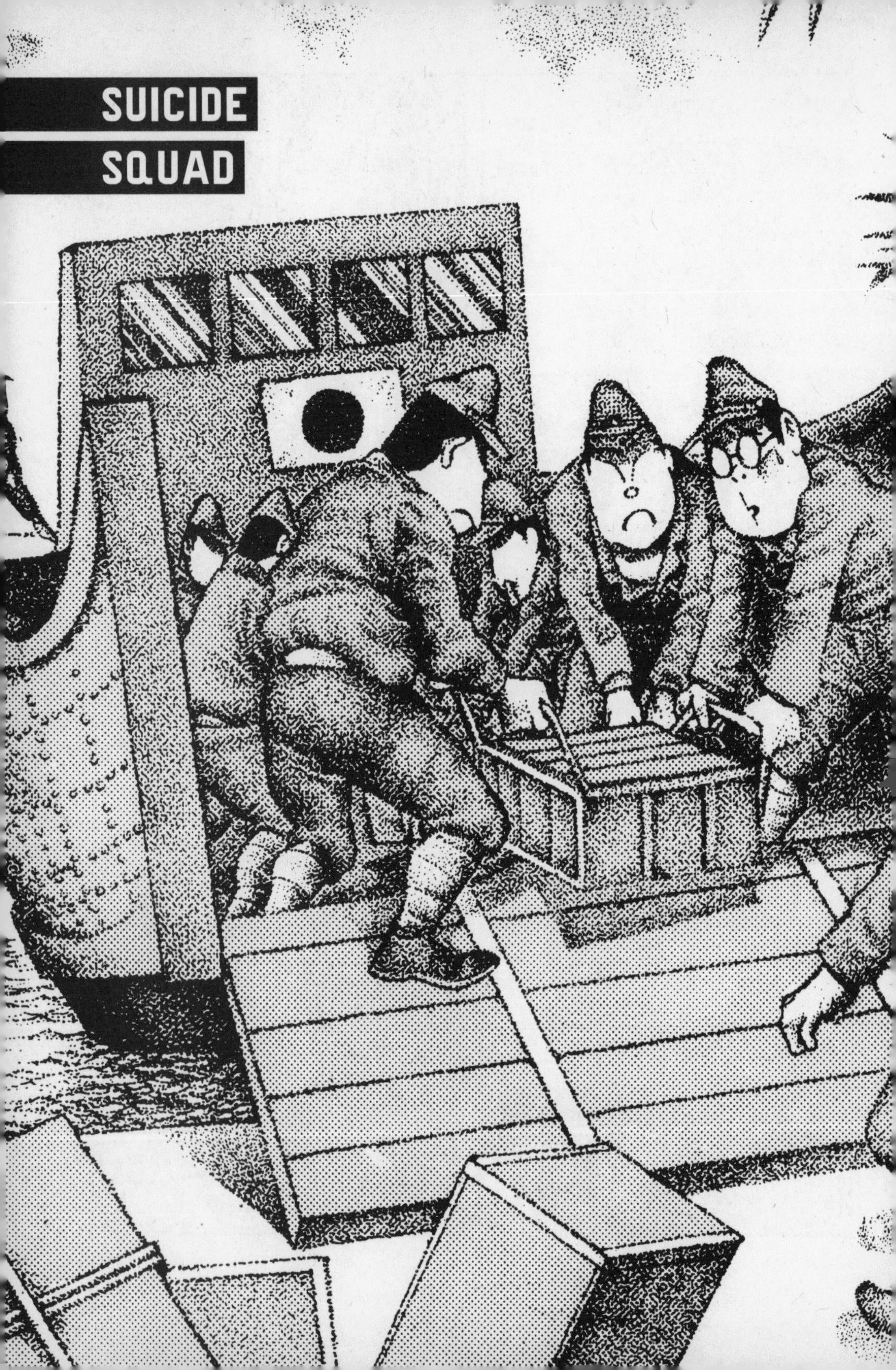

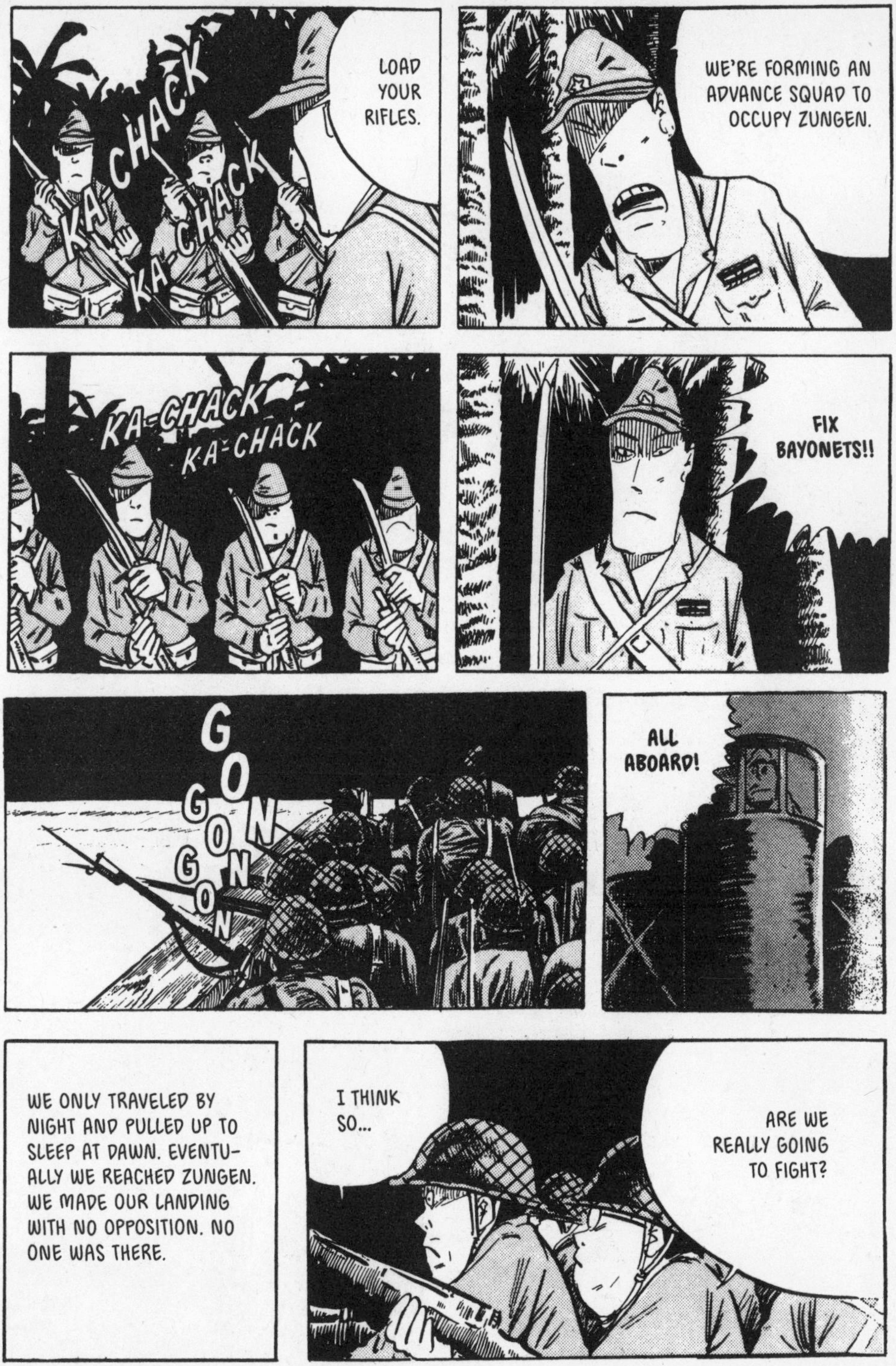
WE'RE FORMING AN ADVANCE SQUAD TO OCCUPY ZUNGEN.
LOAD YOUR RIFLES.
KA-CHACK
KA-CHACK
FIX BAYONETS!!
KA-CHACK
KA-CHACK
ALL ABOARD!
GON
GON
GON
ARE WE REALLY GOING TO FIGHT?
I THINK SO...
WE ONLY TRAVELED BY NIGHT AND PULLED UP TO SLEEP AT DAWN. EVENTUALLY WE REACHED ZUNGEN. WE MADE OUR LANDING WITH NO OPPOSITION. NO ONE WAS THERE.

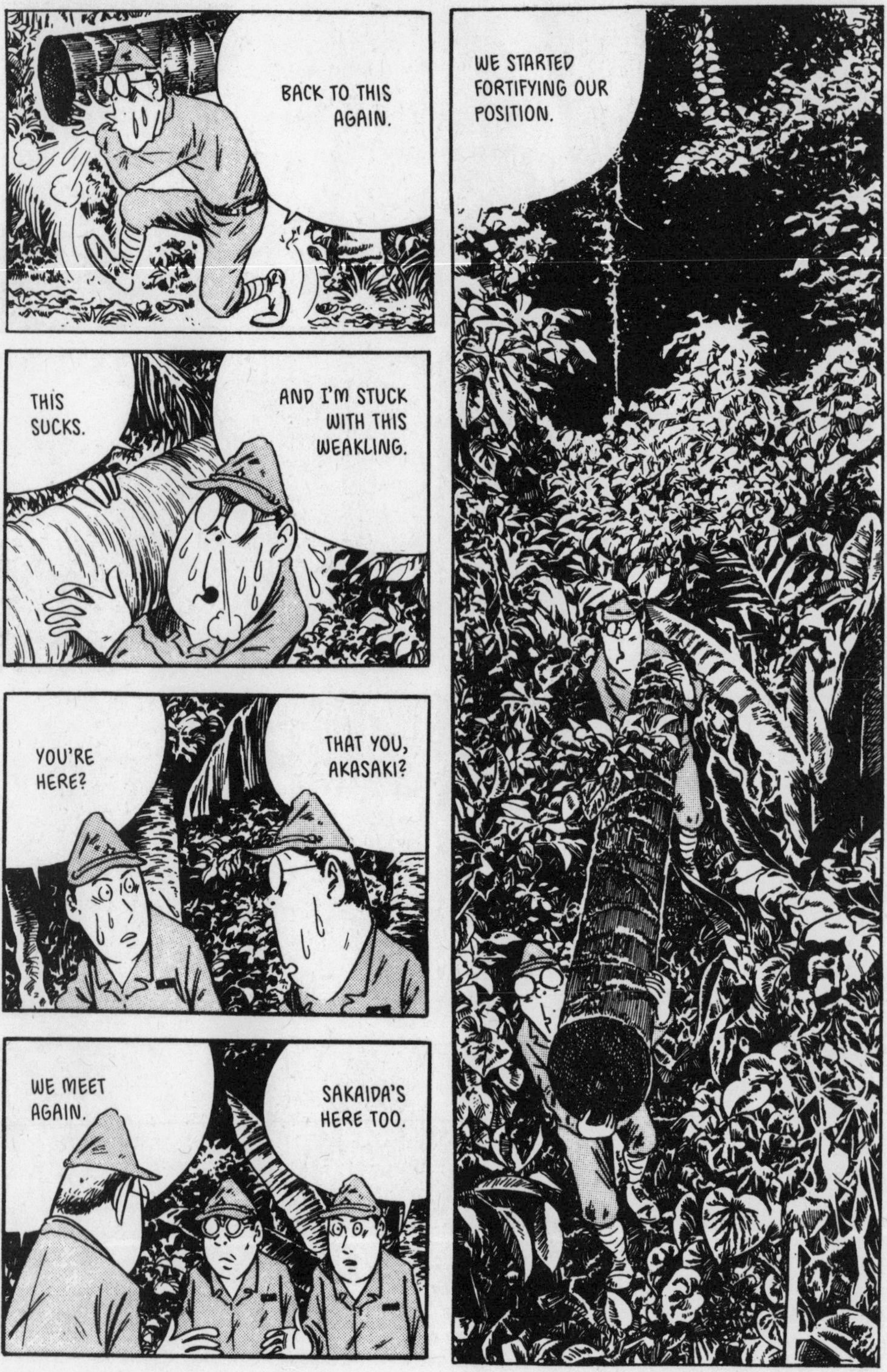
WE STARTED FORTIFYING OUR POSITION.
BACK TO THIS AGAIN.
AND I'M STUCK WITH THIS WEAKLING.
THIS SUCKS.
THAT YOU, AKASAKI?
YOU'RE HERE?
SAKAIDA'S HERE TOO.
WE MEET AGAIN.

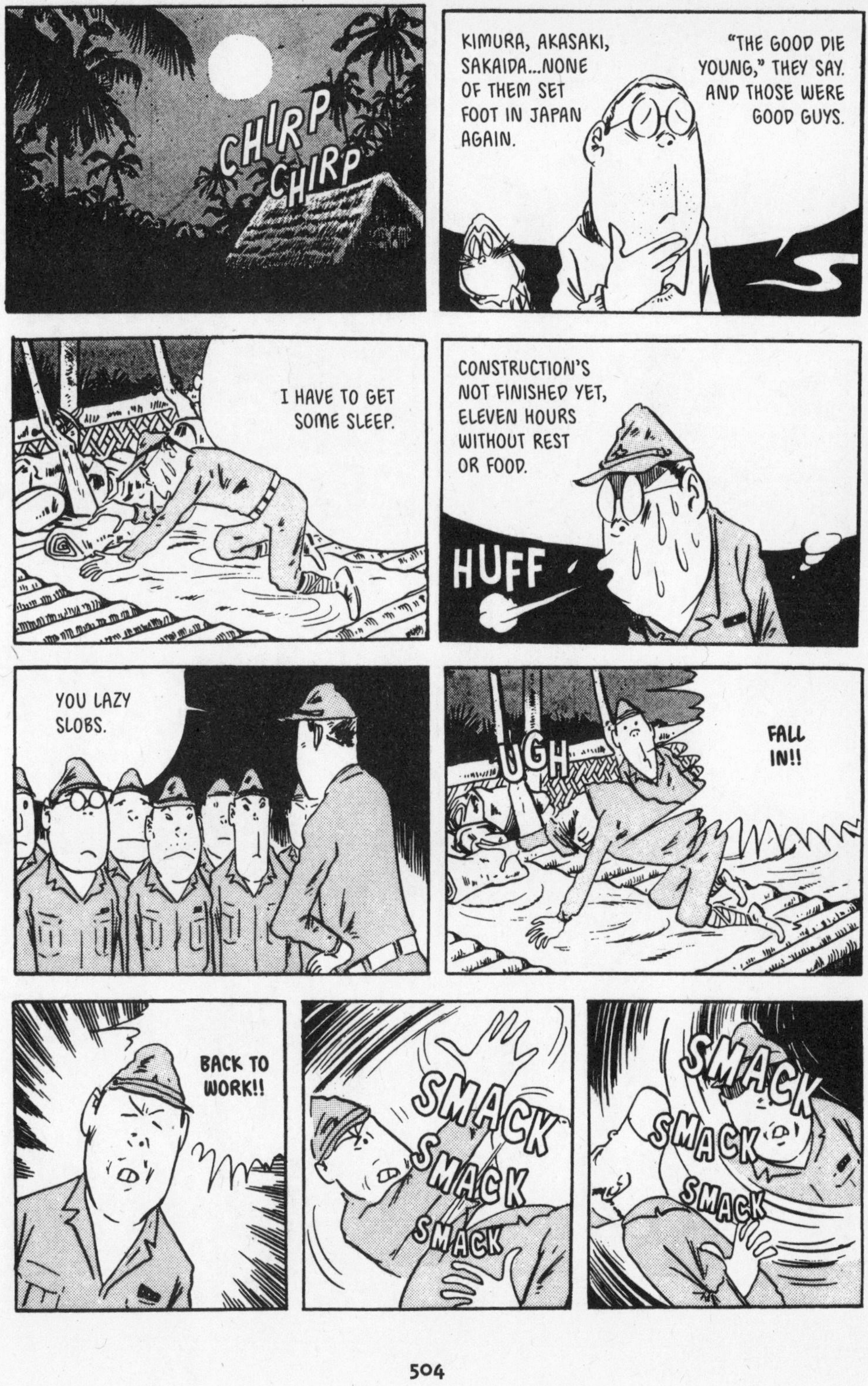
"THE GOOD DIE YOUNG," THEY SAY. AND THOSE WERE GOOD GUYS.
KIMURA, AKASAKI, SAKAIDA...NONE OF THEM SET FOOT IN JAPAN AGAIN.
CHIRP
CHIRP
CONSTRUCTION'S NOT FINISHED YET, ELEVEN HOURS WITHOUT REST OR FOOD.
HUFF
I HAVE TO GET SOME SLEEP.
FALL IN!!
UGH
YOU LAZY SLOBS.
SMACK
SMACK
SMACK
SMACK
SMACK
SMACK
BACK TO WORK!!

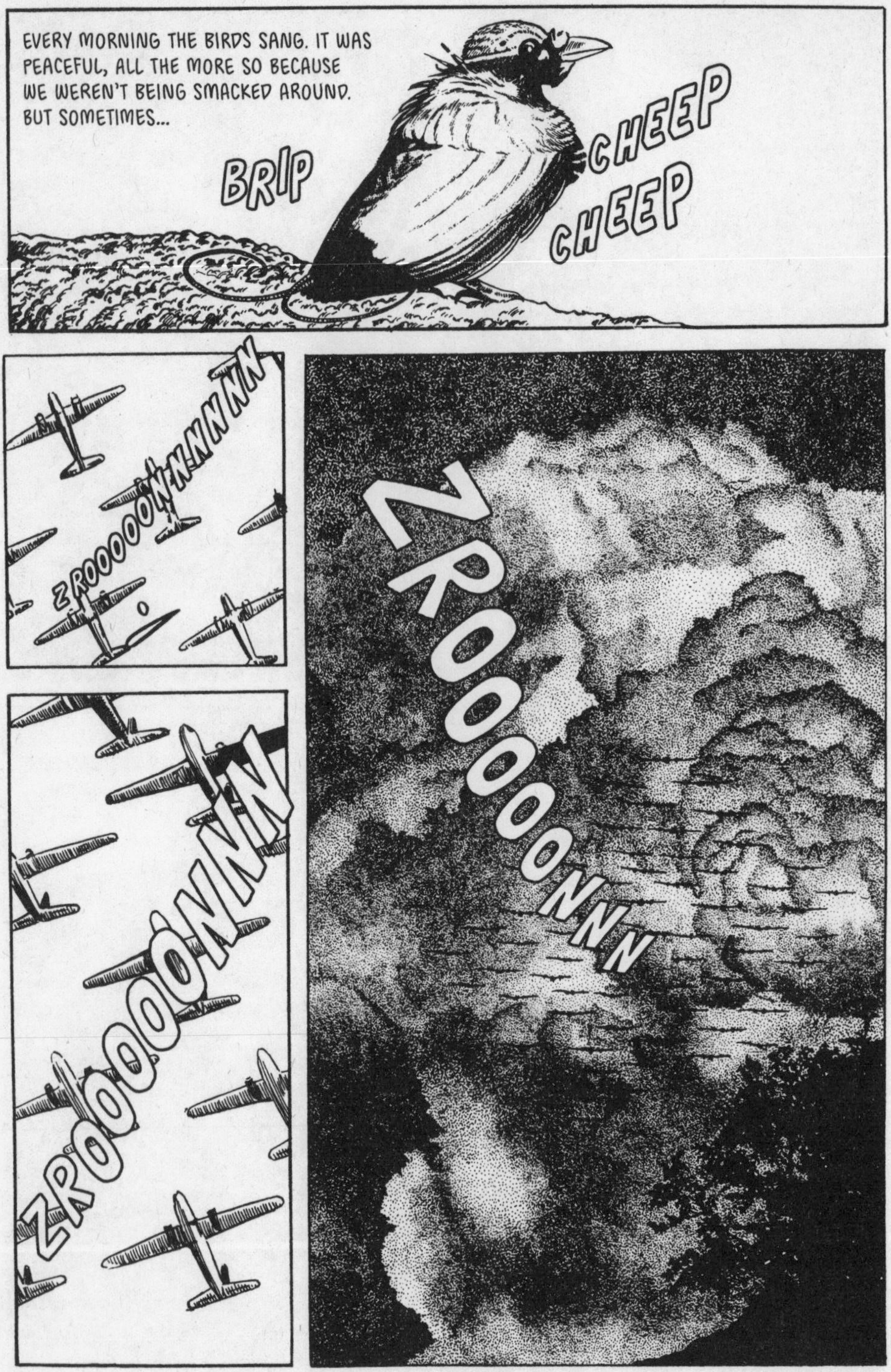
EVERY MORNING THE BIRDS SANG. IT WAS PEACEFUL, ALL THE MORE SO BECAUSE WE WEREN'T BEING SMACKED AROUND. BUT SOMETIMES...
CHEEP
CHEEP
BRIP
ZROOOOOONNN
ZROOOOONNNNNN
ZROOOOONNN

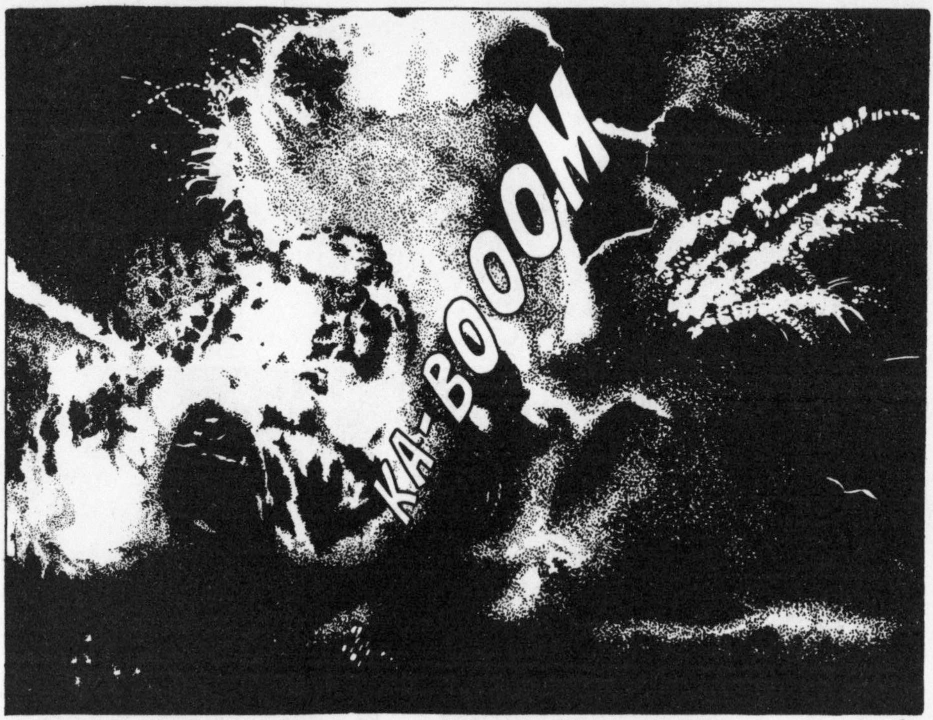
KA-BOOOM

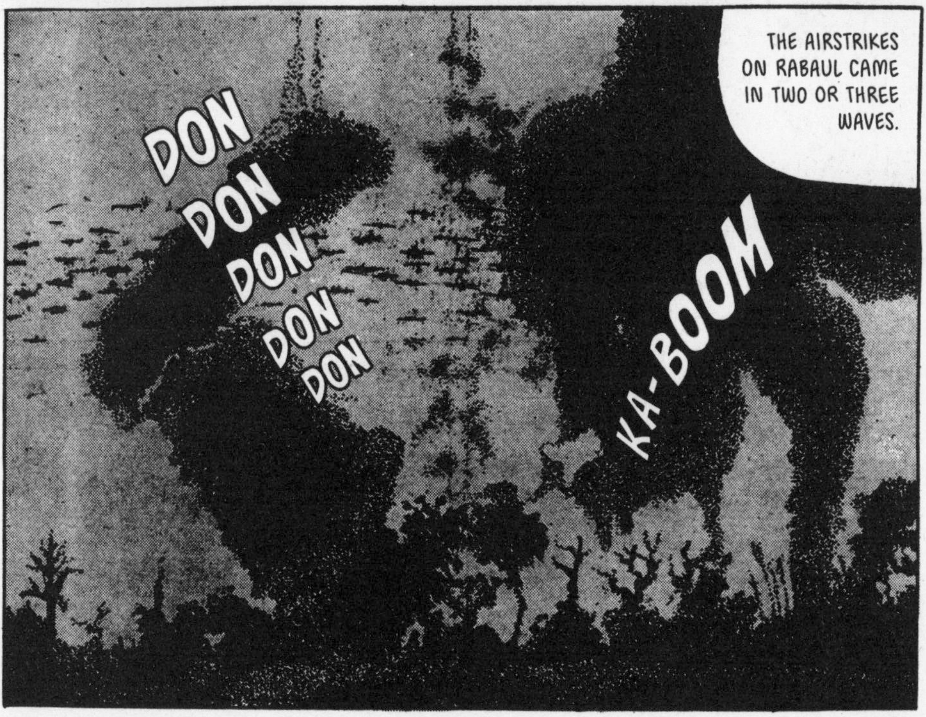
THE AIRSTRIKES ON RABAUL CAME IN TWO OR THREE WAVES.
KA-BOOM
DON
DON
DON
DON
DON

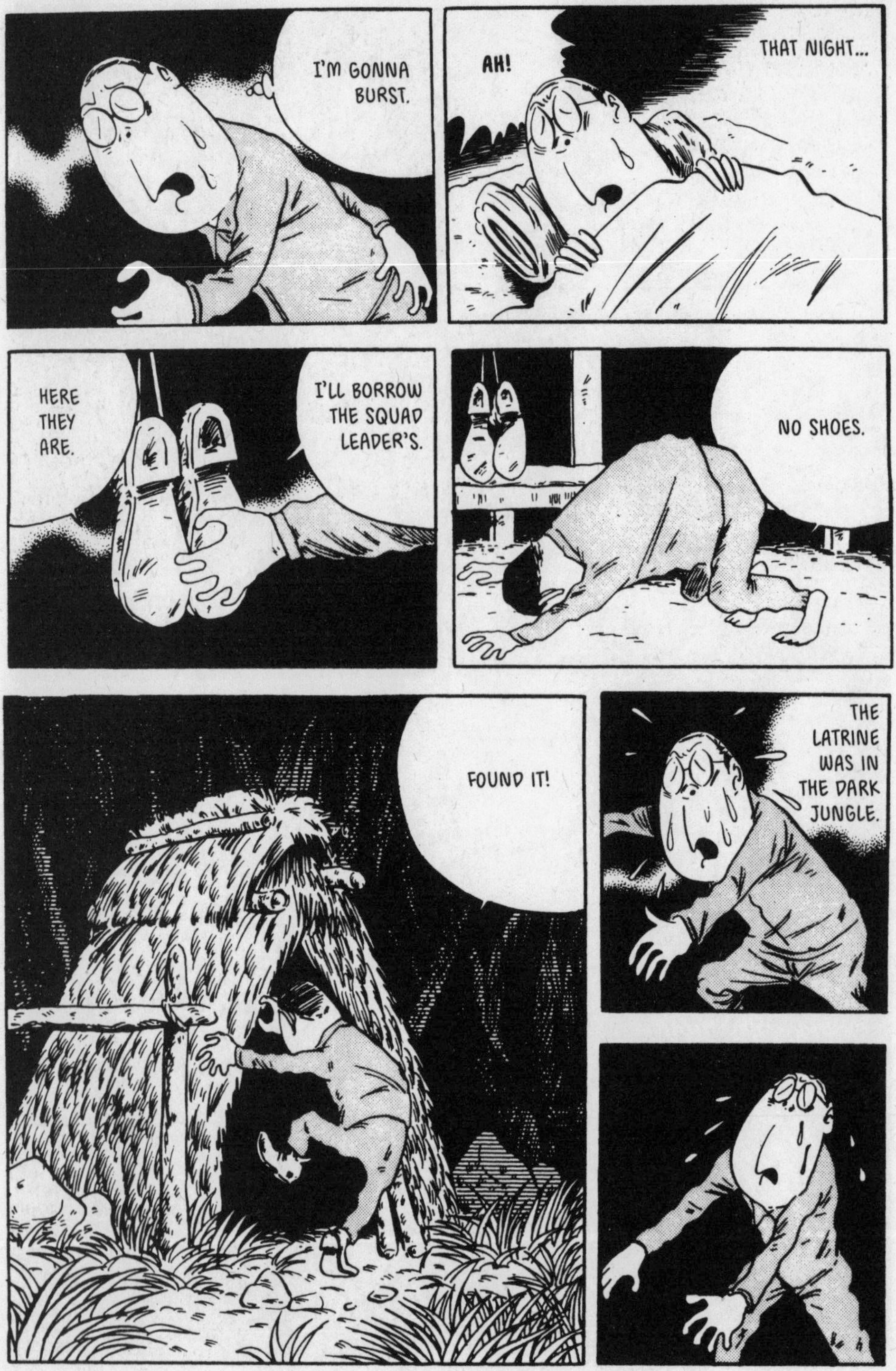
THAT NIGHT...
AH!
I'M GONNA BURST.
NO SHOES.
I'LL BORROW THE SQUAD LEADER'S.
HERE THEY ARE.
THE LATRINE WAS IN THE DARK JUNGLE.
FOUND IT!

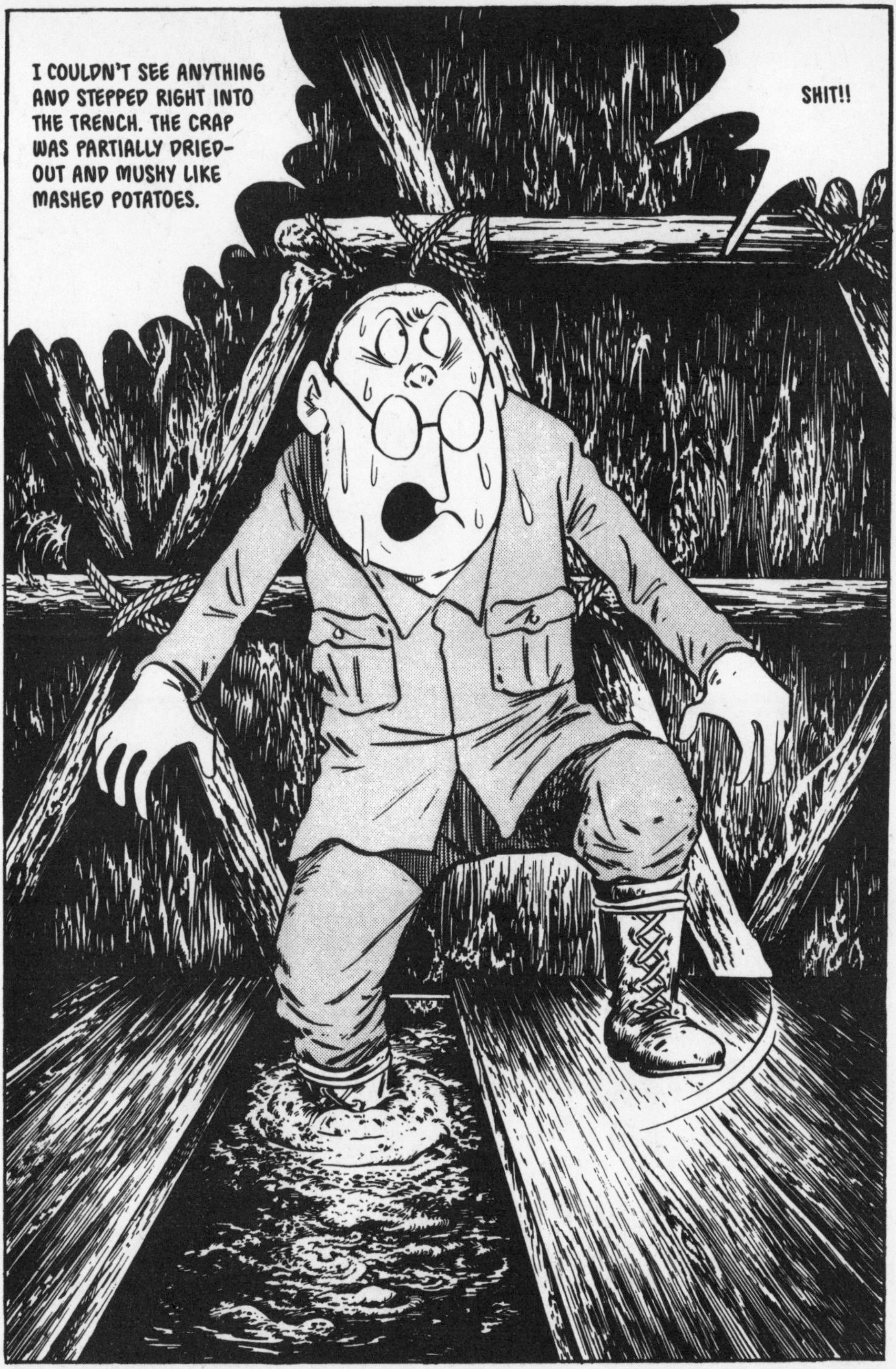
I COULDN'T SEE ANYTHING AND STEPPED RIGHT INTO THE TRENCH. THE CRAP WAS PARTIALLY DRIED-OUT AND MUSHY LIKE MASHED POTATOES.
SHIT!!

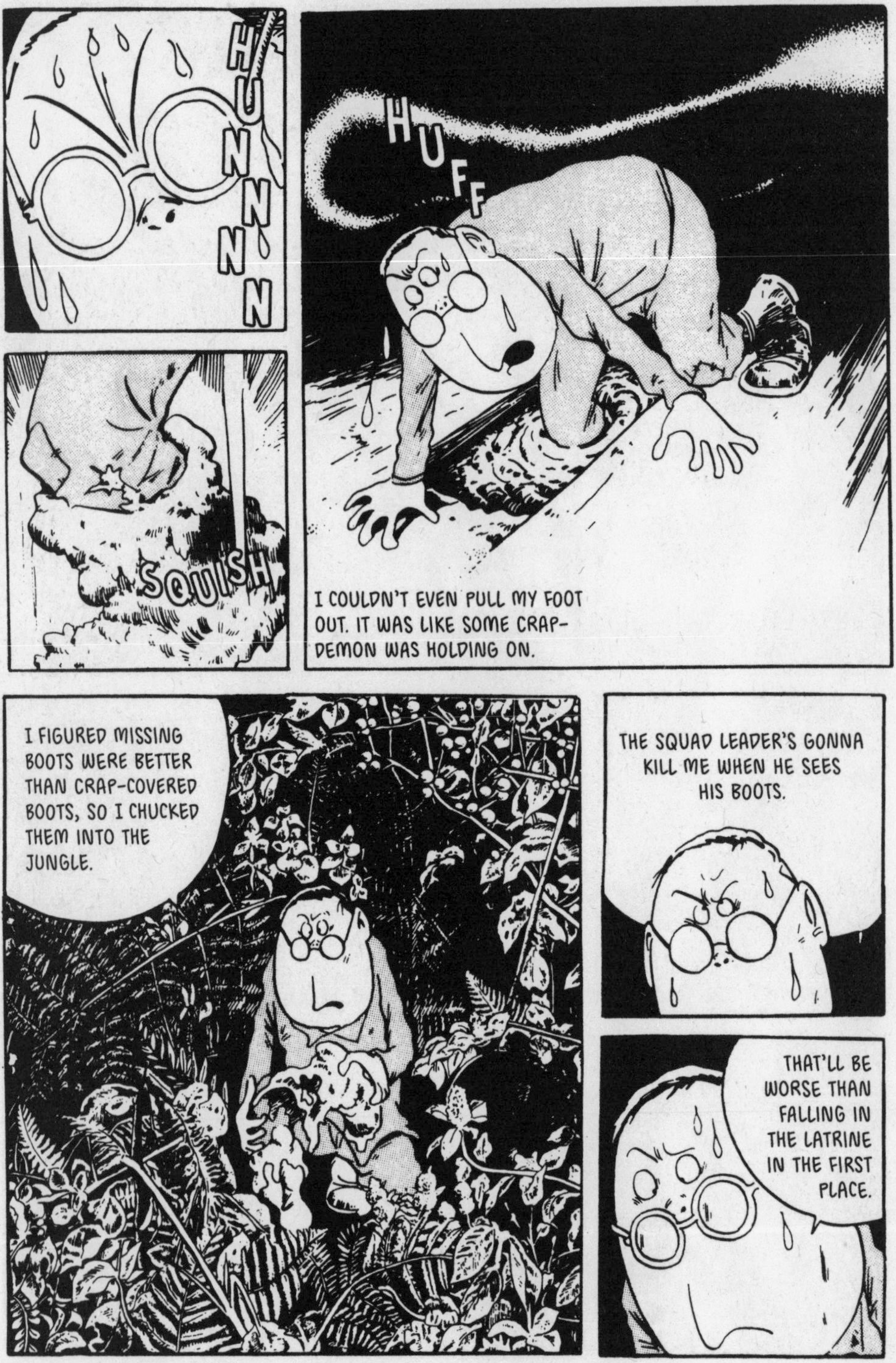
HUFF
I COULDN'T EVEN PULL MY FOOT OUT. IT WAS LIKE SOME CRAP-DEMON WAS HOLDING ON.
HUNNNN
SQUISH
THE SQUAD LEADER'S GONNA KILL ME WHEN HE SEES HIS BOOTS.
THAT'LL BE WORSE THAN FALLING IN THE LATRINE IN THE FIRST PLACE.
I FIGURED MISSING BOOTS WERE BETTER THAN CRAP-COVERED BOOTS, SO I CHUCKED THEM INTO THE JUNGLE.

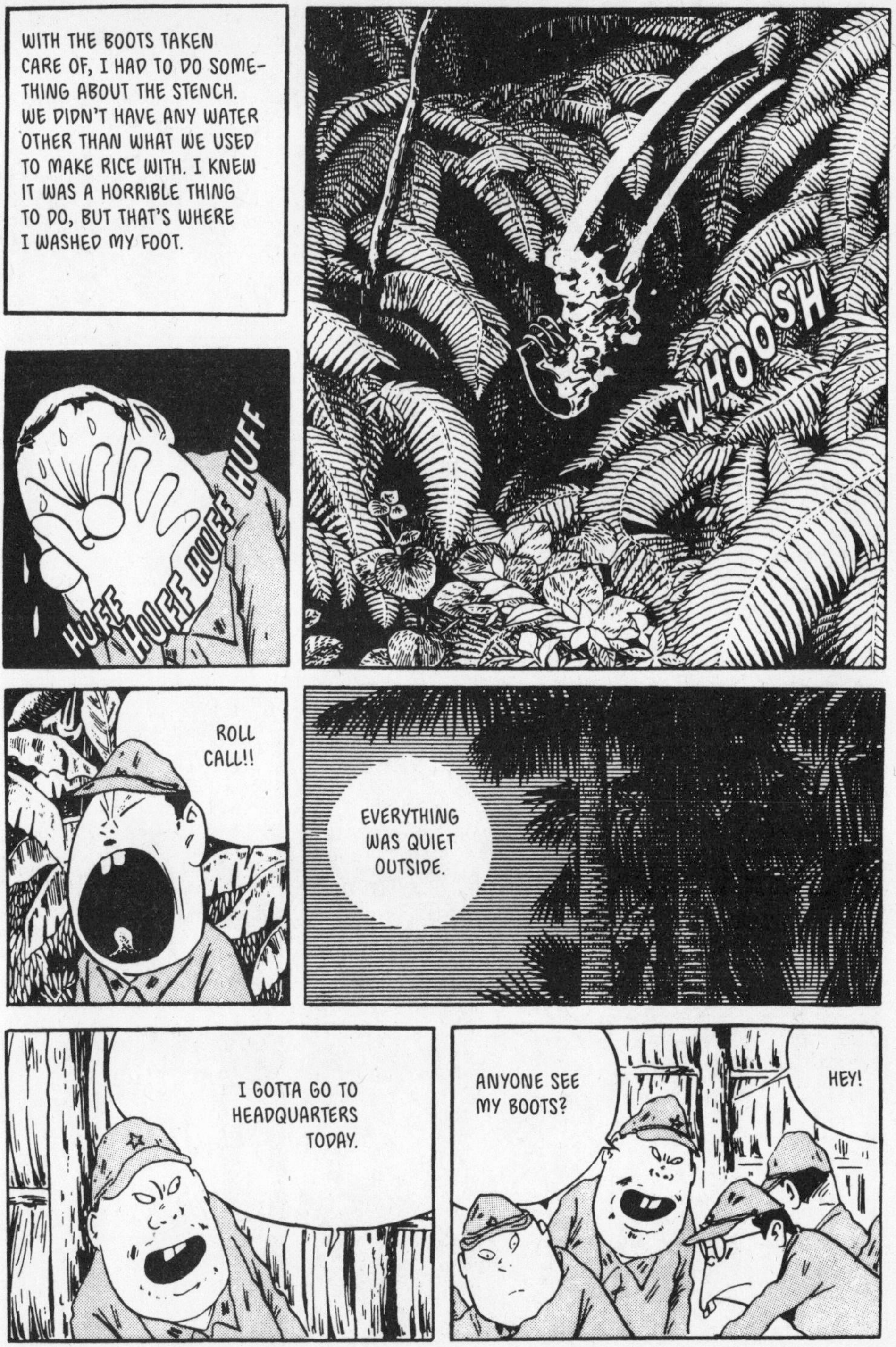
WHOOSH
WITH THE BOOTS TAKEN CARE OF, I HAD TO DO SOMETHING ABOUT THE STENCH. WE DIDN'T HAVE ANY WATER OTHER THAN WHAT WE USED TO MAKE RICE WITH. I KNEW IT WAS A HORRIBLE THING TO DO, BUT THAT'S WHERE I WASHED MY FOOT.
HUFF HUFF HUFF HUFF
EVERYTHING WAS QUIET OUTSIDE.
ROLL CALL!!
HEY!
ANYONE SEE MY BOOTS?
I GOTTA GO TO HEADQUARTERS TODAY.

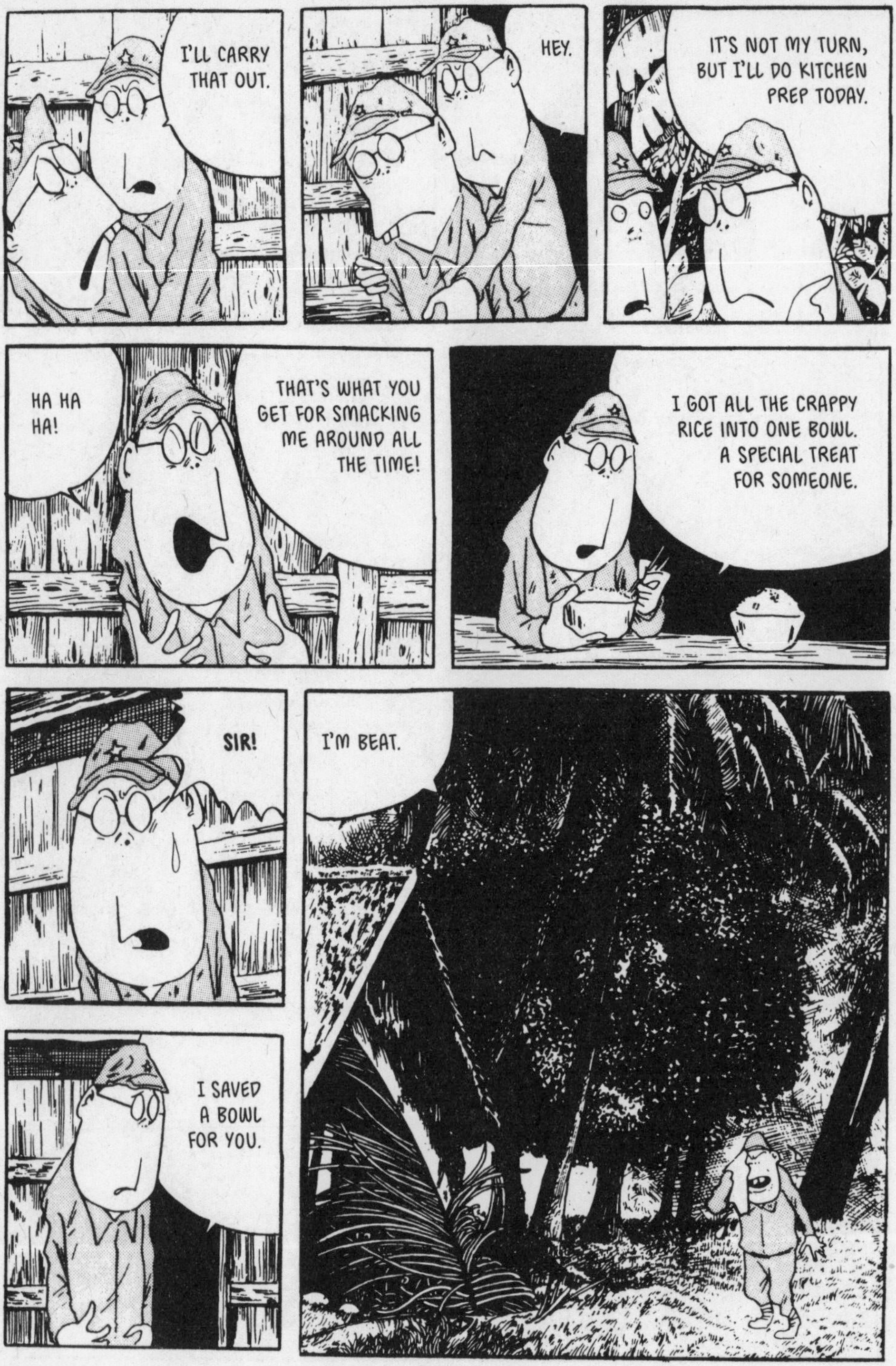
IT'S NOT MY TURN, BUT I'LL DO KITCHEN PREP TODAY.
HEY.
I'LL CARRY THAT OUT.
I GOT ALL THE CRAPPY RICE INTO ONE BOWL. A SPECIAL TREAT FOR SOMEONE.
THAT'S WHAT YOU GET FOR SMACKING ME AROUND ALL THE TIME!
HA HA HA!
I'M BEAT.
SIR!
I SAVED A BOWL FOR YOU.

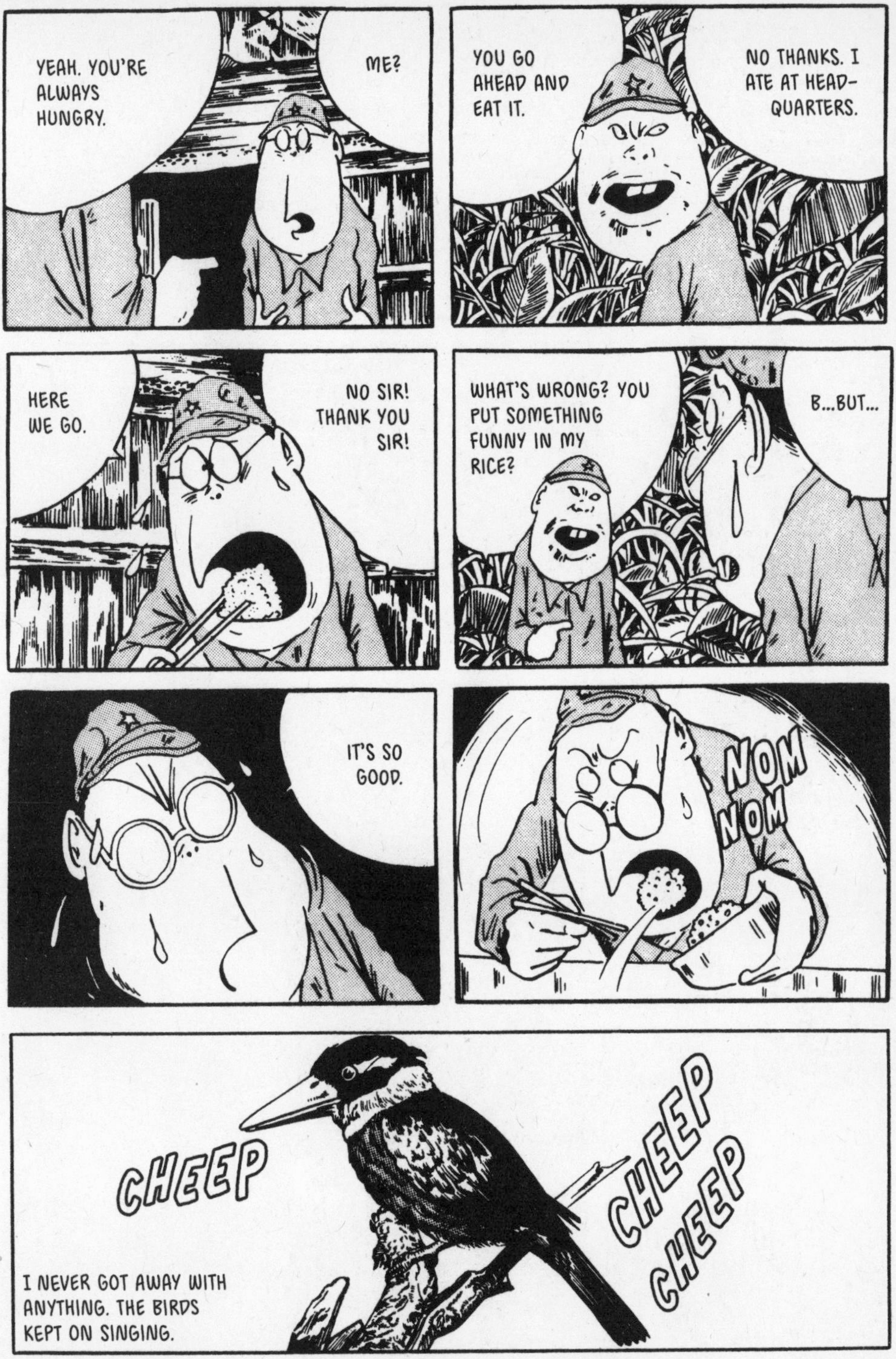
NO THANKS. I ATE AT HEAD-QUARTERS.
YOU GO AHEAD AND EAT IT.
ME?
YEAH. YOU'RE ALWAYS HUNGRY.
B...BUT...
WHAT'S WRONG? YOU PUT SOMETHING FUNNY IN MY RICE?
NO SIR! THANK YOU SIR!
HERE WE GO.
NOM NOM
IT'S SO GOOD.
CHEEP CHEEP
CHEEP
I NEVER GOT AWAY WITH ANYTHING. THE BIRDS KEPT ON SINGING.

THE ALLIGATOR AND THE BOOTS

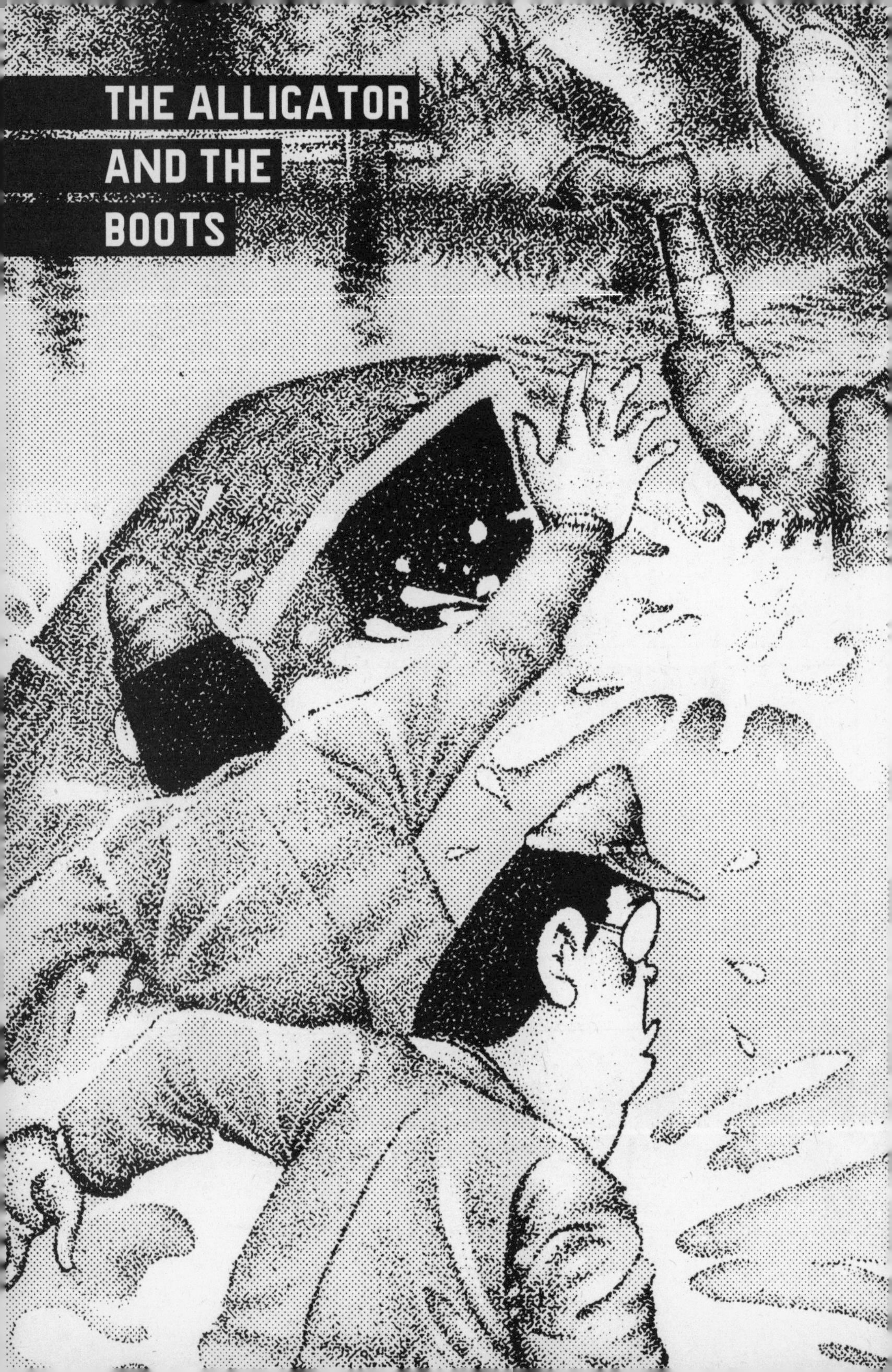

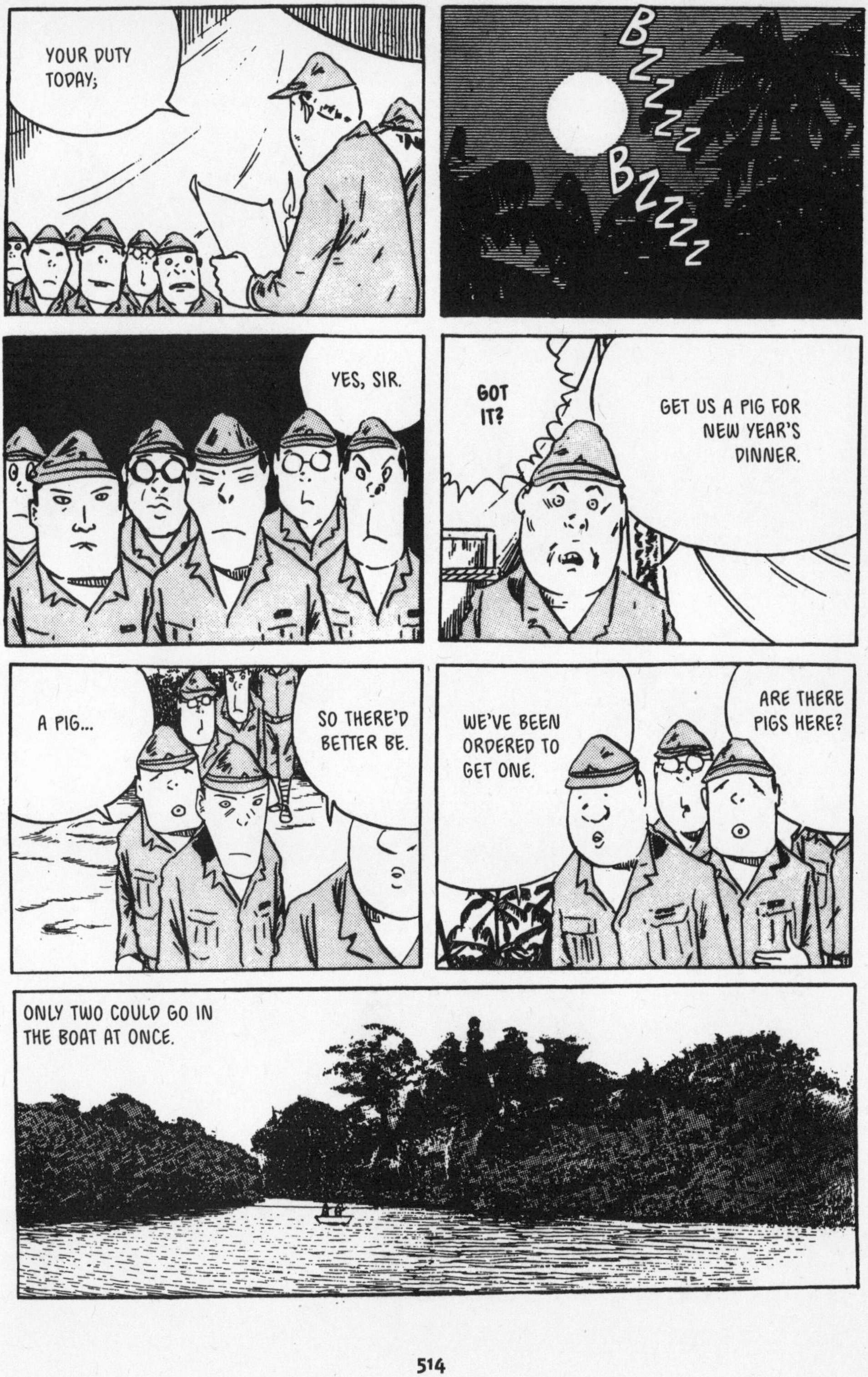
BZZZZ BZZZZ
YOUR DUTY TODAY;
GET US A PIG FOR NEW YEAR'S DINNER.
GOT IT?
YES, SIR.
ARE THERE PIGS HERE?
WE'VE BEEN ORDERED TO GET ONE.
SO THERE'D BETTER BE.
A PIG...
ONLY TWO COULD GO IN THE BOAT AT ONCE.

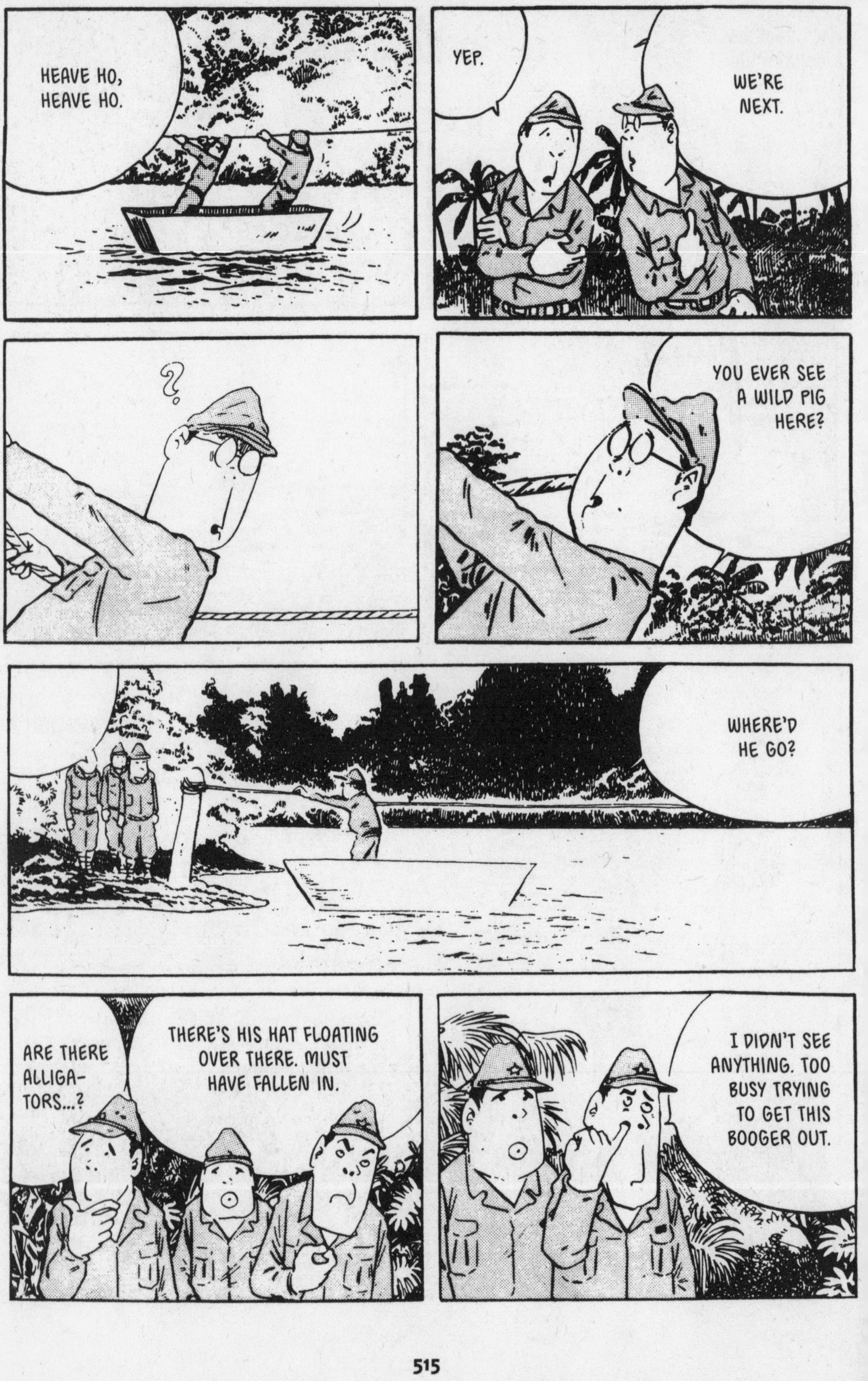
WE'RE NEXT.
YEP.
HEAVE HO, HEAVE HO.
YOU EVER SEE A WILD PIG HERE?
?
WHERE'D HE GO?
I DIDN'T SEE ANYTHING. TOO BUSY TRYING TO GET THIS BOOGER OUT.
THERE'S HIS HAT FLOATING OVER THERE. MUST HAVE FALLEN IN.
ARE THERE ALLIGA-TORS...?

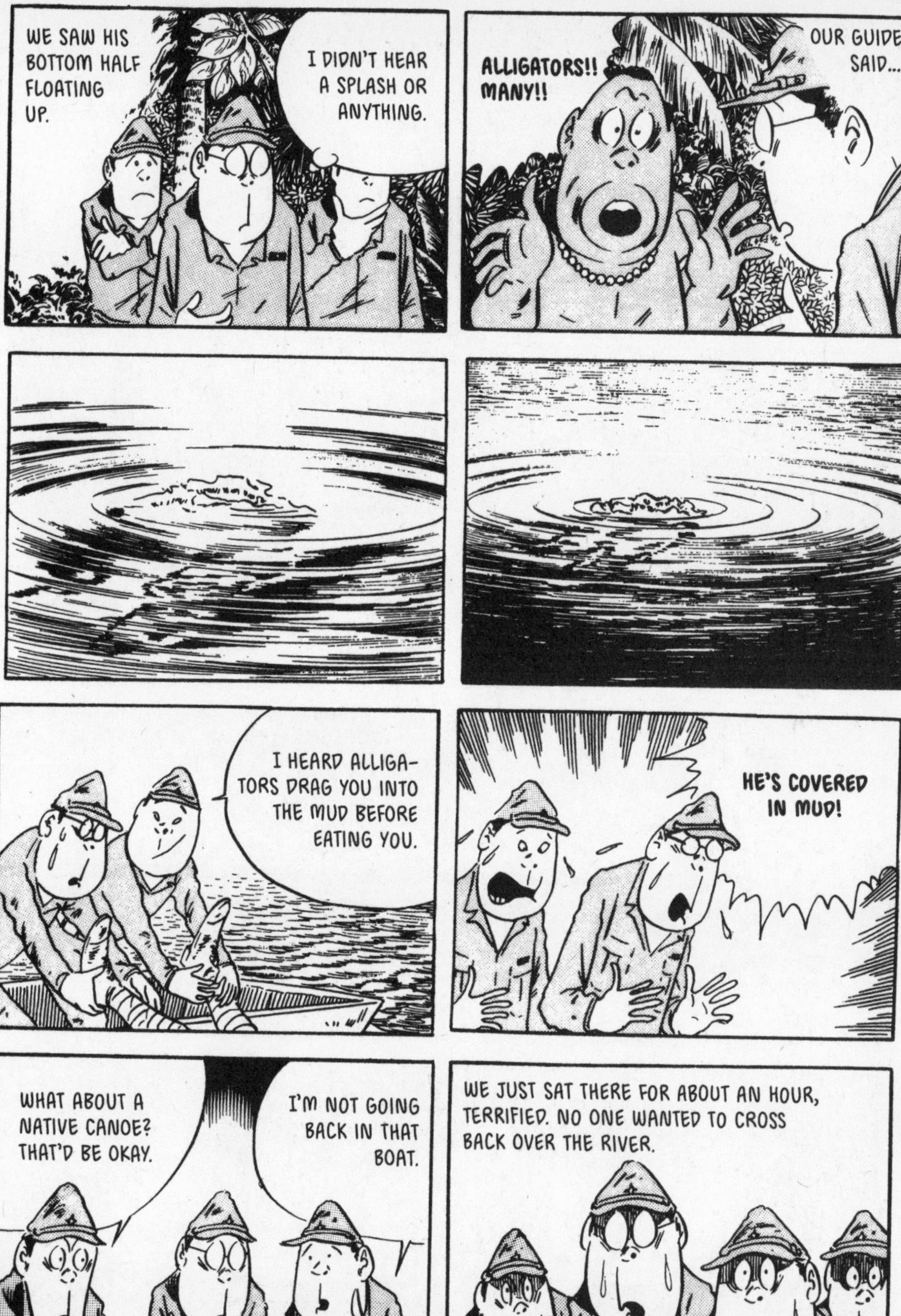
OUR GUIDE SAID...
ALLIGATORS!! MANY!!
I DIDN'T HEAR A SPLASH OR ANYTHING.
WE SAW HIS BOTTOM HALF FLOATING UP.
HE'S COVERED IN MUD!
I HEARD ALLIGATORS DRAG YOU INTO THE MUD BEFORE EATING YOU.
WE JUST SAT THERE FOR ABOUT AN HOUR, TERRIFIED. NO ONE WANTED TO CROSS BACK OVER THE RIVER.
I'M NOT GOING BACK IN THAT BOAT.
WHAT ABOUT A NATIVE CANOE? THAT'D BE OKAY.

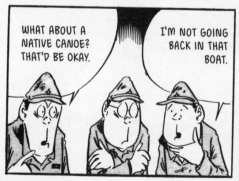

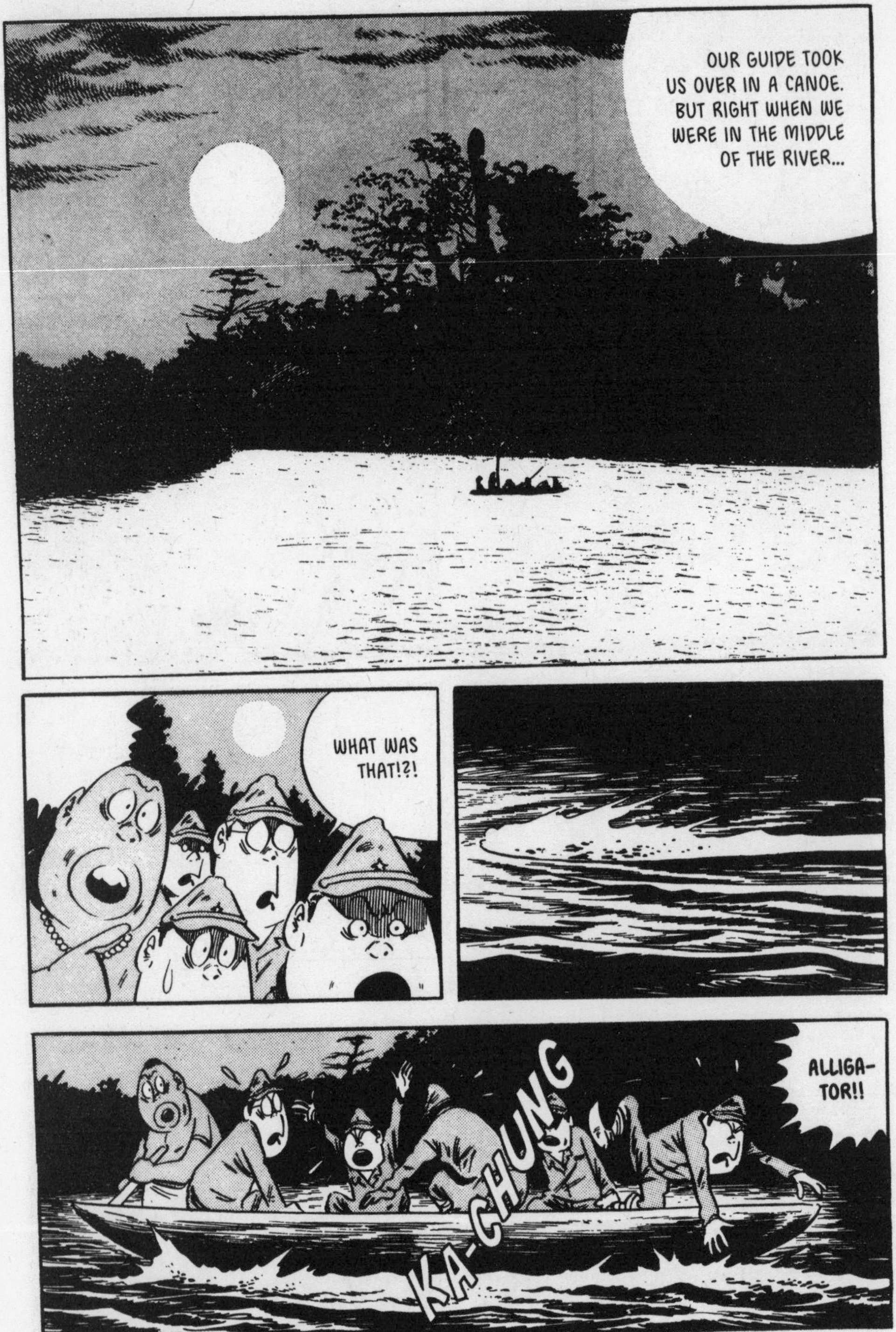
OUR GUIDE TOOK US OVER IN A CANOE. BUT RIGHT WHEN WE WERE IN THE MIDDLE OF THE RIVER...
WHAT WAS THAT!?!
ALLIGA-TOR!!
KA-CHUNG

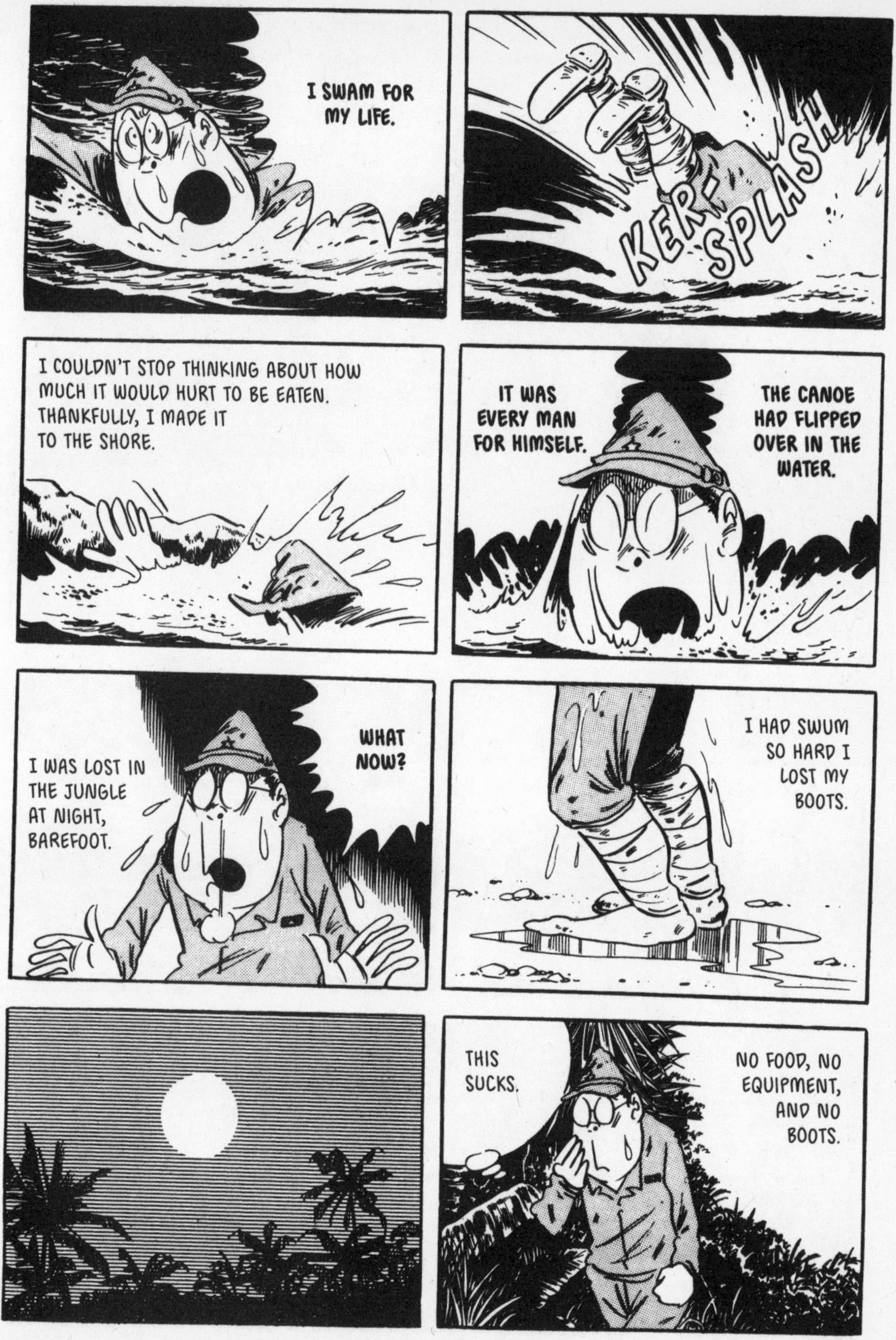
KER-SPLASH
I SWAM FOR MY LIFE.
THE CANOE HAD FLIPPED OVER IN THE WATER.
IT WAS EVERY MAN FOR HIMSELF.
I COULDN'T STOP THINKING ABOUT HOW MUCH IT WOULD HURT TO BE EATEN. THANKFULLY, I MADE IT TO THE SHORE.
I HAD SWUM SO HARD I LOST MY BOOTS.
WHAT NOW?
I WAS LOST IN THE JUNGLE AT NIGHT, BAREFOOT.
NO FOOD, NO EQUIPMENT, AND NO BOOTS.
THIS SUCKS.

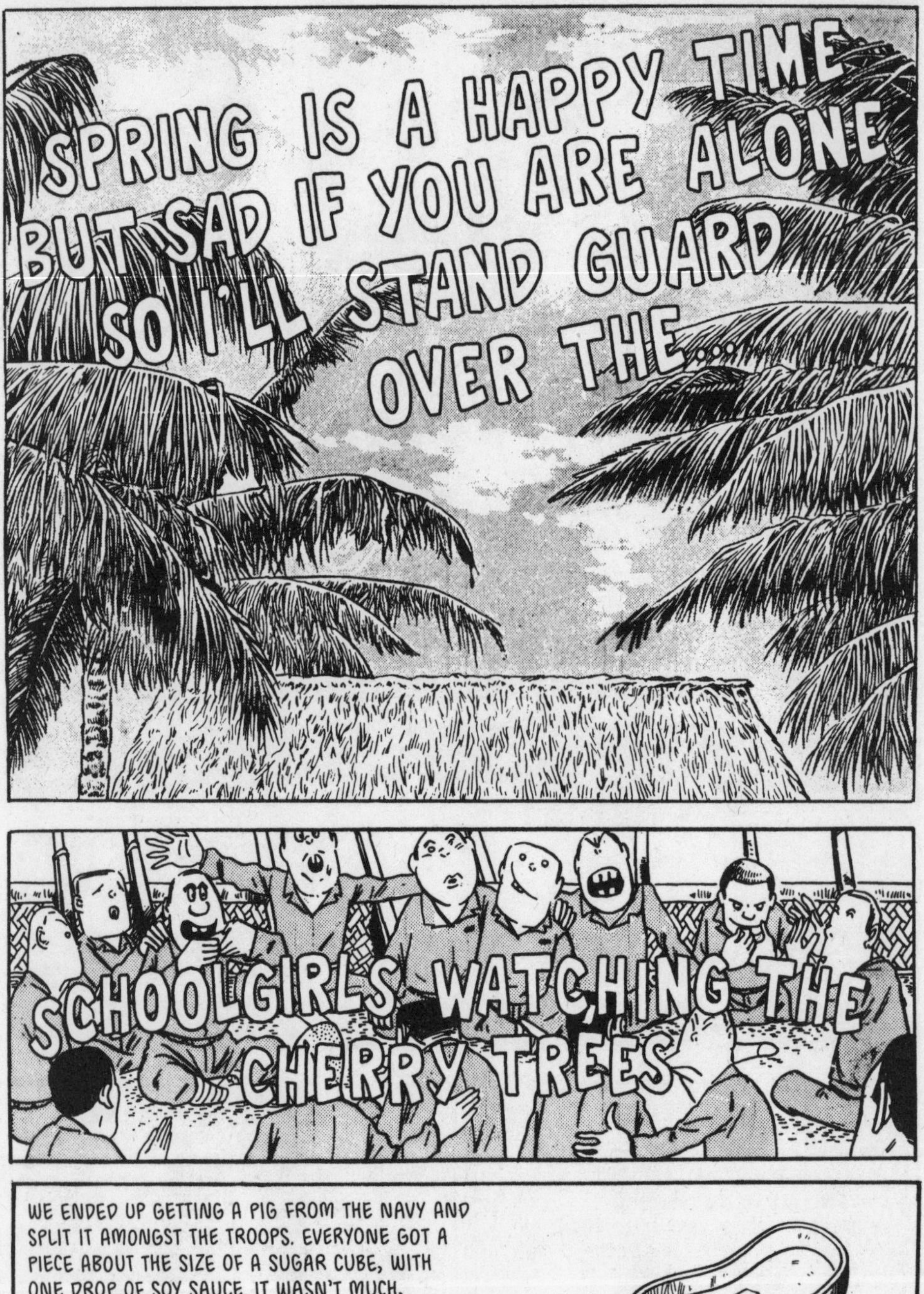
SPRING IS A HAPPY TIME
BUT SAD IF YOU ARE ALONE
SO I'LL STAND GUARD
OVER THE...
SCHOOLGIRLS WATCHING THE CHERRY TREES
WE ENDED UP GETTING A PIG FROM THE NAVY AND SPLIT IT AMONGST THE TROOPS. EVERYONE GOT A PIECE ABOUT THE SIZE OF A SUGAR CUBE, WITH ONE DROP OF SOY SAUCE. IT WASN'T MUCH, BUT IT WAS MEAT.

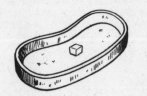

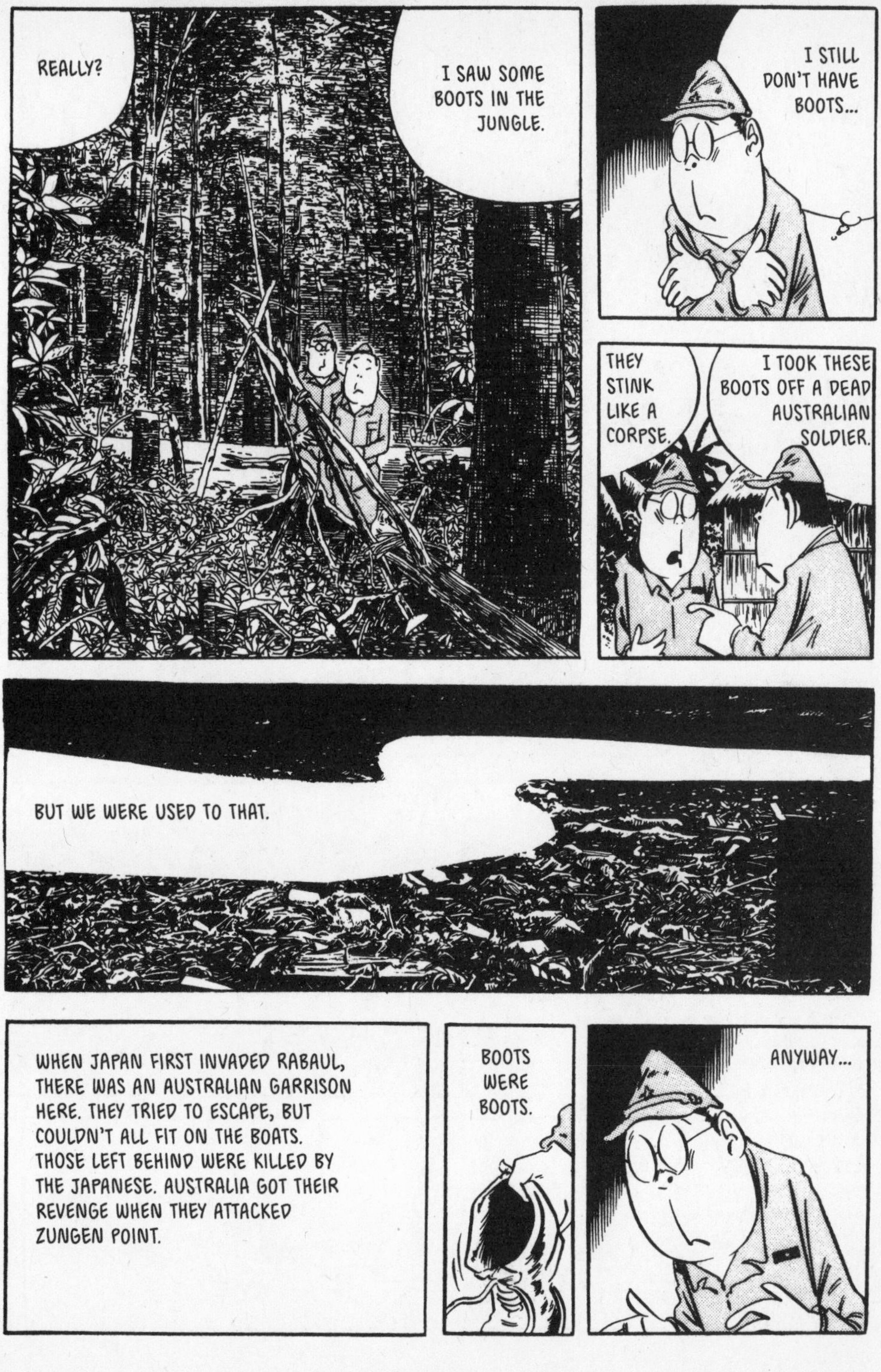
I SAW SOME BOOTS IN THE JUNGLE.
REALLY?
I STILL DON'T HAVE BOOTS...
I TOOK THESE BOOTS OFF A DEAD AUSTRALIAN SOLDIER.
THEY STINK LIKE A CORPSE.
BUT WE WERE USED TO THAT.
WHEN JAPAN FIRST INVADED RABAUL, THERE WAS AN AUSTRALIAN GARRISON HERE. THEY TRIED TO ESCAPE, BUT COULDN'T ALL FIT ON THE BOATS. THOSE LEFT BEHIND WERE KILLED BY THE JAPANESE. AUSTRALIA GOT THEIR REVENGE WHEN THEY ATTACKED ZUNGEN POINT.
BOOTS WERE BOOTS.
ANYWAY...

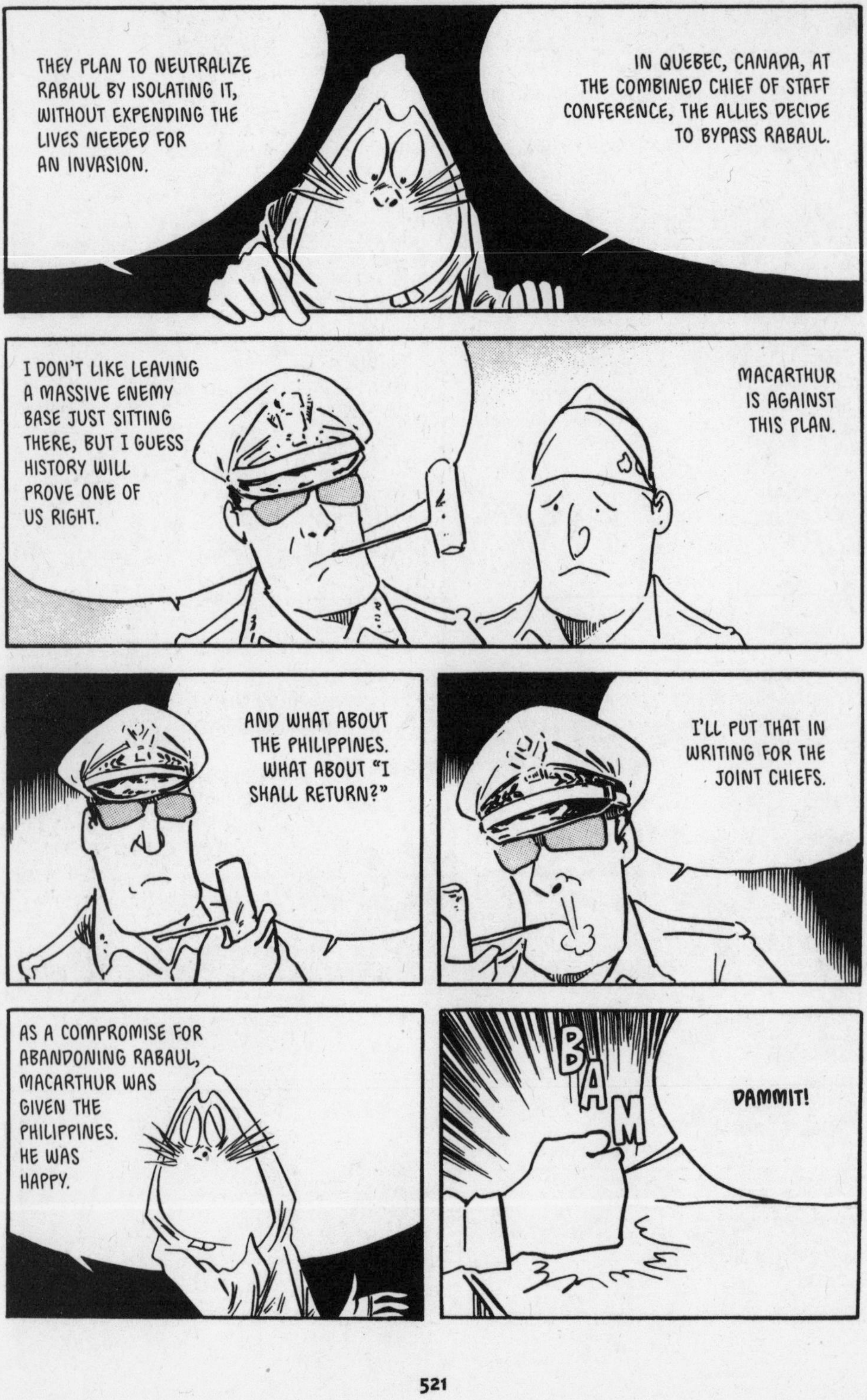
IN QUEBEC, CANADA, AT THE COMBINED CHIEF OF STAFF CONFERENCE, THE ALLIES DECIDE TO BYPASS RABAUL.
THEY PLAN TO NEUTRALIZE RABAUL BY ISOLATING IT, WITHOUT EXPENDING THE LIVES NEEDED FOR AN INVASION.
MACARTHUR IS AGAINST THIS PLAN.
I DON'T LIKE LEAVING A MASSIVE ENEMY BASE JUST SITTING THERE, BUT I GUESS HISTORY WILL PROVE ONE OF US RIGHT.
I'LL PUT THAT IN WRITING FOR THE JOINT CHIEFS.
AND WHAT ABOUT THE PHILIPPINES. WHAT ABOUT "I SHALL RETURN?"
BAM
DAMMIT!
AS A COMPROMISE FOR ABANDONING RABAUL, MACARTHUR WAS GIVEN THE PHILIPPINES. HE WAS HAPPY.

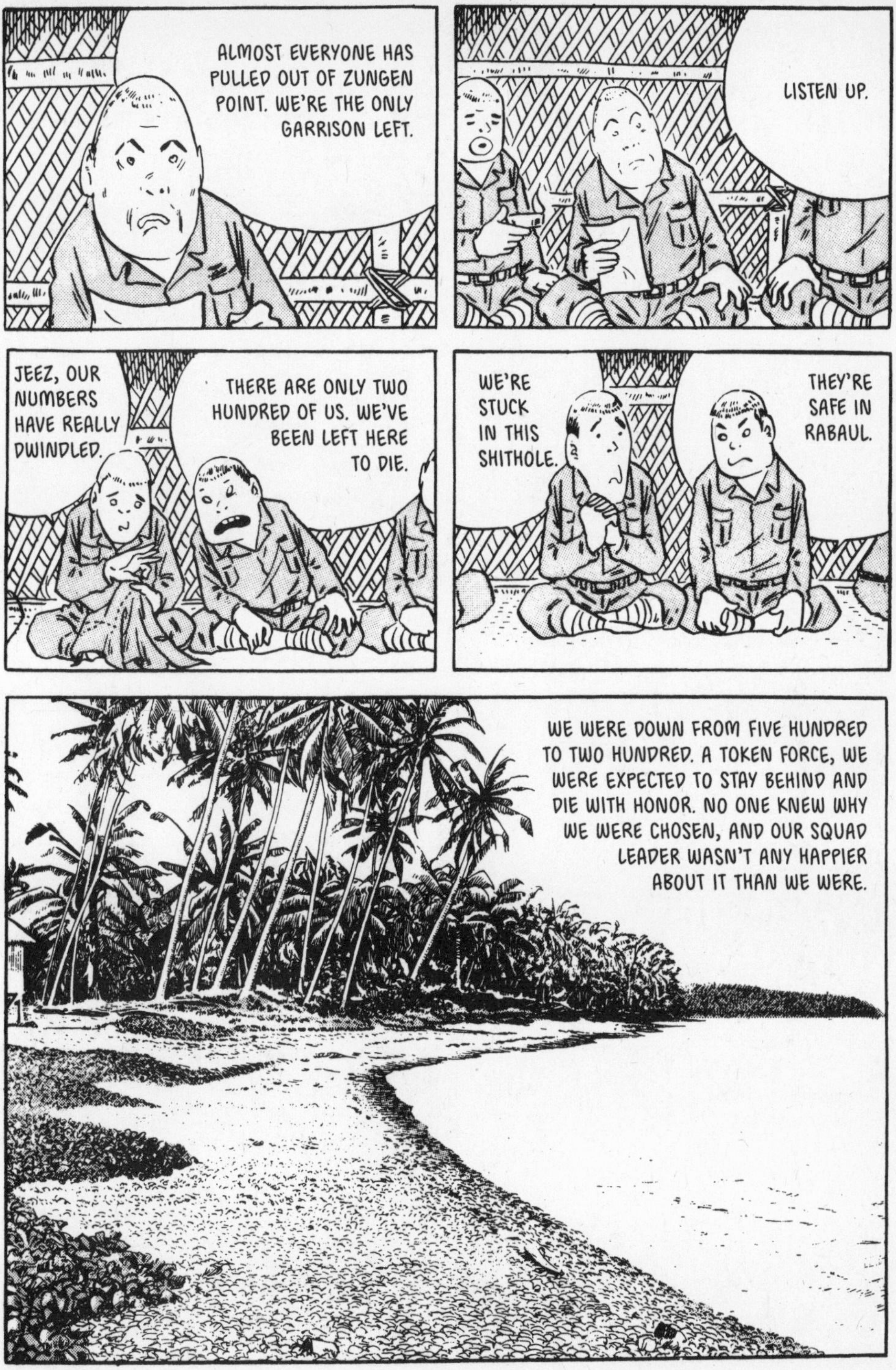
LISTEN UP.
ALMOST EVERYONE HAS PULLED OUT OF ZUNGEN POINT. WE'RE THE ONLY GARRISON LEFT.
THEY'RE SAFE IN RABAUL.
WE'RE STUCK IN THIS SHITHOLE.
THERE ARE ONLY TWO HUNDRED OF US. WE'VE BEEN LEFT HERE TO DIE.
JEEZ, OUR NUMBERS HAVE REALLY DWINDLED.
WE WERE DOWN FROM FIVE HUNDRED TO TWO HUNDRED. A TOKEN FORCE, WE WERE EXPECTED TO STAY BEHIND AND DIE WITH HONOR. NO ONE KNEW WHY WE WERE CHOSEN, AND OUR SQUAD LEADER WASN'T ANY HAPPIER ABOUT IT THAN WE WERE.

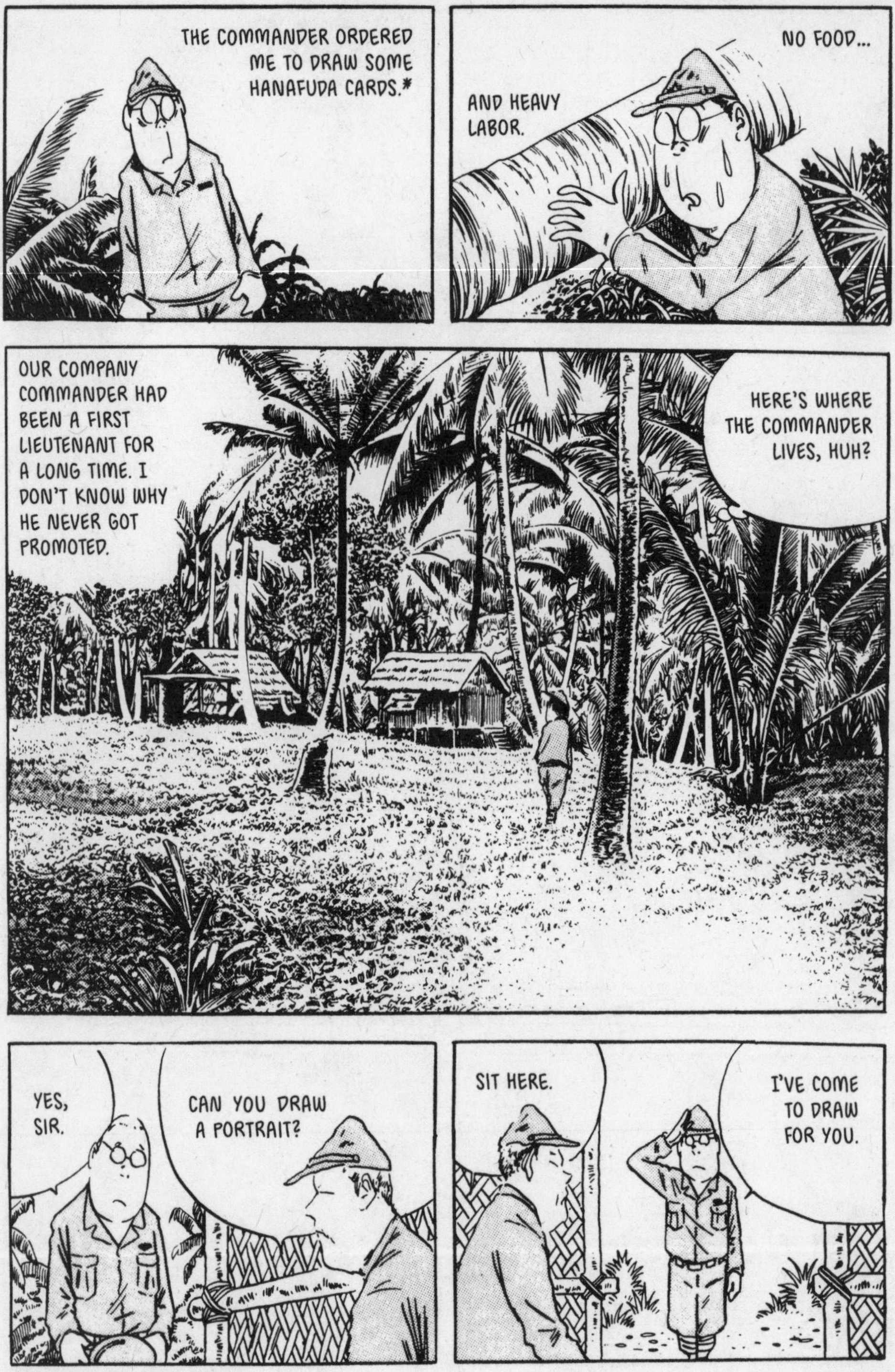
NO FOOD...
AND HEAVY LABOR.
THE COMMANDER ORDERED ME TO DRAW SOME HANAFUDA CARDS.*
HERE'S WHERE THE COMMANDER LIVES, HUH?
OUR COMPANY COMMANDER HAD BEEN A FIRST LIEUTENANT FOR A LONG TIME. I DON'T KNOW WHY HE NEVER GOT PROMOTED.
I'VE COME TO DRAW FOR YOU.
SIT HERE.
CAN YOU DRAW A PORTRAIT?
YES, SIR.

*SEE NOTE ON PAGE 548.

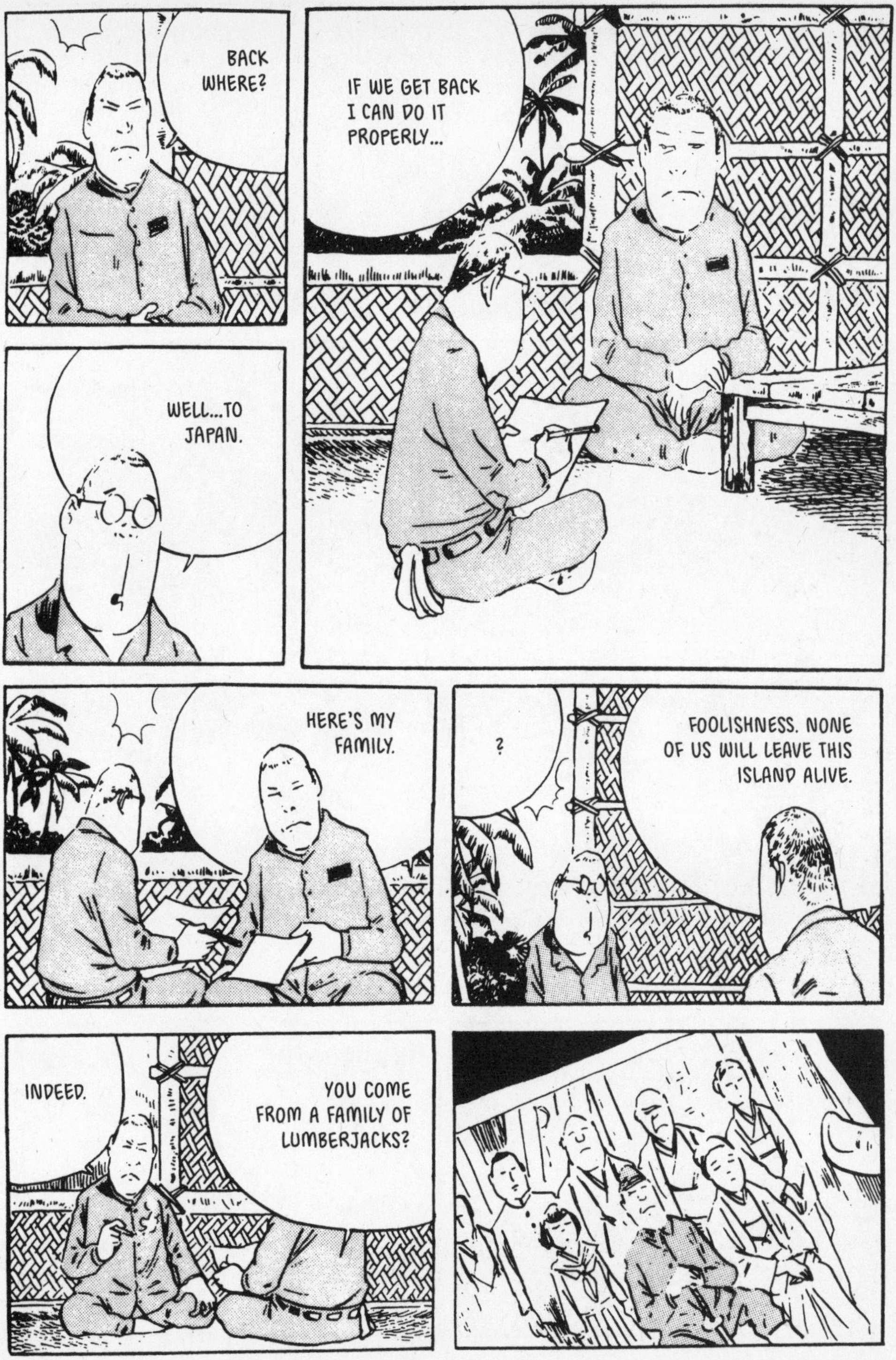
IF WE GET BACK I CAN DO IT PROPERLY...
BACK WHERE?
WELL...TO JAPAN.
FOOLISHNESS. NONE OF US WILL LEAVE THIS ISLAND ALIVE.
?
HERE'S MY FAMILY.
YOU COME FROM A FAMILY OF LUMBERJACKS?
INDEED.

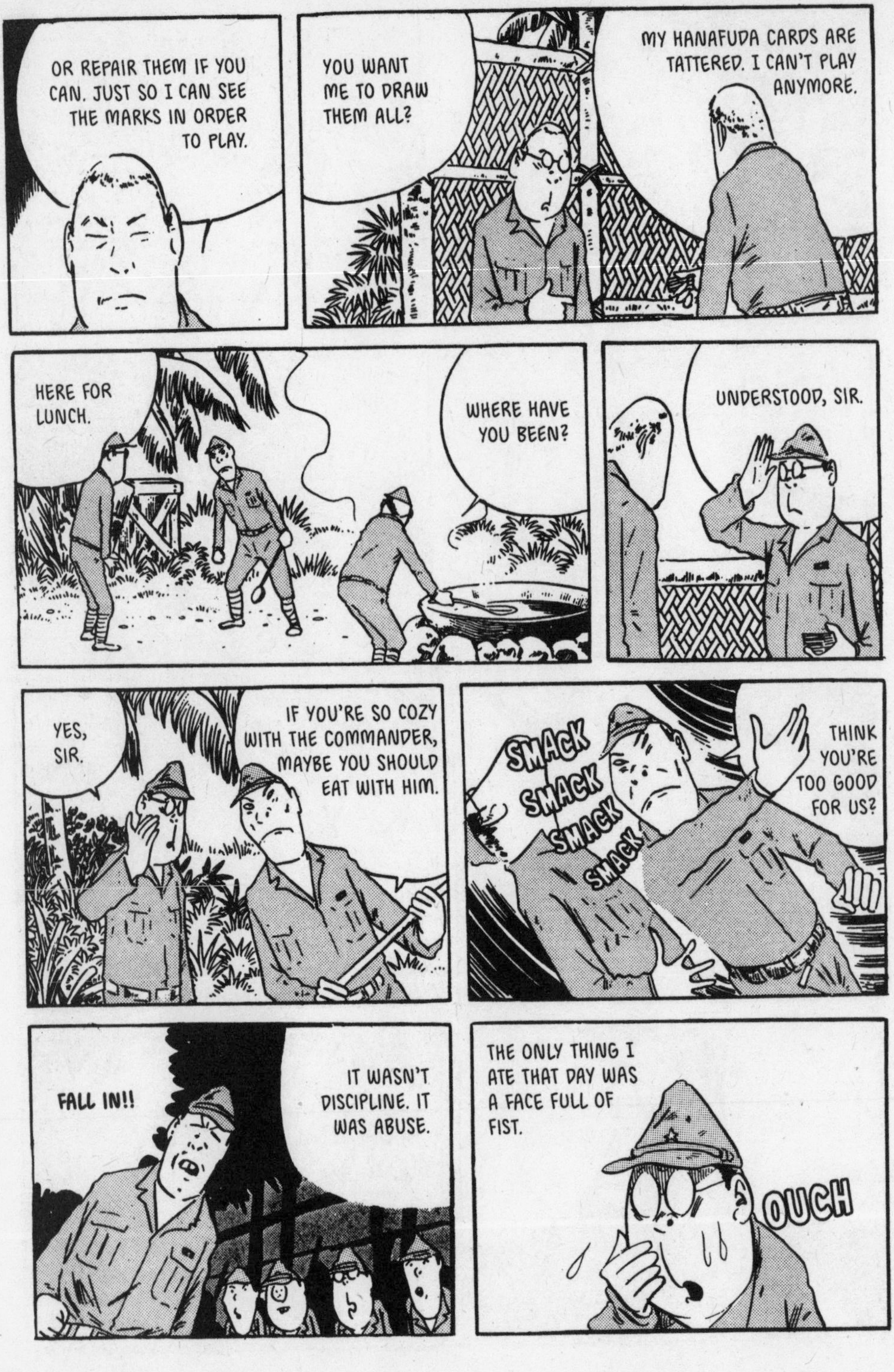
MY HANAFUDA CARDS ARE TATTERED. I CAN'T PLAY ANYMORE.
YOU WANT ME TO DRAW THEM ALL?
OR REPAIR THEM IF YOU CAN. JUST SO I CAN SEE THE MARKS IN ORDER TO PLAY.
UNDERSTOOD, SIR.
WHERE HAVE YOU BEEN?
HERE FOR LUNCH.
THINK YOU'RE TOO GOOD FOR US?
SMACK
SMACK
SMACK
SMACK
IF YOU'RE SO COZY WITH THE COMMANDER, MAYBE YOU SHOULD EAT WITH HIM.
YES, SIR.
THE ONLY THING I ATE THAT DAY WAS A FACE FULL OF FIST.
OUCH
IT WASN'T DISCIPLINE. IT WAS ABUSE.
FALL IN!!

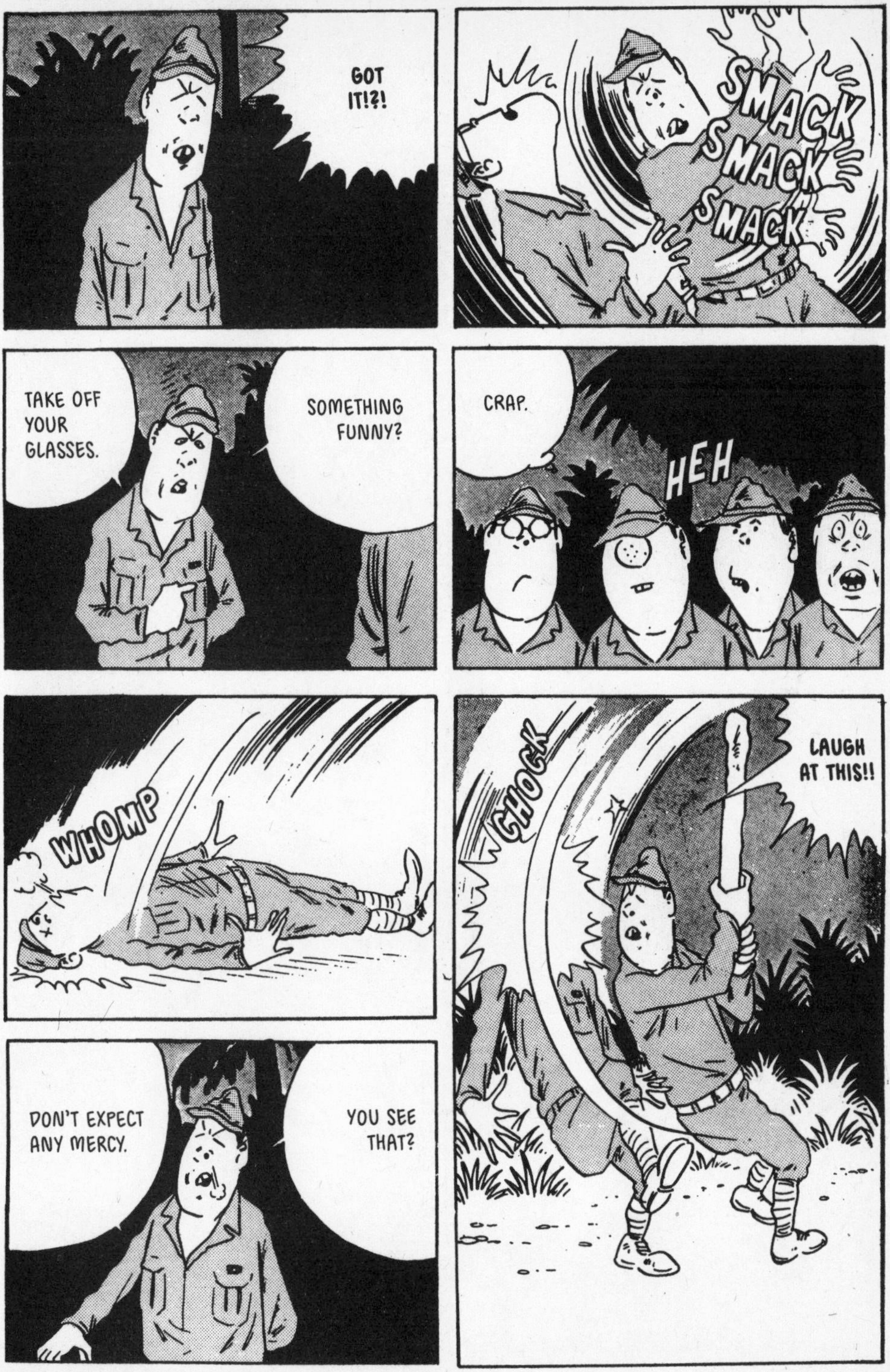
SMACK
SMACK
SMACK
GOT IT!?!
HEH
CRAP.
SOMETHING FUNNY?
TAKE OFF YOUR GLASSES.
LAUGH AT THIS!!
CHOCK
WHOMP
YOU SEE THAT?
DON'T EXPECT ANY MERCY.

BEFORE BAIEN

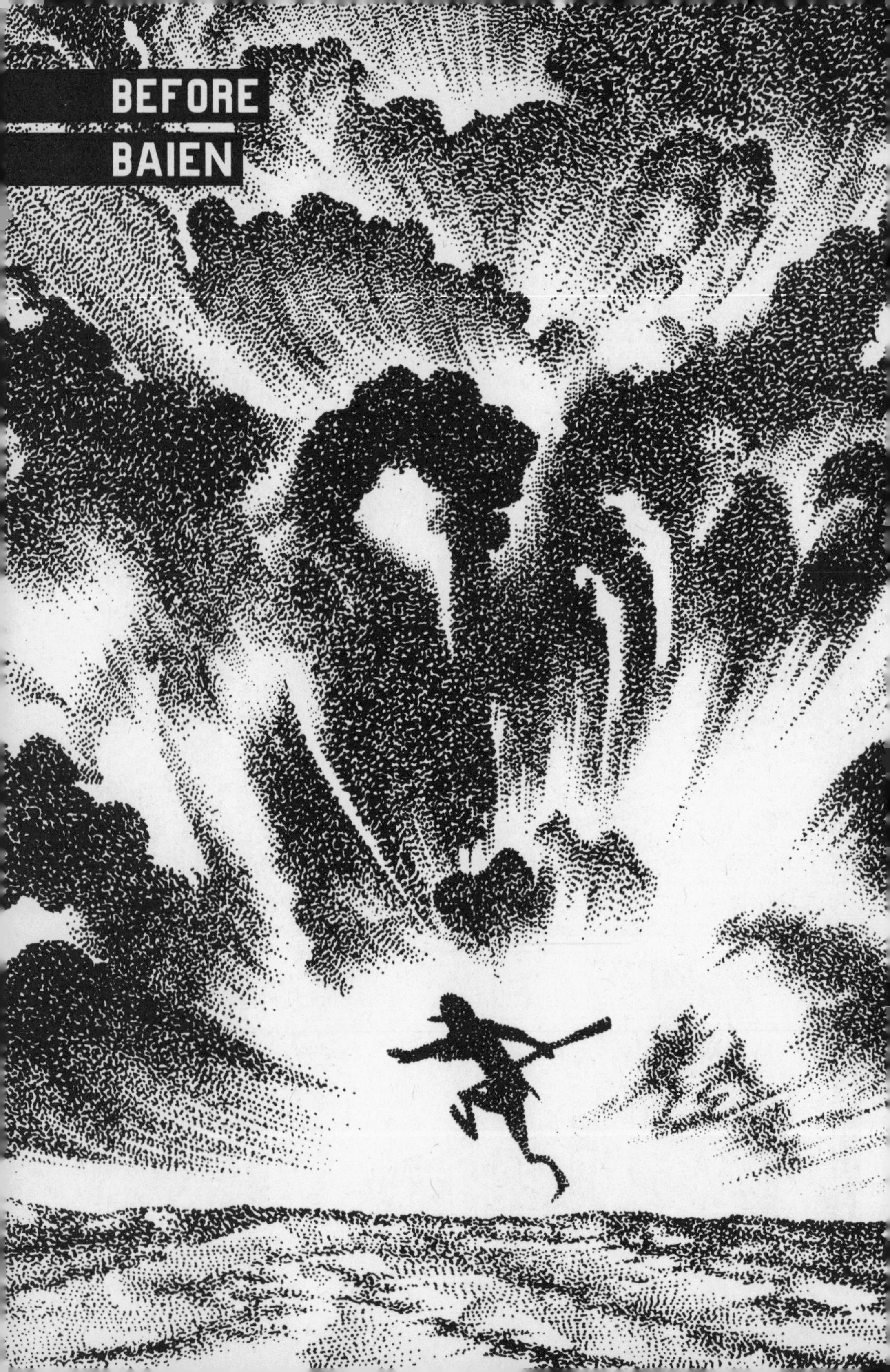

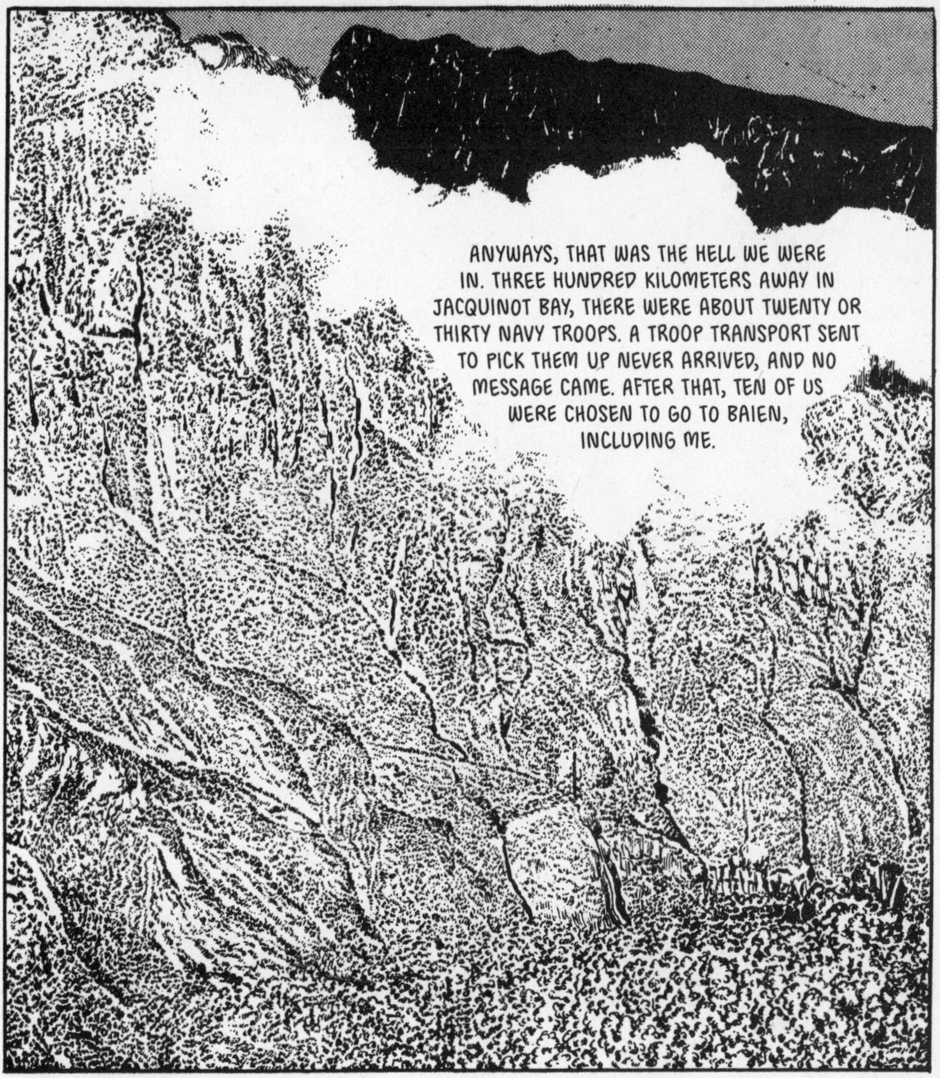
ANYWAYS, THAT WAS THE HELL WE WERE IN. THREE HUNDRED KILOMETERS AWAY IN JACQUINOT BAY, THERE WERE ABOUT TWENTY OR THIRTY NAVY TROOPS. A TROOP TRANSPORT SENT TO PICK THEM UP NEVER ARRIVED, AND NO MESSAGE CAME. AFTER THAT, TEN OF US WERE CHOSEN TO GO TO BAIEN, INCLUDING ME.

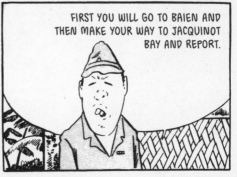

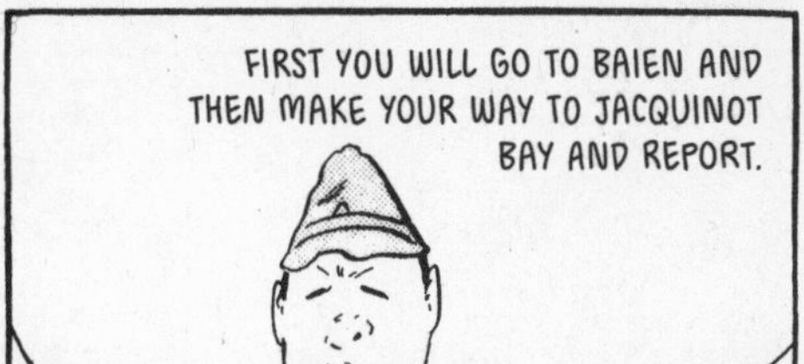
FIRST YOU WILL GO TO BAIEN AND THEN MAKE YOUR WAY TO JACQUINOT BAY AND REPORT.

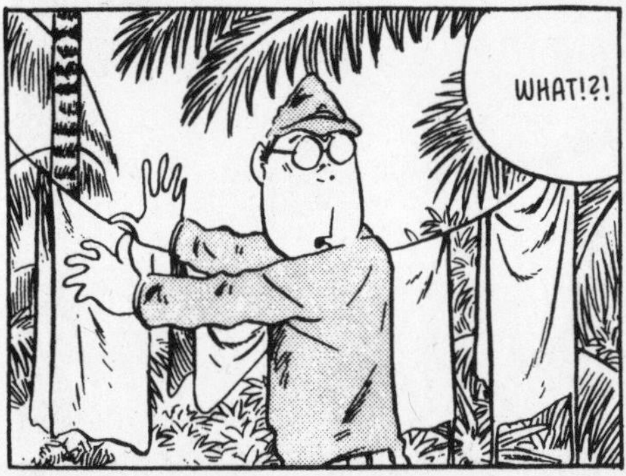
WHAT!?!

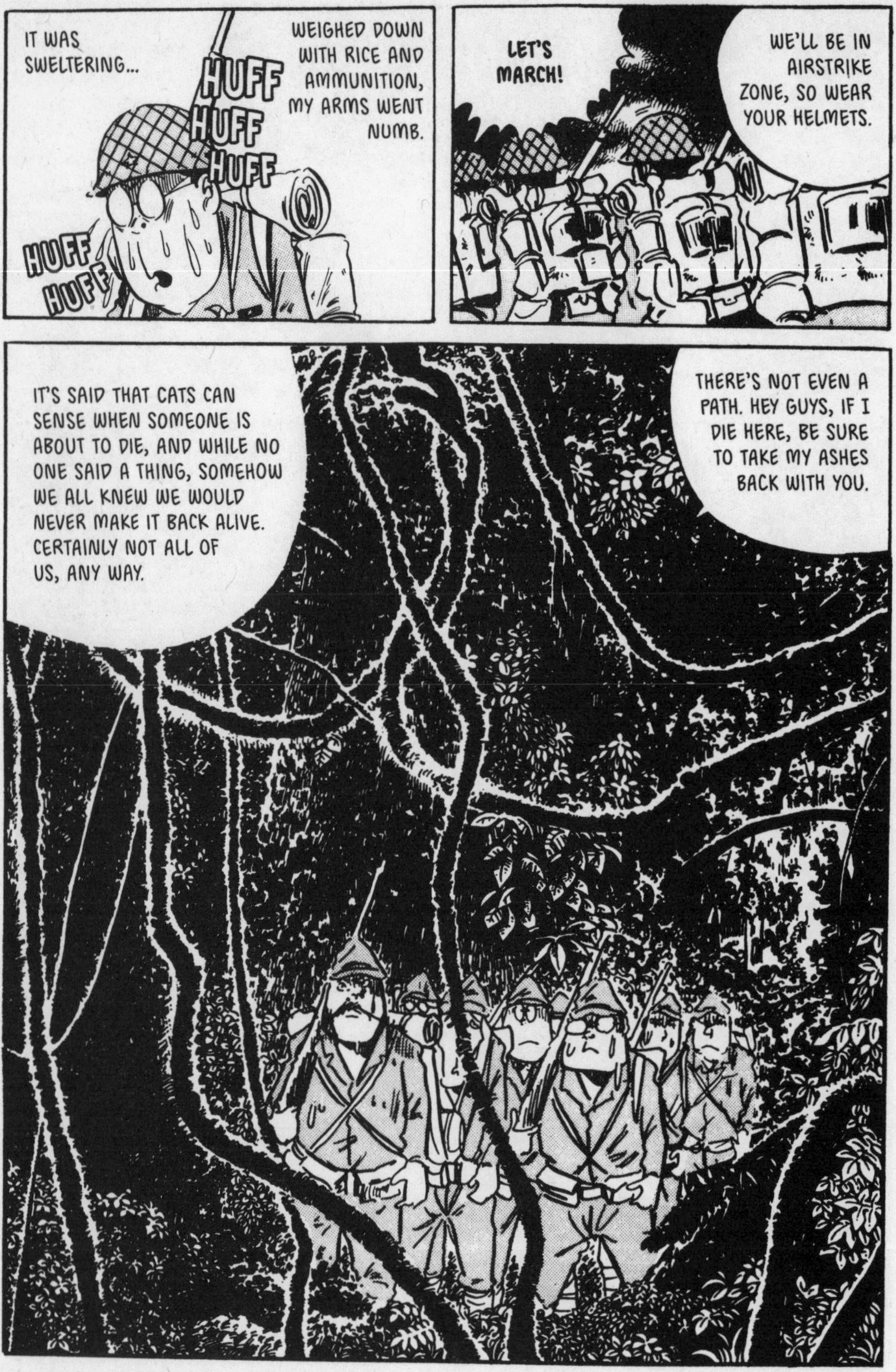
WE'LL BE IN AIRSTRIKE ZONE, SO WEAR YOUR HELMETS.
LET'S MARCH!
WEIGHED DOWN WITH RICE AND AMMUNITION, MY ARMS WENT NUMB.
IT WAS SWELTERING...
HUFF HUFF HUFF
HUFF HUFF
THERE'S NOT EVEN A PATH. HEY GUYS, IF I DIE HERE, BE SURE TO TAKE MY ASHES BACK WITH YOU.
IT'S SAID THAT CATS CAN SENSE WHEN SOMEONE IS ABOUT TO DIE, AND WHILE NO ONE SAID A THING, SOMEHOW WE ALL KNEW WE WOULD NEVER MAKE IT BACK ALIVE. CERTAINLY NOT ALL OF US, ANY WAY.

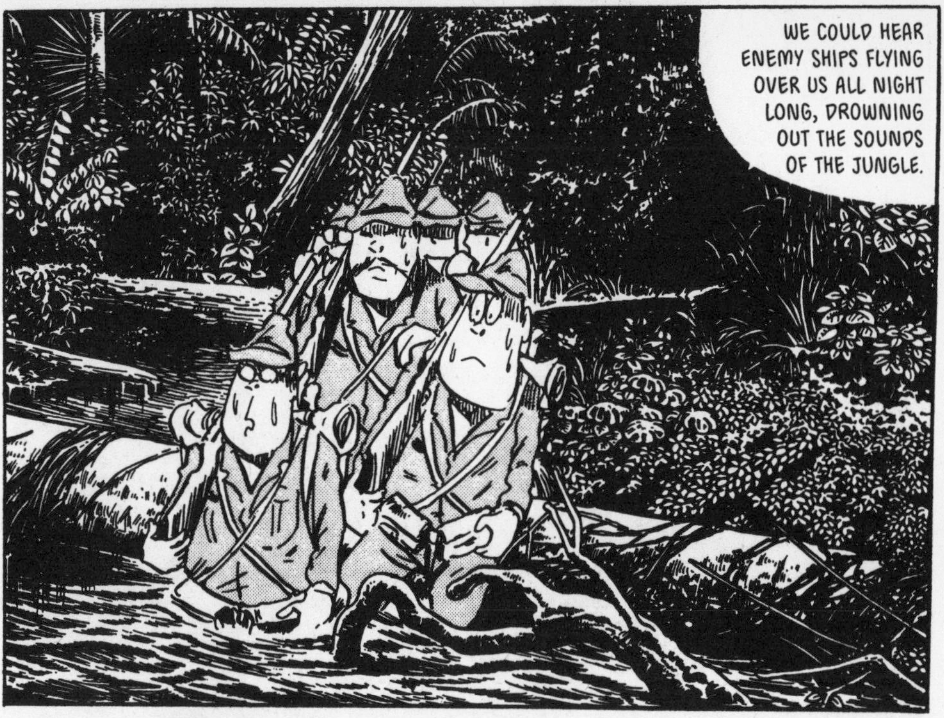
WE COULD HEAR ENEMY SHIPS FLYING OVER US ALL NIGHT LONG, DROWNING OUT THE SOUNDS OF THE JUNGLE.

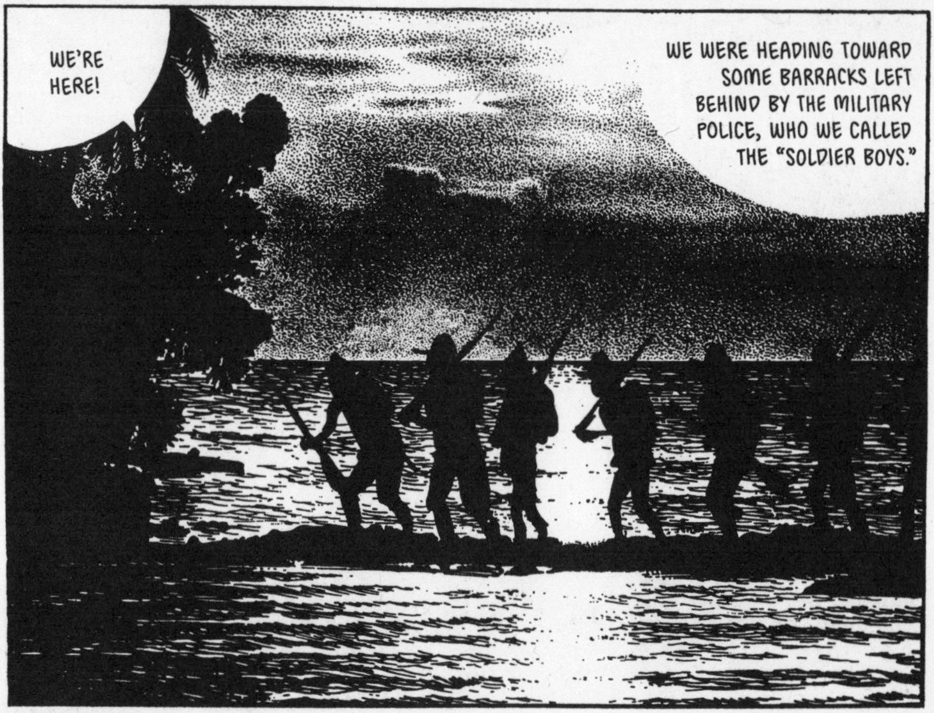
WE WERE HEADING TOWARD SOME BARRACKS LEFT BEHIND BY THE MILITARY POLICE, WHO WE CALLED THE "SOLDIER BOYS."
WE'RE HERE!

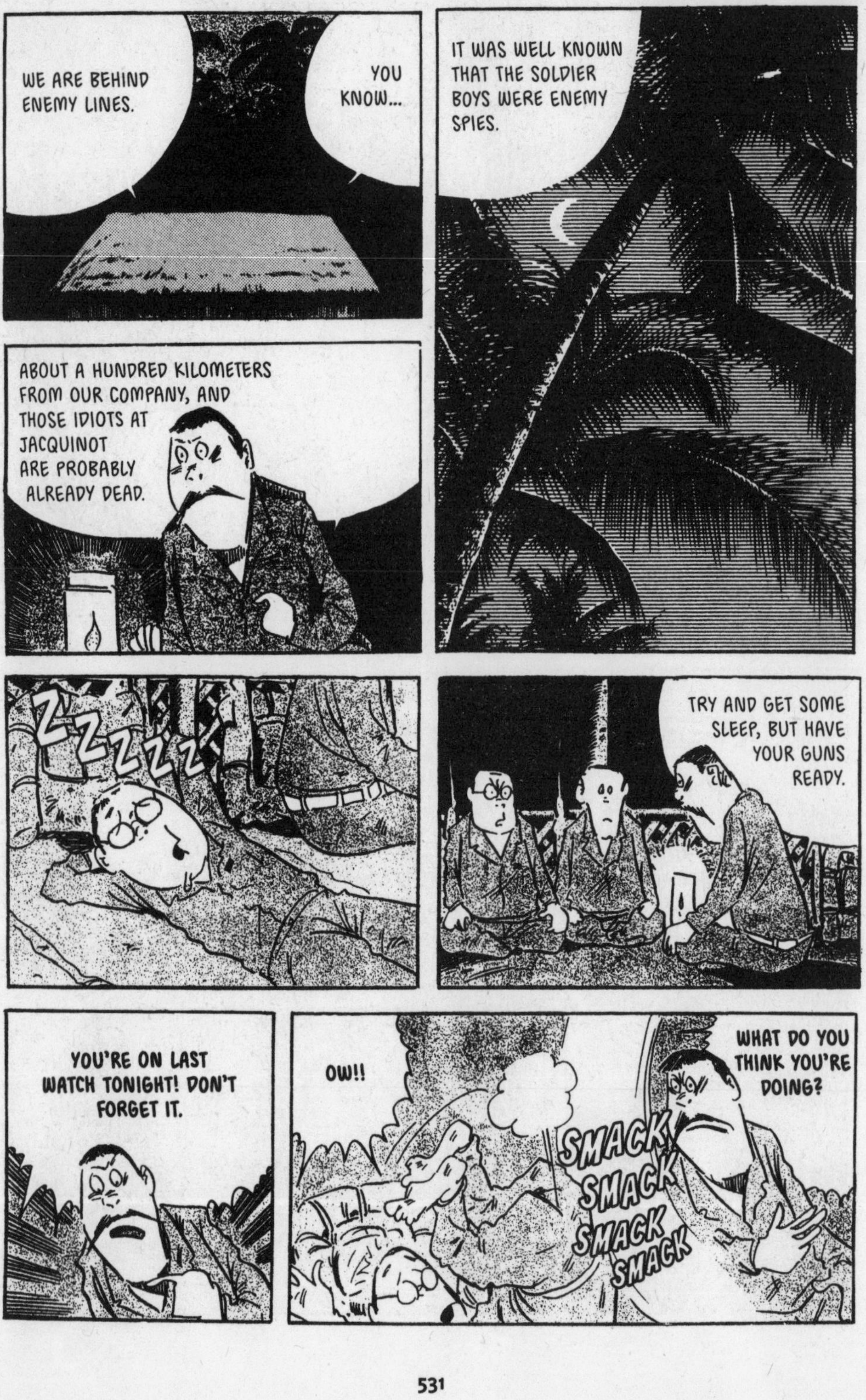
IT WAS WELL KNOWN THAT THE SOLDIER BOYS WERE ENEMY SPIES.
YOU KNOW...
WE ARE BEHIND ENEMY LINES.
ABOUT A HUNDRED KILOMETERS FROM OUR COMPANY, AND THOSE IDIOTS AT JACQUINOT ARE PROBABLY ALREADY DEAD.
TRY AND GET SOME SLEEP, BUT HAVE YOUR GUNS READY.
ZZZZZZ
WHAT DO YOU THINK YOU'RE DOING?
SMACK SMACK SMACK SMACK
OW!!
YOU'RE ON LAST WATCH TONIGHT! DON'T FORGET IT.

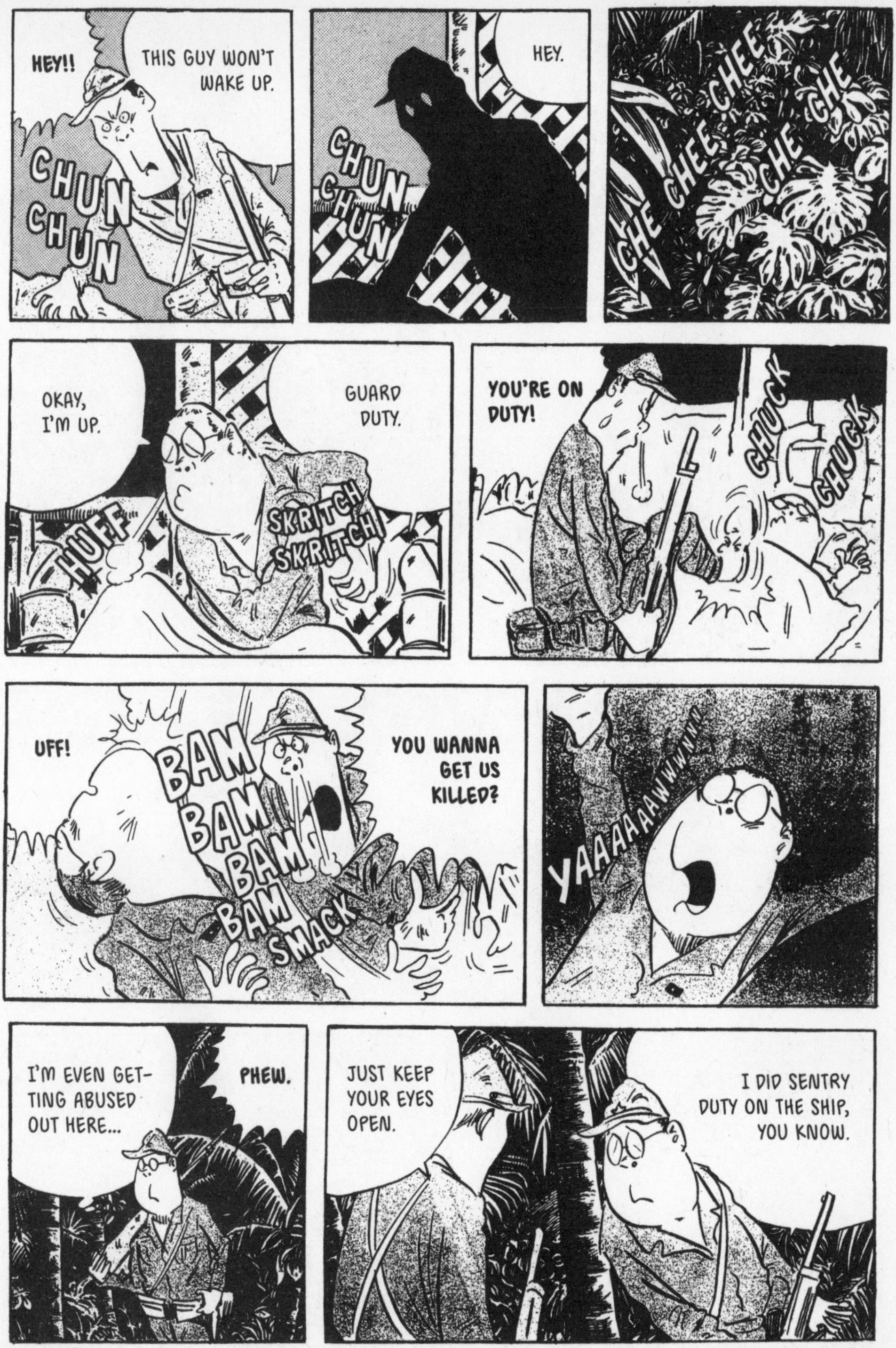
CHE CHEE CHEE
CHE CHE
HEY.
CHUN CHUN
THIS GUY WON'T WAKE UP.
HEY!!
CHUN CHUN
YOU'RE ON DUTY!
CHUCK
CHUCK
GUARD DUTY.
OKAY, I'M UP.
SKRITCH SKRITCH
HUFF
YAAAAAAWWNNN
YOU WANNA GET US KILLED?
UFF!
BAM BAM BAM BAM BAM
SMACK
I DID SENTRY DUTY ON THE SHIP, YOU KNOW.
JUST KEEP YOUR EYES OPEN.
PHEW.
I'M EVEN GET-TING ABUSED OUT HERE...

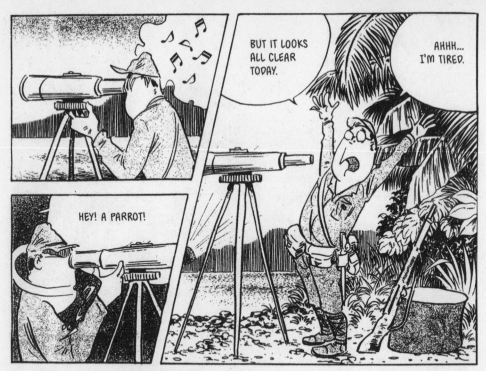

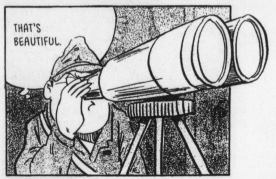

AHHH... I'M TIRED.
BUT IT LOOKS ALL CLEAR TODAY.
HEY! A PARROT!
LOOKING BACK NOW, I'M ASHAMED OF THIS MOMENT. AT TWENTY YEARS OLD, I HAD NO UNDERSTANDING OF LIFE OR DEATH. I WAS INEXPERIENCED. I DIDN'T TAKE ANYTHING SERIOUSLY. (AND MAYBE I HAVEN'T REALLY CHANGED ALL THAT MUCH...)
THAT'S BEAUTIFUL.
IF THERE IS A HEAVEN, I HOPE IT LOOKS LIKE THIS.
MY WATCH SHIFT ENDED FIVE MINUTES AGO...

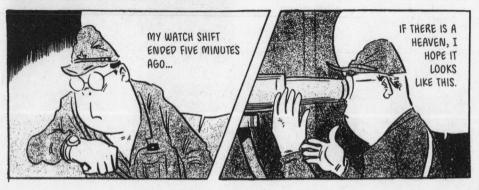

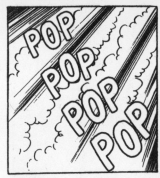

THAT DEVIL SERGEANT OF MINE...
I HAVE TO WAKE UP THAT ASSHOLE.
SHHHHHHHHH
POP POP POP POP
IS THAT FRUIT FALLING FROM THE TREES?
BA BA BA BA BA BA
BOOM
UGH
THEY'RE KILLING US!!
BAM BAM BAM
AHHHH!!

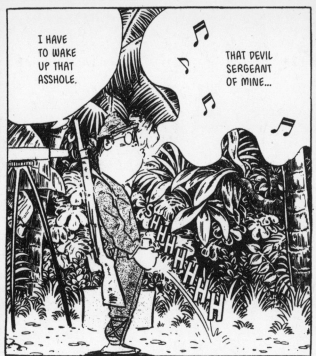

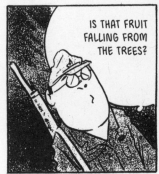

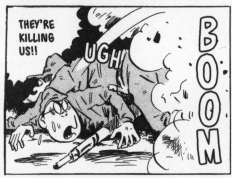

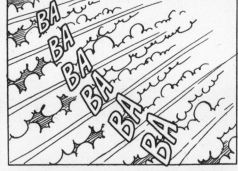

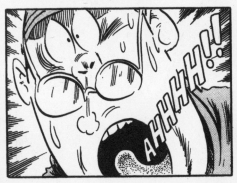

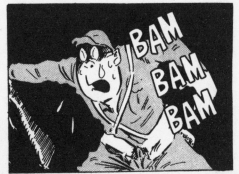

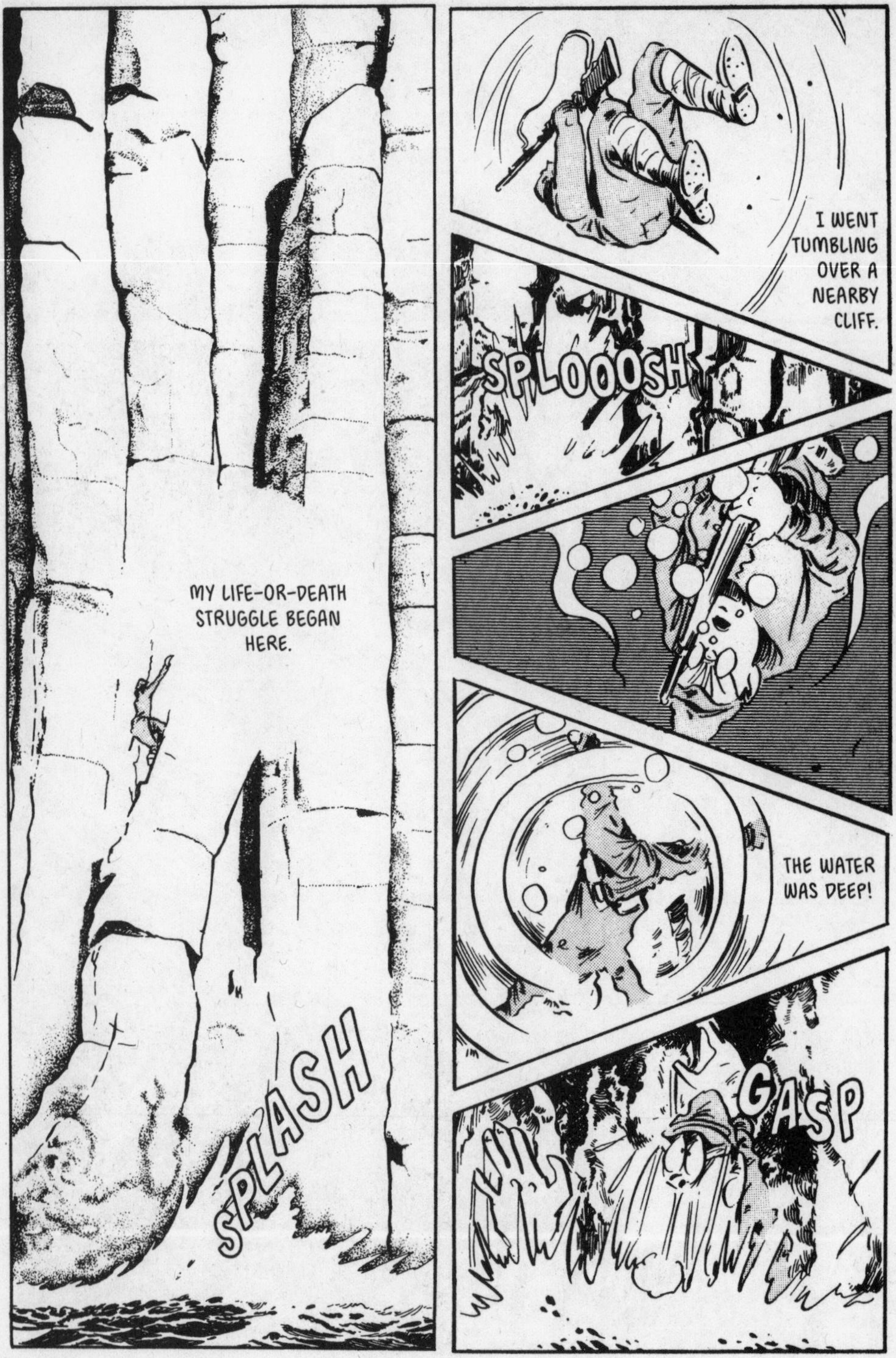
I WENT TUMBLING OVER A NEARBY CLIFF.
SPLOOOSH
THE WATER WAS DEEP!
GASP
MY LIFE-OR-DEATH STRUGGLE BEGAN HERE.
SPLASH

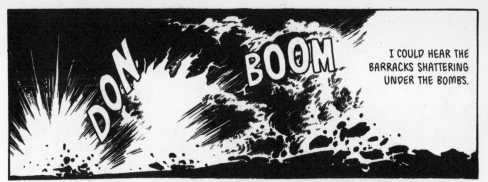

I COULD HEAR THE BARRACKS SHATTERING UNDER THE BOMBS.

I KNEW THE ENEMY WOULD KILL ME IF THEY FOUND ME. THEY DIDN'T LEAVE SURVIVORS. AND I DIDN'T EXPECT TO FIND ANYONE STILL LIVING AT JACQUINOT BAY EITHER.

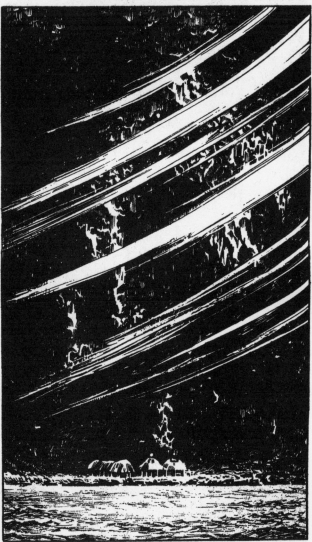

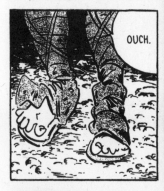

OUCH.

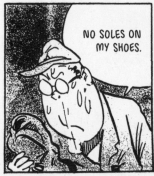

NO SOLES ON MY SHOES.

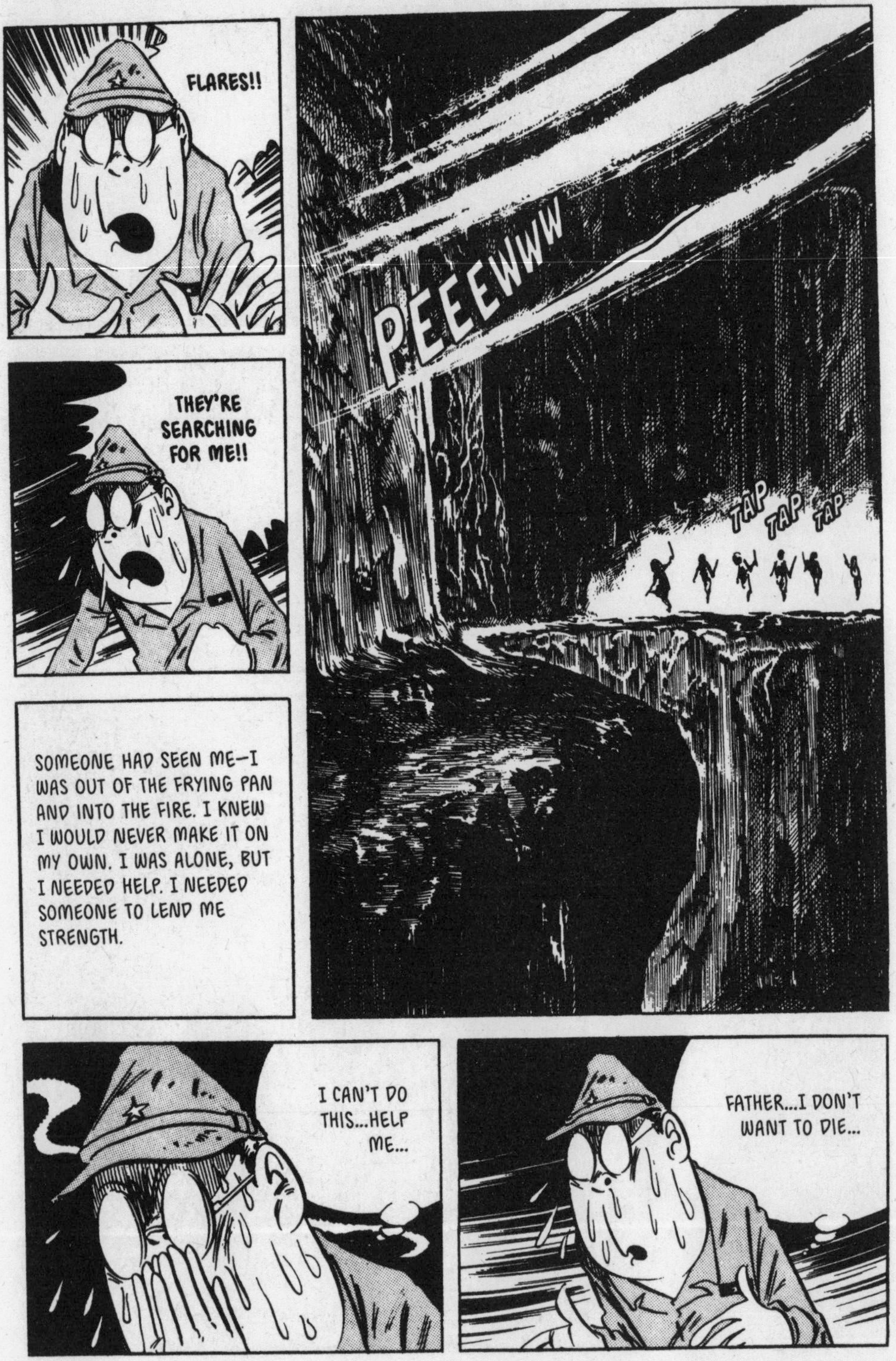
PEEEWWW
TAP TAP TAP
FLARES!!
THEY'RE SEARCHING FOR ME!!
SOMEONE HAD SEEN ME—I WAS OUT OF THE FRYING PAN AND INTO THE FIRE. I KNEW I WOULD NEVER MAKE IT ON MY OWN. I WAS ALONE, BUT I NEEDED HELP. I NEEDED SOMEONE TO LEND ME STRENGTH.
FATHER...I DON'T WANT TO DIE...
I CAN'T DO THIS...HELP ME...

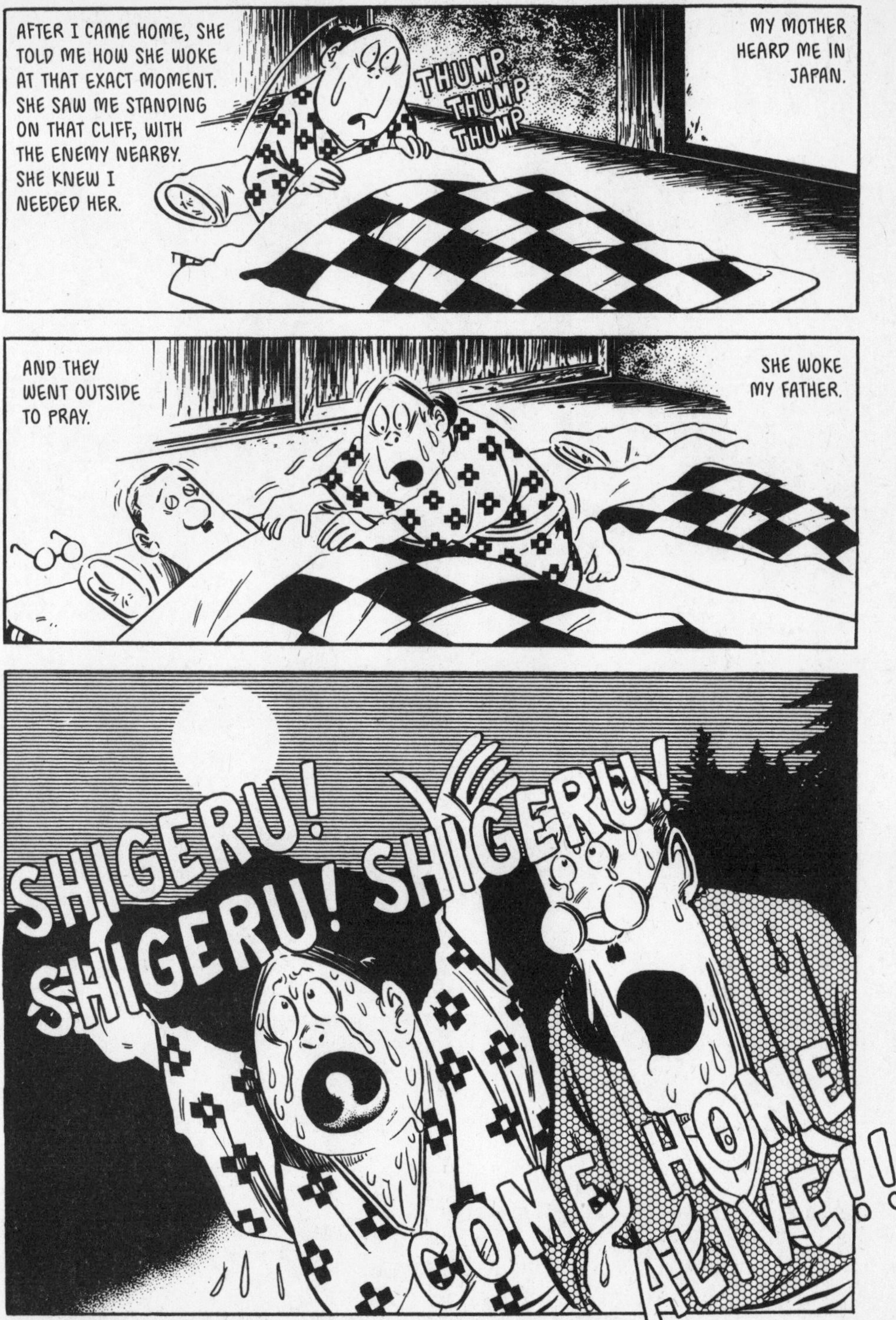
MY MOTHER HEARD ME IN JAPAN.
THUMP THUMP THUMP
AFTER I CAME HOME, SHE TOLD ME HOW SHE WOKE AT THAT EXACT MOMENT. SHE SAW ME STANDING ON THAT CLIFF, WITH THE ENEMY NEARBY. SHE KNEW I NEEDED HER.
SHE WOKE MY FATHER.
AND THEY WENT OUTSIDE TO PRAY.
SHIGERU!
SHIGERU!
SHIGERU!
COME HOME ALIVE!!

STORY CONTINUES IN *SHOWA 1944–1953*.

NOTES

16 Meiji Restoration: (1853–1868) A series of uprisings and events that began with the arrival of Commodore Matthew Perry from the US and culminated in the overthrow of the Tokugawa shogunate and the restoration of imperial rule under the figurehead of Emperor Meiji. This ended Japan's two hundred year policy of strict isolationism.

17 Tenshin Okura: (1863–1913) b. Kanagawa Prefecture. Art historian. Founded the Japan Art Institute. Taught artists Yakoyama Taikan and Hishida Shunso. Published *The Book of Tea* and *Ideals of the Orient*, and introduced Asian and Japanese art and culture to the world.

17 Toten Miyazaki: (1871–1922) b. Kumamoto Prefecture. Philosopher. Pondered deeply on the future of China and Asia. Supported Chinese revolutionary Sun Yat-sen, and was instrumental in the Xinhai Revolution.

19 Wang Jingwei: (1883–1944) b. Sanshui District. Chinese politician. Revolutionary. Along with Sun Yat-sen and Chiang Kai-shek, the driving force behind the Xinhai Revolution and a leader in the Kuomintang. During the Second Sino-Japanese War, signed the Sino-Japanese Treaty and joined forces with Japan. Established the Reorganized National Government of China.

19 Prince Konoe Fumimaro: (1891–1945) b. Tokyo City. Politician. Prince. Elected Prime Minister three times between 1938–1941 (Showa 13–16). A political leader in pre-war Japan. Committed suicide immediately following Japan's defeat.

20 Provisional Government of the Republic of China: From 1937–1939 (Showa 12–14), a puppet government covering Northern and Central China under the control of Japan's military authorities.

23 Chiang Kai-shek: (1887–1975) b. Xikou. Chinese Militant. Politician. Succeeded Sun Yat-sen as leader of the Kuomintang Nationalist Party (KMT). After World War Two, he lost the Chinese Civil War and retreated to Taiwan, where he ruled as the self-declared President of the Republic of China.

34 Continental: This was a popular phrase at the time. It meant someone who couldn't pay attention to details, who only saw things as big as a continent.

36 Nippon Air: A joint sponsorship with Tokyo's *Hibi* and Osaka's *Mainichi* newspapers, the *Japan Air* did one circuit around the globe. The plane took off from Haneda airport on August 1939 (Showa 14) and returned in October.

40 Graveyard scraps: Shigeru is referring to food left as offerings to the dead in graveyards. According to tradition, this food is holy and consumed by the dead. In practice, it was often eaten by Japan's homeless population.

47 Adolf Hitler: (1889–1945) German politician. Leader of the Nazi Party after Paul von Hindenburg. Appointed Chancellor of Germany and Führer in 1934 (Showa 9), and later became a dictator. During Germany's defeat in World War Two, Hitler committed suicide.

47 Benito Mussolini: (1883–1945) Italian politician. Leader of the Fascist party. Becomes dictator of Italy in 1922 (Taisho 11), and inspires Fascist leaders in other countries. In World War Two, allies Italy with Germany and Japan. Executed by firing squad at the end of the war.

48 Francisco Franco: (1892–1975) Spanish militarist. Politician. Leads a rebellion against the Popular Front government in 1936 (Showa 11), wins the civil war in 1939 (Showa 14). He establishes himself as Generalissimo of Spain, a position he holds until death.

49 Comintern: The foreign Communist party. In 1919 (Taisho 8) under Lenin, the Soviets worked to establish an international Communist community.

53 Hiroshi Oshima: (1886–1975) b. Gifu Prefecture. Army Lieutenant General. Ambassador to Germany.

53 Yonai Mitsumasa: (1880–1948) b. Iwate Prefecture. Admiral. Prime Minister. Opposed to the Tripartite Pact. A leading critic of the Pacific War.

53 Yamamoto Isoroku: (1884–1943) b. Nigata Prefecture. Admiral of the Fleet. Commander in Chief of the combined fleet during World War Two. Killed in flight over the Solomon Islands in 1943 (Showa 18).

55 Hiranuma Kichiro: (1867–1952) b. Okayama Prefecture. Elected to Prime Minister January, 1939 (Showa 14). Resigns with his cabinet in August of that same year.

57 Matsuoka Yosuke: (1880–1946) b. Yamaguchi Prefecture. Politician. Diplomat. Presides over Japan's withdrawal from the League of Nations in 1933 (Showa 8). Later, served as Minister of Foreign Affairs.

59 Sensei: An honorific used in Japanese that literally means "One who is born before me" and (very) roughly translates as "teacher." It is used as a title for craftsmen and artists who have achieved a high level of mastery. Because of the esteem the Japanese people have for Shigeru Mizuki, he is never directly addressed by his name and is always called Sensei.

62 Futabayama Sadaji: (1912–1968) b. Oita Prefecture. Yokozuna. Winner of twelve tournament championships. His sixty-nine-bout winning streak is the longest in sumo history. After the war, becomes head of the Japan Sumo Association.

71 The Imperial Rule Assistance Association: Established 1940 (Showa 15) by Prime Minister Konoe Fumimaro. Attempted to force national unity through government control. Dissolved on June 13, 1945 (Showa 20).

73 Ozaki Hotsumi: (1901–1944) b. Gifu Prefecture. Journalist. Advisor to Konoe Fumimaro. Implicated in the Sorge Incident and executed.

74 Showa Research Association: Established in 1936 (Showa 11). Political think tank staffed with scholars and industry and community leaders who discuss Japan's politics. Dissolved in 1940 (Showa 15) following the establishment of the Imperial Rule Assistance Association.

75 Cabinet Planning Board: 1937 (Showa 12). A government organization established to shepherd Japan's economy through wartime. 1943 (Showa 18): merged with the Ministry of Munitions.

77 *The Nihon Shoki*: Translated as *Chronicles of Japan*, *The Nihon Shoki* is the second oldest book on Japanese history. The book was largely a propaganda tool, and mixes fact and fiction. It gives an apocryphal account of early emperors and their divine connections starting with the mythical Jimmu, called the first Emperor of Japan, a direct descendant of the sun goddess, Amaterasu. This was taught as fact in Japan until the end of World War Two, when Emperor Hirohito was required to renounce his divinity.

78 Motoori Norinaga: (1730–1801) b. Mie Prefecture. An Edo period scholar of Kokugaku, which is essentially "Japaneseness." Kokugaku taught the uniqueness of the Japanese people, and was used during World War Two to justify Japan's dominance over the other Asian races. Glorifying the "falling cherry blossoms" is a metaphor for soldiers. A national symbol of Japan, cherry blossoms bloom only for a short time before they wither and fall. Cherry blossoms and soldiers share in common a life that is "short but beautiful."

83 Hideki Tojo: (1884–1948) b. Tokyo city. General of the Imperial Japanese Army. During the War, elected to Prime Minister and Army Minister. President of the Army General Staff. Nagata Tetsuzan's successor to leadership of the Tosei Control Faction. After the war, tried by the Tokyo Tribunal as a Class-A war criminal, and executed by hanging.

83 In Mizuki Shigeru's comic *Ge ge ge no Kitaro*, Nezumi Otoko is known for his terrible stench.

86 Joseph Stalin: (1878–1953) Soviet politician. Dictator. Succeeded Lenin as head of the Communist party in 1922 (Taisho 11). Ruthlessly eliminated any opposition to his rule. Played a pivotal role in World War Two by opposing Nazi forces.

86 Vyacheslav Molotov: (1890–1986) Russian politician. Stalin's right-hand man. Active in foreign diplomacy. After Stalin's death, expelled from the Communist party and banished.

93 Kwantung Army: Before the war, an army group of the Imperial Japanese Army stationed in Manchuria. Responsible for several actions designed to advance Japan's control of Manchuria.

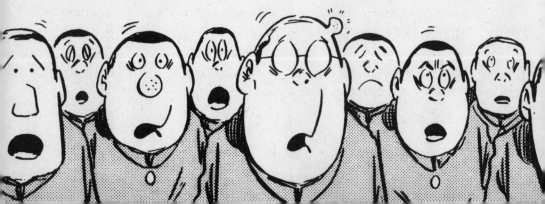

101 Franklin D. Roosevelt: (1882–1945) American politician. President. Overcomes the Great Depression with his New Deal policy. A crucial leader in the Allied victory.

101 Winston Churchill: (1874–1965) British politician. Raised to Prime Minister during World War Two, Churchill oversaw the Allied victory.

104 Nomura Kichisaburo: (1877–1964) b. Wakayama Prefecture. Navy Admiral. Foreign Minister. Ambassador to the US during the Pacific War, engaged in Japanese-American peace negotiations.

104 Cordell Hull: (1871–1955) American politician. Secretary of State at the start of World War Two. Received the Nobel Peace Prize in 1945.

126 Togo Shigenori: (1882–1950) b. Kagoshima Prefecture. Diplomat. Minister of Foreign Affairs at the time of the attack on Pearl Harbor. Tried as a Class-A war criminal and sentenced to twenty years. Died of cholecystitis while in prison.

126 Shimada Shigetaro: (1883–1976) b. Tokyo city. Navy Admiral. Minister of the Navy in Tojo's cabinet. Tried as a Class-A war criminal and sentenced to life imprisonment.

126 Muto Akira: (1892–1948) b. Kumamoto Prefecture. Adjunct General to the Army during the war. Hanged as a Class-A war criminal.

128 December 7, 1941: Although it is the United State's "Day of Infamy," due to datelines and calendar differences Japan considers the attack to have taken place on December 8.

136 Nagumo Chuichi: (1887–1944) b. Yamagata Prefecture. Militarist. Navy Admiral. Fleet Commander of the Kido Butai Carrier Strike Force during the attack on Pearl Harbor. Committed suicide during the Battle of Saipan.

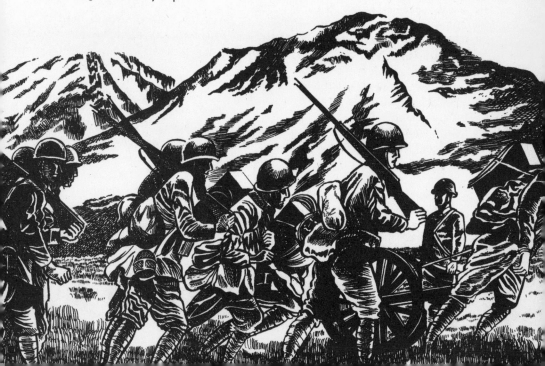

144 Classification of military rankings:

Private (E-1): The raw recruits. They get smacked around every day for about a year.

Private (E-2): A little toughened up, but still pretty green.

Private first-class: They call these guys *kami sama* (see note on page 548). In charge of doing the smacking.

Lance Corporal: One step above private first-class, sometimes promoted to squad leader. Also called *kami sama*.

Corporal: Most of the squad leaders are this rank.

Sergeant: The guys who know everything about military life.

Master Sergeant: In charge of personnel affairs and supplies. The real *kami sama*.

Warrant Officer: The biggest loudmouths of the commissioned officers.

Second Lieutenant: Usually a platoon leader with around forty men.

Lieutenant: Usually a company commander with around two hundred men.

Captain: A company commander with seniority.

Major: Usually a battalion commander with around seven to eight hundred men.

Lieutenant Colonel: When you get here, you can relax a little.

Colonel: A military commander with around three thousand men.

Major General: A brigade commander. Called Your Excellency.

Lieutenant General: Also a brigade commander. Held in high regard.

General: There are lots of Lieutenant Generals, but few Generals.

150 Songkhla: Also known as Singora, a city in Southern Thailand near the Malaysian border.

150 Patani: A southern region made up of the Pattani, Yala, and Narathiwat provinces, as well as part of Songkhla.

156 Empire Day: Now known as "National Foundation Day," Empire Day is an annual holiday that takes place on February 11 and celebrates the foundation of Japan and its first ruler, Emperor Jimmu.

165 Lieutenant-General Takuma Nishimura: (1899–1951) b. Fukuoka Prefecture. Commander of the Imperial Guard Division during the Malayan campaign. Tried as a war criminal for his role in the Sook Ching massacre and the Parit Sulong massacre by the Australian military tribunal on Manus Island, and executed by hanging.

178 General Douglas MacArthur: (1880–1964) American militarist. Field Marshal of the Army. Commander of the American Far East Forces at the beginning of the war. After the war, became Supreme Commander of the Allied Powers and de facto ruler of Japan. In 1953 (Showa 18), he was dismissed from service and sent back to the US.

183 Tsuji Masanobu: (1902–1968) b. Ishikawa Prefecture. Army staff officer specializing in tactics and strategies. Active post-war as a politician and advisor. In 1961 (Showa 36), went missing in Laos and was officially declared dead seven years later, presumed a casualty of the Laotian Civil War.

195 Rabaul: A city on the northwest edge of New Britain, Papua New Guinea. Used by Japanese military as their southern headquarters during World War Two.

195 Seneca: (4 BCE–CE 65) Roman era Stoic philosopher. Author of many books. Forced to commit suicide after arousing the displeasure of the Emperor Nero.

195 Johann Wolfgang von Goethe: (1749–1832) German poet and writer. Along with Johann Christoph Friedrich von Schille, created the philosophy of Weimar Classicism. Author of *The Sorrows of Young Werther* and *Faust*.

205 Otori Shima: This means "Great Bird Island." The island was so named because the Japanese thought Wake Island was bird-shaped. In a bit of sad irony, later in the war starving Japanese troops are thought to have eaten to extinction an endemic bird, the Wake Island Rail.

209 Commissioned Education Officer: During the war, all students after elementary school underwent military training. A special active duty officer was assigned to oversee the training.

212 Imamura Hitoshi: (1886–1968) b. Miyagi Prefecture. Commander of the sixteenth Army during the Dutch East Indies campaign. Jailed as a war criminal, but released after ten years.

221 Sukarno: (1901–1970) Indonesian politician. President. Fought for the independence of Indonesia. Influential in the founding of the Republic of Indonesia, and is known as the Father of Indonesia. Elected first President of Indonesia. Served until retirement in 1967.

222 Air raid drills: During air raid drills, all houses went into total blackout so that incoming bombers couldn't locate their targets. This was practiced by all countries involved in World War Two.

224 Aung San: (1915–1947) Burmese politician. Leader of independence movement. Assassinated in 1947, just before Burma won its independence from Britain.

225 Ba Maw: (1893–1977) Burmese politician. Leader of independence movement. With Japan's help, established the independent State of Burma and became its first head of state.

240 Parade our Battleships: This refers to an official Naval Review, usually performed for the Prime Minister, to demonstrate the power of the fleet.

242 Mitsubishi G4M: A special Naval aircraft used for troop transport.

267 "When a spring breeze blows, I lose my mind:" This phrase has no special meaning. They are just making Shigeru Mizuki do something embarrassing.

272 This song is based on a popular tune from the Kyoto pleasure districts, written in 1896. The original song plays through all of the seasons and celebrates Kyoto's famous four seasons. During World War Two, it was adapted into a soldier's marching song, and the lyrics were changed.

273 Sentinels: Soldiers assigned to the barracks gates, ostensibly for protection, but in practice as ceremonial guards.

286 Chester Nimitz: (1885–1966) American Naval Officer. Admiral of the Fleet for the US's Pacific forces during World War Two.

287 Midway Atoll: A small island in the middle of the Pacific Ocean. Of strategic importance to both Japan and the US during World War Two.

295 Zero Fighters: Japan's main Naval aircraft during the Pacific War. In terms of performance and firepower, they were the most advanced fighters known at the time.

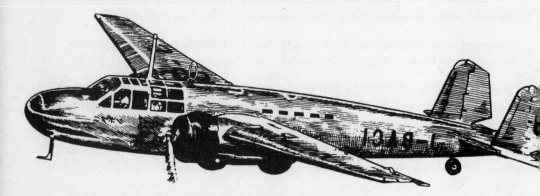

298 Yamaguchi Tamon: (1892–1942) b. Shimane Prefecture. Navy Vice Admiral. Commander of the *Hiryu* aircraft carrier. Died 1942 (Showa 17) at the Battle of Midway.

328 Guadalcanal: In the South Pacific, a small island near the Solomon Islands. The scene of a hard-fought battle between Japan and the US during World War Two.

335 Full uniform: Military lingo. A full uniform of the time included a gun with bayonet, a backpack, a canteen, and a duffle bag. You brought everything with you to the combat zone.

338 Aleutian Islands: A bow-shaped group of islands between the Alaska and Kamchatka Peninsulas. American territories, they are also known as the Volcano Islands. During World War Two, battles were fought on Kiska and Attu Island.

345 Flagship: The personal vessel of the Armada Commander or Fleet Commander. An identifying flag hangs from the mast of this ship.

351 Duel at Ganryu Island: April 13, 1612: Japan's greatest swordsman, Miyamoto Musashi met his rival Kojiro Sasaki on Ganryu Island for a duel. The fight was over in moments when Musashi killed Sasaki with a wooden sword.

356 Palau: An islet of Micronesia in the southwestern Pacific Ocean. Formerly a protectorate of Japan by United Nations mandate, it gained full sovereignty in 1994.

366 Naval superiority: When one force has command of the sea, hosting forces so strong a rival cannot attack directly.

380 Sugiyama Hajime: (1880–1945) b. Fukuoka Prefecture. Chief of the General Staff. Field Marshal. Minister of the Army. Held various other posts in the General Staff. Committed suicide following Japan's defeat.

382 Rationing: Due to limited resources during World War Two, daily living necessities were carefully rationed for the population. Each household was allowed to purchase only a fixed allotment of rationed goods.

385 Cabinet Intelligence Bureau: A government agency established in 1940 to control speech and the press. Abolished at the end of the war.

388 Ugaki Matome: (1890–1945) b. Okayama Prefecture. Navy Vice Admiral. Chief-of-Staff of the Combined Fleet. Committed suicide in a kamikaze attack immediately after receiving news of Japan's surrender.

404 Suicide squad: During the Pacific War, Japanese troops cut off from supplies and ammunition were expected to charge enemy lines with their swords and kill as many enemies as they could before they died.

410 Nagano Osami: (1880–1947) b. Kochi Prefecture. Admiral. Chief of Imperial Japanese Navy General Staff. Charged as a Class-A war criminal, but died while under trial.

429 State Funeral: Reserved for people of particular importance to a nation, a state funeral is given and paid for by the government.

430 Koga Mineichi: (1885–1944) b. Saga Prefecture. Fleet Marshal. Navy Admiral. Took over command of the combined fleet after the death of Yamamoto. Died in battle in May 1944 (Showa 19).

488 Kami Sama: This refers to a spirit in the Shinto religion. It can be translated as "god" or "deity," but those are lazy translations that don't really capture the essence. It would take a book to truly describe what a kami really is—and there are books written on the subject—but for purposes of this comic you could say "one who is so far above me as to be unto a god."

499 Dog tags: Soldiers wear an ID badge that can be used to identify their dead body; these are sent home along with the death notice. The badges are metal and stamped with a serial number.

523 Hanafuda Cards: Translating literally as "flower cards," hanafuda is a point-based card game played with illustrated cards.

This book is presented in the traditional Japanese manner and is meant to be read from right to left. The cover at the opposite end is considered the front of the book.

To begin reading, please flip over and start at the other end, making your way "backward" through the book, starting at the top right corner and reading the panels (and the word balloons) from right to left. Continue on to the next row and repeat.